# ELSEVIER'S DICTIONARY OF ACRONYMS, INITIALISMS, ABBREVIATIONS AND SYMBOLS

Second, Revised and Enlarged Edition

# ELSEVIER'S DICTIONARY OF ACRONYMS, INITIALISMS, ABBREVIATIONS AND SYMBOLS

**Second, Revised and Enlarged Edition**

compiled and edited by

**FIORETTA BENEDETTO MATTIA**
*Milan, Italy*

2003
ELSEVIER
Amsterdam – Boston – Heidelberg – London – New York – Oxford
Paris – San Diego – San Francisco – Singapore – Sydney – Tokyo

ELSEVIER SCIENCE B.V.
Sara Burgerhartstraat 25
P.O. Box 211, 1000 AE Amsterdam, The Netherlands



First edition 1997
Second, revised and enlarged edition 2003

Library of Congress Cataloging in Publication Data
A catalog record from the Library of Congress has been applied for.

British Library Cataloguing in Publication Data
A catalogue record from the British Library has been applied for.

ISBN 0-444-51241-1

∞ The paper used in this publication meets the requirements of ANSI/NISO Z39.48-1992 (Permanence of Paper).
Printed in The Netherlands.

*If you cannot - in the long run -*
*tell everyone what you have been*
*doing, your doing has been worthless.*

Erwin Schrödinger

## TABLE OF CONTENTS

## ABOUT THE AUTHOR

The author has a polyhedric background. She studied *Commercial Science* and *Languages* followed by *Philosophy* and *Psychology*. Next *Journalism*, *Law & Economics of the European Communities* and *Criminal Law*. Last but not least *International Business* (University of Washington).

The above and her in-depth knowledge of the specific terminologies pertaining to the scientific and technical disciplines, plus the several languages that she knows at mother-tongue level, have allowed her to succeed in her career in Translations, Teaching and Consultancy.

She has acquired her expertise and know-how by working with Patent Offices, with the Polytechnic of Milan, with Universities and important concerns, specializing in fields such as: *Chemistry; Criminal Law; Medicine; Nuclear Engineering; Physics; Psychology; Alternative Energies.*

She is a Certified Translator, she writes and runs Post-University Courses, she does Professional Consultancy work for the Milan Court of Law and she is a member of the American Association for the Advancement of Science, Washington D.C. as well as the New York Academy of Sciences.

## PREFACE TO THE FIRST EDITION

This **Dictionary** is the outcome of an idea I had several years ago when, in my Profession, I actually *lived* the difficulty of finding definitions of acronyms, initialisms and abbreviations and possibly additional information. In my daily professional life, same as it may have happened to you, I was also confronted with many acronyms and initialisms that had identical sets of letters but different definitions.

For instance: **AA** in *Computer Programming* stands for: Absolute Address whereas in *Psychology* it stands for: Achievement Age and in *Biochemistry*: Arachidonic Acid.
**BDA** stands for: British Dental Association, but also for: Bomb Damage Assessment.
**CAP** stands for: Civil Air Patrol, but in *Molecular Biology* it stands for: Catabolite Activator Protein, and this goes on and on.

Who is the person on earth that can name them or remember them all?

I found that there was a lot of confusion in this intricate world of acronyms, initialisms, abbreviations, with the thousands of existing ones plus the new ones coined every day. So I realized I had to do something to fill this gap, as no such Dictionary is available. We all know that Dictionaries do not materialize overnight, so armed with determination, perseverance and patience, I started collecting a wealth of information. I literally went through thousands of Scientific and Technical Journals and Periodicals, I scanned a huge amount of reference material, I gathered both historical data as well as recent developments spanning two decades: from 1976 to 1996. I listed thousands of acronyms/initialisms/abbreviations. I added freshly coined ones and updated terms. I coordinated the work and finally assembled the whole lot of acronyms, initialisms, abbreviations, symbols and codes. I re-checked the whole manuscript for accuracy and presented the Dictionary in easily readable form.

This is the result: a **Dictionary** including over 14,000 acronyms, initialisms, abbreviations in English - the language that makes most use of them. However, I have also added French and Italian ones translating them into English whenever applicable. In order to make it more exhaustive and anticipating your need for further details, you will find that many acronyms/ initialisms/abbreviations have, besides the definition itself, also explanations or information such as when or how a substance or material was developed; when and where a certain Plant started operating; when a Program was issued; when and where an Institution was established. I have also made ample use of cross-references for those interested in making a more in-depth study.

I have added several **Appendices** from 1 to 7 including acronyms and initialisms of: Research Institutes, Universities, Foundations, Publications, Awards, Fellowships, Banks, Airport Codes, Chemical symbols, NATO acronyms, International Organizations. They are all in alphabetical order for you to find at a glance the acronym that interests you.

In Appendix 8 I have listed the names of Publishers and Authors who have granted me permission to reprint acronyms and excerpts from their publications. All the other material has not been obtained from copyrighted sources. I have collected it from: broadcastings; brochures; pamphlets;

literature circulated and information disseminated at workshops; seminars; symposia and conferences relating to the various fields and subfields included in my Dictionary.

This **Dictionary** covers over 800 fields and subfields ranging from *Atmospheric Physics* to *Cytokine Biology*, from *Oncology* to *Clone-making*, from *Computer Science* to *Chaotic Dynamics*, from *Apoptosis* to *Paleography*, from *River Morphology* to *Petaflops*, from *Viral Pathogenesis* to *Xenotransplantation*, all of which are listed in Appendix 9.

I know that my efforts and the time I have spent in research will be more than compensated for when you - whether you are a Biologist, a Physicist, a Physician, a Scholar, a Consultant, a Translator, a Business person, a student or a layperson - when in difficulty will consult this **Dictionary** and find the answers to your acronym or abbreviation problems.

Fioretta BENEDETTO MATTIA

Milan, March 1997

## PREFACE TO THE SECOND REVISED AND ENLARGED EDITION

The publication of my dictionary in 1997, diffused throughout the world, elicited so much interest that I was prompted and encouraged to update and enlarge the previous work.

Acronyms/Initialisms/Abbreviations are being coined at a super high pace. I have collected, selected, expanded and assembled for you over 20,000 new ones in addition to the previous 14,000, for a total of more than 34,000.

In order to be able to provide the latest acronyms/initialisms/abbreviations I have explored hundreds of fields and subfields covering in this new enlarged Edition over 3,000 of them.

I have revised the previous work to correct oversights that inadvertently occurred and took this opportunity to update acronyms and initialisms that in the meantime have become obsolete and therefore have been replaced.

In the collection and expansion of acronyms, initialisms and abbreviations as well as in the information I have supplied, I have maintained the same guidelines as in the previous work. However, this time you do not have Appendices as I have merged the acronyms and initialisms with the others of the Volume.

The new 20,000 acronyms/initialisms and abbreviations with relevant expansions that I have added, include new fields/subfields such as: *Angiogenesis*; *Antisense Agents*; *Asteroseismology*; *Bioanthropology*; *Biomedical Optics*; *Copper Metabolism*; *Dopaminergic Neurons*; *Exoplanets Imaging*; *Fish Biology*; *Galaxy Evolution*; *Glacial Cycles*; *Mesenchymal Tumors*; *Monitoring of Volcanoes; Pharmacogenetics*; *Pharmacokinetics*; *Sickle Cell Disease*; *Terrorist Weapons; Transgenic Plants*; *Vaccine Vectors*; *Vasculogenesis*; *Whirling Disease*; *Advection*; *Hypoxia Science*; *Space Weather Modelling; Rare Cancer Cell Strains; Genetically Modified Animals;* etc. where research is undertaken.

Others refer to the *Changeover to the EURO;* to *Banking Integrations*, to *Websites* dealing with Medicine, Biology, etc., to Educational Websites, to Associations, Centers, Research Institutes, Consortia, and many more.

All acronyms/initialisms/abbreviations and symbols are listed in alphabetical order and underneath you will find in italics, for easy reference, the fields and subfields that offer you at a glance, without wasting time, the ones that interest you. Same as in the previous work, in addition to the standard fields/subfields I have added others to give you a clue as to the direction where research is carried out.

Besides the acronyms / initialisms / abbreviations in English and the French and Italian ones translated into English, I have added others in Dutch, German, Portuguese and Spanish with relevant translations into English where applicable.

I have also included NATO acronyms, initialisms and abbreviations according to their updated AAP-15 (2003) both in English and French: the two official languages of the North Atlantic Treaty Organisation.

You will also find of interest the Acronyms / Initialisms of Science Experiments / Initiatives / Programs / Projects worldwide from 2000 up to 2020. These include the European Community & Commission.

Many acronyms/initialisms refer to *Re-emerging Diseases*; to *Nascent Fields*; to new studies in *Mad Cow Disease;* to *Anti-pathogen Programs;* to *Biodefense;* to *Counterterrorism Technologies;* to *Terrorist Weapons*; to *Anthrax Disease*; to *E. Coli Projects* worldwide; to *Emerging Technologies*; to *European/U.S. Missions* (up to 2020); to *Artificial Organs*, to *Metastasis* (New Studies), to *Laser Thermometers* (to prevent spreading of infections such as SARS, etc.) and more.

Where else would you find this wealth of information?

Since there are acronyms deliberately coined for effect, I thought you would like to know about it, so I have included some of them, such as:

**POWER** People Organized and Working for Economic Rebirth;
**MACHO** Men Allied to Combat Hyprocrisy and Oppression;
**BLOSSOM** Basic Liberation Of Smokers and Sympathizers Of Marijuana

and so forth.

All of this has entailed a lot of work in Scientific and Technological research. Much time has also been spent in checking cross-references and in going through information disseminated. Under the heading "Permission to include granted by:" I have listed the names of Academies, Associations, Institutes, Centers, Federations and Organizations who have allowed me to do so. All other material is not from copyrighted sources, same as in the previous work, I have collected it from information disseminated and circulated at seminars, workshops, symposia, conferences, brochures and broadcastings.

I have more than doubled the size of the previous Edition making this one a comprehensive source of information, expanding its scope and enhancing its usefulness.

I sincerely hope that you my Reader, will welcome this Second, Revised and Enlarged Edition and that you will decide to add it to the reference collection of your library. Please accept it as a new Millennium achievement.

Fioretta BENEDETTO MATTIA

Milan, June 2003

## GUIDE TO THE USE OF THE DICTIONARY

1) **Abbreviations not used**

a) In view of the fact that this is meant to be exclusively a Dictionary of acronyms, initialisms, abbreviations, symbols, codes, none of the fields or subfields covered by the Dictionary has been put in abbreviated form.
For example: com.prog. for *Computer Programming;*
geod. for *Geodesy;* med. for *Medicine*, etc.

b) In addition, the usual abbreviations, such as esp. for especially, or ab. for about, have not been abbreviated.

2) **When the fields are not mentioned**

In certain cases the fields or subfields to which the acronym or initialism refers to has not been mentioned. This is because it is obvious or can be derived.

For example: **AGI** - American Geological Institute
In this case it is obvious that the field is *Geology* and therefore there is no need to mention it.

Or, **UPVG**: Utility PhotoVoltaic Group
In this case it can easily be derived that it refers to *Photovoltaics*

3) **When the same acronym/initialism relates to many fields**

When the acronym, initialism or abbreviation is used in several contexts all of the fields and subfields have been mentioned.

For example: **a.** (abbr.) absolute
*Chemistry; Physics; Thermodynamics*
**AC** Anchor Cell
*Cell Biology; Molecular Medicine; Signal Transduction*

4) **When the acronym is purposely coined with a meaning**

When the acronym or initialism has been coined purposely with a meaning, this has been brought to the attention of the person consulting the dictionary.

For example: **PAWS** - Progressive Animal Welfare Society
**paws** actually meaning: the foot of an animal

**HOPE** Health Opportunity for People Everywhere
It is obvious why they have used the word "hope" in the acronym

**STRESS** Structural Engineering System Solver
In this case it is significative that they have used the word "Stress"

**ESPRIT** - European Strategic Program for Research and development in Information Technology
**esprit** actually means in French: mind, intellect, talent, intelligence, brains.

**HANUL** High-energy Astrophysics Neutrino Laboratory (South Korea)
In Korean, the word “hanul” means: sky

**GUTs** - Grand Unified Theories
Surely, it is not a coincidence that the word "**guts**" has been used to coin the acronym

5) **When the acronym accidentally means something in another language**

It may happen that the acronym or initialism accidentally means something in another language. Also in this case it has been brought to your attention as it is only fair that you should know for instance that:

**SEM** - Scanning Electron Microscopy
**sem** actually means in Arabic: poison

**AVIS** - Audiovisual Information System
**avis** actually means in French: notice, opinion, advice, judgement, counsel, etc.

**ASTI** - Association for Science, Technology and Innovation
**Asti** - The name of an Italian town

**BOIA** - Bureau Of Indian Affairs
**boia** actually means in Italian: executioner

6) **Acronyms/initialisms with explanations or additional information**

When deemed necessary, besides the definition, an explanation of the acronym or initialism or details that may interest the person consulting the Dictionary, have been added.

For example: **BESTEST** - Building Energy Simulation Test: is a new diagnostic method to improve the accuracy of computer energy software programs

**PMMA** - Polymethyl Methacrylate: used mainly in lighting fixtures and surgical appliances

**ACM** - Association for Computing Machinery: is located in Washington D.C. (U.S.A.).

**US Pharm.** - U.S. Pharmacopoeia: The first one was published in the U.S.A. in 1820

**PEMFC** - Polymer Electrolyte Membrane Fuel Cell
European Commisssion 5$^{th}$ FP
For further details see under: **5FP**

**PLANMAN Project** After a brief description the date: Launched in September 1996

**MMA** After the expansion: A 1998 U.S. Project

**MPS** After the expansion: The Italian MPS was founded in 1472

**MPS** Materials Processing in Space
Conducted by NASA ever since the late 1960s

7) **The importance of mentioning the fields/subfields**

1) In many cases you will find that there are, besides the standard fields and subfields, also additional ones. This is because I have added them as research progresses and/or according to technological developments in that particular field.

2) In other cases it is important to know the field, as a person not conversant with the subject may be misled.

For instance: **TV** - Tidal Volume relates to *Physiology* and has nothing to do with tides.

**PMD** - Postmortem Dump: has nothing to do with the paraphernalia of a deceased person, but as you will see refers to *Computer Programming*

**PH** - Purpleheart does not relate to medicine or anatomy but is a type of wood to make furniture, so it goes under "*Materials*"

8) **When the definition of an acronym is known with another name**

When the definition of an acronym / initialism is known with another name, this has been mentioned.

For example: **PC** - Program Counter
*Computer Technology*
Program counter is also known as: Control counter or register; instruction counter or register; sequence counter or register

**PMN granulocyte**
*Immunology*
Polymorphonuclear granulocyte is also known as: Neutrophil

**VP** - Vapor Pressure
*Meteorology*
Vapor Pressure is also known as: Vapor Tension

9) **Cross-references**

Whenever applicable cross-references have been used.

For example: **P** Pascal
For further details see under "Pa."

**W** Wait Time
For further details see under: "WT" (Waiting Time)

10) **NATO acronyms/initialisms/abbreviations**

NATO acronyms/initialisms/abbreviations are according to their AAP-15 (2003). Underneath each one you will find the equivalent in French if it has been coined in English, and in English if it has been coined in French. This is because English and French are the two official languages of the North Atlantic Treaty Organisation.

11) **Punctuation and Capitalization**

Acronyms usually do not have periods after each letter, and even though initialisms do have them, this practice is rapidly declining. The use of capital, lowercase or a combination of both is also controversial.

Therefore, since the use of punctuation and capitalization in acronyms and initialisms has never been universally agreed upon, I have used in this Dictionary the most commonly adopted form.

When both forms - with periods and without periods - are used, they have been indicated.

For example: **AA** or **A.A.** Author's Alteration
**AAA** or **A.A.A.** American Association of Anatomists

12) **Why the use of the English language**

a) Because the practice of coining acronyms and initialisms prevails in the English language.

b) Because English, besides being the native language of Great Britain, the United States, Canada and other countries, is also the second language most widely used in the world. As a matter of fact it is used by over 1000 million people around the world.

c) Because it has the role of international language: in the *Computer* field; in *Science*, *Technology* and many more fields.

Fioretta BENEDETTO MATTIA

**PERMISSION TO INCLUDE GRANTED BY:**

AAAS - American Association for the Advancement of Science (U.S.A.)
Agbioworld Foundation, Inc. Tuskegee Institute (Alabama, U.S.A.)
AIDIC - Associazione Italiana Di Ingegneria Chimica (Italy)
AIIA - Associazione Italiana di Ingegneria Agraria (Italy)
AIPND - Associazione Italiana Prove Non Distruttive - Monitoraggio Diagnostico (Italy)
AIT - Associazione Italiana di Telerilevamento (Italy)
AITA - Associazione Italiana di Tecnologia Alimentare (Italy)
AIV - Associazione Italiana del Vuoto (Italy)
APFA - Association pour Promouvoir le Français des Affaires (France)
ATIG - Associazione Tecnica Italiana del Gas (Italy)
BoE - Bank of England (G.B.)
BPB-CV - Banca Popolare di Bergamo - Credito Varesino (Italy)
CIAM - Collegio degli Ingegneri e Architetti di Milano (Italy)
CIB - Center for Integrative Bioscience (Japan)
ESDA - East Sweden Development Agency (Sweden)
Europe Publications (G.B.)
European School of Oncology (Italy)
FAST - Federazione delle Associazioni Scientifiche e Tecniche (Italy)
GRC - Glenn Research Center, NASA (U.S.A.)
GSFC - Goddard Space Flight Center, NASA (U.S.A.)
IntesaBCI (formerly Cariplo and BCI) (Italy)
JSC - Lyndon B. Johnson Space Center - NASA (U.S.A.)
LaRC - Langley Research Center, NASA (U.S.A.)
MJ Research (U.S.A.)
MPS - Monte dei Paschi di Siena (Italy)
MSFC - Mashall Space Flight Center, NASA (U.S.A.)
MSKCC - Memorial Sloan-Kettering Cancer Center (U.S.A)
MSU - Murray State University (U.S.A.)
NASA - National Aeronautics and Space Administration (U.S.A.)
NATO - North Atlantic Treaty Organisation - AAP-15 (2003)
NBB - National Bank of Belgium
NCCAM - National Center for Complementary and Alternative Medicine (U.S.A.)
NCMHD - National Center for Minority Health and Health Disparities - NIH (U.S.A.)
NEI - National Eye Institute - NIH (U.S.A.)
NHGRI - National Human Genome Research Institute - NIH (U.S.A.)
NIA - National Institute on Aging - NIH (U.S.A.)
NIAID - National Institute of Allergy and Infectious Diseases (U.S.A.)
NIDCD - National Institute of Deafness and other Communication Disorders - NIH (U.S.A.)
NIDCR - National Institute of Dental and Craniofacial Research - NIH (U.S.A.)
NIEHS - National Institute of Environmental Health Sciences (U.S.A.)
NIMH - National Institute of Mental Health - NIH (U.S.A.)
NINR - National Institute of Nursing Research - NIH (U.S.A.)

NIPS - National Institute of Physiological Sciences (Japan)
NREL - National Renewable Energy Laboratory (U.S.A.)
NYAS - New York Academy of Sciences (U.S.A.)
SIAM - Società di Incoraggiamento d'Arti e Mestieri (Italy)
SIRI - Associazione Italiana di Robotica (Italy)
Unicredito (formerly Credito Italiano) (Italy)
World Bank

# A

**a** (abbr.) absolute.
*Chemistry* - Absolute in chemistry means: pure.
*Physics* - In physics absolute relates to measurement by means of mass, length and scale units.
*Thermodynamics* - In thermodynamics absolute refers to the absolute temperature scale.
**a** account.
Also: **a/c**; **A/C**; **A/c**; **c/c**; **acct**.
**a** accumulator.
*Aviation; Computer Technology; Electricity; Mathematics; Mechanical Engineering; Petroleum Engineering.*
**a** action.
meaning: share; stock in French.
**a** (abbr.) address.
Address is a symbol, integer or a series of characters indicating a location, or the like where information is stored.
*Computer Technology.*
**A** Agglutinogène.
meaning: Agglutinogen in French.
*Medicine.*
**A** America; American.
Also: **Am**.
**a** (abbr.) analog / analogue.
*Chemistry; Food Technology; Evolution; Metrology.*
**A**; **a** anno.
meaning: year in Italian.
**a** assented.
**a** (abbr.) asynchronous.
*Computer Technology; Science.*
**a** audit; auditor.
**aA** Abampere.
Abampere is the centimeter-gram-second electromagnetic unit of current, equivalent to 10 amperes.
*Electricity.*
**AA** Absolute Address; Machine Address.
Absolute address is the number that identifies a location in computer memory.
*Computer Programming.*
**AA** Absolute Addressing.
*Computer Programming.*
**AA** Accademia Aeronautica (Italy).
Italian initialism meaning: Air Force Academy.
**AA** Access Arm.
*Computer Technology.*
**AA** Achievement Age or Educational Age.
Achievement age or educational age actually refers to the level of educational development of a person measured by means of achievement tests. It is based on the comparison of his/her score with the average score of persons of the same chronological age.
**AA** Active Account; Active Assets; Activity Account.
*Banking; Business; Commerce; Economics.*
**AA** Advertising Association.
**AA** After Arrival.
**AA** Air Attaché.
**AA** Air-to-Air.
Also: **ATA**.
*Ordnance.*
**AA**; **A.A.** Alcoholics Anonymous.
**AA** Always Afloat.
**AA** The airline code for American Airlines.
**AA** Annular Array.
**AA** Antiaerea.
Italian initialism meaning: Antiaircraft.
**AA** Antiaircraft.
*Ordnance* - Antiaircraft is used to destroy enemy aircraft.
**AA** Anxiety Attack.
*Psychology.*
**AA** Arachidonic Acid or Arachidonate.
*Biochemistry* - $C_{20}H_{32}O_2$ - Arachidonic acid is found in animal fats and in view of the fact that it is an unsaturated fatty acid it is necessary in the human diet.
**AA** Architectural Association.
**AA** Arithmetic Average.
**AA** Arma Aeronautica.
Italian initialism meaning: Air Corps.
**aa** (abbr.) arteries.
*Anatomy.*
**AA** Articulated Arm.
*Mechanics.*
**AA** Ascorbic Acid.
*Biochemistry* - $C_6H_8O_6$ - Ascorbic acid: vitamin C, is found in many vegetables and fruits and is indispensable for human growth.
**AA** Assets Accounting.
*Business; Commerce; Finance.*
**AA** Assistant Administrator.
**AA** Assistenza Automobilistica.
Italian initialism meaning: Road Service.
**AA** Associate in Arts.
**AA** Audit Agency.
**AA**; **A.A.** Author's Alteration.
**AA** Automobile Association.
**AAA** Abdominal Aortic Aneurysm.
*Cardiology.*

**AAA** Accademia Arti Applicate - Italy; since 1956.
**AAA** Agricultural Adjustment Administration.
**AAA** Amateur Athletic Association.
**AAA** American Accounting Association.
**AAA** American Arbitration Association.
**AAA**; **A.A.A.** American Association of Anatomists (U.S.A.).
**AAA** American Automobile Association.
**AAA** Antiaircraft Artillery.
*Military Science.*
**AAA** Applied Behavior Analysis.
**AAA** Associazione Analisti Ambientali (Italy).
Italian initialism meaning: Environment Analysts Association.
**AAAA** American Association of Advertising Agents (U.S.A.).
**AAACS** Attitude And Articulation Control Subsystem.
Also: **AACS**.
**AAAD** Aromatic Amino Acid Decarboxylase.
Also: **AADC**.
**AAAF** Association des Assureurs Aviation de France.
**AAAL** American Academy of Arts and Letters.
**AAAL** American Association for Applied Linguistics (U.S.A.).
**AAA pathway** Aminoadipic Acid pathway.
The aminoadipic acid pathway is a chemical pathway for the biosynthesis of the amino acid lysine.
*Mycology.*
**AAAS** American Association for the Advancement of Science (U.S.A.).
Founded in 1848, the AAAS has worked to advance science for human well-being through projects, programs, and publications, in the areas of science policy, science education and international scientific cooperation. The AAAS comprises 10 million individual members and is the world's largest federation of scientists. The Association also publishes **Science**, an editorially independent, multidisciplinary, weekly peer-reviewed journal.
**AAASDoSER Group** AAAS Dialogue on Science, Ethics and Religion Group.
For further details see under: **AAAS**.
**AAB** air assault brigade.
brigade d'assaut aérien.
**AABB** Association des Archivistes et Bibliothécaires de Belgique (Belgium).
*Belgian Association.*
**AABDFC** Association des Archivistes, Bibliothécaires et Documentalistes Francophones de la Caraibe.
**AABW** Antarctic Bottom Water.
Also: **ABW**. The AABW is characterized by temperatures of about -0.4°C.
*Oceanography.*
**AAC** ADP-ATP Carrier.
*Mitochondrial Carriers.*
**AAC** ACCS Advisory Committee [has replaced AIAC and APAC].
Comité consultatif pour l'ACCS [remplace AIAC et APAC].
**AAC** Alaskan Air Command.
**AAC** Automatic Aperture Control.
**AAC** Average Annual Cost.
**AACA** American Association of Certified Appraisers (U.S.A.).
**AACC** ATAF airspace coordination centre.
centre de coordination de l'espace aérien de la FATA.
**AACCLA** Association of American Chambers of Commerce in Latin America.
The AACCLA was founded in 1967.
**aA/cm$^2$** Abampere per square centimeter.
*Electricity.*
**AACP** Allied Acquisition Practices Publication.
publication interalliée sur les pratiques d'acquisition.
**AACP**; **A.A.C.P.** American Academy of Child Psychiatry (U.S.A.).
**AACR** American Association of Cancer Researchers (U.S.A.).
**AACS** Advanced Automatic Compilation System.
**AACS** Attitude and Articulation Control Subsystem.
Also: **AAACS**.
**AACSB** American Assembly of Collegiate Schools of Business (U.S.A.).
**AACSL** American Association for the Comparative Study of Law (U.S.A.).
**AACT** American Association of Commodity Traders (U.S.A.).
**AAD** 1. advanced ammunition depot.
1. dépôt de munition avancé.
2. area air defence.
2. défense aérienne de zone.
**AAD**; **A.A.D.** American Academy of Dermatology (U.S.A.).
**AAD** Appropriation Account Data.
**AAD** At A Discount.
*Business; Commerce.*
**AAD** Australian-Antarctic Discordance.
*Geodynamics; Geology; Geophysics.*
**AADC** All-Application Digital Computer.
**AADC** area air defence commander.
commandant de défense aérienne de zone.
**AADC** Aromatic Amino Acid Decarboxylase.

Also: **AAAD**.
**AADEBUG** Automated and Algorithmic DEBUGging.
**AADGE** ACE Air Defence Ground Environment.
infrastructure électronique de la défense aérienne du CAE.
**AA dip.** Architectural Association diploma.
**AADS**; **A.A.D.S.** American Association of Dental Schools (U.S.A.).
**AADS** Automatic Applications Development System.
**AAE**; **A.A.E.** American Association of Engineers (U.S.A.).
**AA/EO employer** Affirmative Action/Equal Opportunity employer.
**AAES** American Association of Engineering Societies (U.S.A.).
**AAF** Acetylaminofluorene.
**AAF** allied air force.
force aérienne alliée (FAA 1.).
**AAF** Army Air Force.
**AAF** Ascorbic Acid Factor.
**AAF** Association des Archivistes Français.
*French Association.*
**AAF** Auxiliary Air Force.
**AAFCE** Allied Air Forces, Central Europe [obsolete].
Forces aériennes alliées du Centre Europe (FAACE) [obsolète].
**AAFE** Advanced Aircraft Flight Experiment.
**AAFP**; **A.A.F.P.** American Academy of Family Physicians (U.S.A.).
**AAFS** American Academy of Forensic Sciences (Rockville, Maryland, U.S.A).
**AAG** Assistant Adjutant-General.
**AAGR** Average Annual Growth Rate.
**AAH** Advanced Attack Helicopter.
**AAHA** Awaiting Action of Higher Authority.
**AAHL** Australian Animal Health Laboratory (Australia).
**AAHSLD** Association of Academic Health Sciences Library Directors.
**AAI**; **A.A.I.** American Association of Immunologists (U.S.A.).
**AAI** Associate of the Auctioneers' Institute.
**AAI** Associazione Artistica Internazionale.
Italian initialism of the: International Artistic Association.
**AAIA** ACE ACCIS implementation architecture.
architecture de mise en œuvre de l'ACCIS du CAE.
**AAIA** Associate of the Institute of Actuaries.
**AAII** American Association of Individual Inventors.
Founded in 1979. Located in Chicago, Illinois, U.S.A.
**AAIMS** An Analytical Information Management System.
**AAIP** ACE ACCIS implementation plan.
plan de mise en œuvre de l'ACCIS du CAE.
**AAIS** ACE ACCIS implementation strategy.
stratégie de mise en œuvre de l'ACCIS du CAE.
**AAIS** American Association for Information Science (U.S.A.).
**AAI system** Acid-Amplified Imaging system (Polaroid's).
*Printing Applications.*
**AAIW** Antarctic Intermediate Water.
AAIW is characterized by a below-average salinity.
*Oceanography.*
**AAIW** Automotive Aftermarket Industry Week (U.S.A.).
**AAL** Absolute Assembly Language.
**AAL** Aeroacoustic Levitation.
*Engineering; Geology; Geophysics; Materials Science.*
**AAL** artillerie antiaérienne légère.
light anti-aircraft artillery (LAA 1.).
**AAL** Associazione Armatori Liberi (Italy).
**AALC** Amphibious Assault Landing Craft.
**AALCC** Asian-African Legal Consultative Committee.
**AALDI** Association of Agricultural Libraries and Documentalists of India.
*Indian Library Association.*
**AALL** American Association of Law Libraries.
**AALS** Association of American Law Schools (U.S.A.).
**AAM** Air-to-Air Missile.
**AAM**; **A.A.M.** American Academy of Microbiology (U.S.A.).
**AAM** Antiaircraft Missile.
*Ordnance.*
**AAM** Atmospheric Angular Momentum.
**AAMC**; **A.A.M.C.** American Association of Medical Colleges (U.S.A.).
**AAMC** American Association of Medico-legal Consultants.
Philadelphia, Pennsylvania, U.S.A.
**AAME** American Association of Microprocessor Engineers (U.S.A.).
**AAMG** anti-aircraft machine-gun.
mitrailleuse antiaérienne.
**AAMI** Association for the Advancement of Medical Instrumentation.

**AAMS** Azienda Autonoma Monopoli di Stato (Italy).

**AAMSS** Association of Assistant Mistresses in Secondary Schools.

**AAN**; **A.A.N.** American Academy of Neurology (U.S.A.).

**AAN** Assemblée de l'Atlantique Nord.
North Atlantic Assembly (NAA).

**A&D** Accounting and Disbursing.

**A&D** Assets and Depreciation.

**A&E** architecture and engineering (fees).
frais d'étude technique et de surveillance (FETS).

**A&I** audit and inspection.
vérification comptable et inspection.

**A&M** Acquisition and Merger.

**A&M**; **A and M** Agricultural and Mechanical.

**A&M** Ancient and Modern.

**A&M** Arts et Métiers.
French initialism meaning: Arts and Crafts.

**A&P** Anterior & Posterior.
*Medicine.*

**A&P** Auscultation and Percussion.
*Medicine.*

**A&R** Account and Risk.

**AAO**; **A.A.O.** American Academy of Ophtalmology- U.S. A.

**AAO**; **A.A.O.** American Association of Orthodontists (U.S.A.).

**AAOE** Airborne Arctic Ozone Experiment.

**AAOS**; **A.A.O.S.** American Academy of Orthopedic Surgeons (U.S.A.).

**AAP** 1. Allied Administrative Publication.
1. publication administrative interalliée.
2. area air picture.
2. situation aérienne de zone.

**AAP**; **A.A.P.** American Academy of Pediatrics (U.S.A.).

**AAP**; **A.A.P.** American Association of Pathologists (U.S.A.).

**AAP** Analyst Assistance Program.

**AAP** Associative Array Processor.

**AAPA** Advertising Agency Production Association.

**AAPA**; **A.A.P.A.** American Academy of Physician's Assistants (U.S.A.).

**AAPA** American Association of Physical Anthropologists (U.S.A.).

**AAPCC** American Association of Poison Control Centers (U.S.A.).

**AAPG**; **A.A.P.G.** American Association of Petroleum Geologists (U.S.A.).

**AAPI** Associazione delle Aziende Pubblicitarie Italiane (Italy).

**AAPL** Association of Australian Parliamentary Libraries (Australia).
*Australian Library Association.*

**AAPMR**; **A.A.P.M.R.** American Academy of Physical Medicine and Rehabilitation.

**AAPS** American Association of Pharmaceutical Scientists (U.S.A.).
Annual Meeting and Exposition held in New Orleans (LA, U.S.A.) in November 1999.
*Pharmaceutical Science.*

**AAPSO** Afro-Asian People's Solidarity Organization.

**AAPT** American Association of Physics Teachers (U.S.A.).

**AAR** 1. after action report (or review).
1. compte rendu (ou analyse) après action.
2. air-to-air refuelling.
2. ravitaillement en vol.

**AAR** Against All Risks.

**AAR** Alliance for Aging/Ageing Research.
The AAR is a group which promotes research on age-related diseases.

**AAR** Amino Acid Racemization.
*Diagenesis; Geochronological Research; Geology; Geophysics.*

**AARA** air-to-air refuelling area.
zone de ravitaillement en vol.

**AA rating** Average Audience rating.

**AARB** American Association for Research in Baghdad.
Protection of Cultural Property - Hague Convention 1954.
*Cultural Heritage at Risk.*

**AARC** air-to-air refuelling controller.
contrôleur du ravitaillement en vol.

**AARI** Arctic and Antarctic Research Institute (Russian Federation).
*Glaciology.*

**AARS** Automated Aircraft Reporting System.

**aaRS's** Aminoacyl-tRNA Synthetases.
*Biochemistry; Biophysics; Genetic Information Translation; Protein Engineering Research.*

**AartyP** Allied Artillery Publication.
publication interalliée sur l'artillerie.

**AAS** African Academy of Sciences.

**AAS**; **A.A.S.** American Astronomical Society.

**AAS**; **A.A.S.** American Astronautical Society.

**AAS** American Astrophysical Society (U.S.A.).

**AAS** Associate in Applied Science.

**AAS** Atomic Absorption Spectroscopy.
The atomic absorption spectroscopy is the study of absorption spectra.

**AAS** Azienda Autonoma di Soggiorno (Italy).

Italian initialism of the: Tourist Information Office.
**AASE** Airborne Arctic Stratospheric Expedition.
**AASE** Australian Associated Stock Exchanges (Australia).
**AASE I** Airborne Arctic Stratospheric Expedition I.
**AASE II** Airbome Arctic Stratospheric Expedition II.
**AASHTO** American Association of State Highway and Transportation Officials.
**AASL** American Association of School Librarians (U.S.A.).
*American Library Associations.*
**AAS's** Armenian Academy of Sciences.
**AASTP** Allied Storage and Transportation of Ammunition and Explosives Publication.
publication interalliée sur le stockage et le transport des munitions et explosifs.
**AAT** Alpha-1-Antitrypsin (a protein).
**AAT** Anglo-Australian Telescope.
**AAU** Association of American Universities.
**AAUL** Atlantic Association of University Libraries.
**AAUP**; **A.A.U.P.** American Association of University Professors (U.S.A.).
**AAUW**; **A.A.U.W.** American Association of University Women (U.S.A.).
**AAV** Adeno-Associated Virus.
AAV is also known as: Dependovirus.
*Virology.*
**AAV** Airborne Assault Vehicle.
**AAV** amphibious assault vehicle.
véhicule d'assaut amphibie.
**AAV** Assessed Annual Value.
**AAVSP** Allied Avionics Publication.
publication interalliée sur l'avionique.
**A.Av.Tech.** Associate in Aviation Technology.
**AAW** 1. air-to-air warfare.
1. lutte aérienne.
2. anti-air warfare (naval air defence only).
2. lutte antiaérienne (LAA 2.) [défense aérienne navale uniquement].
**AAWACU** anti-air warfare aircraft control unit.
unité contrôleur d'aéronefs de lutte antiaérienne.
**AAWC** 1. anti-air warfare commander.
1. commandant de la lutte antiaérienne.
2. anti-air warfare coordinator.
2. coordonnateur de la lutte antiaérienne.
**AAWCN** anti-air warfare command net.
réseau de commandement de la lutte antiaérienne.
**AAWS** Aerial Artillery Weapons System.
**AB** (abbr.) Abbey.
**ab.** (abbr.) abort.
*Aviation; Biology; Computer Programming; Medicine; Ordnance.*
**ab** (abbr.) abortion.
*Biology; Medicine.*
**AB**; **ab** (abbr.) about.
**ab** (abbr.) abridg(e)ment.
Also: **abr.**
**AB** Absolute Value.
*Computer Programming; Mathematics.*
**AB** Abstract.
Also: **abstr.**; **abs.**
**AB** Account Bought.
*Business; Finance.*
**AB** Adaptive Behaviour.
*Psychology.*
**AB** Address Bus.
*Computer Technology.*
**AB** Advisory Board.
**AB** Aeronautical Board.
*U.S. Air Force.*
**AB** African Bank.
**AB** Aid to Blind.
**AB** airbag / air bag.
The airbag is a bag that inflates automatically in order to protect automobile passengers during the impact of a collision.
*Mechanical Engineering.*
**AB** Air Base.
*Aviation; Aerial Photogrammetry.*
**AB** Air Bearing.
**AB** Air Blast.
*Engineering; Mining Engineering.*
**AB** Airblasting / air-blasting.
*Engineering.*
**AB** Air Board (R.A.F.) (G.B.).
**a/b** (abbr.) Airborne.
For further details see under: **ABN**; **abn.**
**AB** Air Bomber.
**AB** Air Brake.
The air brake is a mechanism operated by means of compressed air.
*Mechanical Engineering.*
**AB** Air Breathing.
Referring to an aerodynamic vehicle or an engine.
*Mechanical Engineering.*
**AB** Air Burst.
*Ordnance; Petroleum Engineering.*
**A/B** Aktiebolaget.
Swedish Limited Co.
**Ab.** (abbr.) Alabamine.
**AB** Amyloid Body.
*Pathology.*
**A/B** Anchor Bolt.

The anchor bolt is used to hold a machine or a structure in place. It is also known as: anchor rod.
*Civil Engineering.*
**Ab** Antibody.
The antibody is a protein in blood serum which reacts to overcome the toxic effects of a particular antigen. The antibody is also known as: Immune Body.
*Immunology.*
**AB** Arterial Blood.
The arterial blood is oxygenated blood bright red in color.
*Hematology.*
**AB** Asymmetric Balance.
**AB; ab** Bachelor of Arts.
**ABA** Abscisic Acid.
$C_{15}H_{20}O_4$ - Abscisic acid, formerly known as abscisin, is a plant hormone having an important role in growth and development.
*Biochemistry.*
**ABA** Activity-Based Anorexia.
**ABA** Amateur Boxing Association.
**ABA** American Bankers/Banking Association.
**ABA** American Bar Association (U.S.A.).
**ABA** American Books Awards (U.S.A.).
**ABA** American Booksellers Association.
**Aba** $\alpha$-Amino butyric acid.
**ABA** Annual Budget Authorization.
**ABA** Applied Behaviour Analysis.
*Psychology.*
**ABA** Arab Bankers Association.
**ABA** Association of British Archaeologists (G.B.).
**A.B.A.** Associazione Balestrieri Arcieri (Italy).
Italian acronym of the: Crossbow Archers Association.
**A.B.A.** Associazione per il Bambino Allergico.
Italian acronym of the: Association for the Allergic Child.
**A.B.A.** Associazione Studio Ricerca su Anoressia Bulimia Disordini Alimentari (Italy).
**ABADCAM** Association des Bibliothécaires, Archivistes, Documentalistes et Muséographes du Camerun.
**ABAI** American Boiler and Affiliated Industries (U.S.A.).
**A.B.A.J.P.** Association Belge des Architectes de Jardins et des Architectes Paysagistes (Belgium).
**ABARE** Australian Bureau of Agriculture and Resource Economics (Australia).
ABARE is a Government-owned Agency.
**ABB** (abbr.) Abbey.
**abb.** (abbr.) abbonamento.
Italian abbreviation meaning: subscription.
**abb.** (abbr.) abbonato.
Italian abbreviation meaning: subscriber.
**abb.** (abbr.) abbuono.
Italian abbreviation meaning: allowance; discount.
**ABB** Ablating Blunt Body.
**ABB** airborne brigade.
brigade aéroportée.
**ABB** Archives et Bibliothèques de Belgique (Belgium).
*Publication.*
**ABB** Array of Building Blocks.
**ABB** Artificial Breeding Box.
**ABB** Automatic Back Bias.
*Radar.*
**ABBB** Association of Better Business Bureaus.
**abbr.**; **abbrev.** abbreviation.
**ABC** Aber Bio Centre (Aberystwyth).
At the University of Wales.
**ABC** Aconite, Belladonna and Chloroform.
ABC is a liniment compound.
**ABC** Active Bioprosthetic Composition.
**ABC** Ahram Beverages Company (Cairo, Egypt).
Producer of "stella" beer. Founded in 1897 with Belgian and local funds. The invention of beer is mentioned in a number of papyri of the Pharaonic period.
**ABC; abc** Airborne Control.
**ABC** Airway, Breathing and Circulating (cardiopulmonary resuscitation).
**A.B.C.** Alcoholic Beverage Control.
**ABC** American Bibliographical Center.
**ABC** American Broadcasting Company.
**ABC** Approach By Concept.
**ABC** Aquaculture genetics and Breeding technology Center.
Virginia Institute of Marine Science (U.S.A.).
**ABC** Arab Banking Corporation.
Headquarters: Bahrain.
**ABC** Argentine, Brazil and Chile.
**ABC** Association of Biotechnology Companies.
**ABC** Associazione Bambini Cardiopatici.
Italian initialism of the: Cardiopathic Children Association (Italy).
**ABC**; **A.B.C.** Atomic, Biological and Chemical (weapons or missile warheads).
*Ordnance.*
**ABC** ATP-Binding Cassette.
*Cell Biology; Medicine; Physiology.*
**ABC** Audit Bureau of Circulation.
**ABC** Australian Broadcasting Corporation (Australia).
**ABC** Automatic Background Control.

For further details see under: **ABC** (Automatic Brightness Control).

**ABC** Automatic Bandwidth Control.

**ABC**; **abc** Automatic Bass Compensation.

**ABC** Automatic Brightness Control.
The automatic brightness control is a circuit used in a television receiver to keep the brightness of the reproduced image constant. The automatic brightness control is also known as: automatic background control.
*Electronics.*

**ABCA** American, British, Canadian and Australian (Armies).

**ABCA** American Business Communication Association (U.S.A.).

**ABCA (nations)** America, Britain, Canada, Australia.
Amérique, Grande-Bretagne, Canada, Australie.

**ABCB** American Board of Clinical Biofeedback (U.S.A.).

**ABCB switch** Air-Blast Circuit Breaker switch.
The ABCB switch is an electric switch that, upon opening, uses a high-pressure gas blast to break the arc.

**ABCC** American Board of Clinical Chemistry.

**ABCC** Association of British Chambers of Commerce (G.B.).

**ABCC** Atomic Bomb Casualty Commission.
The ABCC has been replaced in 1975 by the **RERF** (Radiation Effects Research Foundation).
*Atomic Radiation.*
For further details see under: **RERF**.

**ABCCC** 1. airborne battlefield command and control centre.
1. centre aéroporté de commandement et de contrôle du champ de bataille.
2. airborne command, control and communications (system).
2. (système) aéroporté de commandement, de contrôle et de communications.

**ABCD** Accelerated Business Collection and Delivery.
The ABCD is a U.S. Postal Service.

**ABCD** Agency for Business and Career Development.

**ABCDE** Annual Bank Conference ob Development Economics (World Bank's).
15/16th May 2003 held in Paris, France.
*International flows of People; Trade; Capital; Knowledge.*
21/23rd May 2003 held in Bangalore, India.
*Foresting Entrepreneurship; Innovation & Growth.*

**ABCGC** American Business Council of the Gulf Countries (Saudi Arabia).
The ABCGC was formed in 1989.

**ABC laws** Alcoholic Beverage Control laws.
The ABC laws date back to the Code of Hammurabi (King of Babylonia) almost 4,000 years ago.

**ABC (nations)** America, Britain, Canada.
Amérique, Grande-Bretagne, Canada.

**ABC Powers** Argentina, Brazil and Chile Powers.
Referring to their mediation between the U.S. and Mexico in 1914.

**ABCR gene** ATP-Binding Cassette transporter - Retina gene.
Mutations in the ABCR gene cause Stargardt disease, which is a form of macular degeneration.
*Genetic Epidemiology; Human Genetics; Macular Degeneration; Molecular Genetics; Ophtalmology.*

**ABC transporters** Adenosine triphosphate-Binding Cassette transporters.
*Molecular and Cellular Biology.*

**ABD** airborne division.
division aéroportée.

**ABD** Association Belge de Documentation (Belgium).
*Belgian Library Association.*

**abd**; **AB** (abbr.) abdomen.
The abdomen is the part of the human body between the thorax and the pelvis. Also the cavity of this part of the body containing most of the digestive organs.
*Anatomy.*

**abd** (abbr.) abdominal.
*Medicine.*

**ABDR** aircraft battle damage repair.
réparation des dégâts subis par les aéronefs au combat.

**ABE** Acute Bacterial Endocarditis.
Acute bacterial endocarditis is an abrupt progressive inflammation of the endocardium associated with infection.
*Medicine.*

**ABE** Association Belge de l'Eclairage (Belgium).

**ABE** The airport code for Allentown (Pennsylvania, U.S.A.)

**Abecafe** Brazilian Association of Coffee Exporters.

**ABEF** Association des Bibliothèques Ecclésiastiques de France (France).
*French Library Association.*

**ABEI** Associazione dei Bibliotecari Ecclesiastici Italiani (Italy).
*Italian Library Association.*

**ABEL disorders** Acid-Base Electrolyte disorders.

**abend** abnormal end of task.
*Computer Programming.*
**ABEPP**; **A.B.E.P.P.** American Board of Examiners in Professional Psychology (U.S.A.).
**ABE process** Acetone, Butanol, and Ethanol process.
*Microbiology.*
**ABES** Aerospacc Business Environment Simulator.
A computer-programmed business game.
**ABF** Association des Bibliothécaires Français.
*French Library Association.*
**ABF I** ARS Binding Factor I.
*Biology; DNA Replication; Medicine.*
**ABFD** Affordable Basic Floppy Disk.
**A.B.F.M.** American Board of Foreign Missions.
**ABG** Abnormal Blood Gas.
**ABG** Antibacklash Gear.
**ABG** Arterial Blood Gases.
**ABG** Association Bernard Gregory (France).
The ABG was created in the 1970s. It is an organization devoted to finding jobs for young scientists.
**ABI** Accademie e Biblioteche d'Italia (Italy).
*Publication.*
**ABI** American Biographical Institute (U.S.A.).
**ABI** Associate of the Book-keepers Institute.
**ABI** Association des Bibliothèques Internationales.
**ABI** Association of British Insurers (G.B.).
**ABI** Associazione delle Banche Italiane.
**ABI** Associazione Bancaria Italiana (Italy).
Italian acronym of the: Italian Banking Association.
**AbiH** Army of Bosnia-Herzegovina.
Armée de Bosnie-Herzégovine.
**ABIM** Associate of the British Institute of Management (G.B.).
**ABIOS** Advanced Basic Input / Output System.
**ABIs** Auditory Brainstem Implants.
The ABIs have been under development since the 1970s.
*Neuroscience; Neurosurgery; Otolaryngology.*
**abl.** (abbr.) ablative.
**ABL** Airborne laser.
laser aéroporté.
**ABL** Atmospheric Boundary Layer.
ABL is also known as: Ground Layer; Surface Layer; Friction Layer; Surface Boundary Layer.
*Meteorology.*
**ABLA** American Business Law Association.
Atlanta, Georgia, U.S.A.
**ABLE** Acquisition Based on consideration of Logistic Effects.
*U.S. Air Force.*
**ABLE** Adult Basic Learning Examination.
**ABLE** Agricultural-Biological Literature Exploitation (U.S.A.).
Of the U.S. National Agricultural Library.
**ABLE** Association for Biology Laboratory Education.
**ABLE** Atmospheric Boundary Layer Experiment.
**ABLE-2** Amazon Boundary Layer Experiment.
*Atmospheric Aerosols; Atmospheric Chemistry.*
**ABLP** Air Bearing Lift Pad.
**A.B.L.S.** Bachelor of Arts in Library Science.
**ABM** Acquisition Bus Monitor.
*Data Processing.*
**ABM** Advanced Bill of Materials.
**ABM** Antiballistic missile.
Missile antimissile balistique.
**ABM** Automated Batch Mixing.
**ABMA** American Boiler Manufacturers Association (U.S.A.).
**ABMA** American Brush Manufacturers Association (U.S:A.).
**ABMA** Army Ballistic Missile Agency.
**ABMC** American Battle Monuments Commission (U.S.A.).
**ABMPS** Automated Business Mail Processing System.
**ABMS** Automated Batch Manufacturing System.
**ABN**; **abn** (abbr.) airborne.
*Aeronautics* - Supported by air as an aircraft in flight.
*Biology* - Carried by / in the air, as pollen, and the like.
*Military Science* - Personnel or equipment carried in airplanes.
**ABNI** Available But Not Installed.
*Business; Commerce.*
**ABNOC** Airborne operations centre.
centre d'opérations embarqué.
**ABO** Absent Bed Occupancy.
**ABO** Accessory Boring Organ.
**ABO** American Board of Ophtalmology.
**ABO** Association of British Orientalists (G.B.).
**ABO** Astable Blocking Oscillator.
**ABOL** Adviser Business-Oriented Language.
**ABOM** Australian Bureau Of Meteorology.
**ABP** Absolute Boiling Point.
*Physical Chemistry.*
**ABP** Acetyl Benzoyl Peroxide or Acetozone or Benzozone.
$C_6H_5CO{\cdot}O_2{\cdot}COCH_3$ - ABP is used as a germicide and disinfectant.
*Organic Chemistry.*
**ABP** Actin-Binding Protein.
**ABP** Air Bearing Platform.

**ABP** Airborne Beacon Processor.
**ABP** Aldosterone-Binding Protein.
*Endocrinology.*
**ABP** American Business Press (U.S.A.).
**AβP** Amyloid β Protein.
**ABP** Androgen Binding Protein.
*Endocrinology.*
**ABP** Arabinose Binding Protein.
*Biochemistry.*
**Abp.** (abbr.) Archbishop.
**ABP** Arterial Blood Pressure.
**ABP** Associated British Ports (G.B.).
*Port Operators.*
**ABPA** Allergic Bronchopulmonary Aspergillosis.
**ABPA** American Book Producers Association.
**ABPC** Abelson Plasmacytoma.
*Oncology.*
**ABPC**; **A.B.P.C.** American Book Publishers Council (U.S.A.).
**Aβ peptides** Amyloid-β peptides.
*Medicine; Molecular Biology; Neuroscience; Nervous System Injury; Pharmacology; Psychiatry; Toxicology.*
**ABPF** Audio Bandpass Filter.
**ABPG** Advanced Base Proving Ground.
**ABPI** Association of the British Pharmaceutical Industry (G.B.).
**ABPL** Abelson Plasmacytoid Lymphosarcoma.
*Oncology.*
**ABPS** Automated Bill Payment System.
**ABQ** The airport code for Albuquerque, New Mexico.
**ABR** Abortus Bang Reaction.
*Microbiology.*
**abr.** (abbr.) abridged; abridg(e)ment.
Also: **ab**.
**abr.** (abbr.) abrogato.
Italian abbreviation meaning: abrogated.
**ABR** Absolute Bed Rest.
**ABR** Adhesive Bonding Repair.
**ABR** Agrobiological Resources.
**Abr** All brand removed.
*Textile Industry.*
**ABR** Auditory Brainstem Response.
*Neurophysiology.*
**ABRAC** Agricultural Biotechnology Research Advisory Committee.
**ABRC** Advisory Board for Research Councils (G.B.).
**ABRGT** airborne regiment.
régiment aéroporté.
**ABRIXAS** A Broad Band Imaging X-ray All-Sky Survey.
ABRIXAS is a German X-ray mission.
*Astronomy; Astrophysics.*
For further details see under: **RASS** (ROSAT All-Sky Survey).
**abs.** (abbr.) absence; absent.
**abs.**; **abs** (abbr.) absolute.
*Chemistry; Geology; Meteorology.*
**abs.** (abbr.) abstract.
Also: **AB**; **abs.**; **abstr.**
**ABS** Acute Brain Syndrome.
*Medicine.*
**ABS** Adaptive Behaviour Scale.
*Psychology.*
**ABS** Air-Brake Switch.
The air-brake switch is also known as: air switch.
*Electricity.*
**ABS** Alkyl Benzene Sulfonate.
ABS is used as a nonbiodegradable detergent.
*Organic Chemistry.*
**ABS** Alternative Billing Services.
*Business; Commerce.*
**ABS** American Bible Society (U.S.A.).
**ABS** American Bureau of Shipping (U.S.A.).
**abs** (abbr.) antibodies.
*Immunology.*
**ABS** Architecture for information Brokerage Service.
*European Community Project.*
**ABS** Asset-Backed Security/Securities.
*Banking; Finance.*
**ABS** Associate in Business Science.
**ABS** Association des Bibliothécaires Suisses (Switzerland).
*Swiss Library Association.*
**ABS** Automated Bond System.
**ABS** Aux Bons Soins de.
French acronym meaning: care of (c/o).
**ABSA** Allied Bank South Africa.
**ABSD** Advance-Base Section Dock.
**ABS resin** Acrylonitrile Butadiene Styrene resin.
A blend of the AS copolymer and the BA rubber with a view to obtain a polymer having the properties of the nitrile rubber and the vinyl resin.
*Organic Chemistry.*
**ABSWG** Agricultural Biotechnology Stewardship Working Group (U.S.A.).
A consortium formed by major biotechnology companies.
**abt.** (abbr.) about.
**ABT** Abtesla.
Abtesla is the unit of magnetic induction.
*Electromagnetism.*
**ABT** Air Blast Transformer.

**ABT** Airborne Tracking.
**ABT** American Board of Trade (U.S.A.).
**ABT** Associate in Business Technology.
**ABT** Automatic Battery Test.
**ABT** Auxiliary Ballast Tank.
**ABTA** Association of British Travel Agents.
**ABTAPL** Association of British Theological And Philosophical Libraries.
**ABTIR** Association des Bibliothèques de Théologie et d'Information Religieuse.
*Religious Library Association.*
**ABU** Alliance Biblique Universelle.
French acronym of the: Universal Biblical Alliance.
**ABU** American Board of Urology (U.S.A.).
**A. Bus.** Associate in Business.
**abv.** (abbr.) above.
**ABV** Air Blast Valve.
**ABV** Air Bubble Vehicle.
**ABV** Armed Boarding Vessel.
**ABVC** Absolute Value Computer.
The absolute value computer is a computer that processes the values of the variables instead of their increments.
*Computer Technology.*
**ABV function** Absolute Value function.
*Computer Programming.*
**ABW** Advise By Wire.
*Business; Commerce.*
**ABW** Antarctic Bottom Water.
ABW is also known as: AABW.
For further details see under: **AABW**.
**ABW design** Advanced Boiling Water design.
*Power Generation Equipment.*
**ABWI** American Business Women International (U.S.A.).
**ABYC** American Boat and Yacht Council.
The ABYC is located at Edgewater, Maryland, U.S.A.
**AC** Abdominal Circumference.
**AC** Able Chief.
**AC** Absolute Ceiling.
*Aviation.*
**AC** Acapulco, Mexico.
*Airport Codes.*
**AC** (abbr.) accelerator.
*Mechanical Engineering; Materials Science; Graphic Arts.*
**AC** Access Control.
*Transportation Engineering; Computer Technology.*
**AC** Access Cycle.
**a/c** (abbr.) account; Account current.
Also: **a**; **AC**; **A/c**; **c/c**.
*Commerce.*
**AC**; **ac** Accumulator.
*Aviation; Computer Technology; Electricity; Mathematics; Mechanical Engineering; Petroleum Engineering.*
**AC** Acetate.
*Organic Chemistry* - Either of two compounds derived from acetic acid.
*Textiles* - Acetate, that was known as acetate rayon, is a synthetic fiber.
**Ac** Acetyl.
*Organic Chemistry* - $CH_3CO$- Acetyl is an organic radical which contains a methyl group and a carbonyl group.
**ac** (abbr.) acid.
*Chemistry.*
**ac** acmite.
Acmite is also known as: Aegirine; Aegirite.
*Mineralogy.*
**a/c** acoustic coupler.
*Acoustical Engineering.*
**Ac** Acquisition costs.
**Ac** Acre.
*Metrology.*
**Ac** the chemical symbol for Actinium.
Actinium is a radioactive chemical element, having the atomic number 89, an atomic weight of 227, and a melting point of 1050°C.
*Chemistry; Symbols.*
**AC** Active Capital; Actual Cost.
*Business; Commerce; Finance.*
**AC** Add Carry.
**AC** Address Computation.
Address computation is the process of modification by a computer of the address portion of an instruction. Address Computation is also known as: address modification.
*Computer Programming.*
**AC** Address Constant.
Address constant also known as base address; presumptive address; reference address is the value used as the reference address from which subsequent addresses must be modified.
*Computer Programming.*
**AC** Address Conversion.
*Computer Programming.*
**AC** Address Counter.
*Computer Technology.*
**AC** Adenylate Cyclase.
*Enzymology.*
**A2C** Administration-to-Consumer.
For further details see under: **ACL**.

**AC** The airline code for Air Canada.
**AC**; **A.C.** Air Conditioning.
Air conditioning is a process / system to control the temperature, humidity, flow, or purity of the air in enclosed spaces. Air conditioning is also known as: Climate Control.
*Mechanical Engineering.*
**AC** 1. air coordinator.
1. coordinateur aérien.
2. airspace control.
2. contrôle de l'espace aérien.
3. antichar.
3. antitank / AT.
4. Antigua and Barbuda.
4. Antigua-et-Barbuda.
5. area commander.
5. commandant de zone.
6. army corps.
6. corps d'armée / CA 5. /.
7. (North) Atlantic Council [prefix used for identifying documents of the Council].
7. Conseil de l'Atlantique (Nord) [préfixe utilisé pour les documents du Conseil].
8. see A/C.
8. voir A/C.
**a/c** (abbr.) aircraft.
Also: **acft.**
*Aviation.*
**AC** Allocation Counter.
**AC** Allyl Chloride.
$CH_2$=$CHCH_2Cl$ - Allyl chloride is used mainly in resins and pharmaceuticals.
*Organic Chemistry.*
**AC** Alphabetic Character.
A letter of the alphabet.
*Computer Programming.*
**AC** Alphabetic Coding.
*Computer Programming.*
**AC** Alpine Club.
**A.C.** Alta Corte Costituzionale.
Italian acronym meaning: Supreme Constitutional Court.
Also: **A.C.C.**
**A.C.**; **a.c.** Alternating Current.
The A.C. is an electric current that reverses direction of flow at regular intervals.
*Electricity.*
**AC**; **ac** Alto Cumulus.
*Meteorology.*
**AC** Analog Computer.
An analog computer solves a given problem by using physical analogues.
*Computer Technology.*
**AC** Anchor Cell.
*Cell Biology; Molecalar Medicine; Signal Transduction.*
**ac.** année courante.
French abbreviation meaning: the present year; this year.
**A.C.**; **a.c.** anno corrente.
Italian initialism meaning: current year; the present year; this year.
**AC** Anterior Commissure.
*Anatomy.*
**A/C**; **AC** Appeal Court.
*Law.*
**ac.** argent comptant.
French abbreviation meaning: cash; ready money; cash on the nail.
**AC** Army Council.
**AC** Arterial Compliance.
*Aging; Antiaging; Geriatrics; Gerontology.*
**AC** Asbestos Cement.
*Buildings.*
**AC** as cast.
*Foundry.*
**a.c.** assegno circolare.
Italian initialism meaning: banker's draft.
**AC** Auditory Cortex.
**AC** Autocoder.
An autocoder is an individual or a machine using or producing autocode representing a certain job or a portion thereof.
*Computer Programming.*
**AC** Automatic Check.
The automatic check is an error-detection device operation, without human intervention, unless an error is found.
*Computer Technology.*
**AC** Automatic Computer.
The automatic computer can carry out certain operations without human intervention.
*Computer Technology.*
**AC** Automatic Controller.
The automatic controller is also known as: Automatic Regulator.
*Control Systems.*
**AC** Automation Center.
**AC** Automobile Club.
**aC** avanti Cristo.
Italian initialism meaning: before Christ.
**AC** Aviazione Civile.
Italian initialism meaning: Civil Aviation.
**AC** Azione Cattolica.
Italian initialism meaning: Catholic Action.
**ACA** The airport code for Acapulco, Mexico.

**ACA** 1. agence centrale des approvisionnements.
1. central supply agency / CSA /.
2. airspace coordination area.
2. zone de coordination de l'espace aérien.
3. airspace control authority.
3. autorité de contrôle de l'espace aérien.

**ACA** Agency for Cultural Affairs (Japan).
Of the Japanese Ministry of Education.

**ACA** Agile Combat Aircraft.
The ACA was developed by British Aerospace.

**ACA** American Citizens Abroad.
ACA is an international US citizens' organization. It exists to inform Americans living abroad of their rights and obligations.

**ACA** American Crystallographic Association.

**ACA** Associate of the Institute of Chartered Accountants.

**ACA** Association of Canadian Archivists.

**ACAA** Agricultural Conservation and Adjustment Administration.

**ACAI** Associazione Costruttori Acciaio Italiani.
Italian acronym of the: Association of Italian Steel Manufacturers.

**ACAL** Association of Chinese Agricultural Libraries.

**ACAMP** Allied Camouflage and Concealment Publication.
publication interalliée sur le camouflage et la dissimulation.

**ACAP** Advanced Computer for Array Processing.

**ACAP** American Council on Alcohol Problems.

**ACAPS** Automated Cost and Planning System.

**ACARD** Advisory Council for Applied Research and Development (G.B.).

**ACARS** air concepts and requirements study.
étude sur les concepts et besoins des forces aériennes.

**ACA/S**; **ACAS** Advisory, Conciliation and Arbitration Service (G.B.).

**ACAS** Airborne Collision Avoidance System.
The airborne collision avoidance system is also known as: airborne collision warning system.
*Navigation.*

**ACAS** American Computer Appraisal Service.

**ACAST** (*U.N.*) Advisory Committee on the Application of Science and Technology.

**ACATS** Airborne Chromatograph for Atmospheric Trace Species.

**ACAU** Automatic Calling and Answering Unit.

**ACB** Advertising Checking Bureau.

**ACB** Amphibious Construction Battalion.

**ACB** Associated Credit Bureau.

**ACB** Associazione di Categoria Brokers (Italy).

**ACBA** Allied Command, Baltic Approaches [obsolete].
Commandement allié des approches de la Baltique [obsolète].

**ACBE** Advisory Committee on Business and the Environment.

**ACBI** Association of Consultants to the Bioscience Industries.

**a/c bk** account book.

**ACBM** Association Canadienne des Bibliothèques Musicales (Canada).
French initialism of the: Canadian Music Library Association.

**ACB of A** Associated Credit Bureau of America (U.S.A.).

**ACBs** Associated Credit Bureaus (U.S.A.).

**acc.** accademia; accademico.
Italian abbreviation meaning: academy; academic.

**acc.** (abbr.) accept.
To accept means to receive an input with no errors found.
*Computer Technology.*

**acc.** (abbr.) acceptance.
Also: **acpt.**; **accpt.**

**acc.** (abbr.) accepted.

**acc.** acciaio.
Italian abbreviation meaning: steel.

**acc.** (abbr.) according to.

**acc.** (abbr.) account.
Also: **a**; **A/C**; **A/c**; **c/c**.

**acc.** (abbr.) accumulate.

**acc** (abbr.) accumulator.
*Aviation; Computer Technology; Electricity; Mathematics; Mechanical Engineering; Petroleum Engineering.*

**acc.** accumulatore.
Italian abbreviation meaning: storage battery.

**ACC** Accuracy Control Character.
*Computer Programming.*

**ACC** Acetyl-Co A Carboxylase.
*Lipid Synthesis.*

**ACC** Adaptive Control Constraint.

**ACC** Administrative Committee on Coordination - U.N.

**ACC** 1. air asset coordinator / ACC /.
1. coordonnateur des moyens aériens.
2. air component commander.
2. commandant de composante air.
3. air control centre.
3. centre de contrôle aérien.
4. air (space) coordination centre.
4. centre de coordination de l'espace aérien.
5. alternate control centre.

5a. centre de contrôle de remplacement [QG].
5b. centre de commande secondaire [télécoms].
6. approach control centre.
6. centre de contrôle d'approche / CCA 2. /.
7. area control centre.
7. centre de contrôle régional.
8. automatic code changing.
8. changement de code automatique.

**ACC** Air Combat Command.

**ACC** Alaska Coastal Current.
*Oceanography.*

**ACC**; **A.C.C.** Alta Corte Costituzionale.
Italian initialism meaning: Supreme Constitutional Court.
Also: **A.C.**

**ACC**; **A.C.C.** American College of Cardiology.

**ACC** 1-Aminocyclo-propane Carboxylic Acid.

**ACC** Antarctic Circumpolar Current.
ACC flows eastward around Antarctica.
*Oceanography.*

**ACC** Anterior Cingulate Cortex.
The ACC is a small area of the brain located between the cerebral hemispheres. It is a critical component of the neural circuit for action monitoring.
*Magnetic Resonance; Medicine; Psychiatry; Psychology.*

**ACC** Anthropogenic Climate Change.
*Ecology.*

**ACC** Ascending Chain Condition.
*Mathematics.*

**ACC** Association des Cartothèques Canadiennes (Canada).

**ACC** Automatic Chroma Control.

**ACCA** Accelerated Capital Cost Allowance.

**ACCA** American Corporate Counsel Association (U.S.A.).
The ACCA is located in Washington D.C.

**ACCA** Association of Certified and Corporate Accountants (G.B.).

**acca** The above acronyms were coined accidentally using the Italian word "acca" which means aitch (the letter "h").

**ACCAD** Advisory Committee on Climate Applications and Data.

**ACCAP** ACE CIS contingency assets pool.
pool de moyens SIC de circonstance du CAE.

**ACCB** ACE centralized communications budget.
budget des systèmes de télécommunications centralisés du CAE.

**ACCC** Australian Competition and Consumer Commission (Australia).

**acce.** (abbr.) acceptance.
Also: **accpt.**; **acpt.**

**ACCE** Atlantic Circulation and Climate Experiment.

**ACCESS** Aircraft Communication Electronic Signaling System.

**ACCIS** Automated Command and Control Information System.
système automatisé d'information de commandement et de contrôle.

**ACCL** Alberta Council of College Libraries (Canada).

**ACCLAIM** Automated Circuit Card Layout And IMplementation.

**ACCN** American Court and Commercial Newspapers (U.S.A.).
Founded in 1930. Newspapers of general circulation devoted to the Courts, financial, real estate and business interests.

**ACC oxidase** 1-amynocyclo-propane-1-carboxylate (ACC) oxidase.

**ACCP** Allied Combat Clothing Publication.
Publication interalliée sur les vêtements de combat.

**ACCP** Atlantic Climate Change Program.
Of the U.S. National Oceanic and Atmospheric Administration.

**accpt.** (abbr.) accept; acceptance.
Also: **acce.**; **acpt.**; **acc.**

**ACCR** Annual Cost of Capital Recovery.

**ACCRA** American Chamber of Commerce Researchers Association.

**Accrd.Int.** (abbr.) Accrued Interest.
*Banking; Business; Commerce; Finance.*

**accred.** (abbr.) accredited.

**ACCs** Acetyl-Coenzyme A Carboxylases.
ACCs are needed for the biosynthesis and oxidation of long-chain fatty acids.
*Biological Sciences.*

**ACCS** Air Command and Control System.
Système de commandement et de contrôle aériens.

**ACCS** Associate of the Corporation of Certified Secretaries.

**ACCSA** Allied Communications and Computer Security Agency [obsolete].
Bureau allié de sécurité des transmissions et de l'informatique [obsolète].

**ACC synthase** 1-Aminocyclopropane-1-Carboxylic Acid synthase.

**acct.** (abbr.) account.
Also: **a**; **A/C**; **A/c**; **acct.**

**acct.** (abbr.) accountant.
Also: **actnt.**

**acct.** (abbr.) accounting.

**ACCT** Agence de Coopération Culturelle et Technique (France).
French initialism of the: Cultural and Technical Cooperation Agency.
**ACD** Automatic Call Distributor / Distribution.
**ACDA** Arms Control and Disarmament Agency.
**ACDD** ACCS common data dictionary.
dictionnaire des données communes de l'ACCS.
**ACDMS** Automated Control of a Document Management System.
**ACDs** Automatic Call Distributors.
*Call Center Technology.*
**ACE** Academic Common Experience.
**ACE** Adaptive Computer Experiment.
**ACE** Adenylation Control Element.
**ACE** Advisory Center for Education (G.B.).
**ACE** Agencia de Certificación Electrónica (Spain).
*Certificate Authorities; Digital Signatures.*
**ACE** Allied Command Europe [obsolete - replaced by SC Europe].
Commandement allié en Europe / CAE / [obsolète - remplacé par SC Europe].
**ACE** American Council on Education (U.S.A.).
**ACE** Angiotensin Converting Enzyme.
*Enzymology.*
**ACE** Antarctic Current Experiment.
**ACE** Association of Computer Educators.
**ACE** Associazione Consorzi all'Esportazione (Italy).
**ACE** Atmospheric Collection Equipment.
**ACE** Audit, Control and Evaluation.
**ACE** Automated Computing Engine.
**ACE** Automated Cost Estimates.
**ACE** Automatic Calling Equipment.
**ACE** Automatic Checkout Equipment.
**ACE** Automatic Circuit Exchange.
**ACE-1** Aerosol Characterization Experiment.
*Atmospheric Aerosols; Atmospheric Chemistry.*
**A.C.E.A.** Association des Constructeurs Européens d'Automobiles (Belgium).
**ACEADGE** ACE Air Defence Ground Environment.
infrastructure électronique de la défense aérienne du CAE.
**ACEATM** aimed controlled-effect antitank mine.
mine antichar pointable à effet dirigé (MACPED).
**ACEC** American Consulting Engineers Council (U.S.A.).
**ACED** Advanced communications equipment depot.
dépôt avancé de matériels de télécommunications.
**ACEDB** *A.C. Elegans* Database.
*Genetic Map Data; Physical Map Data.*
**ACEER** Amazon Center for Environmental Education and Research (Foundation) (Peru).
**ACEF** Association of Commodity Exchange Firms (U.S.A.).
**ACEFORSTAN** ACE Forces Standards.
normes de forces du CAE.
**ACEHIGH** ACE Troposcatter Communications System [obsolete].
système de télécommunications troposphériques du CAE [obsolète].
**ACELIP** ACE Long-Term Infrastructure Programme [obsolete - now called LTIP].
Programme d'infrastructure à long terme du CAE [obsolète - maintenant appelé LTIP].
**AcEm** (abbr.) Actinium Emanation.
*Nuclear Physics.*
**ACEMET** ACE Meteorological Services.
service météorologique du CAE.
**ACENET** ACE communications network.
réseau de télécommunications du CAE.
**ACEREP** ACE reporting system.
Système de compte rendu du CAE.
**ACES** Annual Cycle Energy System.
*Energy Conservation.*
**ACES** Arab Center for Energy Studies.
The ACES is located in Kuwait.
**ACES** Automated Code Evaluation System.
**ACESE** Association Catalane pour l'Environnement, la Solidarité et l'Emploi.
**ACE satellite** Advanced Composition Explorer satellite (U.S.A.).
**Acet.** (abbr.) Acetylene.
Acetylene is used mainly in the synthesis of industrial compounds.
*Organic Chemistry.*
**ACEUM** Association Canadienne des Ecoles Universitaires de Musique.
*Canadian Association.*
**ACF** Access Control Field.
**ACF** Administration for Children and Families (U.S.A.).
**ACF** Advanced Communications Function.
**ACF** Aéro-Club de France.
French initialism of the: French Aero Club.
**ACF** Army Cadet Force.
**ACF** Automated Control Function.
**ACF** Automobile Club de France.
French initialism of the: French Automobile Club.
**ACFCI** Assemblée des Chambres Françaises de Commerce et d'Industrie (Belgium).
**ACFEC** Arbitral Centre of the Federal Economic Chamber (Austria).
**ACFL** agreed ceasefire line.
ligne cessez-le-feu agréée.

**acfl** Associazione culturale formazione lavoro (Italy).
**acfm** actual cubic feet per minute.
*Chemical Engineering.*
**acft.** (abbr.) aircraft.
Also: **a/c**.
*Aviation.*
**AcG** Acceleration Globulin.
*Biochemistry.*
**ACG** Advanced Computing Group (U.S.A.).
Of the U.S. Forecast System Laboratory.
**ACG** amphibious combat group.
groupe de combat amphibie.
**ACG** Automatic Code Generator.
**ACG** Guanacaste Conservation Area (Costa Rica).
*Biodiversity; Taxonomy; Tropical Ecology.*
**ACGB** Arts Council of Great Britain (G.B.).
**ACGI** Associate of the City of Guilds of London Institute (G.B.).
**ACGIH** American Conference of Governmental Industrial Hygienists (U.S.A.).
**Ach** Acetylcholine.
$C_7H_{17}O_3N$ - Ach is a derivative of choline.
*Biochemistry.*
**ACH** Adrenal-Cortical Hormone.
ACH is also known as: adrenocortical hormone.
*Biochemistry; Medicine.*
**ACH** Automated Clearinghouse.
**AchE** Acetylcholinesterase.
Acetylcholinesterase is also known as: Choline esterase I; true cholinesterase.
*Enzymology.*
**ACHQ** advanced control headquarters.
quartier général de contrôle avancé (QGCA).
**AchR** Acetylcholine Receptor.
*Neuroscience.*
**ACHRE** Advisory Committee on Human Radiation Experiments (U.S.A.).
**AchRs** Acetylcholine Receptors.
*Neuroscience.*
**AchS** American Chemical Society (U.S.A.).
**ACI** Accordi di Cooperazione Industriale.
Italian acronym meaning: Industrial Cooperation Agreements.
**ACI** Acoustic Comfort Index.
The acoustic comfort index is a scale to indicate the noise inside the passenger cabin of an aircraft.
*Acoustics.*
**ACI** Acoustic Control Index.
**ACI** Action-Centered Learning.
**ACI** Actual Cost Incurred.
**ACI** Adenylate Cyclase Inhibitor.
*Biochemistry.*
**ACI** Adjacent-Channel Interference.
The term adjacent-channel interference refers to an interference that a transmitter operating in an adjacent channel causes.
*Telecommunications.*
**ACI** Aero Club d'Italia (Italy).
Italian acronym of the: Italian Aero Club.
**ACI** airborne control intercept.
interception contrôlée en vol.
**ACI** Air Cargo Incorporated (U.S.A.).
**ACI** Airports Council International (Geneva, Switzerland).
**ACI** Alliance Coopérative Internationale.
**ACI** American Concrete Institute (U.S.A.).
**ACI** Army Council Instruction.
**ACI** Association Cambiste Internationale.
**ACI** Associazione Culturale Italiana (Italy).
Italian acronym of the: Italian Cultural Association.
**ACIA** Associate of the Corporation of Insurance Agents.
**ACIA** Asynchronous Communications Interface Adapter.
*Computers.*
**ACIB** Associate of the Corporation of Insurance Brokers (G.B.).
**ACIBM** American Center for Immuno-Biology and Metabolism (U.S.A.).
**ACIC** Aeronautical Charting and Information Center (U.S.A.).
**ACICAFE** Associazione del Commercio e dell'Industria del Caffè (Italy).
**ACID** Aircraft IDentification.
**ACID** Attempted Corporate Integration of Dividends.
*Economics.*
**ACID** Automatic Classification and Interpretation of Data.
**ACIDUH** Association des Carrefours Interprofessionnels du Droit de l'Urbanisme et de l'Habitat (France).
*French Association.*
**ACIF** Associazione Culturale Italo-Francese.
**ACII** Associate of the Chartered Insurance Institute.
**ACIL** ACE installation list.
liste des installations du CAE.
**ACIL** Amsterdam Classics In Linguistics.
**ACIL** Associazione Concessionari Italiani Lancia (Italy).
**ACIM** American Committee on Italian Migration.
**ACIMALL** Associazione Costruttori Italiani Macchine e Accessori per la Lavorazione del Legno (Italy).

**ACIMGA**; **Acimga** Associazione Costruttori Italiani Macchine Grafiche, Cartotecniche e Affini.
Acimga is located in Milan, Italy.
**ACIMIT** Associazione Costruttori Italiani di Macchinario per l'Industria Tessile.
*Textile Industry Machinery.*
**ACIMM**; **Acimm** Associazione costruttori italiani macchine per marmo ed affini.
Acimm is located in Cinisello Balsamo (Milan), Italy.
**ACINT** acoustic intelligence.
renseignement acoustique.
**ACIP** Active Certificate Information Program.
**ACIP** Advisory Committee on Immunization Practices (U.S.A.).
**ACIS** Advanced Communications and Information Systems.
**ACIS** Alto Commissariato per l'Igiene e la Sanità (Italy).
Italian acronym of the: Office of the High Commissioner of Public Health.
**ACIS** Associate of the Chartered Institute of Secretaries.
**ACIST** Associazione Corsi Istruzione Specializzazione Tecnica (Italy).
**ACI test** Adult-Child Interaction test.
**ACIU** Danish Center for International Training Programs (Denmark).
**ACJS** Academy of Criminal Justice Sciences (U.S.A.).
The ACJS is an international organization established in 1963 to foster professional and scholarly activities in the field of criminal justice.
**ACJS Today** Academy of Criminal Justice Sciences (Publication).
Published quarterly. Provides the current news and activities of ACJS, individual accomplishments, and articles.
**ack**; **ak.** (abbr.) acknowledgement.
Also: **ackt.**
*Telecommunications.*
**ACL** Administration et Consommateur en Ligne.
French initialism meaning: administration-to-consumer (A2C).
**ACL** allowable cabin/cargo load.
charge autorisée de la cabine.
**ACL** All weather Carrier Landing.
**ACL** Association for Computational Linguists.
**ACL** Association of Christian Libraries.
**a.c.l.** assurance contre l'incendie.
French initialism meaning: fire insurance.
**ACL** Audit Command Language.
*Computers.*
**ACL** Automobile Club du Grand-Duché de Luxembourg.
**ACLANT** Allied Command, Atlantic [replaced by SC Atlantic].
Commandement allié de l'Atlantique [remplacé par le SC Atlantic].
**ACLCP** Associated College Libraries of Central Pennsylvania (U.S.A.).
**ACLIS** Australian Council of Libraries and Information Services (Australia).
**ACLM** American College of Legal Medicine.
**ACLO** Associational Church Library Organization.
**ACLR** Apricot Chlorotic Leaf Roll.
**ACLS** American Council of Learned Societies.
**ACLU** American Civil Liberties Union.
**ACM** 1. acoustic countermeasures.
1. contre-mesures acoustiques.
2. air combat manoeuvre.
2. manœuvre de combat aérien.
3. airspace control means.
3. moyens de contrôle de l'espace aérien.
4. airspace control measure.
4. mesure de contrôle de l'espace aérien.
**ACM** Advanced Composite Materials.
**ACM** Air Chief Marshal.
**ACM** Association for Computing Machinery.
The ACM is located in Washington D.C., U.S.A.
**ACM** Atom-Cavity Microscope.
**ACM** Authorized Controlled Material.
**ACMA** Associazione nazionale Ciclo Moto Accessori (Italy).
**ACMC** ACCS Configuration Management Committee.
Comité de gestion de la configuration de l'ACCS.
**ACMC** African Capital Market Conference.
ACMC School of Management - University of Michigan (U.S.A.).
**ACMC** Association of Canadian Medical Colleges (Canada).
**ACME** Advisory Committee on the Marine Environment.
Of the International Council for the Exploration of the Sea.
**ACME** Association of Consulting Management Engineers.
**ACMI** air combat manoeuvring instrumentation.
instrumentation de suivi de la manœuvre de combat aérien.
**ACMI** Associazione Credit Managers Italiani (Italy).
**ACML** Association of Canadian Map Libraries (Canada).
**ACMP** Advisory Committee on Marine Pollution.

Of the International Council for the Exploration of the Sea.

**ACMP** Allied Configuration Management Publication.
publication interalliée - gestion de la configuration.

**ACMR** air combat manoeuvring range.
polygone d'entraînement à la manœuvre de combat aérien.

**ACMRR** Advisory Committee of Experts on Marine Resources Research.

**ACMS** Aerosol Composition Mass Spectrometer.
*Atmospheric Physics; Meteorology; Middle Atmosphere Research.*

**ACMS** automated communications management system.
système automatisé de gestion des télécommunications.

**ACN** Acrylonitrile or Vinylcyanide.
$CH_2$=CHCN. A colorless liquid that is soluble in organic solvents. It is used mainly in acrylic rubber.
*Organic Chemistry.*

**ACN** Air Consignment Note.
*Transportation.*

**ACN** Asian Chemical News.
A weekly news magazine for the Asian Chemical Industry.

**ACNI** Azienda Comunale Navigazione Interna (Italy).

**A.C.N.I.N.** Associazione Culturale Nazionale Igienistiche Naturali (Italy).

**ACNP** American College of Neuropsychopharmacology (U.S.A.).

**AcNPV** *Autographa californica* Nuclear Polyhedrosis Virus.

**ACNS** Advanced Communications Network Service.

**ACNUR** Alto Commissariato delle Nazioni Unite per i Rifugiati - U.N.

**ACO** Adaptible Control Optimization.

**ACO** 1. airspace control order.
1. ordre de contrôle de l'espace aérien.
2. airspace coordination order.
2. ordre de coordination aérienne.

**ACO** Alternating Current Outputs.

**ACO** Association of Commissioned Officers.

**ACO** Average Calculating Operation.
The average calculating operation is used to estimate computers calculation speeds.
*Computer Programming.*

**ACOA** Adult Children Of Alcoholics.

**ACodP** Allied Codification Publication.
publication interalliée sur la codification.

**ACOG** agence civile OTAN du temps de guerre.
NATO civil wartime agency (NCWA).

**ACOH** Advisory Committee for Operational Hydrology.
Of the World Meteorological Organization.

**A.Coll.H.** Associate of the College of Handicraft.

**AComP** Allied Communications Publication.
publication interalliée sur les communications.

**ACOMR** Advisory Committee on Oceanic Meteorological Research.
Of the World Meteorological Organization.

**ACOP** Associação de Conselheiros de Orientação Profissional (Portugal).
*Portuguese Associations; Vocational Guidance.*

**ACOPS** Advisory Committee On Protection of the Sea.

**ACORD** Advisory Council On Research and Development (G.B.).

**ACOS** Assistant Chief of Staff.
sous-chef d'état-major (SCEM 2.).

**ACOST** Advisory Council On Science and Technology (G.B.).

**ACP** Acyl Carrier Protein.
The ACP is a protein in fatty acid synthesis.
*Biochemistry.*

**ACP** 1. advanced command post.
1. poste de commandement de l'avant.
2. airborne command post.
2. poste de commandement volant.
3. airspace control plan.
3. plan de contrôle de l'espace aérien.
4. Allied Communications Publication.
4. publication interalliée sur les communications.

**ACP** African, Caribbean and Pacific (Group of Countries).

**ACP** American College of Physicians (U.S.A.).

**ACP** Archean Churchill Province (Canada).

**ACP** Associate of the College of Preceptors.

**ACP** Association of Correctors of the Press.

**ACP** Automatic Colt Pistol.

**ACPA** Association of Computer Programmers and Analysts.

**A/CPay** Account Payable.

**ACPC** Association of Coffee Producing Countries.

**ACPF approach** Averaged-Coupled Pair Functional approach.

**ACPM** Association de formation pour la Coopération et la Promotion (France).

**acpt.** (abbr.) accept; acceptance.
Also: **acc.**; **accpt.**; **acce**.

**acq.** (abbr.) acquittement.

French abbreviation meaning: (*Law*) acquittal, discharge; (*Commerce*) settlement, balance.
**ACQM** Automatic Circuit Quality Monitoring.
**ACQS** Association of Consultant Quantity Surveyors.
**acqt.** acquit.
French abbreviation meaning: paid for; paid (in full discharge of a debt).
*Business; Commerce; Finance.*
**acquis.** (abbr.) acquisition/s.
**ACR** Accelerated Cost Reçovery.
**ACR** Active Cavity Radiometer.
**ACR** 1. air control and reporting.
1. détection et contrôle aériens.
2. airfield control radar.
2. radar de contrôle d'aérodrome.
**ACR** Alternate Current Recovery.
**ACR**; **A.C.R.** American College of Radiology.
**ACR** American College of Rheumatology.
**ACR** Anomalous Cosmic Rays.
**ACR** Approach Control Radar.
*Electronics.*
**ACRA** Associazione di Cooperazione Rurale in Africa e America Latina (Italy).
Italian acronym of the: Association for Rural Cooperation in Africa and Latin America.
**A.C.R.A.M.** Associazione Culturale per il Recupero delle Arti Minori (Italy).
**ACRC** Arkansas Cancer Research Center (U.S.A.).
**acrd.** (abbr.) accrued.
**ACRE** Advisory Committee on Releases to the Environment (G.B.).
The ACRE and the Advisory Committee on Novel Foods and Processes examine all applications to plant experimental GM crops or sell GM foods.
*Genetically Modified Crops/Foods.*
**ACRE** Associate Citizens for Responsible Education.
A group opposing sex education in U.S. schools.
**ACRE** Automatic Checkout and Readiness Equipment.
**acre** The above acronyms were coined accidentally using the Italian word "acre" which means: acrid (*Biology*).
**A/C Rec.** Accounts Receivable.
**acr-ft.** acre-foot.
**acr-ft./d.** acre-foot per day.
*Metrology.*
**ACRI** American Cocoa Research Institute (U.S.A.).
**ACRI** Association of Crown Research Institutes (New Zealand).
**ACRI** Associazione fra le Casse di Risparmio Italiane (Italy).
Italian initialism of the: Association of Italian Savings Banks.
**ACRIM II** Active Cavity Radiometer Irradiance Monitor II.
ACRIM II was launched in 1991. It is capable of recording solar brightness during an 11-year sunspot cycle.
*Climate; Global Change.*
**acr-in.** acre-inch.
**ACRL** Association of College and Research Libraries.
**ACRN** Acrylonitrile.
For further details see under: **ACN**.
*Organic Chemistry.*
**ACRO** Applicazioni Cliniche della Ricerca Oncologica (Italy).
**ACROSS** ACE Resources Optimization Software System.
système logiciel d'optimisation des ressources du CAE.
**ACRS** Accelerated Capital Recovery System; Accelerated Cost Recovery System.
**ACRS** Advisory Committee on Reactor Safeguards.
**ACRs** Ancient evolutionarily Conserved Regions.
*Biotechnology; Genetics; Medicine.*
**ACRS** Assured Crew Rescue System.
**ACRV** Assured Crew Return Vehicle; Astronaut Crew Return Vehicle.
**ACS** Accuracy Control System.
*Computer Programming.*
**ACS** Adaptive Control System.
*Control Systems; Robotics.*
**ACS** Advances Communications Service.
**ACS** 1. aircraft cross-servicing.
1. services mutuels pour aéronefs.
2. airspace control system.
2. système de contrôle de l'espace aérien.
**ACS** Alaska Clean Seas.
ACS is a Research Cooperative funded by twelve Oil and Gas Companies.
**ACS**; **A.C.S.** American Cancer Society.
**ACS** American Chemical Society; American College of Surgeons (U.S.A.).
**ACS** American Community Survey.
*U.S. Demography.*
**ACS** Antireticular Cytotoxic Serum.
**ACS** Anticoincidence Shield.
*Lunar Research.*
**ACS** ARS Consensus Sequence.
**Acs** Autistics and cousins.
**ACS** Automatic Control System.
**ACSAD** Arab Centre for the Studies of Arid Zones and Dry Lands (Syria).

**ACSEC** Allied Courier Services Executive Committee.
Comité exécutif des services de courrier alliés.
**ACSES** Automated Computer Science Education System.
**ACSF** Association des Centres Serveurs Français.
French initialism of the: Association of French Server Centers.
**ACSF perfusion** Artificial Cerebrospinal Fluid perfusion.
*Biochemistry; Biomedicine; Neurophysiology; Psychiatry.*
**ACSL** Advanced Continuous Simulation Language.
**ACSL** Association of Church and Synagogue Libraries.
**ACSM** American College of Sports Medicine.
**ACSM** American Congress on Surveying and Mapping (U.S.A.).
**ACSM** Assemblies, Components, Spare parts and Materials.
**A/Cs Pay.** Accounts Payable.
**ACSR** Aluminum Cable Steel-Reinforced.
The ACSR is a type of power transmission line comprising an aluminum conductor having a core of steel.
*Electricity.*
**A/Cs Rec.** Accounts Receivable.
**ACSTI** Advisory Committee for Scientific and Technical Information.
**ACSYS** Arctic Climate SYstem Study.
Of the World Climate Research Program.
**act.** (abbr.) acting.
**act.** (abbr.) active.
*Computer Programming; Electronics; Space Technology; Volcanology.*
**act.** (abbr.) actor; actual; actuary.
**ACT** Advance Corporation Tax.
*Business; Finance.*
**ACT** American College Test.
**ACT** Association of Classroom Teachers.
**ACT** Associazione Culturale per il Turismo.
*Italian Association.*
**ACT** Australian Capital Territory.
**ACTA** America's Carriers Telecommunications Association (U.S.A.).
**ACTAS** Alliance of Computer-based Telephony Application Suppliers.
**ACTE** Association of Corporate Travel Executives (U.S.A., Virginia-based).
**ACTEL** Alternating Current Thin-film ELectroluminescence.
**ACTFL** American Council on the Teaching of Foreign Languages (U.S.A.).
**ACTG** AIDS Clinical Trials Group (called Protocol 019) NIAID's, U.S.A.
For further details see under: **NIAID**.
**ACTH** Adrenocorticotropic Hormone.
The ACTH is the secretion of the corticotrophs of the anterior pituitary gland. The adrenocorticotropic hormone is also known as: Adrenotropic Hormone.
*Endocrinology.*
**ACTI** Associazione Campeggiatori d'Italia.
*Italian Association.*
**ACTICE** Agence pour la coordination des transports intérieurs du Centre-Europe.
Agency for the Coordination of Inland Transport in Central Europe.
**Actim** Agence pour la coopération technique, industrielle et économique.
French acronym of the: Agency for technical, industrial and economic cooperation (France).
**ACTIMED** Agence pour la coordination des transports intérieurs en Méditerranée.
Agency for the Coordination of Inland Transport in the Mediterranean.
**ACTL** American Course of Trial Lawyers.
**ACTL** Associazione per la Cultura e il Tempo Libero.
*Italian Association.*
**actnt.** (abbr.) accountant.
Also: **acct**.
**ACTORD** activation order.
Ordre d'activation.
**ACT program** American College Testing program.
**ACTREQ** activation request.
demande d'activation.
**ACTS** Advanced Communications Technologies and Services.
*E.C. Programs.*
**ACTS** Advanced Communications Technology Satellite.
**ACTS** African Center for Technology Studies.
**ACTS** Application Control and Teleprocessing System.
**ACTSU** Association of Computer Time-Sharing Users.
**ACT UP** AIDS Coalition To Unleash Power.
*AIDS Vaccine Research.*
**Act.Val.** (abbr.) Actual Value.
*Business; Commerce; Finance.*
**ACTWARN** activation warning.
avertissement d'activation.
**AcU** Actinouranium.
Actinouranium is now called: uranium-235.
*Nuclear Physics.*

**ACU** air(craft) control unit.
1a. unité contrôleur des aéronefs (ou contrôleur Air).
1b. unité de contrôle aérien.
**ACU** Arithmetic Control Unit.
**ACU** Association of Computer Users.
**ACU** Associazione Consumatori Utenti.
ACU was previously known as: Agrisalus (Associazione Italiana Agricoltura Alimentazione Salute Difesa Consumatori). Created in 1984.
**ACU** Autocycle Union.
**ACU** Automatic Calling Unit.
*Telecommunications.*
**ACUG** Association of Computer User Groups.
**ACULE** Association of Credit Union League Executives.
**ACUM** Annales, Centre Universitaire Mediterranéen (Nice).
*Publication.*
**ACURIL** Association of Caribbean University and Research Libraries.
**ACUS** Administrative Conference of the United States (U.S.A.).
**ACUs** Asian Currency Units.
**ACUTA** Association of College and University Telecommunications Administrators.
**ACUTE** Accountants Computer Users Technical Exchange.
**ACV** Actual Cash Value.
*Business; Finance.*
**ACV** Air-Cushion Vehicle.
ACV is also known as: Ground-Effect Machine.
*Mechanical Engineering.*
**ACV (unità)** (Unità) Analisi Crimine Violento.
Italian initialism meaning: Unit for Violent Crime Analysis.
**ACW** Alternating Continuous Waves.
**ACW** anti-carrier warfare.
lutte anti-porte-avions (LAPA).
**ACW** (abbr.) Anticlockwise.
**ACWA** Amalgamated Clothing Workers of America.
**ACWA** Associate of the Institute of Costs and Works Accountants.
**ACWF** Actual Cost of Work Flow.
*Business; Commerce; Economics; Finance.*
**ACWP** Actual Cost for Work Performed.
*Business; Commerce; Economics; Finance.*
**ACWS** Airborne Collision Warning System.
**ACYF** Administration for Children, Youth, and Families (U.S.A.).
**Acyl-HSL** Acylated Homoserine Lactone.
*Cellular Biology; Microbial Genetics; Microbiology; Molecular Genetics.*
**AD** Accrued Dividend.
*Business; Economics; Finance.*
**AD** Acoustic Detection.
*Acoustical Engineering.*
**AD** Acoustic Dispersion.
*Acoustics.*
**AD** Acqua Dolce.
Italian initialism meaning: fresh water / freshwater / fresh-water.
*Biology; Hydrology.*
**A.D.** Active Duty.
*Military.*
**ad.** (abbr.) advantage.
**ad.** (abbr.) advertisement / advertising.
Also: **advt.**; **adv.**
**AD** After Date.
*Banking; Finance.*
**A.D.** Aggregate Demand.
*Economics.*
**AD** Air Defense.
The term air defense refers to measures to destroy attacks by enemy aircraft or missiles.
*Military Science.*
**AD** Air-Dried.
*Materials Science.*
**AD** Alzheimer's Disease.
The Alzheimer's disease is a progressive, irreversible disease that develops after age 40.
*Medicine.*
**A/D** Analog / Digital.
**AD** Antiproton Decelerator.
At CERN, the European particle physics laboratory near Geneva, Switzerland.
*Antimatter; Mirror-image Atoms; Physics.*
**AD** Anxiety Disorder.
*Psychology.*
**AD** Assistant Director; Associate Director.
**AD** Audio Device.
An audio device can be any of a wide range of computer components that accept or produce sound.
*Computer Technology.*
**AD** Availability Date.
*Business; Commerce.*
**AD** Average Deviation.
Average Deviation is also known as: Mean Deviation.
*Mathematics.*
**AD** Aviation Division.
**ADA** Adenosine Deaminase.
*Enzymology.*

**ADA** Air Defense Artillery.
The term air defense artillery refers to equipment / weapons for combating air targets from the ground.
*Military.*

**ADA** Aluminiurn Dihydroxyaminoacetate.
*Pharmacology.*

**ADA** American Dental Association; American Dermatological Association; American Dietetic Association (U.S.A.).

**ADA** Americans for Democratic Action.

**ADA** Americans with Disabilities Act (U.S.A.).
ADA became law in the summer of 1992. This federal law - often called "the Bill of Rights for the Disabled" - has a part of its stated purpose "to provide a clear and comprehensive national mandate for the elimination of discrimination against individuals with disabilities".
*U.S. Federal Law.*

**ADA** Applied Decision Analysis.

**ADA** Atom Development Administration.

**ADA** Automatic Document Analysis.

**ADA** Average Daily Attendance.

**ADAB** Assistant Director of the Army Budget.

**adab** The above acronym was coined accidentally using the Arabic word "adab" which means: education; good manners; politeness; graciousness.

**ADAC** Art and Design Advisory Council.

**ADAC** Avion à Décollage et Atterrissage Courts.
French acronym meaning: Short Take-Off and Landing Aircraft.

**Adaci** Associazione degli approvvigionatori e compratori italiani.
Italian acronym of the: Association of Italian Suppliers and Buyers. Founded in 1968. Based in Milan (Italy).

**ADA deficiency** Adenosine Deaminase deficiency.
ADA deficiency is a rare severe immune disorder. A patented experimental gene therapy to treat this disorder was developed by U.S. molecular biologists in 1995.
*Gene Therapy; Molecular Biology; Patents.*

**ADAF models** Advection-Dominated Accretion Flow models.
*Advection; Astronomy; Astrophysics; Meteorology.*

**ADAM** Academic Document by Advanced Microprocessor.

**ADAM** Adaptive Arithmetical Method.

**ADAM** ADvanced Architecture in Medicine.

**ADAM** Advanced DAta Management.

**ADAM** Air base Damage Assessment Model.

**ADAM** 1. air defence and airspace management.
1. défense aérienne et gestion de l'espace aérien.
2. area denial artillery munition.
2. munition d'artillerie d'interdiction de zone.

**ADAM** Air Defense Antimissile.

**ADAM** Analog Data Acquisition Module.

**ADAM** Automatic Distance and Angle Measurement.

**ADAMHA** Alcohol, Drug Abuse and Mental Health Administration.
Part of the Public Health Service U.S. Department of Health. ADAMHA has been replaced by SAMHSA.
For further details see under: **SAMHSA**.

**ADAMS** Aggregate DAta Management System.
*European Community Project; Information Processing; Information Systems; Mathematics; Statistics.*

**ADAMS** Allied Deployment and Movement System.
système de soutien interallié des déploiments et des mouvements [anciennement appelé JRMS].

**ADAN** Associazione Degli Albergatori Napoletani (Naples, Italy).

**ADAPT** Accent on Developing Abstract Processes and Thought.

**ADAPT** Active Duty Assistance Program Team.

**ADAPT** ADaptation of Automatically Programmed Tools.
*Data Processing.*

**ADAPT** Alcohol and Drug Abuse Prevention Treatment.

**ADAPT** Analog-Digital Automatic Program Tester.
*Data Processing.*

**ADAR** Advanced Design Array Radar.
*Military.*

**ADARA** American Deafness And Rehabilitation Association (U.S.A.).

**ADARs** Adenosine Deaminases Acting on RNA.
*Human Genetics; Molecular Biology.*

**AD-AS** Aggregate Demand-Aggregate Supply.

**ADAS** Airborne Data Acquisition System.

**ADatP** Allied Data Processing Publication.
Publication interalliée sur le traitement des données.

**ADATS** air defence antitank system.
système de défense antichar et antiaérienne.

**ADAV** Avion à Decollage et Atterissage Verticaux.
French acronym meaning: Vertical Take-Off and Landing Aircraft.

**ADB** Adjusted Debit Balance.

**ADB** Asiatic Development Bank.

**ADBACI** Association pour le Développement de la Documentation, des Bibliothèques et Archives de la Côte d'lvoire (Ivory Coast).

**ADBS** Association des Documentalistes et des Bibliothécaires Spécialisés.
**ADBT** Associate Director for Biomedical Technology.
**ADC** Advanced Development Center.
**ADC** Aid to Dependent Children.
**ADC** Aide-De-Camp.
**ADC** Analog-to-Digital Conversion.
**ADC** Analog-to-Digital Converter.
The ADC is a device that changes continuous analog signals into digital or discrete signals.
Also: **A/D converter**.
*Electronics.*
**ADC** Assistant Division Commander.
**ADCAV** aéronef à décollage court et atterrissage vertical.
Short take-off and vertical landing aircraft (STOVL).
**ADCB** Abu Dhabi Commercial Bank.
United Arab Emirates.
**ADCC** air defence control centre.
centre de contrôle de défense aérienne.
**ADCC** Antibody-Dependent Cell-mediated Cytotoxicity.
*Immunology.*
**ADCCP** Advanced Data Communications Control Procedure.
**ADCC phenomenon** Antibody-dependent Cell-mediated Cytotoxicity phenomenon.
*Immunology.*
**ADCM** Associate Director Comparative Medicine.
**ADCO** Air Defence Coordination Organization.
Organisation de coordination de la défense aérienne.
**ADCOM** administrative command.
commandement administratif.
**ADCON** ADdress CONstant.
*Computer Programming.*
For further details see under: **AC**.
**ADCON** administrative control.
contrôle administratif.
**A/D converter** Analog-to-Digital converter.
For further details see under: **ADC**.
*Electronics.*
**ADCP** Acoustic Doppler Current Profiler.
**ADC2S** ACE Deployable Command and Control System.
système déployable de commandement et de contrôle du CAE.
**ADC values** Apparent Depth of Compensation values.
**ADD** Acoustic Deception Device.
**ADD** Acoustic Detection Device.
**ADD** Acoustic Discrimination of Decays.
**add.** (abbr.) addenda.
**ADD** The airport code for Addis Ababa.
**add.** (abbr.) addressed.
**add.** (abbr.) addition.
*Chemistry; Mathematics.*
**ADD.** (abbr.) adduction.
Adduction is the movement of a body part toward the main axis of the body or toward another part of the body.
*Physiology.*
**ADD.** (abbr.) adductor.
The adductor is a muscle that draws a body part toward the midline axis.
*Anatomy.*
**ADD** Administration on Developmental Disabilities (U.S.A.).
**ADD** Aerospace Digital Development; Aerospace Defense Development.
**ADD** air defence district.
district de défense aérienne.
**ADD** American Dialect Dictionary.
**ADD** Attention Deficit Disorder.
*Medicine; Psychology.*
**ADD** Automatic Distribution of Documents.
Of the U.S. Department of Defense.
**ADDEPOS** Associazione dei Diritti e dei Doveri dei POSitivi e Portatori del Virus dell'AIDS (Italy).
**ADDER** Automatic Digital-Data-Error Recorder.
**addr.** (abbr.) addressing.
*Computer Programming.*
**ADE** Associazione Disabili E Handicappati.
*Italian Association.*
**ADEBIO** French Association for the Development of Biotechnology and the Bioindustry.
**ADEC** Alaska's Department of Environmental Conservation.
**adee** (abbr.) addressee.
**ADEL** Agence pour le Développement de l'Economie Locale (France).
French acronym of the: Agency for Local Economics Development.
**ADEM** Asociación de Empresarias Mexicanas A.C. (Mexico).
*Mexican Association.*
**ADEOS** ADvanced Earth Observing Satellite.
**ADEPA** Association pour le DEveloppement de la Production Automatisée.
**ADEPT** Aerospace Draftsman's Education and Proficiency Training.
**ADEPT** Agricultural and Diary Educational Political Trust.

**ADEPT** Air Force Depot Equipment Performance Tester.
**ADEPT** Automatic Data Extractor and Plotting Table.
**ADEPT** Automatic Dynamic Evaluation by Programmed Tester.
**ADEPT program** Assisting in Deployment of Energy Practices and Technologies program.
Of the U.S. Department Of Energy.
**ADETEM** Association pour le DEveloppement des TEchniques de Marketing.
French acronym of the: Association for the Development of Marketing Techniques.
**ADETIM** Association pour le Développement des Techniques des Industries Mécaniques.
French acronym of the: Association for the DEvelopment of Mechanical Industries Techniques (France).
**ADEW** air defence early warning.
1a. alerte lointaine de défense aérienne.
1b. détection lointaine de défense aérienne.
**ADEX** air defence exercise.
exercise de défense aérienne.
**ADF** Administrator's Discretionary Fund.
**ADF**; **adf** Aircraft Direction Finder.
**ADF** Algorithm Development Facility.
**ADF**; **adf** Automatic Direction Finder or Radio Compass.
*Navigation.*
**ADF branch** Advanced Development Facility branch.
Of the Forecast Systems Laboratory - U.S. National Oceanic and Atmospheric Administration.
**AD(G)** air defence (ground).
défense aérienne (sol).
**ADG** air defence gun.
canon antiaérien.
**ADGB** Air Defence of Great Britain (G.B.).
**ADGE** Air Defence Ground Environment.
infrastructure électronique de défense aérienne.
**adh.** (abbr.) adhesive.
*Materials Science; Physics; Science.*
**ADH** Antidiuretic Hormone.
Antidiuretic Hormone is also known as: Arginine Vasopressin.
*Endocrinology.*
**ADHD** Attention-Deficit Hyperactivity Disorder.
The ADHD is a disorder with genetic as well as environmental determinants manifested by hyperactivity, inattention and impulsivity.
*Cell Biology; Endocrinology; Genetics; Medicine; Neurobiology; Psychiatry; Personality Traits.*
**ADI** Acceptable Daily Intake.
ADI refers to the amount of chemicals as food additives used without harming human beings.
*Food Technology.*
**ADI** air defence interceptor.
intercepteur de défense aérienne.
**ADI** Air Defense Institute; Air Distribution Institute.
**AdI** Alliance des Independants.
French acronym of the: Independent Party (Swiss).
**ADI** Allowable Daily Intake.
**ADI** Altitude Direction Indicator.
**ADI** American Defense Institute (U.S.A.).
**Adi** Associazione del disegno industriale.
Italian acronym of the: Industrial Design Association (Italy).
**ADI** Australian Defence Industries.
**ADI** Average Daily Intake.
**adi** The above acronyms were coined accidentally using the colloquial Arabic word "adi" which means: judge.
**ADIA** Academy of Diplomacy and Intemational Affairs.
ADIA was founded in 1972.
**ADIA** Africa Dissertation Intership Awards.
**ADIBOR** Abu Dhabi Interbank Offered Rate.
*Banking; Business; Finance.*
**Adica**; **ADICA** Associazione Nazionale Distributori Carta (Milan, Italy).
Italian acronym of the: National Association of Paper Distributors.
**Adico** Associazione dei direttori commerciali e Marketing Managers.
Italian acronym of the: Association of Sales Managers and Marketing Managers. Founded in 1964. Based in Milan, Italy.
**ADICOR** Associazione DIfesa COnsumatori e Risparmiatori (Italy).
**ADIEF** Association pour le Développement des Initiatives Economiques pour les Femmes.
French acronym of the: French Association for the Development of Women Economic Initiatives.
**ADIOS** Asian Dust Input to the Oceanic System.
**ADIPs** Accelerated Development and Introduction Plans.
A framework to introduce vaccines into the developing world.
For further details see under: **GAVI**.
**ADivP** Allied Diving Publication.
publication interalliée-plongée.
**ADIZ** air defence identification zone.
Zone d'identification de défense aérienne.
**adj.** (abbr.) adjust.
**adj.** (abbr.) adjustable.
*Mechanical Devices.*

**adj.** (abbr.) adjustment.
*Engineering; Metrology; Psychology.*
**ADK** Adenylate Kinase.
*Biochemistry.*
**ADL** Activities of Daily Living.
The activities of daily living are the routine activities and skills that a normal daily existence entails.
*Medicine.*
**ADL** 1. Ada-based programme and design language [obsolete].
1. langage de programmation et de conception basé sur l'Ada [obsolète].
2. Allied disposition list.
2. liste des forces alliées mises à disposition.
3. automatic data link.
3. liaison automatique de transmission de données.
**ADL** Adductor Longus.
*Muscles.*
**ADL** Application - Development Language.
*Computer Programming.*
**ADL process** Arthur D. Little extractive coking process.
**AdlV** Associazione dipendenti laici del Vaticano (Italy).
**ADM** Acoustic Digital Memory; Activity Data Method.
**ADM** Adaptive Delta Modulation.
**AdM** Adrenal Medulla.
*Anatomy.*
**adm.** (abbr.) administration; administrative.
Also: **admin.**; **admn.**
**ADM**; **adm** (abbr.) Admiral; Admiralty.
**ADM** Advanced Diploma in Midwifery (G.B.).
**ADM** Air Defense Missile.
**ADM** Assistant Deputy Minister (Canada).
**ADM** 1. Atomic demolition munition.
1. charge nucléaire statique.
2. arme de destruction massive.
2. weapon of mass destruction /WMD/.
**ADM** Automated Drafting Machine.
**ADM** Automatic Degreasing Machine.
**ADM** Automatic Detection Mark.
**ADM** Automatic Display Mode.
*Data Processing.*
**ADMD** ADministration Management Domain.
*Computers.*
**ADME studies** Absorption, Digestion, Metabolism, and Excretion studies.
**ADMG** air defence machine gun.
mitrailleuse antiaérienne.
**admin.** (abbr.) administration; administrative.
Also: **adm.**; **admn.**
**admin.** (abbr.) administrator.
Also: **admr.**
**Ad ML** Adenoviral Major Late Py-tracts.
*Cell Biology; Molecular Medicine; Nucleic Acids.*
**ADML** atomic demolition munition location.
emplacement des charges nucléaires statiques.
**AdMLP** Adenovirus Major Late Promoter.
**admn.** (abbr.) administration.
Also: **adm.**; **admin.**
**ADMO** Associazione Donatori Midollo Osseo.
Italian initialism of the: Bone-Marrow Donors Association.
**ADMP** air defence modernization plan.
programme de modernisation de la défense aérienne.
**admr.** (abbr.) administrator.
Also: **admin.**
**ADN** Advanced Digital Network.
**ADNFLE** Autosomal Dominant Nocturnal Frontal Lobe Epilepsy.
*Human Genetics; Medicine; Neurology.*
**ADN Natif** Acide Désoxyribonucléique Natif.
French initialism meaning: Native DNA.
*Medicine.*
**ADNOC** Abu Dhabi National Oil Company.
**ADNOM** (abbr.) ADministrative NOMenclature.
The ADNOM is a Norwegian Project for Multilingual Administrative Nomenclature.
**ADOC** air defence operations centre.
centre d'opérations de la défense aérienne (CODA).
**ADOC** Associazione per la Difesa e l'Orientamento dei Consumatori (Italy).
ADOC was created 16 years ago.
**AdoCbl** Adenosylcobalamin.
*Biochemistry; Chemistry; Cofactor Biochemistry; Spectroscopy.*
**ADOLT** air defence operations liaison team.
équipe de liaison des opérations de défense aérienne.
**ADONAI** Associazione Donne Organizzate Nell'Arte Internazionale.
Italian acronym of the: Association of Women organized in Intemational Art.
**Adonai** The above acronym was coined accidentally using the word "Adonai" which is the name of the God of the Hebrews.
**ADOT** Arizona Department Of Transportation (U.S.A.).
**ADP** Adenosine Diphosphate.
$C_{10}H_{15}N_5O_{10}P_2$ - Adenosine diphosphate is a coenzyme involved in energy metabolism.
*Biochemistry.*
**ADP** Applications Development Program.

**ADP** Automated Data Processing.
**ADP** Automatic Data Processing.
*Computer Technology; Computer Programming.*
**ADPase** Adenosinediphosphatase.
*Enzymology.*
**ADPE** Automatic Data-Processing Equipment.
The ADPE consists of computers and related devices used in data processing.
*Computer Technology.*
**ADPG** Architecte Diplomé Par le Gouvernement (France).
**ADPGP** Adenosine Diphosphate Glucose Pyrophosphorylase.
**ADPKD** Autosomal Dominant Polycystic Kidney Disease.
The appropriate location of the ADPKD gene was identified by U.S. Researchers in 1985.
*Genetics.*
**ADP/O** Adenosine Diphosphate/Oxygen.
**ADR** Accidents et Délits Routiers.
French initialism meaning: Road Accidents and Crimes.
**ADR** 1. aerodrome damage repair.
1. réparation des dégâts subis pas un aérodrome.
2. air defence radar.
2. radar de défense aérienne.
3. air défence region.
3. région de défense aérienne.
**ADR** Aeroporti Di Roma (Italy).
**ADR** Assets Depreciation Range.
*Accounting.*
**ADR** Automatic Dividend Reinvestment.
*Banking; Business; Finance.*
**ADR** Average Discount Rates.
**A-D ratio** Advance-Decline ratio.
**ADREP** air defence representative.
représentant de la défense aérienne.
**ADRIA** Associazione Di Ricerca Intolleranze Alimentari.
Italian acronym of the: Association for Food Allergy Research.
**adrm.** (abbr.) airdrome.
Also: **airport**; **airfield**.
*Aviation.*
**ADROE** air defence rules of engagement.
règles d'engagement de la défense aérienne.
**ADRs** American Depository Receipts; Authorized Depository Receipts (U.S.A.).
*Banking.*
**ADRS** Asset Depreciation Range System.
*Business; Finance.*
**ADRS** automatic data reporting system [obsolete].
système de compte rendu automatique de données [obsolète].
**A.d.S.** Académie des Sciences (France).
French initialism of the: Academy of Sciences.
**ADS** Accertamento Diffusione Stampa.
Italian initialism meaning: Audit Bureau of Circulation.
**ADS** Action Dynamique Spécifique des Aliments.
French initialism meaning: Specific Dynamic Action of Food.
**ADS** Active Directory Service.
A component that allows IT Managers to securely manage IT systems.
*Windows.*
For further details see under: **IT**.
**ADS**; **ads.** Advertisement.
**ADS** Antidiuretic Substance.
**ADS** Archaeology Data Service - Based at the University of York (G.B.).
**ADS** Atmospheric Diving Suit.
**a.d.s.** autograph document, signed.
**ADSAP** Accelerated Degradation of Soil Applied Pesticides.
*European Community Project.*
**ADSC** Air Defence Software Committee.
Comité du logiciel de défense aérienne.
**ADSD** Air Defence Systems Directorate.
Direction des systèmes de défense aérienne.
**ADSET** Association of Databank Services in Education and Training (G.B.).
**ADSF** Adipocyte-specific Secretory Factor.
A recombinant mouse resistin.
*Diabetes; Obesity.*
**ADSID** Air-Delivered Seismic Intrusion Detector.
**ADSL technology** Asymmetric Digital Subscriber Loop technology.
The ADSL is a system which can deliver data to the office or home across existing copper wire instead of requiring fibre.
*Broadband Technologies.*
**ADSM techniques** Active Disassembly using Smart Materials techniques.
*Smart Materials; Recycling.*
For further details see under: **SMAs**; **SMPs** and **WEEE**.
**ADT** Average Daily Traffic.
*Transportation Engineering.*
**Aduc** Associazione per i diritti degli utenti consumatori (Italy).
**ADUS** Associazione Docenti Universitari Subalterni (Italy).
**adv.** (abbr.) advance.
**adv.** (abbr.) advertisement.

Also: **ad.**; **advt.**; **advert.**
**adv.** (abbr.) advice; advise; advisory.
**ADVACAST** ADVanced aluminium-precision CASTing for integrally stiffened net-shape components.
Daimler-Benz Aerospace launched ADVACAST in 1991 in partnership with foundries Ciral (France), Thyssen (Germany), Mirtec (Greece) and the Universities of Lisbon, Munich and Patras (Greece).
*European Community Project.*
**ADVANCE** Association on Development of Vocations And New Creative Employment (Italy).
*Transnational Projects.*
**Adv.Chgs.** (abbr.) Advance Charges.
*Business; Commerce.*
**Ad vector** Adenoviral vector.
*Anatomy; Genetic Therapies; Medicine; Neurobiology.*
**advert.** (abbr.) advertisement.
Also: **ad.**; **adv.**; **advt.**
**Adv.Frt.** (abbr.) Advance Freight.
**Adv.Pmt.** (abbr.) Advance Payment.
**advt.** (abbr.) advertise.
**advt.** (abbr.) advertisement.
Also: **ad.**; **adv.**; **advert.**
**advt.** (abbr.) advertiser.
**ADW** area defence weapon.
arme de défense de zone.
**ADWHQ** air defence war headquarters.
poste de commandement de guerre de la défense aérienne (PCGDA).
**ADZ** air defence zone.
zone de défense aérienne (ZDA 1b.).
**ADZC** air defence zone coordinator.
coordonnateur de zone de défense aérienne.
**AE** Accommodation Endorsement.
*Business; Economics; Finance.*
**AE** Account Executive.
**AE** Accrued Expenditure.
*Business; Commerce; Finance.*
**AE** Adaptive Enzyme.
Adaptive enzyme is also known as: Inducible Enzyme.
*Enzymology.*
**AE** Administration of the Environment (U.S.A.).
**AE** Arithmetical Element.
**A.E.** Associate in Education.
Also: **A.Ed.**
**ae** at the age of; aged.
**A.E.A.** Actors' Equity Association.
**AEA** Agenzia Europea dell'Ambiente.
Italian initialism of the European Environmental Agency.
**AEA** American Economic Association; American Electronics Association (U.S.A.).
**AEA** American Export Airlines (U.S.A.).
**AEA** Atomic Energy Authority.
**AEBS** Anti-Estrogen Binding Site.
**AEC** Additional Extended Coverage.
*Insurance.*
**AEC** Architecture, Engineering and Construction.
*Design Software.*
**AEC** Army Educational Corps.
**AEC** Atomic Energy Commission.
**AEC** Atomic Energy Council.
**AECA** Associazione Emiliana Centri Autonomi di formazione professionale (Bologna, Italy).
*Vocational Training.*
**AECB** Atomic Energy Control Board (Canada).
**Ae.Cl.** Aero Club Italiano (Italy).
**AECL** Atomic Energy of Canada Limited.
**AECMA** Association Européenne de Construction de Matériel Aérospatial.
French initialism of the: European Association of Aerospace Material Construction.
**AECP** Allied Environmental Conditions Publication.
publication interalliée sur les conditions environnementales.
**AECTP** Allied Environmental Conditions Testing Publication.
publication interalliée sur les essais relatifs aux conditions environnementales.
**AED** Academy for Educational Development.
**A.Ed.** Associate in Education.
Also: **A.E.**
**AED** Atlantic Ecology Division (U.S.A.).
Of the U.S. Environmental Protection Agency.
*Anthropogenic Stressors.*
**AEDA**; **A.E.D.A.** Associazione Estimatori d'Arte Antica (Italy).
*Antique Art.*
**AEDA** Autori EDitori Associati (Italy).
**AEDP** Allied Engineering Documentation Publication.
publication interalliée - documentation d'ingénierie.
**AEDS** Atomic Energy Detection System.
**AEE** Atomic Energy Establishment.
**AEEN** Agence Européenne pour l'Energie Nucléaire.
French initialism of the: European Agency for Nuclear Energy.
**AEF** Aviation Engineer Force.

**AEGIS** airborne early warning ground integration segment.
segment d'interface entre l'infrastructure électronique et le système aéroporté de détention lointaine.
**AEHC** Aminoethylhomocysteine.
**AEI** Association of Electrical Industries.
**AEI** Associazione Elettrotecnica ed elettronica Italiana; Associazione Elicotteristica Italiana.
*Italian Associations.*
**AEIDC** Arctic Environmental Information and Data Center (U.S.A.).
**AEL** Audit Entry Language.
**AEL** Average-Edge Line.
*Computer Technology.*
**AELE** Association Européenne de Libre-Echange.
French acronym of the: European Free Trade Association.
**AELS** Associazione Europea di Libero Scambio.
Italian acronym of the: European Free Trade Association.
**AELT** aeromedical liaison team.
équipe de liaison sanitaire aérienne.
**AEM** Azienda Energetica Municipale (Italy).
**AEM** Analytical Electron Microscopy.
AEM is also known as: Energy-Dispersive X-Ray Analysis.
*Optics.*
**AEMI interpretation** Advanced Environment for Medical Image interpretation.
*Medicine.*
**AEMU** Association for European Monetary Union.
**AEN** Agence de l'Energie Nucléaire.
French initialism of the: Nuclear Energy Agency.
**AengrP** Allied Combat Engineer Publication.
publication interalliée sur le génie de combat.
**AEO** Atomic Energy Organization.
**AEODP** Allied Explosive Ordnance Disposal Publication.
publication interalliée sur l'enlèvement et la destruction des explosifs.
**AEOP** Amend Existing Orders Pertaining to.
*Business; Commerce.*
**AEP** Accrued Expenditure Paid.
*Business; Commerce.*
**AEP** Advanced Executive Program.
Of the Northwestern University, U.S.A.
**AEP** Agenzia Europea per la Produttività.
Italian initialism of the: European Agency for Productivity.
**AEP** Aggregate Exercise Price.
*Business; Commerce.*
**AEP** Allied Engineering Publication.
publication interalliée sur l'ingénierie.
**AEPD** 2-Amino-2-Ethyl-1,3 Propanediol.
**AEPI** Atmospheric Emissions Photometric Imaging.
**AEPP** Allied Engineering Practices Publication.
publication interalliée - pratiques en ingénierie.
**AEPS** Arctic Environmental Protection Strategy.
**AER** Apical Ectodermal Ridge.
AER is essential for limb morphogenesis.
*Biology; Development Biology; Genetics; Medicine; Vertebrate Limb Development.*
**AER** Atmospheric and Environmental Research.
**A/E ratio** Absorptivity - Emissivity ratio.
*Astrophysics.*
**AERB** ACE Exercise Review Board.
Commission d'examen des exercises du CAE.
**AERC** Association of Ecosystem Research Centers.
**A.E.R.E.**; **AERE** Atomic Energy Research Establishment.
AERE is based in Harwell, G.B.
**AEROCE** Atmosphere / Ocean Chemistry Experiment.
**AEROMEDEVAC** aeromedical evacuation.
évacuation sanitaire aérienne.
**AER pollutants** Atmospheric Energy - Related pollutants.
**AES** Advanced Encryption Standard.
*Computer Security; Cryptography.*
**AES** aeromedical evacuation system.
chaîne d'évacuation sanitaires aériennes.
**AES** Aerospace Electrical Society.
**AES** Airways Engineering Society.
**AES** American Economic Society (U.S.A.).
**AES** Atmospheric Environment Service (Canada).
**AES** Atomic Emission Spectroscopy.
**AES** Audio Engineering Society.
**AES** AUGER Electron Spectroscopy.
**Aes** Axial lateral elements - Of the synaptonemal complex.
*Cell Biology; Genomics; Molecular Biology.*
**AESB** armament and equipment storage base.
base de stockage des armements et matériels.
**AESOP** Airborne Experiment to Study Ozone Production.
**A.E.T.** Associate in Electrical Technology.
**AEtP** Allied Electronics Publication.
publication interalliée sur l'électronique.
**AEW** Airborne Early Warning.
**AEW&CS** airborne early warning & control system.
système aéroporté de détection lointaine et de contrôle.
**AEWC** Alaska Eskimo Whaling Commission.
**AEWCU** AEW control unit.
unité de contrôle AEW.

**AEWS** Advanced Earth Satellite Weapon System.
**AEWS** airborne early warning system.
système aéroporté de détection lointaine.
**AEWTF** aircrew electronic warfare training facility.
installation de formation aux tactiques de guerre électronique pour équipages.
**AEX** Amsterdam Exchange.
AEX is the operator of the Dutch Securities market.
**aF** abfarad.
The abfarad is the centimeter-gram-second electromagnetic unit of capacitance.
*Electricity.*
**AF**; **af** Absorption Factor.
*Nucleonics.*
**A.F.** Admiral of the Fleet.
**AF** Advance Freight.
**AF** Advancing Fire.
*Ordnance.*
**af.** (abbr.) affix.
*Linguistics.*
**AF** Afghanistan.
**AF** Agricoltura e Foreste (Italy).
**AF** Air Force.
**AF** The airline code for Air France.
**AF**; **af** Alta Frequenza.
Italian initialism meaning: High Frequency.
**A 1/2 F** A mezzo Ferrovia.
Italian initialism meaning: by rail.
**AF** Aminofluorene.
**AF** Anglo-French.
*Languages.*
**AF** Antiferromagnetic.
*Electromagnetism.*
**AF** Army Form.
**AF** Assault Fire or Advancing Fire.
*Ordnance.*
**AF** Assegno Familiare.
Italian initialism meaning: Family Allowance.
**AF** Atrial Fibrillation.
The AF is characterized by irregular and rapid activation of the atrium.
*Heart Research.*
**AF**; **af** Audio Frequency.
The term audio frequency refers to any frequency within the audio frequency range.
*Acoustics.*
**AF** Auricular Fibrillation; Auricular Flutter.
*Medicine.*
**AFA** Advertising Federation of America.
**AFA** Air Force Academy (U.S.A.).
**AFA** Air Force Association (U.S.A.).
**AFA** Allergy Foundation of America (U.S.A.).
**AFA** Amateur Fencing Association; Amateur Football Association (G.B.).
**AFA** American Finance Association; American Forensic Association; American Franchise Association; American Freedom Association (U.S.A.).
**AFA** Armed Forces Act.
**A.F.A.** Associate in Fine Arts.
**AFA** Associate of the Faculty of Actuaries.
**AFA** Association Française des Automobilistes.
French acronym of the: Motorists French Association.
**afa** The above acronyms were coined accidentally using the Italian word "afa" which means: sultriness (*Meteorology*).
**AFAA** Air Force Audit Agency (U.S.A.).
**AFAH** Association pour les Foyers et Ateliers Handicapés (France).
For further details see under: **CPO**.
**AFAIK** As Far As I Know.
**AFAL** Association Francophone d'Amitié et de Liaison.
**A.F.A.M.** Ancient Free and Accepted Masons.
*Freemansonry.*
**AFAN** Association for National Archaeological Excavations (France).
**AFAP** artillery-fired atomic projectile.
munition nucléaire d'artillerie.
**AFAP** Association Française pour l'Accroissement de la Productivité (France).
French acronym of the: French Association for Productivity Increase.
**AFAR** Azores fixed acoustic range.
polygone acoustique fixe des Açores.
**AFAS** Associate of the Faculty of Architects and Surveyors.
**AFAT** Auxiliaire Féminine de l'Armée de Terre (France).
**AFAV** Association Française de la Valeur.
*French Association.*
**AFB** Acid-Fast Bacillus.
**AFB** Acid-Fast Bacteria.
*Microbiology.*
**AFB**; **A.F.B.** Air Force Base (U.S.A.).
**AFB** American Federation for the Blind.
**AFB** Antifriction Bearing.
*Mechanics.*
**AFB** Association Française des Banques.
French acronym of the: French Banks Association (France).
**AFB** Atmospheric Fluidized Bed.
**AFBCMR** Air Force review Board for Correction of Military Records (U.S.A.).

**AFB/CTIU** Atmospheric pressure Fluidized-bed Combustion/Component Test and Integration Unit.
*Boiler Systems.*
**AFBD** Association of Futures Brokers and Dealers (G.B.).
**AFBF** American Farm Bureau Federation (U.S.A.).
**AFC** Air Force Cross.
**AFC** American Football Conference (U.S.A.).
**AFC** Antibody-Forming Cells.
*Immunology.*
**AFC; afc** Automatic Frequency Control.
*Electronics.*
**AFCARA** Air Force Civilian Appellate Review Agency (U.S.A.).
**AFCCE** Association of Federal Communications Consulting Engineers.
**AFCE** Automatic Flight Control Equipment.
**AFCENT** Allied Forces, Central Europe [obsolete - replaced by AFNORTH 1.].
Forces alliées du Centre Europe [obsolète - remplacé par AFNORTH 1.].
**AFCET** Association Française de Cybernétique Economique et Technique (France).
**AFCISS** affordable CIS security.
sécurité abordable pour les SIC.
**AFCR** American Federation for Clinical Research (U.S.A.).
**AFCS** Automatic Flight Control System.
**AFD** Auxiliary Floating Dock.
**AFDB** AFrican Development Bank.
**AFDC** Aid to Families with Dependent Children (U.S.A.).
**AFDCC** Association Française des Directeurs et Chefs de Crédit (France).
**AFDD** Auxiliary Floating Dry Dock.
**AFDF** AFrican Development Fund.
**AFDI** Annuaire Français de Droit International (France).
**AFDL** Alliance of Democratic Forces for the Liberation of Congo (Congo).
**AFE** Association Française de l'Eclairage.
*French Association.*
**AFE** Associazione Fertilizzazione Extracorporea (Italy).
**AFECEI** Association Française des Etablissements de Crédit et des Entreprises d'Investissement (France).
French acronym of the French Association of Credit Institutions and Investment Firms.
**aff.** (abbr.) affiliated; affirmative.
**AFF** Automatic Frequency Follower.
**affil.** (abbr.) affiliation.
**AFF phases** Antiferro-Ferro phases.
**AFG** amended force goal.
objectif de force modifié.
**AFGC** Arabidopsis Functional Genomic Consortium (U.S.A.).
The AFGC is a U.S. National Science Foundation-funded collaboration among several U.S. Academic Institutions working together to develop technologies in *Arabidopsis genomics.*
**aFGF** acidic Fibroblast Growth Factor.
**AFGI** Association Française de Gestion Industrielle.
French acronym of the: French Association for Industrial Management.
**AFGP** Associazione Formazione Giovanni Piamarta (Italy).
**AFGWC** Air Force Global Weather Center (U.S.A.).
**AFH** Acceptance For Honor.
*Business; Commerce; Finance.*
**AFI** Associate of the Faculty of Insurance.
**AFI** Associazione Filatelica Italiana.
Italian acronym of the Italian Philatelists' Association.
**AFI** Associazione Fiscale Internazionale.
Italian acronym of the International Tax Law Association.
**AFICE** Air Forces, Iceland [obsolete].
Forces aériennes de l'Islande [obsolète].
**AFICE** Associazione Fabbricanti Italiani Cavi Elettrici (Italy).
Italian acronym of the: Italian Association of Electric Cables Manufacturers.
**AF in BH** Armed Forces in Bosnia and Herzegovina.
Forces armées en Bosnie-Herzégovine.
**AFIP** Associazione Fotografi Italiani Professionisti (Italy).
**AFIS** American Forces Information Service (U.S.A.).
**AFIS** Associazione Fabbricanti Impianti Sportivi (Italy).
**AFIS** Automatic Fingerprinting Identification System.
**AFITAE** Association Française des Ingénieurs et Techniciens de l'Aéronautique et de l'Espace (France).
*French Association.*
**AFL/CIO** American Federation of Labor / Congress of Industrial Organizations (U.S.A.).
**AFLP** Amplified Fragment Length Polymorphism.
*Forest Genetics; Molecular Biology; Plant Biotechnology.*
**AFM** American Federation of Musicians (U.S.A.).
**AFM** Atomic Force Microscope.

*Atomic Scale Friction; Chemistry.*
**AFME** Asociaciòn de Fabricantes de Material Electrico (Spain).
*Spanish Association.*
**AFMED** Allied Forces, Mediterranean [obsolete].
Forces alliées de la Méditerranée [obsolète].
**AFML** Air Force Materials Laboratory.
**AFMS project** Advanced Flight Management System project.
*European Community.*
**AFN** American Forces Network (U.S.A.).
**AFNON** Allied Forces, North Norway [obsolete].
Forces alliées du nord de la Norvège [obsolète].
**AFNOR** Association Française de NORmalisation (France).
*French Association.*
**AFNORTH** 1. Allied Forces North Europe [obsolete - has replaced AFCENT].
1. Forces alliées Nord-Europe [obsolète - remplace AFCENT].
2. Allied Forces, Northern Europe [obsolete].
2. Forces alliées du Nord-Europe [obsolète].
**AFNORTHWEST** Allied Forces, Northwestern Europe [obsolete - not replaced].
Forces alliées du Nord-Ouest-Europe [obsolète - n'a pas été remplacé].
**AFOD** Association Française des Conseils en Organisation et Direction (France).
**AFORISM** A comprehensive Forecasting system for flood Risk Mitigation and control.
*European Community Project; Meteorology; Safety.*
**AFOS** Automation of Field Operations and Services (U.S.A.).
Of the U.S. National Weather Service.
**AFOSR** Air Force Office of Scientific Research.
The AFOSR is located in Washington, D.C., U.S.A.
**AFP** Agence France-Presse.
**AFP** 1. Allied FORACS Publication.
1. publication interalliée - FORACS.
2. Allied Fuel Publication.
2. publication interalliée sur les carburants.
**AFP** Alpha-Fetoprotein.
Also: $\alpha$ **F.P.**
*Biochemistry.*
**AFP** Anterior Forebrain Pathway.
**AFPA** Association nationale pour la Formation Professionnelle des Adultes.
French initialism of the: National Association for Vocational Training of Adults (France).
**AFPC** Advanced Financial Planning Certificate (Advanced level).
**AFPC** Armed Forces Policy Council (U.S.A.).
**AFPEO** Air Force Program Executive Office (U.S.A.).
**Af Plate motion** African Plate motion.
*Geological Sciences; Terrestrial Magnetism.*
**AFPPS** American Forces Press and Publications Service (U.S.A.).
**AFPRO** Air Force Plan Representative Office (U.S.A.).
**AFPS** Association Française du Génie Parasismique (France).
**AFPS** AWIPS Forecast Preparation System.
For further details see under: **AWIPS**.
**AFQ** Association Française des Qualiticiens (France).
**AFQPL** Air Force Qualified Products List.
**AFR** Accident Frequency Rate.
*Industrial Engineering.*
**AFR** (abbr.) Africa.
**Afr** African.
*Languages.*
**afr** (abbr.) airframe.
*Aviation.*
**AFR** Air-Fuel Ratio.
*Chemistry.*
**AFR** Away From Reactor.
**AFRA** Average Freight Rate Assessment.
*Business; Commerce; Shipping.*
**AFRC** Agriculture and Food Research Council (G.B.).
**AFRF** African Famine Relief Fund.
**AFRIMS** Armed Forces Research Institute of Medical Sciences (Thailand).
The AFRIMS is located in Bangkok. It is a 40-year-old collaboration between the U.S. Walter Reed Army Institute of Research and the Royal Thai Army.
*AIDS Research; AIDS Vaccine; Epidemiology.*
**AFRRI** Armed Forces Radiobiology Research Institute (U.S.A.).
**AFRTS** Armed Forces Radio and Television Service (U.S.A.).
**AFS** ACE forces standards.
normes de forces du CAE.
**A.F.S.** American Field Service (U.S.A.).
**AFS** American Fisheries School (U.S.A.).
**AFS** American Foundrymen's Society (U.S.A.).
**AFS** Army Fire Service.
**AFS** Asian Fisheries Society.
**AFS** Australian Fisheries Service (Australia).
**AFS** Auxiliary Fire Service (U.S.A.).
The AFS has been replaced by the National Fire Service.

**AFSC** Armed Forces Staff College (U.S.A.).
**afsd.** (abbr.) aforesaid.
**AFSONOR** Allied Forces, South Norway [obsolete].
Forces alliées du sud de la Norvège [obsolète].
**AFSOUTH** 1. Allied Forces South Europe [has replaced AFSOUTH 2.].
1. Forces alliées Sud-Europe [remplace AFSOUTH 2.].
2. Allied Forces, Southern Europe [replaced by AFSOUTH 1.].
2. Forces alliées du Sud-Europe [remplacé par AFSOUTH 1.].
**AFSSA** French Food Safety Agency.
**AFSTB** Air Force Science and Technology Board (U.S.A.).
**AFSTN** Augmented Finite State Transition Network.
*Artificial Intelligence.*
**aft.** (abbr.) after; afternoon.
**A.F.T.** American Federation of Teachers.
**AFT** Analog Facility Terminal.
*Computers.*
**AFT**; **aft** Audio Frequency Transformer.
**AFT**; **aft** Automatic Fine Tuning.
*Electronics.*
**AFT** Automatic Fund Transfer.
*Business; Commerce; Finance.*
**AFTA** Acoustic Fatigue Test Article.
**AFTA** American Family Therapy Association.
**AFTA** Atlantic Free Trade Area.
**afta** The above acronyms were coined accidentally using the Italian word "afta" which means: thrush (*Medicine*).
**AFTAD** Analysis-Forecast Transport And Diffusion.
**AFT control** Automatic Fine-Tuning control.
*Electronics.*
**AFTE** Association Française des Trésoriers d'Entreprise (France).
French acronym of the: French Association of Company's Treasurers.
**AFTN** aeronautical fixed telecommunication network.
réseau du service fixe de télécommunications aéronautiques (RSFTA).
**AFTRA**; **A.F.T.R.A.** American Federation of Television and Radio Artists.
**AFTRI** Association Française des Transporteurs Routiers Internationaux.
French initialism of the: French Association of International Road Carriers.
**AFTRP** Agence Foncière Technique de la Région Parisienne (France).
*French Agency.*
**AFU** Air Force Units.
**AFU** American Fraternal Union (U.S.A.).
**AFU** Auxiliary Functional Unit.
**AFV** Armoured Fighting Vehicle.
**AFVP** Aviation Forecast Verification Program (U.S.A.).
**AFWG** AFPS Foreacst Working Group.
For further details see under: **AFPS**.
**AG** Acrosomal Granule.
**A.G.** Adjutant-General.
*Military.*
**ag.** (abbr.) agent; agreement; agriculture.
**AG** Agrigento, Italy.
**A/G** air-to-ground.
air-sol.
**Ag.** Androgenetic.
*Biology.*
**ag.** antigen.
*Immunology.*
**AG** Arabinogalactan.
**AG** army group.
groupe d'armées.
**AG** Attorney General.
**Ag** The chemical symbol for Silver.
Silver is a metallic element having the atomic number 47, an atomic weight of 107.87 and a melting point of 961°C. It is used mainly in jewelry; in medical equipment; in water distillation and for plating.
*Chemistry.*
**AGA**; **A.G.A.** American Gastroenterological Association (U.S.A.).
**A.G.A.** Autorità Giurisdizionale Amministrativa (Italy).
**Agaf; AGAF** Associazione Nazionale fra i Grossisti di Apparecchi Fotografici.
AGAF is located in Milan, Italy.
**AGAL** American Gas Association Laboratories (U.S.A.).
**AGAM** Associazione Giovani Avvocati Milano (Italy).
*Intellectual Property Law.*
For further details see under: **LYSG**.
**AGARD** Advisory Group for Aerospace Research and Development [obsolete - incorporated into RTA].
Groupe consultatif pour la recherche et les réalisations aérospatiales [obsolète - intégré dans l'ART].
**AGAS** Automated Grant Application Systems.
*Electronic Documents.*
**Agas.** Aviation gasoline.

**AGAS-LESS** AGAS-Limited Electronic Submission System (U.S.A.).
For further details see under: **AGAS**.
*Electronic Documents.*

**$Ag_3AsO_3$** Silver Arsenite.
Silver arsenite is used in medicine.
*Inorganic Chemistry.*

**AGASP** Arctic Gas and Aerosol Sampling Program.

**$AgBiS_2$** Matildite.
*Mineralogy.*

**AgBr** Silver Bromide.
Silver Bromide is used in photographic films.
*Inorganic Chemistry.*

**$AgBrO_3$** Silver Bromate.
Silver Bromate is used as a reagent.
*Inorganic Chemistry.*

**AGB stars** Asymptotic Giant-Branch stars.
*Astronomy; Astrophysics; Earth and Planetary Sciences; Nucleosynthesis in Stars; Physics; Space Science.*

**AGC** Advanced Graduate Certificate.

**AGC** Automatic Gain Control.
The automatic gain control consists of a device that automatically changes the gain of a receiver.
*Electronics.*

**$Ag_2C_2$** Silver Acetylide.
Silver Acetylide is used in detonators.
*Inorganic Chemistry.*

**AGCA** Associated General Contractors of America (U.S.A.).

**AGCA** Automatic Ground-Controlled Approach (Radar).

**AGCAS** Association of Graduate Careers Advisory Services (G.B.).

**AGCI** Associazione Generale Cooperative Italiane (Italy).
Italian initialism of the: General Association of Italian Cooperatives.

**AgCl** Chlorargyrite.
Chlorargyrite is also known as: Cerargyrite.
*Mineralogy.*

**AgCl** Silver Chloride.
Silver Chloride is used mainly in optics; silver plating; and as an antiseptic.
*Inorganic Chemistry.*

**AGCMs** Atmospheric General Circulation Models.
The AGCMs incorporate land surface parameterizations.
*Atmospheric Sciences; Biospheric Sciences; Earth and Ocean Sciences; Space Research.*
For further details see under: **LSPs**.

**AgCN** Silver Cyanide.
Silver Cyanide is used mainly in medicines.
*Inorganic Chemistry.*

**Ag85 complex** Antigen 85 complex.

**AGCSI** Association of Graduate Career Services in Ireland.

**AGCT** Army General Classification Test.
A test used in the U.S. Army (World War II).
*Psychology.*

**Agcy** (abbr.) Agency.

**agd** (abbr.) agreed.

**AGDGADU** A Gloria Del Grande Architetto Dell'Universo.
*Freemasonry.*

**AGDI**; **Agdi** Associazione Giovani Diabetici Italiani (Italy).

**AGDS** American Gage Design Standard.

**AGE** Admiralty Gunnery Establishment (G.B.).

**AGE** Advisory Group on Energy.

**AGE** Aerospace Ground Equipment.

**Ag.E.** Agricultural Engineer.

**AGE** Angle of Greatest Extension.

**A.G.E.** Associate in General Education.

**AGE**; **Age** Associazione italiana GEnitori.
*Italian Association.*

**AGE** Attorney-General of England (G.B.).

**AGE** Auditory Gross Error.

**AGE** Automatic Ground Equipment.

**AGE** Automatic Guidance Electronics.

**AGE** Auxiliary Ground Equipment.

**AGED** Advisory Group on Electron Devices.

**AGED** Aerospace Ground Equipment Department.

**AGeoP** Allied Geographic Publication.
publication géographique interalliée.

**AGER** AGricultural Economics Research.
*Publication.*

**Ager** Associazione per la ricerca scientifica e lo studio della longevità (Italy).
Italian acronym of the: Association for scientific research and the study of longevity; based in Milan, Italy.

**AGERI** Agricultural Genetic Engineering Research Institute.
A center for state-of-the-art research in Egypt, focusing on developing pest-resistant and stress-tolerant varieties of crops.

**AGEs** Advanced Glycosylation End products.
*Biochemistry; Biomolecular Engineering; Chemistry; Gerontology; Molecular Biology; Physics; Physiology.*

**AGES** Air-Ground Engagement Simulation.

**AGES** American Gas and Electric Services.

**AGES** American Greek Exchange Society.

**AGES** Aspetti Giuridici, Etici e Sociali.

Italian acronym meaning: Legal, Ethical and Social Aspects.

**A.G.E.T.A.C.** Accord Général sur les Tarifs et le Commerce.
French acronym meaning: General Agreement on Tariffs and Trade (G.A.T.T.).

**AGEX program** Above Ground EXperiments program.

**AGFS** Aviation Gridded Forecast System.

**agg.** aggiunto.
Italian abbreviation meaning: assistant; deputy. Also: added.

**agg.** (abbr.) aggregate.
*Botany; Geology; Materials.*

**AGGG** Advisory Group on Greenhouse Gases.
Of the World Climate Program.

**Ag, Hg** Kongsbergite.
Kongsbergite is a mercurian type of silver.
*Mineralogy.*

**AGI** Adjusted Gross Income.

**AGI**; **A.G.I.** American Geological Institute.

**AGI** Année Géodésique Internationale.
French acronym meaning: International Geodetic Year.

**AgI** Iodargyrite.
AgI is also known as: Iodyrite.
*Mineralogy.*

**AgI** Silver Iodide.
Silver Iodide is used mainly in medicine, and photography.
*Inorganic Chemistry.*

**AGIFAR** Associazione GIovani FARmacisti.
Italian acronym of the: Young Pharmacists Association.

**AGIL** Airborne General Illuminating Light.

**AGIO** Armed Guard Inspection Officer.

**agio** The above acronym was coined accidentally using the Italian word "agio" which means in Italian: ease; comfort; (sometimes): chance.

**$AgIO_3$** Silver Iodate.
Silver Iodate is used in medicine.
*Inorganic Chemistry.*

**AGIP** Azienda Generale Italiana Petroli (Italy).

**A.G.I.R.E.** Azienda Generale Italiana per l'Esportazione del Riso (Italy).
Italian acronym of the: National Italian Rice Export Board.

**AGIS** Associazione Generale Italiana dello Spettacolo (Italy).

**AGL** Above Ground Level.
*Navigation.*

**AGL** Acute Granulocytic Leukemia.
The AGL is a disease characterized by symptoms such as anemia, bleeding, and infection. Acute Granulocytic Leukemia is also known as: Myeloblastic Leukemia.
*Medicine.*

**AGM** Acceleratore a Gradiente Magnetico.
Italian initialism meaning: Magnetic Gradient Accelerator.

**AGM** Air-to-Ground Missile.
*Military.*

**AGM** Annual General Meeting.

**AGMA** American Gear Manufacturers' Association (U.S.A.).

**AGMA**; **A.G.M.A.** American Guild of Musical Artists (U.S.A.).

**AGMK cells** African Green Monkey Kidney cells.
The AGMK cells are used for the growth of certain types of viruses.
*Virology.*

**AGN** Active Galactic Nucleus.
For further details see under: **AGNs**.

**$AgNO_3$** Silver Nitrate.
Silver Nitrate is used mainly to cauterize wounds, in hair dyes, and in ink manufacture.
*Inorganic Chemistry.*

**AGNs** Active Galactic Nuclei.
*Astronomy; Extreme Ultraviolet Astronomy.*

**AGO** Adjutant General's Office.

**ago.** (abbr.) agosto.
Italian abbreviation meaning: August.

**AGO** Air Gunnery Officer.

**AGO** Auditor General's Office.

**ago** The above acronyms were coined accidentally using the Italian word "ago" which means: needle; tongue. Also: crystal (*Chemistry*).

**$Ag_2O$** Silver Oxide.
Silver Oxide, also known as Argentous Oxide, is used mainly to purify drinking water.
*Inorganic Chemistry.*

**AGP** Accordi Generali di Prestito.
Italian initialism meaning: General Arrangements to Borrow.

**$Ag_3PO_4$** Silver Phosphate.
Silver Phosphate, also known as: Silver Orthophosphate, is used mainly in pharmaceuticals.
*Inorganic Chemistry.*

**AGR** Advanced Gas-cooled Reactor.
The AGR is a power-generating nuclear reactor cooled by carbon dioxide gas.
*Nuclear Engineering.*

**agr.** (abbr.) agricultural.

**agr.**; **agric.** (abbr.) agriculture.

**AGR** Association of Graduate Recruiters (G.B.).

**A/G ratio** Albumin-Globulin ratio.
The A/G ratio is the ratio of albumin to globulin in blood serum.
*Medicine.*

**AGRF** Australian Genome Research Facility.
The AGRF is a collaboration of the University of Queensland and the Walter and Eliza Hall Institute, Australia.
*DNA Sequencing; Genotyping; Mutation Detection.*

**AGRICOLA** AGRICultural On line Access (U.S.A.).

**AGRIMED** MEDiterranean AGRIculture.

**AGRIS** AGRicultural Information Service (U.S.A.).

**AGRP** AGouti-Related Protein.
*Obesity Syndrome.*

**AGRTF** Avian Genetic Resources Task Force.
*Animal Sciences; Poultry Genetic Resources.*

**AGS** Alliance ground surveillance.
capacité alliée de surveillance terrestre.

**AGS**; **A.G.S.** American Geriatrics Society.

**ags.** (abbr.) antigens.
*Immunology.*

**A.G.S.** Associate in General Studies.

**AGS** The airport code for Augusta, Georgia, U.S.A.

**AGS** Automatic Gain Stabilization.

**$Ag_2S$** Silver Sulfide.
Silver Sulfide is used mainly in ceramics.
*Inorganic Chemistry.*

**AGSO** Australian Geological Survey Organization (Australia).
*Marine Science.*

**AGSP** Alliance ground surveillance programme.
programme de capacité alliée de surveillance terrestre.

**AGS/PPO** Allied Ground Surveillance Capability Provisional Project Office [obsolete - replaced by AGS/SSC].
Bureau du Programme provisoire de la capacité de surveillance terrestre de l'Alliance (BPO/AGS) [obsolète - remplacé par AGS/SSC].

**AGS/SSC** Alliance Ground Surveillance (Capability)/ Support Staff Cell.
Cellule de soutien pour la capacité alliée de surveillance terrestre.

**agst.** (abbr.) against.

**Agt.**; **agt.** (abbr.) agent; agreement.

**AGTDC** Accord Général sur les Tarifs Douaniers et le Commerce.
French initialism meaning: General Agreement on Customs Tariffs and Trade.
*International Business.*

**$Ag_2Te$** Hessite.
*Mineralogy.*

**AGT gene** Angiotensinogen gene.
*Medicine.*

**AGU** American Geophysical Union (U.S.A.).

**agw** actual gross weight.

**AGWI** Atlantic, Gulf, West Indies.

**Agy.** (abbr.) Agency.

**AGZ** Actual Ground Zero.

**aH** Abhenry.
Abhenry is the centimeter-gram-second electromagnetic unit of inductance.
*Electricity.*

**a.h.** aft hatch.
*Shipping.*

**aH**; **ah** Ampere-Hour.
The AH is the quantity of electricity passing through a circuit in one hour when the rate of flow is one ampere.
*Electricity.*

**AH** Anxiety Hierarchy.
*Psychology.*

**AH** Arts and Humanities.

**AH** attack helicopter.
hélicoptère d'attaque.

**AHA** American Heart Association; American Historical Association (U.S.A.).

**AHA** arrived holding area.
arrivée dans la zone d'attente.

**AHA** Australian Hotels Association (Australia).

**AHAF** American Health Assistance Foundation.

**AH&T** Air Hardened and Tempered.
*Metallurgy.*

**AHB** Allgemeine Hypotheken Bank.
*German Bank.*

**AHC** Accepting Houses Committee.

**AHC** ACCS Hardware Committee.
Comité du matériel de l'ACCS.

**AHC** Acute Hemorrhagic Conjunctivitis.
The AHC is an acute endemic conjunctivitis characterized by swelling of the eyelids, tearing and conjunctival hemorrhages.
*Medicine.*

**AHCPR** Agency for Health Care Policy and Research (U.S.A.).

**AHCs** Academic Health Centers.

**AHCTL** Acetylhomocysteinethiolactone.

**A.H.E.** Associate in Home Economics.

**AHERF** The Allegheny Health Education and Research Foundation (U.S.A.).

**AHF** Antihemophilic Factor.
AHC is also known as: Antihemophilic Globulin Factor VIII, and Thromboplastinogen.
*Hematology.*

**AHG** ad hoc group.
groupe ad hoc.
**AHG** Antihemophilic Globulin.
For further details see under: **AHF**.
**AHG** Antihuman Globulin.
**AHGFC** Ad Hoc Group of Financial Counsellors.
Groupe ad hoc des conseillers financiers.
**AHL** American Hockey League (U.S.A.).
**ahm** ampere-hour meter.
*Engineering.*
**AHM** Association of Headmasters / Headmistresses.
**AHO** Aerobraking Hiatus Orbit.
*Spacecraft Orbital Phases.*
**AHP** Afterhyperpolarization.
**AHP** Allied Hydrographic Publication.
publication interalliée sur l'hydrographie.
**AHP** Analytic Hierarchy Process.
*Economics Calculation System.*
**AhpR** Alkyl Hydroperoxide Reductase.
*Biochemistry; Immunology; Medical Sciences; Microbiology.*
**AHQ** Air Headquarters.
**AHR** Airway Hyperresponsiveness / Hyperreactivity.
*Allergic Asthma; Environmental Health Sciences; Immunology; Medicine; Molecular Microbiology; Ventilation Regulation.*
**AHS** airborne homing system.
système de radioralliement embarqué (ou de bord).
**AHS** Automated Highway System.
**AHSA** American Horse Show Association.
**AHWG** as hoc working group.
groupe de travail ad hoc (GTAH).
**AHYDS** Active HYpermedia Delivery System.
*Multimedia Information.*
**AI** Accrued Interest; Accumulated Interest.
*Banking; Business; Economics; Finance.*
**AI** Adaptive Immunity.
*Immunology.*
**AI** Airborne Intercept.
**AI** The airline code for Air India.
**AI** Air Interception.
**AI** Altesse Impériale.
**AI** Anti-Icing.
*Aviation.*
**AI** Aptitude Index.
**AI** Artificial Insemination.
Artificial Insemination is a process by means of which sperrnatozoa are deposited into the vagina (or cervix) by artificial means.
*Medicine.*
**AI** Artificial Intelligence.
**AIA** Académie Internationale d'Astronautique.
French acronym of the: International Astronautics Academy.
**AIA** Aerospace Industries Association.
**AIA** American Institute of Architects (U.S.A.).
**AIA** Associate In Advertising; Associate of the Institute of Actuaries (G.B.).
**AIA**; **Aia** Associazione Industrie Aerospaziali.
Italian acronym of the: Aerospace Industries Association.
**A.I.A.** Associazione Italiana Arbitri.
Italian acronym of the: Italian Referees' Association.
**AIA** Associazione Italiana di Aerobiologia.
Italian acronym of the Italian Association for Aerobiology.
Founded in 1985 in Bologna where it is based. The AIA holds annual aerobiology monitoring courses, organizes workshops and a biannual National Congress. Publishes the Aerobiology Bulletin.
**AIA** Associazione Italiana per l'Arbitrato.
Italian acronym of the: Italian Arbitration Association. Located in Rome, Italy.
*Law.*
**aia** The above acronyms were coined accidentally using the Italian word "aia" which means: farm-yard; threshing-floor.
**AIAA** American Institute of Aeronautics and Astronautics (U.S.A.).
**AIAA** Architect member of the Incorporated Association of Architects and Surveyors.
**AIAB** Associazione Italiana Agricoltura Biologica.
Italian acronym of the: Italian Biological Agriculture Association.
**AIAC** ACCS Implementation Advisory Committee [obsolete - has merged with APAC to become AAC].
Comité consultatif sur la mise en œuvre de l'ACCS [obsolète - a fusionné avec l'APAC pour devenir l'AAC].
**A.I.A.C.** Associazione Internazionale degli Agenti di Cambio (Italy).
Italian acronym of the: International Stockbrokers' Association.
**AIAC** Associazione Italiana Agenti di Cambio.
Italian acronym of the: Italian Stockbrokers' Association.
**AIAE** Associate of the Institute of Automobile Engineers.
**AIAF**; **Aiaf** Associazione Italiana degli Analisti Finanziari.
Italian acronym of the: Italian Association of Financial Analysts.

**AIAP** Associazione Italiana di Architettura del Paesaggio (Italy).
**AIArb.** Associate of the Institute of Arbitrators.
**AIAS** Associazione Italiana Addetti alla Sicurezza (Italy).
**AIAS** Associazione Italiana per l'Assistenza agli Spastici (Italy).
**AIB** Académie des Inscriptions et Belles Lettres.
**AIB** Academy of International Business.
Founded in 1959. Located in Cleveland, Ohio, U.S.A.
**AIB** Accidents Investigations Branch (Royal Air Force) (G.B.).
**AIB** Allied Irish Banks.
**AIB** American Institute of Banking (U.S.A.).
**AIB** Aminoisobutyric Acid.
*Biochemistry.*
**AIB** Associate of the Institute of Bankers.
**AIB** Association of Investment Brokers.
**AIB** Associazione Italiana Biblioteche.
Italian initialism of the: Italian Libraries Association (Italy).
**AIB1** Amplified In Breast cancer 1.
*Molecular Biology; Molecular Endocrinology.*
**AIBA** Agricultural Information Bank of Asia.
**AIBA** Associazione Italiana di Broker di Assicurazione (Italy).
Italian acronym of the: Insurance Brokers Italian Association.
**AIBD** Associate of the Institute of British Decorators (G.B.).
**AIBD** Association of International Bond Dealers.
**AIBI**; **Ai.Bi.** Associazione Amici dei Bambini.
Italian acronym of the: Friends of Children Association.
**AIBL** Académie des Inscriptions et Belles Lettres (France).
**AIBL** Association of International Business Leaders.
**AIBN** Azobisisobutyronitrile.
AIBN is used mainly as a blowing agent for elastomers and plastics.
*Organic Chemistry.*
**AIBS** American Institute of Biological Sciences (U.S.A.).
**aic** addestramento individuale al combattimento.
**AIC** Associate of the Institute of Chemistry.
**AIC** Associazione Italiana Cineoperatori.
*Italian Association.*
**A.I.C.** Associazione Italiana Cronometristi.
Italian acronym of the: Italian Timekeepers' Association.
**AICA** Alleanza Italiana delle Cooperative Agricole (Italy).
**AICA** Associate of the Institute of Company Accountants.
**AICA** Associazione Italiana Comunicazioni Alternative (Italy).
AICA is an Association dealing with assistance to handicapped children.
**AICA** Associazione Italiana Contro l'Artrite.
Italian acronym of the: Italian Association for the Fight Against Arthritis.
**AICA** Associazione Italiana per l'Informatica e il Calcolo Automatico.
*Italian Association.*
**AICB** International Association Against Noise (Switzerland).
**AICC** Alleanza Italiana Cooperative di Consumo (Italy).
**AICD** Activation-Induced Cell Death.
*Human Genetics; Molecular Biology; Pathology.*
**AICE** American Institute of Consulting Engineers (U.S.A.).
**AICE** Associate of the Institute of Civil Engineers.
**AICE**; **A.I.C.E.** Associazione Italiana per la lotta Contro l'Epilessia.
Italian acronym of the: Italian Association for the fight against Epilepsy.
**AICEL**; **Aicel** Associazione Italiana Commercio Elettronico.
Italian acronym of the: Italian Association for (the development of) Electronic Commerce.
**AICF** ACCS interoperability coordination function.
fonction de coordination de l'interopérabilité de l'ACCS.
**AICO** Association of Iberoamerican Chambers of Commerce (Bogota).
**AICOD** Associazione Italiana Imprese di Consulenza Organizzativa e Direzionale.
*Italian Association.*
**AICPA** American Institute of Certified Public Accountants (U.S.A.).
**AICQ** Associazione Italia Centronord per la Qualità (Italy).
**AICS** Associate of the Institute of Chartered Shipbrokers (G.B.).
**AICS** Association of Independent Computer Specialists.
**AICV** armoured infantry combat vehicle.
véhicule blindé de combat d'infanterie (VBCI).
**AICVF** Association des Ingénieurs de Chauffage et Ventilation de France.
French initialism of the: Association of Heating and Airconditioning Engineers of France.

**AID** Abbreviated Item Description.
**AID** Accident, Incident, Deficiencies.
**AID** Action Item Directive.
**AID** Activation-Induced cytidine Deaminase.
*Antigen Affinity; Antibody Mutation in B Cells; Biology of Disease; Medicine; Medical Chemistry; Molecular Biology; Radioisotope Research.*
For further details see under: **CSR**, **SHM** and **ILFs**.
**AID** Active Integral Defense.
**AID** Acute Infectious Disease.
*Medicine.*
**AID** Adult Information on Drugs.
Referral Service in the U.S.A.
**AID** Advanced Integrated Diagnostics.
**AID** Aerospace Information Division.
Library of Congress U.S.A.
**AID** Agency for International Development.
U.S. Government - The U.S. Agency for International Development was established in 1961.
**AID** American Institute of Decorators; American Institute of Interior Designers.
**AID** Army Intelligence Department (G.B.).
**AID** Artificial Insemination by Donor.
**AID** Association Internationale de Développement.
French acronym of the: International Association for Development.
**AID** ATCA interoperability database [obsolete].
base de données sur l'interopérabilité de l'ATCA [obsolète].
**AID** Automatic Implantable Defibrillator.
*Medicine.*
**AID** Automatic Interaction Detection/Detector.
*Data Processing.*
**AIDA** American Independent Designers Association (U.S.A.).
**AIDA** American Indicator Digest Average.
American Stock Exchange.
**AIDA** Association Internationale de Defense des Artistes.
French acronym of the: International Association for the Defence of Artists.
**AIDA** Association Internationale de la Distribution des Produits Alimentaires et des produits de grande consommation.
French acronym of the: International Association for the Distribution of Food Products.
**AIDA** Association Internationale de Droit de l'Assurance.
French acronym of the: International Association for Insurance Law.
**AIDA** Associazione Industrie Dolciarie Italiane.
Italian acronym of the: Italian Confectioneries Association.
**AIDA** Attenzione, Interesse, Desiderio, Azione.
Italian acronym meaning: Attention, Interest; Desire, Action.
*Marketing.*
**AIDC** Associazione Italiana di Diritto Comparato (Italy).
**AIDD** Associazione Italiana Contro la Diffusione della Droga (Milan, Italy).
**A.I.D.D.A.** Associazione Imprenditrici Donne e Dirigenti d'Azienda.
Italian acronym of the: Association of Women Entrepreneurs and Managers.
**AIDE** Associazione Impiegati dell'Edilizia.
*Italian Association.*
**AID gene** Activation-Induced Deaminase gene.
*Immunoglobulin; Gene Conversion.*
**AIDI** Associazione Italiana Di Illuminazione.
*Italian Association.*
**AIDIC** Associazione Italiana Di Ingegneria Chimica (Milan, Italy).
Italian acronym of the: Italian Association of Chemical Engineering.
**AIDIPP**; **A.I.D.I.P.P.** Associazione Italiana Decoratori e Insegnanti di Pittura su Porcellana (Italy).
Italian Association dealing with porcelain painting, ceramics, glass and metal enameling.
**AIDJEX** Arctic Ice Dynamics Joint EXperiment.
U.S.A. - Canada - Japan.
**AIDL** Arthropod-borne and Infectious Diseases Laboratory (U.S.A.).
**AIDMED** Assistant for Interacting with multi-media MEdical Databases.
*Medicine.*
**AIDOS** Associazione Italiana DOnne per lo Sviluppo (Italy).
Italian initialism of the: Italian Women Association for Development. AIDOS is based in Rome, Italy.
**Aidp** Associazione italiana per la direzione del personale.
Italian initialism of the: Italian Association for Personnel management. Aidp was founded in 1960. Based in Milan, Italy.
**AIDROS** Associazione Italiana per i Diritti di Riproduzione delle Opere a Stampa.
*Italian Association.*
**AIDS** Acquired Immunodeficiency Syndrome.
AIDS is an epidemic retroviral disease due to infection with human immunodeficiency virus (HIV-1).
*Medicine.*

**AIE**; **A.I.E.** Associazione Internazionale degli Economisti (Italy).
Italian acronym of the: International Economists' Association.

**A.I.E.** Associazione Italiana degli Editori.
Italian acronym of the: Italian Publishers' Association.

**AIEA** Agence Internationale pour l'Energie Atomique.
French initialism of the: Atomic Energy International Agency.

**AIED**; **Aied** Associazione Italiana per l'Educazione Demografica.
Italian acronym of the: Italian Association for Demographic Education.

**AIEE** Associate of the Institute of Electrical Engineers.

**AIEE** Association des Instituts d'Etudes Européennes.
Located in Geneva, Switzerland. Founded in 1951 to co-ordinate activities of member institutes in teaching and research, exchange information, provide a centre for documentation.

**AIESEC** Association Internationale des Etudiants de Sciences Economiques et Commerciales (France).
French acronym of the: International Association of Economic and Commercial Science Students.

**Aiesec** Associazione internazionale degli studenti in scienze economiche e commerciali.
Italian acronym of the: International Association of Economic and Commercial Science students. Founded in Italy in 1950. It promotes training within Companies in 74 Countries.

**Aiesee - Esg** Association inter-étudiants en sciences économiques et commerciales et Ecole Supérieure de Gestion -France.

**AIEST** International Association of Scientific Experts in Tourism (Switzerland).

**AIF** Apoptosis-Inducing Factor.
*Caspases; Cellular Immunology.*

**AIF**; **Aif** Associazione Importatori Fertilizzanti.
*Italian Association; Fertilizers.*

**AIF** Associazione Italiana Formatori (Italy).

**AIF** Atomic Industrial Forum.

**AIF** automated intelligence file.
dossier informatisé du renseignement.

**AIFIL** Associazione Italiana Fabbricanti Insegne e Pubblicità Luminose (Italy).

**AIFS** ACE information flow system.
système d'acheminement des informations du CAE.

**AIFV** armoured infantry fighting vehicle.
véhicule blindé de combat d'infanterie (VBCI).

**AIG** address indicator group.
1a. adresses intentionnellement groupées [en abrégé, un AIG].
1b. groupe indicateur d'adresses.

**AIG** Associazione Italiana ostelli della Gioventù (Italy).
Italian initialism of the: Italian Association of Youth Hostels.

**AIGA** Association Internationale de Géomagnetisme et d'Aéronomie.

**AIGCP** Association Internationale des Groupes des Cyclistes Professionnels.

**AIGR** Associazione Italiana di Genio Rurale.
For further details see under: **AIIA**.

**AIH** Artificial Insemination by Husband.

**AIHA** American International Health Alliance.

**AIH Association** American Industrial Hygiene Association (U.S.A.).

**AII** area of intelligence interest.
zone d'intérêt du renseignement.

**AIIA** Associazione Italiana di Ingegneria Agraria.
Italian initialism of the Italian Association of Agricultural Engineering.
A non-profit association, founded in 1959. For the period from the end of the 1960s until 1993 the Association adopted the initialism AIGR and after that date got back to the original one AIIA. Scope and aims: to give its own contribution to the scientific and technical disciplines pertaining to Engineering applied to the development of agricultural and forestry systems; coordinating and carrying out research and teaching courses, promoting events and activities in scientific, cultural and historical fields, keeping in touch with similar Italian and Foreign Institutions.
For further details see under: **AIGR**.

**AI*IA** Associazione Italiana per l'Intelligenza Artificiale (Milan, Italy).
Italian acronym of the: Italian Association for Artificial Intelligence.

**AIIC** Association Internationale des Interprètes de Conférence.
French initialism of the: International Association of Conference Interpreters.

**AIIG** Associazione Italiana di Ingegneria Gestionale.
Italian initialism of the: Italian Association of Management Engineering.

**A.I.I.M.** Associazione Italiana di Informatica Medica (Italy).

**AIIP** Associazione Italiana Internet Providers.
*Italian Association.*

**AIIPA**; **Aiipa** Associazione Italiana Industrie Prodotti Alimentari (Italy).
**AIL** Advance Information Letter.
*U.S. Military.*
**AIL** Aeronautical Instruments Laboratory.
*U.S. Military.*
**AIL** Aerospace Instrumentation Laboratory.
*U.S. Air Force.*
**AIL** Air Intelligence Liaison (G.B.).
**AIL** American Institute of Leisuretime (U.S.A.).
**AIL** Argon-Ion Laser.
For further details see under: **AL**.
**AIL** Associate of the Institute of Linguists.
**AIL** Associazione Italiana contro le Leucemie.
Italian acronym of the: Italian Association Against Leukemias.
**AILE** Association Internationale des Lotteries d'Etat.
French acronym of the: International Association of State Lotteries.
**AILO** Air Intelligence Liaison Officer (G.B.).
**AILOG**; **Ailog** Associazione Italiana di LOGistica (Italy).
AILOG was founded in 1978; based in Milan, Italy.
**AILS** Advanced Integrated Landing Systems.
**AIM** Academy for Interscience Methodology.
**Aim** Achievement integrated methods.
**AIM** Active Inert Missile.
**AIM** Adaptive Injection Molding.
**AIM** Advanced Informatics in Medicine.
**AIM** Aerospace Industrial Modernization.
**AIM** Aid for International Medicine.
**AIM** Airborne Infrared Mapper.
**AIM** air intercept missile.
missile d'interception aérienne.
**AIM** Airmen's Information Manual.
*Navigation.*
**AIM** American Institute of Management.
**AIM** Applied Interactive Marketing.
**AIM** Associazione Italiana di Metallurgia.
Italian acronym of the: Italian Association of Metallurgy (Milan, Italy).
**AIM** Associazione Italiana per la Lotta alla Miastenia (Italy).
Italian acronym of the: Italian Association for the fight against Myasthenia.
**AIM** Astrometric Interferometry Mission.
**AIMA** Associazione Italiana Malattia di Alzheimer.
Italian acronym of the: Alzheimer's Disease Italian Association.
**AIMA** Azienda statale per gli Interventi sui Mercati Agricoli (Italy).
**AIMaC** Associazione Italiana Malati di Cancro (Italy).
**AIMAN** Associazione Italiana fra i tecnici di MANutenzione (Italy).
**AIMAT** Associazione Italiana di Ingegneria dei Materiali.
Italian acronym of the Italian Association for Materials Engineering. AIMAT is a non-profit association founded in 1993. The association promotes and coordinates research relating to the composition, microstructure, properties and applications of materials.
**AIMB** Associazione degli Industriali di Monza e di Brianza (Italy).
**AIMBE** American Institute of Medical and Biological Engineering (U.S.A.).
**AIME** American Institute of Mining, metallurgical and petroleum Engineers.
**AIMI** Associazione Italiana Microfilm.
*Italian Association.*
**AIMS** 1. ACCS Information Management System.
1. système de gestion de l'information de l'ACCS.
2. Allied Information Management System.
2. système interallié de gestion de l'information.
**AIMS** Advanced Integrated Magnetic anomaly detection System.
**AIMS** Advanced Intercontinental Missile System.
**AIMS** Air-launched Intercept Missile record System.
**AIMS** American Institute of Merchant Shipping (U.S.A.).
**AIMS product** Automated Individual Marketing Sales product.
*Campaign Management Software.*
**AIN** Advanced Intelligent Network.
**AIN** Alternative Information Network.
**AIN** American Institute of Nutrition (U.S.A.).
**AIN** Assembly Identification Number.
**AINA** Arctic Institute of North America.
*Arctic Science.*
**AInd** Anglo-Indian.
*Languages.*
**AINS** Anti-Inflammatoire Non Stéroïdien.
French acronym meaning: Nonsteroid Anti-Inflammatory.
**AIntP** Allied Intelligence Publication.
publication interalliée sur le renseignement.
**A.I.O.C.** Anglo-Iranian Oil Company.
**A.I.O.S.** Associazione Italiana Operatori in Sessuologia.
Italian acronym of the: Italian Association of Sexual Therapy Operators.

**AIOSP** Association Internationale d'Orientation Scolaire et Professionnelle.
AIOSP was founded in 1951 to contribute to the development of vocational guidance and promote contact between persons associated with it.
**AIOTE** Associazione Italiana Operatori Titoli Esteri (Italy).
Italian acronym of the: Italian Association of Brokers in Foreign Securities.
**AIP** 1. Aeronautical Information Publication.
1. publication d'information aéronautique.
2. air-independent propulsion.
2. propulsion anaérobie.
**AIP** American Institute of Physics (U.S.A.).
**AIP** Associazione Italiana Pellicciai (Italy).
Italian acronym of the: Italian Furriers Association.
**AIP** Associazione Italiana tra gli addetti ai sistemi Produttivi (Italy).
AIP was founded in 1987. Based in Turin, Italy.
**A.I.P.** Associazione Italiana Parkinsoniani.
*Italian Association.*
**AIPA** Associate of the Institute of Incorporated Practitioners in Advertising.
**AIPA**; **A.I.P.A.** Associazione Italiana Psicologia Analitica (Italy).
Italian acronym of the: Italian Association of Analytic Psychology.
**AIPA**; **Aipa** Autorità per l'Informatica nella Pubblica Amministrazione (Italy).
**AIPAI** Associazione Italiana Periti Assicurativi Incendio e rischi diversi.
*Italian Association.*
**AIPE** American Institute of Plant Engineers.
**AIPE** Associate of the Institution of Production Engineers.
**AIPES** Associazione Italiana per la Promozione dell'Energia Solare (Italy).
Italian acronym of the: Italian Association for the Promotion of Solar Energy.
**AIPEV** Associazione Italiana per la difesa dei Portatori di Epatite Virale.
Italian acronym of the: Italian Association for the protection of Viral Hepatitis Carriers.
**AIPH**; **Aiph** Association Internationale des Producteurs de l'Horticulture.
French initialism of the: International Association of Horticulture Producers.
**AIPnD** Associazione Italiana Prove non Distruttive Monitoraggio Diagnostica.
Italian initialism of the: Italian Society for Non Destructive Testing Monitoring Diagnostics. The AIPnD was established in 1979 and is based in Brescia, Italy. Purpose: the promotion of scientific and technical knowledge in the field of Non-Destructive Testing. Publishes: a Journal on a quarterly basis, congress and symposium proceedings, educational papers and technical and scientific textbooks.
**AIPP** Associazione Italiana Pubblicitari Professionisti.
*Italian Association.*
**AIPPI** Associazione Italiana di Psicoterapia Psicoanalitica Infantile.
Italian acronym of the: Italian Association of Infantile Psychoanalytic Psychotherapy.
**AIPS** Astronomical Image Processing System.
**AIPT** Advanced Image Processing Terminal.
Of the Defence Research Agency.
Algorithms written by Logica Programmers.
*Neural Network Software.*
**AIQF** Associazione Italiana per la Qualità della Formazione (Italy).
**AIR** Acoustic Intercept Receiver.
**AIR** Acute Insulin Response.
*Endocrinology.*
**AIR** After Initial Release.
**AIR** Airborne Intercept Rocket.
**AIR** Air Inflatable Retarder (referring to bombs).
**AIR** Air-Injection Reactor.
*Mechanical Engineering.*
**AIR** Air Intercept Rocket.
**AIR** Annals of Improbable Research.
A 1944 humor publication.
**AIR** 1. annual infrastructure report.
1. rapport annuel d'infrastructure.
2. area of intelligence responsibility.
2. zone de responsabilité du renseignement (ZRR).
**AIR** Army Intelligence Reserve.
**AI radar** Airborne Intercept radar.
*Engineering.*
**AIRBALTAP** Allied Air Forces, Baltic Approaches [obsolete - replaced by AIRNORTH 1.].
Forces aériennes alliées des approches de la Baltique [obsolète - remplacé par AIRNORTH 1.].
**AIRC** Associazione Italiana per la Ricerca sul Cancro (Italy).
Italian initialism of the: Italian Association for Cancer Research.
**AIRCENT** Allied Air Forces, Central Europe [obsolete - replaced by AIRNORTH].
Forces aériennes alliées du Centre-Europe [obsolète - remplacé par AIRNORTH].
**AIRCENTLANT** Maritime Air Central Atlantic Sub-Area [obsolete].

Forces aéromaritimes de la Sous-zone centrale de l'Atlantique [obsolète].

**AIRE** Anagrafe Italiani Residenti all'Estero.
Italian acronym meaning: Register of Italians Residing Abroad.

**AIRE** Association Internationale des Ressources en Eau.
French acronym of the: International Water Resources Association.

**AIRE** Associazione Italiana per la Ricerca e la promozione degli studi per l'Edilizia.
*Italian Association.*

**AIRE; A.I.R.E.** Associazione Italiana Società di Revisione (Italy).
Italian acronym of the: Italian Association of Audit Companies.

**AIRE** Autoimmune Regulator (transcription factor).
A defective form of AIRE in humans results in *Multiorgan Autoimmune Disease.*
*Immunology; Immunogenetics; Molecular Biology.*

**AIREASTLANT** 1. Naval Air Forces, East Atlantic [obsolete - has replaced AIREASTLANT 2.].
1. Forces aéronavales Est de l'Atlantique [obsolète - remplace AIREASTLANT 2.].
2. Naval (Maritime) Air Forces, Eastern Atlantic Area [obsolete - replaced by AIREASTLANT 1.].
2. Forces aéronavales du Secteur oriental de l'Atlantique [obsolète - remplacé par AIREASTLANT 1.].

**AIREX** air exercise.
exercise aérien.

**AIRFA** Associazione Italiana per la Ricerca sull'Anemia di Fanconi (Italy).
Italian acronym of the: Italian Association for Research on Fanconi's Anemia.

**AIRI** Associazione Italiana per la Ricerca Industriale (Italy).
Italian acronym of the: Italian Association for Industrial Research.

**AIRIC** Associazione Italiana per la Ricerca sull'Invecchiamento Cerebrale (Italy).

**AIRIEL** Associazione Italiana per la Ricerca nell'Impiego degli elastomeri.
Italian acronym of the: Italian Association for Research regarding the use of elastomers.

**AIRLORDS** AIRlines Load Optimization Recording and Display System.

**Airmic** Association of insurance and risk managers.

**AIRMoN** Atmospheric Integrated Research Monitoring Network.

**AIRMOVREP** air movement report.
compte rendu de mouvements aériens.

**AIRNON** Alied Air Forces, North Norway [obsolete].
Forces aériennes alliées du nord de la Norvège [obsolète].

**AIRNORTH** 1. Allied Air Forces North [has replaced AIRBALTAP; AIRCENT and AIRNORTHWEST].
1. Forces aériennes alliées Nord [remplace AIRBALTAP, AIRCENT et AIRNORTHWEST].
2. Allied Air Forces, Northern Europe [obsolete].
2. Forces aériennes alliées Nord-Europe [obsolète].

**AIRNORTHWEST** Allied Air Forces, Northwestern Europe [obsolete - replaced by AIRNORTH 1.].
Forces aériennes alliées du Nord-Ouest-Europe [obsolète - remplacé par AIRNORTH 1.].

**AIROFEX** air offensive exercise.
exercice aérien offensif.

**AIRP** Association Internationale des Relations Publiques.
French initialism of the: Public Relations International Association.

**AIRPASS** Airborne Interception Radar and Pilots Attack Sight System.

**AIR project** Agro-Industrial Research project.
*European Community Project.*

**AIRS** Accident Information Retrieval System.

**AIRS** Advanced Inertial Reference Sphere.

**AIRS** Airborne Infrared Radiometer System.

**AIRS** Associazione Italiana Ricerca sulla Sordità.
Italian acronym of the: Italian Association for Deafness Research.

**AIRS** Atmospheric Infrared Sounder.

**AIRS** Automatic Image Retrieval System.

**AIRSONOR** Allied Air Forces South Norway [obsolete].
Forces aériennes alliées du sud de la Norvège [obsolète].

**AIRSOUTH** 1. Allied Air Forces South [has replaced AIRSOUTH 2.].
1. Forces aériennes alliées Sud [remplace AIRSOUTH 2.].
2. Allied Air Forces, Southern Europe [obsolete - replaced by AIRSOUTH 1.].
2. Forces aériennes alliées du sud-Europe [obsolète - remplacé par AIRSOUTH 1.].

**AIRTRANSEX** AIR TRANSportation EXercise.
*Military.*

**A.I.R.U.** Associazione Italiana Riscaldamento Urbano.
Italian initialism of the: Italian Association for Urban Heating.

**AIS** Ablating Inner Surface.
**AIS** Academy of Independent Scholars (U.S.A.).
**AIS** Accounting Information System.
**AIS** Advanced Information Systems.
**AIS** Aeronautical Information Service.
**AIS** Aeronautical Information Specialist.
**AIS** Air-Injection System.
*Mechanical Engineering.*
**AIS** Air Intelligence Service.
**AIS** Alcohol Insoluble Solids.
**AIS** Analog Input System.
**AIS** Androgen Insensitivity Syndrome.
*Endocrinology.*
**AIS** Anti-Icing System.
*Aviation.*
**AIS** Anti-Inflammatoire Stéroïdien.
French acronym meaning: Steroid Anti-Inflammatory.
**AIS** Army Intelligence School.
**AIS** Association Internationale de la Savonnerie et de la Detergence.
French acronym of the: International Association of the Soap and Detergent Industry.
**AIS** Association Internationale de Sociologie.
French acronym of the: International Sociology Association.
**AIS** Association Internationale de la Soie.
French acronym of the: International Silk Association.
**AIS** Associazione Internazionale per lo Sviluppo.
Italian initialism of the: International Development Association. AIS was created in September 1960.
**AIS** Associazione Italiana Strumentisti.
*Italian Association.*
**AIS** Automated Information System.
**AISA** Associate of the Incorporated Secretaries Association.
**AISA** Association Internationale pour la Securité Aérienne.
French acronym of the: International Air Safety Association.
**AISC** Assessment and Information Services Center - Of the U.S. National Environmental Satellite, Data and Information Service.
**AISE**; **A.I.S.E.** Associazione Internazionale delle Science Economiche.
Italian acronym of the: International Association of Economical Sciences.
**AISI** American Iron and Steel Institute.
**AISI** Associazione Italiana per lo Sviluppo Internazionale (Italy).
Italian acronym of the: Italian Association for International Development.
**AISLE** An Intersociety Liaison Committee on Environment.
**AISM** Associazione Italiana per gli Studi di Marketing (Italy).
Italian acronym of the: Italian Association for Marketing Studies.
**AISM** Associazione Italiana Sclerosi Multipla.
Italian acronym of the: Italian Multiple Sclerosis Association.
**AISP** Allied Imagery System Publication.
publication interalliée sur les systèmes d'imagerie.
**AISPO** Associazione Italiana per la Solidarietà tra i Popoli (Italy).
Italian acronym of the: Italian Association for Solidarity among Peoples. AISPO is based in Milan, Italy.
**AIS process** Advanced Isotope Separation process.
*Nuclear Energy.*
**AISS** Association Internationale de Sécurité Sociale.
French initialism of the: International Association for Social Security.
**AIST** Agenzia per l'Innovazione Scientifica e Tecnologica (Italy).
Italian acronym of the: Agency for Scientific and Technological Innovation.
**Aistom** Associazione italiana incontinenti e stomizzati.
*Italian Association.*
**AIT** Academy for Implants and Transplants.
**AIT** Advanced Individual Training.
*U.S. Army.*
**AIT** Agency for Instructional Technology.
**AIT** Agglutination-Inhibition Test.
*Clinical Chemistry.*
**AIT** Alliance Internationale de Tourisme.
French acronym of the: International Tourism Alliance.
**AIT** American Institute in Taiwan.
**AIT** Analytic Intelligence Test.
*Psychology.*
**AIT** Anterior Inferotemporal Cortex.
**AIT** Army Intelligence Translator.
**AIT** Asian Institute of Technology (Thailand).
**AIT** Association Internationale des Travailleurs (France).
French acronym of the: International Association of Workers.
**AIT** Associazione Italiana di Telerilevamento.
*Italian Association.*
**AITA** Association Internationale des Transports Aériens.
**A.IT.A.** Associazione Italiana Afasici.

Italian acronym of the: Aphasics Italian Association.
**AITA** Associazione Italiana di Tecnologia Alimentare.
Italian acronym of the: Italian Association of Food Technology. AITA was founded in Milan, Italy in 1979.
**Aitec** Associazione italiana tecnico economica del cemento (Italy).
**A.I.T.I.** Associazione Italiana Traduttori e Interpreti.
Italian acronym of the: Italian Association of Translators and Interpreters.
**AIT program** Advanced Information Technology program.
*European Union Program.*
**AITIVA** Associazione Italiana Tecnici Industrie Vernici e Affini (Italy).
**AIV** Associazione Internazionale di Vulcanologia.
Italian initialism of the: International Association of Volcanology.
**AIV** Associazione Italiana del Vuoto.
Italian initialism of the Italian Association for Vacuum. A non-profit Association, started its activity in 1962. A member of the IUVSTA, the AIV organizes a national congress every two years. Publishes a Review and textbooks, organizes Courses on vacuum physics and specialized workshops.
For further details see under: **IUVSTA**.
**AIV** Aviation Impact Variable.
**AIX** Astrotech International Corp.
*American Stock Exchange symbols.*
**AIY** The airport code for Atlantic City, New Jersey, U.S.A.
**A.J.** Achilles Jerk.
The Achilles Jerk is also known as: Achilles Tendon Reflex.
*Physiology.*
**AJ** American Journal.
**AJ** Antijamming.
*Electronics.*
**AJ** Azerbaijdzhan.
**aja.** (abbr.) adjacent.
**Aja** American Jail Association (U.S.A.).
**AJA** American Journal of Archaeology.
*Publication.*
**AJA** American Judges Association (U.S.A.).
**Aja** L'Aja - The above acronyms were coined accidentally using the Italian word Aja (L'Aja) which means The Hague in Italian.
**AJAR** Association des Juifs Anciens Resistants (France).
French acronym of the: Association of the Jews in the Resistance.
**AJCMC** ACCS Joint Configuration Management Committee.
Comité de gestion conjointe de la configuration de l'ACCS.
**AJF** Allied joint force.
force interarmées interalliées.
**AJI** area of joint interest.
zone d'intérêt commun.
**AJOD** Allied Joint Operations Doctrine.
doctrine interalliées des opérations interarmées.
**AJP** Allied Joint Publication.
publication interalliée interarmées.
**ak**; **ack** (abbr.) acknowledge.
*Telecommunications.*
**AK** (abbr.) Alaska (U.S.A.).
**AKA** Also Known As.
*Management.*
**AKAPs** A-Kinase Anchoring Proteins.
*Medicine; Molecular Pharmacology; Signal Transduction.*
**A.K.C.** American Kennel Club.
**AKHI** Alaska Historical library and museum.
**akhi** The above acronym was coined accidentally using the Arabic word "akhi" which means: my brother.
**AKtb** Aktiebolaget (Sweden).
Joint Stock Company in Sweden.
**AL** Abnormal Lungs.
*Medicine.*
**AL** Absolute Limen.
*Psychophysics.*
**AL** Accession List.
**AL** Accidental Loss.
*Nuclear Energy.*
**AL** Acoustic Labyrinth.
*Acoustical Engineering.*
**AL** Action for Life.
**AL** Acute Leukemia.
Acute leukemia is a form of leukemia characterized by anemia and hemorrhagic manifestations.
*Medicine.*
**AL** Aeronomy Laboratory (U.S.A.)
Of the U.S Environmental Research Laboratories.
**AL** Air Liaison.
**AL** Air Lock.
*Civil Engineering; Engineering; Mining Engineering.*
**AL** (abbr.) Alabama (U.S.A.).
**AL** Albania.
**AL** Alessandria, Italy.
**Al** the chemical symbol for Aluminum / Aluminium.

Aluminum is a metallic element having the atomic number 13, an atomic weight of 26.9815, and a melting point of 650°C. It is used in alloys mainly for household utensils, beverage cans and electrical equipment.
*Chemistry.*

**AL** American League; American Legion.

**AL**; **A.L.** Anglo-Latin.
*Languages.*

**a.l.** année de lumière.
French initialism meaning: light-year.
*Astronomy.*

**a.l.** après livraison.
French initialism meaning: after delivery.

**AL** Arc Lamp.
Arc lamp is also known as: electric arc lamp.
*Electricity.*

**AL** Argon Laser.
Argon Laser is a laser that uses ionized argon. It is also known as: Argon-Ion Laser.
*Optics.*

**AL**; **A.L.** Artillerie Lourde.
French initialism meaning: Heavy Artillery.
*Ordnance.*

**AL** Assembly Language.
The assembly language is a low-level programming language.
*Computer Programming.*

**AL** Authorized Library.
*Computer Programming.*

**a.l.** Autograph letter.

**ALA** Academy for Lighting Arts.

**ALA** Afrique Littéraire et Artistique.
*Publications.*

**ALA** Air-Land Assault.

**Ala**. (abbr.) Alabama (U.S.A.).

**Ala** (abbr.) Alanine.
*Biochemistry.*

**ALA** American Lawyers Association; American Library Association; American Longevity Association (U.S.A.).

**ALA** Arab Liberation Army.

**ALA** Associate in Liberal Arts.

**ALA** Associate of the Library Association.

**ALA** Associazione Nazionale Italiana Lotta AIDS (Italy).
Italian acronym of the: Italian National Association for the fight against AIDS.

**ALA** Authors League of America (U.S.A.).

**A.L.A.** Automobile Legal Association.

**ala** The above acronyms were coined accidentally using the Italian word "ala" which means: wing *Architecture; Aviation; Geology; Military Science; Zoology.*

**ALAA** American Lands Access Association.

**ALACE** Autonomous LAgrangian Circulation Explorer.

**ALAE** Atmospheric Lyman-Alpha Emissions.

**ALALC** Associazione Latino-Americana per il Libero Commercio.
Italian acronym of the: Latin-American Association for Free Trade.

**ALARA** As Low As Reasonably Achievable.

**ALARM** Airborne LAser Receiver Module.

**ALARM** Air-Launched Advanced Ramjet Missile.

**ALARM** air-launched anti-radar missile.
missile antiradar à lanceur aérien.

**ALARM** Automatic Light Aircraft Readiness Monitor.

**ALAS**; **Alas.** (abbr.) Alaska.

**ALAS** Associate in Letters, Arts and Sciences.

**ALAS** Associate of the Chartered Land Agents' Society (G.B.).

**ALAS** Automated Literature Alerting System.
*Data Processing.*

**ALAS** Auxiliary Loans to Assist Students.

**ALAT** Avion Léger de l'Armée de Terre (France).

**ALB** Academic Libraries of Brooklyn (U.S.A.).

**ALB** Aircraft Launching Bulletin.

**ALB** The airport code for Albany, New York, U.S.A.

**alb.** (abbr.) albumin.
Albumin is a type of plant and animal protein which is soluble in water and coagulates when heated.
*Biochemistry.*

**ALB** Anticipated Level of Business.

**ALBA** (abbr.) Alberta (Canadian province) (Canada).

**ALBA** American Lawn Bowls Association; American Leather Belting Association (U.S.A.).

**Alba** The above acronyms were coined accidentally using the Italian proper name (feminine) Alba. Also: dawn (*Astronomy*).

**ALBI** Air-Launched Ballistic Intercept; Air-Launched Boost Intercept.

**ALBI** ALaska Business and Industry.

**ALBSU** Adult Literacy and Basic Skills Unit (London, G.B.)

**ALB system** Anti-Lock Brake system.
*Mechanical Engineering.*

**ALC** 1. ACCS logistic concept.
1. concept logistique de l'ACCS.
2. ACE Logistic Centre.
2. centre logistique du CAE.

3. Alerts Committee.
3. Comité des alertes.
**alc.** (abbr.) alcohol.
*Organic Chemistry.*
**ALC** Automatic Level Control.
*Electronics; Mechanical Engineering.*
**ALCE** 1. ACE Logistic Control Element.
1. élément de contrôle logistique du CAE.
2. airlift control element.
2. élément de contrôle du transport aérien.
**ALCE** Associazione Lombarda Consorzi Esportazione (Italy).
Italian acronym of the: Lombardy Association of Export Consortia.
**alce** The above acronyms were coined accidentally using the Italian word "alce" which means: elk (*Vertebrate Zoology*).
**$AlCl_3$** Aluminum Chloride.
Aluminum Chloride has many applications in petroleum manufacturing and refining.
*Inorganic Chemistry.*
**ALCM** Air-Launched Cruise Missile.
*Ordnance.*
**ALCO** Associazione Lirico-Concertistica.
*Italian Association.*
**ALCU** Arithmetic Logic and Control Unit.
**ALD** Adrenoleukodystrophy.
ALD is a fatal hereditary brain disease.
*Biochemistry; Medicine; Neurobiology; Neurology; Physiology.*
**ALD** Advanced Learner's Dictionary.
**ALD** (abbr.) Aldehyde.
Aldehyde is a class of organic compounds.
*Organic Chemistry.*
**ald.** (abbr.) alderman.
**ALDA** Aluminum (Dihydroxy) Allantoinate.
*Organic Chemistry.*
**ALDA** American Land Developmental Association.
**ALDAC** Associazione Lombarda Dirigenti Aziende Commerciali (Italy).
**ALDCE** Advanced Learner's Dictionary of Current English.
**ALDF** Animal Legal Defense Fund.
California-based (U.S.A.).
**ALDO** Activity Level Dependent Operations.
**Aldo** Aldosterone.
$C_{21}H_{28}O_5$ - Aldosterone, also known as: Aldocortin, chiefly functions to regulate sodium, potassium, and metabolism.
*Biochemistry.*
**ALDP** Advanced Launch Development Program.
**ALE** Adaptive Line Enhancer.
**ALE** Additional Living Expense.
**ALE** Airport Lighting Equipment.
**ALE** American Lives Endowment.
**ALE** Analysis of Lexical Errors.
**ALE** Atmospheric Lifetime Experiment.
**ALE** Automatic Laser Encoder.
**ALE-B** Average Life Expectancy at Birth.
*Medicine.*
**ALEC** American Legislative Exchange Council.
**ALEC** Associazione Libraria Europea Culturale.
Italian acronym of the: European Cultural Library Association.
**ALEF** Alcor Life Extension Foundation.
**alef** or **alif** The above acronym was coined accidentally using the Arabic word "alef" which is the first letter of the Arabic alphabet.
**ALENA** Accord de Libre-Echange Nord-Americain.
French acronym meaning: North American Free Trade Agreement.
**ALE output** Address Latch Enable output.
*Computers.*
**ALER** Azienda Lombarda Edilizia Residenziale Milano (Italy).
Since April, 1997. Formerly IACP.
For further details see under: **IACP**.
**ALERFA** alert phase.
phase d'alerte.
**ALERT** Alcohol Level Evaluation Road Tester.
**ALERT** American Library for Education, Research and Training (U.S.A.).
**ALERT program** Arctic Long-term Environmental Research Transects program.
Of the U.S. Environmental Protection Agency.
**ALESCO** Arab League Educational, cultural and Scientific Organization.
**ALE technology** Automatic Link Establishment technology.
**ALEX** alert exercise.
exercise d'alerte.
**Alex** short for Alexander / Alexandra.
**ALF** Acute Liver Failure.
*Medicine.*
**ALF** Animal Liberation Front.
**ALFA** Adaptive optics with a Laser For Astronomy.
ALFA was built by the Max Planck Institute.
*Optics.*
**Alfa** Associazione lombarda famiglie audiolesi.
*Italian Association.*
**ALFA Romeo** Anonima Lombarda Fabbrica Automobili Romeo (Italy).
*Car Makers.*
**AlFn** Aluminum Fluoride.
Aluminum Fluoride is a white, crystalline powder slightly insoluble in cold water.

*Inorganic Chemistry.*

**ALFRED** Associative Learning From Relative Environmental Data.

**ALFS** Alaska Landscape Flux Study.

**alg.** (abbr.) algebra.
The word algebra derives from the Arabic term "reduction".
*Mathematics.*

**Alg.** (abbr.) Algerian; Algiers.

**ALG** Antilymphocyte Globulin.
Antilymphocyte globulin, also known as antilymphocytic globulin, is a drug used in transplant surgery. It was developed in the 1960s. Clinical studies were approved in 1971.
*Transplant Surgery.*

**ALGOL**; **Algol** Algorithmic Language.
ALGOL which is no longer widely used is a computer language for communicating algorithms.
*Computer Programming.*

**ALI** American Law Institute.
ALI is located in Philadelphia, Pennsylvania, U.S.A.

**ALI** Arc Lamp Igniter.

**ALI** Associazione Librai Italiani (Italy).
Italian acronym of the: Italian Booksellers Association.

**ALI** Atlante Linguistico Italiano.
Italian acronym meaning: Italian Linguistic Atlas.

**ALIAS instrument** Aircraft Laser Infrared Absorption Spectrometer instrument.

**ALI/ABA Review** American Law Institute/American Bar Association Review.
Founded in 1970. Review of the American Law Institute/American Bar Association Committee on Continuing Professional Education (U.S.A.).
*Publications.*

**Alice** Adiabatic low-energy injection and capture experiment.

**ALICE**; **Alice** ALaska Integrated Communications Exchange.
*Electronics.*

**ALICE** Archivio Libri Italiani su Calcolatore Elettronico (Italy).
Italian acronym meaning: Archives of Italian Books on Computer.

**ALID** Automated Library Issue Document.

**ALIMPREP** alert implementation report.
compte rendu d'exécution des mesures d'alerte.

**ALIR** Associazione per la Lotta all'Insufficienza Respiratoria.
*Italian Association.*

**ALIRT** Adaptive Long range Infrared Tracker.

**ALIT** Automatic Line Insulation Tester.

**ALIVE Study** AIDS Link to Intravenous Experience Study.

**ALJ** (Service de Coordination de) l'Action Locale pour Jeunes (Luxemburg).

**alk.** (abbr.) alkaline; alkalinity.
*Chemistry.*

**ALL** Accelerated Learning of Logic.

**ALL** Address Locator Logic.

**all.** (abbr.) allegato.
Italian abbreviation meaning: enclosed; enclosure.
Also: **alleg.**

**ALLA** 1. Alliance Long Lines Activity.
1. Activité alliée des lignes à grande distance.
2. Allied Long Lines Agency [obsolete].
2. Bureau allié des lignes à grande distance [obsolète].

**ALL cells** Acute Lymphoblastic Leukemia cells.
*Biological Chemistry; Life Sciences.*

**alleg.** (abbr.) allegato.
For further details see under: **all.**

**all'ingr.** (abbr.) all'ingrosso.
Italian abbreviation meaning: by wholesale.

**ALLOYSUPPORT** ALLOY and process development SUPPORT by means of dedicated thermodynamic database.
*European Community Project.*

**ALM** Assurance Longue Maladie (France).
*Insurance.*

**ALMA** Asian Land Mammal Age.
*Paleontology.*

**ALMA** Atacama Large Millimeter Array.
ALMA, built by the United States and Europe, will be located 5000 meters above sea level on the Chajnantor plain in the Chilean Andes. Could be fully operational in 2009.

**alma** The above acronyms were coined using the Spanish word alma which means "soul".

**ALMIS** Associazione per la ricerca sulle Lesioni del Midollo Spinale.
Italian acronym of the: Association for Spinal Cord Injury Research.

**ALMV** air-launched miniature vehicle.
véhicule (ou engin) miniature à lanceur aérien.

**AlN** Aluminum Nitride.
AlN is used in electronics.
*Inorganic Chemistry.*

**ALO** air liaison officer.
officier de liaison air.

**$Al_2O_3$** Activated Alumina.
Activated Alumina is used mainly for water purification.
*Inorganic Chemistry.*

**$Al_2O_3$** Aluminum Oxide.

Aluminum Oxide, also known as: Alumina, is used mainly for the production of aluminum, and for the manufacture of many products such as abrasives, paper, and ceramics.
*Inorganic Chemistry.*
**$Al_2O_3$** Corundum.
*Materials; Mineralogy.*
**ALO** At Least Once.
*Computers.*
**ALOA** Aviation Légère d'Observation d'Artillerie (France).
**ALOFT** Airborne Light Optical Fibre Technology.
**ALP**; **Alp** Adaptable Lending Project.
*Banking; Finance.*
**ALP** Alkaline Phosphatase.
Alkaline phosphatase is also known as: phosphomonoesterase.
*Biochemistry; Enzymology.*
**ALP** Allied Logistic Publication.
publication interalliée sur la logistique.
**ALP** American Labor Party (U.S.A.).
**ALP**; **Alp** Associazione Liberi Professionisti.
Italian acronym of the: Association of Professional Men/Women (Italy).
**ALP** Australian Labor Party (Australia).
**ALPA** Airline Pilot Association.
**ALPH** ALaskan PHilatelist.
*Publications.*
**alph** The above acronym was coined accidentally using the Arabic word "alph" which means: one thousand.
**a**; **al**; **alph** (abbr.) alphabet.
*Computer Programming; Linguistics.*
**a**; **al**; **alph** (abbr.) alphabetical / alphabetic.
**ALPHA** Automatic Literature Processing, Handling and Analysis.
**alpha** The above acronym was coined accidentally using the word "alpha" which is the first letter of the Greek alphabet: $\alpha$.
**Alpi** Associazione laboratori di prova indipendenti (Italy).
Italian acronym of the: Association of independent testing laboratories.
**$AlPO_4$** Aluminum Phosphate.
Aluminum Phosphate, also known as: Aluminum Triphosphate; Aluminum Orthophosphate, is used mainly in ceramics and pharmaceuticals.
*Inorganic Chemistry.*
**ALPS** Advanced Linear Programming System.
**ALPS** Aosta, Liguria, Piemonte System (Italy).
**ALR** Alliance for Lupus Research (U.S.A.).
**ALRI** Acute Lower Respiratory Infection.
*Medicine.*
**ALS** Advanced Launch System.
**ALS** Advanced Light Source.
*Synchrotron Light.*
**ALS** Alternative Line Service.
*Cellular Phones.*
**ALS** American Lung Society (U.S.A.).
**ALS** Amyotrophic Lateral Sclerosis.
Amyotrophic lateral sclerosis, also known as lateral sclerosis is a degenerative disease of the lower motor neurons. ALS is also known as: *Lou Gehrig's disease.*
*Medicine; Neurodegenerative Diseases.*
**ALS** Antilymphocyte Serum.
*Immunology.*
**a.l.s.** autograph letter, signed.
**ALSC** afloat logistics and sealift capability.
capacité de transport et de soutien logistique embarqués.
**ALSE** Applied Language Studies in Education.
*Linguistics.*
**$Al_2SiO_5$** Andalusite.
*Mineralogy.*
**ALSL** Alternative Landing Ship Logistic.
**ALSP** Atmospheric and Land Surface Processes.
**ALSS** Adult Learning Satellite Service.
**ALSS** Advanced Location Strike System.
**ALSS** advanced logistics support site.
site de soutien logistique avancé.
**ALT** aérodyne léger télépiloté.
remotely-piloted vehicle (RPV).
**ALT** Alanine Aminotransferase.
*Enzymology.*
**ALT** (abbr.) Alteration.
*Graphic Arts* - An alteration requested by the author or the publisher, is a change to be made in copy after it has been typeset.
*Petrography* - In petrography, an alteration is a change in a rock's mineral composition.
**ALT**; **alt.** (abbr.) alternate.
**alt.** (abbr.) alternatively.
**ALT** Alternative mechanism for Lenghening of Telomeres.
*Medical Research.*
**ALT** (abbr.) Altimeter.
The altimeter is an instrument for measuring altitude, in relation to sea level or some other fixed level.
*Engineering.*
**alt.** (abbr.) altitude.
*Astronomy; Aviation; Engineering; Mathematics.*
**ALT** Associazione nazionale Lotta alla Trombosi (Italy).

Italian acronym of the: National Association for the fight against Thrombosis.

**ALTA** American Literary Translators Association; American Library Trustee Association (U.S.A.).

**ALTAI** Analisi, Livellamento e Tempificazione Automatici Integrati.
Italian acronym meaning: Automation-Integrated Analysis, Levelling and Timing.
*Business Management.*

**ALTBMD** active layered theatre ballistic missile defence.
défense active contre les missiles balistiques de théâtre.

**ALTE** ALTitude Error; ALtitude Transmitting Equipment.

**ALTEL Companies** Association of Long-distance TELephone Companies.

**Alter-Europe project** Alternative Traffic in Towns project.
Alter-Europe is funded by the U.K.'s environment and transport department. The initiative was launched in April 1998.
*Low Emissions Vehicles.*

**ALT key** ALTernate Key.
*Computer Technology.*

**AL.TOUR.** Accueil Local TOURistique.
Of the NOW Program.
*European Community Program.*

**ALTROCCENT** Alternate Regional Operational Control Centre.
centre de contrôle operationnel régional de rechange.

**ALTS** Associazione per la Lotta ai Tumori del Seno (Italy).
Italian acronym of the: Association for the fight against Breast Cancer.

**ALU** Arab Lawyers Union.

**ALU** Arithmetic Logic Unit.
ALU is a digital circuit or group of circuits within the CPU which carries out a set of arithmetic logic operations. Arithmetic Logic Unit is also known as: Arithmetical Element.
*Computer Technology.*

**ALVF** Artillerie Lourde sur Voie Ferrée (France).

**alw.** (abbr.) allowance.
*Design Engineering; Industrial Engineering.*

**aly.** (abbr.) alloy.
*Foundry; Metallurgy.*

**AL-YD boundary** ALlerød - Younger Dryas boundary.
*Deglacial Records; Geology; Geophysics; Quaternary Geology.*

**a/m** above mentioned.

**AM** Academy of Management.

**AM** Access Management; Access Mechanism; Access Method.
*Computer Technology.*

**AM** Access Matrix; Access Mode.
*Computer Programming.*

**AM** Accounting Machine.
The accounting machine is a keyboard-operated noncomputerized machine used to carry out calculations and provide accounting records.
*Computer Technology.*

**AM** Acoustic-Magnetic.

**AM** Actuator Mechanism.

**AM** Addressing Mode; Address Modification.
*Computer Programming.*

**AM** Address Mark.
*Microprocessors.*

**AM** The airline code for Aeromexico.

**a.m.** air mail.

**AM** Air Mattress.

**AM** Alveolar Macrophage.
The alveolar macrophage is also called dust cell because it absorbs foreign matter.
*Anatomy.*

**Am.** (abbr.) America; American.
Also: **A**.

**A4M** American Academy of Anti-Aging Medicine (Chicago, U.S.A).
Holds annual Conferences and trains doctors in *Antiaging Medicine.*

**Am** The chemical symbol for Americium.
Americium is a chemical element having the atomic number 95, an atomic weight of 243 and a half-life of 475 years. Named for **America** because it was discovered in the United States of America.
*Chemistry; Symbols.*

**AM** Aminophylline.
$C_{16}H_{24}N_{10}O_4$.
*Pharmacology.*

**am.** (abbr.) ammeter.
An instrument to measure the flow rate of an electric current.
*Engineering.*

**Am** ammonium.
*Chemistry.*

**am.** (abbr.) amortissement.
French abbreviation meaning: redemption of stock.
*Business; Economics; Finance.*

**A/m** Ampere per meter.
The Standard International unit of magnetic field strength or magnetization.
*Metrology.*

**am.** (abbr.) amplitude.

*Astronomy; Ecology; Electricity; Geology; Mathematics; Navigation; Physics.*
**AM** Amplitude Modulation.
The amplitude modulation is the variation of the amplitude of a radio wave or carrier for the purpose of transmitting a signal.
*Electronics.*
**Am** Amyl.
Amyl is also known as: Pentyl.
*Organic Chemistry.*
**AM** Anderson Model.
*Physics.*
**AM** Anovular Menstruation.
**AM** Apparent Motion.
*Biophysics; Cognitive Science.*
**AM** Armenia.
**AM** Arousal Mechanism.
*Medicine.*
**A.M.**; **AM** Assistant Manager; Associate Member.
**AM** Assurance Maladie.
French initialism meaning: Medical Insurance.
**AM** Astigmatism, Myopic.
Also: **AsM**.
*Ophthalmology.*
**A/M** Auto/Manual.
**AM** Auxiliary Memory.
Auxiliary Memory is also known as: Auxiliary Storage; Secondary Storage; External Memory.
*Computer Technology.*
**AM** Aviation Medicine.
**A/m$^2$** Ampere per square meter.
The SI unit of current density.
*Metrology.*
**AMA** Acoustical Materials Association.
**AMA** Actual Mechanical Advantage.
*Mechanical Engineering.*
**AMA** Against Medical Advice.
**AMA** Agence Mondiale Antidopage.
**AMA** The airport code for Amarillo, Texas, U.S.A.
**AMA** American Management Association; American Marketing Association; American Medical Association; Assistant Masters' Association (U.S.A.).
**A.M.A.** Archaeology and Museum Association.
**AMA** Automatic Message Accounting.
Automatic message accounting is also known as: Automatic Toll Ticketing.
*Telecommunications.*
**AMA** Automobile Manufacturers Association.
**AMAC** Aeronautica Militare - Aviazione Civile (Italy).
**AMAD** accès multiple avec assignations à (ou par) la demande.
demand-assignment multiple access (DAMA).
**AMANDA** Antarctic Muon And Neutrino Detector Array.
*Astrophysics; Geography.*
**AMANIS** Advanced MANufacturing Information System for the designer.
*European Community.*
**AMAP** Arctic Monitoring and Assessment Program.
The purpose of AMAP was to measure the levels of anthropogenic pollutants and assess their effects in parts of the Arctic Environment.
**AMAST** Algebraic Methodology And Software Technology.
**AMB** AIDS Malignancy Bank.
The AMB opened in October 1995. It is funded by the U.S. National Cancer Institute and comprises repositories in five sites around the United States.
**amb.** (abbr.) ambasciata.
Italian abbreviation meaning: embassy.
**amb.** (abbr.) ambasciatore / ambasciatrice.
Italian abbreviation meaning: ambassador / ambassadress.
**AMBIM** Associate Member of the British Institute of Management (G.B.).
**Ambroveneto** (abbr.) Banco Ambrosiano Veneto (Italy).
Now BancaIntesaBCI with CARIPLO and BCI.
*Banking Integration.*
For further details see under: **CARIPLO** and **BCI**.
**AMC** Advanced Management Course.
**AMC** Agricultural Mortgage Corporation.
**AMC** air mission control.
contrôle de mission aérienne.
**AMC** Army Material Command (U.S.A.).
**AMC** Art Master's Certificate.
**AMC** Atlantic Marine Center.
**AMC** Automatic Message Counting.
**AMC** Automatic Modulation Control.
*Electronics.*
**AMC** Axial Magma Chamber.
*Earth Observations; Geological Sciences; Magmatic Activity; Oceanography.*
**AMCC** Allied Movement Coordination Centre.
Centre interallié de coordination des mouvements.
**AMCM** airborne mine countermeasures mission.
mission antimine aéroportée.
**AMCs** Asset Management Corporations.
**AMD** Acid Mine Drainage.
*Chemistry; Geology; Geophysics.*
**AMD**; **Amd** Advanced Micro Devices.
**AMD** aeromedical.
aéromédical.
**AMD** Age-related Macular Degeneration.

*Genetics; Macular Dystrophy.*
**AMD** Air Movement Data.
**AMD** Automated Multiple Development.
**AMDI** Associazione Medici Dentisti Italiani.
*Italian Association.*
**amdt.** (abbr.) amendment.
**AME** Accordo Monetario Europeo.
Italian acronym meaning: European Monetary Agreement.
**A.M.E.** Advanced Master of Education.
**A.M.E.** African Methodist Episcopal.
**AME** Angle-Measuring Equipment.
**AMEC** Arctic Military Environmental Cooperation.
**AMeDP** Allied Medical Publication.
publication médicale interalliée.
**AMEN** Association Mondiale pour l'Energie Non-pollutante.
French acronym of the: World Association for Clean Energy.
**AMEPP** Allied Maritime Environmental Protection Publication.
publication interalliée sur la protection de l'environnement maritime.
**AMERIEZ program** Antarctic Marine Ecosystem Research at the Ice - Edge Zone program.
*Research Program.*
**AmerInd** American Indian.
*Languages.*
**AmerSp** American Spanish.
*Languages.*
**AMES** accès multiple par étalement du spectre.
spread-spectrum multiple access (SSMA).
**AMESLAN** AMErican Sign LANguage.
For further details see under: **ASL**.
**AMETS** army meteorological system.
système météorologique de l'armée de terre.
**AMEX** American Stock Exchange.
Also: **ASE**.
**AMF** Accordo Multifibre.
AMF is an International Agreement regarding textiles.
**AMF** ACE Mobile Force.
Force mobile du CAE.
**AMF(A)** ACE Mobile Force (Air).
Force mobile du CAE (Air).
**AmFAR** American Foundation for AIDS Research (U.S.A.).
**AMF(L)** ACE Mobile Force (Land).
Force mobile du CAE (Terre).
**AM fungi** Arbuscular Mycorrhizal fungi.
*Biology; Ecology; Hydrology.*
**AMG** Allied Military Government.
**AMG** Assistance Médicale Gratuite (France).
**AMGOT** Allied Military Government.
**AMGRA** American Genetic Resources Alliance.
*Plants Genetics.*
For further details see under: **NPGS** (National Plant Germplasm System).
**AMH** Anti-Müllerian Hormone.
*Developmental Biology; Mammalian Sex Determination; Molecular Biology.*
**AMH** Automated Materials Handling.
**AMHS** automated message handling system.
système automatisé de manipulation de messages.
**AMI** Acute Myocardial Infarction.
**A.M.I.** Aeronautica Militare Italiana.
Italian acronym of the: Italian Air Force.
**AMI** Air Mileage Indicator.
For further details see under: **AMU** (Air Mileage Unit).
**AMI** Alternate Mark Inversion.
*Computers.*
**AMIB** allied military intelligence battalion.
bataillon interallié du renseignement militaire.
**A.M.I.C.I.** Associazione per le Malattie Infiammatorie Croniche dell'Intestino.
Italian acronym of the: Association for Chronic Inflammatory Diseases of the Intestine.
**Amie** Automatisme, mécanique, informatique et électronique.
**AMIES** Animal Monitoring and Identification, the European System.
*European Community Project.*
**AMIES** Automotive Multi-company Integrated Engineering System.
*European Community Project.*
**AMIN** Advertising and Marketing International Network.
**AMINA** Associate Member of the Institution of Naval Architects.
**Amina** The above acronym was coined accidentally using the Arabic word "Amina" which means: honest; faithful; true; loyal. It is also a proper name (feminine).
**AMIP** Atmospheric Model Intercomparison Project.
Of the World Climate Research Program.
**AMIRA** Australian Mineral Industries Research Association (Australia).
**AMIS** automated management information system [obsolete].
système automatisé d'information de gestion [obsolète].
**AMISR** Advanced Molecular Incoherent Scatter Radar.
*Atmospheric Sciences.*
**Amitié** Association for managerial vocational train-

ing in software and information technologies in Europe.
Amitié, a transnational consortium, was founded in 1991.
*European Union Vocational Training Program.*
**am²/Js** ampere square meter per Joule second.
*Metrology.*
**AML** Acute Monocytic Leukemia.
Acute monocytic leukemia is a blood disorder characterized by the symptoms present with other leukemias plus gum bleeding and inflammation.
*Medicine.*
**AML** Acute Myelogenous Leukemia.
**AML** 1. additional military layer.
1. couche militaire additionnelle.
2. aerodrome marking and lighting.
2. marquage et balisage d'aérodrome.
**AML** Adjustable Mortgage Loan.
*Business; Finance.*
**AML** Algebraic - Manipulation Language.
*Computer Programming.*
**AML** Automatic Modulation Limiting.
*Telecommunications.*
**AMLCD** Active Matrix Liquid Crystal Display.
*Applied Physics; Semiconductor Devices.*
**AMLR** Autologous Mixed Lymphocyte Reaction.
**amm.** (abbr.) amministratore.
Italian abbreviation meaning: administrator; (of a Company) director.
Also: **amm.re**.
**amm.** (abbr.) amministrazione.
Italian abbreviation meaning: administration; management.
Also: **amm.ne**.
**amm.** (abbr.) ammiraglio.
Italian abbreviation meaning: admiral.
**AMM**; **amm** Antimissile Missile.
*Ordnance.*
**AMMA** Associazione Metallurgici Meccanici Affini.
*Italian Association.*
**AMMINET** Automated Mortgage Market Information NETwork.
**amm.ne** (abbr.) amministrazione.
For further details see: **amm**.
**ammo.** (abbr.) ammunition.
**amm.re** (abbr.) amministratore.
For further details see: **amm**.
**AMMS** automatic message management system [obsolete].
système de gestion automatique de messages [obsolète].
**AMMSA** Alliance for Microgravity Materials Science and Applications (U.S.A.).
**AMNH** American Museum of Natural History.
**AMO** Administrative Medical Officer (G.B.).
**AMO** Air Ministry Order (G.B.).
**AMO** Allied meteorological office.
**AMO** Alternate Molecular Orbital.
**AMO** Answering Machine Owner.
**AMO** Appareil de Mesure de l'Observation.
French acronym meaning: Observation Measuring Apparatus.
**AMO** Axiomesio-Occlusal.
*Dentistry.*
**AMOA** American Mailorder Association.
Founded in 1982. Located in Washington D.C., U.S.A.
**AMOLED displays** Active Matrix Organic Light-Emitting Diode displays.
*Applied Physics; Semiconductor Devices.*
**AMO physicists** Atomic, Molecular, and Optical physicists.
**amort.** (abbr.) amortissable.
French abbreviation meaning: redeemable.
*Business; Economics; Finance.*
**AMOS** Automated Meteorological Observing System; Automatic Meteorological Observing Station.
**AMovP** Allied Movement Publication.
publication interalliée sur les mouvements.
**AMP** Adenosine Monophosphate.
AMP is also known as: Adenylic Acid.
*Biochemistry.*
**AMP** Advanced Microstructure Prolifer.
The AMP collects data for analysis and interpretation.
**AMP** 1. Allied Mine Warfare Publication.
1. publication interalliée sur la guerre des mines.
2. assisted maintenance period.
2. période de maintenance assistée.
**amp.** (abbr.) amperage.
*Electricity.*
**amp.** (abbr.) ampere.
Named after the French mathematician and physicist André Marie **Ampère**.
*Metrology.*
**AMPA** advanced mission planning aid.
aide perfectionnée à la planification des missions.
**AMPA** Advanced Multimedia Parallel Accelerator.
*European Community Project.*
**AMPA** α-Amino-3-hydroxy-5-methyl-4-isoxazole-Propionic Acid.
**AMPAS** Academy of Motion Picture Arts and Sciences.

**amp-hr** ampere-hour.
For further details see under: **AH**, **ah** (ampere-hour).

**Amplats** Anglo-American platinum Corporation.

**ampR gene** ampicillin Resistance gene.
*Medicine.*

**AMPS** Advanced Mobile Phone Service.

**AMPS** automated message processing system [obsolete].
système automatisé de traitement de messages [obsolète].

**AMPT** α-Methyl-p-Tyrosine.

**AMPTE** Active Magnetospheric Particle Tracer Explorer.

**AMR** Abnormal Mission Routine.

**AMR** Activity Metabolic Rate.

**AMR** Advance Material Request.

**AMR** Advanced Modular Radar.

**AMR** Aerospace Medical Research.

**AMR** Airborne Magnetic Recorder.

**AMR** Alternating Motion Rate.

**AMR** Applied Mechanics Review.

**AMR** Automatic Message Registering.

**AMR** Automatic Message Routing.

**AMR** Automatic Meter Reading.

**amr** The above acronyms were coined accidentally using the Arabic word "amr" which means: order, injuction, prescription.

**AMRAAM** Advanced Medium-Range Air-to-Air Missile.
*Ordnance.*

**AM radio** Amplitude - Modulation radio.
*Telecommunications.*

**AMRC** accès multiple par répartition en code.
code division multiple access (CDMA).

**AMR codes** Adaptive Mesh Refinement codes.
*Astronomy; Physics.*

**AMREF** African Medical and REsearch Foundation.
Located in Nairobi, Kenya. Founded in 1957; independent, non-profit organization working to improve the health of people in Eastern Africa; funds from governmental and non-governmental aid agencies in Africa, Europe and North America, and private donors; official relations with WHO. Activities: primary health care, training, teaching aids, health behaviour and education, *airborne medicine, flying doctor service, medical radio communication, ground mobile medicine, research, consultancies.*

**AMRF** accès multiple par répartition en fréquence.
frequency division multiple access (FDMA).

**AMRI** Association of Missile and Rocket Industries.

**AMRO Bank** AMsterdam-ROtterdam Bank.
*Dutch Bank.*

**AMRS** Automated Merchant Shipping Reporting System.
système automatisé de compte rendu pour la marine marchande.

**AMRT** accès multiple par répartition temporelle.
time-division multiple access (TDMA).

**AMS** Accelerator Mass Spectrometer / Spectrometry.
The Accelerator Mass Spectrometry is a carbon-14 dating technique.
*Archaeobiology; Archaeology.*

**Ams** Accompanying Measures.

**AMS** Aerial Measuring System (U.S.A.).
*Nuclear Defense.*

**AMS** Aerospace Material Specifications.

**AMS** Agricultural Marketing Service.

**AMS** Alpha Magnetic Spectrometer.
NASA's AMS was launched in 2002.
*Cosmic Rays; Physics; Space Technology.*

**AMS**; **A.M.S.** American Mathematical Society; American Meteorological Society (U.S.A.).

**ams** amount of substance.
Ams refers to the amount of a certain component present in a solution or medical preparation.
*Science.*

**AMS** The airport code for Amsterdam (Schiphol) (The Netherlands).

**AMS** Anisotropy of Magnetic Susceptibility.
*Earth Sciences.*

**AMS** Antimatter Magnetic Spectrometer.

**AMS** Army Map Service; Army Medical Service.

**A.M.S.** Army Medical Staff.

**AMS** Assistant Military Secretary.

**AMS** Automatic Music Search.
*Acoustical Engineering.*

**AMSA** Advanced Manned Strategic Aircraft.

**AMSA** Allied Military Security Agency.
Agence alliée de sécurité militaire.

**AMSA** Azienda Municipale Servizi Ambientali (Italy).

**AMSG** Allied military security guidelines.
directive interalliée sur la sécurité militaire.

**AMSIE** Annual Meeting & Science Innovation Exposition.
AAAS's meetings.
For further details see under: **AAAS**.

**AMSL** above mean sea level.
au-dessus du niveau moyen de la mer.

**AMSO** Arab Standardization and Metrology Organization.
The AMSO is based in Amman.
**AMSP** Allied Military Security Publication.
publication interalliée sur la sécurité militaire.
**AMSR** Advanced Microwave Sounding Radiometer.
**AMS radiocarbon method** Accelerator Mass Spectrometer radiocarbon method.
*Anthropology.*
**AMST** Advanced Medium Short-take-off and landing Transport.
**AMSU** Advanced Microwave Sounding Unit.
**A.M.S.W.** Master of Arts in Social Work.
**AMT** Address Mapping Table.
*Computers.*
**a.m.t.** airmail transfer.
**AMT** Alternative Minimum Tax.
**amt.** (abbr.) amount.
**AMT** Appropriate Medical Technologies.
**A.M.T.** Associate in Mechanical Technology.
**A.M.T.** Associate in Medical Technology.
**A.M.T.** Master of Arts in Teaching.
**amtank** (abbr.) amphibious tank.
**AMTEX** Air-Mass Transportation EXperiment (Japan).
**AMTI** airborne moving target indicator.
éliminateur de bord d'échos fixes.
**AMTI** Alternative Minimum Taxable Income (U.S.A.).
**amtrac** (abbr.) amphibious tractor.
*Ordnance.*
**AMTS** Allied Movement and Transportation System.
système de soutien interallié des mouvements et transports.
**AMU** Air Mileage Unit.
The air mileage unit calculates the air distance flown and feeds the resulting data into the air mileage indicator.
*Engineering.*
**AMU** Asian Monetary Unit.
**AMU**; **amu** Atomic Mass Unit.
The atomic mass unit also known as Dalton is a unit of mass to indicate the masses of atoms and molecules.
*Physics.*
**AMU** Auxiliary Memory Unit.
**AMU** Average Monthly Usage.
**AMUE** Association for the Monetary Union of Europe.
**A-MuLV** Abelson Murine Leukemia Virus.
*Virology.*
**A.Mus.** Associate in Music.
**A.Mus.D.** Doctor of Musical Arts.
**AMV** Atterrissage par Mauvaise Visibilité.
French initialism meaning: Poor Visibility Landing.
**AMV** Avian Myeloblastosis Virus.
*Virology.*
**AMVER** automated mutual assistance vessel rescue system.
système automatique d'entraide pour le sauvetage des navires.
**AMVN** Azobis (2,4-dimethylvaleronitrile).
**AMWOP** amphibious warfare operation.
opération de lutte amphibie.
**AMY** (abbr.) Amygdala.
The amygdala is almond-shaped and is located in the lateral ventricle of the brain.
*Anatomy.*
**AMY** (abbr.) Amylase.
*Enzymology.*
**AMY plaques** Amyloid plaques.
*Alzheimer's Research; Neuromolecular Biology; Neuropathology; Neuropsychology of Ageing; Neuroscience.*
**AMZ** Association Mondiale de Zootechnie.
*World Associations.*
**a/n** above named.
**an.** Actinon.
Now called radon-219.
*Nuclear Physics.*
**AN** Ancona, Italy.
**AN** Andorra.
**AN**; **A.N.** Anglo-Norman.
**An** Angstrom / angstrom.
Angstrom is a unit of length to measure wavelengths of light.
*Metrology.*
**AN** Anorexia Nervosa.
AN is characterized by loss of appetite and consequent malnutrition associated with psychological, emotional and physiological disturbances.
*Psychiatry.*
**AN** Army / Navy.
**A.N.** Associate in Nursing.
**ANA** Acoustic Neuroma Association.
**ANA** Administration for Native Americans.
**ANA** Aerojet Network Analyzer.
**ANA** Alanine Nitroanilide.
*Biochemistry.*
**ANA** The airline code for All Nippon Airways.
ANA is Japan's second-largest international airline.
**ANA** Alpha-Naphthyl Acetate.
*Organic Chemistry.*

**ANA**; **A.N.A.** American Nurses' Association.
**ANA** Antinuclear Antibodies.
*Pathology.*
**ANA** Association of National Advertisers (U.S.A.).
**A.N.A.** Associazione Nazionale Alpini.
Italian acronym of the: National Mountain Troops Corps Veterans' Association.
**ana** The above acronyms were coined accidentally using the Arabic word "ana" which means: I, me.
**ANAAO** Associazione Nazionale Aiuti e Assistenti Ospedalieri.
*Italian Association.*
**ANAC** Associazione Nazionale Autoservizi in Concessione.
*Italian Association.*
**Anact** Agence nationale pour l'amélioration des conditions de travail (France).
French acronym of the: National Agency for Improvement of Working Conditions.
**ANAEE**; **Anaee** Associazione NAzionale dell'Editoria Elettronica (Italy).
Italian initialism of the: National Association of Electronic Publishing.
**ANAF** Army, Navy, Air Force.
**A.N.A.G.** Associazione Nazionale Arma del Genio (Italy).
Italian acronym of the: National Pioneer Corps Veterans' Association.
*Military.*
**ANAIP** Associazione Nazionale Amministratori Immobiliari Professionisti.
*Italian Association.*
**ANAL**; **anal.** (abbr.) Analgesic.
An analgesic is a substance or medication that relieves pain.
*Pharmacology.*
**anal.** (abbr.) analogie; analogique.
French abbreviation meaning: analogy; analogic; analogical.
**anal.** (abbr.) analogy.
*Anthropology; Evolution.*
**anal.** (abbr.) analysis.
*Analytical Chemistry; Mathematics; Meteorology.*
**anal.** (abbr.) analyst.
**anal.** (abbr.) analytique.
French abbreviation meaning: analytic(al).
**ANAQ** autorité nationale pour l'assurance de la qualité.
national quality assurance authority (NQAA).
**A.N.A.S.** Azienda Nazionale Autonoma delle Strade (Italy).
Italian acronym of the: National Road Board.
**ANASIN** Associazione Nazionale Aziende Servizi di Informatica e Telematica.
**anat.** (abbr.) anatomical; anatomy.
**ANB** Associazione Nazionale Bersaglieri.
Italian initialism of the: National "Bersaglieri" Association. The Bersaglieri are soldiers of the light infantry of the Italian Army.
**ANBD** Association of National Bond Dealers (U.S.A.).
The ANBD was founded in 1979.
**ANC** Acid-Neutralizing Capacity.
*Acid Rain; Ecosystem Studies; Limnology.*
**ANC** African National Congress.
**ANC** The airport code for Anchorage, Alaska.
**Anc.** (abbr.) ancien.
French abbreviation meaning: old; former.
**anc.** (abbr.) ancient.
**ANC** Army-Navy Civil (Aeronautics Committee).
**ANC** Army Nurse Corps.
**ANCA** Allied Naval Communications Agency [obsolete].
Bureau allié des transmissions navales [obsolète].
**ANCA** Associazione Nazionale Cooperative Agricole (Italy).
**anca** The above acronyms were coined accidentally using the Italian word "anca" which means: buttock (*Anatomy; Mining Engineering)* hip (*Anatomy; Architecture*) ilium (*Anatomy*).
**ANCAD**; **Ancad** Associazione Nazionale Commercianti Articoli Dentari.
*Italian Association.*
**ANCC** Associazione Nazionale delle Cooperative di Consumo.
*Italian Association.*
**ANCE** Agence Nationale pour la Création d'Entreprises.
*French Agency.*
**ANCE** Associazione Nazionale Costruttori Edili.
*Italian Association.*
**Ance**; **ANCE** Associazione Nazionale del Commercio con l'Estero.
Italian acronym of the: National Association of Foreign Trade. ANCE is located in Milan, Italy.
**a/n**; **an. characters** alphanumeric characters.
a/n characters, also known as alphameric characters, are alphabetic or numeric characters such as letters or numerals as well as punctuation marks and symbols used by a computer.
**anch.** (abbr.) anchored.
**ANCI** Associazione Nazionale Comuni Italiani.
*Italian Association.*
**ANCMA** Associazione Nazionale Ciclo, Motociclo e Accessori.

*Italian Association.*

**ANCOVA** ANalysis of COVAriance.
*Statistics.*

**ANCPL** Associazione Nazionale delle Cooperative di Produzione e Lavoro.
*Italian Association.*

**ANCR** Association Nationale des Cabinets de Recouvrement de créances.
*French Association.*

**A.N.C.R.** Associazione Nazionale Combattenti e Reduci (Italy).
Italian initialism of the: National Veterans' Association.
*Military.*

**AND** Air Navigation Directions.

**AND** Airplane Nose Down.

**AND** (abbr.) Andorra.

**And.** (abbr.) Andromeda.
Andromeda is a constellation of the northern sky.
Also: **Andr**.
*Astronomy.*

**Andaf** Associazione nazionale dei direttori amministrativi e finanziari (Italy).
Italian acronym of the: National Association of Directors and Financial Managers. Founded in 1966. Based in Milan, Italy.

**andaf** The above acronym was coined accidentally using the Arabic word "andaf" which means: cleaner than.

**ANDE** Active Nutation Damper Electronics.

**ANDE** Alphanumeric Display Equipment.

**A.N.D.E.** Associazione Nazionale Donne Elettrici (Italy).
Italian acronym of the: Women Voters' National Association.

**Andec; ANDEC** Associazione Nazionale Distributori Elettronica Civile (Italy).

**Andi** Associazione nazionale degli inventori.
Italian acronym of the: National Association of Inventors.

**A.N.D.I.** Associazione Nazionale Dentisti Italiani (Italy).

**ANDP** Association of Neuroscience Departments and Programs (U.S.A.).

**Andr.** (abbr.) Andromeda.
For further details see under: **And**.

**ANDRA** Agence Nationale pour la gestion des Déchets RAdioactifs.
French acronym of the: National Agency for Management of Radioactive Waste. Based in Paris, France. Founded in 1980.

**ANDREE** Association for Nuclear Development and Research in Electrical Engineering.

**ANE** Acoustic Noise Environment.

**ANE** Aerospace and Navigational Electronics.

**ANE** Americans for Nuclear Energy.

**A.N.E.A.** Associazione Nazionale fra gli Enti di Assistenza (Italy).
Italian acronym of the: Welfare Boards' National Association.

**ANED** Associazione Nazionale Emodializzati.
Italian acronym of the: National Association of Hemodialysis patients.

**ANEFLE** Association Nationale des Enseignants de Français Langue Etrangère.
French acronym of the: National Association of Teachers of French as a Foreign language.

**ANELS** Associazione Nazionale Enti Lirici e Sinfonici.
*Italian Association.*

**ANEP** Allied Naval Engineering Publication.
publication interalliée sur l'ingénierie navale.

**ANES** (abbr.) Anesthesiology.
Anesthesiology is the branch of medicine dealing with the administration of anesthetics.
*Medicine.*

**ANF** Air Navigation Facility.
*Transportation Engineering.*

**ANF** Antinuclear Factor.

**A.N.F.** Associazione Nazionale del Fante.
Italian initialism of the: National Infantrymen Association.
*Military.*

**ANF** Atrial Natriuretic Factor.
Atrial natriuretic factor is also known as: Atrial Natriuretic Peptide.
*Endocrinology.*

**ANFI** Associazione Nazionale Finanzieri Italiani.
*Italian Association.*

**ANFFAS**; **Anffas** Associazione nazionale famiglie di fanciulli e adulti subnormali.
*Italian Association.*

**A.N.F.I.A.** Associazione Nazionale fra le Industrie Automobilistiche (Italy).
Italian acronym of the: Motor Industries' National Association.

**ANFP Libraries** Austrian National Focal Point Libraries.
*Austrian Libraries.*

**ANG** Air National Guard.

**Ang.** (abbr.) Angiopoietin.
*Angiogenesis; Medicine; Molecular Medicine.*

**A.N.G.** Associazione Nazionale dei Granatieri.
Italian initialism of the: National Granadier Corps Veterans' Association.
*Military.*

**Angl.** (abbr.) Anglican.
**ANGRY** Antinuclear Group Representing York.
**Ang.-Sax.** Anglo-Saxon.
**ANGTOL** (abbr.) ANGularity TOLerance.
**ANGUS** Air Navigational Guard of the United States.
**ANGUS** A Navigable General-purpose Underwater Surveyor.
**ANI** Automatic Number Identification.
**A.N.I.A.** Associazione Nazionale fra le Imprese Assicuratrici (Italy).
Italian acronym of the: Insurance Companies' National Association.
**ANIAD**; **Aniad** Associazione Nazionale Italiana Atleti Diabetici.
*Italian Association.*
**ANIC** Associazione Nazionale dell'Industria Chimica (Italy).
Italian acronym of the: National Association of the Chemical Industry.
**ANIC** Azienda Nazionale Idrogenazione Carburanti (Italy).
**A.N.I.C.A.** Associazione Nazionale fra gli Istituti di Credito Agrario (Italy).
Italian acronyn of the: National Association of Agrarian Credit Banks.
**ANICA project** Atmospheric Nutrient Input to Coastal Areas project.
**ANIE** Associazione Nazionale Industrie Elettrotecniche ed elettroniche (Italy).
**ANIMA** Associazione Nazionale Industria Meccanica varia e Affine (Italy).
The above acronym was coined accidentally using the Italian word "anima" which means: core (*Foundry; Metallurgy*); web (*Railways*); tube (of a gun) (*Military*).
Also: soul; ghost; spirit.
**ANIPLA** Associazione Nazionale Italiana per l'Automazione (Italy).
Italian acronym of the: Italian National Association for Automation.
**ANIRE** Associazione Nazionale Italiana di Riabilitazione Equestre.
*Italian Association.*
**A.N.L.** Accademia Nazionale dei Lincei (Italy).
Italian initialism of the: Lincei National Academy.
**ANL** Argonne National Laboratory (U.S.A.).
**ANL** arme non létale.
non-lethal weapon (NLW).
**ANL**; **anl** Automatic Noise Limiter.
*Electronics.*
**Anlaids**; **ANLAIDS** Associazione Nazionale per la lotta contro l'AIDS (Italy).
Italian acronym of the: National Association for the fight against AIDS.
**ANLT** (abbr.) ANchor Light.
**ANMC** Alliance Nationale des Mutualité Chrétiennes (Belgium).
**A.N.M.I.G.** Associazione Nazionale Mutilati e Invalidi di Guerra (Italy).
Italian initialism of the: National Association of Disabled Servicemen.
*Military.*
**A.N.M.I.L.** Associazione Nazionale Mutilati e Invalidi del Lavoro (Italy).
Italian initialism of the: National Association of Disabled Workers.
**ANN**; **ann.** (abbr.) Annals.
**ann.** (abbr.) annealed.
*Engineering.*
**ANN**; **ann.** (abbr.) announce.
**ann.** (abbr.) annual.
**ANN** Asia-Pacific News Network.
**ANNA geodetic satellite** Army, Navy, NASA, Air Force geodetic satellite.
**ANNIE** Artificial Neural Networks In Engineering.
**ANNs** Artificial Neural Networks.
*Computational Neuroscience.*
**ANO** Air Navigation Order.
**ANO** Alphanumeric Output.
**ANO basis sets** Atomic Natural Orbital basis sets.
**ANOCOVA** (abbr.) ANalysis Of COVAriance.
*Statistics.*
**ANOD**; **anod.** (abbr.) Anodize.
*Metallurgy.*
**anon.** (abbr.) anonymous.
**ANOVA** (abbr.) ANalysis Of VAriance.
**ANP** Aircraft Nuclear Propulsion.
**ANP** 1. air navigation plan.
1. plan de navigation aérienne.
2. Allied Navigation Publication.
2. publication interalliée sur la navigation.
3. annual national programme.
3. programme national annuel.
**ANP** Atrial Natriuretic Peptide.
Atrial Natriuretic Peptide is also known as: Atrial Natriuretic Factor.
**ANPA** Agenzia Nazionale per la Protezione dell'Ambiente (Italy).
Italian acronym of the: National Agency for Environmental Protection.
**ANPA**; **A.N.P.A.** American Newspaper Publishers' Association (U.S.A.).
**ANPAS** Associazione Nazionale Pubbliche Assistenze.
*Italian Association.*

**ANPE** Agence Nationale Pour l'Emploi.
French acronym of the: National Employment Agency.

**ANPF** Association Nationale pour le "Faites-le vous même" (France).
French initialism of the: Do-It-Yourself National Association.

**A.N.P.I.** Associazione Nazionale Partigiani d'Italia (Italy).
Italian acronym of the: National Association of Italian Partisans.

**AN.P.P.I.A.** Associazione Nazionale Perseguitati Politici Italiani Antifascisti.
Italian acronym of the: National Association of Italian Antifascist political Victims.

**ANPO** $\alpha$-Naphthylphenyloxazole.

**ANPP** Annual Net Primary Productivity.

**ANRAVA** Advanced Noise Reduction using Active Vibration Actuators.
*European Community Project.*

**ANRE** Agency of Natural Resources and Energy (Japan).
*Japanese Agency.*

**ANRS** National Agency for AIDS Research.
*French Agency.*

**ANRT** Association Nationale de la Recherche Technique (France).
French initialism of the: National Association for Technical Research.

**ANS** Academy of Natural Sciences (U.S.A.).

**ANS** Advanced Neutron Source.
*Neutron Science.*

**ANS**; **A.N.S.** American Nuclear Society.

**ans.** (abbr.) answer.

**ANS** Aquatic Nuisance Species.

**ANS** Astronomical Netherlands Satellite (The Netherlands).

**ANS** Autonomic Nervous System.
The autonomic nervous system controls involuntary actions.
*Physiology.*

**A.N.S.A.** Agenzia Nazionale Stampa Associata.
Italian acronym of the: Italian Associated Press Agency.

**ansa** The above acronym was coined accidentally using the Italian word "ansa" which means: handle; hoop; as well as "ansa" (*Anatomy*) in English.

**ANSI** American National Standards Institute.
ANSI is located in New York (U.S.A.).
*U.S. Standards Issuing Institutes.*

**ANSIM** (abbr.) ANalog SIMulation.
*Computer Programming.*

**ANSULF** Association Nationale des Scientifiques pour l'Usage de la Langue Française.
*French Association.*

**ANSWER** Automated Network Schedule With Evaluation of Resources.

**ANT** Adenine Nucleotide Translocator.

**ANT**; **Ant** (abbr.) Antarctic / antarctic.
*Geography.*

**ANT**; **ant** (abbr.) Antenna.
*Electromagnetism* - The antenna is a device that radiates or receives radio waves.
*Invertebrate Zoology* - The antennas are movable sensory receptors on the heads of many insects and crustaceans.

**ANT** Antenna Noise Temperature.

**Ant.** Anthranilic Acid.
The Anthranilic acid is used mainly in the manufacture of dyes and pharmaceuticals. Anthranilic acid is also known as: O-Aminobenzoic acid.
*Organic Chemistry.*

**Ant** Associazione nazionale tumori (Italy).

**ANTA**; **A.N.T.A.** Associazione Nazionale Termotecnici ed Aerotecnici.
*Italian Association.*

**ANTC** Advanced Networking Test Center.

**anthol.** (abbr.) anthology.
An anthology is a book or a collection of selected writings by one author or by various authors.

**ANTI** Associazione Nazionale dei Tributaristi Italiani (Italy).
Italian acronym of the: National Association of Tax Consultants / Advisors.

**ANTU** $\alpha$-Naphthylthiourea.
ANTU is used as a rodenticide.
*Organic Chemistry.*

**ANU** Australian National University.

**ANVAR** Agence Nationale pour la VAlorisation de la Recherche (France).
French acronym of the: National Association for Exploitation of Research.

**A.N.V.G.** Associazione Nazionale Volontari di Guerra (Italy).
Italian initialism of the: National War Volunteers' Association.
*Military.*

**ANWR** Arctic National Wildlife Refuge.

**ANZAC**; **Anzac** Australian and New Zealand Army Corps.

**A/O** Account Of.

**AO** Angola.

**AO** Appel d'Offres.
French initialism meaning: Call For Bids.

**AO** Arctic Oscillation.

*Weather Forecasting.*
**AO** Atomic Orbital.
*Atomic Physics; Physical Chemistry.*
**AO** Aviation Ordnanceman.
**AOA** Administration On Ageing (U.S.A.).
**AOA**; **A.O.A.** American Optometric Association (U.S.A.).
**AOA** 1. amphibious objective area.
1. zone des objectifs d'une opération amphibie.
2. amphibious operations area.
2. zone d'opérations amphibies.
3. area originating authority.
3. autorité origine de zone.
**AOAA** Aminooxyacetic Acid.
**AOAD** army organic air defence.
défense aérienne organique de l'armée de terre.
**AOAs** Amoeboid Olivine Aggregates.
*Earth Sciences; Space Sciences; Geology; Geophysics; Planetology.*
**AOAT** Annuaire Officiel des Abonnés du Téléphone.
French initialism meaning: Telephone Book; Phone Book; Directory.
**AOB** Accessory Olfactory Bulb.
**AOB** air order of battle.
ordre de bataille Air.
**AOB** Any Other Business.
**AOC** Advice Of Charge.
*Cellular Phones.*
**AOC** Aircraft Operations Center.
**AOC** Air Officer Commanding.
**AOC** 1. air operations centre.
1. centre d'opérations aériennes.
2. automatic overload control.
2. régulation automatique de surcharge.
**AOC** Appellation d'Origine Controllée (France). Since 1934.
**AOCC** air operations coordination centre.
centre de coordination des opérations aériennes.
**AOcP** Allied Oceanographic Publication.
publication interalliée sur l'océanographie.
**AOCS** Atmospheric Optical Calibration System.
The AOCS significantly advances the technology of measuring atmospheric optical properties by combining easy-to-use, readily available instruments with a personal computer and special software. Corrections to the ambient solar spectrum are made automatically and in real time. A PV device is placed outdoors with the AOCS close by. While researchers monitor the devices' electrical output, the AOCS measures atmospheric pressure, aerosol and water vapor, and optical properties.
*Atmospheric Optical Calibration System.*
**AOCS** (satellite) attitude and orbital control system.
système de commande de l'attitude et de commande en orbite (des satellites).
**AOD** Advanced Ordnance Depot.
**AOD** Aerosol Optical Depth.
**AOD** Argon-Oxygen Decarburization.
*Metallurgy.*
**AOFLA** Atlantic Offshore Fish and Lobster Association (U.S.A.).
**AOI** Appel d'Offres International.
French initialism meaning: International Call for Tenders.
**AOIPS** Atmospheric and Oceanographic Information Processing System.
**AOL** America Online.
AOL is the world's largest Online Service.
*Online Services.*
**AOM** Anaerobic Oxidation of Methane.
*Biogeochemistry; Marine Chemistry; Marine Microbiology; Microbial Reefs.*
**AOML** Atlantic Oceanographic and Meteorological Laboratory (U.S.A.).
**AON** 1. Agence OTAN de normalisation [a remplacé le BMS 2. et l'ONS].
1. NATO Standardization Agency (NSA 2.) [has replaced MAS and ONS].
2. appel d'offre national.
2. national competitive bidding (NCB 2.).
**AON** Anterior Olfactory Nucleus.
**AON** Autoregulation Of Nodulation.
*Biochemistry; Botany; Microbial Sciences; Nodule Meristems.*
**AOO** American Oceanic Organization (U.S.A.).
**AOO** area of operations.
zone d'opérations.
**AOOI** area of operational interest.
zone d'intérêt opérationnel.
**AOP** Air Observation Post.
**AOP** 1. Allied Ordnance Publication.
1. publication interalliée sur les munitions.
2. area of probability.
2. aire de probabilité.
**AOPI**; **A.O.P.I.** Associazione Orticola Professionale Italiana.
*Italian Association.*
**AOPTS** air operations planning & tasking system.
système d'attribution des tâches et de planifications des opérations aériennes.
**AOQ** Average Outgoing Quality.
**AOQL** Average Outgoing Quality Limit.
**aor.** (abbr.) aortic; aortal.
*Anatomy.*
**AOR** area of responsibility.

zone de responsabilité.
**AORF** Arctic Ocean Radiative Fluxes.
**AOS** Agricultural Organization Society.
**AOs** Atomic Orbitals.
*Atomic Physics; Physical Chemistry.*
**AOS** Average Oxidation State.
**AOSB** Arctic Ocean Science Board (U.S.A.).
**AOSI** area of strategic interest.
zone d'intérêt stratégique.
**AOSP** Atmospheric and Ocean Sciences Program (U.S.A.).
**AOSR** The American Overseas School of Rome (Italy).
**AOSTRA** Alberta Oil Sands Technology and Research Administration (Canada).
**AO systems** Adaptive Optics systems.
*Astronomy.*
**AOT** area of transfer [operations].
zone de transfert [opérations].
**AOTA** American Occupational Therapy Association (U.S.A.).
**AOU** Apparent Oxygen Utilization.
*Oceanography.*
**AP** Absolute Programming.
The term absolute programming actually refers to programming with the use of absolute code.
*Computer Programming.*
**AP** Access Path.
*Computer Technology.*
**AP** Action Potential.
Action potential is also known as: Spike Potential.
*Physiology.*
**AP** Active Program.
The term active program refers to a program in current use.
*Computer Programming.*
**AP** Adaptive Peak.
*Evolution.*
**A.P.**; **a.p.** additional premium.
**AP** Adhesion Proteoglycan.
*Biochemistry; Physics.*
**AP** After-Perpendicular.
*Naval Architecture.*
**AP** (abbr.) airplane.
*Aviation.*
**AP** Alkaline Phosphatase.
For further details see under: **ALP**.
**AP** Alkaline Protease.
*Enzymology.*
**AP** Allophycocyanin.
AP is one of the major species of phycobiliproteins.
*Plant Biology.*
**A.P.** Alta Pressione.
Italian initialism meaning: High Pressure.
*Physics.*
**AP** Amalgamated Press, Ltd.
**AP** American Plan.
**AP** Ammonium Perchlorate.
$NH_4C10_4$. AP is used in explosives, and pyrotechnics.
*Inorganic Chemistry.*
**AP** Angina Pectoris.
AP is characterized by chest pain accompanied at times by a feeling of suffocation due to exertion or stress.
*Medicine.*
**a.p.** année prochaine.
French initialism meaning: next year.
**AP** Anterior Pituitary.
**AP** Anteroposterior.
Anteroposterior actually means: from front to back.
*Anatomy.*
**AP** Antipersonnel.
AP refers to weapons or the like intended to kill people instead of damaging structures.
*Ordnance.*
**AP** Aortic Pressure.
**ap** (abbr.) apothecaries.
**AP** Application Program.
*Computer Programming.*
**AP** Apply Pressure.
**AP** Arithmetic Progression.
Arithmetic progression is also known as: Arithmetic Sequence.
*Mathematics.*
**AP** Armor-Piercing.
Armor-piercing refers to bombs, ammunition and the like that penetrate the armor of targets such as ships.
*Ordnance.*
**AP** Array Processor.
*Computer Technology.*
**AP** Arterial Pressure.
**AP** Assembly Program.
For further details see under: **assm/asbl** (assembler).
**AP** Associated Press (U.S.A.).
**AP** Associative Processor.
The associative processor has an associative or content-addressable memory.
*Computer Technology.*
**AP**; **A.P.** Authority to Pay.
*Business; Finance.*
**AP**; **A.P.** Authority to Purchase.

**a.p.** author's proof.
**AP** Automatic Pagination.
The automatic pagination automatically indicates successive page numbers on a document.
*Computer Programming.*
**AP** Automatic Pistol.
*Ordnance.*
**AP** Automatic Programming.
*Computer Programming.*
**APA** Advance Pricing Agreements.
**APA** air patrol area.
zone de patrouille aérienne.
**APA** Alexandria Port Authority.
**APA** Alkaline Phosphatase Activity.
**APA**; **A.P.A.** American Pharmaceutical Association; American Psychiatric Association; American Psychological Association (U.S.A.).
**APA** American Protective Association; American Protestant Association (U.S.A.).
**Apa** Artigianato piccole aziende (Italy).
**A.P.A.** Associate in Public Administration.
**APA** Association of Public Analysts (G.B.).
**A.P.A.** Associazione Provinciale Artigiani.
*Italian Association.*
**APAAP-staining** Alkaline Phosphatase - Anti-Alkaline-Phosphatase staining.
*Dermatology; Melanoma; Skin Cancer.*
**APAC** ACCS Policy and Advisory Committee [has merged with AIAC to become AAC].
Comité consultatif sur la politique et la planification de l'ACCS [a fusionné avec l'AIAC pour devenir l'AAC].
**APAC** Association Assurance - Peinture Anti-Corrosion (Belgium).
*Belgian Associations.*
**APACHE** Accelerator for Physics And Chemistry of Heavy Metals.
**APACHE** Active thermal Protection for Avionics Crew and Heat-sensitive Equipment.
*U.S. Air Force.*
**APACS** Association for Payment Clearing Services (G.B.).
**Apaf** Associazione per la promozione dell'alta fedeltà (Italy).
Italian acronym of the: Association for the promotion of high-fidelity.
**Apaf-1** Apoptotic protease activating factor-1.
*Apoptosis; Medicine.*
**APAG** Atlantic Policy Advisory Group.
Groupe consultatif de la politique atlantique.
**APAM** Antipersonnel-Antimaterial.
**APAP** Acetyl-p-aminophenol.
**APAR** Absorbed Photosynthetically Active solar Radiation.
*Biological Sciences; Marine and Coastal Sciences; Photosynthesis.*
**APAS** Adaptable Programmable Assembly System.
The APAS is a robotic system to automatically assemble and manufacture parts.
**APAS News** Association of Personal Assistant & Secretaries News.
A publication of the: APAS (G.B.).
*Publications.*
**APATC** Allied Publication - Air Traffic Control.
publication interalliée sur le contrôle de la circulation aérienne.
**APB** Accounting Principles Board (G.B.).
**APB** All Points Bulletin.
**APB** Antiphase Boundary.
APB is also known as: Antiphase Domain.
*Materials Science.*
**APB** Arterial Premature Beat.
**APBA** American Power Boat Association (U.S.A.).
**APC** Adenomatous Polyposis Coli.
*Signal Transduction; Tumor Suppressors.*
**APC** Ammonium Perchlorate.
For further details see under: **AP**.
**APC** Anaphase-Promoting Complex.
*Biochemistry; Biology; Cell Biology; Cell Cycle; Medicine; Molecular and Human Genetics; Molecular Pathology.*
**APC** Antenna Pattern Correction.
**APC** Antigen-Presenting Cell.
*Immunology.*
**a.p.c.** a pronta cassa.
Italian initialism meaning: cash down; ready cash.
**APC** Armored Personnel Carrier.
*Ordnance.*
**APC** Aromatic Polymer Composites.
**APC** Aspirin, Phenacetin and Caffeine.
**APC** Automatic Phase Control.
*Electronics.*
**APC** Average Propensity to Consume.
**APCAC** Asia-Pacific Council of American Chambers of Commerce (Japan).
APCAC was formed in 1968.
**apCAMs** Aplysia Cell Adhesion Molecules.
**APC/C** APC/Cyclosome.
For further details see under: **APC**.
**APCCI** Assemblée Permanente des Chambres de Commerce et d'Industrie.
**APCE** Agence Pour la Création d'Entreprises.
**APCO**; **Apco** Associazione Professionale dei Consulenti di Direzione ed Organizzazione Aziendale (Italy).

*Italian Association; Management Consultants.*

**AP Courses** Advanced Placement Courses.
Courses that high school seniors take in order to gain college credits (U.S.A.).

**APCs** Antigen-Presenting Cells.
*Immunology; Medicine.*

**APD** Antiphase Domain.
APD is also known as: Antiphase boundary.
*Materials Science.*

**APD** Avalanche Photodiode Detector.
*Electronics.*

**APDs** Antiphase Domains.
For further details see under: **APD**.

**APDS** Armor-Piercing Discarding Sabot.
*Ordnance.*

**APE** Advanced Production Engineering.

**APE**; **Ape** Agenzia Provinciale per l'Energia (Italy).
A consortium founded in 1997. Founding members: The Reggio Calabria Province and FAST.
For further details see under: **FAST**.

**APE** Anterior Pituitary Extract.
*Endocrinology.*

**APE** Assemblea Parlamentare Europea.
Italian acronym of the: European Parliamentary Assembly.

**APE** Assistant Project Engineer.

**APE** Auroral Photography Experiment.

**APE** Available Potential Energy.
*Geophysics.*

**APE** Available Power Efficiency.

**ape** The above acronyms were coined accidentally using the Italian word "ape" which means: bee (*Invertebrate Zoology*) as well as the English word "ape" (*Vertebrate Zoology*).

**APEAL** Accrediting Prior Experience, Achievement and Learning.

**APEC**; **Apec** Association Pour l'Emploi des Cadres (France).
French acronym of the: Association for the Employment of Executive / Managerial Staff.

**APECED** Autoimmune Polyendocrinopathy - Candidiasis - Ectodermal Distrophy.
A disease characterized by autoimmune destruction of endocrine organs. The inability to eliminate *Candida* yeast infections and growth of ectodermal dystrophic tissue.
*Cancer; Immunology; Medical Biophysics.*

**APEC Forum** Asia-Pacific Economic Co-operation Forum.

**APEF** Association pour la Promotion Economique de la Femme (Burundi).
French acronym of the: Association for Economic Promotion of Women.

**APEFE** Association pour la Promotion de l'Education et de la Formation à l'Etranger (Belgium).
French acronym of the: Association for the Promotion of Education and Vocational Training Abroad.
*Belgian Association.*

**APEX** Arctic Polynya EXperiment.

**APF** advance(d) planning funds.
fonds d'études préparatoires.

**APF** Animal Protein Factor.

**APF** Antarctic Polar Front.

**APFA** Association pour Promouvoir le Français des Affaires (France).
French acronym of the: Association for the Promotion of the French language in Business.
*French Association.*

**APFIM** Atom-Probe Field-Ion Microscopy.

**APFUC** Association des Professeurs de Français dans les Universités du Canada.
French acronym of the: Association of Professors of French in Canadian Univerisities.
*Canadian Association.*

**APG** Anterior Pituitary Gland.

**APGERN** Asian-Pacific Global Environmental Research Network.

**APGI** Association de Pharmacie Galénique Industrielle (France).
*Galenic Pharmacology.*

**APH** Anterior Pituitary Hormones.
The anterior pituitary hormones are produced and released by the adenohypophysis.
*Endocrinology.*

**APHA** American Pharmaceutical Association; American Public Health Association (U.S.A.).

**APHEA 2** Short-term effects of Air Pollution on Health: a European Approach to methodology, dose response Assessment and evaluation of public health significance.
*European Community Project; Environmental Protection; Meteorology; Safety; Policies.*

**APHIA** Association for the Promotion of Humour in Internationl Affairs.

**APHIS** Animal and Plant Health Inspection Service.
USDA's APHIS funds and administers the Foreign Animal Disease Diagnostic Laboratory.
For further details see under: **USDA**.

**API** Acceptable Periodic Inspection.

**API** Accountants for the Public Interest.

**API** Accurate Position Indicator.

**API** Air-Position Indicator.
*Navigation.*

**API** Alabama Polytechnic Institute (U.S.A.).

**API** Alignment Progress Indicator.
**API**; **A.P.I.** American Petroleum Institute.
**API** Antenna Position Indicator.
**API** Anonima Petroli Italiana (Italy).
**API** Application Program / Programming Interface.
**API** Armor Piercing Incendiary.
*Military.*
**API** Associazione Piccole Imprese (Italy).
Italian acronym of the: Association of Small Enterprises.
**API** Associazione Poliziotti Italiani.
Italian acronym of the: Italian Policemen Association.
**API** Astro-Psychology Institute.
**API** Automated Pronunciator Instructor.
**API** Automatic Priority Interrupt.
*Data Processing.*
**APIC** Allied press information centre.
centre interallié d'information de la presse.
**APICE convention** Anaesthesia, Pain, Intensive Care, Emergency Medicine convention.
APICE was held in Trieste in November 1998.
*Emergency Medicine.*
**apice** The above acronym was coined accidentally using the Italian word "apice" which means: apex; summit.
Also: height.
**APICS** American Production and Inventory Control Society (U.S.A.).
**APID** air photographic interpretation detachment.
détachement d'interprétation de photographies aériennes.
**API-MS** Atmospheric Pressure Ionization Mass Spectrometry.
*Chemistry.*
**APIS** Advanced Papyrological Information System (U.S.A.).
APIS is a consortium of six universities in the United States.
*Archaeology; Papyrology.*
**APIs** Application Program Interfaces.
**API scale** American Petroleum Institute scale.
The API scale is used to measure the specific gravity of liquids.
*Chemical Engineering.*
**APIT** Armor-Piercing Incendiary Tracer.
*Ordnance.*
**APIU** army photo interpretation unit.
unité d'interprétation de photographies des forces terrestres.
**APL** Acceptable Productivity Level.
**APL** Accreditation of Prior Learning.
*Education.*
**APL** Acute Promyelocytic Leukemia.
*Chromosomal Translocations; Human Genetics; Medicine; Pathology.*
**APL** Altered Peptide Ligand.
*Epidemiology; Human Genetics; Infectious Diseases; Molecular Immunology; Molecular Medicine; Tropical Medicine.*
**APL** Applied Physics Laboratory.
**APL** A Programming Language.
*Computer Programming.*
**a/pl** armor plate.
Also: **ARM PL**.
**APLA** American Patent Law Association.
Founded in 1897. Located in Arlington, VA, U.S.A. The APLA is a voluntary Bar Association of lawyers practicing in the field of patents, trademarks and copyrights.
**APLA quarterly** American Patent Law Association quarterly.
Quarterly Journal of the: APLA (U.S.A.).
*Publications.*
**APL hormone** Anterior Pituitary-Like hormone.
**APLP** β-Amyloid Precursor-Like Proteins.
APLP is supposed to stabilize plaques in Alzheimer's disease.
*Brain Research; Cerebellar Pathology; Neurodegenerative Diseases; Neuropathology; Neuroscience.*
**APLS** American Psychology Law Society (Newton, Massachusetts, U.S.A.).
**APM** Absolute Plate Motion.
*Terrestrial Magnetism.*
**APM** acoustic protective measures.
mesures de protection acoustique.
**APM** Anti-Personnel Mine.
*Ordnance.*
**APM** Assistant Provost Marshal.
**APM** Atmospheric Particle Monitor.
**APMF** Association de la Presse Médicale Française (France).
**APMI** American Powder Metallurgy Institute.
**APM-locking** Additive-Pulse Mode-locking.
*Quantum Electronics; Optics.*
**APMM** Association of Policy Market Makers.
**APMS** Automated Personnel Management System.
système automatisé de gestion du personnel.
**ApMV** Apple Mosaic Virus.
*Virology.*
**APN** Asian-Pacific Network - For Global Change Research.
*Environmental Research.*
**APO** Army Post Office.
**APO** Asian Productivity Organization.

**APO** AWIPS Program Office.
For further details see under: **AWIPS**.
**Apoc.** (abbr.) apocalypse.
**Apoc.** (abbr.) apocrypha; apocryphal.
**APOCALIPS** Active and Passive Optical Components based on in-situ formed Anisotropic LIquid crystalline Polymeric Systems.
*European Community Project.*
**APOD** airport of debarkation.
aéroport de débarquement.
**APOE** airport of embarkation.
aéroport d'embarquement.
**APOE gene** Apolipoprotein E gene.
*Alzheimer's Disease; Biochemistry; Genetic Factors; Neurology; Physiology.*
**APOEP** Associação Portuguesa de Professores Peritos de Orientação (Portugal).
*Portuguese Association.*
**ApoJ** Apolipoprotein J.
*Brain Research; Cerebellar Pathology; Neurodegenerative Diseases; Neuropathology; Neuroscience.*
**APO product** Advanced Planning and Optimization product.
The APO product, by SAP was released in December 1998.
**APP** Adenosine Phosphate.
*Biochemistry.*
**APP** Allied Procedural Publication.
publication interalliée sur les procédures.
**APP** Amyloid Precursor Protein.
*Medicine; Neurology.*
**app.** (abbr.) apparato.
Italian abbreviation meaning: apparatus.
**app.** (abbr.) apparente.
Italian abbreviation meaning: apparent.
**app.** (abbr.) appendice.
Italian abbreviation meaning: appendix.
**app.** (abbr.) appendix.
Also: **appx**.
**app.** (abbr.) appointed.
Also: **apptd.**
**app.** (abbr.) apprentice.
**APPA** American Public Power Association.
**APPC** Advanced Program-to-Program Communications.
**APPCA** Assemblée Permanente des Présidents de Chambre d'Agriculture (France).
**appd.** (abbr.) approved.
**APPE** Association of Petrochemical Producers in Europe.
**APPLAUSE** Appeal, Plain facts, Personalities, Local Angle, Action Uniqueness (or Universality), Significance, Energy.
**APPLE** Applied Parallel Programming Language Experiment.
*Data Processing.*
**APPLE** Association of Public and Private Labor Employees.
**APPLES** Asian and Pacific Professional Language and Education Services.
**APPN** Advanced Peer-to-Peer Networking.
**APPORT** Associação dos Psicólogos Portugueses (Portugal).
*Portuguese Association.*
**appr.** (abbr.) approximate; approximation.
**APPR** Army Package Power Reactor.
*Nuclear Physics.*
**appr'l** (abbr.) approval.
Also: **appro.**
**approx.** (abbr.) approximately.
Also: **aprx.**
**appt.** (abbr.) appartement.
French abbreviation meaning: flat; apartment (U.S.).
**appt.** (abbr.) appoint; appointed; appointment.
**apptd.** (abbr.) appointed.
Also: **app.**
**appx.** (abbr.) appendix.
Also: **app.**
**APQ** armaments planning questionnaire.
questionnaire sur les plans d'armements.
**APR** Active Prominence Region.
Active prominence region refers to a region of the sun displaying active prominences.
*Astronomy.*
**APR** Airborne Profile Recorder.
Airborne profile recorder is also known as: Terrain Profile Recorder.
*Engineering.*
**APR** Annualized Percentage Rate (G.B.).
**APR** Annual Percentage Rate.
*Business; Finance.*
**APR** Annual Progress Report.
**apr.** (abbr.) après.
French abbbreviation meaning: after; later on.
**apr.** (abbr.) aprile.
Italian abbreviation meaning: April.
**APRE** Agenzia per la Promozione della Ricerca Europea (Italy).
Italian acronym of the: Agency for the Promotion of European Research. Founded in 1990.
**APRF** Acute-Phase Response Factor.
*Biochemistry.*

**APRIA** Association pour la Promotion Industrie Agriculture.
*French Association.*
**APRIL** Aquaplaning Risk Indicator for Landings.
**APRO** Aerial Phenomena Research Organization.
**APRO** Army Personnel Research Office.
**APROM**; **Aprom** Associazione per il PROgresso del Mezzogiorno (Italy).
Italian acronym of the: Association for Southern Italy Progress.
**APRT** Adenine Phosphoribosyltransferase.
**APRU** Astra Pain Research Unit.
The APRU is based in Montreal, Canada.
**aprx.** (abbr.) approximately.
Also: **approx**.
**APS** Acoustic Polarized Stereo.
**Aps** Action Potentials.
For further details see under: **AP**.
**APS** Adenosine-5'-phosphosulfate.
**APS** Advanced Photon Source.
At Argonne National Laboratory near Chicago, Illinois, USA.
*Synchrotron Research.*
**APS** Aiuto Pubblico alla Sicurezza (Italy).
**APS** Alpha Particle Spectrometer.
*Gas Releases; Lunar Research.*
**A.P.S.** American Peace Society (U.S.A.).
**APS**; **A.P.S.** American Physical Society; American Physiological Society (U.S.A.).
**APS** American Protestant Society (U.S.A.).
**Aps.** (abbr.) Apus.
*Astronomy; Vertebrate Zoology.*
**APS** Armor-Piercing Sabot.
The armor piercing sabot is an armor-piercing projectile that includes a sabot.
*Ordnance.*
**APS** Associazione per la Partecipazione allo Sviluppo.
Italian initialism of the: Association for Participation to Development. The APS is based in Turin, Italy.
**APS** auxiliary power supply.
alimentation électrique auxiliaire.
**APS** Average Propensity to Save.
**APS** Portuguese Insurance Association (Portugal).
**APSA** American Political Science Association.
**APSA** Amministrazione del Patrimonio della Sede Apostolica.
The President of APSA is Cardinal Lorenzo Antonetti.
**APS cameras** Advanced Photo System cameras.
Developed by a camera and film makers consortium, APS cameras, are cameras easier to load than conventional 35mm. ones.
**APSO** Audio Precision System One.
APSO is an accepted industry-standard instrument to generate and analyze test signals.
**APS systems** Advanced Planning and Scheduling Systems.
*APS Software.*
**APSTI** Associazione Parchi Scientifici Tecnologici Italiani.
Italian initialism of the: Association of Italian Scientific and Technological Parks.
**APT** acquisition, pointing and tracking.
acquisition, pointage et poursuite.
**APT** Adaptive Programming Technology.
**APT** Advanced Patent Technique.
**APT** Advanced Pointing Tracking.
**apt.** (abbr.) apartment.
**APT** (abbr.) appoint.
**apt** (abbr. ) aptitude.
The aptitude is the talent or the innate or acquired capacity to learn or perform skillfully a previously unlearned job.
*Psychology.*
**APT** Armor-Piercing Tracer.
*Ordnance.*
**APT** Association for Preservation Technology.
**APT** Automatic Picture Transmission.
**APT** Automatically Programmed Tools.
*Computer Programming.*
**APT** Automation Planning and Technology.
**APT** Azienda di Promozione Turistica (Italy).
**APT**; **Apt** Azienda Provinciale del Turismo (Italy).
**APTES** 3-Aminopropyltriethoxysilane.
**APTIC** Air Pollution Technical Information Center (U.S.A.).
**APT plant** Accelerator Production of Tritium plant.
*Neutron Science.*
**APT projectile** Armor-Piercing Tracer projectile.
**APT system** Automatic Picture Transmission system.
*Electronics.*
**APTT** Activated Partial Thromboplastin Time.
*Medicine.*
**APU** Auxiliary Power Unit.
**APUA** Alliance for the Prudent Use of Antibiotics.
**APUD** Amine Precursor Uptake and Decarboxylation.
*Medicine; Oncology.*
**APV** International Association for Pharmaceutical Technology (Germany).
**APWA** American Public Works Association -U.S.A.
**APXS** $\alpha$-Proton X-ray Spectrometer.

Information from APXS was collected by Mars Pathfinder which landed on the surface of Mars on 4th July 1997.
*Chemistry; Geology; Geophysics; Planetary Exploration; Scientific Instruments.*

**AQ** Accomplishment Quotient.
For further details see under: **AQ** (Achievement Quotient).

**AQ** Achievement Quotient.
The achievement quotient is actually the achievement age divided by the chronological age.
*Psychology.*

**aq.** (abbr.) aqueous.
*Chemistry; Geology; Science.*

**AQ** assurance de la qualité.
quality assurance (QA 2.).

**AQ** L'Aquila (Italy).

**AQAM** Air Quality Assessment Model.

**AQAP** Allied Quality Assurance Publication.
publication interalliée sur l'assurance de la qualité.

**AQC** Automatic Quench Compensation.

**AQIRP** Auto-oil air Quality Improvement Research Program (U.S.A.).
*Chemical Engineering; Environmental Engineering Science.*

**AQL** Acceptable Quality Level.
*Industrial Engineering.*

**Aql** Aquila.
The Eagle is a constellation lying south of Cygnus and Lyra.
*Astronomy.*

**AQPF** Association Québecoise des Professeurs de Français (Canada).
French initialism of the: Quebec Association of Professors of French.

**Aqr** Aquarius.
Aquarius is a constellation located between Pisces and Capricornus.
*Astronomy.*

**AR** Account Receivable.

**AR** Accounts Register.
*Data Processing.*

**AR** Acknowledgement of Receipt.

**AR** Active Resistance.
*Occupational Therapy.*

**AR**; **a.r.** Advice of Receipt.

**AR** Advisory Report.

**AR** 1. air reconnaissance.
1. reconnaissance aérienne.
2. air route.
2. route aérienne.
3a. anti-radar.
3b. anti-radiation.
3a. antiradar.
3b. antirayonnement.
4. Argentina.
4. Argentine.
5. Armour.
5. Arme blindée.

**AR** Allergic Rhinitis.
The allergic rhinitis, also known as hay fever, is the inflammation of the nasal membranes caused by certain plant pollens, by household dust and the like.
*Medicine.*

**A.R.** Aller-Retour (billet d').
French initialism meaning: return (ticket).

**AR** All Rail; All Risks.

**A.R.** Altezza Reale.
Italian initialism meaning: Royal Highness.

**AR**; **a.r.** American Register.

**a.r.** analytical reagent.

**AR** Androgen Receptor.

**AR** Annual Report; Annual Return.

**Ar** Arabic.
Also: **ARA**; **Arab.**
*Languages.*

**AR** Arezzo, Italy.

**Ar** the chemical symbol for Argon.
Argon is a chemical element, having the atomic number 18, an atomic weight of 39.998 and a boiling point of -185.7°C. The word argon derives from the Greek term "idle".
*Chemistry.*

**AR** Arkansas (U.S.A.).

**AR** Arithmetic Register.
*Computer Technology.*

**AR** Army Regulation.

**ar** (abbr.) arrival; arrive.

**Ar** aryl.
*Organic Chemistry.*

**AR** Aspect Ratio.

**ar** as required.

**AR** Automatic Regulator.
For further details see under: **AC** (Automatic Controller).

**AR** Automatic Routine.
The automatic routine automatically performs if certain conditions occur in a program or record.
*Computer Programming.*

**β-AR** β-Adrenergic Receptor.
*Endocrinology; Molecular and Cellular Physiology; Medicine; Thyroid.*

**ARA** Abbreviated Register Address.

**ARA** Acetylene Reduction Assay.
*Botany.*

**ARA** Aerial Rocket Artillery.
**ARA** airborne relay aircraft.
avion-relais en vol.
**ARA** Antibiotic Resistance Analysis.
A library-dependent technique developed by researchers at the James Madison University, Virginia, U.S.A.
*Library-dependent Techniques; Microbial Source Tracking.*
**ARA** (abbr.) Arabic.
Also: **Ar.**; **Arab.**
**ARA** Arab Relief Agency.
**Arab.** (abbr.) Arabian.
**Arab.** (abbr.) Arabic.
Also: **Ar.**; **ARA**.
*Languages.*
**ARAC** AIDS Research Advisory Committee.
*AIDS Vaccine Research.*
**ARAC** Atmospheric Release Advisory Capability.
*Nuclear Accidents and Incidents; Nuclear Defense.*
**ARAM** Antigen Receptor Activation Motif.
*Immunology.*
**Aram** Aramaic.
*Languages.*
**ARAMCO** ARabian-AMerican Oil COmpany.
**AR&D System** Automated Rendezvous and Docking System.
**ARASS**; **Arass** Associazione per il Restauro di Antichi Strumenti Scientifici (Italy).
Italian acronym of the: Association for Restoration of Scientific Instruments. Founded in 1997.
**Arb.** (abbr.) arbitrager, arbitrageur.
**arb.** (abbr.) arbitrary.
**ARBBA** American Railway Bridge and Building Association (U.S.A.).
**ARC** Abnormal (or anomalous) Retinal Correspondence.
**ARC** Accelerating Rate Calorimeter.
*Instrumentation.*
**ARC** Activator-Recruited Cofactor.
*Cell Biology; Medicine; Molecular Biology.*
**ARC** Adult Rehabilitation Centre (Canada).
**ARC** Advanced Reentry Concepts; Advanced Research Center.
*Aerospace.*
**ARC** Aeronautical Research Council (G.B.).
**ARC** Agreements for Recreation and Conservation (Canada).
**ARC**; **arc** AIDS-Related Complex.
AIDS-related complex, is also known as AIDS-related Condition or Syndrome.
*Pathology.*
**ARC** Airlines Reporting Corporation.
ARC is headquartered in Virginia, U.S.A.
**ARC** Air Release Capacity.
*Aviation.*
**ARC** Alberta Research Council (Canada).
**ARC** American Red Cross.
**ARCA** Associate of the Royal Cambrian Academy.
**ARCA** Associate of the Royal Canadian Academy.
**ARCA** Associate of the Royal College of Art.
**ARCA** Associazione nazionale Ricreativa Culturale Assistenziale (Italy).
Italian acronym of the: Recreational, Cultural and Relief National Association.
**ARCA** Attenuated Replication Competent Adenoviruses.
ARCA is a trademark of Calydon Inc. (U.S.A.).
*In Vivo Cancer Therapies.*
**ARCADE** Ampere Remote Control Access Data Entry - E.C.
ARCADE was developed in 1993.
*Research Telematics System for Data Recording.*
**A.R.C.E.** Associazione per le Relazioni Culturali con l'Estero (Italy).
Italian acronym of the: Association for Cultural Relations with Foreign Countries.
**arch.** (abbr.) archaic; archaism.
**Arch.** (abbr.) Archduke.
**arch.** (abbr.) architect; architectural.
**arch.** archivio.
Italian abbreviation meaning: archives; records office.
**Archaeol.** (abbr.) Archaeological; Archaeology.
**Archd.** Archdeacon.
**Archia** Architettura investimenti aggregati.
A consortium founded in 1997. Founding member: FAST (Italy).
For further details see under: **FAST**.
**Archop.** Archbishop.
**ARCI** Addiction Research Center Inventory.
*Psychology.*
**ARCI** American Railway Car Institute (U.S.A.).
**ARCI** Associate of the Royal Colonial Institute (G.B.).
**ARCI** Associazione Ricreativa Culturale Italiana (Italy).
Italian acronym of the:: Italian Recreational Cultural Association.
**arci** The above acronyms were coined accidentally using the Italian word "arci" which means: extremely; absolutely.
**ARCN** air reporting and control net.
réseau de veille et de compte rendu.
**ARCO** Aircraft Resources Control Office.

**ARCO** Airspace Reservation Coordination Office (Canada).
**ARCO** Associate of the Royal College of Organists (G.B.).
**ARCP** air refuelling control point.
point de contrôle du ravitaillement en vol.
**ARCS** Altitude Rate Command System.
**ARCS** Assessment and Remediation of Contaminated Sediments.
**ARCS** Associate of the Royal College of Surgeons (G.B.).
**ARCSS program** ARCtic System Science program.
**ARCT** air refueling control time.
temps de contrôle du ravitaillement en vol.
**ARC W**; **arc w.** Arc Weld.
*Metallurgy.*
**ARD** Absolute Reaction of Degeneration.
**ARD** Acute Respiratory Disease.
The acute respiratory disease is an infection affecting the respiratory system.
*Medicine.*
**ARD** Armament Research Department (G.B.).
**ARD** Association of Research Directors.
**ard** The above acronyms were coined accidentally using the Arabic word "ard" which means: land, soil.
**ARDE** Aircraft and Rocket Design Engineers.
**ARDE** Armament Research and Development Establishment (G.B.).
**ARDF** Alternatives Research and Development Foundation.
**ARDS** Adult Respiratory Distress Syndrome.
For further details see under: **ARD** (Acute Respiratory Disease).
**ARDSNET** Acute Respiratory Distress Syndrome Network.
**ARE** Acoustic Radiation Element.
**ARE** Advanced Real-Time Executive.
**ARE** Aircraft Reactor Equipment.
**ARE** Air Reactor Experiment.
**ARE** Ancient Records of Egypt.
*Publication.*
**ARE** Arab Republic of Egypt.
**A.R.E.** Associate in Religious Education.
**ARE** Asymptotic Relative Efficiency.
*Statistics.*
**ARE** Atmospheric Research Equipment.
**ARE** Automated Responsive Environment.
**ARE** Automatic Record Evaluation.
**AREA** American Railway Engineering Association (U.S.A.).
**AREA** American Recreational Equipment Association (U.S.A.).
**AREA** Arctic Research in Environmental Acoustics.
**AREA** Army Reactor Experirnental Area.
**AREC** air resource element coordinator.
coordonnateur des moyens aériens.
**AREL** Agenzia di Ricerche E Legislazione (Italy).
AREL is an Agency based in Rome, Italy.
**AREP** Atmospheric Research and Environmental Program.
**ARES** Automazione Ricerca e Soccorso.
*Ship Reporting.*
**ARF** ACE Reaction Force.
Force de réaction du CAE.
**ARF** ASEAN Regional Forum.
ARF deals with security issues in Asia-Pacific.
For further details see under: **ASEAN**.
**ARF1** Auxin Response Factor 1.
*Biochemistry.*
**ARFA** Allied Radio Frequency Agency [obsolete].
Bureau allié des fréquences radio [obsolète].
**ARFOR** (abbr.) ARea FORecast.
ARFOR is an intemational code word.
*Meteorology.*
**ARFPS** ACE Reaction Forces Planning Staff [obsolete - see CJPS].
Etat-major de planification des forces de réaction du CAE [obsolète - voir CJPS].
**ARFs** Adenosine diphosphate-Ribosylation Factors.
*Cell Biology; Medicine; Molecular Biology; Molecular Medicine; Physiology; Receptor-Mediated Endocytosis.*
**ARG** Accident Response Group (U.S.A.).
*Nuclear Defense.*
**arg.** (abbr.) argument.
*Computer Programming; Mathematics.*
**arg** arrester gear.
*Aviation.*
**ARGC** Australian Research Grants Committee (Australia).
*Research Grants.*
**ARGOT** Adaptive Representation Genetic Optimizer Technique.
**ARI** Accelerated Research Initiative.
**ARI** Acute Respiratory Infection.
*Medicine.*
**ARI** Air conditioning and Refrigeration Institute (U.S.A.).
**Ari.** (abbr.) Aries.
The Ram is a small constellation located between Pisces and Taurus.
*Astronomy.*
**ARIA** Accounting Researchers International Association.
**ARIA** Adult Reading Improvement Association.

**ARIA** Advanced Range Instrumentation Aircraft.
**ARIA** American Risk and Insurance Association (U.S.A.).
**A.R.I.A.** Aria, Rumore, Informazione, Ambiente. Italian acronym meaning: Air, Noise, Information, Environment.
*Ecology.*
**aria** The above acronyms were coined accidentally using the Italian word "aria" which means: air
*Aviation; Chemistry; Engineering.*
**ARIBA** Associate of the Royal Institute of British Architects (G.B.).
**ARIES** Advanced Radar Information Evaluation System.
**ARIES** Airborne Reconnaissance Integrated Electronic System.
**ARIES** Atmospheric Research Information Exchange Study.
**ARIES** Authentic Reproduction of an Independent Earth Satellite.
**ARIES program** Automated Reliability EStimation program.
*Data Processing.*
**ARIMA** Autoregressive Integrated Moving Average.
**ARIP** air refuelling initial point.
point initial du ravitaillement en vol.
**ARIS** Advanced Range Instrumentation Ship.
**ARIS** Aeronautical Institute of Sweden.
*Swedish Institutes.*
**ARIS** Airborne Range Instrumentation Station.
**ARIS** Aircraft Recording Instrumentation System (G.B.).
**ARIS** Altitude and Rate Indicating System.
**ARIS** Automatic Recording Infrared Spectrometer.
**ARISE** American Renaissance In Science Education.
*U.S. Education Reforms.*
**ARISTOTELES** Applications and Research Involving Space Technologies Observing The Earth's field from Low Earth orbiting Satellite.
**ARISTOTLE** Annual Review and Information Symposium on the Technology Of Training, Learning and Education.
Of the U.S. Department of Defense.
**arith.** (abbr.) arithmetic.
The processes of addition, subtraction, multiplication, and division.
*Mathematics.*
**Ariz.** (abbr.) Arizona (U.S.A.).
**AR-JP** Autosomal Recessive Juvenile Parkinsonism.
*Medicine; Neurobiology.*
**Ark.** (abbr.) Arkansas (U.S.A.).
**ARL** Acceptable Reliability Level.
**ARL** Air Resources Laboratory; Arctic Research Laboratory (U.S.A.).
**ARL** Association of Research Libraries.
ARL is an organization of 121 libraries in North America.
**ARLO** air reconnaissance liaison officer.
officier de liaison de la reconnaissance aérienne.
**ARLTAB** Army Research Laboratory Technical Assessment Board (U.S.A.).
**ARM** Adjustable Rate Mortgage.
**ARM** All Risk Management.
*Insurance.*
**ARM** Antiradiation Missile.
*Ordnance.*
**ARM** Applications Response Measurement (Hewlett-Packard's).
An initiative (1998) to consolidate all the components of a single business transaction into an assessment of end-to-end user response, including every element such as PC, network, local server, mainframe, transatlantic line and so forth.
**ARM** Area Radiation Monitor.
**ARM** Artificial Rupture of Membranes.
*Medicine.*
**ARM** Assistant Regional Manager.
**ARM** Association of Railway Museums.
**ARM** Automatic/Automated Route Management.
**ARM** Automatic Reel Mounting.
**ARMA** Accumulator Reservoir Manifold Assembly.
**ARMA** ARMy Attaché.
*Military.*
**ARMA** Autoregressive Moving Average.
*Statistics.*
**arma** The above acronyms were coined accidentally using the Italian word "arma" which means: firearm; weapon (*Ordnance*).
**ARMINES** Association pour la Recherche et le développement des Méthodes et processus Industriels (France).
French acronym of the: Association for Research and Development of Industrial Methods and processes.
**ARMP** Allied Reliability and Maintainability Publication.
publication interalliée sur la fiabilité et la maintenabilité.
**ARM PL**; **arm pl.** Armor Plate.
Also: **a/pl**.
**ARM program** Atmospheric Radiation Measurement program.
**ARMS** Advanced Receiver Model System.

**ARMS** Aircraft Resources Management System.
**ARMS** Amplification Refractory Mutation System.
**ARMS** Area Radiological Monitoring System.
**ARMS** Associate of the Royal Miniature Painters Society (G.B.).
**armt.** (abbr.) armament.
*Military Science; Ordnance.*
**ARN** Acide Ribonucléique.
French initialism meaning: Ribonucleic Acid.
*Biochemistry.*
**ARNAS** automatic radar navigation system.
système automatique de navigation au radar.
**ARN messager** Acide Ribonucléique messager.
French initialism meaning: messenger Ribonucleic Acid.
*Medicine.*
**ARN ribosomal** Acide Ribonucléique ribosomal.
French initialism meaning: ribosomal Ribonucleic Acid.
*Medicine.*
**ARNt** Acide Ribonucléique de Transfert.
French initialism meaning: transfer Ribonucleic Acid.
*Medicine.*
**Arnt protein** Ah receptor nuclear translocator protein.
*Biomedical and Environmental Sciences; Pathology.*
**ARO** After Receipt of Order.
*Business; Commerce; Finance.*
**ARO**; **Aro** Application Response Option.
**ARO** Army Research Office (U.S.A.).
**ARO** Autorespiratore ad Ossigeno.
**ARP** ACCS rolling plan.
plan à horizon glissant de l'ACCS.
**ARP** Activité Rénine du Plasma.
French initialism meaning: Plasma Renin Activity.
*Medicine.*
**ARP** Address Resolution Protocol.
*Computers.*
**ARP** Advanced Research Project.
**ARP** Air-Raid Precautions.
**ARPA** Advanced Research Projects Agency.
Of the U.S. Defense Department.
ARPA has replaced DARPA (U.S.A.).
For further details see under: **DARPA**.
**ARPA**; **Arpa** Agenzie Regionali per l'Ambiente (Italy).
Italian acronym of the: Regional Agencies for Environment.
**arpa** The above acronyms were coined accidentally using the Italian word "arpa" which means: harp.
**ARPANET** Advanced Research Projects Agency NETwork.
ARPANET became international in 1973 by linking the University College of London with the Swedish Royal Radar Establishment.
**ARPES** Angle-Resolved Photoelectron Spectroscopy.
**ARPS** Advanced Regional Prediction System.
**ARR** Advanced Release Record.
**ARR** Advanced Restricted Report.
**ARR** Airborne Radio Receiver.
**ARR** Alkaline Rust Remover.
*Chemistry.*
**ARR** Antenna Radiation Resistance.
**ARR** Antenna Rotation Rate.
**ARR** Army Readiness Regions (U.S.A.).
**arr.** (abbr.) arranged.
**arr.** (abbr.) arrival; arrived.
Also: **arrd.**
**ARR** Automatic Repeat Request.
The ARR is a request that the receiving unit transmits when an error is found in information, so that the sending unit retransmits.
*Telecommunications.*
**ARRC** ACE Rapid Reaction Corps.
Corps de réaction rapide du CAE.
**ARRCS** air raid reporting control ship.
bâtiment contrôleur des comptes rendus de raids aériens.
**arrd.** (abbr.) arrived.
Also: **arr.**
**ARRE-1** Antigen-Receptor Response Element-1.
**ARRF** ACE Rapid Reaction Force.
Force de réaction rapide du CAE.
**ARRL** American Radio Relay League (U.S.A.).
**ARRT** American Registered Respiratory Therapist.
**ARRT** American Registry of Radiologic Technologists (U.S.A.).
**AR rule** Accept-Reject rule.
*Statistics.*
**ARS** Acid-Rinsing Solution.
**ARS** Advanced Reconnaissance System (U.S.A.).
**ARS** Advanced Reentry System.
*Aerospace.*
**ARS** Aerial Reconnaissance and Security.
**ARS** Aeronautical Research Scientist.
**ARS** Aerospace Research Satellite.
**ARS** Agricultural Research Service (U.S.A.).
Of the U.S. Department of Agriculture.
**ARS** American Rocket Society (U.S.A.).
**ARS** Asbestos Roof Shingle.
**ARS** Autonomously Replicating Sequence.
*Genetics.*

**ARSI** Associazione per la Ricerca Scientifica Italiana.
Italian acronym of the: Association for Italian Scientific Research.
**β-AR signalling** β-Adrenergic Receptor signalling.
*Calcium Homeostasis; Gene Transfer; Myocardial Contractility.*
**ARSR** Air-Route Surveillance Radar.
*Navigation.*
**ARSSA** Agenzia Regionale per i Servizi di Sviluppo Agricolo (Italy).
Italian initialism of the: Regional Agency for Agricultural Development Services.
**AR systems** Augmented Reality systems.
*Computer Technology.*
**ART** Absolute Rate Theory.
*Statistics.*
**ART** Accredit Record Technician.
**ART** Acoustic Reflex Test.
*Audiology.*
**ART** Advanced Reactor Technology.
**ART** 1. Agence de recherche et de technologie [remplace AGARD et GRD].
1. Research and Technology Agency (RTA) [has replaced AGARD and RDA].
2. air-launched radiation thermometer.
2. thermomètre à rayonnement aérolargué.
3. artillery and related equipment.
3. artillerie et matériels connexes.
**ART** Airborne Radiation Thermometer.
The ART measures the ocean surface temperature.
*Oceanography.*
**ART** Alarm Reporting Telephone.
**ART** Alert Reaction Time.
**ART** Applied Research and Technology.
**ART** Armatron International.
*American Stock Exchange Symbols.*
**art.** (abbr.) article.
**art.** (abbr.) artificial.
**art.** (abbr.) artillery.
Also: **arty**.
**art.** (abbr.) artist.
**ART** Assisted Reproductive Technology / Technique.
*Development; Embryology; Endangered Wildlife; Reproductive Physiology; Reproductive Problems.*
**ART** Automatic Ranging Telescope.
**ART** Autorité de Régulation des Télécommunications (France).
**ARTCC** Air Route Traffic Control Center.
Of the U.S. Federal Aviation Administration.
**ARTEMIS** Advanced Relay TEchnology MISsion.
**ARTEMIS** Automatic Retrieval of Text from Europe's Multinational Information Service.
**ARTEX** artillery exercise.
exercice d'artillerie.
**ARTI** Acute Respiratory Tract Illness.
**ARTI** Advanced Rotocraft Technology Integration.
**artic.** (abbr.) articulation.
*Anatomy; Botany; Robotics; Telecommunications.*
**ARTS** Advanced Road Traffic System.
**ARTS** ARmy Training Study.
*U.S. Army.*
**ARTs** Assisted Reproductive Technologies / Techniques.
For further details see under **ART**.
**ARTS** Automated Radar Terminal System.
*Navigation.*
**ARTS** Automatic Resistance Test Set.
**ARTU** Automatic Range Tracking Unit.
**arty.** (abbr.) artillery.
Also: **art**.
*Military Science; Ordnance.*
**ARU** Audio Response Unit.
*Telecommunications.*
**ARV** Armoured Recovery Vehicle.
**ARV therapy** Antiretroviral therapy.
Used for prevention and treatment of HIV infection. It also reduces mother-to-child transmission of HIV.
**ARXPS** Angular Resolved X-Ray PES.
*Chemistry; Physics.*
**AS** 1. airfield services.
1. services des aérodromes.
2. associated support.
2. soutien associé.
3. Australia.
3. Australie.
**AS**; **A.S.** Academy of Sciences.
**A.S.**; **a/s** Account Sales.
*Commerce; Economics; Finance.*
**AS** Accumulated Surplus.
**AS** Acrylic Styrene.
*Plastic Technology.*
**AS** Active Securities.
**AS** Active Sleep.
Active Sleep is also known as: REM Sleep; Dreaming Sleep; Fast Wave Sleep; Desynchronized Sleep; Paradoxical Sleep.
*Neurology.*
**AS** Additional Sources.
**AS** Adociasulfate.
*Marine Sponges; Medicine; Pharmacology.*
**AS** Aeronautical Standard.
**a/s** after sight.

*Commerce; Economics; Finance.*
**AS** Aggregate Supply.
*Economics.*
**AS** Airscoop / Air Scoop.
AS is used for combustion or ventilation.
*Mechanical Devices.*
**AS** Airspeed.
*Aviation.*
**AS** Air-to-Surface.
*Missiles.*
**AS** The airline code for Alaska Airlines.
**AS** Alimentary System.
*Medicine.*
**a/s** (abbr.) alongside.
**A.S.** Altezza Serenissima.
Italian acronym meaning: Most Serene Highness.
**As** Altostratus cloud.
*Meteorology.*
**AS** Ammonium Sulfate.
$(NH_4)_2SO_4$ - AS is used mainly as a food additive, in fermentation processes and in water treatment.
*Inorganic Chemistry.*
**A.S.** Anglo-Saxon.
**AS** Anthranilate Synthase.
AS is a stromal enzyme.
**AS** Antisubmarine.
Also: **A/S.**
*Ordnance.*
**AS** Anxiety Score; Anxiety State.
*Psychology.*
**AS** Aortic Stenosis.
*Medicine.*
**AS**; **as** Application System.
**AS** Arcuated Sulcus.
**AS** Arithmetic Scan.
*Computer Programming.*
**AS** Arithmetic Shift.
Arithmetic shift actually refers to the shift of the digits of a number.
**As** The chemical symbol for Arsenic.
Arsenic is a chemical element having the atomic number 33, an atomic weight of 74.9216 and a boiling point of 613°C.
The word arsenic derives from the Greek term manly / strong.
*Chemistry.*
**AS** Arteriosclerosis.
Arteriosclerosis is a disease of the arteries characterized by thickening and loss of elasticity of arterial walls.
*Medicine.*
**As.** (abbr.) Asian; Asiatic.
**AS** Asperger Syndrome.
AS is a mild version of autism.
**AS** Asserted Securities.
**AS** Assessable Stock.
*Business; Finance.*
**A.S.** Assistant Secretary.
**A.S.** Assurances Sociales.
French initialism meaning: National Insurance.
**As** (abbr.) astigmatism.
*Electronics; Optics; Physiology.*
**AS**; **as** At Sight.
*Business; Commerce; Economics; Finance.*
**AS** Audiogenic Seizure.
AS is a type of reflex epilepsy.
*Medicine; Neurology.*
**AS** Australian Standard.
*Technology.*
**AS** Automatic Sprinkler.
**AS** Auxiliary Storage.
For further details see under: **AM** (Auxiliary Memory).
**a/s** aux soins de.
French initialism meaning: care of; c/o.
**ASA** Accessible Surface Area.
**ASA** Acetylsalicylic Acid.
$CH_3COOC_6H_4COOH$. The trade name of acetylsalicylic acid is aspirin. It has widespread medicinal use as an antipyretic.
*Organic Chemistry.*
**ASA**; **A.S.A.** Acoustical Society of America; American Society of Anesthesiologists; American Surgical Association (U.S.A.).
**ASA** 1. admission au service actif [FR].
1. initial operational capability (IOC 1.).
2. artillerie sol-air.
2. ground-to-air artillery.
3. association de système d'arme.
3. weapon system partnership (WSP).
**A.S.A.** Amateur Swimming Association (G.B.).
**ASA** American Society of Appraisers; American Standards Association (U.S.A.).
**A.S.A.** American Statistical Association (U.S.A.).
**ASA** Area Strategica di Affari.
Italian acronym meaning: Strategic Business Area.
**ASA** Association of South-east Asia.
**ASA** Astronomical Society of the Atlantic (U.S.A.).
**ASA** Atomic Sphere Approximation.
**ASA** Associazione Solidarietà AIDS (Italy).
**ASA** Ausiliario Socio Assistenziale.
**ASAAD** advanced shipborne area air defence.
défense aérienne de zone avancée, embarquée.
**ASAB** Association for the Study of Animal Behavior.
**ASADHA**; **Asadha** Association Syndicale Autorisée

pour l'Aménagement et le Développement des Irrigations des Hautes-Alpes (France).
**ASAE** American Society of Agricultural Engineers (U.S.A.).
**ASAG** air surface action group.
groupe d'action Air de surface.
**ASAL** Annuaire, Société d'Histoire et d'Archeologie de la Lorraine (France).
*Publication.*
**asal** The above acronym was coined accidentally using the Arabic word "asal" which means: honey (*Food Technology*).
**ASALM** Advanced Strategic Air-Launched Missile.
**ASANCA** Advanced Study for Active Noise Control in Aircraft.
*Noise Control in Aircraft.*
**ASAP** Americans for a Sound AIDS/HIV Policy.
**ASAP** Associazione Sindacale per le Aziende Petrolchimiche e collegate a partecipazione statale.
*Italian Association.*
**ASAP** As Soon As Possible.
**ASAR** Advanced Synthetic Aperture Radar.
**ASAT** anti-satellite.
antisatellite.
**ASAU** Air Search Attack Unit.
**ASB** Accounting Standards Board.
**ASB**; **A.S.B.** American Society of Bacteriologists (U.S.A.).
**ASB** Analytical Support Branch.
Of the U.S. National Institute for Occupational Safety and Health.
*Analytical Services; Occupational Diseases; Workplace Hazards.*
**ASB** Army Science Board (U.S.A.).
**asb** (abbr.) asbestos.
*Materials Science; Mineralogy.*
**ASB** Auditing Standards Board.
**ASB agriculture programme** Alternatives to Slash-and-Burn agriculture programme (Kenya).
Of the ICRAF.
For further details see under: **ICRAF**.
**asbl.** (abbr.) assemble.
**asbl.** (abbr.) assembler.
Also: **assm.**; **asmblr.**
For further details see under: **asmblr**.
**ASBMB** American Society for Biochemistry and Molecular Biology (U.S.A.).
**ASBO** Association of School Business Officials International.
*Educational Web Site.*
**ASC** Académie des Sciences Commerciales.
French initialism of the: Academy of Commercial Sciences (France).
**ASC** 1. ACCS Software Committee.
1. Comité du logiciel de l'ACCS.
2. airspace control.
2. contrôle de l'espace aérien.
3. all-source cell.
3. cellule toutes sources.
4. area support commander.
4. commandant de soutien de zone.
5. authorized subordinate command.
5. commandement subordonné autorisé.
6. AUTODIN switching centre.
6. centre de commutation AUTODIN.
**ASC** Administrative Support Center (U.S.A.).
**ASC** Altered State of Consciousness.
**ASC** American Society of Criminology.
The ASC is located in Columbus, Ohio, U.S.A.
**ASC** Analytical Sciences Center (U.S.A.).
The ASC is a state-of-the-art Research Organization serving analytical needs of Monsanto's new Life Sciences Company.
*Analytical Sciences.*
**ASC** Association for Systematics Collections.
*Taxonomy.*
**ASC** Axial Summit Caldera.
The Axial Summit Caldera is a small, narrow depression, often included in the summit region of the axial high.
*Earth Observations; Oceanography.*
**ASCA** Advanced Satellite for Cosmology and Astrophysics - Japan - U.S.A.
*Astronomy; Astrophysics; Cosmology; X-ray Satellites.*
**ASCAP** American Society of Composers, Authors and Publishers (U.S.A.).
**ASCB** American Society for Cell Biology (U.S.A.).
**ASCE** American Society of Civil Engineers (U.S.A.).
**asce** The above acronym was coined accidentally using the Italian word "asce" which means: hatches. (*Engineering; Graphic Arts; Zoology*).
**ASCEND** Advanced System for Communications and Education in National Development.
**ASCET** American Society of Certified Engineering Technicians (U.S.A.).
**ASCI** Accelerated Strategic Computing Initiative.
*Defense; Explosive Testing; Stockpile Stewardship; Weapons Design.*
**ASCI** Advanced Scientific Computing Initiative.
**ASCI** Advanced Speech Call Item.
*Digital Mobiles.*
**ASCI** American Society for Clinical Investigation (U.S.A.).

**ASCII** American Standard Code for Information Interchange.
**ASCM** Archivio Storico Civico di Milano (Italy).
**ASCN** American Society for Clinical Nutrition (U.S.A.).
**ASCO** American Society of Clinical Oncology (U.S.A.).
**ASCO** Arab Satellite Communications Organization (Saudi Arabia).
**ASCOT** Atmospheric Studies in COmplex Terrain (U.S.A.).
**ASCS** Agricultural Stabilization and Conservation Service.
**ASCS** American Society of Corporate Secretaries (U.S.A.).
**ASD** Aide et Soins à Domicile (Belgium).
*Social Institution.*
**ASD** Airport Surface Detection.
*Navigation.*
**ASD** Associazione Separati e Divorziati (Italy).
Italian initialism of the: Association of Separated and Divorced persons.
**ASD** Automation Source Data.
*Computers.*
**ASDAR system** Aircraft-to-Satellite DAta Relay system.
**ASDE** air situation data exchange.
échange de données sur la situation aérienne.
**ASDIC** Allied Submarine Detection Investigation Committee.
**AS disease** Adams-Stokes disease or syndrome.
From the name of two Irish physicians Robert **Adams**, and Robert **Stokes**.
**ASDs** Atrial Septal Defects.
*Artery-Clogging Plaques; Cardiovascular Electrophysiology; Cardiovascular Genetics; Medicine; Mutant Genes.*
**ASE** Advanced Space Engine.
**ASE** Agence Spatiale Européenne.
French acronym of the: European Space Agency.
**ASE** aircraft survivability equipment.
matériel de surviabilité des aéronefs.
**ASE** American Stock Exchange.
Also: **AMEX**.
**ASE** Amplified Spontaneous Emission.
*Electrical Engineering; Optoelectronic Materials; Photonics.*
**ASE** Athens Stock Exchange.
Since 1876.
**ASEA** American Society of Engineers and Architects (U.S.A.).
**ASEAMS** Association of South-East Asian Marine Scientists.
**ASEAN** Association of South East Asian Nations (Jakarta).
**ASEB** Aeronautics and Space Engineering Board (U.S.A.).
**ASEP** Asian Society for Environmental Protection (Thailand).
**ASEPS** Astronomical Studies of Extrasolar Planetary Systems.
ASEPS was one of NASA's multistage programs.
*Astronomical Studies.*
**ASET** Assistant Secretary for Energy Technology (U.S.A.).
**ASEV** Assistant Secretary for Environment (U.S.A.).
**ASF** ACE strike file.
dossier des attaques nucléaires du CAE.
**ASF** Atlantic Salmon Federation (Canada).
**ASFA** Action Sociale des Forces Armées (France).
**ASFA** Aquatic Sciences and Fisheries Abstracts.
**A.S.F.D.** Azienda di Stato per le Foreste Demaniali (Italy).
Italian acronym of the: National Board of State Forests.
**ASFIS** Aquatic Sciences and Fisheries Information System.
*Aquatic Sciences and Fisheries.*
**ASG** Administrative Support Group (U.S.A.).
Of the U.S. Pacific Marine Environmental Laboratory.
**ASG** 1. AFCENT Support Group [obsolete].
1. Groupe de soutien de l'AFCENT [obsolète].
2. Assistant Secretary General.
2. Secrétaire général adjoint.
**asg.** (abbr.) assigned.
Also: **asgd.**
**asg.** (abbr.) assignment.
Also: **asgmt.**
**AsGa** Arséniure de Gallium.
French symbol for Gallium Arsenide.
For further details see under: **GaAs**.
**ASGAMAGE** Air Sea Gas exchange MAGE Experiment.
*European Community Project; Environment Protection; Resources of the Sea; Fisheries.*
**asgd.** (abbr.) assigned.
Also: **asg.**
**asgmt.** (abbr.) assignment.
Also: **asg.**
**ASGPI** Association of Sea Grant Program Institutes (U.S.A.).
**ASH** Academy of Scientific Hypnotherapy.
**ASH** Action on Smoking and Health.
The ASH is an Antismoking Organization.

**ASH** Aldosterone-Stimulating Hormone.
*Endocrinology.*
**ASH**; **A.S.H.** American Society of Hematology (U.S.A.).
**ASH** Armature Shunt.
*Electromagnetism.*
**ASH** Assault Support Helicopter.
**ASH** Assistante Sociale Hospitalière.
French initialism meaning: Hospital Social Worker (France).
**ASH** Assistant Secretary for Health (U.S.A.).
**ASHA** American School Health Association; American Society of Hospital Attorneys (U.S.A.).
**ASHA**; **A.S.H.A.** American Speech and Hearing Association (U.S.A.).
**ASHES** Axial Seamount Hydrothermal Emissions Study.
**ASHG** American Society of Human Genetics.
**ASHOE** Airborne Southern Hemisphere Ozone Experiment.
**ASHRAE** American Society of Heating, Refrigerating, and Airconditioning Engineers (U.S.A.).
Testing will result in an extensive database of desiccant cooling options that can help architects, building managers, and consumers make objective, informed decisions about which technology is appropriate for a specific application.
**ASHVE** American Society of Heating and Ventilating Engineers (U.S.A.).
**ASI** Accumulator Shift Instruction.
*Computer Programming.*
**ASI** Agenzia Spaziale Italiana (Italy).
Italian acronym of the: Italian Space Agency.
**ASI** Airspeed Indicator.
*Aviation.*
**ASI** Assistante Sociale Industrielle (France).
French acronym meaning: Industrial Social Worker.
**ASI** Associazione Sanitaria Internazionale.
Italian acronym of the: International Health Association.
**ASI** Atmosphere Structure Instrument.
The ASI directly measured the temperature of Jupiter's upper atmosphere in december, 1995.
*Meteorology; Space Physics; Space Science.*
**ASI** Audience Surveys Incorporated.
**3ASI** Associazione degli Analisti di Affidabilità e Sicurezza Italia (Italy).
**ASIA** Airlines Staff International Association.
**ASIA** American Society of Industrial Auctioneers (U.S.A.).
**ASIA** American Spinal Injury Association; American Stone Importers Association; Army Signal Intelligence Agency (U.S.A.).
**A.s.i.a.** Associazione per la solidarietà internazionale in Asia (Italy).
**ASIC** Application Specific Integrated Circuit.
*Computer Technology.*
**ASICA** ASsociation Internationale pour le Calcul Analogique.
**Asics** Application specific integrated circuits.
*Computer Technology.*
**ASIECO** Associazione Italiana Imprese Elettrocommerciali.
*Italian Association.*
**ASIEP** Associazione Sindacale dell'Industria dell'Energia e del Petrolio (Italy).
**ASIF** Airlift Service Industrial Fund.
**asif** The above acronym was coined accidentally using the Arabic word "asif' which means: I am sorry.
**a-Si: H** Hydrogenated Amorphous Silicon.
*Applied Physics; Semiconductor Devices.*
**ASIL** American Society of International Law. Northwest, Washington D.C., U.S.A.
**ASIM**; **A.S.I.M.** American Society of Internal Medicine (U.S.A.).
**ASI/MET Experiment** Atmospheric Structure Investigation / METeorology Experiment.
Information from ASI/MET Experiment was collected by Mars Pathfinder which landed on the surface of Mars on 4th July 1997. The Mars Pathfinder is a project of the JPL (U.S.A.).
*Chemistry; Geology; Geophysics; Martian Surface Meteorology; Planetary Exploration.*
For further details see under: **JPL**.
**ASK** Actively Shared Knowledge.
*Data Processing System.*
**ASK** Aircraft Station Keeper.
**ASK** Amplitude Shift Key(ing).
*Telecommunications.*
**ASK** Analog Select Keyboard.
**ASK project** Action South Kildare project (Greece).
**ASL** Above Sea Level.
**ASL** Acceptable Supplier List.
**ASL** Acetone-Soluble Lipids.
*Allergy and Infectious Diseases; Microbiology.*
**ASL** Activity Safety Level.
**ASL** Advanced Systems Laboratory.
**ASL** American Sign Language.
The American sign language is a way to communicate with the deaf by means of hand gestures.
*Linguistics.*
**ASL** Anticodon Stem-Loop.
**ASL** Antistreptolysin.

Antistreptolysin is an antibody that counteracts the streptolysin activity.
*Immunology.*
**ASL** Applied Science Laboratory.
**ASL** Astrosurveillance Science Laboratory.
**ASL** Atmospheric Sciences Laboratory.
**ASL** Authorized Stock Level.
**ASL** Azienda Sanitaria Locale (Italy).
**ASLB** Atomic Safety and Licensing Board.
**ASLE** American Society of Lubrication Engineers (U.S.A.).
**ASLO** American Society of Limnology and Oceanography (U.S.A.).
**ASLO** Antistreptolysin O.
*Medicine.*
**ASLs** Anticodon Stem-Loops.
*Biomolecular Research; Molecular Biology; Molecular Crystallography; Physical Biosciences.*
**ASLV** Assurance Sur La Vie.
French initialism meaning: Life Insurance.
**ASM**; **Asm** Accademia Solare Mondiale.
Italian initialism of the: World Solar Academy.
Founding member: FAST.
For further details see under: **FAST**.
**ASM**; **asm** Air-to-Surface Missile.
*Military.*
**ASM** All Sky Monitor.
The ASM is aboard the orbiting Rossi X-ray Timing Explorer.
*Astronomy; Gamma-Ray Bursts.*
**ASM**; **A.S.M.** American Society for Metals; American Society for Microbiology (U.S.A.).
**ASM** Analyses et Statistiques Monétaires.
French initialism meaning: Monetary Analyses and Statistics.
**ASM** Associazione Studio Malformazioni.
Italian initialism of the: Association for the Study of Malformations (Italy).
**AsM** Astigmatism, Myopic.
Also: **AM**.
*Ophtalmology.*
**ASMA** American Ski Manufacturers' Association; American Society of Music Arrangers (U.S.A.).
**asma** The above acronyms were coined accidentally using the Italian word "asma" which means: asthma (*Medicine*).
**asmblr.** (abbr.) assembler.
Also: **assm.**; **asbl.**
Assembler is also known as: Assembler Program; Symbolic Assembly System.
*Computer Programming.*
**ASMC** American Society of Mature Catholics (U.S.A.).
**ASMC** ASEAN Specialized Meteorological Centre.
For further details see under: **ASEAN**.
**ASMD** anti-ship missile defence.
défense contre (les) missiles antinavires.
**ASMD** Atmospheric Sciences Modeling Division.
**ASMDEX** anti-ship missile defence exercise.
exercice de défense contre missiles antinavires.
**ASME** American Society of Mechanical Engineers (U.S.A.).
**ASMFC** Atlantic States Marine Fisheries Commissions.
**ASMP** air-sol moyenne portée.
medium-range air-to-ground (MRAG).
**ASNE** American Society of Naval Engineers (U.S.A.).
**ASNM** Agenzia Sviluppo Nord Milano (Italy).
**ASNT** American Society for Nondestructive Testing (U.S.A.).
**ASO** Aviation Supply Office.
**$As_2O_3$** Arsenic Trioxide.
Arsenic Trioxide, also known as; Arsenous Acid, is used mainly in herbicides and insecticides, as well as in glass and ceramics.
*Inorganic Chemistry.*
**$As_2O_3$** Arsenolite.
*Mineralogy.*
**$As_2O_3$** Claudetite.
*Mineralogy.*
**ASOC** 1. air support operations centre.
1. centre d'opérations d'appui aérien.
2. alternate sector operations centre.
2. centre d'opérations de secteur de rechange.
**ASOC** Antarctic and Southern Ocean Coalition (U.S.A.).
**ASOG** air support operations group.
groupe d'opérations d'appui aérien.
**ASOS** air support operations squadron.
escadron d'opérations d'appui aérien.
**ASOS** Automated Seismological Observation System.
**ASOS** Automated Surface Observing Systems.
The ASOS report on an almost continuous way, atmospheric pressure, temperature, wind direction, and visibility.
**ASP**; **asp** Accepté Sans Protêt.
French initialism meaning: Accepted without protest.
**ASP** Active Server Pages.
ASP is a technology produced by Microsoft to create dynamic websites.
**ASP** American Selling Price.
**ASP** American Society of Photogrammetry (U.S.A.).

**ASP** ammunition supply point.
point de ravitaillement munitions.
**ASP** Antisubmarine Patrol.
*Ordnance.*
**ASP; asp** Application Service Provider.
**ASP** Associazione italiana Studenti di Psicologia.
Italian initialism of the: Italian Association of Psychology Students.
**ASP** Astronomical Society of the Pacific.
**ASP** Attached Support Processor.
*Computers.*
**ASPA** Association Suisse Pour l'Automatisme (Switzerland).
*Swiss Association.*
**ASPB** American Society of Plant Biologists (U.S.A.).
**ASPE** Associazione Sistemi per la Produzione di Energia.
*Italian Association.*
**ASPE** Associazione Solidarietà Paesi Emergenti (Italy).
Italian acronym of the: Association for Solidarity to Emerging Countries.
**Aspe** Agenzia di stampa sui problemi dell'emarginazione.
**ASPEA** Associazione Svizzera Per l'Energia Atomica.
Italian acronym of the: Swiss Association for Atomic Energy.
**ASPECT** Acoustic Short-Pulse Echo Classification Technique.
**ASPECT** Advanced Security for PErsonal Communications Technologies.
*European Community Project.*
**ASPED** Arizona Strategic Planning for Economic Development (U.S.A.).
**ASPEI** Association of South-Pacific Environmental Institutions.
**ASPEP** Association of Scientists and Professional Engineering Personnel (U.S.A.).
**ASPET** American Society for Pharmacology and Experimental Therapeutics.
ASPET is a society of FASEB (U.S.A.).
*Experimental Therapeutics; Pharmacology.*
For further details see under: **FASEB**.
**A.S.P.H.I.** Associazione per lo Sviluppo di Progetti informatici per gli Handicappati (Italy).
A.S.P.H.I. was founded 22 years ago.
**ASPI** Advanced SCSI Programming Interface.
For further details see under: **SCSI**.
**ASPIC** Author's Symbolic Prepress Interfacing Codes.
**ASPIRE** Achieve Successful Performance, Intensify Reliability Effort.
**ASPIRE** Advanced Special Projects In Radiation Effects.
**ASPIRE** Associated Students Promoting Individual Rights for Everyone.
**ASPPI** Associazione Sindacale Piccoli Proprietari Immobiliari.
*Italian Association.*
**ASPR** Armed Service Procurement Regulations.
**ASPs** Application Service Providers.
*Online Information Technology Applications.*
**ASQC** American Society for Quality Control (U.S.A.).
**ASQDS** American Society of Questioned Documents Examiners.
The ASQDS is located in Houston, Texas, U.S.A.
**ASR** Airport Surveillance Radar.
**ASR** Air-Sea Rescue.
**ASR** 1. Alliance standardization requirements.
1. besoins de l'Alliance en matière de normalisation.
2. area surveillance radar.
2. radar de surveillance de zone.
3. authorized supply rate.
3. taux d'approvisionnement autorisé.
4. available supply rate.
4. taux de ravitaillement consenti.
**ASRAAM** advanced short-range air-to-air missile.
missile air-air perfectionné à courte portée.
**A/S ratio** Advertising-to-Sales ratio.
*Marketing.*
**ASRE** American Society of Refrigerating Engineers (U.S.A.).
**ASRI** Allegheny-Singer Research Institute (U.S.A.).
ASRI is part of the Allegheny Health, Education and Research Foundation, an academic medical center located in Pittsburgh and Philadelphia, Pennsylvania (U.S.A.).
**ASRM** American Society for Reproductive Medicine (U.S.A.).
*Fertility Research; Reproductive Medicine.*
**ASRM** Advanced Solid Rocket Motor.
**asRNA** antisense RNA.
*Genetics; Molecular Biology.*
**ASROC** Antisubmarine ROCket.
*Military.*
**AS/RS** Automated Storage/Retrieval System.
*Design Engineering.*
**ASS** Accessory Supply System.
**ASS** Acquisition Sun Sensor.
**ASS** Action Sanitaire et Sociale.

French initialism meaning: Social and Health Action.
**ASS** Advanced Space Station.
**ASS** Affective Sensitivity Scale.
**ASS** Air Sampling System; Air Surveillance System.
**ASS** Antenna Support Structure.
**ass.** (abbr.) assembly.
*Computer Programming; Mechanical Engineering; Military Science.*
**ass.** assicurata.
Italian abbreviation meaning: insured mail.
**ass.** (abbr.) assistant.
**ASS** Assize Rolls (G.B.).
**A.S.S.** Associate in Secretarial Science.
**A.S.S.**; **ASS** Associate in Secretarial Studies.
**ass.** (abbr.) association.
For further details see under: **assn.**
**ASS** Associazione Solidarietà per lo Sviluppo.
Italian initialism of the: Solidarity for Development Association.
**ass.** (abbr.) assorted.
Also: **asstd.**
**ASS** aviation support ship.
bâtiment de soutien de l'aéronavale.
**$As_2S_2$** Arsenic Disulfide.
Arsenic Disulfide is used mainly in fireworks, and in the leather industry.
*Inorganic Chemistry.*
**$As_2S_5$** Arsenic Pentasulfide.
Arsenic Pentasulfide is used as a pigment.
*Inorganic Chemistry.*
**$As_4S_3$** Dimorphite.
*Mineralogy.*
**Assalzao** (abbr.) Associazione Nazionale tra i Produttori di Alimenti Zootecnici.
Assalzao is located in Rome, Italy.
**ASSASSIN** Agricultural System for Storage And Subsequent Selection of Information (G.B.).
**3-ASSC** 3-A Sanitary Standards Committees (U.S.A.).
**ASSCO** ASSociazione nazionale COnsulenti.
Italian acronym of the: National Association of Consultants.
**ASSD** Association of Stock and Share Dealers.
**ASSE** air servicing and standard equipment.
entretien et équipment standard des aéronefs.
**ASSE** American Society of Safety Engineers; American Society of Sanitary Engineers (U.S.A.).
**ASSE** Automatic System for Scientific Experiments.
**asse** The above acronyms were coined accidentally using the Italian word "asse" which means: board; axis; axle.
**ASS.E.D.I.C.** Association pour l'Emploi dans d'Industrie et le Commerce.
*French Association.*
**ASSESS** Analytical Studies of Surface Effects of Submerged Submarines.
**ASSESSREP** assessment report.
compte rendu d'évaluation.
**ASSET** Air Storage Systems Energy Transfer.
*Energy Transfer.*
**ASSET** American Society of Scientific and Engineering Translators (U.S.A.).
**ASSET** Automated System for Sequential Extraction and Tabulation.
**ASSICC**; **Assicc** Associazione Italiana del Commercio Chimico.
ASSICC is located in Milan, Italy.
**ASSICREDITO** Associazione Sindacale fra le Aziende di Credito (Italy).
Italian abbreviation of the: Italian Bankers' Trade Union.
**ASSIDER** ASsociazione industrie SIDERurgiche Italiane (Italy).
**Assinform** (abbr.) Associazione Costruttori Macchine, Attrezzature per l'Ufficio e per il Trattamento delle Informazioni.
Assinform is located in Milan, Italy. A National Association of the main enterprises of Information Communication Technology operating in the Italian market.
*Italian Association.*
**Assintel** Associazione Nazionale Imprese Servizi Informatica, Telematica, Robotica Eidomatica (Italy).
**ASSIREME** Associazione fra gli Istituti Regionali di Medio Credito (Italy).
Italian abbreviation of the: Association of Medium-Term Regional Credit Institutions.
**ASSIREVI** ASSociazione Italiana REVIsori contabili (Italy).
Italian abbreviation of the: Italian Association of Auditors.
**ASSIST** Army System for Standardized Intelligence Support Terminals (U.S.A.).
**ASSIST** ASSessment of Information Systems and Technologies in medicine.
**ASSIST** Automation Services - System Improvement - Solution and Tracking.
**ASSIST** Automatic System for Surface Inspection and Sorting of Tiles.
*European Community Project.*
**ASSM** anti-surface ship missile.

missile antinavire.

**assm** (abbr.) assembler.
Also: **asbl.**; **asmblr.**
For further details see under: **asmblr.**

**assmt** (abbr.) assessment.

**assn** (abbr.) association.
*Chemistry* - Association in chemistry is the correlation / combination of functions / substances.
*Psychology* - Association in psychology is a connection between two thoughts or images whereby when one takes place, the other is recalled.

**ASSO** American Society for the Study of Orthodontics (U.S.A.).

**ASSO** Archivio Storico per la Sicilia Orientale.
*Publication.*

**asso** The above acronyms were coined accidentally using the Italian word "asso" which means: ace; star; wizard.

**ASSOBANCA** ASSOciazione BANCAria Italiana (Italy).
Italian abbreviation of the: Italian Banker's Association.

**ASSOBAT** ASSociazione Operatori BAncari in Titoli (Italy).

**Assoc.** (abbr.) Association.
Also: **ass.**; **assn**.

**Assocamp.** Associazione nazionale operatori veicoli ricreazionali e articoli per campeggio.
*Italian Association.*

**ASSODEL** ASSOciazione nazionale Distribuzione ELettronica (Italy).
Italian abbreviation of the: National Association for Electronic Distribution.

**ASSODIRECT** ASSOciazione Agenzie di DIRECT Marketing (Italy).
Italian abbreviation of the: Association of Direct Marketing Agencies.

**ASSOFARMA** ASSOciazione fra industrie chimico-FARMAceutiche.

**ASSOFOND**; **Assofond.** (abbr.) ASSOciazione nazionale delle FONDerie.
Italian abbreviation of the: National Foundries Association. Assofond is located in Trezzano sul Naviglio (Milan), Italy.

**ASSOFT** (abbr.) ASsociazione Italiana per la Tutela del SOFTware (Italy).
Italian abbreviation of the: Italian Association for Software Protection.

**ASSOLOMBARDA** Associazione Industriale Lombarda (Italy).
Italian abbreviation of the: Association of the Industrialists of Lombardy.

**Assonime** Associazione tra le società anonime.
Italian acronym coined in 1911 and still currently in use. At the time, the Società per Azioni, Joint-Stock Companies, were called Società Anonime.

**Assorevi** Associazione delle Società di revisione (Italy).
Italian abbreviation of the: Association of auditing Companies.

**ASSP** Aerosol Scattering Spectrometer Probe.

**ASSP** Approved Species-Specific Protocol.

**ASS reactor** Automatic Start-up System reactor.

**ASST** American Society for Steel Treating (U.S.A.).

**Asst.**; **asst.** (abbr.) Assistant.

**asstd.** (abbr.) assented.

**asstd.** (abbr.) assorted.
Also: **ass.**

**ASSU** air support signal unit.
unité de transmissions d'appui aérien.

**assy.** (abbr.) assembly.
For further details see under: **ass.**

**Assyr.** (abbr.) Assyrian.

**A.S.T.** Agenzia della Stampa Tecnica (Italy).
Italian acronym of the: Technical Press Agency.

**ASTA** Aerial Surveillance and Target Acquisition.

**ASTA** American Sail Training Association; American Spice Trade Association; American Surgical Trade Association (U.S.A.).

**ASTC** Association of Science and Technology Centers (U.S.A.).

**ASTE** Aerospace Systems Test Environment.

**ASTE** American Society of Test Engineers; American Society of Tools Engineers (U.S.A.).

**aste** The above acronyms were coined accidentally using the Italian word "aste" which means: rods; bars; lances; auctions.

**ASTEC** Australian Science and TEchnology Council (Australia).

**ASTEF** Association pour l'organisation de Stages de Techniciens Etrangers dans l'industrie Française (France).
French acronym of the: Association for the setting up of training courses / periods for Foreign Technicians in the French Industry.

**ASTER** Advanced Spaceborne Thermal Emission and Reflection.

**ASTER** Agenzia per lo Sviluppo Tecnologico dell'Emilia Romagna (Italy).

**ASTER facility** Atmospheric-Surface Turbulent Exchange Research facility.
*Air-Surface Exchange Processes; Atmospheric Research.*

**ASTER radiometer image** Advanced Spaceborne Thermal Emission and Reflection radiometer image.

For further details see under: **GLIMS**.
**ASTEX** Atlantic Stratocumulus Transition EXperiment.
**ASTF** Arab Science and Technology Foundation (3-year old (2003)).
Held its first international conference end of march 2002 in Abu Dhabi and Sharjah, United Arab Emirates.
**ASTHMA** Aerotherm Axisymmetric Transient Heating and Material Ablation.
**ASTI** antisubmarine target indicator.
indicateur d'objectif anti-sous-marin.
**ASTI** Applied Statistics Training Institute.
**ASTI** Association de Soutien aux Travailleurs Immigrés (Luxemburg).
**ASTI** Association for Science, Technology and Innovation.
**ASTI** Automated System for Transportation Intelligence.
**Asti** The above acronyms were coined accidentally using the name of the Italian town "Asti".
**ASTIO** Advanced Systems Technology and Integration Office.
**astio** The above acronym was coined accidentally using the Italian word "astio" which means: resentment, rancour, grudge.
**ASTM**; **A.S.T.M.** American Society for Testing Materials (U.S.A.).
**ASTME** American Society of Tool and Manufacturing Engineers (U.S.A.).
**ASTOR** airborne stand-off radar.
radar aéroporté à distance de sécurité.
**ASTOR** Antisubmarine TORpedo.
*Ordnance.*
**ASTRA** Application of Science and Technology to Rural Areas.
**ASTRA** Applied Space Technology Regional Advancement.
**ASTRA** Astronomical and Space Techniques and Research on the Atmosphere (U.S.A.).
ASTRA is a U.S. National Science Foundation Project.
**ASTRA** Automatic Sorting, Testing, Recording Analysis.
**ASTRI** Applied Science and Technology Research Institute (Hong Kong).
**ASTRID** Association Scientifique et Technique pour la Recherche en Information Documentaire (Belgium).
**Astrid** The above acronym was coined using the proper name (feminine) Astrid.
**ASTRO** Air Space Travel Research Organization.
**AST/RO** Antarctic Submillimeter Telescope and Remote Observatory.
**ASTRO** Antisubmarine Test Requirement Outline.
**ASTRO** Army Strategic and Tactical Reorganization Objective.
**astro** The above acronyms were coined accidentally using the Italian word "astro" which means: star. Also: planet (*Astronomy*).
**ASTRON** The Netherlands Foundation for Research in Astronomy (Dwingeloo).
**ASU** antenna switch unit.
élément de commutation d'antenne.
**ASU** Arizona State University (U.S.A.).
**ASUW** antisurface warfare.
lutte antinavire (LAN 2.).
**ASUWC** 1. antisurface warfare commander.
1. commandant de la lutte antisurface (antinavire).
2. antisurface warfare coordinator.
2. coordonnateur de lutte antisurface (antinavire).
**ASUWEX** anti surface warfare exercise.
exercice de lutte antinavire.
**ASV** American Standard Version.
**ASVAB** Armed Services Vocational Aptitude Battery (U.S.A.).
The ASVAB, of the U.S. Armed Services, comprises power tests as well as speed tests and is used to select and sort recruits in training programs.
*Education.*
**ASVAHL** ASsociation pour la VAlorisation des Huiles Lourdes (France).
French initialism of the: Association for the Exploitation of Fuel Oils/Heavy Oils.
**ASW** antisubmarine warfare.
lutte anti-sous-marine (LASM).
**ASW** Artificial Sea Water.
*Oceanography.*
**ASW** Association of Scientific Workers (U.S.A.).
**ASWACU** antisubmarine warfare aircraft control unit.
unité contrôleur des aéronefs de lutte anti-sous-marine.
**ASWC** antisubmarine warfare commander.
commandant de la lutte anti-sous-marine.
**ASWEPS** antisubmarine warfare environmental prediction studies.
études sur la prévision des conditions du milieu dans la lutte anti-sous-marine.
**ASWEX** antisubmarine warfare exercise.
exercice de lutte anti-sous-marine.
**ASWFA** antisubmarine warfare free area.
zone d'action anti-sous-marine libre.

**ASWM** Association of State Wetland Managers (U.S.A.).
*Ecology; Environment; Microbiology; Wetlands Vegetation.*
**ASWOC** antisubmarine warfare operations centre.
centre d'opérations de lutte anti-sous-marine.
**async.**; **asynch.** (abbr.) asynchronous.
*Computer Technology; Physics.*
**ASZ** air safety zone.
zone de sécurité aérienne.
**ASZ** American Society of Zoologists (U.S.A.).
Founded 97 years ago.
**AT** Absolute Threshold.
*Physiology.*
**AT** Absolute Title.
**AT** Acceptance Tag.
**AT** Acceptance Test.
The acceptance test is performed on a product in order to assess whether it conforms to certain specifications.
*Industrial Engineering.*
**AT** Access Time.
*Computer Technology; Transportation Engineering.*
**AT** Access Type.
*Computer Programming; Computer Technology.*
**AT** Accident du Travail.
French initialism meaning: industrial accident / injuries; occupational accident.
**AT** Achilles Tendon.
The Achilles tendon is the tendon that connects the calf muscle with the calcaneous bone in the heel.
*Anatomy.*
**AT** Acquisition Tone.
*Computer Technology.*
**AT** Address Translation.
*Computer Programming.*
**AT** Administrative Trainee (G.B.).
**AT** Agglutination Test.
*Virology.*
**AT** Air Temperature.
*Meteorology.*
**at.** (abbr.) airtight.
*Engineering.*
**AT** Air Transport.
**AT** Allergen Tachyphylasis.
*Immunology.*
**AT** Ampere-Turn.
*Electromagnetism.*
**AT** Ammissione Temporanea.
Italian initialism meaning: Temporary Import.
*Business; Commerce.*
**AT** Anaphylatoxin.
*Immunology.*
**AT** Ancient Testament.
French initialism meaning: Old Testament.
**A.T.** Antico Testamento.
Italian initialism meaning: Old Testament.
**A-T** Antitank.
Also: **AT**.
*Ordnance.*
**AT** Antithrombin.
Antithrombin is a plasma protein that inactivates thrombin.
*Biochemistry.*
**AT** Anti-TRAP.
*Biological Sciences.*
For further details see under: **TRAP**.
**AT** Antitrypsin.
*Biochemistry.*
**AT** Appropriate Technology.
**AT** Armoured Tractor; Armoured Train (G.B.).
**At** Astatine.
Astatine is a nonmetallic chemical element having the atomic number: 85; and an atomic weight of 211. The word astatine derives from the Greek term "unstable".
*Chemistry.*
**AT** Asti, Italy.
**A-T** Ataxia Telangelectasia.
Ataxia Telangelectasia is also known as: Louis-Bar Sydrome.
*Pathology.*
**at.** (abbr.) atomic.
*Chemistry; Ordnance.*
**AT** Atopic Dermatitis.
*Medicine.*
**AT** Auroral Time.
*Geophysics.*
**ATA** Actual Time of Arrival.
**ATA** Advanced Tactical Aircraft.
**ATA** Air-To-Air.
Also: **AA**.
*Ordnance.*
**ATA** Air Transport Auxiliary.
**ATA** Aminotriazole.
$C_2H_4N_4$. Aminotriazole is a crystalline solid having a melting point of 159°C. Aminotriazole is also known as: Amitrole.
*Organic Chemistry.*
**ATA** Arte, Turismo, Ambiente.
Italian acronym meaning: Art, Tourism, Environment.
**A.T.A.** Associate Technical Aide.
**ATA** Associazione Tecnica dell'Automobile.
*Italian Association.*

**A.T.A.A.V.** Association Thionvilloise d'Aide Aux Victimes (France).
French initialism of the: Thionville Association for Aid to Victims. Located at Thionville, France.
**ATAC** air tasking authority commander.
commandant de l'autorité d'attribution des missions aériennes.
**A.T.A.C.** Air Transport Advisory Council (G.B.).
**ATACMS** army tactical missile system.
système de missile tactique de l'armée de terre.
**ATAD model** Atmospheric Transport And Dispersion model.
**ATAF** Allied tactical air force [obsolete].
force aérienne tactique alliée (FATA) [obsolète].
**ATAI** Association de Transport Aérien International.
**ATAL** Alternate Transoceanic Abort Landing.
**AT&T** American Telephone and Telegraph.
**ATAOO** air tactical area of operations.
zone d'opérations aérienne tactiques.
**ATAR** Above Transmitted As Received.
**ATAR** Acquisition Tracking And Recognition.
*Aviation.*
**ATAR** Advanced Tactical Avionics Radar.
**ATAR** Air-To-Air visual Recognition.
*Aviation.*
**ATAV** Association Technique pour l'Amélioration de la Viticulture (France).
French acronym of the: Technical Association for Improvement of Viticulture.
**ATB** Across The Board.
**ATB** Advanced Technology and Biotechnology.
**ATB** 1. advanced technology bomber.
1. bombardier de technologie avancée.
2. air technical battalion.
2. bataillon technique des forces aériennes.
**ATBI** All Taxa Biodiversity Inventory.
The ATBI is a survey of the various types of organisms in a limited area.
**ATBM** Antitactical Ballistic Missile.
**ATBMD** active theatre ballistic missile defence.
défense active contre les missiles balistiques de théâtre.
**AT bus** Advanced Technology bus.
**ATC** Air Traffic Control.
*Navigation.*
**ATC** Alcoholic Treatment Center (U.S.A.).
**ATC** All-terrain Cycle.
The ATC is a cycle for off-road use.
*Mechanical Devices.*
**ATC**; **A.T.C.** Ambiti Territoriali di Caccia (Italy).
**ATC** Association of Translation Companies (G.B.).
**ATC** Astronomy Technology Center (G.B.).
The ATC opened in October 1998.
For further details see under: **RGO**.
**ATC** Automatic Train Control.
The automatic train control is a rail system where all operations are controlled automatically.
*Transportation Engineering.*
**ATCA** Advanced Tanker/Cargo Aircraft.
**ATCA** Allied Tactical Communications Agency [obsolete].
Bureau allié des télécommunications tactiques [obsolète].
**ATC array** Australia Telescope Compact array.
The ATC array in Narrabri, Australia, is provided with 6 antennas. Together they form a 54-m. diameter antenna.
*Astrophysics; Geophysics; Radio Astronomy; Space Science.*
**ATCC** air traffic control centre.
centre de contrôle de la circulation aérienne (CCCA).
**ATCC** American Type Culture Collection.
The ATCC is a global bioscience organization for intellectual and economic development.
*Bioresources; Mammalian Gene Collection; Molecular Biology.*
**ATCCIS** Army Tactical Command and Control Information System.
système tactique d'information de commandement et de contrôle de l'armée de terre.
**ATCF** Automobile and Touring Club of Finland.
**ATCP** Antarctic Treaty Consultative Parties.
**ATCRBS** Air-Traffic Control Radar Beacon System.
*Navigation.*
**ATCRU** air traffic control radar unit.
station radar de contrôle de la circulation aérienne.
**ATCS** Active Thermal Control System.
**ATCSCC** ATC Systems Command Center.
**ATCT** Air Traffic Control Tower.
*Navigation.*
**ATCV** antitank combat vehicle.
véhicule de combat antichar (VCAC).
**ATD** Actual Time of Departure.
**ATDC** Advanced Technology Development Center.
The ATDC has been established by the RBSI (Japan).
For further details see under: **RBSI**.
**ATDC** After Top Dead Center.
*Mechanical Engineering; Timing Marks.*
**ATDD** Atmospheric Turbulence and Diffusion Division.
**ATDs** Arrival Time Distributions.
**ATE** automatic test equipment.
matériel d'essai automatique.

**ATEA** Automatic Test Equipment Association.
**atea** The above acronym was coined accidentally using the Italian word "atea" which means: atheist (feminine).
**ATEC** Authorized Technical Education Center. Microsoft's.
**ATEE** Association Technique pour les Economies d'Energie (France).
French initialism of the: Technical Association for Energy Savings.
*French Association.*
**ATEFI** Associazione Tecnica delle società FInanziarie (Italy).
**ATEN** Association TEchnique pour la production et l'utilisation de l'Energie Nucléaire (France).
French acronym of the: Technical Association for the production and use of Nuclear Energy.
**ATENE** Association for Theological Education in the Near East.
**Atene** The above acronym was coined accidentally using the Italian word Atene which means: Athens.
**ATF** 1. allied tactical force.
1. force tactique alliée.
2. amphibious task force.
2. force opérationnelle amphibie.
3. avion de transport futur.
3. future cargo aircraft.
**ATF-2** Activating Transcription Factor-2.
*Biochemistry and Molecular Biology; Molecular Medicine.*
**ATFLIR** Advanced Targeting Forward Looking Infrared.
**ATG** 1. amphibious task group.
1. groupement opérationnel amphibie.
2. antitank gun.
2. canon antichar.
**ATG** Association Technique de l'industrie du Gaz (France).
French initialism of the: Gas Industry Technical Association.
The ATG is based in Paris.
**ATGM** antitank guided missile.
missile guidé antichar.
**ATGW** antitank guided weapon.
arme guidée antichar.
**ATH** The airport code for Athens, Greece.
**ATHS** automated target hand-off system.
système de répartition automatique des cibles.
**A.T.I.** Aero Trasporti Italiani (Italy).
Italian acronym of the: Italian Air Freight Line.
**ATI** Associate of the Textile Institute.
**ATI** Associazione Temporanea d'Impresa.
*Italian Association.*
**ATI** Associazione Termotecnica Italiana.
*Italian Association.*
**A.T.I.** Azienda Tabacchi Italiani (Italy).
Italian acronym of the: Italian State Tobacco Board.
**ATIC** Association Technique de l'Importation Charbonnière (France).
**ATIG; Atig** Associazione Tecnica Italiana del Gas.
Italian acronym of the Italian Technical Gas Association. ATIG is a non-profit Body. Its scope is the promotion and development of technologies in the gas industry as well as the investigation and divulgation of technological and operational know-how in relation to gas. The ATIG organizes: seminars, conventions and events such as International Sitgas (forum).
**ATIL program** Air Target Intelligence Liaison program.
**ATIP** Asian Technology Information Program.
**ATIS** Alliance of Telecommunications Industry Solutions.
**Atl.** (abbr.) Atlantic.
**ATL** Automated Tape Library.
*Computer Technology.*
**ATLAS** Abbreviated Test Language for All Systems.
*Data Processing.*
**ATLAS** Advanced Tactical Lightweight Air Superiority (Radar); Advanced Tactical Lightweight Avionics System.
**ATLAS** Advanced Technology Large Aircraft System.
**ATLAS** ATmospheric Laboratory for Applications and Science - NASA's.
**ATLAS** Automated Tape Label Assignment System.
**ATLAS** Autonomous Temperature Line Acquisition System.
**ATLB** Air Transport Licensing Board.
**ATL RC EAST** Atlantic Regional Command East.
Commandement régional Est de l'Atlantique.
**ATL RC WEST** Atlantic Regional Command West.
Commandement régional Ouest de l'Atlantique.
**ATLS** advanced trauma life support.
1a. matériel de survie de pointe en traumatologie.
1b. soins avancés de réanimation traumatologique.
**ATL SC** Atlantic Strategic Command [formerly called ACLANT].
Commandement stratégique de l'Atlantique [anciennement appelé ACLANT].
**ATM** 1. agent de transfert de messages.
1. message transfer agent (MTA).
2. air task(ing) message.
2. message de mission aérienne.

3. asynchronous transfer mode.
3. mode de transfer asynchrone.
**ATM** Air Target Materials.
**ATM** Air Turbine Motor.
**ATM** Antitactical Missile.
*Ordnance.*
**ATM** Ataxia Telangelectasia Mutated.
For further details see under: **AT**.
**atm.** (abbr.) atmosphere.
*Astronomy; Mechanics; Metorology.*
**atm.** (abbr.) atmospheric.
*Meteorology.*
**ATM** Automated Teller Machine.
The automated teller machine is an electronic machine used by bank customers to automatically carry out transactions.
*Banking; Electronics.*
**ATM** Azienda Trasporti Municipali (Italy).
**ATMES** Atmospheric Transport Model Evaluation Study.
**ATMOS** Atmospheric Trace MOlecule Spectroscopy.
*Experiments.*
**atm. press.** (abbr.) atmospheric pressure.
*Physics.*
**ATMS** Advanced Traffic Management System.
**ATMS** Assumption-based Truth Maintenance System.
*Artificial Intelligence.*
**atn.** attention.
Also: **attn**.
**ATN** Augmented Transition Network.
The augmented transition network is also known as: Augmented Finite State Transition Network.
*Artificial Intelligence.*
**ATNF** Australia Telescope National Facility (Australia).
**at.no.** (abbr.) atomic number.
*Nuclear Physics.*
**ATO** Abort To Orbit.
**ATO** 1. air task(ing) order.
1a. ordre d'attribution de mission aérienne.
1b. ordre de mission aérienne.
1c. ordre opérationnel air.
2. area of tactical operations.
2. zone d'opérations tactiques.
**ATO** At The Opening.
**ATO** Automatic Train Operation.
**ATOC** 1. air tactical operations centre.
1. centre d'opérations tactiques Air (COTA).
2. Allied tactical operations centre.
2. centre interallié d'opérations tactiques.
**ATOC project** Acoustic Thermometry of Ocean Climate project.
*Oceanography; Projects.*
**ATOFMS** Aerosol Time-Of-Flight Mass Spectrometer.
*Chemistry; Environmental Engineering.*
**ATOM** Arizona Trade-Off Model.
The ATOM is a project of the U.S. Department of Commerce and the State of Arizona to resolve conflicts between environmental and economic goals.
*U.S. Project.*
**ATOMS** Automated Technical Order Maintenance Sequence.
**ATP** Adenosine Triphosphate.
The adenosine triphosphate is a coenzyme consisting of adenosine diphosphate and another phosphate group.
*Biochemistry.*
**ATP** Advanced Technology Program.
The Advanced Technology Program is a program of the U.S. Department of Commerce.
**ATP** Advanced Turbo-Prop.
**ATP** Allied Tactical Publication.
publication interalliée sur les questions tactiques.
**ATP** Authority To Purchase.
**ATPase** Adenosinetriphosphatase.
*Enzymology.*
**ATR** Achilles Tendon Reflex.
Achilles Tendon Reflex is also known as: Achilles Jerk.
*Physiology.*
**ATR** Attenuated Total Reflectance.
Attenuated Total Reflectance is also known as: Frustrated Internal Reflectance; Internal Reflectance.
*Spectroscopy.*
**atr.** Attribute.
Also: **att.**; **attr.**
*Archaeology; Computer Programming; Statistics.*
**ATR** automatic target recognition.
reconnaissance automatique des objectifs.
**ATRA** All-*trans*-Retinoic Acid.
*Skin Cancer.*
**Atra** a-trans-retinoico.
(a-retinoid).
**ATREX** Astrophysics TRansient EXplorer.
*Astrophysics.*
**ATRI** Air Transportable Radio Installations.
**ATRI** Artists Technical Research Institute.
**atri** The above acronyms were coined accidentally using the Italian word "atri" which means: atria/atriums; halls; lobbies.

**ATRCC** Air Traffic Route Control Center (U.S.A.).
**ATR tube** Anti-Transmit-Receive tube.
**ATS** Absolute Temperature Scale.
The absolute temperature scale, or Absolute Scale, is a scale based on absolute zero temperature.
*Thermodynamics.*
**ATS** air traffic service.
service de la circulation aérienne.
**ATS** Acceptance Test Specification.
**Ats** Acceptance trials.
*Shipbuilding.*
**ATS** Acoustic Target Sensor.
**ATS** Acoustic Telemetry Subsystem.
**ATS** Acoustic Transmission System.
**ATS** Administrative Terminal System.
*Computers.*
**ATS** Alkali-Tin-Silicate.
*Chemistry; Environmental Protection; Geology; Materials Science; Nuclear Waste.*
**ATS** American Therapeutic Society (U.S.A.).
The American Society for Clinical Pharmacology and Therapeutics was formerly known as: American Therapeutic Society.
**ATS** American Thoracic Society (U.S.A.).
**A.T.S.** American Transport Service (U.S.A.).
**ATs** Anisotropy Telescopes.
**ATS** Antitetanus Serum.
*Medicine.*
**ATS** Anxiety Tension State.
*Psychology.*
**ATS** Applications Technology Satellite.
The applications technology satellite is a NASA satellite used to evaluate new technology and equipment.
*Space Technology.*
**ATS** Asian Test Symposium.
**ATS** Automated Telemetry System.
**ATS** Automated Tracking System.
A science which allows customers to obtain package status information by simply speaking into the telephone.
**ATS** Automatic Train Supervision.
**ATS** Automatic Transfer Service; Automatic Transfer System.
*Accounts; Banking.*
**ATS** Automatic Tuning System.
The automatic tuning system is a mechanical or electrical system which tunes automatically a radio receiver or transmitter to a given frequency.
*Control Systems.*
**ATSDR** Agency for Toxic Substances and Disease Registry.
**ATSR** Along-Track Scanning Radiometer.
**ATSs** Alternative Trading Systems.
**ATSTAT** air transport status report.
compte rendu de situation sur les transports aériens.
**Att.** (abbr.) Attaché.
**att.** (abbr.) attached.
**att.** (abbr.) attivo, attività.
Italian abbreviation meaning: assets.
*Business; Commerce; Finance.*
**Att.** (abbr.) Attorney.
Also: **Atty.**; **atty.**; **att.**
**att.** (abbr.) attribute.
Also: **atr.**; **attr.**
For further details see under: **atr.**
**ATT** Automatic Toll Ticketing.
Automatic toll ticketing is also known as: Automatic Message Accounting.
**attach.** (abbr.) attachment.
**attn.** (abbr.) attention.
Also: **atn.**
**attr.** (abbr.) attribute.
Also: **atr.**; **att.**; **attrib.**
For further details see under: **atr.**
**ATTU** Atlantic to the Urals.
de l'Atlantique à l'Oural.
**Atty.** (abbr.) Attorney.
Also: **Att.**; **att.**; **atty.**
**Atty.Gen.** Attorney General.
**ATUG** Australian Telecommunications Users Group (Australia).
**ATV** Advanced Television.
**ATV** All-Terrain Vehicle.
An all-terrain vehicle is a vehicle, such as a jeep for off-road use.
**ATV** Automatic Transfer Vehicle.
*Astronomy; Particle Physics; Space Science.*
**ATW** Accelerator Transmutation of Waste.
*Nuclear Engineering; Radioactive Waste Management; Technology.*
**ATWC** Alaska Tsunami Warning Center (U.S.A.).
**ATWCS** Advanced Tomahawk Weapons Control System (U.S. Navy).
**at.wt.** atomic weight.
**AT XPL** (abbr.) Atomic Explosion.
*Atomic Physics.*
**ATWCS** Advanced Tomahawk Weapons Control System (U.S. Navy).
**ATZ** Anilinothiazolinone.
*Biochemistry; Pathology.*
**AU** Absorbance Units.
**AU** Accounting Unit.
**AU** Airborne Unit.
**AU** Air University.

**AU** Alignment Unit.
**AU** Allegheny University (of the Health Sciences) (U.S.A.).
Also: **AUHS**.
**AU** American University.
**au** angstrom unit.
For further details see under: **An** (Ångstrom).
**AU**; **au** Antitoxin Unit.
*Immunology.*
**AU** Associated Universities.
**AU** Astronomical Unit.
The astronomical unit is the mean distance from earth to the sun: about 149,600,000 kilometers.
*Astronomy.*
**AU** Austria.
**Au** The chemical symbol for Gold.
*Chemistry* - A metallic element having the atomic number 79, an atomic weight of 196.967 and a melting point of 1063°C.
*Metallurgy* - precious metal used for jewelry and dentistry.
**A.U.A.** American Unitarian Association (U.S.A.).
**AUBER** Association for University Business and Economic Research.
**AUBG** American University in Bulgaria.
**AUC**; **A.U.C.** Allievi Ufficiali di Complemento (Italy).
**AUCI** Associazione Universitaria per la Cooperazione Internazionale.
Italian acronym of the: University Association for Intemational Cooperation.
**$AuCl_3$** Gold Chloride.
Gold Chloride, also known as: Gold Trichloride; Auric Chloride, is used mainly in medicine, ceramics, and gold plating.
*Inorganic Chemistry.*
**aud.** (abbr.) audible.
*Acoustics.*
**aud.** (abbr.) audit; auditor.
**AUDACIOUS** AUtomatic Direct ACcess to Information with the On-line UDC (Universal Decimal Classification) System.
**AUDIT** Aircraft Unitized Diagnostic Inspection and Test.
**AUDIT** Army Uniform Data Inquiry Technique (U.S.A.).
**AUDIT** AUDitory Input Task.
*Data Processing.*
**AUDIT** Automatic Unattended Detection Inspection Transmitter.
**Audio-CASI technology** Audio Computer-Assisted Self-Interviewing technology.
*Computer-Driven Technologies.*
For further details see under: **NSAM** and **SAQs**.
**AUF** augmentation force.
force d'appoint.
**aug** (abbr.) augmentation.
*Astronomy; Navigation.*
**aug.** (abbr.) augmentative; augmented.
**Aug.** (abbr.) August.
**AUHS** The Allegheny University of the Health Sciences (U.S.A.).
Also: **AU**.
**AUI** Associated Universities Inc. (U.S.A.).
**AUI** Attachment Unit Interface.
*Computers.*
**auj.** (abbr.) aujourd'hui.
French abbreviation meaning: today / to-day; nowadays; at present; at the present time.
**AUM** air-to-underwater missile.
missile air-sous-surface.
**$AuNa_3O_6S_4$** Gold Sodium Thiosulfate.
Gold Sodium Thiosulfate also known as: Sodium Aurothiosulfate is used mainly to treat lupus erythematosus.
*Pharmacology.*
**AUNT** Automatic UNiversal Translator.
**$Au_2O_3$** Gold Oxide.
Gold Oxide, also known as: Auric Oxide; Gold Trioxide, is used in gold plating.
*Inorganic Chemistry.*
**$Au(OH)_3$** Gold Hydroxide.
Gold Hydroxide, also known as: Auric Hydroxide, is used in gold plating.
*Inorganic Chemistry.*
**AUPELF** Association des Universités Partiellement ou Entièrement de Langue Française (Canada).
Founded in 1961; aims: documentation, co-ordination, co-operation, exchange.
**Aur** (abbr.) Auriga.
A northern constellation that lies between Perseus and Gemini.
*Astronomy.*
**AURA** Association of Universities for Research in Astronomy (U.S.A.).
Of the U.S. National Science Foundation. AURA operates the U.S. National Optical Astronomical Observatories.
*U.S. Association.*
**AURE** Association pour l'Utilisation Rationnelle de l'Energie (France).
French acronym of the: Association for Rational Use of Energy.
*French Association.*
**AURORA** AUtomated Restoration of ORiginal film and video Archives.

*European Community Project.*
**AUS** The airport code for Austin, Texas, U.S.A.
**AUS** Australia's international vehicle registration letters.
**Aus.** (abbr.) Austria; Austrian.
**Aus CERT** Australian Computer Emergency Response Team (Australia).
*Web Site.*
**AUSM** Adaptive User Selection Mechanism (U.S.A.).
Of the California Institute of Technology.
**Austral.** (abbr.) Australia.
**Austral.** Australian.
*Languages.*
**AUT** Association of University Teachers.
**AuTe$_2$** Calaverite.
Calaverite is a gold ore mineral.
*Mineralogy.*
**auth.** (abbr.) authentic.
**auth.** (abbr.) author; authority.
**auth.** (abbr.) authorization; authorized.
**AUTM** Association of University Technology Managers Inc. (U.S.A.).
*U.S. Association.*
**AUTO** (abbr.) Automatic.
**AUTO** (abbr.) Automobile.
**AUTOBUS** Automated Budget System.
**autobus** The above acronyrn was coined accidentally using the Italian word "autobus" which means: bus.
**AUTOMAP** AUTOmatic MAchining Program.
**automtn.** (abbr.) automation.
The term automation refers to the automatic or remote-controlled operation of machines in order to replace human labor.
*Engineering.*
**AUTO-PROMT** AUTOmatic PROgramming of Machine Tools.
**AUTOPROPS** AUTOmatic PROgramming for Positioning Systems.
**AUTOPSY** AUTomatic OPerating SYstem.
**AUTOSPOT** AUTOmatic System for POsitioning Tools.
**AUVs** Autonomous Underwater Vehicles.
*Automated Docking; Autonomous Oceanography; Autonomous Underwater Vehicles; Oceanographic Experiments.*
**AUW** All-Up-Weight.
**aux.** (abbr.) auxiliary.
**AuxREs** Auxin Response Elements.
*Biochemistry.*
**aV** abvolt.
The abvolt is the centimeter-gram-second electromagnetic unit of electromotive force.
*Electricity.*
**AV** Acrosomal Vesicle.
**AV** Actual Value.
*Business; Finance.*
**AV** Anchoring Villus (placental).
*Anatomy; Biochemistry; Reproductive Medicine; Stomatology.*
**AV** Aortic Valve.
The aortic valve regulates blood flow from the left ventricle into the aorta.
*Anatomy.*
**AV** Armored Vehicle.
*Ordnance.*
**AV** Arteriovenous.
**AV** Atrioventricular.
*Anatomy.*
**AV** Authorized Version.
**av.** (abbr.) available.
**AV** Avellino, Italy.
**av.** (abbr.) avenue.
Also: **Ave.**
**av** (abbr.) average.
Also: **ave.**; **avg.**
**AV** The airline code for Avianca.
**a.v.**; **a/v** a vista.
Italian initialism meaning: on demand; at sight.
*Banking; Commerce; Finance.*
**av.** avoirdupois.
Also: **AVDP**; **AVOIR**.
**av.**; **audvis.** (abbr.) audiovisual.
The term audiovisual refers to an education and training method that uses visual images and audible signals.
*Telecommunications.*
**AVA** Academy of Veterinary Allergy.
**AVA** Activity Vector Analysis.
*Psychology.*
**AVA** Allocation de Vieillesse Agricole (France).
**AVA** American Vecturist Association; American Ventilation Association; American Video Association; American Vocational Association (U.S.A.).
**AVA** Anthrax Vaccine Absorbed.
*Biodefense.*
**AVA** Arteriovenous Anastomosis.
*Anatomy.*
**AVA** Asbestos Victims of America.
**AVA** Associate of the Valuers Association.
**AVA** Automated Vision Association.
**AVAG** Associazione Volontari Assistenza malati Gravi.

*Italian Association.*

**AVAME** Asociaciòn de Mujeres Empresarias de Valladolid (Spain).
*Spanish Associations.*

**AVANT** Association of Voluntary Agencies on Narcotics Treatment.

**avant** The above acronym was coined accidentally using the French word "avant" which means: before; front; forward.

**AVAPO** Associazione Volontari Assistenza Pazienti Oncologici.
*Italian Association.*

**AVC** Automatic Volume Control.
*Electronics.*

**AVC** Average Variable Cost.

**aV/cm** abvolt per centimeter.

**AVCO** (abbr.) AVerage COst.

**AVD** Alternate Voice / Data.

**AVDP** Aided Visual Development Program.

**AVDP** Alaska Village Demonstration Project.
Of the U.S. Environmental Protection Agency.

**AVDP** avoirdupois.
Also: **av.**; **AVOIR**.

**AVE** Aerospace Vehicle Electronics.

**AVe** Anterior Vermis.
*Clinical Psychology; Medicine; Neuroscience of Autism; Radiology.*

**Ave.** (abbr.) Avenue.
Also: **av.**

**ave** (abbr.) average.
Also: **av.**; **avg.**
*Mathematics.*

**AVEC** Automatic Vibration Exciter Control.

**AVES** Associazione Volontariato Extracomunitario Sardegna.
*Italian Association.*

**AVF** Azimuthally Varying Field.

**AVG** Aminoethoxynivyl Glycine.
AVG is an inhibitor of ethylene biosynthesis.
*Crop Biotechnology; Microbiology; Plant Pathology; Rhizobial Infections.*

**avg.** (abbr.) average.
Also: **av.**; **ave.**
*Mathematics.*

**AVGAS** aviation gasoline.
essence (aviation).

**AVGRS** Avian Genetic Resources System.
*Coordination and Living Stocks Conservation.*

**AVHRR** Advanced Very-High Resolution Radiometer.
*Atmospheric Research; Atmospheric Sciences; Land-Atmosphere Interactions; Meteorology.*

**AVI** Aéroasthénie (de l'Aviateur).
French acronym meaning: Aeroasthenia.
*Medicine.*

**AVI** Airborne Vehicle Identification.

**AVI** Air Velocity Index.

**AVI** American Veterans of Israel.

**AVI** Association Universelle d'Aviculture Scientifique.
French acronym of the: World's Poultry Science Association.

**avi** The above acronyms were coined accidentally using the Italian word "avi" which means: grandfathers; ancestors.

**AVICA** Advanced Video endoscopy Image Communication and Analysis.
*Medicine.*

**AVID** Advanced Visual Information Display.

**AVID** Airborne Vehicle IDentification.

**Avigolfe** Association des victimes militaires et civiles de la guerre du Golfe.

**AVIRIS** Airborne Visible and Infrared Imaging Spectrometer.

**AVIS** Active Vibration Isolation System.

**A.V.I.S.** Associazione Volontari Italiani del Sangue.
Italian acronym of the: Association of Voluntary Italian Blood-Donors.

**AVIS** Audiovisual Inforrnation System.

**avis** The above acronyms were coined accidentally using the French word "avis" which means: notice; opinion; advice; judgement; counsel.

**AVLB** armoured vehicle-launched bridge.
véhicule blindé poseur de ponts (VBPP).

**AVLIS system** Atomic Vapor Laser Isotope Separation system.
*Commercial Technologies; Uranium Enrichment.*

**AVM** Arteriovenous Malformation.

**AVMA**; **A.V.M.A.** American Veterinary Medical Association.

**AVMRL** armoured vehicle-mounted rocket launcher.
véhicules blindé lance-roquettes (VBLR).

**AVMs** Arteriovenous Malformations.
*Radiation Oncology; Tumor Biology.*

**avn.** (abbr.) aviation.
Also: **av**.

**AVNIR** Advanced Visible and Near-Infrared Radiometer.
An instrument aboard ADEOS.
For further details see under: **ADEOS**.

**AVO** Alaska Volcano Observatory.
*Volcanology.*

**AVO** Avoid Verbal Orders.

**AVOID** Airfield Vehicle Obstacle Indication Device.

**AVOIDS** AVionic Observation of Intruder Danger Systems.
**AVOIR** Avoirdupois.
Also: **AVDP**; **av.**
**AVP** Arginine Vasopressin.
Arginine Vasopressin is also known as: Antidiuretic Hormone.
*Endocrinology.*
**AVP** The airport code for Wilkers-Barre/Scranton, Pennsylvania, U.S.A.
**AVR** Acute Vascular Rejection.
*Pathology; Immunogenetics; Surgery; Transplantation.*
**AVR** Automatic Voltage Regulator.
**AVR** Automatic Volume Recognition.
**avr.** (abbr.) avril.
French abbreviation meaning: April.
**AVRC** AIDS Vaccine Research Committee (U.S.A.).
AVRC is a NIH advisory group.
*AIDS Vaccine Research.*
For further details see under: **NIH**.
**AVRDC** Asian Vegetable Research and Development Center (Taiwan).
**AVS** Application Visualization System.
*Programs.*
**AVS** avionics system.
système d'avionique.
**AVSI** Associazione Volontari per il Servizio Internazionale.
Italian initialism of the: Association of Volunteers for International Service.
**AVT** All Volatile Treatment.
Westinghouse Commercial.
*Steam Generators.*
**AVT** Arginine Vasotocin.
AVT is a hormone associated with sexual behavior.
*Behavioral Endocrinology; Endocrinology.*
**AVTAG** aviation fuel (gasoline/kerosene).
carburant aviation (essence/kérosène).
**AVTP** Allied Vehicle Testing Publication.
publication interalliée sur les essais de véhicules.
**AV.UR.NAV.** (abbr.) AVis URgent aux NAVigateurs.
**avv.** (abbr.) avvocato.
Italian abbreviation meaning: lawyer; counsel (*Law*); attorney-at-law (U.S.A.); solicitor; barrister (Britain).
**AW** 1. acoustic warfare.
1. lutte acoustique.
2. air warfare.
2a. guerre aérienne.
2b. lutte aérienne [dans le domaine naval].
3. air warning.
3. alerte aérienne.
4. all-weather.
4. tout temps.
5. amphibious warfare.
5. lutte amphibie.
**AW** Active Window.
*Computer Technology.*
**a.w.** actual weight.
**AW** Aircraft Warning.
**a/w** all-weather.
*Aeronautics; Transport.*
**AW** Article of War.
**AW** Automatic Weapon.
The automatic weapon is also known as: Automatic firearm; Automatic gun.
*Ordnance.*
**AW** Automatic Writing.
The automatic writing in psychology refers to writing while in the unconscious state.
*Psychology.*
**AWA** Animal Welfare Act (U.S.A.).
**AWACS** airborne warning and control system.
système aéroporté de détection et de contrôle.
**AWAKE** Association of Women Entrepreneurs Of Karnataka (India).
**AWAR** American Women's Association of Rome (Italy).
**AWARDS** Automated Weather Acquisition and Retrieval Data System.
**AWARE** Academic Women Allied for Rights and Equality.
**AWARE** Advanced Weapon/Aircraft Requirements Evaluation.
**AWARE** Airborne Warning and Recording Equipment.
**AWARE** All Women's Archaeological Research Expedition.
**AWB** Airway-Bill.
**AWB** Asian Wetlands Bureau (Malaysia).
**AWC** Association for Women in Computing.
**AWCIES** ACCS-wide common information exchange system.
normes communes pour l'échange d'informations à l'échelle de l'ACCS.
**AWD** awaiting departure.
en attente de départ.
**AWE** Accepted Weight/Estimate.
*Shipping.*
**AWE** Advise When Established.
*Aviation.*
**AWE** Association for World Education (U.S.A.).
The AWE was formerly known as: AWCU.
**AWE** Average Weekly Earnings.

**AWEA** American Wind Energy Association.
*U.S. Association.*
**AWERS** Association of Women Entrepreneurs of the Republic of Sakha.
Russian Federation.
**AWF** African Wildlife Foundation.
*Endangered Species.*
**AWG** American Wire Gauge.
The American Wire Gauge is also known as: Brown and Sharp Gage (B and S gage).
*Metallurgy.*
**AWGs** Arrayed Waveguide Gratings.
**AWHQ** alternate war headquarters.
quartier général de guerre de rechange (QGGR).
**AWIPS** Advanced Weather Interactive Processing System.
**AWIPS** Automated Weather Information Processing System.
**AWL** Absent With Leave.
**AWM** Advantage West Midlands (G.B.).
A British regional development agency.
*Regional foresight.*
For further details see under: **CLED** and **CUE**.
**AWNIS** Allied Worldwide Navigational Information System (or Service).
système (ou service) interallié mondial d'informations nautiques.
**AWOL** Absent Without Leave.
**AWP** Allied Weather Publication.
publication météorologique interalliée.
**AWR** Association for the study of the World problem of Refugees.
**AWRAP Organisation** Australian Wool Research and Promotion Organisation.
**AWS** Aircraft Weaponization Systems.
**AWS** American Welding Society (U.S.A.).
**AWS** Amphibious Watercraft Systems.
**AWS** Solidarity Electoral Action (Poland).
Trade union-led alliance of right-wing parties.
**AWSM** acoustic warfare support measure.
mesure de soutien de lutte acoustique.
**AWT-27** Advanced Wind Turbine-27.
Advanced Wind Turbine Inc.'s new 275-kilowatt machine uses blades designed with advanced airfoils to increase energy production, an innovative teetered rotor to reduce stress from wind gusts, and a strong but lightweight tube tower.
*Wind Turbines.*
**AWWA** American Water Works Association (U.S.A.).
**AWX** all-weather fighter.
chasseur tout temps.
**awy.** (abbr.) airway.
*Anatomy; Building Engineering; Medicine; Mining Engineering; Navigation.*
**AX** (abbr.) axillary.
*Anatomy* - The term axillary refers to the armpit or to some location near it.
*Botany* - Axillary in botany means growing on the axis of a leaf or a branch.
**ax.** (abbr.) axiom.
*Artificial Intelligence; Mathematics.*
**AX** axion or postulate.
*Mathematics.*
**AX** (abbr.) axis.
*Anatomy; Botany; Geology; Mathematics; Mechanics; Ordnance.*
**AXAF** Advanced X-Ray Astrophysics Facility.
A many-layered mirror telescope which flew on the Shuttle in 1999.
*Astrophysics.*
**AXBT** Airborne Expendable Bathythermograph.
The AXBT is a device used to record temperature at different depths.
*Oceanography.*
**AXCP** Airborne Expendable Current Profiler.
**ax.fl.** (abbr.) axial flow.
*Fluid Mechanics.*
**AXP** Allied Exercise Publication.
publication interalliée sur les exercices.
**AY** Annual Yield.
**AYC** American Youth Congress (U.S.A.).
**AYD** American Youth for Democracy (U.S.A.).
**AYE** Alcohol Education for Youth (U.S.A.).
**AYH** American Youth Hostels (U.S.A.).
**AYSA** American Yarn Spinners Association.
**AZ** Academy of Zoology.
**AZ** Active Zone.
**AZ** The airline code for Alitalia.
**AZ** (abbr.) Arizona (U.S.A.).
**az.** (abbr.) azimuth.
*Astronomy; Cartography; Navigation.*
**az.** (abbr.) azione.
Italian abbreviation meaning: share.
*Business; Commerce; Finance.*
**az.** (abbr.) azionista.
Italian abbreviation meaning: shareholder.
*Business; Commerce; Finance.*
**AZ** Azote.
French symbol meaning: Nitrogen.
**az.** (abbr.) azure.
**AZS** Automatic Zero Setting.
**AZT** Azidothymidine.
*Virology.*
**A-Z test** Aschheim-Zondek test.
In the Aschheim-Zondek test the urine of women

is injected into immature female mice and the reaction is used to ascertain pregnancy in women. *Pathology.*

# B

**B** Bacillus.
*Bacteriology.*
**b** bacillus.
*Microbiology.*
**b** bag.
bag is also known as: multiset.
*Computer Science.*
**B** Baht.
Also: **Bht** (Thailand).
*Currencies.*
**b** bale.
*Agriculture; Industrial Engineering.*
**b** ball.
*Geology; Mathematics; Mechanical Engineering; Oceanography; Ordnance.*
**b** barn.
barn is a unit of measure for nuclear reaction cross sections.
*Agriculture; Nuclear Physics.*
**B** Baron.
Also: **BR.**
**b** (abbr.) base.
*Architecture; Biology; Building Engineering; Chemical Engineering; Chemistry; Electronics; Engineering; Graphic Arts; Mathematics; Military Science; Robotics.*
**b** bass.
*Acoustics.*
**b** bat.
*Building Engineering; Materials Science; Vertebrate Zoology.*
**b** (abbr.) batch.
*Computer Programming; Engineering.*
**B** Battery.
Also: **bty**; **btry**.
*Chemical Engineering; Electricity; Medicine; Military Science; Ordnance.*
**b** (abbr.) bel.
bel is equal to ten decibels.
*Physics.*
**B** Belgium.
Also: **BE**.
**B** Better.
**B** Bible.
**b** bid.
*Business; Finance.*
**b** billion.
*Mathematics.*
**b** (abbr.) binary.
*Computer Programming; Science.*
**b** (abbr.) bit.
*Computer Programming; Mathematics; Mechanical Devices.*
**B** Bolivar.
Also: **Bol.**; **bol** (Venezuela).
*Currencies.*
**b** bond.
Also: **bd**.
*Building Engineering; Business; Chemistry; Civil Engineering; Electricity; Finance; Medicine; Metallurgy.*
**b** book.
**b** bore.
*Design Engineering; Mechanical Engineering; Mining Engineering; Oceanography; Ordnance.*
**b** born.
**B** the chemical symbol for Boron.
The word boron is a combination of the words borax and carbon.
*Chemistry; Symbols.*
**b** brightness.
*Astrophysics; Optics.*
**b** brick.
*Materials.*
**B** British.
**b** bulk.
*Graphic Arts.*
**BA**; **B.A.** Bachelor of Arts.
**BA** Bahrain.
**BA** Banca Antoniana (di Padova e Trieste).
*Italian Bank.*
**BA** Bank Acceptance.
**BA** Bari, Italy.
**Ba** The chemical symbol for Barium.
Barium is a chemical element having the atomic number 56, an atomic weight of 137.34, and a melting point of about 725°C. The word barium derives from the Greek term "heavy".
*Chemistry; Symbols.*
**BA** Base Address.
*Computer Programming.*
**B.A.** Belle Arti.
Italian acronym meaning: Fine Arts.
**BA** Bénéfices Agricoles (France).
**B/A** Billed At.
*Business -Finance.*
**BA** Brewster Angle.
*Optics.*
**Ba**; **B.A.** British Academy.
**BA** The airline code for British Airways.
**BA** British Association (G.B.).
**BA** Brodmann's Areas.

Named after the German neurologist Korbinian **Brodmann**.
*Brain and Cognition; Physiology; Spatial Working Memory.*
**BA** Bronchial Asthma.
*Medicine.*
**BA** Bronchoalveolar.
*Anatomy.*
**BA** Budget Authority (U.S.A.).
**BA** Bundesanstalt für Arbeit (Germany).
**BA** Bureau of Accounts.
**BA** Butyl Acrylate.
**B2A** Business to Administration.
*e-commerce.*
**BAA; B.A.A.** Bachelor of Applied Arts.
**BAA** Barium Arachidate.
**BAA** British Airports Authority (G.B.).
**BAA; B.A.A.** British Astronomical Association.
**BAAE** Bachelor of Aeronautical and Astronautical Engineering.
**BAB** Bureau pour l'Automation des Bibliothèques. French acronym meaning: Office for the Automation of Libraries.
**BAB activity** Blood group Antigen-Binding activity.
*Cancer Epidemiology; Clinical Microbiology; Molecular Microbiology.*
**BABLH** British Association for Better Land Husbandry (Kenya).
**BABS** Beam Approach Beacon System.
*Aviation.*
**BABS** Book Acquisition and Bibliographic Service. National Book Center (Canada).
**BAC** Baccalauréat (France).
**BAC** Bacterial Artificial Chromosome.
The vector BAC was developed at the California Institute of Technology with U.S. Department of Energy funding.
*Clone-making; Genome Research.*
**BAC** Bacterial Antigen Complex.
*Immunochemistry.*
**BAC** Banca Agricola Commerciale della RSM (Italy).
For further details see under: **RSM**.
**BAC** Barometric Altitude Control.
**BA/C** Beverage Analyzer/Controller.
**BAC** bilateral agreement conference.
conférence sur les accords bilatéraux.
**BAC** British Accreditation Council.
**BAC** Bromoacetylcholine.
**BACAT** barge aboard catamaran.
porte-barge catamaran.
**BAcc.; B.Acc.** Bachelor of Accountancy.
**BACC** British America's Cup Challenge.
**BACCHUS** Boost Alcohol Consciousness Concerning the Health of University Students (U.S.A.).
**BACCHUS** British Aircraft Corporation Commercial Habitat Under the Sea.
**BAC crust** Bulk Archean Continental crust.
*Earth Sciences.*
**BACD** British Association of Conference Destinations.
**BACH** (abbr.) Bachelor.
**BACI** Brazilian-American Cultural Institute.
**$Ba(CN)_2$** Barium Cyanide.
Barium Cyanide is used mainly in metallurgy.
*Organic Chemistry.*
**$BaCO_3$** Barium Carbonate.
Barium Carbonate is used mainly in TV picture tubes, optical glass, and ceramics.
*Inorganic Chemistry.*
**$BaCrO_4$** Barium Chromate.
Barium Chromate is used mainly as a pigment.
*Inorganic Chemistry.*
**BACs** Bacterial Artificial Chromosomes.
For further details see under: **BAC**.
**BACs** Bacterial Artificial Clones.
*Genomic Biology; Medicine; Neurology; Psychiatry.*
**BACS** Bankers' Automated Clearing Services.
**bact.** (abbr.) bacterial; bacteriological.
*Bacteriology.*
**bact.** (abbr.) bacteriology.
The term bacteriology refers to the study of bacteria.
*Microbiology.*
**bact.** (abbr.) bacterium.
The singular of bacteria. The word bacterium derives from the Greek term "little rod".
*Microbiology.*
**BACT** Best Available Control Technology (U.S.A.).
**BACV** Budget At Completion Variance.
**BAD** Base Ammunition Depot.
*Military.*
**BAD** Biological Aerosol Detection.
**BADA** Base Air Depot Area.
**BADA** British Antique Dealers' Association.
**bada** The above acronyms were coined accidentally using the Italian word "bada" which means: be careful; take care; mind.
**BADC** British Atmospheric Data Centre (G.B.).
**BADGE** Basic Air Defense Ground Environment.
**BAD tax** Bank Account Debits tax.
**BAE; B.A.E.** Bachelor of Aeronautical Engineering.
**BAE; B.A.E.** Bachelor of Agricultural Engineering.

**BAE**; **B.A.E.** Bachelor of Architectural Engineering.
**BAE** Barium Enema.
Also: **BE**.
For X-ray examination of the intestines.
*Radiology.*
**BAE** battlefield area evaluation.
évaluation de la zone du champ de bataille.
**BAe** British Aerospace (G.B.).
**BAE** Bureau of Agricultural Economics.
**BAE** Bureau of American Ethnology (U.S.A.).
**BAE cells** Bovine Aortic Endothelial cells.
**BAF** Bunker Adjustment Factor.
*Business; Economics; Finance.*
**$BaF_2$** Barium Fluoride.
Barium Fluoride is used mainly in spectroscopy.
*Inorganic Chemistry.*
**BAFI** BAFI is a collection of Statistical Data for the Database on Financial Firms.
**BAFLs** Bands Across all Four Lanes.
**BAG** Beta Absorption Gauge.
**BAGC** Business Alliance on Government Competition.
**BAGS** Bachelor of Arts in General Studies.
**BAHC** Biospheric Aspects of the Hydrological Cycle.
**BAI** ex-Banca d'America e d'Italia.
Deutsche Bank (since 1995).
**BAI** Bank Administration Institute.
**BAI** battlefield air interdiction.
interdiction aérienne du champ de bataille (IACB).
**BAI** Bureau of Animal Industry.
**BAINS** Basic Advanced Integrated Navigation System.
**Ba.Is.** (abbr.) Bahama Islands.
**BAJour**; **B.A. Jour.** Bachelor of Arts in Journalism.
**BAK** backup.
*Computer Technology.*
**bal** (abbr.) balance.
*Acoustics; Aviation; Chemistry; Computer Programming; Electricity; Engineering; Horology; Hydrology; Mining Engineering.*
**BAL** Basic Assembler Language.
*Data Communications.*
**BAL** Bioartificial Liver.
*Artificial Organs; Biosciences; Hepatology; Liver Transplantation; Medicine.*
**BAL** Blood Alcohol Level.
*Medicine.*
**BAL** British Anti-Lewisite / antilewisite.
*Medicine.*
**BAL** Bronchoalveolar Lavage.
*Medicine.*
**BALA** Bulletin, Association Lyonnaise de recherches Archeologiques.
*Publication.*
**BALAD** Bleachable Absorber Laser Amplifier and Detector.
**balad** The above acronym was coined accidentally using the Arabic word "balad" which means: country.
**BALANCE** Basic And Logically Applied Norms - Civil Engineering.
**balce.** (abbr.) balance.
For further details see under: **bal**.
**BALL** (abbr.) ballast.
*Civil Engineering; Electricity; Naval Architecture.*
**BALL** (abbr.) Ballistic.
*Mechanics.*
**BALLOTS** Bibliographic Automation of a Large Library Operations using a Time-Sharing System.
**BALM** Block And List Manipulator.
**balm** The above acronym was coined using the English word "balm" (*Botany; Geology*).
**BALO** Bulletin des Annonces Légales Obligatoires (France).
**BALPA** (abbr.) BALance of PAyments.
**BALTAP** Allied Forces, Baltic Approaches [obsolete - replaced by JCNORTH].
Forces alliées des approches de la Baltique [obsolète - remplacé par JCNORTH].
**BAM**; **B.A.M.** Bachelor of Applied Mathematics.
**BAM**; **B.A.M.** Bachelor of Arts in Music.
**BAM** Banca Agricola Milanese (Italy).
*Italian Bank.*
**BAM** Basic Access Method.
**BAM** British Academy of Management (G.B.).
**BAM** Brooklyn Academy of Music (U.S.A.).
**BAM** Bundesanstalt für Materialforschung und Prüfung (Germany).
**BAMBI** BAllistic Missile Bombardment Interceptor.
BAMBI is also known as: Ballistic Missile Boost Interceptor.
*Military.*
**$BaMnO_4$** Barium Manganate.
Barium Manganate is used as a paint pigment.
*Inorganic Chemistry.*
**$BaMoO_4$** Barium Molybdate.
Barium Molybdate is used mainly in optical equipment.
*Inorganic Chemistry.*
**BAN** Base Activation Notice.
**$Ba(N_3)_2$** Barium Azide.
Barium Azide is used in explosives.
*Inorganic Chemistry.*

**BANA** Benzoylargininenaphthylamide.
**BANCOREX** Romanian Bank for Foreign Trade.
**BAND** Book Action for Nuclear Disarmament (G.B.).
**B&F** Bell and Flange.
**B&PA** Business & Public Affairs (Murray State University, U.S.A.).
*Publication.*
**BANJO/SEDA experiments** Broadband Andean JOint/Seismic Examination of the Deep Altipiano experiments.
*Geophysics; Geosciences; Terrestrial Magnetism.*
**BANKITALIA** Banca d'Italia.
Also: **B.I**.
*Bank of Italy.*
**$Ba(NO_3)_2$** Barium Nitrate.
Barium Nitrate is used mainly in explosives and fireworks.
*Inorganic Chemistry.*
**banq.** (abbr.) banque.
French abbreviation meaning: bank.
Also: **bque**.
**BANR** Board on Agriculture and Natural Resources (U.S.A.).
**BANS** Back, Arm, Neck, Scalp.
*Medicine.*
**BANs** Bond Anticipation Notes (U.S.A.).
**BANW** Business Alert to Nuclear War.
**BaO** Barium Oxide.
BaO is used mainly as a dehydrating agent.
*Inorganic Chemistry.*
**BAO** Boulder Atmospheric Observatory (U.S.A.).
**$BaO_2$** Barium Peroxide.
Barium Peroxide is used mainly in bleaching.
*Inorganic Chemistry.*
**$Ba(OH)_2$** Barium Hydroxide.
Barium Hydroxide is used mainly in sugar refining and water softening.
*Inorganic Chemistry.*
**BAP** β-Amyloid Protein.
*Alzheimer's Research; Medicine; Neuromolecular Biology; Neuropathology; Neuropsychology of Aging.*
**BAP** Basic Assembly Program.
**BAP** Benzyl-p-AminoPhenol.
**BaP** Benzo [*a*] pyrene.
BaP is highly carcinogenic. It is found in cigarette smoke, and in coal tar. BaP is also known as: 3,4-Benzpyrene.
*Organic Chemistry.*
**BAP**; **b.à.p.** Billet à Payer.
French acronym meaning: Bill Payable.
*Business; Finance.*
**BAP** Biotechnology Action Program.
**BAPMoN** Background Air Pollution Monitoring Network - U.N.
**BAPR** Banca Agricola Popolare di Ragusa (Italy). Formerly (1889) established as Banca Popolare Cooperativa di Ragusa.
**BAr.**; **B.Ar.** Bachelor of Architecture.
**BAR** Bacille Acido-Resistant.
French acronym meaning: Acid-Fast Bacillus.
**bar.** (abbr.) barometer.
*Engineering.*
**Bar.** (abbr.) Barone.
Italian abbreviation meaning: Baron.
**bar.**; **brl.** (abbr.) barrel.
*Horology; Mathematics; Mechanical Devices; Metrology.*
*Naval Architecture* - In naval architecture barrel is also known as: Barrel of capstan; Drum.
*Optics; Ordnance.*
**bar.**; **barr.** (abbr.) barrister.
**BAR** Biblical Archeological Review.
**BAR**; **b-a-r** Billet à Recevoir.
French acronym meaning: Bill Receivable.
*Business; Finance.*
**BAR** Browning Automatic Rifle.
*Ordnance.*
**BAR** Budget Adjustment Request.
**barb.** (abbr.) barbiturate.
Barbiturate is a sedative-hypnotic agent.
*Pharmacology.*
**BARB** Bulletin, Academie Royale de Belgique (Belgium).
*Publication.*
**BARC** Bhabha Atomic Research Centre (Mumbai, India).
BARC is India's main nuclear weapons laboratory.
**BARCAP** barrier combat air patrol.
barrage de patrouilles aériennes de combat.
**BARD network** Bay Area Regional Deformation network.
*Earth Engine; Geology; Planetary Science.*
**BARE** Bile Acid Response Element.
*Medicine; Nuclear Receptors; Pharmacology.*
**barg.** (abbr.) bargain.
**BARN** Bombing And Reconnaissance Navigation.
**BAROPS** barrier operations.
opérations de barrage.
**BARRITT diode** BARRier Injection Transit-Time diode.
*Electronics.*
**BARS** Backup Attitude Reference System.
**BARS** Ballistic Analysis Research System.
**BARS** Baseline Accounting and Reporting System.

**BARS** Behaviorally Anchored Rating Scale.
**BARS** Budget Analysis Reporting System.
**BARTOC** Bus Advanced Real Time Operational Control.
**BAS** Bachelor of Agricultural Science.
**BAS**; **B.A.S.** Bachelor of Applied Science.
**BAS**; **B.A.S.** Bachelor of Architectural Science.
**BAS**; **B.A.S.** Bachelor of Arts and Sciences.
**BAS**; **B.A.S.** Bachelor of Arts in Speech.
**BAS** Banca Africana di Sviluppo.
Italian acronym of the: African Development Bank.
**BaS** Barium Sulfide.
BaS is used mainly as a flame retardant.
*Inorganic Chemistry.*
**BAS** Behavioral Approach Scale.
*Psychology.*
**BAS** Block Automation System.
**BAS** British Antarctic Survey (G.B.).
The BAS is a government-funded organisation responsible for a programme in science in the Antarctic and related regions.
*Antarctic Marine Fauna; Benthic Marine Invertebrates; Cladistic Techniques; Marine Biology; Marine Molluscs.*
**BAS** Building Automation Systems.
**Ba.sa** (abbr.) Baronessa.
Italian abbreviation meaning: Baroness.
Also: **b.ssa**.
**BASC** Board on Atmospheric Sciences and Climate (U.S.A.).
**BASDA**; **Basda** Business and Accounting Software Developers' Association.
**Base** Basic semantic element.
*Data Processing.*
**BASE** Brokerage Accounting System Elements.
**BASH** Body Acceleration Synchronous with the Heartbeat.
*Cardiology.*
**BASH** Booksellers' Association Service House (G.B.).
**$BaSi_2$** Barium Silicide.
*Inorganic Chemistry.*
**BASIC** Banking and Securities Industry Committee.
**BASIC** Basic Appraisal System for Incoming Components.
**BASIC** Beginner's All-purpose Symbolic Instruction Code.
**BASIC** British-American Security Information Council.
**BASICS** Battle Area Surveillance and Integrated Communication System.
**$BaSiO_3$** Barium Silicate.
Barium Silicate is used in ceramics.
*Inorganic Chemistry.*
**$BaSi_2O_5$** Sanbornite.
*Mineralogy.*
**BASIS** Bank Automated Service Information System.
**BASIS** Budgetary And Scheduling Information System.
**BASIX** Bay Area Seismic Imaging Experiment.
*Geology; Seismology.*
**$BaSO_3$** Barium Sulfite.
Barium Sulfite is used in the paper manufacturing industry.
*Inorganic Chemistry.*
**$BaSO_4$** Barium Sulfate.
*Inorganic Chemistry.*
**BASR** Bureau of Applied Social Research.
Of Columbia University. BASR is one of the U.S.A.'s oldest university-affiliated social research organizations.
**BASS** 1. barrier ammunition storage site.
1. site de stockage de munitions d'obstacles.
2. base automated support system.
2. système automatisé de soutien des bases.
**BASS** Belgian Archives for the Social Sciences.
*Belgian Information Service.*
**BAST** Board on Army Science and Technology (U.S.A.).
**BAT**; **B.A.T.** Bachelor of Arts in Teaching.
**BAT** Basic Air Temperature.
**BAT** Best Available Technology.
**BAT** Brown Adipose Tissue.
**bat** The above acronyms were coined using the English word "bat" (*Building Engineering; Materials Science; Vertebrate Zoology*).
**BAT industries** British-American Tobacco Industries.
**$BaTiO_3$** Barium Titanate.
*Inorganic Chemistry.*
**BATS** Ballistic Aerial Target System.
**BATS** Basic Additional Teleprocessing Support.
**BATS** Business Air Transport Service.
**BATSE** Burst And Transient Source Experiment.
*Astronomy.*
**batt.** (abbr.) battalion.
Also: **bn**.
*Military Science.*
**BAU** Business As Usual.
*Business; Finance.*
**BAUD** Baudot Code.
*Telecommunications.*
**BAV** Banco Ambrosiano Veneto (Italy).
Now BancaIntesaBCI with CARIPLO and BCI.

*Banking Integrations.*
For further details see under: **CARIPLO** and **BCI**.
**Bav.** (abbr.) Bavaria; Bavarian.
**BAV** Bloc Atrioventriculaire or Auriculo-Ventriculaire.
French acronym meaning: Atrio-Ventricular Heart Block; Auriculo-Ventricular Heart Block; A-V Block; Atrio- or Auriculoventricular Block.
*Medicine.*
**BAW caterpillars** Beet Army Worm caterpillars.
*Agricultural Research; Chemistry; Medical, Agricultural and Veterinary Entomology; Organic Chemistry.*
**$BaWO_4$** Barium Tungstate.
Barium Tungstate is used mainly in X-ray photography.
*Inorganic Chemistry.*
**BB** Baby Bond.
*Business; Finance.*
**BB** Ball Bearing.
*Mechanical Engineering.*
**BB** Banca Brignone SpA (Italy).
Established in 1926 as a private bank including some exclusive international multinationals it remained private and independent being controlled by the Brignone's, a family of third-generation bankers until its incorporation on the $10^{th}$ June 2002 in the BPB-CV.
*Banking Integrations.*
For further details see under: **BPB-CV**.
**BB** Banco de Bilbao (Spain).
*Spanish Bank.*
**BB** Barbados.
**BB** Basic Block.
*Computer Science.*
**b/b** bearer bonds.
**BB** Big Board.
**b/b** billet de banque.
French abbreviation meaning: banknote; bill (U.S.A.).
**BB** Board on Biology (U.S.A.).
**bb** broad band / broadband.
A broad band is actually a band with a broad range of frequencies.
*Telecommunications.*
**BB** Bundle Branch.
*Anatomy.*
**BB** Bureau of the Budget (U.S.A.).
**BB** Buy Back.
*Business; Finance.*
**B2B** Business to Business.
*e-Business.*
**BBA** Bachelor of Business Administration.
**BBA** Banque Belge d'Afrique.
*Belgian Bank.*
**BBA** British Bankers' Association.
**BBB** Banker's Blanket Bond.
**BBB** Better Business Bureau.
**BBB** Bloc de Branche Bilatéral.
French initialism meaning: Bilateral Bundle Branch Block.
*Medicine.*
**BBB** Bundle Branch Block (heart).
*Medicine.*
**BBBD** Blood-Brain Barrier Disruption.
A technique to deliver chemotherapy drugs to brain cancer patients.
**BBB scale** Basso, Bresnahan, and Beattie scale.
*Neurosurgery; Medicine.*
**BBC** British Broadcasting Corporation (G.B.).
**BBC** Bromobenzylcyamide.
*Organic Chemistry.*
**B2B2C** Business to Business to Consumer.
Also: **BtoBtoC**.
*e-Commerce.*
**BBCR** Bellcore Bell Communications Research (U.S.A.).
**BBD** Bank Bumi Daya (Indonesia).
*Indonesian Bank.*
**BBD** Bloc de Branche Droit.
French initialism meaning: Right Bundle Branch Block.
*Medicine.*
**BBD** Bucket-Brigade Device.
The BBD is a semiconductor device.
*Electronics.*
**BBDC** Before Bottom Dead Center.
**BBE** Bachelor of Business Education.
**BBG** Bloc de Branche Gauche.
French initialism meaning: Left Bundle Branch Block.
*Medicine.*
**BBG** Board of Broadcasting Governors.
**BBL** Banque Bruxelles Lambert S.A.
*Belgian Bank.*
**bbl**; **bbl.** barrel.
**BBL** Basic Business Language.
**bbl**; **bbl.** bushel.
**bbls**; **bbls.** barrels.
**bbls**; **bbls.** bushels.
**BBM** Break-Before-Make.
*Electricity.*
**BBO** Billion Barrels of Oil.
**BBP** Butyl Benzyl Phthalate.
**B2BP** Business-to-Business Procurement.
**BBR** Bank Base Rate.

**$BBr_3$** Boron Tribromide.
$BBr_3$ is used to produce diborane.
*Inorganic Chemistry.*
**BBS** Bardet-Biedl Syndrome.
**BBS** Bulletin Board Software.
**BBS**; **Bbs** Bulletin Board System.
**BBS** Business Batch System.
**BBSI** Beauty and Barber Supply Institute (U.S.A.).
**BBSO** Big Bear Solar Observatory.
The BBSO is located in California, U.S.A.
**BBSRC** Biotechnology and Biological Sciences Research Council (G.B.).
**BBT** Basal Body Temperature.
*Medicine.*
**BBVA** Banco Bilbao y Viscaya Argentaria.
*Spanish Bank.*
**BB/W rats** Bio Breeding Worcester rats.
*Medicine; Pathology.*
**BBXRT** Broad Band X-Ray Telescope.
**BC** Bachelor of Commerce.
**BC** Bad Check/Cheque.
*Business; Commerce; Finance.*
**BC**; **B.C.** Bank Clearing.
**B.C.** Bankruptcy Court.
**BC** Before Christ.
**BC** Bibliographic Classification.
**BC**; **B.C.** Bills for Collection.
**BC** Binary Code.
*Computer Programming.*
**BC** Black Carbon.
*Earth System Science.*
**bc** blind copy.
**BC** Bliss Classification.
**BC** Blue Chip.
**BC** Board of Control.
**BC** Bogus Check.
*Business; Commerce; Finance.*
**BC** Botswana.
**BC** British Columbia (Canada).
**BC** (abbr.) broadcast.
**B2C** Business to Consumer; Business to Customer.
Also: **BtoC**.
*e-Commerce.*
**$B_4C$** Boron Carbide.
*Inorganic Chemistry.*
**BCA** Bank Credit Analyst.
*Business Forecast; Global Investments.*
**BCA** Benzene Carboxylic Acid.
*Organic Chemistry.*
**BCA** Biopharmaceutical Characterization and Analysis.
**BCA** 1. border crossing authority.
1.a. autorité pour le franchissement de frontière.
1.b. autorisation de franchissement de frontière.
2. broadcast control authority.
2.a. autorité de contrôle de la radiodiffusion.
2.b. autorité de contrôle de TRAM.
**BCAAW** Bureau for the Coordination of Arabization in the Arab World.
**BCAH** Bureau de la coordination des affaires humanitaires [remplace l'UNDHA].
Office for the Coordination of Humanitarian Affairs (OCHA) [has replaced UNDHA].
**BC&I** Banca Popolare Commercio e Industria.
*Italian Bank.*
**BCAS** Beacon Collision-Avoidance System.
**BCB** Benzocyclobutene.
**BCBA Newsletter** Newsletter of the Broome County Bar Association, N.Y., U.S.A.
**BCC** Block Check Character.
*Data Communications.*
**BCCI** Banca di Credito e Commercio Internazionale (Luxemburg).
**BCCI** British Chamber of Commerce for Italy.
**BCCM** Banque Centrale des Coopératives et des Mutuelles (France).
*French Bank.*
**BCD** Barrels per Calendar Day.
**BCD** Biological and Conservation Database.
**BCD system** Binary-Coded Decimal system.
*Computer Programming.*
**BCE**; **B.C.E.** Bachelor of Chemical Engineering.
Also: **BchE**; **B.Ch.E**.
**BCE**; **B.C.E.** Bachelor of Civil Engineering.
**BCE** Banca Centrale Europea; Banque Centrale Européenne.
Italian and French initialism of the: European Central Bank. The European Central Bank became operative in 1999.
*Changeover to the EURO.*
**BCE** battlefield coordination element.
élément de coordination du champ de bataille.
**BCE**; **B.C.E.** Before the Common Era.
**BCE** Board of Customs and Excise (G.B.).
*Taxation.*
**BCEAO** Banque Centrale des Etats de l'Afrique de l'Ouest.
*Central Bank.*
**BCE cells** Bovine Capillary Endothetial cells.
**BCerE**; **B.Cer.E.** Bachelor of Ceramic Engineering.
**bcf** billion cubic feet.
**BCF**; **B.C.F.** British Cycling Federation (G.B.).
**BCF** budget control figure.
montant de contrôle de la dotation budgétaire.
**BCF** Bureau of Commercial Fisheries (U.S.A.).

The BCF has been replaced by the U.S. **NMFS** (National Marine Fisheries Service).
**BC flux** Biogenic organic Carbon flux.
*Atmospheric Research; Chemistry; Chemical and Physical Oceanography.*
**BCG** Ballistocardiogram.
*Medicine.*
**BCG** Bécégite.
French initialism meaning: BCG infection.
*Medicine.*
**BCG** Bromocresol Green.
BCG is also known as: Bromcresol Green.
*Organic Chemistry.*
**BCG vaccine** Bacillus Calmette-Guérin vaccine.
The BCG vaccine is used for immunization of humans against tuberculosis. Named for Albert **Calmette** and Camille **Guérin**.
*Immunology.*
**Bch**; **B.Ch.** Bachelor of Chemistry.
**BChl a molecules** Bacteriochlorophyll a molecules.
*Photosynthesis.*
**BChE**; **B.Ch.E.** Bachelor of Chemical Engineering.
Also: **BCE**; **B.C.E**.
**BCI** Banca Commerciale Italiana (Italy).
Now: BancaIntesaBCI with CARIPLO and BAV.
*Banking Integrations.*
For further details see under: **CARIPLO** and **BAV**.
**BCI** Banco de Comercio & Industria.
*Angolan Bank.*
**BCI** Battery Council International.
The BCI is based in Chicago, U.S.A.
**BCI** Broadcast Interference.
*Data Communications.*
**BCIP** Bromochloroindoylphosphate.
**BCIS** Biodiversity Conservation Information System.
**BCIs** brain-computer interfaces.
Several laboratories in the United States started developing BCIs in the 1980s and have been improving them ever since. The BCIs read the electrical impulses created by neural activity through the scalp.
*Neuroscience.*
**BCL** Bachelor of Civil Law.
**$BCl_3$** Boron Trichloride.
$BCl_3$ is used mainly to refine copper, magnesium and aluminium.
*Inorganic Chemistry.*
**B-CLL** B-cell Chronic Lymphocytic Leukemia.
**BCLS** Basic Cardiac Life Support.
**BCM**; **B.C.M.** Bachelor of Church Music.
**BCM theory** Bienenstock-Cooper-Munro theory.
*Physiology.*
**BCN** The airport code for Barcelona, Spain.
**bcn.** (abbr.) beacon.
*Navigation.*
**BCN** Beet Cyst Nematode.
*Crop Science; Molecular and Structural Biology; Plant Breeding; Reproduction Research.*
**BC-NET** Business Cooperation NETwork.
*European Community.*
**BCODH** Branched-Chain Oxoacid Dehydrogenase.
**BcomSc**; **B.Com.Sc.** Bachelor of Commercial Science.
**BCoV** Bovine Coronavirus.
*Anti-SARS Drugs; Biochemistry; Molecular Biology; Molecular Biotechnolgy.*
**BCP**; **B.C.P.** Bachelor of City Planning.
**BCP** Banco Comercial Português (Portugal).
The BCP is listed on the New York, Frankfurt and London Stock Exchange. The BCP was granted the Euromoney "Award for Excellence" as the best Portuguese bank 4 years in a row.
*Portuguese Bank.*
For further details see under: **BPA** (Banco Português do Atlântico).
**BCP** Birth Control Pill.
**BCP** Budget Change Proposal.
**BC particles** Black Carbon particles.
*Asian Climate; Soot.*
**BCPs** Block Copolymers.
*Chemical Engineering; Polymeric Materials.*
**BCPT** Breast Cancer Prevention Trial.
The breast cancer prevention trial got under way in the United States and Canada in 1992.
**BCR** Bank Cash Ratio; Bank Cash Reserve.
*Banking; Finance.*
**BCR** B Cell antigen Receptor.
The BCR is a multiprotein complex.
*Biochemistry; Cell Biology; Genetics; Immunology; Medicine.*
**BCS**; **B.C.S.** Bachelor of Chemical Science.
**BCs** Backcrosses.
*Genetics.*
**BCS** Basic Control System.
**BCs** Before Computers.
**BCS** Best Cast Steel.
*Metallurgy.*
**BCS** Boston Computer Society (U.S.A.).
**BCS Award** British Computer Society Award (G.B.).
The BCS in association with The Financial Times runs The Information Systems Management Award.

**BCSD** Business Council for Sustainable Development (Switzerland).

**BCS density of states** Bardeen-Cooper-Schrieffer density of states.
*Physics.*

**BCSE** Board of Civil Service Examiners.

**BCSSE** Board on Behavioral, Cognitive, and Sensory Sciences and Education (U.S.A.).

**BCST** Board on Chemical Sciences and Technology (U.S.A.).

**BCS theory** Bardeen-Cooper-Schrieffer theory.
*Solid-State Physics.*

**BCT** Bank Credit Transfer.

**BC Tel** British Columbia Telecom (Canada).

**BCV** Banque Cantonale Vaudoise.
*Swiss Bank.*

**BCV** Barge-Carrying Vessel.

**BCV** Blister Canker Virus.
*Plant Pathology.*

**BCVB** Birmingham Convention & Visitor Bureau (G.B.).

**BD** Back Deliveries; Bad Delivery.
*Business; Commerce.*

**BD** Bank Dividends.
*Banking; Finance.*

**BD** Bank Draft.
*Banking; Business; Commerce; Finance.*

**BD** Barrels per Day.
Also: **BPD**, **bpd**.

**Bd.** (abbr.) Baud.
*Computer Science* - Bd. is the number of bits transmitted per second.
*Telecommunications* - Bd. is a unit of signaling speed.

**BD**; **b.d.** Bills Discounted.
*Banking; Business; Commerce.*

**BD** Blood Derivatives.

**bd.** (abbr.) board.
*Building Engineering.*
*Computer Technology* - In computer technology board is also known as: plugboard; wire board; panel.
*Electronics* - In electronics board is also known as: circuit board.
*Forestry; Graphic Arts; Naval Architecture; Navigation.*

**BD** Bomb Disposal.
*Ordnance.*

**bd.** (abbr.) bond.
For further details see under: **b**.

**bd.** (abbr.) boulevard.
Also: **Boul**.

**bd.** (abbr.) bound; boundary.

**B/D** Broker-Dealer.
*Business; Commerce.*

**b/d** brought down.

**bd.** (abbr.) bundle.
*Botany; Computer Science; Mathematics; Optics.*

**BDA** Bachelor of Domestic Arts.

**BDA** Bachelor of Dramatic Art.

**BDA** Banque des Nations Unies pour le Développement Africain.
*United Nations Bank.*

**BDA** Bomb Damage Assessment.

**BDA** Booster-Distribution Amplifier.
*Data Communications.*

**BDA** British Dental Association (G.B.).

**BDA** The airport code for Bermuda.

**BDAM** Basic Direct-Access Method.
*Computer Programming.*

**BDB consortium** British Digital Broadcasting consortium (G.B.).

**BdC** Banque du Caire.
*Egyptian Bank.*

**BDC** Bottom Dead Center.
Bottom dead center refers to the point at which a piston is at the end of its downstroke.
*Mechanical Engineering.*

**BD cats** Binocularly Deprived cats.
*Integrative Neuroscience; Physiology.*

**BDDs** Binary Decision Diagrams.
*Computer Science; Logical Structures.*

**Bde**; **bde** (abbr.) brigade.

**BDEs** Bond Dissociation Energies.

**BDF** Banque De France.
For further details see under: **BF**.

**BDF** Base Detonating Fuse.
*Explosives.*

**B/DFT**; **B/Dft** Bank Draft.

**bd.ft.**; **bd ft** board foot; board feet.
For further details see under: **BF** (Board Foot).

**BDGP** Berkeley *Drosophila* Genome Project (U.S.A.).

**BDI** Bearing Deviation Indicator.
*Navigation.*

**BDI** Both Dates Included; Both Days Included.

**BDI** Germany Industry Association.

**BDIC** Bourses de Docteur-Ingénieur Classiques (France).

**BDIE** Bourse de Docteur-Ingénieur cofinancée par les Entreprises (France).

**BDIR** Bourses de Docteur Ingénieur cofinancées par les Régions (France).

**BdL** Banque du Liban (Lebanon).

**BDL** Building Design Language.
*Computer Programs.*

**bdl** bundle.
Also: **bd.**; **bdle**.
**bdls.** (abbr.) bundles.
*Botany; Computer Science; Mathematics; Optics.*
**BDM** Butanedione Monoxime.
**BdN** Banco di Napoli.
*Italian Bank.*
**BDNF** Brain-Derived Neurotrophic Factor.
*Motor Neuron Disease; Neuroscience; Neurobiology.*
**B/DOE** Barrels per Day Oil Equivalent.
**BDP** Biblioteca di Documentazione Pedagogica (Florence, Italy).
**bdp** bilancia dei pagamenti.
Italian initialism meaning: balance of payments.
**BDR** Bangladesh Rifles.
Responsible for guarding the frontier.
**BDR** battle damage repair.
1a. réparation au combat.
1b. réparation des dégâts subis au combat.
**BDR** Bearer Depositary Receipt; British Depository Receipt.
**Bd.Rts.** Bond Rights.
*Business; Finance.*
**BDS**; **B.D.S.** Bachelor of Dental Surgery.
**BDS** Banco di Sicilia (Italy).
The BDS was officially established in 1867. In 1999 became part of Mediocredito Centrale and in 2002 incorporated in Banca di Roma.
*Banking Integrations.*
**BDS.** (abbr.) Barbados International Vehicle Registration letters.
**BDs** Best Delays.
*Biology; Brain Behavior; Neurophysiology.*
**bds.** boards; bundles.
**BDSc**; **B.D.Sc.** Bachelor of Dental Science.
**BDT** Brittle-Ductile Transition.
*Earth and Planetary Sciences; Geological Sciences.*
**BDU** battledress uniform.
tenue de combat.
**BDV** Breakdown Voltage.
Breakdown Voltage is also known as: Zener Voltage.
*Electronics.*
**bdy.** (abbr.) boundary.
*Chaotic Dynamics; Electronics; Mathematics; Military Science; Robotics.*
**BDZ** base defence zone.
zone de défense de bases.
**BE** Bachelor of Education.
Also: **B.E.**; **Bed.**; **B.Ed**.
**BE**; **B.E.** Bachelor of Engineering.
Also: **B.eng.**; **B.Engr**.
**BE** Back End.
**BE** Balanced Error.
*Computer Technology.*
**BE** Band Elimination.
*Data Communications.*
**BE** Barium Enema.
*Radiology* - Also: **BAE**.
**BE** Baron of Exchequer (G.B.).
**Bé**; **Bé.** Baumé (hydrometer) scale.
Named for the French chemist Antoine **Baumé**.
*Physical Chemistry.*
**BE** Belgium.
Also: **B**.
**BE** Bell End.
**BE** Below Elbow.
*Medicine.*
**Be** the chemical symbol for Beryllium.
Beryllium is a chemical element having the atomic number 4, an atomic weight of 9.0122, and a melting point of about 1280°C. Used mainly in lasers, in X-ray tubes and in electronic devices.
*Chemistry; Symbols.*
**BE**; **B/E** Bill of Entry.
**be**; **BE** Bill of Exchange.
**BE** Binding Energy.
In physics and physical chemistry, binding energy is also known as: bond energy.
*Nuclear Physics; Physics; Physical Chemistry.*
**BE** Board of Education.
**BE** Booster Engine.
*Space Technology.*
**B2E** Business to Education.
Also: **BtoE**.
**BEA** Background Equivalent Activity.
**BEA** Bank of East Asia.
It is Hong Kong's third-largest bank.
**BEA** Binary Encounter Approximation.
*Nuclear Physics.*
**BEA** Break Even Analysis.
**BEA** British Electricity Authority; British Engineers Association (G.B.).
**BEA** Broadcast Education Association.
**BEA** Bureau of Economic Analysis (U.S.A.).
**$BeAl_2O_4$** Chrysoberyl.
Chrysoberyl is used as a gemstone.
*Mineralogy.*
**$BeAlSiO_4(OH)$** Euclase.
*Mineralogy.*
**BEAM** Brain Electrical Activity Mapping.
**BEAMA** British Electrical and Allied Manufacturers' Association (G.B.).

**BEAMS** Base Engineering Automated Management System.
**BEAR** Biological Effects of Atomic Radiation.
**BEAST** Business, Engineering, Appropriate technology, and Skilled Trades.
**BEAT** Best Execution Analysis Tabulation.
*Psychology.*
**BEB** British Export Board (G.B.).
**$Be_2BO_3(OH)$** Hambergite.
*Mineralogy.*
**BeC** Beryllium Carbide.
*Inorganic Chemistry.*
**BEC** Bose-Einstein Condensation / Condensate.
*Physics.*
**BEC** Bureau of Employees' Compensation.
**BECA** Banca Europea Centro America.
**$BeCl_2$** Beryllium Chloride.
*Inorganic Chemistry.*
**BECN** Backward Explicit Congestion Notification.
*Computers.*
**BECO** Booster Engine Cutoff.
**BECs** Bose-Einstein Condensates.
*Physics.*
**Bed** Bachelor of Education.
Also: **B.Ed.**; **BE**; **B.E.**
**BED** Basic Engineering Development.
**BED** Box External Data.
**Beds.** (abbr.) Bedfordshire (G.B.).
**beds.** (abbr.) bedrooms.
**BEDT-TTF molecule** [Bis-(Ethylenedithio)-Tetrathiafulvalene] molecule.
*Condensed Matter Physics.*
**BEE**; **B.E.E.** Bachelor of Electrical Engineering.
**BEE** Banca Europea delle Esportazioni.
Italian initialism of the: European Export Bank.
**BEE** Benthic foraminifera Extinction Event.
*Geology; Geophysics; Paleocene Epoch; Oceanography.*
**BEEF** Business and Engineering Enriched FORTRAN.
*Data Communications.*
**BEEP** Battalion Equipment Evaluation Program.
U S. Department of Defense.
**BEEP** Bureau Européen de I'Education Populaire.
French acronym of the: European Bureau of Adult Education.
**BEES** Board on Energy and Environmental Systems (U.S.A.).
**bef.** (abbr.) before.
**BEF** British Expeditionary Force.
*Military.*
**$BeF_2$** Beryllium Fluoride.
Beryllium Fluoride is used mainly in metallurgy.
*Inorganic Chemistry.*
**BEG** Brigade Engineer Group.
*Marine Corps.*
**BEI** Banca Europea per gli Investimenti - Banque Européenne d'lnvestissement.
Italian and French acronym of the: European Investment Bank.
**BEI** Brevet d'Enseignement Industriel (France).
**BEI** Butanol-Extractable Iodine.
*Clinical Chemistry.*
**BELA** Black Entertainment Lawyers Association.
**Bel.Fcs.** Belgian Francs.
Now: EURO/EUR (€). Became ECU (European Single Currency) with effect from January 2002.
*New Currencies.*
**BELL** Bulletin, Société, des études de Lettres - Lausanne, Switzerland.
*Publication.*
**BeLT** Berylliurn Lymphocyte proliferation Test.
The beryllium lymphocyte proliferation test is used to make a specific diagnosis of chronic *beryllium disease*.
**BEM**; **B.E.M.** Bachelor of Engineering of Mines.
**BEM** Boundary Elements Methods.
**BEMA** Business Equipment Manufacturers Association.
**BEMPEX** Barotropic Electromagnetic and Pressure EXperiment.
BEMPEX took place in 1986/87.
**BEMs** Big Emerging Markets.
**BEN** Biased Enhanced Nucleation.
*Chemistry; Materials Science; Physics.*
**BEN** BioSciEdNet.
A AAAS-managed Web site.
*Biological Sciences.*
For further details see under: **AAAS**.
**$Be_3N_2$** Beryllium Nitride.
Beryllium Nitride is used mainly to make rocket fuels.
*Inorganic Chemistry.*
**BENECHAN** Benelux Sub-Area, Channel [obsolete].
Sous-zone Benelux de la Manche [obsolète].
**BENELUX** BElgium, the NEtherlands and LUXemburg.
**B.eng**; **B.Engr.** Bachelor of Engineering.
Also: **BE**; **B.E.**
**BEngS** Bachelor of Engineering Science.
**benz.** (abbr.) benzene.
For further details see under: **$C_6H_6$**.
*Organic Chemistry.*
**benz.** (abbr.) benzoic.
**BeO** Beryllium Oxide.

Beryllium Oxide is used mainly in electron tubes.
*Inorganic Chemistry.*
**BEP**; **B.E.P.** Bachelor of Engineering Physics.
**BEP** Back-End Processor.
*Computer Technology.*
**BEP** Biomolecular Engineering Program.
**BE point** Break-Even point.
*Industrial Engineering.*
**BER** Basic Encoding Rules.
*Computers.*
**BER** The airport code for Berlin, Germany.
**BER** Bit Error Rate.
**BERD** Banque Européenne pour la Reconstruction et le Développement.
French acronym of the: European Bank for Reconstruction and Development.
**BERI** Bog Ecosystem Research Initiative.
*European Community Project.*
**Berks.** (abbr.) Berkshire (G.B.).
**Bers** Banca Europea per la Ricostruzione e lo Sviluppo.
Italian acronym of the: European Bank for Reconstruction and Development.
**BERT** Bit Error Rate Test.
**BERTS**; **Berts** Bangkok Elevated Road and Train System.
**BES** Banco Espirito Santo e Comercial de Lisboa (Portugal).
BES is Portugal's fourth largest bank group. It has its origin in the late 19th century and its title since a merger in 1937. In 1975 it was taken over by the State and was reprivatised in 1992. Espirito Santo is the surname of the family founder of the bank.
Also: **BESCL**.
*Portuguese Bank.*
**BES** budget estimate submission.
1a. document budgétaire.
1b. projet de budget.
**BES** Bureau of Employment Security (U.S.A.).
**BES** Business Expansion Scheme.
*Business; Finance.*
**BESA** Brevet d'Enseignement des Sports Aériens (France).
**BESA** British Engineering Standards Association (G.B.).
**BESAC** Basic Energy Sciences Advisory Committee (U.S.A.).
**BES division** Basic Energy Science division.
Of DOE, U.S.A.
For further details see under: **DOE**.
**BESR** Board on Earth Sciences and Resources (U.S.A.).
**BESS** Binary Electromagnetic Signal Signature.
**BESS** Biomedical Experiment Scientific Satellite.
**BESS** Bottom Environmental Sensing System.
**BEST** Basic Educational Skills Test; Basic Essential Skills Testing.
**BEST** Battery Energy Storage Test.
**BEST** Better Electronic Service Technicians.
**BEST** Board on Environmental Studies and Toxicology (U.S.A.).
**BEST** Board of European Students of Technology.
**BEST** Building Engineering and Science Talent (U.S.A.).
**BEST** Bulletin of European Studies of Time - European Community.
BEST is produced and published by the E.C. Foundation. It refers to part-time work in Europe.
**BEST** Business class versus Economy Syndrome as a cause of Thrombosis.
A project undertaken by King's College London and the University of the Witwatersround in South Africa.
*Blood-clot Study.*
**BEST** Business EDP Systems Technique.
**BEST** Business Electronic Systems Techniques.
**BESTEST** Building Energy Simulation Test.
BESTEST is a diagnostic method to improve the accuracy of computer energy software programs. The BESTEST procedure is part of an overall validation method first developed at NREL in 1983 that combines analytical, empirical, and comparative techniques. BESTEST was developed as part of an International Energy Agency project and has been field tested in several European countries.
*Energy Software.*
For further details see under: **NREL**.
**BET** Bachelor of Engineering Technology.
**BET** Bi-SC Evaluation Team.
Equipe d'évaluation des Commandements stratégiques.
**BET** British Electric Traction.
**BETA** Battlefield Exploitation and Target Acquisition.
**BETA** Billion channel Extraterrestrial Assay.
*Extraterrestrial Intelligence.*
**BETA** Business Equipment Trade Association.
**beta** The above acronyms were coined using the word "beta" which is the second letter of the Greek alphabet: β.
**BET method** Brunauer-Emmett-Teller method.
*Engineering; Intelligent Polymers; Nanotubes.*
**BEUC** Bureau Européen Unions Consommateurs.
French acronym of the: European Bureau of Consumers' Unions.
**BEV**; **bev.** (abbr.) Bevel.

*Building Engineering; Design Engineering; Graphic Arts; Mechanical Engineering.*

**BEV** Blacksburg Electronic Village (Virginia, U.S.A.).
*Community Networks; Electronic Communities.*

**BeV** One billion electron volts, $10^9$ eV.
Also: **GeV**.
*Physics.*

**BEVs** Baculovirus Expression Vectors.
Baculovirus expression vectors are used at present in many basic research laboratories and commercial biotechnology companies for the production of vaccines, therapeutics, and diagnostic reagents.
*Biology; Baculovirology; Biotechnology; Medical Research.*

**$Be_2WO_6$** Russellite.
*Mineralogy.*

**BEX** Broadband Exchange.
*Data Communications.*

**BF**; **B.F.** Bachelor of Forestry.

**BF** Backdoor Financing (U.S.A.).

**BF** Bahamas.

**BF** Balanced Flue.
*Engineering.*

**BF** Balanced Fund.
*Business; Finance.*

**Bf** Bandfilter.

**BF** Banque de France.
Also: **BDF**.
Established on 18th January 1800.

**BF** Base Fuse.

**b.f.**; **b/f** bassa frequenza - basse fréquence.
Italian and French initialism meaning: low frequency.
*Physics.*

**BF** Belgian Francs.
For further details see under: **Bel.Fcs.**

**BF** Blastogenic Factor; Blocking Factor.

**BF** Board-Foot.
Board-foot is a unit of measure equal to 2360 cubic centimeters.
*Engineering.*

**Bf** Boilerfeed.

**b.f.**; **bf** boldface.
Boldface refers to a type having dark lines so as to appear black with respect to other type.
*Graphic Arts.*

**b/f** brought forward.
*Book-Keeping.*

**$BF_3$** Boron Trifluoride.
$BF_3$ is used to catalyze chemical reactions.
*Inorganic Chemistry.*

**BFA**; **B.F.A.** Bachelor of Fine Arts.

**BFA** Brefeldin A.

**BFAR** Bureau of Fisheries and Aquatic Resources. The Philippines.

**BFC** Backup Flight Computer.

**BFC** Budget and Forecast Calendarization.

**BFCE** Banque Française du Commerce Extérieur (France).
*French Bank.*

**BFCS** Backup Flight Control System.

**BFCU** Bureau of Federal Credit Unions (U.S.A.).

**bfcy.** (abbr.) beneficiary.
*Business; Commerce; Finance.*

**BFE** Bromotrifluoroethylene.

**BFEE** Benthic Foraminiferal Extinction Event.
*Earth Science; Geological Sciences; Marine Science.*

**BfG** Federal Institute for Hydrology (Germany).

**bFGF** basic Fibroblast Growth Factor.

**BFI** bulk fuel installation.
installation de carburants en vrec.

**BFL** Back Focal Length.
The back focal length is actually the distance from the rear surface of a lens to its focal plane.
*Optics.*

**BFL** The airport code for Bakersfield, California, U.S.A.

**BfN** Federal Agency for Nature Conservation (Germany).

**BFNC** Benign Familial Neonatal Convulsions.
BNFC is an autosomal dominant epilepsy of infancy.
*Human Genetics; Neonatal Human Epilepsy.*

**BFO** Beat-Frequency Oscillator.
The beat-frequency oscillator is also known as: heterodyne oscillator.
*Electronics.*

**BFP** Biologic False-Positive.
*Medicine.*

**BFP** Boiler Feed Pump.
*Boilers.*

**BFP** Bundle-Forming Pilus (or pili).
*Microbiology.*

**BFRA** Boron Fibers Reinforced Aluminum.
*Metallurgy.*

**BFS**; **B.F.S.** Bachelor of Foreign Service.

**BFS** Backup Flight System.

**BFS** Beam-Foil Spectroscopy.
BFS is a method for the study of atoms and ions.

**BFSP** British and Foreign State Papers.

**BFT**; **B.F.T.** Bachelor of Foreign Trade.

**BFU-E** Burst-Forming Unit Erythroid.

**BFY** Budget Fiscal Year.
*Business; Economics; Finance.*

**bg** (abbr.) background.
*Acoustics; Computer Technology; Geochemistry; Physics; Telecommunications.*
**bg.** (abbr.) bag.
In computer science bag is also known as: multiset.
*Computer Science.*
**BG** Bangladesh.
**BG** Bergamo, Italy.
**BG** Birmingham Gauge.
For further details see under: **BWG**.
**B/G**; **b/g** Bonded Goods.
**BG** Brigadier General.
**BG** Bulgaria's vehicle registration letters.
**B2G** Business to Government.
Also: **BtoG**.
*e-Commerce.*
**BGC** Berkeley Geochronology Center.
The BGC is located at Berkeley, California, U.S.A.
*Anthropology.*
**BGD** Billion Gallons per Day.
**BGG** Bovine Gamma Globulin.
**BGH** Board on Global Health (U.S.A.).
**bGH** Bovine Growth Hormone.
**BGI** Beijing Genomics Institute (China).
**BGI** The airport code for Barbados.
**BGI's** Barclays Global Investors (G.B.).
**BGK** Background Knowledge.
**BGL** Bombe à Guidage Laser.
laser-guided bomb (LGB).
**BGOH** Bureau de gestion OTAN HAWK.
NATO HAWK Management Office (NHMO).
**BGP** Banque de Gestion Privée (France).
**BGP** bureau de gestion de projet.
project management office (PMO).
**BGR** The airport code for Bangor, Maine.
**bgs.** (abbr.) bags.
**BGS** British Geological Survey (G.B.).
**bgt.** (abbr.) bought.
*Business; Commerce.*
**BH** Bank Handlowy (Poland).
*Polish Bank.*
**BH** Bank Holiday.
**BH** Bill of Health.
*Medicine.*
**BH** Black Hole.
**BH** Brinell Hardness.
Named for the Swedish metallurgist Johann **Brinell**.
*Materials Science.*
**$BH_4$** Tetrahydrobiopterin.
**$B_2H_6$** Diborane.
Diborane has many applications in industry.
*Inorganic Chemistry.*
**BHA** Butylated Hydroxyamisole.
BHA is used as an antioxidant for oils and fats.
*Organic Chemistry.*
**B'ham** (abbr.) Birmingham (G.B.).
**BHB motif** Bulge-Helix-Bulge motif.
*Biotechnology; Cellular Biology; Molecular Biology.*
**BHC** Benzene Hexachloride.
Benzene Hexachloride is also known as: Hexachlorocyclohexane.
*Organic Chemistry.*
**BHC** Bosnia-Herzegovina Command.
Commandement de Bosnie-Herzégovine.
**BHCCC** Bosnia-Herzegovina communications control centre.
centre de contrôle des communications de la Bosnie-Herzégovine.
**bhd.** (abbr.) bulkhead.
*Aviation; Building Engineering; Mining Engineering; Naval Architecture.*
**BHE** Bureau of Higher Education.
**B'head** (abbr.) Birkenhead (G.B.).
**BHEW** Board on Higher Education and Workforce (U.S.A.).
**BHF** British Heart Foundation (G.B.).
**BHK cells** Baby Hamster Kidney cells.
*Immunology; Medicine; Microbiology; Tumor Biology; Virology.*
**BHL** Bachelor of Hebrew Letters; Bachelor of Hebrew Literature.
**bHLH motif** basic Helix-Loop-Helix motif.
*Pathology; Transcription Factors.*
**bHLH-PAS domains** basic Helix-Loop - Helix and Per-Arnt-Sim domains.
*Cell Biology.*
**BHN** Brinell Hardness Number.
Named for the Swedish metallurgist Johann **Brinell**.
*Materials Science.*
**BHP**; **bhp** Boiler Horsepower; Brake Horsepower.
*Mechanical Engineering.*
**BHRA** British Hydromechanics Research Association (G.B.).
**BHs** Black Holes.
*Astronomy.*
**Bht**; **B** Baht.
Also: **B** (Thailand).
*Currencies.*
**BHT** Butylated Hydroxytoluene.
BHT is used in petroleum products.
*Antioxidants; Organic Chemistry.*

**B.I.** Banca d'Italia.
Also: **BANKITALIA**.
Italian initialism of the: Bank of Italy.
**Bi** The chemical symbol for Bismuth.
Bismuth is a metallic element, having the atomic number 83, and an atomic weight of 208.980.
*Chemistry; Symbols; Mineralogy.*
**BIA**; **B.I.A.** Bachelor of Industrial Arts.
**BIA** Board of Immigration Appeals (U.S.A.).
**BIA** Braille Institute of America (U.S.A.).
**BIA** Bureau of Indian Affairs.
**BIAC** Business and Industry Advisory Committee (to the OECD) (France).
**BIACTON** Development of Industrial equipment allowing production of a stable and heat resistant mix of bacteria.
*European Community Project.*
**BIAS** Battlefield Illumination Airborne System.
**BIAS** Buoy Integrated Antenna Submarine.
**$BiAsO_4$** Rooseveltite.
Rooseveltite is a mineral of the monazite group.
*Mineralogy.*
**BIATA**; **B.I.A.T.A.** British Independent Air Transport Association (G.B.).
**BIB** Baby Incendiary Bomb.
**BIB** Biographical Information Blank.
**BIB** Board for International Broadcasting (U.S.A.).
**BIB** British Interactive Broadcasting (G.B.).
*Interactive Television Services.*
**bib** The above acronyms were coined using the English abbreviation "bib" (*Medicine*).
**BIBA** British Insurance Brokers' Association.
**BIBB** Bundesinstitut für Berufsbildung.
BIBB is located in Berlin, Germany.
*German Institute.*
**bibl.** biblico.
Italian abbreviation meaning: biblical.
**bibl.** bibliografia; bibliografo.
Italian abbreviation meaning: bibliography; bibliographer.
**bibl.** biblioteca.
Italian abbreviation meaning: library.
**BIC** Banco Internacional de Crédito (Portugal).
*Portuguese Bank.*
**BIC** Bioinformatics Core.
At MSKCC.
For further details see under: **MSKCC**.
**BIC** Business Innovation Center.
**BICA** Biennale Internazionale di Comunicazione Ambientale (Italy).
**BICC** BICES initial core capability.
capacité centrale initiale du BICES.
**BICE** Board on Infracture and the Constructed Environment (U.S.A.).
**BICEMA** British Internal Combustion Engine Manufacturers' Association (G.B.).
**BICES** Battlefield Information Collection and Exploitation System.
système de recueil et d'exploitation des informations du champ de bataille.
**$BiCl_3$** Bismuth Chloride.
Bismuth Chloride is used mainly as a catalyst.
*Inorganic Chemistry.*
**BICs** Business Innovation Centres.
**BICSE** Board on International Comparative Studies in Education (U.S.A.).
**BID**; **B.I.D.** Bachelor of Industrial Design.
**BID** Bacterial IDentification.
**BID** Banque Islamique de Développement.
*Arab Bank.*
**BID**; **Bid** Business Improvement District (U.S.A., New York 1992).
**BIDCO** Business and Industrial Development COrporation.
**BIDS** Base Intrusion Detection System.
**BIDS** British Institute of Dealers in Securities (G.B.).
**BIDS** Broadband Infrastructures for Digital TV and multimedia Services.
*European Community Project.*
**BIE**; **B.I.E.** Bachelor of Industrial Engineering.
**BIE** Bureau International des Expositions.
**BIF** Banded Iron Formation.
For further details see under: **BIFs**.
**BIF** Bank Insurance Fund.
**BIF** Benevolence International Foundation.
*Charities.*
**BIF**; **B.I.F.** British Industries Fair (G.B.).
**BIFA** British International Freight Association (G.B.).
**BIFF** battlefield identification friend-or-foe.
identification ami/ennemi sur le champ de bataille.
**BIFs** Banded Iron Formations.
The BIFs are sedimentary rocks.
*Earth Sciences; Environmental Sciences; Isotope Geology; Geochemistry.*
**BIFU** Banking Insurance and Finance Union (G.B.).
**BIG** Best In Group.
**BIG** Business Investment Game.
**bignum** (abbr.) big number.
*Computer Science.*
**BIH** Beth Israel Hospital (U.S.A.).
**BIH** Bureau International de l'Heure (France).
**BII** Bank International Indonesia.
*Indonesian Bank.*

**BiI** Bismuth Iodide.
*Inorganic Chemistry.*
**BIL** Banca Internazionale Lombarda (Italy).
*Italian Bank.*
**BILE** Balanced Inductor Logical Element.
**BIM** Bataillon d'Infanterie de Marine (France).
**BIM** Beginning-of-Information Marker.
BIM is also known as: Beginning-of-tape marker.
*Computer Technology.*
**bim.** Bimestrale; bimestre.
Italian abbreviation meaning: bi-monthly; a two-months period.
**BIM** British Institute of Management (G.B.).
**BIM** British Institute of Metals (G.B.).
**BIMA** British Interactive Media Association (G.B.).
**BIMA facility** Berkeley - Illinois - Maryland Association facility.
At Hat Creek, California, U.S.A.
*Astronomy.*
**BIMCO** Baltic and International Maritime COuncil.
**BIMDA** Bioserve-Instrumentation technology associates Materials Dispersion Analysis.
*Experiments.*
**bi-MNC** (of the) two Major NATO Commands [obsolete - now replaced by bi-SC].
(des) deux Grands Commandements de l'OTAN (ou GCO) [obsolète - remplacé par bi-SC].
**BIN**; **Bin** Banca di Interesse Nazionale (Italy).
Italian acronym meaning: Nation-Wide Bank.
**BIN** Bureau International de Normalisation.
French acronym of the: International Standardization Bureau.
**BINGO** Beacon INstrumented Guided Ordnance.
**BINOCULARS** Biogeochemical Nutrients Cycling in Large River Systems.
*European Community Project; Environmental Protection; Meteorology; Safety.*
**BIO** Bedford Institute of Oceanography (Canada).
**BIO** Biotechnology Industry Organization.
BIO is based in Washington D.C., U.S.A.
*Biotechnology.*
**$Bi_2O_3$** Bismite.
Bismite is also known as: Bismuth Ocher.
*Mineralogy.*
**$Bi_2O_3$** Bismuth Trioxide.
$Bi_2O_3$ is used mainly to colour ceramics.
*Inorganic Chemistry.*
**BIOC** basic identity object class.
classe d'objets "catégories élémentaires d'identité".
**biochim.** biochimica; biochimico.
Italian abbreviation meaning: biochemistry; biochemist.
**BiOCl** Bismuth Oxychloride.
BiOCl is used mainly in cosmetics.
*Inorganic Chemistry.*
**BIOCOMB** BIOfuel for COMBustion.
Preparation of biofuel for cumbustion - a demonstration project focused on the development of clean technologies for solid fuels.
*European Commission Fifth Framework Programme; Energy.*
**BIODEPTH** BIODiversity and Ecological Processes in Terrestrial Herbaceous ecosystems.
*European Community Project.*
**$Bi(OH)_3$** Bismuth Hydroxide.
*Inorganic Chemistry.*
**biol.** biologia; biologo.
Italian abbreviation meaning: biology; biologist.
**BIOMASS** Biological Investigations Of Marine Antarctic Systems and Stocks.
**BIO/MCD** Bedford Institute of Oceanography / Marine Chemistry Division (Canada).
**BIOS** Basic Input / Ouput System.
*Computer Programming.*
**BIOSIS/CAS** Biosciences Information Service/Chemical Abstracts Service.
**BIO/SPICE** Bioinformatics / SPICE.
For further details see under: **SPICE**.
**biosyn.** (abbr.) biosynthesis.
**BIP** Balanced In Plane.
**BIP** Bipropellant.
*Space Technology.*
**BIP** Bureau of International Programs.
Of the U.S. Department of Commerce.
**BIPM** Bureau International des Poids et Mesures.
French initialism of the: International Bureau of Weights and Measures. The BIPM is located in Sèvres, France.
**$BiPO_4$** Bismuth Phosphate.
Bismuth Phosphate is used to recover plutonium.
*Inorganic Chemistry.*
**BIPOP** Banca Popolare di Brescia (Italy).
BIPOP is a Co-operative limited Liability Company.
*Italian Bank.*
**BIPS** Billion Instructions Per Second.
**BIR** Biological Instrumentation and Resources.
BIR is a Division of the U.S. National Science Foundation.
**BIR** British Institute of Radiology (G.B.).
**BIRA** British Iron Research Association (G.B.).
*Foundry.*
**BIRD** Banque Internationale pour la Reconstruction et le Développement.

French acronym of the: International Bank for Reconstruction and Development.

**BIRN** Biomedical Informatics Research Network.
Mouse models of human neurological diseases.
*Neuroscience.*
For further details see under: **MBIRN**.

**BIRS** Banca Internazionale per la Ricostruzione e lo Sviluppo.
Italian acronym of the: International Bank for Reconstruction and Development.

**BIS** Bachelor of Interdisciplinary Studies.

**B.I.S.** Bank for International Settlements.

**BIS** Battlefield Illumination System.

**BIS** Biographical Inventory for Students.
*Psychology.*

**bis.** bisestile.
Italian abbreviation meaning: bissextile (leap-year).

**BIS** British Information Services; British Interplanetary Society (G.B.).

**BIS** Bureau Interafricain des Sols (et de l'Economie Rurale).

**BIS** Bureau of Inspection and Survey.

**BIS** Business Intelligence System.

**$BiS_3$** Bismuth Sulfide.
Bismuth Sulfide is used for the production of bismuth compounds.
*Inorganic Chemistry.*

**$Bi_2S_3$** Bismuthinite.
*Mineralogy.*

**bi-SC** (of the two) Strategic Commands (des deux) Commandements stratégiques.

**BISCLANT** Bay of Biscay Sub-Area [obsolete].
Sous-zone du golfe de Gascogne [obsolète].

**BISE** Balkans intelligence support element.
élément de soutien du renseignement dans les Balkans.

**$Bi_2Se_3$** Guanajuatite.
Guanajuatite is found in quartz.
*Mineralogy.*

**bisett.** bisettimanale.
Italian abbreviation meaning: bi-weekly.

**$Bi_4(SiO_4)_3$** Eulytite.
*Mineralogy.*

**$Bi_{12}SiO_{20}$** Sillénite.
*Mineralogy.*

**BISO** Board on Intercontinental Scientific Organizations (U.S.A.).

**BISRA** British Iron and Steel Research Association (G.B.).
*Metallurgy.*

**BISTI** Biomedical Information Science and Technology Initiative (U.S.A.).
BISTI is an interdisciplinary program to create academic centers of excellence in biocomputing.

**BIT** Bachelor of Industrial Technology.

**BIT** Boron-Injection Tank.
*Nuclear Energy.*

**BIT** Borsa Internazionale del Turismo (Italy).

**BIT** Bureau International du Travail (France).

**BITE** Built-In Test Equipment.

**$Bi_2Te_3$** Bismuth Telluride.
Bismuth Telluride is used mainly for semiconductors.
*Inorganic Chemistry.*

**$Bi_2Te_3$** Tellurobismuthite.
*Mineralogy.*

**bitn.** (abbr.) bitumen.
bitumen is a flammable substance occurring naturally or obtained pyrolitically.
*Geology; Materials.*

**BITS** Binary Intersystem Transmission Standards.

**BITS** Bureau International du Tourisme Social.

**$BiVO_4$** Pucherite.
*Mineralogy.*

**biz** abbreviation of the word: business.

**BJ** Bachelor of Journalism.

**BJ** Batch Job.
*Computer Programming.*

**BJ** Biceps Jerk.
*Medicine.*

**BJA** Bureau of Justice Assistance (U.S.A.).

**BJP** Bharatiya Janata Party (India).

**BJS** The airport code for Beijing, China.

**BJS** Bureau of Justice Statistics (U.S.A.).

**bk** (abbr.) bank.

**BK** Below Knee.
*Medicine.*

**Bk** The chemical symbol for Berkelium.
The name Berkelium derives from **Berkeley** (University of Califomia, U.S.A.) where it was produced.
*Chemistry.*

**bk** (abbr.) book.

**BK** Bosnia-Herzegovina.

**bk.** brook.
*Hydrology.*

**BK21** Brain Korea 21 (Korea).
*Graduate Training.*

**bkg.** (abbr.) banking.

**bkg.** (abbr.) bookkeeping.
Also: **bkpg.**

**bkgrd.** (abbr.) background.

**BKK** The airport code for Bangkok, Thailand.

**bkpg.** (abbr.) bookkeeping.
Also: **bkg.**

**bkpr.** (abbr.) bookkeeper.
**bkr** (abbr.) Broker.
*Business; Finance.*
**bks.** (abbr.) barracks.
**bks** (abbr.) books.
**BL**; **B.L.** Bachelor of Law.
**BL** Bachelor of Letters.
Also: **BLitt**.
**bl.** (abbr.) balance.
*Banking; Business; Commerce.*
**BL** Bank Larceny; Bank Lending.
**BL** Base Line; baseline.
*Cartography; Electronics; Engineering; Graphic Arts; Ordnance; Science.*
**BL** Belluno, Italy.
**BL**; **B/L** Bill of Lading.
*Business; Commerce.*
**BL** Bolivia.
**BL** Borsa di Lavoro.
**BL**; **B-L** Breadth Length.
**BL** Burkitt's Lymphoma.
Burkitt's lymphoma is a malignant lymphoma.
*Oncology.*
**BLA** Bond Length Alternation.
**BLADE** Basic Level Automation of Data through Electronics.
**blade** The above acronym was coined using the English word "blade".
*Archaeology; Aviation; Botany; Electrical Engineering; Mechanical Devices; Vertebrate Zoology.*
**B.Land.Arch.** Bachelor of Landscape Architecture.
**BLAST** Basic Local Alignment Search Tool.
*Biochemistry; Biophysics; Heuristic Search Algorithms; Medicine; Pathology; Public-Domain Web Tools.*
**BLC** Boundary-Layer Control.
*Aviation.*
**bldg.** (abbr.) building.
**BLEU** Belgium-Luxemburg Economic Union.
**BLEU** Blind Landing Experimental Unit.
*Aviation.*
**BLI**; **B.L.I.** Bachelor of Library Interpretation.
**BLINK** Backward LINKage.
**BLIPS** Benthic Layer Interactive Profiling System.
**BLISS** Balloon-borne Laser In-Situ Sensor (Spectrometer).
**BLISS** Basic Language for the Implementation of System Software; Basic Library Inquiry Subsystem.
**BLISS** Broadband LIghtwave Sources and Systems.
*European Community Project.*
**B. Litt** Bachelor of Letters.
Also: **BL**.
**B. Lit.** Bachelor of Literature.
Also: **Blt**.
**blk.** (abbr.) black.
*Chemistry; Optics; Telecommunications.*
**blk.** (abbr.) block.
*Computer Programming; Computer Technology; Forestry; Mathematics; Mining Engineering; Transportation Engineering.*
**blk.** (abbr.) bulk.
*Graphic Arts.*
**BLKFLT** Black Sea Fleet.
Flotte de la mer Noire.
**B.L.L.**; **BLL** Bachelor of Laws.
**BLL division** British Library Lending division (G.B.).
**BLM** Boundary-Layer Model.
**BLM** Bureau of Land Management.
**B-L membrane** Basal-Lateral membrane.
**BLMRCP** Bureau of Labor Management Relations and Cooperative Programs (U.S.A.).
**BLOB** Binary Large OBject.
The binary large object is essentially a large object stored in binary form.
*Computer Programming.*
**BLOS** beyond line of sight.
au-delà de la portée optique.
**BLOSSOM** Basic Liberation Of Smokers and Sympathizers Of Marijuana.
**BLOWS** British Library Of Wildlife Sound (G.B.).
**BLQ** The airport code for Bogotà, Colombia.
**bls.** (abbr.) bales; barrels.
**BLS** Board on Life Sciences (U.S.A.).
**BLS** Bureau of Labor Statistics (U.S.A.).
**BLSA** Baltimore Longitudinal Study of Aging (U.S.A.).
**BLSP** Brazilian Lithospheric Seismic Program.
*Geophysics; Geosciences; Terrestrial Magnetism.*
**blst.** (abbr.) ballast.
For further details see under: **BALL.**; **ball**.
**Blt** Bachelor of Literature.
Also: **B.Lit**.
**BLT** Battalion Landing Team.
*Military.*
**BLU** à bande latérale unique.
single sideband (SSB 2.).
**BLU** Basic Logic Unit.
**BLU** Bomb, Live Unit.
**BLU data** Basic Link Unit data.
**BLUE** Best Linear Unbiased Estimator.
*Statistics.*
**BM**; **B.M.** Bachelor of Medicine.
**B.M.** Banca Mondiale.

Italian initialism of the: World Bank.
**BM**; **bm** Barrels per Month.
Also: **bpm**.
**BM** Basal Metabolism.
Basal metabolism is actually the minimal energy expended to maintain the vital functions.
*Physiology.*
**BM** Basement Membrane.
BM is also known as: Basilemma.
*Histology.*
**BM** 1. battlefield maintenance.
1. maintenance sur le champ de bataille.
2. Burma [current official name: Myanmar].
2. Birmanie [nom officiel actuel: Myanmar].
**BM** Bear Market.
*Business; Finance.*
**BM** Bench Mark / Benchmark.
*Engineering; Finance; Geology; Science.*
**BM** Bill of Materials.
Also: **BOM**.
**bm**; **b.m.** board measure.
Board feet - To measure lumber.
*Engineering.*
**BM** Bond Maturity.
*Business; Economics; Finance.*
**BM** Bowel Movement.
*Medicine.*
**BM** British Museum (G.B.).
**BM** Bulletin Météorologique (France).
**BM** Business Machine.
**BM** Buyer's Market.
*Business; Commerce.*
**BMA** Banque des Marchés et d'Arbitrage (France).
**BMA**; **B,.M.A.** British Marine Aircraft (G.B.).
**B.M.A.** British Medical Association (G.B.).
**BMAED** Board on Manufacturing And Engineering Design (U.S.A.).
**BMBF** Bundesministerium für Bildung, Wissenschaft, Forschung und Technologie.
The BMBF is Germany's Ministry of Education and Research.
**BMCDB** Biochemistry and Molecular Biology and Cellular and Development Biology.
**BMC3I** battle management command, control, communications and intelligence.
commandement, contrôle, communication et renseignement pour la gestion tactique.
**BMCs** Bone Marrow Cells.
*Basic Medical Sciences; Cancer Chemotherapy; Clinical Transplantation Studies; Immunology; Molecular Biotherapy; Development.*
**BMD** Ballistic Missile Defense.
*Ordnance.*
**BMD** Bone Mineral Density.
*Osteoporosis.*
**BMDEAR** Ballistic Missile Defense Emergency Action Report.
**BMD-NEA Committee** Ballistic Missile Defense - Nuclear Effects and Threat Committee.
**BMDO** Ballistic Missile Defense Office.
The Pentagon's.
**BMDO** Ballistic Missile Defense Operations; Ballistic Missile Defense Organization.
**BMDOA** Ballistic Missile Defense Operations Activity.
**BMDS** Ballistic Missile Defense System.
**BMDSCOM** Ballistic Missile Defense Systems COMmand.
**BME**; **B.M.E.** Bachelor of Mechanical Engineering.
**BME**; **B.M.E.** Bachelor of Mining Engineering.
Also: **B.Min.E.**
**BME** Basement Membrane Extract.
**BMEC** Biomedical Engineering Center (U.S.A.).
**BMEd**; **B.M.Ed.** Bachelor of Music Education.
Also: **B.M.E.**
**BME net** Biomedical Engineering net.
The BME net was launched by the Whitaker Foundation in 1994. The site is managed by Purdue University (U.S.A.).
*Web Sites.*
**BMEP** Brake Mean-Effective Pressure.
The brake mean-effective pressure is actually the hypothetical average pressure on a piston during the power stroke.
*Mechanical Engineering.*
**BMetE**; **B.Met.E.** Bachelor of Metallurgical Engineering.
**BMet**; **B.Met.** Bachelor of Metallurgy.
**BMEWS** Ballistic Missile Early Warning System (U.S.).
**BMF** B-cell Maturation Factor.
*Immunology.*
**BMgtE**; **B.Mgt.E.** Bachelor of Management Engineering.
**BM HSCs** Bone Marrow Hematopoietic Stem Cells.
*Developmental Biology; Pathology.*
**BMI** Battelle Memorial Institute.
**BMI** Body Mass Index.
*Obesity.*
**BMinE**; **B.Min.E.** Bachelor of Mining Engineering.
Also: **B.M.E.**
**BMJ** British Medical Journal.
*Publication.*
**BMLET/R** Ballistic Missile Launch Equipment Technician-Repairman.

**BMLO** Ballistic Missile Logistics Office.
**BMMG** Ballistic Missile Management Group.
**BMN** brigade multinationale.
multinational brigade (MNB).
**B-MOD** Behavior MODification.
**BMP** Barbiturate 5'-Monophosphate.
*Biochemistry; Chemistry.*
**BMP** Biomass Protein.
**BMP** Bone Morphogenetic Protein.
For further details see under: **BMPs**.
**BMPC** Bone Marrow Plasmacytosis.
*Oncology.*
**BMPR** Bimonthly Progress Report.
**BMPs** Bone Morphogenetic Proteins.
BMPs are bone-forming proteins.
*Bone Research; Cell and Developmental Biology; Developmental Genetics; Genetics; Medicine; Orthopedic Surgery; Osteoporosis.*
**BMR** Ballistic Magnetoresistance.
*Condensed-matter Physics.*
**BMR** Basal Metabolic Rate.
*Medicine.*
**BMR** Brookhaven Medical Reactor.
**BMR** Bureau of Mineral Resources (Australia).
**BMRC** Bureau of Meteorology Research Center.
**BMS**; **B.M.S.** Bachelor of Marine Science.
**BMS**; **B.M.S.** Bachelor of Mechanical Science.
**BMS**; **B.M.S.** Bachelor of Medical Science.
**BMs** Basement Membranes.
For further details see under: **BM**.
**BMS** Basic Mapping Support.
*Psychology.*
**BMS** Board on Mathematical Sciences (U.S.A.).
**BM(S)** Boron Measurement (System).
*Nuclear Energy.*
**BMS** British Ministry of Supply; British Music Society (G.B.).
**BMS** 1. battlefield management system.
1. système de gestion du champ de bataille.
2. Bureau militaire de standardisation [remplacé par l'AON 1.].
2. Military Agency for Standardization (MAS) [replaced by NSA 2.].
**BMS sheets** Bright Mild Steel sheets.
*Metallurgy.*
**BMT**; **B.M.T.** Bachelor of Medical Technology.
**BMT** Bollettino Meteo Telefonico (Italy).
**BMT** Bone Marrow Transplant.
**BMTD** Ballistic Missile Terminal Defense.
**BMTs** Bone Marrow Transplants.
*Immunology; Medicine.*
**BMT study** Basic Motion-Time Study.
*Industrial Engineering.*
**BM vibrations** Basilar Membrane vibrations.
The BM supports the organ of Corti. Also known as: Spiral Organ.
*Anatomy; Audiology; Hearing Sciences; Communication Sciences; Communication Disorders; Frequency Tuning; Neuroscience; Physiology.*
**BMWS** Ballistic Missiles Weapon System.
**BN**; **B.N.** Bachelor of Nursing.
**B.N.**; **b.n.** banknote.
**Bn** (abbr.) battalion.
Also: **batt.**; **btn**.
**BN** Benevento, Italy.
**BN** Benin.
**BN** Bibliothèque Nationale.
French initialism meaning: National Library.
**bn** (abbr.) billion.
**BN** Boron Nitride.
Boron Nitride is used for many industrial purposes.
*Inorganic Chemistry.*
**BN** Bulimia Nervosa.
*Psychiatry.*
**BN** Bureau de Normalisation (France).
French initialism meaning: Standardization Office.
**BNA**; **B.N.A.** Bachelor of Navigation.
**BNA** Banca Nazionale dell'Agricoltura.
*Italian Bank.*
**BNA** Bangladesh News Agency.
**BNA** Basle Nomina Anatomica.
Nomenclature adopted in 1895.
**BNA** Beta-Naphthylamine.
*Organic Chemistry.*
**BNA** British North America (Act 1867).
**BNB** Banque Nationale de Belgique.
*Belgian Bank.*
**BNBC** British National Book Center (G.B.).
**BNC** Banca Nazionale delle Comunicazioni (Italy).
*Italian Bank.*
**BNC** Bi-National Commission.
**BNC** Bureau national de codification.
National Codification Bureau (NCB 1.).
**BNCDST** British National Committee on Data for Science and Technology.
**BNCF** Biblioteca Nazionale Centrale Firenze (Italy).
**BNCI** Banque Nationale pour le Commerce et l'Industrie (France).
*French Bank.*
**BNCT** Boron Neutron Capture Therapy.
*Cancer Treatment; Radiation Therapies.*
**bnd.** (abbr.) bond; bonded.
**BNDD** Bureau of Narcotics and Dangerous Drugs.

Formerly, Bureau of Narcotics and Bureau of Drug Abuse Control. Created in 1968, replaced by **DEA** in 1973.
*U.S. Department of Justice.*
**bndg.** (abbr.) bonding.
**BNEC**; **B.N.E.C.** British National Export Council (G.B.).
**BNEL** British National Engineering Laboratory (G.B.).
**BNF** Backus-Naur Form.
BNF is also known as: Backus Normal Form.
*Computer Programming.*
**BNF** besoin net de financement (des administrations publiques).
public sector borrowing requirement (PSBR).
**BNF** British Nuclear Forum; British Nuclear Fuels (G.B.).
**BNF** Bulgarian National Front.
**BNIF** British Nuclear Industry Forum (G.B.).
*Nuclear Energy.*
**BNIST** Bureau National de l'Information Scientifique et Technique (France).
**bnk** (abbr.) bank.
**bnkg.** (abbr.) banking.
**BNL** Banca Nazionale del Lavoro (Italy).
*Italian Bank.*
**BNL** Brookhaven National Laboratory (U.S.A.).
BNL is a multidisciplinary laboratory engaged in basic and applied research.
**BNL/AUI** Brookhaven National Laboratory / Associated Universities Inc. (U.S.A.).
**BNLI** Banque Nicolet Lafanechère et de l'Isère.
*French Bank.*
**BNLS** Botswana National Library Service.
**BNM** Before New Moon.
*Freemasonry.*
**BNM** Bureau National de Métrologie (France).
**BNO** Barrels of New Oil.
**BNO** Bladder Neck Obstruction; Bowels Not Opened.
*Medicine.*
**BN object** Becklin-Neugebauer object.
*Astronomy.*
**BNP** Banque Nationale de Paris (France).
*French Bank.*
**BNR** (abbr.) burner.
*Aviation; Chemical Engineering; Mechanical Engineering.*
**BNS** Biblical Numismatic Society.
**BNS** Biological Nuclear Solvent.
*Physiology.*
**BNS** Bombing-Navigation System.
**BNSC** British National Space Centre (G.B.).
**bnst** bed nucleus of the stria terminalis.
**BNU** Banco National Ultramarino (Portugal).
*Portuguese Bank.*
**BO** Back Order; Bad Order.
*Business; Commerce.*
**BO** 1. Belarus.
1. Bélarus.
2. boarding officer.
2. officier de visite.
3. break-off (position) [navy].
3. (point de) séparation [marine].
**BO** Body Odor.
*Medicine.*
**BO** Bologna, Italy.
**B.O.**; **b.o.** Branch Office.
**BO** Broker's Order; Broker's Option.
*Business; Commerce.*
**BO** Bulletin Officiel (France).
French initialism meaning: Official Gazette.
**BO** Buyer's Option; Buy Order.
**$B_2O_3$** Boric Oxide.
Boric Oxide is also known as: Boron Oxide.
*Inorganic Chemistry.*
**BOA** 1. basic ordering agreement.
1. accord-type de passation de commandes.
2. blanket ordering agreement.
2. accord-cadre de passation de commandes.
3. Board of Auditors.
3. Collège des commissaires aux comptes.
**BOA** Benzoic Acid.
BOA is also known as: Benzenecarboxylic Acid; Phenylformic Acid.
*Organic Chemistry.*
**BOA** Big Optical Array.
**BOA** Bølling - Allerød.
In the late glacial climate sequence the warm BOA was followed by the cold Younger Dryas.
*Biodiversity; Conservation Biology; Environmental Physics; Last Deglaciation.*
For further details see under: **YD**.
**BOA**; **B.O.A.** British Orthopaedic Association (G.B.).
**BOA** Butoxyacetamilide.
*Pharmacology.*
**boa** The above acronyms were coined accidentally using the Italian word "boa" which means: buoy (*Navigation*).
**BO approximation** Born-Oppenheimer approximation.
Also known as: Born-Oppenheimer method.
Named for the German physicist Max **Born** and the American physicist J. Robert **Oppenheimer**.

*Electronic States Calculations; Physical Chemistry; Quantum Mechanics.*
**BOAR** Board Of Action on Redetermination.
*U.S. Navy.*
**BOAT** Better Occupational Awareness Training.
**BOB** Beginning of Business.
**BOB** Bureau Of the Budget (U.S.A.).
**BOB** Business Opportunity Bank (U.S.A.).
Institute for New Enterprise Development.
**BOC** Bank Of China.
*Chinese Bank.*
**BOC** battalion operations centre.
centre d'opérations de bataillon (COB 1.).
**BOC** Bell Operating Company (U.S.A.).
**BOC** Breach Of Contract.
*Business; Economics; Finance.*
**BOCCA** Bureau of Coordination for Civil Aviation.
Bureau de coordination de l'aviation civile.
**bocca** The above acronym was coined using the Italian word "bocca" which means: mouth
*Acoustical Engineering; Geography; Mining Engineering.*
**BOCYF** Board On Children, Youth and Families (U.S.A.).
**BOD** Bacteriological Oxygen Demand.
*Water Pollution.*
**BOD** Bid Opening Date.
*Business; Commerce; Finance.*
**BOD** Biochemical Oxygen Demand.
BOD is also known as: Biological Oxygen Demand.
*Microbiology.*
**BOD** Board Of Directors.
**BODC** Born-Oppenheimer Diagonal Correction.
*Astronomy; Applied Physics; Physics; Theoretical Chemistry.*
**BODC** British Oceanographic Data Centre (G.B.).
**BODS** British Oceanographic Data Services (G.B.).
**BOE**; **B.O.E.** Bachelor of Oral English.
**BoE** Bank of England.
The BoE was founded in 1694 to act as the Government's banker and debt-manager. Since then its role has developed and evolved centred on the management of the nation's currency. The 1998 Bank of England Act made changes to the Bank's governing body. The Court of Directors is now made up of the Bank's Governor and 2 Deputy Governors, and 16 Non-Executive Directors.
**BOE** Barrels of Oil Equivalent.
**BOEC** Beginning Of Equilibrium Cycle.
*Nuclear Energy.*
**BOED** Barrels of Oil Equivalent per Day.
**BOE group** Board of Executors group (South Africa).
**B. of A.** Bank of America (U.S.A.).
*American Bank.*
**B. of E.** Board of Education.
**BOFS** Biogeochemical Ocean Flux Study (G.B.).
**BOG** Board Of Governors.
**BOHS** British Occupational Hygiene Society (G.B.).
**BOI** Bank Of Israel (Israel).
*Israeli Bank.*
**BOI** Board Of Investments.
The BOI is the principal government Agency of The Philippines.
**BOI** The airport code for Boise.
**BOIA** Bulletin, Office International des Instituts d'Archeologie et d'Histoire de l'Art.
*Publication.*
**BOIA** Bureau Of Indian Affairs.
Also known as: **BIA**.
Department of the Interior.
**boia** The above acronyms were coined accidentally using the Italian word "boia" which means: executioner.
**BOIS** Basis Of Issue System.
*Army.*
**BoJ** Bank of Japan.
**BOL**; **B.O.L.** Bachelor of Oriental Language.
**BOL** Basics of Language (Method).
**BOL** Beginning Of Life.
**BOL** Be On the Lookout.
*U.S. Police Terminology.*
**BOL** Biotechnology Orbital Laboratory.
**BOL.**; **bol.** (abbr.) Bolivar.
Also: **B** (Venezuela).
*Currencies.*
**BOL** Bolivia's International vehicle-registration letters.
**BOL** Bologna, Italy.
**BOLD effect** Blood Oxygen Level-Dependent effect.
*Biochemistry; Biophysics; Neuroscience.*
**boll.** (abbr.) bollato.
Italian abbreviation meaning: stamped.
**boll.** (abbr.) bolletta.
Italian abbreviation meaning: bill; note; receipt; voucher.
**boll.** (abbr.) bollettino.
Italian abbreviation meaning: bulletin; gazette.
**BOLT** Basic Occupational Language Training.
**BOLT** Basic Occupational Literacy Test.
**BOLT** Beam Of Light Transistor.
**BOLT** BOmb LASER Tracking.

**BOLT system** Bombay On-Line Trading system (India).
**BoM** Bank of Montreal (Canada).
**BOM** Beginning Of the Month.
*Business; Commerce; Finance.*
**BOM** Bill Of Materials.
Also: **BM**.
**BOM** The airport code for Bombay, India.
**BOM** Buying On Margin.
*Business; Commerce.*
**BOMA** Building Owners Management Association.
**BOMB** (abbr.) Bombardment.
**BOMB** British Overseas Media Bureau.
**BOMBREP** bombing report.
1a. compte rendu de bombardement.
1b. rapport de mission de bombardement.
**BOMEX** Barbados Oceanographic and Meteorological EXperiment.
**BONA** Beta-Oxynaphthoic Acid.
*Organic Chemistry.*
**BONDINOX** In-service qualification of adhesive bonded stainless steel components.
*European Community Research Project.*
**BONUS reactor** BOiling NUclear Superheat reactor.
**BONY** Bank Of New York (U.S.A.).
**BOO** Bond-Orientational Order.
**BOO arrangements** Build-Own-Operate arrangements.
*Power Generation Equipment.*
**BOOK** Bibliographic On-Line Organized Knowledge.
*Psychology.*
**BOOK** Built-in Orderly Organized Knowledge.
*Learning Device.*
**BOONE** BOOster Neutrino Experiment.
*Cosmology; Physics.*
**BOP** Balance Of Payments.
**BOP** Bulletin Officiel des Prix (France).
**B Opt** Bachelor of Optometry.
**BOQ** Bachelor Officers' Quarters.
*Army.*
**BOQ** Beginning Of Quarter.
**bor.** (abbr.) borough.
**BOR** Bureau Of Reclamation.
**BORAM** Block-Oriented Random-Access Memory.
**BORAX** Boiling Reactor Experiments.
*Nuclear Energy.*
**BORE** Beryllium Oxide Reactor Experiment.
*Nuclear Energy.*
**BOREAS** BOReal Ecosystem - Atmosphere Study.
**BORIS** Box-Office Reservation and Information Service.
**BORN FREE** Built Options, Renew Norms, Free Roles through Educational Equity (U.S.A.).
**BORSCHT** Battery feed; Overvoltage protection, Ringing, Supervision, Coding, Hybrid, and Testing.
BORSCHT includes the functions and components used in telecommunications.
*Telecommunications.*
**BOS** The airport code for Boston (U.S.A.).
**BOSC** base operating support cost.
dépense liée au soutien du fonctionnement des bases.
**BOSS** Ballistic Offensive Suppression System (U.S.A.).
*Ordnance.*
**BOSS** Basic Operating Software System.
**BOSS** Book Of The Season Scheme (G.B.).
**BOSS** Bride Of Sevenless.
*Biology; Medicine.*
**BOSS** Broad Ocean Scoring System.
*Missiles.*
**BOSS** Business Operational Support System (Sweden).
Internet-enabled SAS data warehouse application.
**boss** The above acronyms were coined using the English word "boss".
*Biology; Design Engineering; Geology; Graphic Arts; Medicine; Naval Architecture.*
**BOSTID** Board On Science and Technology for International Development.
The BOSTID is based in Washington D.C., U.S.A.
**BOT**; **B.O.T.** Bachelor of Occupational Therapy.
**BOT** Balance Of Trade; Board Of Trade.
**BOT** Beginning Of Tape.
*Data Processing.*
**BOT** Board Of Trustees.
**bot.** (abbr.) botanical; botanist; botany.
**bot.** (abbr.) bottle; bottom; bought.
**BOT** Build, Operate, Transfer.
*Project Financing.*
**BOT** Buoni Ordinari del Tesoro.
Italian acronym meaning: Treasury Bills; Treasury Certificates.
*Finance; Commerce.*
**BOTA** Board On Testing and Assessment (U.S.A.).
**BOT arrangements** Build-Operate-Transfer arrangements.
*Power Generation Equipment.*
**BOTB** British Overseas Trade Board.
**BOT marker** Beginning-Of-Tape marker.
*Computer Programming.*
**Boul.** (abbr.) Boulevard.
Also: **bd**.

**BOY** Beginning Of Year.
**BP**; **B.P.** Bachelor of Pharmacy.
Also: **B.Pharm**.
**BP**; **B.P.** Bachelor of Philosophy.
Also: **B.Ph.**; **B.Phil**.
**BP** Back Pressure.
*Engineering; Mechanical Engineering.*
**BP** Banca Passadore.
*Italian Bank.*
**BP** Band Printer.
*Computer Technology.*
**bp** base pair.
*Genetics.*
**BP** Base Plate.
*Building Engineering; Electronics.*
**bp** basic pairs.
**BP** Basic Protein; Binding Protein.
**BP** Batch Processing.
Batch processing is also known as: batching.
*Computer Programming.*
**B.P.** Before the Present.
**BP** Between Perpendiculars (length).
*Shipbuilding.*
**B/P** Bills Payable.
**BP** Biodegradable Polymer.
For further details see under: **BPs**.
**Bp** (abbr.) Bishop.
**BP**; **B.P.** Blood Pressure.
The term blood pressure refers to the pressure exerted by the blood on the walls of the arteries.
*Physiology.*
**B.P.**; **b.p.** Blueprint.
*Graphic Arts.*
**BP** Boiler Plate / boilerplate.
*Geology; Hydrology.*
In *Metallurgy*, boilerplate is also known as: Boiler Steel.
**bp**; **BP**; **b.p.** Boiling point.
Essentially, the boiling point is the temperature at which a liquid boils.
*Physical Chemistry.*
**B.P.** Boîte Postale.
French initialism meaning: P.O. Box.
**BP** Book Profit.
**BP** Breach of Promise.
**BP** Brevet Professionnel (France).
**BP** British Pharmacopoeia.
**BP** British Pound (G.B.).
*Currencies.*
**BP** Solomon Islands.
**BPA**; **B.P.A.** Bachelor of Professional Arts.
**BPA** Banca Popolare di Abbiategrasso (Italy).
*Italian Bank.*
**BPA** Banco Português do Atlântico.
BPA was acquired in 1995 by the Banco Comercial Português thus becoming Portugal's biggest private-sector financial group.
*Portuguese Bank.*
For further detail see under: **BCP** (Banco Comercial Português).
**BPA** battlefield psychological activities.
activités psychologiques du champ de bataille.
**BPA** Board on Physics and Astronomy (U.S.A.).
**BPA** Bonneville Power Administration.
**BPA** British Paediatric Association; British Parachute Association (G.B.).
**BPAG1** Bullous Pemphigoid Antigen.
BPAG1 mediates linkage between keratin filaments and the hemidesmosomal $\alpha 6\beta 4$ integrins.
*Anatomy; Developmental Biology; Plastic and Reconstructive Surgery; Reepithelialization.*
**BPAM** Banca Popolare Abruzzese Marchigiana (Italy).
*Italian Bank.*
**BPAM** Basic Partitioned Access Method.
**BPAS** British Pregnancy Advisory Service (G.B.).
**BPB-CV** Banca Popolare di Bergamo - Credito Varesino.
Founded in 1869, the BPB-CV heads now a single group with BPCI and BPLV and is listed on the Milan Stock Exchange since 1992.
*Asset Management; Insurance; Leasing; Investment Banking; e-banking; e-commerce; Virtual Banking.*
For further details see under: **BPCI** and **BPLV**.
**BPC** Bonded-Phase Chromatography.
*Analytical Chemistry.*
**BPC** British Productivity Council (G.B.).
**BPCD** Barrels Per Calendar Day.
**BPCF** British Precast Concrete Federation (G.B.).
*Buildings.*
**BPCI** Banca Popolare Commercio e Industria.
For further details see under: **BPB**.
**BPD**; **bpd** Barrels Per Day.
Also: **BD**.
*Chemical Engineering.*
**BPDG** Biochemical Pharmacology Discussion Group.
Of the New York Academy of Sciences.
**BPE**; **B.P.E.** Bachelor of Physical Education.
**B-PER** Bacterial Protein Extraction Reagent.
**BPetE**; **B.P.E.** Bachelor of Petroleum Engineering.
**B.Ph.** Bachelor of Philosophy.
Also: **B.P.**; **B.Phil**.
**BPH**; **B.P.H.** Bachelor of Public Health.
**BPH** Bank Przemyslowo-Handlowy SA.

*Polish Bank.*
**BPH**; **bph** Barrels Per Hour.
**BPH** Benign Prostatic Hypertrophy.
**B.Pharm.** Bachelor of Pharmacy.
Also: **B.P.**
**B.Phil.** Bachelor of Philosophy.
Also: **B.P.**; **B.Ph.**
**BPI** Banca Popolare di Intra (Italy).
*Italian Bank.*
**BPI** Banco Português de Investimento.
*Portuguese Bank.*
**BPI** Bank of The Philippine Islands.
**BPI**; **bpi** Bits per Inch.
*Computer Technology.*
**BPI** Bureau of Public Inquiries.
**BPI** Buying Power Index.
**BPI**; **bpi** bytes per inch.
**BPICA** Bureau Permanent International des Constructeurs d'Automobiles (France).
**BPIF** British Printing Industries Federation (G.B.).
**BPI protein** Bactericidal Permeability-Increasing protein.
**BPL** Banca Provinciale Lombarda.
*Italian Bank.*
**BPL** basic priority list.
liste des priorités essentielles.
**bpl.** (abbr.) birthplace.
**BPLV** Banca Popolare di Luino e di Varese.
For further details see under: **BPB**.
**BPM** Banca Popolare Molise (Italy).
*Italian Bank.*
**bpm** barrels per month.
Also: **bm.**; **BM**.
**BPM** Business Process Management (or Outsourcing).
**BPMC** o-sec-Butylphenyl-N-Methyl Carbamate.
**BPMG** BICES Project Management Group.
groupe de gestion du projet BICES.
**BPN** Banca Popolare di Novara (Italy).
*Italian Bank.*
**BPNL** Battelle Pacific Northwest Laboratories.
**BPO** Benzoyl Peroxide.
Benzoyl Peroxide is used for many purposes such as for bleaching or as an acne treatment.
*Organic Chemistry.*
**BPO** Butyl Peroxide.
**BPO/AGS** Bureau du Programme provisoire de la capacité de surveillance terrestre de l'Alliance [obsolète - voir AGS/SSC].
Allied Ground Surveillance Capability Provisional Project Office (AGS/PPO) [obsolete - see AGS/SSC].
**BPQ** Budgetary and Planning Quotations.
**BPR** Bottom Pressure Recorder.
**BPR** bureau de première responsabilité.
office of primary responsibility (OPR).
**Bpr** Business process re-engineering.
*Management Techniques.*
**BPRF** Bulletproof.
In *Computer Programming* BPRF is also known as: Bombproof.
*Ordnance* - Capable of withstanding the impact of bullets.
**BPS** Banca Popolare di Sondrio (Italy).
Established on the 4th March 1871.
*Italian Bank.*
**BPS** Basic Programming Support.
**BPS** Binary Program Space.
**BPs** Biodegradable Polymers.
*Biocatalysis of Macromolecules; Bioprocessing of Macromolecules.*
**bps** bits per second.
**BPS** Bosnian Patriotic Party.
**bpsa** best power spark advance.
**BPSA** Business Products Standards Association.
**BPSK** Binary Phase-Shift Keying.
**BPT** The airport code for Beaumont-Port Arthur, Texas, U.S.A.
**BPTI** Bovine Pancreatic Trypsin Inhibitor.
*Biochemistry; Molecular Biophysics.*
**BPV** Banca Popolare di Verona (Italy).
*Italian Bank.*
**BPV** Bovine Papilloma Virus.
*Virology.*
**BPVD** Bourses Pour Candidats en provenance des Pays en Voie de Développement (France).
**BPX** Burning Plasma Experiment.
*Fusion Reactors.*
**BQ** Basis Quote.
*Business; Finance.*
**Bq** Becquerel.
*Nucleonics.*
**BQ** Bloc Québecois (Canada).
**bque.** (abbr.) banque.
French abbreviation meaning: bank.
Also: **banq**.
**bR** bacteriorhodospin.
bR is a protein found in certain bacteria membranes.
*Biophysics; Microbiology.*
**BR**; **br** Bank Rate.
**BR** Bank Robbery.
**BR** Baron.
Also: **B**.
**BR** Base Register.
*Computers.*

**BR** Bed Rest.
*Medicine.*
**BR** Belgian Reactor.
**BR** Bill of Rights.
**BR**; **b/r** Bills Receivable.
**BR** Biological Research.
**BR** Bond Rating.
**BR** Borrowed Reserves.
*Banking.*
**br.** (abbr.) branch.
**br.** (abbr.) brass.
Also: **brs.**
*Geology; Metallurgy.*
**BR** Brazil.
**BR** (abbr.) Breakdown.
*Chemistry; Electricity; Metallurgy; Materials Science; Psychology.*
In *Materials Science* breakdown is also known as: Dielectric Breakdown.
In *Psychology* it is also known as: Nervous Breakdown.
**BR** Bright Rock.
*Rock Types.*
For further details see under: **IMP** (Imager for Mars Pathfinder).
**BR** Brindisi, Italy.
**Br.** (abbr.) British.
**BR** British Railways.
**Br** The chemical symbol for Bromine.
Bromine is a chemical element, having the atomic number 35, an atomic weight of 79.904, and a melting point of -7.2°C. It is used mainly in water purification and photography. The word bromine derives from the Greek term "foul odor".
*Chemistry; Symbols.*
**Br** Bromocriptine.
Bromocriptine is used mainly in the treatment of Parkinson's disease.
*Pharmacology.*
**BR** Bronchitis.
*Medicine* - The term bronchitis refers to an inflammation of the bronchi.
**BRA** Bank Restructuring Agency (Indonesia).
**BRA** β-resorcylic acid.
$(OH)_2C_6H_3COOH$. β-resorcylic acid is used mainly in pharmaceuticals, and in the manufacture of chemicals.
*Organic Chemistry.*
**BRA** Bougainville Revolutionary Army.
**BRAC** Britannica Reading Achievement Center.
**BRAD** British Rate And Data.
**BRAD** Bureau of Research And Development.
**BRAID** Bidirectional Referenced Array Internally Derived.
**BRAID** Buying, Receiving, and Accounts payable Integrated Data.
**BRAIN** Basic Research in Aircraft Interior Noise.
*European Community Project.*
**BRAN** BReaking Action Nil.
*Aviation.*
**BRANDS** BRight Alphanumeric Display System.
**BRASS** broadcast and ship-shore (system).
1a. (système de) radiodiffusion et liaison navire-terre.
1b. TRAM et liaison N/T [FR].
**BRAT** Bi-drive Recreational All-terrain Transporter.
**BRATS** Bottom Refraction Acoustic Telemetry System.
**BRAVO** Best Range of Aging Verified Oscillator.
**bravo** The above acronym was coined accidentally using the Italian word "bravo" which means: good; clever; skilful.
**BRB**; **brb** be right back.
**BRC** Biomedical Research Centre.
**BRC** British Retailing Consortium (G.B.).
**BRC** Business Reply Card.
**BRC** (Medtronic's) Bakken Research Centre (The Netherlands).
BRC is located in Maastricht, The Netherlands. Medtronic is the world's largest manufacturer of implantable biomedical devices.
**BRCC** Biodiversity Research Center of the Californias (U.S.A.).
**brch.** (abbr.) branch.
*Botany; Computer Programming; Electricity; Electronics; Hydrology; Mathematics.*
**$BrCH_2COCH_3$** Bromoacetone.
Bromoacetone is used mainly as a tear gas.
*Organic Chemistry.*
**$BrCH_2COOH$** Bromoacetic Acid.
Bromoacetic Acid is used in organic synthesis.
*Organic Chemistry.*
**$Br_3C_6H_3OH$** Bromol.
Bromol is also known as: Tribromophenol.
*Organic Chemistry.*
**BrCl** Bromine Monochloride.
*Inorganic Chemistry.*
**BRCS**; **B.R.C.S.** British Red Cross Society (G.B.).
**BRD** Biological Resources Division.
U.S. Geological Survey's (formerly The National Biological Survey).
*Ecological Surveys; Marine Ecology.*
**BRD-SMB** Romanian Bank for Development - Bucharest Branch.
**BrdU** 5-Bromo-2'-Deoxyuridine.

**BRE** Bachelor of Religious Education.
**BRE** Bank Rozwojn Eksportu SA (Poland).
*Polish Bank.*
**BRE** Bureau de Rapprochement des Enterprises - E.C.
French initialism of the: Office for Cooperation among Enterprises.
**BREC**; **b.rec.** bills receivable.
**BREC** Bills RECoverable.
**BRED** Banque Régionale d'Escompte et de Dépôts (France).
*French Bank.*
**BREMA** British Radio Equipment Manufacturers' Association (G.B.).
**BRER** Board on Radiation Effects Research (U.S.A.).
**brev.** (abbr.) brevetto.
Italian abbreviation meaning: patent.
**$BrF_3$** Bromine Trifluoride.
*Chemistry.*
**$BrF_5$** Bromine Pentafluoride.
*Inorganic Chemistry.*
**brg.** (abbr.) bearing.
*Building Engineering; Mechanical Engineering.*
**BRGGM** Bureau de Recherches Géologiques, Géophysiques et Minières (France).
**BRGM** Bureau de Recherches Géologiques et Minières (France).
**BRHE** Basic Research and Higher Education (Russian Federation).
**B.R.I.** Banca dei Regolamenti Internazionali.
Italian acronym of the: Bank for International Settlements.
**BRI** Banque des Règlements Internationaux.
French acronym of the: Bank for International Settlements.
**BRI** BioResearch Ireland.
BRI is EI's Programme in Advanced Technology for Biotechnology.
For further details see under: **EI**.
**BRIC** Biotech Research and Innovation Centre (Copenhagen).
**BRIC** British Institute of International and Comparative Law (G.B.).
**BRICS** Black Resources Information Coordinating Services.
**Brit.** Britain; British.
**BRITE** Basic Research in Industrial Technologies in Europe.
**Brit. J. of Gen. Prac.** British Journal of General Practice.
*Publication.*
**brkt.** (abbr.) bracket.
*Architecture; Building Engineering; Ordnance; Medicine.*
In *orthodontics*, bracket is also known as: orthodontic attachment; orthodontic bracket.
**brl.** barrel.
For further details see under: **bar.**
**BRL** Bethesda Research Laboratories (U.S.A.).
**BRM** Biological Response Modifier.
The biological response modifier is actually a protein that modifies biological response.
*Immunology.*
**BRMA** Bureau de Recherches Minières Algériennes.
**BRMC** Business Research Management Center.
**BRMP** Biological Response Modifiers Program.
*Cancer Treatment.*
**BRN** Bahrain's International Vehicle registration letters.
**$BrN_3$** Bromine Azide.
Bromine Azide is used in numerous explosive devices.
*Inorganic Chemistry.*
**brok.** (abbr.) broker; brokerage.
**Bros.** (abbr.) Brothers.
**bross.** brossura.
Italian abbreviation meaning: paper-back binding.
**brot.** (abbr.) brought.
Also: **brt**; **bt**.
**brot.fwd.** (abbr.) brought forward.
Also: **Brt.Fwd**.
**BRP** Bacterial Release Protein.
**BRP** Bureau de Recherches des Pétroles (France).
**BRR** Basic Radial Rating (of a bearing).
*Mechanical Engineering.*
**BRS** Bibliographic Retrieval Services.
**BRS** Bilancio Rettificativo e Suppletivo.
*Business; Economics; Finance.*
**brs.** (abbr.) brass.
For further details see under: **br**.
*Metallurgy.*
**BRS** British Road Services (G.B.).
**BRS** Business Radio Service.
*Data Communications.*
**BRSA** Banking Regulation and Supervision Agency.
**brt** (abbr.) brought.
Also: **bt.**; **brot**.
**Brt.Fwd.** Brought Forward.
Also: **brot.fwd.**
*Business; Commerce.*
**B Ru E** Bachelor of Rural Engineering.
**BRWM** Board on Radioactive Waste Management (U.S.A.).

**Brz.** (abbr.) bronzo.
Italian abbreviation meaning: bronze.
*Metallurgy.*
**BRZG** (abbr.) Brazing.
*Materials Science.*
**BS**; **B.S.** Bachelor of Science.
**BS**; **B.S.** Bachelor of Surgery.
**BS** Backspace.
*Computer Technology; Graphic Arts.*
**BS** Back Spread.
*Business; Finance.*
**BS** (abbr.) Bahamas.
**BS** Balance Sheet.
**bs** (abbr.) battleship.
*Naval Architecture.*
**BS** Beam Splitter.
*Optics.*
**BS** Beam Storage.
*Computer Technology.*
**BS**; **B.S.**; **b.s.** Bill of Sale.
**BS** Bill of Store.
**BS** Blood Sugar.
The glucose in the blood.
*Biochemistry; Medicine.*
**BS** Bloom Syndrome.
BS is characterized by immunodeficiency, male infertility, small stature, chromosome breakage, predisposition to cancers.
*Biochemistry; Molecular Genetics; Medicine.*
**BS** Bottom Settlings.
Bottom settlings are also known as: bottoms or basic sediment and water.
*Petroleum Engineering.*
**BS** Bowel Sounds; Breath Sounds.
*Medicine.*
**BS** Bright Soil.
*Soil Types.*
For further details see under: **IMP**.
**BS** British Shipbuilders.
**BS**; **B.S.** British Standard.
**BS** Building Society.
**b/s** bytes per second.
**BSA** Bachelor of Science in Agriculture.
Also: **BSAg**.
**BSA** Bank Secrecy Act.
**BSA** Body Surface Area.
**BSA** Bovine Serum, Albumin.
**BSA** brigade support area.
zone de soutien de brigade.
**BSA** Building Societies Association.
**BSA** Business Software Alliance.
**BSAA**; **B.S.A.A.** Bachelor of Science in Applied Arts.
**BSAC** Biotechnology Science Advisory Committee (U.S.A.).
**BSAE**; **B.S.A.E.** Bachelor of Science in Aeronautical Engineering.
**BSAE**; **B.S.A.E.** Bachelor of Science in Agricultural Engineering.
**BSAE**; **B.S.A.E.** Bachelor of Science in Architectural Engineering.
**BSAF** Bids Solicited As Follows.
*Business; Finance.*
**BSAg.**; **B.S.Ag.** Bachelor of Science in Agriculture.
Also: **BSA**.
**BS&W** Basic Sediment and Water.
Also: **BSW**.
*Petroleum Engineering.*
For further details see under: **BS**.
**BSArch.**; **B.S.Arch.** Bachelor of Science in Architecture.
**BSB**; **B.S.B.** Bachelor of Science in Business.
**BSB** British Standard Beam.
**BSBA** British Standard Bulb Angle.
**BSBP** British Standard Bulb Plate.
**Bsc**; **B.Sc.** Bachelor of Science.
**BSC** Bibliographical Society of Canada.
**BSC** Biological Sciences Curriculum.
**BSC** British Shippers' Council; British Standard Channel (G.B.).
**BSCCO** Bismuth, Strontium, Calcium, Copper, and Oxygen.
BSCCO is a ceramic compound used for conventional high-temperature superconductivity wires.
*Superconducting Wires; Superconducting Technology Programs.*
**BSCh**; **B.S.Ch.** Bachelor of Science in Chemistry.
**BSCH** Banco Santander Central Hispano.
*Spanish Bank.*
**BSCs** Business Service Centers (U.S.A.).
**BSCW** Basic Support for Cooperative Work.
**BSD** Barrels per Stream Day.
*Chemical Engineering.*
**BSD** Berkeley Software Distribution (U.S.A.).
**BSD**; **bsd** Berkeley System Distribution (U.S.A.).
**BSD** Board on Sustainable Development (U.S.A.).
**BSDC** Binary Symmetric Dependent Channel.
*Data Communications.*
**BSE**; **B.S.E.** Bachelor of Science in Education.
Also: **BSEd**.
**BSE** Bombay Stock Exchange (India).
The BSE is the oldest bourse in Asia.
**BSE** Boston Stock Exchange (U.S.A.).
**BSE** Bovine Spongiform Encephalopathy.
The bovine spongiform encephalopathy is also known as: mad cow disease.

**BSEA** British Standard Equal Angle.
**BSEc.**; **B.S.Ec.** Bachelor of Science in Economics.
Also: **BSEcon.**; **B.S.Econ.**
**BSEd.** Bachelor of Science in Education.
Also: **BSE**.
**BSEE**; **B.S.E.E.** Bachelor of Science in Elementary Education.
**BSE images** Backscattered Electron images.
**BSF** Binational Science Foundation (Jerusalem, Israel).
The United States - Israel BSF was established by the two governments with a view to promote cooperation in scientific research.
**BSF** budget submission figure.
1a. montant limite du projet de budget (MLPB).
1b. montant de la dotation budgétaire.
**BSF** busulfan.
For further details see under: **BUS**.
**bsfc** brake specific fuel consumption.
**BS FOCI** Bering Sea FOCI.
For further details see under: **FOCI**.
**BSFS**; **B.S.F.S.** Bachelor of Science in Foreign Service.
**BSFor.**; **B.S.For.** Bachelor of Science in Forestry.
**BSFT**; **B.S.F.T.** Bachelor of Science in Fuel Technology.
**BSF thread** British Standard Fine thread.
**BSG** Blue Supergiant.
*Astrophysics; Communications Research; Geophysics.*
**BSGE**; **B.S.G.E.** Bachelor of Science in General Engineering.
**Bsgsp** Banco S. Giminiano e S. Prospero SpA (Italy).
*Italian Bank.*
**BSH** Federal Maritime and Hydrographic Agency (Germany).
**bsh.** bushel; bushels.
**BSHA**; **B.S.H.A.** Bachelor of Science in Hospital Administration.
**BSI** Banca della Svizzera Italiana.
BSI was acquired by the Swiss Bank Corporation in 1991. It is its Lugano-based private banking subsidiary.
**Bsi** Biogenic Silica.
**BSI** Brain Science Institute.
RIKEN (Japan).
**BSI** British Standards Institution (G.B.).
**BSkyB** British Sky Broadcasting (G.B.).
**BSL**; **B.S.L.** Bachelor of Sacred Literature.
**BSL**; **B.S.L.** Bachelor of Science in Languages.
**BSL**; **B.S.L.** Bachelor of Science in Law.
**BSL**; **B.S.L.** Bachelor of Science in Linguistics.
**BsL**; **Bs/L** Bills of Lading.
*Business; Commerce.*
**BSL** Bit Serial Link.
**BSL4** Biosafety Level 4.
**BSM** Buffer-Stock Money.
*Economics.*
**bsmith.** (abbr.) blacksmith.
**bsmt.** (abbr.) basement.
*Building Engineering; Geology.*
**BSN** Bachelor of Science in Nursing.
**BSN** Brevet Sportif National (France).
**BSN** Brigade Spéciale de Nuit (France).
**BSO** Biosafety Officer.
**BSO**; **bso** Blue Stellar Object.
**BSOT**; **B.S.O.T.** Bachelor of Science in Occupational Therapy.
**BSP** Behaviour Support Plan (G.B.).
*School Improvement.*
**BSP** Business Systems Planning.
**BSPA**; **B.S.P.A.** Bachelor of Science in Public Administration.
**BSPT**; **B.S.P.T.** Bachelor of Science in Physical Therapy.
Also: **B.S.Ph.Th**.
**BSP test** Bromosulphalein test.
*Medicine.*
**BSRec.**; **B.S.Rec.** Bachelor of Science in Recreation.
**BSRet.**; **B.S.Ret.** Bachelor of Science in Retailing.
**BSRN** Baseline Surface Radiation Network.
Of the World Meteorological Organization - U.N.
**BSRT**; **B.S.R.T.** Bachelor of Science in Radiological Technology.
**BSS** Balanced Salt Solution.
*Chemistry.*
**BSS** Block Starting with Symbol.
*Computer Science.*
**BSS** Broadband Satellite Services.
*Satellite Systems.*
**BSSA**; **B.S.S.A.** Bachelor of Science in Secretarial Administration.
**b.ssa** baronessa.
Italian abbreviation meaning: baroness.
Also: **Ba.sa**.
**BSSE** Basis Set Superposition Error.
**BSSRS** British Society for Social Responsibility in Science (G.B.).
**BSSRS** Bureau of Safety and Supply Radio Service.
*Data Communications.*
**BSSS**; **B.S.S.S.** Bachelor of Science in Secretarial Studies.
**BST** Barium Strontium Titanate.
BST is a ceramic compound used by researchers to

replace silicon dioxide, to develop the next generation of DRAMs.
For further details see under: **DRAMs**.
**BST** Beam-Switching Tube.
The BST is actually a multiposition electronic switch.
**B/St** Bill of Sight.
**BST** Blood Serological Test.
**BST** British Standard Tee; British Summer Time.
**BSTDB** Black Sea Trade and Development Bank (Greece).
The BSTDB is based in the southern Greek port of Thessaloniki. Launched in 1998 as the financial arm of the Istambul-based Black Sea Economic Cooperation Organization. Its goals are to finance trade, infrastructure projects and growing businesses from the Balkans to the Caucasus.
**BSTransp.**; **B.S.Transp.** Bachelor of Science in Transportation.
**BSUA** British Standard Unequal Angle.
**BSV** Bark Split Virus.
*Plant Pathology.*
**BSW** Bottom Sediment and Water.
Also: **BS&W**.
For further details see under: **BS**.
*Petroleum Engineering.*
**BSW thread** British Standard Whitworth thread.
Named for the British mechanical engineer Sir Joseph **Whitworth**.
**BSX** Bermuda Stock Exchange (Bermuda).
**BT**; **B.T.** Bachelor of Theology.
Also: **B.Th**.
**Bt** Bacillus thuringiensis.
*Agrobiotechnology; Bacterial Toxins; Microbiology.*
**BT** Bathythermograph.
The BT is used to record water temperature with respect to ocean depth.
*Oceanography.*
**BT** Bedtime.
*Medicine.*
**bt** (abbr.) bent; between.
**b.t.** berth terms.
**BT** Binding Time.
*Computer Programming.*
**BT** Bleeding Time.
Bleeding time is the recording of the time required for the blood to stop flowing after the skin has been pricked for the purpose.
*Physiology.*
**BT** Boat-Tail / boattail.
*Design Engineering.*
**BT** Body Temperature.
**bt.** (abbr.) bought.
**bt.** (abbr.) brought.
Also: **brt.**; **brot**.
**BT** Brain Tumor.
*Medicine.*
**BT** Buoni del Tesoro (Italy).
Italian initialism meaning: Treasury Bonds; Treasury Bills.
**BTB** Buoni del Tesoro Biennali.
Italian initialism meaning: Biennial Treasury Bonds.
**BTC** Bacterial Test Chamber.
**BTC** Bankers Trust Company.
**BTC** Batch Terminal Controller.
**BTC**; **btc** before top center.
**BTC** Bioprocessing Technology Center.
National University of Singapore.
**BTC**; **B.T.C.** British Transport Commission (G.B.).
**BTCh.**; **B.T.Ch.** Bachelor of Textile Chemistry.
**BTDA** Benzophenone Tetracarboxylic Dianhydride.
**BTDC** Before Top Dead Center.
**BTE**; **B.T.E.** Bachelor of Textile Engineering.
**BTE** Buoni del Tesoro in ECU.
Italian initialism meaning: ECU Treasury Bonds.
**BTE** Bureau des Temps Elémentaires (France).
**BTF** Bulk Transfer Facility.
**BTH** (abbr.) berth.
*Naval Architecture; Navigation.*
**BTI** Boyce-Thompson Institute (U.S.A.).
A not-for-profit organization located at the Cornell University Campus.
*Molecular plant-microbe interactions.*
**BTK**, **Btk** Bruton's Tyrosine Kinase.
**BTL** Bell Telephone Laboratories (U.S.A.).
**BTM** Basic Transport Mechanism.
**BTM** The Bank of Tokyo - Mitsubishi Ltd.
*Japanese Bank.*
**BTN** Brussels Tariff Nomenclature.
**BTNS** Basic Terminal Network Support.
**BTO** Bombing Through Overcast.
Bombing through overcast is also known as: blind bombing.
*Military Science.*
**BTO** Buoni del Tesoro Ordinari.
Italian initialism meaning: Ordinary Treasury Bonds /Bills.
**BtoBtoC** Business to Business to Consumer.
Also: **B2B2C**.
*e-Commerce.*
**BTP** Banque du Bâtiment et des Travaux Publics (France).
*French Bank.*
**BTP** Batch Transfer Program.

**BTP** Buoni del Tesoro Poliennali.
Italian initialism meaning: Long-term Treasury Bonds.
**BTPs** Bond-Topological Parameters.
**BTR** Basic Thrust Rating.
*Mechanical Engineering.*
**BTR** The airport code for Baton Rouge, Louisiana, U.S.A.
**btry.** (abbr.) battery.
Also: **B**; **bty.**
**BTS** Bureau of Transportation Statistics (U.S.A.).
**BTSC** BICES Team Steering Committee.
Comité directeur du projet BICES.
**BTU** Basic Tactical Unit.
*Military Science.*
**BTU** Basic Transmission Unit.
**BTU** Board of Trade Unit.
**BTU**; **B.T.U**; **Btu**; **B.t.u.** British Thermal Unit.
**BTV** The airport code for Burlington, Vermont, U.S.A.
**BTW** By The Way.
**BTWC** Biological and Toxin Weapons Convention.
Convention sur les armes biologiques et à toxines.
**BTX** Benzene-Toluene-Xylene.
*Aromatic Chemicals Admixture.*
**bty.** (abbr.) battery.
Also: **B**; **btry.**
*Chemical Engineering; Electricity; Medicine; Military Science; Ordnance.*
**B.U.** Bollettino Ufficiale.
Italian initialism meaning: Official Gazette.
**BU** Boston University (U.S.A.).
**BU** Bulgaria.
**BU** (abbr.) Burnish.
*Engineering.*
**Bu.**; **bu.** (abbr.) bushel.
**BuBa** Bundesbank (Germany).
*German Bank.*
**BUB gene** Budding Uninhibited by Benzimidazole gene.
*Biochemistry; Biomedical Research; Cellular Biology; Developmental Biology; Molecular Biology; Physiology.*
**BUCK** (abbr.) Buckram (fabric).
**BUCKS** (abbr.) Buckinghamshire.
County of England.
**BUCO** Buildings Control Officer.
**buco** The above acronym was coined accidentally using the Italian word "buco" which means: hole.
*Aviation; Solid-State Physics.*
**BUCOP** British Union Catalogue of Periodicals.
**BUD** Beneficial Use Date.
**BUD** The airport code for Budapest, Hungary.
**BUD** (abbr.) Budget.
**bud** The above acronyms were coined using the English word "bud".
*Botany; Invertebrate Zoology.*
**BUDCOM** Budget Communications (System) [replaced by NAFS].
(système) BUDCOM [remplacé par le NAFS].
**BUDFIN** budget and finance.
budget et finances.
**BUDS** Building Utility Design System.
**BUE** The airport code for Buenos Aires, Argentina.
**BUF** The airport code for Buffalo, New York, U.S.A.
**BUFR** Binary Universal Form for Representation.
*Meteorological Data.*
**BUG** BUccal Ganglion.
*Dentistry.*
**BUIA** British United Island Airways.
**BUILD** Base for Uniform Language Definition.
*Psychology.*
**bul.** (abbr.) bulletin.
**Bulbank** Bulgarian Bank.
Bulbank is Bulgaria's biggest bank.
**Bulg.** (abbr.) Bulgarian.
*Languages.*
**BUMC** Boston University Medical Center (U.S.A.).
**BUMP** Boston University Marine Program (U.S.A.).
**bump** The above acronym was coined using the English word "bump".
*Aviation; Geology.*
**BUN** Blood Urea Nitrogen.
**BUNY** Board of Underwriters of New York (U.S.A.).
**BUP** British United Press.
**BUPPIES** Black Yuppies (U.S.A.).
**BUR** Biblioteca Universale Rizzoli (Italy).
**BUR** The airport code for Burbank, California, U.S.A.
**bur.** (abbr.) bureau.
**BUR** Burma's International vehicle-registration letters.
**BURL** Bollettino Ufficiale Regione Lombardia.
Italian acronym meaning: Official Gazette of the Lombardy Region.
**BURST** BICES user requirements studies & trials.
études et essais relatifs aux besoins des utilisateurs du BICES.
**BURY** Backup Rate of Yaw.
**BUS** Bachelor of Urban Studies.
**BUS** Backscatter Ultraviolet Spectrometer.
**BUS** Bank of the United States (U.S.A.).
**Bus** Budget surplus.

**bus.** (abbr.) bushel.
Also: **bush**.
**bus.** (abbr.) business.
**bus** The above acronyms were coined using the English word "bus".
*Computer Technology; Electricity; Transportation Engineering.*
**BUS** (abbr.) Busulfan.
Busulfan is used as an antineoplastic drug.
*Pharmacology.*
**BUSA** Bollettino Ufficiale delle S.p.A.
Italian acronym meaning: Official Bulletin of Joint-Stock Companies.
**BUSARL** Bollettino Ufficiale delle S.r.1.
Italian acronym meaning: Official Bulletin of Limited Companies.
**BUSCI** British-United States Convoy Instructions.
**BUS glands** Bartholin's, Urethral, Skene's glands.
**bush.** (abbr.) bushel.
Also: **bus**.
**BUSS** Backup Scram System.
*Nuclear Energy.*
**BUSS** Backup Study Sheets.
*Military.*
**BUSS** Balloon-borne Ultraviolet Stellar Spectrometer.
**BUSS** Biomedical Urine Sampling System.
**BUSS** Buoy Underwater Sound Signal.
**BUT** (abbr.) button.
*Electricity; Electronics; Metallurgy; Mycology.*
**BV** Blood Vessel.
*Anatomy.*
**BV**; **bv** Book Value.
**BV** Breakdown Voltage.
Breakdown Voltage is also known as: Zener voltage.
*Electronics.*
**BV.**; **B.V.** Bureau Veritas (France).
French Register of Shipping.
*Shipping and Marine Insurance.*
**BVA** Board of Veterans Appeals (U.S.A.).
**BVDU** Bromovinyldeoxyuridine.
*Biochemistry.*
**BVDV** Bovine Viral Diarrhea Virus.
*Virology.*
**BVE** Butyl Vinyl Ether.
**BVL** Bolsa de Valores de Lisboa (Portugal).
Portuguese initialism of the: Lisbon Stock Exchange.
**BVR** beyond visual range.
au-delà de la portée optique.
**BVRT** Benton Visual Retention Time.
*Psychiatry.*
**Bvs** Balanced Voltages.
*Electricity.*
**BVS** Biodegradable Volatile Solids.
*Analytical Chemistry.*
**BW** Bacteriological Warfare.
*Military Science.*
**BW** Baden-Württembergische Bank AG (Guernsey).
**BW**; **bw** Bandwidth.
*Telecommunications.*
**BW** Bids Wanted (U.S.A.).
**BW** Biological Warfare.
*Military Science.*
**BW** Biological Weapons.
*Military.*
**BW**; **B.W.** Black and White.
*Graphic Arts.*
**BW** Bladder Washout.
*Urology.*
**BW** Board of Works.
**BW** Body Water; Body Weight.
*Medicine.*
**BW** Bonded Warehouse.
**BW** British Waterways (G.B.).
**BWA** Backward Wave Amplifier.
**BWC** Biological Weapons Convention.
**BWD** Basic Work Data.
**BWE** Bucket-Wheel Excavator.
*Mechanical Engineering.*
**BWF** Building Wake Factor.
*Nuclear Energy.*
**BWF** Burroughs Wellcome Fund.
*Career Awards;* 1998 *Award Programs* in: *Malaria; Molecular Parasitology; Molecular Pathogenic Mycology.*
**BWG** Birmingham Wire Gauge.
The Birmingham wire gauge is a system of standard sizes of wire, metal tubing, steel plates and the like.
*Design Engineering.*
**BWH** Boston's Brigham and Women's Hospital (U.S.A.).
*Academic Medical Centers; Clinical Research; Pharmaceuticals; Photomedicine Research.*
**BWI** The airport code for Baltimore-Washington International.
**BWIP** Basalt Waste Isolation Project.
Of the U.S. Department Of Energy.
**bwk** (abbr.) brickwork.
*Building Engineering.*
**BWLT** (abbr.) Bow Light.
**BWO** Backward-Wave Oscillator.
*Electronics.*
**BWR** Bandwidth Ratio.

**BWR** Boiling Water Reactor.
*Nuclear Engineering.*
**BWRA** British Welding Research Association (G.B.).
**BWST** Borated Water Storage Tank.
*Nuclear Energy.*
**BW system** Bretton Woods system.
**BWT** Backward Wave Tube.
*Physics.*
**BWT** Birth Weight.
*Medicine.*
**BWTC** Business Woman's Travel Club.
**BWTF** Bank Wire Transfer of Funds.
*Business; Finance.*
**BWTR** Babcock and Wilcox Test Reactor.
**BWU** Blue-Whale Unit.
**BX** Base Exchange.
BX is also known as: Ion Exchange; Cation Exchange.
*Geochemistry.*
**BX**; **bx** biopsy.
Biopsy is actually the removal and examination of the tissue or fluid, taken from the living body in order to establish a correct diagnosis.
*Pathology.*
**Bx** (abbr.) Box.
**BX** Brunei.
**BXC genes** Bithorax Complex genes.
*Molecular Biology; Molecular Genetics; Human Development.*
**BXP** border crossing point.
point de franchissement de frontière.
**by**; **b.y.** billion years.
**BY** Budget Year.
*Business; Finance.*
**BY** Burundi.
**byp.** (abbr.) bypass.
*Electricity; Engineering; Surgery; Transplantation Engineering.*
**bypro.** (abbr.) byproduct.
**Byz.** (abbr.) Byzantine.
**Bz**; **bz** benzene.
$C_6H_6$ - Benzene is also known as: benzol. Benzene is obtained mainly from petroleum and from coal distillation.
Also: **benz.**
For further details see under: $\mathbf{C_6H_6}$.
*Organic Chemistry.*
**BZ** Brillouin Zone.
*Chemical Technology; Materials Science; Solid-state Physics.*
**Bza** Benzimidazole - $C_7H_6N_2$.
*Organic Chemistry.*
**Bza**; **BZA** Board of Zoning Adjustment.
**BZD**; **BZ** Benzodiazepine.
*Pharmacology.*
**BZ effect** Blandford-Znajek effect.
*Astrophysics.*
**bZIP dimerization** basic-region leucine ZIPper dimerization.
*Biology; Biomedical Research.*
**B-Z reaction** Beluzov-Zhabotinsky reaction.
*Chaotic Dynamics.*
**BZT** Barium Zirconate Titanate.
*Applied Physics; Gate Insulators; Semiconductor Devices.*

# C

**C** Calorie (large).
**c** calorie (small).
*Nutrition; Physiology; Thermodynamics.*
**C**; **c** capacity; capacitance; capacitor.
**c** carat (karat).
*Metallurgy.*
**C** The chemical symbol for Carbon.
*Chemistry; Symbols.*
**c** cent.
**c** cento.
meaning: hundred in Italian.
**c** century; chairman; chairperson; chairwoman.
**c** circa.
meaning: about in Italian.
**c** city.
**c** (abbr.) clear.
*Computer Programming; Meteorology; Navigation; Ordnance.*
**C** Code.
*Computer Programming; Telecommunications.*
**c** cold.
*Electricity; Medicine.*
**c** collateral.
**c** compte.
meaning: account in French.
**C** Congress.
**C**; **c** consumer; consumption.
**c** controller.
**c** corrente.
meaning: current in Italian.
*Electricity; Hydrology; Meteorology; Physics.*
**c** cost.
**C** Coulomb.
Named for Charles Augustin **de Coulomb**, the French engineer, for his numerous discoveries in electricity, friction and formulation of Coulomb's law.
*Electricity.*
**C**; **c** Coupon.
**C** Cuba.
**c** cubico.
meaning: cubic in Italian.
**c** curie.
Also: **Ci**.
*Nucleonics.*
**C2** command and control.
commandement et contrôle.
**C3** consultation, command and control.
consultation, commandement et contrôle.
**CA** The airline code for Air China.
**CA** Cagliari, Italy.
**Ca** The chemical symbol for Calcium.
The word calcium derives fron the Greek term lime/limestone.
*Symbols; Chemistry.*
**CA** (abbr.) California (U.S.A.).
**ca** callable (bonds).
*Business; Economics; Finance.*
**CA** 1. Canada.
1. Canada.
2. combat aircraft.
2. avion de combat.
3. contract authority.
3. autorisation de programme (AP 6.).
4. coordinating authority.
4. autorité de coordination.
5. corps d'armée.
5. army corps (AC 6.).
6. counter-air (operation).
6. (opération de) supériorité aérienne.
**CA** CAncel.
*Data Communications.*
**CA** Cancer.
Sarcoma, carcinoma and other malignant tumors.
*Oncology.*
**CA** Capital Account.
**CA** Capital Appreciation.
*Business; Economics; Finance.*
**CA** Capital Assets.
*Banking; Business; Finance.*
**CA** Carbonic Anhydrase.
Carbonic Anhydrase is also known as: Carboanhydrase; Carbonic Acid Anhydrase; Carbonate Dehydratase.
*Enzymology; Physiological Processes.*
**CA** Carcinoma.
Carcinoma is a malignant epithelial cell tumor.
*Oncology.*
**CA** Cardiac Arrest.
A cardiac arrest is actually the heartbeat cessation.
*Medicine.*
**CA** Cash Account.
**CA** Cellulose Acetate.
CA is a used mainly in lacquers, magnetic tapes, and plastic films.
*Organic Chemistry.*
**CA** Central America.
**CA** Certificate Authority.
*Digital Identity Certificates.*
**CA** Chartered Accountant; Chief Accountant.
**CA** Cholic Acid.

Acid in the human bile.
*Biochemistry.*
**CA**; **ca** Chronological Age.
*Psychology.*
**CA** Commercial Agent.
**CA** Complexity Analysis.
*Computer Programming.*
**CA** Comptable Agrée.
French acronym meaning: Chartered Accountant; Certified Accountant.
**CA** Computer Architecture.
*Computer Technology.*
**CA** Consumers' Association.
**CA** Controller of Accounts.
**CA** Cortisone Acetate.
**CA** Cost Account.
**CA** Coupons Attached.
**CA** Court of Appeal.
**CA** Credit Account.
**CA** Crédit Agricole (France).
*French Bank.*
**CA** Creditanstalt (Poland).
Head Office: Warszawa, Poland. Services: Private Banking Products; Syndicated / Project Financing.
*Polish Bank.*
**CA** Credito Artigiano (Italy).
*Italian Bank.*
**CA** Current Account.
**CA** Current Assets.
*Business; Economics; Finance.*
**CAA** Cerebral Amyloid Angiopathy.
*Clinical Neuroanatomy; Medicine; Neuroscience.*
**CAA** Civil Aeronautics Administration; Civil Aviation Administration.
**CAA** Clean Air Act (U.S.A.).
**CAA** Committee on Astronomy and Astrophysics (U.S.A.).
**CAA** 1. Civil Aviation Authority.
1. Direction de l'aviation civile.
2. contrôleur air (ou aérien) avancé.
2. forward air controller (FAC 2.).
3. counter-air attack.
3. attaque de superiorité aérienne.
**CAA**; **C.A.A.** Corte d'Assise d'Appello.
Italian initialism meaning: Criminal Court of Appeal.
*Legal.*
**CAAA** Clean Air Act Amendments.
**CAALS** Consortium on Automated Analytical Laboratory Systems (U.S.A.).
**CAAMI** Caisse Auxiliaire d'Assurance Maladie-Invalidité (Belgium).
**CAAT** Center for Alternatives to Animal Testing (U.S.A.).
**CAAT** computer-assisted audit technique.
technique de vérification informatisée (TVI).
**CAB** Cellulose Acetate Butyrate.
*Organic Chemistry.*
**CAB** Civil Aeronautics Board (U.S.A.).
The CAB has replaced the Federal Administrative Agency in 1985.
*Transportation Engineering.*
**CAB** Codice di Avviamento Bancario.
Italian acronym meaning: Bank's Routing Number.
**CAB** Coronary Artery Bypass.
Coronary artery bypass is also known as: coronary bypass.
*Cardiology.*
**CAB** Credito Agrario Bresciano (Italy).
*Italian Bank.*
**CABA** Charge Account Bankers Association.
**CABB** Centro Analisi Banche e Borsa.
Italian initialism meaning: Banks and Stock Exchange Analysis Centre.
**CABEI** Central American Bank for Economic Integration (U.S.A.).
*Banks; Economic Integration.*
**CABG** Coronary Artery Bypass Graft.
*Cardiology.*
**CABHE** Committee on Agricultural Biotechnology, Health and the Environment (U.S.A.).
Of the National Research Council.
**CABM** Center for Advanced Biotechnology and Medicine (U.S.A.).
**CAB protein** Chlorophyll a/b - Binding protein.
*Arabidopsis Plants; Biological Timing; Plant Molecular Biology.*
**CABRA numbers** Copper And Brass Research Association numbers.
Number Designations for various wrought copper and copper alloy grades.
**CAC** Cardiac Accelerator Center.
*Cardiology.*
**CAC** Citric Acid Cycle.
CAC is also known as: Krebs Cycle; Tricarboxylic Acid Cycle.
*Biochemistry; Organic Chemistry.*
**CAC** Climate Analysis Center (U.S.A.).
**CAC** Compagnie des Agents de Change (France).
**CAC** Computer Advisory Committee; County Agricultural Committee; Currency Adjustment Charge.
**CAC** Contract Awards Committee.
Comité d'adjudication des marchés (CAM 3.).
**Ca-CaM** Calcium-Calmodulin.

*Biological Chemistry; Medicine; Physiology.*
**CACAR II** second Canadian Arctic Contaminants Assessment Report.
The symposium regarding the above was held in Ottawa, Canada, in March 2003 as a result of Canada's 10-year NCP.
For further details see under: **NCP**.
**CACCI** Confederation of Asian Pacific Chambers of Commerce and Industry (Taipei).
**CACG** consolidated Alliance capability goal.
objectif général de capacité de l'Alliance.
**CACGP** Committee on Atmospheric Chemistry and Global Pollution (U.S.A.).
**CACL** Canadian Association of Children's Libraries.
**$CaCO_3$** Calcite.
Calcite is also known as: Calcspar.
*Mineralogy.*
**$CaCO_3$** Calcium Carbonate.
Calcium Carbonate has numerous chemical uses, for example, in tooth powders, in cement, and in white paint.
*Inorganic Chemistry.*
**CACOHIS** Computer-Aided Community Oral Health Information System.
*Medicine.*
**CACUL** Canadian Association of College and University Libraries.
**CAD**; **cad** (abbr.) cadauno.
Italian abbreviation meaning: each.
**CAD** Cartridge Activated Device.
**CAD** Cash Against Documents.
**c.-à-d.** c'est-à-dire.
French initialism meaning: That is to say; i.e.; in other words.
**CAD** Cinnamyl Alcohol Dehydrogenase.
**CAD** Computer-Aided Design; Computer-Assisted Drafting; Computer-Assisted Drawing.
**CAD**; **Cad** Coordinamento Associazioni Diabetici.
c/o Centro Antidiabetico Ospedale Morgagni, Forlì, Italy.
**CAD** Coronary Artery Disease.
*Pathology.*
**CAD2** Capital Adequacy Directive 2.
*European Union Financial Institution.*
**CADA** coordinated air defence area.
zone de défense aérienne coordonnée.
**CADAE** Computer-Aided Design And Engineering.
**CADAM** Computer-graphics Augmented Design And Manufacturing.
**CADAPSO** Canadian Association of DAta Processing Service Organizations.
**Cadcam** Computer-aided design and manufacturing.
**CADCOS** Control and assessment of Agricultural data with a GPS-supported Data COllecting System.
*European Community Project.*
**CADENCE** Computer-Aided DEsign and Numerical Control Effort.
**cadence** The above acronym was coined accidentally using the French word "cadence" which means: beat; cadence; (rhythmic) tread.
**CADF** Commutated Antenna Direction Finder.
*Navigation.*
**CADH** Communications And Data Handling.
**CADIG** Coventry And District Information Group.
**CADIMS** Coordinated Air Defence In Mutual Support (Agreement).
(Accord sur la) coordination de la défense aérienne pour l'appui mutuel.
**CADO** coordinated air defence operations.
opérations coordonnées de défense aérienne.
**CADRE** Collectors, Artists, and Dealers for Responsible Equity (U.S.A.).
**cadre** The above acronym was coined accidentally using the French word "cadre" which means: picture-frame; ambit; circle; framework. Also: executive.
**CADS** Cellular Absorbed Dose Spectrometer.
**CADS** Central Air Data System.
**CADS** Command And Data Simulator.
**CADV** Cash ADVance.
*Business; Economics; Finance.*
**CADV** commande automatique de vol.
automatic flight control system (AFCS).
**CAE** Commandement allié en Europe [remplacé par SC Europe].
Allied Command Europe (ACE) [replaced by SC Europe].
**CAEC** Center for the Analysis of Environmental Change (U.S.A.).
The CAEC is formed cooperatively by Oregon State University; the Pacific Northwestern Experiment station of the U.S. Forest Service; the Environmental Research Laboratory, Corvallis, U.S. Environmental Protection Agency; and Battelle, Pacific N.W. Laboratories.
**CAE** Chinese Academy of Engineering (China).
**CAE** The airport code Columbia, South Carolina, U.S.A.
**CAE**; **cae** Computer-Aided Engineering.
*Industrial Engineering.*
**CAE**; **C.A.E.** Comunità Agricola Europea.
Italian initialism of the: European Agricultural Community - E.C.
**CAeM** Commission for Aeronautical Meteorology.

**CAENEX** Complete Atmospheric ENergetics EXperiment.

**CAENs** Chemically Assembled Electronic Nanocomputers.
*Biochemistry; Chemistry; Nanocomputers.*

**CAESAR** Center of Advanced European Studies and Research (Germany).

**CAETS** Council of Academies of Engineering and Technological Sciences.
Located in Washington DC. U.S.A.. Founded in 1978 to promote the development of engineering and technology throughout the world and to provide an international forum for the discussion of technological and engineering issues; encourages international engineering efforts in order to promote economic growth and social welfare.

**CAF** CD8+ Antiviral Factor.
*AIDS Vaccine Development; AIDS Vaccine Research; Epidemiology; Vaccines and Preventions; Virology.*

**CAF**; **C.A.F.** Commissione di Appello Federale.
Italian acronym of the: Federal Committee of Appeal.
*Sports.*

**CAF** Cost Adjustment Factor.
*Business; Economics; Finance.*

**CAF** Cost And Freight.

**CAF** Cost, Assurance, and Freight.

**CAF** Currency Adjustment Factor.

**CAFE** Computer-Aided Film Editor.

**CAFE standards** Corporate Average Fuel Economy standards.
Became law in the U.S. in 1975.
*Fuel Consumption; Motor Industry.*

**CAFMED** Combined Amphibious Force Mediterranean.
Force amphibie multinationale de la Méditerranée.

**CAFRAD** Centre Africain de Formation et de Recherche Administratives pour le Développement.
Located in Tangier, Morocco. Founded in 1964 by agreement between Morocco and UNESCO; training of African senior civil servants; research into administrative problems in Africa, documentation of results, and the provision of a consultation service for governments and organizations in Africa; holds frequent seminars.
For further details see under: **UNESCO**.

**CAG** 1. carrier air group.
1. groupe aérien embarqué.
2. circulation aérienne générale.
2. general air traffic (GAT).
3. commande automatique de gain.
3. automatic gain control (AGC 2.).

**CAG**; **Cag** Centro Aggregazione Giovanile.
*Italian Centers.*

**CagA protein** Cytotoxin-associated gene A protein.
*Cancer Epidemiology; Clinical Microbiology; Molecular Microbiology.*

**cage.** (abbr.) courtage.
French abbreviation meaning: brokerage.
*Business; Economics; Finance.*

**CAgM** Commission for Agricultural Meteorology.

**CAGS** Chinese Academy of Geological Sciences (China).

**CAH** Congenital lipoid Adrenal Hyperplasia.

**$CaHPO_4$** Monetite.
Monetite is found on many Caribbean islands.
*Mineralogy.*

**CAI** The airport code for Cairo, Egypt.

**CAI** Calcium-Aluminum-rich Inclusion.
For further details see under: **CAIs**.

**CAI** Codon Adaptation Index.
*Cell and Molecular Biology.*

**CAI** Computer-Aided Instruction.

**CAI** Computer-Assisted Instruction.
*Artificial Intelligence; Interactive Dialogues.*

**CAIA** Conference on Artificial Intelligence for Applications.

**CAIC** Computer-Assisted Indexing and Classification.

**CAINS** Computer-Aided INstruction and Classification.

**$Ca(IO_3)_2$** Lautarite.
*Mineralogy.*

**CAIA** Conference on Artificial Intelligence for Applications.

**CAIDA** Cooperative Association for Internet Data Analysis (U.S.A.).

**C.A.I.R.O.S.** Coordinamento Analisti psicologi per l'Intervento e la Ricerca Operativa e Sociale (Italy).

**CAIs** Calcium-Aluminum-rich Inclusions.
CAIs are the first solid particles formed in the solar nebula.
*Asteroids; Early Solar System; Earth and Planetary Sciences; Geophysics; Metamorphism; Meteoritics; Mineralogy.*

**CAIS** Canadian Association for Information Science.

**CAK** CDK-Activating Kinase.

**cal.** (abbr.) calendar.

**cal.** (abbr.) caliber.
*Ordnance.*

**CAL** (abbr.) California (U.S.A.).

Also: **Calif.**
**cal** (abbr.) calorie.
For further details see under: **c** and **C**.
**CAL** Computer-Assisted Learning.
**CAL** Conversational Algebraic Language.
**CAL** Coupling of Atmospheric Layers.
For further details see under: **SPECIAL**.
**CAL** Crescita Apprendimento Lavoro (Italy).
**CALA** Chinese-American Librarians Association.
**CALA** Computer-Aided Loads Analysis.
**CALCO** Capitol Area Library COnsortium (U.S.A.).
**CalCOFI programs** The California Cooperative Oceanic Fisheries Investigations programs (U.S.A.).
The Marine Life Research Group of the Scripps Institution of Oceanography at the University of Califomia San Diego, U.S.A. cooperates with federal and state fisheries agencies in the study of the pelagic ecology of the Califomia Current System - the CalCOFI program.
*Pelagic Ecology.*
**CALENER** Collection d'Aides Logicielles à l'enseignement de l'ENERgétique.
**CalEPA** California Environmental Protection Agency (U.S.A.).
**CALFIN** CALifornia Fisheries Information Network.
**CALI** Chromophore-Assisted Laser Inactivation.
*Cellular Biology; Molecular Biology; Physiology.*
**Calif.** (abbr.) California.
Also: **CAL**.
**CALINCAD** Computer-Aided Learning IN Computer-Aided Design.
**CALIPER** Cost Analysis of Laser Investment, Production, Engineering, and Research.
**calkg.** (abbr.) calking / caulking.
*Building Engineering; Engineering; Naval Architecture.*
**CALL** Canadian Association of Law Libraries.
**CALL** Computer-Augmented Loft Lines.
*Graphics.*
**CALLIOPE** Computer-Assisted Language Learning for Information, Organization and Production in Europe.
*European Community.*
**CALLIOPE** Computer-Assisted Legislative LIaison, On-line Political Evaluation.
**CalM** Calmodulin.
*Biochemistry;* Also: **CaM**.
**CALM** Collected Algorithm for Learning Machines.
*Data Processing.*
**CALM** Computer-Assisted Library Mechanization.
**CALMS** Continuous Automatic Line Monitoring System.
**CAIs** CaAl-rich inclusions.
For further details see under: **CAIs**.
**CALS** College of Agricultural and Life Sciences (U.S.A.).
**CALS** continuous acquisition and life cycle support.
acquisition et soutien en continu pendant la vie des systèmes.
**CALSAT** calibration satellite.
satellite d'étalonnage.
**CALS/CE** Computer-aided Acquisition and Logistic Support / Concurrent Engineer.
**Caltech** California Institute of technology (U.S.A.).
**Caltrans** (abbr.) California Department of transportation (U.S.A.).
**CALURA** Corporations And Labor Union Returns Act (U.S.A.).
**calura** The above acronym was coined accidentally using the Italian word "calura" which means great heat; sultriness.
**CaM** Calmodulin.
Also: **CalM**.
*Biochemistry.*
**cam.** (abbr.) camber.
*Aviation; Design Engineering; Geology; Naval Architecture.*
**Cam.** (abbr.) Camelopardus.
Camelopardus is a large constellation lying near the north celestial pole.
Also: Camelopardalis.
*Astronomy.*
**Cam** Carbamylmethyl.
*Biochemistry.*
**CAM** CArgo Module.
**CAM** Carrier Aircraft Modification.
**CAM** Cell Adhesion Molecule.
For further details see under: **CAMs**.
**CAM** Centro Assistenza Minori (Italy).
*Italian Center.*
**CAM** 1. chemical agent monitor.
1. détecteur d'agents chimiques.
2. circulation aérienne militaire.
2. military air traffic (MAT).
3. Comité d'adjudication des marchés.
3. Contract Awards Committee (CAC).
4. computer-aided manufacturing.
4. fabrication assistée par ordinateur (FAO).
**CAM** Chorioallantoic Membrane.
The CAM is a membrane that lines the hard shell of chicken eggs.

**CAM** Combined Admission Mode (in Biological and Biomedical Sciences).
**CAM**; **cam** Computer-Assisted Manufacturing.
**CAM** Containment Atmospheric Monitoring.
*Nuclear Energy.*
**CAM** Content-Addressable Memory.
Content-addressable memory is also known as: Associative Memory.
*Computer Technology.*
**CAMA** Centralized Automatic Message Accounting.
*Data Communications.*
**CAMARC** Computer-Aided Movement Analysis in a Rehabilitation Context.
*Medicine.*
**CAMBIA** Center for Application of Molecular Biology to International Agriculture (Australia).
**CAMBITAL** Ufficio Italiano Cambi.
Italian abbreviation of the: Italian Bureau of Exchange.
**Cambs.** (abbr.) Cambridgeshire (G.B.).
**CAMD** Computer-Aided Molecular Design.
**CAMEL** Component and Material Evaluation Loop.
*Nuclear Energy.*
**CAMEO** Computer-Aided Management of Emergency Operations.
**CAMEO** Creative Audio and Music Electronics Organization.
**CAMEO system** Covert Active Modular Electro-Optical system.
**CAMERA** Canadian Association of Motion picture and Electronic Recording Artists (Canada).
**CAMKII** Calcium-Calmodulin-Dependent Kinase II.
*Medicine; Neurobiology.*
**CAML** Canadian Association of Music Libraries.
**CAMOS** Committee on Atomic, Molecular, and Optical Sciences (U.S.A.).
**CAMP** Cabin Air Manifold Pressure.
*Aviation.*
**CAMP** Compiler for Automatic Machine Programming.
*Data Communications.*
**CAMP** Computer-Assisted Management of Portfolios.
**CAMP** Computer-Assisted Menu Planning.
**CAMP** Continuous Air Monitoring Program / Project.
Of the U.S. EPA.
For further details see under: **EPA**.
**cAMP** cyclic Adenosine 3',5'-Monophosphate.
Intracellular messenger in the neurons.
*Cell Biology; Neuroscience.*
**CAM plants** Crassulacean-Acid Metabolism plants.
*Carbon Fixation.*
**CAMPS** Centralized Automated Military Pay System (U.S.A.).
**CAMPS** Cooperative Area Manpower Planning System.
Of the U.S. EPA.
For further details see under: **EPA**.
**CAMP test** Christie-Atkins-Munch-Petersen test.
Named for the discoverers of the phenomerion.
*Microbiology; Hemolysis.*
**CAMPUS** Comprehensive Analytical Method of Planning in the University Sphere (U.S.A.).
**CAMS** Cabin Atmosphere Monitoring System - NASA's.
**CAMs** Cell Adhesion Molecules.
*Axon Pathfinding; Cell Biology; Medical Biophysics; Molecular and Structural Biology.*
**CAMS** Center for Accelerator Mass Spectroscopy.
Of the U.S. Lawrence Livermore National Laboratory.
**CAMS** Communications Area Master Station.
**CAMS** Container Automated Marking System.
**CAMT** Center for Advanced Manufacturing Technologies.
*Design Methodologies; Machine Tools; Robotics & Assembly.*
**CAMT** Center for Advanccd Medical Technology (U.S.A.).
**CaMV** Cauliflower Mosaic Virus.
*Virology.*
**CAN**; **can.** (abbr.) cancel.
Also: **canc**.
**CAN.**; **can.** (abbr.) canister; cannon.
*Ordnance.*
**CAN.**; **can.** (abbr.) canopy.
*Aviation; Forestry.*
**CAN** Career Advancement Network.
**CAN** Central Autonomic Nucleus.
*Anatomy; Cell Biology; Neurobiology.*
**CAN** Ceric Ammonium Nitrate.
*Inorganic Chemistry.*
**CAN** Commission d'Amérique du Nord - de la Féderation Internationale des Professeurs de Français.
**CAN** Committee on Animal Nutrition (U.S.A.).
**CAN** Configuration Accounting Number.
**CAN** Conseil de l'Atlantique Nord.
North Atlantic Council (NAC).
**CAN** Cost Account Number.
*Business; Economics; Finance.*
**c.a.n.** costo, assicurazione, nolo.

Italian acronym meaning: cost, insurance, freight.
**CAN** Cure Autism Now.
**CANARIE** CAnadian Network for the Advancement of Research, Industry, and Education (Canada).
CANARIE is a non-profit Industry - Government Consortium, located in Ottawa, Canada.
**canc.** (abbr.) cancel.
Also: **CAN.**; **can**.
**Canc** (abbr.) Cancer.
Cancer is a constellation that lies between Gemini and Leo.
*Astronomy.*
**C&EE** Central and Eastern Europe.
Europe centrale et orientale (ECO).
**C&GC program** Climate and Global Change program (U.S.A.).
**C&GS** Charting and Geodetic Services (U.S.A.).
**C&R** Consulting and Research.
**CANE** Cationic Asphalt-Neoprene Emulsion.
*Dust Control.*
**cane** The above acronym was coined using the English word "cane" (*Botany*) while in Italian "cane" means "dog" (*Vertebrate Zoology*); "hammer" (*Ordnance*).
**CanF** Canadian - French.
French spoken as a native language in Canada, particularly in Quebec province.
*Languages.*
**CANIF** CArbon and NItrogen cycling in Forest ecosystems.
*European Community Project.*
**CANLANT** Canadian Atlantic Sub-Area [obsolete].
Sous-secteur canadian de l'Atlantique [obsolète].
**CANR** Chemically Assisted Nuclear Reaction.
*Cold Fusion (Latest Developments).*
**CANS** Civilian Air Navigation Schools.
**CANS system** Computer-Assisted Network Scheduling system.
**CANTV** Compañia Anônima Nacional Teléfonos de Venezuela.
**CANUS** Canada-United States.
Canada-États-Unis.
**CaO** Calcium Oxide.
Calcium Oxide, also known as: Lime; Quicklime; Burnt Lime; Calx, is used mainly in glass manufacture; in steel manufacturing; in fertilizers and as a water softener.
*Inorganic Chemistry.*
**CAO** Central Applications Office (Ireland).
**CAO** 1. circulation aérienne opérationnelle.
1. operational air traffic (OAT 1a.).
2. conception assistée par ordinateur.
2. computer-aided design (CAD 2.).
3. counter-air operation.
3. opération de supériorité aérienne.
**CAO** Copper Amine Oxidase.
**CAOC** combined air operations centre [has replaced ICAOC].
centre combiné d'opérations aériennes [remplace l'ICAOC].
**CA ordination** Corespondance Analysis ordination.
*Holocene Limnological Changes.*
**CAP** Calcium Assimilation in Plants.
*European Community Project.*
**CaP** Cancer of the Prostate.
*Medicine.*
**cap.** (abbr.) capital; capitalization.
**Cap** (abbr.) capitolo.
Italian abbreviation meaning: chapter.
**Cap** (abbr.) Capricornus.
Capricornus is a large southern constellation that lies between Sagittarius and Aquarius.
*Astronomy.*
**CAP** Catabolite Activator Protein.
*Biochemistry; Molecular Biology; Research in Cancer and Allied Diseases.*
**CAP** Cellulose Acetate Propionate.
*Organic Chemistry.*
**CAP** Circum-Atlantic Project.
**CAP** Civil Air Patrol.
**CAP** Clathrin-Associated Protein.
*Cytology.*
**CAP** Code of Advertising Practices- G.B.
**CAP**; **cap** Codice di Avviamento Postale.
Italian acronym meaning: Postal Code; Zip Code.
**CAP** College of American Pathologists (U.S.A.).
**CAP** combat air patrol.
patrouille aérienne de combat.
**CAP** Common Agricultural Policy.
*Business & the Environment.*
**CAP** Computer-Aided Planning.
**CAP** Consorzio per l'Acqua Potabile.
*Italian Consortium.*
**CAP** Cost Analysis Plan.
*Business; Economics; Finance.*
**CAP** The Committee on Awards and Prizes.
EUFEPS Advisory Panel.
For further details see under: **EUFEPS**.
**cap** The above acronyms were coined using the English word "cap".
*Building Engineering; Engineering; Genetics; Mining Engineering; Mycology; Petroleum Engineering.*
**CAPA** Certificat d'Aptitude à la Profession d'Avocat (France).

**CAPC** Civil Aviation Planning Committee.
Comité d'étude de l'aviation civile.
**CAPCO** capability package coordonination officer.
coordinateur des paquets (ou ensembles) des capacités.
**CAPCU** combat air patrol control unit.
unité de contrôle de patrouille aérienne de combat.
**CAPE** Capacity And Proficiency Evaluation.
**CAPE** CApe Kennedy Precipitation Experiment.
**CAPE** Center for Advanced Professional Education (Canada).
**CAPE** Communication Automatic Processing Equipment.
**CAPE** Computer-Aided Planning and Estimating.
**CAPE** Consortium for the Advancement of Physics Education (U.S.A.).
**CAPE** Convective Available Potential Energy.
**CAPE** Council for American Private Education (U.S.A.).
**CaPEI experiment** Convective and Precipitation / Electrification experiment.
**CAPER** Computer-Aided Pattern Evaluation and Recognition.
**CAPER** Configuration Analysis and PERformance.
**CAPERs** Cost And Performance Effectiveness Ratios.
**CAPEXIL** Chemicals & Allied Products Export Promotion Council (India).
CAPEXIL is an Export promotion council sponsored by the Ministry of Commerce, Government of India and the Private Sector Trade & Industry.
**CAPM** Capital Asset Pricing Model.
*Business; Finance.*
**CAPO** Center Apollo Program Offices - NASA's.
**CAPP** CAD Process Planning.
**CAPP** Ceramide-Activated Protein Phosphatase.
**CAPP** Computer-Aided Process (or Production) Planning.
*Design Engineering.*
**CAPRI** Civil Aircraft PRotection against Ice.
*European Community Project.*
**CAPRI** Compact All-Purpose Range Instrument.
*Radar.*
**caps.** capital letters.
**caps.** (abbr.) capsule.
**CAPS** CAssini Plasma Spectrometer.
**CAPS** Cell Atmosphere Processing System.
*Nuclear Energy.*
**CAPS** Center for AIDS Prevention Studies (U.S.A.).
Of the University of San Francisco.
**CAPS** Center for Analysis and Prediction of Storms (U.S.A.).
**CAPs** Children of Ageing Parents.
**CAPS** Computer-Assisted Problem Solving.
**CAPS** Computer-Assisted Prosthesis Selection.
*Orthopedic Surgery.*
**CAPS** Conventional Armaments Planning System.
système de plans d'orientation pour les armements conventionnels (SPOAC).
**CAPS** Convertible Adjustable Preferred Stocks (U.S.A.).
**CAPSR** Cost Account Performance Status Report.
**CAPT** Coupling Active and Passive Telemetric data collection for monitoring, control and management of animal production at farm and at sectorial level.
*European Community Project.*
**CAPTAIN** Computer-Aided Processing and Terminal Access Information Network.
*Library Computer Network.*
**CAPTAS** combined active / passive towed array sonar.
système d'antenne remorquée.
**CAR** Caisse Autonome de Refinancement (France).
*French Bank.*
**CAR** Capital Authorization Request.
*Business; Economics; Finance.*
**CAR**; **car** (abbr.) carat.
For further details see under: **k**.
**Car.** (abbr.) Carina.
A constellation that lies in the Milky Way.
*Astronomy.*
**CAR** Certification Approval Request.
**CAR** Compounded Annual Rate.
**CAR** Computer-Assisted Research.
**CAR** Conditioned Avoidance Response.
**CAR** Contractor's All Risks.
**CAR** The Committee on Academic Relations.
EUFEPS Advisory Panel.
For further details see under: **EUFEPS**.
**CAR** Coxsackie and Adenovirus Receptor.
**CARA** Cargo And Rescue Aircraft.
**CARA** Center for Astrophysics in Antarctica.
CARA was founded in 1991. It has an 11-year lifetime.
*Astronomy; Astrophysics.*
**CARA** Compagnie d'Aménagement Rural d'Aquitaine (France).
**CARA** Current Aerospace Research Activities.
**CARB** California Air Resources Board (U.S.A.).
**CARB** Center for Advanced Research in Biotechnology.
The CARB is located in Rockville, Maryland, U.S.A.
**CARCAE** Caribbean Regional Council for Adult Education.

Founded in 1978 to promote and facilitate co-operation among national adult education organizations and agencies in non-Spanish-speaking territories of the region; to advocate awareness and recognition of the importance of adult education and to seek funding from governments and other sources; to hold conferences, seminars, training courses, etc.; to advise governments and other bodies on matters relating to adult education.

**CARD** (abbr.) Cardiganshire (G.B.).
Also: **Cards**.

**CARD** CAspase Recruitment Domain.
Caspases are a family of proteases.
*Apoptosis; Biochemistry; Medicine; Molecular Medicine; Pathology.*

**CARD** Channel Allocation and Routing Data.

**CARD** Civil Aviation Research and Development - NASA's.

**CARD** Coastal and Arctic Research Division.
CARD has replaced: **MSRD** (Marine Services Research Division).

**CARD** Compact Automatic Retrieval Device.
*Data Processing.*

**CARD** Compact Automatic Retrieval Display.
*Data Processing.*

**CARD** Coded Automatic Reading Device.

**CARD** conventional armaments review document.
document sur l'examen des armaments conventionnels.

**CARDAN** Centre d'Analyse et de Recherche Documentaire pour l'Afrique Noire.

**CARDS** Card-Automated Reproduction and Distribution System (U.S.A.).
Of the Library of Congress.

**Cards.** (abbr.) Cardiganshire (G.B.).
Also: **CARD**.

**CARDS** Combat Aircraft Recording and Data System.

**CARE** Center for Athletes' Rights and Education (U.S.A.).

**CARE** Coalition of Americans for Research Ethics (U.S.A.).
CARE is a group that opposes the use of embryos in research.

**CARE** Combined Accident Reduction Effort.

**CARE** Computer-Aided Reliability Estimation.

**CaRE** $a^{2+}$ Response Element.

**CARE Act** Comprehensive AIDS Resources Emergency Act (U.S.A.).
The Ryan White CARE Act was created in 1990 in the U.S.A. to help states, families and communities cope with the AIDS problem.

**CAREC** CARibbean Epidemiology Centre.

**CAREIRS** Conservation And Renewable Energy Inquiry and Referral Service.

**CAREL** Centre Audio-Visuel de Royan pour l'Etude des Langues (Royan, France).
*French language Center.*

**CARE system** Clinical and Administrative REcord system (U.S.A.).

**CARI** Comparative Administration Research Institute (U.S.A.).

**CARI** Council of Air-conditioning and Refrigeration Industry (U.S.A.).

**CARIBANK** CARIbbean Development Bank.

**CARICOM** (abbr.) CARIbbean COMmunity.

**CARICOMP** CARibbean COastal Marine Productivity.
Implemented in 1993.

**CARIFE** Cassa di Risparmio di Ferrara.
Established in 1838.
*Italian Savings Bank.*

**CARIGE** CAssa di RIsparmio di Genova.
Established in 1846.
*Italian Bank.*

**CARIM** CArdiovascular Research Institute of Maastricht (The Netherlands).

**CARIPLO** CAssa di Risparmio delle Provincie LOmbarde (Italy).
Founded in 1823.
For further details see under: **BancaIntesaBCI**.

**CARIPOL Monitoring Program** CARIbbean Marine POLlution Monitoring Program.

**CARIRA** Cassa di Risparmio di Ravenna (Italy).

**CARISBO** Cassa di Risparmio di Bologna.
The Fondazione CARISBO is the continuation of CARISBO which was founded in Bologna, Italy, in 1837.
*Social & Economic Development.*

**CARISMA** Computer-Aided Research Into Stock Market Application.

**carisma** The above acronym was coined accidentally using the Italian word "carisma" which means: charisma / charism.

**CARISP.SM** Cassa di Risparmio della Repubblica di San Marino (Italy).
Private banking since 1882.

**CARITRO** Cassa di Risparmio di Trento e Rovereto S.p.A. (Italy).
Established in 1841, since 1st July 2002 part of the UniCredito Italiano Group.
*Italian Savings Bank.*

**CARL** CAlibration Requirement List.

**CARL** Canadian Academic Research Libraries (Canada).

**CARL** Canadian Association of Research Libraries (Canada).
**CARL** Colorado Alliance of Research Libraries (U.S.A.).
**CARL** Comparative Animal Research Laboratory (U.S.A.).
**CARLA** Code Actuated Random Load Apparatus.
**CARLJS** Council of Archives and Research Libraries in Jewish Studies.
**CARM1** Coactivator-Associated Arginine Methyltransferase 1.
*Biochemistry; Enzymes; Medicine.*
**CARO** Combined Arms Research Office (U.S.A.).
**CARP** Center for Advanced Research in Phenomenology (U.S.A.).
**CARS** CAble Relay Stations.
**CARs** Civil Air Regulations.
**CARS** Coherent Anti-stokes Raman Spectroscopy.
*Chemistry; Physics.*
**CARS** Community Antenna Relay Service.
*Data Communications.*
**CARS** Computer-Aided Reference Service.
**CARS** Consortium for Advanced Radiation Sources.
The CARS includes a group of scientists from many U.S. institutions. It is based at the University of Chicago (U.S.A.).
**CARS** Containment Atmosphere Recirculation System.
*Nuclear Energy.*
**CARSO** Center for Advanced Research in Space Optics.
**CARS technique** Coherent Anti-stokes Raman Scattering technique.
The CARS technique was first used for imaging in the 1980s.
*Imaging; Microscopy; Physics.*
**CARSTRIKFOR** carrier striking force.
1a. force d'attaque de porte-avions.
1b. force d'intervention de porte-avions.
**CART** Centralized Automatic Recorder and Tester.
**CARTE** Computer-Aided Reasoning and Tutoring in Engineering.
**CART network** Cloud And Radiation Testbed network (U.S.A.).
**CAS** Cahiers d'Archéologie Subaquatique.
**CaS** Calcium Sulfide.
CaS is used mainly as a flotation agent.
*Inorganic Chemistry.*
**CAS** Calibrated Air Speed / Airspeed.
*Aviation.*
**CAS** California Academy of Sciences (U.S.A.).
**Cas.** (abbr.) Cassiopeia.
*Astronomy.*
**CAS** Central Admissions Services (Ireland).
**CAS** Chemical Abstracts Service.
**CAS** Chicago Academy of Science (U.S.A.).
**CAS** Chinese Academy of Sciences (China).
CAS was founded in 1949.
**CAS** close air support.
appui aérien rapproché.
**CAS** Collision-Avoidance System.
CAS is also known as collision-avoidance radar.
*Engineering.*
**CAS** Commission for Atmospheric Sciences - U.N.
**CAS** Committee on Atmospheric Sciences (U.S.A.).
**CAS**; **cas** Computer-Aided Styling (software).
**CASA** 1. chapitre, article, sous-article.
1. chapter, item, sub-item (CISI).
2. comité d'association de système d'arme [NAMSO].
2. weapon system partnership committee (WSPC) [NAMSO].
**CASA** Computer and Automated Systems Association.
**CASA** Computer-Associated Self-Assessment (G.B.).
**C.A.S.A.**; **CASA** Confederazione Autonoma Sindacati Artigiani (Italy).
**CASA** Custom Automotive Sound Association (U.S.A.).
**casa** The above acronym was coined accidentally using the Italian word "casa" which means: house; home; (at times) firm; business; concern.
**CASA approach** Carnegie-Ames-Stanford approach.
*Biological Sciences; Marine and Coastal Sciences.*
**CASAC** Clean Air Science Advisory Committee (U.S.A.).
Of the U.S. EPA.
For further details see under: **EPA**.
**CASB** Cost Accounting Standards Board.
**CASC** Central Administrative Support Center.
**CASE** Common Access Switching Equipment.
**CASE** Computer-Aided System Evaluation.
**CASE** Computer-Aided Software Engineering.
*Computer Programming.*
**CASE** Confederation for the Advancement of State Education (U.S.A.).
**CASE** Coordinated Air-Sea Experiment.
**CASEVAC** casuality evacuation.
1a. évacuation des pertes.
1b. évacuation des victimes.
**CASEX** combined antisubmarine warfare exercise.
exercice combiné de lutte anti-sous-marine.
**cash.** (abbr.) cashier.

Also: **cashr**.
**CASI** Canadian Aeronautics and Space Institute (Canada).
**CASI** Conditional Amount of Sample Information.
*Statistics.*
**CASLIM** Consortium of Academic and Special Libraries in Montana.
*U.S. Library Association.*
**CASLIS** Canadian Association of Special Libraries and Information Services.
**CASNET** Causal ASsociation NETwork.
*Artificial Intelligence.*
**CASO** Civil Affairs Staff Officer (G.B.).
**$CaSO_4$** Calcium Sulfate.
Calcium Sulfate is used mainly as a food additive, in polishes, paints, and dyes.
*Inorganic Chemistry.*
**CASP** Canadian Atlantic Storm Project (Canada).
**CASP** 1. computer-aided search planning.
1. planification de la recherche assistée par ordinateur.
2. coordinated air / sea procedures.
2. procédures air-mer coordonnées.
**CASP2** second Critical Assessment of Techniques for Protein Structure Prediction.
*Computational Biology; Computer Science; Crystallography; Nuclear Magnetic Resonance; Physical Chemistry; Protein Engineering; Spectroscopy.*
**CAS procedure** Cylindrical Anisotropy Stacking procedure.
**CASREP** casualty report.
1a. compte rendu des pertes [personnel].
1b. compte rendu d'avarie [marine].
**CASS** categories of sensitive subjects.
catégories de questions sensibles.
**CASS** Corte di Cassazione.
Italian abbreviation meaning: Court of Cassation.
Also: **C.C.**
*Law.*
**CASSIOPE** Computer-Aided System for Scheduling Information and Operation of Public transport in Europe - E.C.
**CAST** Center for Application of Sciences and Technology (U.S.A.).
**C.A.S.T.** Centro Assistenza Sociale Territoriale.
*Italian Center.*
**CAST** China Association for Science and Technology (China).
**CAST** Common Access Security Terminal.
**CAST** Computerized Automatic System Tester.
**CAST** Coronary Artery Surgery Trial.
*Medicine.*
**CAST** Council for Agricultural Science and Technology (U.S.A.).
**cast** The above acronym was coined using the English word "cast".
*Engineering; Geology; Medicine; Optics; Paleontology.*
**CASTNet** Clean Air Status and Trends Networks.
Of the U.S. EPA.
*Earth and Atmospheric Sciences; Forest Resources; Rural Air Quality.*
For further details see under: **EPA**.
**CASTS** CAnal Safe Transit System.
**CAT** Cabin Air Temperature.
*Aviation.*
**CAT** California Achievement Test.
*Psychology.*
**CAT** Cambridge Antibody Technology (G.B.).
CAT was founded in 1991.
**CAT** Catecholamine.
Catecholamine is also known as: Adrenergic Amine.
*Biochemistry.*
**cat.** (abbr.) catter.
Catter is also known as: catter pin.
*Design Engineering.*
**CAT** 1. central analysis team.
1. équipe centrale d'analyse.
2. container anchorage terminal.
2. terminal de mouillage pour porte-conteneurs.
**CAT** Chloroamphenicol Acetyltransferase.
**CAT** Choline Acetyl Transferase.
**CAT** Clear-Air Turbulence.
*Meteorology.*
**CAT** Clerical Aptitude Test.
**CAT** Cognitive Ability Test; College Ability Test.
*Education.*
**CAT** College of Advanced Technology.
**C.A.T.** Comando Aereo Tattico.
Italian acronym meaning: Tactical Air Command.
*Military.*
**CAT** Comitato Ambientalista Taxi (Italy).
*Italian Committee.*
**CAT** Computer-Aided (Assisted) Testing.
**CAT** Computer-Assisted Trading.
**CAT** Computer-Assisted Translation.
**CAT** computerized / computed Axial Tomography.
Also known as: CAT scan.
*Radiology.*
**CAT** Cosmic Anisotropy Telescope.
*Astronomy.*
**CAT** Crack Arrest Temperature.
*Nuclear Energy.*
**CAT** Credit Authorization Terminal.

**CATAS** critical angle towed-array system.
système de réseau remorqué à angle critique.

**CATER** Center for Aviation Training at Embry-Riddle (U.S.A.).
CATER has customized programs to meet the specialized continuing education training needs of corporations, governments, agencies and individuals. They include: English language training, flight and ground school instruction, air traffic control training.

**CATF** commander, amphibious task force.
commandant de force opérationnelle amphibie.

**cath.** (abbr.) cathode.
Cathode is also known as: Negative Electrode. At times the abbreviation is: ka.
*Electricity; Electronics; Physical Chemistry.*

**CATI** Centre d'Analyse et de Traitment de l'Information.
French acronym meaning: Center for the Analysis and Processing of Information.

**CATI**; **cati** Computer-Aided Telephone Interviewing.

**cati** The above acronym was coined accidentally using the French word "cati" which means in French "dressing".
*Textile Industry.*

**CATIE** Centro Agronomico Tropical de Investigacion y Enseñanza (Costa Rica).
CATIE has been operating since 1943. It deals with the Development, Conservation, and sustainable use of natural resources in the Americas.

**CATS** Certificates of Accrual on Treasury Securities (U.S.A.).

**CATs** Chloroamphenicol Acetyltransferases.
*Microbiology; Immunology.*

**CATs** Collaborative Access Teams.

**CATS** Committee on Applied and Theorethical Statistics (U.S.A.).

**CATS** Computer-Aided Troubleshooting.

**CATS** Computer-Assisted Trading System.

**CATT**; **CATTT** Controlled Avalanche Transit-Time Triode.
*Electronics.*

**CATV** CAble Television.
*Telecommunications.*

**CATV** Community Antenna Television.

**Cav.** (abbr.) Cavaliere.
Italian abbreviation meaning: knight; knight of labour.

**CAV** Coefficiente di Adeguamento Valutario.
Italian acronym meaning: Currency Adjustment Factor.

**CAW** Center for the Advancement of Women (Poland).

**CAW** Channel Address Word.
*Computer Programming.*

**$CaWO_4$** Cadmium Tungstate.
Cadmium Tungstate is used mainly in the manufacture of fluorescent lamps.
*Inorganic Chemistry.*

**CAX** Community Automatic Exchange.

**CAX** computer-assisted exercise.
exercice assisté par ordinateur.

**CB** Callable Bond.
*Business; Economics; Finance.*

**CB** 1. Cambodia.
1. Cambodge.
2. counter-battery.
2. contrebatterie.

**CB** (abbr.) Campobasso, Italy.

**CB** Cash Book.

**CB** Central Bank.

**CB** Centro Banca (Italy).
*Italian Bank.*

**Cb** Cerebellum.

**CB** Citizens' Band.
The citizens' band is the frequency band used by the citizens' radio service for signal transmission.
*Telecommunications.*

**Cb** The chemical symbol for Columbium.
Niobium was formerly called Columbium.

**CB** Conduction Band.
*Solid-State Physics.*

**CB** Confidential Bulletin.

**CB** Corporate Bonds.
*Business; Economics; Finance.*

**CB** Corporate Budget.

**CB** Coupon Bond.

**CB** Credito Bergamasco (Italy).
*Italian Bank.*

**Cb** Cumulonimbus clouds.
*Meteorology.*

**CB** Currency Bond.

**CB1** Cannabinoid Receptor 1.
Neuromodulatory receptor in the brain.
*Biology; Cellular and Molecular Pharmacology; Physiology.*

**CBA** Centro di Biotecnologie Avanzate.
Italian initialism of the: Advanced Biotechnologies Center.

**CBA** Cost Benefit Analysis.
In the U.S.A., CBA is used for any regulation anticipated to have an impact on the U.S. economy of more than $100m. In Britain, the Health and

Safety Executive uses this method routinely, as does the Department of Transport.
**CBA** Cytometric Bead Array.
*Immunoassays.*
**CBAI** Centre Bruxellois d'Action Interculturelle (Belgium).
**CBASSE** Commission on Behavioral And Social Sciences and Education (U.S.A.).
**CBC** Canadian Broadcasting Corporation (Canada).
**CBC** Carbon-Burnup Cell.
*Fluidized Bed Combustion Technology.*
**CBC** Center for Biodiversity and Conservation (U.S.A.).
**CBC** Certificat de Bonne Conduite (France).
**CBC** Chain Block Controller.
**CBC** Chambre Belge des Comptables (Belgium).
Founded in 1905.
**CBC** Chronic Beryllium Disease.
CBC is also known as: Berylliosis.
*Analytical Chemistry; Immune Reactions; Lymphocyte Proliferation; Workplace Health Studies.*
**CBC** 1. Civil Budget Committee.
1. Comité du budget civil.
2. cross-border connection (circuit).
2. connexion (circuit) transfrontière.
**CBC** Community-Based Care.
*Public Health.*
**CBC** Complete Blood Count.
*Pathology.*
**CBC** County Borough Council (G.B.).
**CBC movement** Community-Based Conservation movement.
*Conservation Biology; Wildlife Conservation.*
**CBC(T)** Customer-Bank Communication (Terminal).
**CBCTR** The Cooperative Breast Cancer Tissue Resource.
Of The U.S. NCI.
For further details see under: **NCI**.
**CBD** Cannabidiol.
Cannabidiol is a solid which is insoluble in water, soluble in alcohol and has a melting point of 67°C.
*Organic Chemistry.*
**CBD** Cash Before Delivery.
*Business; Finance.*
**CBD** Central Business District.
*Business; Finance.*
**CBD** Certificate of Bank Deposit.
*Banking; Business; Finance.*
**CBD** Chitin Binding Domain.
**CBD** Closed Bladder Drainage.
*Medicine.*
**CBD** Common Bile Duct.
The common bile duct connects the cystic duct and the hepatic duct.
*Anatomy.*
**CBD** Convention on Biological Diversity.
The CBD opened for signature at the Earth Summit in Rio de Janeiro in 1992.
For further details see under: **COP**.
**CBDW** Canada Basin Deep Water.
**CBE** Center for Biofilm Engineering (U.S.A.).
*Biofilm Engineering; Chemical Engineering; Environmental Biotechnology; Microbiology.*
**CBE** Center for Biology Education.
**CBE** Commander of the British Empire (G.B.).
**CBED** Convergent Beam Electron Diffraction.
*Chemical Engineering; Chemistry; Materials Science.*
**CBER** Center for Biologics Evaluation and Research (U.S.A.).
Of the U.S. FDA.
For further details see under: **FDA**.
**CBERS** China-Brazil Earth Resources Satellite.
CBERS-1 was launched: October 1999. CBERS-2 was launched: August 2002.
*Earth Remote Sensing Satellites.*
**CBF** Cerebral Blood Flow.
*Medicine.*
**CBF1** C promoter Binding Factor 1.
*Medicine; Molecular Virology; Oncology; Pharmacology.*
**CBFR** Colliding Beam Fusion Reactor.
*Plasma Physics.*
**CBFWCP** Columbia Basin Fish and Wildlife Compensation Program (Athalmere, British Columbia, Canada).
*Habitat Biology; Mountain Ecosystems; Wildlife Management.*
**CBHL** Council of Botanical and Horticultural Libraries.
**CBI** Computer-Based Instruction.
**CBI** Confederation of British Industries (G.B.).
**CBI** Contralateral Bias Index.
*Neurobiology; Psychology.*
**CBI** Cosmic Background Imager.
A telescope in the Atacama Desert of Chile.
*Cosmology.*
**CBI scale** Chronic Brain Injury scale.
The CBI rates symptoms on a scale from 0 to 9.
*Epidemiology; Medicine; Neurology.*
**cbk.** (abbr.) checkbook.
**CBL** Case-Based Learning.
CBL is a type of artificial intelligence.
**CBL** Chesapeake Biological Laboratory (U.S.A.).

**CB/L** Commercial Bill of Lading.
*Business; Commerce.*
**CBL** Convective Boundary Layer.
**CBL** cross-border link.
liaison transfrontière.
**CBM** Carbohydrate-Binding Molecule.
*Biochemistry.*
**C.B.M.** Centro per il Bambino Maltrattato e la cura della crisi familiare (Italy).
*Italian Center.*
**CBM** Chlorobromomethane.
**CBM** Cognitive Behavior(al) Modification.
*Behavioral Changes; Conditioning Techniques.*
**CBM** 1. Comité du budget militaire.
1. Military Budget Committee (MBC).
2. confidence-building measures.
2. mesures de confiance (MDC).
**CBMS** Computer-Based Message Service.
**CBN** Central Bank of Nigeria.
**CBO** Certificate of Beneficial Ownership.
*Business; Finance.*
**CBO** Congressional Budget Office (U.S.A.).
**CBOE** Chicago Board Options Exchange (U.S.A.).
The CBOE is the biggest of the U.S. options markets.
**CBOT** Chicago Board Of Trade (U.S.A.).
Also: **CBT**.
**CBP** Calmodulin Binding Peptide.
**CBP** Clam Breeding Program.
Virginia Institute of Marine Science (U.S.A.).
**CBP** CREB Binding Protein.
CBP is a transcriptional coactivator protein.
For further details see under: **CREB**.
**CBPQ** Corporation des Bibliothécaires Professionnelles du Québec (Canada).
*Canadian Library Association.*
**CBR** Center for Bioenvironmental Research (U.S.A.).
**CBR** Chemical, Biological and Radiological; Chemical, Bacteriological and Radiological.
*Medicine.*
**CBR** Community Bureau of Reference.
Joint Research Center - Commission of the European Communities.
**CBR** Cosmic Background Radiation.
*Astronomy; Astrophysics; Physics.*
**$CBrF_3$** Bromotrifluoromethane.
$CBrF_3$ is used as a fire-extinguishing agent.
*Organic Chemistry.*
**CBRN** chemical, biological, radiological and nuclear.
chimique, biologique, radiologique et nucléaire.
**$CBr_3NO_2$** Bromopicrin.
Bromopicrin, also known as: Nitrobromoform is used for poison gas.
*Organic Chemistry.*
**$CBr_2O$** Carbonyl Bromide.
Carbonyl Bromide, also known as: Bromophosgene, is used as a poison gas.
*Organic Chemistry.*
**CBS** Combined Behavioral Score.
**CBS** Commission for Basic Systems - U.N.
**CBS** Consolidated Balance Sheet.
**CBSO** City of Birmingham Symphony Orchestra (G.B.).
**C.B. system** Central-Battery system.
**CBT** Center for Broadband Telecommunications.
The CBT is based at the Denmark Technical University.
**CBT** Chemical and Biological Terrorism.
**CBT** Chicago Board of Trade (U.S.A.).
Also: **CBOT**.
**CBT** computer-based training.
formation assistée par odinateur.
**CBT** Coulomb Blockade Thermometer.
*Applied Physics; Physics.*
**CB transport** Coulomb Blockade transport.
*Chemistry; Nanoscale Science and Technology; Physics.*
**CBTS** Centers for Basic and Translational Science USA-CRI.
For further details see under: **CRI**.
**CBU** cluster bomb unit.
arme à dispersion.
**CBW** Chemical and Biological Warfare.
*Military Science.*
**CC** 1. cahier des charges.
1. statement of work (SOW 2.).
2. cash credit.
2. crédit de paiement (CP 7.).
3. Complaints Committee.
3. Comité de réclamations (CREC).
4. component command(er).
4. commandement (commandant) de composante.
5. compression chamber.
5. chambre de décompression.
**CC**; **C.C.** Carta Costituzionale.
Italian initialism meaning: Constitutional Charter.
**CC** Cash Commodity.
**CC** Cashier's Check / Cheque.
**CC** Centre de Commutation.
**CC** Certified Check.
*Business; Economics; Finance.*
**C.C.** Chamber of Commerce.
**cc** (abbr.) chapters.
**CC** Charges Collect.

**CC** Chief Complaint.
**C.C.** Circuit Court.
**Cc** cirrocumulus.
*Meteorology.*
**C.C.** City Council.
**CC** Cluster Controller.
**CC** Code Converter.
The Code Converter actually converts information from one coding scheme to another.
*Computer Technology.*
**CC; C.C.** Codice Civile.
Italian initialism meaning: Civil Code.
**CC; C.C.** Codice di Commercio.
Italian initialism meaning: Commercial Code.
**CC** Combinatorial Chemistry.
**CC** Command Chain.
**CC** Command Character.
Command character is also known as: Control Character.
*Computer Programming.*
**C.C.; C.C.** Commissione Centrale.
Italian initialism meaning: Central Commission.
**CC** Communications Controller.
**CC** Companion Cell.
*Botany; Plant Biology; Plant Physiology.*
**CC** Compétence de Communication.
**CC** Computer Center.
**CC** Computerized Conferencing.
**C.C.** Controlled Circulation.
**CC** Conventions Collectives.
French initialism meaning: Collective Agreements.
**cc** (abbr.) copies.
**CC; C.C.** Corrente Continua.
Italian initialism meaning: Direct Current.
*Electricity.*
**CC; C.C.** Corte Costituzionale.
Italian initialism meaning: Constitutional Court.
**C.C.** Corte dei Conti.
Italian initialism meaning: National Audit Office.
**C.C.** Corte di Cassazione.
Italian initialism meaning: Court of Cassation.
Also: **CASS**.
**CC** Counterclockwise.
**CC; C.C.** County Council.
**C.C.** County Court.
**CC** Critical Condition.
*Medicine.*
**c.c.** cubic centimetre.
**CC** Current Complaint.
*Medicine.*
**CCA** Canonical Correlation Analysis.
*Climate.*
**CCA** 1. carrier-controlled approach.
1. approche contrôlée depuis le porte-avions.
2. centre de contrôle d'approche.
2. approach control centre (ACC 4.).
3. contamination control area.
3. zone de contrôle de la contamination.
**CCA** Circuit Court of Appeals.
**CCA** Complementary Chromatic Adaptation.
*Plant Biology.*
**CCA** Controlled Circulation Audit.
**CCA** Current Cost Accounting.
**CCAFS** Cape Canaveral Air Force Station (U.S.A.).
**CC AIR** component command(er) Air.
commandement (commandant) de la composante aérienne.
**CC AIR NORTH** Component Command(er) Allied Air Forces North.
Commandement (commandant) de composante des Forces aériennes alliées Nord.
**CC AIR SOUTH** Component Command(er) Allied Air Forces South.
Commandement (commandant) de composante des Forces aériennes alliées Sud.
**CCAM line** Carbonaceous Chondrite Anhydrous Minerals line.
*Chemistry; Earth and Space Sciences; Mineral Sciences.*
**CCAMLR** Convention of the Conservation of Antarctic Marine Living Resources.
**CCAP-M** Culture Collection of Algae and Protozoa - Marine (G.B.).
*Culture Collections.*
**CCAR** centre de contrôle d'approche radar.
radar approach control centre (RAPCON).
**CCAs** Crystalline Colloidal Arrays.
*Chemistry.*
**CCATF** commander combined amphibious task force.
commandant de force opérationnelle amphibie multinationale.
**CCB** Command Control Block.
**CCB** Compagnie Commerciale de Banque.
*Banks.*
**CCB** Configuration Control Board.
Commission de contrôle de la configuration.
**CCB** Convertible Circuit Breaker.
**CCBR** Centre for Cellular and Biomolecular Research.
A newly formed Center at the University of Toronto (Canada).
**CC brain structures** Central Complex brain structures.
*Biomedical and Life Sciences; Genetics; Molecular Genetics.*

**CCBS** Committee on Capacity Building in Science.
Located in the U.S.A.. Founded in 1993; aims to promote to the public and to decision-makers an understanding and appreciation of the proper role of science in modern society and of building a scientific capacity in all parts of the world.
**CCC** capacity coordination cell [obsolete].
cellule de coordination des capacités [obsolète].
**CCC** cathodal closure contraction.
**CCC; C.C.C.** Central Control Commission.
**CCC; C.C.C.** Central Criminal Court.
**CCC** Chemical Coal Cleaning.
**CCC** Civilian Conservation Corps.
The former U.S. Federal Agency (1933-1943) that instituted and administered projects for the conservation of natural resources.
**CCC** Commodity Credit Corporation (G.B.).
**CCC** Competition and Credit Control (G.B.).
*Banking.*
**CCC** Copyright Clearance Center (U.S.A.).
A not-for-profit Corporation.
**CCC** Customs Cooperation Council (U.S.A.).
**CCCA** centre de contrôle de la circulation aérienne.
air traffic control centre (ATCC).
**CCCA-BTP** Comité Central de Coordination de l'Apprentissage du Bâtiment et des Travaux Publics (France).
**CCCC** Center for Captive Chimpanzee Care (Florida, U.S.A.).
*Animal Research.*
**CCCC** cross-channel coordination centre.
centre de coordination transmanche.
**CCCE** Cassa Centrale Cooperazione Economica.
Italian initialism meaning: Central Fund for Economic Co-operation.
**CCCO** Committee on Climate Changes and the Oceans.
**CCCP** Carbonyl cyanide m-chlorophenylhydrazone.
*Molecular and Cell Biology.*
**CCCS** Consumer Credit Counseling Services.
**CCD** Calcite Compensation Depth.
*Geological Sciences.*
**CCD** Camouflage Concealment and Deception.
*Defence.*
**CCD** Centro Cooperazione Doganale.
Italian initialism meaning: Centre for Customs Co-operation.
**CCD** Charge-Coupled Device.
*Electronics; Superconductor Devices.*
**CCD** Cleidocranial Dysplasia.
CCD is a skeletal disease.
*Bone Research; Cell and Developmental Biology; Developmental Genetics; Genetics; Osteoporosis.*
**CCD** Cold-Cathode Discharge.
**CCD** Confederazione Coltivatori Diretti.
Italian initialism meaning: Farmers' Association.
**CCD** Convention to Combat Desertification.
Held in Geneva, Switzerland in October 2001.
**CCDM** Cold Collisionless Dark Matter.
*Astronomy; Astrophysics.*
**CCDP** Climate Change Detection Project.
**CCDS** Center for the Commercial Development of Space (U.S.A.).
**CCDs** Charge-Coupled Devices.
**CCDU** Comitato dei Cittadini per i Dirittti dell'Uomo.
*Italian Committee.*
**CCE** Contour of Constant Energy.
*Applied Physics; Materials Science; Physics; Superconductivity.*
**CCE** Countries of Central Europe.
**CCEA** Cabinet Council on Economic Affairs (U.S.A.).
**CCEE** countries of Central and Eastern Europe.
pays d'Europe centrale et orientale (PECO).
**CCEI** Conferenza per la Cooperazione Economica Internazionale.
Italian initialism meaning: International Economic Co-operation Conference.
**CCEP** Citrus Canker Eradication Program - Florida's.
A joint effort by the FDACS and USDA-APHIS.
For further details see under: **FDACS**; **USDA**; **APHIS**.
**CCETT** Centre Commun d'Etudes de Télédiffusion et de Télécommunications.
**CCF** conventional counter-force.
contre-force conventionnelle.
**CCF** Crédit Commercial de France.
*French Bank.*
**CCFAS** Compact Colony-Forming Active Substance.
*Biochemistry; Carbohydrates.*
**CCFF** Canadian Cystic Fibrosis Foundation.
**CCFF** Compensatory and Contingency Financing Facility.
In order to increase its activities, the International Monetary Fund has had to create new forms of lending. The standby facilities with which it began now operate alongside the CCFF; the EFF; the SAF; the ESAF and the STF.
*Business; Finance.*
For further information see under: **EFF**; **ESAF**; **SAF** and **STF**.
**CCG** 1. cartesian coordinate grid.
1. carroyage en coordonnées cartésiennes.

2. Coordinating Committee of Government Budget Experts [obsolete - replaced by CCR].
2. Comité de coordination des experts budgétaires gouvernementaux [obsolète - remplacé par CCR].
**CCG** Childhood Cancer Group.
The CCG is a consortium of over 100 institutions in the U.S.A.
**CCG** Consiglio di Cooperazione del Golfo.
Italian initialism of the: Gulf Cooperation Council.
**CCGE** cellule de coordination de la guerre électronique.
electronic warfare coordination cell (EWCC).
**CCGs** Cross-Correlograms.
**CCh** Carbachol.
Carbachol is also known as: Carbamylcholine Chloride.
*Pharmacology.*
**CCH** Channel-Check Handler.
**CCI; C.C.I.** Camera di Commercio Internazionale.
Italian initialism of the: International Chamber of Commerce.
**CCI** Chambre de Commerce et d'Industrie (France).
**CCI** Chambre de Commerce Internationale.
French initialism of the: International Chamber of Commerce.
**CCI** Chronic Coronary Insufficiency.
*Medicine.*
**CCI** Contrôleur des Contributions Indirectes (France).
**CCIAA** Camera di Commercio, Industria, Agricoltura, Artigianato.
Italian intialism of the: Chamber of Commerce for Industry, Agriculture and Handicraft.
**CCIP** Chambre de Commerce et d'Industrie de Paris (France).
French initialism of the: Paris Chamber of Commerce and Industry.
**CCIR** 1. Comité consultatif international des radiocommunications [obsolète].
1. International Radio Consultative Committee (IRCC) [obsolete].
2. commander's critical information request.
2. demande d'informations critiques soumise par le commandant.
3. commander's critical information requirement.
3. besoin du commandant en informations critiques.
**CCIRM** collection, coordination and intelligence requirements management.
gestion de la recherche, de la coordination et des besoins en renseignement.
**CCI(S)** Common Channel Interoffice (Signaling).
**CCITT** Comité Consultatif International Télégraphique et Téléphonique.
French initialism of the: Consultative Committee on International Telegraphy and Telephony.
*Standards-making Organization* (communications) of the United Nations.
**CCIW** Canada Centre for Inland Waters (Canada).
**CCJTF** commander combined joint task force.
commandant de groupe de forces interarmées multinationales.
**CCK** Cholecystokinin.
CCK is one of the numerous peptides secreted from the gut during meals.
*Medicine; Satiety Peptides.*
**CCL** centre de coordination logistique.
logistics coordination centre (LCC 4.).
**CCL** Consorzio Cooperative Lavoratori (Italy).
Italian initialism of the: Workers Cooperatives Consortium.
**CCL** Contratto Collettivo di Lavoro.
Italian initialism meaning: Collective Labour Contract.
**CCLF** commander combined landing force.
commandant de force de débarquement multinationale.
**$CClF_3$** Chlorotrifluoromethane.
*Organic Chemistry.*
**$CCl_3NO_2$** Chloropicrin.
Chloropicrin is used mainly in pesticides and dyes.
*Inorganic Chemistry.*
**$C_6Cl_4O_2$** Chloranil.
Chloranil is used mainly as an agricultural fungicide.
*Organic Chemistry.*
**CCLRC** The Council for the Central Laboratory of the Research Councils (G.B.).
**CCM** Chromatograph Control Module.
**CCM** Community Climate Model.
**CCM** counter-countermeasure.
contre-contre-mesure.
**CCMAR** centre de coordination maritime.
maritime coordination centre (MACC).
**CCME** contre-contre-mesures électroniques [obsolète].
electronic counter-countermeasures (ECCM) [obsolete].
**CCMRI** Central Coal Mining Research Institute (China).
*Chinese Institute.*
**CCMS** Committee on the Challenges of Modern Society.
Comité sur les défis de la société moderne (CDSM).

**CCMS** Commodity Configuration Management System.
*Business; Commerce.*
**CCMV** Cowpea Chlorotic Mottle Bromovirus.
*Agricultural Biotechnology; Transgenic Crop Safety.*
**CCN** Cloud Condensation Nuclei.
*Atmospheric Research; Chemistry; Earth Sciences; Oceanography.*
**CCNA** Conseil de coopération nord-atlantique [obsolète - remplacé par CPEA].
North Atlantic Cooperation Council (NACC) [obsolete - replaced by EAPC].
**CC NAV** component command(er) naval.
commandement (commandant) de composante navale.
**CC NAV NORTH** Component Command(er) Allied Naval Forces North.
Commandement (commandant) de composante des Forces navales alliées Nord.
**CC NAV SOUTH** Component Command(er) Allied Naval Forces South.
Commandement (commandant) de composante des Forces navales alliées Sud.
**CCNE** Comité Consultatif National d'Ethique.
*Genetics; Medicine.*
**CCNL** Contratto Collettivo Nazionale di Lavoro (Italy).
Italian initialism meaning: Collective National Labor Agreement; Collective National Bargaining Agreement.
**CCNY** City College of New York (U.S.A.).
**CCO** Cytochrome C Oxidase.
*Biochemistry; Chemistry.*
**CCOL** Coordinating Committee on the Ozone Layer - U.N.
**$C_1$ compounds** One-carbon compounds.
*Biochemistry; Chemical Engineering; Microbiology.*
**CC.OO.PP.** Consorzio di Credito per le Opere Pubbliche (Italy).
**CCOPE** Cooperative COnvective Precipitation Experiment.
**CCP** 1. Cellule de coordination du partenariat.
1. Partnership Coordination Cell (PCC 1.).
2. configuration change proposal.
2. proposition de modification de la configuration.
3. Conseil conjoint permanent (OTAN - Russie).
3. Permanent Joint Council (NATO - Russia) (PJC).
**CCP; C.C.P.** Chief Commissioner of Police.
**CCP** Code of Civil Procedure.
**CCP, ccp** Commissione Centrale dei Prezzi.
Italian initialism meaning: Central Committee on Prices.
**CCP** compte-chèque postal.
French initialism meaning: Post Office account.
**CCP** Court of Common Pleas.
**CCPC** Civil Communications Planning Committee.
Comité d'étude des télécommunications civiles.
**CCPC** (The Banking Industry's) Co-operative Credit Purchasing Company (Japan).
The CCPC was inaugurated in January 1993.
**CCPCC** Chinese Communist Party Central Committee.
**CCPIT** China Council for the Promotion of International Trade (China).
**CCP-RM** Conseil conjoint permanent au niveau des représentants militaires [OTAN - Russie].
Permanent Joint Council at Military Representatives' Level (PJC-MR) [NATO - Russia].
**CCR** Center for Cancer Research (U.S.A.).
**CCR** 1. centralized control room.
1. salle de contrôle centralisé.
2. Coordinating Committee on Remuneration.
2. Comité de coordination sur les rémunerations.
**CCR** Centro Comune di Ricerca (Italy).
Italian initialism meaning: Common Research Center.
**CCR** Clinical Cancer Research.
*Publication.*
**CCR** Cold-Cathode Rectifier.
CCR is also known as: Gas-Filled Rectifier.
*Electronics.*
**CCR** Commission on Civil Rights (U.S.A.).
**C.C.R.** Consorzio Cooperative Residenziali (Italy).
**CCRI** Climate Change Research Initiative (U.S.A.).
**C.Cr.P.** Code of Criminal Procedure.
**CCRS** Canada Centre for Remote Sensing.
**CCS** The airport code for Caracas, Venezuela.
**CCs** Carbonaceous Chondrites.
*Earth and Space Sciences; Mineral Sciences.*
**C2CS** command and control communication system.
système de communication de commandement et de contrôle.
**CCSA** Common Control Switching Arrangement.
**CCSD** Cardiac Conduction System Disease.
*Genetics; Heart Research.*
**CCSD method** Coupled-Cluster Singles and Doubles method.
**CCSDS** Consultative Committee for Space Data Systems (U.S.A.).
**CCSI** Camera di Commercio Svizzera in Italia.

Italian initialism of the: Swiss Chamber of Commerce in Italy.
**CCSR** Center for Climate System Research (U.S.A.).
**CCSSO** Council of Chief State School Officers (U.S.A.).
**CCST** corps combat support troops.
troupes d'appui tactique de corps.
**CCSU** Central Connecticut State University (U.S.A.).
**CCT** Certificati di Credito del Tesoro.
Italian initialism meaning: Treasury Credit Certificates.
*Commerce; Finance.*
**CCT** Chocolate-Coated Tablet.
*Medicine.*
**CCT** 1. combat-capable trainer.
1. avion d'entraînement apte au combat.
2. combat control team.
2. équipe de contrôle du combat.
**CCTA** Central Computer and Telecommunications Agency.
**CCTA** centre de contrôle tactique Air.
tactical air control centre (TACC).
**C.C.T.E.** Comitato Contro la Tossicodipendenza e l'Emarginazione.
*Italian Committee.*
**CCT images** Constant Current Topographic images.
*Chemistry; Physics.*
**ccTLDS** country code Top Level Domain Names.
**CCTV** closed circuit television (system).
(système de) télévision en circuit fermé.
**CCU** The airport code for Calcutta, India.
**CCU** Cardiac Care Unit.
*Cardiology.*
**CCU** Central Control Unit.
*Control Systems.*
**CCU** Comité Consultatif des Universités (France).
*French Committee.*
**CCU** Communications Control Unit.
*Computer Technology; Telecommunications.*
**CCU** Coronary Care Unit.
*Cardiology.*
**CCU** Critical Care Unit.
*Medicine.*
**CCW** Channel Command Word.
Channel Command Word is also known as: Channel Control Command.
*Computer Programming.*
**ccw.** (abbr.) counterclockwise.
Also: **cckw**.
**CCWCP** Coordinating Committee for the World Climate Program.
**CCZ** Civilian Control Zone (Korea).
**Cd** The chemical symbol for Cadmium.
Cadmium is used mainly to make alloys. The word cadmium derives from the Greek term "earth of Cadmus".
*Chemistry; Symbols.*
**CD** Canadian Dollar.
Also: **CAD**.
*Currencies.*
**cd** (abbr.) candela.
candela is the base unit of luminous intensity.
*Optics.*
**cd.** (abbr.) card.
*Computer Technology; Electronics.*
**CD** Carrier Detection.
**c/d** carried down.
**CD**; **c.d.** Cash Discount.
**CD** Certificate of Deposit.
**CD** 1. Chad.
1.Tchad.
2. civil defence.
2a. défense civile.
2b. protection civile.
**CD** Circular Dichroism.
*Biochemistry; Optics.*
**CD** Civil Defence.
**CD** Classe/Facteur de Différentiation.
French initialism meaning: Cluster of Differentiation.
*Medicine.*
**CD** Closing Date.
*Business; Commerce.*
**CD** Cluster Designation.
*Immunology.*
**CD** Comitato Direttivo.
Italian initialism meaning: Managing Committee.
**CD** Communicable Disease.
The communicable disease is an infectious disease that can be transmitted from one affected individual to another.
*Medicine.*
**CD** Compact Disc/Disk.
*Accounting Engineering; Computer Technology.*
**CD** Consigliere Delegato.
Italian initialism meaning: Managing Director.
**CD** Constant Drainage.
*Medicine.*
**CD** Contagious Disease.
A contagious disease is any of the various diseases that are transmitted through contact or proximity.
*Medicine.*
**CD** Convulsive Disorder.
*Medicine.*

**c.d.** cosiddetto.
Italian initialism meaning: so-called.
**CD** Curative Dose.
*Medicine.*
**CDA** Career Development Award.
**CDA**; **C.D.A.** Centro Discipline Aeronautiche.
*Italian Center.*
**CDA** Command and Data Acquisition.
**CDA** Compound Document Architecture.
**C.d.A.** Consiglio di Amministrazione.
Italian initialism meaning: Board of Directors.
**C.d.A.** Corte d'Appello.
Italian initialism meaning: Court of Appeal.
**C.d.A.** Corte d'Assise.
Italian initialism meaning: Court of Assizes.
**CDB** Cyprus Development Bank (Cyprus).
**CDBG** Community Development Block Grants (U.S.A.).
**$CdBr_2$** Cadmium Bromide.
Cadmium Bromide is used mainly in photography.
*Inorganic Chemistry.*
**CDC** Calculated Date of Confinement.
*Medicine.*
**CDC** Call Directing Code.
*Data Communications.*
**CDC** Centers for Disease Control and prevention (U.S.A.).
**CDC** 1. centre de détection et de contrôle.
1. control and reporting centre (CRC 1.).
2. centre de distribution de clés.
2. key distribution centre (KDC).
3. certificat de conformité.
3. certificate of conformance (COC).
**CDC** Centre des Dirigents de la Construction.
*French Center.*
**C.D.C.** Centro della Cooperazione (Italy).
*Italian Center.*
**CDC** Climate Diagnostics Center (U.S.A.).
**CDC** Constitutional Dynamic Chemistry.
*Supramolecular Chemistry; Supramolecular Science.*
**CDCA** Chenodeoxycholic Acid.
Also known as: Chenic Acid; Chenodiol.
*Biochemistry.*
**CDCC** Caribbean Development and Co-operation Committee.
Of the United Nations.
**CDCIR** Community Documentation Center on Industrial Risk.
The CDCIR was created to collect, classify and disseminate data on safety regulations, technical rules and accidents relevant for the implementation of the Directive Joint Research Center - *Commission of the European Communities.*
**CDC/NCID** Centers for Disease Control and prevention / National Center for Infectious Diseases (U.S.A.).
**$CdCO_3$** Cadmium Carbonate.
Cadmium Carbonate is used as a chemical reagent.
*Inorganic Chemistry.*
**CDD** Contrat à Durée Determinée.
French initialism meaning: Fixed-term contract.
*Employment.*
**CDDI** Copper Distributed Data Interface.
**CDDT** Countdown Demonstration Test.
**CDE** Centre pour le Développement Industriel (France).
French initialism of the: Center for Industrial Development.
**CDE** 1. Conference on Confidence- and Security-Building Measures and Disarmament in Europe.
1. Conférence sur les mesures de confiance et de sécurité, et sur le désarmement en Europe.
2. concept development and experimentation.
2. élaboration et expérimentation de concepts.
3. core deployable element.
3. noyau déployable.
**CDE engine** Concentration Difference Energy engine.
**CDER** Center for Drug Evaluation and Research (U.S.A.).
**CDEs** Conserved DNA Elements.
*Anatomy; Cell Biology.*
**CDF** Collider Detector at Fermilab.
*Physics.*
**CDF** Common Data Format.
**CDF** Consiglio di Fabbrica.
Italian initialism meaning: Shop Committee; Works Council.
**CDF** Cumulative Distribution Function.
**CDFS** Cloud Depiction and Forecast System.
**CDG** The airport code for Charles de Gaulle Airport, Paris, France.
**CDI** California Department of Insurance (U.S.A.).
**CDI** Center for Defense Information (U.S.A.).
*Nuclear Threat Reduction; Policy Analysis.*
**CDI** Centro Diagnostico Italiano (Italy).
*Italian Center.*
**CDI** Centro Di sviluppo Industriale (Italy).
**CDIAC** Carbon Dioxide Information Analysis Center (U.S.A.).
**CDIF** Component Development and Integration Facility.
**CDKs** Cyclin-Dependent Kinases.

*Biochemistry; Biophysics; Molecular Biology; Physiology.*

**CdM** Cassa del Mezzogiomo (Italy).
*Italian Bank.*

**CDM** Code Division Multiplex.
*Telecommunications.*

**CDM** Cold Dark Matter.
*Astronomy; Astrophysics; Physics.*

**C.D.M.** Collettivo Donne Milanesi (Milan, Italy).

**cd/m²** candelas per square meter of surface.

**CDMA** Code Division Multiple Access.
*Next-generation Mobile Phone Technology.*

**CDMS** Cold Dark Matter Search.
At Stanford University, Palo Alto, California, U.S.A.
*Astronomy; Astrophysics; Physics.*

**CDMS** Cryogenic Dark Matter Search.
*Astronomy; Bolometers; Physics.*

**C.d.N.** Codice della Navigazione.
Italian initialism meaning: Navigation Code.

**cDNA** complementary Deoxyribonucleic Acid.
*Genetics.*

**CDNA** Conférence des directeurs nationaux des armements.
Conference of National Armaments Directors (CNAD).

**CdO** Cadmium Oxide.
Cadmium Oxide is used mainly in battery electrodes.
*Inorganic Chemistry.*

**Cdo** (abbr.) Commando.

**CDOA** Cellule Départementale d'Ouvrages d'Art (France).

**CDOM** Colored Dissolved Organic Matter.

**CDOS** combat day of supply.
jour d'approvisionnement de combat.

**CDOW** Colorado Division Of Wildlife (U.S.A.).
*Conservation Biology.*

**CDP** Cassa Depositi e Prestiti (Italy).
Italian initialism meaning: Bank for Deposits and Loans. Founded 150 years ago.
*Italian Bank.*

**CDP**; **Cdp** Customer Dedicated Processor.

**CDPs** Cord Dorsum Potentials.

**C.d.R.** Cassa di Risparmio.
Italian initialism meaning: Savings Bank.

**Cdr** (abbr.) Commander.
Also: **Comdr.**; **Cmdr**; **Comm**.

**CDR** Council for Development and Reconstruction (Lebanon).

**CDR** critical design review.
examen critique de la conception.

**CD28RE** CD28 Responsive Element.
*Flow Cytometry Analysis; Medical Research.*

**CDRI** Central Drug Research Institute (India's Government).

**C.D.R.L.** Centro di Documentazione e Ricerche per la Lombardia (Italy).
*Italian Center.*

**CDRL** contract data requirements list.
liste des données contractuelles.

**CD-ROM** Compact Disk with Read-Only Memory.
The CD-ROM is used for storage of a very large volume of data.
*Computer Technology.*

**CDRs** Complementarity-Determining Regions.

**CD-RW** Rewritable CDs.

**CdS** Cadmium Sulfide.
CdS is used mainly in solar cells, and in ceramic glazes.
*Inorganic Chemistry.*

**CDS**; **C.D.S.** Centro Diagnosi Sterilità.
Italian initialism of the: Center for the Diagnosis of Sterility.
*Italian Center.*

**CDS** 1. Chief of Defence Staff [UK].
1a. Chef d'état-major de la défense (CEMD).
1b. Chef d'état-major des armées (CEMA) [FR].
2. civil direction of shipping.
2. direction civile de la navigation commerciale.

**C.d.S.** Codice della Strada.
Italian initialism meaning: Road Regulations.

**CDS** Command and Data Subsystem.

**CDS** Compatible Duplex System.

**CDS** Comprehensive Display System.

**C.d.S.** Consiglio di Sicurezza.
Italian initialism meaning: Security Council.

**C.d.S.** Consiglio di Stato.
Italian initialism meaning: Council of State.

**CDS** Consolidated Debenture Stock.

**CdSe** Cadmium Selenide.
Cadmium Selenide is used mainly in photoelectric cells.
*Inorganic Chemistry.*

**CDSH** Centre de Documentation en Sciences Humaines (France).
*French Center.*

**CDSL** Consumer Digital Subscriber Line.
*Broadband Technologies.*

**CDSM** Comité sur les défis de la société moderne.
Committee on the Challenges of Modern Society (CCMS).

**CDSORG** Civil Direction of Shipping Organization.
Organisation de la direction civile de la navigation commerciale.

**CD-4 sound** Compatible Discrete Four-Channel sound.
**CDST** Centre de Documentation Scientifique et Technique (France).
*French Center.*
**CDT** Cambridge Display Technology (G.B.).
**CDT** Central Daylight Time.
**Cdt.** (abbr.) commandant.
French abbreviation meaning: commander.
**CdTe** Cadmium Telluride.
Design and production of thin-film modules made of cadmium telluride (CdTe). Areas of special attention include increased module efficiency and lower costs.
*Thin-film modules.*
**CdTe blend** Cadmium and Tellurium blend.
*Photovoltaics; Solar Cells.*
**CDU** Classificazione Decimale Universale.
Italian initialism meaning: Universal Decimal Classification.
**CDW** Charge Density Wave.
For further details see under: **CDWs**.
**$CdWO_4$** Cadmium Tungstate.
Cadmium Tungstate is used mainly in fluorescent paint.
*Inorganic Chemistry.*
**CDWs** Charge Density Waves.
*Astronomy; Atomic-Scale Materials Physics; Physics.*
**CE** Capillary Electrophoresis.
**CE** Capitale d'Esercizio.
Italian initialism meaning: Working Capital.
**CE** Capitale Economico.
Italian initialism meaning: Economic Capital.
**CE** Cardiac Enlargement.
*Medicine.*
**CE** Caserta, Italy.
**CE** Cash Earnings.
*Business; Economics; Finance.*
**CE** Central Element.
Of the synaptonemal complex.
*Genomics; Cell Biology; Molecular Biology.*
**CE** Central Europe.
**Ce** the chemical symbol for Cerium.
Cerium is a rare-earth element having the atomic number 58 and a melting point of 795°C. Cerium is used mainly in the metal industry and in the glass industry.
*Chemistry.*
**CE** Chemical Energy.
*Physical Chemistry.*
**CE** Chemical Engineer.
**CE** Chief Engineer.
**CE** Chief Executive.
**CE** Cholesterol Ester.
*Clinical Chemistry.*
**C.E.**; **CE** Civil Engineer.
**CE** Comitato Esecutivo.
Italian initialism meaning: Executive Committee.
**CE** Commission Européenne.
French initialism meaning: European Commission.
**CE** Commodity Exchange.
**CE** Common Era.
**CE** Conseil d'Europe.
French initialism meaning: Council of Europe.
**CE** Cooperative Extension.
**C.E.** Corps of Engineers.
**CE** Cost Effectiveness.
*Business; Commerce.*
**CE** Council of Europe (Strasbourg).
**CE** Current Efficiency.
*Physical Chemistry.*
**CE** Cytopathic Effect.
Also: **CPE**.
*Virology.*
**CEA** Carcinoembryonic Antigen.
*Medicine.*
**CEA** Center for Extreme ultraviolet Astronomy.
*Extreme Ultraviolet Astronomy.*
**CEA** Center for EUV Astrophysics.
For further details see under: **EUV**.
**CEA** Commissariat à l'Energie Atomique (France).
**CEA** Commission Economique des Nations Unies pour l'Afrique.
**CEA** Commission of Enterprises and Administration.
**CEA** Commodity Exchange Authority.
**CEA**; **C.E.A.** Confederazione Europea dell'Agricoltura.
Italian acronym of the: European Agricultural Federation.
**CEA** Cost Effectiveness Analysis.
*Business; Commerce; Economics; Finance.*
**CEA** Council on Economic Advisers.
**CEA** crisis establishment authority.
authorité responsable du tableau d'effectifs du temps de crise.
**CEA** European Insurance Committee (France).
**CEAC** Committee for European Airspace Coordination.
Comité de coordination de l'espace aérien européen.
**CEAL** Committee on East-Asian Libraries.
**CEAREX** Coordinated Eastern ARctic EXperiment.
**CEAS** Conditioned Equivalence Agreements.
*U.S.-E.C. Business; Transatlantic Issues.*

**CEASI** Concerted European Action on Structural Intermetallics.
*European Community Project.*

**CEAT** Comando Especial Anti-Terrorista (El Salvador).

**CEB** Central Electricity Board.

**CEC** 1. Central European Command [obsolete].
1. Commandement du Centre Europe [obsolète].
2. commandant en chef.
2. Commander-in-Chief (CINC).
3. cooperative engagement capability.
3. moyens d'engagement en coopération.

**CEC** Centre Electronique de Comptabilité.

**CEC** Circulation Extra-Corporelle.
French initialism meaning: Extracorporeal Circulation.
*Medicine.*

**CEC** Commission of the European Community.

**CEC** Commodity Exchange Commission.

**CEC** Council for Exceptional Children (U.S.A.).
*Biomedical Sciences; Psychology.*

**CECA** Communauté Européenne du Charbon et de l'Acier; Comunità Europea del Carbone e dell'Acciaio.
French and Italian acronym of the: European Coal and Steel Community.

**Cecafe** Council of Green Coffee Exporters of Brazil.
Cecafe, the coffee trade group of Brazil was inaugurated on 27th April 1999.

**CECC** Civil Emergency Crisis Cell.
cellule de gestion des crises pour les situations d'urgence dans le domaine civil.

**CECEI** Comité des Etablissements de Crédit et des Entreprises d'Investissement.
*French Committee.*

**$CeCl_3$** Cerium Chloride.
Cerium Chloride is used mainly in spectrography.
*Inorganic Chemistry.*

**CECLANT** commandant en chef (français) pour l'Atlantique.
French Commander-in-Chief Atlantic.

**CECODHAS** Comité Européen de COordination De l'HAbitat Social.

**CECS** Centro de Estudios Cientificos de Santiago (Chile).

**CED** Committee for Economic Development.
*Economics; Finance.*

**CED** Comunità Europea di Difesa.
Italian acronym of the: European Defence Community.

**CEDAC** Cause-Effect Diagram with Additional Cards.

**CEDAW** Committee for the Elimination of Discriminations Against Women.

**CEDB** Component Event Data Bank.
Analysis of operational data stored in the CEDB collected in two of ENEL'S power plants. Joint Research Center - Commission of the European Communities.

**CEDD** Centres of Excellence for Drug Discovery.
Of GlaxoSmithKline.

**CEDDA** Center for Experimental Design and Data Analysis.

**CEDEFOP** Centre Européen pour le DEveloppement de la Formation Professionnelle.
French acronym of the: European Center for the Development of Vocational Training.
*Educational Web Site.*

**CE design** Competitive Equilibrium design.

**Cedex** Courrier d'entreprise à distribution exceptionnelle.
French abbreviation meaning: special postal service for companies.

**CEDF** China Enterprise Development Fund.
*Chinese Fund.*

**CEDI** CEntro di Documentazione e di Informazione (Italy).
*Italian Center.*

**CEDIEP** CEntre de Documentation et d'Information sur les Etudes et les Professions (Belgium).
*Belgian Center.*

**CEDIMON** Centro Europeo per lo Sviluppo Industriale dell'Oltremare.
Italian acronym of the: European Center for Industrial Overseas Development.

**CEDP** common European defence policy.
politique européenne de défense commune (PEDC).

**CEE** Centre d'Etudes de l'Emploi (France).
*French Center.*

**CEE** Committee on Energy and the Environment (U.S.A.).
Of the U.S. NRC.
For further details see under: **NRC**.

**CEE** (international) Commission (on Rules for the Approval of) Electrical Equipment.

**CEE** Communauté Economique Européenne.
French initialism of the: European Economic Community.

**CEE** Conference on English Education.

**CEEF** Compagnie Européenne pour l'Equipement du Foyer.

**CEELI** Centraland East European Law Initiative.
Of the ABA.
*Human Rights.*

For further details see under: **ABA**.
**CEEP** Centro Ecumenico Europeo per la Pace.
*European Center*.
**CEES** Center for Earth and Environmental Sciences (U.S.A.).
Of the IUPUI.
For further details see under: **IUPUI**.
**CEES** Center for Environmental and Estuarine Studies (U.S.A.).
Of the University of Maryland.
**CEF** Centre de Formalités des Entreprises - European Community.
An E.C. Center to simplify formalities for new enterprises.
**CEF** Comité Electrotechnique Français (France).
**$CeF_3$** Cerium Fluoride.
Cerium Fluoride is used mainly to prepare cerium metal.
*Inorganic Chemistry*.
**CEFA**; **Cefa** Comitato Europeo Formazione Agraria.
*Italian Committee*.
**CEFE** Comité d'Etudes sur le Financement des Entreprises.
*French Committee*.
**CEFIC** European Council of Chemical Manufacturers Federations (Brussels, Belgium).
**CEFPI** Council of Educational Facility Planners International.
*Educational Web Site*.
**CEFs** Chicken Embryo Fibroblasts.
*Cancer; Experimental Medicine; Molecular Medicine; Signal Transduction*.
**CEFTA** Central European Free Trade Area.
The five nations of CEFTA are: The Czech Republic, Hungary, Poland, Slovakia and Slovenia - and the Baltic States.
**CEGES** cellule de gestion de l'espace aérien.
airspace management cell.
**CEGT** Centre d'Exploitation et de Gestion Télétex (France).
*French Center*.
**CEI** Comitato Elettrotecnico Italiano.
CEI is located in Milan, Italy.
*Italian Committee*.
**CEI** Communauté des Etats Indépendants.
French acronym meaning: Commonwealth of Independent States.
**CEI** Conferenza Episcopale Italiana.
Italian acronym meaning: Italian Episcopal Conference.
**CEI** Cost Effectiveness Index.
*Business; Economics; Commerce*.
**CEI** Coulomb Explosion Imaging.
CEI is an experimental technique to determine molecular structures.
*Hypercarbon Chemistry; Molecular Spectroscopy; Physics*.
**CEI** Council of Engineering Institutions (G.B.).
**CEIP** Coastal Energy Impact Program.
**CEIPI** Centre d'Etudes Internationales de la Propriété Industrielle (France).
*French Center*.
**Ce.I.S.** Centro Italiano di Solidarietà.
Ce.I.S. is located in Rome, Italy.
*Italian Center*.
**CEL** 1. Combined Events List.
1. liste combinée d'événements.
2. see CINCEASTLANT 1.
2. voir CINCEASTLANT 1.
**CELA** Canadian Environmental Law Association (Canada).
**CELI**; **Celi** Chiesa Evangelica Luterana in Italia (Italy).
**CELL** Continuing Education Learning Laboratory.
**cell** The above acronym was coined using the English word "cell".
*Biology; Computer Technology; Electricity; Engineering; Mathematics; Nucleonics; Physical Chemistry; Telecommunicatians*.
**CELSS** Controlled Ecological Life Support System.
**Celt** (abbr.) Celtic.
Celtic is a branch of the Indo-European family of languages. It includes Irish, Scots Gaelic, Welsh, and Breton.
*Languages*.
**CELT** crypto equipment for low-speed telegraphy.
matériel cryptographique pour télégraphie à faible vitesse de modulation.
**CELTA** CEntre de Linguistique Théorique Appliquée (Zaire).
*Linguistics*.
**cem.** (abbr.) cement.
*Geology; Invertebrate Zoology; Materials* - An adhesive used for binding objects, secreted by some invertebrates.
*Histology* - In histology, cement is also known as: cementum.
**CEM** 1. chef d'état-major.
1. Chief of Staff (COS 2.).
2. compatibilité électromagnétique.
2. electromagnetic compatibility (EMC).
**CEM** Compagnie Electromécanique.
**CEM** Continuous Emissions Monitoring.
**CE.M.A.** CEntro Manageriale Ambrosiano.
*Italian Center*.

**CEMA** Chef d'état-major des armées [FR].
1a. Chief of Defence (CHOD).
1b. Chief of Defence Staff (CDS 1.) [UK].
1c. Joint Chief of Staff (JCS) [US].
**CEMA** Conveyor Equipment Manufacturers Association.
**CEMAT** Mesoamerican Centre for the Study of Appropriate Technology (Guatemala).
**CEMB** Centro di Educazione Musicale di Base.
*Italian Center.*
**CEMD** chef d'état-major de la défense.
Chief of Defence (CHOD).
**C.E.M.E.A.** Centri di Esercitazione nei Metodi dell'Educazione Attiva (Italy).
*Italian Center.*
**CEMF** Counterelectromotive Force.
*Electromagnetism.*
**CEMG** chef d'état-major général.
General Chief of Staff (GCOS).
**CeMM** Center of Molecular Medicine.
New Center that will open in 2004 in Vienna, Austria.
For further details see under: **GMI** and **IMBA**.
**C.E.M.P.** Centro Educazione Matrimoniale e Prematrimoniale (Italy).
*Italian Center.*
**CEN** Centre d'études de l'Energie Nucléaire.
French acronym meaning: Center for Nuclear Energy Studies.
**CEN** Centro Europeo di Normalizzazione.
*European Center.*
**C.E.N.** Centro Studi dell'Energia Nucleare.
Italian acronym meaning: Center for Nuclear Energy Studies.
**CEN** Comitato Europeo di Normalizzazione - European Community.
*Standardization Committee.*
**CENELEC** Comitato Europeo di Normalizzazione nel campo Elettrotecnico ed Elettronico.
*Standardization Committee.*
**CENR** Committee on the Environment and Natural resources Research (U.S.A.).
At the White House.
*Chemistry and Biology of the Oceans; Hypoxia Science.*
**CENSA** Council of European and Japanese National Shipowners' Associations (G.B.).
**CENSHADCOM** Central Shipping Advisory Committee.
Comité consultatif central de la marine marchande.
**CENSIS** Centro Studi Investimenti Sociali.
Italian acronym meaning: Social Investments Study Centre.
**CENT.**; **cent.** (abbr.) Centrifugal.
*Mechanics; Neurology.*
**cent.** (abbr.) century.
**CENTAG** Central Army Group, central Europe [obsolete].
Groupe d'armées centre du Centre Europe [obsolète].
**CENTLANT** Central Atlantic Sub-Area [obsolete].
Sous-secteur central de l'Atlantique [obsolète].
**CENTRC** Central New York Resources Council (U.S.A.).
**CEO** Center of Earth Observation.
**$CeO_2$** Ceric Oxide.
Ceric Oxide is used mainly in ceramics, and in nuclear fuels.
*Inorganic Chemistry.*
**CEO** Chief Executive Officer.
**CEO** Collective - Electronic Oscillator.
*Chemistry; Optical Sciences.*
**CEO** convoy escort oiler.
pétrolier d'escorte de convoi.
**$C_{16}EO_8$** Octaethyleneglycol Monohexadecylether.
**CEOA** Central Europe Operating Agency [obsolete - replaced by CEPMA].
Agence Centre Europe d'exploitation [obsolète - remplacée par CEPMA].
**CEOI** Communications & Electronics Operating Instructions.
**CEOS** Committee on Earth Observation Satellites.
**CEP** Caribbean Environment Program - U.N.
**CEP** Centri per l'Educazione Permanente.
Of the Milan Town Council.
*Italian Center.*
**CEP** 1. circular error probable.
1. écart circulaire probable (ECP).
2. civil emergency planning.
2. plans civils d'urgence (PCU).
3. communications equipment programme.
3. programme d'equipment des télécommunications.
**CEP** Comitato Euro Provinciale (Italy).
**CEP** Committee on Environmental Protection.
**CEPA** Commonwealth Environment Protection Agency (Australia).
**CEPAIM** Consorcío de Entitades Para la Accion Integral con los Migrantes (Madrid, Spain).
*Spanish Consortium.*
**CEPAL**; **Cepal** Commissione Economica Per l'America Latina e i Caraibi - U.N.
**CEPAS** crypto-equipment for packet switching.
matériel de chiffrement pour la commutation par paquets.
**CEPD** Civil Emergency Planning Directorate.

Direction des plans civils d'urgence.
**CEPER** Centro per la Prevenzione dei Rischi.
*Italian Center.*
**CEPES** Centre Européen Pour l'Enseignement Supérieur.
Located in Bucharest, Romania. Founded in 1972.
**CEPES, C.E.P.E.S.** Comitato Europeo per il Progresso Economico e Sociale.
Italian acronym of the: European Committee for Economic and Social Development.
**CEPEX** Central Equatorial Pacific Experiment.
*Atmospheric Research; Geophysics; Meteorology.*
**CEPEX** Controlled Ecosystems Pollution EXperiment.
**CEPH** Centre d'Etude du Polymorphisme Humain (France).
*French Center.*
**CEPI** Capital Expenditure Price Index.
**CE.P.I.** CEntro Psicopedagogico per l'Infanzia.
*Italian Center.*
**CEPIS** Pan American Centre for Sanitary Engineering and Environmental Sciences (Peru).
**CEPM** Centre d'Exploitation Postale Métropolitain (France).
*French Center.*
**CEPMA** Central Europe Pipeline Management Agency.
Agence de gestion des oléoducs en Centre-Europe.
**CEPMO** Central Europe Pipeline Management Organization.
Organisation de gestion des oléoducs en Centre-Europe.
**CEPO** Central European Pipeline Office [obsolete - replaced by CEPMO].
Bureau Centre-Europe des pipelines [obsolète - remplacé par CEPMO].
**CEPP** Committee on Elementary Particle Physics (U.S.A.).
**CEPPC** Central Europe Pipeline Policy Committee.
Comité de gestion Centre-Europe des pipelines.
**CEPQ** civil emergency planning questionnaire.
questionnaire des plans civils d'urgence (QPCU).
**CEPS** Central Europe pipeline system.
réseau Centre-Europe des pipelines.
**CEPT** Conférence Européenne des Administrations des Postes et des Télécommunications.
French acronym meaning: European Conference of Postal and Telecommunications Administrations.
**CEPU** Centro Europeo Preparazione Universitaria.
*Italian Center.*
**CEQ** Council on Environmental Quality.
**CER** Centro Europeo Ricerche.
Italian acronym meaning: European Research Center (Rome, Italy).
**CER** combat effectiveness report.
rapport sur l'efficacité au combat.
**Cer** Comitato per l'edilizia residenziale.
*Italian Committee.*
**CER** Conditioned Emotional Response.
*Medicine.*
**CER** Conti Economici Regionali (reparto).
Italian acronym of the: Central Statistics Institute (department).
**CER** Coordinated Ecosystem Research.
**CERACS** Comparative Evaluation of the different RAdiating Cables and Systems technologies - *European Community.*
**CERAM** Centre d'Enseignement et de Recherche Appliquées au Management.
**CERC** Center for Environmental Research and Conservation (U.S.A.).
CERC is involved in studies to combat loss of biodiversity.
*U.S. Research Center.*
**CERC** Centre d'Etudes des Revenus et des Coûts (France).
*French Center.*
**CERC** Correlated Electron Research Center (Japan).
**CERCA** CEntre de Recherche en Calcul Appliqué (Canada).
CERCA is a Quebec Center created in 1992. Its main objective is to intensify technology transfer from university to industry.
*Computational Fluid Dynamics; Chemistry.*
**CERCHAR** Centre d'Etudes et Recherches de Charbonnages de France.
**cerebellar LTD** cerebellar Long-Term Depression.
*Medicine; Neuroscience.*
**CEREQ** Centre d'Etudes et de REcherches sur les Qualifications (France).
**CERES** Centre d'Etudes et de Recherches En Stratégie (France).
*French Center.*
**CERES** Centro di Ricerche e Studi Economici.
Italian acronym of the: Center for Research and Economic Studies.
**CERES** Clouds and Earth's Radiant Energy System.
**CERFA** Centre d'Enregistrement et de Révision des Formulaires Administratifs - European Community.
CERFA is an E.C. Center which helps new enterprises in the compilation of forms (as far as language, regulations and other details are concerned).

**CE.R.G.E.S.** CEntro Ricerche Giuridiche ed Economico-Sociali (Milan, Italy).
*Italian Research Center.*

**CERI** Center for Educational Research and Innovation (U.S.A.).

**CERI** Center for Environmental Research Information.

**CERI** Central Electrochemical Research Institute (U.S.A.).

**CERI** Centro Europeo delle Relazioni Industriali - European Community.
Italian acronym of the: European Center for Industrial Relations.

**CERI** Clean Energy Research Institute (U.S.A.).

**C.E.R.I.E.S.** Centre de Recherches et Investigations Epidermiques et Sensorielles.
C.E.R.I.E.S. is an autonomous research center based in Paris (France), funded by Chanel.
*Awards; Physiology and Biology of Healthy Skin.*

**CERIF** Common European Research Information Format.
*European Community Research Information.*

**CERL** Central Electricity Research Laboratories.

**CERN** Commission Européenne pour la Recherche Nucléaire.
French acronym of the: European Commission for Nuclear Research.

**C.E.R.N.** Consiglio Europeo per le Ricerche Nucleari.
Italian acronym of the: European Council for Nuclear Research.

**CERNet** China Education and Research Network (China).
*Internet in China.*

**CERP** Centro Europeo di Relazioni Pubbliche.
Italian acronym of the: European Centre of Public Relations.

**CERPOD** CEntre of studies and Research on POpulation for Development.
Sahel Institute, Mali.

**CERT** Centre d'Etude et de Recherche de Toulouse (France).
*French Research Center.*

**cert.** (abbr.) certificate; certification.

**CERT** Council of Education, Recruitment and Training for Hotel and Catering Industry (Ireland).
*Irish Council.*

**CERT e T** Centro di Economia Regionale dei Trasporti e del Turismo (Italy).

**CERTI** CEntro di Ricerche Tributarie dell'Impresa (Italy).
Of the L. Bocconi University (Milan, Italy).
*Italian Research Center.*

**CES** Center for Environmental Studies (U.S.A.).

**CES** Central Excitatory State.
*Medicine.*

**CES; Ces** Circuit Emulation Service.

**CES** coast earth station [INMARSAT].
station terrienne côtière [INMARSAT].

**CES** Comitato Economico e Sociale - E.C.
Italian acronym of the: Economic and Social Committee. Set up by the Treaties of Rome in 1957.

**CES** Committee of European Shipowners.

**CES** Committee on Earth Studies (U.S.A.).

**CES** Confederazione Europea dei Sindacati.
Italian acronym of the: Trade Unions European Confederation.

**CES** Conseil Economique et Social.

**CESA** Canadian Engineering Standards Associations (Canada).

**CESA** Centre d'Enseignement Supérieur des Affaires (HEC - ISA - CFC) (France).

**CESAR** Central European Satellite Advanced Research.
To study *Earth's magnetosphere, Ionosphere and Thermosphere.*

**CESCOT** Centro Sviluppo Commercio, Turismo e Terziario (Italy).
*Italian Center.*

**CESD** Cholesteryl Ester Storage Disease.
*Medicine.*

**CESDP** Common European Security and Defence Policy.
politique européenne commune en matière de sécurité et de défense (PECSD).

**CESEN** CEntro Studi ENnergia (Italy).
Italian acronym of the: Center for Energy Studies.

**CESG** Center for Eukaryotic Structural Genomics.
Funded by NIH (U.S.A.).
For further details see under: **NIH**.

**CESI** Centro Elettronico Sperimentale Italiano
*Italian Center.*

**CESNEF** CEntro Studi Nucleari Enrico Fermi.
Italian acronym of the: Enrico Fermi Nuclear Studies Center, of the Polytechnic of Milan, Italy.

**CESPE** Centro Studi di Politica Economica.
Italian acronym of the: Economic Policy Studies Centre (Italy).

**CESPRI** Centro Studi sui Processi di Internazionalizzazione (Italy).

**CESR** Cornell Electron Storage Ring.

**Cestame** Centre d'études spècialisées des techniques appliquées.

**CESVIT** CEntro per lo SVIluppo della ricerca Tecnologica.

Italian acronym of the: Center for the Development of Technological Research. CESVIT is based in Florence, Italy.

**CESVITEC** CEntro per la promozione e lo SVIluppo TECnologico delle piccole e medie imprese del Mezzogiorno.
Italian acronym of the: Center for the Technological Promotion and Development of small - and medium-sized enterprises of Southern Italy. CESVITEC is based in Naples, Italy.

**CET** combat enhancement training.
entraînement de perfectionnement au combat.

**CETA** Crew and Equipment Translation Aid.

**CETIAT** CEntre Technique des Industries Aéroliques et Thermiques (France).
*French Technical Center.*

**CETIM; Cetim** CEntre Technique des Industries Mécaniques (France).
*French Technical Center.*

**CETOP** Comité Européen des Transmissions Oléohydrauliques et Pneumatiques (France).
*European Committee.*

**CETP** Cholesteryl Ester Transport Protein.

**CETS** Commission on Engineering and Technical Systems (U.S.A.).

**C.E.T.S.** Continuing Education and Training Service (G.B.).

**CEUMC** Chairman of the European Union Military Committee.
président du Comité militaire de l'Union européenne (PCMUE).

**CEV** Citrus Exocortis Viroid.

**CEW** Counter-Electronic Warfare.

**Cf** The chemical symbol for Californium.
Named after **California** because it was discovered by researchers at the University of California, Berkeley, U.S.A.
*Symbols; Chemistry.*

**CF** Carried Forward.

**CF** Carrier Frequency.
Carrier Frequency is also known as: Center Frequency.
*Telecommunications.*

**CF** Cash Flow.
*Business; Economics; Finance.*

**CF** Cement Floor.
*Buildings.*

**CF; cf** Centrifugal Force.
*Mechanics.*

**CF; cf** Centripetal Force.
*Mechanics.*

**CF** Characteristic Frequency.
*Audiology; Hearing Sciences; Communication Sciences; Communication Disorders; Physiology.*

**CF** Christensen Fund (Palo Alto, California, U.S.A.).

**CF** Codice Fiscale.
Italian initialism meaning: Fiscal code; taxpayer's code.

**CF** Complement Fixation.
*Immunology.*

**CF** 1. Congo.
1. Congo.
2. counterforce.
2. contre-force.

**CF** Constant Frequency.

**CF** Counting Factor.
*Polypeptides.*

**CF** Cystic Fibrosis.
Cystic fibrosis is a hereditary disease. It is also known as: mucoviscidosis because the exocrine glands produce mucus of high viscosity.
*Medicine.*

**CFA** Canadian Forestry Association.

**CFA** Carbonate Fluorapatite.

**CFA** ceasefire agreement.
accord de cessez-le-feu.

**CFA; CfA** Center For Astrophysics (Harvard-Smithsonian's).
The CFA is located in Cambridge, Massachusetts (U.S.A.).

**CFA** Colonization Factor Agar.

**CFA** Commission of Fine Arts (U.S.A.).

**CFA** Communauté Financière Africaine.

**CFA** Complete Freund's Adjuvant.

**CF1A** Cleavage Factor 1A.
*Cell Biology; Pathology.*

**CF&I** Cost, Freight and Insurance.
*Commerce; Shipping.*

**CFAO** Compagnie Française de l'Afrique Occidentale.

**CFAR** Center For AIDS Research.
The Great Lakes Regional CFAR is a consortium of scientists of various U.S. Universities.

**CFAR** constant false alarm rate.
taux constant de fausses alertes.

**C-FARR** Center for Fertility And Reproductive Research (U.S.A.).

**CFATG** Centre de Formation Aux Techniques Gazières (France).

**C-FAT loading** Creep-FATigue loading.
Optimisation of methodologies to predict crack initiation and early growth in components under complex creep-fatigue loading.
*European Community Project.*

**CFB** Call For Bids.
**CFB Group** Cytophaga-Flexibacter-Bacterioides Group.
*Biology; Marine Science.*
**CFC** Colony-Forming Cell.
*Hematology.*
**CFC** Combined Federal Campaign (U.S.A.).
**CFC** Controlled Foreign Company.
*Business; Finance.*
**CFCs** Chlorofluorocarbons.
Desiccant systems use materials such as silica gel to remove moisture from the air while cooling it. Solid desiccant materials are often embedded in a rotating wheel, where they can be dried and regenerated for continued use by exposing them to heat. Because desiccants remove water from the air without condensing it, they control humidity more effectively than air conditioners. They also operate without the use of chlorofluorocarbons (CFCs) and can handle the larger flow rates of outside air required by new indoor air quality standards.
*Desiccant Cooling.*
**CFD** Computational Fluid Dynamicist.
**CFD** Corporate Finance Director.
**CFE** Campaign for Free Education (G.B.).
**CFE** Center For Education (U.S.A.).
**CFE** conventional armed forces in Europe.
forces armées conventionnelles en Europe (FCE 1.).
**CFED** Corporation For Enterprise Development (Arizona; U.S.A.)
**CFEM** Compagnie Française d'Entreprises Métalliques (France).
**CFF** Columbus Free Flyer.
**CFF** Cystic Fibrosis Foundation (U.S.A.).
**CFFE** Cantor Financial Futures Exchange.
The CFFE is the first electronic futures market to set up in the U.S.A. (1999).
*Futures Markets.*
**cfh** cubic feet per hour.
**CFHT** Canada-France-Hawaii Telescope.
*Adaptive Optics; Astronomy; Planetary Science.*
**CFI** Canada Foundation for Innovation.
The CFI was created in 1997 with government funds. It is Canada's largest foundation.
*Awards; Grants.*
**CFL** 1. ceasefire line.
1. ligne de cessez-le-feu.
2. coordinated fire line.
2. ligne de tirs coordonnés.
**CFL** Council of Federal Libraries.
**cfm** cubic feet per minute.
**CFMs** Chlorofluoromethanes.
**CFNT** Centro de Formacion en Nuevas Technologias (Spain).
*Spanish Center.*
**CFO** Carrier Frequency Oscillator.
**CFO** Chief Financial Officer.
**CFONB** Comité Français d'Organisation et de Normalisation Bancaires (France).
**CFP** Centro di Formazione Professionale.
Italian initialism meaning: Vocational Training Center.
**CFP** Cyan Fluorescent Protein.
*Biological Imaging; Cell Biology and Metabolism; Human Development.*
**CFPB** Centre de Formation de la Profession Bancaire (France).
*French Center.*
**CFPC** Centre de Formation Professionnelle Continue (Luxemburg).
*Vocational Training Center.*
**CFP-GIAO method** Charge Field Perturbation - Gauge Including Atomic Orbital method.
*Chemistry.*
**CFR** Code of Federal Regulations (U.S.A.).
**cfr.** (abbr. ) confronta.
Italian abbreviation meaning: compare (cf.).
**CFR** Contact Flight Rules.
*Navigation.*
**CFR** 1. (aircraft) crash, fire-fighting and rescue.
1. lutte contre le feu et sauvetage en cas d'accident (d'aéronef).
2. customer-funding regime.
2. régime de financement par le client.
**CFRBCS** The Cooperative Family Registry for Breast Cancer Studies (U.S.A.).
Of the U.S. National Cancer Institute.
**CFR Committee** Cooperative Fuel Research Committee.
**CFRP** Carbon Fibre Reinforced Plastic.
*Materials.*
**Cfs** Carbon fullerenes.
*Materials and Interfaces.*
**CFs** Characteristic Frequencies.
For further details see under: **CF**.
**CFS** Chronic Fatigue Syndrome.
**CFS** Committee on Fundamental Science.
*U.S. Committee.*
**cfs** cubic foot/feet per second.
Also: **CUSEC**.
*Metrology.*
**CFSE** Carboxyfluorescein diacetate Succininyl Ester.
*Biophysics; Neurobiology; Physiology.*

**CFSP** Common Foreign and Security Policy - European Union.
**CFTC** Commodity Futures Trading Commission (U.S.A.).
**CFTR** Cystic Fibrosis Transmembrane conductance Regulator.
**CFTRI** Central Food Technological Research Institute.
**CFTRs** Cystic Fibrosis Transconductance Regulators.
*Cell Biology; Biophysics; Medicine; Physiology; Pulmonary Biology.*
**CFU** Colony-Forming Unit.
*Hematology.*
**CFU-G assay** Colony-Forming-Unit-Granulocyte assay.
*Granulocytic Colonies; Medicine; Oncology; Transcription Research.*
**CFU-S** Colony-Forming Unit Spleen.
*Hematology.*
**CFV** ceasefire violation.
violation du cessez-le-feu.
**CFV** Constant Flow Valve.
**CFV** Credito Fondiario delle Venezie S.p.A.
*Italian Bank.*
**CFX** command field exercise.
exercice de commandement sur le terrain.
**CG** Capital Gain.
*Business; Economics; Finance.*
**CG** Capital Goods.
**C.G.** Captain of the Guard.
**CG**; **cg** center of gravity.
*Mechanics.*
**cg.** (abbr.) centigram / centigramme.
Also: **cgm**.
*Metrology.*
**CG** Chorionic Gonadotropin.
Chorionic Gonadotropin is a glycopeptide hormone.
*Endocrinology.*
**CG** Ciliary Ganglionic.
**cg.** (abbr.) coniugato/a.
Italian abbreviation meaning: married.
**C.G.** Consul General.
**CG** Zaire.
Now: Democratic Republic of Congo.
**CGA** Color Graphics Adapter.
*Computer Programming.*
**CGAP** Cancer Genome Anatomy Project.
The CGAP is funded by the U.S. National Cancer Institute; the U.S. National Library of Medicine; and many U.S. drug and biotechnology Companies.
*Genomics; U.S. Projects.*
**CGAT program** Canadian Genome Analysis and Technology program.
*Canadian Program.*
**CGB** Center for Genomics and Bioinformatics.
At Karolinska Institute.
**CGC** Caenorhabditis Genetics Center (U.S.A.).
The CGC is supported by NIH's National Center for Research Resources.
*Genetic Mapping; Nematodes.*
For further details see under: **NIH**.
**CGCMs** Coupled ocean-atmosphere General Circulation Models.
*Climate Change; Meteorology.*
**CGCP** Climate and Global Change Program.
*U.S. Program.*
**CGCR** Committee on Global Change Research (U.S.A.).
**CGCS** Center for Global Change Science.
Of the Massachusetts Institute of Technology (U.S.A.).
**CGD** Caixa Geral de Depósitos.
*Portguese Bank.*
**CGD** Chronic Granulomatous Disease.
*Immunology; Medicine; Pathology.*
**CG discharge** Cloud-to-Ground discharge.
*Geophysics.*
**cge** (abbr.) carriage.
**CGE** Compagnie Générale d'Electricité.
**CGER** Commission on Geosciences, Environment, and Resources (U.S.A.).
**CGF** Crystal Growth Furnace.
**CGH** Cape of Good Hope (South Africa).
**CGH** Computer-Generated Hologram.
**CGIAR** Consultative Group on International Agricultural Research.
**CGIC** Compressed Gas-Insulated Cable.
**CGII**; **C.G.I.I.** Confederazione Generale Italiana dell'Industria.
Italian initialism of the: Italian Industry Association (Italy).
**CGIL** Confederazione Generale Italiana del Lavoro (Italy).
Italian initialism of the: General Federation of Italian Trade Unions.
**CGI-S scale** Clinical Global Impressions Severity scale.
*Human Behavior; Neuroscience; Psychiatry.*
**CGIT line** Compressed Gas-Insulated Transmission line.
**CGL** Confédération Générale du Logement (France).
**CGM** Cairo Geological Museum (Egypt).

**CGM** Center for Genomics and Bioinformatics.
Launched in 1997 as a new academic department at the Karolinska Institute, Stockholm, Sweden.
**cgm** centigram.
Also: **cg**.
*Metrology.*
**CGM** Chauffage Gaz Modulable.
**cGMP** cyclic Guanosine 3', 5'-Monophosphate.
*Biochemistry; Cell Biology; Neuroscience; Pharmacology.*
**CGMW** Commission for the Geological Map of the World.
**CGN** The airport code for Cologne, Germany.
**CGNPs** Cerebellar Granular Neuronal Precursors.
*Cancer Research; Genetics; Medicine; Molecular Biology; Neurology; Oncology.*
**cgo** (abbr.) cargo.
**CGP** Committee on Gravitational Physics (U.S.A.).
**CGP** coût global de possession.
life cycle cost /LCC 2./.
**CGPS** Convention Générale de Protection Sociale (France).
**CGRO** Compton Gamma Ray Observatory.
The CGRO was launched in April 1991.
*Astrophysics.*
**CGRP** Calcitonin Gene-Related Peptide.
*Biochemistry.*
**CGS**; **C.G.S.** Centimetro; Grammo; Secondo.
Italian initialism meaning: Centimeter; Gram; Second.
Also: **cgs**.
*Metrology.*
**CGS** Centro di Geodesia Spaziale (Italy).
*Italian Center.*
**CGS** Commander General Staff.
commandant de l'état-major général.
**CGS** Committee on Geological Sciences.
Of the U.S. National Academy of Sciences.
**CGSC** Coli Genetic Stock Center (U.S.A.).
The CGSC maintains genotypic descriptions and genetic map information for many *E. Coli* K 12 strains.
**CGSTC**; **C.G.S.T.C.** Centro Giovanile Scambi Turistici.
Italian initialism of the: Youth Center for Tourism and Cultural Exchanges.
**CGS technology** Continuous Grain Silicon technology.
*Ultra-high definition TVs.*
**CGT** Capital Gains Tax.
**CGT** Confédération Générale du Travail.
**CH** Case Hardening / Casehardering.
*Geology; Materials Science; Metallurgy.*
**c.h.** central heating.
**ch** (abbr.) chain (22 yards).
**ch** (abbr.) chapter.
**ch** (abbr.) charge(s).
**ch.** (abbr.) chief.
**CH** Chieti, Italy.
**CH** China.
**C.H.** Clearing House.
**CH** Congenital Hypomyelination.
**CH** Current Hogging.
*Electronics.*
**C.H.** Custom(s) House.
**CH** Switzerland's international vehicle-registration letters.
**$CH_4$** Methane.
**$C_4H_{10}$** Butane.
Butane is used mainly as a fuel for lighters; in many household appliances and for numerous industrial applications.
*Organic Chemistry.*
**$C_9H_8$** Indene.
*Organic Chemistry.*
**$C_{10}H_{18}$** Camphane.
Camphane is also known as: Bornane.
*Organic Chemistry.*
**$C_{15}H_{18}$** Guaiazulene.
*Pharmacology.*
**$C_{15}H_{24}$** Cadinene.
*Organic Chemistry.*
**$C_{18}H_{12}$** Chrysene.
Chrysene is used in organic synthesis.
*Organic Chemistry.*
**$C_{40}H_{56}$** Carotene.
Carotene is also known as: Carotin; Pre-Vitamine H.
*Biochemistry.*
**ChAC** Choline Acetyltransferase.
**Cha clouds** Chamaleon clouds.
*Astronomy; Astrophysics; Space Research.*
**CHAm.**; **cham.** (abbr.) chamfered.
*Engineering.*
**CHAMP** Community Health Air Monitoring Program (U.S.A.).
Of the U.S. Environmental Protection Agency.
**CHAMP satellite** Challenging Minisatellite Payload satellite.
Measures the periodic $M_2$ magnetic-field variations.
*Applied Physics; Ocean Physics.*
**CHAMPVA** Civilian Health And Medical Program of the Veterans Administration (U.S.A.).
**chan.** (abbr.) channel.
*Agronomy; Building Engineering; Chemical*

*Engineering; Computer Technology; Electronics; Geography; Geology; Hydrology; Navigation-Nucleonics; Telecommunications; Transportation Engineering.*

**CHAOS** Cambridge Heart Antioxidant Study.
*Coronary Disease.*

**CHAP** Challenge Handshake Authentication Protocol.
*Computers.*

**CHAPS** Clearing House Automated Payment System (G.B.).

**CHARA** Center for High Angular Resolution Astronomy.
At the Georgia State University (U.S.A.).

**CHARISMA** CHicago-Argonne Resonant Ionization Spectrometer for Microanalysis.
*Chemistry; Geophysical Sciences; Materials Science.*

**CHARM** Coupled Hydrosphere - Atmosphere Research Model.

**CHARMS** CJTF HQ augmentation requirements and manning system [obsolete - now called GEMS].
système de gestion des besoins en effectifs (et moyens) d'appoint des QC de GFIM [obsolète - maintenant appelé GEMS].

**CHASM** Coventry Health And Safety Movement (G.B.).

**chasm** The above acronym was coined using the English word "chasm" (*Geology*).

**ChAT** Choline Acetyltransferase.

**C-H bonds** Carbon-Hydrogen bonds.
*Chemical Biodynamics; Chemistry.*

**$CHBr_3$** Bromoform.
Bromoform is used to separate minerals.
*Organic Chemistry.*

**$CH_2Br_2$** Methylene Bromide.
Methylene Bromide is used mainly as a solvent.
*Organic Chemistry.*

**$CH_3Br$** Methyl Bromide.
Methyl Bromide is used mainly as an extraction solvent for vegetable oils.
*Organic Chemistry.*

**$C_6H_5Br$** Bromobenzene.
Bromobenzene also known as: Phenyl Bromide is used mainly as a solvent.
*Organic Chemistry.*

**$CHCl_3$** Chloroform.
Chloroform also known as: Trichloromethane, is now used as a solvent and insecticide; formerly it was used as an anesthetic.
*Organic Chemistry.*

**$CHClF_2$** Chlorodifluoromethane.
Chlorodifluoromethane is used as a solvent and a refrigerant.
*Organic Chemistry.*

**$CH_2Cl_2$** Methylene Chloride.
For further details see under: **MC**.

**$CH_3Cl$** Methyl Chloride.
Methyl Chloride also known as: Chloromethane is used mainly as a refrigerant.

**$C_3H_5ClO$** Epichlorohydrin.
Epichlorohydrin is used mainly in the manufacture of glycerol, and in resins.
*Organic Chemistry.*

**ChCMV** Chrysanthemum Chlorotic Mottle Viroid.

**CHCs** Cuticular Hydrocarbons.
*Entomology; Environmental Sciences; Zoology.*

**CHD** Childhood Disease.
*Medicine.*

**Chd** Chordin.
*Developmental Biology.*

**CHD** Coronary Heart Disease.

**CHDM** Cold + Hot Dark Matter.
*Astronomy; Particle Astrophysics; Physics.*

**ChE** Cholinesterase.
Cholinesterase is also known as: Pseudocholinesterase; serum cholinesterase.
*Enzymology.*

**CHEC** Commonwealth Human Ecology Council (G.B.).

**chem.** (abbr.) chemical; chemist; chemistry.

**Ches.** (abbr.) Cheshire (England).

**CHESS** Cornell High Energy Synchrotron Source.

**CHEX** Committee on Human Exploration (U.S.A.).

**C/H experiments** Centurion / Halite experiments.
The C/H experiments were underground bomb tests carried out in the 1980s.
*Fusion; Physics.*

**CHF** Congestive Heart Failure.
*Heart Research; Medicine.*

**CHF** Critical Heat Flux.

**$CHF_3$** Fluoroform.
Fluoroform, also known as: Trifluoromethane, is used mainly as a refrigerant.
*Organic Chemistry.*

**ch.fwd.** charges forward.

**chg.** (abbr.) change.

**chg.** (abbr.) charge.
Also: **chge**.
*Electricity; Engineering; Mechanical Engineering; Metallurgy; Military Science; Nucleonics; Ordnance.*

**CHI** The airport code for the city of Chicago, U.S.A.

**$CH_3I$** Methyl Iodide.

Methyl Iodide is used mainly in microscopy.
*Organic Chemistry.*

**$CH_2I_2$** Methylene Iodide.
Methylene Iodide, also known as: Diiodomethane is used mainly to separate mineral mixtures.
*Organic Chemistry.*

**$C_2H_5I$** Ethyl Iodide.
Ethyl Iodide, also known as: Iodoethane is used mainly in medicine.
*Organic Chemistry.*

**CHIC** Community Health Information Classification and Coding - *European Community.*

**CHIL** Current-Hogging Injection Logic.

**CHILD** Council of Historical Libraries of Delaware.

**ChiMP** Chimpanzee Management Program.
*Chimpanzee Colonies; Ethology; Neuroscience.*

**CHIN** Community Health Information Network.

**Chin** (abbr.) Chinese.
Chinese is the standard language of China, based on the speech of Peiping; Mandarin; it is also a group of languages of the Sino-Tibetan family, including standard Chinese and most of the other languages of China.
*Languages.*

**CHINA** CHronic Infectious Neuropathic Agents.
*Medicine.*

**CHIP** CHannel-forming Integral Protein.
*Biological Chemistry; Medicine.*

**CHIP**; **ChIP** Chromatin Immunoprecipitation.
*Biochemistry; Cellular Biotechnology; DNA Replication; Experimental Oncology; Hematology; Histology; Medical Research; Molecular Bioscience; Molecular Genetics.*

**chip** The above acronyms were coined using the English word "chip" (*Archaeology- Electronics; Materials*).

**chir.** (abbr.) chirurgia.
Italian abbreviation meaning: surgery.

**chk.** (abbr.) check.
*Computer Technology.*

**CHL** Current-Hogging Logic.

**CHLA** Canadian Health Libraries Association (Canada).

**CHLAHG** Council High-Level Ad Hoc Group on NATO C3 Restructuring [obsolete].
Groupe ad hoc de haut niveau du Conseil sur le réaménagement de la structure des C3 de l'OTAN [obsolète].

**CHLIC** Coastal Health Library Information Consortium.

**CHM** Complete Hydatidiform Mole.
*Imprinting Mechanisms; Molecular Medicine.*

**Ch mass** Chandrasekhar mass.
*Astronomy; Astrophysics.*

**chmn.** (abbr.) chairman.
Also: **chn**.

**CHMS** Council of Heads of Medical Schools (G.B.).

**chn**. (abbr.) chairman.
Also: **chmn.**

**$C_{12}H_{16}N_2O_3$** Hexobarbital.
Hexobarbital is a barbiturate used as an oral sedative.
*Pharmacology.*

**$C_6H_8O_7$** Citric Acid.
Citric Acid is used mainly as a flavoring agent in food products.
*Biochemistry.*

**$C_{10}H_8O_3$** Hymecromone.
*Organic Chemistry.*

**$C_{10}H_{10}O_4$** Ferulic Acid.
Ferulic Acid is used as a preservative in food products.
*Organic Chemistry.*

**$C_{12}H_{26}O$** Lauryl Alcohol.
*Inorganic Chemistry.*

**$C_{15}H_{10}O_4$** Chrysophanic Acid.
Chrysophanic Acid is used mainly in the treatment of eczema.
*Organic Chemistry.*

**$C_{21}H_{30}O_2$** Hashish.
The word hashish derives from the Arabic term "herb".
*Pharmacology.*

**$C_{24}H_{40}O_4$** Chenodeoxycholic Acid.
$C_{24}H_{40}O_4$ is also known as: Chenodiol; Chenic Acid.
*Biochemistry.*

**CHO cells** Chinese Hamster Ovary cells.
Used to grow numerous viruses.
*Virology.*

**CHOD** Chief of Defence.
1a. chef d'état-major de la défense (CEMD).
1b. chef d'état-major des armées (CEMA) [FR].

**chol.** (abbr.) cholesterol.
*Biochemistry.*

**CHOP** change of operational control.
changement de contrôle opérationnel.

**CHOP** Cyclophosphamide, Hydroxydaunomycin (doxorubicin), Oncovin (vincristine) and Prednisone.
*Cancer Chemotherapy; Oncology.*

**CHP** Children's Hospital of Pittsburgh (U.S.A.).

**CHP technology** Combined Heat and Power technology.

*Energy Technology.*
**CHP** People's Republican Party (Turkey).
**ch.pd.** charges paid.
**ch.ppd.** charges prepaid.
**chq.** (abbr.) cheque.
Also: **ck**.
**CHR** Centre Hospitalier Régional.
French initialism meaning: Regional (general) Hospital.
*Medicine.*
**CHR** Committee on Human Rights (U.S.A.).
**CHRAC** CHRomatin Accessibility Activity.
*Biochemistry; Gene Expression; Medicine; Microchemistry; Molecular Biology.*
**C'HRD** (abbr.) Casehardened.
*Geology; Materials Science; Metallurgy.*
**CHRISTINE** CHaracteristics and Requirements of Information Systems based on Traffic data in an Integrated Network Environment - European Community.
**CHRLA** Center for Human Rights Legal Aid.
*Human Rights.*
**chron.** (abbr.) chronicle; chronological; chronology.
**CHRU** Centre Hospitalier Régional Universitaire (France).
**CHS** Casehardened Steel.
*Metallurgy.*
**CHS** The airport code for Charleston, South Carolina, U.S.A.
**CHTN** The Cooperative Human Tissue Network.
Of the U.S. National Cancer Institute.
**CHU** Centigrade Heat Unit.
**CHU** Centre Hospitalier Universitaire.
French acronym meaning: University (general) Hospital.
*Medicine.*
**CHV** Centre Hospitalier Vaudois (Switzerland).
**CHW** Chilled Water.
**c.h.w.** constant hot water.
**CI**; **c.i.** cast iron.
*Metallurgy.*
**C.I.** Channel Islands.
**CI** Chemical Intolerance.
*Environmental Health.*
**CI** Chemotherapeutic Index.
*Pharmacology; Virology.*
**CI**; **C.I.** Chief Inspector.
**CI** 1. Chile.
1. Chili.
2. counter-intelligence.
2. contre-ingérence.
**CI** The airport code for China Airlines.
**CI** Cirrus.
Also: **Ci**.
*Invertebrate Zoology; Meteorology; Vertebrate Zoology.*
**C.I.** Compulsory Insurance.
**CI** Configuration Interaction.
**CI**; **C.I.** Consular Invoice.
*Commerce.*
**CI** Containment Integrity; Containment Isolation.
*Nuclear Energy.*
**CI** Contamination Index.
*Medicine.*
**CI** Coronary Insufficiency.
*Medicine.*
**CI**; **ci** Corrugated Iron.
**c.i.** cost and insurance.
*Commerce; Shipping.*
**CI** Credito Italiano (Italy).
*Italian Bank; Banking Integrations.*
For further details see under: **UCI**.
**CI** Criminal Investigation.
*Criminal Law.*
**Ci** Curie.
Also: **c**.
*Nucleonics.*
**CI** Cytoplasmic Incompatibility.
*Cell Biology; Developmental Biology; Molecular Biology.*
**CI** Cytotoxic Index.
*Cytochemistry.*
**CI** Ivory Coast's international vehicle-registration letters.
**CIA** California Institute of Arts (U.S.A.).
**CIA** Cash In Advance.
*Business; Commerce.*
**CIA** Central Intelligence Agency (U.S.A.).
**CIA** Ceramics International Association.
**CIA** Clinical Innovator Award.
Novel studies on the effects of exposure to second-hand tobacco smoke. The CIA has been established by FAMRI.
*Award Programs; Novel Medical and Clinical Scientific Research Studies.*
For further details see under: **FAMRI**.
**CIA** Communication Interauriculaire.
Journal de Biophysique & Médecine Nucléaire.
*Publication.*
For further details see under: **CIV**.
**CIA** Confederazione Italiana Agricoltori (Italy).
**CIA** Conseil International des Archives.
*Library Association.*
**CIAB** Conseil international des agences bénévoles [opérations de secours].

International Council of Voluntary Agencies (ICVA) [relief operations].
**CIAD** Climate Impact Assessment Division.
**CIAD** Coalition Internationale pour l'Action au Developpement.
**CIAD** Counterintelligence Analysis Division (U.S.A.).
**CI&Sy** counter-intelligence and security.
contre-ingérence et sécurité.
**CIAO** Congress of Italian-American Organizations.
**CIAR** Center for Inter-American Relations.
**CIAS** Containment Isolation Actuation Signal.
*Nuclear Energy.*
**CIASE** Computer Institute for Applications in Science and Engineering (U.S.A.).
**CIAT** Center for International Tropical Agriculture (Cali, Colombia).
**CIAU** Coordinamento Italiano Aiuti Umanitari (Italy).
**CIAV** persistance du Canal Atrio- ou Auriculo-Ventriculaire Commun.
French acronym meaning: Common Atrioventricular Canal persistent.
*Medicine.*
**CIB** Centre for Integrative Biology (Ireland).
*Proteomics Research Programme.*
**CIB** Chartered Institute of Bankers (G.B.).
**CIB** Comité International des Bibliothèques.
**CIB** Commercial International Bank (Egypt).
*Egyptian Bank.*
**CIB** Compagnie Internationale de Banque (France).
**CIB** Consorzio Interuniversitario per le Biotecnologie (Italy).
*Italian Consortium.*
**CIBC** Canadian Imperial Bank of Commerce.
*Canadian Bank.*
**CIBC** Centres Interinstitutionnels de Bilan des Compétences (France).
*Employment; Vocational Guidance; Vocational Training.*
**CIBC** Confédération Internationale de la Boucherie et de la Charcuterie.
**Ci-Bit** Centro interuniversitario Biblioteca italiana telematica.
Ci-Bit is based in Pisa, Italy.
**CIC** Carcinogen Identification Committee.
*U.S. Committee.*
**CIC** Cardiac Inhibition Center.
*Physiology.*
**CIC** Chemical Institute of Canada.
**CIC** 1. combat information centre.
1. centre d'information de combat (CIC).
2. combined intelligence centre.
2. centre interallié de renseignement.
**CIC** Conseil International des Compositeurs.
French acronym of the: International Council of Composers.
**CIC** Construction Industry Commission (Canada).
**CIC** Consumer Information Center (U.S.A.).
**CICA** counter-intelligence coordinating authority.
autorité de coordination de la contre-ingérence.
**CICC** Collaborative Integrated Communications for Construction.
*European Community Project.*
**CICEP** Conseil Interaméricain du Commerce Et de la Production.
French acronym of the: Inter-American Council for Trade and Production.
**CICERO** Centre for International Climate and Energy Research (Norway).
**CICF** Chambre des Ingénieurs Conseils de France (France).
**CICH** Comité International de la Culture du Houblon.
*International Committee.*
**CICHE** Consortium for International Cooperation in Higher Education.
**CICIN** Conference on Interlibrary Communications and Information Network.
**CICIREPATO** Committee for International Cooperation in Information REtrieval among Examining PATent Offices.
**CICP** Capital Investment Computer Program.
*Business; Economics; Finance.*
**CICP** Committee to Investigate Copyright Problems.
*U.S. Committee.*
**CICP** Communication Interrupt Control Program.
*Data Processing.*
**CICR** Comitato Interministeriale per il Credito e il Risparmio (Italy).
Italian initialism meaning: Credit and Savings Interdepartmental Committee.
**CICR** Comitato Internazionale della Croce Rossa; Comité International de la Croix-Rouge.
Italian and French initialism of the: International Committee of the Red Cross.
**CICRA** Centre International pour la Coordination des Recherches en Agriculture.
French acronym of the: International Center for Coordination of Research in Agriculture.
**CICRIS** Co-operative Industrial and Commercial Reference and Information Services.
*Library Association.*
**CICR process** $Ca^{2+}$-Induced $Ca^{2+}$ Release process.
*Medical Biotechnology; Physiology.*

**CICS** Cooperative Institute for Climate Studies (U.S.A.).
**CICS** Customer Information Central System.
**CICSENE** Centro Italiano di Collaborazione per lo Sviluppo delle Nazioni Emergenti.
CICSENE is based in Turin, Italy.
*Italian Center.*
**cicu** (abbr.) cirrocumulus.
*Meteorology.*
**CICU** Coronary Intensive Care Unit.
**CID** The airport code for Cedar Rapids-Iowa City, U.S.A.
**CID** Central Institute for the Deaf (U.S.A.).
The CID is an affiliate of Washington University Medical Center.
*Sensory Neuroscience.*
**CID** Centro di Informazione per Disoccupati (Rome, Italy).
*Italian Center; Unemployment.*
**CID** Charge-Injection Device.
*Electronics.*
**CID** Civil Investigation Demand.
U.S. Department of Justice.
**CID** Combined Immunological Deficiency.
*Medicine.*
**C.I.D.**; **CID** Criminal Investigation Department (G.B.).
**CiD** Cubic-inch Displacement.
**CID** Cytomegalic Inclusion Disease.
CID is a viral infection affecting newborn infants.
*Medicine.*
**CIDA** Canadian International Development Agency.
*Canadian Agencies.*
**CIDA** Centre International de Développement de l'Aluminium.
French acronym of the: International Center for the Development of Aluminium.
**CIDA** Confederazione Italiana Dirigenti d'Azienda (Italy).
Italian acronym of the: Italian Federation of Business Executives.
**CIDADEC** Confédération Internationale Des Associations D'Experts et de Conseils.
**CID analysis** Collision-Induced Dissociation analysis.
**CIDCO** City & Industrial Development COrporation of Maharashta (India).
**CID disease** Combined Immunological Deficiency disease.
A fatal disorder.
*Medicine.*
**CIDET** Coopération Internationale en matière de Documentation sur l'Economie des Transports (France).
**CIDI** Centro di Iniziativa Democratica degli Insegnanti (Italy).
CIDI's 26$^{th}$ National Convention was held at Montecatini Terme, Italy on 11$^{th}$/13$^{th}$ March 1999.
**CIDI engine** Compression Ignition Direct Injection engine.
*Clean-car Technology; Futuristic Cars; Industrial Research; Pollution Standards.*
For further details see under: **PNGV**.
**CIDJ** Centre d'Information et de Documentation pour la Jeunesse (France).
*French Center.*
**CIDOC** Centre Intercommunautaire de DOCumentation pour la formation professionnelle (Belgium).
*Vocational Training Centers.*
**CIDR** Center for Inherited Disease Research.
The CIDR opened in early 1997. It is a joint effort by eight participating institutes at the U.S. National Institutes of Health.
*Inherited Diseases; Medical Genetics.*
**CIDS** Computer Information Delivery Service (U.S.A.).
**CIDSS** Comité International pour l'Information et Documentation des Sciences Sociales.
*International Committee.*
**CIE** Carbon Isotope Event.
*Geology; Geophysics; Paleocene Epoch; Oceanography.*
**CIE** Carbon Isotope Excursion.
*Earth Sciences; Ecological Analysis; Paleoanthropology; Primate Research; Vertebrate Paleontology.*
**CIE** Commission Internationale d'Eclairage.
*International Commission.*
**CIE** Commonwealth Institute of Entomology (G.B.).
**CIE** Chinese Institute of Engineers (China).
**Cie** (abbr.) Compagnie.
French abbreviation meaning: Company.
Also: house; firm; enterprise.
**CiE** Counter immunoelectrophoresis.
*Immunodiffusion method.*
**CIE** Crossed Immunoelectrophoresis.
**CIEL** Center for International Environmental Law (Washington D.C., U.S.A.).
**CIEL** Centre International d'Etudes des Langues (France).
French acronym of the: International Center for the Study of Languages.

**ciel** The above acronyms were coined using the French word "ciel" which means: sky; vault.
**CI engine** Compression-Ignition engine.
*Mechanical Engineering.*
**CIEP** Council on International Economic Policy.
**CIER** Centre Interaméricain d'Education Rurale.
French acronym of the: Interamerican Center for Rural Education.
**CIER** Conseil International des Economies Régionales.
**CIERSES** Centre International d'Etudes et de Recherches en Socio-Economie de la Santé.
**CIES** Centre for Interdisciplinary Environmental Studies (Italy).
**CIESIN** Consortium for International Earth Science Information Network (U.S.A.).
**CIF** Central Information File.
**CIF** Corporate Information Facility.
*Taxation Systems; Tax Databases.*
**CIF**; **c.i.f.** cost, insurance, freight.
**cif and c** cost, insurance, freight and commission.
**cif and c and i** cost, insurance, freight and commission and interest.
**cif and e** cost, insurance, freight and exchange.
**CIFAR** Cooperative Institute For Arctic Research (U.S.A.).
**CIFI** Collegio Ingegneri Ferroviari Italiani (Italy).
**CIFLT** Cost, Insurance, Freight, London Terms.
**CIFOPE** Centre International de FOrmation en Politique Energétique.
**CIFOR** Center for International FOrestry Research.
CIFOR is located in Bogor, Indonesia. It was founded in 1993 and has regional offices in Latin America and Southern Africa.
**CIFS** close-in fire support.
appui-feu rapproché.
**CIG** Cassa Integrazione Guadagni.
Italian acronym meaning: Unemployment Benefits Fund.
**CIg** Cold-Insoluble globulin.
*Cytochemistry.*
**CIG** Comitato Italiano Gas.
Italian acronym of the: Italian Gas Committee.
CIG is located in Milan, Italy.
*Italian Committee.*
**CIG** Computer Image Generation.
**CIG** Conferenza Intergovernativa.
Italian acronym meaning: Intergovernmental Conference.
**C.I.G.** Corte Internazionale di Giustizia.
Italian initialism of the: International Court of Justice.
**CIG** Current Intelligence Group.
groupe sur le renseignement de situation.
**CIGRE** Conférence Internationale des Grands Réseaux Electriques à haute tension.
Located in Paris, France. Founded in 1921; electrical aspects of electricity generation, sub-stations and transformer stations, high voltage electrical lines, interconnection of systems and their operation and protection.
*Electricity Generation and Sub-stations.*
**CIGS mixture** Copper, Indium, Gallium, and Selenium mixture.
*Photovoltaics; Thin-film Solar Cells.*
**CIHR** Canadian Institutes of Health Research (Canada).
*Research Excellence.*
**CII** Chartered Insurance Institute (G.B.).
**CII** Confederation of Indian Industry (India).
**CIIF** Coconut Industry Investment Fund (The Philippines).
**CIINTREP** counter-intelligence intelligence report.
Compte rendu de renseignement "contre-ingérence".
**CIIT** Chemical Industry Institute of Toxicology (U.S.A.).
*Chemical Carcinogenesis; Endocrine/Reproductive Toxicology; Neurotoxicology; Respiratory Toxicology.*
**CIJ** close-in jamming.
brouillage rapproché.
**CIJL** Centre for the Independence of Judges and Lawyers.
**CIL** Congrès International des Linguistes.
French acronym meaning: International Congress of Linguists.
**CILEA** Consorzio Interuniversitario Lombardo per l'Elaborazione Automatica.
*Italian Consortium.*
**CILER** Cooperative Institute for Limnology and Ecosystems Research.
**CILPE** Conférence Internationale de Liaison entre Producteurs d'Energie électrique.
**CIM** Capital Investment Model.
*Business; Economics; Finance.*
**CIM** Colonic Intestinal Metaplasia.
*Oncology.*
**CIM** Common Interface Model.
**CIM** Computer Input from Microfilm.
**CIM** Computer-Integrated Manufacturing.
*Industrial Engineering.*
**CIM** Conseil International de la Musique.
**CIM** Cortically Induced Movement.
*Medicine.*

**CIMA** Centre pour l'Indépendance des Magistrats et des Avocats.
French acronym meaning: Center for the Independence of Magistrates and Lawyers.
**CIMAC** CIvico Museo di Arte Contemporanea.
*Italian Museum.*
**CIMAC** Conseil International des Machines à Combustion.
**CIMAP** Commission Internationale des Methodes d'Analyse des Pesticides.
**CIMAS** Conférence Internationale de la Mutualité et des Assurances Sociales.
**CIMAS** Cooperative Institute for Marine and Atmospheric Studies.
**CIMBAPP** CIM Building block for the Automated Production of Plastic Parts.
*European Community Project.*
**CIME** Comité Intergouvernemental pour les Migrations Européennes.
**CIMEA** Centro di Informazione sulla Mobilità e le Equivalenze Accademiche (Rome, Italy).
*Italian Center.*
**CIMI** Centre for International and Medical Informatics (G.B.).
Set up by the Nottingham University CIMI has developed a remote ultrasound system for obstetrics.
*Remote Ultrasound Diagnostics; Telemedicine.*
**CIMIC** civil-military cooperation.
coopération civilo-militaire.
**CIMIT** Center for Minimally Invasive Therapy (U.S.A.).
CIMIT has been launched by Brigham Women's Hospital, Massachusetts General Hospital, the Draper Laboratory and Massachusetts Institute of Technology, under the auspices of Partners Healthcare System. It was created to seek new and less invasive ways to perform traditional surgical procedures.
*Minimally Invasive Therapies.*
**CIMM** Canadian Institute of Mining and Metallurgy (Canada).
**CIMMYT** Centro Internacional de Mejoramiento de Maiz Y Trigo (Mexico).
Spanish acronym of the: International Maize and Wheat Improvement Center.
CIMMYT is a Mexico City-based laboratory.
*Agricultural Management Techniques; Crop Improvements.*
**CI-MPR** Cation-Independent Mannose 6-Phosphate Receptor.
The CI-MPR has an important role in the biogenesis of lysosomes.
*Cargo Receptors; Cell Biology; Human Development; Metabolism; Medicine; Molecular Genetics; Pathology.*
**CIMS** Chemical Ionization Mass Spectrometer.
**CIMSS** Center for Intelligence Material Systems and Structures.
At the Virginia Polytechnic Institute (U.S.A.).
**CIMSS** Cooperative Institute of Meteorology Satellite Studies.
**CIM-UCL** Catholic University of Louvain - Centre for Medical Informatics (Belgium).
**CIMV** Cauliflower Mosaic Virus.
*Virology.*
**CIN** Chinese Institute of Neuroscience (China).
**CINC** Commander-in-Chief.
commandant en chef (CEC 2.).
**CINCEASTLANT** 1.Commander-in-Chief, East Atlantic [has replaced: CINCEASTLANT 2].
1. commandant en chef Est de l'Atlantique [remplace CINCEASTLANT 2.].
2. Commander-in-Chief, Eastern Atlantic (Area) [obsolete - replaced by: CINCEASTLANT 1].
2. commandant en chef du Secteur oriental de l'Atlantique [obsolète - remplacé par CINCEASTLANT 1].
**CINCENT** Commander-in-Chief, Allied Forces Central Europe [obsolete - replaced by CINCNORTH 1.].
commandant en chef des Forces alliées du Centre-Europe [obsolète - remplacé par CINCNORTH 1.].
**CINCH** Computerized Information from National Criminological Holdings.
*Information Service.*
**CINCIBERLANT** Commander-in-Chief, Iberian Atlantic Area [obsolete - replaced by CINCSOUTHLANT].
commandant en chef du Secteur ibérique de l'Atlantique [obsolète - remplacé par CINCSOUTHLANT].
**CINCNORTH** 1. Commander-in-Chief North [has replaced CINCENT and CINCNORTHWEST].
1. commandant en chef des Forces alliées Nord-Europe [remplace CINCENT et CIRCNORTHWEST].
2. Commander-in-Chief, Allied Forces Northern Europe [obsolete - replaced by COMJCNORTH].
2. commandant en chef des Forces alliées du Nord-Europe [obsolète - remplacé par COMJCNORTH].
**CINCNORTHWEST** Commander-in-Chief, Allied Forces Northwestern Europe [obsolete - now part of CINCNORTH 1.].
commandant en chef des Forces alliées du Nord-

Ouest-Europe [obsolète - fait maintenant partie de CINCNORTH 1.].

**CINCSOUTH** 1. Commander-in-Chief South [has replaced CINCSOUTH 2.].
1. commandant en chef des Forces alliées Sud-Europe [remplace CINCSOUTH 2.].
2. Commander-in-Chief, Allied Forces Southern Europe [obsolete - replaced by CINCSOUTH 1.].
2. commandant en chef des Forces alliées du Sud-Europe [obsolète - remplacé par CINCSOUTH 1.].

**CINCSOUTHLANT** Commander-in-Chief South Atlantic [has replaced CINCIBERLANT].
commandant en chef Sud de l'Atlantique [remplace CINCIBERLANT].

**CINCUSAREUR** Commander-in-Chief, US Army Europe.
commandant en chef des Forces terrestres américaines en Europe.

**CINCWESTLANT** 1. Commander-in-Chief West Atlantic [has replaced CINCWESTLANT 2.].
1. commandant en chef Ouest de l'Atlantique [remplace CINCWESTLANT 2.].
2. Commander-in-Chief Western Atlantic Area [obsolete - replaced by CINCWESTLANT1.].
2. commandant en chef du Secteur occidental de l'Atlantique [obsolète - remplacé par CINCWESTLANT1.].

**CINTC** Chief, Intelligence Corps.

**CINTEC**; **Cintec** Council for INformation TEChnology (Sri Lanka).

**CINV** Comité international de normalisation de la vérification.
International Auditing Practices Committee (IAPC).

**CINVESTAV** Centro de Investigaciones y Estudios Avanzados (Mexico).
*Genetic Engineering; Mexican Center.*

**CIO** Central Imagery Office (U.S.A.).

**CIO** Chief Information Officer.

**CIO** Church Information Office (G.B.).

**CIO** Comitato Internazionale Olimpico; Comité International Olympique.
Italian and French acronym of the: International Olympic Committee.

**CIO** Community Investment Officer.

**CIO** Conventional International Origin.

**CIOA** Committee on International Ocean Affairs.

**CIOMS** Council for International Organizations of Medical Sciences.
Located in Geneva, Switzerland (c/o WHO). Founded in 1949 to facilitate and co-ordinate the activities of its members, to act as a co-ordinating centre between them and the national institutions, to maintain collaboration with the UN, to promote international activities in the field of medical sciences, to serve the scientific interests of the international biomedical community.
*Medical Sciences.*

**CIOR** Conféderation interalliée des officiers de réserve.
Interallied Confederation of Reserve Officers.

**CIOs** Chief Information Officers.

**C.I.O.S.** Comitato Internazionale Organizzazione Scientifica.
Italian acronym of the: International Committee for Scientific Organization.

**CIOS** Conseil International pour l'Organisation Scientifique.

**CIOSTA** Commission Internationale pour l'Organisation Scientifique du Travail en Agriculture.

**CIP** Calf Intestinal Phosphatase.
*Molecular Biology; Thylakoids.*

**CIP** Capital Investment Program.

**CIP** Carriage and Insurance Paid to.
*Economics; International Trade.*

**CIP** Cast Iron Pipe.

**CIP** Catholic Intercontinental Press.

**CIP** Center for International Policy.

**CIP** Centre d'Information de Presse.
*Belgian Center.*

**CIP** Clean-In-Place.

**CIP**; **C.I.P.** Comitato Interministeriale per i Prezzi.
Italian acronym of the: Interdepartmental Committee on Prices.

**CIP** Committee on International Programs (U.S.A.).

**CIP** communications improvement plan.
plan d'amélioration des télécommunications.

**CIP** Computer-Integrated Production.
A computer-integrated production refers to a manufacturing process where all the phases of the process are computer-controlled.
*Robotics.*

**CIP** Consolidated Instrument Package.
*Atmospheric Research.*

**CIP** Continuation-In-Part.
*Patents.*

**CIP** Contrat d'Insertion Professionnelle (France).
CIP is a French job creation scheme for young people.

**CIP** Current-In-Plane.
*Applied Physics.*

**CIP** International Potato Centre (Peru).

**CIPA** Canadian Institute of Public Affairs.

**CIPA** Centro Italiano di Psicologia Analitica.
*Italian Center.*

**CIPA** Comité International de Photogrammetrie Architecturale.

**CIPA** Commissione Internazionale per la Protezione delle Alpi.
Italian acronym of the: International Commission for Protection of the Alps.

**CIPA** Convenzione Interbancaria per i Problemi dell'Automazione.
Italian acronym meaning: Automation Problems Interbanking Convention.

**CIPACE** counter-intelligence policy, ACE.
politique du CAE en matière de contre-ingérence.

**CIPC** Canadian Institute on Pollution Control (Canada).

**CIPC** Community Intellectual Property Court.
*Community Patents; Infringement Proceedings; Invalidity Proceedings.*

**ciPCR** survey culture-independent PCR survey.
*Biology; Microbiology.*
For further details see under: **PCR**.

**CIPE** Comitato Interministeriale per la Programmazione Economica (Italy).
Italian acronym of the: Economic Planning Interdepartmental Committee.

**CIPE** Conseil International de la Préparation à l'Enseignement.

**CIPF**; **C.I.P.F.** Consorzio Italiano Produttori Fazzoletti (Italy).
*Italian Consortium.*

**CI.PI.ELLE** Consorzio Pellettieri Lombardi (Milan, Italy).

**Cipm** Centro Italiano per la promozione della mediazione (Italy).
Italian initialism of the: Italian Center for Mediation Promotion (Italy).

**CIPM** Comité International des Poids et Mésures.

**CIPs** CLOCK-Interacting Proteins.
*Biological Timing; CLOCK Proteins; Medicine; Neurobiology; Physiology.*

**CIPS** Commonwealth International Philatelic Society.

**CIPSH** Conseil International de la Philosophie et des Sciences Humaines.

**CIPSRO** Comité Intersecrétariat pour les Programmes Scientifiques se Rapportant à l'Océanographie.

**CIR** Canadian Institute of Research (Canada).

**CIR** Center for Inter-American Relations.

**CIR** Center for Individual Rights (U.S.A.).

**CIR** Central Indian Ridge.
*Geology; Geophysics.*

**CIR** Centre International de Reference pour l'Approvisionnement en Eau Collective de l'Assainissement.
French acronym of the: International Reference Center for Community Water Supply and Sanitation.

**Cir.** (abbr.) Circinus.
A small constellation adjoining Centaurus.
*Astronomy.*

**cir.** (abbr.) circle.
*Mathematics.*

**cir.** (abbr.) circuit.
*Cartography; Computer Programming; Electricity; Electromagnetism; Mathematics.*

**cir.** (abbr.) circular.
Also: **circ**.

**cir.** (abbr.) circumference.
*Mathematics.*

**CIR** Commission on Industrial Relations.
Department of Employment (G.B.).

**CIR** Commission on Intergovernmental Relations.

**CIR** Consiglio Italiano per i Rifugiati.
Italian acronym of the: Italian Council for Refugees.

**CIR** Consumer Information Regulation.
U.S. National Highway Traffic Safety Administration.

**CIR** Continuing Intelligence Requirement.

**CIR** Court of Industrial Relations (The Philippines).

**CIR** The Committee on Industrial Relations.
EUFEPS Advisory Panel.
For further details see under: **EUFEPS**.

**CIRA** Centro Italiano Ricerche Aerospaziali.
Italian acronym of the: Italian Center for Aerospace Research. CIRA is located in Capua, Italy.

**CIRA** Cooperative Institute for Research in the Atmosphere.

**CIRAD** Centro de Informação sobre Reconhecimento Académico de Diplomas.
*Portuguese Center.*

**CIRC** Central Information Reference and Control.

**CIRC** Central Intelligence Retrieval Center.

**CIRC** Centre International de Recherche sur le Cancer.
French acronym of the: International Center for Research on Cancer.

**circ.** (abbr.) circular.
Also: **cir**.

**CIRCE** Central Italy innovation Relay CEntre.
CIRCE is located in Rome, Italy.
*Italian Center.*

**CIRCEA** College of Investigative Remedial and Consulting Engineers of Australia.

**CIRCLE** Cylindrical Internal Reflectance Cell for Liquid Evaluation.
The CIRCLE cell is used for rapid, nondestructive, and reproducible analysis of liquids. It is a device patented by Spectra - Tech (U.S.A.).
**CIREP** Centro de Informação e Relações Públicas (Portugal).
*Portuguese Center.*
**CIRES** Cooperative Institute for Research in Environmental Sciences (U.S.A.).
The CIRES is an institute engaged in research in various fields within the Geophysical Sciences.
**CIRF** Centre International d'Information et de Recherche sur la Formation Professionnelle.
**CIRFI** Centre International de Recherche sur le Financement des Investissements.
*International Center.*
**CIRL** Committee of Industrial Relations Librarians.
**CIRM** Centro Internazionale Radio-Medico.
CIRM gives emergency medical advice to ships at sea.
*International Center.*
**CIRM** Centro Italiano Radio Mobile (Italy).
**C.I.R.M.** Comitato Internazionale Radio-Medico.
Italian acronym meaning: International Radio-Medical Committee.
**CIRP** Centres d'Information des Relais d'opinion et de la Presse (France).
**CIRRIS** Cryogenic Infrared Radiance Instrument for Shuttle.
**CIRRPC** Committee on Interagency Radiation Research and Policy Coordination.
Created in 1984 by former President Ronald Reagan.
**CIRS** Containment Iodine Renewal System.
*Nuclear Energy.*
**CIRs** Corotating Interactive Regions.
*Astronomy; Astrophysics.*
**CIRSF** Centre for Interdisciplinary Research on Structure Formation (Bielefeld, Germany).
**CIRSI** Centro Internazionale di Ricerca in Strategia d'Impresa (Milan, Italy).
*International Center.*
**CIRT** Conference on Industrial Robot Technology.
**CIRUR** Comité Intergouvernemental de Recherches Urbaines et Régionales (Canada).
**CIS** Cancer Information Service.
Of the U.S. National Cancer Institute.
**CIS** Central Immune System.
*Immune System.*
**CIS** Centro Investigazioni Scientifiche.
Italian acronym of the: Scientific Investigations Center (Italy).
**CIS** Clinical Information Scientist.
**CIS**; **Cis** Comitato Interministeriale per la Sicurezza (Italy).
*Italian Committee.*
**CIS** Comitato Internazionale per gli Scambi.
Italian acronym of the: International Exchange Committee.
**CIS** 1. Commonwealth of Independent States.
1. Communauté des États indépendants (CEI 1.).
2. communication and information systems.
2. systèmes d'information et de communication (SIC 2.).
**CIS** Community Improvement Scale.
*Psychology.*
**CIS** Community Innovation Survey.
European Community.
**CIs** Confidence Intervals.
**CIS** Consorzio Impianti Smaltimento (Italy).
*Italian Consortium.*
**CIS**; **cis** contact image sensor.
**CIS** Containment Isolation Signal.
*Nuclear Energy.*
**CIS** Copper Indium Diselenide.
*PV modules.*
**CIS** Credito Industriale Sardo (Italy).
*Italian Bank.*
**C2IS** command and control information system.
système d'information de commandement et de contrôle.
**CISA** Centro Italiano Studi Aziendali.
Italian acronym of the: Italian Centre for Business Management Studies.
**CISAC** Committe on International Security and Arms Control (U.S.A.).
**Cisai** Consiglio italiano per la scienza applicata e l'ingegneria.
Italian acronym of the: Italian Council for Applied Science and Engineering. Cisai was formed on the 26th February 1992 to promote studies and cooperation in the fields of applied sciences and engineering.
**CISAP** Congrès International des Sciences de l'Activité Physique (Canada).
**CISBH** Comité International de Standardisation en Biologie Humaine.
*International Committee.*
**CISC** Complex Instruction Set Computer.
*Computer Technology.*
**CISCC** Communication and Information Systems Coordinating Committee.
Comité de coordination des systèmes d'information et de communication.
***cis*-DCE** *cis*-Dichloroetene.

**CISDO** Centro Italiano Studi e Documentazione in Omeopatia (Italy).
*Italian Center.*
**CISE** Centro Informazioni, Studi, Esperienze - Segrate (Milan), Italy.
*Italian Center.*
**CISE** (Directorate for) Computer and Information Science and Engineering.
Of the U.S. National Science Foundation.
**CISEM** Centro per l'Innovazione e la Sperimentazione Educativa Milano (Italy).
*Italian Center.*
**CIS-ESG** Communication and Information Systems Executive Steering Group.
Comité directeur des systèmes d'information et de communication.
**CISGEM** Centro Informazioni e Servizi GEMmologici (Milan, Italy).
*Italian Center.*
**CISHEC** Chemical Industries Association's Safety and Health Council (G.B.).
**CISI** chapter, item, sub-item.
chapitre, article, sous-article (CASA 1.).
**CISI**; **Cisi** Compagnie Internationale de Services en Informatique (France).
**CISID** Computerized Information System for Infectious Diseases.
The CISID, of the World Health Organization, began in 1998.
**CISL**; **C.I.S.L.** Confederazione Internazionale dei Sindacati Liberi.
Italian acronym of the: International Federation of Free Trade Unions (Italy).
**CISL**; **C.I.S.L.** Confederazione Italiana Sindacati Lavoratori.
Italian acronym of the: Federation of Italian Trade Unions (Italy).
**CISM** Centre International des Sciences Mécaniques.
*International Center.*
**CISMEC** Centro Informazioni e Studi sul MCE.
Italian acronym of the: Centre for Information and Studies on ECM.
For further details see under: **ECM**.
**CISPEL** Confederazione Italiana dei Servizi Pubblici ed Enti Locali (Italy).
Italian acronym of the: Italian Federation of Public Utilities and Local Authorities.
**CISQ** Certificazione Italiana dei Sistemi di Qualità (Italy).
**CISS** Cooperazione Internazionale Sud Sud (Palermo, Italy).
**CIST** Centro Internazionale per la Scienza e la Tecnologia.
Italian acronym of the: International Center for Science and Technology.
**CISTI** Canada Institute for Scientific and Technical Information (Canada).
**cisti** The above acronym was coined accidentally using the Italian word "cisti" which means: cyst.
*Biology; Pathology.*
**CISUPINTREP** counter-intelligence supplementary report.
compte rendu supplémentaire de renseignement “contre-ingérence”.
**CIT** California Institute of Technology (U.S.A.).
**CIT** Center for Information Technology (U.S.A.).
CIT, formerly known as: DCRT, OIRM, TCB, was established in 1964. The Center incorporates the power of modern computers into the biomedical programs of the NIH by focusing on three primary activities: conducting-*computational biosciences research*, developing *computer systems* and providing *computer facilities*.
For further details see under: **NIH**.
**CIT** Centre International de Toxicologie (France).
*International Center.*
**CIT** Chartered Institute of Taxation (G.B.).
**CIT** Commerciale Italo - Tedesca.
*Commercial Bank.*
**CIT** Compact Ignition Torus.
CIT is a program conducted at Princeton University, U.S.A., proposed by milanese physicist Bruno Coppi in 1984.
**CIT** Conditions Internationales de Transit.
French acronym meaning: Combiterms.
**CIT** Controlled Interceptor Trainer.
*Aerospace.*
**CIT** Cyprus Institute of Technology.
**CIT** International Rail Transport Committee (Switzerland).
**CITA** Canadian Institute for Theoretical Astrophysics (Canada).
*Astronomy; Astrophysics; Planet Search.*
**CITA** Comité International de l'Inspection Technique Automobile.
*International Committee.*
**CITA** Commission Internationale de Tourisme Aérien.
*International Commission.*
**CITA** Confédération Internationale des Ingénieurs Agronomes.
**CITA** Corporate Income Tax Act.
**CITA** Court Interpreters and Translators Association.

**CITE** Carence Immunitaire T Epidémique.
French acronym meaning: Acquired Immunodeficiency Syndrome (AIDS).
*Medicine.*

**CITE** Cargo Integration Test Equipment.

**CITE** Centre for Information Technologies and Electronics.

**CITE**; **Cite** Centro per l'Innovazione Tecnico-Educativa (Italy).
*Italian Center.*

**CITE** Chemical Instrumentation Test and Evaluation - NASA's.

**CITE** Consortium for graphic Information Tehnology training in Europe.
*European Community Consortium.*

**CITERE** Centre d'Information en Temps Réel pour l'Europe (France).

**CITES** Convention on International Trade in Endangered Species of Wild Fauna and Flora.
28 year-old.

**CITI** Confédération Internationale des Travailleurs Intellectuels.

**Citic** China international trust and investment corporation (China).
A state investment Body.

**CITIL** Citicorp Information Technologies Ltd.

**CITP** Comité International des Télécommunications de Presse.
*International Committee.*

**CIUS**; **C.I.U.S.** Consiglio Internazionale delle Unioni Scientifiche.
Italian acronym of the: Iternational Council of Scientific Unions.

**civ.** (abbr.) civilian.

**CIV** Communication Interventriculaire.
Journal de Biophysique & Médecine Nucléaire.
*Publication.*
For further details see under: **CIA**.

**CIVAB** Centro Informazione e Valutazione delle Apparecchiature Biomedicali (Italy).
*Italian Center.*

**CIVES** Commissione Italiana Veicoli Elettrici Stradali.
*Italian Commission; Electric Vehicles.*

**CIVIS**; **C.I.V.I.S.** Centro Italiano per i Viaggi d'Istruzione per Studenti.
Italian acronym of the: Italian Center for Students' Educational Travels (Italy).

**CIVPOL** civilian police.
police civile.

**CIWO** civil works.
travaux de génie civil.

**CIWS** close-in weapon system.
système d'arme de combat rapproché.

**CJCCC** combined joint communications coordination centre.
centre interarmées multinational de coordination des communications.

**CJCMTF** combined joint civil military task force.
groupe interarmées multinational pour la coopération civilo-militaire.

**CJD** Creutzfeldt-Jakob Disease.
For further details see under: **GSS disease** (Gertsmann-Straussler-Sheinker disease).

**CJFCC** combined joint force component command.
commandement de composante de force interarmées multinationale.

**CJHQ** combined joint headquarters.
1a. quartier général interarmées multinational.
1b. poste de commandement interarmées multinational.

**CJICTF** combined joint information campaign task force [replaced by CJPOTF].
groupe interarmées multinational pour la campagne d'information [remplacé par CJPOTF].

**CJIE** Criminal Justice Information Exchange.

**CJMCRTF** combined joint military-civilian relations task force.
groupe interarmées multinational pour les relations militaro-civiles.

**CJPOTF** combined joint psychological operations task force.
groupe interarmées multinational pour les opérations psychologiques.

**CJPS** Combined Joint Planning Staff [has replaced ARFPS].
État-major de planification interarmées multinational [remplace l'ARFPS].

**CJS** College of Judea and Samaria (Ariel, Israel).
Established by the Israeli Government, CJS opened in 1983.

**CJSOTF** combined joint spécial operations task force.
groupe interarmées multinational pour les opérations spéciales.

**CJTF** combined joint task force.
groupe de forces interarmées multinationales (GFIM).

**ck** (abbr.) check; cheque.
Also: **chq.**

**ck.** (abbr.) cork.
*Materials.*

**ck.** (abbr.) countersink.
*Mechanical Devices.*

**CK** Creatine Kinase.
*Enzymology.*

**ckd.** (abbr.) checked.
**CKD** Completely Knocked Down.
**CKI** Cheung Kong Infrastructure (China).
**CKII** Casein Kinase II.
*Livestock Research; Theileriosis.*
**CL** Cabbage Looper.
*Entomology.*
**CL** Cathodoluminescence.
*Electrical and Computer Engineering; Electronics; Industrial Science; Material Science; Quantized Electronic Structures.*
**CL** Caltanissetta, Italy.
**CL** Center Line / Centerline.
*Cartographgy.*
**cl**; **cl.** (abbr.) Centiliter / centilitre.
*Metrology.*
**Cl** The chemical symbol for Chlorine.
The word chlorine means in Greek greenish-yellow.
*Symbols; Chemistry.*
**CL** Circular List.
Circular List is also known as: Ring.
*Computer Programming.*
**cl.** (abbr.) class.
*Anthropology; Artificial Intelligence; Computer Science; Mathematics; Systematics.*
**cl.** (abbr.) clavicle.
*Anatomy.*
**cl.** (abbr.) clearance.
*Aviation; Mechanical Engineering; Military Science; Ordnance; Transportation Engineering.*
**CL** Cleistogamus.
*Botany.*
**cl.** (abbr.) clinic.
*Medicine.*
**cl.** (abbr.) closure.
*Artificial Intelligence; Aviation; Building Engineering; Cartography; Geology; Mathematics; Psychology.*
**CL** 1. combat load.
1. charge de combat.
2. confidence level.
2.niveau de confiance.
3. confrontation line.
3. ligne de confrontation.
4. coordination level.
4. échelon de coordination.
**CL** Commissione Legislativa.
Italian initialism meaning: Legislative Committee.
**CL** Corpora Lutea.
**CL** Cost of Living.
*Economics.*
**CL** Course Line.
*Aviation.*
**C/L** Craft Loss.
*Shipping.*
**CL** Crédit Lyonnais (France).
*French Bank.*
**CL** Critical List.
**CL** Sri Lanka international vehicle-registration letters.
**CLA** California Library Association (U.S.A.).
**CLA** Canadian Library Association (Canada).
**CLA** Catholic Library Association.
**CLA** Center-Line Average.
**CLA** Certified Laboratory Assistant.
**CLA** Chinese Library Association (China).
**CLA** Colorado Library Association (U.S.A.).
**CLA** Common Leucocyte Antigen.
*Immunology.*
**CLA** Conjugated Linoleic Acid.
**CLA** Curtin Labor Alliance (Australia).
**CLAES** Cryogenic Limb Array Etalon Spectrometer.
*Geophysics; Meteorology; Physics.*
**CL angiogenesis** Corpus Luteum angiogenesis.
*Cardiovascular Research; Molecular Oncology; Pathology.*
**CLANN** College Libraries Activity Network in New South Wales.
**CLARINET** Contaminated Land Rehabilitation Network for Environmental Technologies in Europe.
*European Project.*
**CL arm** Chest and Left arm.
*Medicine.*
**CLASS** California Library Authority for Systems and Services (U.S.A.).
**Cl atoms** Clorine atoms.
*Chemistry.*
**CLAW hypothesis** Charlson, Lovelock, Andreae, and Warren hypothesis.
*Chemistry.*
**CLBE** Core-Level Binding-Energy.
**CLC** Confirmed Letter of Credit.
*Banking; Business; Commerce; Finance.*
**CLD** Chronic Lyme Disease.
CLD causes inflammation and joint pain.
**cld** (abbr.) cleared (through customs).
**CLD** communications logistics depot.
dépôt logistique des télécommunications.
**cld.** (abbr.) cooled.
**CL-DNA** Cationic Liposomes Complexed with DNA.
*Biochemistry; Gene Therapies; Molecular Biology.*

**CLE** The airport code for Hopkins International airport, Cleveland, Ohio, U.S.A.
**CLEAN** Case-based Learning Environment for plant process management.
*European Community Project.*
For further details see under: **CBL** (Case-Based Learning).
**CLED** Centre for Local Economic Development.
Industrial sector specialist, AWM's partner.
For further details see under: **AWM**.
**CLEFIN** Corso di Laurea in Economia delle Istituzioni e dei mercati Finanziari.
The course was presented on 1st April, 1992 at the Bocconi University, Milan, Italy.
**CLENE** Continuing Library Education Network and Exchange.
**CLEOs** Collateralized Lease Equipment Obligations (U.S.A.).
**CLEOS** Conference on Laser and Electro-Optical Systems.
**CLF** Christian Librarians' Fellowship.
**CLF** commander landing force.
commandant de la force de débarquement.
**CLF** Crédit Local de France (France).
*French Bank.*
**$ClF_3$** Chlorine Trifluoride.
$ClF_3$ is used mainly as an oxidizer.
*Inorganic Chemistry.*
**clg.** (abbr.) ceiling.
*Aviation; Meteorology.*
**CLGI** City & Guilds of London Institute (G.B.).
*British Institutes.*
**CLI** Caller Identification.
*Cellular Phones.*
**CLIA** Clinical Laboratory Improvement Act (1988) (U.S.A.).
**CLIBCON** Chiropractic Library Consortium.
**CLIC** College Libraries Consortium.
**CLIC** Compact Linear Collider.
*Particle Physics* - Laboratory: CERN.
**CLICOM** (abbr.) CLImate COMputing.
**CLIMAP project** Climate Long-range Investigation MApping and Prediction project.
*Geosciences; Projects.*
**CLIP** Caribbean Large Igneous Province.
The oceanic plateau that became the Caribbean plate.
*Geochemistry; Geology.*
**CLIP** CLass II-associated Invariant chain Peptide.
*Immunology; Medicine.*
**CLIP** Corticotropin-Like Intermediate lobe Peptide.
**CLIVAMP** Climatic Variability of Mediterranean Paleo-Circulation.
*European Community Project; Environmental Protection; Resources of the Sea; Fisheries.*
**CLIVAR Project** CLImate VARiability and Predictability Project.
*Atlantic Climate Variability; Earth and Environmental Sciences.*
**CLK** Chek Lap Kok (Hong Kong).
The new CLK airport started operations on Monday 6th July 1998.
*Airport Code.*
**clk phenotype** Clock phenotype.
*Biology.*
**CLL** Chronic Lymphocytic Leukemia.
*Medicine.*
**CLL** Committee on Legal Liability.
**CLMC** Combined Loyalist Military Command (Ireland).
The main loyalist paramilitary groupings: The Ulster Defense Association, the Ulster Volunteer Force and the Red Hand Commando are allied under the CLMC.
**CLNP** Connectionless Network Protocol.
**ClO** Chlorine Monoxide.
Chlorine Monoxide is used in chlorination reactions.
*Inorganic Chemistry.*
**CLO** Cod-Liver / codliver Oil.
*Materials; Medicine.*
**$ClO_2$** Chlorine Dioxide.
$ClO_2$ is used mainly in water treatment.
*Inorganic Chemistry.*
**CLOD** Coralline Lethal Orange Disease.
The coralline lethal orange disease is a bacterial pathogen of coralline algae that was initially observed in 1993.
*Biological Sciences.*
**CLOS** Common Lisp Object System.
*Artificial Intelligence.*
**CLP** Centrifuged Liquid Product.
**CLP** China Light & Power (China).
**CLPC** Central Lunar Processing Complex.
*Lunar Development.*
**CLPV** Carta di Localizzazione Probabile delle Valanghe.
**clr.** (abbr.) clear.
*Computer Programming; Meteorology; Navigation; Ordnance.*
**CLRC** Central Laboratory of the Research Councils (G.B.).
**CLRV** Cherry Leaf Roll Virus.
*Plant Pathology.*
**CLs** Cationic Liposomes.

*Biochemistry; Gene Therapies; Molecular Biology.*
**CLS** Characteristic Loss Spectroscopy.
**CLS** Commission on Life Sciences (U.S.A.).
**CLS** contractor logistic support.
soutien logistique fourni par le contractant.
**CLSA** Crédit Lyonnais Securities Asia.
CLSA is a securities and investment banking house in Greater China.
**CLSM** Confocal Laser Scanning Microscopy.
**$ClSO_2OH$** Chlorosulfonic Acid.
Chlorosulfonic Acid is also known as: Sulfuric Chlorohydrin.
*Inorganic Chemistry.*
**CLSP** composite launch sequence plan.
plan mixte d'ordre de succession des lancements.
**CLSS** Circumlunar Space Station.
*Lunar Development.*
**CLT** The airport code for Charlotte, North Carolina, U.S.A.
**CLUE** Changing Land Usage Enhancement of biodiversity and ecosystem development.
*European Community Project.*
**CLUP** Costo di Lavoro per Unità di Prodotto.
Italian acronym meaning: Labor Cost per Unit Produced.
**CLWG** CLear Wire Glass.
**CLX** command live exercise.
exercice de commandement réel.
**CM** Cardiomyopathy.
**cm** (abbr.) centimetre / centimeter.
*Metrology.*
**cM** centiMorgan.
*Genetics.*
**CM** Chinese Medicine.
**CM** Chorismate Mutase.
*Chemical Engineering; Enzymes; Protein Design.*
**C.M.** Circolare Ministeriale.
Italian initialism meaning: Ministry Circular Letter.
**CM** Circular Mil.
CM is the area of a circle 1 mil in diameter.
*Metrology.*
**CM** 1. Cameroon.
1. Cameroun.
2. Comité militaire.
2. Military Committee (MC).
3. configuration management.
3. gestion de la configuration.
4. crisis management.
4. gestion des crises.
5. cruise missile.
5. missile de croisière.
**CM** Chemically Modified.
**CM** Command Module.
*Space Technology.*
**CM** Common Meter.
**CM** Conditioned Medium.
*Medicine.*
**Cm** The chemical symbol for Curium.
*Symbols; Chemistry.*
**CMA** Capital Market Authority (Egypt).
*Capital Market Regulations.*
**CMA** Cash Management Account.
*Finance.*
**C.M.A.** Certificato di Management Alberghiero.
Of the International School of Tourism, Italy.
**CMA** Certified Medical Assistant.
**CMA** contact motion analysis.
analyse des mouvements du contact.
**CMA** Corticomedial Amygdala.
**CMAFs** Co-operatives, Mutuals, Associations and Foundations.
**C-MAN** Coastal Marine Automated Network (U.S.A.).
**CM angle** Center-of-Mass angle.
**CMB** Cell and Molecular Biology.
**Cmb** Compagnie Monégasque de Banque.
*Monegasque Bank.*
**CMB** Core-Mantle Boundary.
*Geology; Geophysics; Planetary Physics; Earth Sciences.*
**CMB** Cosmic Microwave Background.
*Cosmology; Physics.*
**CMB** configuration management board.
commission de gestion de la configuration.
**CMB arrangement** Crossed Molecular Beam arrangement.
**CMBOD** Center for Molecular Biology of Oral Diseases (U.S.A.).
Of the University of Illinois at Chicago.
**CMBR** Cosmic Microwave Background Radiation.
*Astronomy; Particle Astrophysics; Physics.*
**CMC** Canadian Meteorological Centre (Canada).
**CMC** Carbon Modeling Consortium.
The CMC is based in Princeton, U.S.A.
*Climate Change.*
**CMC** Carboxymethyl Cellulose.
Carboxymethyl cellulose, also known as cellulose gum; sodium cellulose glycolate; and sodium carboxymethylcellulose, is an acid ether derivative of cellulose.
*Organic Chemistry.*
**CMC** Cell-Mediated Cytotoxicity.
*Immunology.*
**CMC** 1. centre militaire de contrôle.

1. military control centre (MCC 3.).
2. Chairman of the Military Committee.
2. président du Comité militaire.
3. command meteorological centre.
3. centre météorologique du commandement.
4. crisis management centre.
4. centre de gestion des crises.
5. see CIMIC.
5. voir CIMIC.

**CMC** Critical Micelle Concentration.
For further details see under: **CMCs**.

**CMCC** Central Mission Control Centre.
*European Community.*

**Cmdr.** Commander.
Also: **Comdr.**; **Comm.**; **Cdr**.

**CMC method** Correlation Metric Construction method.
*Chemistry; Chemical Kinetics; Electrophoresis; Physical Chemistry.*

**CMCs** Critical Micelle Concentrations.
*Biochemistry; Chemistry; Chemical Engineering; Marine Biology; Physical Chemistry.*

**CMD** Color-Magnitude Diagram.
*Astronomy; Astrophysics; Galaxy Evolution.*

**cmd.** (abbr.) command.
Also: **comd**.

**CMDL** Climate Monitoring and Diagnostics Laboratory (U.S.A.).
*Atmospheric Research; Earth, Ocean, and Space Studies; Natural Resource Ecology.*

**Cmdr.** (abbr.) Commander.
Also: **Comdr.**; **Comm.**; **Cdr**.

**Cmdt** (abbr.) commandement.
French abbreviation meaning: command.

**CME** Center for Microbial Ecology (U.S.A.).

**CME** Centre de Microencapsulation.
*French Center.*

**CME** Chicago Mercantile Exchange.

**CME** CNS Midline Element.
*Biological Timing; Cell Biology; Physiology.*
For further details see under: **CNS**.

**CME** Community Modeling Effort.

**CME** Conseil Mondial de l'Energie.
French initialism meaning: Energy World Council.

**CME** 1. combined METOC element.
1. élément multinational METOC.
2. contre-mesures électroniques.
2. electronic countermeasures (ECM).

**CME** Coronal Mass Ejection.
*Astronomy; Astrophysics; Geophysics; Space Science; Solar Physics.*

**CMEA** Council for Mutual Economic Assistance.

**CMED** contre-mesures électroniques de déception [obsolète].
deceptive electronic countermeasures (DECM) [obsolete].

**CMEs** Coronal Mass Ejections.
For further details see under: **CME**.

**C.Mezz.** (abbr.) Cassa del Mezzogiorno.
Italian abbreviation of the: Fund for the Improvement of Southern Italy.

**CMF** conceptual military framework.
cadre conceptuel militaire.

**CMF** Conseil des Marchés Financiers.
France's financial market Regulator.

**CMF** cyclosphamide, Methotrexate, and 5-Fluoromacil.
*Breast-cancer Chemotherapy; Oncology.*

**CMFU** combined METOC forecast unit.
unité multinationale de prévisions METOC.

**CMGR** Committee on Microgravity Research (U.S.A.).

**CMGR** Constant Money Growth Rule.
*Monetary Policy.*

**CMH** Commission on Macroeconomics and Health.
Of the World Health Organization (Geneva, Switzerland).

**CMH** Complexe Majeur d'Histocompatibilité.
French initialism meaning: Major Histocompatibility Complex.
*Medicine.*

**CMH** The airport code for Port Columbus International, Columbus, Ohio, U.S.A.

**CMHEC** Carboxymethyl Hydroxyethyl Cellulose.

**cmHg** centimeter of Mercury.

**CMHS** Center for Mental Health Services (U.S.A.).

**CMI** Caribbean Meteorological Institute.

**CMI** Cell-Mediated Immunity.
*Anatomy and Biology; Dental Research; Medicine; Molecular Microbiology and Immunology.*

**CMI** Climate Modeling Initiative.
Of the Massachusetts Institute of Technology (U.S.A.).

**CMI** Computer-Managed Instruction.
*Computer Programming.*

**CMI** International Maritime Committee (Belgium).

**CMIA** captured / missing in action.
capturé / disparu au combat.

**CMIAG** Chemical Measuring Instruments Advisory Group.

**CMIP** Common Management Information Protocol.

**CMIS** Common Management Information Service.

**CMJ** Craniomandibular Joint.
*Evaluation and Development of the Mammalian*

*Middle Ear; Phylogenetic Analysis; Vertebrate Paleontology.*

**CML** Chemical Markup Language.
*Computer Science.*

**CML** Chronic Myeloid Leukemia.
CML is a type of leukemia that affects the myeloid.
*Medicine.*

**cml** (abbr.) commercial.
Also: **coml.**

**CML** Coupled Map Lattice.
*Biological Networks.*

**CMLA** Canadian Medical Library Association.

**CMLEA** California Media and Library Educators' Association (U.S.A.).

**CMM** Chinese Medical Materials.

**CMM** Committee on Membership Management.
EUFEPS Advisory Panel.
For further details see under: **EUFEPS**.

**CMM** Computational Melting Model.
*Computational Models; Geological Sciences.*

**CMM** Coordinate Measuring Machine.

**CMM** Corporación Mundial de la Mujer Medellin (Colombia).

**CMM** Crisis Management Manual.
Manuel de gestion des crises.

**CMMP** (Committee on) Condensed-Matter and Materials Physics (U.S.A.).

**CMMs** crisis management measures.
mesures de gestion des crises.

**Cmn** Centro di medicina nucleare.
Italian initialism of the: Nuclear Medicine Center (Italy).

**CMN** Cerium Magnesium Nitrate.

**CMO** Cardiomyopathie Obstructive.
French initialism meaning: (Hypertrophic) Obstructive Cardiomyopathy.
*Medicine.*

**CMO** Caribbean Meteorological Organization.

**CMO** Collateralized Mortgage Obligations (U.S.A.).
*Finance.*

**CMO** 1. civil-military operations [obsolete].
1. opérations civilo-militaires [obsolète].
2. communications management organization [obsolete].
2. organisation de gestion des télécommunications [obsolète].
3. configuration management office (organization).
3. bureau (organisation) de gestion de la configuration.
4. coverage mission order.
4. ordre de mission de couverture.
5. crisis management organization.
5. organisation de gestion des crises.

**CMOC** 1. civil-military object class.
1. classe d'objets civils/militaires.
2. civil-military operation cell.
2. cellule d'opérations civilo-militaires.

**CMOP** configuration management operating plan.
plan fonctionnel de gestion de la configuration.

**C-MOPP** Cyclophosphamide, Mechlorethamine, Oncovin, Procarbazine, and Prednisone.
*Cancer Chemotherapy; Oncology.*

**CMOREP** civil-military operations report.
compte rendu d'opérations civilo-militaires.

**CMOS device** Complementary MOS device.
*Electronics.*
For further details see under: **MOS**.

**CMP** Capillary Melting Point.

**CMP** Coastal Management Programs.

**CMP** Common Midpoint Profiles.

**CMP** configuration management plan.
plan de gestion de la configuration.

**CMP** Corrugated Metal Pipe.

**CMP** Cytidine Monophosphate.
CMP is also known as: Cytidylic Acid.
*Biochemistry.*

**CMPEA** Comité militaire de partenariat euro-atlantique.
Euro-Atlantic Partnership Military Committee (EAPMC).

**CMPEA/CEM** Comité militaire de partenariat euro-atlantique en session des chefs d'état-major.
Euro-Atlantic Partnership Military Committee in Chiefs-of-Staff Session (EAPMC/CS).

**cmps** centimeters per second.

**CMPs** Common Myeloid Progenitors.
*Biology; Cardiology; Cardiovascular Medicine.*

**cmptr.** (abbr.) computer.
Also: **CP**.

**cmq** centimetro quadrato.
Italian abbreviation meaning: square centimeter.

**CMR** Center for Medicines Research.

**CMR** Colossal Magnetoresistance.
*Magnetoresistance; Metals Research.*

**CMR** contre-mesures radar.
radar countermeasures (RCM).

**CMRA** Chemical Marketing Research Association.

**CMRB** Crisis Management Resource Board.
Commisssion des ressources pour la gestion des crises.

**CMS biology** Cell, Molecular and Structural biology.

**CMSG** Configuration Management Steering Group.
Groupe directeur de la gestion de la configuration.

**CMT** Cadmium Mercury Telluride.
**CMT** Chromomethylase.
**C.M.T.** Comando Militare Territoriale.
Italian initialism meaning: Zone of the Interior Headquarters.
*Military.*
**CMT disease** Charcot-Marie-Tooth disease.
Charcot-Marie-Tooth disease is a disorder that causes progressive degeneration of peripheral nerves.
*Genetics; Medicine; Neurobiology; Neurology.*
**CMTF** civil-military task force.
groupe civilo-militaire.
**CMTX** X-linked Charcot-Marie-Tooth disease.
X-linked Charcot-Marie-Tooth disease is a form of hereditary neuropathy with demyelination.
*Genetics; Medicine; Neurobiology; Neurology.*
**CMU** Carnegie-Mellon University.
**CMU** Chlorophenyldimethylurea.
**CMU** Conventional Mission Upgrade.
**CMUE** Comité militaire de l'Union européenne.
European Union Military Committee (EUMC).
**CMV** Cucumber Mosaic Virus.
*Virology.*
**CMV** Cytomegalovirus.
**CMVM** Comissào do Mercado de Valores Mobiliários (Portugal).
CMVM is Portugal's financial markets Regulator.
**CMX** crisis management exercise.
exercice de gestion des crises.
**CN** Capitale Netto.
Italian initialism meaning: Net Capital.
**CN** Comoros.
**CN** Condensation Nucleus.
*Meteorology.*
**C/N** Consignment Note.
**c/n** conto nostro.
Italian initialism meaning: our account.
**C/N** Credit Note.
**CN** Cuneo, Italy.
**CN** Cyanide.
*Inorganic Chemistry.*
**CNA** Caisse Nationale des Autoroutes (France).
**CNA** Center for Naval Analysis (U.S.A.).
**CNA** computer network attack.
attaque contre les réseaux informatiques.
**CNA**; **C.N.A.** Confederazione Nazionale dell'Artigianato.
Italian initialism of the: National Federation of Craftsmen / Craftswomen.
**CNAD** Conference of National Armaments Directors.
Conférence des directeurs nationaux des armaments (CDNA).
**CNAF** Centro Nazionale Analisi Fotogrammi.
Italian initialism of the: National Center for Photogram Analysis (Italy).
**CNAM** Conservatoire National des Arts et Métiers (France).
**CNAP** Centre for Novel Agricultural Products.
The CNAP is an academic research Centre at the University of York, G.B.
*Fundamental Molecular Science.*
**CNAS** College of Natural and Agricultural Sciences.
Of the University of California Riverside (U.S.A.).
**CNB** Congenital Night Blindness.
*Neuroscience.*
**CNB** National Biotechnology Center.
The CNB is located in Madrid (Spain).
**CNBA** Coordinamento Nazionale Biblioteche di Architettura (Italy).
*Italian Library Association.*
**CNBC** Center for the Neural Basis of Cognition (U.S.A.).
Of the Carnegie-Mellon University.
*Cognitive Neuroscience.*
**CNb domain** Cyclic Nucleotide-binding domain.
*Medicine; Molecular Biology and Genetics; Neurobiology; Neuroscience.*
**CNC** Computer Numerical Control.
*Control Systems.*
**CNCA** Caisse Nationale de Crédit Agricole (France).
**CNCA** Centre National de Coopération Agricole (France).
*French Center.*
**C.N.C.A.** Coordinamento Nazionale Comunità di Accoglienza (Italy).
**CNCF** Chambre Nationale des Conseils et Experts Financiers (France).
**CND** computer network defence.
défense des réseaux informatiques.
**CNDS**; **cnds.** (abbr.) condensate.
*Science.*
**CNED** Centre National de l'Enseignement à Distance (France).
*France Center.*
**CNEL** Consiglio Nazionale dell'Economia e del Lavoro.
Italian acronym of the: National Council of Economics and Labor.
*Italian Council.*
**CNEME** Centre National d'Etudes, de Mesures et d'Expertise (France).

*French Center.*
**CNEN** Comitato Nazionale per l'Energia Nucleare.
Italian acronym of the: National Committee for Nuclear Energy.
**CNES** Centre National d'Etudes Spatiales.
French acronym of the: National Center for Space Studies (France).
**CNET** Centre National d'Etudes des Télécommunications (France).
**CNETO** Centro Nazionale Edilizia e Tecniche Ospedaliere.
*Italian Center.*
**CNF** Centre National de Formation (France).
*French Center.*
**CNF** Conjunctive Normal Form.
*Artificial Intelligence.*
**CNF** Cyanogen Fluoride.
CNF is used mainly as a tear gas.
*Inorganic Chemistry.*
**CNFPT** Centre National de la Fonction Publique Territoriale (France).
*French Center.*
**CNG** Compressed Natural Gas.
**CNG** Cyclic Nucleotide-Gated Channels.
*Medicine; Molecular Biology and Genetics; Neurobiology; Odorant Signals.*
**CNGE** Corpo Nazionale Giovani Esploratori (Italy).
**CNI** Chemical News & Intelligence.
Online information resources for the Chemical Industry.
**CNI** Communications Navigation-Identification.
**CNIE** Committee for the National Institute for the Environment (U.S.A.).
**CNIIC** China National Internet Information Center (China).
*China Internet.*
**CNIJ** Centro Nacional de Informação para a Juventude (Portugal).
*Portuguese Center.*
**CNIO** National Cancer Research Center.
*Spanish Center.*
**CNLA** China National Library Association.
**CNLA** Council of National Library Associations.
**CNM** Certified Nurse-Midwife.
**CNMCA** Centro Nazionale Meteorologia Climatologia Aeronautica (Italy).
Located in Rome, Italy. The Aeronautics service is part of the OMM.
For further details see under: **OMM**.
**CNME** Caisse Nationale des Marchés de l'Etat (France).
**CNMR** Centro Nazionale Materiali di Riferimento (Italy).
*Italian Center; Reference Materials.*
**CNN** Cable News Network (U.S.A.).
**cnn.** (abbr.) connector.
*Design Engineering; Electrical Engineering; Industrial Engineering.*
**CNNS** Connectionless Network Services.
**CNO** Chief of Naval Operations.
**CNO cycle** Carbon-Nitrogen-Oxygen cycle.
High-temperature *thermonuclear reactions in stars - Astronomy.*
**CNODC** China National Oceanographic Data Center.
*Chinese Center.*
**CNOF** Conseil National de l'Organisation Française (France).
*French Council.*
**CNOS** Centro Nazionale Opere Salesiane.
*Italian Center.*
**CNOSF** Comité National Olympique et Sportif Français (France).
**CNP** 2', 3'-cyclic-nucleotide 3'-phosphohydrolase.
**CNP** Caisse Nationale de Prévoyance (France).
French initialism of the: National Provident Fund.
**CNP** Committee on Nuclear Physics (U.S.A.).
**CNP** Continuous Negative Pressure.
*Medicine.*
**CNPP** Centre National de Prévention et de Protection (France).
French initialism of the: National Center for Prevention and Protection.
**CNPS** Centre National des Ponts de Secours (France).
**CNPSVER** Centre National des Ponts de Secours à Verneuil-l'Etang (France).
**CNR** combat net radio.
radio de réseau de combat.
**CNR** Committee on Natural Resources - U.N.
**CNR; C.N.R.** Consiglio Nazionale delle Ricerche (Italy).
Italian initialism of the: National Research Council.
**CNRF** Cold Neutron Research Facility.
**CNS** Center for Neuroscience (U.S.A.).
**CNS** Central Nervous System.
The CNS comprises the brain, eyes, and spinal cord.
*Anatomy; Brain and Cognitive Sciences; Neurophysiology; Neurology.*
**CNS** see COMNAVSOUTH.
voir COMNAVSOUTH.
**CNSA** National Centre for Environmental Health (Spain).

**CNSD** Computer and Network Services Division (U.S.A.).
CNSD has replaced: **CSG** (Computer Support Group).
**CNSI** California NanoSystems Institute (U.S.A.).
**CNSI** Comunità Nuovi Stati Indipendenti.
**CNST** Consiglio Nazionale della Scienza e della Tecnica (Italy).
Italian initialism of the: Science and Technique National Council.
**CNSTAT** Committee on National STATistics (U.S.A.).
**CNT** Conseil National du Travail (Belgium).
*Belgian Council.*
**CNTF** Ciliary Neurotrophic Factor.
*Obesity.*
**CNT-FETs** Carbon Nanotube Field-Effect Transistors.
*Applied Physics.*
**CNTR** (abbr.) Container.
**CNTS** Center for Nuclear Technology and Society.
At Worcester Polytechnic Institute.
*Nanoscience; Physics.*
**CNUL** Council of National University Libraries.
**CNVA** Capitale Normalizzato di Valutazione Analitica.
Italian initialism meaning: Standardized Capital of Analytical Evaluation.
**CNVR** (abbr.) conveyor.
**CO** Call Option.
*Banking; Business; Finance.*
**CO** Carbon Monoxide.
Carbon Monoxide is a poisonous and inflammable gas. If inhaled it can cause asphyxiation.
*Inorganic Chemistry.*
**CO** Cardiac Output.
*Physiology.*
**c/o** care of; carried over.
**CO** Cash Order.
*Business; Commerce.*
**CO** Central Office.
**CO** Certification Officer (G.B.).
**Co** Cleanout.
**Co** The chemical symbol for Cobalt.
Cobalt is used mainly in alloys and ceramics production.
*Symbols; Chemistry.*
**Co** Coenzyme.
*Enzymology.*
**CO** Coinsurance.
**CO** Colombia's international vehicle-registration letters.
**CO** Colonial Office (G.B.).
**CO** (abbr.) Colorado (U.S.A.).
**C/O** Commanding Officer.
**CO** Communications Officer.
**CO** Como, Italy.
**Co.** (abbr.) Company.
Also: **Coy**.
**CO** The airline code for Continental Airlines.
**Co** (abbr.) County.
**CO** Covered Option.
*Banking; Business; Finance.*
**CO** Cytochrome Oxidase.
CO is a mitochondrial enzyme.
*Neuroscience.*
**$CO_2$** Carbon Dioxide.
$CO_2$ is used mainly: in refrigeration systems, carbonated beverages, aerosols and fire extinguishers.
*Inorganic Chemistry.*
**CoA** Coenzyme A.
Coenzyme A is essentially a coenzyme that is found in the cells of living organisms.
**COA** Contract Of Affreightment.
**COA** course of action.
1a. mode d'action.
1b. plan d'action.
**COAM**; **Coam.** (abbr.) coaming.
*Naval Architecture.*
**COAP** Center for Ocean Analysis and Prediction (U.S.A.).
**COAP** Cyclophosphamide, Oncovin, Ara-C, and Prednisone.
*Oncology.*
**COAPEC** Coupled Ocean Atmosphere Processes and European Climate (G.B.).
COAPEC is a 5-year programme funded by NERC.
*Air-Sea flux Analysis; Evolution of Ocean Heat Anomalies; Ocean and Climate Modelling; Tropical Atlantic Warm Events.*
For further details see under: **NERC**.
**COAR** centre d'opérations aériennes régional.
regional air operations centre (RAOC).
**COARE** Coupled Ocean-Atmosphere Response Experiment.
The COARE is an international TOGA program of oceanic and atmospheric observations in the western tropical pacific.
**COAS** Cooperativa Olbiense Artigianato Senegalese (Olbia, Italy).
**COAST** Cambridge Optical Aperture Synthesis Telescope.
*Astronomy.*
**COB** 1. centre d'opérations de bataillon.
1. battalion operations centre /BOC/.

2. co-located operating base.
2. base opérationnelle coïmplantée.
**CoB** Cobaltic Boride.
Cobaltic Boride is used mainly in ceramics.
*Inorganic Chemistry.*
**COB** Commission des Opérations de Bourse.
French acronym of the: Securities and Investments Board (G.B.); Securities and Exchange Commission (U.S.).
**COBAC** COmitati di Base per l'Assemblea Costituente (Italy).
**COBCOE** The Council Of British Chambers Of Commerce in COntinental Europe.
**COBE satellite** COsmic Background Explorer satellite - NASA's.
*Astronomy; Astrophysics; Cosmology.*
**COBMAM** Cyclophosphamide, Oncovin, Bleomycin, Methotrexate, Adriamycin, and MeCCNU.
*Oncology.*
**COBNET** Corporate Optical Backbone NETwork.
*European Community Project.*
**COBOL** COmmon Business Oriented Language.
*Computer Programming.*
**COBRA** Common Open Brokerage Architecture.
*European Community Project.*
**COBRA** counter-battery radar.
radar de contrebatterie.
**COBUCO system** COrdless BUsiness COmmunication system.
*European Community Project.*
**COC** Cathodal Opening Contraction.
*Medicine.*
**COC** 1. certificate of conformance.
1. certificat de conformité (CDC 3.).
2. change of command.
2. passation de commandement.
3. combat operations centre.
3. centre des opérations de combat.
**COCC** Center for Ocean Climate Chemistry (Canada).
**$COCl_2$** Carbonyl Chloride.
Carbonyl Chloride, also known as: Phosgene, is used mainly as a herbicide, and pesticide.
*Organic Chemistry.*
**$CoCl_2$** Cobaltous Chloride.
*Inorganic Chemistry.*
**$CoCO_3$** Cobaltous Carbonate.
*Inorganic Chemistry.*
**co.co.co.** collaboratori coordinati e continuativi (Italy).
*Working Conditions in Italy.*
**COCOMO** (abbr.) COnstructive COst MOdel.
**$CoCrO_4$** Cobaltous Chromate.
*Inorganic Chemistry.*
**COCTA** Conceptual and Terminological Analysis.
**COD** carrier onboard delivery.
livraison à bord.
**COD** Cash On Delivery.
**cod.** (abbr.) codex.
*Archaeology.*
**cod.** (abbr.) coding.
*Computer Programming.*
**C.O.D.** Collect On Delivery.
**CODA** Cash On Deferred Arrangement.
**CODA** centre d'opérations de la défense aérienne.
air defence operations centre (ADOC).
**coda** The above acronyms were coined accidentally using the Italian word "coda" which means in Italian: tail; queue.
**CODAG** combined diesel and gas (propulsion).
(propulsion) combinée diesel et (turbine à) gaz.
**CODAR** Coastal Ocean Dynamics Applications Radar.
**CODAR** COrrelation, Detection, And Ranging.
CODAR is a submarine detection method.
*Acoustical Engineering.*
**CODASYL** COnference on DAta Systems Languages.
*Computer Programming.*
**CODATA** Committee On DAta for Science and Technology.
Founded in 1966 by ICSU to improve the quality, reliability and accessibility of scientific data, including not only quantitative information on the properties and behavior of matter, but also other experimental and observational data.
**CODIAC** COoperative Distributed Interactive Atmospheric Catalog.
**CODIS** Clip On Demand Interactive System.
*European Community Project.*
**CODOG** combined diesel or gas (propulsion).
(propulsion) combinée diesel ou (turbine à) gaz.
**COE** Council Of Europe.
**COE** Crude Oil Equivalent.
**COE** Current Operation Expenditure.
**COEC** Council Operations and Exercise Committee.
Comité des opérations du Conseil et des exercices.
**coeff**; **coeff.** (abbr.) coefficient.
**COEs** Centers Of Excellence.
**COESA** Committee on Extension to the Standard Atmosphere (U.S.A.).
**CoF** Cobaltous Hydroxide.
Cobaltous Hydroxide is also known as: Cobalt Hydrate; Cobalt Hydroxide.

*Inorganic Chemistry.*
**$COF_2$** Carbonyl Fluoride.
Carbonyl Fluoride, also known as:
Fluorosphosgene is used in organic synthesis.
*Organic Chemistry.*
**$CoF_2$** Cobaltous Fluoride.
Cobaltous Fluoride is also known as:
Cobalt(di)Fluoride.
*Inorganic Chemistry.*
**$CoF_3$** Cobaltic Fluoride.
Cobaltic Fluoride is also known as: Cobalt Trifluoride.
*Inorganic Chemistry.*
**COFACE** Compagnie Française d'Assurances pour le Commerce Extérieur.
French acronym of the: Export Credit Guarantee Department.
**COFACE** Confederation of Family Organizations in the European Community.
**COFC** Container-On-Flatcar.
**C of Engrs.** Chief of Engineers.
**COFF., coff.** (abbr.) cofferdam.
*Naval Architecture.*
**COFFA** certificate of final financial acceptance.
certificat d'acceptation financière finale.
**COFI** COmmittee on FIsheries.
Of the U.N. FAO.
For further details see under: **FAO**.
**COFO** Certificate OF Occupancy.
**CO-FTIR** CO Fourier Transform Infrared Spectroscopy.
**COG** Center Of Gravity.
*Mechanics.*
**COGA** COllaborative study on the Genetics of Alcoholism.
*Behavioral Genetics.*
**COGAG** combined gas and gas (propulsion).
(propulsion) combinée (turbine à) gaz et (turbine à) gaz.
**COGEMI** COntractants GEnéraux de Maisons (France).
**COGENE** Committee On GENetic Experimentation.
Located in Paris, France. Founded in 1976 to serve as a non-governmental interdisciplinary and international council of scientists and as a source of advice for the benefit of governments, intergovernmental agencies, scientific groups and individuals concerning recombinant DNA activities.
**CO gene** Cytochrome Oxidase gene.
*Biomedical Chemistry; Cardiac Hypertrophy; Medicine.*
**COGO** (abbr.) Coordinate Geometry.
*Computer Programming.*
**COGOG** combined gas or gas (propulsion).
(propulsion) combinée (turbine à) gaz ou (turbine à) gaz.
**COH** cessation of hostilities.
cessation des hostilités.
**COHA** cessation of hostilities agreement.
accord de cessation des hostilités.
**Coho** Coherent oscillator.
*Electronics.*
**COHR** Center for Oral Health Research.
University of Kentucky (U.S.A.).
**COI** Central Office of Information.
**COI** 1. Commission océanographique intergouvernementale.
1. Intergovernmental Oceanographic Commission (IOC 2.).
2. community of interest.
2. communauté d'intérêts.
**COIC** Careers and Occupational Information Centre (G.B.).
*British Center.*
**COIE** Centro de Orientación e Información de Empleo (Spain).
**COIN** Centre for Organic INformatics.
Established in East Sweden.
*Organic and Polymer Electronics.*
**COIN** COnsorzio cooperative INtegrate.
*Italian Consortium.*
**COIN** counter-insurgency.
contre-insurrection.
**COINOP** counter-insurgery operation.
opération de contre-insurrection.
**COINS** COmputerized INformation Systems.
**Col.** (abbr.) Columbia (U.S.A.).
**Col.**; **Colo.** (abbr.) Colorado (U.S.A.).
**col.** (abbr.) column.
*Architecture; Chemical Engineering; Computer Programming; Engineering; Mathematics; Nucleonics.*
**COL** Cost-Of-Living.
**COL** Council on Ocean Law.
**COLA** Cost-Of-Living Adjustment.
**COLA** Cost Of Living Allowance.
**CO laser** Carbon Monoxide laser.
*Optics.*
**COLA Studies** Center for Ocean-Land-Atmosphere Studies.
**Cold** Computer output to laser disk.
**COLD** Council on Oceanographic Laboratory Directors.
**COLDIRETTI** Confederazione Nazionale Coltivatori Diretti.

Italian acronym of the: Italian Farmers' National Federation.
**CO-LEARN** (abbr.) COoperative LEARNing.
**coll.** (abbr.) collision.
**COLOC** change of location of command.
1a. bascule de PC [FR].
1b. changement d'emplacement du commandement.
**COLOS** COncept Learning Of Science.
**COLPRO** collective protection [NBC].
protection collective [NBC].
**COLT** City Of London Telecommunications.
*Conferences.*
**COM** circulation opérationnelle militaire.
operational air traffic (OAT).
**COM** Claquement d'Ouverture de la Mitrale.
French acronym meaning: Mitral Opening Snap.
*Medicine.*
**COM** Computer Output on Microfilmer.
**COMA** COmmittee on the Medical Aspects of Food and Nutrition Policy (G.B.).
**COMAIRBALTAP** Commander Allied Air Forces Baltic Approaches [obsolete - now part of COMAIRNORTH].
commandant des Forces aériennes alliées des approches de la Baltique [obsolète - fait maintenant partie de COMAIRNORTH].
**COMAIRCENT** Commander Allied Air Forces, Central Region [obsolete].
commandant des Forces aériennes alliées de la Région Centre [obsolète].
**COMAIRCENTLANT** Commander Maritime Air Central Atlantic Sub-Area [obsolete].
commandant des Forces aéromaritime de la Sous-zone centrale de l'Atlantique [obsolète].
**COMAIREASTLANT** Commander Naval Air Forces East Atlantic [has replaced COMMARAIREASTLANT].
commandant des Forces aéronavales Est de l'Atlantique [remplace COMMARAIREASTLANT].
**COMAIRNORTH** Commander Allied Air Forces North.
commandant des Forces aériennes alliées Nord.
**COMAJF** commander allied joint force.
commandant de force interarmées interalliée.
**COMAMF(A)** Commander ACE Mobile Force (Air).
commandant de la Force mobile du CAE (Air).
**COMAMF(L)** Commander ACE Mobile Force (Land).
commandant de la Force mobile du CAE (Terre).
**COMAO** composite air operations.
opérations aériennes combinées.
**COMARAIRMED** Commander Maritime Air Force Mediterranean.
commandant des Forces aéromaritimes de la Méditerranée.
**COMARRC** Commander ARRC.
commandant de l'ARRC.
**COMB** Center Of Marine Biotechnology.
Of the University of Maryland (U.S.A.).
*Bioremediation; Fish Endocrinology; Genetics of Archaeal Organisms; Marine Microbial Products; Molecular Biology.*
**COMB** Cyclophosphamide, Oncovin, MeCCNU, and Bleomycin.
*Oncology.*
**comb** The above acronyms were coined using the English word "comb" (*Molecular Biology; Invertebrate Zoology; Vertebrate Zoology*).
**COMBALTAP** Commander Allied Forces Baltic Approaches [obsolete - now part of CINCNORTH].
commandant des Forces alliées des approches de la Baltique [obsolète - fait maintenant partie du CINCNORTH].
**COMBEX** combined exercise.
exercice multinational.
**COM Center** Communication, Optics and Materials Center.
Of the Denmark Technical University.
**COMCHECK** communications check.
vérification des transmisssions.
**Comdr.** (abbr.) Commander.
Also: **Comm.**; **Cmdr.**; **Cdr**.
**comdt** (abbr.) Commandant.
**COMECON**; **Comecon** Council for Mutual Economic Assistance.
**COMEDS** Committee of the Chiefs of Military Medical Services in NATO.
Comité des chefs des services de santé militaires au sein de l'OTAN.
**COMEFOT** COnsorzio MEditerraneo di FOrmazione Tecnologica.
*Italian Consortium.*
**COMESA**; **Comesa** Common Market for Eastern and Southern Africa.
**COMET** COnsortium for Microelectronics Training.
**COMETT** Community action programme for Education and Training for Technology.
*European Community Program.*
**COMEX** 1. commence exercise.
1. commencer l'exercice.
2. communications exercise.

2. exercice de transmissions (ou télécommunications).
**COMEX** COMmittee on EXchanges (U.S.A.).
**COMEX** COMmodity Exchange (New York, U.S.A.).
**COMINT** communications intelligence.
renseignement transmissions.
**COMINTREP** communications intelligence report.
compte rendu du renseignement transmissions.
**COMINTSUM** communications intelligence summary.
synthèse de renseignement transmissions.
**COMJAM** communications jamming.
brouillage transmissions (ou des télécommunications).
**COMJCCENT** Commander Joint Command Centre.
commandant du Commandement interarmées Centre.
**COMJCNORTH** Commander Joint Command North.
commandant du Commandement interarmées Nord.
**COMJCNORTHEAST** Commander Joint Command North-East.
commandant du Commandement interarmées Nord-Est.
**COMJCSOUTH** Commander Joint Command South.
commandant du Commandement interarmées Sud.
**COMJCSOUTHCENT** Commander Joint Command South-Centre.
commandant du Commandement interarmées Sud-Centre.
**COMJCSOUTHEAST** Commander Joint Command South-East.
commandant du Commandement interarmées Sud-Est.
**COMJCSOUTHWEST** Commander Joint Command South-West.
commandant du Commandement interarmées Sud-Ouest.
**COMKFOR** Commander of the Kosovo Force.
commandant de la Force pour le Kosovo.
**coml.** (abbr.) commercial.
Also: **cml**.
**COMLA** COMmonwealth Library Association.
**COMLNDJUT** Commander Allied Land Forces Schleswig-Holstein and Jutland.
commandant des Forces terrestres alliées du Schleswig-Holstein et du Jutland.
**COMLANDSOUTH** Commander Allied Land Forces Southern Europe.
commandant des Forces terrestres alliées du Sud-Europe.
**COMLANDSOUTHCENT** Commander Allied Land Forces South Central Europe.
commandant des Forces terrestres alliées du Centre-Sud-Europe.
**COMLOGSITREP** communications logistic situation report.
compte rendu de situation logistique sur les transmissions.
**COMM** Chemistry Of Metals in Medicine.
*European Community Project.*
**comm.** (abbr.) commander.
Also: **Cdr.**; **Comdr.**; **Cmdr**.
**comm.** (abbr.) commercio.
Italian abbreviation meaning: trade; commerce; business; trading; market.
**comm.** (abbr.) commission.
**comm.** (abbr.) commodore.
Also: **com**.
**comm.** (abbr.) communication.
**COMMAIRNORLANT** Commander, Maritime Air Northern Atlantic Area.
commandant des Forces aéronavales du Secteur septentrional de l'Atlantique.
**COMMARAIREASTLANT** Commander Maritime Air Eastern Atlantic Area [obsolete - replaced by COMAIREASTLANT].
commandant des Forces aéronavales du Secteur oriental de l'Atlantique [obsolète - remplacé par COMAIREASTLANT].
**COMMARAIRNORTH** 1. Commander Maritime Air Forces North.
1. commandant des Forces aéronavales Nord.
2. Commander Maritime Allied Naval Forces North.
2. commandant des Forces aéronavales alliées Nord.
**COMMZ** communications zone.
zone des communications.
**COMNAVNORTH** Commander Allied Naval Forces North.
commandant des Forces navales alliées Nord.
**COMNAVNORTHWEST** Commander Allied Naval Forces Northwestern Europe [obsolete].
commandant des Forces navales alliées du Nord-Ouest-Europe [obsolète].
**COMNAVSOUTH** 1. Commander Allied Naval Forces South [has replaced COMNAVSOUTH 2.].
1. commandant des Forces navales alliées Sud [remplace COMNAVSOUTH 2.].
2. Commander Allied Naval Forces Southern Europe [replaced by COMNAVSOUTH 1.].

2. commandant des Forces navales alliées du Sud-Europe [remplacé par COMNAVSOUTH 1.].
**COMNORHAG** Commander Northern Army Group [obsolete].
Commandant du Groupe d'armées Nord [obsolète].
**COMOPS** commander of operations.
commandant des opérations.
**comp.** (abbr.) compound.
Also: **cpd**.
*Biology; Chemistry; Petroleum Engineering.*
**COMPAG; Compag** Federazione Nazionale Commercianti Macchine e Prodotti per l'Agricoltura (Italy).
*Italian Federation; Agricultural Products.*
**Compander** (abbr.) Compressor Expander.
*Electronics.*
**COMPILE** COMpact disc Publishing for Interactive Language Learning.
*European Community Project.*
**COMPLAN** communications plan.
plan des transmissions.
**COMPLEX** COMmittee on Planetary and Lunar EXploration (U.S.A.).
**compr.** (abbr.) compratore.
Italian abbreviation meaning: buyer; purchaser; vendee.
**compr.** (abbr.) compravendita.
Italian abbreviation meaning: buying and selling; marketing; purchase and sale.
**COMPSAC** COMPuter Software and Applications Conference.
**COMPTEL** (abbr.) COMPton TELescope.
**COMPUSEC** computer security.
1a. sécurité des systèmes informatiques.
1b. sécurité informatique.
**COMSAT** (abbr.) COMmunications SATellite (Corporation).
COMSAT is a common carrier created under the provisions of the U.S. Communications satellite Act of 1962 to provide Communications Satellite service.
**COMSEC** communications security.
securité des communications.
**COMSFOR** Commander of the Stabilization Force.
commandant de la Force de stabilisation.
**COMSITREP** communications situation report.
compte rendu de situation des télécommunications.
**COMSTRIKFLTLANT** Commander Striking Fleet Atlantic (afloat).
commandant de la Flotte d'intervention de l'Atlantique (à la mer).
**COMSTRIKFLTSOUTH** Commander Naval Striking Fleet Southern Europe.
commandant de la Flotte d'intervention du Sud-Europe.
**COMSTRIKFORSOUTH** Commander Naval Striking and Support Forces Southern Europe.
commandant des Forces navales d'intervention et de soutien du Sud-Europe.
**COMSUBACLANT** 1. Commander Submarines Atlantic [has replaced COMSUBACLANT 2.].
1. commandant des Forces sous-marines de l'Atlantique [remplace COMSUBACLANT 2.].
2. Commander Submarines, Atlantic Area [obsolete - replaced by COMSUBACLANT 1.].
2. commandant des Forces sous-marines de l'Atlantique [obsolète - remplacé par COMSUBACLANT 1.].
**COMSUBEASTLANT** 1. Commander Submarines East Atlantic [has replaced COMSUBEASTLANT 2.].
1. commandant des Forces sous-marines Est de l'Atlantique [remplace COMSUBEASTLANT 2.].
2. Commander Submarines Eastern Atlantic Area [obsolete - replaced by COMSUBEASTLANT 1.].
2. commandant des Forces sous-marines du Secteur oriental de l'Atlantique [obsolète - remplacé par COMSUBEASTLANT 1.].
**COMSUBMED** Commander Submarines Mediterranean.
commandant des Forces sous-marines de la Méditerranée.
**COMSUBNORTH** Commander Submarines North.
commandant des Forces sous-marines Nord.
**COMSUBWESTLANT** Commander Submarines Western Atlantic Area [obsolete].
commandant des Forces sous-marines du Secteur occidental de l'Atlantique [obsolète].
**COMT** Catechol-*O*-Methyl Transferase / Methyltransferase.
*Behavioral Sciences; Breast Cancer; Medicine; Metabolism; Neuroscience; Pharmacogenetics; Psychiatry; Schizophrenia.*
**COMTECH** (abbr.) COMmunication TECHnology.
**Con.** (abbr.) Consols.
**Con.** (abbr.) Consul.
**ConA** Concanavalin A.
*Human Genetics; Molecular Biology; Pathology.*
**CONAES** Committee On Nuclear and Alternative Energy Systems.
**CONAD** COnsorzio NAzionale cooperative Dettaglianti.
Italian acronym of the: National Co-operative Society of Retail Traders.

**CONAG** COnsiglio NAzionale Geofisico.
Italian abbreviation of the: National Geophysics Council (Italy).
**CONBLS** Consortium of Southern Biomedical Libraries.
**conc.** (abbr.) concentrate.
*Chemistry; Food Technology; Mining Engineering.*
**conc.** (abbr.) concentric / concentrical.
*Science.*
**conc.** (abbr.) concrete.
*Materials.*
**cond** (abbr.) condensed.
*Graphic Arts; Science.*
**cond** (abbr.) condenser.
*Mechanical Engineering; Optics.*
*Electricity* - In electricity condenser is also known as: capacitor.
**cond** (abbr.) condition.
*Behavior; Mathematics.*
**cond** (abbr.) conductivity.
*Electricity.*
**cond** (abbr.) conductor.
*Electricity; Physics; Surgery.*
**condis crystal** conformationally disordered crystal.
*Materials Science.*
**Conelrad** (abbr.) Control of electromagnetic radiation (U.S.A.).
Conelrad was a former U.S. broadcasting system intended to provide control in case of nuclear attacks.
*Telecommunications.*
**conf.** (abbr.) confidential.
**CONI**; **C.O.N.I.** Comitato Olimpico Nazionale Italiano.
Italian acronym of the: Italian Committee for the Olympic Games.
**CONICET** Consejo Nacional de Investigaciones Cientificas y Técnicas (Argentina).
CONICET is Argentina's National Council for Scientific and Technical Research.
**CoNISMa** Consorzio Nazionale Interuniversitario per le Scienze del Mare.
*Italian Consortium.*
**CONMAROPS** concept of marine operations.
concept d'opérations maritimes.
**CONOPLAN** contingency operation plan.
plan d'opérations des circonstances.
**CONOPS** concept of operations.
1a. concept de l'opération (idée de manœuvre).
1b. concept d'opération.
**CONPLAN** contingency plan.
plan de circonstance.

**CONS** Connection Oriented Network Services.
**Cons.** (abbr.) Conservative.
**cons.** (abbr.) consigliere.
Italian abbreviation meaning: adviser; councillor; director.
*Legal;* Judge (of a Court of Appeal; etc.).
**Cons.** (abbr.) Constitution.
**Cons.** (abbr.) Consul.
**cons.** (abbr.) consulting.
**CONSA** consular shipping advisor.
conseiller consulaire pour la navigation commerciale.
**CONSAL** CONference of South-East Asian Libraries.
**consgt.** (abbr.) consignment.
**CONSOB** COmmissione Nazionale per le SOcietà e la Borsa.
Italian abbreviation of the: National Commission for Listed Companies and the Stock Exchange.
**const.** (abbr.) constable.
**const.** (abbr.) constant.
*Artificial Intelligence; Mathematics; Science.*
**const.** (abbr.) constitution; constitutional.
**const.** (abbr.) constituency.
**cont.** (abbr.) contact.
*Aviation; Electricity; Geology; Medicine; Telecommunications.*
**cont.** (abbr.) container.
*Transportation Engineering.*
**cont.** (abbr.) content.
*Linguistics; Mathematics.*
**Cont.** (abbr.) Continent.
**cont.** (abbr.) continued.
Also: **contd**.
**cont.** (abbr.) control.
*Aviation; Cartography; Computer Programming; Computer Technology; Control Systems; Electronics; Science; Statistics.*
**contd**. (abbr.) continued.
Also: **cont**.
**contg.** (abbr.) containing.
**CON TOL** (abbr.) CONcentricity TOLerance.
**CONTOUR** COmet Nucleus TOUR.
The spacecraft operated after launch but blew apart in August 2002 when it rocketed out of the Earth orbit.
**contr.** (abbr.) contract; contractor.
**CONUS** Continental United States.
**CONVAIR** CONsensus and Validation in ACTS Results exploitation.
*European Community Project.*
**CONVEX** convoy exercise.
exercice de navigation en convoi.

**COO** Chief Operating Officer (U.S.A.).
**CoO** Cobaltous Oxide.
CoO, also known as: Cobalt Oxide, is used mainly as a pigment.
*Inorganic Chemistry.*
**$CO_2O_3$** Cobaltic Oxide.
Cobaltic Oxide is used mainly as a pigment.
*Inorganic Chemistry.*
**COOC** Contact with Oil or Other Cargo.
*Insurance; Transportation.*
**$Co(OH)_2$** Cobaltous Hydroxide.
Cobaltous Hydroxide is also known as: Cobalt Hydrate; Cobalt Hydroxide.
*Inorganic Chemistry.*
**co-op** co-operative.
**COOP** craft of opportunity.
navire utilisé de manière occasionnelle.
**COOS** Committee On Opportunities in Science.
**COP** Coastal Ocean Program.
**COP** Coefficient Of Performance.
*Thermodynamics.*
**COP** 1. common operational picture.
1. situation opérationnelle commune.
2. see CONOPLAN.
2. voir CONOPLAN.
**COP** Conference Of the Parties (biennial).
The CBD parties make commitments through the COP which is the political decision-making body.
For further details see under: **CBD**.
**cop.** (abbr.) copper.
Also: **cpr**.
For further details see under: Symbol **Cu**.
**COP** Cyclophosphamide, Oncovin, and Prednisone.
*Oncology.*
**COP II** Coat Protein complex II.
*Biochemistry; Cargo Proteins; Eukaryotic Cells.*
**COPA** Comitato delle Organizzazioni Professionali Agricole - *European Community.*
**COP-BLAM** Cyclophosphamide, Oncovin, Prednisone, BLeomycin, Adriamycin, and Matulane.
*Oncology.*
**COPD** Chronic Obstructive Pulmonary Disease.
*Medicine.*
**copd.** (abbr.) coppered.
**COPE** Chronic Obstrusive Pulmonary Emphysema.
*Medicine.*
**COPE** Coastal Ocean Probing Experiment.
**COPE** Committee On Publication Ethics (G.B.).
Formed by British Journal Editors (1997).
**COPE Program** Coastal Oregon Productivity Enhancement Program (U.S.A.).
**CO.P.E.V.** COmitato per la Prevenzione dell'Epatite Virale.
Italian acronym of the: Committee for the Prevention of Viral Hepatitis. Founded in 1987 in Milan, Italy.
**COPIAT** COalition to Preserve the Integrity of American Trademarks (U.S.A.).
COPIAT is an association of U.S. trademark-owning companies.
**COPLIN** Committee of Polytechnic Librarians In Nigeria.
**COPP** Cyclophosphamide, Oncovin, Procarbazine, and Prednisone.
*Oncology.*
**COPQ** Cost Of Poor Quality.
**COPR** Center for Overseas Pest Research (G.B.).
**COPROM** computer-supported COllaborative PROcess Management - *European Community.*
**COPS** Comité politique et de sécurité.
Political and Security Committee (PSC).
**COPSCAULS** Council Of Pennsylvania State College And University Library Directors (U.S.A.).
**COPSI** Comité politique et de sécurité intérimaire (COPSI) [obsolète - maintenant appelé COPS].
Interim Political and Security Committee (IPSC) [obsolete - now called PSC 1.].
**COPS Program** Coastal Ocean Prediction Systems Program (U.S.A.).
**COPUL** Council Of Prairie University Libraries.
**COPUS** Committee On the Public Understanding of Science (G.B.).
**CoPUST** Committee on the Public Understanding of Science and Technology.
**COR** Career Opportunities in Research.
*Education and training.*
**cor.** (abbr.) corner.
*Cartography.*
**CORA** Centri Orientamento Retravailler Associati (Italy).
**CORAL** Council Of Research and Academic Libraries.
**coral** The above acronym was coined using the English word "coral" (*Invertebrate Zoology*).
**CORBA**; **Corba Standard** Common Object Request Broker Architecture Standard.
Corba, by OMG, defines the format and rules governing the passage of messages betweeen software programs.
*Bioinformatics; Database Interactions; Information Technology.*
For further details see under: **OMG**.
**cor.bd.** (abbr.) corner bead.

*Building Engineering.*
**CORCEN** correlation centre [air defence].
centre de corrélation [défense aérienne].
**CORD** Chronic Obstructive Respiratory Disease.
**CORDIS** COmmunity Research and Development Information Service - *European Community.*
**CO.RE.CO.** COmitato REgionale di COntrollo (Italy).
**COREIS** COmunità REligiosa ISlamica.
Italian acronym meaning: Islamic Religious Community (Italy).
**CORELAP** (abbr.) COmputerized RElationship LAyout Planning.
*Industrial Engineering.*
**Co.Re.Ma.** (abbr.) Consumer Relationship Marketing.
*Novel Software Systems.*
**COREP** COnsorzio per la Ricerca e l'Educazione Permanente.
COREP is located in Turin, Italy.
*Italian Consortium.*
**COREPLA** COnsorzio nazionale per la Raccolta, il Riciclaggio e il Recupero dei Rifiuti di Imballaggi in PLAstica.
*Italian Consortium.*
**COREs** Centers Of Research Excellence (U.S.A.).
**COREVE** (abbr.) COnsorzio REcupero VEtro.
*Italian Consortium; Glass Recovery.*
**CORF** Committee On Radio Frequencies (U.S.A.).
**COR genes** COld-Regulated genes.
*Plant Biology; Crop and Soil Sciences.*
**CoRI** Coatings Research Institute (Belgium).
**CORINE** Coordination of Information on the Environment.
*European Community Program.*
**CORISS** COoperative RIunite Socio-Sanitarie (Italy).
**CORK Observatory** Circulation Obviation Retrofit Kit Observatory.
To study the biogeochemical properties and microbial diversity in circulating fluids from aging Ocean crust.
*Microbiology; Ocean and Earth Science; Ocanography.*
For furthe rdetails see under: **ODP** and **JFR**.
**Corn.** (abbr.) Cornwall (G.B.).
**Corp.** (abbr.) Corporation.
**corr.** (abbr.) corrispondente.
Italian abbreviation meaning: correspondent, corresponding.
**corr.** (abbr.) corrispondenza.
Italian abbreviation meaning: correspondence.
**corr.** (abbr.) corrugated.
**CORRONOISE** Electrochemical Noise for field Corrosion measurements.
*European Community Project.*
**CORTAC** corrected tactical (procedure message).
(message de procédure) tactique corrigée.
**COS** Camere Operatorie Sicure.
Italian acronym meaning: Safe Operating Rooms / Theaters.
*Medicine.*
**COS** Carbonyl Sulfide.
*Chemistry.*
**COS** Cash On Shipment.
*Commerce; Shipping.*
**COS** Chief Of Staff.
Also: **C.S.**
**Cos.** (abbr.) Companies.
**COS** The airport code for Colorado Springs, Colorado, U.S.A.
**COS** Control Air Support.
*Military Science.*
**cos.** (abbr.) cosine.
*Mathematics.*
**cos.** (abbr.) countries.
**COSA** Cost Of Sales Adjustment.
*Business; Commerce; Economics.*
**COSE** COllege of Science and Engineering (U.S.A.).
**COSE** Committee on Optical Science and Engineering (U.S.A.).
**cosec.** (abbr.) cosecant.
Also: **csc**.
*Mathematics.*
**COSELs** Circular Grating Coupled Surface-Emitting Lasers.
*Electrical Science; Engineering Science.*
**COSEUP** Committee On Science, Engineering, and Public Policy (U.S.A.).
**COSI** Center Of Science & Industry (U.S.A.).
**COSMAT** COmmittee on the Survey of MATerials Science and Engineering.
**COSNA** Composite Observing System for the North Atlantic.
**$CoSO_4$** Cobaltous Sulfate.
*Inorganic Chemistry.*
**COSPAR** Committee On SPAce Research.
Located in Paris, France. Founded in 1958 to continue and foster, after the end of IGY, international co-operation in all sciences that make use of the new research tools of rockets, satellites and balloons.
For further details see under: **IGY**.
**Cospe**; **COSPE** Cooperazione per lo Sviluppo dei Paesi Emergenti (Florence, Italy).

*Non-governmental Organization.*
**Cospes**; **COSPES** Centro Orientamento Scolastico, Professionale e Sociale (Italy).
**COSPIN** COsmic ray and Solar Particle INvestigations.
*Astronomy; Astrophysics; Space Science.*
**COST** COoperation in the field of Scientific and Technical Research.
*European Community.*
**COST** COoperazione europea nel settore della ricerca Scientifica e Tecnica.
Italian acronym meaning: European Cooperation in the field of Scientific and Tecnical Research.
**COSTAR** Corrective Optics Space Telescope Axial Replacement.
**COSTED** COmmittee on Science and Technology in Developing Countries.
**COSTED-IBN** Committee On Science and Technology in Developing Countries and International Biosciences Networks.
Located in India. Founded in 1966 (reconstituted in 1972, 1993) for the encouragement of science and technology in developing countries, the organization of meetings, seminars and symposia related to *science teaching* and *natural resources*, and the identification of problems of relevance to developing countries.
**COSTEX** command and staff exercise.
exercice de commandement et d'état-major.
**costr.nav.** (abbr.) costruzione navale.
Italian abbreviation meaning: shipbuilding.
**COSU** COllaboration with the former Soviet Union in Radiation Protection.
*European Community.*
**COSY** Correlated Spectroscopy.
**COSYS** Design and implementation of a computer-based COurse production and delivery SYStem.
*European Community Project.*
**cot** cotangent.
*Mathematics* - The cotangent is actually the reciprocal of the tangent.
**Cot.** (abbr.) cotter.
Cotter is also known as: Cotter pin.
*Design Engineering.*
**COTA** centre d'opérations tactiques air.
air tactical operations centre (ATOC 1.).
**COTAT**; **cotat** COrrelation Tracking And Triangulation.
*Engineering.*
**COTDS** CO Thermal Desorption mass Spectroscopy.
**CO-TECH** (abbr.) COoperation TECHnology.
*European Community Project.*
**COTOREP** COmmission Technique d'Orientation et de REclassement Professionnel.
*Technical Commission.*
**CO-TRAO** COmmunauté du TRavail des Alpes Occidentales.
**COTS** commercial off-the-shelf.
commercial sur étagère (ou commercial standard).
**Cots doctrine** Commercial off-the-shelf doctrine.
*Computer Security; Information Technology Development.*
**COUP-TF II** Chicken Ovalbumin Upstream Promoter - Transcription Factor II.
*Biology; Cell Biology; Genetics; Medicine.*
**court.** (abbr.) courtage.
French abbreviation meaning: brokerage.
**COVEN** COllaborative Virtual ENvironments.
*European Community Project.*
**COVIP** COmmissione di VIgilanza sui fondi Pensione (Italy).
*Italian Commission; Pension Funds.*
**COVIRA** (abbr.) COmputer VIsion RAdiology.
*Medicine.*
**COWL pattern** Cold Ocean-Warm Land pattern.
*Climate Change; Geophysics; Polar Science.*
**COWRR** Committee On Water Resources Research.
**COx** Cholesterol Oxidase.
*Environmental Molecular Sciences; Flavoenzymes.*
**cox.** (abbr.) coxswain.
**COX** Cytochrome-c-OXydase.
*Medicine; Molecular Biology.*
**COX-2 enzymes** Cyclooxygenase-2 enzymes.
COX-2 are enzymes that promote fever, pain and inflammation.
*Anti-inflammation Research; Biochemistry; Molecular Biophysics; Pharmaceutics.*
**COXII** Cytochrome Oxidase Subunit II.
*Biochemistry and Biophysics; Genetics and Development.*
**Coy** Company.
Also: **Co**.
**COZI** COmmunications Zone Indicator.
*Telecommunications.*
**CP** Calorific Power.
**CP** The airline code for Canadian Airlines International Ltd.
**CP**; **cp** Candlepower.
*Optics.*
**CP** 1. capability package.
1. paquet (ou ensemble) de capacité.
2. command post.
2. poste de commandement (PC 2.).
3. control point.

3. point de contrôle.
4. Cooperation Partner [PfP].
4. Partenaire de la coopération [PPP].
5. coordination post.
5. poste de coordination.
6. counter-proliferation.
6. contre-prolifération.
7. crédit de paiement.
7. cash credit (CC 2.).
8. see COLPRO.
8. voir COLPRO.

**CP**; **C.P.** Cape Province.

**CP** Capillary Pressure.
*Fluid Mechanics; Physiology.*

**CP**; **C.P.** Carriage Paid.

**C.P.**; **c.p.** Casella Postale.
Italian initialism meaning: Post Office Box.

**Cp** Caudate-putamen.

**CP** Center of Pressure.
*Aviation.*

**CP** Certificate of Purchase.
*Business; Commerce; Finance.*

**cp** Ceruloplasmin.
Ceruloplasmin is also known as: Ferroxidase.
*Biochemistry; Copper Metabolism.*

**CP** Chartered Party.

**CP**, **cp** Chemically Pure.
Chemically pure actually means without impurities detectable by means of analysis.
*Chemistry.*

**CP**; **C.P.**; **c.p.** Chief of Police.

**CP** Circular Pitch.

**CP**; **C.P.** Civil Procedure.

**CP** Closing Price; Closing Purchase.
*Business; Finance.*

**CP**; **C.P.** Code of Procedure.

**CP**; **C.P.** Codice Penale.
Italian initialism meaning: Penal Code.

**CP** Cold-Punched.

**CP** Commercial Paper.
*Banking; Business; Finance.*

**CP**; **C.P.** Communist Party.

**CP**; **cp** (abbr.) compare.

**CP** (abbr.) computer.
Also: **cmptr**.

**CP**, **C.P.** Consiglio Provinciale.
Italian initialism meaning: District Council.

**CP** Constant Pressure.
*Medicine.*

**CP**; **C.P.** Contract Price.
*Business; Commerce; Finance.*

**CP** Cortical Plate.

**CP**; **cp** Counterpoise.
*Electricity; Ordnance.*
*Mechanical Engineering* - In mechanical engineering, counterpoise is also known as: counterweight; counterbalance.

**CP** Cross-Polarization.
*Electromagnetism.*

**CPA** Centre de Perfectionnement aux Affaires.
French initialism of the: Center for Business improvement.

**CPA** Certified Public Accountant.
*Accounts; Finance.*

**CPA** Chirped Pulse Amplification.
*Laser Chemistry; Physics.*

**CPA** Claims Payable Abroad.

**CPA** closest point of approach.
point d'approche le plus rapproché.

**cpa** color-phase alternation.
*Telecommunications.*

**CPA** Corte Permanente d'Arbitrato.
Italian initialism meaning: Permanent Arbitration Court.

**CPA** Critical Path Analysis.

**cPABP** chloroplast Polyadenylate - Binding Protein.
*Cell Biology; Chemical Biology.*

**CPAP** Continuous Positive Airway Pressure.

**CPAPOC** Comité permanent des associations du personnel des organisations coordonnées [obsolète - remplacé par CRP 1.].
Standing Committee of the Staff Asssociations of the Coordinated Organizations [obsolete - replaced by CRP 1.].

**CPB** Bureau of Economic Policy (The Netherlands).

**CPB** Cartagena Protocol on Biosafety.
The CPB will come into force in September 2003 and will establish modalities for safe transfer, handling and use of LMOs.
For further details see under: **LMOs**.

**CPB** Competitive Protein Binding.
*Medicine.*

**CPB** Cooper Pair Box.
*Nanoscience; Physics.***CPBS** Para-Chlorophenylbenzenesulfonate.
*Organic Chemistry.*

**CPBW** charged particle beam weapon.
arme à faiseau de particules chargées.

**CPC** Caspian Pipeline Consortium.

**CPC** Cement Plaster Ceiling.
*Masonry.*

**CPC** Central Product Classification.
*European Community.*

**CPC** Chronic Passive Congestion.
*Medicine.*

**CPC** 1. Civil Protection Committee.
1. Comité de la protection civile.
2. Conflict Prevention Centre.
2. centre de prévention des conflicts.
**CPC** Cleaning and Polishing Compound.
**CPC** Climate Prediction Center (U.S.A.).
Of the U.S. NOAA.
For further details see under: **NOAA**.
**CPC** Codice di Procedura Civile.
Italian initialism meaning: Code of Civil Law Procedure.
**CPC** Cœur Pulmonaire Chronique.
French initialism meaning: Chronic Pulmonary Heart.
*Medicine.*
**CPC** Condensation Particle Counter.
**CPCG** Commercial Protein Crystal Growth.
*Experiments.*
**CPCRA** Community Programs for Clinical Research on AIDS (U.S.A.).
NIAID-sponsored clinical trials network.
For further details see under: **NIAID**.
**CPCSEA** Committee for the Purpose of Control and Supervision of Experiments on Animals (India).
*Animal Welfare.*
**CPCU** Compagnie Parisienne de Chauffage Urbain (France).
**CPD** Chemicals Plants Division.
**cpd** (abbr.) compound.
Also: **comp.**
*Biology; Chemistry; Petroleum Engineering.*
**CPD** Continuing Professional Development.
**cPDI** chloroplast Protein Disulfate Isomerase.
*Cell Biology; Chemical Biology.*
**CPDL** Cumulative Population Doubling Levels.
*Antiaging; Cellular Aging; Molecular and Structural Biology; Molecular Gerontology.*
**cpDNA** Chloroplast DNA.
*Coding Sequences; Genetics; Green Plants.*
**CPDS** Commerce Procurement Data System.
**CPDW** Circumpolar Deep Water.
*Geological Sciences; Marine Science.*
**CPE** Centrally Planned Economy.
**CPE** Chimie Physique Electronique de Lyon (France).
**CPE** 1. collective protection equipment [NBC].
1. matériel de protection collective [NBC].
2. contact point embassy.
2. ambassade point de contact.
3. coopération politique européenne.
3. European political cooperation (EPC).
4. see CPX.
4. voir CPX.
**CPE** Common Professional Examination.
The CPE replaced the intermediate Examination in 1980 and is taken only by aspiring solicitors.
**CPE** Computer Performance Evaluation.
Essentially, the CPE is the evaluation of a computer's performance, as well as the cost and waste involved in the data-processing services.
*Computer Technology.*
**CPE** Continuing Professional Education.
**CPE** Cooperazione Politica Europea - E.C.
**CPE** Cytopathic Effect.
Also: **CE**.
*Virology.*
**CPE** Cytoplasmic Polyadenylation Element.
**CPEA** Conseil de partenariat euro-atlantique [remplace CCNA].
Euro-Atlantic Partnership Council (EAPC) [has replaced NACC].
**CPEM** Conference on Precision Electromagnetic Measurements.
The CPEM was held in Washington, D.C., U.S.A. in July 1998.
**CPEP** Contemporary Physics Education Project.
Lawrence Berkeley Laboratory, Berkeley, California, U.S.A.
*U.S. Projects.*
**C peptide** Connecting peptide.
*Biochemistry.*
**CPER** Central Plains Experimental Range.
*Food Webs; Environmental Sciences; Veterinary Medicine.*
**CPF** Collective Peacekeeping / Peacemaking Forces (of the CIS).
forces collectives de maintien de la paix et de rétablissement de la paix (de la CEI).
**CPFA** Cyclopropanoid Fatty Acid.
**CPF method** Coupled Pair Functional method.
**CPFP** Cancer Prevention Fellowship Program.
Of the Division of Cancer Prevention and Control of the U.S. National Cancer Institute.
*U.S. Fellowship Program.*
**CPG** CNAD Partnership Group.
Groupe du Partenariat de la CDNA.
**CPG** Consumer Packaged Goods.
**CPG circuits** Central Pattern Generating circuits.
*Zoology.*
**CPGs** Central Pattern Generators.
The CPGs are local spinal neuronal networks that generate locomotion.
*Medical Biochemistry; Neuroscience.*
**CPH** Characters Per Hour.
**CPH** The airport code for Copenhagen, Denmark.

**CPHST** Center for Plant Health Science and Technology.
U.S. Department of Agriculture.
**CPI** California Personality Inventory.
*Psychology.*
**CPI** Communist Party of India.
**CPI** Consumer Price Index.
*Economics.*
**CPIC** 1. Coalition Press Information Centre [SFOR].
1. Centre des informations de presse de la coalition [SFOR].
2. combined public information centre.
2. centre multinational d'information publique.
**CPI-M** Communist Party of India - Marxist.
**CPIN; cpin** (abbr.) crankpin.
*Mechanical Devices.*
**CPK** Créatine-Phospho-Kinase.
French initialism meaning: Creatine Phosphokinase.
*Medicine.*
**CPL** Cement PLaster.
*Masonry.*
**CPL** Circular Polarized Light.
*Molecular Inorganic Chemistry.*
**CPL** Common Programming Language; Conversational Programming Language.
**CPL** Council of Planning Librarians.
**cPLA$_2$** Cytoplasmic Phospholipase $A_2$.
*Cancer Research; Signal Transduction.*
**cplg.** (abbr.) coupling.
*Computer Programming; Electricity; Engineering; Mechanical Engineering.*
**CPLR** Coalition for Public Library Research.
**CPM** Cairo Peace Movement.
To save the Middle East peace process.
**CPM** Conseil de la Politique Monétaire.
French initialism of the: Monetary Policy Council.
Of the BDF.
For further details see under: **BDF**.
**CP/M** Control Program for Microprocessors.
*Computer Programming.*
**CPM; cpm** costo per mille.
Italian initialism meaning: cost per one thousand.
**CPM; cpm** counts per minute.
**CPM** Critical Path Method.
The critical path method is also known as: Critical Path Technique.
*Industrial Engineering.*
**cpm** cycle per minute.
*Physics.*
**CP market** Commercial Paper market.
**CP-MAS** Cross-Polarization Magic Angle Spinning.
**CPMC** California Pacific Medical Center (U.S.A.).
The Geraldine Brush Cancer Research Institute is a division of CPMC.
**CPME** Charged Particle Measurement Experiment.
*Applied Physics; Physics; Space Science.*
**cpn** (abbr.) coupon.
**CPO** Centre de Pre-Orientation.
CPO is managed by AFAH.
For further details see under: **AFAH**.
**CPO** 1. Centre de programmation de l'OTAN.
1. NATO Programming Centre (NPC 2.).
2. civilian personnel office (or officer).
2. Bureau (ou responsable) du personnel civil.
**CPO** Commissione Pari Opportunità.
Italian initialism of the: Equal Opportunity Commission.
**CPO; Cpo** Conferenza Provinciale Organizzativa.
**CPOA; C.P.O.A.** Consorzio Produttori Orafi Aretini (Italy).
*Italian Consortium.*
**CPOP** Committee on POPulation (U.S.A.).
**CPOS** Centre de Psychologie et d'Orientation Scolaires (Luxemburg).
Of the Ministry of Education.
**CPP** Codice di Procedura Penale.
Italian initialism meaning: Code of Criminal Law Procedure.
**CPP** Current Perpendicular to the bilayer Plane.
*Applied Physics.*
**CPP** Current Purchasing Power.
**CPPA** Canadian Pulp and Paper Association (Canada).
**CPPA** Constant-Parameter Prediction Algorithm.
*Bioengineering.*
**CP propeller** Controllable-Pitch propeller.
*Mechanical Engineering.*
**CPPS** Permanent South Pacific Commission (Chile).
**CPR** Cardiopulmonary Resuscitation.
*Medicine.*
**CPR** Circular Polarization Ratio.
*Astronomy; Space Research; Space Science.*
**CPR** Civilian Personnel Regulations.
Règlement du personnel civil (RPC 2.).
**c.p.r.** con preghiera di restituzione.
Italian initialism meaning: please return.
**CPR** Continuous Plankton Recorder.
**CPRE** Council for the Protection of Rural England (G.B.).
**CPRI** Central Power Research Institute (India).
**CPRO-DLO** DLO-Centre for Plant Breeding and Reproduction Research (The Netherlands).
**cps** (abbr.) centipoise.

Also: **cp**.
*Fluid Mechanics.*
**CPS** Code Penal Suisse.
French initialism meaning: Swiss Penal Code.
**CPS** Controlled-Path System.
*Robotics.*
**CPS** Convertible Preferred Stock.
*Banking; Business; Finance.*
**CPs** Critical Points.
**CPs** Cryptopatches.
*Allergology; Medicine; Microbiology; Immunology.*
**CPS** Cumulative Preferred Stock.
*Banking; Business; Finance.*
**c.p.s.** cycles per second.
For further details see under: **Hz**.
**CPSC** Consumer Product Safety Commission.
**CPSE** corps PSYOPs support element.
élément de soutien des opérations psychologiques de corps.
**CPSMA** Commission on Physical Sciences, Mathematics, and Applications (U.S.A.).
**CPSS** Centre de Préparation Supérieure au Secrétariat.
*French Center.*
**CPST** Commission on Professionals in Science and Technology (U.S.A.).
The CPST is an affiliated organization of the AAAS.
For further details see under: **AAAS**.
**CPT** Camptothecin.
*Anticancer Drugs; Biology; Medicine.*
**CPT** Capacité Pulmonaire Totale.
French initialism meaning: Total Lung Capacity.
*Medicine.*
**CPT** Carriage Paid To.
*Economics; International Trade.*
**CPT** 1. central planning team [obsolete - replaced by CPT 2.].
1. groupe central de planification [obsolète - remplacé par CPT 2.].
2. core planning team.
2. groupe noyau de planification.
**CPT** Centre de Perfectionnement Technique.
French initialism of the: Center for Technical Improvement (France).
**CPT** Centre Parisien de Technologie (France).
**CPT** Charged Particle Telescope.
*Ballistic Missiles; Naval Research; Science Applications.*
**cpt** (abbr.) comptant.
French abbreviation meaning: cash.
**CPT** Continuous Performance Test.
**CPT** Cost-Per-Thousand.
**CPT** Critical-Path Technique.
Critical-Path Technique is also known as: Critical Path Method.
*Industrial Engineering.*
**cpte** (abbr.) compte.
French abbreviation meaning: account.
**CPT Theorem** Charge, Parity, and Time reversal theorem.
*Physics.*
**CPU** Central Processing Unit.
The central processing unit, also known as frame or main frame is the computer portion comprising the circuits necessary for the execution of instructions.
*Computer Technology.*
**CPUE** Capacité Pulmonaire Utilisable à l'Effort.
French initialism meaning: Timed Vital Capacity.
*Medicine.*
**CPUE** Catch-Per-Unit-Effort.
**cpv** (abbr.) capoverso.
Italian abbreviation meaning: paragraph.
**CPX** command post exercise.
exercice de poste de commandement.
**cpx crystals** clino pyroxene crystals.
*Mineralogy.*
**CPY** Carboxypeptidase Y.
**CPZ** Chlorpromazine.
*Pharmacology.*
**CQ** Clioquinol.
CQ is a copper / zinc chelating antibiotic.
*Alzheimer's Disease; Amyloid Pathology; Clinical Trials.*
**CQIB** Centre Québécois d'Innovation en Biotechnologie (Canada).
**CQMS** Circuit Quality Monitoring System.
**CR** Caloric Restriction.
*Animal Health; Biomedical Sciences; Geriatric Research; Medicine; Nutritional Sciences.*
**CR** Cardiorespiratory.
*Medicine.*
**CR** Carriage Return.
Carriage return is actually the operation that enables printing of the next character at the left margin.
*Computer Programming.*
**CR** Carrier's Risk.
**CR** Cash Receipt.
**CR** Catalytic Reforming.
*Organic Chemistry.*
**CR** Cathode Ray.
*Electronics.*
**CR** 1. Central Region [obsolete].

1. Région Centre (RC) [obsolète].
2. control and reporting.
2. contrôle et détection.
**CR** Centre de Réservation (France).
**CR** Cerenkov Radiation.
*Electromagnetism; Materials Science and Engineering; Phyiscs.*
**Cr** the chemical symbol for Chromium.
Chromium is used in chrome plating and in alloys. The word chromium derives from the Greek term "color".
*Chemistry.*
**CR** Clot Retraction.
*Medicine.*
**CR**; **C.R.** Conditioned Response.
*Behavior.*
**CR** Conseiller de la Reine.
French initialism meaning: Queen's Counsel.
**CR**; **C.R.** Continuous Reinforcement.
*Behavior.*
**CR**; **cr** Credit.
**cr** (abbr.) crédit.
French abbreviation meaning: credit.
**CR** Cremona, Italy.
**cr** (abbr.) crew.
**CR** Cold-Rolled.
*Metallurgy.*
**CR** Company's Risk.
**CR** Conditioned Reflex.
CR is also known as: Conditioned Response.
*Behavior.*
**CR** Correlation Radiometer.
**CR** Croce Rossa.
Italian initialism of the: Red Cross.
**CR2** Complement Receptor 2.
*Biochemistry; Molecular and Medical Genetics.*
**Cr**; **cr** Current Rates.
**CRA** Communications Regulatory Agency.
Agence de régulation des communications.
**CRA** Consiglio per le Ricerche Astronomiche.
Italian acronym of the: Council for Astronomical Research (Italy).
**CRA** Conventional Radiocarbon Ages.
*Anthropology; Archaeology.*
**CrA** Corona Australis.
A constellation lying between Sagittarius and Scorpius.
*Astronomy.*
**CRAA** CECLANT routine activity area.
zone d'activité de routine (du CECLANT) (ZAR).
**CRABS** Cellular Radio Access for Broadband Services.
*European Community Project.*
**CRAC** Careers Research and Advisory Centre.
*British Centers.*
**CRAC channel** Calcium Release-Activated $Ca^{2+}$ channel.
*Animal Physiology; Zoology.*
**CRADA** Cooperative Research and Development Agreement.
Under a CRADA signed in late 1991, engineers have tested two new versions of the 8-meter (26-foot) blade currently used on more than 4000 operating machines. They are also testing a 17-meter (54-foot) fiberglass blade for an advanced prototype turbine.
*Wind Turbine Blades.*
**CRADAs** Cooperative Research And Development Agreements.
Created in the U.S.A. by a 1986 Technology Transfer Law.
*Technology Transfer; U.S. Government/Industry Collaboration.*
**CRADO** Chief Research And Development Officer.
**Crae** Centro Ricerche Attività Ecumeniche.
Italian acronym meaning: Ecumenical Activity Research Center (Udine, Italy).
**CRAF** Comet Rendezvous / Asteroid Fly-by.
*Space Probes.*
**CRAi** Comptes Rendus des Séances de l'Académie des Inscription et Belles-Lettres.
**CRAI** Consorzio per la Ricerca e le Applicazioni di Informatica.
CRAI is located in Cosenza, Italy.
*Italian Consortium.*
**CRAL** Circolo Ricreativo-Assistenziale per Lavoratori (Italy).
Italian acronym meaning: Recreational and Welfare Center for Workers.
**CRAM**; **C.R.A.M.** Consorzio Regionale Accessori Macchine (Italy).
*Italian Consortium.*
**CRAMPS** Combined Rotation And Multiple Pulse Sequence.
*Biomaterials; Medicine; Orthopaedic Surgery; Radiology; Skeletal Disorders.*
**CR arm** Chest and Right arm.
*Medicine.*
**CRATOS** Center for Research on the Applications of Telematics to Organizations and Society.
Of the College of Economics, Università Cattolica del Sacro Cuore at Piacenza, Italy and the SIMS, U.S.A.
For further details see under: **SIMS**.
**CRAZED sequence** COSY Revamped with Asymmetric *z*-gradient Echo-Detection sequence.

*Chemistry; Pharmaceuticals.*
**CrB** Corona Borealis.
A small constellation lying between Bootes and Hercules.
*Astronomy.*
**CRBR** Clinch River Breeder Reactor.
**CRBRP** Clinch River Breeder Reactor Plant.
**Crb transmembrane protein** Crumbs transmembrane protein.
A regulator of epithelial polarity in *Drosophila.*
*Cell Biology; Molecular Genetics; Epithelial Cell Polarity; Photoreceptor Morphogenesis.*
**CRC** Cancer Research Campaign.
**CRC** Cardiac Calcium Release Channel (ryanodine receptor).
*Biochemistry; Biophysics; Medicine; Physiology.*
**CRC** Colorectal Cancer.
**CRC** 1. control and reporting centre.
1. centre de détection et de contrôle (CDC 1.).
2. Crisis Response Cell [obsolete - replaced by JOC].
2a. cellule de réaction aux crises [obsolète - remplacé par JOC].
2b. cellule de crise.
3. Crisis Response Centre [obsolete - replaced by JOC].
3. centre de crise [obsolète - remplacé par JOC].
**$Cr_3C_2$** Chromium Carbide.
*Inorganic Chemistry.*
**CRC method** Coordinating Research Council method.
A research technique formulated, approved and published by the Coordinating Research Council, Inc. (U.S.A.).
**CRC Programme** Canada Research Chairs Programme.
Established by the Government of Canada.
**CRCs** Cooperative Research Centres (Australia).
The CRCs were set up in 1991 to unite academic, government, and industry researchers.
**CRD** Carbohydrate Recognition Domain.
*Biochemistry; Glycobiology; Medicine; Molecular and Cellular Physiology; Structural Biology.*
**CRD** commander's required date.
date d'échéance fixée par le commandant.
**CRDC** Climate Research Data Center.
**CRDC** Cotton Research and Development Corporation.
**CRDF** Cathode Ray Direction Finder.
**CRDF** Civilian Research and Development Foundation (U.S.A.).
The CRDF is a Virginia-based nonprofit Foundation that supports research in the former Soviet Union.
*Collaborative U.S.; F.S.U. Projects.*
**CRDO** Chief Research and Development Officer.
**CRDP** Centres Régionaux de Documentation Pédagogique (France).
**CRD system** Control Rod Drive system.
**CRE** cAMP Response Element.
*Neurobiology; Neurology; Neuroscience; Signal Transduction.*
**CRE** Centro Ricerche Europeo.
Italian acronym of the: European Research Center.
**CRE** Commission for Racial Equality (G.B.).
**CRE** Cosmic-Ray Exposure.
**CRE** Cyclic AMP Response Element.
**CRE** Standing Conference of Rectors, Presidents and Vice-Chancellors of the European Universities.
Geneva, Switzerland. Founded in 1959 to develop co-operation between the executive heads of all European universities; to represent the universities' points of view to governmental and non-governmental bodies concerned with higher education in Europe.
**CREAM** Cosmic Radiation Effects and Activation Monitor.
**CREB protein** Cyclic AMP-Response Element-Binding protein.
*Molecular Biology; Neuroscience; Transcription Factors.*
For further details see under: **CBP** and **cAMP**.
**CREC** Colorado River Extensional Corridor.
*Geological Sciences.*
**CREC** Comité de réclamations.
Complaints Committee (CC3.).
**CREDC** Capital Region Economic Development Corporation.
CREDC is located in Harrisburg, Pennsylvania, U.S.A.
**CREDEM** (abbr.) CREDito EMiliano.
*Italian Bank.*
**CREDIOP** Consorzio di Credito per le Opere Pubbliche (Italy).
Italian acronym of the: Credit Consortium for Public Works.
Established in 1919, in 1999 became part of the Gruppo Dexia, since May 2001 the corporate name is Dexia Crediop.
**CREDO** Cluster of Research on Endocrine Disruption in Europe.
A new (2003) European Union 4-year Research Program.
*Hormone-mimicking Chemicals; Toxicology.*

**CREFAC** Centre d'Etude et de Formation pour l'Accompagnement des Changements.
**C region** Constant region.
*Immunoglobulin Molecules.*
**CREHA**; **Creha** Centres Régionaux pour l'Energie et l'HAbitat (France).
*French Center.*
**CREME** conclusions and recommendations on maritime exercises [obsolete - replaced by NLLDB].
conclusions et recommandations relatives aux exercises maritimes [obsolète - remplacé par NLLDB].
**CRES** Center for Reproduction of Endangered Species (U.S.A.).
*Cloning; Conservation Biology; Conservation Programs/Projects; Genetics; Molecular Genetics; Population Biology; Population Genetics; Reproductive Biology; Zoology.*
**CRES** Centro per la Ricerca Elettronica in Sicilia.
Italian acronym of the: Center for Electronic Research in Sicily.
CRES is based in Palermo, Italy.
**Cres.** (abbr.) crescent.
*Astronomy; Invertebrate Zoology; Science.*
**CRE segment** Camp Rock-Emerson segment.
*Crustal Studies.*
**CRESME** Centro Ricerche Economiche Sociologiche e di Mercato Edilizio (Italy).
*Italian Research Center.*
**CRESP** crisis response prototype.
prototype de réponse aux crises.
**CRESST project** Cryogenic Rare Event Search with Superconducting Thermometers project (Germany).
*Astronomy; Bolometers; Physics.*
**CREST** Core Research for Evolutional Science and Technology (Japan).
*Research Projects.*
**CRF** Capacité Résiduelle Fonctionnelle.
French initialism meaning: Functional Residual Capacity; Functional Residual Air.
*Medicine.*
**CRF** Centro Ricerche FIAT.
Italian initialism of: FIAT Research Center (Turin, Italy).
**CRF** Classical Receptive Field.
*Computation and Neural Systems; Neuroscience; Psychiatry; Psychology.*
**CRF** Cloud Radiation Feedback.
**CRF** contingency reaction force.
force de réaction pour les situations de circonstance.
**$CrF_2$** Chromous Fluoride.
$CrF_2$ is used as a catalyst.
*Inorganic Chemistry.*
**CRF** Corticotropin-Releasing Factor.
CRF is a peptide.
*Brain Chemistry; Neuroscience; Neurotransmitters.*
**CR-FFT technique** Cyclic Reduction-Fast Fourier Transform technique.
**$CRF_{lw}$** long-wave Cloud Radiative Forcing.
*Atmospheric Sciences; Cloud Microphysics; Geophysics.*
**CRFP**; **Crfp** Centri Regionali di Formazione Professionale (Italy).
*Italian Centers; Vocational Training.*
**crg.** (abbr.) carriage.
*Engineering; Graphic Arts; Ordnance.*
**CRG** communication reporting gate.
seuil de compte rendu.
**CRGR** Coalition for Responsible Genetic Research.
**CRH system** Corticotropin-Releasing Hormone system.
*Mammalian Genetics; Mental Health; Psychiatry.*
**CRI** Centrale des Règlements Interbancaires (France).
French initialism of the: Center for Interbank Settlements. Referring to settlements by the TBF system.
For further details see under: **TBF**.
**CRI** Christensen Research Institute (Madong, Papua New Guinea).
**CRI** Commission Rogatoire Internationale.
French acronym meaning: International Rogatory Commission; Judicial Commission.
**CRIA**; **Cria** Community Research Initiative on Aids (U.S.A.).
**CRIADS** Central Region Integrated Air Defence System [obsolete].
système de défense aérienne intégrée de la Région Centre [obsolète].
**CRIAI** Consorzio campano di Ricerca per l'Informatica e l'Automazione Industriale.
CRIAI is located in Naples, Italy.
*Italian Consortium.*
**CRICS** Central Region Integrated Communications System [obsolete].
système intégré de télécommunications de la Région Centre [obsolète].
**CRIM** Commercial Refrigerator Incubator Module.
**CRINCA** Central Region Intelligence Communications Architecture [obsolete].
architecture des communications pour le renseignement de la Région Centre [obsolète].

**CRIPG** Central Region Interface Planning Group [obsolete].
Groupe de planification sur l'interface de la Région Centre [obsolète].
**CRIs** Crown Research Institutes (New Zealand).
**CRISTA** CRyogenic Infrared Spectrometers and Telescopes for the Atmosphere.
*Physics; Space Research.*
**CRISTA-SPAS Experiment** CRISTA-Shuttle Pallet Satellite Experiment.
For further details see under: **CRISTA**.
**crit. mass** (abbr.) critical mass.
*Nucleonics.*
**CRJ** Canadair Regional Jet - Bombardier's.
**CRL** Center for Research Libraries.
**CRL** Charles River Laboratory (U.S.A.).
**CRL** ChemBridge Research Laboratories (U.S.A.).
**CRL** Communication Research Laboratory.
Of the Ministry of Posts and Telecommunications (Japan).
**CRM** Carimonte Banca SpA (Italy).
*Italian Bank.*
**CRM** Cassa di Risparmio di Modena (Italy).
*Italian Bank.*
**CRM** Caveolae-Rich Membrane.
*Biomedical Sciences.*
**CRM** Centre de Recherches Metallurgiques.
CRM is a metallurgical research centre in Liège, Belgium.
**CRM** Certified Reference Material.
*European Community.*
**CRM** Counter-Radar Measures.
*Ordnance.*
**CRM** Cross-Reacting Material.
*Biochemistry.*
**CRM** Cultural Resource Management.
*Archaeology.*
**CRM**; **Crm** Customer Relationship Management.
*Business to Consumer; Software Development.*
**C2RM** command and control resource management.
1a. gestion des ressources C2.
1b. gestion des moyens C2.
**cRNA molecules** copy RNA molecules.
*Plant Biology; Plant Physiology; Plant Sciences.*
**CRNL** Chalk River Nuclear Laboratories.
**CRO** Cathode-Ray Oscillograph.
**CRO** Cathode-Ray Oscilloscope.
The cathode-ray oscilloscope, also known as oscilloscope or scope is actually an instrument that comprises a cathode-ray tube to display signal waveforms on a fluorescent screen.
*Electronics.*
**CRO** Centri di Riferimento Oncologico.
*Italian Centers.*
**CRO** Companies Registration Office.
**CRO** crisis response operation.
opération de réponse aux crises.
**$CrO_3$** Chromic Acid.
Chromic Acid also known as Chromium Trioxide; Chromic Anhydride is used mainly in medicine and chromium plating.
*Inorganic Chemistry.*
**$Cr_2O_3$** Chromic Oxide.
Chromic Oxide is also known as: Chromium Sesquioxide; Chromium Oxide. It is used mainly as a pigment and a catalyst.
*Inorganic Chemistry.*
**$CrO_2$** Chromium Dioxide.
$CrO_2$ is used mainly in magnetic tapes.
*Inorganic Chemistry.*
**CROM** Control and Read-Only Memory.
**CROs** Contract Research Organizations.
**CROSS**; **Cross** Centro di Ricerca sull'Orientamento Scolastico, professionale e sullo Sviluppo delle organizzazioni (Italy).
*Italian Research Center.*
**CROW** Condition of ROad and Weather monitoring system.
*European Community.*
**CRP** cAMP Receptor Protein.
An activator of transcription.
For further details see under: **cAMP**.
**CRP** Cardiovascular Research Program.
*U.S. Program.*
**CRP** Centre de Rééducation Professionnelle VIVRE (France).
**CRP** 1. Comité des représentants du personnel [remplace le CPAPOC].
1. Committee of Staff Representatives [has replaced CPAPOC].
2. control and reporting post.
2. poste de détection et de contrôle.
**CRP** The airport code for Corpus Christi International.
**CRP** C-Reactive Protein.
A liver-derived inflammatory protein.
*Biochemistry; Clinical Medicine; Heart Disease; Pathology.*
**CRPE** Centre de Recherches en Physique de l'Environnement terrestre et planétaire.
**$CrPO_4$** Chromic Phosphate.
Chromic Phosphate is also known as: Chromium Phosphate.
*Inorganic Chemistry.*
**CRPV** Cottontail Rabbit Papillomavirus.
*Virology.*

**CRRB** Change Request Review Board.
**CRREL** Cold Regions Research and Engineering Laboratory.
The CRREL is a Research, Development and Engineering facility.
**CRRES** Combined Release / Radiation Effects Satellite.
**CRRN** centre de réduction du risque nucléaire.
Nuclear Risk Reduction Centre (NRRC).
**crs.** (abbr.) centers.
**CRS** 1. coast radio station.
1. station radio côtière.
2. control and reporting system.
2. réseau de détection et de contrôle.
**CRS** Cold-Rolled Steel.
*Metallurgy.*
**CRS** Common Registration System.
*Taxation Systems; Tax Databases.*
**CRS** Community Relations Service; Congressional Research Service (U.S.A.).
**CRSG** 1. Comité des représentants des secrétaires généraux.
1. Committee of Representatives of the Secretaries General.
2. Central Region Signal Group [obsolete].
2. Groupe de transmissions de la Région Centre [obsolète].
**CRSP** Cofactor Required for Sp1 Activation.
*Medicine; Cell Biology; Molecular Biology.*
**CRT** Cassa di Risparmio di Torino (Italy).
*Italian Bank.*
**CRT** Cassa di Risparmio di Trieste (Italy).
*Italian Bank.*
**CRT** Cathode-Ray Tube.
*Electronics.*
**CRT** Choice Reaction Time.
*Aging; Antiaging; Geriatrics; Gerontology.*
**CRT** Clot Retraction Time.
*Pathology.*
**CRT** communications receiver / transmitter.
émetteur-récepteur de télécommunications.
**CRT** Complex Reaction Time.
*Medicine.*
**CRT** Composite Reaction Texturing.
CRT is a novel fabrication process for high-temperature high current superconductor wires and shaped components.
*European Community Project.*
**CRT** Connexion au Réseau Terrestre.
**crt** (abbr.) crater.
*Astronomy; Geology; Mechanical Engineering; Metallurgy.*
**CRT/DRE** C-Repeat / Drought-Responsive Element.
*Crop and Soil Sciences.*
**CRTS** casualty receiving triage ship.
bâtiment de réception et de triage des pertes.
**CRTT** Certified Respiratory Therapy Technician.
*Medicine.*
**CRUEI; C.R.U.E.I.** Centro Italiano per le Relazioni Universitarie con l'Estero.
Italian acronym of the: Italian Center for University Relations with Foreign Countries.
**CRUI** Conferenza dei Rettori delle Università Italiane.
Italian acronym meaning: Conference of the Rectors* of Italian Universities. * Chancellors (G.B.). * Presidents (U.S.A.).
**CRUP** Cassa di Risparmio di Udine e Pordenone (Italy).
*Italian Savings Bank.*
**Crv** Corvus.
*Astronomy* - Corvus is a small constellation lying west of Spica.
**CRV** Crew Return Vehicle.
*Astronomy; Particle Physics; Science Program; Space Science.*
**CRW** The airport code for Charleston, West Virginia.
**CRWG** The Center for Research on Women and Gender.
The CRWG was established in 1991. The University of Illinois at Chicago, U.S.A.
**CRY2** Cryptochrome 2.
*Botany.*
**Cryo-EM** Cryo-Electron Microscopy.
*Crystallography; Imaging technologies; Molecular Biology; Protein Synthesis; Ribosomal; Structures.*
**Crypto** (abbr.) cryptographic.
*Linguistics; Communications.*
**CRZ** Core Rigidity Zone.
*Earth Sciences.*
**C/S** call sign.
indicatif d'appel.
**CS** Carbon Monosulfide.
**CS** Carbon Steel.
*Metallurgy.*
**cs.** (abbr.) case / cases.
**cs** casein.
Casein is found in milk.
*Organic Chemistry.*
**CS** Cast Steel.
*Metallurgy.*
**cs** centistoke.
*Fluid Mechanics.*

**cs** cesarean section.
*Medicine.*
**Cs** the chemical symbol for Cesium.
Cesium is a chemical element having the atomic number 55 and a melting point of 28°C. The word cesium derives from the Latin term "blue".
*Chemistry.*
**C.S.** Chief of Staff.
Also: **COS**.
**CS** Chief Scientist.
**CS**; **C.S.** Chief Secretary.
**Cs** Cirrostratus cloud.
The cirrostratus cloud occurs at heights of about 36,000 feet.
*Meteorology.*
**CS** Citrate Synthase.
*Biochemistry.*
**CS** Civil Servant.
**CS**; **C.S.** Civil Service.
**CS** Cold Start.
Cold Start is also known as: Cold Boot.
*Computer Technology.*
**CS**; **C.S.** Collegio Sindacale.
Italian initialism meaning: Board of Auditors.
U.S.A.: Audit Committee.
**CS**; **C.S.** Comando Supremo.
Italian initialism meaning: Supreme Headquarters.
*Military.*
**CS** 1. combat support.
1. appui tactique.
2. Costa Rica.
2. Costa Rica.
**c.s.** come sopra.
Italian abbreviation meaning: as above.
**CS** Committee on Seismology.
**CS** Commonwealth Secretariat (G.B.).
**CS** Community Survey.
*Human Development; Sociology.*
**CS**; **C.S.** Conditioned Stimulus.
*Behavior.*
**cs** (abbr.) consciousness.
*Neurology; Psychology.*
**CS**; **C.S.** Consiglio di Sicurezza.
Italian initialism meaning: Security Council.
**CS**; **C.S.** Consiglio Superiore.
Italian initialism meaning: High Council.
**CS**; **C.S.** Co-operative Society.
**CS**; **C.S.** Corte Suprema.
Italian initialism meaning: Supreme Court.
**cs** corticosteroid.
Corticosteroid is also known as: Adrenocorticosteroid.
*Endocrinology.*
**CS** Cosenza, Italy.
**CS** Credito Svizzero.
**cs** current strength.
*Medicine.*
**c/s** cycle per second.
Also known as Hertz.
*Metrology.*
**C2S** command and control system.
système de commandement et de contrôle.
**C3S** consultation, command and control systems.
systèmes de consultation, de commandement et de contrôle.
**$CS_2$** Carbon Disulfide.
Carbon Disulfide is used mainly in the production of rayon, and soil disinfectants. Carbon Disulfide as a molecule can be present in many cosmochemical environments.
*Organic Chemistry.*
**CSA** Canadian Space Agency (Canada).
**CSA** 1. central supply agency.
1. agence centrale des approvisionnements (ACA 1.).
2. civilian staff association.
2. association du personnel civil (APC).
**CSA** Chemical Shift Anisotropy.
*Biochemistry; Cellular Biology; Chemistry; Molecular Biology.*
**CSA** Chief Scientists' Assembly (Japan).
Since 1959 the CSA acts as an advisory body to RIKEN's President and Board of Executive Directors.
For further details see under: **RIKEN**.
**CSA** Community Services Administration (U.S.A.).
**CSA** Cross-Sectional Area.
**CsA** Cyclosporin A.
Cyclosporin A is a cyclic peptide. It is used as an immunosuppressive agent.
*Biochemistry; Immunobiology; Immunology.*
**CSAP** Center for Substance Abuse Prevention (U.S.A.).
**CSAR** combat search and rescue.
recherche et sauvetage de combat (RESCO).
**CSAT** Center for Substance Abuse Treatment (U.S.A.).
**CSATI** Centro Studi ed Applicazioni sulle Tecnologie dell'Informazione.
*Italian Center; Information Technologies.*
**CSB** Center for Surface Biotechnology.
At the Uppsala Biomedical Center (Sweden).
*Surface Biotechnology.*
**CSBC** The Center for the Study of Biological Complexity.
Virginia Commonwealth University, U.S.A.

**CSBM** Committee on Space Biology and Medicine (U.S.A.).
**CSBM** confidence- and security-building measures.
mesures de confiance et de sécurité (MDCS).
**CsBr** Cesium Bromide.
Cesium Bromide is used mainly in medicine.
*Inorganic Chemistry.*
**CSBs** Competence Standards Bodies.
**CSC** China Scholarship Council (China).
**CSC** Computer Science Corporation.
**CSC** Cooperativa per lo Spettacolo Culturale (Italy).
**csc.** cosecant.
Also: **cosec.**
*Mathematics.*
**CSCAP** Council for Security Co-operation in Asia-Pacific.
**CSCB** Centre for Synthesis and Chemical Biology (Ireland).
*Cancer; Neuroscience; Vascular Biology.*
**CSCE** Conference on Security and Cooperation in Europe.
As of January 1995, renamed Organization for Security and Cooperation in Europe (OSCE).
**CSChE** Canadian Society for Chemical Engineering (Canada).
**CsCl** Cesium Chloride.
Cesium Chloride has many applications, it is used for example in mineral waters, in brewing, and photoelectric cells.
*Inorganic Chemistry.*
**CSCL** Computer-Supported Collaboration Learning.
**$CsClO_4$** Cesium Perchlorate.
Cesium Perchlorate is used mainly in optics.
*Inorganic Chemistry.*
**$Cs_2CO_3$** Cesium Carbonate.
Cesium Carbonate is used mainly in brewing and mineral waters.
*Inorganic Chemistry.*
**CSCP** Comité de surveillance de la caisse de prévoyance.
Board of Supervisors of the Provident Fund.
**CSCPA** California Society of Certified Public Accountants (U.S.A.).
**CSCS** Consolidated Scientific Computing System.
**CSCW** Computer-Supported Co-operative Work.
**CSD** Cambridge Structural Database.
**CSD** Chromosomal (Genetic) Sex Determination.
*Population Biology; Zoology.*
**C.S.D.** Commissione Suprema Difesa.
Italian initialism meaning: Supreme Defense Board.
*Military.*
**CSD** Console de Supervision et de Dialogue.
**CSD** Cotton Seed Distributors.
CSD is a grower-controlled organization based in Wee Waa, New South Wales, Australia.
**C.S.d.P.I.** Consiglio Superiore della Pubblica Istruzione.
Italian initialism of the: High Board of the Ministry of Education.
**CSDR** combined ship destination room.
chambre combinée de destination des navires.
**C/SDW compounds** Charge- and Spin- Density Wave compounds.
*Physics.*
**CSE** Centre for Science and Environment (India).
*Air Pollution.*
**CSE** Certificate of Secondary Education (G.B.).
**CSE** communication support element.
élément de soutien des transmissions.
**CSE** Consortium for Superconducting Electronics.
The CSE is a group of U.S. companies and institutions working in the field.
*Basic Physics; High-Temperature Superconductivity.*
**CSEC** Centre for Science at Extreme Conditions (G.B.).
**CSEMS** Computer Science, Engineering, and Mathematics Scholarships.
*U.S. Scholarships.*
**CSEOL** Center for the Study of Evolution and the Origin of Life.
The CSEOL, at the University of California, Los Angeles, U.S.A. has held meetings every week ever since 1981.
*Evolution; Origin of Life.*
**CSERGE** Centre for Social and Economic Research on the Global Environment (G.B.).
**CSES** Center for Social and Economic Studies (U.S.A.).
**CSES** Center for the Study of Earth from Space.
**CSF** central supply facility.
installation centrale de soutien.
**CSF** Cerebrospinal Fluid.
**CsF** Cesium Fluoride.
CsF is used mainly in optics.
*Inorganic Chemistry.*
**CSF** Colony Stimulating Factor.
*Endocrinology; Immunology.*
**CSF** Cytostatic Factor.
*Embryology; Mitosis; Nuclear Trafficking; Microtubule Polymerization.*
**CSFB** Credit Suisse First Boston.

CSFB entered the world of high technology financing in March 1997.
*Advisory Services; Corporate Finance; Swiss Bank.*
**CSFR** Committee on Scientific Freedom and Responsibility.
Of the AAAS.
For further details see under: **AAAS**.
**CSFS** see COMSTRIKFORSOUTH.
Voir COMSTRIKFORSOUTH.
**CSG** 1. Civil Sealift Group.
1. Groupe sur le "Sealift" civil.
2. course and speed made good over the ground.
2. route et vitesse sur le fond.
**CSG** Computer Support Group (U.S.A.).
CSG has been replaced by: **CNSD** (Computer and Network Services Division).
**CSG** Contribution Sociale Généralisée.
French initialism meaning: Social Security Contribution.
**CSGE** Conformation-Sensitive Gel Electrophoresis.
*Collage Research; Diagnostic Radiology; Gene Therapy; Genetics; Medical Biochemistry; Medicine.*
**CS gene** Citrate Synthase gene.
*Plant Molecular Biology; Plant Physiology.*
**CSH** combat support helicopter.
1a. hélicoptère d'appui au combat.
1b. hélicoptère de soutien au combat.
**CSHAFT** (abbr.) Crankshaft.
*Mechanical Engineering.*
**CSH Laboratory** Cold Spring Harbor Laboratory (U.S.A.).
Also: **CSHL**.
**CSI** Centro per lo Sviluppo Industriale.
Italian initialism of the: Center for Industrial Development.
**CSI**; **C.S.I.** Centro Sportivo Italiano.
Italian initialism of the: Italian Sport Center.
**CsI** Cesium Iodide.
CsI is used mainly for infrared spectroscopy. It is now used for the study of dielectric-to-metal transition.
*Engineering Science; Inorganic Chemistry; Materials Science; Metallization; Physical Science.*
**CSI**; **C.S.I.** Codice Sportivo Internazionale.
Italian initialism meaning: International Sport Code.
**CSI** Computational Sciences and Informatics.
The CSI is at George Mason University. It was established in 1993. It is one of the first PhD programs in bioinformatics and computational biology in the United States.
*Bioinformatics; Computational Biology.*
**CSI** Comunità degli Stati Indipendenti.
Of the Former Soviet Union.
**CSI** Conditional Symmetric Instability.
**CSI** CRC/SAM interface.
interface CDC/SAM.
**CSIC** Spanish National Research Council.
*Spanish Councils.*
**CSICOP** Committee for the Scientific Investigation of Claims Of the Paranormal (U.S.A.).
**CSIO** Central Scientific Instruments Organization (India).
**CSIR** Council of Scientific & Industrial Research (India).
**CSIRO** Commonwealth Scientific and Industrial Research Organization (Australia).
**CSIS** Center for Strategic and International Studies (U.S.A.).
**csk** countersink.
*Mechanical Devices.*
**CSL** Central Science Laboratory.
The CSL is located near York (G.B.). It is an Executive Agency of MAFF.
*Food Safety; Safeguarding of Food Supply; Protection of the Environment.*
For further details see under: **MAFF**.
**CSL** Consorzio Scuola e Lavoro (Italy).
*Projects.*
**CSLA** Church and Synagogue Library Association.
**CSM** Centro Sviluppo Materiali.
Italian initialism of the: Materials Development Center (Rome, Italy).
**CSM** Cerebrospinal Meningitis.
*Medicine.*
**CSM** Climate System Model; Climate System Monitoring.
**CSM** Command and Service Module.
**CSM** continental shelf mine.
mine pour le plateau continental.
**CSMA** Centre for Surface and Materials Analysis (G.B.).
*Biomedical Devices; Surface Analysis.*
**CSMA/CD** Carrier-Sense Multiple Access with Collision Detection.
*Telecommunications.*
**CSMB** Consiglio degli Stati del Mar Baltico.
**CSMEE** Center for Science, Mathematics, and Engineering Education (U.S.A.).
**CSN** Carotid Sinus Nerve.
**CSNCRA** Chambre Syndicale Nationale du

Commerce et de la Réparation Automobile (France).
**CSNET** Computer Science NETwork.
**CSNIS** (Steering Committee on) Communication Systems Network Interoperability [obsolete].
(Comité directeur du project d') interopérabilité des réseaux de systèmes de communication [obsolète].
**CSNLV** Chambre Syndicale Nationale des Loueurs de Véhicules Industriels (France).
**$CsNO_3$** Cesium Nitrate.
*Inorganic Chemistry.*
**CSO** Central Selling Organization.
**CSO** Central Statistics Office (Ireland).
**CSO** Chief Scientific Officer.
**CSO** Committee of Senior Officials.
**$Cs_2O$** Cesium Oxide.
*Inorganic Chemistry.*
**$Cs_2O_2$** Cesium Peroxide.
*Inorganic Chemistry.*
**CsOH** Cesium Hydroxide.
CsOH is also known as: Cesium Hydrate.
*Inorganic Chemistry.*
**Csp**; **CSP** Camera Sindacale Provinciale (Italy).
**CSP** Chiral Stationary Phase.
**CSP** Circumsporozoite Protein.
*Malaria Vaccine.*
**CSP** 1. Commandement (commandant) subordonné principal [obsolète - remplacé par SRC].
1. Principal Subordinate Command (Commander) /PSC/ [obsolete - replaced by SRC].
2. commence search point.
2. point de commencement de la recherche.
**CSP** Consulenza per lo Sviluppo della Produttività (Italy).
**CSP** Control Switching Point.
**CSPGs molecules** Chondroitin Sulphate Proteoglycans molecules.
*Brain Research; Neuroscience; Neurosurgery; Spinal-cord Injuries.*
**CSPI** Center for Science in the Public Interest (U.S.A.).
**CS protein** Circumsporozoite protein.
*Epidemiology; Human Genetics; Infectious Diseases; Molecular Immunology; Molecular Medicine; Tropical Medicine.*
**CSPRP** Committee on Scholarly Communication with the People's Republic of China.
**CSPs** Corporate Service Providers.
**C-SPT** commander for support.
commandant chargé du soutien.
**CSR** Center for Scientific Review (U.S.A.).
The CSR was established in 1946. The Center is the focal point at NIH for the conduct of initial peer review, the foundation of the NIH grant and award process. To this end, the Center develops and implements innovative, flexible ways to conduct referral and review for all aspects of science.
For further details see under: **NIH**.
**CSR** Class Switch Recombination.
For further details see under: **AID**.
**CSR** combat stress reaction.
1a. réaction de stress de combat.
1b. stress suite au combat.
**CSR** Committee for Scientific Research.
**CSR** Customer Service Representative.
**CSRC** China Securities Regulatory Commission (China).
*Chinese Commissions.*
**CSREES** Cooperative State Research, Education, and Extension Service.
Of the U.S.D.A.
For furthe rdetails see under: **U.S.D.A**.
**CSRF** common source route file.
fichier commun des routages d'origine.
**CSRI** Council of Scientific and Industrial Research.
*Indian Council.*
**CSRS** Center for Science Research and Statistics.
*Former Soviet Union.*
**CSRS** Coherent Stokes-Raman Spectroscopy.
**CSRS** common security requirement statement.
énoncé des impératifs de sécurité communs.
**CSRS** Cooperative State Research Service.
**CSRs** Customer Service Representatives.
**CSs** Central Stars.
The CSs are so called because of their location near or in the centres of the Planetary Nebulae.
*Astronomy; Astrophysics.*
**CSS** Chaotic Strain Structure.
CSS is also known as: Cyclical Strain Structure.
*Epidemiology.*
**CSS** combat service support.
soutien logistique du combat.
**CSSA** Computing Services and Software Association.
**CSSA** Crop Science Society of America (U.S.A.).
**CSSE** Conference of State Sanitary Engineers.
**CSSL** Continuous System Simulation Language.
**$Cs_2SO_4$** Cesium Sulfate.
Cesium Sulfate is used mainly in brewing and mineral waters.
*Inorganic Chemistry.*
**cSt.** Centistoke.
*Fluid Mechanics.*
**CST** Cervical Corticospinal Tract.
**CST** 1. Collective Security Treaty [CIS].

1. Traité de sécurité collective [CEI].
2. Conventional Stability Talks.
2. entretiens (ou pourparlers) sur la stabilité des armements conventionnels.

**CST** Corticospinal Tract.

**CSTB** Computer Science and Telecommunications Board (U.S.A.).

**CSTD** Center for Science and Technology Development - U.N.

**cstg.** (abbr.) casting.
*Metallurgy.*

**cstms.** (abbr.) customs.

**CST Net** China Science and Technology Network (China).
*Internet in China.*

**C.S.T.O.** Certificato Superiore di Turismo Operativo.
Of the International school of Tourism, Italy.

**CSTR** Continuous-flow, Stirred - Tank Reactor.
*Chemical Kinetics; Chemistry; Electrophoresis; Physical Chemistry.*

**CSU** California State University (U.S.A.).

**CSU** casualty staging unit.
unité de transit des malades et blessés.

**CSU** Christian Social Union (Germany).

**CSU** Colorado State University- (U.S.A.).

**CSU**; **C.S.U.** Constant Speed Unit.

**CSV** Chrysanthemum Stunt Viroid.

**CSW** Channel Status Word.

**CSW** course and speed made good through the water.
route et vitesse sur l'eau.

**CSWR** Center for the Study of World Religions.
At Harvard Divinity School, Harvard University.

**CSWs** Commercial Sex Workers.
The so-called "direct" commercial sex workers are the ones who work in brothels, and the "indirect" commercial sex workers are the ones who work in massage parlors, and the like.

**CSWS** corps support weapon system.
système d'arme de soutien de corps d'armée.

**CSZ** Cascadia Subduction Zone.
*Earth and Environmental Sciences; Oceanic and Atmospheric Sciences.*

**CT** Cable Transfer.

**ct.** (abbr.) carat.
Also: **k**.

**CT** Catania, Italy.

**ct.** (abbr.) cent.

**CT** Center Tap.
*Electricity.*

**CT** Central African Republic.

**CT** Cholera Toxin.
*Genomics; Microbiology; Immunology.*

**CT** Circulation Time.
*Medicine.*

**CT** Coated Tablet.
*Medicine.*

**CT**; **C.T.** Commissario Tecnico.
Italian initialism meaning: Coach.
*Sports.*

**CT** Computerized Tomography.

**CT** Condensed Tannin.
For further details see under: **CTs**.

**CT** Conference Terms.

**CT** (abbr.) Connecticut (U.S.A.).

**CT** Constitutive Transcript.

**CT** Consulente Tecnico.
Italian initialism meaning: Consulting Engineer.

**CT** Corporation Tax.

**CT** (abbr.) Counter.

**CT** Critical Theory.

**CT** (Endocardial) Cushion Tissue.

**CTA** Center for Technology Assessment.
The CTA is a Washington D.C.-based information Clearinghouse (U.S.A.).

**CTA**; **Cta** Centro di Terapia dell'Adolescenza.
*Italian Center.*

**CTA** Common Training Architecture.
*European Community Project.*

**CTA** Council for Technological Advancement (U.S.A.).

**CTAB** Cetyltrimethylammonium Bromide.
*Chemistry.*

**CTAC/OH** Cetyltrimethylammonium Chloride/Hydroxide.
*Chemistry.*

**CTAK** Cipher Text Auto Key.

**CTAPS** contingency theatre automated planning system.
système automatisé de planification des opérations de circonstance à l'échelon du théâtre.

**Ctas** Chrysler technologies airborne systems.

**CTB** Cancer Training Branch.
Of the U.S. National Cancer Institute.

**CTB** Centro Teatrale Bresciano.
*Italian Center.*

**CTB** Comprehensive Test Ban.

**CTB column** Cytotrophoblast column.
*Anatomy; Biochemistry; Reproductive Medicine; Stomatology.*

**CtBP** Carboxyl-terminal Binding Protein.
*Pkant Biology.*

**CTB-subunit** Cholera Toxin B-submit.
*Brain Research; Neuroscience; Neurosurgery; Spinal-cord Injuries.*

**CTBT** Comprehensive Test Ban Treaty (1996). Signed but never ratified by the United States (2002).
**CTC** Centralized Traffic Control.
**CTC** Central Training Council.
**CTC** Chinook Technical Committee.
*Marine Biology.*
**CTC** Chlorotetracycline.
*Microbiology.*
**CTCA**; **C.T.C.A.** Commission for Technical Co-operation in Africa.
**CTCB** Consorzio per la Tutela dei formaggi Valtellina, Casera e Bitto.
An Italian organization dealing with cheese promotion and technical assistance to producers.
**CTCS** Category Theory and Computer Science.
**CTCs** Clinical Trials Coordinators.
**CTD** Carboxyl Terminal repeat Domain.
*Biochemistry; Cell Biology; RNA Processing.*
**CTD** Combined Transport Document.
**CTD** Conductivity-Temperature-Depth.
**CTD** COOH-Terminal repeat Domain.
*Cancer Research; Medicine; Microbiology; Structural Biology.*
**CTD de l'UIC** Commission Technique Documentation de l'Union Internationale des Chemins de fer.
**CTE** Certificato del Tesoro in ECU.
Italian initialism meaning: ECU Treasury Certificate.
*Commerce; Finance.*
**CTE** Coefficient of Thermal Expansion.
*Electronics; Lightwave Technology; Materials Science; Physics.*
**CTE** commander task element.
commandant d'élément opérationnel.
**CTE** Committee on Training and Education.
EUFEPS Advisory Panel.
For further details see under: **EUFEPS**.
**CTE** Constitutive Transport Element.
*Biology; Medicine; Neurosciences; Peptide Biology.*
**CTE** Corsi Tecnici Esterni.
**CTF** 1. combined task force.
1. force opérationnelle interalliée (ou multinationale).
2. commander task force.
2. commandant de force opérationnelle.
**CTF** Controlled Thermonuclear Fusion.
*Nucleonics.*
**CTF** COOH-Terminal Fragment.
*Apoptosis; Genetics; Life Sciences; Medicine; Neurology.*
**CTFE polymer** Chlorotrifluoroethylene polymer.
CTFE polymer is also known as: Fluorothene. It is used mainly in pipes and electronic compounds.
*Organic Chemistry.*
**CTFS** Center for Tropical Forest Science.
**ctg.** (abbr.) cartridge.
*Electronics; Engineering; Ordnance.*
**CTG** commander task group.
commandant de groupe opérationnel.
**ctg.** (abbr.) cutting.
**ctge.** (abbr.) cartage.
*Commerce.*
**CTGF** Connective-Tissue Growth Factor.
*Anatomy; Developmental Biology; Plastic and Reconstructive Surgery; Reepithelialization.*
**CTHK** China Telecom Hong Kong.
**CTI** Centre de Traitement de l'Information.
French initialism meaning: Data Processing Center.
**CTI** Comitato Termotecnico Italiano.
*Italian Committee.*
**CTI** Computer-Telephone Integration.
*Computer-Supported Telephony.*
**CTI** Credito Totale Interno.
Italian initialism meaning: Total Internal Credit.
**CTI** Critical Technologies Institute (U.S.A.).
**CTIAC** Concrete Technology Information Analysis Center.
**CTICM** Centre Technique Industriel de la Construction Métallique (France).
**CTIF** Centre Technique des Industries de la Fonderie.
*French Center.*
**CTIFL** Centre Technique Interprofessionnel des Fruits et Légumes (France).
**CTIO** Cerro Tololo Inter-American Observatory.
**CTIU** Component Test and Integration Unit.
**CTL** Complementary Transistor Logic.
**CTL** Constructive Total Loss.
*Insurance.*
**CTL clones** Cytotoxic T Lymphocyte clones.
*Human Immunology; Microbiology; Molecular and Cellular Biology.*
**CTLO** Constructive Total Loss Only.
*Insurance.*
**CTM** Centro informazioni Terzo Mondo (Italy).
Italian initialism meaning: Third World Information Center.
**CTM** Computational Thermal Model.
*Computational Models; Geological Sciences.*
**CTMBL** Cloud-Topped Marine Boundary Layer.
**CTMT** Combined Thermomechanical Treatment.
**ctn.** (abbr.) cotangent.

For further details see under: **cot.**

**CTNS** Center for Theology and the Natural Sciences.

**CTNT** Cardiac Troponin T.
*Medicine; Pathology.*

**CTO** Campaign for Take-Off-European Union.
*Renewable Energy Sources.*

**CTO** Certificato del Tesoro con Opzione.
Italian initialism meaning: Option Treasury Certificate.

**C to C** Center to Center.

**CTOs** Certified Tradable Offsets (Costa Rica).
CTOs are environmental bonds created by the Government of Costa Rica, guaranteed under an independent verification service for forestry offsets. Countries which buy the bonds use these carbon credits as a bargaining chip in international climate negotiations. This pilot scheme (end of 1997) to trade permits for carbon dioxide emission is created under the auspices of UNCTAD.
*International Climate Negotiations; Environmental Bonds.*
For further details see under: **UNCTAD**.

**CTP** Cytidine 5' Triphosphate.
*Biochemistry.*

**CTR** Calcitonin Receptor.

**CTR** Cardiothoracic Ratio.

**ctr.** (abbr.) center.

**CTR** Centro Territoriale Riabilitativo (Italy).
*Italian Center.*

**CTR** Certificato del Tesoro Reale.
Italian initialism meaning: Real Treasury Certificate.

**CTR** Controlled Thermonuclear Reactor.
*Nuclear Energy.*

**CTR** Council for Tobacco Research (U.S.A.).
The CTR was founded 46 years ago.

**ctr.** (abbr.) counter.
*Computer Technology; Engineering; Electrical Engineering.*

**CTR** Crystal Truncated Rod.

**ctr.** (abbr.) cutter.
*Acoustical Engineering; Engineering; Naval Architecture.*

**CTRA** Coal Tar Research Association (G.B.).

**CTRL** (abbr.) Control.

**CTS** Cab-Tyre-Sheathed.

**CTS** 1. Centre technique du SHAPE [obsolète - intégré dans la NC3A].
1. SHAPE Technical Centre (STC 2.) [obsolete - incorporated into NC3A].
2. COSMIC Top Secret.
2. COSMIC Très Secret.

**cts.** (abbr.) cents.

**CTS** Certificato del Tesoro a Sconto.
Italian initialism meaning: Issue Discount Treasury Certificate.
*Commerce; Finance.*

**CTS** Clear To Send.
*Computers.*

**CTS** Communications Technology Satellite (Canada).

**CTS** Component Test System.

**CTs** Condensed Tannins.
CTs are also known as: Proanthocyanidins.
*Natural Products Research; Plant Biology.*

**CTS** Confederazione Europea dei Sindacati.
Italian acronym of the: Trade Unions European Confederation.

**cts.** (abbr.) crates.

**CTSA** Center for Tropical and Subtropical Aquaculture (U.S.A.).

**CTSA** COSMIC Top Secret ATOMAL.
COSMIC Très Secret ATOMAL.

**CTSCREEN model** Complex Terrain SCREENing model.

**CTSR** Crosstie wall magnetic Shift Register.

**CTSs** Cardiotonic Steroids.
CTSs are used therapeutically to increase the strength of contraction of the heart.
*Biophysics; Medicine; Molecular Biology; Physiology.*

**CTS test** Controlled Thermal Severity test.

**CTT** Capital Transfer Tax.
*Banking; Finance.*

**CTT** Consorzio Tutela Taleggio (Italy).
*Italian Consortium.*

**CTTC** Colorado Technology Transfer Center (U.S.A.).

**cTTs** classical T Tauri stars.
*Astronomy; Astrophysics.*

**CTU** Centigrade Thermal Unit.

**CTU** commander task unit.
commandant d'unité opérationnelle.

**CTU** Constitutive Transcription Unit.

**CTU** Consulente Tecnico d'Ufficio (Italy).
*Law.*

**CTW**; **ctw** (abbr.) counterweight.
CTW is also known as: counterbalance; counterpoise.
*Mechanical Engineering.*

**CTW** course made good through the water.
route sur l'eau.

**CTWG** C3 Terminology Working Group.
Groupe de travail sur la terminologie des C3.

**CTX** Ciguatoxin.

*Applied Bioorganic Chemistry; Biochemistry; Chemistry.*

**Ctx** (abbr.) Cortex.

**CTZ** control zone.
zone de contrôle.

**CU** Clinical Unit.
*Medicine.*

**CU** Close-Up.

**CU** Commercial Union.

**C.U.** Consumers' Union.

**CU** Control Unit.
*Computer Technology.*

**Cu** The chemical symbol for Copper.
Copper is used as a base in many alloys.
*Chemistry; Mineralogy; Symbols.*

**CU** Crystal Unit.
*Electronics.*

**CU** Cuba.

**cu.** (abbr.) cubic.
*Mathematics.*

**cu** (abbr.) cumulative; cumulus.

**CuAsS** Lautite.
*Mineralogy.*

**$CuBr_2$** Cupric Bromide.
Cupric Bromide is used mainly in photography, and as a wood preservative.
*Inorganic Chemistry.*

**CuBr** Cuprous Bromide.
*Inorganic Chemistry.*

**CUBS**; **Cubs** Committee of University Book Sellers.

**CUC** Chronic Ulcerative Colitis.
*Medicine.*

**CUC** Computer Users Committee.

**Cu-CATH** Cathode Copper.
*Metallurgy.*

**$CU(C_{17}H_{33}COO)_2$** Copper Oleate.
Copper Oleate is also known as: Cupric Oleate.
*Organic Chemistry.*

**CUD** Consorzio per l'Università a Distanza (Rome, Italy).
*Distant Learning.*

**Cu-DHP** Deoxidized High Phosphorous Copper.
*Metallurgy.*

**Cu-DLP** Deoxidized Low Phosphorous Copper.
*Metallurgy.*

**CUE** Coventry University Enterprises.
CUE which has a considerable SME experience is AWM's partner.
For further details see under: **AWM** and **SME**.

**CUEA** Coastal Upwelling Ecosystems Analysis.

**CUEP** Central Unit on Environmental Pollution (G.B.).

**CUESP** Cooperativa Universitaria Editrice Scienze Politiche (Milan, Italy).

**Cu-ETP** Electrolytic Tough Pitch Copper.
*Metallurgy.*

**CUF** Commissione Unica per il Farmaco (Italy).

**$CuFeS_2$** Chalcopyrite.
*Mineralogy.*

**Cu-FRHC** Fire Refined High Conductivity Copper.
*Metallurgy.*

**CUFT** Center for the Utilization of Federal Technology (U.S.A.).

**CUG** Closed User Group.
*Cellular Phones.*

**CUHK** The Chinese University of Hong Kong.
Founded in 1963.

**Cu-HSTP** High Silver Tough Pitch Copper.
*Metallurgy.*

**CUIL** common user item list.
liste d'articles communs à plusieurs utilisateurs.

**cu.in.** cubic inch.
Equal to 16.4 cubic centimeters.
*Metrology.*

**CUIP** Chicago Public Schools / University of Chicago Internet Project.
*Internet Training.*

**Cu-LSTP** Low Silver Tough Pitch Copper.
*Metallurgy.*

**CUM**; **Cum** Club Universitari Marketing.
Of the Turin Industrial Union. CUM deal with the impact of new technologies on the economic system, the communication world and marketing.

**cum.** (abbr.) cumulative.

**Cumatex** Associazione Nazionale Rappresentanti e Commercianti Macchine e Accessori per l'Industria Tessile, Maglierie e per Cucire.
Cumatex is located in Milan, Italy.
*Italian Association; Textile Machinery.*

**CUMC** Cornell University Medical College (U.S.A.).

**$CuMnO_2$** Crednerite.
*Mineralogy.*

**cum.pref.** cumulative preference.
*Shares.*

**CUN** The airport code for Cancun, Mexico.

**CUN** Consiglio Universitario Nazionale.
Italian acronym of the: National University Council (Italy).

**CUNA** Commissione tecnica di UNificazione nell'Autoveicolo.
CUNA is located in Turin, Italy.
*Italian Standards Issuing Organization.*

**Cunico** Copper alloy with nickel and cobalt.
*Alloy.*

**Cunife** Copper alloy with nickel and iron.
*Alloy.*
**cunit** cubic unit.
**$Cu_2O$** Cuprous Oxide.
Cuprous Oxide, also known as: Copper Oxide Red, is used mainly in electroplating, and in ceramics.
*Inorganic Chemistry.*
**CUOA** Consorzio Universitario per gli studi di Organizzazione Aziendale (Italy).
**Cu-OF** Oxygen-Free Copper.
*Metallurgy.*
**CUP** Centro Unico Prenotazione.
*Italian Center.*
**CUPAV** Centro Universitário Padre António Vieira (Portugal).
*Portuguese Center.*
**CUPLE project** Comprehensive Unified Physics Learning Environment project.
The CUPLE is sponsored by the U.S. American Association of Physics teachers.
*U.S. Project.*
**CUR** Council on Undergraduate Research (U.S.A.).
**cur.** (abbr.) currency.
**$CuSbS_2$** Chalcostibite.
*Mineralogy.*
**CUSE** Committee on Undergraduate Science Education (U.S.A.).
**CUSEC** cubic foot per second.
*Metrology* - Also: **cfs**.
**CUSL** Cooperativa Universitaria Studio e Lavoro (Milan, Italy).
**$Cu^{+2}SO_4$** Chalcocyanite.
*Mineralogy.*
**CUSRPG** Canada-United States Regional Planning Group.
Groupe stratégique régional Canada / États-Unis.
**CV** 1. aircraft carrier.
1. porte-avions.
2. Cape Verde Islands.
2. îles du Cap-Vert.
**CV** Cardiovascular.
The structures including the heart and blood vessels.
*Anatomy.*
**C.V.** Cavallo Vapore.
Italian initialism meaning: Horse-Power.
*Mechanics.*
**CV** Check Valve.
The check valve, also known as clack valve or non-return valve consists of a pipe valve that limits the flow of fluid to a single direction.
*Engineering.*
**CV** Combat Vehicle.
*Ordnance.*
**CV** Commercial Value.
**C.V.**; **CV** Conto Vendite.
Italian initialism meaning: Sales Account.
**Cv** Coxsackie virus.
Coxsackie virus is one of a group of enteroviruses.
*Virology.*
**CV** Crystal Violet.
*Biochemsitry; Biological Sciences; Cytotoxic Agents; Molecular Biology.*
**CV** Curriculum Vitæ.
**CVA** Cerebrovascular Accident.
The cerebrovascular accident is characterized by a sudden loss of consciousness resulting from embolism or thrombosis of the cerebral vessels. It is also known as: Apoplexy; Stroke.
*Medicine.*
**CVB** CCNU, Vinblastine and Bleomycin.
*Oncology.*
**CVBG** aircraft carrier battle group.
groupe aéronaval (GAN).
**CVC** Conserved Vector Current.
*Particle Physics.*
**CVCP** Committee of Vice Chancellors and Principals.
**CVD** Cardiovascular Disease.
**cvd** cash against (versus) document.
**CVD** Chemical Vapor Deposition.
The chemical vapor deposition is essentially a technique for coating the surface of a solid by exposing it to a vapor, while the latter undergoes thermal decomposition.
*Applied Physics; Chemistry; Materials Science.*
**CVF** Cobra Venom Factor.
**CVG** The airport code for Greater Cincinnati, U.S.A.
**CVGT** Constant-Volume Gas Thermometer.
*Applied Physics; Primary Electronic Thermometry; Physics.*
**CVI** Children's Vaccine Initiative.
Of the U.S. IOM.
*Immunization; International Campaign.*
For further details see under: **IOM**.
**$C^2$VIP** Centre for Computer Vision and Image Processing.
At Cranfield University (G.B.).
*Computer Vision; Image Processing.*
**CVM** Center for Veterinary Medicine.
The CVM is part of the U.S. Department of Health and Human Services, Food and Drug Administration and is located in Rockville, Maryland, U.S.A.

**CVM** Securities Exchange Commission (Brazil).
**CVM technology** Cardholder Cerification Method technology.
**CVOs** Circumventricular Organs.
**CVP** Central Venous Pressure.
**CVP** Cyclophosphamide, Vincristine, and Prednisone.
*Oncology.*
**CVPR** Computer Vision and Pattern Recognition.
**CVR** Cardiovascular Renal; Cardiovascular Respiratory; Cerebrovascular Resistance.
*Medicine.*
**CVRC** Cardiovascular Research Center.
At the University of Michigan (U.S.A.).
**CV redox cycle** Cyclic Voltametric redox cycle.
*Intelligent Polymers Research.*
**CVRT** combat vehicle, reconnaissance tracked.
véhicule de combat à chenilles pour la reconnaissance.
**CVS** Cathodic Voltametry Stripping.
**CVS** Clean Voided Specimen.
*Medicine.*
**CVS** Comunicazione Valutaria Statistica.
Italian initialism meaning: Currency Report for Statistical Purposes.
**CVS** Consorzio Viterbo Servizi (Italy).
*Italian Consortium.*
**CVS** Corrigées des Variations Saisonnières.
French initialism meaning: Seasonally Adjusted Figures.
**cvt.** (abbr.) convert; convertible.
**CVTG** aircraft carrier task group.
groupe opérationnel aéronaval.
**CVU** Coût Variable Unitaire.
French initialism meaning: Variable Unit Cost.
*Business; Commerce; Economics.*
**cvy** (abbr.) convoy.
**CW** Carrier Wave.
**CW** Chemical Warfare.
Chemical warfare is also known as: Chemical Operation.
*Military Science.*
**CW** Chemical Weapon.
**CW** Circular Wait.
Circular Wait is also known as: Mutual Deadlock.
*Computer Programming.*
**CW**; **cw** (abbr.) clockwise.
**CW** Cold Water.
**CW** Comparable Worth.
*Economics; Statistics.*
**c/w** complete with.
**CW** Continuous wave.
The continuous wave is also known as type A wave.
*Electromagnetism.*
**CW** Crutch Walking.
*Medicine.*
**C2W** command and control warfare.
guerre du commandement et du contrôle.
**CWA** chemical warfare agent.
agent de guerre chimique.
**CWC** 1. Chemical Weapons Convention.
1. Convention sur les armes chimiques.
2. composite warfare commander.
2. commandant des luttes coordonnées.
**CWD** Chronic Wasting Disease.
In wild deer and elk areas, it is a sort of "mad deer" disease similar to the mad cow disease: a transmissible spongiform encephalopathy.
**CWDM** Coarse Wavelength-Division Multiplexing.
**CWF group** Compassion in World Farming group.
*Biotechnology.*
**CWIP** Construction-Work-In-Progress.
**CWL** Council of Wisconsin Libraries (U.S.A.).
**CW laser** Continuous-Wave laser.
*Optics.*
**CWM** Convertible Wraparound Mortgage.
*Business; Commerce; Finance.*
**CWO**; **cwo** Cash With Order.
*Business; Commerce.*
**CWPS** Council on Wage and Price Stability.
**CWQC** Company-Wide Quality Control.
**CWQM** Company-Wide Quality Management.
**CWR** coastal warning radar.
radar d'alerte côtier.
**CW radar** Continuous-Wave radar.
CW radar is also known as: Continuous-Wave Doppler radar.
*Engineering.*
**CWRU** Case Western Reserve University (U.S.A.).
**CWS** Canadian Wildlife Service.
Of the Simon Fraser University (Canada).
**CWS** Central Weather Bureau (Taiwan).
**CWS** Co-operative Wholesale Society (G.B.).
**CWSE** Committee on Women in Science and Engineering (U.S.A.).
U.S. NAS.
For further details see under: **NAS**.
**CWSU** Central Weather Service Unit - Of the U.S. FAA.
For further details see under: **FAA**.
**CWT** Carrier Wave Telegraphy.
**cwt** hundredweight.
**CWTS** Constructed Wetland Treatment Systems.
**CX** The airline code for Cathay Pacific Airways.

**CX** Cycloheximide.
*Molecular Biology.*
**Cx43** Connexin 43.
*Developmental Biology.*
**CXE** Charge Exchange Excitations.
*Aerospace Engineering; Space Physics.*
**CXO** Chandra X-ray Observatory.
*Planetary Science.*
**CY** Calendar Year.
**cy.** currency.
**CY** Current Year.
**CY** Current Yield.
*Business; Commerce; Finance.*
**cy.** (abbr.) cyanogen.
Cyanogen is also known as: Dicyan(ogen).
*Inorganic Chemistry.*
**cy.** (abbr.) cycle.
*Engineering; Fluid Mechanics; Industrial Engineering.*
**CY** Cyprus's International vehicle-registration letters.
**cyborg** (abbr.) Cybernetic Organism.
*Robotics.*
**CYCLES** CYCLonic Extratropical Storms.
*Program.*
**Cyg** Cygnus.
Cygnus is a constellation of the Northern Hemisphere lying in the Milky Way.
*Astronomy.*
**cyl.** (abbr.) cylinder.
*Computer Technology; Engineering; Mechanical Engineering; Mathematics.*
**CyP40** Cyclophilin-40.
*Biochemistry; Cell Biology; Medicine; Molecular Biology.*
**Cys.** (abbr.) Cysteinate.
**CYSB** Cape York Space Base (Australia).
**CYSF** Cape York Space Facility (Australia).
**CYSP** Cape York Space Port (Australia).
**CYT** Cytoplasm.
*Cell Biology.*
**CYTA** CYprus Telecommunications Authority.
**CyVADIC** Cyclophosphamide, Vincristine, Adriamycin and Imidazole Carboxamide.
*Oncology.*
**CZ** Catanzaro, Italy.
**CZ** 1. combat zone.
1. zone de combat.
2. Czech Republic.
2. République tchèque.
**CZCS satellite** Coastal Zone Color Scanner satellite.
*Biological Sciences; Marine and Coastal Sciences; Marine Ecology; Plant Biology.*
**CZE** Capillary Zone Electrophoresis.
*Chemical Kinetics; Chemistry; Electrophoresis; Physical Chemistry.*
**CZM** Coastal Zone Management.
Of the U.S. National Ocean Service.
**CZMA** Coastal Zone Management Act.
**CZR** communication zone, rear.
zone arrière des communications.

# D

**d** data; date.
**D**; **d** daughter (Company).
**d** day; debenture.
**d** degree.
*Mathematics; Metrology.*
**d** delivered.
**D**; **d** density.
*Computer Technology; Ecology; Graphic Arts; Mechanics; Optics; Transportation Engineering.*
**D**; **D.** derivative.
*Chemistry; Mathematics.*
**D** Détenu.
meaning in French: detained in custody.
**D**; $^{2}$**H** The chemical symbol for Deuterium.
Deuterium is also known as: Heavy Hydrogen.
*Chemistry; Symbols.*
**d** deviation.
*Engineering; Navigation; Optics; Ordnance; Psychology; Statistics.*
**d**; **d.** diameter; distance; distal.
**D** Digit.
*Anatomy; Mathematics.*
**D** Digital.
*Computer Technology; Engineering.*
**d** dime.
**D** Diode.
*Electronics.*
**d** diopter.
*Optics.*
**D** Diretto.
*Railways* - Through train in Italian.
**d** disease.
*Medicine.*
**d** discount.
**D** Display.
*Behavior; Computer Science; Electronics.*
**D**; **d** dividend.
**D** Doctor.
**D** Dollar.
Also: **dol.**; **dlr.**
**D** Domenica.
Sunday in Italian.
**d** (abbr.) dorsal.
*Anatomy.*
**d** (abbr.) dose.
*Medicine; Nucleonics.*
**D** Drum.
*Architecture; Chemical Engineering; Computer Technology; Mechanical Devices; Mechanical Engineering; Mining Engineering.*
**D** Duchess; Duke.
**d** duration.
*Oceanography; Science.*
**D** Dutch.
The Germanic language of the Netherlands.
*Languages.*
**d** penny / pence.
**DA** 1. damage assessment.
1. évaluation des dommages.
2. défense aérienne.
2. air defence (AD 2.).
3. Denmark.
3. Danemark.
4. direct action.
4. action directe.
**DA** Denmark.
Also: **Den.**; **Dk**.
**DA** Data Acquisition.
*Computer Programming; Telecommunications.*
**DA** Data Available.
**da**. day; days.
**DA** Days after Acceptance.
*Business; Commerce.*
**DA** Decimal Address.
*Data Communications.*
**DA** Deductible Average.
**DA** Deed of Agreement.
**DA** Delayed Action.
*Ordnance.*
**D/A** Delivery against Acceptance.
**DA** Denmark.
**DA**; **D.A.** Dental Assistant.
**DA** Department of the Army (U.S.A.).
**DA** Depletion Allowance.
**DA** Deposit Account.
**DA** Design Automation.
*Computer Technology.*
**DA**; **D.A.** Developmental Age / Development Age.
*Psychology.*
**DA** Differential Analyzer.
DA is also known as: Electronic Differential Analyzer.
*Computer Technology.*
**DA** Diploma in Anaesthetics.
**DA** Diritti d'Autore (compensi).
Italian initialism meaning: Royalties.
**DA** Diritto d'Autore.
Italian acronym meaning: Copyright.
*Law.*
**D/A** District Attorney (U.S.A.).
**DA** Doctor of Arts.

**DA** Documenti contro accettazione.
Italian acronym meaning: Documents against acceptance.

**D/A** Documents Attached.

**DA** Do not Answer.

**DA** Dopamine.
*Biochemistry* - Dopamine is also known as: 3,4-Dihydroxyphenylethylamine.

**DA** Dormant Account.
*Business; Finance.*

**D/A** Double Action.

**DAA** Data-Access Arrangement.

**DAA** Diacetone Acrylamide.

**DAA** Diploma of the Advertising Association.

**DAA** Documents Against Acceptance.
*Business; Commerce.*

**DAAC** Distributed Active Archive Center.

**DAAD** 2,6-diazaanthracene-9, l0-dione (a compound).

**DAB** Daytona Beach, Florida, U.S.A.
*Airport Code.*

**DAB** Diaminobenzidine.

**DAB** Dictionary of American Biography.

**DAB** Digital Audio Broadcasting.
*Digital Radios.*

**DAB** Distributeur Automatique de Billets (de banque).
French acronym meaning; Automated Teller Machine; Cash dispenser; cashpoint.
*Banking Technology.*

**DAB** Distributeur Automatique de Billets (de parking).
French acronym meaning: Ticket machine.

**DABS** Discrete-Address Beacon Systems.

**DAC** Data Assembly Center.

**DAC** Delayed Action Command.
*Ordnance.*

**DAC** 1. deployable ACCS component.
1. composante déployable de l'ACCS.
2. disarmament and arms control.
2. désarmement et maîtrise des armements.

**DAC** Diamond Anvil Cell.
For further details see under: **DACs**.

**DAC**; **dac** Digital-to-Analog Converter.
The digital-to-analog converter actually changes digital input signals to proportional analog signals.
*Electronics.*

**DACAN** Military Committee Distribution and Accounting Agency.
Bureau de distribution et de comptabilité du Comité militaire.

**DACAR** Data Acquisition and Communication techniques and their Assessment for Road transport.
*European Community Project.*

**dac gene** dachshund gene.
The dac gene is a fly gene.
*Biology; Developmental Biology; Developmental Genetics; Genetic Engineering.*

**D/A converter** Digital-to-Analog converter.
For further details see under: **DAC**.

**DACOS** Deputy Assistant Chief of Staff.
sous-chef d'état-major adjoint (SCEMA).

**DACS** Data Acquisition and Control Subsystem.

**DACs** Diamond Anvil Cells.
*Engineering Science; Materials Science; Physical Science.*

**DACs** Digital-to-Analog Converters.
For further details see under: **DAC**.

**DACT** (abbr.) Dactinomycin.
*Pharmacology.*

**DAD**; **dad** Database Action Diagram.

**DAD** Deputy Assistant Director [IMS].
directeur adjoint délégué [EMI].

**DAD** Desktop Applications Director.

**DAD** Documents Against Discretion.

**DADR** deployable air defence radar.
radar de défense aérienne déployable.

**DAE** Dictionary of American English.

**DAE** Director of Army Education.

**DAF** Decay Accelerating Factor.
*Hepatology; Immunology; Pathology; Surgery; Transplantation Biology- Xenotransplantation.*

**DAF** Delivered At Frontier.
*Business; Commerce; International Trade.*

**DAF** Dissolved Air Flotation.
*Chemical Engineering.*

**DAF** Dry, Ash-Free.

**DAG** Diacylglycerol.
*Endocrinology.*

**DAG** Direct Access Gateway (Ericsson's & Sunet).
DAG was released in June 1998. The project is supported by the Swedish Foundation for Knowledge and Competence Development.
*e-mail Directory Services.*
For further details see under: **Sunet**.

**DAG** Directed Acyclic Graph.
*Computer Science.*

**DAGC** Delayed Automatic Gain Control.
DAGC is also known as: Delayed Automatic Volume Control.
*Electronics.*

**DAH** Dictionary of American History.

**DAH** Disordered Action of the Heart.
*Medicine.*

**D&J** December and June.
*Securities.*
**DAL** Data Access Line; Data/Address Line.
**DAL** The airport code for Love Field, Dallas, Texas, U.S.A.
**DAM** DAVIC Accompanying Measures.
*European Community Project.*
**DAM** Descripter/Attribute Matrix.
**Dam** DNA adenine methylase.
*DNA Repair; Genetics; Infectious Diseases; Microbiology.*
**DAMA** demand assignment multiple access.
accès multiple avec assignation à (ou par) la demande (AMAD).
**DAMA experiment** (abbr.) DArk MAtter experiment.
At Gran Sasso National Laboratory (Italy).
*Astronomy; Astrophysics; Cosmology; Physics.*
**DAME** Digital Automatic Measuring Equipment.
**DAML**; **Daml** DARPA Agent Markup Language.
A language (devised in 2000) allowing nontraditional programs and browsing devices to understand Web sites.
*Semantic Web.*
For further details see under: **DARPA**.
**DAMREP** damage report.
1a. compte rendu d'avarie [marine].
1b. compte rendu de dommages [armée de terre].
**Dan.** (abbr.) Danish.
Danish is a Germanic language, spoken in Denmark, closely related to Norwegian, Swedish and Icelandic.
*Languages.*
**DAN** dépenses administratives nationales.
national administrative expenses (NAE).
**DAN** Deposit Account Number.
*Banking; Finance.*
**DAN** Divers Alert Network.
**D and C**; **D & C** Dilation and Curettage.
*Surgery.*
**D and D** Decommissioned and Decontaminated.
**DA neurons** Dopaminergic neurons.
*Anatomy; Genetic Therapies; Medicine; Neurobiology.*
**DANS acid** 5-dimethylamino-1-naphthalenesulfonic acid.
*Organic Chemistry.*
**DAO** Data Assimilation Office - NASA's.
**DAO** Departmental Administrative Order.
**DAO** Dessin Assisté par Ordinateur.
French acronym meaning: Computer-Assisted Design.
**DAP** Data Access Protocol.
**DAP** 1. date d'achèvement prévue.
1. estimated date of completion (EDC).
2. departure and arrival point.
2. point de départ et d'arrivée.
**DAP** Diallyl Phthalate.
$C_6H_4(COOCH_2CH{=}CH_2)_2$. DAP is used as a plasticizer and for polymerization, purposes.
*Organic Chemistry.*
**DAP** Diammonium Phosphate.
DAP is also known as: Ammonium Phosphate.
*Inorganic Chemistry.*
**DAP** Dipartimento dell'Amministrazione Penitenziaria (Italy).
**DAP** Documents Against Payment.
*Business; Commerce.*
**3DAP** three-Dimensional Atom Probe.
**DAPA ATase** 7,8-Diaminopelargonic Acid Aminotransferase.
**DAPI** 4',6-Diamino-2-Phenylindole.
*Chemistry.*
**DAR** Damage Assessment Routine.
**D.A.R.** Daughters of the American Revolution (U.S.A.).
D.A.R. was organized in 1890.
**DAR** Defense Acquisition Regulations.
**DAR** Defense Aid Reports.
**DAR** disabled aircraft recovery.
récupération d'aéronefs hors service.
**dar** The above acronyms were coined accidentally using the Arabic word "dar" which means: house, abode.
**DARA** Deutsche Agentur für Raumfahrtangelegenheiten (Germany).
DARA was merged with DLR.
For further details see under: **DLR**.
**DARC** Device for Automatic Remote data Collection.
**DARC** Direct Access Radar Channel.
**DARES** Direction de l'Animation, de la Recherche, des Etudes et des Statistiques (France).
**DARHT facility** Dual-Axis Radiographic Hydrotest Facility.
**DARPA** DOD's Advanced Research Projects Agency (U.S.A.).
DARPA has been replaced by: **ARPA**.
*U.S. Defense.*
For further details see under: **DOD** and **DAML**.
**DARS** Data Acquisition and Reduction System.
**DART** Deployable Automatic Relay Terminal.
**DART campaign** Depression Awareness, Research and Treatment campaign.
Of the U.S. National Institute of Mental Health.
**DARTS** Distributors Automated Real-Time System.

**DAS** Days At Sea.
**DAS** defence and space.
défense et espace.
**DASA** Daimler-Benz Aerospace.
**DASA** Defense Atomic Support Agency.
Of the U.S. Department Of Defense.
**DAS** Department of Drug Addiction Services (1973 - U.S.A.).
**DAS** Differential Absorption and Scattering.
**DAS**; **das** Direct-Access Storage.
*Computer Technology.*
**DAS** Direct Attached Storage.
**DASC** direct air support centre.
centre d'appui aérien direct.
**DASD** Direct Access Storage Device.
*Computer Technology.*
**DASG** Directeur des Affaires Sociales Générales (France).
**DASH** Dietary Approaches to Stop Hypertension (U.S.A.).
DASH is a study advocating that blood pressure can be lowered by means of a low-fat diet.
*Cardiology; Hypertension; Medical Research; Nutrition.*
**DASH** drone antisubmarine helicopter.
hélicoptère anti-sous-marin télécommandé.
**DASI** Degree Angular Scale Interferometer.
A microwave telescope located near the South Pole.
**DASN** Differenziale di Appetibilità Strategica Normalizzata.
Italian acronym meaning: Standard Strategic Desirability Differential.
**DAST** Direction des Affaires Scientifiques et Techniques (France).
**DAT** Delayed Action Tablet.
*Medicine.*
**DAT** Differential Aptitude Test.
**DAT** Digital Audiotape.
*Acoustical Engineering.*
**DAT** Direct Antiglobulin Test.
*Chemotherapy; Immunology; Medicine; Microbiology.*
**DAT** Dynamic Address Translator.
Dynamic Address Translator is also known as: Relocation Hardware.
*Computer Technology.*
**DATACOMM** (abbr.) DATA COMMunications.
Data Communications is also known as: Data Transmission.
*Computer Technology.*
**DATAR**; **D.A.T.A.R.** Délégation à l'Aménagement du Territoire et à l'Action Régionale (France).
**DAV.**; **D.A.V.** Disabled American Veterans.
**DAWN** Drug Abuse Warning Network (U.S.A.).
**DAY** The airport code for Dayton, Ohio, U.S.A.
**DB** Data Bank.
Data bank, also known as Data base, is an exhaustive collection of information from computer disks, libraries, or other sources and in various forms for numerous applications.
*Computer Programming.*
**DB**; **db** Database.
*Computer Programming.*
For further details, see under: **DB** (Data Bank).
**DB** Data Bus.
*Computer Technology.*
**DB**; **db.** (abbr.) daybook.
**db.** (abbr.) debenture.
*Commerce; Finance.*
**db.** (abbr.) debit.
**dB**; **db** decibel; decibels.
*Metrology; Physics.*
**DB** division blindée.
armoured division.
**D/B** Documentary Bill.
**dBa** Adjusted Decibels.
*Electronics.*
**DBA** Data-Base Administrator.
*Computer Technology.*
**DBA** Doctor of Business Administration.
**DBA** Doing Business As.
*Management.*
**DBASSE** Division of Behavioral and Social Sciences and Education (U.S.A.).
**DBBS** Division of Biology and Biomedical Sciences.
**DBC** Data Broadcasting Corporation.
The DBC provides real-time market data to the investor.
**DBC** Decussation of the Brachium Conjunctivum.
**DBCP** 1,2-dibromo-3-Chloropropane.
DBCP is used as a pesticide and nematocide.
*Organic Chemistry.*
**DBD** DNA Binding Domain.
*Cancer Research; Medicine; Molecular Biology; Cell Biology.*
**DBDE** Database Design Evaluator.
**DB diffusion** Dangling Bond Diffusion.
*Chemistry; Dangling Bond Dynamics.*
**DBE** Dame Commander of the Order of The British Empire (G.B.).
**DBE** Data Bus Enable.
**DBE** Dibasic Ester.
*Chemistry.*
**dBf** decibels above 1 femtowatt.

**DBF** Detail Digital Beamforming.
*Mobile Communications Systems.*
**DBH** Diameter at Breast Height.
**DBIR** Directory of Biotechnology Information Resources.
**DBK** Dibenzyl Ketone.
**dbk.** (abbr.) drawback.
**DBL** development (allocated) baseline.
référence de développement.
**dbl.**; **dbl** (abbr.) double.
**DBM** Database Machine.
*Computer Technology.*
**DBM** Dibutyl Maleate.
$C_4H_9OOCCH{=}CHCOOC_4H_9$. DBM is used mainly in copolymers and plasticizers.
*Organic Chemistry.*
**DBM** Donor Bone Marrow.
*Medicine; Transplantation Tolerance.*
**DBMS**; **dbms** Database Management System.
Essentially, DBMS is a collection of programs and includes storage, and retrieval software.
*Computer Programming.*
**DBO** Demande Biologique en Oxygène.
French initialism meaning: Biological Oxygen Demand.
*Medicine.*
**DBOA** Dioptrician of the British Optical Association (G.B.).
**dBp** decibels above 1 picowatt.
**DBP** Diastolic Blood Pressure.
*Physiology.*
**DBP** Dibutyl Phthalate.
Dibuthyl Phthalate is used mainly as a plasticizer, and insecticide.
*Organic Chemistry.*
**DBP** Direction de la Balance des Paiements (France).
**DBPs** Disinfection Byproducts / by-products.
*Health Risks.*
**DBR** Division of Basic Research.
**DBR lasers** Distributed Bragg Reflector lasers.
*Applied Physics.*
**DBRN**; **dBrn** Decibels above Reference Noise.
*Electricity.*
**DBRTS** (abbr.) Debenture Rights.
**DBS** Database Server.
*Computer Programming.*
**Dbs**; **dbs** Direct-Broadcast satellite.
**Dbt.** (abbr.) debit.
**DBT** Dry-Bulb Thermometer.
*Engineering.*
**DBT protein** Double-Time protein.
*Mammalian Clock Genes.*
**dBV** decibels above 1 volt.
*Electricity.*
**dBw** decibels above 1 watt.
*Electricity.*
**dBx** decibels above reference coupling.
*Electricity.*
**DC** Data Cartridge.
*Computer Technology.*
**DC** Data Center.
*Computer Technology.*
**DC** Data Channel.
*Computer Technology.*
**DC** Data Code.
*Computer Programming.*
**DC**; **D.C.** Data Communications.
**DC** Data Conversion.
*Computer Programming.*
**DC** Debit Collection.
*Business; Commerce; Finance.*
**DC** Decimal Classification.
**DC** Delta Clipper.
**DC** 1. Democratic Centre (Croatia).
1. Centre démocratique (Croatie).
2. disarmament commission.
2. commission pour le désarmement.
**DC** Dental Corps.
**DC** Design Change.
**DC** Detail Condition.
**D.C.** Developed Country.
**DC** Diagnostic Center.
**DC** Digital Computer.
Essentially, the digital computer is a computer which can accept digital data and perform on the data arithmetic and logic processes.
*Computer Technology.*
**D.C.** Direct Costs.
**DC**; **D.C.**; **dc**; **d.c.** Direct Current.
**DC** Direct Cycle.
**DC** Direction Cycle.
*Data Communications.*
**D.C.** Direttore Centrale.
Italian initialism meaning: Central Manager.
**D.C.** Direzione Centrale.
Italian initialism meaning: Central Management.
**DC** Display Console.
**DC**; **D.C.** District Court.
**DC** (abbr.) District of Columbia (U.S.A.).
**DC** Divisional Court.
**DC** Doctor of Chiropractice.
**D.C.**; **DC** Double Convex.
**DC** Dyskeratosis Congenita.
*Premature Aging; Cancer Susceptibility; Nail Dystrophy.*

**DCA** Defense Communications Agency.
DCA has been replaced by: **DISA**.
**DCA** 1. defensive counter-air (operation).
1. (opération) défensive contre le potentiel aérien.
2. dual-capable aircraft.
2. avion à double capacité.
**DCA** Deoxycholic Acid.
*Medicine; Pharmacology.*
**DCA** Dichloroanthracene.
**DCA** Direct-Coupled Amplifier.
*Electronics.*
**DCA** National Airport Washington, D.C., U.S.A.
*Airport Code.*
**DCAA** Defense Contract Audit Agency.
**DC amplifier** Direct-Current amplifier.
**DCAOC** deployable combined air operations centre.
centre combiné d'opérations aériennes déployable.
**DCase** Decarboxylase.
**DCB** Data Control Block.
**DCB** 2,6-Dichlorobenzonitrile.
**DCB** Division of Cancer Biology.
Of the U.S. National Cancer Institute.
**DCC** damage control centre.
1a. centre de contrôle des avaries [marine].
1b. PC organisation sécurité [FR].
**DCC** Devon Consuls Crustal Contaminants.
*Earth Sciences.*
**D.Cc**; **DCc** double concave.
**DCCA** Department of Commerce and Community Affairs (Illinois, U.S.A.).
**dc casting** direct-chill casting.
Direct-chill casting, which is also known as semi-continuous casting is essentially a process wherein the metal is poured into molds and then cooled in a water bath.
*Metallurgy.*
**DCC gene** Deleted in Colon Carcinoma gene.
**DCCI** Dicyclohexylcarbodiimide.
DCCI is used in peptide synthesis.
*Organic Chemistry.*
**DC content** Detrital Carbonate content.
**DCCS** Dynamic Cell Culture System.
**DCD** Data Carrier Detect.
**DCDS** Digital Control Design System.
**DC dump** Direct-Current dump.
*Electricity.*
**DCE** Data Circuit terminating Equipment.
**DCE**; **dce** Data Communications Equipment.
**DCE** Discounted Cash Equivalent.
**DCE** Domestic Credit Expansion.
**DCEF** Discounted Cash Equivalent Flow.
**DCEG** Division of Cancer Epidemiology and Genetics.
**DCF** democratic control of forces and defence structures.
contrôle démocratique des forces et structures de défense.
**DCF** Discounted Cash Flow.
*Cash-Flows; Valuation Methods.*
**DCF** Dose Commitment Factors.
**DCFM** Discounted Cash Flow Method.
*Business; Commerce; Finance.*
**DCG** deception group [navy].
groupe de déception [marine].
**DCH** Data CHannel.
*Computer Technology.*
**DchE**; **D.Ch.E.** Doctor of Chemical Engineering.
**DCI** Defence Capabilities Initiative.
Initiative sur les capacité de défense.
**DCINC** Deputy Commander-in-Chief.
commandant en chef adjoint.
**DCIS** Ductal Carcinoma In Situ.
*Breast Cancer; Medicine; Pathology.*
**DCIT** Direzione Centrale Informatica e Telecomunicazioni (Italy).
**D.C.J.**; **DCJ** District Court Judge.
**DCL** Discretionary Credit Limit.
*Business; Commerce; Finance.*
**DCL**, **D.C.L.** Doctor of Civil Law.
**DCL**, **D.C.L.** Doctor of Common Law.
**DCL** Dynamic Combinational Library.
For further details see under: **DCLs**.
**DCLA** District of Columbia Library Association (U.S.A.).
*U.S. Library Association.*
**DCLs** Dynamic Combinatorial Libraries.
*Development of Artificial Receptors; Drug Discoveries.*
**DCM** deployable CIS module.
module SIC déployable.
**DCM** Dichloromethane.
DCM also known as: Methylene Chloride is used mainly in paint removers.
*Organic Chemistry.*
**DCM** Dilated Cardiomyopathy.
The most common cause of CHF.
*Cardiology; Genetics; Medicine; Mutant Genes; Heart Research.*
For further details see under: **CHF**; **FDCM** and **IDCM**.
**DCM**; **D.C.M.** Distinguished Conduct Medal (G.B.).
**DCM** District Court Martial.
**DCM** Double-Chirped Mirror.

**DCMC** Deputy Chairman Military Committee.
président délégué du Comité militaire.
**DCMs** Double Chirped Mirrors.
*Optics; Quantum Electronics.*
**DCN** Dicyanate.
**DCN** Direction des Constructions Navales.
**DCN** Dorsal Column Nuclei.
**DCNA** 2,6-dichloro-4-nitroaniline.
$C_6H_4Cl_2N_2O_2$ - DCNA is used as a fungicide for vegetables and fruits.
*Organic Chemistry.*
**DCOFS** see DCOS.
voir DCOS.
**DCOMARRC** Deputy Commander ACE Rapid Reaction Corps.
commandant adjoint du Corps de réaction rapide du CAE.
**DCOMOPS** Deputy Commander of Operations.
commandant adjoint des opérations.
**DCOS** Deputy Chief of Staff.
chef d'état-major adjoint.
**DCP** Data Communications Processor.
*Computer Technology.*
**DCP** date de commencement prévue.
estimated date of start (EDS 1.).
**DCP** Doped Conjugated Polymer.
*Materials.*
**DCPC** Division of Cancer Prevention and Control (U.S.A.).
Of the U.S. National Cancer Institute.
**DCR** Data Conversion Receiver.
*Data Communications.*
**DCR** Deglaciation Climatic Reversal.
*Paleoclimate Changes.*
**DCR** Digital Cassette Recorder.
**DCR** Direct Critical Response.
*Medicine.*
**DCR** Direct-Cycle Reactor.
*Nucleonics.*
**DcR1** Decoy Receptor 1.
*Cancer Research; Medicine.*
For further details see under: **TRID**.
**DCRDO** Deputy Chief Research and Development Officer.
**DCS** Data Collection System.
**DCS** Defense Communication System.
**DCs** Dendritic Cells.
*Immunology Research; Medicine.*
**DCS** Differential Cross Section.
**DCS** Digital Computer System.
**DCS** Distributed Computer Systems.
**DCS** Doctor of Commercial Science.
**DC-SIGN** Dendritic Cell Specific Intracellular adhesion molecule-3 Grabbing Nonintegrin.
*Biochemistry; Glycobiology; Medicine; Molecular and Cellular Physiology; Structural Biology.*
**DCSs** Differential Cross Sections.
**DCTL** Direct-Coupled Transistor Logic.
The direct-coupled transistor logic is essentially a logic circuit making use only of transistors and resistors with direct conductive coupling between the transistors.
*Electronics.*
**DCTs** Discourse Completion Tests.
*Linguistics.*
**DCVs** Dense Core Vesicles.
*Anatomy; Cell Biology; Medicine.*
**dcwv** direct-current working voltage.
**DD** Dangerous Deck.
**DD** Data Definition.
*Computer Programming.*
**DD** Data Dictionary.
The data dictionary is actually a catalog making available names and structures of all data types contained in a database.
*Computer Programming.*
**DD** Data Division.
*Computer Programming.*
**dd.** datato.
dated in Italian.
**DD** Days after Date.
**DD** Deferred Delivery; Delayed Delivery.
*Business; Commerce.*
**dd.** (abbr.) delivered.
Also: **delv'd**; **dld.**
**D/D** Demand Deposit.
**DD** Demand Draft.
**DD** Demonstration Division.
**DD** destroyer.
destroyer.
**DD** Developmentally Disabled.
**dd** direttissimo.
Express train; fast train in Italian.
*Railways.*
**DD** Dishonorable Discharge.
**DD** Doctor of Divinity.
**DD** Due Date.
**DDA** Dangerous Drug Act (U.S.A.).
**DDA** Demand Deposit Accounting.
*Banking.*
**DDA** Digital Differential Analyzer.
**DDA** Direction Déléguée à l'Automatisme (France).
**DDB** Den Danske Bank.
DDB is Denmark's largest bank.
*Danish Bank.*

**DDB** DNA Data Bank.
**DDB** Dodecylbenzene.
Dodecylbenzene, also known as detergent alkylate is used in certain types of detergents.
*Organic Chemistry.*
**DDBJ** DNA Data Bank of Japan.
**DDC** Dewey Decimal Classification.
**DDC** Direct Digital Control.
Direct digital control is used in the petroleum, chemical, and other industries for process control.
*Control Systems.*
**DDCCRF** Direction régionale De la Concurrence, de la Consommation et de la Répression des Fraudes (France).
**DDD** Desired Deposit of Dividends; Direct Deposit of Dividends.
*Business; Finance.*
**DDD** Direct Distance Dialing.
*Telecommunications.*
**DDD simulations** Discrete Dislocation Dynamic simulations.
*Materials Science.*
**DDG** Deputy Director General.
**DDG**; **D.D.G.** Diplomé/e du Gouvernement (France).
**DDGS** Distiller's Dried Grains and Solubles.
Starch makes up only about 72% of the corn kernel. The material remaining at the bottom of the distillation column such as: cellulose, hemicellulose, lignin proteins, and fat, is dried into an animal feed known as distiller's dried grains and solubles.
**DDH and DS** Digital Data Handling and Display System.
**D.D.I.**; **DDI** Due Diligence Investigation.
*Business Intelligence; Law.*
**DDL** Data Definition Language.
**DDL** Data Description Language.
*Computer Programming.*
**DDL** Disegno Di Legge.
Italian initialism meaning: Parliamentary Bill; Bill; Government Bill.
**DDM** Decaying Dark Matter.
*Astronomy; Astrophysics.*
**DDM** Discreet Decision Making.
*Cryptography; Private Communication.*
**DDM** Distributed Data Management.
**DDM** Dodecyl Mercaptan.
DDM is also known as: Lauryl Mercaptan; Thiododecyl Alcohol.
*Organic Chemistry.*
**DDMS** Deputy Director of Medical Services.
**DDN** Defense Department Network (U.S.A.).
**DDN** Documented Discount Notes.
*Business; Commerce.*
**DDOS**; **Ddos** Distributed Denial-Of-Service.
**DDP** detailed deployment plan.
plan de déploiement détaillé.
**DDP** Direct Deposit of Payroll.
**DDP** Drug Discovery Program (U.S.A.).
**DDPAC** Disinhibition-Dementia-Parkinsonism-Amyotrophy Complex.
*Geriatric Medicine; Gerontology; Medicine; Neurodegenerative Diseases; Neurology; Pathology.*
**DDPS** Digital Data-Processing System.
**DDR**; **Ddr** Dial-up on Demand Routing.
**DDR** DNA Damage Response.
*Biochemistry; Medical Genetics; Human Cancer; Microbiology; Molecular Biology.*
**DDR** Dynamic Device Reconfiguration.
*Data Communications.*
**DDR&E** Director of Defense Research and Engineering.
*Defense Science.*
**DDRI** Danube Delta Research Institute (Tulcea).
*Romanian Institute.*
**DDRT-PCR analysis** Differential Display combined with Reverse Transcription-Polymerase Chain Reaction analysis.
*Biological Sciences; Plant Biology.*
**DDS** Dataphone Digital Service.
**DDS** Denys-Drash Syndrome.
**DDS** Deway Decimal System.
**DDS** Diaminodiphenylsulfone.
**DDS** Digital Data Service; Digital Data System.
**DDS**; **D.D.S.** Doctor of Dental Science.
**DDS**; **D.D.S.** Doctor of Dental Surgery.
**DDS** Dust Detector on the Galileo Spacecraft.
*Atmospheric and Space Physics; Jovian Magnetosphere.*
**DD scenario** Double-Degenerate scenario.
**DDT** Dichlorodiphenyltrichloroethane.
DDT is used as a pesticide and an insecticide.
*Organic Chemistry.*
**DDTs** Double Drive-Throughs (U.S.A.).
**DDU** Delivered Duty Unpaid.
*Business; Commerce.*
**DE** 1. damage expectancy.
1a. dégâts escomptés.
1b. prévision de dommages.
2. directed energy.
2. énergie dirigée (ED 2.).
**DE** Data Encryption.
*Computer Programming.*
**DE** Data Entry.

*Computer Programming.*
**DE** Decision Element.
*Electronics.*
**DE** (abbr.) Delaware (U.S.A.).
Also: **Del.**
**DE** Digital Element; Display Element; Display Equipment.
*Data Communications.*
**DE** Division Entry.
*Data Communications.*
**DE**; **D.E.** Doctor of Engineering.
**DE** Double Entry.
*Bookkeeping.*
**DEA** Diethanolamine.
$(HOCH_2CH_2)_2NH$ - DEA is used mainly in polishes, cleaners and as a chemical intermediate.
*Organic Chemistry.*
**D.E.A.** Dipartimento Emergenza e Accoglienza - Policlinico Gemelli (Rome, Italy).
**DEA** Diplôme d'Etudes Agricoles (France).
**DEA** Diplôme d'Etudes Approfondies.
Of the I.H.E.E. (Strasbourg, France).
For further details see under: **I.H.E.E.**
**DEA** Drug Enforcement Administration (U.S.A.).
**DEAE** Diethylaminoethyl.
**DEAP** Department of Emissions and Air Pollution.
Of NERI, Denmark.
For further details see under: **NERI**.
**DEB** Data Extent Block.
**deb.** (abbr.) debenture.
**DEB** Diplôme d'Etudes Bibliothécaires (France).
**6-dEB** 6-deoxyerythronolide B.
*Chemical Engineering; Chemistry.*
**DEBA** Direccion de la Energia de la provincia de Buenos Aires.
DEBA was founded in the early 1950s.
**DEBS** Deoxyerythronolide B Synthase.
*Chemical Engineering; Chemistry; Pharmacy.*
**dec** (abbr.) December.
**dec**; **dec.** (abbr.) decimeter, decimeters.
**dec.** (abbr.) declaration.
**dec.** (abbr.) decoder.
*Computer Technology; Electronics; Telecommunications.*
**dec.** (abbr.) decorated.
**dec.** (abbr.) decotto.
Italian abbreviation meaning: decoction.
*Medicine.*
**dec.** (abbr.) decrease.
**DEC** dernière estimation de coût.
latest cost estimate (LCE 1.).
**DEC** Detroit Edison Company (U.S.A.).
**DEC** Diarrheagenic *E. Coli.*
**DEC** Diethylcarbonate.
Diethylcarbonate is used mainly as a solvent.
*Organic Chemistry.*
**DEC** Digital Equipment Corporation.
**DEC** Dominant Energy Condition.
*Physics.*
**DECM** deceptive electronic countermeasures [obsolete].
contre-mesures électroniques de déception (CMED) [obsolète].
**DECO** (abbr.) DEnominazione COmunale (Italy).
**DECs** District Export Councils.
The 25th Anniversary Conference of the District Export Councils and the World Trade Symposium was held in New York on the 3rd of June, 1998.
**DECT**; **Dect** Digital Enhanced Cordless Telecommunications.
*Cordless Telecommunications; Cellular Phones.*
**DED** Data Element Dictionary; Data Element Directory.
**DED** Death Effector Domain.
*Apoptosis; Biochemistry.*
**DEDICATED** DEvelopment of a new DImension in Europe Computer-Aided Teaching and EDucation.
*European Community Project.*
**DEEP** Development of a data handling Environment for Exploration and exploitation of mining Projects.
*European Community Project.*
**def.** (abbr.) default.
**def.** (abbr.) defense / defence.
**def.** (abbr.) deferred.
**def.** (abbr.) definite.
**DEFCON** (abbr.) DEFense CONdition.
*Ordnance.*
**DEFRA** Department for Environment, Food & Rural Affairs (G.B.).
**DEFT** Direct Epifluorescent Filter Technique.
*Microbiology.*
**deg.** (abbr.) degree / degrees.
*Mathematics; Metrology.*
**2DEG** two-Dimensional Electron Gas.
*Physics.*
**DEGs** Degenerins.
*Neurobiology; Neurology; Medicine.*
**DEI** Dizionario Enciclopedico Italiano.
**DEIH**; **D.E.I.H.** Diplôme d'Etat d'Infirmière Hospitalière (France).
**DEIS** Draft Environmental Impact Statement.
**Del.** (abbr.) Delaware (U.S.A.).
Also: **DE**.
**Del.** (abbr.) Delegate.

**del**; **del.** (abbr.) delete.
*Computer Technology.*
**del.** (abbr.) deletion.
**DEL** The airport code for Delhi, India.
**del** (abbr.) delta.
*Electronics; Geology; Mathematics; Science.*
**DELHP** Division on Education, Labor, and Human Performance (U.S.A.).
**DELS** Division on Earth and Life Studies (U.S.A.).
**delv'd** (abbr.) delivered.
Also: **dd.**; **dld**.
**DEM** Data-Entry Machine.
**dem.** (abbr.) demand.
**DEM** DEModulator.
*Electronics* - In electronics demodulator is also known as: Decommutator.
*Telecommunications.*
**dem.** (abbr.) demurrage.
Also: **demur**.
**DEM**; **D.E.M.** Détection Electro-Magnétique.
**DEM** Deutsche Mark.
Also: **DM**.
Now: EURO/EUR (€). Became ECU (European Single Currency) with effect from January 2002).
**DEM** Diethyl Maleate.
DEM is used mainly in flavorings.
*Organic Chemistry.*
**DEM** Digital Elevation Map.
*Earth and Planetary Science.*
**DEM** Digital Elevation Model.
For further details see under: **DEMs**.
**Demarrage** Development of multimedia applications in remote sensing, risk assessment, geography and environment.
**DEMETER** Development of a European Multi-model Ensemble System for Seasonal to Interannual Predictions.
*European Union Project.*
**DEMOD.** (abbr.) DEMODulator.
For further details see under: **DEM**.
**DEMR** Department of Energy, Mines and Resources (Canada).
**DEMS** Débit Expiratoire Maximum Seconde.
French initialism meaning: Timed Vital Capacity.
*Medicine.*
**DEMS** defensively equipped merchant ship.
navire de commerce doté d'un équipment défensif.
**DEMS** Digital Electronic Message System (Service).
**DEMs** Digital Elevation Models.
*Geophysics and Planetary Physics; Oceanography.*
**demur.** (abbr.) demurrage.
Also: **dem**.
**Den**. (abbr.) Denmark.
Also: **Dk.**; **DA**.
**DEN** Department of ENergy (G.B.).
**DEN** The airport code for Stapleton International, Denver, Colorado, U.S.A.
**DENI** Department of Education for Northern Ireland.
**denom.** (abbr.) denomination.
**dent** (abbr.) dental; dentist; dentistry.
**dep.** (abbr.) department.
Also: **dept.**
**dep.** (abbr.) dependent.
**dep.** (abbr.) deposit.
**dep.** (abbr.) deputy.
**DEP** Diethylphthalate.
DEP is used mainly in insecticides and perfumes.
*Organic Chemistry.*
**DEPC** Diethyl Pyrocarbonate.
DEPC is used mainly as a fermentation inhibitor.
*Organic Chemistry.*
**Dep.Ctf.** (abbr.) Deposit Certificate.
**DEP effect** Dielectrophoresis effect.
**DEPEX** deployment exercise.
exercice de déploiement.
**depr.** (abbr.) depreciation.
**DEPS**; **D.E.P.S.** Dernier Entré, Premier Sorti.
French acronym meaning: Last In, First Out (L.I.F.O.).
**DEPS** Division on Engineering and Physical Sciences (U.S.A.).
**dept.** (abbr.) department.
Also: **dep.**
**DEQ** Delivered Ex Quay.
*Business; Commerce; International Trade.*
**DER** DEgeneration Reaction.
**der** (abbr.) derivative.
Also: **deriv.**
*Chemistry; Mathematics.*
**der.** (abbr.) derivato.
Italian abbreviation meaning: by-product.
*Commerce.*
**DER** *Drosophila* Epidermal growth factor Receptor.
**DERA** Defence Evaluation and Research Agency (G.B.).
With effect from July 2001 DERA has become G.B.'s largest independent science and technology agency.
For further details see under: **DST**.
**deriv.** (abbr.) derivative.
Also: **der.**
*Chemistry; Mathematics.*
**DERV** Diesel Engined Road Vehicle.

**DES** Data Encryption Standard; Data Encryption System.

**DES** décharge électrostatique.
electrostatic discharge (ESD).

**DES** Delivered Ex Ship.
*Business; Commerce; International Trade.*

**DES** Density of Electronic States.

**DES** DEterminant Séculaire.

**DES** Diethylstilbestrol.
$C_{18}H_{20}O_2$ - Diethylstilbestrol, which is also known as stilbestrol, is a crystalline, nonsteroid estrogen used for natural estrogenic hormones replacement in therapeutic treatments.
*Biochemistry.*

**DES; D.E.S.** Diplôme d'Etudes Supérieures (France).

**DES** Division of Earth Sciences.
Of the U.S. National Research Council.

**DES** Division of Environmental Sciences.
Of the U.S. National Science Foundation.

**Desat.** (abbr.) Desaturation.

**DESG; D.E.S.G.** Diplôme d'Etudes Scientifiques Générales (France).

**DEST; D.E.S.T.** Diplôme d'Etudes Supérieures Techniques (France).

**DESTEMA** DEvelopment of STEels for non-polluting MAnufacturing.
*European Community Project; Industrial Manufacture; Materials Technology.*

**DESY** Deutsches Elektronen SYnchrotron (Germany).

**DET** Data-Entry Terminal.
*Computer Technology.*

**det.** (abbr.) detached.

**det.** (abbr.) detachment.
In geology, detachment is also known as: décollement.
*Geology.*

**det.** (abbr.) detachment.
*Military Science.*

**det.** (abbr.) detail.
*Military Science.*

**det.** (abbr.) determine.

**DET** The airport code for Detroit City, Michigan, U.S.A.

**DETAB** (abbr.) DEcision TABle.
*Computer Programming.*

**DETCs** Dendritic Epidermal T Cells.
Activated DETCs produce KGFs and chemokines.
*Cell Biology; Immunology; Molecular Genetics; Tissue Repair.*
For further details see under: **KGFs**.

**detd.** (abbr.) determined.

**DETDA** Diethyl Toluene Diamine.

**DETR** Department of Environment, Transport and the Regions (G.B.).

**DETRASFA** distress phase.
phase de détresse.

**dett.** (abbr.) dettagliante.
Italian abbreviation meaning: retailer; retail dealer.

**dett.** (abbr.) dettaglio.
Italian abbreviation meaning: retail. Also: detail.
*Commerce; General.*

**DEUS** Developing EUropean SMEs.
*European Community Project.*

**DEUS TRAINET** Danish Enterprise University Systems TRAIning NETwork.

**dev.** (abbr.) development.

**dev.** (abbr.) deviation.

**DEV** Duck Embryo (rabies) Vaccine.

**DEVAL** DELTA EVALuation.
*European Community Project.*

**Devon.** (abbr.) Devonshire (G.B.).

**DEW** 1. defensive electronic warfare [obsolete].
1. guerre électronique défensive [obsolète].
2. directed energy weapon.
2. arme à énergie dirigée.

**DEW line** Distant Early Warning line.
*Military Science.*

**DEXA** Dual Energy X-ray Absorptiometry.
*Endocrinology; Medicine; Metabolism; Molecular Physiology; Visceral Obesity.*

**DF** Damage-Free.

**DF** Data Field.
Data field refers to the space in the computer main memory where records are contained.
*Computer Programming.*

**DF** Dataflow / data flow.
*Computer Programming.*

**DF** Dead Freight.

**DF** 1. defensive fire.
1. tir défensif.
2. direction finding.
2. radiogoniométrie.

**DF** Destination Field.
*Computer Technology.*

**DF** Device Flag.
*Computer Technology.*

**DF** Direction Finder.
*Navigation.*

**DF** Doctor of Forestry.

**DF** Don't Fragment.
*Computers.*

**df** (abbr.) draft / draught.
*Civil Engineering; Engineering; Fluid Mechanics;*

*Mechanical Devices; Metallurgy; Naval Architecture.*
**D/F**; **d/f** drinking fountain.
**DFA** Deposit Fund Account.
*Business; Commerce; Finance.*
**DFA** Deterministic Finite Automation.
*Computer Science.*
**DFA** Doctor of Fine Arts.
**DFAIT** Department of Foreign Affairs & International Trade (Canada).
**DFB laser diodes** Distributed Feedback laser diodes.
**DFC** Data Flow Control.
**DFC** Development Finance Company.
**DFC** Distinguished Flying Cross.
**DFCG** (Association Nationale des) Directeurs Financiers et de Contrôle de Gestion (France).
*French Association.*
**DFD** data fusion demonstrator.
démonstrateur de fusion de données.
**DFDEL** (abbr.) Deferred Delivery.
**DFE** Department For Education (London, G.B.)
**DFELL** Duke Free-Electron Laser Laboratory.
**DFG** Deutsche Forschungsgemeinschaft (Germany).
DFG is Germany's main research funding agency.
**DFG** Diode Function Generator.
*Electronics.*
**DFL** Degree of Financial Leverage.
*Business; Finance.*
**DFL** Department of Foreign Languages.
At the U.S. Air Force Academy.
**DFM**; **D.F.M.** Director of Freight Movement.
**DFM** Distinguished Flying Medal.
**DFMO** Difluoromethylornithine.
*Biochemistry; Clinical Pharmacology; Molecular Pharmacology.*
**DFO** Department of Fisheries and Oceans (Canada).
**DFP** Diisopropyl Phosphorofluoridate.
$C_6H_{14}FO_3P$ - Diisopropyl phosphorofluoridate is also known as diisopropyl fluorophosphate; diisopropyl fluorophosphonate; fluostigmine; isopropyl-fluophosphate. It is used mainly as a cholinergic drug in eye diseases.
*Pharmacology.*
**DFR** Dihydroflavonol Reductase.
*Natural Products Research; Plant Biology.*
**DFS** Decoherence-Free Subspace.
*Physics.*
**2dFSurvey** 2-degree Field Survey.
*Physics.*
**DFT**; **dFt** Discrete Fourier Transform.
**DFT/A** Draft Attached.
*Business; Commerce.*
**DFT/C** Clean Draft.
*Business; Commerce.*
**DFT calculations** Density Functional Theory calculations.
*Physics; Steam; Reforming Processes.*
**DFW** The airport code for Dallas/Ft. Worth International Airport, Texas, U.S.A.
**DFWL** direct fire weapons line.
ligne des armes à tir direct.
**Dfz2 protein** Drosophila frizzled 2 protein.
*Developmental Biology.*
**dg.** decigram / decigramme.
*Metrology.*
**DG** Dentate Gyrus.
**dG** deoxyguanosine.
**DG** Differential Generator.
*Electricity.*
**DG** Directeur Général.
French initialism meaning: Chief Executive Officer; Managing Director.
**DG** Direction Générale.
French initialism meaning: Headquarters.
**D.G.**; **DG** Director General.
**2DG** 2-Deoxy-D-Glucose.
**3DG** 3-Deoxyglucosone.
**DGA** Direction Générale des Armements (France).
**DGAC** French Civil Aviation Authority (France).
**DG Bank** Deutsche Genossenschaftsbank.
*German Bank.*
**DGCCRF** Direction Générale de la Consommation, de la Concurrence et de la Répression des Fraudes.
Of the Ministère de l'Economie et des Finances (France).
**DGCR** DiGeorge Syndrome minimal Critical Region.
*Cancer; Genome Research; Genetics.*
**DGDG** Digalactosyl Diacyl Glycerol.
**DGE** Doppler Gravity Experiment.
*Lunar Research.*
**DGI** digital geographic information.
informations géographiques numériques.
**DGI** Direction Générale des Impôts.
French initialism meaning: General Tax Authority; Inland Revenue.
**DGLF** Délégation Générale à la Langue Française (Paris, France).
**DGM** Deputy General Manager.
**DGP** Senior Defence Group on Proliferation.
Groupe defense de haut niveau sur la prolifération.
**DGPI** Direzione Generale Produzione Industriale (Rome, Italy).
**DGRST** Délégation Générale à la Recherche Scientifique et Technique (France).

**DGS** Density Gradient Sedimentation.
**DGT** Direction Générale des Télécommunications (France).
**DGZ** Desired Ground Zero.
*Ordnance.*
**DGZ** Deutsche Girozentrale (Germany).
DGZ is specialized in public-sector lending.
*German Bank.*
**DH** Dbl Homology.
*Biochemistry; Biophysics; Molecular Genetics; Neurology; Neuroscience; Signal Transduction.*
**DH**; **dh** Delayed Hypersensitivity.
DH is a reactivity in a sensitized person that occurs several hours after contact with the allergen.
*Immunology.*
**DH** dual-hatted (post).
(poste) à double fonction.
**DHA** departure holding area.
départ de la zone d'attente.
**DHA** Dihydroxyacetone.
Dihydroxyacetone, which is also known as: dihydroxypropanone, is used in medicine, cosmetics, and in fungicides.
*Organic Chemistry.*
**DHA** Double Hemagglutinin.
**DHAS** Dehydroepiandrosterone Sulfate.
**DHase** Dehydrogenase.
*Enzymology.*
**DHBV** Duck Hepatitis B Virus.
*Virology.*
**DHCP**; **Dhcp** Dynamic Host Configuration Protocol (Cisco).
**DHEA** Dehydroepiandrosterone.
*Age-related Disorders; Anti-Aging Drugs; Endocrinology; Reproductive Medicine.*
**DHEAS** Dehydroepiandrosterone Sulfate (serum).
*Anti-aging Medicine; Caloric Restrictions.*
**DHF** Dengue Hemorragic Fever.
*Infectious Diseases; Medicine.*
**DHFR** Dihydrofolate Reductase.
*Biochemistry; Enzymology; Medicine; Molecular Microbiology.*
**DHFR-TS** Dihydrofolate Reductase-Thymidylate Synthase.
*Biomedical Research; Chemistry; Malaria Parasites.*
**DHg**; **D.Hg** Doctor of Hygiene.
**DHGP** German Human Genome Program.
**DHI** Danish Hydraulic Institute.
*Urban Wastewater.*
**DHL** Doctor of Hebrew Letters; Doctor of Hebrew Literature.
**DHLA** Dihydrolipoic Acid.
**DHLRI** Dorothy M.Davis Heart and Lung Research Institute.
At the Ohio State University (U.S.A.).
**DHOD** deputy head of delegation.
chef adjoint de délégation.
**DHPLC** Denaturing High-Pressure Liquid Chromatography.
**DHPys** 5,6-Dihydropyrimidises.
**D/H ratio** Deuterium/Hydrogen ratio.
**DHS** Department of Homeland Security.
Created in 2002 (U.S.A.).
**DHS** Desert Hot Springs.
**DHS** Dihydrostreptomycin.
$C_{21}H_{41}O_{12}N_7$ - Dihydrostreptomycin is essentially a derivative of streptomycin.
*Microbiology.*
**DHSP** Directorate of Health Standards Programs (U.S.A.).
**DHT** Dihydrotestosterone.
*Endocrinology.*
**DHT** 5,6-Dihydrothymine.
**DHU** 5,6-Dihydrouracil.
**DHy**; **D.Hy** Doctor of Hygiene.
**DI** Decreto Interministeriale.
Italian initialism meaning: Interdepartmental Decree.
**DI** Détroit Inférieur.
French initialism meaning: Inferior Strait (of the pelvis).
*Medicine.*
**DI** Device Independence.
*Computer Technology.*
**DI**; **D.I.** Diabetes Insipidus.
Diabetes insipidus is actually due to a dysfunction of the hypothalamus.
*Medicine.*
**D.I.** Disposable Income.
**DI** division d'infanterie.
infantry division (ID 2.).
**DI**; **D.I.** Drill Instructor.
**di.**; **dia.** (abbr.) diameter.
**DIA** Defense Intelligence Agency (U.S.A.).
**Dia** Dichiarazione d'inizio attività.
Italian acronym meaning: beginning of activity declaration.
**DIA** Direzione Investigativa Antimafia (Italy).
**DIA** Distance Interatomique.
**DIA**; **D.I.A.** Division d'Infanterie Alpine (France).
**DIA** Due In Assets.
*Business; Finance.*
**DIABLO** Direct IAP-binding Protein with Low pI.

*Cancer Research; Molecular Biology; Pharmaceutical Research; Structural Biology.*
For further details see under: **IAPs**.

**Diad** Delivery information acquisition device.
Developed by United Parcel Service to capture delivery information electronically by drivers at the point of arrival.
*Hand-held Computers.*

**diag** (abbr.) diagonal; diagnosis; diagram.

**dial**. (abbr.) dialect.

**DIAL** DIfferential Absorption by Lidar.
*Environmental Technology; Medicine; Science.*

**DIANE** Design, Implementation and operation of a distributed ANnotation Environment.
*European Community Project.*

**DIANE** Direct Information Access Network for Europe.

**DIATM** Delegazione Italiana di Assistenza Tecnico Militare in Marocco.

**DIB** Directory Information Base.

**DIBIT** Department of Biological and Technological Research.
At San Raffaele Hospital (Milan, Italy).

**DIBs** Diffuse IS absorption Bands.
*Astrophysics; Space Science.*

**DiC** Dicarboxylate Carrier.
*Mitochondrial Carriers.*

**DIC** Differential Interference Contrast.

**DIC** Disseminated Intravascular Coagulation.

**DIC** Dissolved Inorganic Carbon.

**DICASS** DIrectional Command Activated Sonobuoy System.

**DICBR** Division of Intramural Clinical and Biological Research.

**DICE** Digital Interface Countermeasures Equipment.

**DICONSTAFF** directing, controlling staff.
état-major de direction et de contrôle.

**DICS** Deficit Immunitario Combinato Severo.
Italian initialism meaning: Severe Combined Immunodeficiency.

**dict**. (abbr.) Dictionary.
*Computer Programming; Linguistics.*

**DID** Direct Inward Dialing.
*Telecommunications.*

**DIDA** Diisodecyl Adipate.
DIDA is used mainly as a plasticizer for polymers.
*Organic Chemistry.*

**DIDC** Depository Institutions Deregulation Committee (U.S.A.).
*Business; Economics; Finance.*

**DIDP** Diisodecyl Phthalate.
DIDP is a clear liquid boiling al 250-257°C and used as a plasticizer.
*Organic Chemistry.*

**DIE** Delegazione Italiana Esperti (Albania).

**DIEB** Department of the Interior Energy Board.

**DIF** Data-Interchange Format.
*Computer Technology.*

**dif.** (abbr.) difetto.
Italian abbreviation meaning: defect; flaw; imperfection.

**diff.** (abbr.) differenziale.
Italian abbreviation meaning: differential.
*Mathematics; Mechanical Engineering.*

**DIFFERENCE** DIssemination and Facilitation for European Research in Selected chains.
*European Community Project.*

**Diff.Serv.** (abbr.) Differentiated Services.
Diff. Serv. is a standard of I.E.T.F.
For further details see under: **I.E.T.F.**

**DIG** Deputy Inspector-General.

**dig.** (abbr.) digest.

**DIGISAT** advanced DIGItal SATellite broadcasting and interactive services.
*European Community Project.*

**DIH** droit international humanitaire.
international humanitarian law (IHL).

**DIHT** German Chamber of Industry and Commerce (Germany).

**dil.** (abbr.) dilute.

**DILCS** dedicated intelligence loop-circuit system.
système à circuits en boucle réservés au renseignement.

**DILS** Domestic Indexed Lira Swap.

**dim.** (abbr.) dimension.

**DIM**; **D.I.M.** Division d'Infanterie Motorisée (France).

**DIMACS** DIscrete MAthematics and Computer Science.

**DIME** Dual Independent Map Encoder.

**DIMMI project** Digital Interactive Multimedia Made in Italy project (Italy).

**dimmi** The above acronym was coined using the Italian word "dimmi" which means: tell me.

**DIN** Do It Now.

**DINFOS** Defense INFOrmation School (U.S.A.).

**din gene** damage-inducible gene.
*Genetics.*

**DINKS** Double Income, No Kids (U.S.A.).

**dinucl.** (abbr.) dinucleotide.
*Biochemistry.*

**DIO** Department of Interdisciplinary Oncology.
Ministry of South Florida (U.S.A.).

**Dio** The above acronym was coined accidentally using the Italian word: Dio which means God.
**DIO mice** Diet-Induced Obese mice.
*Metabolic Diseases; Obesity.*
**diP** Diphosphate.
*Chemistry.*
**DIP** Dissolved Inorganic Phosphorus.
**DIP** Dual In-line Package.
DIP is an enclosure containing integrated circuits.
*Electronics.*
**DIPA** Delta-Interacting Protein A.
**DIPA** Diisopropanolamine.
DIPA is used as an emulsifying agent for insecticides and polishes.
*Organic Chemistry.*
**DIPC** Diisopropyl Carbodiimide.
**DIPJ** Distal Interphalangeal Joint.
**DIPP Study** DIabetes Prediction and Prevention Study (Finland).
The DIPP was launched in 1994.
**DIP switch** Dual In-line Package switch.
*Computer Technology.*
**Dir.**; **dir.** (abbr.) Director; directory.
**DIRAC** (abbr.) DIRect ACcess.
Direct access, also known as Random Access is actually the ability to write or read data anywhere within a storage device regardless of the location of data previously accessed.
*Computer Technology.*
**DIRANI** 1. direction de l'animation d'exercise [FR].
exercise directing staff [FR].
**DIRBE** Diffuse Infrared Background Experiment.
*Astronomy; Astrophysics; Cosmology.*
**DIRLAUTH** direct liaison authorized.
liaison directe autorisée.
**DIRP** Division of Intramural Research Programs (U.S.A.).
Of the U.S. NIH.
*Research Programs.*
For further details see under: **NIH**.
**DIRPAT** Director Permanent (Exercise) Analysis Team [obsolete].
directeur de l'équipe permanente d'analyse (des exercices) [obsolète].
**DIS** Defense Investigative Service (U.S.A.).
**dis**; **dis.** (abbr.) discharge.
**dis.** (abbr.) discount.
**DIS** Disseminated Intravasculate Coagulation.
**dis**; **dis.** (abbr.) distance.
**DIS** Distributed Interactive Simulation.
DIS was invented in 1983 by the U.S. Department of Defense.
*Simulation Software.*
**DIS** Draft International Standards.
**DIS** Driver Information Systems.
*European Community.*
**DISA** Data Interchange Standards Association.
**DISBEE** digital intermediate-speed bulk encryption equipment.
matériel numérique de chiffrement global à moyenne vitesse.
**DISC** Death-Inducing Signal Complex.
*Apoptosis; Caspases; Human Genetics; Immunology.*
**disc.** (abbr.) discount.
Also: **disct.**; **dist.**
**DISC** Disrupted In Schizophrenia.
*Medical Research; Psychiatry; Psychological Medicine.*
**DISC** Domestic International Sales Corporation.
*International Business.*
**DISC-1** Diagnostic Interview Schedule for Children.
*Medicine; Psychiatry.*
**DISCLIMAX** (abbr.) DISturbance Climax.
*Ecology.*
**DISCOURSE** Design and Interactive Specification of COURSEware.
*European Community.*
**disct.** (abbr.) discount.
Also: **disc.**; **dist.**
**DISE** direct intelligence support element.
élément de soutien direct du renseignement.
**DISMA**; **Disma** Distributori Italiani Strumenti Musicali e Artigianato.
DISMA is located in Milan, Italy.
**displ.** (abbr.) display.
*Computer Science; Electronics.*
**DisS** Disturbed Soil.
*Soil Types.*
For further details see under: **IMP** (Imager for Mars Pathfinder) and **ASI/MET experiment** (Atmospheric Structure Investigation / METeorology experiment).
**DISSUB** disabled / distressed submarine.
sous-avion en avarie / en détresse.
**DIST** Direction de l'Information Scientifique et Technique (France).
**dist.** (abbr.) discount.
Also: **disct.**; **disc.**
**dist.** (abbr.) distinguished.
**DISTAFF** directing staff.
1a. direction de l'animation d'exercice (DIRANI) [FR].
1b. état-major de direction d'exercice.
**DistEdNet** Global Distance Education Net.

Of the World Bank.
*Human Development.*
**DIT** Diet-Induced Thermogenesis.
*Anti-obesity Therapies; Biomedicine; Medicine.*
**DIT** Diiodotyrosine.
*Endocrinology.*
**DIT**; **Dit** Dual Income Tax.
**DIU** Data Information Unit.
**DIV** DIsposition de Valence.
**div.** (abbr.) divided.
**div.** (abbr.) dividend.
Also: **divd.**
**div.** (abbr.) division.
*Computer Programming; Mathematics; Military Science; Systematics.*
**div.** (abbr.) divorced.
**DIVA** Digital Inquiry - Voice Answerback.
*Computers.*
**DIVA** Digital Intravenous Angiography.
*Medicine.*
**divd.** (abbr.) dividend.
Also: **div**.
**DIVINE** Deployment of Interpersonal Videoconferencing systems on IBC NEtworks.
*European Community Project.*
**divs.** (abbr.) dividends.
**DIY** Do-It-Yourself.
**diz.** (abbr.) dizionario.
Italian abbreviation meaning: dictionary.
**DJ** Disc Jockey.
**DJ** District Judge.
**DJ** Djibouti.
**DJ** Doctor of Jurisprudence.
**DJ** Dow-Jones.
*Business; Finance.*
**DJA** Dow-Jones Averages.
*Business; Finance.*
**DJD** Degenerative Joint Disease.
*Medicine.*
**DJF** December-January-February.
**DJI** Dow-Jones Index.
*Business; Finance.*
**DJIA** Dow-Jones Industrial Average.
**dk.** (abbr.) dark; deck; dock.
**Dk** (abbr.) Denmark.
Also: **Den.**; **DA**.
**DKB** Dai-Ichi Kangyo Bank.
Head Office: Tokyo, Japan.
*Japanese Bank.*
**DKFZ** The Deutsches Krebsforschungszentrum (Germany).
German Cancer Research Center.
**dkg**; **dkg.** dekagram; dekagrams.
**DKK** Danish Krone.
Also: **Dkr**.
*Currencies.*
**dkl**; **dkl.** dekaliter; dekaliters.
**dkm**; **dkm.** dekameter; dekameters.
**DL** Danger List.
**DL** Data Link.
Data Link, also known as Information Link; Tie-Line; Tie-Link; Communication Link; consists of the equipment for automatically transmitting and receiving information.
*Telecommunications.*
**DL** Day Letter.
**DL** dead light.
**dl**; **dl.** deciliter; deciliters.
**DL** The airline code for Delta Air Lines.
**DL** demarcation line.
ligne de démarcation.
**DL** Disturbance Lines.
**DL** Dorsolateral.
*Anatomy;* Referring to the back and the side.
**DL** Doxorubicin and Lomustine.
*Oncology.*
**DL50** Dose Léthale 50.
French initialism meaning: Lethal Dose 50; Median Lethal Dose.
*Toxicology.*
**DLA** data link address.
adresse de liaison de données.
**DLA** Defense Logistics Agency (U.S.A.).
**DLA** Delaware Library Association (U.S.A.).
**DLA model** Diffusion-Limited-Aggregation model.
*Engineering; Growth Atomistic Mechanisms; Materials Science; Physics.*
**DLB** division légère blindée.
light armoured division.
**DLBCL** Diffuse Large B-Cell Lymphoma.
A common lymphoid cancer in adults which causes death in about 50% of affected persons.
*Gene Expression.*
**DLC** Data Link Control.
*Data Communications.*
**DLC**; **dlc** Deadweight Loading Capacity.
**DLC1** Dynein Light Chain.
*Medical Research.*
**dld.** (abbr.) delivered.
Also: **dd.**; **delv'd**.
**DLE** Data Link Escape (character).
*Data Communications.*
**DLE** Disseminated Lupus Erythematosus.
*Medicine.*
**DLG** Discs-Large.
DLG is a fly protein.

*Developmental Neuroscience.*
**DLG maps** Digital Line Group maps.
**DLGN** Dorsal Lateral Geniculate Nucleus.
**DLH** Delhi's Lieutenant Governor (India).
**DLH** Direct Labour Hours.
**DLI** Digital Library Initiative - NASA's.
The DLI is a program for computer scientists that began in 1994. It is funded by the U.S. National Science Foundation.
*Digital Libraries; Information Sciences.*
**DLI**; **D.L.I.** Division Légère d'Intervention (France).
**DLL** Data Link Layer.
*Computer Technology.*
**DLM** depot-level maintenance.
maintenance à l'échelon dépôt.
**DLM**; **D.L.M.** Division Légère Motorisée (France).
**DLMO** Dim Light Melatonin Onset.
*Extraocular Circadian Phototransduction; Human Chronobiology; Psychiatry.*
**DLNR** Department of Land and Natural Resources (Hawaii).
**DLO** detachment liaison officer.
officier de liaison du détachement.
**DLO** Dispatch Loading Only.
**DLP** Diffusing Light Photography.
*Ripple-Wave Turbulence.*
**DLPFC** Dorsolateral Prefrontal Cortex.
*Medicine; Psychiatry; Psychology; Radiology.*
**dlr.** (abbr.) dealer.
**dlr.** (abbr.) dollar.
Also: **dol.**; **D**.
*Currencies.*
**DLR** German Aerospace Center (Germany).
DLR deals also with Germany's Space Program.
For further details see under: **DARA**.
**DLRP** data link reference point.
point de référence de transmission de données (PRTD).
**DLS** Debt Liquidation Schedule.
*Business; Commerce; Finance.*
**DLS** Doctor of Library Science.
**dls.** (abbr.) dollars.
Also: **dolls.**
*Currencies.*
**DLSA** Defense Legal Services Agency (U.S.A.).
**DLT** Data Loop Transceiver.
*Data Communications.*
**DLTP** defence long-term planning.
plans de défense à long terme.
**Dlvo.** (abbr.) Documento legislativo.
**DM** Data Management.
*Computer Programming.*
**DM** Data Manipulation.
Data manipulation actually refers to the sorting, merging, and editing functions.
*Computer Programming.*
**DM** Debit Memorandum.
**dm**; **dm.** decimeter; decimeters.
**DM** Decreto Ministeriale.
Italian initialism meaning: Minister's Decree.
**DM** deployability and mobility.
aptitude au déploiement et mobilité.
**DM** Destroyer Minelayer.
*Military; Weapons.*
**DM** Deutschmark / Deutsche Mark.
Also: **DEM**.
Now: EURO/EUR (€). Became ECU (European single currency) with effect from january 2002.
*Currencies.*
**DM** Diabetes Mellitus.
Diabetes Mellitus is a metabolic disorder due to a deficiency of insulin secretion by the pancreas.
*Medicine.*
**DM** Diastolic Murmur.
*Medicine.*
**DM** District Manager.
**DM** Dry Matter.
*Medicine.*
**DM** Myotonic Dystrophy.
DM is a congenital disease.
*Medicine; Pathology.*
**DM1** Myotonic Dystrophy type 1.
*Molecular Medicine.*
**DMA** Defense Mapping Agency (U.S.A.).
Of the U.S. DOD.
For further details see under: **DOD**.
**DMA** Differential Mobility Analyzer.
*Chemistry.*
**DMA** Dimethylamine.
$(CH_3)_2NH$ - DMA is used mainly in pharmaceuticals, dyes, and surfactants.
*Organic Chemistry.*
**DMA** Dimethylarsenic Acid.
**DMA**; **dma** Direct-Memory Access.
*Computer Technology.*
**DMA** Disodium Methylarsonate.
Disodium Methylarsonate, also known as Disodium Methane Arsonate, is used mainly in pharmaceuticals and as an herbicide.
*Organic Chemistry.*
**DMA** Dynamic Mechanical Analysis.
**DMAA** Direct Mail Advertising Association.
**DMAC** Direct-Memory Access Channel.
*Computer Technology.*

**DMAHP** Dystrophia Myotonica-Associated Homeodomain Protein.
**DMB** datum marker buoy.
bonée marqueur.
**DMC** Developmental Medicine Center.
At Children's Hospital, Boston, U.S.A.
**DMC** Dichlorophenyl Methyl Carbinol.
**DMC** Digital Micro-Circuit.
**DMC** Dimethyl Carbonate.
DMC also known as: Methyl Carbonate is used mainly in organic synthesis and as a solvent.
*Organic Chemistry.*
**DMC** Direct Manufacturing Cost.
*Business; Commerce.*
**DMD** Dark Mantling Deposit.
*Astronomy; Planetary Geoscience; Terrestrial Physics.*
**DMD**; **D.M.D.** Doctor of Dental Medicine.
**DMD** Duchenne type Muscular Dystrophy.
DMD is an incurable human genetic disease which affects particularly boys.
*Muscular Dystrophy.*
**DME** Decentralized Market Economy.
**DME** Distance-Measuring Equipment.
*Navigation.*
**DME** Dropping Mercury Electrode.
*Physical Chemistry.*
**DMEM** Department of Marine Ecology and Microbiology.
Of NERI, Denmark.
For further details see under: **NERI**.
**DMEM** Dulbecco's Minimum Essential Medium.
**DMEs** polymorphic Drug-Metabolizing Enzymes.
*Medicine; Pharmacogenetics; Pharmacology.*
**DMEWSG** Director MEWSG.
directeur du MEWSG.
**DMF** Decayed, Missing and Filled (referring to teeth).
**DMF** Digital Matched Filters.
**DMF** Dimethylformamide.
**DMF** Dimethylfuran.
**DMFT** Dynamical Mean Field Theory.
*Astronomy; Materials Theory; Physics.*
**DMG** Deutsche Morgan Grenfell (Germany).
**DMI technology** Desktop Management Interface technology.
DMI is a technology that defines a standard mechanism for accessing and configuring data in any piece of hardware or software.
*Network Management Software.*
**DMI**; **D.M.I.** Division Motorisée d'Infanterie (France).
**DM Industry** Document Management Industry.
**DMJS** December, March, June, September.
*Securities.*
**DML** Data-Manipulation Language.
For further details see under: **DM** (Data Manipulation).
**DML** Dimyristoyl Lecithin.
**DML** Doctor of Dental Medicine.
**D.M.L.** Doctor of Modern Languages.
**DMM** Digital Multimeter.
**DMMC** Dublin Molecular Medicine Centre (Ireland).
**DMMP** Dimethyl Methylphosphonate.
**DMN** division multinationale.
multinational division (MND 2.).
**DMNPAA** 2,5-Dimethyl-4-*p*-Nitrophenylazoanisole.
**Dmo** Developing markets operations.
**DMOS** Diffused Metal-Oxide Semiconductor.
*Electronics.*
**DMPA** Dimyristoylphosphatidic Acid.
**DMPI** desired mean point of impact.
point moyen d'impact souhaité.
**DMPK** Drug Metabolism and Pharmacokinetics.
**DMPK** Dystrophia Myotonica Protein Kinase.
*Genome Mapping; Medicine; Molecular Biology; Molecular Genetics.*
**$DMQ_9$ intermediate** Demethoxy-$Q_9$ intermediate.
*Aging; Ecology; Evolutionary Biology.*
**DMR** Differential Microwave Radiometer.
**DMRs** Differentially Methylated Regions.
*Imprinting Mechanisms; Molecular Medicine.*
**DMS** Data Management System.
*Data Communications.*
**DMS** Dimethyl Sulfide.
**DMS** Dipole Moment Surface.
*Astronomy; Chemistry; Physics.*
**DMS** document management system.
système de gestion des documents.
**DMSO** Dimethyl Sulfoxide.
$(CH_3)_2SO$ - DMSO is used as a local analgesic, as a solvent, and in chemical reactions.
*Organic Chemistry.*
**DMSP** Defense Meteorological Satellite Program.
**DMSP** Dimethylsulfoniopropionate.
**DMST** Division of Military Science and Technology (U.S.A.).
**DMT** Dimethyl Terephthalate.
Dimethyl Terephthalate is used mainly to make polyester fibers.
*Organic Chemistry.*
**DMT** 4-Dimethyltryptamine.
*Hallucinogen.*
**DMT** Director of Military Training.

**DMTS technique** Delayed-Matching-To-Sample technique (or procedure).
*Behavior.*
**DMU** Dimethylolurea.
Dimethylolurea is used mainly in plywood manufacture.
*Organic Chemistry.*
**DMX** Document Manager for Microsoft Exchange.
**DMZ** Demilitarized Zone.
*Military Science.*
**DMZ explants** Dorsal Marginal Zone explants.
*Medical Science.*
**DN** Debit Note.
*Business; Commerce; Finance.*
**DN** Directorate for Nature Management (Norway).
**DNA** Defense Nuclear Agency (U.S.A.).
**DNA** Deoxyribonucleic Acid.
DNA is the carrier of genetic information.
*Biochemistry.*
**DNA** Digital Network Architecture.
**DNA** Direttore/Direzione Nazionale degli Armamenti (Italy).
**DNA** Direzione Nazionale Antimafia (Italy).
Since October 1991.
**DNA** Does Not Apply.
**DNACI** DNA Copyright Institute (U.S.A.).
*DNA Copyright.*
**DNA-PK** DNA-activated Protein Kinase.
**DNAT** Division Nationale Antiterroriste (France).
**DNB** Den Norske Bank (Norway).
DNB is Norway's largest bank.
**DNB** Departure from Nucleate Boiling.
*Energy.*
**DNB** Dictionary of National Biography.
**DNB**; **D.N.B.** Diplomate of the National Board (of Medical Examiners).
**DNBA** Diplôme National des Beaux-Arts (France).
**DNBI** disease and non-battle injury (rate).
(taux de) maladies et blessures reçues hors combat.
**DNC** Democratic National Committee (U.S.A.).
**DNC** Direct Numerical Control.
*Computer Technology.*
**DNC** Distributed Numerical Control.
*Control Systems.*
**DNCS** data net control station.
station de contrôle du réseau de liaison de données.
**DNDI** Drugs for Neglected Diseases Initiative.
The DNDI was launched in New York in March 2002. Its aim is to create a not-for-profit pharmaceutical industry to develop and produce drugs for neglected diseases that afflict people in poor countries.
**Dnmt's** DNA methyltransferases.
*Cellular Biotechnology; Experimental Oncology; Hematology; Histology; Medical Embryology.*
**DNP** Deoxyribonucleoprotein.
*Biochemistry.*
**DNP** Dinitrophenol.
*Organic Chemistry.*
**DNP** Dynamic Nuclear Polarization.
*Applied Physics; Chemistry; Physics.*
**DNP-Ficoll** Dinitrophenyl-conjugated Ficoll.
*Immunology; Medical Biophysics; Medicine; Oncologic Pathology; Oncology.*
**DNP-KLH** Dinitrophenyl-conjugated Keyhole Limpet Hemocyanin.
*Immunology; Medical Biophysics; Medicine; Oncologic Pathology; Oncology.*
**DNR** Department of Natural Resources (U.S.A.).
**DNR** Do Not Reduce.
*Stock Exchange / Bourse.*
**DNR**; **D.N.R.** Do Not Resuscitate.
**DNRC** Division of Nutrition Research Coordination.
Of the U.S. NIDDK.
For further details see under: **NIDDK**.
**DNS** Democratic People's Alliance (RS).
Alliance démocratique du peuple (RS).
**DNS** Domain Name Service.
**DNS** Domain Name System (Microsoft).
**DN stage** Double Negative stage.
**DNT** Dinitrotoluene.
Dinitrotoluene is used mainly in dyes and explosives.
*Organic Chemistry.*
**DN thymocytes** Double-Negative thymocytes.
*Genetics; Immunology; Medicine; Microbiology; Pediatrics.*
**dNTPs** deoxynucleoside Triphosphates.
**DN values** Data Number values.
**DNVT** digital non-secure voice terminal.
terminal numérique en phonie non protégé.
**DNZ** Democratic People's Union (FbiH).
Union démocratique du peuple (FbiH).
**D/O** Delivery Order.
**DO** Densité Optique.
French acronym meaning: Optical Density.
*Optics.*
**$D_2O$** Deuterium Oxide (heavy water).
*Inorganic Chemistry.*
**DO** Dissolved Oxygen.
**DO**; **D.O.** Doctor of Optometry.
**DO**; **D.O.** Doctor of Osteopathy.

**DO** Dominica.
**DOA**; **D.O.A.** Dead On Arrival.
**DOA** Department Of Agriculture (U.S.A.).
**DOA** Department Of Aviation (Australia).
**DOA** Desired Order of Arrival.
**DOA** Dioctyl Adipate.
**DOALOS** Division for Ocean Affairs and the Law Of the Sea - U.N.
DOALOS has replaced: **OALOS** (Office for Ocean Affairs and the Law Of the Sea).
**DOAS analysis** Differential Optical Absorption Spectroscopy analysis.
*Analysis Techniques; Environmental Technology.*
**DOB**; **D.O.B.** Date Of Birth.
**DOB** Decade Of the Brain.
The U.S. Congress designated the 1990s the DOB. The proclamation was signed by President George Bush in July 1990.
*Brain Research; Neuroscience.*
**DOB** 1. deployment operating base.
1. base opérationnelle de déploiement.
2. depth of burst.
2. profondeur d'explosion.
3. dispersal operating base.
3. base opérationnelle de dispersion.
**DOC** Denominazione di Origine Controllata.
Italian acronym meaning: Authenticated Trade-Mark; Controlled Denomination of Origin.
**DOC** Department Of Commerce (U.S.A.).
**DOC** Department Of Communications (Canada).
**DOC** Detergent Deoxycholate.
**DOC** Dissolved Organic Carbon.
*Earth System Science.*
**DOC** Dissolved Oxygen Concentration.
*Biotechnology.*
**doc.** (abbr.) doctor.
Also: **Dr**.
**doc.** (abbr.) document.
**DOCERPO** DOped CERamic POwders.
Development of Doped Ceramic Powders and Processing for the Production of High Power - High Energy Non-Ohmic Resistors.
*European Community Project.*
**DOCSIS** Data Over Cable Service Interface Specification.
*Broadband Access by Cable.*
**DOCUP** DOCumenti Unici di Programmazione.
*European Community.*
**DOD** Department Of Defense (U.S.A.).
**DoE** Department of Education (U.S.A.).
**DOE** Department Of Energy (U.S.A.).
**DOE** Dyspnea On Extention.
*Medicine.*
**D-O events** Dansgaard-Oeschger events.
*Climatology; Environmental Science; Geological Sciences; Geocryology; Glaciology; Paleoceanography.*
**DOF** Degrees Of Freedom.
**D. of the Crown** Demesne of the Crown (G.B.).
**DOG** Days Of Grace.
*Business; Commerce.*
**DOG** Difference Of Gaussians.
*Applied Physics; Neural Computation.*
**DOI** Department Of the Interior (U.S.A.).
**DOI** Digital Object Identifier (AGU's).
For further details see under: **AGU**.
**DOI Foundation** (International) Digital Object Identifier Foundation.
Near Oxford, G.B. Established in 1998 with the help of major publishers.
**DoIT** Division of Information Technology.
**DOJ** Department Of Justice (U.S.A.).
**DOL** Department Of Labor (U.S.A.).
**DOL** dispensed operations location.
emplacement d'opérations dispersé.
**dol.** (abbr.) dollar.
Also: **dlr.**; **D**.
*Currencies.*
**DOLCE** digital on-line crypto equipment.
matériel numérique de chiffrement en ligne.
**dolce** The above acronym was coined accidentally using the Italian word dolce which means: sweet; gentle, mild; dulcet; soft (material); balmy (air).
**dolls.** (abbr.) dollars.
Also: **dls.**
**DOLMEN** service machine Development for an Open Long-term Mobile and fixed network Environment.
*European Community Project.*
**DOM** Départements (français) d'Outre-Mer.
French acronym meaning: French Overseas Departments.
**DOM** Dissolved Organic Matter.
**dom.** (abbr.) domestic; dominant; dominion.
**DOMES** Deep Ocean Mining and Environmental Study (U.S.A.).
**DO.M.IN.A.E.** DOnne Miglioramento INformazione Attraverso Europa.
*European Project.*
**DOMI program** Diseases Of the Most Impoverished program.
Undertaken by IVI.
For further details see under: **IVI**.
**DOMP** Département des opérations de maintien de la paix.
Department of Peacekeeping Operations (DPKO).

**DOMS** Diploma in Ophthalmic Medicine and Surgery.
**DOMSAT** (abbr.) DOMestic SATellite.
**DOM-TOM** Départements d'Outre-Mer - Territoires d'Outre-Mer.
French acronym meaning: French Overseas Departments - French Overseas Territories.
**DON**; **DoN** Department Of the Navy (U.S.A.).
**DON** Dissolved Organic Nitrogen.
**DOO** Departmental Organization Order.
**DOP** Degree Of Pyritization.
**DOP** Denominazione di Origine Protetta (Italy).
**DOP** Dioctyl Phthalate.
Dioctyl Phthalate also known as di-(2-ethylhexyl)phthalate is used mainly as a plasticizer.
*Organic Chemistry.*
**DOPAC** 3,4-Dihydroxyphenylacetic Acid.
**DOPE** Department Of Freshwater Ecology.
Of NERI, Denmark.
For further details see under: **NERI**.
**DOPE liposomes**
Dioleoylphosphatidylethanolamine liposomes.
*Cell Biology; Pathology.*
**D.O.P.O.** Drop Out Placement Objectives.
*Transnational Projects.*
**DOR** Differenced One-way Range.
**DORIS system** Doppler Orbitography and Radiopositioning Integrated Satellite system.
*Space-Based Geodetic Techniques.*
**DORO** (abbr.) DOcument ROuting.
**DOS** Date Of Shipment; Day Of Sale.
*Business; Commerce.*
**DOS** 1. day of supply.
1. jour d'approvisionnement.
2. director of staff.
2. directeur de l'état-major.
**DOS** Density Of States.
*Solid-State Physics.*
**DOS** Department Of State (U.S.A.).
**DOS** Director of Ordnance Services.
**DOS** Director Of Studies.
**DOS** Disk/Disc Operating System.
*Computer Technology.*
**DOSO** director of staff operations.
directeur des activités de l'état-major.
**DOST** Department Of Science and Technology (The Philippines).
**DOT** Date Of Trade.
*Business; Commerce.*
**DOT** Department Of Telecommunications (India).
**DOT** Department Of Transportation; Department Of Treasury (U.S.A.).
**DOT** Designated Order Turnaround.
**DOT** Dictionary of Occupational Titles.
*Human Resources.*
**DOT** Dissolved Oxygen Tension.
**DOTAP** Dioleoyl Trimethylammonium Propane.
**DOTE** Department Of Terrestrial Ecology.
Of NERI, Denmark.
For further details see under: **NERI**.
**DOTH** désignation d'objectif(s) transhorizon.
over-the-horizon targeting OTHT.
**DOTREX** Deep Ocean TRacer EXperiment.
**DOTS** Directly Observed Treatment (Therapy) - Short-course.
DOTS has been a 6-months course of 4 drugs, so-called because health workers stand over patients when they take the pills -Resurgence of TB in Russia.
*Drug-resistant Strains; Epidemiology; Microbiology; Reemerging Diseases; Tuberculosis.*
For further details see under: **PHRI** and **MERLIN**.
**Double-B** Double-Banked; Double-Bonded.
**DOVAP** DOppler Velocity And Position.
*Electronics.*
**DOW** Doppler On Wheels.
*Analysis and Prediction of Storms; Mesoscale Meteorological Studies; Meteorology; Weather Radar.*
**DOWE** Department Of Wildlife Ecology.
Of NERI, Denmark.
For further details see under: **NERI**.
**DOW production** DOmestic hot Water production.
*European Union.*
The annual installation rate (1999) of 1 million $m^2$ solar collectors will be brought to a total installed capacity of 100 million $m^2$ by 2010.
*Solar Thermal Heating Technology.*
**DOXP pathway** 1-Deoxy-D-Xylulose 5-Phosphate pathway.
DOXP pathway is also called the methylerythritol phosphate pathway.
*Biomedicine; Tropical Diseases.*
**doz.** (abbr.) dozen.
**DP**; **dp** Data Processing or data-processing.
Data processing, also known as information processing refers to an operation carried out on data by a computer system.
*Computer Technology.*
**DP** Data Processor.
A data processor is a person carrying out operations on data or a device used to carry out these operations.
*Computer Technology.*

**D.P.** Decreto Penale.
Italian initialism meaning: Penal Writ.
*Law.*
**D.P.** Decreto Presidenziale.
Italian initialism meaning: Presidential Decree.
**DP** Deferred Payment.
*Business; Commerce.*
**DP; dp** Degree of Polymerization.
*Organic Chemistry.*
**DP** Détention Provisoire (France).
*Criminal Law.*
**DP; dp** Dew Point.
*Chemistry* - Dew point is the temperature at which air or a gas begins to condense to a liquid.
*Meteorology* - Dew point, in meteorology, is also known as dew-point temperature.
**DP** 1. directeur de projet.
1. project manager (PM 5.).
2. distribution point.
2. point de distribution.
3. see IDP.
3. voir IPD.
**DP** Direct Price.
**DP; D/P** Displaced Person.
**DP; D.P.** Doctor of Pharmacy.
**DP; D.P.** Doctor of Podiatry.
**D/P** Documenti contro Pagamento.
Italian initialism meaning: Documents against Payment.
**DP** Double Play.
**DP** Due Process.
**DP** Draft Proposal.
**DP; D/P** Duty Paid.
**DP** Dynamic Programrning.
*Industrial Engineering; Mathematics.*
**DPA** Dayton Peace Agreement.
Accord de paix de Dayton.
**DPA** Diphenylamine.
$(C_6H_5)_2NH$ - Diphenylamine is also known as phenylaniline. It is used mainly in propellants, pharmaceuticals, pesticides, and dyes.
*Organic Chemistry.*
**DPA** 9,10-Diphenylanthracene.
*Chemiluminescence; Chemistry.*
**DPA** Diploma in Public Administration.
**DPA** Directory and database Publishers Association.
**DPA** Displaced Persons Act (U.S.A.).
Enacted in the U.S.A. in 1948.
**DPAS** Direction du Personnel et des Affaires Sociales (France).
**DPB** Deposit Pass Book.
**DPC** Data Processing Center.
**DPC** Defence Planning Committee.
Comité des plans de défense.
**DPC** Differential Photocalorimetry.
**DPC** Domestic Policy Council (U.S.A.).
**DPC** Duke Primate Center.
**DP cells** Double-Positive cells.
*Genetics; Immunology; Medicine; Microbiology; Pediatrics.*
**dPC12 cells** differentiated PC12 cells.
*Alzheimer Biology; Cellular Neurobiology; Clinical Sciences; Gerontology; Neurology.*
**DPCM** Differential Pulse-Code Modulation.
DPCM is used for television transmission.
*Electronics.*
**DPD** dépôt permanent désigné.
designated permanent storage site /DPSS/.
**DPD** DNA Patent Database.
**DPDA** date prévue de la demande d'authorisation.
estimated date of authorization request /EDAR/.
**dpdt switch** double-pole double-throw switch.
*Electricity.*
**DPE** Data Processing Equipment.
**DPE** Downstream Promoter Element.
*Biology; Cell Biology; Molecular Genetics; Transcription.*
**DPEs** Downstream Promoter Elements.
**DPF** Deferred Pay Fund.
**DPG** Differential Pressure Gauge.
The DPG is used to record pressure variations.
**DPG** 2,3-Diphosphoglycerate.
*Biochemistry.*
**DPG** Diphenylguanidine.
Diphenylguanidine, also known as Melaniline, is used as a rubber accelerator.
*Organic Chemistry.*
**DPH** 1,6-Diphenylhexatriene.
**DPH; D.P.H.** Department of Public Health (U.S.A.).
**DPH** Diploma in Public Health.
**DPH** Doctor of Philosophy.
**DPH; D.P.H.** Doctor of Public Health.
**DPI** Diagnostic Préimplantatoire.
French initialism meaning: Preimplantation Diagnostic.
*Human Embryos; Medicine.*
**DPI** Digital Photon Integration.
**DPI** Dry Powder Inhaler.
**DPICM** dual purpose improved conventional munition.
munition classique bivalente améliorée.
**DPIP** 2,6-Dichlorophenolindophenol.
**DPJ** Democratic Party of Japan (Japan).
**DPJ** Division de Police Judiciaire (France).
**DPKO** Department of Peacekeeping Operations.

Département des opérations de maintien de la paix (DOMP).
**DPLG; D.P.L.G.** Diplômé/e Par Le Gouvernement (France).
**DPM; D.P.M.** Diploma in Psychological Medicine.
**DPM; D.P.M.** Doctor of Podiatric Medicine.
**DPM** Drop Physics Module.
**DPM** Dynamically Preformed Morpha.
*Epithelial Cells.*
**DPMCH** Department of Preventive Medicine and Community Health.
Virginia Commonwealth University (U.S.A.).
**DPN** Dip-Pen Nanolithography.
*Chemistry; Microfabrication; Molecular Electronics; Nanoscale Devices- Nanotechnology.*
**DPO** Direction Par Objectifs.
French initialism meaning: Management By Objectives.
**DPP** Decepentaplegic.
*Molecular Biology.*
**DPP** Democratic Progressive Party (Taiwan).
**DPP** Diabetes Prevention Program.
*U.S. Programs.*
**DPP** Direction of Public Prosecutions.
**DpP** Direzione per Politiche.
Italian initialism meaning: Management by Policies.
**DPP Commission** Disaster Prevention and Preparedness Commission (Ethiopia).
**DPP IV** Dipeptidyl Peptidase IV.
**DPPC** Dipalmitoylphosphatidylcholine.
**DPP protein** Decapentaplegic protein.
**DPQ** defence planning questionnaire.
questionnaire pour les plans de défense.
**DPR** Decreto del Presidente della Repubblica.
Italian initialism meaning: Presidential Decree.
**DPR** Demonstration Power Reactor.
**DPR** Domestic Policy Review (U.S.A.).
*Solar Energy.*
**DPRE** displaced persons and refugees.
personnes déplacées et réfugées.
**DPRK** Democratic People's Republic of Korea.
**DPS** 1. defence policy and strategy.
1. politique et stratégie de défense.
2. Democratic Patriotic Party (RS).
2. Parti démocratique patriotique (RS).
**d-PS** deuterio Polystyrene.
**DPS** Distributed Processing System.
DPS is also known as: Distributed Data-Processing System.
*Computer Technology.*
**DPS** Division for Planetary Sciences.
**DPS provision** Distinct Population Segment provision (U.S.A.).
*Wildlife Biology.*
**DPSS** Data Processing Services Subsystem.
**DPSS** designated permanent storage site.
dépôt permanent désigné (DPD).
**DP stage** Double Positive stage.
**dpst switch** double-pole single-throw switch.
*Electricity.*
**dpt.** (abbr.) department.
Also: **dep**.
**DPT** Dipropyltryptamine.
*Synthetic Hallucinogen.*
**DPT** Direzione Promozione coordinamento Tecnico (Italy).
**DPTS** 4-(N-N-Dimethylamino)Pyridinium-4-Toluenesulfonic acid.
**DPT vaccine** Diphtheria-Pertussis-Tetanus vaccine.
**DPV** Differential Pulse Voltametry.
*Chemistry; Chemical Engineering; Nano-and Molecular Science and Technology.*
**DPV** Discounted Present Value.
*Business; Commerce.*
**Dq** Dequalinium.
*Biochemistry; Biological Sciences; Cytotoxic Agents; Molecular Biology.*
**DQDB** Distributed Queue Dual Bus.
*Broadband Technologies.*
**DQFCOSY** Double-Quantum Filter COrrelated Spectroscopy.
**DQMC** Diffusion / Quantum Monte Carlo.
**DQSI** Direction de la Qualité et de la Sécurité Industrielles (France).
Of the French Ministry of Industry.
**DR** Daily Report.
**DR** Dark Rock.
*Rock Types.*
For further details see under: **IMP** (Imager for Mars Pathfinder).
**DR** Data Report.
**DR** Dead Reckoning.
*Navigation.*
**dr.** (abbr.) debtor.
**DR; D.R.** Degeneration Reaction.
**DR** Delivery Room.
*Medicine.*
**DR** Dietary Restriction.
*Biological Aging; Genetic Toxicology.*
**DR** Dining Room.
**DR** Discount Rate.
*Banking; Finance.*
**DR** Dissociative Recombination.

*Molecular Ions; Particle Physics; Plasma and Radiation Physics.*
**dr** (abbr.) divisor.
*Mathematics.*
**Dr** (abbr.) doctor.
Also: **doc.**
**DR** Dominican Republic.
**DR** Dorsal Raphe.
**DR**; **dr** Dose Rate.
**dr** (abbr.) dram; drams.
**DR**; **Dr** Drawer.
**dr.** (abbr.) dressing.
*Medicine.*
**dr.** (abbr.) drive.
*Behavior; Computer Technology; Electronics; Engineering.*
**dr.** (abbr.) drum.
*Architecture; Chemical Engineering; Computer Technology; Mechanical Devices; Mining Engineering.*
**D8R** Double 8-Rings.
*Chemistry; Materials.*
**DRA** Danish Research Agency.
**DRA** Defense Research Agency (G.B.).
DRA is a semi-autonomous body which is part of G.B.'s Ministry of Defense.
**DRACO** DRiving Accident Coordinating Observer.
*European Community.*
**DRAF** draft resource allocation figure.
1a. montant de la dotation proposée.
1b. montant proposé des ressources à affecter.
**DRAM** Dynamic Random Access Memory.
*Computer Technology.*
**D-RAM chips** Dynamic Random Access Memory chips.
D-RAM chips are the most widely used type of data storage.
**DRASER** Doppler Radar And Storm Electricity Research.
Of the U.S. Environmental Research Laboratory.
**DRAW** Direct Read After Write.
**DRC** Democratic Republic of Congo.
Formerly Zaire.
**DRC** Device Research Conference.
The DRC was held in Santa Barbara, California, U.S.A. in June 1996.
**DR calculations** Dissociative Recombination calculations.
*Astronomy; Physics.*
**DRDO** Defence Research and Development Organisation (India).
**DRE** Direction Régionale de l'Equipement (France).
**DRE** DNA Response Elements.
**DREN** Defense Research and Engineering Network (U.S.A.).
Of the U.S. Department of Defense. DREN was implemented in 1997.
**DRF** Deputy to SACEUR for Russian forces in SFOR and KFOR.
Adjoint du SACEUR pour les forces russes de la SFOR et de la KFOR.
**DRF** Direct Radiative Forcing.
*Atmospheric Sciences.*
**DRFM** Digital Radio Frequency Memory.
**DRG** Defence Research Group [obsolete - incorporated into RTA].
Groupe sur la recherche pour la défense (GRD) [obsolète - intégré dans l'ART].
**DRG**; **D.R.G.** Diagnosis Related Group.
**DRG** Division of Research Grants (U.S.A.).
Of the U.S. National Institutes of Health.
**DRG** Dorsal Root Ganglion.
*Cell Biology; Neurology.*
**DRGs** Delayed Response Genes.
*Neuroscience; Signal Transduction.*
**DRGs**; **D.R.Gs** Diagnosis Related Groups.
**DRI** Defense Reinvestment Initiative (U.S.A.).
**DRI** Desert Research Institute (U.S.A.).
DRI is a large multidisiplinary Environmental Research Organization.
*Research Projects.*
**DRIA**; **Dria** Dinamometria per la Ricerca di Intolleranze Alimentari (Italy).
**D.R.I.D.E.** Direction des Relations Internationales / Direction de l'Enseignement.
Chambre de Commerce et de l'Industrie de Paris (France).
**DRIRE** direction régionale de l'industrie de la recherche et de l'environnement des Pays de la Loire (France).
**DRK** German Red Cross.
**DrKW** Dresdner Kleinwort Wasserstein (Germany).
*Investment Bank.*
**DRLM** Depolarized Reflected Light Microscopy.
**DRM** Detergent-Resistant membrane.
*Biomedical Sciences.*
**DRME** Direction des Recherches et Moyens d'Essais (France).
**DRMs** Detergent-Resistant Membranes.
*Biochemistry; Cell Biology.*
**DROPS** demountable rack off-loading and pick-up system.
système de chargement et de déchargement à crémaillère démontable.
**dRP** deoxyribose 5'-phosphate.

**DRP** Distribution Reinvestment Program; Dividend-Reinvestment Plan.
*Banking; Business; Finance.*
**DRP2** Dystrophin-Related Protein 2.
*Microbiology; Physiology; Demyelination.*
**DRR** defence requirements review.
examen des besoins de défense.
**DRR** Discounted Rate of Return.
**DR rats** Diabetes-Resistant rats.
**DRS** Data Receiving System.
**DRS** Debtor Reporting System - W.B.'s.
For further details see under: **W.B.**
**DRSS** Data Relay Satellite System - *European Community.*
**DRT** Department of Research Technologies.
**DRTC** Diabetes and Research Training Center.
At Vanderbilt University (U.S.A.).
**DRW** Daily Routine Work.
**DS** Dark Soil.
*Soil Types.*
For further details see under: **IMP** (Imager for Mars Pathfinder).
**DS** Data Set.
DS is a collection of related data records in computer-readable form.
*Computer Programming.*
**DS** Data Station.
*Computer Technology.*
**DS** Data Structure.
*Computer Programming.*
**DS** Days after Sight.
**DS** Debenture Stock.
*Business; Commerce.*
**DS** 1. decision sheet.
1. compte rendu de décisions.
2. declared site.
2. site déclaré.
3. Democratic Party (RS).
3. Parti démocratique (RS).
4. direct support.
4a. appui direct.
4b. soutien direct (SD 1.).
**DS** Democratici di Sinistra.
Italian initialism meaning: Democrats of the Left (Italy).
**DS**; **D.S.** Department of State (U.S.A.).
**DS**; **D.S.** Deputy-Secretary.
**ds.** (abbr.) destro.
Italian abbreviation meaning: right.
*Medicine.*
**DS** Detached Service.
**DS** Détroit Supérieur.
French initialism meaning: Superior Strait (of the pelvis).
*Medicine.*
**DS** Déviation Standard.
French initialism meaning: Standard Deviation.
*Statistics.*
**DS** Directional Solidification.
*Metallurgy.*
**DS** Directory Services.
**DS** Direct Sequence.
**DS** Document Signed.
**ds** double stranded.
**DS** Down Syndrome.
*Cell Biology; Genetics; Neurosciences.*
**DS** Dropsiding / drop siding.
Dropsiding is also known as: Novelty Siding.
*Building Engineering.*
**DSA** 1. Defence Shipping Authority.
1a. Autorité des transports maritimes.
1b. Direction de la navigation commerciale pour la défense.
2. detailed support arrangements.
2. arrangements détaillés en matière de soutien.
**DSA** Destination Software Address.
**DSA** Digital Substraction Angiography.
*Medicine.*
**DSA**; **D.S.A.** Diplôme Supérieur Agricole (France).
**DSA** Directory System Alert.
**DSA** Direct Sales Association.
**DSAA** Defense Security Assistance Agency (U.S.A.).
**DSACEUR** Deputy SACEUR.
SACEUR adjoint.
**DSARC** Defense Systems Acquisition Review Council.
**DSB** DNA double-strand Break.
For further details see under: **DSBs**.
**DSBs** DNA double-strand Breaks.
*Biochemistry; Cell Biology; DNA Damage; Developmental Biology; Genetics; Molecular Biology; Oxidative Metabolism.*
For further details see under: **NER**; **NHEJ**; **IR**.
**DSC** Defence Shipping Council.
Conseil de la navigation commerciale pour la défense.
**DSC** Detroit Stock Exchange (U.S.A.).
**DSC** Differential Scanning Calorimetry.
*Materials Science.*
**DSC** Digital-to-Synchro Converter.
Also: **D/S Converter**.
**DSC** Distinguished Service Cross.
**Dsc**; **D.Sc.** Doctor of Science.
**DSC**; **D.S.C.** Doctor of Surgical Chiropody.

**DSCB** Data Set Control Block.
*Data Communications.*
**DSCF** Doppler-Shifted Constant-Frequency.
**DSCS** Defense Satellite Communications System.
**DSD** Director of Staff Duties.
**DSD** Dry Sterile Dressing.
**dsDNA** double-stranded DNA.
For further details see under: **DNA**.
*Biochemistry.*
**DSDP** Deep Sea Drilling Project (Site 607).
Located on the West flank of the Mid-Atlantic Ridge.
*Applied Systems Analysis; Glacial Cycles; Paleoceanography; Physics.*
**DSE** Data Set Extension.
**DSE** Data Switching Equipment; Data Switching Exchange.
**DSE** Depolarization-induced Suppression of Excitation.
*Biology; Cellular and Molecular Pharmacology; Physiology; Postsynaptic Depolarization.*
**DSE** Dipartimento Scuola Educazione (Italy).
**DSE** Diplôme de Sciences Economiques (France).
**DSE** Dispositifs de Sécurité par Equilibrage.
**DSE** Distributed Systems Environment.
**DSEB** Defence Shipping Executive Board.
Bureau éxecutif des transports maritimes.
**DSES** Division on Social and Economic Studies (U.S.A.).
**DSF** deployed SHED facility.
installation de SHED déployé.
**DSG** 1. Deputy Secretary General [HQ NATO].
1. Secrétaire général délégué [siège de l'OTAN].
2. divisional support group.
2. groupe de soutien divisionnaire.
**DSHEA** Dietary Supplements Health and Education Act (U.S.A.).
Passed by the U.S. Congress in 1994.
**DSHV** Democratic Union of Croats in Vojvodina [FRY].
Union démocratique des Croates de Voïvodine [RFY].
**DSI** declared site inspection.
inspection de site déclaré.
**DSI** Depolarization-induced Suppression of Inhibition.
*Biology; Cellular and Molecular Pharmacology; Postsynaptic Depolarization; Physiology; Retrograde Signaling in the Brain.*
**DSIOP** Direcçáo de Serviços de Informação e Orientação Profissional (Portugal).
**DSIP** Digital Signal and Image Processing.
**DSIR** Department of Scientific and Industrial Research.
**DS6K** *Drosophila* S6 Kinase.
A signaling molecule.
*Biochemistry; Cancer Research; Molecular Biology.*
**DSL** Data Set Label.
*Data Communications.*
**DSL** Deep-Scattering Layer.
*Oceanography.*
**DSL** Digital Subscriber Line.
**DSL** Dutch State Treasury.
**DSM** The airport code for Des Maines, Iowa, U.S.A.
**DSM** Detergent-Soluble Membrane.
*Biomedical Sciences.*
**DSM** Diagnostic and Statistical Manual (of Mental Disorders).
DSM is the Standard Classification text of the American Psychiatric Association.
**DSM** Distinguished Service Medal.
**DSMB** Data and Safety Monitoring Board.
**DS1 Mission** Deep Space 1 Mission.
NASA-JPL ion-propulsion spacecraft launched in October 1998.
*NASA's New Millennium Program.*
For further details see under: **NASA** and **JPL**.
**DSM programs** Demand-Side Management programs.
Traditionally, these programs have encouraged consumers to use less energy by adding insulation to their homes, improving the efficiency of industrial processes, or installing energy-wise lighting systems.
**DSN** Deep Space Network.
*Astronomy; Earth and Planetary Sciences; Earth and Space Sciences; Terrestrial Physics.*
**DSN** Digital Switched Network.
**DSO** Detailed Supplementary Objective.
**DSP** Defense Support Program.
**DSP** Dibasic Sodium Phosphate.
Also known as: Disodium Phosphate; Secondary Sodium Phosphate.
*Inorganic Chemistry.*
**DSP** Digital Signal Processing.
**DSP** Diritti Speciali di Prelievo.
Italian initialism meaning: Special Drawing Rights.
**DSP** 1. Democratic Socialist Party (RS).
1. Parti socialiste démocratique (RS).
2. drift start position.
2. position initiale de dérive.
**DSPC** Distearoylphosphatidylcholine.

**DSPs** Digital Signal Processors / Processing.
**DSR** Data Set Ready.
**DSRE** Direzione Sviluppo e Relazioni Esterne (Italy).
**dsRNA** double-stranded RNA.
For further details see under: **RNA**.
**DSRV** deep submergence rescue vehicle.
sous-marin de recherche et de sauvetage à grande profondeur.
**DSS** Decision Support Systems.
*Data Warehouses; Next Generation Programs.*
**DSS** Deep Space Station.
**DSS** Dejerine-Sottas Syndrome.
*Neurobiology; Neuroscience.*
**DSS** Democratic Party of Serbia.
**DSs** Depolarization Shifts.
**DSS** Discrete Strain Structure.
*Epidemiology.*
**DSS** Disuccinimidyl Suberate.
**DSS** Dynamic Support System.
*Data Communications.*
**DSSC** Deep Space Station Complex.
**DSS reversal** Dosage-Sensitive Sex reversal.
*Biological Chemistry; Mammalian Sex Determination; Medicine; Molecular Pharmacology; Surgery.*
**DSSTID** Danish Society for Scientific and Technological Information and Documentation.
**DST** Daylight Saving Time.
**DST** 1. Defence and Space Talks.
1. pourparlers sur la défense et l'espace.
2. direct support team.
2. équipe de soutien direct.
**DST** Direction de la Sécurité du Territoire (France).
**DST** Director of Supplies and Transport.
**DST** Doctor of Sacred Theology.
**DS telescope** Deep Survey telescope.
*Astronomy; Astrophysics.*
**DSTL** Defence Science and Technology Laboratory (G.B.).
Part of DERA.
*Armaments; Chemical and Biological Research; Naval Research.*
For further details see under: **DERA**.
**dstr.** (abbr.) distribution; distributor.
**DSU** 1. direct support unit.
1. unité en appui direct.
2. direct support unit [logistics].
2. unité de soutien direct [logistique].
**Dsurg**; **D.Surg** Dental Surgeon.
**dsx** doublesex.
**DT** Data Terminal.
*Computers.*
**DT** Daylight Time.
**DT** Delirium Tremens.
Delirium Tremens is known as the DTs.
*Medicine.*
For further details see under: **DTs**.
**DT** Destination Time.
*Computer Technology.*
**DT** Deutsche Telekom.
**DT** Dial Tone.
*Telecommunications.*
**DT** Diphtheria and Tetanus (vaccine).
**DT** Diphtheria Toxin.
Diphteria toxin is also known as: diphtherotoxin.
*Toxicology.*
**DT** Distance Test.
*Medicine.*
**DT** Doctor of Theology.
Also: **DTH**.
**DT** Double Time.
**DT** Duration of Tetany.
*Medicine.*
**DTA** Differential Thermal Analysis.
*Thermodynamics.*
**DTAA** Direction des Techniques et Automatismes Avancés (France).
**DTAS** depressed towed-array system.
système d'antenne remorquée par dépresseur.
**DTase** Dehydratase.
Also: Hydrolyase.
*Enzymology.*
**DTB** Deutsche Terminbörse (Germany).
DTB is the Frankfurt-based Derivatives Exchange.
**DTB** Drug and Therapeutics Bulletin (G.B.).
*Publication.*
**DTC** Department of Trade and Commerce (G.B.).
**DTC** Depositary Trust Company (U.S.A.).
**DTC** Deposit-Taking Company.
**DTC** Desktop Computer.
The DTC is a small computer to be used on an office desk.
*Computer Technology.*
**DTC** Development Through Conservation.
DTC is a program in Kabale, Uganda, that is run by the international aid organization CARE.
*Conservation Biology.*
For further details see under: **CARE**.
**dtd.** (abbr.) dated.
**DTD** Data Transfer Device.
**DTD**; **dtd.** Document Type Definition.
The DTD is an optical portion of an XML document.
**DTE**; **dte** Data Terminal / Terminating Equipment.
**DTF** Daily Transaction File.

**DTF** Define The File.
*Data Communications.*
**DTF** Diagnostic Turbulent Flux.
**DTF** Digital Tape Format.
**DTG** Date-Time Group.
*Telecommunications.*
**DTH** Delayed-Type Hypersensitivity.
*Cell Biology.*
**DTH** Diploma in Tropical Hygiene.
**DTH** Direct-To-Home.
**DTH**; **Dth** Doctor of Theology.
Also: **DT**.
**DTI** Department of Trade and Industry (G.B.).
**DTI** Diffusion Tensor Imaging.
A type of magnetic resonance imaging.
*Neurology.*
**DTI** dispositif de test intégré (ou équipement de test intégré).
built-in test equipment (BITE).
**DTL** Diode-Transistor-Logic.
*Electronics.*
**DTM** Department of Terrestrial Magnetism.
Of the Carnegie Institution of Washington (U.S.A.).
**DTM** Digital Terrain Model.
**dTMP** deoxythymidine Monophosphate.
**DTN** Diphtheria Toxin Normal.
*Medicine.*
**DTN** Direction Technique Nationale (France).
**DTP** Desk-Top Publishing.
**DTP**; **Dtp** Developmental Therapeutics Program.
Of the U.S. N.C.I.
*Drug Discovery Programs; Information Sciences; Molecular Cell Biology.*
For further details see under: **N.C.I**.
**DTP** Distal Tingling on Percussion.
*Medicine.*
**DTP/A** Diethylenetriaminepentaacetic (Acid).
**DTR** Data loop TRansceiver.
*Data Communications.*
**DTR** Data Terminal Reader.
**DTR** Data Transmit Ready.
**DTR**; **dtr** Deep Tendon Reflex.
**DTR** Distribution Tape Reel.
*Data Communications.*
**DTR** Diurnal Temperature Range.
*Biological Sciences; Climatic Research; Hydrometeorology.*
**DTRA** Defence Threat Reduction Agency (U.S.A.).
*Chemical and Biological Agents; Counterterrorism.*
**DTs** Delirium Tremens.
Also: **DT**.
Caused by excessive comsumption of alcohol.
*Medicine.*
**DTS**; **dts** Digital Termination Service.
**DTS** Dispositivo Telefonico per Sordomuti.
A device for deaf-mute persons provided by the Italian Telephone Company.
**DTS** Droits de Tirage Spéciaux.
French initialism meaning: Special Drawing Rights.
**DTSA** Defense Technology Security Administration (U.S.A.).
**DTSI** Defense Trade Security Initiative [US].
Initiative sur la sécurité du commerce de défence [US].
**DTT** The airline code for the city of Detroit, Michigan, U.S.A.
**DTT** Digital Terrestrial Television.
The DTT lauched in Britain in 1998 offers new services, for example: near video-on-demand and pay-per view.
**DTT** Dithiothreitol.
$C_4H_{10}O_2S_2$ - DTT is used mainly in biochemical research and as a reducing agent.
*Organic Chemistry.*
**DTU** Denmark Technical University (Lynghy, Denmark).
**DTW** The airport code for Detroit-Wayne County (Michigan, U.S.A.).
**DU** Diagnosis Undetermined.
*Medicine.*
**DU** Dobson Unit.
Used to measure ozone concentration.
**DU** Depleted Uranium.
*Nucleonics.*
**Du** (abbr.) Dutch.
**DUA** Directory User Agent.
**DUB** Depleted Uranium Block.
*Energy.*
**Dub.** (abbr.) Dublin.
**DUC** Danish Underground Consortium.
**DuDat.** Due Date.
*Business; Commerce.*
**DUE** Development of Undergraduate Education (Indonesia).
DUE is funded by the World Bank.
*World Bank Program.*
**DUEL** Diplôme Universitaire d'Enseignement Littéraire (France).
**DUES** Diplôme Universitaire d'Enseignement Scientifique (France).
**DUF** Drug Use Forecasting (U.S.A.).
**DUI of drugs** Driving Under the Influence of drugs.
**DUM** Dorsal Unpaired Median.

**DUMP** Disposal of Unused Medicine and Pills.
**DUP** Disk Utility Program.
*Data Communications.*
**DUP** District à Urbaniser en Priorité (France).
**dup.** (abbr.) duplex; duplicate.
**dup.** (abbr.) duplication.
*Molecular Biology.*
**Dur.** (abbr.) Durham (G.B.).
**DUS** Diploma Universitario di Statistica (Italy).
**DUS** The airport code for Düsseldorf, Germany.
**DUT**; **D.U.T.** Diplôme Universitaire de Technologie (France).
**dUTP** deoxyuridine 5'-Triphosphate.
**DUV** Damaging Ultraviolet.
**DUV** Data Under Voice.
*Telecommunications.*
**DV** Dilute Volume.
*Medicine.*
**DV** distinguished visitor.
visiteur de marque.
**DV** Dorsoventral / dorso-ventral.
**DV**; **D.V.** Double Vibrations.
Also: **dv**; **d.v**.
**DVB** Digital Video Broadcast.
*Digital Broadcasting.*
**DVB** Divinylbenzene.
$C_6H_4(CH=CH_2)_2$ - Divinylbenzene, also known as vinylstyrene is used mainly to make rubbers and polymers.
*Organic Chemistry.*
**DVBIRD** Digital Video Broadcasting Integrated Receiver Decoder.
*European Comunity Project.*
**DVD** Digital Video Disc/Disk.
DVD players relay films at a higher quality than video cassettes.
*Consumer Electronic Industry.*
**DVDs** Digital Video Disks.
For further details see under: **DVD**.
**DVD technology** Digital Versatile Disk technology.
The DVD can be formatted in many different ways in order to handle a variety of contents.
*Digital Movie Players; Digital Versatile Disks.*
**DVL muscle** Deep Vastus Lateralis muscle.
**DVM**; **dvm** Digital Voltmeter.
*Electronics.*
**DVM** Doctor of Veterinary Medicine.
**DVM** Dorsal Ventral Muscle.
**DVMM** Débit Ventilatoire Maximum Minute.
French initialism meaning: Maximum breathing / ventilatory Capacity.
**DVP** Distributed Video Production.
*European Community Project.*
**DVP-CBER** Division of Viral Products - Center for Biologics Evaluation and Research.
The DVP-CBER is the branch of the U.S. Food and Drug Administration that reviews *Viral Vaccines.*
**DVP system** Delivery Versus Payment system.
All DVP systems for wholesale and retail securities transactions started operating in € with effect from 1999.
*Business; Commerce.*
**DVR** Discrete Variable Representation.
*Astronomy; Chemistry; Physics.*
**DVS**; **dvs** Doctor of Veterinary Science.
**DVST**; **dvst** Direct-View Storage Tube.
*Electronics.*
**DVU** German People's Union.
**DW** Daisy Wheel.
The DW, also known as Print Wheel, is a disk having printing characters on its circumference.
*Computer Technology.*
**DW** Dead Weight.
Dead weight in mechanics is known as: Static Load.
*Mechanics.*
**DW**; **dw** Dead Weight.
*Transportation Engineering.*
**DW** Delayed Weather.
**DW**; **dw** Distilled Water.
*Chemistry.*
**DW** Dividend Warranty.
*Business; Economics; Finance.*
**d.w.**, **D.W.**, **D/W** dock warrant.
**DW** Double-Word.
*Data Communications.*
**DW** Dust Wrapper.
**DWA** Damaging Winds Algorithm.
**DWA** Department of Water Affairs (Botswana).
Ministry of Mineral Resources.
**DWB** Driving While Black / Brown (U.S.A.).
**DWBA** Distorted-Wave Born Approximation.
*Nuclear Reactions; Physics.*
**DWBC** Deep Western Boundary Current.
**DWDM** Dense Wavelength Division Multiplexing.
The DWDM uses individual colors of light to carry information.
**DWE** Deglacial Warm Event.
*Geology; Geophysics.*
**DWG** distributed wargame.
jeu de guerre réparti.
**DWI** Driving While Intoxicated.
**DWI** Dutch West Indies.
**DWM** deep-water mine.
Mine de haut fond.

**DWM** Destination Warning Marker.
*Data Communications.*
**DWS** Diffusing-Wave Spectroscopy.
DWS is a multiple-light-scattering technique.
*Astronomy; Diffusing-Wave Spectroscopy; Microscopic Dynamics of Grains; Physics.*
**DWS** distributed wargaming system.
système de jeu de guerre réparti.
**DWSNET** distributed wargaming system network.
réseau de jeu de guerre réparti.
**DWT**; **dwt** Deadweight Ton; deadweight tonnage.
**DX** The airline code for Danair.
**DX** Diagnosis.
*Artificial Intelligence; Computer Technology; Medicine; Systematics.*
**DX** Direct Expansion.
*Mechanical Engineering.*
**DXA** Dual-energy X-ray Absorptiometry.
*Obesity; Osteoporosis; Physiology.*
**DXC** Data Exchange Control.
**DXM** Dexamethasone.
*Immunology; Molecular and Cellular Biology; Molecular Signal Transduction.*
**dy.** (abbr.) delivery.
**dy.** (abbr.) deputy.
**D.Y.** Dockyard.
**dy.** (abbr.) duty.
**Dy** The chemical symbol for Dysprosium.
Dysprosium was discovered by the French chemist Paul Emile Lecoq de Boisbaudran.
*Chemistry; Symbols.*
**DYANA** DYnamic Algorithm for NMR Applications.
**dyn.** (abbr.) dynamics.
Also: **dynam.**
**dyn.** dyne; dynes.
**DYSTAL** Dynamic Storage Allocation.
Dynamic storage allocation is also known as Dynamic Allocation; Dynamic Memory Allocation.
*Computer Programming.*
**DZ** Algeria's international vehicle registration letters.
**DZ** Dizygous.
**DZ** Doctor of Zoology.
**dz.** (abbr.) dozen.
**DZ** drop zone.
zone de largage.
**DZAAS** Drop Zone Assembly Air System.
*Avionics.*
**DZ twins** Dizygotic twins.
Also known as: Fraternal Twins.
*Genetics.*

**E** Earl; Earth; East.
**e** earnings.
*Business; Finance.*
**e** eccentricity.
*Astronomy; Mathematics.*
**E**; **E.** Eddy diffusivity.
*Fluid Mechanics.*
**E** élastance.
meaning: elastance in French.
*Electricity; Medicine.*
**e** elasticity.
*Materials Science; Mathematics.*
**e** electron.
*Electricity; Physics.*
**e** emissivity.
*Thermodynamics.*
**e** (abbr.) enable.
Also: **enbl.**
*Computer Programming; Computer Technology.*
**e** energy.
*Engineering; Physics.*
**E** English.
The Germanic language of the British Isles, standard also in the United States.
*Languages.*
**E** Enzyme.
The word enzyme means in Greek: "in yeast".
*Enzymology.*
**E** epinephrine.
*Endocrinology; Pharmacology.*
**e** (abbr.) error.
*Computer Programming; Medicine; Science.*
**e** estimate.
**E** Ethane.
Ethane is a flammable, colorless gas, insoluble in water and soluble in alcohol.
*Organic Chemistry.*
**E** Excellency; Excellent.
**e** (abbr.) execute; execution.
*Computer Programming.*
**E**; **e** Expectations.
**E** experimenter.
**e** (abbr.) expression.
The expression in chemical engineering is also known as: mechanical expression.
*Chemical Engineering.*
**E** eye.
*Anatomy* - The eye contains the following layers: sclera and cornea, choroid, and retina.
*Meteorology* - In meteorology, the eye is the eye-shaped area at the center of a tropical cyclone.
**E** Spain - International vehicle registration letter.
**E3** electromagnetic environmental effects [naval operations].
effets de l'environnement électromagnétique [opérations navales].
**E-3** NATO E-3A Component [Component of the NAEW&C Force based at Geilenkirchen].
Élement E-3A de l'OTAN [élément de la Force NAEW&C basé à Geilenkirchen].
**ea** (abbr.) each.
**EA** Educational Age.
**EA** Educazione Ambientale.
Italian initialism meaning: Environmental Education.
**EA** Effective Address.
*Computer Programming.*
**EA** 1. electronic attack.
1. attaque électronique.
2. emergency action.
2. mesure d'urgence.
3. evolutionary acquisition.
3. acquisition évolutive.
**EA** Ellipsoid Algorithm.
**EA** Enemy Aircraft.
**E.A.** Energia Atomica.
Italian initialism meaning: Atomic Energy.
**EA** Energy Analysis.
**E.A.** Ente Autonomo.
Italian initialism meaning: Independent Body; Autonomous Agency.
**EA** Enthalpimetric Analysis.
*Analytical Chemistry.*
**EA** Environmental Analysis.
**EA** Erythrocyte-Antibody.
**EA** Erythrocyte-Anticorps.
French initialism meaning: Erythrocyte-Antibodies.
*Medicine.*
**EA** The airline code for Eastern Air Lines.
**EAA** East African Airways.
**E.A.A.** Engineer in Aeronautics and Astronautics.
**EAA** Environmental Assessment Association (U.S.A.).
**EAA** Ethyl Acrylic Acid.
**EAA** European Aluminium Association.
**EAAA** European Association of Advertising Agencies.
*Belgian Association.*
**EAC** East African Community.
Tanzania, Uganda and Kenya reestablished their EAC in November 1999. It was ratified within 6

months and enactement and implementation were completed by November 2000.

**EAC** Erythrocyte-Anticorps-Complément.
French initialism meaning: Erythrocyte-Antibody-Complement.
*Medicine.*

**EAC** European Accident Code.

**EAC** Executive Advisory Committee.

**EAC** Exercise and Activities Conference [PfP] [obsolete - now called PAC].
Conférence sur les exercices et activités [PPP] [obsolète - maintenant appelé PAC].

**EACEM** European Association of Consumer Electronics Manufacturers.

**EACN** European Air Chemistry Network.

**EACOS COOP** Executive Assistant to the Chief of Staff for Cooperation.
officier général délégué du CEM pour la coopération.

**EACR** European Association for Cancer Research.

**EACSO** East African Common Services Organization.
The EACSO has replaced EAHC.
For further details see under: **EAHC**.

**EAD** Elaborazione Automatica dei Dati.
Italian initialism meaning: Automatic Data-Processing.

**EAD** Electroantennographic GC Detection.
*Electrophysiological Techniques.*

**EAD** extended air defence.
défense aérienne élargie.

**EADB** East African Development Bank.
1967 Treaty for East African Cooperation.

**EADC** Ethylaluminum Dichloride.

**EADRCC** Euro-Atlantic Disaster Response Coordination Centre.
Centre euro-atlantique de coordination des interventions en cas de catastrophe.

**EADRU** Euro-Atlantic Disaster Response Unit.
Unité euro-atlantique d'intervention en cas de catastrophe.

**EADS Group** European Aeronautics Defense and Space Group.

**EAE** Experimental Allergic Encephalomyelitis.
*Immunobiology; Immunology; Medicine; Neurotransplants.*

**EAE** Experimental Autoimmune Encephalomyelitis.
*Biochemistry; Cell Biology; Medicine; Neurologic Diseases; Neuropathology; Rheumatology.*

**EAEC** East Asia Economic Caucus.

**EAEC** European Atomic Energy Community.

**EAEG** East Asian Economic Grouping.

**EAF** Entity Armed Forces.
Forces armées des Entités.

**EAF** EPEC Adherence Factor.
For further details see under: **EPEC**.

**EAFB** Edwards Air Force Base (U.S.A.).

**EAG** (single-cell) Electroantennography.
*Electrophysiological Techniques.*

**EAGGF** European Agricultural Guidance and Guarantee Fund.
*European Union.*

**EA2H** Segunda Escuadrilla Aeronaval de Helicòpteros (Argentina).

**EAHC** East African High Commission.
The EAHC was established in 1948. It has been replaced by the EACSO in 1963.
For further details see under: **EACSO**.

**EAHC** East Asia Hydrographic Commission (Monaco).

**EAHIL** European Association for Health Information and Libraries.

**EAHSW** European Agency for Health and Safety at Work.
*European Community Program.*

**EAI** Engineers and Architects Institute.

**EAK** Ethyl Amyl Ketone.
Ethyl amyl ketone, also known as octanone-3 is used mainly in perfumery.
*Organic Chemistry.*

**EAK** Kenya - International vehicle registration letters.

**EALG** European Aquatic Libraries Group.

**EAM** Electric Accounting Machine.

**EAM** Embedded-Atom-Method.
*Physics.*

**EAM** emergency action message.
message de mesure d'urgence.

**E.A.M.** Ente Autotrasporti Merci.
Italian initialism meaning: Freight Transport Board.

**EAMST** European Association for Marine Sciences and Techniques.

**EAN** European Aeroallergen Network.

**EAN** European Article Numbering.

**EAN** Expenditure Account Number.
*Business; Commerce.*

**EAN** Experimental Allergic Neuritis.
*Medicine; Neurology.*

**E&C** Engineering and Construction.

**e&e** each and every.
*Accounting; Commerce.*

**E. and P.** Extraordinary and Plenipotentiary.

**E&O.E.** Errors and Omissions Excepted.
*Accounting; Commerce.*

**EANHS** East Africa Natural History Society (Kenya).
**eaon** except as otherwise noted.
**EAOSS** Ente Autonomo Orchestra Sinfonica Siciliana (Sicily, Italy).
**EAP** Ecole Européenne des Affaires de Paris.
French initialism of the: Paris European Business School (France).
**EAP** emergency action plan.
plan d'action d'urgence.
**EAP** Employee Assistance Program.
**EAP** Evoked Action Potential.
**EAPC** Euro-Atlantic Partnership Council [formerly called NACC].
Conseil de partenariat euro-atlantique (CPEA) [anciennement appelé CCNA].
**EAPC/COEC** Euro-Atlantic Partnership Council in Council Operations and Exercise Committee.
Conseil de partenariat euro-atlantique en session du Comité des opérations du Conseil et des exercices.
**EAPMC** Euro-Atlantic Partnership Military Committee.
Comité militaire de partenariat euro-atlantique (CMPEA).
**EAPMC/CS** Euro-Atlantic Partnership Military Committee in Chiefs of Staff Session.
Comité militaire de partenariat euro-atlantique en session des chefs d'état-major (CMPEA / CEM).
**EARA** Environment Auditors Registration Association (G.B.).
**EARL** Easy Access Report Language.
**EARN** European Academic & Research Network.
EARN was launched in 1984.
For further details see under: **TERE NA**.
**EAROM** Electrically Alterable Read-Only Memory.
*Computer Technology* - The EAROM is used on IBM computers.
**EARRN** European Artificial Reef Research Network.
*Artificial Reef Research; European Community Project.*
**EARSEF** European Airborne Remote SEnsing Facility.
**EAS** Electronic Automatic Switch.
**EAS** Equivalent Airspeed.
*Aviation.*
**EAS** European Astronomical Society.
Formed in 1992, the European Astronomical Society sponsors meetings and encourages contact among scientists.
**EAS** Extended-Area Service.
*Telecommunications.*
**EASC** Eastern Administrative Support Center.
**EASC** Ethylaluminum Sesquichloride.
**EASD** European Association of Securities Dealers.
*European Community.*
**EASDAQ** European Association of Securities Dealers Automated Quotation.
**EASI** Estimate of Adversary Sequence Interruption.
*Graphics.*
**EASN** European Aeronautical Supercomputing Network.
**Easoe** European arctic stratospheric ozone experiment.
**EAST** Educational Access and Support Tools.
*European Community.*
**EASTLANT** 1. East Atlantic [has replaced EASTLANT 2.].
1. Est de l'Atlantique [remplace EASTLANT 2.].
2. Eastern Atlantic Area [obsolete - replaced by EASTLANT 1.].
2. Secteur oriental de l'Atlantique [obsolète - remplacé par EASTLANT 1.].
**EASY** Exception Analysis SYstem.
**EAT** Eating Attitudes Test.
*Psychology.*
**EAT** Tanzania - International vehicle registration letters.
**EATCHIP** European Air Traffic Control Harmonization and Integration Programme.
Programme européen d'harmonisation et d'intégration du contrôle de la circulation aérienne.
**EATMS** European Air Traffic Management System.
**EAU** emergency action unit.
unité d'intervention d'urgence.
**EAU** Extended Arithmetic Unit.
**EAW** The Electric Association for Women (U.S.A.).
The EAW was organized in 1924.
**EAW** Electronic and Acoustic Warfare.
*Military Science.*
**EAWAG** Swiss Federal Institute of Environmental Science and Technology (Switzerland).
**EAX** Electronic Automatic Exchange.
**EB** Early Burst.
**EB** Elementary Body.
*Virology.*
**EB** Encyclopaedia Britannica.
**EB** Epidermolysis Bullosa.
Epidermolysis Bullosa is a congenital disease of the skin and is characterized by the development of blisters at times following trauma.
*Medicine.*
**EB** Ethylbenzene.
EB is used mainly to produce styrene and as a solvent.

*Organic Chemistry.*
**EB** Eurobank.
**EB; E.B.** Excess Baggage.
**EBAM** Electron-Beam Addressable Memory.
**EBC** European Boxing Club.
**EBCDIC** Extended Binary Coded Decimal Interchange Code.
The EBCDIC is a binary code in which each character is represented by eight bits.
*Computer Programming.*
**EBCE** Electron-Beam Control Electronics.
**EBD cells** Embryoid Body-Derived cells.
*Stem Cell Therapies.*
**Eben** European business ethics network.
*International Association.*
**EBI** Electron Beam Irradiation.
**EBI** European Bioinformatics Institute.
EBI is the primary provider of public genome-sequence data in Europe. It is located near Cambridge (G.B.).
**EBIOC** extended basis entity object class.
class élargie d'objects "catégories élémentaires d'identité".
**EBIS** Electron-Beam Ion Source.
*Electronics.*
**EBIT** Earnings Before Interest and Taxes.
*Business; Finance.*
**EBITDA** Earnings Before Interest, Taxes, Depreciation and Amortization.
*Business; Depreciation Policies; Finance; Valuation Methods.*
**EBL** Explanation-Based Learning.
*Artificial Intelligence.*
**EBM** Electron-Beam Machining.
*Metallurgy.*
**EBN** European BIC Network.
For further details see under: **BIC**.
**EBNA2** Epstein-Barr virus Nuclear Antigen 2.
*Medicine; Molecular Virology; Oncology.*
**e-book** electronic book.
**EBP** EPO Binding Protein.
For further details see under: **EPO**.
**EBPR** Enhanced Bottom Pressure Recorder.
**EBR** Electron-Beam Recorder / Recording.
*Electronics.*
**EBRA** European Biomedical Research Association.
EBRA was launched in Strasbourg in November, 1994.
*Biomedical Research; European Associations; Information Networks; Non-animal Alternatives; Research Animals.*
**EBRD** European Bank for Reconstruction and Development.
**EBs** Elementary Bodies.
**EBS** Emergency Broadcast System.
The EBS informs listeners in case of a natural disaster or war.
*Telecommunications.*
**EBS** Engineered Barrier System.
**EBS** Epidermolysis Bullosa Simplex.
*Dermatology; Medicine.*
**EBS** European Business School.
**EB services** Electronic Banking services.
**EBSLG** European Business School Librarians Group.
**EBS-WC** EBS-Weber-Cockayne.
**EBU** European Blind Union.
EBU deals with special assistance of visually impaired.
*European Community.*
**EBV** Epstein-Barr Virus.
Named for the British physician Michael Anthony **Epstein** and the British virologist Y.M. **Barr**.
*Virology; Medicine.*
**EBW** Electron Beam Welding.
**EBWR** Experimental Boiling Water Reactor.
*Nuclear Engineering.*
**EC** East Caribbean; East Coast.
**ec.** (abbr.) economics.
**EC** Ecuador.
**EC** Education Committee.
**EC** Electrical Conductivity.
**EC** Electric Current.
*Electricity.*
**EC** Electron Capture.
Electron capture is also known as: electron attachment.
*Atomic Physics.*
**EC** Endothelial Cell.
Essentially, the endothelial cell is a squamous epithelial cell forming the endothelium.
*Histology.*
**EC** Enzyme Classification.
The naming and classification of enzymes of the Nomenclature Committee of the International Union of Biochemistry.
*Enzymology.*
**EC** Error Correction.
*Computer Programming.*
**EC** Ethylcellulose.
EC is used mainly in hot-melt adhesives and coatings, and printing inks as well as in food and feed additives.
*Organic Chemistry.*
**EC** Ethylene Carbonate.

EC also known as: Dioxolone-2 is used mainly as a plasticizer and a solvent.
*Organic Chemistry.*
**EC** European Commission.
**EC** European Community.
**EC** Ex-Coupon.
**E.C.** Exhaust Closes.
**EC** Expert Consultant.
**EC** Extended Coverage.
**ECA** Economic Commission for Africa.
**ECA** Economic Cooperation Administration.
**ECA** Employment Conditions Abroad (G.B.).
**E.C.A.** Ente Comunale di Assistenza.
Italian acronym meaning: Municipal Relief Board.
**ECA** European Cocoa Association.
**ECA** Europe and Central Asia.
**ECAC** European Civil Aviation Conference (Paris, France).
**ECACC** European Council of American Chambers of Commerce.
The ECACC was founded in 1963.
**ECAI** European Conference on Artificial Intelligence.
**ECAO-CIN** Environmental Criteria and Assessment Office in CINcinnati (U.S.A.).
**ECARDA** European Coherent Approach to Research and Development in ATC.
**ECARP** European Computational Aerodynamics Research Project.
*European Community Project.*
**ECar $** East Caribbean Dollar.
*Currencies.*
**ECB** Environmental Chemistry and Biology.
**ECB** European Central Bank.
**ECB** expendable communications buoy.
bouée de télécommunications consommable.
**ECC** Earth Continuity Conductor.
**Ecc.** (abbr.) Eccellenza.
Italian abbreviation meaning: Excellency; Lordship.
**ecc.** (abbr.) eccetera.
Italian abbreviation meaning: etcetera; and so on.
**ECC** Emergency Core Coolant.
**ECC** Error Checking and Correction.
**ECC** Error-Correcting Code.
The error-correcting code, also known as: self-correcting code, is a data representation that enables detection and correction of specific errors.
*Computer Programming.*
**ECCC** European Communities Chemistry Committee.
**ECCIA** Environmental and Cultural Conservation in Inner Asia.
A U.K.-based (Cambridge) research project (1992-1995).
*Grassland Productivity; Pasture Degradation; Social Anthropology.*
**ECCIP** Ecole Commerciale de la Chambre de Commerce et d'Industrie de Paris (France).
**ECCM** electronic counter-countermeasures [obsolete].
contre-contre-mesures électroniques (CCME) [obsolète].
**ECCNP** European Conference on Computer Network Protocols.
**ECCO** Extremely heavy Cosmic-ray Observatory.
ECCO will reach the ISS in 2003.
*Cosmic Rays; Physics; Space Technology.*
**EC coupling** Excitation-Contraction coupling.
*Medicine; Physiology.*
**ECCS** Emergency Core-Cooling System.
*Nucleonics.*
**ECD** *E. Coli* Database.
**ECD** Electron Capture Detector.
The electron capture detector is actually a sensitive detector used in gas chromatography.
*Analytical Chemistry.*
**ECD** Estimated Completion Date.
**ECD** Extracellular Domain.
**ECDIN** Environmental Chemical Data Information Network.
**ECDIS** Electronic Chart Display Information System.
**ECE** Economic Commission for Europe (Geneva, Switzerland).
**ECEs** Extrachromosomal Elements.
*Evolution; Genome Science; Microbial Genome Initiative; Origins of Life.*
**ECETOC** European Chemical Industry Ecology and TOxicology Centre (Belgium).
**ECF** essential command function.
fonction essentielle de commandement.
**ECF** Extended Care Facility.
**ECF** Extracellular Fluid.
The extracellular fluid essentially consists of ultrafiltrates of blood plasma and transcellular fluid.
*Anatomy.*
**ECFA** European Committee for Future Accelerators.
**ECFMG Certification** Educational Commission for Foreign Medical Graduates Certification (U.S.A.).
**ECFP** Enhanced Cyan Fluorescent Protein.
*Biochemistry; Chemistry.*
**ECG** Electrocardiogram; Electrocardiograph.
Also: **EKG**.
**EC-GC** Electron Capture - Gas Chromatography.

**ECGD** Export Credits Guarantee Departrnent.
G.B.'s official Insurer.
**ECGF-1** Endothelial Cell Growth Factor 1.
For further details see under: **TP** and **PD-ECG F**.
**ECHO** European Commission Host Organization.
*European Community.*
Head Office: Luxembourg.
**ECHO** European Community Humanitarian Office.
*European Community.*
**ECHO** evolutionary capability for HQ operations.
capacité évolutive pour les opérations de QG.
**ECHO virus** Enteric Cytopathogenic Human Orphan virus.
The ECHO virus is also known as: Enterovirus.
*Virology.*
**ECI** Environmental Change Institute (Ireland).
At NUI.
*Biodiversity; Climate Change; Marine Environment; Modelling Systems; Social and Economic Impact.*
For further details see under: **NUI**.
**ECI** European Cooperation in Informatics.
**ECIF** Electronic Components Industry Federation.
**ECIN** (abbr.) ECconomic INdicators.
*Economics.*
**ECIP** European Community Investment Partners.
*European Community Program.*
**ECL** Electrogenerated Chemiluminescence or Electrochemiluminescence.
*Physical Chemistry.*
**ECL** Emitter-Coupled Logic.
*Electronics.*
**ECL** Enhanced Chemiluminescence.
**ECL** Executive - Control Language.
The term executive-control language refers to a set of instructions enabling a programmer to run a program satisfactorily.
*Computer Programming.*
**ECLA** English Cathedral Libraries Association.
**ECLA** Evangelical Church Library Association.
**ECLAC** Economic Commission for Latin America and the Caribbean (Santiago).
**ECLAIR Programme** European Collaborative Linkage of Agriculture and Industry through Research programme.
*European Community Program.*
**ECM** Electrochemical Machining.
**ECM** Electronic Countermeasures.
contre-mesures électroniques (CME 2.).
**ECM** Enterprise Customer Management.
*Software Development.*
**ECM** Error Correction Mode.
**ECM** European Common Market.
**ECM** Extracellular Matrix.
*Anatomy; Biological Chemistry; Development; Medicine; Orthopedic Surgery.*
**ECMA** European Computer Manufacturer's Association.
**ECMM** European Community Monitoring Mission.
Mission de vérification de la Communauté européenne.
**ECMM** European Community Multinational Monitors.
**ECMSA** European Chemical Marketing And Strategy Association.
**ECMT** European Conference of Ministers of Transports (Paris, France).
**EC-MWF** European Center for Medium-range Weather Forecasting.
The ECMWF is located in Reading (G.B.).
*Atmospheric Research; Meteorology.*
**ECN** Energie Centrum Nederland.
The ECN is the Dutch National Energy Research center.
*Dutch Center.*
**ECN** European Chemical News (G.B.).
*Publication.*
**ECNs** Electronic Communications Networks.
**ECO** Electron-Coupled Oscillator.
The Electron-Coupled Oscillator is also known as: Dow Oscillator.
*Electronics.*
**ECO** Engineering Change Order.
**ECO** European Coal Organization.
**ECO** Europe centrale et orientale.
Central and Eastern Europe (C&EE).
**ECOA** Equal Credit Opportunity Act (U.S.A.).
**ECOFIN** (abbr.) ECOnomia e FINanza.
Italian abbreviation meaning: Economics and Finance.
**ECOLE** European COllaborative Learning Environment.
*European Community.*
**ECOMA** European COmputer Measurement Association.
**ECOMAG** ECOlogical Management Advisory Group.
**econ.** (abbr.) economics; economist; economy.
**ECOOP** European Conference on Object-Oriented Programming.
*Object-Oriented Programming.*
**ECOR** Engineering Committee on Oceanic Resources.
**ECORD** European Consortium for Ocean Research Drilling.
For further details see under: **OCP** and **IODP**.

**ECOSOC** U.N. ECOnomic and SOcial Council (New York, U.S.A.).
**ECOS Program** Environmental, Coastal and Ocean Sciences Program.
*Multidisciplinary Program.*
**ECOSS** European Conference On Surface Science.
**ECOTOX** (abbr.) ECOlogical TOXicity.
Database of the U.S. Environmental Protection Agency.
*Database; Pollutants; Toxic Substances.*
**ECP** écart circulaire probable.
circular errror probable (CEP 2.).
**ECPM** European Center for Pharmaceutical Medicine.
**EcR** Ecdysteroid Receptor.
*Larval Development.*
**ECR** Efficient Consumer Response.
**ECR** Electronic Cash Register.
The electronic cash register actually consists of a device to scan packages and read symbols on labels and a computer to convert this information in order to indicate prices of items and at times keep a record of sales and inventories.
*Engineering.*
**ECR** enemy contact report.
compte rendu de contact avec l'ennemi.
**ECRB** European Cancer Resources Bank - European Community.
Centralises a number of rare cancer cell strains.
*E.C. Cancer Banks.*
**ECRC** Engineering College Research Council.
**ECREEA** European Conference of Radio and Electronic Equipment Association.
*European Association.*
**ECR source** Electron Cyclotron Resonance source.
*Electronics.*
**ECs** Endothelial Cells.
**ECS** Environmental Control System.
The ECS is intended for environment modification of a closed space.
*Engineering.*
**ECS** European Collaborative Study.
*AIDS Research.*
**ECSC** European Coal and Steel Community.
**ECSC-STEELDEM** Pilot and Demonstration Projects in the Iron and Steel Industry.
*European Community Project.*
**ECSC-WORK SAFE** Safety in the European Coal and Steel Community Industries.
*European Community Program.*
**ECSEC** European Center for Scientific and Engineering Computing.
ECSEC is an IBM's European center with Head Office in Rome, Italy.
**ECSS** European Computing System Simulator.
**ECSW** Extended Channel Status Word.
**ECSZ** Eastern California Shear Zone.
**ECT** Earliest Completion Time.
**ECT** Electroconvulsive / Electro-Convulsive Therapy.
*Psychiatry; Psychology; Psychopharmacology.*
**ECT** Energy Charter Treaty.
The ECT, which promotes long-term co-operation in the energy field, was opened for signature on the $17^{th}$ December 1994.
**ECT** Environmental Control Table.
*Data Communications.*
**ECT** Estimated Completion Time.
**ECTA** Error-Correcting Tree Automation.
**ECTA** estimation de coût de type "A".
type "A" cost estimate [TACE].
**ECTB** Engineering and Control Technology Branch (U.S.A.).
Of the U.S. Occupational Safety and Health within the Centers for Disease Control and Prevention.
**ECTB** estimation de coût de type "B".
type "B" cost estimate [TBCE].
**ECTC** estimation de coût de type "C".
type "C" cost estimate [TCCE].
**ECTFE** Ethylene Chlorotrifluoroethylene.
**ECTL** Emitter-Coupled Transistor Logic.
**eCTLs** Cytotoxic T Lymphocyte effectors.
*Immunology.*
**ECTN** Episcopal Cathedral Teleconferencing Network.
**ECU** East Carolina University (U.S.A.).
**E.C.U.** English Church Union.
**ECU** European Currency Unit.
The EURO/EUR (€). Single currency with effect from january 2002.
*Finance; International Business.*
**Ecua.** (abbr.) Ecuador.
**ECVAM** European Center for the Validation of Alternative Methods.
The ECVAM is located at Ispra (Italy).
**ECWA** Economic Commission for Western Asia (Bagdad).
**ECZ** N-Ethylcarbazole.
**E.D.** Eastern Department.
**ed.** (abbr.) edited; edition.
**ed.** (abbr.) editor.
Also: **edit.**; **edt.**
The editor is a person who edits a manuscript or a publication.
**ED** Effective Dose.

*Medicine.*
**ED** Elasticity of Demand.
*Business; Economics; Finance.*
**E.D.** Electron District.
**ED** 1. electronic deception.
1. déception électronique.
2. énergie dirigée.
2. directed energy (DE).
3. exposure draft.
3. exposé-sondage.
**ED** Electronic Dummy.
*Acoustical Engineering.*
**ED** Encryption Device.
**ED** End Delimiter.
**ED** Erythema Dose.
*Medicine.*
**E.D.** Ex Dividend.
**ED** Extra Dividend.
Also: **EDD**.
**ED** Extra Duty.
**E-3D** NATO E-3D Component [Component of the NAEW&C force based at RAF Waddington].
Élément E-3D de l'OTAN [élément de la Force NAEW&C basé à la RAF Waddington].
**EDA** Economic Development Administration (U.S.A.).
**EDAC** Ethylene Diamine Carbodiimide.
**EDA Program** Excess Defence Articles Program.
**EDAR** estimated date of authorization request.
date prévue (ou probable) de la demande d'autorisation (DPDA).
**EDAS 120** Electrophoresis Documentation and Analysis System 120.
*Kodak Digital Science.*
**EDASI** European Development And Social Integration.
**Ed.B.** Bachelor of Education.
**EDB** Economic Development Board (Singapore).
**EDB** Ethylene Dibromide.
$BrCH_2CH_2Br$ - Ethylene dibromide is used mainly as a solvent in organic synthesis.
*Organic Chemistry.*
**EDBT** European Doctor in Biotechnology.
**EDC** Economic Development Committee.
**EDC** Economic Development Company.
Of Lancaster County ( U.S.A.). EDC is a private non-profit organization.
For further details see under: **IBEC**.
**EDC** Electronic Digital Computer.
**EDC** Energy Distribution Curve.
*Materials; Superconductivity Physics.*
**EDC** Environmental Data Centre (Finland).
**EDC** Estimated Date of Completion.
**EDC** European Defense Community.
**EDC** Expected Date of Confinement.
The EDC refers to the expected date of delivery for pregnant women.
*Medicine.*
**EDCTP** EU&DCs Clinical Trials partnership.
**Ed.D.** Doctor of Education.
**EDD** Earliest Due Date.
*Industrial Engineering.*
**EDD** Economic Development Department (Dubai).
**EDD** End Delivery Date.
*Business; Commerce.*
**Edd** Endodermin.
*Cellular Biology; Endoderm Development; Medicine; Molecular Biology.*
**EDD** Engineering Development Division.
Of the U.S. Pacific Marine Environmental Laboratory.
**EDD** Envelope Delay Distortion.
**EDD** Estimated Delivery Date; Expected Date of Delivery.
*Business; Commerce.*
**EDD** Extra Dividend.
Also: **ED**.
*Business; Commerce; Finance.*
**EDDA** Ethylenediamine Diacetic Acid.
**EDELWEISS** Experience pour DEtecter Les Wimps E, Site Souterrain (France).
The French EDELWEISS collaboration: building a germanium bolometer in the Fréjus undergroud laboratory.
*Astronomy; Bolometers.*
**EDF** Environmental Defense Fund; European Development Fund.
**EDFA** Erbium-Doped Fiber Amplifier.
*Chaotic Lasers; Chaotic Optical Waveforms.*
**EDFAs** Erbium-Doped Fibre Amplifiers.
**EDFRL** Erbium-Doped Fiber Ring Laser.
*Chaotic Lasers; Chaotic Optical Waveforms.*
**EDGAR**; **Edgar** Electronic Data Gathering And Retrieval.
**EDI** Economic Development Institute.
*World Bank Institute.*
**EDI**; **Edi** Electronic Data Interchange.
*Enterprise Computing.*
**EDI** Engineering Department Instruction.
**EDIMS** Environmental Data and Information Management Systems.
**Edin.** (abbr.) Edinburgh.
**EDIN** Ente nazionale per la Diffusione e l'Incremento della Nautica.
EDIN is located in Rome, Italy.
**EDIP** European Defence Improvement Programme.

programme d'amélioration de la défense européenne.
**EDIS** Environmental Data and Information Service (U.S.A.).
**EDI Service** Electronic Data Interchange Service.
**E.Di.S.U.** Ente regionale per il Diritto allo Studio Universitario (Italy).
**edit.** (abbr.) edited; edition; editor.
Also: **ed**.
**edit.** editore.
Italian abbreviation meaning: publisher.
**EDL** Entry, Descent, and Landing.
For further details see under: **ASI/MET**.
**EDL** Essential Drugs List.
**EDL muscles** Extensor Digitorum Longus muscles.
*Medicine; Muscle Aging; Kinesiology; Physiology.*
**EDM** Electron-Discharge Machining.
Electron-discharge machining is also known as electrical discharge machining; electroerosive machining; electrospark machining, electric spark machining.
*Metallurgy.*
**EDM** Electronic Distance Meter.
*Eruptive Activities; Field measurements of Deformations; Geophysics; Seismic Research; Volcanic Hazards; Volcanology.*
**EDM** Event-Driven Monitor.
The event-driven monitor actually carries out actions when certain events take place.
*Computer Technology.*
**EDMED** European Directory of Marine Environmental Data.
**EDO** Extended Duration Orbiter.
**EDOMP** EDO Medical Project.
**EdP** Electricidade de Portugal.
EdP is the national power utility.
**EDP** Electron Degeneracy Pressure.
*Astronomy; Mathematics; Physics.*
**EDPM** Electronic Data-Processing Machine.
**EDPS** Electronic Data-Processing System.
The electronic data processing system is used for high-speed data processing.
*Computer Technology.*
**EDPs** Employee Development Programs.
**EDR** European Depositary Receipt.
**EDRA** Environmental Design Research Association.
*Educational Web Sites.*
**EDRF** Endothelium-Derived Relaxing Factor.
Also: Endothelial-Dependent Relaxing Factor.
**EDRS** European Data Relay Satellite.
**EDS** Energy-Dispersive Spectroscopy (x-ray Spectrometer).
*Earth and Planetary Sciences; Geology; Ion Microprobe Analysis; Petrographic Studies.*
**EDS** Electronic Data Systems (U.S.A.).
**EDS** Energy Dispersive System.
**EDS** Engineering Design Specification.
**EDS** Environmental Data Service (U.S.A.).
Of the U.S. NOAA.
For further details see under: **NOAA**.
**EDS** estimated date of start.
1a. date de commencement prévue (DCP).
1b. date de début probable.
**EDS** Exchangeable Disk Storage.
*Computer Technology.*
**EDSES** European Data System for Energy Saving.
**EDSP** Endocrine Disruptor Screening Program (U.S.A.).
**EDT** Eastern Daylight Time.
**edt.** (abbr.) editor.
For further details see under: **ed**.
**EDT** Engineering Design Text.
**EDTA** Ethylenediaminetetraacetic Acid.
EDTA is used mainly as a chelating agent, and a food preservative.
*Organic Chemistry.*
**EDTAN** Ethylenediaminetetraacetonitrile.
**educ.** (abbr.) educated; education; educational.
**EDVAC** Electron Discrete Variable Automatic Compiler.
EDVAC became operational in 1952.
*Computer Technology.*
**EDW** effective downwind.
vent effectif de retombée (VER).
**EDWA** Erbium-Doped Waveguide Amplifier.
For metro-area networks.
**EDX analysis** Electron-induced X-ray fluorescence analysis.
*Chemistry; Chemical Biology.*
**EDX spectra** Energy-Dispersive X-ray spectra.
**EE** East(ern) European.
**EE** Electrical Engineer.
**EE** emergency establishment.
tableau d'effectifs d'urgence (TEU).
**EE** Employment Exchange.
**E-E** End-to-End.
**EE** Environmental Education.
**EE** Equity Earnings.
*Business; Finance.*
**EE** Errors Excepted.
*Commerce; Finance.*
**EEa** atipical Early Endosome.
**EEA** Egyptian Electricity Authority (Egypt).
**EEA** Electronic Engineering Association.
**EEA** Ethylene Ethyl Acrylate.

**EEA** European Economic Area.
**EEA** European Environment Agency.
**EEA countries** European Economic Area countries - European Community.
**EEb** basolateral Early Endosome.
**EEB**; **E.E.B.** European Environmental Bureau.
**EEC** European Economic Community.
**EECA** European Electronic Component Manufacturers' Association.
The EECA represents European Union Semiconductor Manufacturers.
*European Association.*
**EED** electron-explosive device.
dispositif électro-explosif.
**EEE** Encéphalite équine de type Est.
French initialism meaning: Eastern Equine Encephalomyelitis or Encephalitis.
*Medicine.*
**EEEM department** Environmental Economics and Environmental Management department.
University of York (G.B.).
**EEFI** essential elements of friendly information.
éléments essentiels d'informations amies.
**EEG** Electroencephalogram; Electroencephalograph.
*Medicine.*
**EEG activation arousal** Electroencephalographic activation arousal.
*Biomedicine; Psychiatry.*
**EEI** Edison Electric Institute.
**EEI** Exo-Earth Imager.
*Astronomy.*
**EEI** Essential Elements of Information.
**EEIB**; **E.E.I.B.** Environmental Engineering Intersociety Board, Inc.
**EEIG** European Economic Interest Group.
*European Community.*
**EELS** Electron Energy Loss Spectra / Spectroscopy.
EELS is also known as: Electron Impact Spectroscopy.
**E.E.N.T.** Eye-Ear-Nose-Throat.
**EEO** Equal Employment Opportunity.
**EEOC** Equal Employment Opportunity Commission (U.S.A.).
**EEOH unit** Environmental Epidemiology and Occupational Health unit.
**E.E.P.** Ente Europeo per la Produttività.
Italian initialism meaning: European Board for Productivity.
**EEP** Export Enhancement Program (U.S.A.).
**EE.PP.** Enti Pubblici.
Italian initialism meaning: Public Bodies.
**EE.PP.TT.** Enti Provinciali per il Turismo.
Italian initialism meaning: District Offices for the Promotion of Tourism.
**EEPROM** Electrically Erasable Programmable Read-Only Memory.
The EEPROM can be electrically erased and reprogrammed.
**EER** explosive echo-ranging.
localisation d'échos par charge explosive.
**EERI** Earthquake Engineering Research Institute.
*Seismology.*
**EERO** European Environmetal Research Organization (The Netherlands).
**EEROM** Electrically Erasable Read-Only Memory.
The EEROM contents can be erased and reprogrammed as many times as desired without damaging the device.
**EETC** Electronic Equipment Technical Committee.
*Electronics.*
**EETIS** Electrical / Electronic / Telecommunications / Information technology Sectors.
*U.S.; E.C. Business.*
**EEX** European Emergency Exchange.
The Frankfurt-based Electricity Trading Market.
**EEZ** Exclusive Economic Zone.
**EF** Edema Factor.
*Anthrax Toxin; Biochemistry; Cell Biology; Dental Research; Medicine.*
**EF** Emitter Follower.
The emitter follower in its operations is similar to the cathode follower.
*Electronics.*
**EF**; **E.F.** Engineering Foundation.
**EF** Europe Fund.
**EF** Execution Function.
**EF** 1. enemy forces.
1. forces ennemies.
2. exercice financier.
2. financial year (or fiscal year).
3. external forces.
3. forces extérieures.
**EF** Extended Facility.
**EFA** European Fertility Association.
**EFA** European Fighter Aircraft.
avion de combat européen.
**EFAs** Essential Fatty Acids.
The EFAs are polyunsaturated fatty acids that have to be included in mammals diets.
**EFC** Estimated Final Cost.
*Business; Commerce.*
**EF coils** Equilibrium Field coils.
**EFDA** European Federation of Data Processing.
**EFE** Einstein Field Equations.
*Physics.*

**EFEDA** Echivial Field Experiment in Desertification-threatened Areas.
*European Community Program; Environmental Protection; Meteorology.*
**EFESO** Ente di Formazione per l'Economia SOciale.
EFESO is located in Bologna, Italy.
**eff.** (abbr.) effettivo.
Italian abbreviation meaning: actual; effective.
**eff.** (abbr.) effetto.
Italian abbreviation meaning: bill; promissory note.
**eff.** (abbr.) efficiency.
**EFF** Empirical Force Field.
*Chemical Physics; Chemistry; Macromolecular Science; Polymer Research.*
**EFF** Exchange For Futures.
*Business; Economics; Finance.*
**EFF** Experimental Forecast Facility (U.S.A.).
**EFF** Extended Fund Facility.
For further details see under: **CCFF**; **ESAF**; and **SAF**.
**effect.** (abbr.) effective.
**EFFOST** European Federation of FOod Science and Technology.
**Efg** Enhanced filamentous growth.
*Cell Biology; Genetics; Microbiology; Transcription.*
**EFH** Echo-Free Hole.
**EFI** Electronic Fuel Injection.
*Motor Vehicles.*
**EFI** Ente Finanziamenti Industriali.
Italian acronym meaning: Industrial Financing Board.
**EFI probes** Electric Field Instrument probes.
*Geophysics; Space Science.*
**EFID** European network of Food Intolerance Databanks.
*European Community Project; Food Allergy and Intolerance.*
**EFINP** Ente di Formazione Impresa No Profit (Italy).
**EFISH generation experiments** Electric Field-Induced Second Harmonic Generation experiments.
*Optical Sciences.*
**EFL** Error Frequency Limit.
*Computer Technology.*
**EFL** established financial limit.
limite financière établie (LFE).
**EFL** External Finance Limit.
**EFLA** Educational Film Library Association.
**EFM** Electronic Fetal Monitor.
The EFM is used during labor to monitor fetal heart-beat and uterine contractions.
*Medicine.*
**EFMD** European Foundation for Management Development.
Located in Brussels, Belgium. Founded in 1971; an international network with a mixed membership of corporations, public and private organizations and educational institutions, aiming to be a focal point for information, research and discussion on best practice, creativity and innovation in human resource development in Europe.
*Management Development.*
**EFOA**; **Efoa University** European Federation of Oriental Arts University.
EFOA is a registered trademark.
**EFP** Exchange For Physicals.
**efph** equivalent full-power hour.
**EFQM**; **E.F.Q.M.** European Foundation for Quality Management.
The EFQM set a European Model (in 1988) for Total Quality Management used as a valuation model.
**EFS** Ecological Farming Systems.
*European Community Project.*
**EFSA** European Food Safety Authority.
EFSA is an independent Body established in January 2002.
**EFSR** Emergency Food Security Reserve (Ethiopia).
**EFT** Electronic Financial Transaction.
**EFT**; **Eft** Electronic Funds Transfer.
The electronic funds transfer is actually a method of transferring bank funds by electronic means.
*Banking.*
**EFTA** European Free Trade Association (Geneva).
**EFTPOS** Electronic Funds Transfer at Point Of Sale.
**EFTS** Electronic Funds Transfer System.
For further details see under: **EFT**.
**EFY** End of Fiscal Year.
*Business; Finance.*
**Eg** (abbr.) Egypt; Egyptian.
**EG** Exhaust Gas.
The term exhaust gas refers to spent gas from a gas turbine or an internal combustion engine.
*Mechanical Engineering.*
**e.g.** for example.
**EGA** Enhanced Graphics Adapter.
The EGA is a second-generation color video display.
*Computer Technology.*
**EGA** Evolved Gas Analysis.

**EGAL** European Group of Astronomy Librarians.
*Library Association.*
**EGAT** Electricity Generating Authority of Thailand.
**EG cells** Embryonic Germ cells.
**EGD** Electrogas Dynamics.
**EGD** Evolved Gas Detection.
**EGDN** Ethylene Glycol Dinitrate.
**EGF** Epidermal Growth Factor.
*Endocrinology.*
**EGGs** Evaporating Gaseous Globules.
**E-G GSSP** Eifelian-Givetian GSSP.
*Geology; Geophysics.*
For further details see under: **GSSP.**
**EGL** External Germinal Layer.
**EGM** Enhanced Graphics Module.
**EGM** Extraordinary General Meeting.
**Egmc** East Germanic.
*Languages* - No longer extant.
**EGO** Eccentric orbiting Geophysical Observatory.
**EGP** Extramural Grant Program.
*U.S. Grant Programs.*
**EGP** Extrasolar Giant Planet.
**EGPs** Extrasolar Giant Planets.
*Astronomy; Astrophysics; Planetary Science.*
**EGR** Etang de la GRuère.
In the Jura mountains, Switzerland.
**EGR** Exhaust Gas Recirculation.
**EGRET** Energetic Gamma Ray Experiment Telescope.
*Astronomy; Space Physics.*
**EGS** European Geophysical Society.
**EGS** External Guide Sequence.
The EGS is a short piece of DNA.
*Bacterial Resistance; Microbiology; Molecular Biology.*
**EGSA** Educational Guidance Services for Adults (G.B.).
**EGT** Ethylene Glycol bis(Trichloroacetate).
EGT is used as an herbicide.
*Organic Chemistry.*
**EGT** European Gas Turbines (G.B.).
*Gas Turbine Manufacture.*
**EGT gene** Ecdysteroid UDP-Glucosyl-Transferase gene.
*Biology; Biotechnology; Environmental Science, Policy and Management Baculovirology; Medical Research.*
**Egypt** (abbr.) Egyptian.
Egyptian is the Afro-Asiatic language of the ancient Egyptians.
*Languages.*
**EH** Early Holocene.
**EH** Eclosion Hormone.
*Biology; Ecdysis Control; Zoology.*
**EH** Epidermolytic Hyperkeratosis.
*Cancer Research; Keratin Mutations; Medicine; Molecular Genetics; Skin Disorders.*
**EH domains** Eps 15 homology domains.
*Biochemistry; Biophysics; Cell Biology; Molecular Biology.*
**EHE** Enterprise in Higher Education.
**EHEC** Ethyl Hydroxyethyl Cellulose.
**EHESS** Ecole des Hautes Etudes en Sciences Sociales (France).
**EHF; ehf** Extremely High Frequency.
The extremely high frequency is in the range from 30 to 300 MHz.
*Telecommunications.*
**EHIP** European HAWK Improvement Programme.
Programme d'amélioration du HAWK européen.
**EHLASS** Community System of information on Home and Leisure Accidents.
*European Community Project.*
**EHMA** European Hotel Managers' Association.
**EHP; ehp** Effective Horsepower.
Effective horsepower is also known as: Towrope Horsepower.
*Telecommunications.*
**EHP; ehp** Electric Horsepower.
**EHR programs** Education and Human Resource programs (U.S.A.).
Of the AAAS.
For further details see under: **AAAS**.
**EHV; ehv** Extra-High Voltage or extra-high tension.
EHV is a voltage above 340 kilovolts.
*Electricity.*
**EI** The airline code for Aer Lingus.
**EI** Earned Income.
*Business; Finance.*
**e.i.** East Indian.
**E.I.** East Indies.
**EI** Echo Intensity.
The E.I. is the brightness degree of a radar echo signal.
*Electronics.*
**EI** Electron Ionization.
**E.I.** Enciclopedia Italiana.
Italian initialism meaning: Italian Encyclopaedia.
**EI** Energy Intensity.
**EI** Enterprise Integration.
**EI** Enterprise Ireland.
An enterprise development Agency.
*Advanced Technology for Biotechnology.*
For further details see under: **BRI**.
**E.I.** Esercito Italiano.
Italian initialism meaning: Italian Army.

**EI** Exact Interest; Ex-Interest.
*Business; Finance.*
**EI** Exposure Index.
*Graphic Arts.*
**EI** Ireland.
**EIA** Electronic Industries Association.
**EIA** Energy Information Administration (U.S.A.).
**EIA** Energy Information Agency (U.S.A.).
**EIA** Environmental Impact Assessment.
Issued in the U.S.A. 27 years ago, the National Environmental Policy Act introduced for the first time the concept of *Environmental Impact Assessment.*
**EIA** Enzyme Immunoassay.
**EIA**; **Eia Center** European Impact Assessment Center.
**EIADS** extended integrated air defence system.
système de défense aérienne intégrée élargie.
**EIAJ** Electronic Industries Association of Japan.
**EIB** European Investment Bank.
**EIB** Experimental Immunology Branch.
Of the U.S. NCI.
For further details see under: **NCI**.
**EIB** Export-Import Bank - U.S.A. and Japan.
*Banks.*
**EIBA** Ethylene Isobutyl Acrylate.
**EIBW** Export-Import Bank of Washington (U.S.A.).
Also: **EXIMBANK**; **EXIMBK**.
**EIC** Engineering Institute of Canada.
**EIC** Equipment Identification Code.
**EICMA** East India Cotton Mills Association.
*Indian Association.*
**EICs** Euro-Info-Centers - E.C.
The EICs are part of a E.C. network for small and medium size enterprises.
*European Community Network.*
**EID** Emerging Infectious Disease.
**EIDs** Emerging Infectious Diseases.
**E.I.E.** Ente Internazionale delle Esposizioni.
Italian acronym of the: International Trade Fair Board.
**EIEMA** Electrical Installation Equipment Manufacturers Association.
**EIES** Electronic Information Exchange System.
**EIES** European Information Exchange Service.
*European Community Project.*
**EIF** entry-into-force (day).
(jour d') entrée en vigueur.
**EIF** Eukaryotic Initiation Factor.
*Medicine; Molecular Pharmacology; Oncology.*
**EIF** European Investment Fund - *European Community.*
**EIFAN** European Independent Financial Advisers Network.
**E.I.M.** Ente Italiano della Moda.
Italian acronym meaning: Italian Fashion Board.
**EIMI** Euler International Mathematical Institute.
EIMI located in St. Petersburg, Russia, was founded in 1989. Named for the Swiss mathematician Leonhard **Euler**.
*International Institute; Mathematics.*
**EIMS** European Innovation Monitoring System - *European Community.*
**EIN** European Informatics Network.
**EINECS** European INventory of Existing Chemical Substances.
**EIODI** External Independent Organization of the Defense Industry.
**EIOM** Ente Italiano Organizzazione Mostre (Italy).
**EIP**; **Eip** Enterprise Information Portal.
**EIRENE** European Information REsearchers NEtwork.
**EIRMA** European Industrial Research Management Association.
**EIRP** equivalent isotropically radiated power.
puissance isotrope rayonnée équivalente (PIRE).
**EIS** Enterprise Information Systems.
*Data Warehouses; Next Generation Programs.*
**EIS** Environmental Impact Statement.
**EI source** Electron Ionization source.
**EISs** Executive Information Systems.
Comprehensive EISs can supply executives with a vast array of both external data and internal data. A properly designed system enables management to monitor current operations relative to worldwide competition, to resolve short-term issues of the firm, and to plan for the future.
*Executive Tools.*
**EIT** Electromagnetically Induced Transparency.
*Optics.*
**EIT** Emplacement, Installation, and Testing.
**EIT** Extreme-ultraviolet Imaging Telescope.
**EITB** Engineering Industry Training Board (G.B.).
**EITC '98** 1998 European Information Technology Conference.
The EITC '98 was held in Vienna on 30th November / 2nd December 1998.
**EITO** European Information Technology Observatory.
*European Observatories.*
**EITS** Express International Telex Service.
**EIU** (the) Economist Intelligence Unit.
**EJ** Electronic Jamming.
**EJASA** Electronic Journal of the ASA.
For further details see under: **ASA**.

**EJB**; **Ejb** Enterprise Java Beans.
*Application Servers.*
**EJC** Engineers Joint Council.
**EJC** European Journal of Cancer.
*Publication.*
**EJTN**; **Ejtn** European Jewellery Technology Network.
Project started in September 1998.
*European Project.*
**EJV** Equity Joint Venture.
*Business; Economics; Finance.*
**EK** Equatorial Guinea.
**EKB** Edgeworth-Kuiper Belt.
*Planetary Science.*
**EKD** Electronic Key Distribution.
**EKG** Electrocardiogram; Electrocardiograph.
Also: **ECG**.
**EKOs** Edgeworth-Kuiper belt Objects.
*Earth and Planetary Sciences.*
**EKP**; **Ekp** Enterprise Knowledge Portal.
**EL** Elastic Limit.
The elastic limit is also known as: Yield Point Load.
*Mechanics.*
**EL** Electroluminescence.
**EL** Employers' Liability.
**EL**; **el** Enamel Lined.
**EL** End of the Line.
**EL** Even Lots.
**EL** External Label.
*Computer Programming.*
**ELA** Education Library Association.
**ELA** Equipment Leasing Association.
**ELA** Ethiopian Library Association.
**ELAM-1** Endothelial Leukocyte Adhesion Molecule-1.
**ELAN** Error Logging and Analysis.
**élan** The above acronym was coined accidentally using the French word "élan" which means: rush, impetus, impulse, outburst.
**ELAs** Equilibrium Line Altitudes.
*Geosciences.*
**ELATT** East London Advanced Technology Training (G.B.).
**ELAV system** Embryonic Lethal Abnormal Visual System.
*Biochemistry; Medicine; Physiology.*
**ELCA** Eastern Atlantic Coordination Agreement [obsolete].
Accord de coordination dans le Secteur oriental de l'Atlantique [obsolète].
**ELCA** European Landscape Contractors Association.
**ELCs** Europe's Largest Companies.
**E.L.D.O.** European Launcher Development Organization.
**ELDOR** Electron-electron DOuble Resonance.
**elettr.** elettricità; elettrico.
Italian abbreviation meaning: electricity; electrical.
**elettr.** elettronica; elettronico.
Italian abbreviation meaning: electronics; electronical.
**elettrochim.** elettrochimica; elettrochimico.
Italian abbreviation meaning: electrochemistry; electrochemist; electrochemical.
**elettromecc.** elettromeccanica; elettromeccanico.
Italian abbreviation meaning: electromechanics; electromechanical.
**elev.** (abbr.) elevation.
*Cartography; Engineering; Ordnance.*
**ELF** Electronic Location Finder.
**ELF** Essences et Lubrifiants de France.
**ELF** Extensible Language Facility.
**ELF** Extra Low Frequency.
**ELF** Extremely Low Frequency.
ELF is a radio frequency in the range from 30 to 300 Hz.
*Telecommunications.*
**ELFAP; Elfap** Ente Lombardo Formazione e Aggiornamento Professionale (Italy).
*Vocational Training.*
**ELG** Electrolytic Grinding.
The term electrolytic grinding refers to a combined grinding and machining operation.
*Mechanical Engineering.*
**ELH** Early Life History.
**ELI** Expression Library Immunization.
*Biochemistry; Gene Vaccine; Immunology.*
**ELINT**; **elint** electronic intelligence.
**ELISA** Enzyme-Linked Immunosorbent Assay.
ELISA is also known as: Immunosorbent assay.
*Immunology.*
**ELISPOT assay** Enzyme-Linked Immunospot assay.
**elix.** (abbr.) elixir.
*Chemistry; Pharmacology.*
**Eliz.** Elizabethan.
**ell.** (abbr.) ellisse.
Italian abbreviation meaning: ellipse.
*Mathematics.*
**ELM** Electrochemical Machining.
*Metallurgy.*
**ELMs** Edge Localised Modes.
*Fusion.*
**ELN** National Liberation Army.
ELN is Colombia's second-largest guerrilla group.

**ELOG substrate** Epitaxially Laterally Overgrown substrate.
*Applied Physics.*
**ELOIS** European Land-Ocean Interaction Studies.
**ELP** Electronic Line Printer.
**ELP** The airport code for El Paso, Texas, U.S.A.
**EL railroad** (abbr.) ELevated railroad.
**ELR scale** Equal-Listener Response scale.
*Acoustics.*
**ELS** Emitter Location System.
**ELS** Encyclopaedia of Life Sciences.
*Publication.*
**ELS** Esercito del Libano del Sud.
Italian acronym meaning: Southern Lebanon Army.
**ELSD** Evaporation Light Scattering Detector.
*Anions and Cations Analysis.*
**ELSEC** electronic security.
sécurité électronique.
**ELSI** Ethical, Legal and Social Implications.
Research Program: 1998-2003.
**ELS model** Economic Lot-Size model.
*Production.*
**ELSS** emergency life-support system.
système de réanimation en cas d'urgence.
**ELSS** Extravehicular Life Support System.
**ELSSE COTAR system** ELectronic Sky Screen Equipment Correlated Orientation Tracking and Range system.
*Electronics.*
**elt.** (abbr.) element.
*Chemistry; Computer Programming; Computer Technology; Electromagnetism; Statistics.*
**ELT** Emergency Locator Transmitter.
*Navigation.*
**ELT** English Language Training.
**ELT** Equipment Limité par le Traité.
**ELV** Expendable Launch Vehicle.
*Space Technology.*
**E.M.** Earl Marshal.
**EM** Electromagnetic.
*Physics.*
**E.M.** Electromotive.
*Physical Chemistry.*
**EM** Electron Microscope.
The electron microscope is actually an instrument which uses electrons focused by electron lenses to magnify small objects.
*Electronics.*
**EM** Electronic Mail.
Also: **e-mail**.
*Telecommunications.*
**EM** Electrophoretic Mobility.
*Biochemistry; Physical Chemistry.*
**Em.** (abbr.) emanation.
**EM** Engineer of Mines.
**EM** Enlisted Man; Enlisted Men.
**EM** Environmental restoration and waste Management.
**EM** Equine Morbillivirus.
*Emerging Viruses.*
**EM** Excerpta Medica.
**EMA** Enterprise Management Architecture.
**EMA** European Monetary Agreement.
**EMAD** Engine Maintenance, Assembly, and Disassembly.
**E-Mail**; **e-mail** Electronic Mail.
Also: **EM**.
**EM&S** Equipment Maintenance and Support.
**EMAP** Environmental Monitoring and Assessment Program.
**EMAS** ECO Management and Audit Scheme - *European Community.*
*Ecological Management.*
**Emb.** (abbr.) Embankment.
**Emb.** (abbr.) Embassy.
**EMB** Explosive Motor Behavior.
**EMB agar** Eosin-Methylene Blue agar.
*Microbiology.*
**EMBC** European Molecular Biology Conference.
**EMBL** European Molecular Biology Laboratory.
**EMBO** European Molecular Biology Organization.
An international Research Organisation Headquartered in Heidelberg, Germany.
**EnBW** Energie Baden-Württenberg.
Germany's third biggest electricity supplier.
**EMC** Electromagnetic Compatibility.
*Electronics.*
**EMC** Encephalomyocarditis.
Encephalomyocarditis is a human infection that may range from a mild febrile illness to a severe encephalomyelitis.
*Medicine.*
**EMC** Equivalent Mécanique de la Chaleur.
French initialism meaning: Mechanical Equivalent of Heat.
*Thermodynamics.*
**EM character** End-of-Medium character.
**EMCON** emission control.
contrôle d'émission.
**EMCV** Encephalomyocarditis Virus.
*Virology.*
**EMD NAPOCOR** Environmental Managemeent Department - NAtional POwer CORporation (The Philippines).

**EMEA** European Medicines Evaluation Agency - European Community.
Also: European Medicinal Products Evaluation Agency. The EMEA deals with the registration of new drugs.
*Medicines Evaluation.*
**EMF** Electromagnetic Frequency.
**EMF**; **emf** Electromotive Force.
Electromotive force is also known as: electromotance.
*Physical Chemistry.*
**EMF** Executive Mortgage Facilities.
**EMFs** Electromagnetic Fields.
*Electromagnetism.*
**EMG** Electromyograph.
The electromyograph is an instrument to make electromyograms.
*Medicine.*
For further details see under: **EMG** (Electromyogram).
**EMG** Electromyogram.
The electromyogram is a graphic record of the electric impulses or eye movements during reading.
*Medicine.*
**EMG** état-major général.
general staff (GS 1.).
**EMG recording** Electromyographic recording.
**E.M.I.** Edizioni Musicali Italiane.
Italian acronym meaning: Italian Musical Publications.
**EMI**; **emi** Electromagnetic Interference.
*Electricity.*
**EMI** European Monetary Institute.
The EMI is the forerunner of the European Central Bank. Under the Treaty the European Monetary Institute has the role of preparing an operational ESCB for stage three.
For further details see under: **ESCBs**.
**EMIND** European Modular Interactive Network Designer.
**EMIT**; **E.M.I.T.** Ente Morale "Giacomo Feltrinelli" per l'incremento dell'Istruzione Tecnica (Italy).
*Technical Education.*
**EML** Estimated Month of Loss.
*Business; Economics.*
**EML** European Medical Lexicon.
**EMMA**; **Emma** Ermes Manufacturers' Marketing Association.
**EMMA** European Mouse Mutant Archive.
A facility near Rome, Italy, was set up using seed money provided by Framework 4.
*European Union.*
**EM method** Expectation Maximization method.
**EMMF** European Multinational Maritime Force.
Force maritime multinationale européenne.
**Em.mo** Eminentissimo.
Italian abbreviation meaning: Most Eminent.
**EMMS** Electronic Mail and Message System.
**EMOP** Enhanced and More Operational Partnership.
Partenariat renforcé et plus opérationnel.
**EMORBs** Element-enriched Mid-Ocean Ridge Basalts.
*Earth Sciences; Geological Sciences; Space Science.*
**EMP** Electro-Magnetic/Electromagnetic Pulse.
*Electromagnetism.*
**EMP** End-of-Month Payment.
**EMP** Environmental Monitoring and Prediction.
**EMP** EPO Mimetic Peptide.
**EMPA** Electron Microprobe Analysis.
**EMPA** European Military Press Association.
**EMPAS** Environmental Management and Protected Areas Services (The Philippines).
**empl.** (abbr.) employee; employer; employment.
**EMPP** electromagnetic pulse protection.
protection contre l'impulsion électromagnétique.
**EMPS**; **Emps** Electronic Mobile Payment System.
**EMQ** Economic Manufacturing Quantity.
**EMRLB** East Midland Regional Library Bureau.
**EMS** electromagnetic spectrum.
spectre électromagnétique.
**EMS** Electronic Mail System.
**EMS** Electronic Message Service.
**EMS** Engineering Material Specification.
**EMS** Environmental Management Systems.
**EMS** Ethyl Methanesulfonate.
**EMS** European Monetary System.
**EMS** Eurotra Morphological Structure.
**EMSA** Electrophoretic Mobility Shift Analysis.
**EMSAs** Electrophoretic Mobility-Shift gel Assays.
**EMSEC** emission security.
sécurité des émissions.
**EMSIWARN** emitter simulation warning message.
message de préavis de simulation d'émetteurs.
**EMSL** Environmental Molecular Sciences Laboratory (U.S.A.).
**EMSL** European Microwave Signature Laboratory.
*Microwave Technology.*
**EMSL-LV** Environmental Monitoring Systems Laboratory - Las Vegas (Nevada, U.S.A.).
**EMSS** Electronic Message Service System.
**EMT** Emergency Medical Technician.
*Medicine.*
**EMT** End of Magnetic Tape.

**EMTS** Electronic Money Transfer System.
**EMTS** Ethylmercury-p-Toluene Sulfonamide.
**EMTS Acid** Ethylmercurithiosalicyclic Acid.
**EMU**; **emu** Electromagnetic Unit.
EMU is a unit based primarily on the magnetic effect of an electric current.
*Electromagnetism.*
**EMU** European Monetary Union - *European Community.*
**EMU** Extravehicular Mobility Unit.
**EMUA** European Monetary Unit of Account - *European Community.*
**EMX service** Electronic Message Exchange service.
**E.N.** Educazione Nazionale.
Italian initialism meaning: National Education.
**EN** 1. electronic neutralization.
1. neutralisation électronique.
2. Estonia.
2. Estonie.
**en-** prefix having different meanings.
May be used for example in: enarthrosis; encapsulate; enthrone; enslave; etc.
*Prefixes.*
**ENA** Ecole Nationale d'Administration (Paris, France).
Founded in 1945. Managed by the State.
**ENA** European Neuroscience Association.
**ENAC** Energetic Neutral Atom Camera.
**ENaC** Epithelial Sodium Channel.
*Mechanosensory Transduction; Medicine.*
**ENaCs** Epithelial Sodium Channels.
*Medicine; Neurobiology; Neurology.*
**ENADEL** Ente Nazionale Assistenza Dipendenti Enti Locali (Italy).
Italian acronym of the: National Association for the Assistance of Local Authorities Workers.
**ENAIP** Ente Nazionale Acli Istruzione Professionale (Italy).
**E.N.A.L.** Ente Nazionale Assistenza Lavoratori (Italy).
Italian acronym of the: National Association for Assistance to Workers.
**ENAM** Ente Nazionale di Assistenza Magistrale (Italy).
*Italian Board.*
**ENAP** Energetic Neutral Atom Precipitation.
*Space plasma physics experiment.*
**E.N.A.P.I.** Ente Nazionale per l'Artigianato e le Piccole Industrie (Italy).
Italian acronym of the: National Organization of Craftsmen and Owners of Small Industries.
**ENAS** Ente Nazionale di Assistenza Sociale (Italy).
**ENASARCO** Ente Nazionale di Assistenza agli Agenti e Rappresentanti di COmmercio (Italy).
Italian acronym of the: National Board for the Assistance to Commercial Agents and Representatives.
**E.N.A.T.** Ente Nazionale Assistenziale agli addetti ai Trasporti (Italy).
Italian acronym of the: National Teamster's Welfare Board.
**enbl.** (abbr.) enable.
Also: **e**.
**E.N.B.P.S.** Ente Nazionale per le Biblioteche Popolari e Scolastiche (Italy).
Italian initialism of the: National Organization of Popular and School Libraries.
**ENCARS** Ente Nazionale CAse a Riscatto Statali (Italy).
**ENCIP** ENte Case Impiegati e Professionisti (Italy).
**encl.** (abbr.) enclosed; enclosure.
**ENCODE** Encyclopedia Of DNA Elements.
ENCODE, a NHGRI's new genome projet, has been launched in February 2003.
*Functional Genomics.*
For further details see under: **NHGRI**.
**ency.** (abbr.) encyclopaedia; encyclopaedic.
**end.** (abbr.) endorsement.
**ENDEX** end of exercise.
fin d'exercice (FINEX).
**ENDOR** Electron Nuclear DOuble Resonance.
*Spectroscopy.*
**ENE** East-Northeast.
**ENEA** Ente Nazionale per l'Energia Atomica e alternativa (Italy).
*Atomic Energy.*
**ENEA** Ente per le Nuove tecnologie l'Energia e l'Ambiente (Italy).
*New Technologies.*
**E.N.E.L.** Ente Nazionale per l'Energia Elettrica (Italy).
Italian acronym of the: National Board for Electric Power.
**ENG** Electro Nystagmographie.
French initialism meaning: Electronystagmography. ENG is a method to assess and record the eye movements.
*Medicine.*
**eng.** (abbr.) engine; engineer; engineering.
**Eng.** (abbr.) England; English.
**eng.** (abbr.) engraved; engraving.
**eng.** (abbr.) engraver.
The term engraver refers to the tool used, as well as to the person working in engraving.
*Graphic Arts.*

**ENHA** en-route holding area.
zone d'attente (en déplacement).
**E.N.I.** Ente Nazionale Idrocarburi (Italy).
Italian acronym of the: National Hydrocarbon Board.
**ENIAC** Electronic Numerical Integrator And Calculator.
The ENIAC was developed in 1942/1945.
*Computer Technology.*
**E.N.I.C.** Ente Nazionale Industrie Cinematografiche (Italy).
Italian acronym of the: National Association of Film Producers.
**E.N.I.C.** Ente Nazionale della Cinofilia Italiana.
Italian acronym of the: National Italian Dog Breeders and Lovers' Associations.
**ENIL** European Network on Independent Living.
*Handicapped Persons.*
**E.N.I.M.** Ente Nazionale dell'Istruzione Media.
Italian acronym of the: National Board for Secondary Schools (Italy).
**E.N.I.O.S.** Ente Nazionale Italiano per l'Organizzazione Scientifica del Lavoro.
Italian acronym of the: Italian Board for the Scientific Organization of Work.
**ENIPG** Ente Nazionale Istruzione Professionane Grafica (Italy).
**E.N.I.T.** Ente Nazionale per le Industrie Turistiche (Italy).
Italian acronym of the: Italian State Tourist Office.
**ENITA** European Network for Information Technology in Agriculture.
*European Community Initiative.*
**ENMOC** El Niño MOnitoring Center.
**ENO** English National Opera (G.B.).
**eNOS** endothelial Nitric Oxide Synthase.
*Cell Biology; Lipid Biology.*
**E.N.P.A.** Ente Nazionale per la Protezione degli Animali (Italy).
Italian acronym of the: National Society for the Prevention of Cruelty to Animals.
**ENPALS** Ente Nazionale Previdenza ed Assistenza Lavoratori Spettacolo (Italy).
**E.N.P.A.S.** Ente Nazionale di Previdenza e Assistenza per i dipendenti Statali.
Italian acronym of the: National Board of Social Insurance and Welfare for Civil Servants.
**ENPC** Ecole Nationale des Ponts et Chaussées (Paris, France).
ENPC was founded in 1747. It is the oldest "grande école" of Engineering Expertise in international marketing, management technology, business strategies, finance.
*Engineering Expertise.*
**E.N.P.I.** Ente Nazionale Prevenzione Infortuni.
Italian acronym of the: National Institution for the Prevention of Accidents (Italy).
**enq.** (abbr.) enquiry.
**ENR** ENoyl Reductase.
ENR is an enzyme involved in fatty acid biosynthesis.
*Biological Sciences; Biomolecular Research; Genetics; Molecular Biology; Plant Sciences.*
**ENRI** Environment and Natural Resources Institute.
Of the University of Alaska Anchorage School of Public Affairs.
**ENRICH** European Network for Research In global CHange.
*Environmental Research.*
**ENS** Ecoles Normales Supérieures (France).
**ENS.** (abbr.) ensign.
**ENS** European Network for Science.
*European Community.*
**ENS** European Network for Services - E.C.
*European Community.*
**ENSA** Ecole Nationale Supérieure de l'Aéronautique (France).
**ENSAE** Ecole Nationale Supérieure de l'Aéronautique et de l'Espace (France).
**ENSEEIHT** Ecole Nationale Supérieure d'Electrotechnique, d'Electronique, d'Informatique et d'Hydraulique de Toulouse (France).
**ENSO events** El Niño-Southern Oscillation events.
In the Galapagos Islands.
**ENSTA** Ecole Nationale Supérieure des Techniques Avancées (France).
**ENT**; **E.N.T.** ear, nose, and throat.
**entd.** (abbr.) entered.
**ENTEL - Chile** Empresa Nacional de TELecommunicaciones S.A. (Chile).
**ENTPE** Ecole Nationale des Travaux Publics de l'Etat (France).
**ENU** N-ethyl-N-Nitrosourea.
**env.** environ.
French abbreviation meaning: about; around; approximately.
**ENVDC** ENVironmental measures in Developing Countries - *European Community.*
**ENVNGO** Community action program promoting Non-Governmental Organizations primarily active in the field of ENVironmental protection.
*European Community Program.*
**EO** Electro-optics; electro-optical.
**EO**; **E.O.** Executive Order.
**EO** Exempt Organization.
*Social Services.*

**EOA** Emissioni Otoacustiche.
*Hearing Tests.*
**EOA** End Of Address.
**EOB** electronic order of battle.
ordre de bataille électronique (ODBE).
**EOB** End Of Block.
**EOB** Expense Operating Budget.
*Business; Economics; Finance.*
**EOB character** End-Of-Block Character.
*Computer Programming.*
**EOC** Economic Opportunity Commission.
**EOC** (the) Equal Opportunities Commission.
**EOC** essential operational capability.
capacité opérationnelle essentielle.
**EOCCM** electro-optical counter / countermeasures.
contre-contre-mesures optoélectroniques.
**EOCM** electro-optical countermeasures.
contre-mesures optoéelectroniques.
**EOCY** End Of Calendar Year.
**EOD** End Of Data.
*Data Communications.*
**EOD** End-Of-Day.
**EOD** Explosive Ordnance Disposal.
*Ordnance.*
**EODC** Earth Observation Data Centre (G.B.).
**EODT** explosive ordnance disposal team (navy).
équipe d'intervention sur le matériel explosif [marine].
**EOE** Equal Opportunity Employer.
**EOE** European Options Exchange.
**EOF** Electro-Osmotic Flow.
The EOF is the flow of electrolyte through the capillary.
*Bioanalytical Chemistry; Biochemical Engineering; Medicine; Pharmaceutical Sciences.*
**EOF** End Of File.
*Computer Programming.*
**EOF** essential operating facility.
installation essentielle d'exploitation.
**EOF analysis** Empirical Orthogonal Function analysis.
*Climate / Ocean Variability; Geoscience; Oceanography.*
**EOF gap** End-Of-File gap.
Essentially the end-of-file gap is a fixed dimension gap that indicates the file end on a tape.
*Computer Programming.*
**EOFY** End Of Fiscal Year.
*Business; Economics; Finance.*
**EOG** Electrooculogram.
The electrooculogram is used for retinal dysfunction detection.
*Medicine.*
**EOG experiments** Electro-Olfactogram experiments.
*Aquaculture Science; Biochemistry; Molecular Biology.*
**EOHR** Egyptian Organization for Human Rights (Egypt).
**EOI** End-Of-Inquiry.
**EOIS** Electro-Optical Imaging Sensor.
*Robotics.*
**EOL** End-Of-Line.
**E-OLM** Electro-Optical Light Modulator.
The electro-optical light modulator comprises an electrooptical device which modulates the amplitude, phase, or direction of a light beam.
*Optics; Telecommunications.*
**EOLSS** Encyclopaedia Of Life Support Systems.
**EOM** Earth Observation Mission.
**EOM** End Of Message.
*Telecommunications.*
**EOM** End Of Month.
*Finance.*
**EOM** European Options Market.
**EOM** Every Other Month.
**EO materials** Electrooptic materials.
*Biochemistry; Chemistry; Optoelectronic Computing Systems.*
**EON** End-Of-Number.
**EONR** European Organization for Nuclear Research.
**EOP; eop** Efficiency Of Plating.
*Virology.*
**EOP** emergency offtake point.
point d'extraction d'urgence.
**EOP** End-Of-Page.
**EOQ** Economic Order Quantity.
EOQ is also known as: Economic Purchase Quantity.
*Industrial Engineering.*
**EOQ** End Of Quarter.
**EOQ** End-Of-Query.
**EOQ; E.O.Q.** European Organization for Quality.
The EOQ is a federation of over 30 European Quality Associations.
**EOR** Earth Orbital Rendez-vous.
**EOR** End-Of-Record.
**EOR** Enhanced Oil Recovery.
*Petroleum Engineering.*
**EOR** explosive ordnance reconnaissance.
1a. reconnaissance d'explosifs et de munitions.
1b. reconnaissance de munition explosive.
**EORC** Earth Observation Research Center.
**EOR gap** End-Of-Record gap.

The end-of-record gap is actually a gap of precise length indicating the end of a record on a tape.
*Computer Programming.*
**EORA** Explosive Ordnance Reconnaissance Agent.
*Military.*
**EORSAT** ELINT ocean reconnaissance satellite.
satellite ELINT de reconnaissance océanique.
**EORTC** European Organization for Research and Treatment of Cancer - European Community.
The EORTC was set up 40 years ago.
*Clinical Trial Startegies; New Drugs Development; Oncology.*
**EOS** Earth Observation Satellite - NASA.
**EOS** Earth Observing System.
**EOS** Electronic Office System.
**EOS** end of set.
fin de bloc.
**EOS** Equation Of State.
*Physical Chemistry.*
**EOSDIS** Earth Observing System Data Information System.
EOSDIS, a network of data storage centers, was built by NASA scientists in 1992.
**EOSM** electro-optical support measures.
mesures de soutien optoélectroniques.
**EOSP** Earth Observing Scanning Polarimeter.
**EOSS** European Sea Level Observing System.
*European Community Project; Mean Sea Level Determination; Sea Surface Topography.*
**EOT** End of Tape; End Of Text.
**EOT** end of tour.
fin d'affectation.
**EOT mark** End-Of-Tape mark.
*Computer Programming.*
**EOT recognition** End-Of-Transmission recognition.
The term end-of-transmission recognition refers to the ability of a computer to recognize the end of a data transmission, even if the buffer is not filled.
*Computer Programming.*
**EOUSA** Executive Office for United States Attorneys (U.S.A.).
**EOV** End-Of-Volume.
**EOW** End-Of-Word.
**EOY** End Of Year.
**EP** Earning Power.
*Business; Economics; Finance.*
**EP** Earnings Price.
**EP** Eastern Pacific.
**EP** Editor Program.
The editor program enables a computer user to perform deletions, modifications, or corrections in an existing file or program.
*Computer Programming.*
**EP** Effective Par.
*Banking; Business; Finance.*
**EP** Electrostatic Potential.
*Electricity.*
**EP** Emulator Program.
**e.p.** ends per inch.
*Textiles.*
**EP** Enterprise Portal.
**EP** Entry Point.
Entry point is also known as: entrance, and refers to the point of execution.
*Computer Programming.*
**EP** Entry Portion.
*Computer Programming.*
**Ep.** Epistle.
**EP** Estimated Position.
*Navigation.*
**EP** Ethylene Propylene.
**EP** European Pharmacopoeia.
**EP** European Plan.
**EP** Evoked Potential.
The evoked potential is essentially a neuron's electrical response to stimuli.
*Physiology.*
**EP** Extended Play.
*Acoustical Engineering; Mechanical Engineering.*
**EP** Extra Play.
*Mechanical Engineering.*
**EPA** Economic Planning Agency (Japan).
**EPA** Ente Protezione Ambientale.
Italian acronym of the: Environmental Protection Agency (Italy).
**EPA** Environmental Protection Agency.
The EPA, created in 1970, is a U.S. Federal Agency, which establishes rules and standards for pollution-control and environmental protection.
For fruther details see under: **STAR fellowship program**.
**EPA** Ethiopian Privatization Agency.
*Ethiopian Agency.*
**EPAC instrument** Energetic PArticle Composition instrument.
*Astronomy; Astrophysics; Geophysics; Space Science.*
**EP Act** Energy Policy Act (U.S.A.).
**EPAM** Esercizi Pubblici Associati Milanesi (Milan, Italy).
**EPASA** Ente Per l'Assistenza Sociale agli Artigiani e commercianti (Italy).
**EPB** East Pacific Barrier.
*Oceanography.*
**EPB approach** Extant Phylogenetic Bracket approach.

*Biomedical Sciences; Extant Organisms; Ichthyology; Herpetology; Medicine.*
**EPBN** European Plant Biotechnology Network.
**EPC** Economic Policy Council.
**EPC** Editorial Processing Center.
**EPC** impulse-Evoked Postsynaptic Current.
**EPC** European Patent Convention.
**EPC** European Political Cooperation.
**EPC** Extra-Pair Copulation.
*Avian Behavioral Ecology; Avian Monogamy; Biology.*
**EPCR** Endothelial cell PC Receptor.
*Cancer Biology; Immunology; Molecular Medicine; Physiology.*
**EPD** Energetic Particles Detector.
**EPDM rubbers** Ethylene-Propylene-Diene Monomer rubbers.
The EPDM rubbers are used as components mainly in roofing, tires and weather stripping in view of the fact that they are highly weather-resistant and present good electrical insulating properties.
**EPEC** Enteropathogenic *Escherichia Coli.*
EPEC causes diarrhea in children in developing countries.
*Microbiology.*
**EPFL** Ecole Polytechnique Fédérale de Lausanne (Switzerland).
French initialism of the: Swiss Federal Institute of Technology (Lausanne, Switzerland).
**EPFs** Extra-Pair Fertilizations.
*Avian Behavioral Ecology; Avian Monogamy; Biology.*
**EPG**; **Epg** Electronic Program Guide.
**EPG** Eminent Persons Group.
**EPG** 1. employment planning guide [NAEW].
1. guide pour la planification d'utilisation [NAEW].
2. exercise planning guide.
2. guide de planification des exercices.
**EPG electrode** Edge-Plane Graphite electrode.
**Eph.** (abbr.) Ephesians.
**EPI** Echo Planar Imaging.
*Biodiagnostics; Chemistry; Magnetic Resonance Research.*
**EPI** Electronic Position Indicator.
*Navigation.*
**EPI** Expanded Program on Immunization.
The EPI was launched by W.H.O. and UNICEF in 1981.
*Microbiology; Medicine; Immunology.*
For further details see under: **W.H.O.** and **UNICEF**.
**EPIA** European Photovoltaics Industries Association.
**EPIAIM** A knowledge-based system for EPIdemiology in AIM.
*European Community Project.*
**EPIC**; **Epic** Electronic Privacy Information Center.
**EPIC** Equatorial Pacific Information Collection.
**EPICA** Electrically Powered Integrated Control Actuators.
*European Community Project; Aerospace Technology.*
**EPICS** Engineering Projects In Community Service.
A U.S. Program that begun in 1995.
**EPIET** European Programme in Intervention Epidemiology Training.
*Communicable Disease Surveillance; Epidemiology.*
**EPILOG Program** Environmental Processes of the Ice age: Land, Oceans, Galciers program.
Originated in 1998 under the aegis of the IMAGES program of IGBP/PAGES - LGM.
For further details see udner: **IMAGES**; **IGBP/PAGES**; **LGM**.
**EPIRB** electronic position-indicating radio beacon.
radiobalise de localisation des sinistres.
**EPIRB** Emergency Position-Indicating Radio Beacon.
*Navigation.*
**Epis.** (abbr.) Episcopal; Episcopalian; Epistle.
**Episc.** (abbr.) Episcopal; Episcopalian.
Also: **Epis.**
**epit.** (abbr.) epitaph; epitome.
**EPI technique** Echo Planar Imaging technique.
**EPL** External Plexiform Layer.
**EPLANS** Engineering, Planning and Analysis Systems.
**EP lubricant** Extreme-Pressure lubricant.
**EPM** electronic protective measures.
mesures de protection électroniques (MPE).
**EPM**; **Epm** Enterprise Performance Management.
**EPMA** Electron Probe Microanalysis.
**EPNL** Effective Perceived Noise Level.
**EPO** Erythropoietin.
*Molecular Mimicry; Protein Engineering.*
**EPOC** Eastern Pacific Oceanic Conference.
**EPO-R** Erythropoietin Receptor.
**EPOS** Earthquake Phenomena Observation System (Japan).
**EPOS**; **Epos** Electronic Point-Of-Sale.
**EPOX** (abbr.) Epoxide.
*Organic Chemistry.*
**EPP** Estimated Price Policy.

**EPP** exercise planning process.
processus de planification d'exercice.
**EPPDyL** Electric Propulsion and Plasma Dynamics Laboratory.
At Princeton University, U.S.A.
**EPPK** Epidermolytic Palmoplantar Peratoderma.
*Cancer Research; Keratin Mutations; Medicine; Molecular Genetics; Skin Disorders.*
**EPQ** Economic Purchase Quantity.
*Industrial Engineering.*
**EPR** Earnings-Price Ratio.
**EPR** East Pacific Rise.
**EPR** Electron Paramagnetic Resonance.
Electron paramagnetic resonance is also known as: Electron Spin Resonance; Paramagnetic Resonance.
**EPR** Estimated Price Request.
*Business; Commerce; Finance.*
**EPR** Ethylene-Propylene Rubber.
**EPR** Experimental Power Reactor.
*Nuclear Energy.*
**EPR** Exxon Production Research.
*Geological Sciences.*
**EPR fluid compositions** East Pacific Rise fluid compositions.
*Aquarium Research; Biogeology; Earth Sciences.*
**EPR frequency** Electron Paramagnetic Resonance frequency.
*Chemistry; Physics.*
**EPRI** Electric Power Research Institute (U.S.A.).
**EPRIWATCH** European Parliament Research Initiative WATCH.
*European Community Project.*
**EPROM** Erasable Programmable Read-Only Memory.
*Computer Technology.*
**EPR pairs** Einstein Podolsky-Rosen pairs.
*Physics; Quantum Cryptography; Quantum Mechanics.*
**EPS** Earnings-Per-Share.
*Business; Economics; Finance.*
**EPS** Ecole Professionnelle de Soudure.
French initialism of the: Soldering / Welding Professional School (France).
**EPS** Ecole Professionnelle Supérieure (France).
**EPS** Epidemiology and Population Studies.
The Division of International Epidemiology and Population Studies of the FIC plans, designs, and conducts studies to examine factors affecting the application of *health science advances* for the benefit of populations, particularly in developing countries. EPS develops strategic partnerships with the categorical institutes of the NIH and other governmental and non-governmental organizations to advance a common research agenda.
For further details see under: **FIC** and **NIH**.
**EPS** exercise planning staff.
état-major de planification d'exercice.
**EPS** Extracellular Polymeric Substances.
*Aquatic Chemistry; Biomineralization; Cell Biology; Geology; Palaeontology.*
**EPSC** Excitatory Postsynaptic Current.
*Neurobiology; Neurophysiology; Psychiatry; Physiology.*
**EPSCoR** Experimental Program to Stimulate Competitive Research (U.S.A.).
EPSCoR is a U.S. National Science Foundation 18-year-old program intended to help states lacking a strong research base.
*U.S. Program.*
**EPSCs** Excitatory Postsynoptic Currents.
For further details see under: **EPSC**.
**EPSDT** Early Periodic Screening, Diagnostic and Treatment.
*Disabilities; Control Transmissible Illness.*
**EPSI** Earnings Per Share Issued.
*Business; Economics; Finance.*
**EPS matrix** Extracellular Polysaccharide matrix.
*Biofilm Engineering; Microbiology.*
**EPSPs** Excitatory Postsynaptic Potentials.
*Biology.*
**E.P.T.** Ente Provinciale per il Turismo (Italy).
Italian initialism of the: District Office for the Promotion of Tourism.
**EPT** Excess-Profits Tax.
*Business; Finance.*
**EPT** Execution Processing Unit.
**EPT** External Pipe Thread.
**EPTC** Ethyl Dipropylthiocarbamate.
**EPU** European Payment Union.
**EPW** earth penetrator weapon / warhead.
arme / tête explosive à forte pénétration dans le sol.
**EPW** Electron Plasma Wave.
*Ultrafast Optical Science.*
**EQ** Educational Quotient.
**eq.**; **eql**; **equ.** (abbr.) equal.
*Mathematics.*
**eq.** (abbr.) equal; equation.
**Eq.** (abbr.) equator.
*Anatomy; Astronomy; Cartography.*
**eq.** equazione.
Italian abbreviation meaning: equation.
**eq.** (abbr.) equivalent.
**EQ.** (abbr.) Equities.
**EQA** European Quality Award.

**EQB** European Quality Beef.
*European Union Labels.*
**EQEs** External Quantum Efficiencies.
**eql.** (abbr.) equal.
Also: **eq.**; **equ**.
**EqPac project** Equatorial Pacific project.
**eqpt.** (abbr.) equipment.
**EQUIS**; **Equis** European QUality Improvement System.
*Management Schools.*
**equiv.** (abbr.) equivalent.
*Chemistry; Geology; Mathematics; Medicine.*
**ER** Earnings Record; Earnings Report.
*Business; Finance.*
**E.R.** East Riding (Yorkshire) (G.B.).
**E.R.** East River (New York City) (U.S.A.).
**ER** Echelle Réaumur.
French initialism meaning: Réaumur temperature scale.
*Thermodynamics.*
**ER** Electroreflectance.
*Spectroscopy.*
**E.R.** Queen Elizabeth (Elizabeth Regina).
**ER** Emergency Room.
*Medicine.*
**ER** Endoplasmic Reticulum.
*Cell Biology.*
**ER** Energy Research.
**ER** Environmental Reports.
**ER** Equatorial Ring.
**Er** The chemical symbol for Erbium.
Erbium is a metallic element having the atomic number 68, an atomic weight of 167.26, and a melting point in the range of 1400/1500°C. It is used mainly in nuclear reactors and lasers.
*Chemistry; Symbols.*
**er** (abbr.) error.
**ER** Estrogen Receptor.
*Adult Oncology; Medicine.*
**ER** Excess Reserves.
**ER** Expense Report.
**ER** Ex-Rights.
*Business; Finance.*
**ER** extended range.
portée prolongée.
**ERA** Economic Regulatory Administration (U.S.A.).
**ERA** Electrical Research Association (G.B.).
**ERA** Electron Ring Accelerator.
*Nuclear Engineering.*
**ERA** Electronic Representatives Association.
**ERA** Energy Research Abstracts.
Of the U.S. Department of Energy.
**ERA** Engineering Research Association (G.B.).
**E.R.A.** Ente Riforma Agraria (Italy).
Italian acronym of the: Organization for Agrarian Reform.
**ERA** 1. entity-relationship analysis.
1. analyse des rapports entre entités.
2. explosive reactive armour.
2. blindage réactif par explosion.
**ERA** European Research Area.
Conceived in 1999 by the European Commission.
**ERA** Expense Reduction Analysts.
Milan, Italy.
**ERAD** ER-Associated Degradation.
*Cell Biology.*
For further details see under: **ER**.
**ERATO** Exploratory Research for Advanced Technology (Japan).
**ERBE** Earth Radiation Budget Experiment.
*Atmospheric Sciences; Climate; Cloud Microphysics; Geophysics.*
**ERBPs** Event-Related Brain Potentials.
*Neuroscience.*
**ERBS** Earth Radiation Budget Satellite.
**ERBSS** Earth Radiation Budget Satellite System.
**ERCC designations** Excision Repair Cross Complementing designations.
*Biochemistry; Biophysics.*
**ERCIM** European Research Consortium for Informatics and Mathematics.
**ERCS** ECM-resistant communications system [obsolete].
système de communication insensible aux CME [obsolète].
**ERCs** Engineering Research Centers.
The ERCs are centers for instructing engineering students. A program sponsored in 1992 by the U.S. NSF.
For further details see under: **NSF**.
**ERCs** Extrachromosomal Ribosomal DNA Circles.
*Cell Biology; Genetics; Gerontology; Molecular Biotechnology; Oxidative Damage.*
**ERDA** Energy Research Development Administration.
Successor to AEC.
For further details see under: **AEC**.
**ERDF** European Regional Development Fund - *European Community.*
**ERDC** Engineer Research and Development Center.
*U.S. Army.*
**ERE** Estrogen Response Element.
*Biological Regulation and Development; Endocrine Research; Endocrinology; Steroid Biochemistry.*

**EREC** Energy efficiency and Renewable Energy Clearinghouse.
The EREC was established by the U.S. Department of Energy, which consolidated two previous services: **CAREIRS** and **NATAS**.
**ERED** Economics, Research and Evaluation Division.
Of Employment Departments.
**EREP** Earth Resources Experiment Package.
**E.R.F.** Ente Riforma Fondiaria (Italy).
Italian initialism of the: Organization for the Reform of Land Property.
**ERF** European Research Forum - *European Community.*
**ERFAP** Ente Regionale per la Formazione e l'Aggiornamento Professionale (Italy).
*Vocational Training.*
**ER fluids** Electrorheological fluids.
**ERGO** European Research Gateways On-line.
*European Community Project.*
**ERGS** Electronic Route Guidance System.
**ERGs** Electroretinograms.
*Medicine; Neurobiology; Neurology.*
**ERI** Elevato Rischio Industriale.
Italian acronym meaning: High Industrial Risk.
**Eri** Eridanus.
Also: **Erid.**
Eridanus is also known as River Po. It is a southern constellation that winds southwest from Orion.
*Astronomy.*
**ERIC** Educational Resources Information Center.
**ERICA** Experiment on Rapidly Intensifying Cyclones over the Atlantic (U.S.A.).
**Erid.** Eridanus.
For further details see under: **Eri**.
**ERIM** Environmental Research Institute of Michigan (U.S.A.).
**ERIM** Ex Repubblica Iugoslava di Macedonia.
**ERIN** Environmental Resources Information Network (U.S.A.).
**ERISA** Employee Retirement Income Security Act.
*Human Resources.*
**ERK** Extracellular signal-Regulated Kinases.
*Basic Science; Biomedical Sciences; Immunology; Pharmacology; Respiratory Medicine.*
**ERK pathway** Extracellular signal-Regulated Kinase pathway.
*Signal Transduction.*
**ERL** Environmental Research Laboratories.
Of the U.S. NOAA.
For further details see under: **NOAA**.
**ERL-C** Environmental Research Laboratory - at Corvallis, Oregon (U.S.A.).
**ERM** Enteric Redmouth.
**ERM** Exchange Rate Mechanism.
*European Monetary Union.*
**ERMES**; **Ermes** European Radio Messaging System.
*Information Exchange (by radio).*
**ERN** Error-Related Negativity.
*Anterior Cingulate Cortex; Magnetic Resonance; Medicine; Neuroscience; Psychiatry; Psychology.*
**ERNACT** European Regions Network for the Application of Communication Technology - European Community.
**ERNIE** Electronic Random Number Indicator Equipment.
**ERO** Executive Records Office (U.S.A.).
**$Er_2O_3$** Erbium Oxide.
Erbium Oxide, also known as Erbia, is used mainly as a phosphor activator.
*Inorganic Chemistry.*
**EROM** Erasable Read-Only Memory.
**EROS** Earth Resources Observations System; Observing Satellite.
**EROS** Expérience de Recherches d'Objets Sombres.
*Astronomy; Astrophysics; Cosmology; Dark Matter; Physics; Planetary Systems.*
**ERP** Effective Radiated Power.
*Electromagnetism.*
**ERP** Emergency Recorder Plot.
*Navigation.*
**ERP**; **Erp** Enterprise Resource Planning.
**ERP** Error Recovery Procedures.
**ERP**; **E.R.P.** European Recovery Program.
The European Recovery Program was a plan proposed by the U.S.A. in 1947 to aid European nations in economic recovery (after World War II).
**ERP** Event-Related brain Potential (human).
*Anterior Cingulate Cortex; Cognitive Neuroimaging; Magnetic Resonance; Medicine; Psychiatry; Psychology.*
**ERP** Exported Repetitive Protein.
*Biological Sciences; Cell Biology; Medicine; Molecular Bacteriology.*
**ERP(F)** Effective Renal Plasma (Flow).
*Medicine.*
**ERPs** Event-Related brain Potentials (human).
For further details see under: **ERP**.
**ERP software** Enterprise Resource Planning software.
ERP software is used by companies to plan and manage business functions.
*International Business.*
**ERR** engineering release record.
dossier de diffusion technique.

**E.R.R.** Ente Radio Rurali.
Italian initialism meaning: Organization for the spreading of Wireless Radios in Rural Areas.

**err.** (abbr.) errata; error.

**ERRAC** European Rail Research Advisory Council.
Launched by the European Union in 2002.
*Rail Research.*

**ERS** Earth Resources Satellite - NASA's.

**ERS** Economic Research Service.

**ERS** Economic Retention Stock.

**ERS** emergency relocation site.
emplacement de repli en cas d'urgence.

**ERs** Engineering Reports.

**ERS** Environmental Research Satellite.

**ERS-1** European Remote Sensing Satellite 1 - ESA.
The ERS-1 was launched in 1991.
For further details see under: **ESA**.

**ERSEP** Electronic Retrieval System on Employment Policies.

**ERT** Estrogen Replacement Therapy.

**ERT** European Round Table.
ERT is a high-level lobby of industrialists, 46 of them from all over Europe, who meet at least twice a year.

**ERT** execution reference time.
temps de référence pour l'éxécution.

**ERTA** Economic Recovery Tax Act (U.S.A.).

**ERTC** Environmental Research and Training Centre - Department of Environmental Quality (Thailand).

**ERTICO** European Road Transport Telematic Implementation Coordination Organization.

**ertor** effective radiational temperature of the ozone region.
*Meteorology.*

**ERTS** Earth Resources Technology Satellite.

**E.R.V.** English Revised Version.

**ERV** Expiratory Reserve Volume.
ERV is also known as: Reserve Air; Supplemental Air.
*Medicine.*

**ERVs** Endogenous Retroviruses.
*Medicine; Xenotransplantation; Xenovirology.*

**ERW** enhanced-radiation weapon [neutron weapon].
arme à effets de radiation renforcés [arme à neutrons].

**ES** Earned Surplus.
*Business; Finance.*

**Es** The chemical symbol for Einsteinium.
Named after the German physicist Albert **Einstein**.
*Symbols; Chemistry.*

**ES** Electrical Stimulation.

**ES** El Salvador - International vehicle registration letters.

**ES** End System.

**ES** Engine Speed.

**es.** esempio.
Italian abbreviation meaning: example.

**es.** (abbr.) estimated.

**ES** Executive Secretariat.

**ES** Exempt Securities.
*Banking; Business; Finance.*

**ES** Expert System.
*Artificial Intelligence.*

**ES** Extension Service.

**ES** telomeric Expression Site.
*Molecular Parasitology.*

**ES** External Store.
*Aviation.*

**ESA** Ecological Society of America (U.S.A.).
*Environment; Fellowship Programs.*

**ESA** Employment Standards Administration (U.S.A.).

**ESA** Endangered Species Act (U.S.A.).
*Biology; Ecology; Environment; Habitat Conservation; Zoology.*

**ESA** European Space Agency.
The ESA is the intergovernmental organization responsible for Europe's collaborative civilian space operations.

**ESAE** European Society for Atomic Energy.

**ESAF** Enhanced Structural Adjustment Facilities.
*Business; Finance.*
For further details see under: **CCFF**; **EFF**; and **SAF**.

**ES&E Program** Environmental Science and Engineering Program.
At the Harvard School of Public Health (Boston, Massachusetts, U.S.A.).

**ESA project** Endogenous Skill Anticipating project.
Promoter: Pavia University (Italy).
*Endogenous Development.*

**ESARDA** European SAfeguards Research and Development Association.

**ESATRI** (abbr.) ESAzione TRIbuti.
Italian abbreviation meaning: exaction / collection of taxes.

**ESB** Encefalopatia Spongiforme Bovina (malattia della mucca pazza).
Italian initialism meaning: Bovine Spongiform Encephalopathy (mad cow disease).
*Medicine.*

**ESC** Embryonic Stem Cell.

**esc.** (abbr.) escape.
*Computer Programming; Space Technology.*

**ESC** European Shippers' Councils.
**ESCAP** Economic and Social Commission for Asia and the Pacific.
Formerly called the Economic Commission for Asia and the Far East, ESCAP was founded in Shangai in 1947. The 48th Session of the ESCAP opened in Beijing on the 15th April, 1992, with a speech from Chinese Premier Li Peng.
**ESCBs** European System of Central Banks.
The ESCBs primary objective is to maintain price stability and to formulate a monetary policy strategy for this purpose.
**ESCEP** Ecole Supérieure de Tourisme, de Commerce et de Publicité (France).
**ESCIM** European Short Course In Mechatronics - European Community.
**ESCMID** The European Society of Clinical Microbiology and Infectious Diseases (Switzerland).
**ESCP** Ecole Supérieure de Commerce de Paris (France).
**escl.** esclusivo.
Italian abbreviation meaning: exclusive.
**ESCs** Embryonic Stem Cells.
*Cell Biology.*
**ESD** Edizioni Studio Domenicano (Italy).
*Publications.*
**ESD** Electron-Stimulated Desorption.
**ESD** Electrostatic Discharge.
**Esd.** (abbr.) Esdras.
**ESD** Estimated Shipping Date.
*Business; Commerce; Shipping.*
**ESD** Experimental Sterilizing Dose.
**ESD** Ex-Stock Dividend.
*Business; Finance.*
**ESD** External Symbol Dictionary.
**E.S.D.A.** East Sweden Development Agency.
*Science & Technology Parks.*
**ESDI** European Security and Defence Identity.
Identité européenne de sécurité et de défense (IESD).
**ESDIAD** Electron-Stimulated Desorption Ion Angular Distribution.
**ESDP** European Security and Defence Policy.
politique européenne en matière de sécurité et de défense (PESD).
**ESE** Ecole Supérieure d'Electricité (France).
**ESE** European School of Economics.
*Economics; Finance; Management.*
**ESEEM** Electron Spin Echo Envelope Modulation.
**e segg.** e seguenti.
Italian abbreviation meaning: and the following ones.
**ESEM** Ente Scuola Edile Milanese (Milan, Italy).
*Italian School.*
**ESEs** Exonic Splicing Enhances.
*Biology; Cancer Research; Chemical Processes; Exons; Oligonucleotide Motifs.*
**ESF** Erythropoietic Stimulating Factor.
**ESF** European Science Foundation.
The European Science Foundation is an association of national research councils and academies from European countries, founded in 1974.
**ESF** European Security Forum.
Forum européen de sécurité.
**e sg.** e seguente.
Italian abbreviation meaning: and the following one.
**ESHA** European Small Hydropower Association.
**ESI** Electrospray Ionization.
*Biochemistry; Chemistry; Chemical Biology.*
**ESI** European Software Institute.
**ESIEE** Ecole Supérieure d'Ingénieurs en Electrotechnique et Electronique (France).
**ESI-MS** Electrospray-Ionization Mass Spectrometry.
**ESIS** ESA Space Information Systems.
For further details see under: **ESA**.
**ESJ** EW stand-off jammer.
brouilleur de GE à distance de sécurité (de l'objectif).
**ESL** European Systems Language.
**ESM** Electronic Support Measure.
**ESM** electronic warfare support measures.
mesures de soutien de guerre électronique (MSE 2.).
**ESM** Electron-Stimulated Migration.
*Electronics; Surface Chemistry; Physics.*
**ESM** Erreur Standard sur la Moyenne.
French initialism meaning: Standard Error of the Mean.
**ESM** European Single Market.
*International Business.*
**ESMR** Electrically Scanning Microwave Radiometer.
**ESN** English-Speaking Nation.
**ESN**; **esn** Erasmus Student Network.
**ESnet** Energy Sciences network (U.S.A.).
**ESNS** (The Brookhaven) Energy System Network Simulator.
**ESO** European School of Oncology.
Headquartered in Milan, Italy with Offices worldwide, it was founded in 1982 by Prof. Umberto Veronesi. It is a non-profit private organization.
*Cancer Prevention, Diagnosis and Cure.*
**ESO** European Southern Observatory.

**ESOC** European Space Operation Center.
**E.S.O.M.A.R.** European Society for Opinion Surveys and Market Research.
The ESOMAR is located in Belgium.
**ESOP** Employee Share Ownership Plan; Employee Share Ownership Programme.
**ESOP** External Sensory Organ Precursor.
**ESOPs** Employee Stock Ownership Plans (U.S.A.).
In 1974 it was estimated that there were approximately 300 ESOPs in the United States. By 1992 more than 10 million employees and 9600 companies participated in ESOPs. ESOPs can serve as a source of corporate financing from asset acquisition to leveraged buyouts.
**ESOR** emergency stand-off range.
distance de sécurité d'urgence.
**ESP** Electrosensitive Paper.
**ESP** Electrostatic Precipitator.
The electrostatic precipitator is a device for removing fine particles from a gas by electrically charging the particles and then collecting them on highly charged plates.
*Engineering.*
**ESP**; **Esp** Enterprise Server Procedures.
**esp.** (abbr.) especially.
**ESP** European Science Foundation.
**ESP** Evoked Synaptic Potential.
**ESP** Extrasensory Perception.
*Psychology.*
**ESP** Spanish peseta.
Now: EURO/EUR (€). Became ECU (European Single Currency) with effect from January 2002.
**ESPC** European Space Power Conference.
**ESPE** end state peacetime establishment.
tableau final d'effectifs du temps de paix.
**ESPS2** Second European Stroke Prevention Study.
*Clinical Trials; European Studies; Neurological Research; Stroke Research.*
**ESPRIT** European Strategic Program for Research and Development in Information Technology.
**esprit** The above acronym was coined accidentally using the French word "esprit" which means: mind; intellect; talent; intelligence; brains.
**ESPRO** European SPace Research Organization.
Also: **ESRO**.
**ESQC calculations** Elastic Scattering Quantum Chemistry calculations.
*Astronomy; Physics.*
**ESR** Early Storage Reserve.
**ESR** Electronic Send/Receive.
**ESR** Electron Spin Resonance.
Electron spin resonance is also known as: Electron Paramagnetic Resonance.
**ESR** Electrosensitive Recording.
*Electronics.*
**ESR** Erythrocyte Sedimentation Rate.
**ESRC** Economic and Social Research Council (G.B.).
**ESRF** European Synchrotron Radiation Facility.
The European Synchrotron Radiation facility began operation in Grenoble, France in 1994.
**ESRIN** European Space Research INstitute.
ESRIN is located in Frascati, Italy.
*European Institute.*
**ESRO** European Space Research Organization.
Also: **ESPRO**.
**ESR process** Electroslag Refined process.
**ESS** ecologically-sound system.
système non polluant.
**ESS** electronic switching system.
*Telecommunications.*
**ess.** (abbr.) essence.
**Ess** (abbr.) Essex.
**ESS** European Spallation Source.
The European Spallation Source, not using reactors to produce neutrons, but relying on a newer *particle-accelerator technology*, will begin to operate in 2010.
**ESS** Evolutionary Stable Strategy.
**ESSA** Ecole Supérieure de Soudure Autogène.
French acronym of the: High School for Autogen Welding (France).
*Metallurgy.*
**ESSA** Environmental Survey SAtellite.
**ESSEC** Ecole Supérieure des Sciences Economiques et Commerciales (France).
**ESSENCE** Program Equation of State SupErNovae trace Cosmic Expansion Program.
Under way at the Cerro Tololo Inter-American Observatory, the program will be completed by 2006.
**ESSI** European System and Software Initiative.
*European Community Initiative.*
**ESSM** Evolved Sea Sparrow Missile.
**ESSP** Elephant Species Survival Pan (U.S.A.).
The ESSP was set up by the American Zoo and Aquarium Association in 1985.
*Elephant Survival; Elephant Crack Necroscopy.*
**EST** Eastern Standard Time.
**EST** Electroshock Therapy.
The EST is also known as: Electroconvulsive Therapy.
*Psychology.*
**est.** (abbr.) established; estate; estimated; estuary.
**ESTA** European Science and Technology Assembly.
ESTA is an advisory body to the European

Commission. ESTA held its first meeting in September 1994.
*Research and Development.*
**estab.** (abbr.) established.
**ESTEC** European Space research and TEchnology Center.
ESTEC is located in Noordwijk, The Netherlands.
**ESTHER** Exploitation of Soliton Transmission Highways for the European Ring.
*European Community Project.*
**ESTI** European Solar Test Installation.
**ESTIM** Engineering Stress Tolerance In Maize.
*European Community Project.*
**ESTs** Expressed Sequence Tags.
The term expressed sequence tags refers to gene fragments that may have many uses, such as the tracking down of genes presenting potential pharmaceutical importance.
**ESU**; **esu** Electrostatic Unit.
*Electricity.*
**ESU** Evolutionarily Significant Unit.
*Wildlife Biology.*
**ESV** Earth Satellite Vehicle.
**ESV** Error Statistics by Volume.
*Data Communications.*
**ET**; **e.t.** Eastern Time.
**e.t.** electrical transcription.
**ET** Electron Transfer.
*Physics.*
**ET** Emerging Technologies / Technology.
**ET** End of Text.
**ET** Ephemeris Time.
*Horology.*
**ET** Estate Tax.
**ET** Ethiopia.
**Et.** Ethyl.
The hydrocarbon radical $CH_3$ $CH_2$, usually written $C_2H_5$.
*Organic Chemistry.*
**ET** Egypt - International vehicle registration letters.
**ET** Executive Team.
**ET** External Tank.
**ET** Symbol for Total Thoracic Elastance.
**ETA** Employment and Training Administration (U.S.A.).
**ETA** Energy Tax Act (U.S.A.).
**ETA** Estimated Time of Arrival.
*Navigation.*
**eta** The above acronyms were coined accidentally using the seventh letter of the Greek alphabet "eta": $\eta$.
**ETACS** Extended Total Access Communications System.
*Cellular Phones.*
**ETAD** Ecological and Toxicological Association of Dyes and Organic Pigments Manufacturers (Switzerland).
**ETAN** European Technology Assessment Network.
*European Community Network.*
**ETB** End-of-Transmission Block.
**ETC** Electron Transport Chain.
*Mitochondrial Aging; Molecular and Cell Biology.*
**ETC** Estimated Time of Completion.
**etc.** et cetera.
**ETC** European Travel Commission.
**ETC** Export Trading Company.
*Business; Commerce.*
**ET chemistry** Electron-Transfer chemistry.
**ETD** Estimated Time of Departure.
*Navigation.*
**ETD** European Telework Development.
*European Community Project.*
**ETEC** Enterotoxigenic *E. Coli.*
ETEC is the main cause of diarrhea in developing countries.
**ETE Program** Evolution of Terrestrial Ecosystems Program (U.S.A.).
**ETE test** End-to-End test.
**ETF** Engineering Test Facility.
**ETFE** Ethylene Tetrafluoroethylene.
**ETFI** European Technology Fund & Investment.
ETFI is based in Manno (Italian-speaking region of Switzerland).
*Technology; Telecommunications.*
**ETFRN** European Tropical Forest Research Network.
*International Cooperation.*
**ETHEL** European Tritium Handling Experimental Laboratory.
**ETHZ** Eldgenössische Technische Hochschule Zürich (Switzerland).
German initialism of the: Federal Institute of Technology Zurich.
**ETI** Ente Tabacchi Italiano (Italy).
**E.T.I.** Ente Teatrale Italiano (Italy).
Italian acronym of the: Board for the Promotion of Theatrical performances.
**ETI activities** Economic and Technological Intelligence activities.
ETI activities aim at facilitating the participation of SMEs and SME groupings in FP6, the creation of groupings or clusters, the promotion of *transregional co-operation*, and the *stimulation of networks* of *industrial incubators.*
For further details see under: **FP6** and **SMEs**.

**ETICA** European Trade of Information, Communication and Advertising (Italy).
**E-TIME** Execution Time.
*Computer Programming.*
**ETL** Electrotechnical Laboratory.
The ETL is located in Tsukuba, Japan.
*Microelectronics; Transistor Architecture.*
**ETL** Environmental Technology Laboratory (U.S.A.).
**ETL** Equilibrio Termodinamico Locale.
Italian initialism meaning: Local Thermodynamic Equilibrium.
*Physics.*
**ETLT** Equal To or Less Than.
**ETM** Enhanced Thematic Mapper.
**ETMA project** Efficient Turbulence Models for Aeronautics project.
*European Community Project.*
**ETNO Association** European public Telecommunications Network Operators' Association.
**ETP** Eastern Tropical Pacific.
**ET polymers** Electron Transport polymers.
**ETR** Eastern Test Range.
**ETR** 1. estimated time of restoration.
1. heure prévue (ou probable) pour le rétablissement de la communication.
2. estimated time of return.
2. heure prévue (ou probable) de retour (HPR).
**ETR** Expected Time of Response.
**ETRI** Enhanced Threat Reduction Initiative.
Initiative élargie pour la réduction de la menace.
**ETRO** Estimated Time of Return to Operation.
**ETS** Educational Testing Service (U.S.A.).
Assessment of Education Progress.
**ETS** Environmental Tobacco Smoke.
**ETSI** European Telecommunications Standards Institute.
*European Institute.*
**ETSU** East Tennessee State University (U.S.A.).
**ETSU** Energy Technology Support Unit.
**Ett** European transactions on telecommunications and related technologies.
*Publication.*
**ETT** Expected Test Time.
**ETTNA** European Training, for Trainers, Network, Action.
*European Community Project.*
**ETTU** east of (the) Urals.
à l'est de l'Oural.
**ETU** Ethylene Thiourea.
**ETUC** European Trade Union Confederation.
**ETV** Educational Television.
**ETX** Ethosuximide.
**etym.**; **etymol.** (abbr.) etymological; etymology.
**ETZ** Electron Transparent Zone.
**EU** Early Uptake.
**EU** Enriched Uranium.
Enriched uranium contains more than 0.711% by weight of uranium-235.
*Nuclear Engineering.*
**E.U.** Etats Unis.
United States in French.
**EU** European Union.
**Eu** The chemical symbol for Europium.
Europium is a rare-earth element, atomic number: 63, atomic weight: 151.96. Named for the continent **Europe**.
*Chemistry; Symbols.*
**EUAC** Equivalent Uniform Annual Cost.
*Business; Commerce; Finance.*
**EUC** Equatorial Undercurrent.
The EUC is also known as: Cromwell Undercurrent.
*Atmospheric Science; Climatology; Meteorology; Oceanography.*
**EUCLIDES** A EUropean standard for Clinical Laboratory Data Exchange between Independent Information Systems.
*European Community Project.*
**EUDAC** European Distribution and Accounting Agency.
Bureau européen de distribution et de comptabilité.
**EUDG** European Datamanager User Group.
**euf.** eufemismo.
Italian abbreviation meaning: euphemism.
**EUFEPS** EUropean FEderation for Pharmaceutical Sciences (Stockholm, Sweden).
Founded 21st September 1991. Inaugural meeting held in Strasbourg Congress Centre. Its mission is to serve and advance excellence in the pharmaceutical sciences and innovative drug research in Europe.
**EUFORES**; **Eurofores** EUropean FOrum for Renewable Energy Sources (Luxemburg).
EUROFORES promotes renewable energies in all the European countries.
*Renewable Energies; European Project.*
**EUI** European University Institute.
**EUMC** European Union Military Committee.
Comité militaire de l'Union européenne (CMUE).
**EUMET SAT** (abbr.) EUropean METerological SATellite.
**$Eu_2O_3$** Europium Oxide.
Europium Oxide is also known as: Europia.

*Inorganic Chemistry.*
**EUP** Early Upper Paleolithic.
*Anthropology; Neandertal Arms; Primate Birth.*
**EUP** Estimated Unit Price.
*Business; Commerce.*
**EUP** Experimental Use Permit.
*Field Trials.*
**EUR** euro (European Single Currency: €
).
With effect from January 2002.
**Eur.** (abbr.) Europe; European.
**EURACS** European Radar Cross Section database.
**EURADA** EURopean Association of Development Agencies.
**EurALMF** European Advanced Light Microscopy Facility.
*Short-term Fellowships.*
**EURANDREF** EURopean ANDalusite purified by original processes and industrial testing as high quality REFractory.
*European Community Project.*
**EURATOM** European Atomic Energy Community.
**EURECA** (abbr.) EUropean REtrievable CArrier.
**EUREKA** European Co-operation Advanced Technology.
**EUREPP** EURopean Education Production Programme.
*European Community Program.*
**EURES** EURopean Employment Services - *European Community.*
**EURESCO** EUropean RESearch COnference (France).
With European Community support from the High Level Scientific Conferences Activity.
**Euro-CASE** European Council of Applied Sciences and Engineering (Paris, France).
The Euro-CASE is a European non-profit organization. It consists of Academies of Applied Sciences and Engineering from 14 European countries. Founded in December 1992, it represents 19 nations and deals with the problems related to engineering and its implications on politics, society and economy.
**EUROCOAST** EUROpean COastal Zone Association for Science and Technology (France).
**EURO-ENVIRON** EUREKA Environmental Umbrella Project.
**EUROFRET** EUROpean system for International Road Freight Transportation operations - European Community.
*Road Frieght Transportation.*
**EUROMICRO** European Association for Microprocessing and Microprogramming.
**EURONET** European Information Network.
**EURONET DIANE** Direct Information Access Network for Europe.
**EURONETT** Evaluating User Responses On New European Transport Technologies - *European Community.*
**EUROPOEM database** EUROpean Predictive Operator Exposure Model database.
*European Community Project.*
**Europol** (abbr.) Ufficio Europeo di Polizia.
Abbreviation of the: European Police Bureau.
**EURORIM** EUROpean Research and consensus Interactive Multimedia.
*European Community Project.*
**EUROSTAT** European Statistical Office.
**EUROTOPP** European Transport Planning Process - *European Community.*
**EUROTRAC** European Experiment on Transport and Transformation of Environmentally relevant trace constituents in the troposphere.
*EUREKA project.*
**EUROTRIP** European Trip planning system - *European Community.*
**EUSEC** European Communications Security and Evaluation Agency.
Bureau européen de sécurité et d'évaluation des transmissions.
**EUSIDIC** European Association of Scientific Information Dissemination Centers.
**EUTELSAT** (abbr.) EUropean TELecommunications SATellite.
**EUV** Extreme Ultraviolet.
**EUVE satellite** Extreme Ultraviolet Explorer satellite.
*Planetary Science.*
**E.V.** Eccellenza Vostra.
Italian initialism meaning: Your Excellency.
**EV** Economic Value.
**eV** electron Volt or electronvolt.
*Physics.*
**EV** Epidermodysplasia Verruciformis.
Epidermodysplasia Verruciformis is also known as: Lewandowsky-Lutz Disease.
*Medicine.*
**E.V.** Era Volgare.
Italian initialism meaning: in the year of the Lord, Anno Domini.
**EV** Expected Value.
*Mathematics.*
**EV** Exposure Value.
**EVA** Economic Value Added.
In view of the fact that shareholder value can only be measured at the consolidated level of a compa-

ny, EVA is a measure of internal operating performance that is highly correlated with MVA.
For further details see under: **MVA** (Market Value Added).
*Business; Economics; Finance.*
**EVA** Error Volume Analysis.
**EVA** Ethylene Vinyl Acetate.
**EVA** Extravehicular Activity.
**EVASAN** evacuation sanitaire.
medical evacuation (MEDEVAC).
**EVCA** European Private Equity and Venture Capital Association.
*European Technology.*
**EVE** Ethyl Vinyl Ether.
**evid.** (abbr.) evidence.
**EVMS** Eastern Virginia Medical School (U.S.A.).
**evo-devo biology** evolutionary developmental biology.
**EVOP** (abbr.) EVolutionary OPeration.
*Industrial Engineering.*
**EVR** Electronic Video Recording.
*Electronics.*
**EVs** Electric Vehicles.
**EVT** Equiviscous Temperature.
*Chemical Engineering.*
**EW** 1. early warning.
1a. alerte lointaine.
1b. détection lointaine.
2. electronic warfare.
2. guerre électronqiue (GE 3.).
**EW** Ex-Warrants.
*Business; Finance.*
**EW** Symbol for Thoracic Wall Elastance.
**EWAM** electronic warfare approved message.
message approuvé de guerre électronique.
**EWC** electronic warfare commander (coordinator).
commandant (coordonnateur) de la guerre électronique.
**EWCC** electronic warfare coordination cell.
cellule de coordination de la guerre électronique (CCGE).
**EWDLS measurements** Evanescent-Wave Dynamic Light-Scattering measurements.
*Macromolecules; Physics; Polymers.*
**EWDT** early-warning data transmission.
transmission de données de détection lointaine.
**EWEX** electric warfare exercise.
exercice de guerre électronique.
**EWG** Environmental Working Group.
Washington, D.C., U.S.A.
**EWG** executive working group.
groupe de travail exécutif.
**EWGRB** European Working Group on Research and Biodiversity.
*European Community Environment and Climate Program.*
**EWHCI Conference** East-West Human-Computer Interaction Conference.
**EWMS** electronic warfare mutual support.
appui réciproque de guerre électronique.
**EWOS** electronic warfare operational support.
soutien opérationnel de guerre électronique.
**EWOS** European Workshop for Open Systems.
**EWR** 1. early warning radar.
1. radar de détection lointaine.
2. electronic warfare range.
2. polygone de guerre électronique.
**EWR** The airport code for Newark International Airport, Newark, New Jersey, U.S.A.
**EWRS** early warning reporting system.
système de comptes rendus de détection lointaine.
**EWRTM** electronic warfare request / tasking message.
message de demande et d'attribution de mission de guerre électronqiue.
**EWSs** Earthquakes early Warning Systems.
*Geology; Geophysics; Oncoming Ground Motion Warnings.*
**EWX** see EWEX.
voir EWEX.
**ex** (abbr.) examined; example.
**ex** (abbr.) except; exception.
**ex.** (abbr.) exchange; exchequer; excluding; excursion.
**ex.** (abbr.) execute; executed; executive; executor.
**EX** Executive Airlines.
**ex** (abbr.) exempt.
**ex** (abbr.) exercise.
**EX** (abbr.) Exeter.
*Geography.*
**Ex.** (abbr.) Exodus.
**Ex.** (abbr.) Expense.
**ex** (abbr.) export.
**ex** (abbr.) external.
**ex.** without.
**ex-** prefix having different meanings.
May be used for example in: ex-dock; exhale; ex-member; ex-president; etc.
*Prefixes.*
**Ex Acct.** Expense Account.
**EXAFS** Extended X-ray Absorption Fine Structure.
**EXASYSDE** new methodologies for EXhaust SYStem DEsign.
*European Community Project.*
**Ex B/L** Exchange Bill of Lading.

*Business; Commerce.*
**EXBRIEF** exercise brief.
exposè d'exercice.
**Exc.** (abbr.) Excellency.
**exc.** (abbr.) excellent.
**exc.** (abbr.) except; excepted; exception.
**exc.** (abbr.) exchange.
Also: **exch**.
**exc.** (abbr.) excudit.
**exc.** (abbr.) excursion.
Also: **ex.**
**exch.** (abbr.) exchequer.
**EXCON** exercise control.
contrôle de l'exercice.
**Ex Cp** Ex Coupon.
**EXCP** Execute Channel Program.
**exctr.** (abbr.) executor.
Also: **ex.**; **exr.**
**Ex D** Ex Dividend.
Also: **Ex. Div**.
**EXD** External Device.
*Computer Technology; Engineering.*
**EX-DC** External-Device Control.
The term external-device control refers to the capability of an external device to bring about an interrupt in the course of job execution.
*Computer Technology.*
**Ex Div.** Ex Dividend.
Also: **Ex D**.
**Ex. Doc.** Executive Document.
**EX-DR** External-Device Response.
EX-DR is a response signal from an external device.
*Computer Technology.*
**exec.** (abbr.) execute; executive.
Also: **ex.**
**Exec.Program** Executive Program.
*Computer Programming.*
**execs** (abbr.) executives.
**exes** (abbr.) expenses.
Also: **exs.**; **exps**.
**EXIMBK** EXport-IMport Bank.
United States or Japan.
Also: **EXIMBANK**; **EIB**.
**EXINST** exercise instruction.
instruction d'exercice.
**ex.int.** without interest.
**EXNOR gate** Exclusive-NOR gate or XNOR gate.
*Computer Technology.*
**ExNPS** Exploration of Neighboring Planetary Systems.
*Astronomy.*
**Ex.O** Executive Officer; Executive Order.
**Exo I** Exonuclease I.
*Cancer Research.*
**EXODUS** EXperiments On the Development of UMTS.
*European Community Project.*
**EXOPLAN** exercise operational plan.
plan d'opération d'exercice.
**EXOPORD** exercise operation order [obsolete - replaced by EXOPLAN].
ordre d'opération d'exercice [obsolète - remplacé par EXOPLAN].
**EXOR** EXclusive OR.
*Computer Programming.*
**EXORDER** exercise order [obsolete].
ordre d'exercice [obsolète].
**EXOR gate** EXclusive-OR gate or XOR gate.
The EXclusive-OR gate is essentially an electronic gate that carries out exclusive-OR operations.
*Computer Technology.*
**exp.** expéditeur / expéditrice.
French abbreviation meaning: consignor; sender; dispatcher.
**exp.** (abbr.) expense.
**exp.** (abbr.) export; exporter.
**exp.** (abbr.) express; expression.
For further details see under: **e**.
**expend.** (abbr.) expenditure.
Also: **expnd**.
**EXPER technique** EXtended Program Evaluation and Review technique.
**EXPI** exercise planning instruction [has replaced EXPLANDIR].
directive de planification d'exercice [remplace EXPLANDIR].
**ExPlan** (abbr.) Exercise Plan.
**EXPLANDIR** exercise planning directive [obsolete - replaced by EXPI].
directive de planification d'exercice [obsolète - remplacé par EXPI].
**EXPLANREC** exercise planners recommandation [obsolete].
recommendation pour les planificateurs d'exercice [obsolète].
**EXPLANSUPP** exercise planning supplement.
supplément de planification d'exercice.
**expnd.** (abbr.) expenditure.
**expo.** (abbr.) exposition.
**EXPORT Project** Excellence In Partnerships for Community Outreach, Research on Health Disparities and Training Project.
For further details see under: **NCMHD**.
**expr.** (abbr.) expression.
For further details see under: **e**.

**EXPROG** exercise programme.
programme d'exercice (ou de manœuvre).
**EXPRESS** EXPerimental REentry Space Vehicle.
**exps.** (abbr.) expenses.
Also: **exs.**; **exes**.
**exr.** (abbr.) executor.
Also: **ex.**; **exctr.**
**ExR** Ex-Rights.
**EXRAP** exercise remedial action programme.
programme de mesures correctives de l'exercice.
**Ex Rights** Without the Rights.
**exs.** (abbr.) expenses.
Also: **exps.**; **exes**.
**EXSPEC** exercise specification.
spécification d'exercice.
**EXSUPP** exercise supplement [obsolete].
supplément d'exercice [obsolète].
**ext.** (abbr.) extension.
French abbreviation meaning: prolongation; extension.
**ext.** (abbr.) external.
*Anatomy; Pharmacology.*
**ext.** (abbr.) extinct.
**ext.** (abbr.) extra; extract.
**EXTAC** experimental tactics.
tactique expérimentale.
**extd.** (abbr.) extruded.
**extve.** (abbr.) executive.
Also: **ex**.
**Ex W** Ex-Warrants.
**EXW** EX Works.
*Economics; International Trade.*
**Ex-Warrants** Without Warrants.
Also: **Ex W**.
**EYFP** Enhanced Yellow Fluorescent Protein.
*Medicine; Neurobiology; Pharmacology; Toxicology.*
**ey gene** eyeless gene.
*Biology; Developmental Biology; Developmental Genetics; Genetic Engineering.*
**EYP** English Yellow Pages.
**EZ** 1. engagement zone.
1. zone d'engagement.
2. exclusion zone.
2. zone d'exclusion.
3. extraction zone.
3. zone d'extraction.
**Ez.**; **Ezr.** Ezra.
**e-zine** electronic magazine

# F

**f** farthing.
coins (G.B). (demonetized in 1961).

**F**; **f** Fellow.

**f** fetch.
In Oceanography fetch is also known as: fetch length.
*Computer Programming; Oceanography.*

**F** The chemical symbol for Fluorine.
Used mainly in fluoride production. The word fluorine derives from a Latin term meaning "flowing".
*Symbols; Symbols.*

**f** force.
*Computer Programming; Mechanics; Military Science.*

**f** fraction.
*Chemistry; Mathematics; Petroleum Engineering; Science.*
*Metallurgy* - In metallurgy, fraction is also known as: cut.

**f** fractional.
*Mathematics.*

**F** French.
A Romance language, spoken in France, parts of Belgium and Switzerland. French is used as an international language for scholarship, science, and diplomacy.
*Languages.*

**f** frequency.
Also: **freq.**
*Acoustics; Mathematics; Physics; Statistics.*

**f** function.
*Chemistry; Computer Programming; Mathematics; Physiology; Psychology.*

**FA** Face Amount.
*Business; Finance.*

**F.A.** Factory Acts.

**FA** Fanconi's Anemia.
Named for the Swiss pediatrician Guido **Fanconi**. FA is a rare autosomal recessive cancer susceptibility syndrome.
*Genetics; Medicine; Oncology; Pathology.*

**FA** Fatty Acid.
Fatty acids are used mainly in cooking and food engineering. They are also used to produce cosmetics and soaps.
*Organic Chemistry.*

**fA** femtoampere.
*Electricity.*

**FA** Field Artillery.

**FA** Fielding Average.

**FA** Fixed Assets.
*Business; Finance.*

**FA** Floating Assets.
*Business; Finance.*

**F.A.** Forze Armate.
Italian acronym meaning: Armed Forces.
*Military.*

**FA** Free Alongside.
*Business; Commerce.*

**FA** Freund's Adjuvant.
*Immunology.*

**FAA** Federal Aviation Administration (U.S.A.).

**FAA** 1. force aérienne alliée.
1. allied air force (AAF).
2. forward assembly area.
2. zone de ressemblement avancée.

**FAACE** Forces aériennes alliées du Centre Europe [obsolète].
Allied Air Forces, Central Europe (AAFCE) [obsolete].

**FAAH** Fatty Acid Amide Hydrobase.
*Biology; Brain Anandamide; Physiology; Neuroscience; Signal Lipids.*

**FAAWC** force anti-air warfare commander.
commandant de lutte antiaérienne de la force.

**FAB** Forestry Association of Botswana.

**FABI**; **Fabi** Federazione Autonoma Bancari Italiani (Italy).
Italian acronym of the: Free Association of Italian Bank Employees.

**FABMS** Fast Atom Bombardment Mass Spectrometry.

**FABP** Fatty Acid-Binding Protein.

**fac.** (abbr.) facsimile.

**fac.** (abbr.) factory.

**f.a.c.** fast as can.

**FAC** Field-Aligned Current.
For further details see under: **FACs**.

**FAC** 1. force aérienne de combat.
1. combat air force.
2. forward air controller.
2. contrôleur aérien (ou Air) avancé (CAA 2.).

**FACA** Federal Advisory Committee Act.
FACA is a U.S. 1972 law.

**FACA** 1. force air coordination area.
1. zone de coordination aérienne de la force.
2. force aircraft control area.
2. zone de contrôle des aéronefs de la force.

**f.a.c.a.c.** fast as can as customary.

**FACE technology** Fluorophore Assisted Carbohydrate Electrophoresis technology.

**FACP** forward air control post.
poste avancé de direction tactique Air (PADTA).
**FACs** Field-Aligned Currents.
*Astronomy; Geophysics; Planetary Physics; Physics; Space Science.*
**FACS** Fluorescence-Activated Cell Sorting.
*Biotechnology; Immunobiology; Medicine; Pharmaceuticals.*
**fact.** (abbr.) factory.
Also: **facty.**; **fac.**; **fcty**.
**FACT** Financial Advisers Core Test.
**FACTE** Finnish ACademies of TEchnology (Finland).
**FACT project** Feasibility Ascension Cape Town project.
**FacTs** Facsimile Transmission.
**FACTS** Florida Atlantic Coast Transport Study (U.S.A.).
**facty.** (abbr.) factory.
Also: **fac.**; **fact.**; **fcty**.
**FAD** Familial Alzheimer's Disease.
*Medicine; Biology.*
**FAD** Fish Aggregating Device.
**FAD** Flavin Adenine Dinucleotide.
$C_{27}H_{33}N_9O_{15}P_2$ - Flavin adenine dinucleotide is a coenzyme.
*Biochemistry.*
**FAD** Fondo Africano di Sviluppo.
Italian acronym of the: African Development Fund.
**FADBEN** Fédération des Amicales de Documentalistes et Bibliothécaires de l'Education Nationale.
**FADD protein** Fas Associated-Death Domain protein.
*Apoptosis Research; Immunology.*
**FaDOL** Formatori a Distanza On Line.
**FADs** First Appearance Datums.
*Fossil Mammals; Paleontology.*
**FAE** Fetal Alcohol Effects.
FAE is a neurotoxic syndrome.
*Medicine; Pediatric Neurobiology; Psychiatry.*
**FAE** Fuel-Air Explosive.
*Ordnance.*
**FAF** Financial Analysts Federation.
**FAG** Force Allotment Group [NAEW].
Groupe d'affectation de la Force [NAEW].
**FAGE** Fluorescence Assay with Gas Expansion.
FAGE was pioneered in the 1980s.
*Environmental Technology; Medicine; Science.*
**FAGS** Federation of Astronomical and Geophysical Services.
The FAGS was founded in 1956.

**fAHP** fast component Afterhyperpolarization.
**Fahr.** (abbr.) Fahrenheit.
*Thermodynamics.*
**FAHSLA** Fint Area Health Sciences Libraries Association.
**Fai**; **FAI** Federazione Associazioni Industriali.
FAI is located in Milan, Italy.
**FAI** Federazione Autotrasportatori Italiani.
*Italian Federation.*
**FAI** Fellow of the Auctioneers' Institute.
**FAI** final acceptance inspection.
inspection de réception définitive.
**FAIP** Farm Animal Industrial Platform.
*European Community Biotechnology Programs.*
**FAIR** Forecast and Assessment of socio-economic Impact of advanced communications and Recommendations.
*European Community Project.*
**FAISBI** Federazione delle Associazioni della Spina Bifida e dell'Idrocefalo (Italy).
Italian acronym of the: Federation of the Bifid Spine and Hydrocephalus Association.
**FAK** Focal Adhesion Kinase.
*Cell-Matrix Adhesions.*
**FAL** File Access Listener.
**FAL**; **F.A.L.** Foglio Annunci Legali.
*Law* - Italian acronym meaning: Law Announcements Bulletin.
**FALS** Familial form of ALS.
For further details see under: **ALS**.
**FAMD** Fondation pour l'Assistance Morale aux Détenus (Belgium).
*Belgian Foundation.*
**FAME** Fatty Acid Methyl Ester.
*Microbiology.*
**FAME** Full-sky Astrometric Mapping Explorer.
FAME, which was due to launch in 2004 to map the position of 40 million stars has been (temporarly) cancelled due to NASA's withdrawal of support and difficulty in obtaining CCD detectors.
*Astrometry Missions.*
For further details see under: **CCD**.
**FAMOUS** French-American Mid-Ocean Undersea Study.
**FAMRI** Flight Attendant Medical Research Institute.
Sponsor of scientific and medical research.
*Clinical Research Awards.*
**FAMS** force assessment and management systems.
système d'évaluation et de gestion des forces.
**FAMU** Florida A&M University (U.S.A.).
**FAN** Facteur Antinucléaire.
French acronym meaning: Antinuclear Factor.

*Medicine.*
**FAND**; **Fand** Federazione Associazioni Nazionali Diabetici (Italy).
**F&A** February and August.
*Securitites.*
**F&A** Finance and Accounting.
**F&D** Freight and Demurrage.
*Business; Commerce; Shipping.*
**f.&f.** fixtures and fittings.
**F&WS** Fish and Wildlife Service (U.S.A.).
The F&WS is a U.S. Federal Agency dealing with the protection of threatened and endangered species.
*Threatened and Endangered Species.*
**FANS** Farmaci Antiinfiammatori Non Steroidei.
Italian acronym meaning: Non Steroidal Anti-Inflammatory Drugs.
*Alzheimer Disease Research; Drugs Testing; Epidemiological Studies.*
**FAO** fabrication assistée par ordinateur.
computer-aided manufacturing (CAM 4.).
**FAO** Flatland Atmospheric Observatory.
**FAO** Food and Agriculture Organization - U.N.
**fao** for the attention of.
**FAP** Familial Adenomatous Polyposis.
*Molecular Genetics; Oncogenesis.*
**FAP** Familial Amyloidotic Polyneuropathy.
**FAP** Fibroblast Activation Protein.
**FAP** First Aid Post.
**FAP** Freedom Attached Payloads.
**FAPAV** Federazione Anti Pirateria Audiovisiva (Italy).
*Italian Federation.*
**FAPC** Food and Agriculture Planning Committee.
Comité d'étude pour le ravitaillement et l'agriculture.
**FAPS** Financial Application Preprocessor System.
**FAQ** Fair Average Quality.
**FAQ** Foire Aux Questions.
French initialism meaning: Frequently Asked Questions.
The French equivalent mentioned above has been coined and published by the French General Commission on terminologies and neologisms in the French Official Gazette of the 14th March 1999.
**FAQ** Free Alongside Quay; Free At Quay.
*Business; Commerce; Shipping.*
**FAQ**; **Faq** Frequently Asked Questions.
**FAR** Federal Acquisition Regulation (U.S.A.).
**FAR** Federal Aviation Regulations (U.S.A.).
**FAR** File Address Register.
**FAR** Financial Accounts Receivable.
*Business; Finance.*
**FAR** Finite Automation Recognizable.
*Computer Science.*
**FAR** Fisheries and Aquaculture Research.
**FAR** Fondation André Renard (Belgium).
*Belgian Foundation.*
**FAR** Forces Armées Rwandaises.
**FARA program** French-American Ridge Atlantic program.
**FARB** Federal Assistance Review Board.
U.S. Department of Commerce.
**FARC**; **Farc** Revolutionary Armed Forces of Colombia.
**FARE** Fonti Alternative e Risparmio Energetico.
Italian acronym meaning: Alternative Sources and Energy Savings.
**farm.** (abbr.) farmacia; farmacista.
Italian abbreviation meaning: pharmacy; pharmacist.
**FARMERS** Multimedia distance-learning for FARMERS and rural development - E.C.
**FAR** Fisheries and Aquaculture Research.
*European Community Program.*
**FARS** Financial Accounting and Reporting System.
**FAS** Faculty of Arts and Sciences.
FAS is the largest of Harvard University's nine faculties.
**FAS**; **F.A.S.** Federation of American Scientists (U.S.A.).
**FAS** Fellow of the Antiquarian Society.
**FAS** Fetal Alcohol Syndrome.
*Medicine.*
**FAS** Financial Accounting Standards.
**FAS** Financial Analysis System.
*Business; Finance.*
**FAS** Firsts And Seconds.
**FAS** Fondo Africano Sviluppo.
Italian acronym of the: African Development Fund.
**FAS** Foreign Agricultural Service (U.S.A.).
**FAS** Free Alongside Ship.
**FAS** functional area services [ACCIS].
services de domaine fonctionnel [ACCIS].
**FASB** Financial Accounting Standards Board.
The FASB issued The Statement of Financial Accounting Standards n° 117 titled *Financial Statements of Not-for-Profit Organizations.* This pronoucement immediately follows the issuance of SFAS N° 116, *Accounting for Contributions Received and Contributions Made.* Both of these pronouncements have a major impact on the financial statements of not-for-profit colleges and universities.

For further details see under: **SFAS**.
**FASC** forward air support centre.
centre d'appui aérien avancé.
**FASE** Fellow of the Antiquarian Society Edinburgh.
**fase** The above acronym was coined accidentally using the Italian word "fase" which means: phase
*Archaeology; Astronomy; Cartography; Chemistry- Mathematics; Materials Science; Metallurgy; Physics.*
**FASEB** Federation of American Societies for Experimental Biology (U.S.A.).
**FASEM** Fabrication and Architecture of Single-Electron Memories.
FASEM will create a working chip in which each bit of data is stored with a single electron.
*European Union Science Program; Microelectronics.*
**FASI**; **Fasi** Fondo di Assistenza Sanitaria Integrativa (Italy).
**FASINEX** Frontal Air-Sea INteraction EXperiment.
**FasL**; **fasL** fas Ligand.
For further information see under: **HT** (Hashimoto's Thyroiditis).
**FASS** functional area sub-system [obsolete - see FAS].
sous-système de domaine fonctionnel [obsolète - voir FAS].
**FAST** Federazione delle Associazioni Scientifiche e Tecniche (Milan, Italy).
Italian acronym of the: Federation of the Scientific and Technical Associations. Founded in 1897.
**FAST** Fluoroaluminate Amplifiers for Second Telecom window.
*European Community Project.*
**FAST** Fore-Aft Scanning Technique.
**FAST** Forecasting and Assessment in Science and Technology.
**fast** The above acronyms were coined using the English word "fast" (*Graphic Arts; Materials Science*).
**FASTEX** Fronts and Atlantic Storm Track Experiment.
*European Community Project; Environmental Protection; Meteorology; Safety; Policies.*
**FASWC** force antisubmarine warfare commander.
commandant de lutte anti-sous-marine de la force.
**FAT** Fixed Asset Transfer.
*Business; Finance.*
**FATA** force aérienne tactique alliée [obsolète].
Allied tactical air force (ATAF) [obsolete].
**FATMA** (Prevenzione e Controllo dei) FATtori di MAlattia.
*Italian Project.*
**FAU** Faujasite.
*Chemistry; Materials.*
**FAUL** Fife Associated University Libraries.
**FAWEU** forces answerable to the WEU [obsolete].
forces relevant de l'UEO (FRUEO) [obsolète].
**fax** facsimile.
**FB** Fidelity Bond.
*Business; Finance.*
**FB** Fire Brigade.
**FB** Fixed-Block.
*Computer Technology.*
**FB** Flying Boat.
*Aviation.*
**F/B** Foreground/Background.
**FB** Foreign Bond.
*Business; Finance.*
**FB** Franc Belge.
French initialism meaning: Belgian Franc (obsolete).
Now: EURO/EUR (€). Became ECU (European Single Currency) with effect from January 2002.
*Currencies.*
**FB** Free Bill.
**FB** Freight Bill.
*Business; Commerce.*
**FB** see BEF.
voir BEF.
**FBA** Federal Bar Association (U.S.A.).
**F.B.A.** Fellow of the British Academy (G.B.).
**FBA** fighter-bomber, attack.
chasseur-bombardier tactique.
**FBA** Fixed-Block Architecture.
*Computer Technology.*
**FBA** Flexible Benefit Account.
*Banking; Business; Finance.*
**FBA** Franco-British Aviation.
**FBB** Fluidized-Bed Boiler.
**FBBF** Fast Breeder Blanket Facility.
**FBC** Fluidized Bed Combustion.
**FBD** Full Business Day.
**FBDC** Fort Bonifacio Development Corporation.
The FBDC is a consortium which is redeveloping the former U.S. airbase.
**FBE** Free Buffer Enquiry.
**FBG** Fibre Bragg Grating.
to dampen dispersion.
**FBI** Federal Bureau of Investigation (U.S.A.).
The FBI is the U.S. Federal Agency that safeguards national security and is charged with investigations.
**FBI** Federation of British Industries (G.B.).
**FbiH** Federation of Bosnia and Herzegovina.
Fédération de Bosnie-Herzégovine.

**FBJ murine sarcoma virus** Finkel-Biskis-Jinkins murine sarcoma virus.
*Virology.*
**FBM** fleet ballistic missile.
missile balistique de la flotte.
**FBMM** Fundación Banco Mundial de la Mujer (Argentina).
**FBPs** Fructose 1,6-biphosphate Aldolases.
*Chemistry; Chemical Biology; Molecular Biology.*
**FBR** Fast Breeder Reactor.
The fast breeder reactor uses highly enriched fuel in the core - and fertile material in the blanket.
*Nuclear Engineering.*
**FBR** Fast Burst Reactor.
**fbr.** (abbr.) fiber.
**FBS** Fetal Bovine Serum.
**FBS** fighter-bomber, strike.
chasseur-bombardier d'attaque (nucléaire).
**FBV** Fuel Bleed Valve.
**FC** Facilities Committee.
**FC** 1. fighter controller.
1. contrôleur d'interception.
2. financial controller.
2. contrôleur des finances (ou financier).
3. fire control.
3. conduite de tir.
4. force commander.
4. commandant de la force.
**FC** Finance Charge.
*Business; Finance.*
**FC** Fire Controlman.
**FC** Fixed Capital.
*Business; Finance.*
**FC** Fixed Charges.
**FC** Flame Cutting.
*Metallurgy.*
**FC** Floating Capital.
*Business; Finance.*
**FC** Follow Copy.
**FC** Food Control.
**FC** Football Club.
**FC**; **f.c.** Footcandle.
Also: **ftc**.
*Optics.*
**FC** Foreign Currency.
*Banking; Commerce.*
**Fc** Fragment cristallisable.
French initialism meaning: Crystallizable Fragment; Fc fragment.
**FC** Free Church (of Scotland).
**FC** Full Charge.
**FC** Function Code.
The function code controls device functions.
*Computer Technology.*
**FC** Fuori Corso (studente).
Italian initialism meaning: an undergraduate who has failed to get a degree in the time prescribed.
**FC** Futures Contract.
*Banking; Business; Finance.*
**FCA** Farm Credit Administration.
**FCA** Fellow of the Chartered Accountants.
**FCA** Free CArrier.
*Economics; International Trade.*
**FCA** functional configuration audit.
audit de la configuration fonctionnelle.
**FCB** Free-Cutting Brass.
*Metallurgy.*
**FCB** Frequency Control Board.
**FCBA** Fair Credit Billing Act (U.S.A.).
**FCC** Familial Colon Cancer.
**FCC**; **F.C.C.** Federal Communications Commission (U.S.A.).
**FCC** Fluid Catalytic Cracking.
**FCCAO** Federation of West African Chambers of Commerce (Lagos).
**FCCC** Fox Chase Cancer Center (U.S.A.).
**FCCC** Framework Convention on Climate Change - U.N.'s.
*Atmospheric Sciences; Environmental Sciences; Geosciences; Oceanography; Space Studies.*
For further details see under: **U.N**.
**fcc phase** face-centered-cubic phase.
*Geophysics.*
**FCCSET** Federal Coordinating Council for Science, Engineering and Technology (U.S.A.).
**FCC system** Fluid Catalytic Cracking system.
**FC curve** Field-Cooled curve.
*Chemistry; High Magnetic Field; Physics.*
**FCDU** Foreign Currency Deposit Units.
**FCE** Femmes Chefs d'Entreprises.
French initialism meaning: Women Company Heads.
**FCE** 1. forces armées conventionnelles en Europe.
1. conventional armed forces in Europe (CFE).
2. forward command element.
2. élément de commandement avancé.
**FCE** Foreign Currency Exchange.
*Business; Finance.*
**FCE1** First Commodities Exchange (India).
**FCEM** Femmes Chefs d'Entreprises Mondiales.
French initialism meaning: Women Company Heads Worldwide.
**FCF** Free Cash Flow.
**FCFS** First Come, First Served.
*Computer Programming.*
**fcg.** (abbr.) facing.

*Building Engineering; Mechanical Engineering; Metallurgy.*

**FCG** Federal Coordinator for Geology (U.S.A.).

**$FC_6H_4NH_2$** p-fluoroaniline.
p-fluoroaniline is used mainly in herbicides.
*Organic Chemistry.*

**FCI** Faculty of Computing Information.
At Cornell University, N.Y., U.S.A.
*Computer Science; Scientific Communication.*

**FCI** Federal Crime Insurance.

**FCI** Fellow of Commerce Institute.

**FCIA** Foreign Credit Insurance Association.

**FCIC** Federal Crop Insurance Corporation (U.S.A.).

**FCIP** Fibre Channel over Internet Protocol.

**fCJD** familial Creutzfeldt-Jakob Disease.
*Biochemistry; Biophysics; Neurology; Neuropathology; Pathology; Prion Diseases.*

**FCMAREP** Federal Coordinator for MARine Environmental Prediction (U.S.A.).

**FCMs** Fuel Containing Masses.
*Nuclear Accidents; Nuclear Physics.*

**FCMSSR** Federal Coordinator for Meteorological Services and Supporting Research (U.S.A.).

**FCN** Free Core Nutation.
*Geomagnetism; Paleomagnetism; Physics.*

**FCNR deposit** Foreign Currency Non-Resident deposit (India).
*Investment Schemes.*

**FCO** Fiumicino Airport (Leonardo da Vinci) Rome, Italy.

**FCOMP** Federal Coordinator for Ocean Mapping and Prediction (U.S.A.).

**FCP** Fonds Commun de Placement.
French initialism meaning: Unit Trust, Mutual Fund (U.S.).

**fcp.** (abbr.) foolscap.

**FCPA** Foreign Corrupt Practices Act.
The FCPA bans U.S. Companies from paying bribes.

**FCR** fire control radar.
radar de conduite de tir.

**FCR** Forwarding agent's Certificate of Receipt.
*Business; Commerce; Shipping.*

**FCRA** Fair Credit Reporting Act (U.S.A.).

**FCRDC** Frederick Cancer Research and Development Center.
The FCRDC is located in Frederick, MD, U.S.A.

**FCS** Federal Counterintelligence Service (U.S.A.).

**FCS** Fetal Calf Serum.
*Biotechnology.*

**FCS** fire-control system.
système de conduite de tir.

**FCS** Flagellate Caudal Seta.
*Agricultural Research; Entomology.*

**FCS** Fluorescence Correlation Spectroscopy.
*Biological Imaging; Cell Biology; Human Development; Metabolism.*

**FCS** Frame Check Sequence.

**fcs.** (abbr.) francs (obsolete).
Now: EURO/EUR (€). Became ECU (European Single Currency) with effect from January 2002.
*Currencies.*

**FCSC** Foreign Claims Settlement Commission (U.S.A.).

**FCS cable** Force Cooled Superconducting cable.

**FCST** Federal Council for Science and Technology (U.S.A.).

**FCT** Fundamentals of Computation Theory.
*Computation Theory.*

**FCTF** Forced Convection Test Facility.

**fcty.** (abbr.) factory.
Also: **facty.**; **fact.**; **fac.**

**FCU** Federal Credit Union.

**FCU** fuel consumption unit.
unité de consommation de carburant.

**FCUS** Federal Credit Union System (U.S.A.).

**FCZ** Fishery Conservation Zone.

**FCZ** forward combat zone.
zone avant des combats.

**FD** Facility Division; Factory Department.

**F.D.**; **fd.** Federal Debt.

**FD** Federal Department.

**FD** Filodiffusione.
Italian initialism meaning: cable radio.

**FD** Fire Department.

**FD** Floppy Disk.
FD is also known as: Diskette; Flexible Disk.
*Computer Technology.*

**FD** Flying Dutchman.

**FD** Focal Distance.
Focal distance is also known as: Focal Length.
*Optics.*

**FD** Forced-Draft.
*Mechanical Engineering.*

**FD** framework document.
document-cadre.

**FD** Free Delivery; Free Dock.

**fd.** (abbr.) fund.
*Business; Commerce; Economics; Finance.*

**fd.** (abbr.) funding.
Also: **fdg**.

**FDA**; **F.D.A.** Food and Drug Administration (U.S.A.).

**FDACS** Florida's Department of Agriculture and Consumer Services (U.S.A.).
For further details see under: **CCEP**.

**FDAMA** Food and Drug Administration Modernization Act (2003) (U.S.A.).
**FDC** fire direction centre.
poste central de tir.
**FDC** Floppy Disk Controller.
**FDC** Flow Duration Curve.
**FDCM** Familial Dilated Cardiomyopathy.
*Genetics; Heart Research.*
**FDCPA** Fair Debt Collection Practices Act (U.S.A.).
**FDCs** Follicular Dendritic Cells.
**FDD** First Flowering Date.
*Biology; Biometeorology; Ecology.*
**FDDI** Fibre Distributed Data Interface.
The FDDI is a Token Ring Structure.
**FDEANST** 3-Fluoro-4-N,N-Diethylamino-β-Nitrostyrene.
**FDE experiments** Frequency-Dependent Ellipsometry experiments.
*Optical Sciences.*
**FDG**; **Fdg.** Federazione nazionale Diabete Giovanile (Italy).
*Italian Federation.*
**fdg.** (abbr.) funding.
Also: **fd**.
**FDI** Foreign Direct Investment.
**FDIC** Federal Deposit Insurance Corporation (U.S.A.).
**FDL** Forms Description Language.
**FDM** Finite Differences Method.
**FDM**; **fdm** Frequency Division Multiplexing.
FDM, also known as: Frequency Multiplexing, uses a different frequency band for each signal transmitted over a common path.
*Telecommunications.*
**FDM** Fuzzy Dark Matter.
*Astronomy; Astrophysics.*
**FDMA** Frequency Division Multiple Access.
**FDMA** Frequency-Domain Multiple Access.
*Telecommunications.*
**fdn.** (abbr.) foundation.
*Building Engineering; Civil Engineering.*
**FDO** fire direction officer.
officier responsable de la direction des tirs.
**FDP** Fertilizing Promoting Factor.
**FDP** Free Democratic Party (Germany).
**FDP** Fructose 1,6-Diphosphate aldolase.
*Protein Aldolases.*
**FDPA** Foundation for the Development of Polish Agriculture (Poland).
**FDR.** (abbr.) feeder.
*Agriculture; Electricity; Geology; Mechanical Engineering; Metallurgy; Ordnance.*
**FDRAKE** First Dynamic Response And Kinematics Experiment.
**fdry.** (abbr.) foundry.
*Engineering.*
**FDS** Floppy Disk System.
**FD statistics** Fermi-Dirac statistics.
*Quantum Mechanics.*
**FDW** (abbr.) Feedwater.
*Mechanical Engineering.*
**FDX** Full-Duplex Transmission.
**FE** Far East.
**F.E.** Federal Estimates.
**FE** Federal Exchange.
**FE** Ferrara, Italy.
**FE** Field Editor; Field Engineering.
**FE** Fire Extinguisher.
*Engineering.*
**FE** Foreign Exchange; Futures Exchange.
**Fe** The chemical symbol for Iron.
*Chemistry; Symbols; Metallurgy; Mechanical Engineering.*
**FEA** Federal Energy Administration.
The FEA is located in Washington D.C., U.S.A.
**FEACO** European Federation of Management Consultancy Associations.
**$Fe^{+2}Al_2O_4$** Hercynite.
Hercynite is also known as: Ferrospinel; Iron Spinel.
*Mineralogy.*
**FEANTSA** European Federation of National Organizations Working with the Homeless.
**FEAOG** Fondo Europeo Agricolo di Orientamento e di Garanzia (Italy).
*European Fund.*
**FeAsS** Arsenopyrite.
*Mineralogy.*
**FEB** Far Eastern Branch.
Of the Russian Academy of Sciences.
**Feb., feb.** (abbr.) February.
**FEB** forward employment base.
base d'emploi avancée.
**FEB** Functional Electronic Block.
**FEBA** forward edge of the battle area.
limite avant de la zone de bataille.
**$FeBr_3$** Ferric Bromide.
Ferric Bromide also known as: Ferric Tribromide is used mainly in chemistry and medicine.
*Inorganic Chemistry.*
**FEBs** Federal Executive Boards (U.S.A.).
**FEBS** Federation of European Biochemical Societies.
**FEBT** Far East Bank & Trust (The Philippines).
**FEC** Federal Election Commission (U.S.A.).

**FEC** Forward Error Correction.
*Computer Programming.*
**FEC** (Institut) Français de l'Emballage e du Conditionnement (France).
*French Institute.*
**$FeCl_3$** Ferric Chloride.
Ferric Chloride is also known as: Ferric Trichloride.
*Inorganic Chemistry.*
**FECN** Forward Explicit Congestion Notification.
*Computers.*
**FECO** Fringes of Equal Chromatic Order.
**$FeCO_3$** Ferrous Carbonate.
Ferrous Carbonate is used in iron deficiency anemia.
*Inorganic Chemistry.*
**$Fe(CO)_4$** Iron Tetracarbonyl.
*Inorganic Chemistry.*
**$Fe(CO)_5$** Iron Pentacarbonyl.
Iron Pentacarbonyl is used mainly as a catalyst.
*Inorganic Chemistry.*
**$Fe_2(CO)_9$** Iron Nonacarbonyl.
Iron Nonacarbonyl is also known as: Iron Enneacarbonyl.
*Inorganic Chemistry.*
**FECOM** Fondo Europeo di COoperazione Monetaria.
Italian acronym of the: European Fund for Monetary Cooperation - E.C.
**FECS** Federation of European Chemical Societies - E.C.
**Fed.** (abbr.) Federal; Federalist; Federation.
**FEDAP** FEDerazione Associazioni Professionali Ambiente e Paesaggio (Italy).
*Italian Federations.*
**FEDARENE**; **Fedarene** European Federation of Regional Energy and Environment Agencies (Brussels, Belgium).
*Energy Management; Environment Protection; Waste Management.*
**FEDER** Fonds Européen de Développement Régional.
French acronym of the: European Regional Development Fund.
**Federcomated** Federazione Nazionale Commercianti Laterizi, Cementi, e materiali Edili (Italy).
*Italian Federation; Building Materials.*
**Federolio** Federazione Nazionale del Commercio Oleario (Italy).
*Italian Federation; Edible Oils.*
**FEDERTERME** Federazione Italiana delle Industrie Termali e delle Acque Minerali Curative (Italy).
*Italian Federation.*
**Federtessabb** Federazione Nazionale Operatori Commerciali Ingrosso e Trasformatori Tessili, Abbigliamento, Mercerie e Affini.
Located in Milan, Italy.
*Italian Federation; Textiles.*
**Fed Funds** (abbr.) Federal Funds (U.S.A.).
**FEDLINK** Federal Library committee / Federal Library and Information Network.
**FEDUCI** Fondation pour l'Etude du Droit et des Usages du Commerce International.
*French Foundation.*
**FEE** Fédération des Experts comptables Européens - E.C.
*European Federation.*
**$FeF_2$** Ferrous Fluoride.
Ferrous Fluoride is used mainly in ceramics.
*Inorganic Chemistry.*
**$FeF_3$** Ferric Fluoride.
Ferric Fluoride is used mainly in ceramics.
*Inorganic Chemistry.*
**FEFC**; **Fefc** Far Eastern Freight Conference.
**FEGG** Foetal Electrocardiogram.
A foetal heart-monitoring system developped by Noeventa Medical of Sweden, which monitors and interprets a particular section of the foetal electrocardiofram.
*European Community Project; Foetal heart-monitoring Technology; Health Professionals Training; Obstetrics Devices.*
**FEG-SEM** Field-Emission Gun-Scanning Electron Microscope.
*Ceramics Materials; Earth Sciences; Geology; Mechanical Engineering.*
**FEI** Federal Executive Institute.
**FEI** Financial Executives Institute.
**FEI** Fondo Europeo per gli Investimenti.
Italian acronym of the: European Investment Fund - *European Community.*
**FEIA** Foreign Earned Income Act (U.S.A.).
**FEIP** Front-end for Echographic Image Processing.
*Medicine.*
**FELABAN** FEderation of Latin American BANks (Bogota).
**FEL Laboratory** Free Electron Laser Laboratory.
At Duke University (U.S.A.).
**FELs** Free-Electron Lasers.
*Computer Engineering; Electrical Engineering; Physics; Plasma Research.*
**FELSI** Fédération de l'Enseignement Libre Subventionné Indépendant (Belgium).

*Belgian Federation.*
**fem.** (abbr.) female.
*Biology; Botany; Engineering.*
**fem.** (abbr.) feminine.
**fem.** (abbr.) femur.
*Anatomy* - Femur is also known as: Thigh Bone.
*Invertebrate Zoology* - In invertebrate zoology, femur is also known as: Meropodite.
**FEM** Field-Emission Microscope.
*Electronics.*
**FEM** Finite Element Modeling; Finite Elements Method.
**FEM** Flight-Engineering Model.
**fem.** forza elettro-motrice.
Italian abbreviation meaning: electromotive force.
*Electricity.*
**FEMA** Federal Emergency Management Agency.
**FEMA** Flavor and Extract Manufacturers' Association.
**FEMIRCs** FEllow Members to the IRC Network.
**FENACA**; **Fenaca** Federazione Nazionale distributori all'ingrosso di Articoli di Cancelleria.
FENACA is located in Milan, Italy.
*Italian Federation.*
**Fe,Ni** Kamacite.
Kamacite is found in meteorites.
*Mineralogy.*
**$(Fe,Ni,Co)_3$** Cohenite.
Cohenite is also known as: cementite.
*Mineralogy.*
**Fe-Ni-S alloy** Iron-Nickel Sulfide alloy.
*Alloys.*
**$FeNNF_2$** Tetrafluorohydrazine.
Tetrafluorohydrazine is used mainly as a rocket fuel.
*Inorganic Chemistry.*
**FEO** Federal Energy Office.
**FeO** Ferrous Oxide.
Ferrous oxide is also known as: Iron Monoxide; Black Iron Oxide.
*Inorganic Chemistry.*
**$Fe_2O_3$** Ferric Oxide.
Ferric Oxide is also known as: Ferric Trioxide.
*Inorganic Chemistry.*
**FEOF** Foreign Exchange Operations Fund (U.S.A.).
**$Fe(OH)_3$** Ferric Hydroxide.
Ferric Hydroxide, also known as: Ferric Hydrate is used mainly in water purification.
*Inorganic Chemistry.*
**$Fe_2P$** Ferrous Phosphide.
Ferrous Phosphide is used in the manufacture of steel and iron.
*Inorganic Chemistry.*
**FEP** Fluorinated Ethylene-Propylene.
**FEP** Front-End Processor.
Front-End Processor is also known as: Front-End Computer.
*Computer Technology.*
**FEPA**; **Fepa** Federazione Europea per la Protezione delle Acque.
*European Federation; Waters Protection.*
**FEPC** Fair Employment Practices Commission (U.S.A.).
**$Fe^{+3}PO_4$** Heterosite.
*Mineralogy.*
**fEPSPs** field Excitatory Postsynaptic Potentials.
**FER** 1. final exercise report.
1. compte rendu final d'exercice.
2. force effectiveness report.
2. rapport sur l'efficacité des forces.
**FERA** Federal Emergency Relief Administration (U.S.A.).
**FeRAM** Ferroelectric Random Access Memory.
*Emerging Electronic Technology.*
**FERC** Federal Energy Regulatory Commission (U.S.A.).
**FES** Family Expenditure Survey.
**FES** Fellow of the Entomological Society.
**FES** Fellow of the Ethnological Society.
**FES** Fondo Europeo per lo Sviluppo.
Italian acronym of the: European Development Fund.
**FeS** Iron Sulfide.
Iron Sulfide also known as: Ferrous Sulfide is used mainly in ceramics.
*Inorganic Chemistry.*
**$FeS_2$** Pyrite.
Pyrite is also known as: Mundis; Iron Pyrite.
*Mineralogy.*
**FESAC** Fusion Energy Sciences Advisory Committee - U.S. DOE's.
For further details see under: **DOE**.
**FeSbS** Gudmundite.
Gudmundite is found in sulfide deposits.
*Mineralogy.*
**FE-SEM** Field-Emission Scanning Electron Microscope.
**FESEM** Forcible Entry Safeguards Effectiveness Model.
*Energy.*
**FESR** Fondo Europeo di Sviluppo Regionale.
Italian initialism of the: European Fund for Regional Development - E.C.
**FESS** Flywheel Energy Storage System.
**F.E.T.** Federal Excise Tax.
**FET** Field-Effect Transistor.

*Electronics; Physics.*
**FET** Fisher's Exact Test.
*Medicine.*
**FET** Fluorescence Energy Transfer.
*Chemistry.*
**$Fe^{+2}TiO_3$** Limenite.
Limenite is also known as: Mohsite; Titanic Iron Ore.
*Mineralogy.*
**FETS** frais d'étude technique et de surveillance.
architecture and engineering (fees) (A&E).
**FEV** Forced Expiratory Volume (for the first second).
*Medicine.*
**$Fe(VO_3)_3$** Ferric Vanadate.
Ferric Vanadate is used mainly in metallurgy.
*Inorganic Chemistry.*
**$Fe^{+2}WO_4$** Ferberite.
*Mineralogy.*
**FEX** (abbr.) Foreign EXchange.
**FEZ** 1. fighter engagement zone.
1a. zone d'engagement d'arme.
1b. zone d'engagement d'avions de combat.
1c. zone d'engagement des intercepteurs.
**FEZ** Frontonasal Ectodermal Zone.
*Development Embryogenesis; Quail and Chick Embryos.*
**fez** The above acronyms were coined accidentally using the word "fez" which is: a cone-shaped hat of red felt usually with a black tassel worn by men in eastern mediterranean countries.
**f.f.**; **ff.** facente funzione.
Italian initialism meaning: acting as; deputy; serving as; locum tenens; pro.
**FF** Fast Forward.
**FF** Fat Free.
*Medicine.*
**FF** Filtration Fraction.
**FF** Fixed-Focus.
*Optics.*
**FF** Flip-Flop.
Flip-Flop is also known as: Bistable Multivibrator.
*Electronics.*
**FF** Forced Flue.
*Engineering.*
**FF** Ford Foundation.
**FF** Form Feed.
*Computer Programming.*
**FF** Fossil Fuel.
*Geology.*
**FF** Franc Français.
French initialism meaning: French Franc (obsolete).
Now: EURO/EUR (€). Became ECU (European Single Currency) with effect from January 2002.
*Currencies.*
**f.f.** the following.
**FFA** free-fire area.
zone de tir libre (ZTL).
**FFA-1** Foci-Forming Activity 1.
*Biology; Cell Biology.*
**FF.AA.** Forze Armate.
Italian initialism meaning: Armed Forces.
*Military.*
**FF&C** Full Faith and Credit.
Also: **FFC**.
*Business; Finance.*
**FF&P** Falsification, Fabrication, and Plagiarism.
**FFAs** Freight Forward Agreements.
FFAs are principal-to-principal contracts based on specific routes rather than an index.
*Freight Brokers.*
**FFB** Federal Financing Bank.
**FFC** Federal Facilities Council (U.S.A.).
**FFC** Fonds de Formation professionnelle de la Construction (Belgium).
*Belgian Funds; Constrution.*
**FFC** Foreign Funds Control.
**FFC** Full Faith and Credit.
Also: **FF&C**.
*Business; Finance.*
**FFC** Free From Chlorine.
**FFCB** Federal Farm Credit Bureau (U.S.A.).
**FFCC** Free-Flyer Control Centre.
**FFD** Failed Fuel Detector.
**FFDCA** Federal Food, Drug, and Cosmetic Act (U.S.A.).
**FFE** fire for effect.
tir d'efficacité.
**FFF** Fédération Française de Football.
*French Federation.*
**FFF-RC** Field-Flow Fractionation Research Center.
Of the University of Utah, U.S.A.
**FFG** Functional Feeding Groups.
*Biology; Detritus; Ecology; Entomology; Ecosystems; Steam Ecology.*
**FFI** Fatal Familial Insomnia.
**FFI** Finance For Industry (G.B.).
**FFI** Free From Infection.
**FFIB lithography** Finely Focused Ion Beam lithography.
*Biophysical Dynamics; Chemistry; Nanofabrication.*
**FFM** Fat Free Mass.
*Hypocaloric Dieting; Obesity.*
**FFPI** Flip-Flop Position Indicator.

**FFR** free-flight rocket.
roquette à vol libre.
**FFRFRL Project** Federalism and Regional Fiscal Reform Loan Project (Russian Federation).
*World Bank Project.*
**FFS** Formatted File System.
**FFS** Front des Forces Socialistes (Algeria).
French initialism meaning: Socialist Forces Front.
**FFS** funded feasibility study.
étude de faisabilité à financement assuré.
**FF.SS.** Ferrovie dello Stato.
Italian initialism meaning: (Italian) State Railways.
Also: **F.S**.
**FFT** Fast Fourier Transform.
*Acoustics; Mathematics.*
In *Computer Science*, Fast Fourier Transform is also known as: Discrete Fourier Transform.
**FFTF** Fast Flux Test Facility (U.S.A.).
The FFTF was shut down in 1993. It was used for over 10 years as a research and materials-testing reactor.
*Nuclear Science.*
**FG** Field Gun.
Field Gun, also known as: Field Piece, is used for field operations.
*Ordnance.*
**FG** Fire Guards.
**FG** Flue Gas.
*Engineering.*
**FG** Fluorogold.
**FG** Foggia, Italy.
**FG** force goals.
objectifs de forces.
**FGA** fighter, ground attack.
1a. chasseur d'appui tactique.
1b. chasseur d'attaque au sol.
**FGCZ** Functional Genomics Center Zurich (Switzerland).
**FGD** Flue-Gas Desulfurization.
*Energy.*
**FGF** Fibroblast Growth Factor.
**FGFR** Fibroblast Growth Factor Receptor.
*Biological Chemistry; Life Sciences.*
**FGFs** Fibroblast Growth Factors.
*Development; Medical research.*
**FGGE** First GARP Global Experiment.
For further details see under: **GARP**.
**FGIS** Federal Grain Inspection Service (U.S.A.).
**FGL** force generation level.
niveau de constitution d'une force.
**FGM** Foundation for Genetic Medicine, Inc. (U.S.A.).
Workshop held at Anaheim, California, U.S.A. on 23rd January 1999.
*New Genetic Technologies.*
**fgn.** (abbr.) foreign; foreigner.
**FGS** Fellow of the Geological Society.
**FH** Familial Hypercholesterolemia.
FH is a genetic defect.
*Genetics.*
**FH** Fire Hose or firehose.
*Engineering.*
**FH** Fire Hydrant.
Fire Hydrant is also known as: Fire Plug.
*Civil Engineering.*
**FH** Frequency Hopping.
*Telecommunications.*
**FHA** Federal Housing Administration (U.S.A.).
**FHA domains** Forkhead-Associated domains.
*Cell Cycle; Medicine; Pathology; Pharmacology.*
**FHAF** Fonds Haitien d'Aide à la Femme (Haiti).
**FHB** Federal Home Bank.
*Federal Bank.*
**FHCRC** Fred Hutchinson Cancer Research Center (U.S.A.).
**FHD** Fixed-Head Disk.
FHD is a disk unit wherein the read-write heads are permanently fixed.
*Computer Technology.*
**FHFB** Federal Housing Finance Board (U.S.A.).
**FhG-IUCT** Fraunhofer Institute for Environmental Chemistry and Ecotoxicology (Germany).
*Environmental Chemistry; Ecotoxicology.*
**FHIT protein** Fragile HIstidine Triad protein.
*Biochemistry; Genomics; Molecular Biophysics.*
**FHLB** Federal Home Loan Bank (U.S.A.).
**FHP**; **fhp motor** Fractional Horsepower motor.
*Electricity.*
**FHP** Friction Horsepower.
*Mechanical Engineering.*
**FHS** Fellow of the Historical Society.
**FH systems** Frequency Hopping systems.
*Wireless Communications.*
**FHV** Flock House Virus.
*Plant Cell Biology; Plant Pathology; RNA Silencing.*
**FHWA** Federal Highway Administration (U.S.A.).
**F1 hybrid plants** First-generation hybrid plants.
*Agronomy; Crop Science; Crop Yield; Heterosis.*
**FI** 1. Finland.
1. Finlande.
2. firing (or fire) incident.
2. incident de tir.
**FI** Firenze, Italy.
**FI** Foreign Investment.

*Business; Finance.*
**FI** Forza Italia (Italy).
*Italian Political Party.*
**FI** Fuel Injection.
FI is a system used in gasoline engines and diesel engines.
*Mechanical Engineering.*
**FI** The airline code for Icelandair.
**FIA** Families In Action.
FIA was founded in Georgia, U.S.A, in 1977 (against drug abuse).
**FIA** Federal Insurance Administration (U.S.A.).
**FIA** Fédération Internationale de l'Automobile.
*International Federation.*
**FIA** Fédération Internationale des Acteurs.
*International Federation.*
**FIA** Fellow of the Institute of Actuaries.
**FIA** Fluoroimmunoassay.
**FIABCI**; **Fiabci** Federazione Internazionale delle Professioni Immobiliari.
FIABCI is located in Milan, Italy.
*International Federation.*
**FIABQUAL** (abbr.) FIABilité et QUALité.
French abbreviation meaning: Reliability and Quality.
**FIAE** Federazione Italiana Artigiani Edili (Italy).
**FIAF** Fédération Internationale des Archives du Film.
**FIAM** Federazione Italiana Aero Modellismo.
*Italian Federation.*
**FIAMS** Flinders Institute for Atmospheric and Marine Sciences (Australia).
**FIAT** Fabbrica Italiana Automobili Torino (Italy).
**FIAT** Fonds d'Intervention pour l'Aménagement du Territoire (France).
**FIA technique** Flow Injection Analysis technique.
For further details see under: **SIA**.
**FIAU** Fialuridine.
*Hepatic Toxicity.*
**FIB** Fellow of the Institute of Bankers.
**FIBS** Field by Information Blending and Smoothing.
**FIBV** Fédération Internationale des Bourses de Valeurs.
French initialism of the: International Federation of Stock Exchanges.
*Stock Exchanges.*
**FIC** Federal Insurance Contribution (U.S.A.).
**F.I.C.** Fédération des Instituteurs Chrétiens.
*Belgian Federation.*
**FIC** Federation of Insurance Counsel (U.S.A.).
**FIC** Federazione Italiana Canottaggio (Italy).
Italian acronym of the: Italian Boating Association.
**FIC** Federazione Italiana Cronometristi (Italy).
Italian acronym of the: Italian Time-Keepers Association.
**FIC** Fellow of the Institute of Chemists.
**FIC** Flight Information Center.
**FIC** Freight, Insurance, Carriage.
*Business; Commerce; Shipping.*
**FIC** John E. Fogarty International Center.
Of NIH, U.S.A. The FIC was established in 1968. The Center promotes and supports scientific research and training internationally to reduce disparities in global health.
For further details see under: **EPS** and **NIH**.
**F.I.C.A.** Federal Insurance Contributions Act.
**FICB** Federal Intermediate Credit Bank.
**FICE** Federazione Internazionale Comunità Educative.
Founded in 1948 under the auspices of UNESCO.
For further details see under: **UNESCO**.
**FICM** Fatal Infantile Cardiomyopathy.
*Medicine.*
**FICN** Free Inner Core Nutation.
*Geomagnetism; Paleomagnetism; Physics.*
**FICO** Financial & Intermediaries Claims Office (G.B.).
**FICO** (abbr.) FInancing COrporation.
**FICs** Federal Information Centers (U.S.A.).
**FICS** Financial Information and Control System.
*Business; Finance.*
**FICT** Federazione Italiana delle Comunità Terapeutiche (Italy).
*Italian Federation.*
**FICV** future infantry combat vehicle.
futur véhicule de combat d'infanterie (FVCI).
**FICYT** Fundación para el fomento en Asturias de la Investigación Cientifica aplicada y la Tecnologia - E.C.
**FID** Fédération Internationale de Documentation.
*International Federation.*
**FID** Federation of International Documentation.
**FID** Federazione Internazionale di Documentazione.
*International Federation.*
**FID**; **Fid** Federazione Italiana Diabete (Italy).
*Italian Federation.*
**FID** Fellow of the Institute of Directors.
**fid.** (abbr.) fidelity; fiduciary.
**FIDAL** Federazione Italiana di Atletica Leggera (Italy).
*Italian Federation.*
**F.I.D.A.P.A.** Federazione Italiana Donne Arti Professioni Affari (Italy).

*Italian Federation.*
**FIDE** Fédération Internationale pour le Droit Européen.
Located in Rome, Italy. Founded in 1961 to advance studies on European law among members of the European Community by co-ordinating activities of member societies and by organizing regular colloquies on topical problems of European law.
*European Law.*
**FIDELF** Fédération Internationale Des Ecrivains de Langue Française (Canada).
French acronym of the: International Federation of French Language Writers.
**FIDES** Forecaster's Intelligent Discussion Experiment System.
**FIDI** Fishery Information, Data and Statistics Service.
Of the U.N. Food and Agriculture Organization.
**FIDIC** Fédération Internationale des Ingénieurs Conseils (Switzerland).
French acronym of the: International Federation of Consulting Engineers.
**FIDO** Fog, Intense, Dispersal, Of.
FIDO is a method of dispersing fog over airfield (World War II).
**FIDO**; **fido** Fog Investigation Dispersion Operations.
*Meteorology.*
**fido** The above acronyms were coined accidentally using the Italian word "fido" which means: credit (*Economics; Banking*) and as an adj.: loyal; faithful; devoted.
**FIDS** force identification system.
système d'identification de forces.
**FIDs** Foreign Income Dividends.
**FIEE** Fédération des Industries Electriques et Electroniques.
**FIEO** Federation of Indian Export Organizations.
The FIEO is located in New Delhi, India, and works as a partner of the Government of India to promote India's foreign trade.
**FIEP** Forest Industry Energy Program.
**FIFO** First-In, First-Out.
*Computer Programming; Industrial Engineering.*
**FIFRA** Federal Insecticide, Fungicide and Rodenticide Act (U.S.A.).
**FIG** Fishing Industry Grants.
*Grants.*
**FIG** Fosse Iliaque Gauche.
French acronym meaning: Left Iliac Fossa.
*Medicine.*
**FIGO**; **F.I.G.O.** International Federation of Gynecology and Obstetrics.
**FIGS** FIGures Shift.
**Figs**; **FiGs** Financial industrial groups.
*Russian Federation.*
**FIH** Federazione Internazionale di Hockey.
*International Federation.*
**FIH** Fellow of the Institute of Hygiene.
**FIJ** Fellow of the Institute of Journalists (G.B.).
**fil.** filiale.
Italian abbreviation meaning: branch office.
**fil.** (abbr.) filter.
*Acoustical Engineering; Computer Programming; Control Systems; Electronics; Engineering; Graphic Arts; Mathematics.*
**FILA** Fellow of the Institute of Landscape Architects.
**fila** The above acronym was coined accidentally using the Italian word "fila" which means: queue; line; rank.
**FILO** First-In, Last-Out.
*Computer Programming.*
**filo** The above acronym was coined accidentally using the Italian word "filo" which means: thread; wire; cable; edge.
**filol.** filologia; filologo.
Italian abbreviation meaning: philology; philologist.
**FIM** Federazione Internazionale Metalmeccanici.
Italian acronym of the: International Federation of Metallurgists and Mechanics.
**FIM** Federazione Italiana Motonautica (Italy).
Italian acronym of the: Italian Motor-Boating Association.
**FIMA system** (abbr.) FInancial MAnagement system.
**FIMBRA** Financial Intermediaries, Managers and Brokers Regulatory Association (G.B.).
**FIMI** Federazione Industria Musicale Italiana.
FIMI is located in Milan, Italy.
*Italian Federation.*
**FIMIS** FIshery Management Information System.
Of the Food and Agriculture Organization - U.N.
**FIMP** Federazione Italiana Medici Pediatri.
*Italian Federation.*
**FIMU** 13[e] Festival International de Musique Universitaire (Belfort, France).
Held on 23[rd] May 1999.
**fin.** (abbr.) financial.
**Fin.** (abbr.) Finland.
**FINCON** see FC 2.
voir FC 2.
**FINEP** Financiadora de Estudos e Projetos (Brazil).

**FINEX** fin d'exercice.
end of exercise (ENDEX).
**FINMAN** (abbr.) FINancial MANagement.
**Finn** (abbr.) Finnish.
Finnish is the main language of Finland, it is a Uralic language closely related to Estonian.
*Languages.*
**FIO** Fleet Intelligence Officer.
**FIO** Florida Institute of Oceanography (U.S.A.).
**FIO** Foreign Intelligence Office.
**FIO** For Information Only.
**FIO** Free-In-and-Out.
*Business; Commerce; Shipping.*
**FIOCES** Fédération Internationale des Organisations de Correspondance et d'Echanges Scolaires.
Located in Turin, (Ivrea) Italy. Founded in 1929, aims: to contribute to the knowledge of *foreign languages and civilizations* and to bring together young people of all nations by furthering *international scholastic correspondence.*
**FIP** Fédération Internationale Pharmaceutique.
*International Federation.*
**FIP** Fédération Internationale de Philatélie.
*International Federation.*
**FIP** Fellow of the Institute of Physics.
**f.i.p.** finite intersection property.
*Mathematics.*
**FIPA** Fellow of the Institute of Practitioners in Advertising.
**FIPART** (abbr.) (La banque de) FInancement de PARTicipations (France).
*French Bank.*
**FIPF** Fédération Internationale des Professeurs de Français.
French initialism of the: International Federation of Professors of French.
**FIPPA**; **Fippa** Federazione Italiana Panificatori, Pasticceri e Affini (Italy).
*Italian Federation.*
**FIPS** Fellow of the Incorporated Phonographic Society.
**FIPS** Fellow of the Incorporated Photographic Society.
**FIPS** Foreign Interest Payment Security.
**FIR** Federazione Italiana Rugby (Italy).
Italian acronym of the: Italian Rugby Association.
**FIR** File Indirect Register.
**FIR** 1. first impression report.
1. compte rendu de première impression.
2. flight information region.
2. région d'information de vol.
**FIRC** Federazione Italiana per la Ricerca sul Cancro (Italy).
Italian acronym of the: Italian Federation for Cancer Research.
**FIRCA** The Fogarty International Research Collaborative Award (U.S.A.).
**FIRE** Fusion Ignition Research Experiment (U.S.A.).
**FIRP** Federazione Italiana Riflessologia del Piede (Italy).
*Italian Federation.*
**FIRS** Federal Information Relay Service (U.S.A.).
**FIRST** Far Infrared and Submillimeter Space Telescope.
The FIRST and Planck will be on a single spacecraft. The launch of the FIRST/Planck combined mission will take place in 2005.
*Astronomy; Space Science Mission.*
**FIRST** Flexible Integrated Radio Systems Technology.
*European Community Project.*
**FIRST Award** First Independent Research Support and Transition Award (U.S.A.).
*U.S. Awards.*
**f.i.s.** family income supplement.
**FIS** flight information service.
service d'information de vol.
**FIS** Front Islamique du Salut (Algeria).
**fis.atom.** fisica atomica.
Italian abbreviation meaning: atomic physics.
**FISE** Fellow of the Institution of Structural Engineers.
**FISH** Fluorescent in Situ Hybridization.
*Biological Sciences; Medicine; Molecular Biology; Radiation Oncology.*
**FIST** Feasible Ideal System Target.
**FIT** Federal Income Tax (U.S.A.).
**FIT** Fondo per l'Innovazione Tecnologica.
Italian acronym of the: Fund for Technological Innovation (Italy).
**FIT** Free In Truck.
*Commerce.*
**FIT** Free of Income Tax.
**FITO** Federation of International Trade Organizations (U.S.A.).
**FITS** Flexible Image Transport System.
**FIU** Food Irradiation Update.
A periodic source of information on all aspects of food irradiation. Date started: July-August 1993.
**FIUC** Fédération Internationale des Universités Catholiques.
Located in Paris, France. Founded in 1949 to ensure a strong bond of mutual assistance among

all Catholic universities in the search for truth to help solve problems of *growth* and *development*, and to co-operate with other international organizations.
**FIV** Feline lmmunodeficiency Virus.
*Virology.*
**FIV** Fertilisation In Vitro.
French acronym meaning: In Vitro Fertilization.
*Medicine.*
**FIV** Venezuelan Investment Fund (Venezuela).
**FJ** Fiji.
**FK5** The Fifth Fundamental Katalog.
*Astronomy.*
**FKBP12** FK506 Binding Proteins 12.
Intracellular Receptor.
*Animal Biology; Biochemistry; Biological Sciences; Biomedical Sciences; Biophysics; Molecular Physiology; Veterinary Medicine.*
**FL** Flight Level.
*Aviation.*
**fl.** (abbr.) floor.
*Architecture; Mining Engineering; Naval Architecture.*
*Geology* - In geology, floor is also known as: bottom.
**FL** (abbr.) Florida (U.S.A.).
**Fl** Florin.
French abbreviation meaning: guilder (obsolete). Now: EURO/EUR (€). Became ECU (European Single Currency) with effect from January 2002.
*Currencies.*
**fl** (abbr.) fluid.
*Physics; Science.*
**FL** Focal Length.
Focal length is also known as: Focal Distance.
*Optics.*
**FLA** Fiji Library Association.
**FLA** Florida Library Association.
**FLA** Future Large Aircraft.
futur avion gros porteur.
**FLAJA** Latin American Federation of Young Environmentalists (Colombia).
**FLAME project** Future Laser Atmospheric Measurement Equipment project.
*European Community Project; Laser Atmospheric Measurement Equipment.*
**FLAP method** Fluorescence Localization After Photobleaching method.
*Biochemistry; Biophysics; Cancer Research.*
**FLAPW** Full-Potential Linear Augmented Plane Wave.
*Materials Science and Engineering.*
**FLAR** forward-looking airborne radar.
radar de bord à vision frontale.
**F.L.B.** Federal Land Bank (U.S.A.).
**FLB** Federal Loan Bank (U.S.A.).
**FLB** Franco le Long du Bateau.
French initialism meaning: Free Alongside Ship (**FAS**). The above expansion has replaced: FLB - Franco Long du Bord.
*Economics; International Trade.*
**FLC** Federal Library Committee.
**FLC** force logistic coordinator.
coordonnateur de soutien logistique de la force.
**FLCs** Ferroelectric Liquid Crystals.
**fld.** (abbr.) field; fluid.
**fl.dr.** fluid dram / fluiddram.
*Metrology.*
**FLEET** Freight and Logistics Efforts for European Traffic - *European Community.*
**Flem** Flemish.
Flemish is one of the official languages of Belgium, it is a Germanic dialect mutually intelligible with Dutch.
*Languages.*
**FLET** forward line of enemy troops.
ligne avant des forces ennemies.
**FLETC** Federal Law Enforcement Training Center (U.S.A.).
**FLEX** fleet exercise.
exercice des forces navales.
**FLF** Federazione Lucio Fontana (Italy).
*Italian Federation.*
**FLIC** Film Library Information Council.
**flic** The above acronym was coined accidentally using the word "flic" which means in French: policeman; cop (USA).
**FLIERs** Fast Low-Ionization Emission Regions.
*Astronomy; Astrophysics.*
**FLIH** First-Level Interrupt Handler.
*Computer Technology.*
**FLIP** flight information publication.
publication d'information de vol.
**FLIP** Fluorescence Loss In Photobleaching.
*Biological Imaging; Cell Biology; Human Development; Metabolism.*
**FLIPs** FADD-Like ICE Inhibitory Proteins.
For further details see under: **FADD**.
**FLIR imager** Forward-Looking Infrared imager.
*Engineering.*
**FLIR(S)** forward-looking infrared (system).
(système) infrarouge à vision frontale.
**FLK** Frida Leakey Karongo.
*Anthropology.*
**FLL** Flux Line Lattice.
*Superconductivity.*

**FLL** The airport code for Ft. Lauderdale International (Florida, U.S.A.).
**FLN** Front de Libération Nationale (Algeria).
French initialism meaning: National Liberation Front.
**FLNC** The National Front for the Liberation of Corsica.
**FLO** 1. faction liaison officer.
1. officier de liaison faction.
2. French liaison officer.
2. officier de liaison français (OLF).
**FLOPS** Floating Point Operations Per Second.
FLOPS is a measure of a computer's speed of operation.
*Computer Programming.*
**FLORAL** Financement Local et Régional (France).
**FLOT** forward line of own troops.
ligne avant des forces amies.
**FLOT** Front Line Of Troops.
*Ordnance.*
**fl oz**; **fl.oz.** fluid ounce.
*Metrology.*
**FLP** (abbr.) flameproof.
**FLR** Fixed Loan Rate.
*Business; Finance.*
**FLR** force of lower readiness [proposed new force structure].
force à niveau de préparation moins élevé [proposition de nouvelle structure de forces].
**FLRA** Federal Labor Relations Authority (U.S.A.).
**FLRT** Federal Librarians Round Table.
**FLS** forward logistic site.
site logistique de l'avant.
**FLSA** Federal Labor Standards Act (U.S.A.).
**FLSO** future less-manned aerospace operations.
opérations aérospatiales menées dans un environnement plus robotisé.
**flt.** (abbr.) flight.
**flu** short for influenza.
*Medicine.*
**FLV** Friend Leukemia Virus.
FLV is also known as: Friend Virus.
*Virology.*
**FLY** Formations LYonnaises (France).
**fm** fathom.
Also: **fth**.
Marine unit of measure, equal to 1.829 meters.
*Oceanography.*
**fm.** (abbr.) farm.
**FM** Fat Mass.
*Obesity.*
**Fm** The chemical symbol for Fermium.
Fermium is a synthetic radioactive element having the atomic number 100. Named for the American physicist (Italian-born) Enrico **Fermi**.
*Chemistry; Symbols.*
**FM** Field Manual.
**FM** Field Marshal.
*Ordnance.*
**FM** Financial Management.
**FM** Flusso Monetario.
Italian initialism meaning: Cash Flow.
**F.M.** Foreign Mission.
**fm.** (abbr.) form.
**F.M.**; **f.m.** Forza Motrice.
Italian initialism meaning: Driving Power.
**FM** Frequency Modulaton; Frequency Modulated.
*Telecommunications.*
**fm.** (abbr.) from.
**FMB** Federal Maritime Board (U.S.A.).
**FMB** forward mounting base.
base de préparatifs de l'avant.
**FMBT** future main battle tank.
futur char de bataille.
**FMC** Federal Maritime Commission (U.S.A.).
**FMC** Financial Management Center.
**FMC** framework multinational corps.
corps-cadre multinational.
**FMCG Companies** Fast-Moving Consumer Goods Companies.
**FMCS** Federal Mediation and Conciliation Service (U.S.A.).
**FMD** force mix data.
données sur les forces en présence.
**FMD virus** Foot-and-Mouth Disease virus.
Also known as: Hoof-and-Mouth Disease.
*Veterinary Medicine; Biological Weapons Agent; Socioeconomic Weapon.*
**FMDZ** forward missile deployment zone.
zone avant de déploiement des missiles.
**FMEA** Failure Mode and Effect Analysis.
**FMF** Fièvre Méditerranéenne Familiale.
French initialism meaning: Familial Mediterranean Fever.
FMF is also known as: Periodical Disease.
**FMI** Fondo Monetario Internazionale; Fonds Monétaire International.
Italian and French initialism meaning: International Monetary Fund.
**FMIS** Financial Management Information System.
**F.MK.**; **FMk** Finnish Mark (obsolete).
Now: EURO/EUR (€). Became ECU (European Single Currency) with effect from Janaury 2002.
*Currencies.*
**FMK**, **fmk** Fluoromethyl Ketone.
**FMLA** Florida Medical Library Association.

**FMM** 1. force mix matrix.
1. table des forces en présence.
2. French military mission.
2. mission militaire française (MMF).
**FMM** Fundación Mundial de la Mujer (Bucaramanga, Colombia).
**FMM** Fundación Mundo Mujer (Popayán, Colombia).
**FMMS** Functionalized Monolayer on Mesoporous Supports.
*Chemistry; Solid-State Materials.*
**FMN** Flavin Mononucléotide.
French initialism meaning: Flavin Mononucleotide.
*Biochemistry* - Flavin mononuclotide is a phosphoric ester of riboflavin.
**FMO** Flatland Meteorological Observatory.
**FMP** Fisheries Management Plan.
**FMPEC** financial management procedures under emergency conditions.
procédures de gestion financière en situation d'urgence.
**FMR** 1. force mix ratio.
1. rapport des forces en présence.
2. forward maintenance and repair.
2. maintenance et réparation de l'avant.
**FMRB** Financial Management and Resource Board.
Bureau de la gestion financière et des ressources.
**fMRI** functional Magnetic Resonance Imaging.
*Cognitive Neurology; Cognitive Neuroscience.*
**FMS** File-Management System.
*Computer Programming.*
**FMS** Financial Management Service; Financial Management System.
**FMS** Flexible Manufacturing System.
**FMS** foreign military sales [US].
ventes militaires à l'étranger [US].
**FMT** frequency-managed training (net).
(réseau) d'instruction à gestion de fréquences.
**FMTC** Familial Medullary Thyroid Carcinoma.
*Endocrinology; Oncology.*
**FMV**; **Fmv** Full Motion Video.
**FMY** The airport code for Page Field, Fort Myers, Florida, U.S.A.
**Fn** Fibronectin.
*Animal Science; Cell Biology; Genetics; Heritable Disorders; Mammalian Genetics; Veterinary and Tumor Pathology.*
For further details see under: **UG** (Uteroglobin).
**fn.** (abbr.) footnote.
**FNA** final network acceptance.
réception définitive du réseau.
**FNAARC**; **Fnaarc** Federazione Nazionale Associazione Agenti e Rappresentanti di Commercio (Italy).
*Italian Federation.*
**FNB** Food and Nutrition Board (U.S.A.).
**FNCS** full naval control of shipping [obsolete].
contrôle naval global de la navigation commerciale [obsolète].
**FNEGE** Fondation Nationale pour l'Enseignement de la Gestion des Entreprises.
*French Foundation.*
**FNI** forces nucléaires de portée intermédiaire.
intermediate-range nuclear forces (INF).
**FNIH** Foundation for the National Institutes of Health (U.S.A.).
For further details see under: **NIH**.
**FNIII repeats** Fibronectin type III repeats.
*Cell Biology; Medicine; Protein Biophysics.*
**FNMA** Federal National Mortgage Association (U.S.A.).
**FNP** Frontonasal Process.
*Development Embryogenesis; Quail and Chick Embryos.*
**fnp** (abbr.) fusion point.
The term fusion point actually refers to the temperature above which nuclear fusion energy generation exceeds energy depletion.
*Nuclear Engineering.*
**FNPF** Fédération Nationale des Producteurs de Fruits.
*French Federation.*
**FNS** Food and Nutrition Service.
**FNS** full NAEGIS site.
station NAEGIS intégrale.
**FNSA** French National Safety Area.
Zone de sécurité nationale française (ZSNF).
**FNSEA** Fédération Nationale des Syndicats d'Exploitants Agricoles.
*French Federation.*
**FNT** The airport code for Flint, Michigan, U.S.A.
**FO** Fellowship Office (U.S.A.).
**FO** Field Officer.
**fo.** (abbr.) firmato.
Italian abbreviation meaning: signed.
**f.o.** firm offer.
*Commerce.*
**FO** Firm Order.
*Business; Commerce.*
**FO** Flying Officer.
**fo** folio.
**FO** Fond d'Oeil.
French acronym meaning: eyeground; fundus of the eye; fundus oculi.
**FO** Fond d'Oeil (examen du).

French acronym meaning: funduscopy; funduscopic examination; ophtalmoscopy.
**FO** Forlì-Cesena, Italy.
**fo.** (abbr.) formato.
Italian abbreviation meaning: size.
**FO** forward observer.
observateur de l'avant.
**FOA** 5-Fluoro-Orotic Acid.
*Molecular Biology.*
**FOA$^R$ cells** FOA-resistant cells.
*Molecular Biology.*
For further details see under: **FOA**.
**FOB** Fiber Optics Board.
**FOB** forward operating base.
base d'opérations avancée.
**FOB**; **fob** free on board.
**FOB** Freight On Board.
*Business; Commerce; Shipping.*
**FOB** Fuel On Board.
*Aviation.*
**FOBS** Fractional Orbital Bombardment System.
*Ordnance.*
**FOBTE** forward operating base test equipment.
équipement d'essais pour la base d'opérations avancé.
**FOC** full operational capability.
capacité opérationnelle totale.
**FOCAL program** French Ocean - Climat Atlantique equatorial program.
**FOCCR** Forza Operativa Cancro Colon Retto.
**FOCI** Fisheries-Oceanography Cooperative Investigations (U.S.A.).
**FOC images** Faint Object Camera images.
*Atmospheric and Planetary Physics; Space Astrophysics; Space Telescope Science.*
**FOCS** Foundations Of Computer Science.
**FOCUS** Fisheries Oceanography Cooperative Users System.
**FOD** foreign object damage.
dégâts causés par un corps étranger.
**f.o.d.** free of damage.
**FOE** Friends Of the Earth.
**FOF** Flow Of Funds.
**FOFA** follow-on forces attack.
attaque des forces d'exploitation et de remplacement.
**FOFs** Futures and Option Funds.
**FOIA** Freedom Of Information Act (U.S.A.).
The FOIA is a 35-year-old law that requires the U.S. Federal Government to disclose a certain number of documents.
**FOL** Fédération des Oeuvres Laïques.
*French Federation.*
**FOL** First-Order Logic.
**FOL**; **fol.** (abbr.) following.
**FOL** forward operating location.
emplacement d'opérations avancé.
**FOL** Friends Of Libraries.
**FOLD** Federally-Owned LANDSAT Data.
**foll.** (abbr.) following.
**FOM** 1. figure of merit.
1. facteur de mérite.
2. freedom of movement.
2a. liberté de circulation [civils].
2b. liberté de mouvements [militaires].
**FOMC** Federal Open Market Committee (U.S.A.).
**FONSPA** Credito FONdiario e Industriale SpA.
*Italian Bank.*
**FOO** forward observation officer.
officier observateur avancé.
**FOODPRO** (abbr.) FOOD PROcessing.
The Food Processing International Exhibition & Conference was held on 10th/13th December 1997 in Chennai (India).
**FOOTSIE** Financial Times and London Stock Exchange Index (G.B.).
**FOP** Fibrodysplasia Ossificans Progressiva.
In Fibrodysplasia Ossificans Progressiva severe inflammation can result from injuries to tendons, ligaments, or muscles.
*Developmental Genetics; Genetic Diseases; Medicine; Orthopedic Surgery.*
**FOP** Free On Plane.
**FOPA**; **Fopa** FOrmazione Professionale Artigiani (Italy).
Italian acronym meaning: Artisans Vocational Training.
**FOPC** First-Order Predicate Calculus.
*Artificial Intelligence.*
**FOQ** Free On Quay.
*Business; Commerce; Shipping.*
**for.** (abbr.) foreign; forestry.
**FOR** freedom of return.
liberté de retour.
**f.o.r.** free on rail.
**FORACS** see NATO FORACS.
voir FORACS OTAN.
**FORACS OTAN** site de contrôle de précision des armes et des détecteurs des forces navales de l'OTAN.
NATO naval forces sensors and weapons accuracy check site (NATO FORACS).
**FORCEPREP** force preparation.
préparation des forces.
**FORDEPRENU** force de deploiment préventif des Nations Unies.

United Nations Preventive Deployment Force (UNPREDEP).

**FORECAP** force combat air patrol.
patrouille aérienne de combat de la force.

**FOREM** Fundacion Formacion y Empleo.
*Spanish Foundation.*

**FOREX** (abbr.) FOReign EXchange.

**FORMAPELEC** Formation Professionnelle continue dans l'Equipement Electrique (France).
*Continuous Vocational Training.*

**FORMETS** message text formatting system.
système de formatage de textes de messages.

**FORPRONU** Force de protection des Nations Unies [obsolète - remplacée par l'IFOR].
United Nations Protection Force (UNPROFOR) [obsolete - replaced by IFOR].

**FORTRAN** (abbr.) FORmula TRANslation.
*Computer Programming.*

**FOS** Faint Object Spectrograph.
*Astronomy; Physics; Space Telescope Science.*

**f.o.s.** free overside ship.
*Business; Commerce; Shipping.*

**FOSDIC II** Film Optical Sensing Device for Input to Computers.
*Computer Technology.*

**FOSFA** Federation of Oil, Seed and Fats Association.

**FOSS** Federal Intelligence Service [FBiH].
Service de renseignement fédéral [FBiH].

**FOSS** Fiber Optic Solar Simulator.
FOSS is a 1992 invention (Bhushan Sopori's) to measure the performance of a photovoltaic cell. The conventional method relies on a single xenon arc lamp, whose output has strong emission lines along the spectrum and does not quite match the standard spectrum. Consequently, corrections have to be made and must be calculated. This process can take up to two days for multijunction devices. The FOSS can accomplish the same task in only five minutes with comparable accuracy. It achieves this by using two light sources. One is an infrared source with no emission lines. The other is split into an ultraviolet beam and a visible beam, both of which are passed through filters to block unwanted emission lines.
*Photovoltaic Measurements.*

**FOT** force opérationnelle terrestre.
land task force.

**FOT**; **f.o.t.** Free On Truck.
*Business; Commerce; Shipping.*

**FOTC** force over-the-horizon track coordinator.
coordonnateur des pistes transhorizon de la force.

**FOV** Field Of View.
*Optics.*

**FOW** Free On Wagon.
*Business; Commerce.*

**FOX** Fishery - Oceanography Experiment.
*U.S. Experiment.*

**FOX** Futures and Options Exchange.
*Commercial.*

**FP** Facist Party.

**F.P.** Fire Plug.

**FP** Fission Product.
*Energy.*

**FP** Fixed Price.

**FP**; **F.P.** Floating Point; Floating Policy.

**FP** 1. force proposal.
1. proposition de forces.
2. force protection.
2. protection des forces.

**F.P.** Foreign Policy.

**FP**; **fp**; **f.p.** Freezing point.
The freezing point is the temperature at which a substance in a liquid phase freezes.
*Physical Chemistry.*

**FP**; **fp** foot-pound.
*Metrology.*

**fp** fully paid.

**FP5** Fifth Framework Programme.
To support cross-border R&D Collaborations.
*European Union Program.*

**FP6** Sixth Framework Programme.
European Research 2000-2006.
For further details see under: **ETI**.

**FPA** Foreign Press Association.

**FPA** Free of Particular Average.

**FPA model** Fixed Principal Axis model.
*Physics.*

**FPAR** Fraction of the incident Photosynthetically Active Reaction.
*Atmospheric Research; Atmospheric Sciences; Environmental Science and Management; Land-Atmosphere Interactions; Meteorology; Plant Biology.*

**FPB** fast patrol boat.
vedette rapide.

**FPB** Floating Point Board.

**FPC**; **F.P.C.** Federal Power Commission.
The Federal Power Commission is a board established in the U.S.A., mainly to regulate electric power and natural gas industries involved in interstate commerce.

**FPC** 1. final planning conference.
1. conférence de planification finale.
2. force planning cycle.
2. cycle de planification des forces.

**FPC** Financial Planning Certificate.
**FPC** Fish Protein Concentrate.
**FPC** Fixed Price Contract.
*Business; Commerce; Finance.*
**FPCA** Functional Programming languages and Computer Architecture.
**FPD** Flight Projects Directorate (U.S.A.).
**FPDI** Flat Panel Display Interface.
*Monitors; Portables.*
**FPDs** Flat-Panel Displays.
*Chemical Engineering; Liquid Crystals; Materials Science.*
**FPF** final protective fire.
tir d'arrêt.
**FPG** functional planning guide.
guide de planification fonctionnelle.
**FPGAs** Field-Programmable Gate Arrays.
The FPGAs are fully reconfigurable chips.
**FPI** force de protection internationale.
international protection force (IPF).
**FPI** Islamic Defenders Front (Jakarta).
**FPIL** Full Premium If Lost.
**FPL** Forest Products Laboratory.
*Chemistry; Materials Science; Paper Industry.*
**FPLA** Field-Programmable Logic Array.
*Electronics.*
**FPLC** Fast Protein Liquid Chromatography.
**FPL tendon** Flexor Pollicis Longus tendon.
*Anatomy; Paleoanthropology; Physical Anthropology.*
**FPM** Federal Personnel Manual (U.S.A.).
**FPM**; **F.P.M.** Federazione contro la Pirateria Musicale.
FPM is located in Milan, Italy.
**fpm**; **f.p.m.** feet per minute.
**FPM** Fiber Pulling in Microgravity.
*Materials; Microgravity.*
**FPNU** forces de paix des Nations Unies.
United Nations peace forces (UNPF).
**FPO** The airport code for Freeport, Bahamas.
**FPP** Farnesyl Diphosphate.
*Biochemistry; Chemistry.*
**FPP** Floating Point Processor.
*Computer Technology.*
**FPP** force planning process.
processus de planification des forces.
**FPR** Federal Procurement Regulations (U.S.A.).
**FPR** Fixed Price Redeterminable.
*Business; Commerce; Economics; Finance.*
**FPRS** Forest Products Research Society.
**fps**; **f.p.s.** feet per second.
**FPS** Financial Planning System.
*Business; Finance.*
**FPS** Fluid Power Society.
**FPS**; **fps** foot-pound-second.
*Metrology.*
**Fps**; **fps**; **f.p.s.** frames per second.
**FPS-LA** Free Piston Stirling - Linear Alternator.
*Energy Conversion System.*
**FPSO** Floating Production Storage and Offloading.
The FPSO allows exploitation of oil fields located in deep water areas.
*European Commission Project.*
**FPT** force protection team.
équipe de protection d'une force.
**FQH effect** Fractional Quantum Hall effect.
**FQR** final qualification review.
étude finale des qualifications.
**FR** Federal Register; Federal Reserve (U.S.A.).
**F.R.** File Register.
**F.R.** Final Report.
**FR** Flocculation Reaction.
**FR** Fogging Resistance.
**fr**; **fr.** (abbr.) fragment.
**fr.** (abbr.) franc (obsolete).
Now: EURO/EUR (€). Became ECU (European Single Currency) with effect from January 2002.
*Currencies.*
**FR** (abbr.) France.
**Fr** The chemical symbol for Francium.
Francium is a radioactive alkali-metal element having the atomic number 87, and an atomic weight of 223. The word francium derives from **France** where it was discovered.
*Chemistry; Symbols.*
**Fr** franco.
**fr** (abbr.) franklin (statacoulomb).
**FR**; **fr** Freight Release.
**Fr.** (abbr.) French.
**Fr.** (abbr.) Friday.
**FR** Frosinone, Italy.
**FRA** Fondo Ricerca Applicata (Italy).
*Italian Fund.*
**FRA** The airport code for Frankfurt (Germany).
**FRA** Future Rate Agreement.
**F.R.Ae.S.** Fellow of the Royal Aeronautical Society (G.B.).
**FRAGO** fragmentary order.
ordre simplifié.
**FRAL** Federazione Regionale Artigianato Lombardo (Italy).
*Italian Federation.*
**FRAM** Fine Resolution Antarctic Model (G.B.).
**FRAM** Fleet Rehabilitation And Modernization.
**FRAM** Fleet Replacement And Modernization.

**FRAME** Fund for the Replacement of Animals in Medical Experiments.
**frame** The above acronym was coined using the English word "frame".
*Artificial Intelligence; Building Engineering; Computer Programming; Electronics; Graphic Arts; Mathematics.*
**FRAMES** Future RAdio wideband Multiple access Systems.
*European Community Project.*
**FRANS** Fibre Radio ATM Network and Services.
*European Community Project.*
**FRAP** FKBP-Rapamycin-Associated Protein.
*Chemistry; Chemical Biology.*
**FRAP** Fluorescence Recovery After Photobleaching.
*Biological Imaging; Cell Biology; Human Development; Metabolism.*
**FRB** Federal Reserve Bank (U.S.A.).
Also: **FRBK**.
**FRB**; **F.R.B.** Federal Reserve Board (U.S.A.).
**FRBK** Federal Reserve Bank (U.S.A.).
Also: **FRB**.
**FRC** Federal Radio Commission (U.S.A.).
**FRC** Federal Records Center (U.S.A.).
**FRC** Field-Reversed Configuration.
*Fusion Reaction.*
**FRC** Financial Reporting Council.
**FRC** Functional Residual Capacity.
Functional Residual Capacity is also known as: Functional Residual Volume.
*Physiology.*
**FRCD** Floating-Rate Certificates of Deposit.
**FRCS** Federal Reserve Communications System (U.S.A.).
**FRD** Field Research Division (U.S.A.).
**FRD** Forecast Research Division (U.S.A.).
**FRDA** Friedreich's Ataxia.
Friedreich's ataxia is an autosomal recessive, degenerative disease involving the heart and the central and peripheral nervous systems. Named after the German Physician Nikolaus **Friedreich**.
*Genetics; Medicine; Molecular and Cellular Biology; Neurology.*
**FRE** future regional engagement.
engagement régional du futur.
**F.R.Econ.Soc.** Fellow of the Royal Economic Society (G.B.).
**freq.** (abbr.) frequency.
Also: **f**.
*Acoustics; Mathematics; Physics; Statistics.*
**FRESC** Forest and Rangeland Ecosystem Science Center.
FRESC is a unit of the Biological Resources Discipline of the U.S. Geological Survey.
**FRET** Fluorescence Resonant Energy Transfer.
*Biochemistry; Cell Signaling; Chemistry; Medicine; Pharmacology.*
**FRF** Flight Readiness Firing.
**FRF** Freedom to Read Foundation.
**Fr.F.** French Franc.
For further details see under: **FF**.
**FRG** Federal Republic of Germany.
**frgt.** (abbr.) freight.
Also: **frt.**
*Business; Commerce; Shipping.*
**FRI** fundamental review of infrastructure (programme).
réexamen fondamental (du programme) de l'infrastructure.
**FRIC** Forest Resource Inventory of China.
**FRICT** Flexibility, Risk, Income, Control and Time.
**FRIDA** FRamework for Integrated Dynamic Analysis of travel and traffic - *European Community.*
**Fris** Frisian.
Frisian is a Germanic language closely related to English. It is spoken in Friesland.
*Languages.*
**FRMAC** Federal Radiological Monitoring and Assessment Center (U.S.A.).
The Federal Radiological Monitoring and Assessment Center was created after the Three Mile Island incident.
*Nuclear Defense; Radiological Monitoring and Assessment.*
**FRMB** fundamental review of military budget.
réexamen fondamental du budget militaire.
**FRMR** (abbr.) frame reject.
*Computers.*
**FRN** Floating-Rate Note.
*Business; Economics; Finance.*
**FROG**; **Frog** Free Rocket Over Ground.
*Ordnance.*
**FROG** Frequency-Resolved Optical Gating.
*Optics; Quantum Electronics.*
**frog** The above acronyms were coined using the English word "frog".
*Agriculture; Design Engineering; Transportation Engineering; Vertebrate Zoology.*
**FRP** financial rules and procedures.
règles et procédures financières.
**FRR** Flight Readiness Review.
**FRRF** Fast Repetition Rate Fluorometry.
*Botany; Coastal Sciences; Environmental Biophysics; Photosynthesis Research.*

**FRS** Federal Reserve System (U.S.A.).
**FRS** Fellow of the Royal Society (G.B.).
**FRS** Financial Reporting System.
*Business; Finance.*
**frs.** (abbr.) francs (obsolete).
Now: EURO/EUR (€). Became ECU (European Single Currency) with effect from January 2002.
*Currencies.*
**FRSI** Flexible Reusable Surface Insulation.
*Insulating Materials.*
**frt.** (abbr.) freight.
Also: **frgt.**
**Frt Ppd** (abbr.) Freight Prepaid.
*Business; Commerce; Shipping.*
**FRUEO** forces relevant de l'UEO [obsolète].
forces answerable to the WEU/FAWEU [obsolete].
**FRV** Functional Residual Volume.
*Physiology.*
**FRW cosmology** Friedmann-Robertson-Walker cosmology.
**FRY** Federal Republic of Yugoslavia (Serbia and Montenegro).
**F.S.** Ferrovie dello Stato.
Italian initialism meaning: (Italian) State Railways.
Also: **FF.SS.**
**FS** Field Service.
**FS** File Separator.
**F.S.**; **f.s.** film strip.
**F.S.**; **f.s.** Final Statement.
**FS** Financial Statement.
*Business; Commerce; Finance.*
**FS** 1. fire support.
1. appui-feu.
2. flight safety.
2a. sécurité aérienne.
2b. sécurité des vols.
3. force standards.
3. normes de forces.
4. functional service.
4. service fonctionnel.
**FS** Frame Status.
**FS** Franc Suisse.
French initialism meaning: Swiss Franc.
*Currencies.*
**F.S.**; **f.s.** Free of Station.
**FS** Free Surface.
*Materials Science and Engineering.*
**FS** Futures Spread.
*Banking; Business; Finance.*
**FSA** 1. final site acceptance.
1a. réception définitive de la station [radar].
1b. réception définitive du site.
2. forward support area.
2. zone avancée de soutien.
**FSA** Financial Supervisory Agency (Japan).
The FSA is Japan's main Banking Regulator.
**FSA** Food Standards Agency (G.B.).
*Food Safety and Standards.*
**FSAP** Financial Services Action Plan.
Single market in financial products.
Implementation by 2005.
**FSAR** Final Safety Analysis Report.
**FSAS** force selection and activation system.
système de sélection et d'activation des forces.
**FSB** (Russian) Federal Security Service.
Service fédéral (russe) de sécurité.
**FSB** Federal Specifications Board.
**FSC** Federal Securities Commission (Russian Federation).
**FSC** Financial Supervision Commission.
**FSC** 1. fire support coordination (coordinator).
1a. coordination (coordonnateur) de l'appui-feu.
1b. coordination (coordonnateur) des tirs (d'appui).
2. Forum for Security Cooperation [OSCE].
2. Forum pour la coopération en matière de sécurité [OSCE].
**FSC** Foreign Sales Corporation.
*Customs.*
**FSC** Forest Stewardship Council.
**FSc** forward scattering.
prodiffusion.
**F-scale** Fascist scale.
*Psychology.*
**FSCC** fire support coordination centre.
centre de coordination des feux d'appui (ou des armes d'appui).
**FSCL** fire support coordination line.
ligne de coordination des feux d'appui (LCFA).
**FSCM** fire support coordination measure.
mesure de coordination des feux d'appui.
**FSC Replacement Act** Foreign Sales Corporation replacement Act.
*Export Subsidy System (U.S.).*
**FSCWG** Future Command Structure Working Group [obsolete].
Groupe de travail sur la future structure de commandement [obsolète].
**FSE** fire support element.
élément d'appui-feu.
**F.S.E.**; **FSE** Fondo Sociale Europeo.
Italian initialism of the: European Social Fund.
The FSE has funded specific projects in favour of women ever since 1978.
**FSF** fire support facility.
installation de soutien de l'avant.

**FSG** forward support group.
groupe de soutien de l'avant.
**FSH** Follicle-Stimulating Hormone.
*Endocrinology.*
**FSI** Federazione Scacchistica Italiana (Italy).
Italian initialism of the: Italian Chess Federation.
**FSI** Federazione Scacchisti Italiani (Italy).
Italian initialism of the: Italian Chess-Players.
**FSI** Fellow of the Chartered Surveyors' Institution.
**FSI** Fellow of the Sanitary Institute.
**FSIS** Finnish Society for Information Services.
**FSIS** Food Safety and Inspection Service (U.S.A.).
**FSK** Frequency-Shift Keying.
*Telecommunications.*
**FSL** Forecast Systems Laboratory (U.S.A.).
**FSL** Formal Semantic Language.
**FSLA** Federal Savings and Loan Association (U.S.A.).
**FSN** French-Speaking Nation.
**FSP** forward support point.
point de distribution avancé.
**FSR** Field Service Regulations.
**FSR** force structure review.
examen de la structure des forces.
**FSR** Full Scale Range.
**FSRD** (Committee on) Federal Support of Research and Development (U.S.A.).
**FSS** Federal Supply Service (U.S.A.).
**FSS** Forensic Scientific Service (G.B.).
**FSS** 1. forward scatter system (or site).
1. système (ou station) de prodiffusion.
2. forward support site.
2. site de soutien avancé.
**FS sheets** Fermi Surface sheets.
*Materials Science; Physics; Superconductivity Research.*
**FSSL** fire support safety line.
ligne de sécurité des feux d'appui.
**FSSP** Forward-Scattering Spectrometer Probe.
**FSSR** Forest Sector and Strategy Review.
*World Bank Publication.*
**FSTI** Fund for International Therapeutic Solidarity (France).
**FSTS** Federal Secure Telephone Service (U.S.A.).
**FSU** Florida State University (U.S.A.).
Founded in 1857.
**FSU** Former Soviet Union.
**FSV Plant** Fort St. Vrain Plant.
**ft.** feet; foot.
**F/T** Financial Times.
Daily Financial Newspaper.
**FT** Frascati Tokamak.
*Physics.*
**FTA**; **Fta** Free To Air.
**FTA** Freight Transport Association (G.B.).
**FTAA** Free Trade Area of the Americas.
**FTA-abs test** Fluorescent Treponemal Antibody absorption test.
*Medicine.*
**FT and A project** Field Tests and Applications project.
**Ftase** Farnesyltransferase.
**FTC** Fair Trade Commission (South Korea).
**FTC** Federal Trade Commission (U.S.A.).
**ftc** footcandle.
Also: **FC**; **f.c.**
*Optics.*
**FTC** force track coordinator.
coordonnateur des pistes de la force.
**FTC** Foreign Trading Company.
**FTC-A** force track coordinator air.
coordonnateur des pistes Air de la force.
**FTC-S** force track coordinator-surface.
coordonnateur des pistes Surface de la force.
**FTC-SS** force track coordinator subsurface.
coordonnateur des pistes sous-marines de la force.
**FTDP-17** Frontotemporal Dementia and Parkinsonism linked to chromosome 17.
*Geriatric Medicine; Gerontology; Medicine; Neurodegenerative Diseases; Neurology; Pathology; Pharmacology.*
**FTE** Full Time Equivalent.
*Employment.*
**fth** fathom.
Also: **fm**.
Marine unit of measure.
*Oceanography.*
**FTI** Financial Times Index (G.B.).
**FTI** Flanders Technology International.
*Technology Fair* held in Ghent (Belgium).
**FTI** Forum per la Tecnologia dell'Informazione.
Italian initialism meaning: *Information Technology Forum.*
**FT-IR** Fourier Transform, Infrared Region.
**ft-L** foot-Lambert.
*Optics.*
**ft lb**; **ft-lb** foot-pound.
**FTM** Flat Tension Mask (picture tube).
**f.to** (abbr.) firmato.
Italian abbreviation meaning: signed.
**FTO** Freedom To Operate.
**FTP** Federal Test Procedure (U.S.A.).
*Car Certification.*
**FTP**; **Ftp** File Transfer Protocol.
**FTP** final technical proposal.
offre technique finale.

**ft-pdl** foot-poundal.
*Metrology.*
**FTR** Foreign Trade Reports (U.S.A.).
**FTR** Funds TRansfer.
*Business; Commerce; Finance.*
**FTS** Federal Telecommunications Systems (U.S.A.).
**FTSE index** Financial Times Stock Exchange index (G.B.).
**FTSR** Foreign Trade Statistics Regulations.
*U.S. Federal Register.*
**FTT** Financial Transaction Terminal.
*Business; Commerce; Finance.*
**FTTH network** Fibre To The House network.
*Broadband Internet Access.*
**FTX** field training exercise.
exercice d'entraînement sur le terrain.
**FTZ** Foreign-Trade Zone.
**FU** Finsen Unit.
A unit of ultraviolet radiation intensity.
*Electromagnetism.*
**FU** Fluoro-Uracile.
meaning in French: Fluorouracil. Used for the treatment of skin cancers and in chemotherapy (with other drugs).
*Oncology.*
**fu** flux unit.
**FUAAM** Fundación Uruguaya de Ayuda y Asistencia a la Mujer.
*Uruguayan Foundation.*
**FUCI** Federazione Universitaria Cattolica Italiana.
*Italian Federation.*
**Fuc*p*** Fucopyranosyl.
**FUDR** floxuridine.
Antineoplastic drug - $C_9H_{11}FN_2O_5$.
*Pharmacology.*
**FUK** The airport code for Fukuoka, Japan.
**FUM** follow-up meeting.
conférence-bilan.
**FUNBODEM** Fundación Boliviana para el Desarrollo de la Mujer.
*Bolivian Foundation.*
**F-U-N- dating** or **F.U.N. dating** Fluorine, Uranium, and Nitrogen dating techniques.
*Archaeology.*
**FUNHDEMU** Fundación Hondurena para el Desarrollo de la Mujer (Honduras).
**FUO** Fever of Undetermined Origin.
**FUP** forming-up point.
point (ou zone) de démarrage.
**FURAD** Forum of the Universities Research Authorities (Israel).
**FUS** Fondo Unico per lo Spettacolo.
*Italian Fund.*
**FUSE** Far Ultraviolet Spectroscopy Explorer (U.S.A.).
FUSE was launched in 1999 on a 3-year mission, extended for 2 more years. It includes Canadian and French participation.
*Astronomy; Astrophysics; Galaxy's Gas Circuit; Physics; Quasars.*
**FUV radiation** Far Ultraviolet radiation.
In the ultraviolet range of: 50 to 200 x $10^{-9}$ meters.
*Electromagnetism.*
**FV** Face Value.
*Banking; Finance.*
**fV** femtovolt.
fV is a unit of voltage that equals $10^{-15}$ V.
*Electricity.*
**FV** Fibrillation Ventriculaire.
French initialism meaning: Ventricular Fibrillation.
*Cardiology.*
**F/V** fishing vessel.
navire de pêche.
**FV** Floating Villus.
*Anatomy; Biochemistry; Reproductive Medicine; Stomatology.*
**FVCI** futur véhicule de combat d'infaterie.
future infantry combat vehicle (FICV).
**FVIF** Future Value Interest Factor.
**FVM** Finite Volume Method.
**FVOG program** Fishing Vessel Obligation Guarantee program.
**FW** fixed-wing.
à voilure fixe.
**FWA** Federal Works Agency (U.S.A.).
**FWA technology** Fixed-Wireless Access technology.
**FWC** fleet weather centre.
centre météorologique de la flotte.
**fwdr.** (abbr.) forwarder.
**FWF** Austrian Science Fund.
**FWHM** Full Width at Half Maximum.
*Physics.*
**FWIW** For What It's Worth.
**FWPCA** Federal Water Pollution Control Act.
A 1972 U.S. Act.
**FWS** Fish and Wildlife Service.
**FWWB** Friends of Women's World Banking (India).
**FX** Foreign Exchange.
**FXR** Farnesoid X Receptor.
*Biochemistry; Cancer Research; Medical Nutrition; Medicine; Metabolism; Nuclear Receptors; Pharmacology.*
**FY** Fiscal Year / Financial Year.
**FY** Former Yugoslav Republic of Macedonia.
Also: **FYROM**.

**FYI** For Your Information.
**FYIG** For Your Information and Guidance.
**FYO** Fiscal Year Option.
*Business; Finance.*
**FYR** Former Yugoslav Republic.
**FYTQ** Fiscal Year Transition Quarter.
*Business; Finance.*
**F.Z.S.** Fellow of the Zoological Society.
**F.Z.S.L.** Fellow of the Zoological Society, London.
**Fzs** Fracture Zones.
*Bathymetry; Oceanography; Seismology.*

# G

**g** (abbr.) gain.
*Control Systems; Design Engineering; Electromagnetism; Electronics.*
**g** gale (Beaufort letter).
*Meteorology.*
**g** gauge / gage.
*Building Engineering; Civil Engineering; Engineering; Electromagnetism; Mechanical Devices; Ordnance.*
**G** Germany.
Also: **GE**; **Ger**.
**g** giga-.
**G** Gold.
**g** gram / gramme.
*Metrology.*
**g** gravity.
*Mechanics.*
**G** Grind.
**G**; **g** Guardian.
**g** Acceleration of gravity.
*Physics.*
**G** Constant of gravitation.
*Physics.*
**G** Gauss.
*Electromagnetism.*
**g** gender.
*Biology; Electricity.*
**g.** gingival.
*Anatomy;* Referring to the gums.
**g.** glucose.
*Biochemistry.*
**G** Guanine.
*Biochemistry.*
**G** specific gravity.
*Mechanics.*
**g** the Greek letter gamma $\gamma$.
**G** Whole Gale (Beaufort letter).
*Meteorology.*
**3G** Third Generation.
**G5** Group of Five.
**G7** Group of Seven.
**Ga** the chemical symbol far Gallium.
Its compounds are used as semiconductors.
*Chemistry; Symbols.*
**GA** Gastric Analysis.
**ga** gauge.
**GA** General Account; General Agent.
**GA** 1. Gambia.
1. Gambie.
2. general agreement.
2. accord général.
3. general alert.
3. alerte générale.
4. ground attack.
4. attaque au sol.
**GA** General Assembly - U.N.
**GA** General Average.
*Commerce.*
**GA** General of the Army.
**G.A.** Genio Aeronautico.
Italian initialism meaning: Aeronautical Engineers.
**GA** Geographical Association.
**GA** (abbr.) Georgia (U.S.A.).
**GA** Gibberellic Acid.
$C_{18}H_{22}O_6$. GA is a crystalline acid which occurs in plants and is similar to the gibberellins.
*Biochemistry.*
**G.A.** Giunta Amministrativa.
Italian acronym meaning: Administrative Council.
**GA** Glide Angle.
**GA** Golfing Association.
**GA** Golgi Apparatus.
Named after the Italian physician Camillo **Golgi** (1844-1926).
*Cell Biology.*
**GA** Gross Asset.
*Business; Finance.*
**GA** Ground-to-Air (referring to a missile).
*Military.*
**GA** Gum Arabic.
A branched arabinogalactan polysaccharide used mainly in the manufacture of pharmaceuticals and inks.
**g,a.&s.** general average and salvage.
*Sea Transport.*
**GAAP** Generally Accepted Accounting Principles.
**GaAs** Gallium Arsenide.
With minor modifications, the SDMS could be used to analyze materials other than silicon. Of particular importance is gallium arsenide (GaAs), a semiconductor material for high-efficiency solar cells and high-speed microelectronics. The SDMS could be used to improve the prospects for GaAs technologies.
*Semiconductor Materials; Solar Cells.*
For further details see under: **SDMS**.
**GaAs** Gallium Arsenide.
Gallium arsenide is a crystalline material having a melting point of 1238°C.
*Inorganic Chemistry.*
**GAAS** Generally Accepted Auditing Standards.
**GAB** General Agreement to Borrow.

**GAB** Guichet Automatique de Banque.
French acronym meaning: Automated Teller Machine.
*Banking Technology.*
For further details see under: **DAB** (Distributeur Automatique de Billets (de banque).
**GABA** γ-Aminobutyric Acid.
**GAC** General Acceptance Corporation.
**GAC** Global Area Coverage.
**g.a.con.** general average contribution.
*Sea Transport.*
**GAD** Geocentric Axial Dipole.
*Geology; Geophysics.*
**GAD** Glutamic Acid Decarboxylase.
**GAD** Glyceraldehyde-Dehydrogenase.
**Gael.** (abbr.) Gaelic.
**GAF** Gesellschaft für Angewadte Fernerkundung (Germany).
**GAF** Guanylyl cyclase-Activating Factor.
**GAFTA** Grain And Feed Trade Association.
**GAG** Gambe, Addominali e Glutei.
**GAG** Glycosaminoglycan.
*Molecular Biology.*
**GAGE** Global Atmospheric Gases Experiment.
**GAI**; **Gai** Giustizia e Affari Interni (Italy).
**GAI** Guaranteed Annual Income.
**GAIC** Genetics And Insurance Committee (G.B.).
**Ga.InP** Gallium-Indium-Phosphide.
**GAINS** Growth And INcome Securities (U.S.A.).
**GaK** Galactokinase.
Galactokinase is an enzyme which catalyzes the phosphorylation of galactose.
*Enzymology.*
**gal.** (abbr.) galactose.
*Biochemistry* - $C_6H_{12}O_6$.
**gal** (abbr.) gallon.
Also: 1) Standard Gallon (U.S.A.); 2) Imperial Gallon (G.B.).
*Metrology.*
**GAL** global address list.
liste globale d'adresses.
**GAL** Globuline Antilymphocyte.
French acronym meaning: Antilymphocyte Globulin.
*Medicine.*
**GAL**; **gal** Gruppi di Azione Locale (Italy).
Italian acronym meaning: Local Action Groups. Partially funded by the European Community to safeguard local products such as: culture; human resources; handicrafts; tourism.
**gal/d** gallons per day.
**GalD** Galactonate Dehydratase.
*Biochemistry; Pharmaceutical Chemistry; Pharmacy.*
**GALE** Genesis of Atlantic Lows Experiment.
**Gal*p*** β-D-Galactopyranosyl.
**gals** (abbr.) gallons.
For further details see under: **gal**.
**GALT** Gut-Associated Lymphoid Tissue.
*Medicine; Primate Research.*
**GALV**; **galv** (abbr.) galvanized.
*Metallurgy.*
**GAM** Guided Aircraft Missile.
**GAMES** General Architecture for Medical Expert Systems.
*Medicine.*
**GaN** Gallium Nitride.
**GAN** group aéronaval.
aircraft carrier battle group (CVBG).
**GAN** Groupe des Assurances Nationales (France).
**GANIL** Large National Accelerator for Heavy Irons (Caen, France).
**GAO** General Accounting Office (U.S.A.).
**GAO** Groupe Aérien d'Observation (France).
**GaP** Gallium Phosphide.
GaP is used in semiconductor devices.
*Inorganic Chemistry.*
**GAP** groupe auxiliaire de puissance.
auxiliary power unit (APU).
**GAPA**, **gapa** Ground-to-Air Pilotless Aircraft.
*Military.*
**GAPDH probe** Glycerol Aldehyde Phosphate Dehydrogenase probe.
*Biotechnology; Molecular Biology.*
**GAPs** GTPase Activating Proteins.
*Molecular Physiology.*
**GAQ** Good Average Quality.
*Business; Commerce.*
**GAR** general assessment report.
rapport d'évaluation générale.
**GAR** Guided Aircraft Rocket (U.S.A.).
*Military; Weapons.*
**GARP** Global Atmospheric Research Program.
For further details see under: **FGGE**.
**GARS** Geological Applications of Remote Sensing.
**GAS** General Adaptation Syndrome.
*Behavior.*
**GASP** GPCR-Associated Sorting Protein.
For further details see under: **GPCR**.
**GASPEC** Gas Filter Correlation Spectrometer.
**GASTEM** GAS Turbine Health Monitoring demonstrator.
*European Community Project; Gas Turbines.*
**GAT** general air traffic.
circulation aérienne générale (CAG 2.).

**GAT** Greenwich Apparent Time.
**GAT** Gruppo Anticrimine Tecnologico (Italy).
**GATB** General Aptitude Test Battery.
**GATC**; **gatc** Guanine, Adenine, Thymine, and Cytosine.
GATC are nitrogenous bases constituting the genetic code in the DNA molecule.
*Genetics.*
**GATE** GARP Atlantic Tropical Experiment.
For further details see under: **GARP**.
**gate** The above acronym was coined using the English word "gate".
*Computer Technology; Electronics; Engineering; Nuclear Engineering; Ordnance.*
**GATS** General Acceptance Test Software.
**GATT** General Agreement on Tariffs and Trade.
GATT was formed in 1948. It has been replaced by the World Trade Organization in 1995.
**GAUGE** General Automation Users Group Exchange.
**gauge** The above acronym was coined using the English word "gauge".
*Building Engineering; Civil Engineering; Electromagnetism; Engineering; Mechanical Devices; Ordnance.*
**GAVI** Global Alliance for Vaccines and Immunization.
Established in January 2000, GAVI is a public-private partnership focused on increasing access to vaccines among children in poor countries. A framework for ADIPs for each vaccine has been developed.
For further details see under: **ADIPs**.
**GAW** Guaranteed Annual Wage.
**GAW program** Global Atmospheric Watch program.
Of the WMO.
For further details see under: **WMO**.
**Gaz.** (abbr.) Gazeteer; gazette.
**Gazz. Uff.** (abbr.) Gazzetta Ufficiale.
Italian abbreviation meaning: Offical Gazette.
**GB** Gabon.
**GB** Gallbladder / Gall Bladder.
Gallbladder is also known as: Cholecyst.
*Anatomy.*
**GB** General Broadcast.
*Telecommunications.*
**gB** gigaBIT.
One billion bits.
*Computer Technology.*
**gb** gigabyte.
Gigabyte is a unit of storage capacity equal to about one billion bytes.
*Computer Technology.*
**Gb** (abbr.) gilbert.
Named after the English scientist William **Gilbert**.
*Electromagnetism.*
**GB** Glass Bottle.
**GB** Glide Bomb.
*Ordnance.*
**GB** Gold Bond; Government Bond.
*Business; Finance.*
**GB** Gould's Belt.
*Astronomy; Astrophysics.*
**GB** Grain Boundary.
*Materials Science and Engineering.*
**GB** Great Britain.
**GB** Grid Battery.
*Radio.*
**GB** Guaranteed Bond.
**G.B.a.I.** Great Britain and Ireland.
**GBAD** ground-based air defence.
défense aérienne basée au sol.
**GB&E Research** Gravitational Biology and Ecology Research.
**GBB** Groningen Biomolecular Sciences and Biotechnology Institute (The Netherlands).
**GBCRI** Geraldine Brush Cancer Research Institute.
The GBCRI is a division of California Pacific Medical Center (U.S.A.).
**GBF** Granular-Bed Filter.
**GBIF** The Global Biodiversity Information Facility.
The GBIF was established on 1st March 2001. It is a body based on a multilateral agreement between countries, economics and relevant international organizations. Its purpose is to make computerized *Scientific Biodiversity Data* freely available via the Internet.
**GBIT** GigaBIT.
For further details see under: **gb**.
**GBL** Groupe Bruxelles Lambert.
*Belgian Group.*
**GBL** Growth Biology Laboratory.
Of the U.S. Department of Agriculture's Agricultural Research Service.
**GBM** Glioblastoma Multiforme.
A human malignant form of brain tumor.
*Biomedicine.*
**GBM** Glomerular Basement Membrane.
The GBM is a sort of filter in the kidneys that allows excess water loss without valuable protein loss.
**GBMI** Guilty But Mentally Ill.
*Criminology.*
**GBN** Golden Bridge Net (China).
*Internet in China.*

**gbo**; **g.b.o.** goods in bad order.
*Commercial; Transportation.*
**GBP** D-Galactose Binding Protein.
**GBP** Gain-Bandwidth Product.
**GBP** pound sterling.
*Currencies.*
**Gbps** Gigabits per second.
*Computer Technology.*
**GBR** Great Barrier Reef (Australia).
**GBRI** Geneva Biomedical Research Institute (Switzerland).
*Molecular Biology.*
**GBS** General Business System.
*Business; Finance.*
**GBS** Guillain-Barre Syndrome.
**g-byte** gigabytes.
For further details see under: **gb**.
**GC** Garbage Collection.
Garbage Collection is also known as: Reclaimer.
*Computer Programming.*
**GC** Gas Chromatography.
*Analytical Chemistry.*
**GC** Gene Conversion.
*Medical Chemistry; Medicine.*
**GC** General Counsel.
**GC** Germinal Center.
For further details see under: **GCs**.
**GC** Giga Cycle.
**gC** Glycoprotein C.
*Medicine.*
**GC** Golf Club.
**GC** Gonococcus.
Gonococcus also known as *Neisseria gonorrhoeae*, causes gonorrhea.
*Bacteriology.*
**GC** Group Captain.
*Military.*
**GC** Guanylate Cyclase.
For further details see under: **GCAP**.
**GC** Guarded Command.
*Computer Programming.*
**GC** Gun Control.
*Weapons.*
**GCA** Ground-Controlled Approach.
*Aviation.*
**g. cal**; **g-cal.** gram calorie.
**GC analysis** Gas Chromatographic analysis.
**GCAP** GC-Activating Protein.
*Signaling Molecules.*
For further details see under: **GC**.
**GCAW** Gas Carbon Arc Welding.
**GCC** Global Climatic Change.
**GCC** Global Climate Coalition.
The GCC, Washington, D.C.-based is a group supported by oil and coal producers and utilities.
*Global Warming.*
**GCC** Gore-Chernomyrdin Commission.
U.S.-Russia Joint Efforts in areas such as: *Disease Surveillance; International Space Stations; Nuclear Disarmament.*
**GCC** groupe consultatif commun.
joint consultative group (JCG).
**GCC** Gulf Cooperation Council.
For further details see under: **GIB** (Gulf International Bank).
**G-C content** Guanosine-Cytosine content.
*Biochemistry; Biophysics.*
**GCCS** global command and control system.
système mondial de commandement et de contrôle.
**GCD** Greatest Common Divisor.
*Mathematics.*
**GCDCA** Glycine CDCA.
For further details see under: **CDCA**.
**GCDIS** Global Change Data and Information System.
**GCE** General Certificate of Education (G.B.).
**GC-ECNCIMS** Gas Chromatography.-Electron Capture Negative Chemical Ionization Mass Spectrometry.
**GCF**; **G.C.F.** Greatest Common Factor.
**GCFI** Gulf and Caribbean Fisheries Institute.
**GCFR** Gas-Cooled Fast Reactor.
**GCG** Genetics Computer Group (U.S.A.).
**GC hormones** Glucocorticoid hormones.
*Biological Sciences; Endocrinology.*
**GCI** General Cognitive Index.
**GCI** Global Commerce Initiative.
The GCI was set up in October 1999 as a forum for technological cooperation between leading suppliers and retailers.
*Technological Cooperation.*
**GCI radar** Ground-Controlled Intercept radar.
*Military Science.*
**GCL** Ganglion Cell Layer.
*Biological Timing; Medicine; Neurobiology; Physiology.*
**GCL** Ground-Controlled Landing.
**GCM** General Circulation Model.
GCM is also known as: Global Circulation Model.
For further details see under: **GCMs**.
**g-cm** gram-centimeter.
**GCM** The airport code for Grand Cayman, East Indies.
**G.C.M.**; **g.c.m.** Greatest Common Measure.
**GCMD** Global Change Master Directory - NASA's.

*Earth Science.*
**GC-MS** Gas Chromatography-Mass Spectrometry.
*Analytical Chemistry.*
**GCMs** General Circulation Models.
*Atmospheric Physics; Climatology; Meteorology.*
For further details see under: **GCM**.
**GCO** Grand Commandement (commandant) de l'OTAN [obsolète - remplacé par SC].
Major NATO Command (commander) (MNC) [obsolete - replaced by SC].
**GC of the spleen** Germinal Center of the spleen.
*B Cell Survival; Medical Research; Pathology.*
**GCOS** General Chief of Staff.
chef d'état-major général (CEMG).
**GCOS** Global Climate Observing System.
**GCPS** Global Climate Perspectives System.
**GCR** Galactic Cosmic Rays.
*Geosciences; Physics; Space Sciences.*
**GCR** Great Central Railway.
**GCR** Ground-Controlled Radar.
**GCR** Group-Coded Record.
*Computer Technology.*
**GCRC** General Clinical Research Center (U.S.A.).
**GC reaction** Germinal Center reaction.
*Cell Biology; Genetics; Immunology; Medicine; Microbiology; Molecular Biology; Oncology.*
**GCRMN** Global Coral Reef Monitoring Network.
The GCRMN is part of the International Coral Reef Initiative, a multilateral agreement signed in 1994.
*Coastal Zone Management; Coral Reef Science; Monitoring Programs.*
**GCRP** Global Change Research Plan.
GCRP is also known as: Global Change Research Program.
The GCRP began in 1989.
**GCS** Gate-Controlled Switch.
**GCS** Gas-Controlled Switch.
*Electronics.*
**GCs** Germinal Centers.
*Autoimmunity; Biology; Biophysics; Cell Biology; Medicine; Microbiology; Pathology.*
**GCs** Globular Clusters.
*Astronomy; Astrophysics; Galaxy Evolution.*
**GCS** Globular Cluster System.
*Astronomy; Astrophysics; Galaxy Evolution.*
**G-CSF** Granulocyte-Colony-Stimulating Factor.
*Chemotherapy.*
**GCT** Galactic Center Transient.
**GCT** Giro Credit Transfer.
*Banking; Finance.*
**GCT**; **G.C.T.** Greenwich Civil Time.
**GCTE project** Global Change and Terrestrial Ecosystem project.
*Ecology.*
**GCTM** Global Chemical Transport Model.
Of the U.S. Environmental Research Laboratories (U.S.A.).
**GCU** guidance and control unit.
section de guidage et de commande (SGC).
**GCV** Green Crinkle Virus.
*Plant Pathology.*
**Gd** the chemical symbol for Gadolinium.
Named after the Finnish chemist Johan **Gadolin**.
*Chemistry; Symbols.*
**GD** Global Data.
**GD** Good Delivery.
*Business; Commerce.*
**G.D.** Grand Duchess; Grand Duchy; Grand Duke.
**gd** (abbr.) guard.
**GDA** Global Data Administrator.
**GDB** Genome Data Base.
*Bioinformatics; Genome Mapping; Positional Cloning.*
**GDC** Generation Data Group.
*Computer Programming.*
**GDCh** Society of German Chemists (Germany).
**GDE** Group for Development and Environment (University of Bern, Switzerland).
**G.d.F.** Guardia di Finanza.
Italian initialism meaning: Revenue Guard Corps.
**GDF database** Global Development Finance database.
Of the World Bank.
**GDH** groupe date-heure.
date-time group (DTG).
**GDI** Gaze Direction Index.
*Brain and Cognitive Sciences; Neuroscience.*
**GDL** Graphic Display Library.
**GDL** The airport code for Guadalajara, Mexico.
**GDM** Group on Defence Matters.
groupe sur les questions de défense.
**GDME** Glycol Dimethyl Ether.
**GDMS** Glow-Discharge Mass Spectrometry.
**gDNA** mutant genomic DNA.
*Cellular Biology; Molecular Biology.*
**GDNF** Glial-Derived Neurotrophic Factor.
The GDNF is a protein that was isolated by U.S. researchers at Synergen Inc. in Colorado, U.S.A. in 1993.
*Biotechnology; Dopaminergic Neurons; Parkinson's Disease.*
**Gdn-HCl** Guanidinium Hydrochloride.
**GDO** Grid-Dip Oscillator.
**$Gd_2O_3$** Gadolinium Oxide.

Gadolinium Oxide is used mainly in lasers.
*Inorganic Chemistry.*
**GDP** Government Development Platform.
**GDP** Gross Domestic Product.
**GDP** Guanosine Diphosphate.
**GDPR** Group of Deputy Permanent Representatives on the Public Disclosure of NATO Documents.
Groupe des représentants permanents suppléants sur la mise en lecture publique de documents OTAN.
**GDPS** Global Data-Processing System.
**GDR** German Democratic Republic.
**GDR** Geophysical Data Record.
**GDRs** Global Depositary Receipts.
*Banking; Finance.*
**GDS** Civil Democratic Party of BiH (FBiH).
parti démocratique civil de Bosnie-Herzégovine.
**GDS** General Data Stream.
*Computers.*
**GDS** Graphic Data System.
**GDS** Graphic Design System.
**GDSIDB** Global Digital Sea Ice Data Bank.
**GDSs** Guanosine Diphosphate-dissociation Stimulators.
For further details sec under: **GRFs** (Guanine-Nucleotide Releasing Factors).
**GE** Gastroenterology.
*Medicine.*
**GE** General Expenses.
**GE** Genetic Engineering; Genetically Engineered.
**GE** Genova, Italy.
**Ge** The chemical symbol for Germanium.
Named for **Germany** where it was discovered.
*Chemistry; Symbols.*
**GE** Germany.
Also: **G**; **Ger**.
**GE** Gross Earnings.
*Business; Finance.*
**GE** Guide Edge.
The term guide edge refers to the edge of a paper tape, a punch card, or other means for alignment use.
*Computer Technology.*
**GEADGE** German Air Defence Ground Environment.
infrastructure électronique de la défense aérienne de l'Allemagne.
**GEBA** Global Energy Balance Archive.
*Earth and Planetary Sciences.*
**GEC** Global Environmental Change.
**GEE** Generalized Estimating Equation.
**GE-EP** Group of Experts on Effects of Pollutants.
**GEF** Global Environmental Facility.
GEF was established in 1991 to coordinate the environmental activities of UNEP, the WB, and the U.N. Development Program. The GEF is charged with demonstrating the value of promising technologies. One of its aims is to reduce the emission of greenhouse gases through *Renewable Energy Projects.*
For further details see under: **UNEP** and **WB**.
**GEFRKA** Genetically Engineered Food Right to Know Act (U.S.A.).
*Bioengineered Foods.*
**GEFs** Guanine nucleotide Exchange Factors.
**GEFSA** Genetically Engineered Food Safety Act (U.S.A.).
*Bioengineered Foods.*
**GEG** The airport code for Spokane, Washington, U.S.A.
**GE-GLOSS** Group of Experts on the Global Sea-level Observing System.
Of the Intergovernmental Oceanographic Commission.
**$GeH_4$** Germanium Tetrahydride.
*Inorganic Chemistry.*
**GEIE** Gruppo Europeo di Interesse Economico.
Italian acronym of the: European Group of Economic Interest - E.C.
**GEIP** Groupe éuropéen indépendant de programme.
Independent European Programme Group (IEPG).
**GEK** Geomagnetic Electrokinetograph.
GEK is an instrument used to calculate the speed and direction of ocean currents.
*Engineering.*
**GEL** General Emulation Language.
**GEM** Graded test for English Majors.
*Linguistics.*
**GEM** Graduated Equity Mortgage.
*Business; Commerce; Economics.*
**GEM** Ground Effect Machine.
*Mechanical Engineering.*
**GEM alliance** Global Equity Market alliance.
Formed in 2000.
*Equity Exchanges.*
**GEM detector** Gammas, Electrons, and Muons detector.
**GE-MIM** Group of Experts on Marine Information Management.
**GEMS** (American) Gas Exchange Measurement System.
*Environment Monitoring.*
**GEMS** generic establishment management system [formerly called CHARMS].
système générique de gestion des effectifs [anciennement appelé CHARMS].

**GEMS** Glass with Embedded Metal and Sulfides.
GEMS are 10-nm-diameter FeNi metal and sulfide grains embedded in silicate glass.
*Astronomy; Interplanetary Dust Particles.*
**GEM(S)** Global Environmental Monitoring (System).
Of the U.N. Environment program and the WHO.
For further details see under: **WHO**.
*Environmental Quality.*
**GEMs** Growing-Equity Mortgages (U.S.A.).
**GEMS/MARC** Global Environment Monitoring System / Monitoring and Assessment Research Centre (G.B.).
**gen.** (abbr.) gender.
*Biology; Electricity.*
**gen.** (abbr.) general.
Also: **gn.**
**GEN** Generate.
*Chemistry; Computer Programming.*
**gen.** (abbr.) generated; genetics.
**gen.** (abbr.) generation.
*Artificial Intelligence; Biology; Computer Technology.*
**gen.** (abbr.) generator.
*Computer Science; Electrical Engineering; Electronics; Mathematics.*
**gen.** (abbr.) genus (plural: genera).
The term genus means the main family subdivision.
*Systematics.*
**GEND** General Electric Neutron Devices.
**Gen.Led.** (abbr.) General Ledger.
**Gen.Mtge.** (abbr.) General Mortgage.
**Genn.** (abbr.) Gennaio.
Italian abbreviation meaning: January.
**gent.** (abbr.) gentleman/gentlemen.
**GEO** Gene Expression Omnibus.
At the National Center for Biotechnology Information, Bethesda, Maryland, U.S.A.
*Embryonic Databases.*
**GEO** Geosynchronous Earth Orbit.
**$GeO_2$** Germanium Oxide.
Germanium Oxide is also known as: Germanium Dioxide.
*Inorganic Chemistry.*
**geod.** (abbr.) geodesy; geodetic.
**GEODAS** (abbr.) GEOphysical DAta System.
**GEODSS** Ground-base Electro-Optical Deep Space Surveillance.
GEODSS is a system used for tracking objects in space.
*Ordnance.*
**geofis.** (abbr.) geofisica; geofisico.
Italian abbreviation meaning: geophysics; geophysicist.
**geog.** (abbr.) geographic; geographical; geography.
**geol.** (abbr.) geologic; geological; geology.
**geom.** (abbr.) geometra.
Italian abbreviation meaning: land surveyor; geometer; geometrician.
*Zoology* - spon-worm (U.S.A.).
**GE-OPC** Group of Experts on Ocean Processes and Climate.
**GEOREF** world geographic reference system.
système mondial géographique de référence.
**GEOS** Geodynamics Experimental Ocean Satellite.
**GEOSAT** (abbr.) GEOdetic SATellite (U.S.A.).
**GEOSECS** GEOchemical Ocean SECtions Study.
**GEOSITREP** geographic situation report.
compte rendu de situation géographique.
**GEP** generic plan.
plan générique.
**GE plants** Genetically Engineered plants.
*Biosafety; Forest Science; Genetic Technologies; Gene Function; Plant Development.*
**Ger.** (abbr.) German.
**Ger.** Germany.
Also: **G**; **GE**.
**GE-RCDS** Group of Experts on Responsible National Oceanographic Data Centers and Climate Data Services.
Of the Intergovernmental Oceanographic Commission.
**GERD** Gross Expenditure on Research & Development.
**GERL** Golgi Endoplasmic Reticulum Lysosomes.
Named for the Italian physician Camillo **Golgi**.
**GES** Gilt-Edged Securities.
*Business; Finance.*
**GES** Gold Exchange Standard.
**GESO** Graduate Employees and Students Organization (U.S.A.).
**GEST Center** Goddard Earth Sciences and Technology Center.
At NASA's GSFC in Greenbelt, Maryland, U.S.A.
For further details see under: **GSFC**.
**GESTECs** GEnome Science and TEchnology Centers.
**GET** Greenwich Electronic Time (G.B.).
Has replaced GMT with effect from 2000.
For further details see under: **GMT**.
**GETA**; **Geta** Global Electronic Trade Association.
**GETAP** Gabinete de Educação Tecnológica, Artistica e Profissional (Portugal).
**GETOL** Ground Effect for Take-Off and Landing.
**GEU** Grossesse Extra-Utérine.

French acronym meaning: Extra-uterine / Extrauterine Pregnancy.
**GeV**; **Gev** Giga Electron Volt / giga-electron volt.
**GEV** Guardia Ecologica Volontaria (Italy).
*Ecology; Environment.*
**GEWEX** Global Energy and Water cycle EXperiment.
**GF** Germ-Free.
*Immunology; Immunobiology.*
**gf** gram-force.
**GF** Growth Factor.
*Biochemistry; Oncology.*
**GFA** 1. gunfire area.
1. zone de tirs d'artillerie.
2. see GFAP.
2. voir GFAP.
**GFA** Gust Front detection Algorithm.
Also: **GFDA**.
**GFAAS** Graphite Furnace Atomic Absorption Spectrometry.
**GFAP** General Framework Agreement for Peace in Bosnia-Herzegovina (commonly called "Dayton Agreement").
Accord-cadre général pour la paix en Bosnie-Herzégovine (communément appélé "Accord de Dayton").
**GFAP** Glial Fibrillary Acidic Protein.
A marker for astrocytes.
*Brain Research; Cerebellar Pathology; Neurodegenerative Diseases; Neuropathology; Neuroscience.*
**GFCF** Gross Fixed Capital Formation.
**GFD** Geophysical Fluid Dynamics.
**GFDA** Gust Front Detection Algorithm.
Also: **GFA**.
**GFDL** Geophysical Fluid Dynamics Laboratory.
The GFDL is located in Princeton, New Jersey, U.S.A.
*Atmospheric Sciences; Climate Change; Geophysics; Meteorology; Space Physics.*
**GFE** Government-Furnished Equipment.
*Military.*
**GFFATM** Global Funds to Fight AIDS, Tuberculosis and Malaria.
The GFFATM was established in January 2002.
*Funds.*
**GFIM** groupe de forces interarmées multinationales.
combined joint task force (CJTF).
**GFLV** Grapevine Fan-Leaf Virus.
*Virology.*
**GFM** Grupo Ferroviario Mexicano.
GFM is a *U.S.; Mexican consortium.*
**GF model** Growth-Factor model.
*Transportation Engineering.*
**GFO** GEOSAT Follow On.
For further details see under: **GEOSAT**.
**GFOFs** Geared Futures and Option Funds.
*Business; Economics; Finance.*
**GFP** Government-Furnished Property.
*Military.*
**GFP** Green Fluorescent Protein.
The GFP was first cloned by reasearchers at WHOI in Massachusetts, U.S.A. in 1992.
*Molecular and Cell Biology; Molecular Genetics; X-Ray Crystallography.*
For further details see under: **WHOI**.
**GFR** gas-filler radar.
radar de couverture.
**GFR** Glomerular Filtration Rate.
*Biochemistry.*
**GFS** General Financial System.
**GFs** Growth Factors.
*Biochemistry; Oncology.*
**GFSC** Guernsey Financial Services Commission (Guernsey).
**GFZ** GeoForschungs Zentrum (Germany).
**GG**; **G.G.** Gamma Globulin.
*Immunology.*
**GG** Georgia.
**gg** (abbr.) giorni.
Italian abbreviation meaning: days.
**GG** Ground-to-Ground (referring to a missile).
Also: **G/G**.
*Military.*
**GGAs** Golgi-localized, *y*-ear-containing, ARF-binding proteins.
*Cell Biology; Human Development; Metabolism; Molecular Genetics.*
**GGA theory** Generalized Gradient Approximation theory.
*Geophysics; High-Pressure Research; Mathematics; Planetary Physics.*
**GG.FF.** Guardie Forestali.
Italian initialism meaning: Ranger Corps.
**GGPP** Geranylgeranyl Diphosphate.
*Biochemistry; Chemistry.*
**GGPPs** Giant Gaseous Protoplanets.
*Terrestrial Magnetism.*
**g.gr.** great gross (144 dozens).
**GGT** Genomics-Guided Transgenes.
*Abiotic Stress Tolerance (of crops); Biosafety Mechanisms; Forest Science; Genetic Technologies.*
**GGTase I** Geranylgeranyltransferase I.

**GH** Ghana - International vehicle registration letters.

**GH** Growth Hormone.
The growth hormone, also known as somatotropin is a protein hormone that promotes growth in body size.
*Endocrinology.*

**GHA** Greenwich Hour Angle.

**GHCN** Global Historical Climate Network.

**GHF** Gold Hill Fault.
*Earth Sciences; Geopjysics; Geological Sciences.*

**GHG** Greenhouse Gas.
GHG is a gas that traps solar electromagnetic radiation.
*Decarbonization; Ecology; Energy; Environment.*

**GHGs** Greenhouse Gases.

**GHQ**; **G.H.Q.** General Headquartes.
*Military.*

**GHMA** Global Humanitarian Mine Action.
action humanitaire mondiale de lutte contre les mines.

**GH-RH** Growth Hormone-Releasing Hormone.
GH-RH is also known as: Somatoliberin; Somatotroprin-Releasing Factor.
*Endocrinology.*

**GHRIH** Growth Hormone-Release Inhibiting Hormone.

**GHRP** Growth Hormone-Release Peptide.
*Health Sciences; Medicine; Pharmacology; Physiology; Primate Research.*

**GHRS** Goddard High-Resolution Spectrograph.
The Goddard High-Resolution Spectrograph is an instrument, that was replaced in 1997. It has recorded ultraviolet light spectra from stars and planets.
*Astronomy.*

**GHSLA** Georgia Health Science Libraries Association.

**Ghz** gigahertz.
One billion hertz.

**GI**; **G.I.** Galvanized Iron.
*Metallurgy.*

**GI**; **G.I.** Gastrointestinal.
*Anatomy; Medicine.*

**GI**; **G.I.** General Issue; Government Issue.

**GI** Genetics Institute.

**GI** gestion de l'information.
information management (IM 1.).

**G.I.** Giudice Istruttore.
Italian initialism meaning: Inquiring Magistrate.

**GI** Gross Inventory.

**GI** Gross Investment.

**$GI_{50}$** 50-percent Growth Inhibitory concentration.

**GIA** Groupes Islamiques Armés.

**GIA** Gruppo Islamico Armato.

**GI absorption spectrum** Grazing-Incidence absorption spectrum.
*Polymer Chemistry.*

**GIAP** Glaxo Institute of Applied Pharmacology.
GIAP is fully integrated with the Department of Pharmacology in Cambridge University. The main areas of research within GIAP are in novel aspects of characterization and classification of *Receptors for Somatostatin and ATP.*

**GIA process** Glacial Isostatic Adjustment process.
*Physics.*

**Gib.** (abbr.) Gibraltar.

**GIB** Gulf International Bank.
Head Office: Manama, Bahrain. GIB is a wholesale commercial bank based in Bahrain. It is wholly owned by GIC, the international investment banking Corporation owned equally by the governments of the six member states of the GCC (Bahrain, Kuwait, Oman, Qatar, Saudi Arabia) and the United Arab Emirates.
For further details see under: **GIC** and **GCC**.

**GIC** Gulf Investment Corporation.
For further details see under: **GIB** and **GCC**.

**GIC conditions** Global Instrument of Certificates conditions.

**GICCS** Georgetown Institute in Cognitive and Computational Sciences.
*Brain Imaging; Computational Neuroscience; Cognitive Science.*

**GICs** Graphite Intercalation Compounds.

**GICs** Guaranteed Income Contracts; Guaranteed Investment Contracts.

**GIF** General Image Format.

**GIF** Graphics Interface Format.
*Computer Science.*

**GIFA** Governing International Fisheries Agreement.

**GIFCO** Gruppo Italiano Fabbricanti Cartone Ondulato (Italy).
Italian acronym of the: Italian Group of Corrugated Board Manufacturers.
*Paper Manufacturing.*

**GIFI** Gruppo Imprese Fotovoltaiche Italiane.
*Italian Group; Photovoltaics.*

**GIFT** Gamete Intra-Fallopian Transfer.
*Genetics.*

**GigE interfaces** Gigabit Ethernet interfaces.
*Ethernet.*

**GIGO** Garbage In, Garbage Out.
The term garbage in, garbage out means that correctness of a computer's output depends on the input correctness.

*Computer Programming.*
**GII** Global Information Infrastructure (U.S.A.).
**GILA** Government of India Librarians' Association.
**GIMPS** Great Internet Mersenne Prime Search.
*Computing Project.*
**GIN** Greenland-Iceland-Norway.
**GINO** Graphical INput and Output.
**giorn.** (abbr.) giornaliero.
Italian abbreviation meaning: daily.
**giov.** (abbr.) giovedì.
Italian abbreviation meaning: Thursday.
**GIP** Gastric Inhibitory Peptide.
*Endocrinology.*
**GIP** Gastric Inhibitory Polypeptide.
**GIP** 1. generic intelligence plan.
1. plan générique de renseignement.
2. Groupe international de police.
2. International Police Task Force (IPTF).
**GIP** Giudice per le Indagini Preliminari.
*Law* (Italy) - Italian acronym meaning: Judge for Preliminary Investigations.
**g.i.p.** glazed imitation parchment.
**GIPLs** Glycoinositolphospholipids.
**GIPME** Global Investigation of Pollution in the Marine Environment.
**GIPSY** General Information Processing System.
**Gir** (abbr.) Gironde (Department) ( France).
**GIR** Groupes d'Intervention Régionaux (France).
**GIRIO** Government Industrial Research Institute (Japan).
**GIRL** Generalized Information Retrieval Language.
**GIRLS** Graphical data Interpretation and Reconstruction in Local Satellite.
**GIRS** Global Integrated Rating System.
**GIS** Generalized Information System.
*Data Communications.*
**GIS** Geographic Information System.
An Oracle database management system supports data analysis as well as GIS functions. Analysts can also access a powerful mainframe computer to produce contour maps of the solar resource or topographical features such as hilly terrain or groundwater contamination.
For further details see under: **MSW** (Municipal Solid Waste).
**GISLA** University of Utrecht, Department of Physical Geography (The Netherlands).
**GISP2** Greenland Ice Sheet Project two.
*Climate Change; Cold Regions Research; Earth, Oceans, and Space Science; Geophysics; Quaternary Isotopes.*
**GISS** NASA's Goddard Institute of Space Studies (U.S.A.).
**GISSI** Gruppo Italiano per lo Studio della Sopravvivenza nell'infarto (Italy).
Italian acronym of the: Italian Group for the Study for Outliving Infarct.
**GIST** Gastrointestinal Stromal Tumor.
GIST is a rare stomach cancer.
*Medicine; Mesenchymal Tumors; Oncology; Pathology.*
**GIST** Grazing-Incidence Solar Telescope.
*Astronomy.*
**GITMO** Gruppo Italiano Trapianti Midollo Osseo (Italy).
*Bone-Marrow Transplantation.*
**Giu.** (abbr.) Giugno.
Italian abbreviation meaning: June.
**GIUK** Greenland - Iceland - United Kingdom (Gap).
(passage) Groenland - Islande - Royaume-Uni.
**GIXD** Grazing-Incidence X-ray Diffraction.
*Materials; Solid-State Physics.*
**GJ** Grenada.
**GJP** Graphic Job Processor.
**GK** Glucokinase.
*Enzymology.*
**GK** (abbr.) Greek.
**4-GL** Fourth-Generation (compter) Language.
**GL** General Ledger; General Length.
**gl.** (abbr.) gill.
*Metrology* - Gill is also known as: Imperial gill.
*Mycology* - In mycology gill is also known as: lamella.
**gl.** (abbr.) gill.
*Vertebrate Zoology.*
**gl.** (abbr.) glass.
*Materials.*
**gl.** (abbr.) gloss.
*Optics.*
**Gl** Glucinium.
Glucinium is the former name for beryllium.
*Chemistry.*
**GL** Grosch's Law.
Grosch's Law is a law of the 1940s stating that a computer processing power is proportional to the square of the cost.
*Computer Technology.*
**GL** Ground Level.
Ground level is also known as: Ground State.
*Quantum Mechanics.*
**GLA** General Ledger Account.
**GLA** Georgia Library Association.
**GLA** Ghana Library Association.
**GLABC** Government Libraries Association of British Columbia.

**GLAD technique** GLancing Angle Deposition technique.
*Applied Physics; Photonic Crystals.*
**GLAM** Grey, Leisured, Affluent, Married (U.S.A.).
**GLAMIS** Grants and Loans Accounting and Management Information System.
**GLAS** Goddard Laboratory of Atmospheric Sciences.
**GLASS** Graphical Language for Assembly of Secondary Structure.
GLASS enables reading of data from different sources generating a 3D image.
**GLAST** Gamma-ray Large Area Space Telescope.
Planned for launch by 2005.
*Astronomy; Cosmology; Gamma-ray Bursts; Physics; Supernova Remnants.*
**glb** (abbr.) glass block.
*Buildings.*
**GLC** Gas-Liquid Chromatography.
Gas-Liquid chromatography, also known as: Gas-Liquid Partition Chromatography is a gas chromatography wherein the fixed phase is a liquid solvent on an inert solid support and the moving phase is a gas.
*Analytical Chemistry.*
**Glc.** (abbr.) Glucose.
French abbreviation meaning: Glucose. Glucose is also known as: Dextrose; Cerelose; D-Glucopyranose.
*Biochemistry.*
**GLC** Greater London Council (G.B.).
**GLC** Green Light Committee.
The GLC is a multi-institutional body comprising the following institutions: Royal Netherlands TB Association; Harvard Medical School; National TB Program (Peru); U.S. Centers for Disease Control and Prevention; Médecins sans Frontières; and WHO.
For further details see under: **WHO**.
**GLC** group logistic coordinator.
coordonnateur de la logistique de groupe.
**GlcCer** Glucosylceramide.
**GLCFS** Great Lakes Coastal Forecasting System.
**GLCM** Ground-Launched Cruise Missile.
*Ordnance.*
**GlcNac** N-acetylglucosamine.
**Gld.** Guilder [Obsolete].
Now: EURO/EUR (€). Became ECU (European single currency) with effect from January 2002.
*Currencies.*
**GLEMEDS** Great Lakes Embryo Mortality Edema and Deformities Syndrome.
*Biology; Environmental Health; Toxicology.*
**GLFC** Great Lakes Fisheries Commission (U.S.A.).
**GLFS** Great Lakes Forecasting System.
**GLGM2** Goddard Lunar Gravity Model-2.
**GLIM** Geographical and Land Information Management.
**GLIMS project** Global Land Ice Measurement from Space project.
The GLIMS provided the ASTER image taken on the 21st September 2001.
For further details see under: **ASTER**.
**GLIN** Georgia Library, Information Network.
**GLIN** Great Lakes Information Network.
**GliRE** Gli Response Element.
*Biology; Cell Biology; Genetics; Medicine; Molecular Biology.*
**GLM** General Linear Model.
**GLO** ground liaison officer.
officier de liaison-terre.
**GLOBE** GLObal Backscatter Experiment.
**GLOBE** Global Learning and Observations to Benefit the Environment.
**GLOBE** Global Legislators Organization for a Balanced Environment (Belgium).
**GLOBE** GLobal Opportunities for Business and the Environment (Canada).
*International Trade Fairs.*
**GLONASS** global navigation satellite system.
système mondial de navigation par satellite.
**GLOSS** Global sea Level Observing System.
**GLP** Gas Liquido di Petrolio.
Italian initialism meaning: Liquid Petroleum Gas.
**GLP-1** Glucagon-Related Peptide-1.
**GLPC** Gas-Liquid Partition Chromatography.
For further details see under: **GLC** (Gas-Liquid Chromatography).
**GLP regulations** Good Laboratory Practices regulations - FDA's (U.S.A.).
For further details see under: **FDA**.
**GLTM-1** Goddard Lunar Topography Model 1.
**glu.** (abbr.) glutamate; glutamine.
*Biochemistry.*
**GluRS** Glutamyl-tRNA Synthetase.
**GluTR** Glutamyl-tRNA Reductase.
*Biochemistry.*
**gly.** (abbr.) glycine.
*Organic Chemistry* - Glycine is used mainly as a nutrient.
In *Biochemistry* glycine is also known as: Aminoacetic Acid.
**GlyR** Glycine Receptor.
GlyR is an abundant inhibitory neurotransmitter receptor in the spinal cord.
*Brain Research; Neurochemistry.*

**GM** Generalized Mystonia.
GM is an autosomal recessive disease.
*Medicine.*
**GM** General Manager.
**GM** General Mortgage.
*Business; Commerce.*
**GM** Geological Museum.
**Gm** gigameter.
**gm** gram / grams.
Also: **gramme/s**.
*Metrology.*
**GM** Greenwich Meridian.
*Cartography.*
**GM** Gross Margin.
**G.M.** Guardia Medica.
Italian initialism meaning: First Aid Station.
**GM** Guided Missile.
*Space Technology.*
**GM** Gun Metal / Gunmetal.
Also: **G.MET**.
*Metallurgy.*
**GMAG** Genetic Manipulation Advisory Group (G.B.).
**GMAN** Global Microlensing Alert Network (U.S.A.).
*Astronomy.*
**GM animals** Genetically Modified animals.
Transgenic animals have not been approved yet (2003) for human consumption.
*Transgenic Animals.*
**GMAT** Graduate Management Admission Test.
**GMAT**; **G.M.A.T.** Greenwich Mean Astronomical Time.
**GMB** General Merchandise Brand; Good Merchandise Brand.
*Business; Commerce.*
**GMC** Geological Museum of China.
**GMCC** Geophysical Monitoring for Climatic Change.
**GM counter** Geiger-Müller counter.
Also: Geiger-Müller tube.
*Nucleonics.*
**GM crops** Genetically Modified crops.
*Altered Foods; Biochemistry; Genetically Modified Foods.*
**GMCs** Ganglion Mother Cells.
*Cell and Structural Biology.*
**GMCs** Giant Molecular Clouds.
*Astrophysics.*
**GM-CSF** Granulocyte-Macrophage Colony-Stimulating Factor.
*Immune System Messengers; Macrophage Reproduction.*
**GMDSS** global maritime distress and safety system.
système mondial de détresse et de sécurité en mer.
**GMES** Global Monitoring for Environment and Security System.
Financed by the European Commission and the ESA; Access to this system from 2008.
*Global Security Monitoring.*
For further details see under: **ESA**.
**G.MET** (abbr.) Gun Metal / gunmetal.
Also: **GM**.
*Metallurgy.*
**G-Mex** Guernsey Manufacturing and Export Services.
**GMF** Galactic Magnetic Field.
*Astrophysics.*
**GMF** ground mobile force.
force terrestre mobile.
**GM foods** Genetically Modified foods.
*Altered Foods; Biochemistry; Novel Foods.*
**GMG** Giornata Mondiale della Gioventù.
Italian initialism meaning: World Youth Day. Held in Toronto, Canada on the 25th July 2002.
**GMHC** Gay Men's Health Crisis (U.S.A.).
*Activist Groups.*
**GMHT crops** Genetically Modified Herbicide-Tolerant crops.
*Plant Genetics.*
**GMI** Gregor Mendel Institute for Plant Molecular Biology.
The GMI will open in Vienna. Austria in 2004. Named for the Austrian monk and botanist Johann Gregor **Mendel**.
*Plant Molecular Biology.*
**GMIS** Grants Management Information System.
**GML** Generalized Markup Language.
**GMM** Glucose Monomycolate.
*Immunology; Lymphocyte Biology; Microbiology; Rheumatology.*
**Gmo** General markets operations.
**GMOs** Genetically Modified Organisms.
**GMP** Guanosine Monophosphate.
Also: cyclic GMP.
*Biochemistry.*
**GMP** Good Manufacturing Practices.
**GMPc** Guanosine Monophosphate Cyclique.
French initialism meaning: Cyclic GMP.
*Biochemistry.*
**GMPCS** Global Mobile Personal Communication Services.
*Satellite Systems.*
**g.m.q.** good merchantable quality.
**GMR** Giant Magnetoresistance.
*Magnetoresistance; Metals Research.*

**GMROI** Gross Margin Return On Investment.
*Business; Finance.*
**GMRT** Giant Meter-wave Radio Telescope.
The GMRT is located near Pune, India. It is provided with 30 antennae and is designed to explore the early universe.
*Astronomy.*
**GMS** Geostationary Meteorological Satellite (Japan).
**GMS** Greater Mekong Subregion.
**GMT** Generic Mapping Tools.
**GMT**; **G.M.T.** Greenwich Mean Time.
Also: **Universal Time**.
Has been replaced by: **GET**.
*Horology.*
**GMU** Gadjah Mada University.
**GMU** George Mason University (U.S.A.).
**GMV** Guaranted Minimum Value.
**GMW** Gram-Molecular Weight.
*Chemistry.*
**GMWL** Global Meteoric Water Line.
**gn.** (abbr.) general.
Also: **gen.**
**G.N.** Genio Navale.
Italian initialism meaning: Navy Engineers.
**GN** Glomérulonéphrite.
French initialism meaning: Glomerulonephritis.
Also known as: Glomerular Nephritis is a chronic or acute kidney disease.
*Medicine.*
**G.N.** Guardia Nazionale.
Italian initialism meaning: National Guard.
**gn.** (abbr.) guinea.
**GNAI/DW** Glacial North Atlantic Intermediate / Deep Water.
*Earth System Science; Geology; Geophysics.*
**GNBPs** Guanine Nucleotide-Binding Proteins.
*Molecular Physiology.*
**gnd** (abbr.) ground.
*Aviation; Electricity; Geology; Materials Science; Military Science; Navigation.*
**GNEF** Guanine Nucleotide Exchange Factor.
**GNF** Genomics Institute of the Novartis Research Foundation (U.S.A.).
**GNI** Gross National Income.
**GNMA** Government National Mortgage Association (U.S.A.).
**GNP** Grand National Party (Korea).
**GNP** Gross National Product.
**GNR** general nuclear response.
riposte nucléaire généralisée.
**GnRH** Gonadotropin-Releasing Hormone.
GnRH is also known as: Luteinizing Hormone-Releasing Horrnone.
*Endocrinology.*
**GNS** Global Network Service.
**GO** General Office; General Order.
**GO** General Organization.
**GO** Glyoxal.
GO is used mainly for leather tanning.
*Organic Chemistry.*
**GO** Government Obligations.
**Goal**; **GOAL** Gruppo Orientamento Adolescenti Lavoro (Italy).
**GOALS program** Global Ocean-Atmosphere-Land System program.
**Goase** Galactose Oxidase.
*Chemistry.*
**GOB** ground order of battle.
ordre de bataille Terre.
**GOCO complex** Government Owned - Contractor Operated complex.
**GOD** Glucose Oxidase.
GOD is used for the estimation of glucose concentration in samples of urine or blood.
*Enzymology.*
**GOE** Gaussian Orthogonal Ensemble.
*Physics.*
**GOES-Next** Next Generation GOES.
For further details see under: **GOES-8**.
**GOES-8** Geostationary Operational Environmental Satellite.
GOES-8 was launched in 1994.
*Atmospheric Science; Earth Science; Planetary Physics; Space Physics.*
**GOEWDS** Group of Experts on Warning and Detection Systems.
Groupe d'experts sur les systèmes d'alerte et de détection.
**GOEZS** Global Ocean Euphotic Zone Study.
*Global Change.*
**GOF** Goodness Of Fit.
**GOF** group of forces.
groupe de forces.
**GOFS** Global Ocean Flux Study.
**GOG** The Gynecologic Oncology Group (U.S.A.).
*Tissue Banks.*
**GOIN** Global Observation Information Network.
**GoK** Government of Karnataka (India).
**GOL** Goal Oriented Language.
**GOLD** Glyoxal-Lysine Dimer.
**GOM** groupement opérationnel de manœuvre.
operational manoeuvre group (OMG).
**GOME** Global Ozone Monitoring Experiment.

**GOMOS** Global Ozone Monitoring by Occultation of Stars.
**GOMS** Geostationary Operational Meteorological Satellite.
**GONG** Global Oscillation Network Group.
GONG is a network of telescopes.
*Astronomy.*
**GOODS Program** Great Observatories Origins Deep Survey Program.
*Astronomy; Astrophysics.*
**GOOS** Global Ocean Observing System.
*Observational Campaigns; Tropical Atlantic Variability.*
For further details see under: **(Atlantic) MOC** and **CLIVAR**.
**GOOS** Global Ozone Observing System.
Also known as: GO3OS.
**GOP** guidelines for operational planning.
directive de planification opérationnelle.
**GOPP** Goal-Oriented Project Planning.
GOPP is a technique to help Europe's regions coordinate their innovation and technology transfer development.
**GOR** Gas-Oil Ratio.
*Petroleum Engineering.*
**GOS** Global Observing System.
**GOS** grade of service.
qualité d'écoulement du trafic.
**GOS** Gruppi Operativi Speciali (Italy).
**GOSP** Gas-Oil Separation Plant.
**GOSR** Gruppo Oncologico per lo Studio dei Retinoidi (Italy).
Italian acronym of the: Oncological Group for the Study of Retinoids.
**GOSTA database** Global Ocean Surface Temperature Atlas database.
**GOT** Glutamic-Oxaloacetic Transminase.
**GOTS** government off-the-shelf.
gouvernemental sur étagère (ou gouvernemental standard).
**GOWON** Gulf Offshore Weather Observing Network.
**G.P.** Gallup Poll.
**gp** gene product.
**GP**; **G.P.** General Practice; General Practitioner.
**GP**; **G.P.** Geometric Progression.
Geometric progression is also known as: Geometric Sequence.
*Mathematics.*
**GP** General-Purpose.
The term general-purpose in computers refers to a program or system which may be used for many functions or applications.
*Computer Science.*
**GP** Global Processing.
**GP** Glycogen Phosphorylase.
*Biochemistry; Biophysics.*
**GP** Going Public.
*Business; Finance.*
**GP** Gold Points.
**GP** Grace Period.
*Business; Commerce; Finance.*
**GP** Grand Prix.
**GP** Gratuito Patrocinio.
Italian initialism meaning: Legal Aid in forma pauperis.
*Legal.*
**GP** Gross Profits.
*Business; Commerce; Finance.*
**gp.** (abbr.) group.
**GPA** Gestione Patrimoni Assicurativi.
*Banking; Finance; Insurance.*
**GPA** Giunta Provinciale Amministrativa.
Italian initialism meaning: District Administrative Council.
**GPA** Global Programme on AIDS.
GPA, of the WHO, was created in 1986. It has been replaced by UNAIDS, a program sponsored by six U.N. agencies, including the WHO.
For further details see under: **WHO**.
**GPA countries** Government Procurement Agreement Countries - *European Community.*
**GPALS** global protection against limited strikes.
protection à l'échelle mondiale contre des attaques limitées.
**GPB** Gravity Probe-B.
NASA's GPB mission, to test Einstein's general theory of relativity will be launched at the end of 2003.
*Space Physics.*
**GPC** Gel Permeation Chromatography.
In gel permeation chromatography, which is also known as: Gel Exclusion Chromatography, Size-Exclusion Chromatography, the moving phase is a liquid and the stationary phase comprises porous polymeric beads.
*Analytical Chemistry.*
**GPCC** Global Precipitation Climatology Center (Germany).
**GPCP** Global Precipitation Climatology Project.
**GPCR** G Protein-Coupled Receptor.
For further details see under: **GPCRs** and **GASP**.
**GPCRs** G-Protein-Coupled Receptors.
*Biology; Cell Biology; Drug Development Programs; Medicine; Molecular Medicine;*

*Neuroscience; Ophthalmology; Retinal Degeneration; Visual Phototransduction.*
**GPD**; **gpd** gallons per day.
**gpd** grams per denier.
*Textiles.*
**G6PD** Glucose-6-Phosphate Dehydrogenase.
**GP/DC** General-Purpose Digital Computer.
**GPDH** D-glyceraldehyde-3-phosphate Dehydrogenase.
**GPEP** Graduate Professional Education Program (U.S.A.).
*Professional Education Programs.*
**GPF** gasproof.
**GPF** general-purpose-force.
Force polyvalente.
**GpF** Gestione patrimoni in Fondi.
*Banking.*
**GPG** general political guidelines.
directives politiques générales.
**GPGM** general-purpose ground mine.
mine de fond universelle.
**gph** gallons per hour.
**GPI** Global Power Investments.
An Open-end Investment Fund for Private Power Projects.
**GPI** Glucose-6-Phosphate Isomerase.
A glycolytic enzyme.
*Biomedicine; Enzymology.*
**GPI** Ground Point of Intercept.
**GPI** Ground Position Indicator.
**GPI moiety** Glycosylphosphatidylinositol moiety.
*Cell Signaling; Medicine; Molecular Cancer Biology and Biochemistry.*
**GPK** GPCR Kinase.
For further details see under: **GPCRs** (G Protein-Coupled Receptors).
**GPL** General Price Level.
*Accounting; Business; Commerce.*
**GPL** General Purpose Language.
**GPLA** General Price Level Adjusted.
*Accounting; Business; Commerce.*
**gpm** gallons per minute.
**GPM** Gestione del Portafoglio Immobiliare.
Italian initialism meaning: Management of customers' securities portfolio.
*Banking.*
**GPM** Graduated-Payment Mortgage.
*Business; Commerce.*
**GPN** Groupe des plans nucléaires.
Nuclear Planning Group (NPG).
**GPO** General Post Office.
**GPO** Government Printing Office.
The GPO is controlled by the U.S. Congress.
**GPP** Gross Primary Production.
*Climate.*
**GPRA** Government Performance and Results Act (U.S.A.).
GPRA was passed in 1993.
**GPCRs** G Protein-Coupled Receptors.
*Biochemistry; Cell Biology; Medicine; olecular Biology; Ophtalmology; Physiology; Retinal Degeneration; Visual Phototransduction.*
**GPRD Group** General Practice Research Database Group (G.B.).
**GPRS** General Packet Radio Services.
A standard for the transmission of large quantities of data via the mobile telecommunication network. This technology - marketed commercially in 2000 - is used to increase the speed of the GSM network.
*Mobile Telecommunications.*
For further details see under: **GSM**.
**gps** gallons per second.
**GPs** General Practitioners.
**GPS** General-Purpose Problem Solver.
GPS is the outcome of research carried out during the 1950s in the U.S.A.
*Artificial Intelligence.*
**GPS** Global Positioning System.
*Geophysics and Planetary Physics; Oceanography.*
**GPSS** General-Purpose Systems Simulator.
*Computer Programming; Industrial Engineering.*
**GPT** Gas Phase Titration.
**GPT** Glutamic-Pyruvic Transaminase.
*Medicine.*
**GPTS** Geomagnetic Polarity Time Scale.
**gpu** geopotential unit.
**GPX** Glutathione Peroxidase.
*Enzymatic Antioxidants.*
**G.P. zones** Guinier-Preston zones.
*Metallurgy.*
**GQA** government quality assurance.
assurance officielle de la qualité.
**GR** General Records; General Register.
**G.R.** General Reserve.
**GR** Globule Rouge.
French initialism meaning: Red Blood Cell.
*Medicine.*
**GR** Glucocorticoid Receptor.
*Cancer Biology; Gene Expression; Medicine; Pharmacology; Receptor Biology.*
**GR** Glutathione Reductase.
**G.R.** Gold Reserve.
**gr** (abbr.) grain.
**gr** (abbr.) gram / gramme.

Also: **gm.**
*Metrology.*
**gr** (abbr.) gravity.
*Mechanics.*
**gr** (abbr.) great.
**GR**; **Gr.** (abbr.) Greece; Greek.
**GR** Gross Receipts; Gross Revenue.
**Gr.** (abbr.) Gunner.
**GRA** Gamma-Ray Astronomy.
GRA is the branch of astronomy studying gamma-rays.
*Astronomy.*
**GRA** Georgia Research Alliance (U.S.A.).
*Eminent Scholar Program.*
**GRA** Government Reports Announcements (U.S.A.).
**GRA** Graduate Research Assistantship (U.S.A.).
**GRACE** GRaphic Arts Composing Equipment.
**GRACE** Gravity Recovery And Climate Experiment.
GRACE was launched on 16th March 2002 from Russia's Plesetsk rocket facility. It is a 5-year mission to produce an accurate map of Earth's gravity and its changes over time.
*Climate Change; Earth Science Mission; Geophysics; Polar Science.*
**grad.** (abbr.) gradient; graduate.
**GRAIN** Graphics-oriented Relational Algebraic Interpreter.
**grain** The above acronym was coined using the English word "grain".
*Botany; Forestry; Materials Science; Metrology.*
**GRANADA** GRAmmatical Nonalgorithmic Data Description.
**Granada** The above acronym was coined using the name of the city Granada (Spain).
**GRAO** Gamma-Ray Astronomy Observatory.
**GRAPES** Groundwater and river resources Action Programme on a European Scale.
*European Commission Project; Environmental Protection; Meteorology; Safety; Policies.*
**GRAS** Generally Recognized As Safe.
*Biotechnology.*
**GRASP** Great Apes Survival Project.
A U.N. Science-based Project.
*Ape Conservation; Primate Species Extinction.*
**GRASS** Geographic Resources Analysis Support System.
**GRB** The airport code for Green Bay, Wisconsin, U.S.A.
**Grb2** Growth factor receptor-bound protein 2.
*Cancer Research; Pharmaceuticals; Signal Transduction.*
**GRBs** Gamma Ray Bursts.
The gamma ray bursts were detected by the Burst and Transient Source Experiment.
*Astronomy; Astrophysics; Physics.*
**GRC** Gendarmerie Royale du Canada.
**GRC** Gerontology Research Center (U.S.A.).
**GRC** Gordon Research Conferences.
**GRC** Government Research Corporation.
**GRD.**; **Grd.** Drachma (obsolete).
Now: EURO/EUR (€). Became ECU (European single currency) with effect from January 2002.
*Currencies.*
**GRDC** Geological Research and Development Center (U.S.A.).
**GRDC** Global Run-off Data Centre (Germany).
**GRE** Graduate Record Examination (U.S.A.).
**GRECC** Geriatric, Research, Education, and Clinical Center (U.S.A.).
**GREs** Glucocorticoid Response Elements.
*Biochemistry.*
**GRF** graduated readiness force.
force à niveau de préparation gradué.
**GRFs** Guanine-Nucleotide Releasing Factors.
GRFs are also known as: Guanine Diphosphate Dissociation Stimulators.
**GR-GFP** Glucocorticoid Receptor-Green Fluorescent Protein.
*Cell Signaling; Medicine; Pathology.*
**GRI** Gas Research Institute (U.S.A.).
The GRI is the scientific arm of the U.S. gas industry.
**GRI** Glaxo inc. Research Institute.
**GRIB** GRIdded Binary.
**GRID** Global Resource Information Database.
**GRIP** Graphics Interactive Programming.
**GRIP** GReenland Icecore Project.
Also: Greenland Icesheet Project.
**GRIP** GReenland Icesheet Program - Europe.
GRIP is also known as: *Greenland Icecore Project.*
**grip** The above acronyms were coined using the English word "grip".
*Medicine; Ordnance; Physiology.*
**GRIST** Grazing-Incidence Solar Telescope.
**GRKs** GPCR Kinases.
For further details see under: **GPCRs**.
**GRL** Geophysical Research Letters.
*Publication.*
**GRM** Geophysical Research Mission (U.S.A.).
**GRM** Grande Ragnatela Mondiale.
New Italian initialism meaning: World Wide Web.
**GRMV** Green Ring Mottle Virus.
*Plant Pathology.*
**gRNAs** guide RNAs.

*Biological Chemistry; Medicine.*
**GRNET** Greek Research and Technology Network.
GRNET is a leading consortium to extend GÉANT connectivity into the Balkans.
*European Commission.*
**GRNN** General Regression Neural Network.
**GRO** Gamma Ray Observatory.
**gro.** gross (12 dozens).
**GROBAT** see GRORBAT.
voir GRORBAT.
**GRORBAT** ground order of battle.
ordre de bataille Terre.
**GRP** Glass-Reinforced Plastic / Polyester.
**GRPs** General Receptors for Phosphoinositides.
*Biochemistry; Molecular Biology; Molecular Medicine.*
**GRR** Genotypic Relative Risks.
*Epidemiology; Genetics; Medicine; Psychiatry.*
**GRR** The airport code for Grand Rapids, Michigan, U.S.A.
**GRS** Gamma Ray Spectrometer.
The GRS is a collection of three instruments which are used to determine the composition of the martian surface.
*Lunar Research; Space Research.*
For further details see under: **HEND**.
**GR-S** Government Rubber and Styrene.
*Chemical Industry.*
**GRS** Great Red Spot.
The GRS is a region in Jupiter's South Equatorial Belt.
*Astronomy.*
**GRT** GReater Than.
Also: **GT**.
**grt**; **GRT**; **gro.t.** gross register tonnage.
**GRT** Group Rapid Transit.
*Transportation Engineering.*
**GRU** grid reference unit.
unité de référence de grille (UREF).
**GRUMPIES** Grown-Up, Mature Persons (U.S.A.).
**gr.wt** gross weight.
**Gs** Gauss.
Named for the German mathematician Karl Friedrich **Gauss**.
*Electromagnetism.*
**GS** General Secretary; General Staff.
**GS** Glamour Stock.
*Business; Finance.*
**GS** Glutamine Synthetase; Glycogen Synthetase.
*Enzymology.*
**G.S.** Gold Standard.
**GS** Goods and Services.
**GS** Government Securities; Government Stock.
**GS** Gross Sales.
*Business; Commerce.*
**GS** Gross Spread.
*Business; Finance.*
**GS** Ground Speed.
Also: Speed over the ground.
*Aviation.*
**GS** Group Separator.
**GS** Growth Stock.
*Business; Finance.*
**gs.** guineas.
**GS** Gulf Shelf.
**GSA** General Services Administration (U.S.A.).
**GSA** Geological Society of America.
**GSA** Great Salinity Anomaly.
**GSAC** The Genome Sequencing and Analysis Conference (U.S.A.).
*Genomics.*
**GSAM** Glutamate-1-semialdehyde Aminomutase.
*Biochemistry.*
**GSAT** Global Satellite data Acquisition Team (U.S.A.).
**GSC** Gas-Solid Chromatography.
Gas-solid chromatography is a chromatography wherein the stationary phase is a surface-active sorbent and the mobile phase is a gas.
*Analytical Chemistry.*
**GSC** General Staff Corps.
**GSC** Geological Survey of Canada.
**GSC** Global Supply Chain.
The GSC is an Information Technology project that Glaxo Wellcome has initiated in 1995.
**GSCI** Goldman Sachs Commodity Index.
Gives a representation of the economic importance of commodities in the world economy.
**GSCs** Germline Stem Cells.
*Cell Biology; Development; Embryology.*
**GSD** Groupe Sanitaire Divisionnaire (France).
**GSE** Ground Support Equipment.
GSE is also known as: Ground Handling Equipment.
*Aviation.*
**GSE longitude** Geocentric Solar Ecliptic longitude.
*Lunar Research.*
**GSES** Government-Sponsored Enterprises.
*Business; Commerce.*
**GSFC** Goddard Space Flight Center - NASA's.
*Extraterrestrial Physics; Space Research; Nanosatellite Technology.*
For further derails see under: **GEST**.
**GSI** Institute for Heavy Ion Research (Darmstadt, Germany).
*Heavy-Ion Physics.*

**GSK3** Glycogen Synthase Kinase 3.
*Developmental Biology; Medicine; Signal Transduction; Tumor Suppression.*

**gskt** (abbr.) gaskket.
A gasket, which is also known as static seal is a pressure-tight ring or sheet made of deformable material which is used to make a joint.
*Engineering.*

**G.sil.** (abbr.) German silver (alloy).
Also: Nickel Silver.
An alloy not containing silver.
*Materials.*

**GSL** Generalized Simulation Language.

**GSL** Guaranteed Student Loans (U.S.A.).

**GSLA** Ghana School Libraries Association.

**GSL lysosomal storage diseases** Glycosphingolipid lysosomal storage diseases.
*Biochemistry; Diabetes and Digestive and Kidney Diseases; Glycobiology.*

**GSM communications** Global System for Mobile communications.
GSM is a digital cellular technology which has become the standard for new European digital mobile telephone services.

**GSM1** Global System for Mobiles One.
Egyptian Mobile Telephone Services.

**GSN** Global Seismic Network.
*Geophysics; Oceanography; Planetary Physics; Seismology.*

**GSNO** S-Nitrosoglutathione.

**GSO** General Staff Officer.

**GSO** geostationary orbit.
orbite géostationnaire.

**GSO** Geosynchronous Orbit.
*Astronomy.*

**GS OSRH** General Staff of the Armed Forces of the Republic of Croatia.
État-major général des Forces armées de la République de Croatie.

**GSP** general strike plan.
plan général d'attaque nucléaire.

**GSPD** Genetic Susceptibility in Parkinson's Disease.

**GSR** Galvanic Skin Response.
GSR is also known as: Electrodermal Response.
*Physiology.*

**GSR** general support reinforcing.
renforcement de l'appui général.

**GSR** Global-Shared Resources.

**GSS** Civil Alliance of Serbia (FRY).
Alliance civique de Serbie (RFY).

**GSS** General Social Survey.

**GSS disease** Gertsmann-Sträussler-Sheinker disease.
GSS is a rare form of Creutzfeldt-Jakob disease.
*Brain Research; Cerebellar Pathology; Neurodegenerative Diseases; Neuropathology; Neuroscience.*

**GSSP** Global boundary Stratotype.
*Geology; Geophysics.*
For further details see under: E-G.

**GSSPS** Gravitationally Stabilized Solar Power System.

**GSS syndrome** Gerstmann-Sträussler-Scheinker syndrome.
The GSS syndrome is an inherited form of spongiform encephalopathy.
*Medicine.*

**GST** Glutathione Sulfur-Transferase.

**GST** Greenwich Sideral Time.

**GSV** Guided Space Vehicle.
*Space Technology.*

**GS VRS** General Staff of the Army of the Republika Srpska.
État-major général de l'armée de Republika Srpska.

**GSZ** ground safety zone.
zone de sécurité terrestre (ZST).

**GT** Gastight.

**GT** Gift Tax.

**Gt** Gigatons.

**gt.** (abbr.) gilt.

**GT** Giudice Tutelare.
Italian initialism meaning: Tutelary Judge.

**g.t.** goods train.

**GT** Grand Touring.

**gt.** (abbr.) great.

**GT** Greater Than.
Also: **GRT**.

**GT** Gross Ton.
Also: Long Ton.
*Metrology.*

**GT** Gross Tonnage.
Not a measure of weight.
*Naval Architecture.*

**GT** 1. groupe de travail.
1. working group (WG).
2. groupe tactique.
2. task group (TG).
3. Guatemala.
3. Guatémala.
4. gun-target (line).
4. (ligne) pièce-but.

**GTAC** Gene Therapy Advisory Committee (G.B.).

**GTAH** groupe de travail ad hoc.

ad hoc working group (AHWG).
**GTC** gain time control.
1a. atténuateur sélectif.
1b. régulation du gain en fonction du temps.
**GtC** Gigatons of Carbon.
*Earth and Environmental Engineering.*
**G.T.C.**; **g.t.c.** Good Till Cancelled.
**G.T.C.**; **g.t.c.** Good Till Countermanded.
**gtd.** (abbr.) guaranteed.
**gtee.** (abbr.) guarantee.
**GT engine** Gas Turbine engine.
**GTF** Generalized Trade Facility.
**GTFs** General Transcription Factors.
*Biochemistry; Cell Biology; Medicine; Transcription.*
**GTI technology** Graphic Target Imaging technology.
Patented by Garrett Electronics (U.S.A.).
**GTL** Georgia Tech Lorraine.
GTL is located in Metz, France. It is a branch of Georgia Institute of Technology, Atlanta, Georgia, U.S.A.
**GTL projects** Gas To Liquids projects.
**GTMA** Gauge and Tool Makers' Association.
**GT-MHR** Gas-Turbine Modular Helium Reactor.
**GTM order** Good-This-Month order.
*Business; Commerce.*
**GTN** Global Trends Network.
**GTOS** Global Terrestrial Observing System.
**GTP** Global Transfer Pricing.
**GTP** Guanosine Triphosphate.
Needed during translation.
*Biochemistry.*
**GTPase** Guanosine Triphosphatase.
*Endocrinology; Neuroscience.*
**GTR** Government Transportation Request (U.S.A.).
**GTR techniques** Geoid-Topography Ratio techniques.
*Lunar Research.*
**GTS** General Theological Seminary.
**GTS** global telecommunications system.
réseau mondial de télécommunications.
**GTV** Gate Valve.
A gate valve is a valve presenting a closing element that controls fluid flow.
*Mechanical Devices.*
**GTW** Good Through Week.
*Business; Commerce; Finance.*
**GTW** Gross Trailer Weight.
*Vehicle-Transportation.*
**GU** Genitourinary.
Genitourinary is also known as: urogenital.
*Anatomy.*
**guar.** (abbr.) guarantee; guaranteed; guarantor.
**GUCE** Gazzetta Ufficiale della Commissione Europea.
Italian acronym meaning: Official Gazette of the European Commission.
**GuCl** Guanidine Hydrochloride.
*Protein Science.*
**GUI** Graphical User Interface.
**GUIRR** Government-University-Industry Research Roundtable (U.S.A.).
**GuK** Guanylate Kinase.
**GUMC** Georgetown University Medical Center (U.S.A.).
**GUN converter** Golder UNits converter (Golder Associates, U.S.A.).
GUN is a scientific calculator software program that automatically converts engineering and scientific units for multiple uses.
*Automatic Units Converters.*
**GUP** Giudice dell'Udienza Preliminare.
*Law* (Italy) - Italian acronym meaning: Judge of the Preliminary Hearing.
**GURTs** Gene Use Restriction Technologies.
*Biotechnologies; Plant Sciences.*
**GUSTO** Globus Ubiquitous Supercomputing Test-Bed.
GUSTO is a grid linking more than 3,000 processors at 15 sites in the United States and Europe.
*Supercomputers Grids.*
**GUTs** Grand Unified Theories.
*Physics Cosmology.*
**guts** The above acronym was coined using the English word "guts".
**GV** Germinal Vesicle.
*Cell Biology.*
**GV** Granulosis Virus.
Granulosis virus is a disease of the lepidopteran larvae.
**GV** Guinea.
**GVA** The airport code for Geneva, Switzerland.
**GVA** Glatt Valley Aquifer (Switzerland).
**GVBD** Germinal Vesicle (nuclear envelope) Breakdown.
*Biochemistry; Cell Biology; Medicine.*
**GVD** Group Velocity Dispersion.
**GVG** Gamma Vinyl-GABA.
*Epilepsy Drugs; Neurobiology.*
**GVHD** Graft-Versus-Host Disease.
*Clinical Medicine; Clinical Immunology; Experimental Medicine; Hematology; Oncology.*
**GVH reaction** Graft-Versus-Host reaction.
Graft-Versus-Host reaction is also known as: Graft-Versus-Host disease.

*Immunology.*
**gvl** (abbr.) gravel.
*Buildings.*
**GVL effect** Graft-Versus Leukemia effect.
*Clinical Medicine; Clinical Immunology; Experimental Medicine; Hematology; Oncology.*
**GVO** Gross Value of Output.
**GVT** à gain variable dans le temps.
sensitivity time control (STC 1.).
**GVW** Gross Vehicle Weight.
**GW** 1. gateway.
1. passerelle.
2. guided weapon.
2. engin guidé.
**GW** gigawatt.
**GW** ground water / groundwater.
Also: Underground Water; Phreatic Water.
*Hydrology.*
**GWAT** Grinding Wheel Abrasion Test.
**GWE** Global Weather Experiment.
**GWEN** Ground-Wave Emergency Network.
*Telecommunications.*
**GWFA** The Gambia Women's Finance Association.
**GWI** Greenhouse Warming Index.
**GWIN** Glaxo Wellcome International Network.
**GWP** Gift With Purchase.
*Marketing.*
**GWP** Global Warming Potential.
**GWP** Gross World Product.
**GWPAS** General Work force Performance Appraisal System.
**GWUMC** George Washington University Medical Center (U.S.A.).
**Gy**; **gy** (abbr.) gray / grey.
*Histology; Optics; Radiology.*
**GY** Guyana.
**Gya** Gigayears ago.
**GYE** Greater Yellowstone Ecosystem.
**gym.** (abbr.) gymnasium; gymnastics.
**GYN**; **gyn** Gynecology.
Gynecology is the branch of the medical science dealing with the diseases that affect the sexual organs of women.
*Medicine.*
**Gyr** Giga-year.
**gyro.** (abbr.) gyrocompass; gyroscope.
*Navigation.*
**gyro.** (abbr.) gyroplane.
*Aviation.*
**GZ** ground zero.
1a. point zéro (PZ).
1b. surface zéro.
**GZT** Greenwich Zone Time.

**H** Half-Adder.
Also: **HA**.
*Computer Technology.*
**H**; **h** harbour; hardness.
**h** (abbr.) hardware.
*Mechanical Engineering* - In mechanical engineering the term hardware comprises: tools, fasteners, hinges, and other metal parts.
*Computer Technology* - In computer technology the term hardware refers to the physical components of which a computer is made up.
*Ordnance* - In ordnance the term hardware refers mainly to metal parts, used in combat.
**h** heat.
*Engineering; Meteorology; Physiology; Thermodynamics.*
**h**; **h.** height.
Also: **ht**; **ht.**
**H**; **h** Heir.
**H** Henry.
**H** Heroin.
Heroin is also known as: Diacetylmorphine.
*Pharmacology.*
**h** (abbr.) Hierarchy.
*Behavior.*
**h** high.
High in meteorology is also known as: high-pressure system; anticyclone.
*Meteorology.*
**h** home.
*Behavior; Computer Technology; Electricity; Electronics; Navigation.*
**h**; **h.** horizontal.
**h** host.
*Biology; Virology.*
**H**; **h** Hot.
**H**; **H.**; **h**; **h.** hour or hours.
Also: **hr.**; **hrs.**
**h**; **h.** humidity.
**h**; **h.** hundred.
**H** Hungary International vehicle registration letter.
**H** Hydrant.
*Civil Engineering.*
**H** Hydraulics.
*Fluid Mechanics.*
**H** The chemical symbol for Hydrogen.
*Chemistry; Symbols.*
**h** coefficient of viscosity.
**h** electrolytic polarization.
**HA** 1. Haiti.
1. Haïti.
2. holdind area.
2. zone d'attente.
**HA** Half-Adder.
Also: **H**.
*Computer Technology.*
**HA** Half-Adjust.
*Computer Programming.*
**H-A** Hautes-Alpes (France).
**HA** Heavy Artillery.
**ha**; **ha.** hectare; hectares.
*Metrology.*
**HA** Home Address.
*Computer Technology.*
**HA**; **HA.** Hour Angle.
**HA** House Account.
**HA** Hyaluronic Acid.
HA also known as: Hyaluronan belongs to the glycosaminoglycan family. It is an essential polysaccharide.
*Biochemistry and Molecular Biology; Health Sciences; Plant Pathology.*
**HAA** heavy anti-aircraft artillery.
artillery antiaérienne lourde.
**HAA** Height Above Airport.
**HAARP** High-frequency Active Auroral Research Program (U.S.A.).
The HAARP project was launched in 2002.
*Atmospheric Physics; Fundamental Physics and Chemical Processes; Plasma Physics; Upper Atmosphere Studies.*
**HAART** Highly Active Antiretroviral Treatment / Therapy.
HAART is a combination of antiretroviral drugs to treat HIV-infected patients.
*AIDS Therapies; Antiretroviral Drugs; HIV Vaccines; Immunology; Infectious Diseases; Treatment of Infections; Virology.*
**HAB** High-Angle grain Boundary.
**HABCIT** High-Altitude Balloon Circumstellar Imaging Telescope.
*Bioastronomy; Exoplanets Imaging.*
**HACC** Harrisburg Area Community College.
HACC is located in Harrisburg, Pennsylvania, U.S.A. It provides customized training in: English as a second language; Hazardous Materials; Police and Firefighting; Heating, AC & Refrigeration; etc.
**HACCP analysis** Hazard Analysis Critical Control Point analysis.
**HACMP** High Availability Cluster Multi-Processing - IBM system.

**HA crystals** Hydroxyapatite crystals.
*Chemistry; Engineering; Materials Science; Medicine.*

**HACs** Human Artificial Chromosomes.
*Biochemistry; Molecular Biology.*

**HACTL** Hong Kong Air Cargo Terminals Limited (Hong Kong).

**HACV** heavy armament combat vehicle.
véhicule de combat à armement lourd (VCAL).

**HAD** Health Assessment Document.

**HAD** Herein After Described.

**HAD** HIV-Associated Dementia.
*Aging Research; Neuroscience.*

**HAER** Historic American Engineering Record.
HAER is a Division of the U.S. Interior's Office of Archaeology and Historic Preservation (U.S.A.).

**HAF black** High-Abrasion Furnace black.

**HAG** helicopter action group.
1a. groupe d'action d'hélicoptères.
1b. groupe de combat d'hélicoptères.

**HAGC** helicopter action group commander.
1a. commandant de groupe d'action d'hélicoptères.
1b. commandant de groupe de combat d'hélicoptères.

**HAI** Helicopter Association International.

**HAI test** Hemagglutination-Inhibition test.
HAI test is also known as: **HI test**.
*Immunology.*

**Hal** Hardware abstraction layer.

**HAL-CA** Highly Advanced Laboratory for Communications and Astronomy.
The HAL-CA is a radio telescope put into orbit by the Japanese Space Agency in 1997.
*Astrophysics; Radio Telescopes.*
For further details see under: **MUSES-B**.

**HALOE** HALogen Occultation Experiment (U.S.A.).
HALOE measures solar observation by the upper atmosphere.
*Atmospheric Chemistry; Meteorology; Physics.*

**HAM-A** HAMilton Anxiety.
*Human Behavior; Neuroscience; Psychiatry.*

**HAMB** HIV and AIDS Malignancy Branch.
Of the U.S. NCI.
For further details see under: **NCI**.

**HAM-D** HAMilton Depression.
*Human Behavior; Neuroscience; Psychiatry.*

**H amino acids** Hydrophobic amino acids.

**hand.** (abbr.) handling.

**H&E** Hematoxylin and Eosin.

**H&SE** Health and Safety Executive (G.B.).

**HANE** high-altitude nuclear explosion.
explosion nucléaire à haute altitude.

**HANPP** Human Appropriation of Net Primary Production.
*Agronomy; Bioscience; Social Ecology.*

**HAN projects** Highly Advanced National projects.
*U.S. Project.*

**HANUL** High-energy Astrophysics Neutrino Laboratory (South Korea).
*Astronomy; Astrophysics; Particle Physics; Physics.*

**hanul** The above acronym was coined using the Korean word "hanul" which means: sky.

**HAP** Hazardous Air Pollutant.
For further details see under: **HAPs**.

**HAPEX** Hydrological Atmospheric Pilot Experiment.

**h.app.** heir apparent.
*Law.*

**HAPs** Hazardous Air Pollutants.
HAPs include a wide range of industrial and agricultural chemicals, as well as mixtures of polycyclic organic matter.
*Chemistry.*

**HAR** Harbor Advisory Radar.

**HAR** helicopter assault regiment.
régiment d'hélicoptères d'assaut.

**HAR** The airport code for Harrisburg, Pennsylvania, U.S.A.

**HAR** Hyperacute Rejector.
*Medicine; Xenotransplantation; Xenovirology.*

**HARM** Hazardous Atmospheric Release Model.

**HARM** High-velocity Anti-Radiation Missile.
HARM is a U.S. air-to-surface anti-radiation missile.
*Ordnance.*

**HARP** Heteroaromatic Polycycles.
*Molecular Biology; Antibacterial Research.*

**HAS** hardened aircraft shelter.
abri durci pour avion(s).

**HAS** Helicopter Armament Subsystem.

**HAS** Helium Atom beam Scattering.
*Applied Physics; Lasers.*

**HAS** Hydroxylamine Acid Sulfate.

**HASP** Houston Automatic Spooling Program (U.S.A.).
*Computer Programming.*

**HASs** HA Synthases.
HASs are integral membrane proteins that polymerize the HA molecule.
For further details see under: **HA** (Hyaluronic Acid).

**HAT** Haley Advanced Technology (Canada).

**HAT** Height Above Touch-down.

*Navigation.*
**Hat A gene** Histone Acetyltransferase Type A gene.
*Cell Biology; Developmental Genetics; Medicine; Molecular Biology.*
**HATRICS** HAmpshire Technical, Research, Industrial and Commercial Service.
**HATs** Histone Acetyltransferases.
The HATs are histone-modifying enzymes.
*Molecular Medicine.*
**HAUs** Hemagglutinating Units.
**HAUSP** Herpesvirus-Associated Ubiquitin-Specific Protease.
*Biochemistry; Biology; Cancer Genetics; Deubiquitination; Medicine; Pathology.*
**HAV** The airport code for Havana, Cuba.
**HAV** Hepatitis A Virus.
Hepatitis A Virus is also known as: Infectious Hepatitis Virus; Epidemic Jaundice Virus.
*Virology.*
**HA virus** Hemadsorption virus.
**HAZCON** hazardous conditions.
conditions dangereuses.
**HAZMAT** (abbr.) HAZardous MATerials.
**HB** Half Block.
*Computer Programming.*
**Hb** Hemoglobin.
Also: **hgb.**
*Hematology.*
**HB** Hepatitis B.
Hepatitis B is also known as: Serum Hepatitis.
*Medicine.*
**HBA** Honest Ballot Association (U.S.A.).
**HbCO** Carboxyhemoglobin.
**HBCs** High-Burden Countries Tuberculosis.
*Tuberculosis Control.*
**HBD** Hormone-Binding Domain.
*Medicine; Oncology.*
**HBEF** Hubbard Brook Experimental Forest (New Hampshire, U.S.A.).
**HBES** Human Behavior and Evolution Society.
**$HBF_4$** Fluoroboric Acid.
Fluoroboric Acid is used for many purposes, for instance for the production of fluoroborates.
*Inorganic Chemistry.*
**HBM** Her Britannic Majesty (G.B.).
**HBMIs** Hybrid Brain-Machine Interfaces.
*Biomedical Engineering; Bionic Technologies; Spinal cord-Injuries.*
**hBMP-2** human Bone Morphogenic Protein-2.
*Genetics.*
**HbO** Oxyhemoglobin.
*Biochemistry.*
**$H_3BO_3$** Boric Acid.
Boric Acid is used mainly as an eyewash.
*Inorganic Chemistry.*
**$H_3BO_3$** Sassolite.
Sassolite is also known as: Sassolin; Sassoline.
*Mineralogy.*
**HBOCs** Hemoglobin-Based Oxygen Carriers.
*Artificial Blood; Blood Substitutes; Cell-free Hemoglobin; Clinical Trials; Transfusion Medicine.*
**HBOI** Harbor Branch Oceanographic Institution.
**H-bomb** Hydrogen Bomb.
*Ordnance.*
**HB population models** Horizontal Branch population models.
*Clusters; Space Astrophysics.*
**HBR** high bit-rate.
débit binaire élevé.
**HBS** Harvard Business School (U.S.A.).
**HbS** Sickle Hemoglobin.
*Sickle Cell Disease.*
**Hbss** Hank's balanced salt solution.
**HbSS** Homozygous Sickle Cell.
*Biochemistry; Dentistry; Medicine; Molecular Genetics; Sickle Cell Disease.*
**HBTs** Heterojunction Bipolar Transistors.
*Circuit Designing; Device Engineering; Device Physics.*
**HBV** Hepatitis B Virus.
Hepatitis B Virus also known as: Serum Hepatitis Virus, is a para-retrovirus.
*Virology.*
**H.C.** Habitual criminal.
*Criminal Law.*
**HC** Hair Cell.
**HC** Half Carry.
*Computer Programming.*
**HC** Hardware Compatibility.
*Computer Technology.*
**HC** Heat Coil.
*Electricity.*
**H.C.** High Church.
**H.C.** High Commissioner.
**HC** High Court.
**HC** Hippocampus.
*Anatomy; Vertebrate Zoology.*
**HC** Holding Company.
**HC** Home Computer.
HC is a PC to be used at home not for professional jobs.
*Computer Technology.*
**h.c.** honoris causa.
**HC**; **H.C.** Hospital Corps.
**HC** Host Computer.

HC is also known as: Host Processor.
*Computer Technology.*
**HC** House of Commons.
**HC** Hybrid Computer.
*Computer Technology.*
**HC** Hydrocarbon.
*Organic Chemistry.*
**HCA** Head of Contracting Activity.
**HCB** Hexachlorobenzene.
*Organic Chemistry.*
**HCBP** Hexachlorobiphenyl.
**HCC** Hepatocellular Carcinoma.
**HCCH** 1,2,3,4,5,6-Hexachlorocyclohexane.
*Organic Chemistry* - $C_6H_6Cl_6$.
**HCCLs** Human Colon Cancer Cell Lines.
**HCDA** Hypothetical Core-Disruptive Accident.
**HCF**; **H.C.F.**; **hcf**; **h.c.f.** Highest Common Factor.
**HCFA** Health Care Financing Administration (U.S.A.).
**HCFCs** Hydrochlorofluorocarbons.
*Chemistry; Chlorofluorocarbons Substitutes; Climate Change.*
**HCG** Human Chorionic Gonadotropin.
HCG, also known as: Chorionic Gonadotropin is produced by the chorionic vesicle.
*Biochemistry.*
**H-chain** Heavy chain.
*Immunology.*
**HCHs** Hexachlorocyclohexanes.
**HCHWA-D** Hereditary Cerebral Hemorrhage with Amyloidosis-Dutch type.
HCHWA-D is a form of β-amyloid-related disease.
**HCI** human-computer interface.
interface homme-machine.
**HCL** High Cost of Living.
**$HClO_2$** Chlorous Acid.
*Inorganic Chemistry.*
**HCM** Hybrid Coupled Model.
**HCM** Hypertrophic Cardiomyopathy.
HCM is characterized by hypertrophy of the heart.
*Cardiology; Medicine; Mutant Genes; Pathology.*
**HCM** Research and technological development program in the field of Human Capital and Mobility.
*European Community Program.*
For further details see under: **HMC Programme**.
**HCN** Hydrocyanic Acid.
HCN also known as: Prussic Acid; Hydrogen Cyanide; is used mainly in insect poisons.
*Inorganic Chemistry.*
**HCO** Head of Contracting Office.
**$H_2CO_3$** Carbonic Acid.
*Inorganic Chemistry.*
**$HCO_2H$** Formic Acid.
*Organic Chemistry* - Formic Acid is used mainly in treating leathers, and for the production of insecticides.
*Biology* - Formic Acid is also known as: Methanoic Acid.
**HCoV** Human Coronavirus.
For further details see under: **HCoVs**.
**HCoVs** Human Coronaviruses.
*Upper Respiratory Tract Illnesses.*
For further details see under: **SARS-CoV**.
**HCP** Habitat Conservation Plan.
For further details see under: **HCPs**.
**HCP** Human Circadian Pacemaker.
*Medicine; Sleep Medicine.*
**hcp 6** holocentric protein 6.
*Molecular Biology.*
**HCP arrangements** Hexagonal Close Packing arrangement.
**HCPI** Harmonized Consumer Price Index.
HCPI, the economic statistic for the euro-zone, is published monthly by Eurostat.
**HCPs** Habitat Conservation Plans (U.S.A.).
The HCPs were created by a 1982 amendment to the U.S. Endangered Species Act.
*Animal Physiology; Biology; Conservation Biology; Ecology; Environment; Wildlife Biology.*
**hcp structure** hexagonal close-packed structure.
*Crystallography.*
**$H_2CrO_7$** Dichromic Acid.
*Inorganic Chemistry.*
**HCs** Hair Cells.
**HCS** Haut Commandement (commandant) subordonné [obsolète - remplacé par RC].
Major Subordinate Command (commander) (MSC 1.) [obsolete - replaced by RC].
**HCS** (Division of) Health Care Services (U.S.A.).
**HCS** High Content Screening.
**HCS** Human Chorionic Somatomammotropin.
*Endocrinology.*
**HCs** Hydrocarbons.
*Organic Chemistry.*
**HCT**; **HT** Hematocrit.
*Pathology.*
**HCU** helicopter control unit.
unité contrôleur d'hélicoptères.
**HCV** Hepatitis C Virus.
*Liver Disease; Immunology.*
**HD** Half Duplex.
**hd.** (abbr.) hand.
**HD** Hansen's Disease.
Hansen's disease is also known as: Leprosy.
*Medicine.*
**HD** (abbr.) Hardened.

**HD** Hardware Diagnostic; Hardware Division.
*Computer Technology.*
**hd.** (abbr.) head.
**HD** Hearing Distance.
**HD** Heavy-Duty.
The term heavy-duty, also known as: heavy-service, refers to the long-wearing resistance of objects as well as their ability to withstand excessive strain.
*Engineering.*
**HD** High Density.
**HD** Huntington's Disease.
HD is a neurodegenerative disorder characterized by progressive neurodegeneration of strial neurons in the brain that leads to death. Named after the American physician George **Huntington**.
*Neurodegeneration.*
**HDA** Hail Detection Algorithm.
**HDA** Hepatitis Delta Agent.
**HDAC** Histone Deacetylase.
For further details see under: **HDACs**.
**HDACs** Histone Deacetylases.
*Biochemistry; Epigenetics; Histone Deacetylation; Molecular Biology.*
**HDAg** Hepatitis Delta Antigen.
**HAD ice** High-Density Amorphous ice.
For further details see under: **LDA ice**.
**hdbk.** (abbr.) handbook.
**HDC** helicopter direction centre.
centre de direction des hélicoptère.
**HDF** Hierarchical Data Format.
**HDF** Hubble Deep Field.
A space telescope exposure (10-days) - NASA's.
*Astronomy.*
**HD gene** Histone Deacetylase gene.
*Medicine; Microbiology.*
**HDI** Human Development Index.
*Public Health.*
**H disease** Hartnup disease.
*Medicine.*
**hdkf.** (abbr.) handkerchief.
**HDL** Hardware Description Language.
*Computer Technology.*
**HDL** High-Density Lipoprotein.
*Biochemistry.*
**HDLC** High-Level Data Link Control.
**HDML**; **Hdml** Handheld Device Markup Language.
**HDN** Hemolytic Disease of the Newborn.
**HDN** Hexadecimal Notation.
*Computer Programming.*
**hDNA** Hybrid DNA.
*Molecular Biology.*
**HDNSW** High-Density Nuclear Shock Wave.
**HDP-CDV** Hexadecyloxypropyl-Cidofovir.
*Antiviral Research.*
**HDPE**; **hdPE** High-Density Polyethylene.
HDPE is also known as: Low-Pressure Polyethylene; Linear Polyethylene.
*Materials.*
**hdq**; **hdq.** (abbr.) headquarters.
Also: **HQ**; **H.Q**.
**HDS** Hitachi Data Systems.
**HDS** Human Development Services.
**HDSL**; **Hdsl** High bit rate Digital Subscriber Line.
**HDT** Hypersensitivity of the Delayed Type.
**HDTV** High-Definition Television.
*Telecommunications.*
**HDV** Hepatitis Delta Virus.
*Biochemistry; Medicine; Virology.*
**HDvV exchange** Heisenberg-Dirac-van Vleck exchange.
*Biochemistry; Chemical Biology; Chemistry; Enzyme Research.*
**hdw.**; **hdwe.** (abbr.) hardware.
For further details see under **h**.
**hdwd** (abbr.) hardwood.
The term hardwood refers to the wood of many broad-leaved or deciduous trees.
*Materials.*
**HDX** Half Duplex.
*Telecommunications.*
**HDZ** Croatian Democratic Union (Croatia).
Union démocratique croate.
**He** the chemical symbol for Helium.
Helium is a gaseous element - atomic number: 2; atomic weight: 4.0026, boiling point: -268.9°C; it is the first element in the noble gas group.
*Chemistry; Symbols.*
**HE**; **H.E.** High Explosive.
*Materials; Ordnance.*
**HEA** Higher Education Authority (Ireland).
**HEA** Hydroxyethyl Acrylate.
**HEADTS** helicopter and aircraft detection training system.
système de formation à la détection d'hélicoptères et d'avions.
**HEAO** High-Energy Astronomical Observatory.
**HEAO3** Third High Energy Astrophysics Observatory.
**HEASD** Human Exposure and Atmospheric Sciences Division.
At NERL (U.S.A.).
*Human Exposure Research.*
For further details see under: **NERL**.
**HEAT** High Explosive Anti-Tank.

*Ordnance.*

**Heb** Hebrew.
Hebrew is a semitic language of the Afro-Asiatic family, the language of the ancient Hebrews, now the national language of Israel.
*Languages.*

**HEBMs** Hot Electron Bolometer Mixers.
*Applied Solid State Physics; Heterodyne Receivers; Instrumentation.*
For further details see under: **HTS HEBM**.

**Hebr** (abbr.) Hebrews.

**Hebr** (abbr.) Hebrides.

**HEC** Ecole des Hautes Etudes Commerciales (France).

**HEC** helicopter element coordinator.
1a. coordonnateur des moyens hélicoptères.
1b. coordonnateur de l'élément hélicoptère.

**HED meteorites** Howardite, Eucrite, and Diogenite meteorites.
*Geochemistry; Geophysics; Meteoritics; Planetary Science.*

**HEDTA Acid**.
Hydroxyethylethylenediaminetriacetic Acid.

**HEduBT** Higher Education in Biotechnology.

**HEED** High-Energy Electron Diffraction.
HEED is the diffraction of electrons with high energies in the range from 30,000 to 70,000 electron volts.
*Physics.*

**HEFA** Higher Education Facilities Act.

**HEF antennas** High Efficiency antennas.

**HEFCE** Higher Education Funding Council for England (G.B.).
HEFCE is the Government body that distributes infrastructure and teaching funding to English Universities.

**HEGRA project** High-Energy Gamma-Ray Astronomy project.
HEGRA, a German-Spanish-Armenian facility project, was completed in 1997.
*Gamma-rays Studies.*

**HEI** Hall-Effect Imaging.
*Cardiac Imaging; Imaging Technology; Magnetic Resonance in Medicine- Medical Imaging.*

**HEI** Health Effects Institute.
The HEI, of Cambridge, MA, U.S.A. is a non-profit organization that serves as an independent source of information on the health effects of motor vehicle emissions and the like.

**HEK** Human Embryonic Kidney.
*Biochemistry; Biology; Medical Sciences.*

**HEL** The airport code for Helsinki, Finland.

**HEL** Hen Egg Lysozyme.
*CancerResearch; Cell Biology; Immunology; Medicine; Microbiology.*

**HEL** High-Energy Laser.

**HEL cell** Human Erythroleukemia cell.

**HELD** Health Effects Laboratory Division.

**HELIOS** Hospital Environment Language within an Information Object System.
*Medicine.*

**HeLLIS** Health Literature, Library and Information Services.

**HELP** Homophile Effort for Legal Protection (U.S.A.).

**HEM** Hostile-Environment Machine.
*Mechanical Engineering; Robotics.*

**HEMA** Hydroxyethylmethacrylate.

**HEMT** High Electron Mobility Transistor.
*Applied Physics; Microelevtronics; Nanoscience; Physics.*

**HEND** High Energy Neutron Detector.
HEND which began mapping in February 2002, is part of the GRS on the Mars Odyssey Mission.
*Nuclear Research; Space Research.*
For further details see under: **GRS**.

**HEP** High Egg Passage.
*Virology.*

**HEP** high-explosive plastic.
explosif brisant plastic.

**HEPA inlet filter** High-Efficiency Particulate Air inlet filter.

**HEPAP** High-Energy Physics Advisory Panel.

**HEPAT charge** High-Explosive Plastic Antitank charge.
*Ordnance.*

**HEPES acid** 4-(2-Hydroxyethyl)-1-Piperazineethanesulfonic acid.
$C_8H_{18}N_2O_4S$, crystals that are soluble in alcohol and water; having a melting point of 234°C.
*Organic Chemistry.*

**HEPnet** High Energy Physics network.

**HEPP** High-Explosive Plastic Projectile.
*Ordnance.*
For further details see under: **HESH**.

**hER** human Estrogen Receptor.

**HER2** Human Epidermal growth factor Receptor 2.
*Medicine; Tumor Biology.*

**HERA** Hadron-Electron Ring Accelerator.
*Particle Physics.*

**Heref(s)** (abbr.) Herefordshire (G.B.).

**HERL** Health Effects Research Laboratory.

**HERTIS** Hertfordshire County Technical Information Service.

**Herts** (abbr.) Hertfordshire (G.B.).

**HESCs** Human Embryonic Stem Cells.

*Human Embryology; Regenerative Medicine.*
**HESCA** HEalth Sciences Communications Association.
**HESH** High-Explosive Squash Head.
HESH is also known as: High-Explosive Plastic Projectile.
*Ordnance.*
**HET** heavy equipment transport.
équipement (matériel) lourd.
**HET** High-Energy Telescope.
University of Chicago (U.S.A.).
**HET** Hot Engineering Tests.
**HetCor experiments** Heteronuclear Correlation experiments.
*Biomaterials; Medicine; Orthopaedic Surgery; Radiology; Skeletal Disorders.*
**HETE** High-Energy Transient Experiment.
A 2002 satellite dedicated to the study of GRBs.
*Astronomy; Astrophysics; Physics.*
For further details see under: **GRBs**.
**HETE Acid** 12-Hydroxyeicosatetraenoic Acid.
**HETP** Height Equivalent of Theoretical Plate.
*Chemical Engineering.*
**HETP** Hexaethyltetraphosphate.
**HE-TPP** Hydroxyethylidene-Thiamine Pyrophosphate.
*Biochemistry.*
**HEU** Highly Enriched Uranium.
*Nucleonics.*
**HEV** porcine Hemagglutinating Encephalomyelitis Virus.
**HEVs** High Endothelial Venules.
*Blood Research; Newborn Medicine; Pathology; Pediatrics.*
**HEW** (Department of) Health, Education and Welfare (U.S.A).
**HEX** Helsinki Stock Exchange and Finnish derivatives Exchange.
A July 1997 merged operation.
**Hf** The chemical symbol for Hafnium.
Hafnium is used mainly in lightbulb filaments and nuclear reactors.
*Chemistry; Symbols.*
**HF** Hageman Factor.
**HF**; **hf**; **hf.** (abbr.) half.
**HF** Height Finder.
*Engineering.*
**H/F** Held For.
**HF** High-frequency.
The range of frequencies from 3 to 30 megahertz.
*Telecommunications.*
**HF** Hydrogen Fluoride.
HF is used mainly as an additive in liquid rocket propellants.
*Inorganic Chemistry.*
**$H_4F$** Tetrahydrofolate.
**HFA** Helsinki Final Act.
Acte final d'Helsinki.
**HFBR** High-Flux Beam Reactor (U.S.A.).
The HFBR is a neutron-scattering facility at the U.S. Brookhaven National Laboratory. It is on indefinite stanby since January 1997.
*Energy; Nuclear Physics; Radioactive Isotopes.*
**HFBR** Hollow Fiber Bioreactors.
**HFC** Hydrofluorocarbon.
**HFCs** Hydrofluorocarbons.
**HF/DF** High-Frequency Direction Finding.
*Ordnance.*
**HFEA** Human Fertilization and Embryology Authority.
The HFEA is an Agency that regulates the use of human reproductive technology in G.B.
*Bioethics.*
For further details see under: **HGAC**.
**HFIR** High-Flux Isotope Reactor.
The high-flux isotope reactor is located at the Oak Ridge National Laboratory, Tennessee, U.S.A.
*Nucleonics.*
**hFIX** human Factor IX.
*Medicine; Human Genetics.*
**HFM** Hold For Money.
*Business; Commerce.*
**HFM disease** Hand-Foot and Mouth disease.
The HFM disease is caused by Coxsackie A16 and other enteroviruses.
**hFn** human Fibronectin.
For further details see under: **Fn** (Fibronectin).
**HFO** Hydrous Ferric Oxide.
**HFP** Hardware Floating Point.
*Computer Technology.*
**HFPE** Hexafluoropropylene Epoxide.
**Hfr**; **hfr** High-Frequency Recombination.
*Microbiology.*
**HFR** High Flux Reactor (Petten).
The 42-year-old HFR owned by the European Union's Joint Research Centre is used for energy-related research.
*Medical Isotopes.*
**HFR** Hold For Release.
*Business; Commerce.*
**HFSP** Human Frontier Science Program.
The HFSP was founded in 1989. A Japanese Prime Minister proposed its creation in 1987 at the G7 economic summit. The HFSP has awarded grants and fellowships to thousands of scientists around

the world. The aim of the U.S. HFSP is to promote *basic research* regarding the complex mechanisms of *living organisms.*

**HFT** High-Flux Telescope.
Herzberg Inst. of Astrophysics (Canada).

**HFT** High Frequency Transformer.
*Electronics.*

**HFT fault** Himalayan Frontal Thrust fault.
*Seismic Hazards.*

**H-G** Haute-Garonne (Department) (France).

**hg; hg.** (abbr.) hectogram; hectograms.

**Hg** Heliogram.
*Telecommunications.*

**Hg** Heliograph.
*Engineering; Meteorology.*

**hg; hg.** Hemoglobin.

**HG** Her Grace.

**HG** High German.
High German is the group of West Germanic languages including German, Yiddish, Bavarian, Alemannic, and the dialects of central Germany.
*Languages.*

**HG** Holy Ghost.

**HG; H.G.** Horse Guards (G.B.).

**Hg** The chemical Symbol for Mercury.
Mercury is used mainly in thermometers and in mercury vapor lamps. In view of the fact that it flows easily and quickly, it was named after the Greek god **Mercury**.
*Symbols; Chemistry.*

**HGAC** Human Genetics Advisory Commission.
The HGAC is a Commission that regulates the use of human reproductive technology in G.B.
*Bioethics.*
For further details see under: **HFEA**.

**HgAc derivative** Mercury Acetate derivative.

**hgb.** (abbr.) hemoglobin.
Also: **Hb**.
*Hematology.*

**$Hg_2Br_2$** Mercurous Bromide.
*Inorganic Chemistry.*

**$HgCl_2$** Calomel.
Calomel is used mainly as a fungicide.
*Mineralogy.*

**$HgCl_2$** Mercuric Chloride.
*Inorganic Chemistry.*

**$Hg_2Cl_2$** Mercurous Chloride.
*Inorganic Chemistry.*

**$Hg(CN)_2$** Mercuric Cyanide.
Mercuric Cyanide is used mainly as an antiseptic.
*Inorganic Chemistry.*

**HGCR** Heterogeneous Gas Core Reactor.

**$Hg_2CrO_4$** Mercurous Chromate.
*Inorganic Chemistry.*

**HGDP** Human Genome Diversity Project.
*Population Genetics.*

**HGDS** Hemophilia Growth and Development Study.

**$HgF_2$** Mercuric Fluoride.
$HgF_2$ is used in organic synthesis.
*Inorganic Chemistry.*

**HGF receptor** Hepatocyte Growth Factor receptor.
*Biochemistry; Biology; Genetics; Molecular Oncology; Protein Engineering.*
For further details see under: **LSECs** and **VEGF**.

**HGF/SF** Hepatocyte Growth Factor / Scatter Factor.
*Dermatology; Immunology; Medicine; Photobiology.*

**HGG** Human Gamma Globulin.

**HGH** Human Growth Hormone.

**$Hg_2I_2$** Mercurous Iodide.
Mercurous Iodide is also known as: Yellow Mercurous Iodide.
*Inorganic Chemistry.*

**HGMS** High-Gradient Magnetic Separation.

**HgO** Red Mercuric Oxide.
Red Mercuric Oxide is used mainly in cosmetics, pharamceuticals, and perfumes.
*Inorganic Chemistry.*

**HgO** Yellow Mercuric Oxide.
Yellow Mercuric Oxide is used mainly to make mercury compounds.
*Inorganic Chemistry.*

**$Hg_2O$** Mercurous Oxide.
*Inorganic Chemistry.*

**HGP** Haber Gold Process.
The HGP was invented by Norman **Haber** of Haber Inc. (U.S.A.).
*Gold Mining Processes.*

**HGP** Human Genome Project.
The HGP began in 1990.
*Genetic Maps; Physical Maps.*

**HGPRT** Hypoxanthine-Guanine Phosphoribosyl-Transferase.
*Enzymology.*

**HGPS** Hutchinson-Gilford Progeria Syndrome.
*Cell Biology; Molecular Biology.*

**hGR** human Glucocorticoid Receptor.

**HgS** Cinnabar.
*Mineralogy.*

**HGS** Human Genome Sciences.

**$HgSb_4S_8$** Livingstonite.
*Mineralogy.*

**$Hg(SCN)_2$** Mercuric Thiocyanate.
Mercuric Thiocyanate, also known as: Mercuric

Sulfocyanate; Mercuric Sulfocyanide is used mainly in fireworks.
*Inorganic Chemistry.*
**$HgSO_4$** Mercuric Sulfate.
$HgSO_4$ is used in many chemical processes.
*Inorganic Chemistry.*
**$Hg_2SO_4$** Mercurous Sulfate.
Mercurous Sulfate is used in batteries.
*Inorganic Chemistry.*
**hgt.**; **hgt** (abbr.) height.
**HgTe** Coloradoite.
Coloradoite is found in telluride ores.
*Mineralogy.*
**HGV** Heavy Goods Vehicle.
**hgwy.**; **hgwy** (abbr.) highway.
**HH** Her Highness.
**HHC** Hand Held Computer.
**Hhd**; **hhd.**; **hhd** (abbr.) hogshead; hogsheads.
Equal to about 238 litres.
**HHDN** Hexachlorohexahydrodimethanonaphtalene.
**HHFA** Housing and Home Finance Agency.
**HHG** High order Harmonic Generation.
*Physics; Theoretical Physics.*
**HHMI** Howard Hughes Medical Institute.
Headquartered at Chevy Chase, Maryland, U.S.A.
**HH object** Herbig-Haro object.
*Astronomy; Astrophysics.*
**HHS** (The U.S. Department of) Health and Human Services (U.S.A.).
**HHV** Higher Heating Value / High Heating Value.
*Thermodynamics.*
**HHV-8** Human Herpes Virus-8.
**HI** (abbr.) Hawaii (U.S.A.).
**HI** Hawaiian Islands.
**HI** High Intensity.
**HI** Horizontal Instruction.
*Computer Programming.*
**HI** Hot Issue.
*Business; Finance.*
**HI**; **H.I.** Humidity Index.
*Meteorology.*
**HI** Hybrid Interface.
*Computer Technology.*
**HI** Hydrogen Iodide.
HI is used mainly to make Hydriodic Acid.
*Inorganic Chemistry.*
**HIA** Horological Institute of America (U.S.A.).
**HIAA** Health Insurance Association of America (U.S.A.).
**HIAPER** High-performance Instrumented Airborne Platform for Environmental Research (U.S.A.).
HIAPER will explore the tropopause (the area between the upper and lower atmospheres).
*Atmospheric Research; Experimental Aircraft; Jet Designs.*
**Hib** *Hemophilus influenzae* type b.
*Clinical Medicine; Pediatrics.*
**HIBU** Hydrological Institute and Belgrade University.
**HICAP** high combat air patrol.
patrouille aérienne de combat à haute altitude.
**hid** head involution defective.
hid is an apoptotic activator.
*Biology; Brain and Cognitive Sciences; Genetics; Medicine.*
**HIDACZ** high-density airspace control zone.
zone de contrôle de l'espace aérien à forte densité.
**HIDO** Highway Industry Development Organization (Japan).
The HIDO was founded in 1984.
*Japanese Organization.*
**HIF** Health Information Foundation (U.S.A.).
**HIF-1** Hypoxia-Inducible factor-1.
The HIF-1 is a transcription factor.
*Aging Research; Cerebrovascular Research; Neuroscience.*
**HIFO** Highest-In, First-Out.
**HIFR** helicopter in-flight refuelling.
ravitaillement en vol d'hélicoptères.
**HIG** Hawaii Institute of Geophysics.
**HII** Health Insurance Institute (U.S.A.).
**HILEX** high-level exercise.
exercice de haut niveau.
**HIM** Her Imperial Majesty.
**HIMAC** Heavy-Ion Medical Accelerator in Chiba (Japan).
HIMAC began operating in 1995 at NIRS. It is the world's only heavy-ion accelerator dedicated to medical use.
*Cancer Therapies; Radiation Oncology.*
For further details see under: **NIRS**.
**HIMEZ** high missile engagement zone.
zone d'engagement des missiles à haute altitude.
**HINA** Croatian Information News Agency.
Agence de presse croate.
**Hind** (abbr.) Hindustani.
Hindustani is the standard language of northern India. It is based on a dialect of Western Hindi spoken in Delhi.
*Languages.*
**HinDC** Holder in Due Course.
*Business; Finance.*
**HINS** helicopter integrated navigation system.
système de navigation intégré pour hélicoptère.
**$HIO_3$** Iodic Acid.
$HIO_3$ is used mainly in medicine.

*Inorganic Chemistry.*
**HIP** Health Insurance Plan.
**HIP** Hot Isostatic Pressing.
**HIPACS** Hospital Integrated Picture Archiving and Communication System.
*Medicine.*
**HIPAR** high-power acquisition radar.
radar d'acquisition de grande puissance.
**HIPCs** Highly Indebted Poor Countries.
**HIPed** Hot Isostatically Pressed.
*Nuclear Science.*
**HIPing** Hot Isostatically Pressing.
*Nuclear Science.*
**HIPIR** high-power illumination radar.
radar d'illumination de grande puissance.
**HIR** hydrostatic impact rocket.
roquette percutante à armement hydrostatique.
**HIRIS** HIgh-Resolution Imaging Spectrometer.
**HIRS** High-Resolution Infrared Radiation Sounder.
**HIS** High-resolution Interferometer Spectrometer.
**His** Histidine.
$C_6H_9O_2N_3$. Histidine is an essential amino acid which contains the imidazole ring system.
*Biochemistry.*
**HIS** Hospital Information Systems.
*Medicine.*
**HIS** 1. Croatian Information service.
1. Service d'information croate.
2. hostile intelligence service.
2. service de renseignement ennemi.
**HIS** House Information Service (U.S.A.).
**HISAM** high-altitude surface-to-air missile.
missile surface-air haute altitude.
**HISCALE** Heliosphere Instrument for Spectrum, Composition, and Anisotropy.
**His6-Plx1** Six-Histidine fusion protein.
**HISS** Hospital Information Support System.
**hiss** The above acronym was coined using the English word "hiss".
*Telecommunications.*
**Hi-tech** High technology.
*Biotechnology; Internet; Software Development; Medical Technology; Telecommunications.*
**HI test** Hemagglutination-Inhibition test.
HI test is also known as: **HAI test**.
*Immunology.*
**HIT protein** HIstidine Triad protein.
*Biochemistry; Genomics; Molecular Biophysics.*
**HITRAN** High resolution TRANsmission.
**HITS**; **Hits** Hypertext Induced Topic Search - I.B.M.
*Clever Technologies.*
**HIUI** Health Institute of the Uranium Industry.
The Health Institute of the Uranium Industry, which is State-run, was established in 1954 in the mining town of Pfibram.
**HIV** Human Immunodeficiency Virus.
The HIV belongs to the subfamily Lentivirinae and is the causative agent of AIDS disease.
*Virology.*
**HIV/CAT reporter** Human Immunodeficiency Virus Chloramphenicol Acetyltransferase reporter.
*Biological Chemistry; Medicine.*
**HIVNET** HIV Vaccine Efficacy Trials Network.
The HIVNET is a Group proposed to oversee and reshape various aspects of AIDS Research.
**HK** Hefner Candle.
HK, also known as Hefnerkerze is a unit of luminous intensity used in the early 1900s in Germany.
*Optics.*
**HK** High molecular weight Kininogen.
*Protein Science.*
**HK** Hexokinase.
*Enzymology.*
**HK** Hong Kong (China).
**HKBU** Hong Kong Baptist University (Hong Kong).
**HKD** Hyperkinetik Disorder.
*Cell Biology; Endocrinology; Medicine; Psychiatry.*
For further details see under: **ADHD**.
**HKE** Hong Kong English.
**HKG** The airport code for Hong Kong, China.
**HKIB** Hong Kong Institute of Biotechnology.
HKIB is a non-profit Research and Development Center.
**HKIBOR** Hong Kong Inter-Bank Offered Rate.
*Banking; Finance.*
**HKLM** Heat-Killed *Listeria Monocytogenes.*
*Immunobiology; Immunology Programs; Medicine.*
**HKMA** Hong Kong Monetary Authority.
**HKR** Hydrolytic Kinetic Resolution.
*Chemical Biology; Chemistry.*
**HKT** Hong Kong Telecom.
**HKTDC** Hong Kong Trade Development Council (Hong Kong).
**HKU** Hong Kong University.
**HKUST** Hong Kong University of Science and Technology.
**hl**; **hl.** (abbr.) hectoliter / hectoliters.
**HL** Home Language.
**H.L.** Honours List.
**HL** House of Lords.
**HLA** Hawaii Library Association.
**HLA** Human Leukocyte Antigen.

HLA is an immune system protein.
*Immunology.*
**HLAs** Human Leukocyte Antigens.
**HLCC** Hawaiian Lee Counter Current.
*Earth Sciences; Oceanography.*
**HLDA** Hold Acknowledge.
*Business; Commerce.*
**HLDLC** High-Level Data-Link Control.
*Computer Technology.*
**HLF** Heart and Lung Foundation (U.S.A.).
**HLG** high-level group.
groupe de haut niveau.
**HLH** Heavy-Lift Helicopter.
**HLI** High-Level Index.
*Computer Programming.*
**HLLV** Heavy-Lift Launch Vehicle.
**HLM** Hématies-Leucocytes-Minute ou Compte d'Addis.
French initialism meaning: Addis count. Named after the American physician Thomas **Addis**.
*Pathology.*
**HLM** High-Level Modulation.
*Telecommunications.*
**HLMS** High Latitude Monitoring Station.
**HLS** Holograph Letter Signed.
**HLS** Huntingdon Life Sciences.
*Drug-testing Group.*
**HLSG** high-level steering group.
groupe directeur de haut niveau.
**HLST** high-level study team.
équipe d'étude de haut niveau.
**HLT** High-Leveraged Takeover.
**HLT** Highly Leveraged Transaction.
*Business; Finance.*
**HLTF** 1. high-level task force.
1. groupe de travail de haut niveau.
2. High-Level Task Force on Conventional Arms Control.
2. Groupe de travail de haut niveau sur la maîtrise des armements conventionnels.
**HLTF/R** reinforced high-level task force.
groupe de travail élargi de haut niveau.
**HLTFST** high-level task force support team.
équipe de soutien du groupe de travail de haut niveau.
**HLWG** high-level working group.
groupe de travail de haut niveau.
**HlyA** Hemolysin.
*Biochemistry; Pathology.*
**HLZ** helicopter landing zone.
zone (aire) de poser d'hélicoptère.
**Hm** hand-made.
**HM** Haute-Marne (France).
**hm**; **hm.** (abbr.) hectometer / hectometers.
**HM** Her Majesty / His Majesty.
**Hm** Manifest Hypothermia.
**HMBC** Heteronuclear Multiple-Bond Correlation.
**HMC** Harvey Mudd College.
The HMC, Claremont, California, U.S.A., is a small private college of science and engineering; member of the Claremont Colleges.
**HMC** Her Majesty's Customs (G.B.).
**HMC** Heroin, Morphine, and Cocaine.
**HMC programme** Human Capital and Mobility programme.
The E.U. HMC programme has been replaced by the TMR programme.
For further details see under: **TMR programme**.
**HMD** Hexamethylenediamine.
Hexamethylenediamine is used to produce nylon.
*Organic Chemistry.*
**HMD** Hyaline Membrane Disease.
The hyaline membrane disease is a disorder of newbom babies.
*Medicine.*
**HMDE** Hanging Mercury Drop Electrode.
**HMDs technology** Helmet-Mounted Displays technology.
*Advanced Optics; Computing; Electronics.*
**HMF** Her Majesty's Forces (G.B.).
**HMFG** Heavy Metal Fluoride Glasses.
**HMG** heavy machine-gun.
mitrailleuse lourde.
**HMG** Her Majesty's Government (G.B.).
**HMG** Human Menopausal Gonadotropin.
*Medicine.*
**HMG-domain proteins** High Mobility Group-domain proteins.
*Biochemistry; Biophysics.*
**HMG-CoA reductase** 3-Hydroxy-3-Methylglutaryl-CoA reductase.
*Chemistry; Cholesterol Biosynthesis; Endocrinology; Pharmacy.*
**HMG protein** High-Mobility Group protein.
*Biochemistry.*
**HMI** Her Majesty's Inspectorate (G.B.).
**HMI** human-machine interface.
interface homme-machine.
**HMIP** Her Majesty Government's Inspectorate of Pollution (G.B.).
**HMK** Heart Muscle Kinase.
**HML** Hybrid Manipulation Language.
*Computer Programming.*
**HMM** Heavy Meromyosin.
*Biochemistry.*
**HMM** Hexamethylmelamine.

**HMMFC** House Merchant Marine and Fisheries Committee.
**HMMs** Hidden Markov Models.
HMMs are algorithms deriving from the statistics work of the Russian mathematician Andrei Andreyevich **Markov** (1856-1922). HMMs were first used in speech recognition programs in the 1960s and can now be used by computational biologists.
*Computational Biology; Speech Recognition Programs.*
**HMMWV** high-mobility multipurpose wheeled vehicle.
véhicule sur roues polyvalent à grande mobilité.
**$HMnO_4$** Permanganic Acid.
*Chemistry.*
**HMO** Health Maintenance Organization.
**HMO** Heart Minute Output.
*Medicine.*
**H-mode operation** High energy confinement mode operation.
*Fusion.*
**HMOs** Health Maintenance Organizations.
**HMO theory** Hückel Molecular Orbital theory.
**Hmp** Heterogeneous multi processing.
**HMPA** Hexamethylphosphoramide.
**$H_4MPT$** Tetrahydromethanopterin.
**HMQC** Heteronuclear Multiple-Quantum Coherence.
**HMQC-TOCSY spectrum** Heteronuclear Multiple-Quantum Coherence-Total Correlation Spectroscopy spectrum.
**HMR** Hoechst Marion Roussel (Germany).
HMR is the drug division of Germany's chemical Company Hoechst.
**HMS** Harvard Medical School (U.S.A.).
**HMS** Her Majesty's Service (G.B.).
**HMSC** Hatfield Marine Science Center.
**HMS-PCI** High-throughput Mass Spectrometric Protein Complex Identification.
*Biochemistry; Cancer; Medical Genetics; Microbiology; Molecular Biology.*
**HMS technology** Helmet-Mounted Sights technology.
*Advanced Optics; Computing; Electronics.*
**HMT** Hazardous Materials Technology.
**HMTA** Hexamethylenetetramine.
**HMT activity** Histone Methyltransferase activity.
*Biochemistry; Biophysics; Cellular Biology; Medicine; Molecular Biology; Molecular Genetics.*
**HMV** high-mobility vehicle.
véhicule à grande mobilité.
**HMWK** High Molecular Weight Kininogen.
**HN** Hopfield Network.
*Biological Networks.*
**HN** host nation.
pays hôte.
**HN** Host-to-Network.
**HNAB** Hexanitroazobenzene.
**Hnble** (abbr.) Honourable.
**HN=C=O** Isocyanic Acid.
Used mainly in the production of urethanes (as an intermediate).
*Organic Chemistry.*
**HND** The airport code for Haneda, Tokyo, Japan.
**HND Department** Human Nutrition and Dietetics Department.
**HNE** 4-Hydroxynonenal.
**HNF** Hepatocyte Nuclear Factor.
*Biotechnology; Molecular Biology.*
**HNIL** High Noise Immunity Logic.
**HNIP** host nation in-place (forces).
(forces) en place du pays hôte.
**HNL** The airport code for Honolulu, Hawaii.
**HNLC** High Nitrate Low Chlorophyll.
*Biochemistry; Chemistry; Chemical Engineering; Marine Biology.*
**HNLC regions** High-Nutrient, Low-Chlorophyll regions.
*Chemistry and Biology of the Oceans; Geology; Marine and Coastal Sciences.*
**HNM** Hexanitromannite.
**$H_2NNH_2$** Hydrazine.
Hydrazine is used mainly as a rocket fuel and corrosion inhibitor.
*Inorganic Chemistry.*
**HNPCC** Hereditary Nonpolyposis Colorectal Cancer.
**HNR** Human Nutrition Research.
**hnRNA** Heterogeneous nuclear Ribonucleic Acid.
*Molecular Biology.*
**hnRNP** heterogeneous nuclear Ribonucleoprotein.
*Medicine.*
**HNS** Hexanitrostilbene.
**HNS** 1. Croatian People's Party.
1. Parti du peuple croate.
2. host nation support.
2. soutien fourni par le pays hôte.
**HNSA** host nation support agreement (arrangement).
accord (arrangement) de soutien fourni par le pays hôte.
**HNT** Homogeneous Nucleation Temperature.
*Thermodynamics.*
**HNZ** Croatian People's Union.

Union du peuple croate.
**HO** Head Office.
**Ho** The chemical symbol for Holmium.
Holmium is a rare-earth metallic element used in spectroscopy and electrochemistry.
*Chemistry; Symbols.*
**HO** Home Office.
**HO** Honduras.
**Ho** (abbr.) house.
**$H_2O$** The chemical formula for water.
*Chemistry.*
**$H_2O_2$** Hydrogen Peroxide.
Used mainly in dyes, antiseptics, and bleaches.
*Inorganic Chemistry.*
**HOB** height of burst.
1a. hauteur d'éclatement.
1b. hauteur d'explosion.
**HOBOS** HOming BOmb System.
*Ordnance.*
**HOC** Hydrophobic Organic Compound.
**$HOCH_2CH_2OC_4H_9$** 2-Butoxyethanol.
2-Butoxyethanol is used mainly in dry cleaning.
*Organic Chemistry.*
**HOCl** Hypochlorous Acid.
HOCl is used mainly as a bleach and disinfectant.
*Inorganic Chemistry.*
**HOD** head of delegation.
chef de délégation.
**HOHAHA spectroscopy** HOmonuclear HArtman - HAhn spectroscopy.
**HOI** House Of Issue.
**HOIS** see HIS.
voir HIS.
**HOJ** home-on-jamming.
ralliement sur brouillage.
**HOL** Higher-Order Logic.
*Computer Science.*
**HOL** High-Order Language.
**HOM** head of mission.
chef de mission.
**HOME** Highly Optimized Microscope Environment.
*Medicine.*
**HOMO-LUMO gap** Highest-Occupied Molecular Orbital - Lowest Unoccupied Molecular Orbital gap.
**hon.** (abbr.) honorary; honourable.
**hon'd** (abbr.) honored.
*Business; Commerce; Finance.*
**$HOOC(CH_2)_6COOH$** Suberic Acid.
Suberic acid, also known as: Octanedioic acid, is used in organic synthesis.
*Organic Chemistry.*
**HOP** High Oxygen Pressure.
**HOP** Hydroxydaunomycin, Oncovin, and Prednisone.
*Oncology.*
**HOPE** Health Opportunity for People Everywhere.
**HOPG** Highly Oriented Pyrolytic Graphite.
*Biochemistry; Chemistry; Optoelectronic Computing Systems; Physics.*
**HOR** Holder Of Record.
**hort.**; **hort** (abbr.) horticulture; horticultural.
**HOS organ culture** High-Oxygen Submersion organ culture.
*Medicine.*
**hosp.**; **hosp** (abbr.) hospital.
**HOTO** Health Of The Oceans.
**HOT Series** Hawaiian Ocean Time Series.
Station ALOHA.
*Marine Sciences; Ocean Sciences.*
**HOU** The airport code for Hobby Airport, Houston, U.S.A.
**HOU** The airport code for Houston, Texas, U.S.A.
**HOV** Norwegian Marine Monitoring and Forecasting Centre (Norway).
**Hox genes** Homeobox genes.
*Developmental Biology.*
**Hp** Haptoglobin.
*Hematology.*
**HP** Hautes Pyrénées (France).
**HP** Heatable Plastic.
**HP** Hematoporphyrin.
Hematoporphyrin is also known as: Hemoporphyrin.
*Biochemistry.*
**HP**; **H.P.** High Power.
**HP**; **H.P.** High Pressure.
**HP**; **H.P.** Horsepower.
Also: **hp**; **h.p.**
Horsepower is the unit of power equal to 550 foot-pounds or approximately 746 watts.
*Metrology.*
**HP**; **H.P.** House Physician.
*Medicine.*
**HP1** Heterochromatin Protein 1.
*Biochemistry; Biophysics; Cellular Biology; Medicine; Molecular Biology; Molecular Genetics.*
**HPA** High Power Amplifier.
**HPA** Hybrid Problem Analysis.
*Computer Programming.*
**HPA axis** Hypothalamic-Pituitary-Adrenal axis.
**HPAEC analysis** High pH Anion Exchange Chromatographic analysis.
**HPAP** Human Placental Alkaline Phosphatase.

**HPAs** Heteropolyanions.
The HPAs are large cluster anions.
*Catalysis; Environmental Cleanup.*
**HPBWs** Half-Power Beam Widths.
**HPC** Hippocampal Pyramidal Cell.
**HPCC Program** (Federal) High Performance Computing and Communications Program.
The HPCC Program is a U.S. Program having the aim of promoting the progress of future generations of high-performance computers.
*Computational Bioscience and Engineering; Computer Research and Technology.*
**HpD** Hematoporphyrin Derivative.
**HPD** heure prévue (ou probable) de départ.
estimated time of departure (ETD).
**HPD** Hourly Precipitation Data.
**HPDP** (Division of) Health Promotion and Disease Prevention (U.S.A.).
**HPE** Holoprosencephaly.
*Cyclopia; Defective Genes; Developmental Biology; Human Genetics; Medicine; Molecular Biology.*
**HPEs** Heat-Producing Elements.
*Earth, Atmospheric, and Planetary Sciences.*
**HPF**; **H.P.F.** Highest Possible Frequency.
**HPF**; **H.P.F.** High-Power Field.
Also: **hpf** or **h.p.f.**
**HPFC** High Performance Functional Computing.
**HP filter** High-Pass filter.
*Electronics.*
**HPGC** Heading Per Gyrocompass.
**HPGL** Hewlett-Packard Graphics Language.
**HPI** High-Positive Indicator.
*Computer Technology.*
**hPL** human Placental Lactogen.
**HPLC** High-Performance Liquid Chromatography.
*Analytical Chemistry.*
**HPLC FT-IR** High-Performance Liquid Chromatography Fourier Transformation-Infrared.
*Spectroscopy.*
**HPMS** High-Pressure Mass Spectrometer.
**$H_2PO_3F$** Fluorophosphoric Acid.
Fluorophosphoric Acid is used mainly in metal cleaners.
*Inorganic Chemistry.*
**HPPF** (Office of) Health Policy Programs and Fellowships (U.S.A.).
**HPPS** high-pressure pump station.
station de pompage haute pression.
**HPR** heure prévue (ou probable) de retour.
estimated time of return (ETR 2.).
**HPr** Histidine-contaning Protein.
*Medicine.*
**H.pre** Heir presumptive.
*Law.*
**HPRT** Hypoxanthine Phosphoribosyl Transferase.
**HPS** Hybrid Processing System.
*Computer Technology.*
**HPT** high-payoff target.
objectif à haut rendement.
**$H_2PtCl_6$** Hexachloroplatinic Acid.
**HPV** Human Papilloma Virus.
Transmission of HPV can take place through sexual contact.
*Cell Biology; Epidemiology; Oncology; Virology.*
**hPXR** human nuclear Pregname X Receptor.
*Biochemistry; Biophysics; Cancer; Chemistry; Endocrinology; Genes Development.*
**HQ**; **H.Q.** Headquarters.
Also: **hdq**; **hdq**.
**HQ** High Quality.
**HQ AIRNORTH** Headquarters Allied Air Forces North.
Quartier général des Forces aériennes alliées Nord.
**HQ AIRSOUTH** Headquarters Allied Air Forces South.
Quartier général des Forces aériennes alliées Sud.
**HQGW** Hyperquenched Glassy Water.
*Biochemistry; Chemistry; Hyperquenching.*
**HQ NAEW&C FC** Headquarters NATO Airborne Early Warning and Control, Force Command [when referring to the Headquarters situated at SHAPE, in Belgium].
Quartier général du Commandement de la Force aéroportée de détection lointaine et de contrôle de l'OTAN [désigne le quartier général implanté au SHAPE, en Belgique].
**HQ NAVNORTH** Headquarters Allied Naval Forces North.
Quartier général des Forces navales alliées Nord.
**HQ NAVSOUTH** Headquarters Allied Naval Forces South.
Quartier général des Forces navales alliées Sud.
**HQ NORTH** Headquarters Allied Forces Northern Europe [obsolete].
Quartier général des Forces alliées Nord-Europe (QG Nord) [obsolète].
**HQ SACLANT** Headquarters Supreme Allied Commander Atlantic.
Quartier général du commandant suprême allié de l'Atlantique.
**HQ STRIKFLTLANT** Headquarters Striking Fleet Atlantic.
Quartier général de la Flotte d'intervention de l'Atlantique.

**HQ SUBACLANT** Headquarters Submarines Atlantic.
Quartier général des Forces sous-marines de l'Atlantique.
**HR** Croatia.
**HR** Heart Rate.
*Physiology.*
**HR** Hellenic Register.
*Shipping.*
For further details see under: **HRS**.
**hr** (abbr.) here.
**HR** Highland Railway.
**HR** High-Representative.
**HR** Home Record.
*Computer Programming.*
**H.R.** Home Rule (Ireland).
**hr**; **hr.** (abbr.) hour.
A unit of time equal to 60 minutes or 3600 seconds.
Also: **H**; **H.**; **h**; **h.**
**HR** House of Representatives.
**HR** Human Relations.
**HR** Hypersensitive Response.
*Biological Sciences; Biology; Disease Resistance; Molecular Pharmacology.*
**HRA** Health Resources Administration.
**HRAF** Human Relations Area Files.
HRAF is a cross-cultural reference system giving data on a great number of world cultures.
*Anthropology.*
**HRB** Health Research Board (Dublin, Ireland).
The HRB is the leading agency supporting health research in Ireland.
*Health Research; Research Projects.*
**HRB** Highway Research Board (U.S.A.).
**HRCC** Human Rights Coordination Centre.
**hRCC1** human RCC1.
*Biochemistry; Cell Biology; Medicine; Moleular Biology.*
**HRD** Hurricane Research Division.
Of the U.S. Atlantic Oceanographic and Meteorological Laboratory.
**H-R diagram** Hertzsprung-Russell Diagram.
*Astrophysics.*
**hrdwre** (abbr.) hardware.
For further details see under: **h**.
**HREE** Heavy Rare Earth Element.
*Geology; Geosciences.*
**HREELS** High-Resolution Electron Energy Loss Spectroscopy.
**HREM** High-Resolution Electron Microscope.
**H Rept** House Report.
**H Res.** House Resolution.
**HRF** high-readiness force.
force à haut niveau de préparation.
**HRF** Histamine-Releasing Factor.
**HRF** Human Research Facility (U.S.A.).
**HRG** Herbicide Resistance Gene.
*Biotechnology.*
**HRG** Hochschulrahmengesetz (Germany).
HRG is the federal framework law on universities.
*University Reforms.*
**HRH** Her/His Royal Highness.
**HRI** Height-Range Indicator.
*Electronics.*
**HRI** human-readable interpretation.
traduction en clair (TC 3.).
**HRIR** High Resolution Infrared Radiometer.
**HRIS** Human Resources Information Systems.
**HRK** Croatian kuna.
kuna croate.
**HRL** The airport code for Harlingen, Texas, U.S.A.
**HRM** Croatian Navy.
Marine croate.
**HRO** High-Representative's Office [UN].
Bureau du Haut-Représentant [ONU].
**HRP** 1. helicopter reference point.
1. point de référence de l'hélicoptère (PRH).
2. human remains pouch.
2. housse à restes humains.
**HRP** High Resolution Profiler.
*Oceanography.*
**HRP** Horseradish Peroxidase.
*Enzymology.*
**HRPT** High-Resolution Picture Transmission.
**HRS** Health and Rehabilitative Services.
**HRS** Hellenic Register of Shipping.
The HRS deals with certification of industrial installations and products and certification of quality systems as well as surveys and classification of ships.
**HRS technique** High Resolution Separation technique.
**HRS** High-Resolution Spectrometer.
**HRS** High Rise Site.
**HRS** Historical Records Survey.
**hrs.**; **hrs** (abbr.) hours.
Also: **H**; **H.**; **h**; **h.**
**HRT** Croatian Radio and TV.
Radio-télévision croate.
**HRT** Hormone Replacement Therapy.
For further details see under: **WISDOM** and **WHI**.
**HRTEM** High-Resolution Transmission Electron Microscopy.
*Engineering; Materials Science.*

**hrz.**; **hrz** (abbr.) hertz.
**hrz.**; **hrz** (abbr.) horizon; horizontal.
**HRZ I PZO** Croatian Air Force and Anti-Aircraft Defence.
Armée de l'air et défense antiaérienne croates.
**hrzn.** (abbr.) horizon.
Also: **hrz.**; **hrz**.
*Archaeology; Astronomy; Cartography; Developmental Biology; Geology; Navigation.*
**HS**; **H.S.** Harbour Service.
**HS** Heparin or Heparan Sulfate.
*Biochemistry; Molecular Biology; Molecular Biophysics; Pharmacology.*
**HS**; **H.S.** High School.
**HS** High Sensitivity.
**HS** High Side.
*Computer Technology.*
**HS** High Speed.
*Computer Technology.*
**HS** Home Secretary.
**HS** Honorary Secretary.
**HS** Hospital Ship.
*Nautical.*
**H.S.**; **HS** House Surgeon.
**HS** Human Society (U.S.A.).
**HS** Hydrogen Swelling.
**$H_2S$** Hydrogen Sulfide.
$H_2S$, also known as: Sulfuretted Hydrogen, is used mainly as a reagent.
*Inorganic Chemistry.*
**HSA** Heat-Stable Antigen.
**HSA** Human Serum Albumin.
*Medicine.*
**HSAA** Health Sciences Advanced Award.
**HSAM** high-range surface-to-air missile.
missile surface-air à grande portée.
**HSBC** Hongkong & Shanghai Banking Corporation.
**HSBK** Halyk Savings Bank of Kazakhstan.
**HS buffer** High Salt buffer.
**HSC** Health Sciences Center - Kuwait University.
**HSC** Hematopoietic Stem cell.
For further details see under: **SCs**.
**HSC** High Speed Carry.
*Computer Technology.*
**HSC** Hospital for Sick Children.
Located in Toronto, Ontario, Canada.
**HSC73** Heat Shock Cognate protein of 73 kD.
**hsCD2d1** soluble nonglycosylated human CD2 domain 1.
**HSCs** Hematopoietic Stem Cells.
Viral elements in bone-marrow transplantation.
*Basic Medical Sciences; Cancer Biology; Cancer Chemotherapy; Clinical Transplantation Studies; Developmental Biology; Immunology; Molecular Biotherapy.*
**HSCSD technology** High Speed Circuit Switched Data technology.
*Cellular Networks.*
**HSCT** High Speed Civil Transport.
**HSDA** High Speed Data Acquisition.
*Data Communications.*
**HSE** Health and Safety Executive.
**HSE** Heat Shock Element.
**HSE** Highly Siderophile Elements.
*Earth Sciences; Geophysics; Isotope Geochemistry.*
**$H_2SeO_4$** Selenic Acid.
*Chemistry.*
**$H_2SeO_3$** Selenious Acid.
Selenious Acid, also known as: Selenous Acid, is used mainly as an analytic reagent.
*Chemistry.*
**HSGPC** High-Speed Gel Permeation Chromatography.
**HSGT** High-Speed Ground Transportation.
**HSI** Horizontal Situation Indicator.
*Navigation.*
**$H_2SiF_6$** Fluorosilicic Acid.
Fluorosilicic Acid is used mainly in ceramics, and in electroplating.
*Inorganic Chemistry.*
**HSK** Herpes Stromal Keratitis.
HSK is an autoimmune disease of the eye caused by Herpes Simplex Virus.
*Ocular Immunology; Ophthalmology; Viral Immunology.*
**HSL** Health and Safety Laboratory (G.B.).
**HSL** High-Speed Launch.
**HSLA steel** High-Strength Low-Alloy steel.
HSLA is a low-alloy steel that has a yield strength higher than that of carbon steel.
*Metallurgy.*
**HSLC** Health Sciences Libraries Consortium.
**HSLC** High-Speed Liquid Chromatography.
**HSLIC** Health Sciences Library and Information Co-operative.
**HSLS** Croatian Liberal Party.
Parti libéral croate.
**HSM** High-Speed Memory.
**HSMHA** Health Services and Mental Health Administration.
**HSO** heure sur l'objectif.
time on target (TOT 2.).
**$H_2SO_3$** Sulfurous Acid.

$H_2SO_3$ is used mainly as an antiseptic, a preservative, and in the production of wines.
*Inorganic Chemistry.*

**$H_2SO_4$** Sulfuric Acid.
Sulfuric acid, also known as: Dipping Acid is used mainly in the chemicals and explosives manufacturing industries.

**$H_2S_2O_3$** Trisulfuric Acid.
*Inorganic Chemistry.*

**$H_2S_2O_6$** Dithionic Acid.
*Inorganic Chemistry.*

**HSOs** Health Service Organizations.

**HSP** Croatian Party of Rights.
Parti des droits croate.

**HSP** (Division of) Health Sciences Policy.

**HSPs** Heat Shock Proteins.
*Evolution; Chemical Ecology.*

**HSPGs** (Cell-surface) Heparan Sulfate Proteoglycans.
*Medicine.*

**HSPN** Hellenic Society for the Protection of Nature (Greece).

**HSQC** Heteronuclear Single-Quantum Correlation.

**HSR** Heterochromatically Staining Region.

**HSR** Homogeneous Staining Region.
*Molecular Biology.*

**HSR&D** Health Services Research and Development.

**HSRP** High Speed Research Program.
*NASA Programs.*

**HSR-TIGET** Hospital San Raffaele - Telethon Institute for GEne Therapy (Milan, Italy).
*Biochemistry; Bone Marrow Transplantation; Gene Therapy; Pediatrics.*

**HSSI**; **Hssi technology** High-Speed Serial Interface technology.

**HS state** High-Spin state.
*Molecular Chemistry.*

**HSSTD** Historical Sea Surface Temperature Dataset.

**HSSTs** High Speed Streams.
*Astronomy; Astrophysics; Atmospheric, Oceanic and Space Sciences; Geophysics; Physics.*

**HSSV** high-speed surface vessel.
bâtiment de surface à grande vitesse.

**HST** Hawaiian Standard Time.

**HST** (Division of) Health Sciences and Technology (U.S.A.).
Massachusetts Institute of Technology.

**HST** Hubble Space Telescope.
*Astrophysics; Atmospheric and Planetary Physics; Space Telescope Science.*

**HST** Hypersonic Transport.

**HSTF** Heat Shock Transcription Factor.

**HST/STIS** Hubbe Space Telescope / Space Telescope Imaging Spectrograph.
*Astronomy; Atmospheric and Environmental Research; Earth and Planetary Science; Physics; Solar Physics.*
For further details see under: **STIS**.

**HSUS** Humane Society of the United States (U.S.A.).

**HSV** Herpes Simplex Virus.
Herpes simplex Virus is a virus of the Herpesviridae family.
*Virology.*

**HSV** The airport code for Huntsville/Decatur, Alabama, U.S.A.

**HSV-1** Herpes Simplex Virus type 1.

**HSV-TK gene** Herpes Simplex Virus Thymidine Kinase gene.
*Cell Biology.*

**HT** Half-Time / halftime.
*Physical Chemistry.*

**HT** Halftone / half tone.
In acoustics, halftone is also known as: Semitone.
*Acoustics.*

**HT** Halftone / half tone.
*Graphic Arts.*

**HT** Hardtop.

**HT** Hashimoto's Thyroiditis.
HT is an autoimmune disease characterized by the gradual destruction of thyroid tissue.
*Apoptosis; Autoimmune Diseases; Clinical Immunology; Endocrinology; Experimental Medicine; Immunology.*

**HT** Hawaiian Time.

**ht**; **ht.** (abbr.) height.
Also: **h**; **h.**
*Mathematics; Metrology.*

**HT**; **HCT** Hematocrit.
*Pathology.*

**HT**; **H.T.** High Tension.

**HT**; **H.T.** High Tide.
For further details see under: **HW** (High Water).

**HT**; **H.T.** High Treason.

**HT** Holy Trinity.

**HT** Horizontal Tabulation (character).
*Data Communications.*

**HT** Hors Taxe.
French initialism meaning: duty-free; exclusive of tax.

**Ht** Hydrotherapy.
The term hydrotherapy refers to a therapeutic treatment for disease by application of water usually externally.

*Medicine.*
**Ht** total Hypothermia.
**5-HT** 5-Hydroxytryptamine.
*Medicine; Molecular Neuroscience; Pharmacology.*
**HTA** Hypertension Artérielle.
French initialism meaning: High Blood Pressure; Hypertension.
*Medicine.*
**HTAP** Hypertension Artérielle Pulmonaire.
French initialism meaning: Pulmonary Hypertension.
*Medicine.*
**HTC** Hungarian Telecommunications Co. Ltd.
**HTCF** Hold Till Called For.
**$H_2TeO_3$** Tellurous Acid.
*Inorganic Chemistry.*
**$H_6TeO_6$** Telluric Acid.
Telluric Acid is also known as: Hydrogen Tellurate.
*Inorganic Chemistry.*
**HTF** Headline Task Force [EU].
Groupe spécial sur l'objectif global [UE].
**HTFFR** High-Temperature Fast-Flow Reactor.
**HTFMI** Heat Transfer and Fluid Mechanics Institute.
**HTGR** High-Temperature Gas-cooled Reactor.
*Energy; Nuclear Engineering.*
**HTG technique** Holographic Time Gating technique.
*Ballistic Light; Optical Sciences.*
**HTL** High Threshold Logic.
**hTLR2** human Toll-Like Receptor 2.
*Medicine; Microbial Pathogenesis; Microbiology; Molecular Biology.*
**HTLV-III** Human T-Lymphotropic Virus Type III.
HTLV-III is the term formerly used for human immunodeficiency virus.
*Virology.*
**HTML** Hypertext Markup Language.
The standard for formatting documents on the World Wide Web.
**HTO** Hellenic Tourism Organization (Greece).
**HTP** High Temperature Photolysis.
**HTPB** Hydroxyl-Terminated Polybutadiene.
**HTPF** High Throughput Factory.
At RIKEN Harima Institute (Japan).
For further details see under: **RIKEN**.
**HTR** High-Temperature Reactor.
**HTR** High-Temperature Reservoir.
*Thermodynamics.*
**hTRβ** human Thyroid hormone Receptor-β.
**hTRT subunit** human Telomerase Reverse Transcriptase subunit.
*Cell Biology; Neuroscience.*
**HTS** Heat Transfer System.
**HTS** High-Temperature Superconductivity / Superconductor.
Also: **HTSC**.
*Solid-State Physics.*
**HTS** High Throughput Screening.
**HTSC** High-Temperature Superconductivity.
Also: **HTS**.
**HTSCs** High-Temperature Superconductors.
*Superconductivity.*
**HTSEC** High-Temperature Size-Exclusion Chromatography.
**HTS HEBM** High Temperature Superconductor Hot Electron Bolometer Mixer.
For further details see under: **HEBMs**.
**HTST** High-Temperature Short-Time.
**HTT** highly transportable terminal.
terminal très facilement transportable.
**Htt** Huntington (abnormal protein).
*Biology; Cell Biology; Cellular Medicine; Human Behavior; Huntington's Disease; Molecular Medicine; Neurology.*
**HTTMT** High-Temperature Thermomechanical Treatment.
**HTTP** Hypertext Transfer Protocol.
*Internet.*
**HTVA** Hors TVA.
French initialism meaning: exclusive of VAT.
**HTWS** Hawaii Tsunami Warning System (U.S.A.).
**HU** Hebrew University (Jerusalem).
**HU** Hungary.
Also: **Hun**.
**HU** Hydroxyurea.
HU is used mainly to treat certain types of leukemia.
*Biology; Medicine; Pathology; Pharmacology.*
**HUD** Head Up Display.
*Optics.*
**HUD** Housing Urban Development.
**HUFIS** HUman Factors in Information Services.
*European Community Project.*
**hUG** human Uteroglobin.
For further details see under: **UG**.
**HUGO** HUman Genome Organization.
**human IUGTEs** human In Utero Gene Transfer Experiments.
For further details see under: **IUGTEs**.
**HUMF** HUman Mammary Fibroblasts.
**HUMINT** human intelligence.
1a. renseignement humain.

1b. renseignement d'origine humaine (ROHUM) [FR].

**HUM project** Helicopter Health and Usage Monitoring project.
*European Community Project.*

**Hun** (abbr.) Hungary.
Also: **HU**.

**hund.** (abbr.) hundred.

**Hung** (abbr.) Hungarian.
Hungarian, also called Magyar, is the language of Hungary, of the Uralic family of languages.
*Languages.*

**HUNSAT** (abbr.) HUNgarian SATellite Communications Association (Hungary).

**HUNTEX** minehunting exercise.
exercice de chasse aux mines.

**Hunts** (abbr.) Huntingdonshire.

**HUPO** HUman Proteome Organization.
The proteome: the pattern of proteins produced by a cell under certain conditions. HUPO, an international alliance of industry, academic and government members, was created at the end of 2001.
*Human Proteome.*

**HURL** Hawaii Underwater Research Laboratory.

**HUSLE** helicopter underslung load equipment.
transport d'équipement à l'élingue par hélicoptère (ou équipement d'elingage).

**HUT** Helsinki University of Technology (Finland).

**HUVECs** Human Umbilical Vein Endothelial Cells.
*Angiogenesis; Anti-angiogenesis; Tumor Angiogenesis; Tumor Vasculature.*

**hv** (abbr.) have.

**HV**; **H.V.** High Velocity.
*Ordnance.*

**HV**; **H.V.** High Voltage.
*Electricity.*

**HVA** High Voltage-Activated.

**HVA** Homovanillic Acid.
*Biochemistry* - $C_9H_{10}O_4$.

**HVAC** Heating, Ventilating, and Air-Conditioning.
Energy-10 is extremely easy to use. The designer inputs floor area, the building's use, the number of stories, and the type of heating, ventilating, and air-conditioning (HVAC) system. Energy- 10 also performs hour-by-hour calculations of thermal, HVAC, and lighting behavior, through a complete year of operation. Energy-10 was released in late 1995.
*New Computer tool: Energy-10.*

**HVAC system** Heating, Ventilation, and Air-Conditioning system.
The potential for gas-fired desiccant cooling is illustrated by a recent study of a 346,000-square-foot office building in Houston, Texas, U.S.A.
*Gas-Fired Desiccant cooling; New standards for indoor air quality.*

**HVAP** Hypervelocity Armor-Piercing.
*Ordnance.*

**HVAR** High-Velocity Aircraft Rocket.

**HVAs** High-Velocity Anomalies.
*Seismology.*

**HVAT** Hypervelocity Antitank.

**HVB** Hypovereins Bank.
HVB is Germany's second biggest bank.

**HVC** High Vocal Center.
The HVC is a brain area in canaries that helps produce their song.

**HVCs** High Vocal Centers.
For further details see under: **HVC**.

**HVD** Hyperthrophie Ventriculaire Droite.
French initialism meaning: Right Ventricular Hypertrophy.
*Medicine.*

**HVDC** High-Voltage Direct-Current.
HVDC is a long-distance direct-current power transmission system.

**HVDCT** High-Voltage Direct-Current Transmission.

**hVDR** human Vitamin D Receptor.

**HveB** Herpesvirus entry mediator B.
*Dental Medicine; Microbiology; Immunology; Oral Health.*

**HVEM** High-Voltage Electron Microscope.

**HVG** Hypertrophie Ventriculaire Gauche.
French initialism meaning: Left Ventricular Hypertrophy.
**HvG reaction** Host-versus-Graft reaction.
*Immunology.*

**HVL** Half-Value Layer.
*Radiology.*

**HVO** Hawaiian Volcano Observatory.
*Eruption Predictions; Seismic Patters; Geophysics.*

**HVRI** Hypervariable Region I.
*Biological Sciences; Earth Sciences; Molecular Biosciences.*

**HVs** Hybrid Vehicles.
HVs of the future will depend on at least two different kinds of propulsion systems to operate. An internal combustion engine might be just one of two or more propulsion systems modified to work in a hybrid design. The Midwest Research Institute (MRI) of Kansas City, MO, U.S.A., will manage the *U.S. Government's Hybrid Vehicle Program.*
*Hybrid Vehicles; Propulsion Systems.*

**HVT** high-value target.
objectif précieux.
**HVU** high-value unit.
unité précieuse.
**hvy** (abbr.) heavy.
**HW** Half-Word.
*Computer Technology.*
**HW** Hardware.
For further details see under: **h**.
**HW** hazardous waste.
déchets dangereux.
**HW**; **H.W.** High Water.
High Water, also known as: High Tide, refers to the highest point reached by a rising tide.
*Oceanography.*
**HW** Highway.
HW is a public road, on which vehicles are allowed to travel at a speed higher than on local streets.
*Civil Engineering.*
**HW** Hot Water.
**hw** (abbr.) how.
**HWC** Hurricane Warning Center.
**HWE principle** Hardy-Weinberg Expectation principle.
**HWK** Henrietta Wilfrida Karongo.
*Anthropology.*
**HWM** High Water Mark.
*Computer Programming; Oceanography.*
**HWO** Hurricane Warning Office (U.S.A.).
Of the U.S. NWS.
For further details see under: **NWS**.
**$H_2WO_4$** Tungstic Acid.
Tungstic Acid, also known as: Orthotungstic Acid; Wolframic Acid is used mainly in plastics, and textiles.
*Inorganic Chemistry.*
**HWWBA** Hungarian Women's World Banking Association (Hungary).
**HXD** Hard X-ray Detector.
**HXRBs** Hard X-Ray Bursts.
*Astronomy; Physics.*
**hy**; **hy.** henry; henries.
*Electromagnetism.*
**HYDO** High-Yield Discount Obligation.
**HYDROLANT** Hydrographic Office and Atlantic Ocean.
*Navigation.*
**HYDROPAC** Hydrographic Office and Pacific Ocean.
*Navigation.*
**Hz.**; **Hz**; **hz.** (abbr.) Hertz.
Hertz, also known as cycle per second, is the standard unit of measurement for frequency.
*Metrology.*

# I

**I** electric current.
**I** (abbr.) Independent.
**i** (abbr.) indicated.
**I** Information.
*Science* - In science, information is the data classified, recorded, or interpreted so that the result is meaningful.
*Telecommunications* - In telecommunications, it is the information transmitted by signals through telecommunication channels.
**I** Input.
*Computer Programming; Electronics.*
**I** (abbr.) Inspector.
**I** (abbr.) Institute.
**I** Instruction.
*Computer Programming; Science.*
**I** Intelligence.
**I** Intensity.
**I** Interrupt.
The term interrupt in computers, is a stoppage in a working program that can resume operation at a later stage.
*Computer Programming.*
**I**; **i** investment.
**I** The chemical symbol for Iodine.
The word iodine derives from the Greek "iodés" which means violet.
*Symbols; Chemistry; Pharmacology.*
**I** Ireland; Irish.
**I** Italy's international vehicle-registration letter.
**IA** Immediate Address.
Immediate address is also known as: Zero-Level Address.
*Computer Programming.*
**IA** Immediately Available.
**IA** Immune Adherence.
*Immunology.*
**IA** Inactive Account.
*Banking; Business; Finance.*
**IA** Income Averaging.
**IA** Incorporated Accountant.
**IA** Indexed Address.
The term indexed address refers to an address modified by an index register before or during the course of an instruction.
*Computer Programming.*
**IA** Indirect Address.
Indirect address is also known as: Multilevel Address; Second-Level Address.
*Computer Programming.*
**IA** Input Area.
Input area is also known as: Input Storage, Input Block; Input Section.
*Computer Programming.*
**IA** Instruction Address.
*Computer Programming.*
**IA** Insuffisance Aortique / Régurgitation Aortique.
French initialism meaning: Aortic Insufficiency/Regurgitation.
*Medicine.*
**IA** Intangible Asset.
*Banking; Business; Finance.*
**IA** Intelligenza Artificiale.
Italian initialism meaning: Artificial Intelligence.
**IA** Interim Audit.
**IA** International Angstrom.
Named for the Swedish physicist and astronomer Anders Jonas **Ångström**.
*Physics.*
**IA** (abbr.) Iowa (U.S.A.).
**IAA** Indoleacetic Acid.
Indoleacetic acid is used as a hormone to stimulate plant growth.
*Biochemistry.*
**IAA** International Academy of Astronautics.
For further details see under: **IAF**.
**IAA** International Advertising Association; International Aerospace Abstracts (U.S.A.).
**IAA** International Association for Aerobiology.
**IAA** Investment Advisers Act (U.S.A.).
**IAA** Israel Archives Association.
**IAA**; **I.A.A.** Italian Association of Accountants.
**IAALD** International Association of Agricultural Librarians and Documentalists.
**IAAPA** International Association of Amusement Parks and Attractions (U.S.A.).
**I.A.B.** Institut Van de Accountants en de Belastingconsulenten.
*Belgian Institute.*
**IAB** Inter-American Bank.
**IAB** Internet Activities Board.
Founded in 1983. Now Internet Architecture Board.
**IAB** Internet Architecture Board.
Has replaced **IAB**.
**IABB** Indian Association of Blood Banks (India).
**IABB** Inter-American Bank Bonds.
*Banking; Business; Finance.*
**IABG** International Association of Biomedical Gerontology.
The 7$^{th}$ Congress of the IABG was held on 15$^{th}$/18$^{th}$ August 1997.

**IABIN** Inter-American Biodiversity Information Network.
**IABO** International Association of Biological Oceanography.
**IAC** Inter-Academy Council (Switzerland).
A Body proposed in 2000 as an international version of the U.S. National Research Council.
**IAC** International Analysis Code.
The International Analysis Code is used worldwide to communicate information.
*Meteorology.*
**IACA** International Air Charter Association.
**IACA** Investigation of the Aerodynamics and Coding of Advanced engine turbine components.
*European Community Project.*
**IACB** interdiction aérienne du champ de bataille.
battlefield air interdiction (BAI).
**IACC** International America's Cup Class.
**IACCMD** Italy-America Chamber of Commerce Maryland (Naples, Italy).
**IACME** International Association of Crafts and small- and Medium-sized Enterprises.
Located in Berne, Switzerland. Founded in 1947. IACME'S goal is to maintain and develop in all countries high-quality individual work and services as well as to insure freedom for individual initiative.
**IACOMS** International Advisory COmmittee on Marine Sciences.
IACOMS has been replaced by: SCOR.
For further details see under: **SCOR**.
**IACP** International Association of Computer Programmers.
**IACP** Intra-Allerød Cold Period.
*Biodiversity; Conservation Biology; Environmental Physics; Last Deglaciation.*
**IACP** Istituto Autonomo Case Popolari (Italy).
Italian acronym meaning: Autonomous Board for Tenement Flats/Apartments. Has been replaced by: ALER.
For further details see under: **ALER**.
**IACR** Institute of Arable Crops Research (G.B.).
The IACR conducts fundamental and applied strategic research to optimise existing and novel crop production systems and their interactions with the environment.
**IACR** Integrated Approach to Crop Research, Long Ashton, G.B.
*Introgressive Hybridization; Hybrid Populations; Microsatellite Marker Assays; Polyploid Genomes.*
**IACS** International Annealed Copper Standard.
*Metallurgy.*
**IACUCs** Institutional Animal Care and Use Committees.
*Animal Research Protocols; Surgery; Xenotransplantation.*
**IAD** The airport code for Dulles International Airport, Washington D.C., U.S.A.
**IAD** Institute for Addictive Disorders (U.S.A.).
**IAD** Inter-American Dialogue.
**IAD** interface adaptor device.
adaptateur d'interface.
**IAD** International Astrophysical Decade.
**IAD** Istituto Accertamento Diffusione (Italy).
Italian initialism meaning: Audit Board of Circulation.
**IADB** Inter-American Defense Board (U.S.A.).
**IADB** Inter-American Development Bank (U.S.A.).
**IADL** International Association of Democratic Lawyers (Belgium).
Founded in 1946; aims to facilitate contacts and exchanges of view between lawyers and lawyers' associations and to foster understanding and goodwill; to work together to achieve the aims of the Charter of the United Nations.
**IADLC**; **Iadlc** Integrated Access Digital Loop Carrier.
**IADO** Instituto Argentine de Oceanografia (Argentina).
**IADR** (abbr.) Instruction Address.
**IADS** integrated air defence system.
système de défense aérienne intégrée.
**IAEA**; **I.A.E.A.** International Atomic Energy Agency - Vienna, Austria.
**IAEH** International Association for Environmental Hydrology (U.S.A.).
**IAESTE** International Association for the Exchange of Students for Technical Experience (France).
Founded in 1948 to organize exchange of students for *on-the-job training*.
**IAF** Inter-American Foundation.
*Partnership Poverty Reduction.*
**IAF**; **I.A.F.** International Astronautical Federation.
Paris, France. Founded in 1950; Constitution adopted at the XII Congress in Washington 1961; to foster the development of astronautics for peaceful purposes at national and international levels; the IAF created the IAA, the IISL, and committees on activities and membership.
*Astronautics; Space Law.*
For further details see under: **IAA** and **IISL**.
**IAFE** International Association of Fairs and Expositions.
Located in Springfield, Missouri, U.S.A.
**IAG** Insurance Australia Group.

**IAG** International Association of Geodesy.
**IAG** International Association of Gerontology (Mexico).
Founded in 1950 to promote contacts between people and organizations interested in the study of *gerontology* and to organize meetings and congresses every 4 years.
**IAG** international auditing guideline.
norme de vérification internationale (NVI).
**IAGA** International Association of Geomagnetism and Aeronomy.
Founded in 1919; aims: the study of *magnetism* and *aeronomy* of the earth and other bodies of the solar system and of the interplanetary medium and its interaction with these bodies.
**IAGLR** International Association for Great Lakes Research.
**IAH** Institute for Animal Health (G.B.).
The IAH is an international center for research on the diseases of farm animals.
*Farm Animals; Immunology; Epidemiology; Molecular Biology.*
**IAHA** Immune Adherence Hemmaglutination Assay.
*Immunology.*
**IAHS** International Association of Hydrological Sciences.
**IAHT** The airport code for Intercontinental Airport, Houston, Texas, U.S.A.
**IAI** Inter-American Institute (for Global Change Research) (U.S.A.).
*Environmental Research.*
**IAI** International African Institute (G.B.).
Founded in 1926 to facilitate the study of *African societies and cultures* and the dissemination of the results of that research.
**IAIA** International Association for Impact Assessment (U.S.A.).
**IAIMS** Integrated Advanced Information Management Systems (U.S.A.).
**IAL** International Algebraic Language.
**IALC** Instrument Approach and Landing Chart.
**IALCE** international airlift control element.
élément international de contrôle du transport aérien.
**IALL** International Association of Law Libraries.
Located in Chicago, Illinois, U.S.A. Founded in 1959 to offer worldwide co-operation in the development of law libraries and the collection of legal documentation.
**IALS** International Association of Legal Science.
**IALTA** International Association of Language Travel Advisers.
**IAM** Institute for Advanced Materials - Petten, The Netherlands.
*Dutch Institute.*
**IAM** Instituto Andaluz de la Mujer.
*Spanish Institute.*
**IAM** International Agencies Meeting.
réunion des agences internationales.
**I.A.M.** International Association of Machinists.
**IAMAM** International Association of Museums of Arms and Military History.
Located in Helsinki, Finland. Founded in 1957; organization to establish contact between museums and other scientific institutions with collections of *arms* and *armour*, *military equipment*, *uniforms*, etc., which may be visited by the public; to promote the study of relevant groups of objects; triennial conferences.
**IAMAP** International Association of *Meteorology and Atmospheric Physics.*
**IAMAS** International Association of Meteorology and Atmospheric Sciences.
Founded in 1919 to organize research symposia and co-ordinate research in *atmospheric science fields*; an Association of the International Union of Geodesy and Geophysics.
**IAML** International Association of Music Libraries, Archives and Documentation Centres.
Located in Stockholm, Sweden. Founded in 1951 to facilitate co-operation between music libraries and information centres, compile *music bibliographies*, and to promote the professional training of music librarians and documentalists; national branches in 19 countries.
**IAMS**; **I.A.M.S.** International Association of Microbiological Societies.
**IAMSLIC** International Association of Marine Science Libraries and Information Centres.
**IAN** Indoleacetonitrile.
*Biochemistry.*
**IAN** Istituto per l'Automazione Navale.
*Italian Institute.*
**IANA**; **Iana** Internet Assigned Numbers Authority.
**I&D** Incision and Drainage.
**I&E** Income and Expense.
**I&I** Imaging and Information (Fujifilm).
*Imaging Systems.*
**I&I** interoperability and integration.
interopérabilité et intégration.
**I&O** Intake and Output.
**I&W** 1. indications and warning.
1. indices et critères d'alerte.
2. indicators and warnings.
2. indices et indicateurs d'alerte.

**IAO** International Antarctic Observatory.
*Astronomy; Astrophysics.*

**IAOL** International Association of Orientalist Librarians.

**IAP** Inhibitor of Apoptosis Protein.
For further details see under: **IAPs**.

**IAP** instrument approach procedure.
procédure d'approche aux instruments.

**IAP** Inter-Academy Panel on International Issues.
The IAP is an Association of about 80 national science academies that holds conferences and provides statements on issues of common interest.

**IAP** International Airport.

**IAPA** International Airline Passengers Association.

**IAPAC** International Association of Physicians in AIDS Care (U.S.A.).
*AIDS Research; AIDS Vaccine.*

**IAPC** International Auditing Practices Committee.
Comité international de normalisation de la vérification (CINV).

**IAPG** Interagency Arctic Policy Group.

**IAPH** International Association of Ports and Harbours (Japan).

**IAPIP** International Association for the Protection of Industrial Property (Switzerland).
*Patents; Trademarks.*

**IAPO** International Association for Physical Oceanography.
IAPO has been replaced by: IAPSO.
For further details see under: **IAPSO**.

**IAPs** Inhibitor of Apoptosis Proteins.
IAPs are proteins discovered by researchers of the University of Georgia, Athens, U.S.A. in 1993.
*Apoptosis; Biochemistry; Medicine.*
For further details see under: **DIABLO**.

**IAPS** International Association for People-environment Studies.
*Educational Web Sites.*

**IAPSO** International Association for the Physical Sciences of the Ocean.
California, U.S.A. Founded in 1919 to promote the study of scientific problems relating to the Oceans, chiefly in so far as such study may be carried out by the aid of mathematics, physics and chemistry; to initiate, facilitate and co-ordinate research; to provide for discussion, comparison and publication.

**IAR** intelligence area of responsibility.
zone de responsabilité du renseignement (ZRR).

**IARC** International Agency for Research on Cancer.
*Cancer Risks.*

**IARC** International Arctic Research Center.
A (1999) Japan-United States facility.
*Global Change; Global Climate; Sea Ice; Vegetation.*

**IARCC** Interagency Arctic Research Coordination Committee.

**IARD** Incendi, Accidenti, Rischi Diversi.
Italian acronym meaning: Fire, Accidents, Sundry Risks.
*Insurance.*

**IARI** Indian Agricultural Research Institute - New Delhi, India.

**IARPC** Interagency Arctic Research Policy Committee (U.S.A.).

**IARU** International Amateur Radio Union (U.S.A.).

**I.A.S.** Indian Administrative Service (India).
Formerly the Indian Civil Service (I.C.S.). IAS members are recruited through an annual entrance test.

**IAS** Indicated Airspeed.
*Aviation.*

**IAS** Institute for Advanced Studies.

**IAS** Institute of Aerospace Sciences.

**IAS** Institute of Aeronautical Sciences.

**IAS** Internal Audit System.
*Accounts.*

**IASA** International Association of Sound Archives.

**IASAP** International Arctic Seas Assessment Project.

**IASC** International Accounting Standards Committee.

**IASC** International Arctic Service Committee (Norway).

**IASI** International Association for Sports Information.

**IASI** Istituto di Analisi ed Informatica.
*Italian Institute.*

**IASL** International Association of School Librarianship.

**IASLIC** Indian Association of Special Libraries and Information Centres.

**IASMAL** International Academy of Social and Moral Sciences, Arts and Letters.

**IASP** International Association of Science Parks.

**IASPEI** International Association of Seismology and Physics of the Earth's Interior.

**IASSIST** International Association for Social Sciences Information Services and Technology.

**IASSW** International Association of Schools of Social Work.
c/o University of Toronto, Canada. Founded in 1928 to provide international leadership and encourage high standards in *social work education.*

**IAT** Indirect Antiglobulin Test.

*Chemotherapy; Medicine; Microbiology; Immunology.*
**IATA** International Air Transport Association (Canada).
**IATO** interim approval to operate.
approbation provisoire d'exploitation.
**IATS** Implicit Association Tests.
*Social Psychology.*
**IATSE** International Alliance of Theatrical Stage Employees.
**IATTC** Inter-American Tropical Tuna Commission (U.S.A.).
**IATUL** International Association of *Technological University Libraries.*
Located in The Netherlands. Founded in 1955 to promote co-operation between member libraries and conduct research on library problems.
**IAU** infrastructure accounting unit [obsolete - replaced by NAU].
unité de compte d'infrastructure (UCI) [obsolète - remplacé par NAU].
**IAU** International Association of Universities.
**IAU** International Astronomical Union.
**IAVCEI** International Association of Volcanology and Chemistry of the Earth's Interior.
Canberra, Australia. Founded in 1919 to promote scientific investigation and discussion on *volcanology* and in those aspects of *petrology* and *geochemistry* relating to the composition of the interior of the Earth.
**IAVI** International AIDS Vaccine Initiative (U.S.A.).
New York-based.
*AIDS Research; AIDS Vaccine; Immunology.*
**IAW** In Accordance With.
**IAWQ** Intercontinental Association on Water Quality (G.B.).
**IB** The airline code for Iberia.
**I.B.** In Bond.
**I.B.** Inclusion Body.
*Virology.*
**IB** Income Bond.
*Business; Finance.*
**I.B.**; **I/B** Inland Bill.
**IB** Input Block.
For further details see under: **IA** (Input Area).
*Computer Programming.*
**IB** Insurance Broker.
**IB** Interbanca (Italy).
**IB** Investment Banker; Investment Banking.
**I.B.**; **I/B** Invoice Book.
**IBA** Independent Bankers Association of America (U.S.A.).
**IBA** Industrial Biotechnology Association.
**IBA** International Banking Act.
**IBA** International Bar Association (G.B.).
**IBA** International Board of Auditors for NATO.
Collège international des commissaires aux comptes de l'OTAN.
**IBA** Investment Bankers Association (U.S.A.).
**IBAA** Independent Bankers Association of America (U.S.A.).
**I-BABP** Intestinal Bile Acid-Binding Protein.
*Cell Biology; Medicinal Chemistry; Molecular Biochemistry; Molecular Endocrinology; Orphan Nuclear Receptors; Physiology.*
**IBAD** Ion Beam-Assisted Deposition.
*Materials Science.*
**IBAM** Institute of Business Administration and Management.
*Japanese Institute.*
**IBAMA** Brazilian Environment Protection Agency (Brazil).
**IBAN** see IBA.
voir IBA.
**IBB** International Bank Bonds.
*Banking; Business; Finance.*
**IBBYP** International Board on Books for Young People.
Located in Basel, Switzerland. Founded in 1953 to support and unify those forces in all countries connected with children's book work; to encourage the production and distribution of good children's books especially in the developing countries; to promote scientific investigation into problems of *juvenile books.*
**IBC** Illinois Benedictine College (U.S.A.).
**IBC** Institute for Biomedical Computing (U.S.A.).
In June 1996 the IBC hosted the 4$^{th}$ International Conference on ISBM.
*Computational Biology.*
**IBC** Integrated Block Channel.
**IBC** International Bathymetric Chart.
**IBC** International BRCA Consortium.
*Breast Cancer.*
**IBC** International Business Communications.
5$^{th}$ Annual World Congress August 2000, Boston, MA, U.S.A.
*Drug Discovery Technology 2000.*
**IBC act** International Business Companies Act.
The International Business Companies Act was introduced in The Bahamas in 1990.
**IBCEA** International Bathymetric Chart of the Central Eastern Atlantic.
**IBCOBN** Integrateed Broadband Communications On Broadcast Networks.

*European Community Project.*

**IBCWIO** International Bathymetric Chart of the Western Indian Ocean.

**IBCWP** International Bathymetric Chart of the Western Pacific.

**IBD** Infectious Bursal Disease Virus.
*Veterinary Medicine.*

**IBE** International Bureau of Education.
Located in Geneva, Switzerland. Founded in 1925, the IBE became an intergovernmental organization in July 1929 and was incorporated into UNESCO in January 1969 as an international centre of *comparative education.*
For further details see under: **UNESCO**.

**IBE** Interval Between Eruptions.
*Terrestrial Magnetism.*

**IBEA** Institute for Biological Energy Alternatives (U.S.A.).
*Clean Energy Products; Microbial Genomics.*

**IBEC** International Bank for Economic Cooperation.

**IBEC** International Business Education Consortium.
IBEM is located in Lancaster, Pennsylvania - U.S.A. It is a coalition of higher education institutions, trade service providers and private businesses in the Mid-Atlantic region. IBEC is administered by the EDC.
For further details see under: **EDC**.

**IBEC** Irish Business and Employers Confederation (Ireland).
For further details see under: **IBIA**.

**IBELs** Interest-Bearing Eligible Liabilities (G.B.).
*Banking.*

**IBERLANT** Iberian Atlantic Area [obsolete - see SOUTHLANT].
Secteur ibérique de l'Atlantique [obsolète - voir SOUTHLANT].

**IBEW** International Brotherhood of Electrical Workers.

**IBEXs** International Buyers' EXhibitions.
IBEX is an EC-Initiative for Enterprise Co-operation.

**IBF** Immunoglobulin-Binding Factor.

**IBF** Input Buffer Full.

**IBF** International Banking Facility (U.S.A.).

**IBFs** International Banking Facilities (U.S.A.).

**IBG** Integrated Business Programme.
At Guinness, the brewing division of the Diageo food and drinks group.
*New Electronic Systems.*

**IBG** Inter Block Gap.

**IBGE** Brazilian Institute of National Statistics and Geography (Brazil).

**IBI** Intergovernmental Bureau for Informatics.

**IBI** Istituto Bancario Italiano (Italy).

**IBIA** The Irish Bio-Industries Association (Ireland).
The IBIA was established by the IBEC in November 1997 for the needs of Biotechnology Industries.
For further details see under: **IBEC**.

**IBIB** Isobutyl Isobutyrate.
IBIB is used mainly in insect repellants, and flavorings.
*Organic Chemistry.*

**IBIRU** Institutional Building and Interactive Research Unit.
For further details see under: **ICIPE**.

**IBIS** Improved monitoring for Brain dysfunction in Intensive care and Surgery.
*European Community Project.*

**IBIS** Integrated Ballistic Identification System.

**IBJ** Industrial Bank of Japan (Japan).

**IBL** see IBERLANT.
voir IBERLANT.

**IBM** Individual-Based Model.

**IBM** Instituto de Biologia Marina.
Spanish initialism meaning: Institute for Marine Biology.

**IBM** International Business Machines (U.S.A.).
IBM is the world's largest computer company.

**IBMX** Isobutyl-Methylxanthine.

**IBN** Institut Belge de Normalisation.
French initialism of the: Belgian Institute for Standardization (Belgium).

**IBN** Integrative Biology and Neuroscience.
U.S. NSF's division.
For further details see under: **NSF**.

**IBO** International Baccalaureate Organization.
Geneva, Switzerland. Founded as International Schools Examination Syndicate in 1964, as IBO in 1968. Aims: the planning of curricula and an international university entrance examination, the *International Baccalaureate*, acceptable to universities throughout the world.

**IBOA** see IBA.
voir IBA.

**IBOR** Interbank Offered Rate.
*Economics; Finance.*

**IBP** Indo-British Partnership - India / G.B.
*Bilateral Business Cooperation; Scientific Education and Technology Progress.*

**IBP** International Biological Program.

**IBr** Iodine Monobromide.
IBr is used in organic synthesis.
*Inorganic Chemistry.*

**IBRA** Indonesia's Bank Restructuring Agency.

**IBRD** International Bank for Reconstruction and Development.
For further details see under: **WB**.
**IBRO** International Brain Research Organization.
Located in Paris, France. Founded in 1958 to assist all branches of *neuroscience*.
**IBS** industrial benefits sharing.
1a. partage des avantages industriels.
1b. répartitions des retombées industrielles.
**IBS** Institute of Biopharmaceutical Sciences (Ireland).
**IBS** International Bank for Settlements.
**IBS** International Beauty Show.
Held in New York $6^{th}/9^{th}$ March 1999 at the Jacob Javits Convention Center.
**IBS** International Biometric Society.
Gödöllö, Hungary. Founded in 1947; an international society for the advancement of *quantitative biological science* through the development of quantitative theories and the application, development and dissemination of effective *mathematical and statistical techniques*.
**IBSFC** International Baltic Sea Fisheries Commission.
**IBSS** Infrared Background Signature Survey.
**IBSS** Institute of Biology of the Southern Seas (Sevastopol, Ukraine).
**IBT** Isatin-β-thiosemicarbazone.
*Biochemistry*.
**I.B.T.C.H.W.** International Brotherhood of Teamsters, Chauffeurs, Helpers and Warehousemen of America (U.S.A.).
**IB-TV** Interactive Business Television.
**IBV** Infectious Bronchitis Virus.
**IBY** International Biodiversity Year.
*Oceans and Security*.
**IBY** International Biological Year.
**IBZM** Iodobenzamide.
**IC** 1. Iceland.
1. Islande.
2. information campaign.
2. campagne d'information.
3. Infrastructure Committee.
3. Comité d'infrastructure.
4. invited country.
4. pays invité.
**i/c** in charge.
**IC** Income Capital.
**IC** Indirect Control.
*Computer Technology*.
**IC** Inferior Colliculus.
**IC** Inspiratory Capacity.
*Physiology*.
**IC** Instruction Counter.
Instruction Counter is also known as: Instruction Register; Program Counter.
*Computer Technology*.
**IC** Instruction Cycle.
*Computer Programming*.
**IC** Integrated Circuit.
The integrated circuit is also known as: integrated semiconductor.
*Electronics*.
**IC** Integrated Console.
*Telecommunications*.
**IC** Interface Card.
*Computer Technology*.
**IC** Internal Combustion; Internal Connection.
**IC** International Cooperation.
**IC** Investment Counselor.
*Business; Finance*.
**IC** Ion Chromatography.
Ion Chromatography is used mainly to separate and precisely identify carbon cluster ion structures as a function of cluster size.
**IC** Irritable Colon.
Irritable colon is also known as: Adaptive Colitis; Mucous Colitis; Unstable Colon; Spastic Colon.
*Medicine*.
**ICA** Institute for Computational Astrophysics (Canada).
Launched in 2002 within the Department of Astronomy and Physics.
**ICA**; **Ica** Institute of Contemporary Art (G.B.).
**ICA** International Commercial Arbitration.
**ICA** International Communication Agency.
**ICA** International Cooperation Administration.
The International Cooperation Administration has been superseded by the AID.
*U.S. Government*.
For further details see under: **AID**.
**ICA** International Cooperative Alliance (Switzerland).
**ICA** Interstate Commerce Act (U.S.A.).
**ICA** Investment Company Act (U.S.A.).
**ICA** Islet Cell Antibodies.
*Immunopathology; Medicine*.
**ICA** Islet Cell Antigen.
**ICACGP** International Commission on Atmospheric Chemistry and Global Pollution.
**ICAEC** International Confederation of Associations of Experts and Consultants (Belgium).
The ICAEC was founded in 1953. Its members are Appraisers, Consultants, and Experts in numerous countries. Its goal is to bring into accord the Professions of *Experts* and *Technical Consultants*.

**ICAEW** Institute of Chartered Accountants in England and Wales.

**ICAF** Industrial College of the Armed Forces (U.S.A.).

**ICAI** Intelligent Computer Assisted-Instruction.
*Artificial Intelligence.*

**ICALPE** International Centre for ALPine Environment (France).

**ICAM-1** Intercellular Adhesion Molecule-1.
*Cell Biology; Medicine; Molecular Biophysics and Biochemistry.*

**ICAMR** Interdepartmental Committee for Applied Meteorological Research.

**ICANN** Internet Corporation for Assigned Names and Numbers.
Founded in 1998.

**ICAO** International Civil Aviation Organization (Canada).

**ICAOC** interim combined air operations centre [obsolete - replaced by CAOC].
centre combiné provisoire d'opérations aériennes [obsolète - remplacé par CAOC].

**ICAPS** integrated command antisubmarine warfare prediction system.
système de prévisions du commandement intégré de lutte anti-sous-marine.

**ICAR** Indian Council for Agricultural Research (India).

**ICARDA** International Center for Agricultural Research in the Dry Areas.
Located in Aleppo, Syria. Founded in 1977, designated a world international center for barley, lentils and faba beans. Serves as a regional center for *the improvement of wheat and chickpeas*; sponsored by 16 countries and international organizations.

**ICAS** Interdepartmental Committee for Atmospheric Sciences.

**ICAT** Impacts of elevated $CO_2$ levels, Climate change and Air pollutants on Tree physiology.
*European Community Project.*

**ICB** Inner Core Boundary.
*Geophysics; Oceanography; Planetary Physics.*

**ICB** International Commercial Bank.

**ICB** international competitive bidding.
appel d'offres international (AOI 1.).

**ICB** Istituto per la Cibernetica e la Biofisica.
Italian initialism of the: Institute for Cybernetics and Biophysics (Italy).

**ICBM** intercontinental ballistic missile.
missile balistique intercontinental.

**ICC** Income-Consumption Curve.

**ICC** Institute Cargo Clauses.

**ICC** integrated command and control.
commandement et contrôle intégrés.

**ICC** International Centre on Censorship.

**ICC** International Chamber of Commerce (France).

**ICC** International Color Consortium.
The ICC was founded by: Abode, Agfa-Gevaert, Apple, Kodak, Fogra, Microsoft, Silicon Graphics and Sun.
*Graphic Files.*

**ICC** International Convention Centre - Birmingham, G.B.

**ICC** International Coordinating Committee for the Presentation of Science and the Development of Out-of-School Scientific Activities.
Brussels, Belgium. Founded in 1962 to co-ordinate and promote on an international level *out-of-school scientific activities* in co-operation with other international organizations; non-governmental, UNESCO consultative status 1967.
For further details see under: **UNESCO**.

**ICC** Interstate Commerce Commission.

**ICCA** International Consumer Credit Association.

**ICCA** International Council for Commercial Arbitration.

**ICCAT** International Commission for the Conservation of Atlantic Tunas.
The ICCAT was formed in 1982. It is a coalition of over 20 nations including the United States.
*Fisheries Management.*

**ICCD** Intensified Charge-Coupled Device.
*Chemistry; Energy.*

**ICCF-7** Seventh International Conference on Cold Fusion.
The ICCF-7 was held in Vancouver, Canada on 19-24 April 1998.
*Cold Fusion Latest Developments; International Conferences.*

**ICCH** International Commodities Clearing House.

**$I_2C$=$CI_2$** Tetraiodoethylene.
Tetraiodoethylene is used mainly as a fungicide.
*Organic Chemistry.*

**ICCON** The International Commercial CONstruction Exposition.
Debut $15^{th}/18^{th}$ January 1999; held at the Dallas Convention Center - Texas, U.S.A.

**ICCREA** Istituto di Credito delle Casse Rurali Ed Artigiane.
*Italian Bank.*

**ICCRI** Istituto di Credito delle Casse di Risparmio Italiane (Italy).
Italian acronym of the: Credit Institute of Italian Savings Banks.

**ICCROM** International Centre for the Study of the

Preservation and Restoration of Cultural Property - Located in Rome, Italy.
Founded in 1959; inter-governmental institution; assembles documentation and disseminates knowledge by way of publications and meetings; coordinates research, organizes training of specialists and short courses; offers technical advice.
*Cultural Property.*
**ICCs** Interstitial Cells of Cajal.
*Medicine; Oncology; Pathology.*
**ICCV** International Conference on Computer Vision.
**ICCVAM** Interagency Coordinating Committee for the Validation of Alternative Methods (U.S.A.).
*Biological Chemistry; Biophysics; Medicine; Molecular Pharmacology; Test-tube Alternatives; Toxicological Test Methods; Veterinary.*
**ICD** Industry Council for Development (U.S.A.).
**ICD** initial communications deception.
déception des communications initiales.
**ICD** Interface Control Document.
**ICD** International Classification of Diseases.
**ICD** Intracellular Domain.
*Cellular Signaling.*
**ICDDR-B** International Centre for Diarrhoeal Disease Research - Bangladesh.
The ICDDR-B is a non-profit international medical research institution located in Dhaka, Bangladesh. It is established under a Charter of the Government of Bangladesh and conducts research and training in *diarrhoeal disease* and related areas of public health, nutrition, and reproductive health.
**ICDP** International Career Development Program.
**ICDPs** Integrated Conservation and Development Projects (Indonesia).
**Ice** (abbr.) Iceland.
**ICE** Institution of Civil Engineers.
**ICE** Interleukin-1β Concerting Enzyme.
*Apoptosis Research; Immunology.*
**ICE** Internal-Combustion Engine.
In the internal-combustion engine the combustion process occurs in the cylinders, and the combustion products serve as the thermodynamic fluid.
*Mechanical Engineering.*
**ICE** International Commerce Exchange (U.S.A.).
*Business; Finance.*
**ICE** Istituto per i Circuiti Elettronici.
*Italian Institute.*
**ICE** Istituto per il Commercio Estero (Italy).
Italian acronym of the: Foreign Trade Institute.
**ICECCS** International Conference on Engineeering of Complex Computer Systems.
**ICEI** Istituto Cooperazione Economica Internazionale.
Italian acronym of the: Institute for International Economic Cooperation.
**Icel** (abbr.) Icelandic.
Icelandic is the language of Iceland, a North Germanic language.
*Languages.*
**ICEP** Investimentos, Comércio E Turismo de Portugal.
**ICEPS** Istituto per la Cooperazione Economica Internazionale e i Problemi dello Sviluppo (Italy).
Italian acronym of the: Institute for International Economic Cooperation and Development Problems.
**ICES** Integrated Community Energy Systems.
**ICES** International Council for the Exploration of the Sea.
Copenhagen, Denmark. Founded in 1902 to promote and encourage research and investigations for the study of the sea, particularly those related to the living resources thereof; area of interest: the Atlantic Ocean and its adjacent seas, and primarily the North Atlantic.
*Sea Exploration.*
**ICESat** Ice, Cloud, and Land Elevation Satellite.
NASA's ICESat will increase measurement accuracy and extend surveys to the interior regions and to the ice-sheet margins. Uses a technology called "lidar" to map the Earth same as the one used to map Mars.
*Climate Change; Geophysics; Polar Ice-Sheets; Space Studies.*
**ICF** Inertial Confinement Fusion.
*Fast Ignition; Fusion Reactions; Physics.*
**ICF** International Congress on Fracture.
Japan. Founded in 1965; aims to foster research in the mechanics and phenomena of fracture, fatigue, and strength of materials; to promote co-operation among scientifists in the fields. Holds International Conference every four years.
*Materials Fracture & Fatigue.*
**ICF** International Consultants Foundation.
The ICF was founded in 1973. Its members are national and multinational Professional and Experienced Consultants, Authors, Researchers and Educators.
Located in Bethesda, Maryland (U.S.A.).
**ICF** Istituto Italiano di Credito Fondiario.
Italian initialism of the: Land Credit/Farm Loan Italian Institute (Italy).
**ICFAC** Inertial Confinement Fusion Advisory Committee.

**ICFAM** Istituto di Chimica Fisica Applicata ai Materiali (Italy).
Italian initialism of the Institute of Physical Chemistry applied to materials.
**ICFC** Industrial and Commercial Finance Corporation.
**ICFI** International Company for Finance and Investments.
Joint-Stock Commercial Bank - Established in 1992 - Moscow (Russian Federation).
**ICF program** Inertial Confinement Fusion program.
The Civilian ICF program at the U.S. Department of Energy.
**ICFY** International Conference on Former Yugoslavia.
Conférence internationale sur l'ex-Yougoslavie.
**ICG** Indocyanine Green.
**ICG** [new member nations] Integration and Coordination Group.
Groupe Intégration et coordination [de nouveaux pays membres].
**ICG** International Commission on Glass.
Venezia-Murano, Italy. Founded in 1933 in Venice to promote the dissemination of information on the *art, history, science and technology of glass.*
**ICG** International Coordination Group.
**ICGEB** International Center for Genetic Engineering and Biotechnology (India).
The ICGEB is located in New Delhi.
**ich** (abbr.) ichthyophthiriasis.
Ichthyophthiriasis is a fish infection due to the protozoan parasite *Ichthyophthirius Multifilis.*
*Veterinary Medicine.*
**ICHCA** International Cargo Handling Coordination Association (G.B.).
Founded in 1952 to foster economy and efficiency in the movement of goods from origin to destination.
**ICI** Imposta patrimoniale Comunale sugli Immobili.
Italian acronym meaning: Local Property Tax.
**ICI** Interassociazione della Comunicazione d'Impresa (Italy).
**ICI** International Cometary Explorer.
For further details see under: **ISEE-3**.
**ICI** Investment Company Institute.
**ICI** Istituto Culturale Italiano.
Italian acronym of the: Italian Cultural Institute.
**ICIB** International Cargo Inspection Bureau.
**ICICI** Industrial Credit and Investment Corporation (India).
ICICI is India's second-biggest financial institution.
**ICIE** Istituto Cooperativo per l'Innovazione.
*Italian Institute.*
**ICIM; Icim** Istituto di Certificazione Industriale per la Meccanica.
*Italian Institute.*
**ICIPE** International Centre of Insect Physiology and Ecology (Kenya).
The ICIPE is an international Institution headquartered in Nairobi, Kenya. It carries out advanced research in *insect science* and *pest management.* It offers high-level training to insect scientists and technologists from Africa and other developing countries.
**ICITA** International Cooperative Investigation for the Tropical Atlantic.
**ICJ** International Commission of Jurists (Switzerland).
Founded in 1952 to promote and strengthen the Rule of Law in all its practical manifestations - institutions, legislations, procedures, etc. - and to defend it through the mobilization of world legal opinion in cases of general and systematic violation of, or serious threat to, such principles of justice.
**ICJ** International Court of Justice.
**ICL** Instrument Control Language.
**ICl** Iodine Monochloride.
ICl is used mainly in analytical chemistry.
*Inorganic Chemistry.*
**ICL** Isentropic Condensation Level.
The isentropic condensation level is also known as: lifting condensation level.
*Meteorology.*
**ICL** Isocitrate Lyase.
**ICL4** Fourth Intracellular Loop of CFTR.
*Medicine.*
For further details see under: **CFTR**.
**ICLARM; I.C.L.A.R.M.** International Centre for Living Aquatic Resources Management.
**ICLAS** International Council for Laboratory Animal Science.
**ICLEI** International Council for Local Environmental Initiatives.
**ICLP** International Conference on Logic Programming.
**ICLQ** International and Comparative Law Quarterly.
**ICM** Image Color Matching.
ICM is a technology based on Eastman Kodak licence.
**ICM** Importi Compensativi Monetari.
Italian initialism meaning: Monetary Equalization Amounts.

**ICM** improved conventional munitions.
munitions classiques (ou conventionnelles) améliorées.
**ICM** Inner Cell Mass.
The inner cell mass is also known as: Embryonic Mass.
*Developmental Biology; Placental Development (mammalian); Placental Insufficiencies (mammalian); Trophectoderm; Veterinary Medical Science.*
**ICM** Institute of Chinese Medicine (Hong Kong).
Established in January 2000.
**ICM** Institute of Credit Management.
**ICM** Instituto de Ciencias del Mar.
*Spanish Institute.*
**ICM** Instruction Control Memory.
**ICM** Integrated Coverage Measurement (U.S.A.).
*Censuses; Demography.*
**ICM** Intracluster Medium.
*Astronomy; Physics.*
**ICMAREP** Interagency Committee on MARine Environmental Prediction.
**ICMF** Indian Cotton Mills Federation (India).
**ICMI** International Commission on Mathematical Instruction.
An affiliate of IMU.
For further details see under: **IMU**.
**ICMM** Istituto per la Corrosione Marina dei Metalli (Italy).
Italian initialism of the Institute for Marine Corrosion of Metals.
**ICMP** Internet Control Message Protocol.
**ICMQ** Istituto Certificazione Marchio Qualità.
*Italian Institute.*
**ICMR** Indian Council of Medical Research.
**ICMS** Interdepartmental Committee for Meteorological Services.
**ICMSE** Interagency Committee on Marine Science and Engineering.
**ICMS techniques** Intracortical Microstimulation techniques.
*Anatomy; Neurobiology; Neurophysiology; Restorative Neurology; Psychiatry.*
**ICN** Institute for the Conservation of Nature (Portugal).
**ICN** Integrated Computer Network.
**ICN**; **I.C.N.** International Council of Nurses.
**ICNAF** International Convention of the Northwest Atlantic Fisheries.
**ICO** International Coffee Organization.
**ICOD** International Center for Ocean Development (Canada).
**ICOG-8** Eighth International Conference on *Geochronology, Cosmochronology* and *Isotope Geology.*
**ICOGRADA** International Council Of GRAphic Design Associations (G.B.).
Founded in 1963 to raise the standards of graphic design and professional practice and the professional status of graphic designers to collect and exchange information relating to graphic design; to organize exhibitions and congresses and to issue reports and surveys.
**ICOLC** International Coalition Of Library Consortia.
The ICOLC was created in 1997. It consists of 42 groups which represent over 5,000 academic libraries.
**ICOMOS** International Council On MOnuments and Sites (France).
Founded in 1965 to promote the study and preservation of monuments and sites; to arouse and cultivate the interest of the authorities and people of every country in their *monuments and sites* and in their *cultural heritage*; to involve those public authorities, departments, institutions and individuals interested in the preservation and study of monuments and sites.
**ICO** International Commission on Optics.
An affiliate of IUPAP.
For further details see under: **IUPAP**.
**iCON** international Community Network.
A U.S.-based marketing Organization.
*Eco-Village Development; Organic Farming; Solid Waste Conversion; Water Incombent.*
**ICON**; **Icon** Italian Culture On the Net (Italy).
Three-year University courses on the Net that started in 1999.
**ICOS molecule** Inducible COStimulatory molecule.
*Transplant Technology.*
**ICP** 1. infrastructure capability package [obsolete - see CP].
1. paquet (ou ensemble) de capacités d'infrastructure [obsolète - voir CP].
2. inventory control point.
2. point de contrôle des stocks (PCS).
**ICP** Istituti Clinici di Perfezionamento.
*Italian Institutes.*
**ICP atomic emission** Inductively Coupled Plasma atomic emission.
*Applied Physics; Atom Technology.*
**ICP-AES** Inductively Coupled Plasma - Atomic Emission Spectroscopy / Spectrometry.
**ICPHS** International Council for Philosophy and Humanistic Studies.

**ICP-MS** Inductively-Coupled Plasma Mass Spectrometry.
**ICPP** International Conference on Parallel Processing.
**ICPR** International Conference on Pattern Recognition.
**IC process** Inverse Compton process.
*Astronomy; Astrophysics.*
**ICR** Ion Cyclotron Resonance.
**ICRA** International Conference on Robotics and Automation.
**ICRAF** International Centre for Research in Agroforestry (Kenya).
Founded in 1977 to mitigate tropical deforestation, land depletion and rural poverty through *improved agroforestry systems.*
**ICRC** International Committee of the Red Cross.
Comité international de la Croix-Rouge (CICR 1.).
**ICRF** Imperial Cancer Research Fund (G.B.).
For further details see under: **ICRT**.
**ICRI** International Coral Reef Initiative.
*Environment; Marine Ecology; Meteorology; Oceanography.*
**ICRISAT** International Crops Research Institute for the Semi-Arid Tropics (India).
Founded in 1972 as world center for genetic improvement of sorghum, millets, pigeonpea, chickpea and groundnut, and for research on the management of resources in the world's semi-arid tropics; research covers all physical and socio-economic aspects of improving the entire system of agriculture on non-irrigated land.
*Crop Research.*
**ICRP** International Commission on Radiological Protection.
*Environmental Control; Environmental Radioactivity; Radioecology.*
**ICRR** Institute for Cosmic Ray Research.
University of Tokyo, Japan.
**ICRSDT** International Committee on Remote Sensing and Data Transmission.
**ICRT** Imperial Cancer Research Technology.
The ICRT is the commercial arm of the ICRF, one of Europe's largest cancer charities (G.B.).
*Commercial Development of Discoveries.*
For further details see under: **ICRF**.
**ICS** in-country support.
soutien à l'intérieur du pays.
**I.C.S.** Indian Civil Service.
For further details see under: **I.A.S.**
**ICS** Indice di Coinvolgimento Seminari.
**ICS** Institute of Chartered Shipbrokers.
**ICS** Institute of Social Sciences (Portugal).
At Lisbon University.
**ICS** Integral Cross Section.
**ICS** Integrated Communications System.
**ICS** International Chamber of Shipping.
**ICS** International Cogeneration Society.
The ICS was founded in 1978. It serves as a focal point of industrial, utility, public, and government activities dealing with *cogeneration* and *decentralized power* with a view to obtain a more efficient use of fuel by employing heat otherwise wasted in electrical generation for industrial steam and home heating.
It is located in Washington D.C., U.S.A.
**I.C.S.** International College of Surgeons.
**I.C.S.** International Correspondence School.
**ICS** Issued Capital Stock.
*Banking; Business; Finance.*
**ICS** Istituto Centrale di Statistica (Italy).
Italian initialism of the: Central Statistics Institute.
**ICS** Istituto per il Credito Sportivo (Italy).
**ICS** Issued Capital Stock.
*Banking; Business; Finance.*
**ICSA**; **Icsa** International Computer Security Association.
**ICSB** International Council for Small Business.
The ICSB is located in St. Louis, Missouri, U.S.A.
**ICSE** International Conference on Software Engineering.
**ICSEAF** International Commission for the South-East Atlantic Fisheries.
**ICSECA Program** Intercontinental Contributions for Scientific, Educational and Cultural Activities Program.
*U.S. Federal Program* for Organizations engaging in *UNESCO-related Programs.*
For further details see under: **UNESCO**.
**ICSEM** International Commission for the Scientific Exploration of the Mediterranean Sea.
**ICSH** Interstitial-Cell-Stimulating Hormone.
**ICSI** International Commission on Snow and Ice.
**ICSI** Intracytoplasmic Sperm Injection.
*Assisted Reproductive Technology; Biology; Embryology; Gynecology; Obstetrics; Reproductive Physiology; Veterinary.*
**ICSIC** Integrated Communication System for Intensive Care.
*Medicine.*
**ICSID** International Center for the Settlement of Investment Disputes.
**ICSM** Imperial College of Science, Technology & Medicine (G.B.).
*British Colleges.*

**ICSU**; **I.C.S.U.** International Council of Scientific Unions.
ICSU was founded in 1931, succeeding the International Research Council founded in 1919, to coordinate international efforts in the different branches of science and its applications; to initiate the formation of international associations or unions deemed to be useful to the *progress of science*; to enter into relations with the governments of the countries adhering to the Council in order to promote investigations falling within the competence of the Council.
ICSU is the main international federation of *scientific societies*.

**ICT** Information and Communication Technology.

**ICT** Institute of Chemical Toxicology.
Wayne State University, Detroit, Michigan, U.S.A.

**ICT** international call for tenders.
appel d'offres international (AOI 1.).

**ICT** International Critical Tables.

**ICT** Intramolecular Charge Transfer.
*Chemistry; Molecular Electronics and Photonics; Optics and Lasers Research.*

**ICT** The airport code for Wichita, Kansas, U.S.A.

**ICTAC** International Confederation for Thermal Analysis and Calorimetry.
Jerusalem, Israel. Founded in 1968.

**ICTI** International Corporation for Trade and Industry.

**ICTP** International Center for Theoretical Physics.
The ICTP is also known as: Trieste Center.

**ICTS** Intermediate Capacity Transit System.

**ICTY** International Criminal Tribunal for the Former Yugoslavia.
Tribunal pénal international pour l'ex-Yougoslavie (TPI).

**ICU** Instruction Control Unit.
*Control Systems.*

**ICU** Intensive Care Unit.
*Medicine.*

**ICU** Intercultural Understanding.
*Linguistics.*

**ICU** International Credit Union.

**ICV** infantry combat vehicle (see also IFV).
véhicule de combat d'infanterie (VCI 1.).

**ICVA** International Council of Voluntary Agencies [relief operations].
Conseil international des agences bénévoles (CIAB) [opérations de secours].

**ICVGAN** International Committee on Veterinary Gross Anatomical Nomenclature.
Department of Veterinary Anatomy, University of Zürich, Switzerland. Founded in 1957.

**ICW** Interrupted Continuous Wave.
*Telecommunications.*

**ICWF** Interactive Computer Worded Forecast.

**ICWG** International Coordination Working Group.

**ICWWP** Interagency Committee for the World Weather Program.

**ICX**; **Icx neuron** Inferior Colliculus neuron.
*Neurobiology; Medicine.*

**ICZM** Integrated Coastal Zone Management.

**ICZN** International Commission on Zoological Nomenclature.

**ID** (abbr.) Idaho (U.S.A.).
Also: **Ida**.

**ID**; **id.** (abbr.) identification.

**ID** Identification Division.
*Computer Programming.*

**ID** Image Dissection.
*Computer Technology.*

**ID** Immediate Data.
*Computer Programming.*

**ID** Immediate Delivery; Import Duty.
*Business; Commerce.*

**ID** Income Debenture.

**ID** Incremental Dump.
*Computer Programming.*

**ID** Indice di Diffusione.

**ID** Indonesia.

**ID**; **I.D.** Infantry Division.

**ID** Initial Dose.

**ID** Inner Diameter.

**ID** Input Device.
*Computer Technology.*

**ID** Inside Diameter; Inside Dimensions; Internal Diameter.

**I.D.** Intelligence Department.

**ID** Intelligent Design.

**ID** Interim Dividend.

**ID** Intradermal.

**Ida** (abbr.) Idaho (U.S.A.).
Also: **ID**.

**IDA** Indice Di Abbandono.

**IDA** Industrial Development Agency.
*Irish Agency.*

**IDA** Initial Denial Authority.

**IDA** Institute for Defense Analyses (U.S.A.).

**IDA** Integrated Digital Access.

**IDA** Interchange of Data between Administrations.
IDA is a multiannual (1993-1998) program to support the implementation of trans-European networks for the Interchange of Data between Administrations.
*European Community Program.*

**IDA** International Development Association.

**IDA** Iron Deficiency Anemia.
*Food Sciences; Human Nutrition; Medicine.*
**IDAC** Import Duties Advisory Committee.
**IDAC** interim deployable ACCS component.
composante déployable provisoire de l'ACCS.
**IDAM** Integrated Direct Access Method.
**IDATE** Institut De l'Audiovisuel et des Télécommunications en Europe.
**I.D.B.** Illicit Diamond-Buying.
**IDB** Industrial Development Bond.
**IDB** InterAmerican Development Bank.
**IDBI** Industrial Development Bank of India.
**IDBR** Input Data Buffer Register.
**IDC** Idiopathic Dilated Cardiomyopathy.
IDC is a heritable form of heart failure.
*Cardiology; Dilated Cardiomyopathy; Medicine; Pathology.*
**IDC** Internal Data Channel.
**IDC** International Data Center (U.S.A.).
*Seismology.*
**IDCA** International Development Cooperation Agency (U.S.A.).
**IDCM** Idiopathic DCM.
The IDCM is characterized by increased ventricular chamber size and reduced pumping of the heart.
*Heart Research.*
For further details see under: **DCM**.
**IDCP** identification data combining process.
processus de combinaison des données d'identification.
**IDD** Insulin-Dependent Diabetes.
**IDD** Integrated Drug Development.
*Global Pharmaceutical Awards.*
**IDD** International Data and Development, Inc. U.S.A.
**IDD** International Direct Dialling.
**IDDM** Insulin-Dependent Diabetes Mellitus.
**IDE** Imprenditori Dirigenti Europei.
Italian acronym meaning: European Executive Entrepreneurs.
**IDE** Insulin-Degrading Enzyme.
*Diabetes (Type II); Hyperinsulinemia; Insulysin; Neuroscience.*
**IDEA** Istituto per la Ricerca e la Prevenzione della Depressione e dell'Ansia.
*Italian Institute.*
**IDEAL** International Decade for the East African Lakes.
*Biodiversity; Climatology; Geography; Limnology; Paleoclimatology; Sedimentation.*
**IDEAS** Initiative to Develop Education through Astronomy and Space Science - NASA's.
*Science Education.*
**IDEC** Industrial Development and Education Center (Greece).
**ident.** (abbr.) identification.
*Control Systems; Military Science; Psychology.*
**IDF** interceptor day fighter.
chasseur - intercepteur de jour.
**IDG** Interdialog Gap.
**IDH reaction** Isocitrate Dehydrogenase reaction.
*Advanced Materials; Basic Sciences; Cancer Research; Molecular and Cell Biology; Structural Biology.*
**IDI** Istituto Dermopatico Immacolata (Rome, Italy).
*Italian Institute.*
**IDIDAS** Interactive Digital Image Display and Analysis System.
**idl.** (abbr.) idle.
*Mechanical Engineering* - In mechanical engineering the term idle refers to an engine or a machine working without a load.
*Science* - In science the term idle means inactive.
**IDL** Interactive Data Language.
**IDL** Intermediate-Density Lipoprotein.
**I.d.L.** Ispettorato del Lavoro.
Italian initialism meaning: Inspectorate of Labor.
**I.D.L.I.** International Development Law Institute (Rome, Italy).
**IDMS** International Directory of Marine Scientists.
**IDMS** Isotope Dilution Mass Spectrometry.
**IDN** International Directory Network.
**iDNAs** information DNAs.
*Long-term storage of information.*
**IDO** Indoleamine 2,3-Dioxygenase.
**IDOE** International Decade of Ocean Exploration. From 1971 to 1980.
**I.DO.LA.** Imprese, DOnne, LAvoro.
*Projects.*
**Idonea** Impresa donne e artigianato.
*Projects.*
**idonea** The above acronym was coined using the Italian word "idonea" (feminine) which means: suitable, qualified; proper; well fitted for; eligible. At times also: capable; expert; experienced; skilled.
**IDP** Institute of Data Processing (G.B.).
**IDP** Integrated Data Processing.
*Computer Programming.*
**IDP** internally displaced person.
personne déplacée à l'intérieur du territoire.
**IDPs** Interplanetary Dust Particles.
*Cosmochemistry; Microscopy; Solar System.*
**iDQCs** intermolecular Double-Quantum Coherences.

*Biodiagnostics; Chemistry; Magnetic Resonance Research; Radiology.*

**idr.** idraulica.
Italian abbreviation meaning: hydraulics.

**idr.** idraulico.
Italian abbreviation meaning: (a) hydraulic; (m) plumber.

**IDR** Institute for Diagnostic Research, Inc.
The IDR is located in Branford, Connecticut (U.S.A.).

**IDR** Institute for Drug Research (Hungary).
IDR, located in Budapest, was created by the Hungarian Government in 1950.

**IDRO** international disaster relief operation.
opération internationale de secours en cas de catastrophe.

**Ids** Independent distributors.

**IDS** Indice di Successo.

**IDS** Internet Demographic Study.
*Race and Ethnicity Data.*

**IDS** intrusion detection system.
système de détection des intrusions.

**IDSL**; **Idsl** Internet Digital Subscriber Line.

**IDTN** Interdiction Du Territoire National.
French initialism meaning: Interdiction from the National Territory.
*Criminal Law.*

**IDU** Idoxuridine.
$C_9H_{11}IN_2O_5$ - IDU is a substance used as an antiviral agent for eye treatment.
*Pharmacology.*

**IDU** Injecting Drug User.
*AIDS Research; AIDS Vaccine; Epidemiology.*

**idu** The above acronyms were coined accidentally using the Arabic word "idu" which means in Arabic: his hand.

**IDUR** Idoxuridine.
For further details see under: **IDU** (Idoxuridine).

**IDUs** Injection Drug Users.
For further details see under: **IDU**.

**IDV sources** Intra-Day Variable sources.
*Astronomy; Astrophysics.*

**IDX** 4'-Iodo-4'-Deoxydoxorubicin.

**IE** Indo-European.
Indo-European is a family of languages that includes several languages, particularly those of the Germanic, Italic, Hellenic, Slavic and Indo-Iranian branches.
*Languages.*

**IE** Industrial Engineer.

**IE** Internationale de l'Education.
For further details see under: **EI** (Education International).

**IEA** Institute for Economic Affairs.

**IEA**; **I.E.A.** International Energy Agency.

**IEAK** Internet Explorer Administration Kit (Microsoft).

**IEBL** inter-entity boundary line.
ligne de demarcation entre entités.

**IEC** Inhibiteur d'Enzyme de Conversion de l'angiotensine.
French initialism meaning: Angiotensin Converting Enzyme Inhibitor.
*Medicine.*

**I.E.C.** Institut des Experts-Comptables et des Conseils Fiscaux (Belgium).

**IEC** International Electrotechnical Commission.

**IEC** International Executive Council (Sweden).

**IECA** International *E.Coli* Alliance.
Launched in August 2002.
*Cell Biology; E.Coli Projects.*

**IECC** International Express Couriers Conference.

**I.E.C.P.R.E.** Istituto Europeo di Chirurgia Plastica e Ricostruttiva Estetica (Italy).
*Italian Institute; Plastic Surgery.*

**IECs** International Education Centers (U.S.A.).

**IED** improvised explosive device.
dispositif explosif de circonstance.

**IEEE**; **I.E.E.E.** Institute of Electrical & Electronics Engineers (U.S.A.).

**IEF** 1. initial entry force.
1. force d'entrée initiale.
2. in-transit evacuation facility.
2. centre de transit pour évacuation sanitaire.

**IEF** Isoelectric Focusing.
Isoelectric focusing is also known as: electrofocusing.
*Physical Chemistry.*

**IEFE** Istituto di Economia delle Fonti di Energia (Italy).
Università Commerciale Luigi Bocconi, Milano, Italy.

**IEFP** Instituto do Emprego e Formação Profissional (Portugal).
*Portuguese Institute; Vocational Training.*

**IEG** information exchange group [obsolete - replaced by NG 1.].
groupe d'échange d'informations [obsolète - remplacé par NG 1.].

**IEGs** Immediate - Early Genes.
*Neuroscience; Neurobiology; Signal Transduction.*

**IEHEI** Institut Européen des Hautes Etudes Internationales (France).

**IELs** Intestinal Intraepithelial Lymphocytes.
*Medicine; Molecular Biology; Primate Research; Immunology.*

**IEM** impulsion électromagnétique.
electromagnetic pulse (EMP).
**IEN** Istituto Elettrotecnico Nazionale "G. Ferraris" (Italy).
*Italian Institute.*
**IEO** Istituto Europeo di Oncologia (Italy).
Founded in Milan in 1991. It is a Comprehensive Cancer Center with Research Laboratories fully operational since 1994/1996.
**IEP** Immunoelectrophoresis.
*Immunology.*
**IEP** International Experience Program.
**IEP** Institute of Experimental Physics.
Warsaw University.
**IEPG** Independent European Programme Group.
Groupe européen indépendant de programme (GEIP).
**IEPR** initial exercise press release.
communiqué de presse préalable à l'exercice.
**IER** information exchange requirements.
besoins (ou exigences) en matière d'échange d'informations.
**IES; I.E.S.** Illuminating Engineering Society.
**IES** Income and Expense Statement.
**IES** Institute for Environmental Studies.
*Conservation Biology; Environment; Health Services.*
**IES** Institute of Ecosystem Studies.
**IES** International Education of Students.
IES was founded in 1950 and serves 18 International Academic Centers in Europe, Asia, Australia and South America.
**IESD** Identité européenne de sécurité et de défense.
European Security and Defence Identity (ESDI).
**IESN** Institut d'Enseignement Supérieur de Namur (Belgium).
**IET** Interest Equalization Tax.
**IETF; Ietf** Internet Engineering Task Force.
Founded in 1986 in the U.S.A. It is now an international forum.
**IETF 1999** The Indian Engineering Trade Fair 1999 (India).
The 13th IETF was held in New Delhi, India on 12th/17th February, 1999.
*International Fairs.*
**IETS** Inelastic Electron Tunneling Spectroscopy.
**IEV** The airport code for Kiev, Ukraine.
**IEVS** Income Eligibility Verification Systems (U.S.A.).
**IEVs** Intracellular Enveloped Virus Particles.
*Vaccinia Virions.*
**IEX** Institute of EXport.
**IF** Inorganic Fullerene.
*Chemistry.*
**IF** Instruction Format.
*Computer Programming.*
**I.F.** Insufficient Funds.
**IF** Integrazione nella Fabbricazione.
**IF** Intendenza di Finanza.
Italian initialism meaning: Internal Revenue Office.
**If** Interface.
*Computer Programming; Computer Technology; Meteorology; Physical Chemistry.*
**IF** Iron-Formation.
**IFA** Intensive Flux Array.
**IFA** International Fiscal Association.
**IFA** International Franchise Association (Washington, D.C., U.S.A.).
**IFA** Irish Farmers' Association.
**IFABP** Intestinal Fatty Acid Binding Protein.
*Cellular Biology; Medicine; Molecular Biology; Small Intestine Markers.*
**IFAC** International Federation of Accountants.
**IFAD** International Fund for Agricultural Development.
**IFB** Institut Français de Bricolage (France).
*French Do-it-yourself Institute.*
**IFB** Invitation For Bids.
**IFBERD** Industry-Financed Business Enterprise Research & Development.
**IFBPW** International Federation of Business and Professional Women (G.B.).
IFBPW was founded in 1930. It is a Federation of organizations of business and professional women in numerous countries.
**IFC** Industrial Finance Corporation (India).
The IFC is one of India's long-term lenders.
**IFC** International Finance Corporation (U.S.A.).
The IFC is the WB's private investment arm.
For further details see under: **WB**.
**ifcad** institut de formation de cadres pour le développment (Brussels, Belgium).
*Belgian Institute.*
**IFCC; Ifcc** International Federation of Clinical Chemistry.
**iFCP** internet Fibre Channel Protocol.
**IFCS** improved fire-control system.
système de conduite de tir amélioré.
**IFCS** Intelligent Flight Control Program.
Of NASA Ames (U.S.A.).
*Aerospace Engineering.*
**IFE** Institute of Financial Education.
**IFE** Institut Français de l'Energie (France).
French acronym of the: French Energy Institute.
**IFE** International Faculty for Executives.

**IFEA** Integrated Furnace Experiment Assembly.
**IFEBS** Integrated Foreign Exchange and Banking System.
**IFEN** Institut Français de l'ENvironnement.
French acronym of the: French Environment Institute (France).
**IFER** International Foundation for Ethical Research.
**IFF** Identification, Friend or Foe.
*Engineering; Military Science.*
**IFFTU** International Federation of Free Teachers' Unions.
**IFG** Institut Français de Gestion (France).
French initialism of the: French Management Institute.
**IFG** The Interface Financial Group (U.S.A.).
Located in Florida, U.S.A., the 30-year-old organization that provides working capital for small businesses to enhance their growth.
**IFG** Interframe Gap.
**IFGO**; **I.F.G.O.** International Federation of Gynecology and Obstetrics.
**IFI** International Financial Institution.
**IFIAS** International Federation of Institutes for Advanced Study.
**IFIB** invitation for international bidding.
appel d'offres international (AOI).
**IFIP** International Federation for Information Processing.
**IFL** Indagine Comunitaria sulla Forza di Lavoro - *European Community.*
**IFL** Infralow Frequency.
*Telecommunications.*
**IFL** international frequency list.
liste des fréquences internationales.
**IFLA** International Federation of Library Associations and Institutions.
Located in The Netherlands. Founded in 1927 to promote international library co-operation in all fields of library activity, and to provide a representative body, in matters of international interest.
**IFM** instantaneous frequency measurement.
mesure de fréquence instantanée.
**IFMA** International Facility Management Association.
IFMA is a non-profit association founded in the U.S.A. in 1980.
**IFMC** Indian Forward Markets Commission.
*Indian Commission.*
**IFMO** Institut de Formation à la Maitrise d'Ouvrage (France).
*French Institute.*
**IFMSA** International Federation of Medical Students' Associations.
Amsterdam, The Netherlands. Founded in 1951 to serve medical students worldwide and to promote international co-operation; organizes professional exchanges in *preclinical* and *clinical fields* of *medicine*, and *primary health care projects.*
**IFN** International Friends of Nature (Austria).
**IFNs** Interferons.
IFNs are cytokines that, among other things, block cells viral infection. They are necessary for host defense.
*Medicine; Molecular Microbiology; Molecular Immunology; Pathology.*
**IFO** Identified Flying Object.
While the IFO is "identified", the UFO is "unidentified".
*Systematics.*
**IFOA** Istituto Formazione Operatori Aziendali.
IFOA is located at Reggio Emilia, Italy.
*Italian Institute; Vocational Training.*
**IFOLD** Istituto FOrmazione Lavoro Donne.
IFOLD is located in Sardinia, Italy.
*Italian Institute; Vocational Training for Women.*
**IFOOM**; **Ifoom** International Federation Of Organic Movements.
**IFOP** Institut Français de l'Opinion Publique.
French acronym of the: French Institute of Public Opinion (France).
**IFOR** Istituto per la FORmazione Imprenditoriale (Italy).
**IFORS** International Federation of Operational Research Societies.
Lyngby, Denmark. Founded in 1959, aims: the development of *operational research* as a unified science and its advancement in all nations of the world.
**IFP** Inkatha Freedom Party (South Africa).
**IFP** Interstitial Fluid Pressure.
*Molecular Medicine; Pathology; Radiation Oncology.*
**IFPI** International Federation of the Phonographic Industry.
The IFPI is the London-based body which represents the world's record Companies.
For further details see under: **ISC**.
**IFPM** Institut de Formation Post-scolaire de l'Industrie du Métal (Belgium).
*Belgian Institute; Metal Industry.*
**IFPMA** International Federation of Pharmaceutical Manufacturers Associations (Geneva, Switzerland).

**IFPME** Institut de Formation Permanente pour les classes Moyennes et les PME (Belgium).
*Belgian Institute.*
**IFPMM** International Federation of Purchasing and Materials Management.
**IFPRI** International Food Policy Research Institute.
The IFPRI is located in Washington D.C., U.S.A.
**IFR** Instrument Flight Rules.
*Aviation.*
**IFRB** International Frequency Registration Board.
**IFREMER** Institut Français de Recherche pour l'Exploitation de la MER (France).
French acronym of the: French Research Institute for Exploitation of the Sea.
**IFRI** Institut Français des Relations Internationales.
French acronym of the: French Institute for International Relations.
**IFS** Institutions Financières Spécialisées (France).
**IFs** Intermediate Filaments.
*Cancer Research; Cell Biology; Medicine; Molecular Genetics; Neuroscience.*
**IFS** International Foundation for Science.
**IFS** Irish Free State.
**IFS/PPPL** Institute for Fusion Studies - Princeton Plasma Physics Laboratory (U.S.A.).
**IFT** Institute of Food Technology.
**IFTF** Institute For The Future (U.S.A.).
IFTF is a California-based Research Institute.
**IFTIM** Institut de Formation aux Techniques d'Implantation et de Manutention (France).
**IFTU** International Federation of Trade Unions.
**IFU** Fraunhofer Institute for Atmospheric Environmental Research (Germany).
**IFV** infantry fighting vehicle.
véhicule de combat d'infanterie (VCI 1.).
**IFW** Institute for Production Engineering and Machine Tools (Germany).
**IFYGL** International Field Year for the Great Lakes.
**Ig** Immunoglobulin.
*Immunology.*
**i.g.** in gold.
**IG** Inspector General.
**IGAC Program** International Global Atmospheric Chemistry Program.
**IGAD** Inter-Governmental Authority on Development.
**IGADD** Inter-Governmental Authority on Drought and Development.
**IGAME** Inspecteur Général de l'Administration en Mission Extraordinaire (France).
**IGAS** Interactive General Accounting System.
**IGBMC** Institut de Génétique et Biologie Moléculaire et Cellulaire.
French initialism of the: Institute of Genetics and Molecular and Cellular Biology. IGBMC is a public research institute near Strasbourg (France).
**IGBP** International Geosphere-Biosphere Program.
University Corporation for Atmospheric Research, Boulder, Colorado, U.S.A. The IGBP is also known as: Global Change Program.
*U.S. Program.*
**IGBP/PAGES** International Geosphere-Biosphere Programme / PAst Global Changes.
For further details see under: **EPILOG**; **IMAGES** and **LGM**.
**IGC** International Genomics Consortium.
The IGC is now located in Scottsdale, Arizona, U.S.A.
*Biomedical Research; Genome Research; Gene Expression Information.*
**IGC** International Geological Congress.
**IGCC** Integrated Gasification Combined Cycle.
*Energy.*
**IGCP** International Gorilla Conservation Program.
*Conservation Biology.*
**IGCs** Interchromatin Granular Clusters.
*Cell Biology; Cytology; Developmental Biology; Molecular Biology; RNA Processing.*
**IGCs** Inter-Governmental Conferences.
**IGD** Institute of Grocery Distribution (G.B.).
**IGDOD** Inspector General - Department Of Defense (U.S.A.).
**IGE** Imposta Generale sull'Entrata.
Italian acronym meaning: purchase tax; sales tax; turnover tax.
**IGERT** Integrating Graduate Education and Research Training.
IGERT is a U.S. National Science Foundation program.
*U.S. Programs.*
**IGF** Impôt sur les Grosses Fortunes.
French initialism meaning: Wealth Tax.
**IGF** International Genetics Federation.
*Eugenics; Population Genetics.*
**IGF-1** Insulin-like Growth Factor 1.
The IGF-1 activates the protein kinase Akt.
*Biochemistry; Biology; Signal Transduction.*
**IGF2 gene** Insulin-like Growth Factor II gene.
For further details see under: **LOI**.
**IgG2a** Immunoglobulin G 2a.
*Immunology.*
**IGFBP** Insulin-like Growth Factor Binding Protein.
*Medicine.*
**IGFETs** Insulated Gate Field-Effect Transistors.

*Applied Physics; Organic Devices.*
**IGG-SF** Immunoglobulin Gene-Super Family.
**IGH** Icy Grain Halo.
*Astronomy; Optical Astronomy; Space Astronomy; Space Physics Research.*
**IGIER** Innocenzo Gasparini Institute for Economic Research.
Università Commerciale Luigi Bocconi, Milano, Italy.
**IGL** Intergeniculate Leaflet.
**IGM** Intergalactic Medium.
*Astronomy; Astrophysics; Physics; Space Sciences.*
**IGM** Interplanetary Global Model.
**I.G.M.** Istituto Geografico Militare (Italy).
Italian initialism of the: Military Survey Office.
**IgM$^+$ memory B cells** Immunoglobulin M-positive memory B cells.
*Immunology; Medicine; Rheumatology.*
**IGN**; **Ign** IBM Global Network.
**IGN** Institut Géographique National (France).
**IGOM** Integrated Global Ocean Monitoring.
**IGOSS** Integrated Global Ocean Services System.
**IGP** Igneous and Geothermal Processes.
**I.G.P.**; **IGP** Indicazione Geografica Protetta.
**IGP** Integrated Graduate Program (U.S.A.).
**IGPP** Institute of Geophysics and Planetary Physics (U.S.A.).
**IGRC** International Geodynamics Research Center.
The IGRC is based at a Russian field station outside Bishkek, Krygyzstan.
**IGRP** Interior Gateway Routing Protocol.
IGRP is a routing protocol of the distance-vector type developed by CISCO System.
**IGS** IBM Global Services.
IGS has created one of the largest Sans in the world.
For further details see under: **Sans**.
**IGS** Inner Gulf Shelf.
**IGS** Institute of Geological Sciences (G.B.).
**IGS** Internal Guide Sequence.
**IgSF domains** Immunoglobulin Superfamily domains.
*Cellular Immunology; Clinical Medicine; Molecular Sciences.*
**IGSP** International Greenland Sea Project.
**IGSS** interim geographic support system.
système provisoire de soutien géographique.
**IGT** Impaired Glucose Tolerance.
**IGT**; **I.G.T.** Institute of Gas Technology.
**IGU** International Gas Union.
**IGU** International Geographical Union.
Founded in 1922 to encourage the study of problems relating to *geography*, to promote and co-ordinate research requiring international co-operation, and to organize international *congresses* and *commissions*.
**IGY** International Geophysical Year.
The IGY is the period from July 1, 1957 to December 31, 1958.
**IH** Infectious Hepatitis.
Infectious hepatitis is also known as: hepatitis A.
*Medicine.*
**IH** Institute of Hydrology (G.B.).
**IHAs** Indian Housing Authorities (India).
**I-HAWK** Improved HAWK.
HAWK amélioré.
**IHB** International Hydrographic Bureau.
The IHB has been replaced by the IHO.
For further details see under: **IHO**.
**IHCP**; **ihcp** Institute for Health and Consumer Protection - *European Commission.*
**IHC procedures** Immunohistochemistry procedures.
*Brain Chemistry; Medical Devices; Tumor Growth.*
**IHD** International Hydrological Decade.
The IHD is the period from 1965-1974 when hydrology research was carried out by the participating nations.
**IHD** Ischemic Heart Disease.
*Cardiology.*
**IHDP** International Human Dimensions of Global Change Program.
*Programs.*
**IHE** Integrated Health Environment.
*Medicine.*
**IHEE**; **I.H.E.E.** Institut des Hautes Etudes Européennes de Strasbourg (France).
Founded in 1953. I.H.E.E. organizes post-university courses. One of them leads to the "Certificat d'études européennes". Others to the "Diplôme d'études approfondies".
**IHEP** Institute of High Energy Physics - Of the Chinese Academy of Sciences.
**IHF** Integration Host Factor.
**Ihh** Indian hedgehog.
The Ihh is a signaling molecule.
*Endocrinology; Genetics; Medicine; Molecular Biology.*
**IHL** International Humanitarian Law.
**IHM** Institute of Hydrometeorology (Albania).
**IHMO**; **I.H.M.O.** International Homeopathic Medical Organization.
**IHO** Institute of Human Origins.
*Paleoanthropology.*

**IHO** International Hydrographic Organization (Monte Carlo, Monaco).
IHO has replaced **IHB**.
**IHP** Indicated Horsepower.
*Mechanical Engineering.*
**IHS** Indian Health Service (India).
**IHS** Institut d'Hygiène Sociale (Senegal).
*Sexually Transmitted Diseases.*
**IHV** Institute of Human Virology.
**II** Indice di Innovazione.
**II** Institutional Investor.
*Business; Finance.*
**IIA** Indian Institute of Astrophysics (India).
**IIA** Institute of Internal Auditors (U.S.A.).
**IIA** Insurance Institute of America (U.S.A.).
**IIA** Istituto Internazionale dell'Agricultura.
Italian initialism of the: International Agriculture Institute (Italy).
**IIASA** International Institute for Applied Systems Analysis.
Founded in 1972 on the initiative of the U.S.A. and the then U.S.S.R.: non-governmental research organization; conducts and supports collaborative and individual research in relation to problems of modern societies arising from scientific and technological development, and undertakes its own studies into both methodological and applied research in the fields of *environment* (acid rain, etc.), *economy*, *population* (ageing, heterogeneity, dynamics), *systems and decision sciences.*
**IIB** Institut International des Brevets (France).
French initialism of the: International Institute of Patents.
**IIE** Institute for International Economics.
The IIE is based in Washington D.C. (U.S.A.).
**IIE** Institute of International Education (New York, U.S.A.).
*Study Abroad Programs.*
**IIED** International Institute for Environment and Development (G.B.).
**IIF** Institute of International Finance.
The IIF is a private sector thinktank, owned by International Banks and other financial institutions.
**IIG** Istituto per l'Imprenditoria Giovanile.
*Italian Institute.*
**III** Inter-American Indian Institute (Mexico).
**IIL** Integrated Injection Logic.
Integrated injection logic is also known as: Merged-Transistor Logic.
*Electronics.*
**IIN** Immune Idiotypic Network.
*Biological Networks.*
**IIO** Interallied Insurance Organization.
Organisation interalliée d'assurance.
**IIP** intelligent interface processor.
processeur d'interface intelligent.
**IIP** International Institute of Philosophy (France).
Founded in 1937; aims to clarify fundamental issues of *contemporary philosophy* in annual meetings, and, by several series of *publications*, to promote mutual understanding among thinkers of different traditions and cultural backgrounds.
**IIP** Investors In People.
**IIPF** International Institute of Public Finance.
**IIPLR** Insurance Institute of Property Loss Reduction (U.S.A.).
**IIPP** Islamic Iranian Participation Party.
**IIR** Istituto Internazionale del Risparmio.
Italian initialism of the: International Savings Institute (Italy).
**IIR** Istituto Italiano del Rame.
The IIR is an Italian Association for the *technological development and applications of copper.*
**IIS** International Informatics Solutions plc (G.B.).
*Applications Management; Project Software Services; Software Development.*
**IIS**; **Iis** Internet Infomation Server - Microsoft.
**IIS**; **I.I.S.** Istituto Internazionale di Statistica.
Italian initialism of the: International Statistics Institute (Italy).
**IIS** Investment Income Surcharge.
**IISI** International Iron and Steel Institute (Belgium).
Founded in 1967 to promote the welfare and interests of the world's *steel industries*; to undertake research in all aspects of steel industries; to serve as a forum for exchange of knowledge and discussion of problems relating to steel industries; to collect, disseminate and maintain statistics and information; to serve as a liaison body between international and national steel organizations.
**IISL** International Institute of Space Law.
For further details see under: **IAF**.
**II.SS.I.MA.** Iniziative Solidali di Inserimento con Modalità di Autoimprenditorialità (Italy).
*Projects.*
**IISU** Istituto Italiano per le Scienze Umane.
Italian initialism of the: Italian Institute for Human Sciences (Naples, Italy).
**IIT** Indian Institute of Technology (India).
**IITA** Information Infrastructure Technology Applications.
**IITA** International Institute of Tropical Agriculture.
Headquartered in Ibadan, Nigeria, it is a consortium of 16 centers co-sponsored by the WB; FAO; UNDP and UNEP.

For further details see under: **WB**; **FAO**; **UNDP** and **UNEP**.
**IITC** Insurance Industry Training Council.
**IITF** Information Infrastructure Task Force.
**IITS** Improved quality of service in Ionospheric Telecommunication Systems planning and operation.
*European Community Project.*
**IITs** Indian Institutes of Technology (India).
**IJAL** International Journal of American Linguistics (U.S.A.).
**IJC** International Joint Commission.
The IJC was established by the U.S. and Canadian Governments for waters management in the Great Lakes Region.
**IJCAI** International Joint Conference on Artificial Intelligence.
**IJCNN** International Joint Conference on Neural Networks.
**IJK subduction** Izu-Japan-Kurile subduction.
*Geological Sciences; Tectonics.*
**IJMS** interim JTIDS message standard.
norme de message provisoire JTIDS.
**IJN** Imperial Japanese Navy (Japan).
**IKI** Institute for Space Research (Russia).
**IKPK** Forests and Pastures Research Institute (Albania).
**IL** (abbr.) Illinois (U.S.A.).
Also: **Ill.**
**IL** Instruction Length.
The term instruction length refers to the number of bits or bytes which define an instruction.
*Computer Programming.*
**IL** Instrumentation Laboratory (Italy).
*Diagnostics & Research.*
**IL** Interactive Language; Interactive Learning.
*Computer Programming.*
**IL** Intermediate Language.
Intermediate language is also known as: Intermediate Code.
*Computer Programming.*
**IL-6** Interleukin-6.
**IL-12** Interleukin-12.
**ILA** Idaho Library Association (U.S.A.).
**ILA** Illinois Library Association (U.S.A.).
**ILA** Indian Library Association.
**ILA** Indiana Library Association (U.S.A.).
**ILA** International Law Association.
**ILA** International Leprosy Association.
**ILA** International Longshoremen's Association (U.S.A.).
**ILA** Iowa Library Association (U.S.A.).
**ILA cooperation** International Laboratory Accreditation cooperation.
**ILAR** Institute for Laboratory Animal Research (U.S.A.).
**ILAS** Improved Limb Atmospheric Spectrometer.
*Earth Science.*
**ILC** International Law Commission.
**ILC** International Legal Center.
The ILC was established in 1966.
**ILC** Irrevocable Letter of Credit.
*Business; Commerce; Finance.*
**ILCA** International Livestock Centre for Africa (Ethiopia).
Founded in 1974 as an interdisciplinary research and information centre to promote and improve *livestock production* in sub-Saharan Africa.
For further details see under: **ILRI**.
**ILCEP** Infrastructure, Logistics and Civil Emergency Planning [obsolete - now called SILCEP].
infrastructure, logistique et plans civils d'urgence [obsolète - maintenant appelé SILCEP].
**ILD** Inspection Laser Diode.
**ILD** Interaural Level Difference.
*Neurobiology.*
**ILDP** inter-look dormant period.
période d'insensibilisation entre impulsions.
**IleRS** Isoleucyl-tRNA Synthetase.
*Biochemistry; Biology; Microbiology; Translation.*
For further details see under: **tRNA**.
**ILEWG** International Lunar Exploration Working Group.
The 2nd ILEWG meeting was held in Kyoto, Japan in October 1996.
**ILFs** Isoled Lymphoid Follicles.
Hyperplasia of ILFs develops when AID is deficient.
For further details see under: **AID**.
**ILI** Institute of Life Insurance (U.S.A.).
**ILIAS** Implanted LIver Assist System.
*European Community Projetc.*
**ILITE** Iowa Library Information Teletype Exchange (U.S.A.).
**Ill.** (abbr.) Illinois (U.S.A.).
Also: **IL**.
**ILL** Institut Laue-Langevin.
The ILL located in Grenoble, France, is a powerful source of neutrons for research.
*Nuclear Reactors.*
**ILLINET** Illinois Library and Information Network.
**ILMH** Institut Libre Marie Haps (Belgium).
*Language Institute.*

**ILMI** Istituto Lombardo per la Medicina Iperbarica (Italy).
Italian acronym of the: Lombard Institute for Hyperbaric Medicine.
*Pharmacology.*
**ILO** International Labour Organization (Switzerland).
Founded in 1919, became specialized Agency of UN in 1946; aims to build a code of *international labour law* and practice, is concerned with the safety, health and social security of workers and provides technical experts where needed by member countries, sets out to improve labour conditions, raise living standards and promote productive employment in all countries.
**ILOR** Imposta LOcale sui Redditi.
Italian abbreviation meaning: Local Income Tax.
**ILPS** International Logic Programming Symposium.
**ILQ** International Law Quarterly.
*Publication.*
**IL-1R** Interleukin-1 Receptor.
*Human Genome Sciences; Pathology.*
**ILR** International Law Reports.
**ILRAD** International Laboratory for Research on Animal Diseases (Kenya).
Founded in 1973. Research programmes on control of *trypanosomiasis* and *theileriosis*.
For further details see under: **ILRI**.
**ILRI** International Livestock Research Institute.
ILRI incorporates the resources of the ILRAD and ILCA.
For further details see under: **ILRAD** and **ILCA**.
**ILS** Instrument Landing System.
*Aviation.*
**ILs** Interlanguages.
*Linguistics.*
**ILSA**; **Ilsa** Iran-Libya Sanctions Act.
**ILSI** International Life-Sciences Institute.
**ILSP** integrated logistics support plan [NACMO].
plan de soutien logistique intégré [NACMO].
**ILSS** Interlaminar Shear Strength.
*Materials Science.*
**ILT** Institute for Low-Temperature Physics and Engineering.
The ILT is located in Kharkov, Ukraine.
**ILTAB** International Laboratory for Tropical Agriculture and Biotechnology (U.S.A.).
ILTAB was originally based in La Jolla, California. Moved to the Donald Danforth Plant Science Center in St. Louis (U.S.A.).
**ILT model** Interlayer Tunneling model.
*Condensed Matter Physics.*
**ILU** Institute of London Underwriters (G.B.).
**IM** Immunoassay.
*Immunology.*
**IM** Imperia, Italy.
**I.M.** Imperial Measure.
**IM** Information Management.
*Telecommunications.*
**IM** Ingénieur Mécanicien.
French initialism meaning: Mechanical Engineer.
**IM** Insoluble Matrix.
**IM** Instruction Modification.
The instruction modification actually consists of an instruction change, so that the computer will carry out a different operation when the instruction is repeated.
*Computer Programming.*
**IM** Insuffisance Mitrale or Régurgitation Mitrale.
French initialism meaning: Mitral Insufficiency / Mitral Regurgitation.
*Medicine.*
**IM** Intermediate Modulus.
**IM** Intermodulation.
**IM** Interrupt Mask.
IM is also known as: Mask Register.
*Computer Technology.*
**I.M.** Intramuscularly.
**IM** Isle of Man.
**IM$^3$** Institute for Multifunctional Macromolecular Materials.
At Stevens Institute of Technology, New Jersey, U.S.A.
**IMA** implementation management authority [ACCIS].
autorité chargée de la gestion de la mise en œuvre [ACCIS].
**IMA** Indian Military Academy (India).
**IMA** Institute of Molecular Agrobiology (Singapore).
*Agricultural Bioiogy; Molecular Agrobiology; Molecular Biology.*
**IMA** Istituto per la Matematica Applicata.
*Italian Institute.*
**IMAG** Istituto di Studi chimico-fisici di Macromolecole Sintetiche e Naturali.
*Italian Institute.*
**I.M.A.G.E.**; **IMAGE Consortium** Integrated Molecular Analysis of Genomes and their Expression Consortium (U.S.A.).
*cDNA Clone Sets; Microarray Studies.*
**IMAGES** Integrated Modular Avionics General Executive Software - *European Community.*
**IMAGES program** International MArine Global Change Study program.

Of IGBP/PAGES.
For further details see under: **EPILOG**; **IGBP/PAGES** and **LGM**.
**IM&T** Information Management and Technology.
**IMAO** Inhibiteur de la Mono-Amine Oxydase.
French acronym meaning: Monoamine Oxidase Inhibitor.
*Medicine; Pharmacology.*
**IMARPE** Instituto del MAR del Perù (Peru).
**IMAT** independent maritime analysis team.
équipe indépendante d'analyses maritimes.
**IMAZON** Instituto do Homen e Meio Ambiente da Amazônia (Brazil).
**IMB** Institute of Molecular Biotechnology.
The Institute of Molecular Biotechnology was created in 1993. Its goal is to promote the development of new means to improve biotechnology in the $21^{st}$ century.
*Biology; Economic Development; Technology.*
**IMBB** Institute of Molecular Biology and Biochemistry (Canada).
**IMBB** Institute of Molecular Biology and Biotechnology (Greece).
**IMB detector** Irvine-Michigan-Brookhaven detector.
**IMBHs** Intermediate-Mass Black Holes.
*Astrophysics.*
**IMBN** International Molecular Biology Network for Asia and the Pacific Rim.
The IMBN was launched at the beginning of 1997 at a meeting in Tokyo, Japan.
**IMBRO** Investment Management Regulatory Organization (G.B.).
**IMC** instrument meteorological conditions.
conditions météorologiques de vol aux instruments.
**IMC** International Marine Centre (Oristano, Italy).
**IMC** International Music Council (France).
Founded in 1949 under the auspices of UNESCO to foster the exchange of musicians, music (written and recorded), and information; to support contemporary composers, traditional music, and young professional musicians; to foster appreciation of music by the public.
For further details see under: **UNESCO**.
**IMCE** Intercontinental Space Station Management and Cost Evaluation.
**IMCL content** Intramyocellular Lipid content.
*Cellular and Molecular Physiology; Diagnostic Radiology; Epidemiology.*
**IMCO** Intergovernmental Maritime Consultative Organization - U.N.
**IMD** India Meteorological Department.
*Climate Forecasting.*
**IMDG** International Maritime Dangerous Goods (Code).
(Code) international du transport maritime de marchandises dangereuses.
**IME** Institute of Makers of Explosives (U.S.A.).
*Bomb Detection; Chemistry; Explosives; Forensics; Tagging Schemes.*
**IME**; **I.M.E.** Institution of Mechanical Engineers.
Also: **IMech.E**.
**IME** Istituto Monetario Europeo - E.C.
Italian acronym of the: European Monetary Institute.
**iMED** istituto per il MEDiterraneo (Italy).
**IMEKO** International Measurement Confederation (Hungary).
Founded in 1958, promotes the international exchange of scientific and technical information relating to developments in *measuring techniques*, *instrument design* and manufacture and in the application of instrumentation in scientific research and industry; promotes cooperation among scientists and engineers in the field, and with other international organizations; organizes congresses, symposia, etc.
**IMEO**; **I.M.E.O.** Istituto Italiano per il Medio ed Estremo Oriente (Italy).
Italian acronym of the: Italian Institute for the Middle and Far East.
**IMER** Institute for Marine Environmental Research (G.B.).
**Imer** Istituto di mediocredito regionale.
*Italian Bank.*
**IMF** Initial Mass Function.
*Astronomy; Astrophysics; Galaxy Evolution.*
**IMF** International Monetary Fund.
*International Business.*
**IMG** Institute of Molecular Genetics.
Of the Czech Academy of Sciences.
**IMG** Interferometric Monitor for Greenhouse Gases.
An Instrument aboard ADEOS.
For further details see under: **ADEOS**.
**IMG** International Management Group [for reconstruction in Bosnia].
Groupe international de gestion [pour la reconstruction en Bosnie].
**IMGG** Institute of Marine Geology and Geophysics (Former Soviet Union).
**IMI** International Meteorological Institute.
**IMI** Istituto Mobiliare Italiano (Italy).
Italian acronym of the: Italian Financing Institute.
**IMINT** imagery intelligence.

renseignement (par) imagerie.
**IMIS** Integrated Management Information System.
**IML-1** International Microgravity - Laboratory-1.
*Space Research.*
**imm.** (abbr.) immediate.
**IMM** Institute of Mathematical Modelling.
Of the Technical University of Denmark.
**IMM** integrated material management.
gestion intégrée des matériels.
**IMM** Intelligent Memory Manager.
**IMM** International Monetary Market.
**IMM** International Money Management.
**IMME 1998** International Mining Machinery Exhibition (India).
The IMME was held in India (New Delhi) on 26-29 October 1998.
**IMMM** International (Conference on) Microcomputer Minicomputers Microprocessors.
**IMMP** Integrated Multimedia Project.
*European Community Project.*
**IMMS** International Material Management Society.
**immun.** (abbr.) immunity.
*Immunology; Metallurgy.*
**immun.** (abbr.) immunization.
*Immunology.*
**IMnet** Interministry Network.
*Computer Networks.*
**IMO** In My Opinion.
**IMO** International Maritime Organization.
The IMO is a UN-backed body which regulates the World's shipping.
**IMO** International Meteorological Organization.
**IMO** International Money Order.
**I.M.O.** Istituto di Medicina Omeopatica (Italy).
Italian acronym of the: Institute for Homeopathic Medicine.
**IMP** Imager for Mars Pathfinder.
*Aeronomy; Applied Physics; Chemistry; Geology; Geophysics; Planetary Exploration; Scientific Instruments.*
For further details see under: **APXS** and **ASI/MET**.
**imp.** (abbr.) import; importer.
**IMP** Industry Market Potential.
**IMP** initial military programme.
programme militaire initial.
**IMP** Inosine Monophosphate.
**IMP** Institute of Molecular Pathology (Vienna, Austria).
**IMPACT** Interactions between Microbial inoculants and resident Populations in the rhizosphere of Agronomically important Crops in Typical soils - *European Community.*
**IMPG** International Press Marketing Group.
**imposs.** (abbr.) impossible.
**IMPREP** implementation report.
compte rendu de mise en œuvre.
**I.M.P.R.E.S.A.** Itinerari Multiculturali per la Progettazione, Realizzazione E Sviluppo di Attività imprenditoriali.
*Projects.*
**IM programs** Inspection and Maintenance Programs.
**IMPROVE** Interagency Monitoring of PROtected Visual Environments.
**IMQ** Istituto del Marchio di Qualità (Italy).
Italian initialism of the: Quality Mark Institute.
**iMQCs** intermolecular Multiple-Quantum Coherences.
*Biodiagnostics; Chemistry; Magnetic Resonance Research; Radiology.*
**IMR** Institute of Marine Research (Norway).
**IMRA** Institute of Minoru Research Advancement (Japan).
The IMRA is owned by an affiliate of Toyota.
**IMRE** Institute of Materials Research and Engineering (Singapore).
**IMRG** Interactive Media in Retail Group.
A forum of electronic commerce. IMRG represents over 200 retailers in 20 countries.
**IMRO** Investment Management Regulatory Organization (G.B.).
**IMRT** Intensity-Modulated Radiotherapy.
*Radiotherapy Treatments.*
**IMS** Information Management System.
**IMS** Ion Mobility Spectrometry.
A detection technique for the chemical identification of explosive materials.
**IMS** Institute of Museum Services (U.S.A.).
**IMS** Intermembrane Space.
**IMS** International Magnetosphere Study.
**IMS** International Metallographic Society.
**IMS** International Military Staff.
État-major militaire international (EMI).
**IMS** International Monitoring System.
The IMS, which is a 321-station network of detectors, was launched in 1995 and will be fully working by 2007.
*Monitoring Stations; Seismology.*
**IMS** Ion Mobility Spectrometer.
The ion mobility spectrometer is an analytical device which operates at atmospheric pressure and may be used for many environmental and other problems.
**IMSAT** imagery satellite.
satellite photographique.

**IMSL** International Mathematics and Statistics Library.
**IMSTI** Institute of Marine Scientific and Technological Information (China).
**IMT** Industrial and Materials Technologies.
**IMTC** International Multimedia Teleconferencing Consortium.
The IMTC is the industry co-ordinating body.
**IMTs** Innovation Management Techniques - *European Community.*
**IMTs** Innovation Management Tools.
**IMU** Inertial Measurement Unit.
**IMU** International Mathematical Union.
**IMV** Intermittent Mandatory Ventilation.
**IMVIC tests** Indole, Methylred, Voges - Proskauer, and Citrate tests.
IMVIC tests are biochemical tests.
*Microbiology.*
**I.M.V.S.** Institute of Medical & Veterinary Science (Australia).
**in.**; **in** inch.
*Metrology.*
**in.** (abbr.) income.
**IN** (abbr.) Indiana (U.S.A.).
Also: **Ind**.
**In** The chemical symbol for Indium.
Indium is a metallic element having the atomic number 49, and a melting point of 156°C.
*Chemistry.*
Indium is used mainly in precious-metal alloys for dentistry and jewelry.
*Metallurgy.*
**IN** 1. India.
1. Inde.
2. inertial navigation.
2a. navigation inertielle.
2b. navigation par inertie.
**IN** Instalment Note.
*Business; Commerce; Finance.*
**INA** Institution of Naval Architects (U.S.A.).
**INA** Institut National Agronomique (France).
**INA** Institut National de l'Audiovisuel.
*French Institute.*
**INA** International Neurological Association.
**INA** Istituto Nazionale Assicurazioni (Italy).
**INAF** Istituto Nazionale di Astrofisica (Italy).
Italian acronym of the: National Institute of Astrophysics.
Headquartered in Rome. Approved by the Government in July 1999. Fully operational summer 2000. It embraces all of Italy's 12 observatories.
**INAIL** Istituto Nazionale per l'Assicurazione contro gli Infortuni sul Lavoro.
Italian abbreviation of the: National Insurance Institute for Industrial Accidents.
**INAMI** Institut National d'Assurance Maladie-Invalidité.
*Belgian Institute.*
**INAO** Institut National des Appellations d'Origine (France).
**INAPE** Instituto NAcional de Pesca (Uruguay).
**InAs** Indium Arsenide.
Metallic crystals, having a melting point of 943°C.
*Inorganic Chemistry.*
**INAS** inertial navigation and attack system.
système de navigation par inertie et d'attaque.
**INAS** Interbank National Anthorization System (U.S.A.).
**INBEL** INstitut BELge d'Information et de Documentation.
*Belgian Institute.*
**INBio** National Institute for Biodiversity (Costa Rica).
*Biodiversity; Taxonomy; Tropical Ecology.*
**inc.** (abbr.) including; inclusive (of); income; incorporate; increase.
**Inc.** (abbr.) Incorporated.
**INC** International Negotiating Committee.
**INC** Interstitial Nucleus of Cajal.
*Midbrain Control; Neurobiology; Physiology; Torticollis.*
**INCAP**; **I.N.C.A.P.** Institute of Nutrition for Central America and Panama.
**INCB** International Narcotics Control Board.
Vienna-based, the INCB monitors compliance with U.N. drug control treaties.
**INCE** INiziativa Centro-Europea.
**INCE** Istituto Nazionale di Credito Edilizio (Italy).
**INCE** University Institute for Exact Sciences (Dominican Republic).
**INCINC** International Copyright Information Centre.
The INCINC, located in Washington D.C., U.S.A, was founded in 1970.
**incl.** (abbr.) including; inclusive.
**$InCl_3$** Indium Chloride.
*Inorganic Chemistry.*
**INCO** INtegrated Communications Officer.
**INCO** INternational Cocoa Organization.
**INCRA** Brazil's Land Reform Agency.
**Ind.** (abbr.) Independent.
**ind.** (abbr.) index.
**Ind.** India.
Also: IN.

**Ind.** Indian (Informal).
Indian includes the indigenous languages of the American Indians.
*Languages.*
**Ind.** (abbr.) Indiana (U.S.A.).
Also: **IN**.
**IND** The airport code for Indianapolis, Indiana, U.S.A.
**IND.** India's international vehicle-registration letters.
**ind.** (abbr.) indicator.
*Analytical Chemistry; Aviation; Computer Technology; Electronics.*
**ind.** (abbr.) industrial.
Also: **indus**.
**Ind.** (abbr.) Industry.
**INDA** Investigational New Drug Applications.
DTP Program of the NCI, U.S.A.
*Therapeutics Program.*
For further details see under: **DTP** and **NCI**.
**indiv.** (abbr.) individual.
**indn.** (abbr.) indication.
**INE** Industria Nazionale Elettrodi (Italy).
*Electrodes.*
**INE** National Institute of Ecology (Mexico).
INE is the research arm of the Mexican Ministry of the *Environment* and *Natural Resources.*
**INEEL** Idaho National Engineering and Environmental Laboratory (U.S.A.).
**INERIS** National Institute for Industrial Environment and Risks (France).
**INET** Institute of Nuclear Energy Technology (Beijng).
**INETI** Instituto Nacional de Engenharia e Tecnologia Industial (Lisbon, Portugal).
**INETOP** Institut National d'Etudes du Travail et d'Orientation Professionnelle (France).
*French Institute; Vocational Guidance.*
**inf.** (abbr.) infantry; infirmary; information; infusion.
**INF** intermediate-range nuclear forces.
forces nucléaire de portée intermédiaire (FNI).
**inFire** Consortium of fire protection / fire science libraries and infornnation Centres.
**INFIS** Indonesian Aquatic Sciences and Fisheries Information System.
**INFM** Istituto Nazionale per la Fisica della Materia.
*Italian Institute.*
**INFN** Istituto Nazionale di Fisica Nucleare.
Italian initialism of the: National Institute of Nuclear Physics.
*High-energy Physics Research.*
**info.** (abbr.) inform; information.
**INFO OP** information operation.
opération d'information.
**INFOSEC** (electronic) information security.
sécurité des informations (électroniques).
**INFOWIN** multimedia INFOrmation WINdow for national hosts.
*European Community Project.*
**INFREP** Institut National de Formation et de Recherche sur l'Education Permanente.
*French Institute.*
**INFUB** INdustrial FUrnaces and Boilers.
**ing.** ingegnere; ingegneria.
Italian abbreviation meaning: engineer; engineering.
**InGaAs cells** Indium Gallium Arsenide cells.
InGaAs cells were originally developed as the bottom subcell of a record-setting tandem cell. In this design, a top cell captures the energy of shorter-wavelength radiation. Longer wavelengths pass through the top cell to be captured by a bottom cell with a lower band gap.
*Indium Gallium Arsenide cells.*
**ing.chim.** ingegnere chimico; ingegneria chimica.
Italian abbreviation meaning: chemical engineer; chemical engineering.
**ing.civ.** ingegnere civile; ingegneria civile.
Italian abbreviation meaning: civil engineer; civil engineering.
**INGEBI** Institute of Research in Genetic Engineering and Molecular Biology (Brazil).
**ing.ind.** ingegnere industriale; ingegneria industriale.
Italian abbreviation meaning: industrial engineer; industrial engineering.
**Ingl.** inglese.
Italian abbreviation meaning: English.
**INH** Isonicotinic acid Hydrazide.
Isoniazid [Isonicotinic acid Hydrazide] is a widely used antitubercular drug administered orally or intermuscularly.
*Pharmacology.*
**inher.** (abbr.) inheritance.
**INHS** Illinois Natural History Survey (U.S.A.).
**INI** Istituto Nazionale dell'Informazione.
Italian acronym of the: National Information Institute.
**INIDN** Indonesian National Information and Documentation Network.
**INIS** International Nuclear Information System.
**init.** (abbr.) initial.
**init.** (abbr.) initialize.
*Computer Programming.*

**INJEP** Institut National de la Jeunesse et de l'Education Populaire.
*French Institute.*

**INL** Inner Nuclear Layer.
*Biological Timing; Medicine; Neurobiology; Physiology.*

**INM** Inner Nuclear Membrane.

**INMARSAT** International Mobile Satellite Organization [formerly called International Maritime Satellite Organization].
Organisation internationale de télécommunications mobiles par satellite [anciennement appelée Organisation internationale des satellites maritimes].

**INMG** National Institute of Meteorology and Geophysics (Portugal).

**INN**; **I.N.N.** Istituto Nazionale della Nutrizione.
The INN is located in Rome, Italy.
*Italian Institute.*

**I.N.N.A.** Istituto Nazionale del Nastro Azzurro.
Italian acronym of the: National Blue Ribbon Institute (Italy).
*Military.*

**INO** Institute for Naval Oceanography.
The Institute for Naval Oceanography is located at the Stennis Space Center near Bay St. Louis Mississippi, U.S.A. and is sponsored by the U.S. Navy.

**iNOS** inducible Nitric Oxide Synthase.
*Biochemistry; Mitochondria; Structural Biology.*

**INOXSAFE** Establishment of anti-crash / anti-intrusion solutions based on high-strength stainless steels to increase the passive safety of vehicles - *European Community.*

**InP** Indium Phosphide.
Indium phosphide is a brittle, metallic mass, having a melting point of 1070°C. It is used mainly in semiconductors, and solar cells.
*Inorganic Chemistry.*

**InP** Indium Phosphide.
Indium Phosphide resists the degrading effects of the intense radiation found in space. When paired with gallium indium arsenide in a tandem cell, this material is also an excellent choice for terrestrial concentrator systems. Indium phosphide is 50% more resistant to radiation damage than silicon and about 15% more resistant than gallium arsenide.
*Tandem cells; Terrestrial Concentrator Systems.*

**INPA** Instituto Nacional de Pesquisas de Amazônia (Brazil).
*Tropical Silviculture.*

**I.N.P.A.P.**; **INPAP** Istituto Nazionale Previdenza Amministrazioni Pubbliche (Rome, Italy).

**INPDAI** Istituto Nazionale di Previdenza dei Dirigenti di Aziende Industriali (Italy).
Italian initialism of the: Social Security Institute for Industrial Executives.

**INPFC** International North Pacific Fisheries Commission.

**INPGI** Istituto Nazionale di Previdenza dei Giornalisti Italiani (Italy).
Italian initialism of the: Social Security Institute for Italian Professional Journalists.

**INPI** Institut National de la Propriété Industrielle.
*French Institute.*

**I.N.P.I.** Istituto Nazionale per la Prevenzione degli Infortuni (Italy).
Italian acronym meaning: National Institute for the Prevention of Accidents.

**INPS** Istituto Nazionale della Previdenza Sociale (Italy).

**INQUA** International Union for Quaternary Research.
Founded in 1928; field of activities:.
*Geology; Geography; Prehistory; Paleontology; Palynology; Pedology.*

**INR** Institute of Nuclear Research (Moscow).

**INR** INsulin Receptor.
*Biochemistry; Cancer Research; Molecular Biology.*

**INRA** Institut National de la Recherche Agronomique.
*French Institute; Agronomy.*

**INRAN** Istituto Nazionale di Ricerca per gli Alimenti e la Nutrizione (Italy).
*Food & Nutrition Research.*

**INRCA**; **Inrca** Istituto Nazionale di Ricerca sugli Anziani.
*Italian Institute.*

**INRIA**; **Inria** Institut National de Recherche en Informatique et en Automatique (France).

**INS** Immigration and Naturalization Service (U.S.A.).

**INS** 1. improved NADGE station.
1. station NADGE améliorée.
2. inertial navigation system.
2a. système de navigation à inertie.
2b. système de navigation par inertie.

**INS** Inelastic Neutron Scattering.
*Chemical Engineering; Materials Science.*

**INS** Institut National des Statistiques.
*Belgian Institute; Statistics.*

**ins.** (abbr.) insurance; insured.

**INS** International News Service.

**INSA** Institut National des Sciences Appliquées.
*French Institute.*

**InSAR** Synthetic Aperture Radar Interferometry.
*Geophysics and Planetary Physics; Oceanography.*

**INSAT** (abbr.) INdian geostationary SATellite.

**InSb** Indium Antimonide.
InSb is used mainly in computer applications.
*Inorganic Chemistry.*

**insce.** (abbr.) insurance.
Also: **ins**.

**INSD** International Nucleotide Sequence Databases.
A 15-years international collaboration between: DDBJ; EMBL and GenBank.
For further details see under: **DDBJ**; and **EMBL**.

**INSDC** Indonesian National Scientific Documentation Centre.

**INSDOC** Indian National Scientific DOcumentation Centre (India).

**Insd.Val.** (abbr.) Insured Value.

**INSEA** International Society for Education through Art (Sweden).
Founded in 1951 to unite art teachers throughout the world, to exchange information and co-ordinate research into art education.

**INSEE** Institut National de la Statistique et des Etudes Economiques.
*French Institute.*

**INSERM** Institut National de la Santé et de la Recherche Médicale (France).
French acronym of the: National Institute of Health and Medical Research.

**INSIG** Institut de Formation Interbancaire.
*French Institute.*

**Insp.** (abbr.) Inspector.

**INRO** International Natural Rubber Organization.

**INSRP** Interagency Nuclear Safety Review Panel.

**INSs** Isolated Neutron Stars.
INSs in our galaxy are believed to be active for a small fraction of their lifetime of $\sim 10^{10}$ years.
*Astrophysics; Astronomy.*

**inst.** (abbr.) instalment / installment.
Also: **instl.**
*Banking; Business; Finance.*

**inst.** (abbr.) instant.

**instl.** (abbr.) instalment / installment.
Also: **inst**.

**INSTM**; **Instm** (Consorzio) Interuniversitario Nazionale per la Scienza e la Tecnologia dei Materiali.

**instr.** (abbr.) instruction; instructor.

**instr.** (abbr.) instrument.
*Acoustical Engineering; Aviation; Engineering; Mechanical Devices.*

**INSURED** INtegrated Satellite UMTS Real Environment Demonstrator.
*European Community Project.*

**int.** (abbr.) intelligence; intercept; interest; interim; interior; intermediate; internal; international; interpreter; intersection; interval.

**INT** Istituto Nazionale Trasporti.
Italian acronym of the: National Transport Institute (Italy).

**INTA** INternational Trademark Association.

**INTAF** international affairs.
affaires internationales.

**INTAMEL** INTernational Association of MEtropolitan City Libraries (Switzerland).
Founded in 1967 to encourage *international co-operation between large city libraries*, and in particular the exchange of books, exhibitions, staff and information and participation in the work of the International Federation of Library Associations.

**INTAP** Interoperability Technology Association for information Processing.

**INTAS** (abbr.) INTernational ASsociation.
For the promotion of cooperation with scientists from the independent states of the Former Soviet Union.
*European Community.*

**$In_2Te_3$** Indium Telluride.
Indium Telluride is used in semiconductors.
*Inorganic Chemistry.*

**INTEGER** International Neural Tube Embryology Genetics and Epidemiology Research.

**INTELCAM** International TELecommunications Organization of CAMeron (Cameron).

**INTELSAT Consortium** INternational TELecommunications SATellite Consortium.

**inter.** (abbr.) intermediate.

**inter.** (abbr.) interrogative.

**INTERASMA** International Association of Asthmology (France).
Founded in 1954 to advance medical knowledge of bronchial asthma and allied disorders.

**INTERMAC** International Association of Merger and Acquisition Consultants.
The INTERMAC is located in Dallas, Texas, U.S.A.

**intermed.** (abbr.) intermediate.
*Chemistry.*

**Internet** (abbr.) International network.

**INTER.POL** (abbr.) INTERnational POLice.

**INTERSIND** Sindacato delle Aziende a Partecipazione Statale (Italy).

Italian abbreviation of the: Union of State-Controlled Industries.
**Intex** International buyers' exhibition.
**INTREP** intelligence report.
compte rendu de renseignement.
**INTREQ** intelligence request.
demande de renseignement.
**intl.** (abbr.) international.
Also: **int**.
**Int. L.R.** International Law Reports.
**intr.** (abbr.) introduction.
**in trans.** in transit.
**intra(d)** (abbr.) introduced; introduction; introductory.
**INTSUM** intelligence summary.
synthèse de renseignement.
**intsv.** (abbr.) intensive.
**inv.** (abbr.) invented; inventor.
**inv.** inventory.
*Commerce.*
**inv.** invoice.
*Commerce.*
**INVIM** Imposta locale sull'Incremento di Valore degli IMmobili.
Italian abbreviation meaning: Local Tax on the Increased Value of Immovable Property.
**INVITEX** invitation to a (national) exercise.
invitation à un exercice (national).
**IO** Immediate Order.
*Business; Commerce; Finance.*
**IO** Institut Océanographique (France).
French initialism of the: Oceanographic Institute.
**IO** 1. international organization.
1. organisation internationale (OI).
2. interoperability objective.
2. objectif d'interopérabilité.
**IOBC** International Organization for Biological Control of Noxious Animals and Plants (Switzerland).
Founded in 1956 to promote and co-ordinate research on biological and integrated control of *pests* and *weeds*.
**IOBM** In Ocean By Mistake.
**IOC** Immediate-Or-Cancel.
**IOC** Indirect Operating Costs.
**IOC** In-Orbit checkout and Calibration.
**IOC** Intergovernmental Oceanographic Commission.
**IOC** International Olympic Committee.
**IOCS** Input / Output Control System.
**IOCU** International Organization of Consumer Unions (G.B.).
**IOD**; **IoD** Institute Of Directors (G.B.).
**IODE** International Oceanographic Data and information Exchange.
**IODP** Integrated ODP.
The IODP will take over from the 19-year old ODP, on 1st October, 2003.
For further details see under: **ODP** and **ECORD**.
**IOE** International Organization of Employers (Geneva, Switzerland).
**IOF** International Oceanographic Foundation.
**IOFCs** International Offshore Financial Centres.
**IOI** Indication Of Interest.
*Business; Commerce; Finance.*
**IOLR** Israel Oceanographic and Limnological Research (Israel).
**IOM** Institute of Medicine (U.S.A.).
**IOM** International Organization for Migration.
**IoM** Isle of Man.
**I-O.**; **I/O mortgage** Interest-Only mortgage.
**ION**; **Ion** Integrated On-demand Network.
**ION** International Optical Network (U.S.A.).
*U.S. Networks.*
**IONS** Institute of Oceanography (Nova Scotia, Canada).
**IOOS** Integrated Ocean Observing System (U.S.A.).
*Oceanography; Ocean Research.*
**IOP** Intensive Observation Period.
**IOP** Intraocular Pressure.
*Physiology.*
**IOS** Institute of Oceanographic Sciences (G.B.).
**IOS** Institute of Ocean Sciences (Canada).
**IOS** Inter-Organizations Section.
Section interorganisations (SIO).
**IOSCO** International Organization of Securities COmmissions.
**IOSDL** Intitute of Oceanographic Sciences - Deacon Laboratory (G.B.).
**IOSS** Inter-Organizations Study Section on Salaries & Prices.
Section interorganisations d'étude des salaires et des prix.
**IOTF** International Obesity Task Force.
**I/O Time** Input /Output Time.
*Computer Science.*
**IoW**; **I.O.W.** Isle of Wight.
**IP** Immunoprecipitation.
**IP** Incentive Pay.
**IP** Initial Point.
*Cartography; Ordnance.*
**IP**; **I.P.** Institute of Petroleum.
**IP** Institut Pasteur.
**IP** Integrated Project.
**IP** Intermediate Pressure.
**IP** Internet Protocol.

**IP** Ionization Potential.
IP is also known as: Ion Potential.
*Atomic Physics.*
**IP** Iron Pipe.
**IP** Issued Price.
*Business; Finance.*
**IP$_3$** Inositol triphosphate.
**IPA** Institute of Practitioners in Advertising.
**IPA** Instruction and Practical Advice.
**IPA** Insurance and Pensions Authority (G.B.).
**IPA** Intergovernmental Personnel Act (U.S.A.).
**IPA** International Phonetic Alphabet.
**IPA** International Phonetic Association (G.B.).
Founded in 1886 to promote the scientific study of *phonetics* and its applications.
**IPAA; I.P.A.A.** International Psychoanalytical Association.
**IPAB** Information Technology Association of America (U.S.A.).
**IPAB** International Program for Antarctic Buoys.
**IPACE** intelligence policy ACE.
politique du CAE en matière de renseignement.
**IPA features** Instrument Performance Assessment features.
**IPAI** International Primary Aluminium Institute.
**IPAL** Iowa Private Academic Library (U.S.A.).
**IPAnet** Investment Promotion Network.
World Bank Group.
**IPAR** improved pulse acquisition radar.
radar d'acquisition à impulsions amélioré.
**IPASS** Interagency Panel on Advanced Science Security (U.S.A.).
**IPB** intelligence preparation of the battlefield.
préparation du champ de bataille pour le renseignement.
**IPBI** International Paper Board Industry (G.B.).
**IPC** 1. Industrial Planning Committee.
1. Comité de planification industrielle.
2. initial planning conference.
2. conférence de planification initiale.
**IPCC** Intergovernmental Panel on Climate Change.
Sponsored by the U.N.
*Anthropogenic Global Warming; Climatology; Greenhouse Science.*
For further details see under: **U.N.**
**IPCC** International Petroleum Clearing Corporation.
**iPCR** inverse PCR.
*Biodiversity.*
For further details see under: **PCR**.
**IPCs** Insulin-Producing Cells.
*Biology; Medicine; Oncology.*
**IPCs** Interferon-Producing Cells.
*Immunology; Viral Replication.*
**IPD** Incubation Period Distribution.
*Biological Sciences; Ecology; Epidemiology.*
**IPD** Institute of Personnel and Development (G.B.).
**IPE** individual protective equipment [NBC].
équipement individuel de protection [NBC].
**IPE** International Petroleum Exchange (London, G.B.).
**IPE regulations** International Petroleum Exchange regulations.
*Oil Trading.*
**IPF** 1. in-place force.
1. force en place.
2. international protection force.
2. force de protection internationale.
**IPFC** Indo-Pacific Fisheries Commission.
Of the U.N. Food and Agriculture Organization.
**IPG** 1. initial partnership goal.
1. objectif initial du Partenariat.
2. international planning group.
2. groupe de planification international.
**IPGRI** International Plant Genetic Resources Institute.
Of the CGIAR.
IPGRI's mission is to encourage, support and engage in activities to strengthen the conservation and use of plant genetic resources wordwide.
*Plant Genetic Resources.*
For further details see under: **CGIAR**.
**IPHC** International Pacific Halibut Commission.
**IPHT** Institute of Physical High Technology.
**IPI** Implicit Price Index.
*Business; Commerce.*
**IPI** International Press Institute.
**IPI** Istituto per la Promozione Industriale.
Italian acronym of the: Institute for Industrial Promotion.
**IPIECA** International Petroleum Industry Environmental Conservation Association (G.B.).
**IPIR** initial programmed interpretation report.
compte rendu initial d'interprétation.
**IPK** Institute of Plant Genetics and Crop Plant Research (Germany).
*Molecular Plant Pathology; Plant Functional Genomics.*
**IPL** Initial Program Load.
*Computer Programming.*
**IPL** Intraperiod Line.
*Medicine.*
**IPL** Ispettorato Provinciale del Lavoro.
Italian initialism of the: District Labor Inspectorate.
**ipm; i.p.m.** inches per minute.

**IPM** Integrated Pest Management.
*Biological Control; Ecology; Environmental Science; Host Plant Resistance.*
**IPM** Intelligent Processing Materials.
**IPM** International Partnership for Microbicides.
Established in January 2003 (U.S.A.).
*HIV Infection Barriers; Microbicides; Pathogen-stopping creams/gels.*
**IPM** Interplanetary Medium.
**IPM** inventory of preventive measures.
inventaire des mesures préventives.
**IPMA** International Primary Markets Association.
**IPMP** Investigations into Polymer Membrane Processing.
**IPMS** Institute for Problems of Materials Sciences (Ukraine).
**IPMS** Institution of Professionals, Managers and Specialists (U.S.A.).
**IPNS** Intense Pulsed Neutron Source (U.S.A.).
The IPNS, at Argonne National Laboratory, was built in 1981.
**IPNV** Infectious Pancreatic Necrosis Virus.
*Virology.*
**IPO** Initial Public Offer / Offering.
*Finance.*
**IPOD** International Program of Ocean Drilling.
France - FSU - G.B. - Germany - Japan (U.S.A.).
**IPOs** Initial Public Offerings.
*Business; Finance.*
**IPP** Incapacité Permanente Partielle de travail.
French initialism meaning: Permanent-Partial Disability.
*Medicine.*
**IPP** Independent Power Producer.
The Public Utilities Regulatory Policy Act (U.S.A.) in part requires utilities to buy power from qualified IPPs if the energy is generated from renewable sources.
**IPP** Individual Partnership Programme.
Programme de partenariat individuel.
**IPP** Industrial Partnering Program (U.S.A.).
The U.S. Industrial Partnering Program was started by the U.S. Department of Energy and the State Department. Its aim is to employ former Soviet weapons scientists on technologies suitable for commercialization and joint ventures.
*Joint Ventures; Nuclear Materials; Weapons.*
**IPP** Initiative for Proliferation Prevention.
Date started: 1994.
For further details see under: **NCI**.
**i-PP** isotactic Polypropylene.
*Chemistry.*
**I.P.P.A.I.** Istituto Provinciale di Protezione e Assistenza all'Infanzia (Italy).
**IPPB** Intermittent Positive Pressure Breathing.
**IPPC** Infrastructure Payments and Progress Committee.
Comité des paiements et de l'avancement des travaux d'infrastructure.
**IPPS** International Parallel Processing Symposium.
**IPR** Industrial Property Rights; Intellectual Property Rights.
**$IP_3R$** Inositol 1,4,5-Triphosphate Receptor.
**IPrA** International Pragmatics Association (Belgium, University of Antwerp).
Founded in 1986; aims to search for a framework for the discussion and comparison of results of research in all aspects of *language use* or *function of language*, to stimulate the various fields of application, and to disseminate knowledge about *pragmatic aspects of language.*
**IPRA** International Public Relations Association (G.B.).
**IPRB** Infrastructure (Priority) Project Review Board.
Commission d'examen des projets d'infrastructure (prioritaires).
**IPRI** Intelligent Polymer Research Institute (Australia).
**Ips** Immunoprecipitates.
*Molecular Biology.*
**ips**; **i.p.s.** inches per second.
**IPS** Indice di Presenza Seminari.
**IPs** Inositol Phosphates.
**IPs** Integrated Projects - *European Commission.*
**IPS** Intermolecular Potential energy Surface.
**IPS** International Publishers Service.
**IPS** Interplanetary Scintillation.
**IPS**; **I.P.S.** Istituto Poligrafico dello Stato.
Italian initialism of the: State Printing and Stationery Office (Italy).
**IPSA** International Political Science Association.
**IPSC** Interim Political and Security Committee [obsolete - now called PSC 1.].
Comité politique et de sécurité intérimaire (COPSI) [obsolète - maintenant appelé COPS].
**IPSec** Internet Protocol Security.
**IPSFC** International Pacific Salmon Fisheries Commission.
**IPSI** Istituto per la Promozione e lo Sviluppo Industriale (Milan, Italy).
Italian acronym of the: Institute for Industrial Promotion and Development.
**IPSLN** Indo-Pacific Sea Level Network.
**IPSPs** Inhibitory Postsynaptic Potentials.

**IPST** Institute of Paper Science and Technology (U.S.A.).
**IPSTA** Indian Pepper and Spice Trade Association (India).
**IPT** Incapacité Permanente Totale de travail.
French initialism meaning: Permanent-Total Disability.
*Medicine.*
**IPT** integrated project team [submarine SAR].
équipe de project intégré [SAR de sous-marins].
**IPTF** International Police Task Force.
Groupe international de police (GIP 2.).
**IPTG** Isopropyl-β-D-Thiogalactopyranoside.
A compound that inactivates Lac repressor.
*Genetics; Molecular Biology; Physics.*
**IPTO** Information Processing Techniques Office (U.S.A.).
**IPTRP** Improving Psychiatric Treatment in Residential Programmes for newly dependent groups through relapse Prevention.
*European Community Program.*
**IPTS** International Practical Temperature Scale.
*Thermodynamics.*
**IPV** Inactivated Poliovirus Vaccine.
*Immunology.*
**IPY** International Polar Year.
**IPX** Internetwork Packet Exchange.
**IPZ** Insuline Protamine-Zinc.
French initialism meaning: Protamine Zinc Insulin.
**IQ** Import Quota.
**IQ** Intelligence Quotient.
*Psychology.*
**IQHE** Integral Quantum Hall Effect.
**IQRS** International Quality Rating System.
**I.R.** Infantry Reserve.
**IR** Information Retrieval.
*Computer Programming.*
**IR** 1. infra-red.
1. infrarouge.
2. intelligence request.
2. demande de renseignement.
**I.R.** Inland Revenue.
**IR**; **I.R.** Intelligence Ratio.
**I.R.** Intermediate Reserve.
**IR** Internal Revenue.
**IR** Internetwork Router.
**IR** Intracellular Receptor.
**IR** Investor Relations.
**IR** Ionizing Radiation.
*Cancer Research; DNA Double-Strand Breaks; Developmental Biology; Oxidative Metabolism.*
For further details see under: **NER**; **NHEJ** and **DSBs**.
**IR** Iran's International vehicle-registration letters.
**Ir** (abbr.) Ireland.
**Ir** The chemical symbol for Iridium.
Iridium is used mainly as a catalyst.
*Chemistry.*
Used for the manufacture of superconductor crystals.
*Metallurgy.*
**Ir** (abbr.) Irish.
Irish is the Celtic language of Ireland.
*Languages.*
**IRA** Indian Rights Association.
**IRA** Individual Retirement Account.
**IRA** Inflammatory Research Association (U.S.A.).
*Anti-Inflammatory Drugs; Inflammatory Diseases; Osteoarthritis; Rheumatoid Arthritis.*
**IRA** International Recreation Association.
**IRA** Irish Republican Army (Ireland).
**IRAC**; **I.R.A.C.** Information Resource and Analysis Center (U.S.A.).
**IRAC** Interdepartment Radio Advisory Committee.
**IRAK** Interleukin-1Receptor-Associated Kinase.
*Human Genome Sciences; Pathology.*
**IRAM** Institut de Radio Astronomie Millimétrique (Plateau de Bure, France).
IRAM is run jointly by (Germany's) Max Planck Society and CNRS (the French basic Research Agency) as well as the National Geographical Institute (Spain).
*Millimetric Radioastronomy.*
**IR&DG** Industrial Research & Development Group (Ireland).
**IRAP** Imposta Regionale sulle Attività Produttive (Italy).
Italian acronym meaning: New (1998) Regional Tax on Productive Activities.
**IRAS** Infrared Absorption Spectroscopy.
**IRAS** Infra-Red Astronomy Satellite.
**IRB** Infrastructure Review Board.
Comité d'examen de l'infrastructure.
**IRB** Institutional Review Board.
For further details see under: **IRBs**.
**IRB** Istituto Ricerche Breda (Italy).
*Italian Research Institute.*
**IRBM** Intermediate-Range Ballistic Missile.
*Ordnance.*
**IRBs** Institutional Review Boards (U.S.A.).
The IRBs are safety panels that must approve all research involving human subjects.
**IRBs** Interest Reduction Bonds.
*Banking; Finance.*
**IRBTs** Infrared Brightness Temperatures.
*Atmospheric Sciences; Oceanography.*

**IRC** Industrial Reorganization Corporation.
**IRC** Infrared Colour.
**IRC** International Research Council.
**IRC** Internet Relay Chat.
A program developed in 1988.
**IRCC** International Radio Consultative Committee.
Comité consultatif international des radiocommunications (CCIR).
**IRCC** Istituto di Ricerca per la Cura del Cancro.
Italian initialism of the: Institute for Cancer Research and Treatment, University of Torino Medical School, Italy.
**IRCCS** Istituto di Ricerca e Cura a Carattere Scientifico (Italy).
The IRCCS, Institute of Medical Sciences, of the Ospedale Policlinico is located in Milan, Italy.
**IRCE**; **I.R.C.E.** Istituto per le Relazioni Culturali con l'Estero (Italy).
Italian acronym of the: Institute for Cultural Relations with Foreign Countries.
**IRCJS** International Research Center for Japanese Studies (Kyoto, Japan).
**IRCM** infrared countermeasure(s).
contre-mesure(s) infrarouge(s).
**IRCM** Institut de Recherches Cliniques de Montréal (Canada).
*Biomedical Research; Cellular Imaging; Cytofluorometry; Histology; Molecular Biology; Transgenesis.*
**IRCP** International Research Cooperation Project.
The IRCP is a 3-year project which began in spring 1996.
*AAAS Programs.*
For further details see under: **AAAS**.
**IRC PS** International Regulations for Prevention of Collisions at Sea.
règlement international pour prévenir les abordages en mer.
**IRCs** Innovation Relay Centers - *European Community.*
**IRCS** international radio call sign.
indicatif d'appel radio international.
**Ircs** Istituto di ricerche e comunicazioni.
Italian initialism of the: Institute of Research and Communications.
**IRD** Ice-Rafter Debris.
*Applied Marine Research; Geology; Geophysics; Glacial Marine Sedimentation; Marine Micropaleontology; Oceanography; Pleistocene Deglaciations.*
**IRD** infrared decoy.
leurre infrarouge.
**IRD** Inland Revenue Department.
**IRD** International Radiation Detectors.
**IRD** International Research & Development.
**IRDA** Infrared Data Association.
**IRDA** Insurance Regulatory and Development Authority (India).
**IRDAC** Industrial Research and Development Advisory Committee - *European Community.*
**IRDS** infrared detection system.
système de détection infrarouge.
**IRDU** Infrared Detection Unit.
**IRE** Istituzioni di Ricovero e di Educazione.
*Italian Institutes.*
**IREC** Institut pour la Recherche et l'Enseignement dans la Confection.
*Belgian Institute.*
**IRECOOP** Istituto Regionale per l'Educazione e studi COOPerativi.
IRECOOP is located in Sardinia, Italy.
**IREE** Initiatives en Réseau pour Entreprendre au féminin en Europe.
*Projects; Women Entrepreneurship.*
**IREE 1997** International Railway Equipment Exhibition.
September 1997 (India).
*International Exhibitions.*
**IRELA**; **Irela** Istituto di Relazioni Europeo - Latinoamericane.
Italian acronym of the: Institute for European - Latin-American Relations.
**I.R.E.N.**Interservice Renewable Energies Newsletter - *European Community.*
**IRENE** Italian Relay Centre for North-Eastern Regions (Italy).
**IRE network** Innovating Regions in Europe network.
As part of the Research and Innovation activities within the Sixth Framework Programme of the European Community, the network of IRE aims to facilitate the exchange of experiences between regions developing *regional innovation policies, strategies and schemes*, and to improve their access to *good practice.*
**IRER** Istituto REgionale di Ricerca.
*Italian Research Institute.*
**IREs** Iron-Responsive Elements.
*Biochemistry; Chemistry and Chemical Biology; Enzyme Research.*
**IRES elements** Internal Ribosome Entry Site elements.
*Biochemistry; Biophysics; Genetics; Health Sciences; Molecular Biology.*
**IRF** immediate reaction force.
force de réaction immédiatel.

**RF** International Road Federation (Geneva, Switzerland).

**IRFA** Institut de Recherches sur les Fruits et Agrumes.
*French Research Institute.*

**IRFA** Institut Régional de Formation pour Adultes (France).

**IRFE**; **I.R.F.E.** Ispettorato generale per i Rapporti Finanziari con l'Estero (Italy).
Italian acronym of the: General Inspectorate for Financial Relations with Foreign Countries.

**IrGael** Irish Gaelic.
Irish Gaelic is Gaelic used in Ireland.
*Languages.*

**IRGC** Islamic Revolutionary Guard Corps (Iran).

**IR gene** Immune-Response gene.
*Genetics.*

**IRGs** Initial Review Groups (U.S.A.).
*Glycobiology.*

**IRGSP** International Rice Genome Sequencing Project.
The IRGSP is an international consortium of publicly funded laboratories led by Japanese Researchers.
*Projects.*

**IRI** Industrial Research Institute.

**IRI** Integrity Research Institute (U.S.A.).
IRI is based in Washington, D.C.
*Conferences; Free Energy.*

**IRI** International Research Institute (N.Y., U.S.A.).
*Climate Prediction.*

**IRI** Istituto per la Ricostruzione Industriale.
Italian acronym of the: Institute for Industrial Reconstruction (Italy).

**IRIA** Institut de Recherches d'Informatique et d'Automatique (France).

**IRIB** Islamic Republic of Iran Broadcasting (Iran).

**IRICP** International Research Institute for Climate Prediction.

**irid.** (abbr.) iridescent.
*Optics.*

**IRIDE** Interfaccia Ricerca Industria a Diffusione Europea (Italy).

**IRIS** Incorporated Research Institutions for Seismology.
IRIS is a consortium of 91 Seismological Research Institutions based in Washington, D.C., U.S.A.
*Seismological Research.*

**IRIS** Integrated Risk Information System.
U.S. EPA's.
*Carcinogens; Hazardous Chemicals; Toxins.*
For further details see under: **EPA**.

**IRL** Ireland's international vehicle-registration letters.

**IRLA** Independent Research Libraries Association.

**IRLC** Illinois Regional Library Council (U.S.A.).

**IRLS** infrared linescan system.
analyseur infrarouge à balayage linéaire.

**IRM** Imagerie par Résonance Magnétique nucléaire.
French initialism meaning: Nuclear Magnetic Resonance Imaging.
*Physics; Radiology.*

**IRM** Information Resources Management.

**IRM**; **irm** Innate Releasing Mechanism.
*Behavior.*

**IRM** Inspection, Repair and Maintenance of offshore structures carried out by remotely operated vehicles.
European Commission Fifth Framework Programme.
*Energy.*

**IRM** integrated resource management.
gestion intégrée des ressources.

**IRM** Isothermal Remanent Magnetization.

**IRMA** Immuno Radiometric Assay.
*Immunology.*

**IRMB** Institute for Research in Molecular Biology.

**IRMC** Information Resources Management College (U.S.A.).

**IRMM** Institute for Reference Materials and Measurements.
The IRMM is located in Geel, Belgium.

**IRMS** Information Resources Management Service (U.S.A.).

**IRNA** IRanian News Agency.

**I.R.O.** Inland Revenue Office.

**IRO** Internal Revenue Office (U.S.A.).

**IROS** Intelligent RObots and Systems.

**IRP** interference reporting point.
poste de compte rendu des interférences.

**IRPEF** Imposta sul Reddito delle PErsone Fisiche (Italy).
Italian abbreviation meaning: Personal Income Tax.

**IRPEG** Imposta sul Reddito delle PErsone Giuridiche (Italy).
Italian abbreviation meaning: Corporate Income Tax.

**IRPS** Institute of Reconstructive Plastic Surgery (U.S.A.).

**IRPTC** International Register of Potentially Toxic Chemicals.

**IRPTS** IR-Induced Population Transfer Spectrology.

*Chemistry.*
For further details see under: **IR**.
**IRQ** Iraq's International vehicle-registration letters.
**IRR** Internal Rate of Return.
*Finance.*
**IR radiation** Infrared radiation.
*Electromagnetism.*
**IRRB** Infrastructure Requirements Review Board.
Comité d'examen des besoins d'infrastructure.
**IRRC** Investor Responsibility Research Center.
Washington-based (U.S.A.).
**irred.** (abbr.) irredeemable.
*Commerce; Finance.*
**irreg.** (abbr.) irregular.
**IRRI**; **I.R.R.I.** International Rice Research Institute.
**IRRMA** Institut Romand de Recherche numérique en physique des MAtériaux (Switzerland).
**IRRV** Institute of Revenues, Rating & Valuation (G.B.).
**IRS** Information Retrieval Service (ESA's).
For further details see under: **ESA**.
**IRS** Internal Revenue Service (U.S.A.).
**IRS** Istituto per la Ricerca Sociale.
Italian initialism of the: Institute for Social Research (Milan, Italy).
**IRS-1** Insulin Receptor Substrate 1.
*Biochemistry; Cancer Research; Medicine; Molecular Biology; Signal Transduction; Tumor Suppressor.*
**IRSA** Irish Research Scientists Association (Ireland).
**IRSA** Istituto per la Ricerca e lo Sviluppo delle Assicurazioni (Italy).
Italian acronym of the: Institute for Insurance Research and Development.
**IRSI** Infrared Space Interferometer - ESA.
The IRSI will be launched in 2009.
*Extrasolar Planetary Systems.*
For further details see under: **ESA**.
**IRSM** Impact sur la Rentabilité de la Stratégie Mercatique.
French initialism meaning: Profit Impact of Marketing Strategy.
*Business; Marketing.*
**IRS satellites** - India Remote Sensing satellites.
**IRST** infrared search and track (system).
(système de) recherche et poursuite infrarouge.
**IRST** Istituto per la Ricerca Scientifica e Tecnologica (Trento, Italy).
Italian initialism of the: Institute for Scientific and Technological Research.
The IRST deals with microelectronics and artificial intelligence.
**IRT** immediate response team.
équipe de réponse immédiate.
**IRTA** Intramural Research Training Award (U.S.A.).
*Awards.*
**I.R.T.A.** Istituto di Rilievi Terrestri ed Aerei.
Italian acronym of the: Ground and Aerial Survey Institute (Italy).
**IRTF** Infrared Telescope Facility - NASA's.
*Astronomy.*
**IRTF(L)** Immediate Reaction Task Force (Land).
force opérationnelle terrestre de réaction immédiate.
**IRTM observations** Infrared Thermal Mapper observations.
*Chemistry; Geology; Geophysics; Planetary Exploration.*
**IRTS** Institut Régional de Travail Social.
French initialism of the: Regional Institute for Social Work.
**IRU** International Road transport Union (Geneva, Switzerland).
**IR-UV** Infrared-Ultra-Violet.
**IRV** Inspiratory Reserve Volume.
IRV is also known as: Complemental Air / Complementary.
*Medicine; Physiology.*
**IR Workshop** Intermediate Representations Workshop.
**IS** Iceland's international vehicle-registration letters.
**IS** Income Statement.
**IS** Income Stocks.
**IS** Indosuez Bank.
**IS** Information Separator.
*Computer Programming.*
**IS** Information System.
*Computer Technology; Telecommunications.*
**IS** Inorganic Semiconductor.
**IS** Integrated Software.
*Computer Programming.*
**IS** Intermediate System.
**IS** Isernia, Italy.
**IS** Israel.
**ISA** Information System Architecture.
*Computer Technology.*
**ISA** Institut Supérieur des Affaires.
*French Institute.*
**ISA**; **I.S.A.** Instrument Society of America (U.S.A.).
**ISA** integrated support area.
zone de soutien intégré.
**ISAAA** International Service for the Acquisition of Agri-Biotech Applications.
The ISAAA is a not-for-profit international organi-

zation co-sponsored by the public and private sector institutions. Its aim is to facilitate the acquisition and transfer of proprietary *agricultural biotechnology* applications from the industrial countries, for the benefit of the developing world.

**ISABP** International South Atlantic Buoy Program.
Of the U.S. Data Buoy Cooperation Council.

**ISACF** Institut Supérieur d'Architecture de la Communauté Française (Belgium).
*Architecture Institute.*

**ISAD** Istituto Superiore di Architettura & Design (Italy).
*Architecture & Design.*

**ISAE** Istituto di Studio e Analisi Economica.
*Italian Economics Institute.*

**ISAF** International Security Assistance Force [Afghanistan].
Force internationale d'assistance à la sécurité [Afghanistan].

**ISAM**; **Isam** Integrazione Statistica Area Milanese (Italy).
*Statistics.*

**ISA method** Indexed Sequential Access method.
*Computer Programming.*

**ISAMS** Improved Stratospheric And Mesospheric Sounder.
ISAMS is an instrument aboard UARS.
For further details see under: **UARS**.

**ISAS** Institute for Space and Aeronautical Science (Japan).
ISAS is a National Inter-University Research Institute under the jurisdiction of the Ministry of Education, Science, and Culture. ISAS merged with NASDA and NAL in 2002.
For further details see under: **NASDA** and **NAL**.

**ISASST** International School on the Science Techniques.

**ISAWIP** Integrate Soil And Water Improvement Program.

**ISB** intermediate staging base.
base d'étape intermédiaire.

**ISBA** Incorporated Society of British Advertisers (G.B.).

**ISBC** International Small Business Consortium (U.S.A.).

**ISBL** Information System Base Language.

**ISBN** International Standard Book Number.

**ISC** Institut Supérieur de Commerce Saint-Louis (Belgium).
*Belgian Institute.*

**ISC** International Scientific Cooperation.

**ISC** International Seismological Centre.
*Earth and Planetary Sciences; Geology; Geophysics; Seismology.*

**ISC**; **I.S.C.** International Society of Chemotherapy.

**ISC** International Steering Committee (of senior executives).
The ISC was formed by the IFPI to oversee development of DVD Audio Technology.
For further details see under: **DVD** and **IFPI**.

**ISC** Interoperability Sub-Committee.
Sous-comité de l'interopérabilité.

**ISC** Inter-System Crossing.

**ISCA** Indian Science Congress Association.

**ISCAR** Information Storage, Curation, Analysis and Retrieval.
*Bioinformatics.*
For further details see under: **BISTI** and **BIO/SPICE**.

**ISCC** 1. Information Systems Coordination Committee.
1. Comité de coordination des systèmes d'information.
2. Information Systems Sub-Committee.
2. Sous-comité des systèmes d'information.

**ISCCP** International Satellite Cloud Climatology Project.
*Atmospheric Profile Data; Earth and Planetary Sciences; Ozone; Projects.*

**ISC-CT** International Scientific Cooperation - Contract.

**ISCEH** International Scientific Committee on Environmental Health.

**ISCO** Innermost Stable Circular Orbit.
*Astrophysics.*

**ISCO** Istituto Nazionale per lo Studio della COngiuntura (Italy).
Italian acronym of the: National Institute for the Study of Economic Trends.

**ISCOMGREENLAND** Island Comman of Greenland [obsolete].
Commandement du Groenland [obsolète].

**ISCOMICELAND** Island Command Iceland [obsolete - now subsumed as an element of RC EAST].
Commandement de l'Islande [obsolète - maintenant incorporé comme élément au sein du RC EAST].

**ISCOMMADEIRA** Island Command of Madeira [obsolete - now subsumed as a detachment of RC EAST].
Commandement de l'archipel de Madère [obsolète - maintenant incorporé comme détachement au sein du RC EAST].

**ISCP**; **I.S.C.P.** International Society of Comparative Pathology.

**ISCPB** Israel Society of Clinical Pharmacy and Biopharmaceutics (Israel).
**ISCs** Irreversible Sickled Cells.
*Sickle Cell Disease; Subcellular Structures.*
**iSCSI** internet Small Computer Systems Interface.
**ISCu** Indice di Soddisfazione Clienti - utenti (Italy).
**IS curve** Investment-Saving curve.
**ISD** in-service date.
date de mise en service.
**ISD** Investment Services Directive.
*Finance.*
**ISDA** International Swap Dealers Association (U.S.A.).
**ISDA** International Swaps and Derivatives Association.
**ISDN**; **Isdn** Integrated Services Digital Network.
ISDN is an international standard to convey voice, video and data in digital form on the telephone line.
*Internet Services; Telecommunications.*
**ISDR** international ship(ping) destination room.
chambre internationale de destination des navires.
**IS dust** Interstellar dust.
*Astrophysics; Molecular Astrophysics; Molecular Physics; Space Science.*
**ISE** Institute for Solar Energy systems.
*German Institute.*
**ISE** International Securities Exchange.
**ISEC** Integrated Science for Ecosystem Challenges.
*Habitat Destruction; Invasive Species.*
**ISEC** International Society for Endangered Cats (U.S.A.).
**ISED** Information System for Education.
For further details see under: **EUD/ISED**.
**ISEE-3** International Sun-Earth Explorer-3.
ISEE-3 was launched in 1978.
**ISEF** International Science and Engineering Fair (U.S.A.).
**ISEF**; **I.S.E.F.** Istituto Superiore di Educazione Fisica (Italy).
Italian acronym of the: Italian Higher School of Physical Training.
**ISEI** Institute for Systems Engineering and Informatics (Ispra, Italy).
**I.S.E.I.** Institut Supérieur d'Enseignement Infirmier (Belgium).
**I.S.E.L.** Istituto per lo Sviluppo dell'Educazione Linguistica (Italy).
Italian acronym of the: Institute for the Development of Linguistic Education.
**Isemar** Institut Supérieur d'Economie Maritime (France).
**ISEO** Istituto per gli Studi Economici e Organizzativi (Italy).
Italian acronym of the: Institute for Economics and Business Management Studies.
**ISEP** Institut Supérieur d'Electronique de Paris.
*French Institutes.*
**ISERD Contact Centre** ISrael EU Research and Development Contact Centre.
**ISEP** Isolated / Stabilized Exercise Platform.
**ISESAO** Istituto di Studi Economico Sociali per l'Asia Orientale.
Università Commerciale Luigi Bocconi, Milano, Italy.
**ISESCO** ISlamic Educational, Scientific and Cultural Organization (Morocco).
Founded in 1982 under the aegis of the Islamic Conference Organization to strengthen co-operation between member states in the fields of *education*, *culture* and *science*.
**ISET** International Solar Electric Technology (U.S.A.).
For further details see under: **CIS**.
**ISF** Impôt de Solidarité sur la Fortune.
French initialism meaning: Capital Levy; Wealth Tax.
**ISF** International Science Foundation.
The ISF was founded in 1992 by George Soros, the Hungarian-American financier.
**ISFOR** Istituto per lo Sviluppo, Formazione, Organizzazione e Ricerca.
Italian abbreviation of the: Institute for Development, Vocational Training, Organization and Research.
**ISGE**; **I.S.G.E.** International Society of Gastro-Enterology.
**ISGs** IFN-Stimulated Genes.
For further details see under: **IFNs**.
**ISH** In Situ Hybridization.
*Molecular Biology.*
**ISH**; **I.S.H.** International Society of Hematology.
**ISHAGE** International Society for Hematology And Graft Engineering (Memphis, Tennessee, U.S.A.).
**ISHAM** International Society for Human and Animal Mycology.
Founded in 1954 to encourage the practice and study of all aspects of *medical and veterinary mycology*.
**ISHTAR** Inner SHelf Transfer And Recycling.
**ISHTEEC** International Symposium on Heat Transfer Enhancement and Energy Conservation.
**ISI** Imposta patrimoniale Straordinaria sugli Immobili (Italy).

Italian acronym meaning: Extraordinary local Property Tax.
**ISI** Institute for Scientific Information (Philadelphia, U.S.A.)
Publisher of ScienceWatch.
**ISI**; **I.S.I.** International Standards Institute.
**ISI** Inter-Services Intelligence.
**ISI** Interstimulus Interval.
**ISIC** International Student Identity Card.
**ISIDA** Istituto Superiore per Imprenditori e Dirigenti d'Azienda (Italy).
*Entrepreneurs & Managers.*
**ISIS** Independent Schools Information Service (G.B.).
**ISIS** Integrated Surface Irradiance Study.
**ISIS** International Security Information Service.
**ISISC** Istituto Superiore Internazionale di Scienze Criminali.
Italian initialism of the: International Institute of Higher Studies in *Criminal Sciences.*
**ISK** Iceland Krona.
Also: **IKr**.
*Currencies.*
**ISKO** International Society for Knowledge Organization (Germany).
Founded in 1989 to promote research, development, and application of all methods for the *organization of knowledge*; gives advice on the construction, perfection and application of classification systems, thesauri, terminologies, etc.; organizes international conference every two years.
**ISLA** Illinois Special Library Association (U.S.A.).
**ISLA** Islamic Library Association.
**ISLA** Istituto di Studi Latino-Americani.
Università Commerciale Luigi Bocconi, Milano, Italy.
*Latin-American Studies.*
**ISLE** Institute of Sociology of Law for Europe.
*Belgian Institute.*
**ISLIC** Israel Society of Libraries and Information Centres.
**IS-LM model** Investment-Saving / Liquidity-Money model.
**ISLSCP** International Satellite Land Surface Climatology Project.
**ISLU** Israel Special Libraries Union.
**ism** industriali, scientifici e medici (usi).
Italian initialism meaning: industrial, scientific and medical (uses).
**ISM**; **Ism** Integrated Services Module.
**ISM**; **I.S.M.** International Society of Microbiologists.
**ISM** Interstellar Medium.
The ISM is the space between the stars.
*Astronomy; Astrophysics; Physics; Space Science.*
**ISMA** International Securities Market Association.
**ISMB** Intelligent Systems in Molecular Biology.
*Computational Molecular Biology.*
**ISMERI Europa** Interdisciplinary Research Institute European Network.
**ISMES** Istituto Sperimentale Modelli E Strutture.
Head Office: Bergamo, Italy.
**ISMET** IStituto MEditerraneo Trapianti (Palermo, Italy).
With the University of Pittsburg, Pennsylvania.
*Research; Transplants.*
**ISMIBM** 6$^{th}$ International Symposium on Metal Ions in Biology and Medicine.
Held on 7$^{th}$ October 2000 in San Juan, Puerto Rico, U.S.A.
*Metal Ions.*
**ISMS** International Seismic Monitoring System.
**ISN** Initial Sequence Number.
**ISN** Intersegmental Nerve.
**I.S.N.A.** Istituto di Studi Nucleari per l'Agricoltura (Italy).
Italian acronym of the: Institute of Nuclear Studies for Agriculture.
**ISNPS** Institute for Space and Nuclear Power Studies (U.S.A.).
**ISO** Imaging Spectrometric Observatory.
**ISO** Incentive Stock Option (U.S.A.).
**ISO** Industry Solutions Operations.
**ISO** Infrared Space Observatory.
ISO was launched by ESA in 1994.
*Infrared Astronomy.*
For further details see under: **ESA**.
**ISO** International Standards Organization.
International Organization for Standardization.
Founded in 1947. Head Office: Geneva, Switzerland.
**Iso** In Greek is a prefix meaning "equal".
**ISO** Intraseasonal Atmospheric Oscillation.
**ISO** Istituto Superiore di Osteopatia (Italy). Set up in Milan in 1993.
**ISO** Istituto Superiore Olistico (Italy).
**ISOC**; **Isoc** Internet SOCiety.
Founded in January 1992.
**ISODE** ISO Development Environment.
**ISOLA**; **I.S.O.L.A.** Istituto Sardo Organizzazione Lavoro Artigiano (Italy).
*Italian Institute.*
**ISOLE** Island Satellite Observation for Local Exploitation.
*Ecosystems; Projects.*

**ISOL facility** Ion Separator On-Line facility (U.S.A.).
Nuclear Physics.
**isoln.** (abbr.) isolation.
**ISO/OSI**; **Iso/Osi** International Standards Organization / Open System Interconnection.
**ISOS** International Southern Ocean Studies.
**ISOS solutions** Integrated Software On Silicon solutions.
*High-Speed Connection Technologies; System Integration.*
**ISOTCO** Italian-Saudi Organization for Trading and Contracting (Milan, Italy).
**ISP** 1. identification safety point.
1. point de sécurité d'identification.
2. individual security programme.
2. programme de sécurité individuelle.
**ISP** Internet Service Provider.
**ISP** Iron-Sulfur Protein.
**ISPA** Istituto Sperimentale Psicodinamica Applicata.
*Italian Institute.*
**ISPAI** IStituto Panafricano d'Italia (Italy).
**ISPE** initial state peacetime establishment.
tableau initial d'effectifs du temps de paix.
**ISPE** Istituto Studi Politici ed Economici.
Italian acronym of the: Institute for Political and Economic Studies (Italy).
**ISPESL** Istituto Superiore per la Prevenzione E la Sicurezza del Lavoro.
*Italian Institute.*
**ISPI** Istituto per gli Studi di Politica Internazionale (Italy).
ISPI was founded in the years 1933/34 by Scholars of the Universities of Milan and Pavia using as a model the Royal Institute of International Affairs of London.
**ISPM** International Solar Polar Mission.
ISPM has been replaced by Ulysses.
**ISPM** Interplanetary Shock Propagation Model.
**ISPO** Information Society Project Office -
*European Community.*
**ISPO** Istituto per gli Studi sulla Pubblica Opinione (Italy).
Italian acronym of the Institute for Studies on Public Opinion.
**ISPRS** International Society for Photogrammetry and Remote Sensing (Japan).
**ISPs** Internet Service Providers.
**ISR** Ice Sounding Radar.
**ISR** 1. identification safety range.
1. distance de sécurité d'identification.
2. implementation status report [CP].
2. rapport sur l'avancement des travaux [CP].
**ISR** Institute for Social Research.
*Social Science.*
**ISR** International Society of Radiology.
*Physics.*
**ISR**; **isr** Interrupt Service Routine.
**ISR**; **isr** Intersecting Storage Rings.
*Nuclear Engineering.*
**ISREC** Swiss Institute for Experimental Cancer Research.
Lausanne, Switzerland.
**ISREs** Interferon Stimulated Response Elements.
*Cytokine Biology.*
**ISRO** Indian Space Research Organization (India).
**ISRS** Impulsive Stimulated Raman Scattering.
**ISRT** International Spinal Research Trust (G.B.).
The ISRT is a grant-giving charity with the purpose of funding research aimed at resolving the non- or partial-functioning of the injured spinal cord.
*Spinal Cord Research.*
**ISS** Immunostimulatory DNA Sequences.
*Medicine.*
**ISS** Integrated Sounding System.
**ISS** International Space Station.
*Space Technology.*
**ISS**; **Iss** Internet Security Systems.
**I.S.S.** Istituto Sperimentale della Strada (Italy).
Italian initialism of the: Institute for Road Construction Research.
**ISS** Istituto Superiore della Sanità (Italy).
Italian initialism meaning: National Health Institute.
**ISSC** Integrated System Support Centre.
Centre de soutien des systèmes intégrés.
**ISSC** International Social Science Council.
Founded in 1952 for the advancement of the *social sciences* throughout the world and their application to the major problems of the world and to spread co-operation at an international level between specialists in the social sciences.
*Councils.*
**ISSMB** Information Systems Standards Management Board (U.S.A.).
**ISSN** International Standard Serial Number.
**ISSOL** International Society for the Study of the Origin of Life.
**IST** 1. information systems technology.
1. technologie des systèmes d'information.
2. inter-switch trunk.
2. liaison de jonction entre commutateurs.
**IST** Ingegneria e Servizi Tecnici.

Italian initialism meaning: Engineering and Technical Services.
**IST** Institute for Safety Technology (Ispra, Italy).
**IST** Insulin Shock Therapy.
The insulin shock therapy is a psychosis treatment used in certain cases in psychiatric therapy.
*Medicine.*
**IST** The airport code for Istanbul, Turkey.
**ist.** istituto.
Italian abbreviation meaning: institute.
**ISTAR** intelligence, surveillance, target acquisition and reconnaissance.
renseignement, surveillance, acquisition d'objectifs et reconnaissance.
**ISTAT** Istituto Centrale di Statistica (Italy).
Italian abbreviation of the: Central Statistics Institute.
**ISTC** International Science and Technology Center.
The ISTC began operating in 1994. It is coordinated by the U.S. State Department.
*U.S.; FSU projects.*
**ISTC** International Student Travel Confederation.
**ISTC** Iron and Steel Trades Confederation.
*British Confederations.*
**ISTCRAD** International Society for Tropical Crop Research And Development (India).
Founded in 1990; provides a forum for *interaction among scientists, progressive farmers and entrepreneurs.*
**ISTE** International Society for Tropical Ecology (India).
**ISTEC** International Superconductivity Technology Center (Japan).
ISTEC runs the Superconducting Research Laboratory.
**ISTM**; **I.S.T.M.** International Society for Testing Materials.
**ISTP** Institut Supérieur des Techniques de Production.
**ISTPOWP** International Society for the Prevention Of Water Pollution (G.B.).
**ISTR** International Society for Third sector Research (U.S.A.).
Founded in 1992; encourages research relevant to *nonprofit organizations, voluntarism and philanthropy.*
**ISTRC** International Society for Tropical Root Crops (The Netherlands).
Founded in 1964.
**ISTS** Institute for Space and Terrestrial Science (Canada).
**ISTUD**; **Istud** Istituto STUdi Direzionali.
Italian acronym of the: Institute for Management Studies. ISTUD is locatd at Stresa (Verbania), Italy.
**ISTUR** IStituto TUrismo e Ricerca.
Italian acronym of the: Institute of Tourism and Research (Italy).
**ISU** Illinois State University (U.S.A.).
**ISU**; **I.S.U.** International Society of Urology.
**ISU** International Space University.
**ISU**; **Isu** Istituto per il diritto allo Studio Universitario.
*Italian Institute.*
**ISV**; **Isv** Independent Software Vendor; Internet Software Vendor.
**ISV** International Scientific Vocabulary.
**ISVAP** Istituto per la Vigilanza sulle Assicurazioni Private (Italy).
*Private Insurance.*
**ISVB** Ideal Society of Vascular Biomechanics (Naples, Italy).
**ISVEIMER** Istituto per lo Sviluppo Economico dell'Italia Meridionale.
Italian acronym of the: Institute for the Economic Development of Southern Italy. Head Office: Naples, Italy.
**Isvet** Istituto per gli studi sullo sviluppo economico e il progresso tecnico.
Italian acronym of the: Institute for studies on economic development and technical progress.
**ISY** International Space Year (1992).
**IT** Inclusive Tours.
*Tourism.*
**I.T.** Income Tax.
**IT** Information Technology.
**IT** Input Transformer.
*Electricity.*
**IT** Insuffisance Tricuspidienne or Régurgitation Tricuspidienne.
French initialism meaning: Tricuspid Regurgitation.
*Medicine.*
**IT** Intelligent Terminal.
**IT** Interactive Terminal.
*Computer Technology.*
**IT** International Trade.
*Business; Finance.*
**i.t.** in transit.
**It** Italian.
Italian is a Romance language, the language of Italy. Official also in Switzerland.
*Languages.*
**it.** italiano.
Italian abbreviation meaning: Italian.
**IT**; **It.** (abbr.) Italy.

**ITA** Independent Television Authority (G.B.).
**ITA** Information Technology Agreement.
**ITA** Institut International du Transport Aérien.
**ITA** Interface Test Adapter.
**ITA** Interim Type Approval (for Telephone Equipment Manufacturers).
**ITA** International Trade Administration.
**ITA** International Trademark Association.
**ITA**; **I.T.A.** International Tuberculosis Association.
**ITAA** Information Technology Association of America (U.S.A.).
**ITALCASSE** Istituto di Credito delle Casse di Risparmio Italiane (Italy).
Italian abbreviation of the: Credit Institute of Italian Savings Banks.
**ITAMs** Immune receptor Tyrosine-based Activation Motifs.
**ITAR** International Traffic in Arms Regulations (U.S.A.).
**IT&T** Information Technology and Telecommunications.
**ITB** Institute of Technology at Bandung (Indonesia).
**ITB** Invisible Trade Balance.
*Business; Commerce; Finance.*
**ITBA** Istituto di Tecnologie Biomediche Avanzate (Italy).
Of the Italian National Research Council.
**ITBTP** Institut Technique du Bâtiment et des Travaux Publics (France).
*French Technical Institute.*
**ITC** Income Tax Code; Income Tax Credit.
**ITC** International Tin Agreement.
**ITC** International Trade Center (Geneva, Switzerland).
**ITC** International Trade Commission.
**ITC** Investment Tax Credit.
**I.T.C.** (Compagnia) Italiana dei Cavi Telegrafici Sottomarini (Italy).
Italian initialism of the: Italian Underwater Telegraph Cable Company.
**ITCA** Independent Television Companies Association.
**ITCB** Institut du Textile et de la Confection Belge.
*Belgian Institute; Textiles.*
**ITCNM** International Trade Council of New Mexico.
**IT cortex** Inferior Temporal cortex.
*Neuropsychology.*
**ITCZ** Intertropical Convergence Zone.
The ITCZ is also known as: Equatorial Convergence Zone. It is where tropical easterly winds converge over the oceans.
*Climatology; Geology; Meteorology.*
**ITD** Interaural Time Difference.
For further details see under: **ITDs**.
**ITD** Istituto per le Tecnologie Didattiche.
*Italian Institute.*
**ITDs** Interaural Time Differences.
*Auditory Space Processing; Medicine; Neurobiology.*
**ITE** Institute of Terrestrial Ecology (G.B.).
Merlewood Research Station.
**ITE** International Trade and Exhibitions.
**ITEC** improved theatre nuclear forces emergency communications.
communications de secours améliorées des forces nucléaire de théâtre.
**ITEC-2** Innovation and Technology Equity Capital.
*European Project.*
**ITEP** Institute of Theoretical and Experimental Physics (Moscow).
ITEP was founded in 1943. The Institute formerly dealt with *nuclear reactor technologies* and later, *particle physics.*
**ITER** International Thermonuclear Experimental Reactor.
ITER is a project sponsored by the United States, Russia, Europe and Japan. Construction of ITER will begin in 2003. It will be completed and operating by 2010.
*Fusion Reactors; Fusion Research; Physics; Plasma Physics; Science & Technology; Projects.*
**ITG**; **Itg** Istituto Tecnico Geometri (Italy).
*Italian Institute of Surveyors.*
**ITG waves** Ion-Temperature-Gradient waves.
*Fusion Research; Physics; Plasma Physics.*
**ITI**; **I.T.I.** Istituto Terapeutico Italiano.
Italian acronym of the: Italian Therapeutic Institute.
**ITICs** International Trust and Investment Corporations (China).
China has six regional ITICs.
**ITIM** Immune receptor Tyrosine-based Inhibitor Motif.
**IT instillation** Intratracheal instillation.
**ITIS**; **Itis** Istituto Tecnico Industriali Statali (Italy).
**ITL** Italian Lira.
Also: **L**; **l**.
Now: EURO/EUR (€). Became ECU (European single currency) with effect from January 2002.
*Currencies.*
**ITMA** Incentive Travel & Meetings Association (G.B.).
**ITO** Illinois Trade Office (U.S.A.).
**ITO** Income Tax Office.

**ITO** Indium Tin Oxide.
*Organic Materials.*
**ITO** International Trade Organization.
**ITOS** Improved Television and infrared Observation Satellite.
**ITP** Idiopathic Thrombocytopenic Purpura.
*Medicine.*
**ITP** Incapacité Temporaire Partielle de travail.
French initialism meaning: Temporary Partial Disability.
*Medicine.*
**ITP** Income Tax Plan.
**ITP** Institute for Theoretical Physics (U.S.A.).
*Programs; Workshops.*
**ITP** International Training Program.
**ITPA**; **Itpa** Istituto Tecnico Periti Aziendali.
*Italian Technical Institute.*
**ITP/HCPs** Incidental Take Permit / Habitat Conservation Plans.
*Habitat Conservation; Integrative and Comparative Biology; Molecular and Cellular Biology; Threatened and Endangered Species.*
**ITPO** India Trade Promotion Organisation.
ITPO deals with the *transaction of products, technologies and services.*
**ITPR** Infra-red Temperature Profile Radiometer.
**ITQ** Individual Transferable Quota.
**ITR** Ignition Test Reactor.
**ITS** Industrial Training Service (G.B.).
**ITS** Information Technology Service.
**ITS** Institute for Telecommunication Science.
**ITS** Intelligent Transportation Systems.
*Positioning Systems; System Engineering; Transportation Planning.*
**ITS** Intermarket Trading System.
**ITSEC** information technology securtity evaluation criteria.
critères d'évaluation de la sécurité des technologies de l'information.
**ITSEF** Information Technology Security Evaluation Facility.
**ITSEM** Information Technology Security Evaluation Manual.
**ITSS** Information Technology and Scientific Services (Raytheon's).
**ITT** Incapacité Temporaire Totale de travail.
French initialism meaning: Temporary Total Disability.
*Medicine.*
**ITT** Innovation and Technology Transfer.
**ITT** Invitation To Transmit.
**ITTC** International Towing Tank Conference.
*Naval Hydrodynamics.*
**ITTO** International Tropical Timber Organization (Japan).
*Biodiversity; Silviculture; Tropical Forest Ecology.*
**ITU** International Telecommunications Union (Switzerland).
The ITU became particularly important after the invention of the telephone in 1876. The acronym now still used, was coined in 1934. Since 1947 it is an agency of the United Nations Organization.
**ITU** Istanbul Technical University (Turkey).
**ITV** Independent Television Companies.
**ITV** Institut Technique du Vin (France).
*French Wine Institute.*
**iTV** interactive Television.
**ITWS** Integrated Terminal Weather System.
**ITX** Iberiotoxin.
**IU**; **I.U.** Immunizing Unit.
**IU** Indiana University (U.S.A.).
**IU** Information Unit.
*Telecommunications.*
**I.U.** International Unit.
*Metrology.*
**IUA** Interlibrary Users Association.
**IUAES** International Union of *Anthropological and Ethnological Sciences.*
**IUAV** Istituto Universitario di Architettura di Venezia (Italy).
*Italian Architecture Institute.*
**IUB** International Universities Bureau.
The IUB was created in 1949.
**IUBMB** International Union of Biochemistry and Molecular Biology.
**IUBS** International Union of Biological Sciences.
**IUC** Informatica Universitaria Campana (Naples, Italy).
**IUCD** Intrauterine Contraceptive Device.
The IUCD is a metal or plastic device inserted within the uterus to prevent pregnancies.
*Medicine.*
**IUCN** International Union for Conservation of Nature and natural resources.
The IUCN is also known as: World Conservation Union.
**IUCR** Industry University Cooperative Research.
The IUCR consists of projects to be developed by academic researchers and businesses.
**IUCr** International Union of Crystallography.
**IUD** Intrauterine Device.
For further details see under: **IUCD**.
**IUDR** Idoxuridine.
For furhter details see under: **IDU**.
**IUE satellite** International Ultraviolet Explorer satellite.

*Atmospheric and Planetary Physics; Space Astrophysics; Space Telescope Science.*

**IUF** Institut Universitaire de France.
*French Institute.*

**IUFoST** International Union of Food Science and Technology.

**IUFRO** International Union of Forestry Research Organizations (Austria).

**IUGG** International Union of Geodesy and Geophysics (France).

**IUGS** International Union of Geological Sciences.

**IUGTEs** (human) In Utero Gene Transfer Experiments.
*Human Gene Therapies; Medical Experiments; Prenatal Gene Trasfer Research.*

**IUHPS** International Union of the History and Physiology of Science.

**IUIS** International Union of Immunology Societies.

**IUKADGE** Improved UK Air Defence Ground Environment.
infrastructure électronique améliorée de la défense aérienne au Royaume-Uni.

**IULM** Istituto Universitario di Lingue Moderne (Italy).
*Italian Language Institute.*

**IUM** Independent University of Moscow.

**IUMI** International Union of Marine Insurance (Switzerland).

**IUMS** International Union of Microbiological Societies.
Located in Strasbourg, France. Founded in 1930.
*Microbiology.*

**IUNS** International Union of Nutritional Sciences.
Founded in 1946.

**IUPAB** International Union of Pure and Applied Biophysics.

**IUPAC**; **I.U.P.A.C.** International Union of Pure and Applied Chemistry.
Founded in 1919 to promote continuing co-operation among chemists of the member countries; to study topics of international importance which require regulation, standardization or codification; to co-operate with other international organizations which deal with topics of a chemical nature; to contribute to the advancement of *pure and applied chemistry* in all its aspects.

**IUPAP** International Union of Pure and Applied Physics.

**IUPESM** International Union for Physical and Engineering Sciences and Medicine.

**IUPHAR** International Union of Pharmacology.
Founded in 1959 as a section of The International Union of Physiological Sciences; independent 1966; promotes international co-ordination of research, discussion, symposia, and publication in the field of *pharmacology*; co-operates with WHO in matters concerning drugs and *drug research*, and with related international unions; four-yearly international congresses.
For further details see under: **WHO**.

**IUPS** International Union of Physiological Sciences.

**IUPsyS** International Union of Psychological Science.

**IUPUI** Indiana University - Purdue University at Indianapolis, U.S.A.
For further details see under: **CEES**.

**IUR** International Union of Radioecology.

**IUR** International Union of Railways.

**IUS** Inertial Upper Stage.

**IUSS** Integrated Undersea Surveillance System.
*Marine Biology.*

**IUSS** International Union of Soil Science.

**IUTAM** International Union of Theoretical and Applied Mechanics.

**IUTOX** International Union of TOXicology.

**IUVDT** International Union against Venereal Diseases and Treponematoses (G.B.).
Founded in 1923; administrative and educational activities, public health, and technical aspects of *sexually transmitted diseases* and AIDS.

**IUVSTA** International Union for Vacuum Science Technique and Applications.
For further details see under: **AIV**.

**i.v.** increased value.

**i.v.** initial velocity.

**I.V.** Intravenous; intravenously.

**I.V.**; **i.v.** invoice value.

**IV** Ivory Coast.

**IVA** Imposta sul Valore Aggiunto (Italy).
Italian acronym meaning: Value Added Tax.

**IVA** Inventory Valuation Adjustment.
*Business; Finance.*

**IVC** immediately vital cargo.
cargaison immédiatement vitale.

**IVC** Intelect Visual Communications.
*Videoconferencing Systems.*

**IVC** Intravenous Cholangiogram.
*Radiology.*

**IVCC** Institut technique des Vins de Consommation Courante (France).
*French Wine Institute.*

**IVCP** illegal vehicle checkpoint.
poste de contrôle illégal des véhicules.

**IVCSM** Wholesale Tax (Venezuela).
IVA (Value-Added Tax) will replace IVCSM.

**IVD** Insuffisance Ventriculaire Droite.
French initialism meaning: Right Ventricular Insufficiency.
*Medicine.*
**IVET** In Vivo Expression Technology.
*Microbiology; Molecular Genetics.*
**IVF** In Vitro Fertilization.
*Gynaecology; Medicine; Obstetrics.*
**IVG** Insuffisance Ventriculaire Gauche.
French initialism meaning: Left Ventricular Insufficiency.
*Medicine.*
**IVHS** Intelligent Vehicle Highway System.
**IVI** International Vaccine Institute (Seoul).
IVI, an autonomous not-for-profit Institute, sponsored a symposium on vaccines for the 21st Century, held in November 1996. The IVI has undertaken in 2002 a program called DOMI.
*Vaccine Development.*
For further details see under: **DOMI**.
**IVIG** (pooled human) Intravenous Immunoglobulins.
IVIG is used to treat TEN patients.
*Biochemistry; Dermatology; Lyell's Syndrome.*
For further details see under: **TEN**.
**IVLS** Illinois Valley Library System (U.S.A.).
**IVP** Intravenous Pyelogram.
*Radiology.*
**IVPN** international virtual private network.
réseau privé virtuel international.
**IVPP** Institute of Vertebrate Paleontology and Paleoanthropology (Beijing, China).
**IVR** Intramolecular Vibrational energy-Redistribution.
*Chemical Reactions; Chemistry; Molecular Structure; Reactive Systems.*
**IVR system** Interactive Voice Response system.
*Call Center Technology.*
**I.V.R.T.** Istituti di Vigilanza Riuniti d'Italia.
*Italian Institute.*
**IVs** Instrumental Variables.
*Statistics.*
**IVSs**; **ivs** Intervening Sequences.
*Genetics and Cell Biology; Molecular Biophysics and Biochemistry.*
**IVS** (assicurazione) Invalidità, Vecchiaia e Superstiti.
Italian initialism meaning: Old Age, Survivors and Disability insurance.
**IVSN** initial voice switched network.
réseau téléphonique commuté initial.
**IVT** Interface Verification Test.
**IVTAN** Institute of High Temperatures (Moscow, Former Soviet Union).
**IVU** International Vegetarian Union (G.B.).
**IW** Identifier Word.
*Computer Programming.*
**IW** individual weapon.
arme individuelle.
**IW**; **I.w.** Inside Width.
**IW** Instruction Word.
*Computer Programming.*
**IW** Internal Writer.
*Computer Technology.*
**IW**; **i.w.** Isotopic Weight.
**IWB** Interactive WhiteBoard.
**IWC** International Whaling Commission.
*Biological Sciences; Whale Species Protection; Zoology.*
**IWG** Investigators Working Group.
**IWI** Inventors Workshop International.
The IWI was founded in 1971.
*Inventions; Publications.*
**IWMI** International Water Management Institute.
*Water Policy Reforms.*
**IWMM** International Workshop on Memory Management.
**IWPCLDO** International Working Party of Cooperative Librarians Documentation Officers.
**IWRA** International Water Resources Association.
**IWRB** International Waterfowl and Wetlands Research Bureau (G.B.).
**IWS** International Wool Secretariat (G.B.).
**IWT** inland waterways transport.
transport par voies navigables intérieures.
**IWU** Intermediate Working Unit.
**IXM** Index Manager.
**IXP** International Executive Program.
*Programs.*
**IXS** Inelastic X-ray Scattering.
*Condensed Matter Physics.*
**IYHF** International Youth Hostel Federation (Denmark).
**IYKWIM** If You Know What I Mean.
**IZ** Intermediate Zone.
**IZ** Iraq.
**iZQCs** intermolecular Zero-Quantum Coherences.
*Biodiagnostics; Chemistry; Magnetic Resonance Research; Radiology.*

# J

**J** Japan.
Also: **JA**.
**J**; **j** jet.
*Fluid Mechanics; Mechanical Engineering.*
**J** Jew; Jewish.
**j** (abbr.)job.
*Computer Programming; Industrial Engineering.*
**J** joint staff.
état-major interarmées.
**J**; **j** journal.
**J**; **j** Judge; Judgement.
*Law.*
**J**; **j** The symbol for joule.
Joule is also known as: Newton-meter of energy.
*Metrology.*
**JA** Japan.
Also: **J**.
**JA** Jeunes Agriculteurs.
French initialism meaning: Young Agriculturers.
**JA** Job Analysis.
Job analysis is also known as: Job Study.
*Industrial Engineering.*
**JA**; **J/A** Joint Account.
**JA** Judge Advocate.
**J.A.** Justice of Appeal (G.B.).
**JAA** joint action area.
zone d'action conjointe.
**JAA** Joint Aviation Authority.
**JAALD** Japan Association of Agricultural Librarians and Documentalists.
*Japanese Association.*
**JAAT** joint air-assault (or air-attack) team.
groupe d'assaut aérien (ou d'attaque aérienne) interarmées.
**JAAWSC** joint AAW support and coordination (net).
(réseau de) coordination et soutien de la LAA combinée.
**JABEX** The Japan Association of Bioindustries EXecutives (Japan).
**JAC** Joint Astronomy Counter (Hawaii).
**JAC** Junior Association of Commerce (U.S.A.).
**JACC** Joint Automatic Control Conference.
**JACM** Journal of the Association for Computing Machinery.
*Periodical.*
**JACS** Journal of the American Chemical Society.
*Periodical.*
**JAEL** JSC Avionics Engineering Laboratory.
For further details see under: **JSC**.
**JAERI** Japan Atomic Energy Research Institute (Japan).
*Atomic Energy; Electrical Engineering; Japanese Institutes; Laser Acceleration; Plasma Physics; Short-pulse Laser Physics.*
**JAFCIS** joint armed forces of the CIS.
1a. forces armées conjointes de la Communauté des États indépendants.
1b. forces interarmées, de la Communauté des États indépendants.
**JAFZ** Jebel Ali Free Zone.
**JAG** Judge Advocate General.
**JAIDS** Journal of Acquired Immune Deficiency Syndrome.
**JAJO** January, April, July, October.
JAJO are the expiry months of many premium contracts.
*Finance.*
**Jak-STAT pathway** Janus Kinase-STAT pathway.
*Cell Biology; Medicine; Molecular Biology.*
**JAL** Journal d'Annonces Légales (France).
*Publication.*
**JAL** The airline code for Japan Air Lines.
**JALLC** Joint Analysis and Lessons Learned Centre [has replaced PAT].
Centre interarmées d'analyse et d'enseignements (tirés) [a remplacé la PAT].
**Jam.** (abbr.) Jamaica.
**JAM** Japanese Association for Microbiology.
**JAM** Journal of Applied Mechanics.
**JAM** Juge des Affaires Matrimoniales.
French acronym meaning: Judge for Matrimonial Affairs (France).
*Law.*
**JAM** Junctional Adhesion Molecule.
*Cell Biology.*
**jam** The above acronyms were coined using the English word "jam" (*Food Technology; Military Science; Ordnance*).
**JAMA** Journal of the American Medical Association (U.S.A.).
**JAMRI** Japan Maritime Research Institute (Japan).
**JAMSTEC** Japan's Marine Science and TEchnology Center (Japan).
JAMSTEC was formed in 1971. In 1995 JAMSTEC launched *Kaiko*, the world's deepest diving submersible.
*Marine Science and Technology; Oceanography.*
**Jan.** (abbr.) January.
**JAN** The airport code for Jacksonville International Airport.
**J&D** June and December.

*Securities.*
**JAPACS** JApanese PAcific Climate Study.
Of the Japanese Maritime Safety Agency.
**JAR** Japanese Association of Refrigeration (Japan).
**JAR** Joint Airworthiness Requirements.
**JAR** Jump Address Register.
**jar** The above acronyms were coined using the English word "jar" (*Chemistry; Electronics; Petroleum Engineering).*
**JARC** joint air reconnaissance centre.
centre interarmées de reconnaisssance aérienne.
**JARPA** JApanese Whale Research Program under Special Permit in the Antarctic.
**JARPN** JApanese Whale Research Program in the North Pacific.
*Japan's Scientific Whaling Program.*
**Jas** (abbr.) James.
**JASIN Experiment** Joint Air-Sea Interaction Experiment (U.S.A.).
The JASIN was a surface observation experiment conducted in July/August 1978 in the Eastern Atlantic (near Scotland).
*Experiments.*
**JASIS** Journal of the American Society for Information Science (U.S.A.).
**JASSW** Joint Air-to-Surface Stand-off Weapon.
**JAT** Juste-A-Temps.
French acronym meaning: Just In Time.
**JATO** Jet-Assisted TakeOff.
The jet-assisted take-off uses one or several jet-producing units for extra thrust.
*Aviation.*
**Jav** (abbr.) Javanese.
**JAWF** Joint Agriculture-Weather Facility.
**JAX** The airport code for Thompson Field, Jackson, Mississippi, U.S.A.
**JB** Junior Bond.
*Business; Finance.*
**JBCoB** Julius Baer Bank (Switzerland).
*Swiss Banks.*
**JBIRC** Japan Biological Information Research Center (Japan).
*Bioinformatics Databases; Bioinformatics Analysis; Molecular Biology; Population Genetics.*
**JBL** Journal of Business Law.
The JBL was founded in 1957.
*Publication.*
**J bolt** The J bolt is so called because it is shaped like the letter J. It presents threads on the longer leg of the J.
*Mechanical Devices.*
**J box** Junction box.
*Electricity.*
**JBS** Japanese Broadcast Satellite.
**JBS** John Birch Society.
**JBTC** joint blood transhipment centre.
centre interarmées de transbordement de sang.
**JC** Jesus Christ.
**JC** Job Class.
Job Class is also known as: Job Family; Job Grade; Labor Grade.
*Computer Programming.*
**J.C.** Jurisconsult.
**JC** Justice Clerk.
**JC** Juvenile Court.
**JCA** jamming control authority.
autorité de contrôle du brouillage.
**JCAH** Joint Commission of Accreditation of Hospitals.
**JCB** Jena Centre for Bioinformatics (Germany).
*Molecular Communication Processes.*
**JCB** Job Control Block.
**JCB** Joint Consultative Board.
Comité mixte de consultation.
**JCB** Junior College of Business.
**JCB** The Journal of Cell Biology.
*Periodical.*
**JCC** joint civil commission.
commission civile mixte.
**JCC** Junior Chamber of Commerce.
**JCCENT** Joint Command Centre [has replaced LANDCENT].
Commandement interarmées Centre [remplace LANDCENT].
**JCCEWS** Joint Command, Control, and Electronic Warfare School (U.S.A.).
**JCCFEP** Joint Commission on Cooperation in the Field of Environmental Protection - U.S.A. / F.S.U.
**JCCSWO** Joint Committee on Cooperation in Studies of the World Ocean - U.S.A. / F.S.U.
**JCEWS** Joint Command, Control, and Electronic Warfare School (U.S.A.).
**JCFC** Japan - China joint Fisheries Commission.
**JCG** joint consultative group.
Groupe consultatif commun (GCC).
**JCIE** Japan Center for International Exchange (Japan).
**JCL** Job-Control Language.
Job-control language is also known as: Command Language.
*Computer Programming.*
**JCMMG** Joint Civil/Military Medical Group.
Groupe médical mixte civilo-militaire.
**JCMT** James Clerk Maxwell Telescope.
**JCN** Journal of Cognitive Neuroscience.

*Periodical.*
**JC NORTH** Joint Command North.
Commandement interarmées Nord.
**JC NORTHEAST** Joint Command North-East.
Commandement interarmées Nord-Est.
**JCP** Job Control Processor.
**JCP** Joint Committee on Proliferation.
Comité mixte sur la prolifération.
**JCP** Journal de Chimie Physique (France).
*Periodical.*
**JCS** Job-Control Statement.
*Computer Programming.*
**JCS** Joint Chief of Staff (US).
**JCSOS** Joint and Combined Staff Officer School (U.S.A.).
**JC SOUTH** Joint Command South.
Commandement interarmées Sud.
**JC SOUTHCENT** Joint Command South-Centre [has replaced LANDSOUTHCENT].
Commandement interarmées Sud-Centre [remplace LANDSOUTHCENT].
**JC SOUTHEAST** Joint Command South-East.
Commandement interarmées Sud-Est.
**JC SOUTHWEST** Joint Command South-West.
Commandement interarmées Sud-Ouest.
**JCT** Joint Committee on Technology (for Space Science and Applications) (U.S.A.).
**jct.** (abbr) junction.
Also: **jctn.**
**JCU** John Cabot University (Rome, Italy).
*U.S. University.*
**JD** Job Description.
The job description describes the basic activities needed to carry out a job.
**Jd.** (abbr.) joined.
**JD** Jordan Dinar.
*Currencies.*
**JD** Julian Date.
Julian date is also konwn as Julian day and refers to the number of days elapsed since January 1, 4713 BC.
*Astronomy.*
**JD** June and December.
*Securities.*
**JD** Junior Dean.
**JD** Justice Department.
**J.D.** Juvenile Delinquency; Juvenile Delinquent.
*Criminal Law.*
**JDC**; **Jdc** Juvenile Diabetes Center (Italy).
*Islet Cell Transplants; Juvenile Diabetes Research.*
**JDF** Juvenile Diabetes Foundation.
**JdFR** Juan de Fuca Ridge.
**JDI** Joint Declaration of Intent.
*Business; Finance.*
**JDI** Journal du Droit International (France).
*Publication.*
**JDRMA** Japan Digital Road Map Association.
The Japan Digital Road Map association was organized in Japan by the Ministry of Constructions. Its aim is to create and maintain a *digital cartographical database of all Japan roads.*
**JE** Job Evaluation.
*Industrial Engineering.*
**JE** Josephson Effect.
The Josephson effect is also known as: Josephson Tunneling.
*Materials Science.*
**JEA** Jersey European Airways.
U.K. Regional Carrier.
**JEB** Junctional Epidermolysis Bullosa.
*Biochemistry; Human Genetics; Medicine; Molecular Genetics; Pediatrics.*
**JECFA** Joint (FAO/WHO) Expert Committee on Food Additives.
*Applied Nutrition; Food Safety; Hepatocarcinogens.*
For further details see under: **FAO** and **WHO**.
**JECS** Job Entry Central Services.
**JECSS** Japan and East China Seas Study.
**JED** Joint Epicentral Determination.
*Seismology.*
**JEDA Center** Joint Environmental Data Analysis Center (U.S.A.).
**JEDEC** Joint Electronic Device Engineering Council.
**JEIDA** Japan Electronic Industry Development Association.
**JEL** Jeunesse Européenne Libérale.
French acronym meaning: European Liberal Youth.
**JEM** Japanese Experiment Module.
**JEMDES** Joint European METOC Data Exchange System.
système interarmées d'échange de données METOC en Europe.
**JENEX** Japanese El Niño Experiment.
**JEP** Joint Educational Project.
*European Community Project.*
**JEPS** jont exercise planning staff.
état-major interarmées (mixte) de planification d'exercice.
**JERS-1** Japan Earth Resources Satellite.
**JES** Job Entry Subsystem.
*Computer Programming.*
**JESSI** Joint European Submicron Silicon Initiative.
*European Community Initiative.*

**JET** Joint European Tokamak.
**JET** Joint European Torus.
The Joint European Torus consists of fusion experiments. Commercial fusion reactors are supposed to operate after year 2040.
*Fusion Reactors; Plasma Physics.*
**JET** Journal Entries Transfer.
**JET** Journalisme Electronique.
French acronym meaning: Electronic Gathering News.
**jet** The above acronyms were coined using the English word "jet"
*Aviation; Fuid Mechanics; Geology; Mechanical Engineering.*
**JETAI** Journal of Experimental & Theoretical Artificial Intelligence.
**JETP** Journal of Experimental and Theoretical Physics.
The JETP is being published by the American Institute of Physics.
*Physics Publishing.*
**JETT** Journal of Educational Techniques and Technologies (Georgia, U.S.A.).
**JEV** Japanese Encephalitis Virus.
The mosquito-borne JEV is a flavivirus allied to the West Nile virus.
*Epidemic Encephalitis.*
**JEV** Joint European Venture - E.C.
For Small and Medium size Enterprises.
**JEWC** Joint Electronic Warfare Coordination (Cell / Committee).
(Cellule/Comité) interarmées de coordination de la guerre électronique.
**JFA** Japan Fisheries Agency (Japan).
**JFA** Journée du Français des Affaires (France).
French initialism meaning: the Day devoted to Business French. The first JFA was held on Wednesday 28th October 1987.
**JFACC** joint forces air component command(er).
commandement (commandant) de composante aérienne de force interarmées.
**JFAI** 1. joint final acceptanmce inspection [obsolete - replaced by JFAI 2.].
1. inspection mixte de réception définitive.
2. joint formal acceptance inspection.
2. inspection mixte de réception officielle.
**JFAP** Joint Faculty Appointment Program (U.S.A.).
Of the U.S. NSF.
For further details see under: **NSF**.
**JFC** Job-Flow Control.
*Computer Programming.*
**JFCB** Job File Control Block.
**JFC** joint force commander.
commandant de la force interarmées.
**JFCs** Jupiter-Family Comets.
The JFCs are the 160 comets discovered that are dynamically controlled by Jupiter.
*Astronomy; Astrophysics; Physics; Space Science.*
**JFET** Junction Field-Effect Transistor.
The junctions field-effect transistor is also known as: Depletion-mode Field-Effect Transistor.
*Electronics.*
**JFG** Joint Frequency Group.
Groupe mixte sur les fréquences.
**JFK** The airport code for John F. Kennedy International Airport, New York, U.S.A.
**JFPAA** Japan Federation of Practicing Attorneys' Associations (Japan).
**JFPF** Joint Federal Police Force [SFOR].
Force de police mixte fédérale [SFOR].
**JFR** Juan de Fuca Ridge.
For further details see under: **ODP** and **CORK**.
**JFSP** Joint Forecast System Project.
**JFTC** Japan Foreign Trade Council.
**jg** junior grade.
**JGB** Japanese Government Bond.
*Banking; Finance.*
**JGI** Joint Genome Institute (U.S.A.).
U.S. DOE's JGI was formed in 1997.
*Computational Genomics; Functional Genomics; Genome Diversity Studies; Genome Institutes.*
For further details see under: **DOE**.
**JGOFS** Joint Global Ocean Flux Study.
**JH** Juvenile Hormone.
*Entomology.*
**JHA** Juvenile Hormone Analogs.
**JHE** Journal of Human Evolution.
*Periodical.*
**JHNSP** joint host nation support plan.
plan interarmées de soutien fourni par le pays hôte.
**JHQ CENT** Joint Headquerters Centre.
Quartier général interarmées Centre.
**JHQ NORTH** Joint Headquarters North.
Quartier général interarmées Nord.
**JHQ NORTHEAST** Joint Headquarters North-East.
Quartier général interarmées Nord-Est.
**JHQ SOUTH** Joint Headquarters South.
Quartier général interarmées Sud.
**JHQ SOUTHCENT** Joint Headquarters South-Centre.
Quartier général interarmées Sud-Centre.
**JHQ SOUTHEAST** Joint Headquarters South-East.
Quartier général interamées Sud-Est.

**JHQ SOUTHWEST** Joint Headquarters South-West.
Quartier général interarmées Sud-Ouest.
**JHS** Jackson Heart Study.
Chief Sponsor of the JHS is the ORMH.
For further details see under: **ORMH**.
**JHSBC** The Johns Hopkins Singapore Biomedical Centre.
An academic affiliate of JHUSOM.
For further details see under: **JHUSOM**.
**JHU** John Hopkins University (U.S.A.).
**JHUSOM** The Johns Hopkins University School Of Medicine (Baltimore, Maryland, U.S.A.).
For further details see under: **JHSBC**.
**JIAMCATT** The Joint Inter-Agency Meeting on Computer-Assisted *Translation and Terminology.*
JIAMCATT was created in 1987 at the U.N. Office in Geneva, Switzerland.
**JIB** Jordans International Bulletin (G.B.).
**JIC** John Innes Centre (G.B.).
The JIC is a government-funded plant and microbial science laboratory in Norwich.
*Bioinformatics; Biological Computing; Life Sciences; Microbial Science; Oilseeds Research.*
**JIC** Joint Ice Center (U.S.A.).
Of the U.S. Navy / U.S. National Oceanic and Atmospheric Administration.
**JIC** 1. Joint Implementation Commission.
1. Commission mixte d'application.
2. Joint Implementation Committee.
2. Comité interarmées (ou mixte) de mise en œuvre.
3. joint intelligence centre.
3. centre de renseignement interarmées.
**JIC** Joint Information Center.
**JICC** Joint Information Coordination Committee.
Comité interarmées de coordination de l'information.
**JICS** Japan International Cooperation Systems (Tokyo, Japan).
**JICST** Japan Information Center for Science and Technology (Japan).
**JILA** Joint Institute for Laboratory Astrophysics.
*Astronomy; Experimental Programs; Laboratory Astrophysics; Laser Physics; Laser Frequency Stabilization; Quantum and Atom Optics.*
**JIM** Judge Institute of Management.
University of Cambridge, G.B.
**JIMAR** Joint Institute of Marine and Atmospheric Research.
**JINR** Joint Institute for Nuclear Research.
The JINR is located in Russia (Dubna) where a joint U.S. - Russian team works.
*Nuclear Physics.*
**JINS** Japan Institute of Nuclear Safety (Japan).
**JIP** joint implementation plan.
plan interarmées (ou mixte) de mise en œuvre.
**JIPID** Japan International Protein Information Database.
**JIRA**; **J.I.R.A.** Japan Industrial Robot Association.
**JIRCAS** Japan International Research Center for Agricultural Sciences (Japan).
**JIS** Japanese Industrial Standard.
**JIS** Japanese Institute for Standards.
**JISAO** Joint Institute for the Study of the Atmosphere and Ocean.
University of Washington (U.S.A.).
**JISC** Japanese Industrial Standards Committee.
**JISTEC** Japan International Science and Technology Exchange Center (Japan).
**JIT**; **Jit** Just In Time.
*Logistic Systems.*
**Jitic** Jiangsu international trust and investment corporation.
*State Investment Bodies.*
**JJ** January and July.
*Securities.*
**JJ** Josephson Junction.
**JJ.** Justices.
**JJA** June-July-August.
**JKFC** Japan-Korea joint Fisheries Commission.
**JKT** The airport code for Jakarta, Indonesia.
**JL** Job Library.
*Computer Programming.*
**JL** Job Lot.
*Industrial Engineering.*
**JL** The airline code for Japan Airlines.
**JLA** Jamaica Library Association.
**JLA** Japan Library Association.
**JLA** Jordan Library Association.
**JLC** Japan Linear Collider.
*Particle Physics.*
**JLG** Japan Library Group.
**JLOC** joint logistic operations centre.
centre interarmées d'opérations logistiques.
**JLP** joint logistic plan.
plan logistique interarmées (ou mixte).
**JLPG** Joint Logistic Planning Group.
Groupe interarmées (ou mixte) de planification logistique.
**JLSP** joint logistic support plan.
plan de soutien logistique interarmées.
**JM** Jamaica.
**JM** Job Memory.
**JM** Job Mix.
*Computer Programming.*

**JMA** Japan Meteorological Agency.
*Earthquake Prediction Information; Seismology.*
**JMAPS** joint message-processing system.
système interarmées de traitement de messages.
**JMC** 1. Joint Medical Committee.
1a. Comité interarmées des services médicaux.
1b. Comité mixte médical.
2. joint military commission.
2. commission militaire mixte.
**JMCC** joint movement coordination centre.
centre interarmées de coordination des mouvements.
**JMCIS** joint maritime command information system.
système commun d'information pour le commandement maritime.
**JMETL** joint mission-essential task list [PCC].
liste commune des tâches essentielles à la mission [PCC].
**JMEX** joint movement exercise.
exercice de mouvements interarmées.
**JMLA** Japan Medical Library Association.
**JMMD** Journal of Multilingual & Multicultural Development.
**JMP** Job-Management Program.
*Computer Programming.*
**JPM** joint movement plan.
plan de mouvements interarmées.
**jmp** (abbr.) jump.
Jump is also known as: Branch or Transfer.
*Computer Programming.*
**JMSA** Japan Marine Safety Agency.
**JMSDF** Japanese Maritime Self-Defense Force.
**JMU** James Madison University (U.S.A.).
**jn.** (abbr.) junction.
Also: **Junc.**; **jnc**.
**JNAF** Japanese Naval Air Force (Japan).
**JNB** The airport code for Johannesburg, South Africa.
**jnc.** (abbr. ) junction.
Also: **junc.**; **jn**.
**JNCI** Journal of the National Cancer Institute (U.S.A.).
**JNCL** Joint National Committee for Languages (U.S.A.).
**JND** Just Noticeable Difference.
Just-noticeable difference is also known as: Difference Threshold; Difference Limen.
*Psychology.*
**JNICT** Junta Nacional Investigaçao Científica e Tecnológica (Portugal).
**JNIH** Japan National Institute of Health.
The JNIH has been replaced by: NIID.
For further details see under: **NIID**.
**JNKs** a -Jun $NH_2$ - terminal kinases.
*Pharmacology; Health Scinces; Signal Transduction.*
**JNLWP** Joint Non-Lethal Weapons Program - U.S. DOD's.
*Hostages Rescue; Rioters Dispersion.*
For further details see under: **DOD**.
**JNOC** Japan National Oil Corporation (Japan).
*Energy Research.*
**Jnr.** (abbr.) Junior.
Also: **Jun.**; **Jr**.
**JNT STK** (abbr.) Joint Stock.
**JO** Joint Ownership.
*Business; Finance.*
**JO** Jordan.
**JO** Journal Officiel (France).
**JOA** Joint Oceanographic Assembly.
**JOA** joint operations area.
zone d'opérations interarmées.
**JOAG** Juvenile Open Angle Glaucoma.
*Glaucoma; Medicine; Ophtalmology; Pediatrics.*
**JOC** Jeunesse Ouvrière Chrétienne.
French acronym meaning: Christian Worker Youth.
**JOC** joint operations centre [has replaced CRC 2. & 3.].
centre d'opérations interarmées [remplace CRC 2. & 3.].
**JOC** Joint Organizing Committee.
**JOCE** Journal Officiel des Communautés Européennes.
French acronym meaning: Official Journal of the European Communities.
**JODC** Japan Oceanographic Data Center (Japan).
*Oceanography.*
**JOI** Joint Oceanographic Institutions, Inc. (U.S.A.).
**JOIDES** Joint Oceanographic Institutions for Deep Earth Sampling.
JOIDES is a group of committees and panels with representatives from the participating countries.
*Oceanography.*
**JOIN** Japan Organization InterNetwork (Japan).
**JOINTEX** joint exercise.
exercice interarmées.
**JOJA** July, October, January, April.
*Securities.*
**JOLIS** JOint LIbraries.
*World Bank.*
**JONSDAP** JOint North Sea Data Acquisition Project.
**JONSIS** JOint North Sea Information System.
**JONSWAP** JOint North Sea Wave Atmosphere Project.

**JOP** Joint Optoelectronics Project.
**JOP** JOint-venture Programme.
**JOP** Jupiter Orbiter Probe.
**JOPP** JOint-venture PHARE Programme.
**JOR** Jordan's international vehicle-registration letters.
**JOSS** Johnniac Open-Shop System.
*Computer Programming.*
**JOT** Job-Oriented Terminal.
*Computer Technology.*
**jour.** (abbr.) journal.
**JOVIAL** Jules' Own Version of International Algorithmic Language.
*Computer Programming.*
**JP** jet propellant.
carburéacteur.
**JP**; **J.P.** Jet Propulsion.
*Aviation; Space Technology.*
**JP** Job Press.
*Graphic Arts.*
**JP**; **J.P.** Justice of the Peace.
*Law.*
**JPA** Job Pack Area.
**JPC** Japan Productivity Center.
**JPC** Job-Processing Control.
*Computer Programming.*
**JPC** 1. joint planning commission.
1. commission mixte de planification.
2. joint planning committee.
2. comité mixte de planification.
**JPEG algorithm** Joint Photographic Experts Group algorithm.
The JPEG algorithm is used to encode images for transmission across the Internet.
**JPF** joint police force [SFOR].
force de police mixte [SFOR].
**JPG** joint planning group.
groupe mixte de planification.
**JPIC** joint precision interdiction concept.
concept d'interdiction de précision interarmées.
**JPL** Jet Propulsion Laboratory.
California Institute of Technology, Pasadena, California, U.S.A. The JPL is NASA's center *for Planetary Exploration.*
**JPL** Journal of planning and Property Law.
The JPL was founded in 1954.
*Publication.*
**JPLA** Japan Pharmaceutical Library Association.
**JPNIC** Japan Network Information Center.
**JPO** joint petroleum office.
bureau interarmées des carburants.
**JPOTS** Joint Panel on Oceanographic Tables and Standards.
**JPS** Jewish Publication Society.
**JPSs** Juvenile Polyposis Syndromes.
*Molecular Genetics; Oncogenesis.*
**JPWHQ** joint primary war headquarters.
quartier général de guerre principal interarmées (QGGPI).
**JQP** Josephson-QuasiParticle.
*Nanoscience; Physics.*
**Jr**; **jr** (abbr.) Journal.
**Jr** (abbr.) Junior.
Also: **Jnr.**; **Jun**.
**Jr** (abbr.) Juror.
*Law.*
**JRC** 1. joint reconnaissance centre.
1. centre interarmées de reconnaissance.
2. joint rescue centre.
2. centre interarmées des opérations de sauvetage.
**JRC** Junior Red Cross.
**JRCC** joint rescue coordination centre.
centre interarmées de coordination des opérations de sauvetage.
**JRC-CEC** Joint Research Centre - Commission of the European Communities (Italy).
**JRC-CEO** Joint Research Centre - Centre for Earth Observation - *European Community.*
**JRC-ENDWEL** Joint Research Centre-management of ENergy in DWELlings.
*Euratom / E.C. Program.*
**JRC-HCM** Joint Research Centre - Human Capital and Mobility.
*E.C. Research Program.*
**JRC-HFR** Joint Research Centre - High Flux Reactor.
Euratom research program on the operation of the HFR to be implemented by the JRC.
*Euratom Research Program.*
**JRC-HTM** Joint Research Centre - High-Temperature Materials.
*Euratom / EEC Research Program.*
**JRC-HYDPROD** Joint Research Centre - HYDrogen PRODuction, energy storage and transport.
*Euratom / EEC Research Program.*
**JRC-INDHAZ** Joint Research Centre - INDustrial HAZards.
*E.C. Research Program.*
**JRC-IT** Joint Research Centre - Information Technologies (1995-1998).
*European Community Program.*
**JRC-MEASTEST** Joint Research Centre - MEASurements and TESTing (1995-1998).
*European Community Program.*

**JRC-NNE** Joint Research Centre - Non-Nuclear Energy (1995-1998).
*European Community Program.*
**JRC-NUMEAS** Joint Research Centre - NUclear MEASurements and reference materials (1984-1987).
*Euratom / EEC Research Program.*
**JRC-RADIOMON** Joint Research Centre - Evaluation and MONitoring of RADIOactivity.
*Euratom Research Program.*
**JRC-REMSENS** Joint Research Centre - Application of REMote-SENSing techniques.
*Euratom / EEC Research Program.*
**JRC-SAFEFM** Joint Research Centre - SAFEguarding and management of Fissile Materials (1988-1991).
*Euratom Research Program.*
**JRC-SOLARTEST** Joint Research Centre - technique for SOLAR energy TESTs.
*Euratom / EEC Research Program.*
**JRC-TSER** Joint Research Centre - Targeted Socio-Economic Research (1995-1998).
*European Community Program.*
**JRI** J. Rothschild International.
*Banks.*
**JRMS** Joint Reception and Movements System [obsolete - now called ADAMS].
système d'accueil et de mouvements interarmées [obsolète - maintenant appelé ADAMS].
**JRO** Jicamarca Radar Observatory.
The Jicamarca Radar Observatory is located outside Lima. It was built by the U.S. Government in 1960 and later donated to Peru. It is used to study the upper atmosphere.
**JS** Job Stacking.
*Computer Programming.*
**JS** Job Step.
*Computer Programming.*
**JS** Job Stream.
*Computer Programming.*
**JSA** Japanese Standard Association.
**JSB** Joint Service Board [NSA].
Bureau interarmées [AON].
**J.S.B.** Joint-Stock Bank.
**JSBG** Joint Structural Biology Group.
**JSC** Johnson Space Center.
The JSC, originally named the Manned Spacecraft Center when it opened in September 1963, was renamed the Lyndon B. Johnson Space Center in honor of the late President Johnson in 1973. The JSC is a field center of the National Aeronautics and Space Administration, a federal agency of the United States Government.
*Analytical Chemistry; Biomineralogy; Electron Microscopy; Exobiology; Geochemistry; Geology; Interplanetary Dust Particle Science; Meteoritics.*
**JSC** Joint Scientific Committee.
**JSC** 1. joint spectrum centre.
1. centre interarmées (de gestion) du spectre.
2. joint steering committee.
2. comité directeur mixte.
3. joint sub-committee.
3. sous-comité mixte.
**JSC** Joint Stock Company.
**JSCNOET** Joint Standing Committee on Nuclear and Other Energy Technologies - U.S.A.-Korea.
**JSDM** June, September, December, March.
*Securities.*
**JSE** Johannesburg Stock Exchange.
**JSEA** Japan Ship Exporters' Association.
**JSF** Joint Strike Fighter.
The JSF, a manned combat aircraft, is scheduled to enter operational service in 2008. It will replace many aircraft in service at the U.S. Air Force, the U.S. Marines and the Royal Navy.
*Manned Combat Aircraft.*
**JSF Program** Joint Strike Fighter Program.
Fully operational by 2008.
**JSIA** Japan Software Industry Association.
**JSK** Jidosha Soko densigijutsu Kyokai.
JSK is a Japanese Association for electronic technology. It was founded in 1979 under the supervision of the Ministry of Foreign Trade.
**JSLA** Japan Special Libraries Association.
**JSME** Japan Society of Mechanical Engineers.
**JSME** Joint Soil Moisture Experiment.
**JSMF** James S. McDonnell Foundation (U.S.A.).
The 21st Century Science Initiative.
*Brain Cancer Research; Brain, Mind and Behavior Bridging; Complex Systems.*
**JSMS** joint spectrum management system.
système interarmées de gestion du spectre.
**JSOTF** joint special operations task force.
groupe opérationnel interarmées pour les opérations spéciales.
**JSP** joint support plan.
plan interarmées (ou mixte) de soutien.
**JSPS** Japan Society for the Promotion of Science (Japan).
The JSPS was founded in 1932. It has an important role in the administration of many scientific and academic programs. The "Research for the Future" Program is funded by the JSPS.
**JSRC** Joint Sub-Regional Command.
Commandement interarmées sous-régional.

**JSRC CENTRE** Joint Sub-Regional Command Centre.
Commandement interarmées sous-régional Centre.
**JSRC NORTH** Joint Sub-Regional Command North.
Commandement interarmées sous-régional Nord.
**JSRC NORTHEAST** Joint Sub-Regional Command North-East.
Commandement interarmées sous-régional Nord-Est.
**JSRC SOUTH** Joint Sub-Regional Command South.
Commandement interarmées sous-régional Sud.
**JSRC SOUTHCENTRE** Joint Sub-Regional Command South-Centre.
Commandement interarmées sous-régional Sud-Centre.
**JSRC SOUTHEAST** Joint Sub-Regional Command South-East.
Commandement interarmées sous-régional Sud-Est.
**JSRC SOUTHWEST** Joint Sub-Regional Command South-West.
Commandement interarmées sous-régional Sud-Ouest.
**JST** Japan Standard Time.
**JSTARS** Joint Surveillance and Target Attack Radar System.
système radar interarmées de surveillance et d'attaque d'objectifs.
**JSTPS** joint strategic target planning staff.
état-major interarmées de planification des objectifs stratégiques.
**JST Corporation** Japan Science and Technology Corporation (Kyoto, Japan).
**JS theory** Jacobson-Stockmayer theory.
**JT** Japan Tobacco.
**jt** (abbr.) joint.
**JT** Joint Tenancy.
**JTAA** see JAA.
voir JAA.
**Jt/Ac** Joint Account.
**JTB** joint transportation board.
comité mixte des transports.
**JTCA** Japan Transport Consultants Association.
**JTC3A** Joint Tactical Command, Control, and Communications Agency.
**JTCC** joint transportation coordination centre.
centre de coordination interarmées des transports.
**JTFP** joint tactical fusion programme.
programme interarmées de fusionnement tactique.
**JTIDS** Joint Tactical Information Distribution System.
**JTLS** joint theatre-level simulation.
simulation interarmées à l'échelle du théâtre.
**JTMS** joint theatre movement staff.
état-major interarmées des mouvements sur le théâtre.
**JTMTA** Japan Traffic Management Technology Association.
The JTMTA is a Japanese Association organized by the Japanese National Policy Agency. It operates in contact with the Japanese National Institute of Policy Science.
**Ju** (abbr.) June.
Also: **Jun**.
**JUG** Joint Users Group.
**Jul.** (abbr.) July.
Also: **Jy.**
**Jun.** (abbr.) June.
Also: **Jn**.
**Jun.** (abbr.) Junior.
Also: **Jnr.**; **Jr**.
**Junc.** (abbr.) junction.
Also: **jn.**; **jnc**.
**jurisp.** (abbr.) jurisprudence.
**jus.** (abbr.) justice.
**JUSE** Japanese Union of Scientists and Engineers (Japan).
**JV** Joint Venture.
*Business; Finance.*
**JV** Junior Varsity.
**JVMs** Java Virtual Machines.
Java is a programming language pioneered by Sun Microsystems.
**JWB** Jewish Welfare Board.
**JWID** Joint Warrior interoperability demonstration.
démonstration d'interopérabilité "Joint Warrior".
**Jy.** (abbr.) July.
Also: **Jul.**
**JYI** Journal of Young Investigators.
The JYI began in 1997.

**k**; **k.** karat.
*Metallurgy.*
For further details see under: **Kt**.

**K** Kelvin; kelvin.
*Thermodynamics.*

**K** Kent.

**k** (abbr.) key.
*Building Engineering; Computer Programming; Electricity; Electronics; Graphic Arts; Mechanical Devices; Systematics; Telecommunications.*

**k** (abbr.) keyboard.
The keyboard is a set of levers or keys which are used to operate a typewriter, a machine, a computer, or a piano.
*Mechanical Engineering.*

**k** kilo.

**K** King.
Also: **Kg.**

**K** Knight.
Also: **Knt.**

**K** The chemical symbol for Potassium.
Potassium is a metallic element having the atomic number 19, an atomic weight of 39.100 and a melting point of 63°C. Potassium is also known as: Kalium. It is used in industry for many purposes.
*Chemistry; Symbols.*

**ka** (abbr.) cathode.
*Electricity; Electronics; Physical Chemistry.*

**KA** Key Access.
*Computer Programming.*

**kA** kiloampere.
kiloampere is a metric unit of electrical current equivalent to 1000 amperes.
*Metrology.*

**KA** Kinase Activity.

**KAB** Keep America Beautiful.

**$KAg(CN)_2$** Potassium Argentocyanide.
Potassium Argentocyanide, also known as: Cyanoargenate; Silver Potassium Cyanide, is used mainly in silver plating.
*Inorganic Chemistry.*

**$KAg(CN)_2$** Silver Potassium Cyanide.
Silver Potassium Cyanide is used mainly as an antiseptic and in silver plating.
*Organic Chemistry.*

**KAIST** Korea Advanced Institute of Science and Technology (Taejon, Korea).

**KAK** Key-Auto-Key.

**KAL** Knowledge About Language.

**$KalSiO_4$** Kaliophilite.
Kaliophilite also known as: Facellite; Phacellite, is found in basement rocks at Mt. Somma, Italy.
*Mineralogy.*

**$KalSi_2O_6$** Leucite.
Leucite is also known as: Grenatite; White Garnet.

**$KalSi_3O_8$** Microcline.
*Mineralogy.*

**KamLAND** Kamioka Liquid scintillator Anti-Neutrino Detector.
KamLAND is a collaboration of 3 Japanese and 10 U.S. Institutions. The experiment may be running till 2010.
*Antineutrinos; Antineutrinos Detection; Neutrino Research; Nuclear Reactors; Particle Physics; Solar Neutrinos.*

**KAM tori** Kolmogorov-Arnold-Moser tori.
*Biochemical Engineering; Chemical Engineering.*

**Kan.** (abbr.) Kansas (U.S.A.).
Also: **Kans.**; **KS**.

**KAPL** Knoll Atomic Power Laboratory (U.S.A.).

**KARMEN experiment** KArlsruhe Rutherford Medium Energy Neutrino experiment.
*Cosmology; Physics.*

**KASLIB** Kanagawa Association of Special Libraries and Information Bureaus.

**kat** katal.
*Enzymology.*

**KAU** Keystation Adapter Unit.

**KAU** 1a. kilo accounting unit.
1b. thousand accounting units.
1a. kilo-unité de compte.
1b. million d'unités de compte.

**KAVAS** Knowledge Acquisition, Visualization and Assessment Study.

**kb** (abbr.) keyboard.
Also: **keybd.**; **kbd**.
For further details see under: **k**.

**KB** Key Bounce.
*Computer Technology.*

**kb** kilobar.
kilobar is a unit of pressure equal to one thousand bars.
*Metrology.*

**Kb**; **kb** Kilobase.
The kilobase is equal to one thousand bases.
*Genetics.*

**Kb** Kilobit.
*Computer Technology.*

**KB** Kilobyte.
Also: **Kbyte**; **kbyte**.

**kbd** (abbr.) keyboard.

Also: **kb**; **keybd**.
For further details see under: **k**.
**KBE** Keyboard Entry.
The keyboard entry is the information manually fed into a computer memory from a typewriter keyboard or other keyboard.
*Computer Programming.*
**KBE** Knight Commander of the Order of the British Empire (G.B.).
**KBI** Keyboard Inquiry.
The keyboard inquiry is an inquiry regarding particular aspects of the computer system made by means of a keyboard.
*Computer Programming.*
**K/BIS MHW** Kitchen/Bath Industry Show / Multihousing World.
Held at Orlando, FL, Orange County Convention Center on $16^{th}/18^{th}$ April 1999.
*U.S. Annual Shows.*
**Kbit** Kilobit.
*Computer Technology.*
**KBOs** Kuiper Belt Objects.
KBOs have a size less than a few hundred kilometers in diameter. Named after the Dutch-American astronometer Gerard **Kuiper** (1905-1973).
*Astronomy; Astrophysics; Lunar and Planetary Sciences.*
For further details see under: **JFCs** and **TNOs**.
**kbp** kilobase pair.
**kbps** kilobit per second.
1,024 bits/second.
**KBr** Potassium Bromide.
Potassium Bromide is used mainly in spectroscopy and in photography.
*Inorganic Chemistry.*
**KBS** Kay Behrensmeyer Site (East Africa).
*Anthropology.*
**KBS** Knowledge-Based Systems.
Knowledge-based systems are also known as: Expert Systems.
**KBSI** Korea Basic Science Institute.
**KBV** Physicians' Association (Germany).
**KByte**; **kbyte** Kilobyte.
Also: **KB**.
**KC** Kansas City, U.S.A.
**KC** Key Change.
*Computer Programming.*
**KC** Key Compression.
Key compression is a technique for the reduction of bits in a key.
*Computer Programming.*
**kc** kilocurie.
For further details see under: **kCi**.
**KC** King's Counsel.
**KC** Kiting Cheek.
**KC** Knights of Columbus.
The Knights of Christopher Columbus are members of a fraternal society of Roman Catholic men.
**KC** Knowledge Coding.
*Artificial Intelligence.*
**kcal** kilocalorie.
For further details see under: **kg-cal** (kilogram-calorie).
**KCB** Knight Commander of the Order of the Bath.
**KCC** Kisan Coordination Committee (India).
**Kcell** Killer cell.
*Immunology.*
**KCF** Kayack Club de France (France).
**$KC_2H_3O_2$** Potassium Acetate.
Potassium Acetate is used mainly in medicine.
*Organic Chemistry.*
**kCi** Kilocurie.
The kilocurie is equivalent to one thousand curies.
*Metrology.*
**KCl** Potassium Chloride.
Potassium Chloride is used mainly in pharmaceuticals.
*Inorganic Chemistry.*
**KCl** Sylvite.
Sylvite, also known as: Sylvine, is used for fertilizers.
*Mineralogy.*
**KCM** Kirchhoff Coda Migration.
*Earth Sciences.*
**K.C.M.G.** Knight Commander of the Order of St. Michael and St. George.
**KCMIA** killed / captured / missing in action.
tué / capturé / disparu au combat.
**KCMSD** Kansas City Metropolitan School District (U.S.A.).
**KCN** Potassium Cyanide.
KCN is used mainly in electroplating and in insecticides.
*Inorganic Chemistry.*
**$K_2CO_3$** Potassium Carbonate.
Potassium Carbonate, also known as: Salt of Tartar; Pearl Ash; Potash, is used in colour TV tubes.
*Inorganic Chemistry.*
**KCOM** Kinksville College of Osteopathic Medicine (U.S.A.).
**KCR** Kimberlite-Clan Rock.
For further details see under: **KCRs**.
**KCRC** Kowloon Canton Railway Company (Hong Kong).
**$K_2CrO_4$** Tarapacàite.

Tarapacàite is found in nitrate deposits in Chile.
*Mineralogy.*
**KCRs** Kimberlite-Clan Rocks.
*Earth Science; Geosciences; Materials Science; Planetary Science.*
**KCs** Kenyon Cells.
*Biology; Insect Olfactory System; Neuroscience; Physiology; Neurophysiology.*
**kc/s** kilocycles per second.
**KCSC** Kinetic City Super Crew (U.S.A.).
KCSC is a production of the AAAS.
For further details see under: **AAAS**.
**K.C.S.I.** Knight Commander of the Order of the Star of India.
**K.C.V.O.** Knight Commander of the (Royal) Victorian Order.
**KD** Kiln Dried.
**kD** kilodalton.
**KD** Kuwait Dinar.
*Currencies.*
**KDC** key distribution centre.
centre de distribution de clés (CDC).
**KDC** Key-Driven Calculator.
A former electromechanical desk calculator.
*Computer Technology.*
**KDCD** Kuwait Dinar Certificate of Deposit.
*Banking; Business; Finance.*
**KDH** $\alpha$-Ketoglutarate Dehydrogenase.
**KDI initiative** Knowledge and Distributed Intelligence initiative.
*U.S. Initiatives.*
**KDM** Key-Disk Machine.
*Computer Technology.*
**KDOM** Kosovo Diplomatic Observation Mission.
Mission d'observation diplomatique au Kosovo.
**KDPG** D-2-Keto-3-Deoxy-6-Phosphogluconate aldolase.
**KD price** Knocked Down price.
*Business; Finance.*
**KDS** Keyboard Display Station.
**KDS** Key-to-Disk System.
*Computer Technology.*
**KDT** Key Data Terminal.
**KdV equation** Korteveg and deVries equation.
*Materials Science; Mathematical Physics; Optical Physics; Solitary Waves (Solitons).*
**KE** Kenya.
**KE** Kinetic Energy.
*Mechanics.*
**KEB** Korea Exchange Bank (Korea).
**KEGG** Kyoto Encyclopedia of Genes and Genomes.
*Computer Networks; Genetics.*
**KEK** High-Energy Accelerator Research Organization (Tsukuba, Japan).
The Institute for Nuclear Studies of the University of Tokyo was merged into KEK in 1997.
**KEK** key-encryption key.
clé de chiffrement de clés.
**KEMRI** KEnya Medical Research Institute.
*Medical Research.*
**Ken.** (abbr.) Kentucky (U.S.A.).
**KEOPS** KEys to Optical Packet Switching.
*European Community Project.*
**KEP** Key Entry Processing.
**KEPCO** Korea Electric Power COrporation.
**Ker** (abbr.) Kerry.
County Kerry, Ireland.
**KET** Kiel Electron Telescope.
University of Kiel and Centre d'Etude Nucléaire de Saclay.
**KEUR** thousand euros (European single currency).
Also: **K€**.
**kev** kilo electron Volt.
kilo electron volt is a unit of energy equal to one thousand electron volts.
*Metrology.*
**KEW** kinetic energy weapon.
arme à énergie cinétique.
**keybd** (abbr.) keyboard.
Also: **kbd.**; **kb**.
For further details see under: **k**.
**KF** Key Field.
*Computer Programming.*
**KF**; **kF** Kilo Franc.
One thousand francs.
**KFAS** Keyed File Access System.
**KFAS** Kuwait Foundation for the Advancement of Sciences (Kuwait).
**KFB** Korea First Bank (Korea).
**KfK PEF** Nuclear Research Centre (Karlsruhe, Germany).
**KFOR** Kosovo Force.
Force pour le Kosovo.
**KfW** Kreditanstalt für Wiederaufbau.
*German Export Bank.*
**Kg.** Kilogram / Kilogramme.
*Metrology.*
**Kg** King.
Also: **K**.
**KG**; **K.G.** Knight of the Order of the Garter.
**KG** Kyrgyz Republic [formerly known as Kyrgyzstan].
République kirghize [anciennement appelée Kirghizistan].
**kg-cal** kilocalorie.

kilogram-calorie is a unit of energy equal to one thousand small calories.
*Metrology.*
**KGFs** Keratinocyte Growth Factors.
*Cell Biology; Molecular Genetics; Immunology; Tissue Repair.*
For further details see under: **DETCs**.
**KGI** Keck Graduate Institute (U.S.A.).
*Applied Life Sciences.*
**KGS** Kansas Geological Survey.
*Geosciences.*
**KGy** Kilogray.
**KGZ** see KG.
voir KG.
**$KHCO_3$** Kalicinite.
Kalicinite is also known as: Kalicine; Kalicite.
*Mineralogy.*
**$KHF_2$** Potassium Bifluoride.
Potassium Bifluoride, also known as: Fremy's Salt, is used mainly in solder flux, and in etching glass.
*Inorganic Chemistry.*
**kHz** kilohertz.
kilohertz is a unit of frequency equal to one thousand hertz. kHz is also known as: **kc** (kilocycle).
*Physics; Metrology.*
**KI** Karolinska Institutet (Stockholm, Sweden).
**KI** Kingpin Inclination.
**KI** Potassium Iodide.
KI is used mainly as a reagent, and in spectroscopy.
*Inorganic Chemistry.*
**KIA** killed in action.
tué au combat.
**KIAS** Knot Indicated Airspeed.
**Kid** Killing determinant.
*Apoptosis; Cell Biology; Eukaryotic Cells.*
For further details see under: **Kis**.
**KID** Kinase Inducible Domain (of CREB).
*Biological Chemistry; Peptide Biology; Regulatory Biology.*
For further details see under: **CREB**.
**KIE** Kinetic Isotope Effect.
**KIMSAC** Kiosk based Integrated Multimedia Service Access for Citizens.
*European Community Project.*
**KIN** The airport code for Kingston, Jamaica.
**Kinc** (abbr.) Kincardineshire.
**KIO** Kuwait Investment Office (G.B.).
**KIPS** Kilowatt Isotope Power System.
The KIPS was founded by the U.S. Energy Research and Development Administration (Washington, D.C., U.S.A.).
*Turbine Power Systems.*
**KIPS** Knowledge Information Processing System.
*Artificial Intelligence.*
**KIR** Kyocera Image Refinement.
**KIRs** Killer cell Inhibitory Receptors.
*Immunology.*
**KIS** Keyboard Input Simulation.
**Kis** Killing suppressor.
*Apoptosis; Cell Biology; Eukaryotic Cells.*
For further details see under: **Kid**.
**KISS** Keep It Simple Stupid.
*Management.*
**KISS** Keyed Indexed Sequential Search.
**KISS** Knowledge-based Interactive Signal monitoring System.
**KIST** Korea Institute of Science and Technology.
**KITA** Kick In The Ass.
*Management.*
**kJ** Kilojoule.
kJ is a unit of energy equal to one thousand joules.
*Metrology.*
**KJ** Knee Jerk.
**KJV** King James Version.
(Authorized Version) A revision of the English Bishops' Bible carried out under James I. (James I of England).
**K-KILL** complete kill.
destruction totale.
**KKK** Ku Klux Klan.
In the U.S.A. the KKK is a secret fraternal society advocating white supremacy.
**Kkt** King's Knight.
*Chess.*
**KKtP** King's Knight's Pawn.
*Chess.*
**kl** kiloliter / kilolitre.
kl is a unit of capacity equal to one thousand litres.
*Metrology.*
**KL** Kuala Lumpur.
**KL** The airline code for KLM Royal Dutch Airlines.
**KLA** Kansas Library Association (U.S.A.).
**KLA** Kentucky Library Association (U.S.A.).
**KLA** Kenya Library Association (Kenya).
**KLA** Korean Library Association (Korea).
**KLA** Kosovo Liberation Army.
**KLCE** Kuala Lumpur Commodity Exchange.
**KLF6** Kruppel-Like Factor 6.
A zinc finger transcription factor.
*Biochemistry; Cancer; Human Genetics; Medicine; Molecular Biology; Tumor Suppressor Genes.*
**KLH** Keyhole Limpet Hemocyanin.
KLH is a carrier protein.
*Chemical Biology; Chemistry.*

**KLH** Knight of the Legion of Honour (France).
**KLM** Kerr-Lens Mode-locking.
*Optics; Quantum Electronics.*
**KL nebula** Kleinmann-Low Nebula.
*Astronomy.*
**klooj** kludge.
The term kludge in computers refers to a poor-performance device, computer, or system made of mismatched components.
*Computer Technology.*
**KLTN** Potassium Lithium Tantalate Niobate.
**km**; **km.** Kilometer.
km is the basic unit of length equal to 1000 meters.
*Metrology.*
**KM** Knowledge Management.
**KMA** Korea Medical Association (Korea).
**KMC** key mission component.
composante clé de la mission.
**kMc** Kilomegacycle.
**KMC simulations** Kinetic MonteCarlo simulations.
**kmole** kilomole.
**KMUs** Kleine und Mittlere Unternehmen.
German initialism meaning: Small and Medium-sized Enterprises.
**kn** knots.
For further details see under: **kt.**
**KN** Korea (North).
**KNAW** The Royal Netherlands Academy of Arts and Sciences (Amsterdam, The Netherlands).
*Dutch Academy.*
**KNCS** Potassium Thiocyanate.
KNCS is used mainly in textiles and in medicine.
*Inorganic Chemistry.*
**KNET** Kyrgyz broadband Seismic NETwork (Krygyzstan).
*Geology; Geophysics; Seismology.*
**KNM-ER** Kenya National Museum, East Rudolf.
*Anthropology.*
**KNMI** Royal Netherlands Meteorological Institute (The Netherlands).
*Dutch Institute.*
**KNP** King's Knight's Pawn.
*Chess.*
**Knt.** (abbr.) Knight.
Also: **K.**
**Ko** kilo-octet.
Kilobyte in French.
**k/o** knockout.
*Mechanical Engineering.*
**KODC** Korea Oceanographic Data Center.
*Korean Center.*
**K of C** Knights of Columbus.
For further details see under: **KC**.
**K of P** Knights of Pythias.
The Knights of Pythias are members of a secret fraternal order.
**KOH** Potassium Hydroxide.
KOH, also known as Potassium Hydrate, is used mainly as a food additive, and in soap manufacture.
*Inorganic Chemistry.*
**kohm** kilohm.
kilohm is the metric unit of electrical resistance which is equal to one thousand ohms.
*Metrology.*
**KOL** Knowledge and Opinion about Law.
*Sociology of Law.*
**KOMRL** Kentucky-Ohio-Michigan Regional Medical Library (U.S.A.).
**KOMSAT System -** Korea Multi-purpose SATellite System.
**KORDI** Korea Ocean Research and Development Institute.
**KORSTIC** Korea Science and Technological Information Center.
**KOSEF** KOrea Science and Engineering Foundation.
**KP** Keyboard Printer.
*Computer Technology.*
**kp** keypunch.
The keypunch is a keyboard-operated device which punches holes in cards.
*Computer Technology.*
**K.P.** King's Pawn.
*Chess.*
**KP**; **K.P.** Kitchen Police.
**K.P.** Knight of the Order of St. Patrick.
**KPB** Potassium Phosphate Buffer.
**KPBRS** Korean Peace Bioreserves System.
The KPBRS preserves the biodiversity of the Korean Demilitarized Zone.
*Biodiversity Research; Environmental Resources Research.*
**kpc**; **kparsec** kiloparsec.
A distance of 3260 light-years.
*Astronomy.*
**kph** kilometers per hour.
**KPH fat** Kidney, Pelvic and Heart fat.
**KPSS** Kosovo Police Service School.
École de police du Kosovo.
**kr** kilorad.
**KR** King's Rook.
*Chess.*
**KR** Kiribati.
**KR** Knowledge Refining.

*Artificial Intelligence.*
**KR** Knowledge Representation.
*Artificial Intelligence.*
**kr.** krona, pl: kronor.
The currency unit of Sweden (SK) and Iceland (IK).
*Currencies.*
**kr.** krone, pl: kroner.
The currency unit of Denmark (DKr).
*Currencies.*
**Kr** The chemical symbol for Krypton.
Krypton is a gaseous element having the atomic number 36, an atomic weight of 83.80, and a melting point of -156.6°C. The word Krypton derives from a Greek term meaning "secret".
*Chemistry; Symbols.*
**KRISS** Korean Research Institute of Standards and Science (Korea).
**KRP** King's Rook's Pawn.
*Chess.*
**krs** kurus.
Kurus is the 100th part of a Turkish lira.
*Currencies.*
**KRV** Kilham's Rat Virus.
*Virology.*
**KS** β-Ketoacyl Synthase.
*Chemistry; Pharmaceutical Sciences.*
**KS** (abbr.) Kansas (U.S.A.).
Also: **Kan.**; **Kans**.
**KS** Kaposi's Sarcoma.
Kaposi's Sarcoma is a tumor characterized by purple blotches on the skin. It affects mainly elderly gay men.
*Epidemiology; Pathology.*
**KS** Knowledge Source.
*Artificial Intelligence.*
**KS** Korea (South).
**$K_2S$** Potassium Sulfide.
$K_2S$ is used mainly in medicine.
*Inorganic Chemistry.*
**KSA** Kingsford Smith Airport - Sidney, Australia.
KSA is operated by SACL.
For further deqails see under: **SACL**.
**KSA** Knowledge, Skills and Ability.
**KSAM** Keyed Sequential Access Method.
*Computer Programming.*
**KSAs** Knowledge, Skills and Abilities.
*Employment; Qualification Requirements for Positions.*
**$KSbO_3$** Potassium Antimonate.
Portassium Antimonate is also known as: Potassium Stibnate.
*Inorganic Chemistry.*
**KSF** Korea Science Foundation.
**KSHV** Kaposi's Sarcoma-associatcd Herpesvirus.
KSHV is a non-integrated, episomal DNA virus.
**$K_2SiF_6$** Hieratite.
*Mineralogy.*
**$K_2SO_4$** Arcanite.
Arcanite has properties resembling those of mascagnite.
*Mineralogy.*
**$K_2SO_4$** Potassium Sulfate.
Potassium Sulfate is used mainly in medicine and in glass manufacture.
*Inorganic Chemistry.*
**KSR** Keyboard Send/Receive.
The keyboard send/receive is also known as: Keyboard Teleprinter.
*Electronics.*
**KSS** Kearns-Sayre Syndrome.
**KST** Known Segment Table.
**KSTAR facility** Korea Superconducting Tokamak Advanced Research facility.
Completed in 2002.
*Fusion Research; Physics; Superheated Plasmas.*
**KSU** Kansas State University (U.S.A.).
**kt.**; **kt** karat.
karat is the unit for measuring the fineness of gold in an alloy.
*Metallurgy.*
**KT** Key Tape.
**KT** Key Transformation.
*Computer Programming.*
**kt.** kiloton.
kiloton is equal to the explosive power of one thousand metric tons of TNT.
*Metrology.*
For further details see under: **TNT**.
**Kt.** Knight.
*Chess.*
**kt.** (abbr.) knot.
Also: **kn**.
*Anatomy; Chemistry; Engineering; Forestry; Mathematics; Metrology.*
**KT** Korea Telecom.
KT is State-run.
**K-T boundary** Cretaceous-Tertiary boundary.
*Paleontology.*
**KTDS** Key-To-Disk Software.
**KTH** Kungl Tekniska Högskolan (Sweden).
Royal Institute of Technology.
*Technical Universities.*
**KTP** Potassium Titanyl Phosphate.
**KTS** Key-to-Tape System.
*Computer Technology.*

**KTS transition** Kosterlitz-Thouless transition.
*Physics; Superfluid Transition.*
**KU** Kansas University (U.S.A.).
**KU** Kuwait.
**KUB** Kidney, Ureter, and Bladder.
**KU Brussel** Katholieke Universiteit Brussel.
*Belgian University.*
**KUL** Katholieke Universiteit Leuven.
*Belgian University.*
**KULOP** Kent Union List Of Periodicals.
**KV** Key Value.
*Computer Programming.*
**KV** Key Verify.
*Computer Programming.*
**kV**; **kV**; **kv** kilovolt.
kV is a unit of potential difference equal to one thousand volts.
*Metrology.*
**kVA**; **kva** kilovolt-ampere.
kVA is a metric unit of apparent power in alternating-current equal to one thousand volt-amperes.
*Metrology.*
**KVL** The Royal Veterinary and Agricultural University.
*Danish University.*
**KVM** Kosovo verification mission.
Mission de vérification au Kosovo.
**kVp** kilovolts peak.
**KW** Keyword or Key Word.
*Computer Programming.*
**kW.**; **kW**; **kw** kilowatt.
kW is equal to one thousand watts.
*Metrology.*
**KWD** Kidney Worm Disease.
KWD is also known as: Swine Kidney Worm Infection.
*Veterinary Medicine.*
**KWh**; **KW/hr** kilowatt-hour.
Kwh is equal to 1000 watt-hours.
*Metrology.*
**KWIC index** - Key-Word-In-Context index.
*Computer Programming.*
**KWOC index** Key-Word-Out-of-Context index.
*Computer Programming.*
**KWP** Keyword Parameter.
*Computer Programming.*
**KWS** Kenya Wildlife Service.
*Wildlife Conservation.*
**KWS** Keyword Search.
*Computer Programming.*
**Ky**; **KY** (abbr.) Kentucky (U.S.A.).
**kyB.P.** thousand years Before the Present.
**KYC** Know Your Customer.
*Business; Commerce.*
**KWFT** Kenya Women Finance Trust (Kenya).
**KZ** Kazakhstan.

# L

**L, l** labour.
*Medicine.*
**L** Lambert.
Lambert is a unit of brightness.
*Optics.*
**L** Langrangian.
*Mechanics.*
**l** language.
*Computer Programming; Linguistics.*
**L** Latin.
*Languages.*
**L, l** league.
*Metrology.*
**L, l** learner.
**L** Legge.
Law in Italian.
**l** length.
*Metrology.*
**l** levorotatory.
*Science.*
**l** light.
*Architecture; Optics.*
**L** Liner.
**l** link.
Also: **lk.**
*Cartography; Civil Engineering; Design Engineering; Telecommunications; Transportation Engineering.*
**l** liquid.
*Physics.*
**L; l** lira.
Also: **ITL.**
Now: EURO/EUR (€). Became ECU (European single currency) with effect from January 2002.
*Currencies.*
**L** Listed.
*Securities.*
**l** liter / litre.
*Metrology.*
**l** local.
*Mathematics; Medicine; Science; Transportation Engineering.*
**L** London.
**L** Lord.
**l** lumber.
*Materials.*
**L; l** Lunedì.
Monday in Italian.
**L** Luxemburg's international vehicle-registration letter.
**L** the Roman numeral for 50.
**La** The chemical symbol for Lanthanum.
Lanthanum is a metallic element having the atomic number 57 an atomic weight of 138.91 and a melting point of 920°C.
*Chemistry; Symbols.*
**LA** Laos.
**LA** Law Agent.
**LA** Law Association.
**L.A.** Lega Araba.
Italian acronym meaning: Arab League.
**LA** Legal Assets.
*Business; Finance.*
**LA** Legislative Assembly.
**LA** Letter of Authority.
*Business; Finance.*
**LA** Library Association.
**L.A.** Light Alloy.
**L.A.** Liquid Assets.
*Business; Finance.*
**LA** Local Accuracy.
*Robotics.*
**L.A.** Local Authority.
**LA; La** Louisiana (U.S.A.).
**LA** Los Angeles (U.S.A.).
**LAA** Library Association of Alberta (Canada).
**LAA** 1. light anti-aircraft artillery.
1. artillerie antiaérienne légère (AAL).
2. lutte antiaérienne [défense aérienne navale uniquement].
2. anti-air warfare (AAW 2.) [naval air defence only].
**LA&R** logistics, armaments and resources.
logistique, armements et ressources.
**LAAPDs** Large Area Avalanche Photodiodes.
*Color Scanning; Emission Spectroscopy; Medical Instrumentation; Scintillation Detection.*
**LAAS** Laboratoire d'Automatique et d'Analyse des Systèmes (France).
Of the CNR (Toulouse, France).
**LAAWC** local anti-air warfare coordinator.
coordonnateur local de la lutte antiaérienne.
**Lab.; lab.** (abbr.) laboratorio.
Italian abbreviation meaning: laboratory.
**L.A.B.** Laboratorio Analisi Biomediche (Italy).
**lab.** (abbr.) labour.
*Medicine.*
**Lab** (abbr.) Labrador (Canada).
**LAB** Library Association of Barbados.
**LAB** low-altitude bombing.
bombardement à basse altitudine.

**LAB** Low-Angle Boundary.
**LABTICO** LABoratorio Tecnologie COgnitive (Italy).
*Italian Laboratory.*
**LAC** Language Acquisition Center.
University of Texas, at Arlington (U.S.A.).
**LAC** Large-Area proportional Counter.
**LAC** Lega per l'Abolizione della Caccia (Italy).
**LAC** Library Association of China (Taiwan).
**LAC** see LOAC.
voir LOAC.
**LAC** Local Area Coverage.
**LAC** London Athletic Club.
**LACEF** Laboratorio per la Comunicazione Economica e Finanziaria (Italy).
Italian acronym of the: Laboratory for Economic and Financial Communication, Università Commerciale Luigi Bocconi, Milano, Italy.
**$LaCl_3 \cdot 7H_2O$** Lanthanum Chloride.
Lanthanum Chloride is used to prepare lanthanum.
*Inorganic Chemistry.*
**Lacma** Los Angeles County Museum of Art (U.S.A.).
**LA.CO.M.** LAboratorio COntrollo Microbiologico (Italy).
*Microbiological Control.*
**LACT** Lease Automatic Custody Transfer.
*Petroleum Engineering.*
**LAD** Language Acquisition Device.
**LAD** Large Area Detector.
**LADB** Laboratory Animal Data Bank.
**LADs** Last Appearance Datums.
*Fossil Mammals; Paleontology.*
**LADS** limited air defence system.
système de défense aérienne limitée.
**LADSIRLAC** Liverpool And District Scientific, Industrial and Research Library Advisory Council.
**LAF** Lance Armstrong Foundation.
The LAF is located in Texas, U.S.A.
*Awards; Fellowships; Urologic Cancer.*
**LaF** Louisiana French.
French as spoken in Louisiana.
*Languages.*
**LAF** Lymphocyte Activating Factor.
*Medicine.*
**LAFTA** Latin-American Free Trade Association.
**LAGEOS** LAser Geodetic Earth Orbiting Satellite.
**LAH** lithium aluminum hydride.
*Inorganic Chemistry.*
**LAI** Leaf Area Index.
The leaf area index is actually the one-sided area of a leaf per unit of ground area.
*Atmospheric Research; Atmospheric Sciences; Land-Atmosphere Interactions; Meteorology; Plant Biology.*
**LAI** Library Association of Ireland.
**LAI** The airline code for Linee Aeree Italiane.
**LA-ICPMS** Laser-Ablation Inductively Coupled Plasma Mass Spectroscopy.
*Earth Sciences; Isotope Geochemistry; Petrography.*
**LALC** local air logistic coordinator.
coordonnateur local de la logistique aérienne.
**LALF** Limulus Anti-LPS Factor.
*Biochemistry; Molecular Medicine; Structural Biology.*
For further details see under: **LPS**.
**LALLS detector** Low-Angle Laser Light-Scattering detector.
**LAM** Laboratorio Analisi Mediche (Italy).
*Italian Laboratory.*
**LAM** LAboratorio di ricerca sul Mutamento sociale.
Italian acronym meaning: Research Laboratory on Social Change.
**LAM** Library Association of Malaysia.
**LAM** Limited Area Model.
**LAM** Lipoarabinomannan.
*Immunology; Lymphocyte Biology; Microbiology; Rheumatology.*
**LAM** Longitudinal Acoustic Mode.
**lam** The above acronyms were coined accidentally using the Arabic word "lam" which is the twenty-third letter of the Arabic alphabet.
**LAMA** Large-Aperture Mirror Array.
18 identical telescopes in a 60-meter-wide circular array.
*Astronomy.*
**LA-MC-ICPMS isotopic analyses** Laser Ablation, Multiple-Collector, Inductively Coupled Plasma Mass Spectrometry isotopic analyses.
*Geological Sciences; Lead Isotope Stratigraphy; Paleoceanography.*
**LAMEF** Los Alamos Medium Energy Facility.
**LAMOST** Large Area, Multi-Object fiber Spectroscopic Telescope (China).
LAMOST is a powerful instrument - a H-meter field telescope - for collecting spectra from numerous galaxies, constructed at Xinglong Station (China).
*Astronomy; Galaxies.*
**LAMP** Legal Authority and Mental Patient (U.S.A.).
**LAMP-1** Lysosome-Associated Membrane Protein-1.
**LAMP facility** Los Alamos Meson Physics facility.

Also: **LAMPF**.
*Proton Accelerators*.
**LAMPCAL** LAMinated Plate CALculations.
**LAMPS** light airborne multi-purpose system.
système léger polyvalent aéroporté.
**LAMS** local area missile system.
système de missile de défense de zone rapprochée.
**LAN**; **Lan** Local Area Network.
*Computer Science*.
**LAN** The airport code for Lansing, Michigan, U.S.A.
**LANA** Latency Associated Nuclear Antigens.
*AIDS Research; Medicine*.
**Lanc.** (abbr.) Lancaster / Lancashire (G.B.).
**Lancs** (abbr.) Lancashire (G.B.).
Also: **Lanc**.
**LANDCENT** Allied Land Forces, Central Europe [obsolete].
Forces terrestres alliées du Centre-Europe [obsolète].
**L&D** Loans and Discounts.
*Business; Commerce*.
**LANDJUT** Allied Land Forces, Schleswig-Holstein and Jutland [obsolete].
Forces terrestres alliées du Schleswig-Holstein et du Jutland [obsolète].
**LANDSAT** (abbr.) LAND SATellite.
**LANDSOUTH** Allied Land Forces, Southern Europe [obsolete - replaced by JSRC SOUTH].
Forces terrestres alliées du Sud-Europe [obsolète - remplacé par JSRC SOUTH].
**LANDSOUTHCENT** Allied Land Forces South-Central Europe [obsolete - replaced by JHQ SOUTHCENT].
Forces terrestres alliées du Centre-Sud-Europe [obsolète - remplacé par JHQ SOUTHCENT].
**LANDSOUTHEAST** Allied Land Forces South-Eastern Europe [obsolete - replaced by JSRC SOUTHEAST].
Forces terrestres alliées du Sud-Est-Europe [obsolète - remplacé par JSRC SOUTHEAST].
**LanE** Lan Emulation.
*Protocols*.
For further details see under: **Lan**.
**lang.** (abbr.) language.
**LANGTAG** LANGuage plan TAsk Group (South Africa).
**LANL** Los Alamos National Laboratory - Bioscience Division (U.S.A.).
*Computational Biology; Environmental Biology; Genomics; Measurement Science & Diagnostics; Medical Applications; Molecular Synthesis; Structural Biology*.
**LANs**; **Lans** Local Area Networks.
**LANSCE** Los Alamos Neutron Scattering Center (U.S.A.).
*Defense; Explosive Testing; Stockpile Stewardship; Weapons Design*.
**LANTIRN** Low-Altitude Navigation and Targeting Infrared for Night.
*Aviation*.
**LAO** Lao's international vehicle-registration letters.
**LAO** Left Anterior Oblique.
**LAO** Left Associative Operator.
*Computer Science*.
**$La_2O_3$** Lanthanum Oxide.
Lanthanum Oxide is used mainly in optical glass.
**LAP** Leukocyte Alkaline Phosphatase.
**LAP** Local Analysis and Prediction.
**LAPA** lutte anti-porte-avions.
anti-carrier warfare (ACW).
**LAPB** Link Access Protocol - Balanced.
**LAPD** Link Access Protocol - Digital.
**LAPIS** Libera Associazione per il Progresso dell'IStruzione (Italy).
Italian acronym of the: Free Association for the Progress of Education.
**lapis** The above acronym was coined using the Italian word "lapis" which means pencil Also: matita.
**LAPO** Los Angeles Philharmonic Orchestra (U.S.A.).
**LAPS** Light-Addressable Potentiometric Sensor.
**LAPS** Local Analysis and Prediction System.
**LAP tissue** lyophilized anterior pituitary tissue.
**LAPW calculations** Linearized Augmented Plane Wave calculations.
*Geophysics; High Pressure Research*.
**LAPW electronic structure methods** Linearized Augmented Plane Wave electronic structure methods.
*Chemical Engineering; Geology; Geophysics; High-Pressure Research; Materials; Mathematics; Planetary Physics; Supercomputers*.
**LAPzβ** Lamin-Associated Polypeptide 2β.
*Cytomegalovirus; Electron Microscopy*.
**LAQ** Laboratori di ricerca Alta Qualità (Italy).
*Italian Research Laboratories*.
**LAR** Leucoanthocyanidin Reductase.
*Biochemistry; Cell Biology*.
**LAR** local acquisition radar.
radar d'acquisition local.
**L.A.R.A.L.** Libera Associazione Ricerca Applicata Lettura e Letteratura (Italy).
*Italian Research Association*.
**LARC** Langley Research Center (U.S.A.).

NASA's LARC has been dealing with new technologies ever since 1917. Many LARC innovations show promise as commercial products for everyday use. The Center works to improve the economy, security and quality of life. LARC programs include *Structures and Materials Research, Aviation Safety and Efficiency, Space Access, Technology Transfer.*

**LARC** Lighter Amphibious Resupply Craft.

**LARICE** Lombardy ARea Innovation Centre, Milan, Italy.

**LARN** Livelli di Assunzione Raccomandati di energia e Nutrienti.
*Food Intake.*

**larr** linear accelerator - regenerator reactor.
*Nucleonics.*

**LARS** 1. laser-aided rocket system.
1. système de roquettes assisté par laser.
2. light artillery rocket system.
2. système de roquettes d'artillerie légère.
3. low-altitude radar system.
3. système de radar à basse altitude.

**LAS** Laboratory Animal Science.

**LAS** Library Association of Singapore.

**LAS** Libretti ASsegni.
Italian acronym meaning: check-books / cheque-books.

**LAS** Linear Alkyl Sulfonate.

**LAS** Linfo-Adenopatia Sistemica.
*Medicine.*

**LAS** Low-Angle X-ray Scattering.

**LAS** The airport code for Las Vegas, Nevada, U.S.A.

**LASA** Large-Aperture Seismic Array.

**LASCO** LAboratory for Surveillance and COntainment.
Construction started end 1989. The first experimental set up in a simulated storage area was designed using robots and surveillance devices for inventory verifications. Joint Research Center - Commission of the European Communities.

**LASCO instrument** Large-Angle Spectrometric Coronagraph instrument - SOHO's.
*Planetary Science.*
For further details see under: **SOHO**.

**lasco** The above acronyms were coined accidentally using the Italian word "lasco" which means in Italian: slack; loose.

**LASCR** Light-Activated Silicon Controlled Rectifier.
The LASCR is also known as: Photothyristor; Photo-SCR.
*Electronics.*

**LASCS** Light-Activated Silicon Controlled Switch.
*Electronics.*

**LASER** Light Amplification by Stimulated Emission of Radiation.

**LASER** London And South East Regional System.

**LASF** lutte (au-dessus) de (la) surface.
surface warfare (SW 2.).

**LASH** lighter aboard ship.
Navire porte-barges.

**LASIE** Library-Automated Systems Information Exchange.

**LAS journal** Laboratory Animal Science journal.
Of the American Association for Laboratory Animal Science.

**LASL** Los Alamos Scientific Laboratory (U.S.A.).

**LASM** lutte anti-sous-marine.
antisubmarine warfare (ASW).

**LASS** Labile Aggregating Stimulating Substance.

**LASSOR** Los Alamos Solid-State Optical Refrigerator.
*First-Generation Laser Cryocoolers.*

**LASWC** local antisubmarine warfare commander (or coordinator).
commandant (ou coordonnateur) de lutte anti-sous-marine.

**Lat** (abbr.) Latin.

**lat** (abbr,) latitude.

**Lat** (abbr.) Latvia.

**LAT** Linker for Activation of T Cells.
*Cancer Research; Cellular Biology; Molecular Biology; Human Development.*

**LAT** Local Apparent Time.

**LATEX** Louisiana - Texas Experiment.
*U.S. Experiments.*

**LATIN** (abbr.) LATeral INitiation (Molecular Control of) - *European Community.*

**LATs** Latency-Associated Transcripts.

**LATS** Long-Acting Thyroid Stimulator.
*Endocrinology.*

**LATT** Library Association of Trinidad and Tobago.

**LAUD** Linguistic Agency, University of Duisburg (Germany).

**LA/UK** Library Association (G.B.).

**LAURA** Look-Ask-Use-Review-Associate.
A Management method (1988) of Time Management International.

**LAUTRO** Life Assurance and Unit Trust Regulatory Organisation (G.B.).

**LAV** Leukemia/lymphotropic Virus.
*Virology.*

**LAV** light armoured vehicle.
véhicle blindé léger (VBL).

**LAV** Lymphadenopathy-Associated Virus.

The AIDS virus is also known as: LAV.
*Virology.*
**LAW** light antitank weapon.
arme antichar légère.
**LAWS** Laser Atmospheric Wind Sounder.
**LAX** The airport code for Los Angeles International Airport, Los Angeles, California, U.S.A.
**LB** Lavatory Basin.
*Buildings.*
**LB** Legal Bond.
*Business; Finance.*
**LB** Local Battery.
The term local battery refers to the battery used for telegraphic station recording means.
*Electricity.*
**LB** Logic Bomb.
**lb** pound.
**L-Bank** Landeskredietbank Baden-Württenberg (Germany).
**LBB** The airport code for Lubbock, Texas, U.S.A.
**LBC** Lebanese Broadcasting Company (Lebanon).
**LBD** Ligand-Binding Domain.
*Medicine; Menopause; Pharmacology.*
**LBE** Long Bill of Exchange.
**lbf** pound force.
*Metrology.*
**L-B film** Langmuir-Blodgett film.
The L-B film may be used as a biosensor; and in fields such as nonlinear optics; molecular electronics; and others.
*Biochemistry; Chemistry; Nuclear Engineering; Physical Chemistry.*
**LBG** The airport code for Le Bourget, Paris, France.
**LBHB** Low Barrier Hydrogen Bond.
**LBI** Legge sui Brevetti Industriali.
Italian initialism meaning: Law concerning Industrial Patents.
**LBI** Lloyds Bank International.
**LBIC** Light Beam Induced Current.
**lbl** label.
*Architecture; Computer Programming.*
**LBL** Lawrence Berkeley Laboratory (U.S.A.).
The LBL is a U.S. national laboratory affiliated with the University of California and funded by the U.S. DOE.
For further details see under: **DOE**.
**LBM** Laser-Beam Printer.
*Graphic Arts.*
**LBM** Legge sui brevetti a Marchi (d'impresa).
Italian initialism meaning: Law concerning Patents and Trademarks.
**LBO** Leveraged BuyOut (U.S.A.).
*Finance.*
**LBO** Lithium Triborate.
**LBP** Lipopolysaccharide Binding Protein.
For further details see under: **LBPs**.
**LBP** LPS-Binding Protein.
*Biochemistry; Molecular Medicine; Structural Biology.*
For further details see under: **LPS**.
**LBPs** Lipopolysaccharide Binding Proteins.
*Biochemistry; Molecular Medicine; Structural Biology.*
**LBS** Land-Based Sources (of marine pollution).
**LBS** London Business School (G.B.).
**LBT** Laboratorio Biopolimeri Tecnologici.
Italian initialism of the: Technological biopolymers Laboratory.
**LBT** Large Binocular Telescope.
A joint project with the Arcetri Observatory in Italy; the Research Corporation of Tucson, Arizona; and Ohio State University (U.S.A.).
*Astronomy; Ecology; Endangered Species; Environment.*
**LBTM** Large Basin Turnoff Model.
**LBW** Low Birth Weight.
*Medicine.*
**LC** Language Converter.
Essentially, Language Converter is a device which translates a certain form of data into another.
*Computer Technology.*
**LC** Late Charge.
*Business; Commerce.*
**LC** Lecco, Italy.
**LC** Legal Capital.
*Business; Finance.*
**LC** Legge sulla Cambiale.
*Italian Laws.*
**LC** Letter Code.
The letter code is a Baudot code function which is used to cancel errors so that the receiving terminal prints nothing.
*Computer Technology.*
**L.C.; L/C; l.c.; l/c** Letter of Credit.
*Banking; Commerce.*
**l.c.** leur compte.
French initialism meaning: their account.
**LC** Level Converter.
*Electronics.*
**lc** level crossing.
**LC** Leverage Contract.
*Business; Finance.*
**LC** Liberation Committee.
**LC** Library of Congress (U.S.A.).
**LC** Life Cycle.

*Biology.*
**LC** Linear Control.
*Telecommunications.*
**LC** Line of Credit.
*Business; Finance.*
**LC** Liquid Cromatography.
*Analytical Chemistry.*
**LC** Liquid Crystal.
For further details see under: **LCs**.
**LC** Listed Company.
*Business; Finance.*
**LC** Loan Capital.
*Business; Finance.*
**LC** Local Cable.
*Telecommunications.*
**LC** Local Control.
*Telecommunications.*
**LC** Location Counter.
*Computer Programming.*
**LC** Logical Construction.
*Computer Programming.*
**L.C.**; **L/C** London Clause.
*Shipping.*
**L.C.**; **L/C** Lord Chancellor (G.B.).
**L/C**; **l.c.** lower case.
**LCA** Last Common Ancestor.
*Phylogenetic Tree.*
**LCA** launch control area.
zone de contrôle de lancement.
**LCA** Lithocholic Acid.
The LCA is the secondary bile acid which is hepatoxic and an enteric carcinogen.
*Biochemistry; Gene Expression; Medicine; Molecular Biophysics; Pharmacology.*
**LCA** London Court of Arbitration (G.B.).
**LCAC** landing craft, air cushion.
engin de débarquement sur coussin d'air.
**LCAO** Linear Combination of Atomic Orbitals.
**LCAR** low-coverage acquisition radar.
radar d'acquisition basse couverture.
**LCAT** Lecithin-Cholesterol Acyltransferase (enzyme).
**LCB** Line Control Block.
**LCC** 1. land component command(er).
1. commandement (commandant) de composante terrestre.
2. life cycle cost.
2. coût global de possession (CGP).
3. local control centre.
3. centre de direction locale.
4. logistics coordination centre.
4. centre de coordination logistique (CCL).
**LCC** Language and Conversational Computing.
**LCC** Library of Congress Classification (U.S.A.).
**LCC** Life Cycle Cost.
**L.C.C.** London Chamber of Commerce (G.B.).
**L.C.C.**; **LCC** London County Council (G.B.).
**LCD** Least Common Denominator.
*Mathematics.*
**LCD** Liquid-Crystal Display.
*Applied Physics; Embryonic Science; Macromolecules.*
**LCD** Low-Cost Drifter.
**LCE** latest cost estimate.
1a. dernière estimation de coût (DEC).
1b. estimation de coût la plus recente.
**LCE** London Commodity Exchange (G.B.).
**LCFA** ligne de coordination des feux d'appui.
fire support coordination line (FSCL).
**LCFA** Long Chain Fatty Acid.
**LCF life** Low Cycle Fatigue life.
**LCGU** Local Cerebral Glucose Utilization.
*Auditory Processing; Neuroscience; Psychology.*
**LCH** London Clearing House (G.B.).
**LCH** Life Cycle Hypothesis.
**LCHQ** local command headquarters.
quartier général de commandement local.
**LCIC** Leverhulme Centre for Innovative Catalysis (G.B.).
*Catalyst Characterization; Genito-urinary Medicine; Innovative Catalysis; Medical Microbiology; Molecular Immunogenetics; Nanostructure Preparation.*
**LCL** less than carload.
**LCL** Lifting Condensation Level.
Lifting Condensation Level is also known as: Isentropic Condensation Level.
*Meteorology.*
**LCL** Lymphoblastoid Cell Lines.
**LCLA** Lutheran Church Library Association.
**LC-LE phases** Liquid Condensed-Liquid Expanded phases.
*Organic Chemistry.*
**LCLS** Linac Coherent Light Source.
An X-ray FEL scheduled for 2008.
For further details see under: **FEL** and **linac**.
**LCLs** Lymphoblastoid Cell Lines.
**LCM** Laser Capture Microdissection.
*Malignant Pancreatic Cancer Cells.*
**LCM** Least Common Multiple.
*Mathematics.*
**LCM** Link Control Message.
*Telecommunications.*
**LCM** Logic-Controlled Mechanism.
**LCM** Lowest Common Multiple.
**LCM** Lymphocytic Choriomeningitis.

**LC materials** Liquid Crystalline materials.
**LCMV** Lymphocytic Choriomeningitis Virus.
*Medicine; Microbiology; Virology.*
**LCN** La Cosa Nostra (Italy).
Italian initialism meaning: The mafia.
**LCN** Linked Cluster Network.
*Chemical Engineering; Electrical and Computer Engineering.*
**LCN** load classification number.
1a. indice de force portante.
1b. numéro de classification de charge.
**LC neurons** Locus Coeruleus neurons.
*Neuroscience.*
**LCNTR** (abbr.) Location Counter.
**LCO** (superconducting) Lanthanum Copper Oxide.
*Superconductivity.*
**LCP** leased circuit programme.
programme de location de circuits.
**LCPM** Laboratoire de Chimie Physique Moléculaire (Lausanne, Switzerland).
*Swiss Laboratory.*
**L/CR** Letter of CRedit.
**LCR** Lettre de Charge Relevée.
*Business; Commerce.*
**LCR** Ligase Chain Reaction.
**LCR** Liquide Céphalorachidien.
French initialism meaning: Cerebrospinal Fluid.
*Physiology.*
**LCR** Locus Control Region.
*Transcription.*
**LCR** London and Continental Railways.
LCR is the sponsor of the link from London to the channel.
**LCRC** Lake Champlain Research Consortium.
**LCs** Langerhans Cells.
Named for the German anatomist Paul **Langerhans**.
*Histology; New Vaccines.*
**LCS** Language and Communication Training (Belgium).
**LCS** Large-capacity Core Storage.
**LCS** Letto, Confermato e Sottoscritto.
Italian initialism meaning: read, confirmed and undersigned. Usually put at the bottom of legal deeds before the signature, for instance: cross-examination/questioning minutes, and the like.
**LCs** Linear Combinations.
*Physics.*
**LCS** Linear Control System.
**LCs** Liquid Crystals.
Liquid crystals present important properties such as high resolution and sensitivity. They are therefore materials that yield good results when used for optical switching and image storage.
*Applied Physics; Biochemistry; Chemistry; Crystallography; Macromolecules; Materials Science.*
**LCSSAP** Low-Cost Silicon Solar Array Project.
**LCT-RTS** Languages, Compilers, and Tools for Real-Time Systems.
**LCTs** Large Cutting Tools.
*Bose Lithic Technology; Geology; Geophysics; Physical Anthropology; Paleoanthropology; Vertebrate Paleontology.*
**LCU** Lake County Uplift.
**LCU** Landing Craft, Utility.
**LCV** Landing Craft, Vehicle.
**LCV** Lymphocryptovirus.
*Immunology; Medicine; Virology.*
**LCVD** Laser-assisted Chemical Vapor Deposition.
**LCVs** Large Compound Vesicles.
*Chemistry.*
**LD** Doctor of Letters.
**LD** Langue de Départ.
French initialism meaning: source language.
*Translation.*
**LD** Latissimus Dorsi.
The LD is the widest muscle of the body.
*Anatomy.*
**LD** Learning Disabilities.
*Biomedical Sciences; Psychology.*
**LD** Lethal Dose.
LD is also known as: Fatal Dose.
*Toxicology.*
**L.D.** Letter of Deposit.
**Ld.** (abbr.) Limited.
Also: **Ltd.**; **ltd**.
**LD** Line Driver.
Line driver is also known as: Limited-Distance Modem.
*Computer Technology.*
**LD** Linkage Disequilibrium.
*Epidemiology; Genome Research; Genetics; Medicine; Molecular Biology.*
**Ld.**; **ld** liquidità differite.
Italian initialism meaning: deferred assets.
*Business; Economics; Finance.*
**LD** Logic Design; Logic Diagram.
*Computer Technology.*
**LD** Logical Device.
Logical device is also known as: Logical Unit.
*Computer Programming.*
**L.D.** London Docks (G.B.).
**LD** Long Day.
**Ld.** (abbr.) Lord.

**LD** Lybian Dinar.
*Currencies.*
**LDA** Linear Discriminant Analysis.
LDA is a linear statistical technique.
**LDA** Local Density Approximation.
*Geophysics; High-Pressure Research; Mathematics; Planetary Physics.*
**LDA** Localizer-type Directional Aid.
*Navigation.*
**LDA** London Development Agency.
The LDA is conducting research to identify where gaps exist in the design and creative industries, education, finance, media, medicine, biotechnology and manufacturing. Its innovation strategy is focused on creating a culture of innovation amongst small- and medium-sized enterprises and universities.
**LDA ice** Low-Density Amorphous ice.
*Thermodynamics.*
For further details see under: **HDA ice**.
**LDAP**; **Ldap** Local Directory Access Protocol.
**LD Banque** LD-Louis Dreyfus Banque.
**LDC** Least-Developed Country; Less Developed Country.
**LDC** (The International) London Dumping Convention.
*Nuclear Waste.*
**LD conditions** Light-Dark conditions.
*Biological Timing.*
**LDCs** Least-Developed Countries; Less Developed Countries.
**LD cycles** Light-Dark cycles.
**LDD** (aerial) Long-Distance Dispersal.
*Agricultural Sciences; Epidemiology; Plant Protection; Stress Biology.*
**l.d.d.** loss during discharge.
*Insurance; Sea Transport.*
**LDDN** Laboratory for Drug Discovery in Neurodegeneration (U.S.A.).
The LDDN is a not-for-profit biotechnology laboratory operating under the Harward Medical School umbrella.
*Alzheimer's Disease; Amyotrophic Lateral Sclerosis; Multiple Sclerosis; Parkinson's Disease.*
**LDF** Legal Defense Fund - N.Y., U.S.A.
**LDF** Lyme Disease Foundation.
The Lyme Disease Foundation is located at Hartford, Connecticut (U.S.A.).
*Allergy; Infectious Diseases; Lyme Disease; Microbiology.*
**ldg.** (abbr.) landing.
*Sea Transport.*
**ldg.** (abbr.) loading.
**ldg. & delry** landing and delivery.
*Sea Transport.*
**LDGO** Lamont Doherty Geological Observatory.
**LDH** Lactate Dehydrogenase.
Lactate Dehydrogenase is also known as: Lactic Dehydrogenase. It was discovered in the 1960s by a biochemist of the Northwestern University, Illinois, U.S.A.
*Enzymology.*
**LDK** Democratic League of Kosovo.
**LDKS** Lovastatin Diketide Synthase.
*Bacteriology; Chemistry; Lovastatin Biosynthesis; Pharmacy; Polyketide Synthase.*
**l.d.l.** loss during loading.
*Insurance; Sea Transport.*
**LDL** Low-Density Lipoprotein.
*Biochemistry; Structural Biology.*
**LD-LISC** Ligand-Driven Light-Induced Spin Changes.
*Applied Physics; Crystallography; Inorganic Chemistry; Magnetism; Optics.*
**LDLR** LDL receptor.
The LDLR among other things regulates cholesterol homeostasis in mammalian cells.
For further details see under: **LDL**.
**LDM** Luminescent Dish Monitor.
*Biology; Biology Informatics; Bioluminescence.*
**LD method** Linear Dichroism method.
**LDMS** Laser-Desorption Mass Spectrometry.
**L-DOPA** L-dihydroxyphenulalanine.
L-DOPA is used to treat Parkinson's disease, which occurs from degeneration of dopaminergic neurons.
**LDOS** Local Density Of States.
*Applied Physics; Microscopy; Physics.*
**LDP** Liberal Democratic Party (Japan).
**LDR**; **ldr** Linear accelerator-Driven Reactor.
*Nucleonics.*
**LD ratio** Length to Diameter ratio.
*Engineering.*
**LDRCs** Learning Disability Research Centers.
The network of LDRCs was created in the U.S.A. in 1987 with a view to improve knowledge of the diagnosis and treatment of learning disability.
*Biomedical Sciences; Psychology.*
**LDRD** Laboratory Directed Research and Development.
**LDRD fund** Laboratory Directed Research and Development fund.
An account created by the U.S. Congress in 1991.
**LDRR** Laboratory of Diagnostic Radiology Research.
Of the U.S. NIH.

*Diagnostic Radiology Research.*
For further details see under: **NIH**.
**LDS** launch detection satellite.
satellite de détection de lancement.
**LDS** Licentiate in Dental Surgery.
**LDS** Local Distribution System.
**LD-SSE source** Laser Desorption and Supersonic Expansion source.
**LDT** Label Data Type.
*Computer Programming.*
**LDT** Licensed Deposit-Taker.
*Banking; Finance.*
**LDTF** Large Dynamic Test Facility (Ispra, Italy).
**ldv.** lagged dependent variables.
*Statistics.*
**LDX** Levitated Dipole Experiment.
The LDX, a collaboration between MIT and Columbia University, began operation in mid-2000.
*Fusion; Plasma Science.*
**LE** Leading Edge.
*Design Engineering; Physics.*
**LE** Lebanon.
**LE** Lecce, Italy.
**Le** leone.
The currency unit of Sierra Leone.
*Currencies.*
**LE** Line Editor.
*Computer Technology.*
**LE** Linkage Editor.
Linkage Editor is also known as: Link Editor.
*Computer Programming.*
**LE** Linkage Equilibrium.
**LE** Logic Element.
*Computer Technology.*
**LE** Logic Error.
*Computer Programming.*
**LE**; **L.E.** Low Explosive.
*Materials Science.*
**LE** Lyapunov Exponents.
*Nonlinear Dynamics; Population Dynamics.*
**LE** Lycopersicon Esculentum.
**LEA** Law Enforcement Associates (U.S.A.).
*Under Vehicle Inspection System.*
**lea.** (abbr.) league.
*Metrology.*
**lea.** (abbr.) leave.
**LEA** Local Education Authority (G.B.).
**LEA** Low-Excess Air.
**LEAA** Law Enforcement Assistance Administration (U.S.A.).
**LEAD** Leadership Education and Advocacy Development (U.S.A.).
*Biomedical Research; Breast Cancer.*
**LEAD** Lupus Erythémateux Aigu Disséminé.
For further details see under: **LED**.
**LEADEX** (abbr.) LEAD EXperiment.
**LEAG** London & East Anglian Examining Board.
**LEAR** Low-Energy Antiproton Ring.
*Antimatter; Physics.*
**LEBM** Laboratorio Europeo di Biologia Molecolare - E.C.
Italian initialism of the: European Laboratory for Molecular Biology.
*European Laboratories.*
**LEC** Lan Emulation Client.
**LEC** locally-employed civilian [also called LEP - specific to SFOR/KFOR].
civil employé localement [aussi appelé LEP - propre à la SFOR/KFOR].
**LECAM-1** Lectin-Cellular Adhesion Molecule-1.
**LECP instrument** Low-Energy Charged-Particle instrument.
Instrument aboard Voyager.
**LECs** Local Enterprise Councils (G.B.).
*British Councils.*
**lect.** (abbr.) lecture; lecturer.
**led.** (abbr.) ledger.
**LED** Light-Emitting Diode.
LED signs use only about 5 watts and last 20 years. The life-cycle cost of LED signs is about 50% less than a compact fluorescent lamp and about 25% less than an incandescent lamp.
*LED Signs.*
**LED** Lobby Europea delle Donne.
Italian acronym meaning: Women European Lobby. LED was founded in 1990 and funded by the *European Community*.
**LED** Lupus Erythémateux aigu Disséminé.
French acronym meaning: Systemic Lupus Erythematosus.
*Medicine.*
**LEDA** Lunar European Demonstration Approach.
*Lunar Programs.*
**LEDs** Light-Emitting Devices.
**LEED**; **Leed** Local Economic and Employment Development.
LEED is an initiative of OECD.
*Local Development.*
For further details see under: **OECD**.
**LEED** Low-Energy Electron Diffraction.
*Solid-State Physics.*
**LEE initiative** Life and Earth Environments initiative (U.S.A.).
*Environmental Research.*
**LEEM** Low-Energy Electron Microscopy.

**LE/ES** Leucoemeraldine / Emeraldine Salt.
**LEF** Life Extension Foundation.
LEF is based in Fort Lauderdale, Florida, U.S.A.
**LE factor** Lupus Erythematosus factor.
*Medicine.*
**LEFM** Linear Elastic Fracture Mechanics.
*Materials Science.*
**leg.** (abbr.) legal.
**leg.** legale.
Italian abbreviation meaning: legal.
**leg.** (abbr.) legate; legation.
**legn.** legno.
Italian abbreviation meaning: wood.
**legn.** legname.
Italian abbreviation meaning: lumber; timber.
**LEI** Liquid Eurobond Index International.
*Bond Index.*
**LEI** Local Employment Initiatives.
**Leics.** (abbr.) Leicestershire (G.B.).
**LEIE** Loi sur l'Examen de l'Investissement Etranger.
*Canadian Laws.*
**LEIFS** Lake Erie Information Forecasting System.
**LEL** Lower Earnings Limit.
**LEM** Lunar Excursion Module.
**LEMSIP** Laboratory for Experimental Medicine and Surgery In Primates.
**LEO** Low Earth Orbit.
**LEOS** Low Earth Orbiting Satellite.
**LEP** Large Electron Positron.
**LEP** locally-employed personnel [also called LEC - specific to SFOR/KFOR].
personnel employé localement [aussi appelé LEC - propre à la SFOR/KFOR].
**LEP** Low Egg Passage.
*Virology.*
**LEPOR** Longterm and Expanded Program of Oceanic exploration and Research.
*Research Programs.*
**LERB** ACLANT Exercise Review Board.
Commission d'examen des exercices de l'ACLANT.
**LES** Large Eddy Simulations.
**LES** Licensing Executives Society (G.B.).
*Intellectual Property Protection; Licensing Diffusion.*
**LES** Lincoln Experimental Satellite.
**LES** Lupus Eritematoso Sistemico.
Italian acronym meaning: Systemic Lupus Erythematosus.
*Medicine.*
**LESIAC** LES International Affairs Committee.
For further details see under: **LES**.
**LESO** Laboratoire d'Energie SOlaire.
French acronym of the: Solar Energy Laboratory.
LESO is located in Lausanne (Switzerland).
**LESS** Least cost EStimating and Scheduling.
*Business; Economics; Finance.*
**LEST** Large Earth-based Solar Telescope.
**LEST** Law-Enforcement Support Team [Dayton Agreement].
Équipe d'appui à l'pplication des lois [Accord de Dayton].
**let.** (abbr.) letter.
The letter is a character of an alphabet usually representing one or several sounds of a spoken language.
*Linguistics.*
**LET** Linear Energy Transfer.
**LET** Low-Energy Telescope.
**LETM** Lake Evaporation and Thermodynamics Model.
**LETS glycoprotein** Large-External-Transformation-Sensitive glycoprotein.
**lett.** lettera.
Italian abbreviation meaning: letter.
**lett.** letterale.
Italian abbreviation meaning: literal.
**lett.** letterario.
Italian abbreviation meaning: literary.
**lett.** letteratura.
Italian abbreviation meaning: literature.
**leu** (abbr.) leucine.
$C_6H_{13}O_2N$ - Leucine is obtained from the hydrolysis of protein-containing substances. It is essential for infants as well as for adults.
*Biochemistry.*
**LEU** Low-Enriched Uranium.
**LEV** laser-enhanced viewer.
tomoscope.
**lev.** (abbr.) level.
*Acoustical Engineering; Acoustics; Civil Engineering; Computer Programming; Electricity; Engineering; Mechanical Devices; Metrology; Mining Engineering.*
**LEV requirements** Low Emission Vehicle requirements.
**LEX** The airport code for Lexington, Kentucky, U.S.A.
**LExEn initiative** Life in Extreme Environments initiative (U.S.A.).
Of the U.S. National Science Foundation. The aim of the LExEn initiative is to study organisms as far as pH levels, salinity, temperature and pressure are concerned.

**LExSWG** Lunar Exploration Science Working Group - NASA's.
*Lunar Research.*
**LF** Lactoferrin.
LF is an iron transport protein.
*Biochemistry.*
**LF** landing force.
force de débarquement.
**LF** Language Family.
*Linguistics.*
**LF** Ledger Folio.
**LF** Lethal Factor.
LF is a toxic protein produced by the anthrax bacillus.
*Anthrax Disease; Macrophages Destruction; Medicine; Microbiology.*
**LF** Line Feed.
*Computer Technology.*
**LF** Link Field.
*Computer Programming.*
**LF** Loi Fédèrale.
French initialism meaning: Federal Law.
**LF** Low Frequency.
Low frequency is a band of frequencies ranging from 30 kHz to 300 kHz.
*Telecommunications.*
**LFA-1** Leukocyte Function-associated Antigen-1.
**LFABP** Liver Fatty Acid Binding Protein.
*Cellular Biology; Liver Markers; Medicine; Molecular Biology.*
**LFA position** Left Fronto-Anterior position.
*Medicine.*
**LFAS** low-frequency active sonar.
sonar actif à basse fréquence.
**LFC** Level of Free Convection.
*Meteorology.*
**LFE** limites financières établies.
established financial limits /EFL/.
**LF loran** Low-Frequency loran.
LF loran is also known as: Cycle-Matching loran.
**LFLOW** Linearized high-resolutiuon wind-field Flow model.
**LFM** Lateral Force Microscopy.
**LFM** Limited-area Fine-mesh Model.
**lFng** lunatic Fringe.
lFng is a vertebrate signaling molecule.
*Anatomy; Medicine; Neurobiology.*
**LFP** Ligue de Football Professionnel (France).
**LFP** Low-Frequency Prediction.
**LFP oscillations** Local Field Potential oscillations.
*Biology; Insect Olfactory System; Neurophysiology; Physiology.*
**LFP position** Left Fronto-Posterior position.
*Medicine.*
**L Fr.** The Luxemburg franc.
Also: **LUF**.
Now: EURO/EUR (€). Became ECU (European single currency) with effect from January 2002.
*Currencies.*
**LFRA** Leatherhead Food Research Association - Surrey, G.B.
The LFRA is an independent research facility providing *Research Consultancy; Information* and *Training.*
**LFRIL** land forces reportable item list.
liste des articles à suivre des forces terrestres.
**LFS** (The) Labour Force Survey.
**LFS** Li-Fraumeni Syndrome.
The LFS is a rare familial multicancer syndrome.
*Hereditary Cancer Susceptibilities.*
**LFS** Low-Frequency Stimulation.
*Biological Sciences; Bioregulation; Medicine; Neurophysiology.*
**LFT** Leapfrog Test.
*Computer Programming.*
**LFT position** Left Frontotransverse position.
*Medicine.*
**LfU** Bavarian-State Office for Environmental Protection (Germany).
**L.G.** Landing Ground.
**LG** Lateral Gastroenemius.
The LG is a sensory nerve in the calf muscle.
*Anatomy; Locomotor System; Neurophysiology.*
**LG** Latvia.
**L/G** Lettre de Garantie.
*Banking; Business; Commerce.*
**L.G.** Life Guards (G.B.).
**LG** Linkage Group.
**LG** Low German.
Low German comprises the West Germanic languages not included in the High German group, as English, Dutch, Flemish, Plattdeutsch.
*Languages.*
**LgA** Long Access.
*Drug Addiction; Drug Intake; Neuropharmacology; Psychopharmacology.*
**LGA** The airport code for La Guardia, New York, New York, U.S.A.
**LGB** laser-guided bomb.
bombe à guidage laser /BGL/.
**LGCAs** Land-Grant Colleges of Agriculture (U.S.A.).
**LGF** Large Granule Fraction.
**LGF** Liver Growth Factor.
*Medicine.*

**LGFSTF** Liquefied Gaseous Fuels Spill Test Facility.

**LGGE laboratory** Glaciology and Geophysics of the Environment laboratory.
The LGGE laboratory il located in Grenoble, France.

**LGk** Late Greek.
Late Greek is the Greek of the early Byzantine Empire, from about A.D. 300 to 700.
*Languages.*

**LGMD** Limb-Girdle Muscular Dystrophy.

**LGM experiments** Last Glacial Maximum experiments.
*Earth, Atmospheric and Planetary Sciences.*

**LGN** Lateral Geniculate Neurons.

**LGN** Lateral Geniculate Nucleus.

**LGR** Loop Gap Resonator.

**LGS** Late Glacial Stage.
*Geological Sciences; Paleoclimate Changes.*

**LGS** Lithogenic Grain Size.
*Deep-Sea Sediments; Geological Sciences.*

**LGT** Lateral Gene Transfer.

**LGU Project** Urban Water and Sanitation Project (The Philippines).
*World Bank Projects.*

**LGUs** Land-Grant Universitites (U.S.A.).

**LGV** Lymphogranuloma Venereum.
LGV is also known as: Venereal Bubo; Lymphopathia Venereum; Lymphogranuloma Inguinale.
*Medicine.*

**LGW** The airport code for Gatwick, London, G.B.

**LH** Lateral Hypothalamus.
*Obesity Research.*

**LH** Left Hand.

**L.H.** Legion of Honour.

**L.H.** Light Horse.
*Ordnance.*

**L.H.** Lighthouse.
*Navigation.*

**LH** Lithuania.

**LHA** 1. amphibious assault ship.
1. bâtiment d'assaut amphibie.
2. landing helicopter assault.
2. hélicoptère d'assaut.

**LHBP** Laboratory of Human Bacterial Pathogenesis (U.S.A.).
*Genome Analysis; High Throughput; DNA Sequencing; Imaging Techniques.*

**LHC** Large Hadron Collider.
LHC is a European mega-accelerator under construction at CERN which will begin to operate in 2007.

**LHC II** Light-Harvesting Complex II.
The LCH II is found in the chloroplasts of plants and green algae.
*Biochemistry; Botany.*

**LHCP** Light-Harvesting Chlorophyll-binding Protein.
*Molecular Biology; Plant Biology.*

**LHCs** Light-Harvesting Centers.
For further details see under: **LHCs** (Light-Harvesting Complexes).

**LHCs** Light-Harvesting Complexes.
*Plant Biochemistry; Plant Biology; Photosynthesis; Structural Biology.*

**LHD** landing ship dock.
navire d'assaut amphibie.

**LHD** Large Helical Device.
The helical coils of the LHD create a strong magnetic field to confine burning plasma thus allowing a continuous fusion reaction.
*Alternative Energy Sources; Fusion Science; Helical Devices; Plasma Physics.*

**LHD** Left-Hand Drive.

**LHON** Leber's Hereditary Optic Neuropathy.
*Molecular Genetics; Molecular Medicine.*

**LHR** The airport code for Heathrow, London, G.B.

**LHRH** Luteinizing Hormone - Releasing Hormone.
LHRH is also known as: Gonadotropin-Releasing Hormone.
*Endocrinology.*

**LHS**; **l.h.s.** Left Hand-Side.

**LH synthesis** Lutenizing Hormone synthesis.

**LHW** Leading Hotels of the World.
*Business Travel.*

**LHX** Light Helicopter Experimental.

**LI** Lead Isotope.
*Archaeological Materials; Geology; Materials Science and Engineering.*

**L/I** Letter of Intent.
*Business; Finance.*

**li** (abbr.) liability / liabilities.

**LI** Liberia.

**LI** Line Item.
*Computer Programming; Industrial Engineering.*

**LI** Liquidità Immediata.
Italian acronym meaning: Quick Assets.

**Li** The chemical symbol for Lithium.
*Chemistry; Pharmacology; Symbols.*

**LI** Livorno, Italy.

**LI** Load Intelligence.
*Computer Technology.*

**LI** Logical Instruction.
*Computer Programming.*

**L.I.** Lombardia Informatica.

**LI** Long Island (U.S.A.).
**LIA** Licensing Industry Association.
An association located in New York, U.S.A.
**LIA** Life Insurance Association (G.B.).
**LIA** Little Ice Age.
*Climate Change; Earth, Oceans and Space; Paleoclimatic Records.*
**$LiAlH_4$** Lithium Aluminum Hydride.
*Inorganic Chemistry.*
**Lib.** (abbr.) liberal.
**Lib.** (abbr.) librarian; Library.
**LIBE** LIBrary Editor.
**LIBER** LIgue des Bibliothèques Européennes de Recherche (Germany).
Located in Bremen, Germany. Founded in 1971 to establish close collaboration between the general research libraries of Europe, and national university libraries in particular; and to help in finding practical ways of *improving the quality of the services* these libraries provide.
**$LiBH_4$** Lithium Borohydride.
*Inorganic Chemistry.*
**LIBID** London Interbank Bid Rate (G.B.).
**lib.-lab.** liberal-labour.
**LIBOR** London Interbank Offered Rate (G.B.) (now: EURIBOR).
**libr.** libraio; libreria.
Italian abbreviations meaning: bookseller; bookshop.
**LiBr** Lithium Bromide.
LiBr is used mainly in pharmaceuticals.
*Inorganic Chemistry.*
**LIBRIS** LIBRary/ LIBRaries Information System.
**LIC** League International for Creditors.
**LIC** Less Industrialized Country.
**LIC** Light-Induced Current.
**LIC** Loi sur l'Investissement au Canada.
*Canadian Laws.*
**LIC** low-intensity conflict.
conflict de faible intensité.
**LiCl** Lithium Chloride.
LiCl is used mainly in the production of mineral waters and soft drinks.
*Inorganic Chemistry.*
**$LiClO_4$** Lithium Perchlorate.
*Inorganic Chemistry.*
**$Li_2CO_3$** Lithium Carbonate.
Lithium Carbonate is used mainly in the paint industry.
*Inorganic Chemistry.*
**LICP** Laboratory of Intracellular Parasites.
*U.S. Laboratories; Genome Analysis; High Throughput DNA Sequencing; Imaging Techniques.*
**LICS** Logic In Computer Science.
**LICTA** Lega Italiana Controlli Trasporto Aereo.
*Italian League.*
**Lid.** (abbr.) Lidocaine.
Lidocaine is also known as: Lignocaine.
*Organic Chemistry.*
**LIDAR system** Laser Identification, Detection And Ranging system.
**L.I.D.U.** Lega Internazionale dei Diritti dell'Uomo.
Italian acronym of the: International League for Man's Rights.
**LIESST** Light-Induced Excited Spin State Trapping.
*Applied Physics; Crystallography; Inorganic Chemistry; Optics; Magnetism.*
**LIF** Laser-Induced Fluorescence.
*Anatomy; Cell Biology; Chemistry; Medicine; Secretory Vesicles.*
**LIF** Left Iliac Fossa.
*Anatomy; Medicine.*
**LIF** Leukemia Inhibitory Factor.
**LiF** Lithium Fluoride.
Lithium Fluoride is used mainly in ceramics.
*Inorganic Chemistry.*
**LIFFE; Liffe** London International Financial Futures and Options Exchange (G.B.).
**LIFO** Last In, First Out.
*Computer Programming; Industrial Engineering.*
**LIFR** Leukemia Inhibitory Factor Receptor.
*Immunology; Medicine.*
**LIG** London International Group (G.B.).
**LIGASF** LIquefaction and GAsification of Solid Fuels.
Financial support for pilot industrial projects and demonstration projects relating to LIGASF.
*European Community Project.*
**ligg.** (abbr.) ligaments / ligamenta.
*Histology.*
**LIGO** Laser Interferometry Gravitational-wave Observatory.
*Astrophysics; Cosmology; Gravitational-wave Detectors.*
**LiH** Lithium Hydride.
LiH is used mainly in organic synthesis.
*Inorganic Chemistry.*
**$LiI \cdot 3H_2O$** Lithium Iodide.
Lithium Iodide, also known as: Lithium Iodide Trihydrate, is used mainly in air conditioning.
*Inorganic Chemistry.*
**LIL** Laboratory Interface Language.
**Lil** Learning and innovation loan.

*Banking; Finance.*
**LILA** Lega Italiana Lotta contrio l'AIDS.
Italian acronym of the: Italian League for the fight against AIDS.
**LILCO** Long Island Lighting Company (U.S.A.).
**LILEs** Large-Ion Lithophile Elements.
*Geology; Mineral Sciences; Subduction zone metamorphism.*
**LIL Project** Enterprise Incubator Project (Armenia).
*World Bank Projects.*
**LILRC** Long Island Library Resources Council (U.S.A.).
**Lim** Laboratorio di informatica musicale.
*Italian Laboratory.*
**LIM** Linear-Induction-Motor.
The LIM capsule pump has been invented at the University of Missouri, Columbia (U.S.A.).
**LIM** Line Interface Module.
**LIM** Liquid Injection Molding.
**LIM** The airport code for Lima, Peru.
**LIMB** Limestone Injection Multistage Burner.
**LIMB** Listing of Molecular Biology Databases.
**limb** The above acronyms were coined using the English word "limb".
*Anatomy; Astronomy; Botany; Design Engineering; Geology.*
**LIMBS** Ligand-Associated Metal Binding Site.
*Biomedical Research; Biosciences; Leukocyte Biology; Oncology.*
**LIMCO** Lake Ice Microbial COmmunity.
*Autotrophic Organisms; Limnology; Microbial Communities; Heterotrophic Organisms.*
**LIMEAN** London Interbank Mean Rate (G.B.).
**$LiMn^{+2}PO_4$** Lithiophilite.
Lithiophilite is found in granite pegmatites.
*Mineralogy.*
**$Li_2MoO_4$** Lithium Molybdate.
*Inorganic Chemistry.*
**LIMS** Laboratory Information Management System.
**LIMTV** Linear Induction Motor Test Vehicle.
**lin.** (abbr.) linear; lineal.
**Linac** (abbr.) linear accelerator.
For further details see under: **SLAC** and **LCLS**.
**$LiNbO_3$** Lithium Niobate.
**LINC** Language In the National Curriculum.
**Lincs.** (abbr.) Lincolnshire (G.B.).
**LINEAR project** Lincoln Near-Earth Asteroid Research project.
LINEAR identifies and catalogs NEAs.
*Asteroid Population.*
For further details see under: **NEAs**.
**LINEs** Long Interspersed Nucleotide Elements.
*Genomic Biology; Biology; Medicine; Molecular Biotechnology; Neurology; Psychiatry.*
**$LiNH_2$** Lithium Amide.
Lithium Amide is used mainly in pharmaceuticals such as antihistamines.
*Inorganic Chemistry.*
**$LiNO_3$** Lithium Nitrate.
Lithium Nitrate is used mainly in ceramics and in pyrotechnics.
*Inorganic Chemistry.*
**LINOSCO** Libraries In North Staffordshire in Co-operation.
**LINS** Long INterspersed Sequence.
**LINUS** Local Independently Nucleated Units of Structure.
*Physical Chemisry; Protein Engineering; Computer Science; Computational Biology; Crystallography; Nuclear Magnetic Resonance Spectroscopy.*
**$Li_2O$** Lithium Oxide.
Lithium Oxide, also known as: Lithia, is used mainly in ceramics.
*Inorganic Chemistry.*
**LIOCS** Logical Input/Output Control System.
*Computer Programming.*
**LiOH** Lithium Hydroxide.
LiOH is used mainly in storage batteries.
*Inorganic Chemistry.*
**LIP** Lateral Intraparietal Area.
The LIP is a subregion of the parietal lobes.
*Neurobiology; Psychology.*
**LIP**; **L.I.P.** Life Insurance Policy.
**LIPI** Indonesian Academy of Sciences.
**LIPL** Linear Information Processing Language.
*Data Communications.*
**LIPs** Large Igneous Provinces.
*Geoscience.*
**LIPS** Logical Interferences Per Second.
*Artificial Intelligence.*
**LIPU** Lega Italiana Protezione Uccelli.
Italian acronym of the: Italian League for Protection of Birds.
**liq.** (abbr.) liquid; liquor.
**liq.pt.** (abbr.) liquid point.
**liquid.** (abbr.) liquidation.
**LIRC** Low Interest Rate Currency.
**Lirma** London international insurance and reinsurance market association (G.B.).
**LIRTS** Large Infrared Telescope.
**LIS** Larsen Ice Shelf.
*Geophysics; Glaciology.*
**LIS** Laser Isotope Separation.

**LIS** Library & Information Service.
**LISA** Laser Interferometer Space antenna.
Joint European-U.S. Mission. Launch planned in 2011.
*Astrophysics.*
**LISA** Librarians and Information Specialists in Addictions.
**LISA** Library and Information Science Abstracts.
**LISA** Life Insurance Savings Account (U.S.A.).
**LISA** Linked Index Sequential Access.
**LISA** Long-term Isolation Safety Assessment.
**LISD** Library and Information Services Division.
Of the U.S. NOAA.
For further details see under: **NOAA**.
**LISE** Libraries of Institutes and Schools of Education.
**LISP** Laser Isotope Separation Program.
**LISP** LIbero Sindacato di Polizia (Italy).
*Police Union.*
**LISP language** LISt Processing language.
**LIST** Library and Information Services, Teesside.
**LIT** Life Insurance Trust.
**L.it.** Lire Italiane.
Italian Lire (obsolete).
Now: EURO/EUR (€). Became ECU (European single currency) with effect from January 2002.
**lit.** (abbr.) literal.
**LIT** Liver-Infusion Tryptose.
**LIT** Local Income Tax.
**LIT** The airport code for Little Rock, Arkansas, U.S.A.
**Lith** (abbr.) Lithuanian.
Lithuanian is a Baltic language, the official language of Lithuania.
*Languages.*
**$Li_2TiO_3$** Lithium Titanate.
Lithium Titanate is used in glazes and enamels.
*Inorganic Chemistry.*
**LIU** Line Interface Unit.
**LIVEX** live exercise.
exercice réel.
**LJ** Life Jacket.
**L.J.** Lord Justice (G.B.).
**LJF** least-jammed frequency.
fréquence la moins brouillée.
**LJV segment** Landers-Johnson Valley segment.
*Crustal Studies.*
**lk.** (abbr.) link.
For further details see under: **l.**
**lkd.** (abbr.) locked.
**LKFM basalt** Low-K Fra Mauro basalt.
*Applied Coherent Technology; Geophysics; Planetology.*
**lkg.** (abbr.) leakage.
Also: **lkge.**
*Engineering; Physical Chemistry.*
**lkg.** (abbr.) locking.
*Electronics.*
**lkg. & Bkg.** Leakage and Breakage.
*Insurance; Transport.*
**lkge.** (abbr.) leakage.
Also: **lkg.**
**LKKR techique** Layer-Korringa-Kohn-Rostoker technique.
The LKKR technique is used for treating isolated interfaces or surfaces.
*Computational Metallurgy.*
**LL** Late Latin.
Late Latin is the Latin of the late Western Roman Empire, from about A.D. 300 to 700.
*Languages.*
**L.L.** Lending Library.
**LL** 1. lessons learned.
1. enseignements (tirés).
2. lower-layer (defence).
2. (défense de la) couche inférieure.
3. low-level.
3. basse altitude.
**L.L.** Limited Liability.
**LL** Lincoln Laboratory.
**LL** Line Level.
*Telecommunications.*
**LL** Line Link.
Line Link is also known as: Line-Link Frame.
*Telecommunications.*
**LL** Link List.
*Computer Programming.*
**LL** Live Load.
Live load is also known as: Moving Load.
*Mechanics.*
**LL** Lloyd's of London (G.B.).
*Insurance; Shipping.*
**LL** Loudness Level.
*Acoustics.*
**LLA** Louisiana Library Association (U.S.A.).
**LL.AA.** Loro Altezze.
Italian initialism meaning: Their Highnesses.
**LLAD** low-level air defence.
défense antiaérienne à basse altitude.
**LLAW** Law Librarians' Association of Wisconsin (U.S.A.).
**LL.B.** Bachelor of Laws.
**LLC** Limited Liability Company.
**LLC** Liquid-Liquid Chromatography.
**LLC** Local Link Control.
**LLCOF** Land Lines COmmunication Facilities.

**LLCs** Lyotropic Liquid Crystals.
*Chemical Engineering; Chemistry; Materials Research.*
**LL.D.** Legum Doctor; Doctor of Laws.
**LLD** Long-Lasting Depolarization.
**LLD factor** Lactobacillus Lactis Dorner's factor.
*Medicine.*
**lldPE** linear low density Polyethylene.
**Llds.** Lloyd's.
*Insurance.*
**LL.EE.** Loro Eccellenze.
Italian initialism meaning: Their Excellencies.
**LL.EEm.** Loro Eminenze.
Italian initialism meaning: Their Eminencies.
**LL frame** Local Level frame.
**LLG equation** Landau-Lifshitz-Gilhert equation.
*Magnetism.*
**LLJ** Low-Level Jet.
**LLL** Lawrence Livermore Laboratory (U.S.A.).
**LLL** Left Lower Lobe.
Also: **L.L.L.**
**LLL circuit** Low-Level Logic circuit.
*Electronics.*
**LLLTV** Low-Level Light Television.
**LLMC** low-level military commission.
commission militaire de bas niveau.
**LL.MM.** Loro Maestà.
Italian initialism meaning: Their Majesties.
**LLNE** Law Librarians of New England.
**LLNL** Lawrence Livermore National Laboratory (U.S.A.).
**LLP** leased long lines programme.
programme de location de lignes à grande distance.
**LLP** Limited Liability Partner.
**L-L phase** Liquid-Liquid phase.
*Chemical Physics.*
**LL.PP.** Lavori Pubblici.
Italian initialism meaning: Public Works.
**LLPs** Limited Liability Partnerships.
**LLR** low-level radiation.
radiation à bas niveau.
**LLR** Lunar Laser Ranging.
*Geophysics; Lunar Research.*
**LLR Center** Language Learning Resource Center.
Washington State University (U.S.A.).
**LLRS** low-level radar system.
système de radar à basse altitude.
**LLRV** Lunar Landing Research Vehicle.
**LLS** low-level support.
appui à basse altitude.
**LLSEE** Linguistics and Literary Studies in Eastern Europe.
**LLSUA** limiting line of submerged approach.
ligne limite d'approche en plongée.
**LLTR** low-level transit route.
route de transit à basse altitude.
**LLTV** Low-Light Television.
**LLWAS** Low-Level Windshear Alert System.
**LM** Langmuir Monolayer.
Named for the American chemist Irving **Langmuir**.
*Applied Sciences; Physics.*
**LM** Learning Machine.
The learning machine is a computer that can improve its performance by learning from its past errors.
*Computer Technology.*
**LM** Light Microscopy.
*Materials Science and Engineering.*
**LM** Linear Modulation.
*Telecommunications.*
**LM** Linguistic Model.
*Computer Programming.*
**l.m.** livello del mare.
Italian initialism meaning: sea level.
**LM** Lower Mantle (Earth's).
**lm** (abbr.) lumen.
*Anatomy; Optics.*
**LM** Lunar Module.
Lunar module is also known as: Lunar Excursion Module.
*Space Technology.*
**LMA position** Left Mento-Anterior position.
*Medicine.*
**LMB** Laboratory of Molecular Biology (Cambridge).
**LMB** Leptomycin B.
**LMC** Large Magellanic Cloud.
*Astronomy; Astrophysics; Galaxies; Globular Clusters.*
**LMCB** (MRC) Laboratory for Molecular Cell Biology.
Based at the University College London.
**LMCC** LOCE mobile communications centre.
centre de communications mobile du LOCE.
**LMCs** Low-Mass Compounds.
**LMCT** Ligand-Metal Charge Transfer.
**LME** Large Marine Ecosystem.
**LME** Livelli Massimi di Esposizione.
**LME** London Metal Exchange (G.B.).
**LMEC** Liquid Metal Engineering Center.
Located at Canoga Park, California, U.S.A.
**LMER network** Land Margin Ecosystem Research network.
Of the U.S. NSF.

*Chemistry and Biology of the Oceans; Coastal Studies.*
For further details see under: **NSF**.
**LMEs** Large Marine Ecosystems.
**LMEX** London Metal Exchange Index (G.B.).
**LMF** Linear Magnetic Fusion.
*Energy.*
**LMFBR** Liquid-Metal Fast-Breeder Reactor.
*Energy.*
**LMFR** Liquid-Metal Fuel Reactor.
**LMG** Laboratory of Molecular Genetics.
At the U.S. National Institute of Aging.
*U.S. Laboratories.*
**LMG** light machine-gun.
mitrailleuse légère.
**LMGP** Laboratoire des Matériaux et du Génie Physique (France).
The LMGP is a CNRS-affiliated Laboratory in *Materials Science.*
**lm-hr** lumen-hour.
*Optics.*
**LMI** Link Management Interface.
**LMICs** Low- and Middle-Income Countries.
**LML** Lean Misfire Limit.
**LMN** Library Management Network.
**LMNA** Long-Range Multipurpose Naval Aircraft.
**LMOs** Living Modified Organisms.
For further details see under: **CPB**.
**LMP** Latent Membrane Protein.
**LM-PCR** Ligation-Mediated Polymerase Chain Reaction.
*Immunology; Genetics; Molecular Immunology.*
**LMP position** Left Mento-Posterior position.
*Medicine.*
**LMR** Large Marine Resource.
**LMR** Liquid Metal Reactor.
**LMs** Langmuir Monolayers.
For further details see under: **LM**.
**lm-sec** lumen-second.
*Optics.*
**LMT** Large Millimeter Telescope.
Completed in 2000.
*Millimeter-Wave Astronomy.*
**L.M.T.**; **LMT** Length, Mass, Time.
*Physics.*
**LMT** Local Mean Time.
*Navigation.*
**LMTO** Linear Muffin-Tin Orbital.
*Electronic Structure Methods; Geophysics; High-Pressure Research; Mathematics; Planetary Physics.*
**LMT presentation** Left Mentum Transverse presentation.
*Medicine.*
**LMV** Long Market Value.
**LMW** Low Molecular Weight.
**lm/w** lumen per watt.
*Optics.*
**LMWHC** Low-Molecular-Weight Hydrocarbon.
**LMXBs** Low-Mass X-ray Binaries.
**LN** lead nation.
1a. pays chef de file [SFOR].
1b. pays pilote.
**L.N.** Lega Nazionale.
Italian initialism meaning: National League.
**LN** Line Number.
*Computer Programming.*
**Ln** Logaritmo naturale.
Italian initialism meaning: natural logarithm.
Also known as: Napierian Logarithm.
*Mathematics.*
**LN** Lymph Node.
LN is also known as: Lymph Gland.
*Anatomy.*
**Ln-5** Laminin-5.
*Cancer Research; Cell Biology; Pathology.*
**LNA** Lega Navale Italiana (Italy).
**LN-A**; **Ln-a** Lotta alla Non Autosufficienza.
An Italian not-for-profit Foundation.
**LNADW** Lower North Atlantic Deep Water.
**LNC** Lymph Node Cell.
**LNE** Laboratoire National d'Essai (France).
**LNG** Liquefied Natural Gas.
Liquefied natural gas is also known as: LN gas.
*Petroleum Engineering.*
**LNGS** Laboratori Nazionali del Gran Sasso.
*Italian Laboratory.*
**L.N.I.** Lega Navale Italiana.
Italian initialism of the: Italian Naval League.
**LNKS** Lovastatin Nonaketide Synthase.
*Bacteriology; Chemistry; Lovastatin Biosynthesis; Pharmacy; Polyketide Synthase.*
**LNKS** Low Natural Killer Syndrome.
LNKS is a subcategory of chronic fatigue.
**LNO** limited nuclear option.
option nucléaire limitée.
**LNPF** Lymph Node Permability Factor.
**LNT model** Linear No-Threshold model.
*Ionizing Radiation; Population Studies; Radion Effects Research; Radiation Risks.*
**LNTCs** (primary) Lymph Node T Cells.
**LNTS** League of Nations Treaty Series.
**LO**; **L/O** Letter of Offer.
*Business; Commerce.*
**LO**; **L.O.** Liaison Officer.
**LO** Limited Order.

*Business; Finance.*
**LO** Local Oscillator.
**LO; L.O.** Lock-Out.
**LO** Lodi, Italy.
**LO; L.O.** London Office.
**LO** Longueur d'Onde.
French acronym meaning: wavelength.
*Physics.*
**lo** (abbr.) low.
**LO** Lowest Offer.
*Business; Finance.*
**LO** Lubricating Oil.
*Materials Science.*
**LO** Lysyl Oxidase.
LO is also known as: Protein Lysine 6-Oxidase.
*Biochemistry; Chemistry; Medicine; Molecular and Cell Biology; Pharmaceutical Chemistry.*
**LO** Slovakia.
**LOA** Length Overall.
**LOA** 1. letter of agreement.
1. lettre d'accord.
2. letter of assistance [PSO].
2. lettre d'attribution [PSO].
**LOA** Location avec Option d'Achat (Location avec promesse de vente - particuliers).
French acronym meaning: Leasing.
**LOAC** law of armed conflict.
droit des conflicts armés.
**LOACREP** law of armed conflict report.
compte rendu sur le droit des conflicts armés.
**LOAD** Laser Optoacoustic Detection.
**load** The above acronym was coined using the English word "load".
*Computer Programming; Electrical Engineering; Electricity; Engineering; Industrial Engineering; Mechanics; Ordnance; Telecommunications.*
**LOA position** Left Occipito-Anterior position.
*Medicine.*
**LOB** Line Of Balance.
**LOC** Letter Of Credit.
*Banking; Commerce.*
**LOC** 1. level of operational capability.
1. niveau de capacité opérationnelle.
2. limited operational capability.
2. capacité opérationnelle limitée.
3. lines of communications.
3. lignes de communication.
**LOC** Line of Code.
*Computer Programming.*
**LoC** Line Of Control.
Separating the Indian and Pakistani parts of Kashmir.
**loc.** (abbr.) local; location.
**LOCA** Loss-Of-Coolant Accident.
*Nuclear Engineering.*
**LOCE** 1. limited operational capability, Europe.
1. capacité opérationnelle limitée en Europe.
2. linked operational intelligence centres, Europe.
2. réseau des centres de renseignement opérationnel en Europe.
**LOCPOD** low-cost powered dispenser.
distributeur propulsé à faible coût.
**LOCPOL** local police [SFOR - Bosnian police force].
police locale [SFOR - police bosniaque].
**LOCS** Land-Ocean-Climate Satellite.
**LOD** Logarithm of the ODds.
**LODYC** Laboratoire d'Océanographie DYnamique et de Climatologie (France).
*French Laboratory.*
**LOEX** Library Orientation-Instruction Exchange.
**LOF** Line Of Fire.
**LOFA** Loss-Of-Flow Accident.
**LOFL** Log Of Fluorescence.
**log** (abbr.) logaritmo.
Italian abbreviation meaning: logarithm.
**Log** (abbr.) logistics.
logistique.
**LOGASREQ** logistic assistance request.
demande d'aide logistique.
**LOGASSESSREP** logistic assessment report.
compte rendu d'évaluation logistique.
**LOGDEF** logistic deficiency.
insuffisance logistique.
**LOGDEFICIENCY** see LOGDEF.
voir LOGDEF.
**LOGDEPLAND** logistic depot report, land forces.
compte rendu des dépôts logistiques des forces terrestres.
**LOGEX** logistic exercise.
exercice logistique.
**LOGFAS** logistic functional area services.
services du domaine fonctionnel logistique.
**LOGFASS** logistics functional area sub-system [obsolete - see LOGFAS].
sous-système de domaine fonctionnel "logistique" [obsolète - voir LOGFAS].
**LOGREQ** 1. logistic request.
1. demande de soutien logistique.
2. logistic requirement.
2. besoin logistique.
**LOGSITLAND** logistic situation report; land forces.
compte rendu de situation logistique des forces terrestres.
**LOGSITREP** logistic situation report.

compte rendu de situation logistique.
**LOGSTAR** logistic status report.
compte rendu de situation logistique.
**LOGSUMREP** logistic summary report.
compte rendu logistique sommaire.
**LOGSURPLUS** logistic surplus.
surplus logistique.
**LOH** light observation helicopter.
hélicoptère léger d'observation.
**LOH** Loss Of Heterozygosity.
**loh** The above acronym was coined accidentally using the Arabic word "loh" which means: block; board; slab; panel; platform.
**LOI** Letter Of Instruction; Letter Of Intent.
**LOI** Loss Of Imprinting (of the IGF2).
*Cancer; Embryonic Development; Epigenetic Alterations.*
For further details see under: **IGF2**.
**LOICZ** Land-Ocean Interactions in the Coastal Zone.
**LOIFO** Lowest-In; First-Out.
**LOJI** loss of job indemnity.
indemnité de perte d'emploi.
**LOLITA system** Language of the Online Investigation and Transformation Abstractors system.
**LOMEZ** low missile engagement zone.
zone d'engagement des missiles à basse altitude.
**LOMI** Letter Of Moral Intent.
*Business; Finance.*
**Lon.** (abbr.) London, G.B.
Also: **Lond.**
**LON** The airport code for the city of London, England.
**Lond.** (abbr.) London, G.B.
Also: **Lon.**
**long.** (abbr.) longitude.
**LOP** Line Of Position.
**LOPAR** low-power acquisition radar.
radar d'acquisition de faible puissance.
**LOPI** Loss Of Piping Integrity.
**LOP position** Left Occipito-Posterior position.
*Medicine.*
**LORAD** long-range active detection (system).
(système de) détection active à longue distance.
**LORAN** long range navigation.
radionavigation à longue distance.
**Lors** Lloyd's outward reinsurance scheme.
Outward reisurance debit and credit notes processed electronically since December 1993.
*Insurance.*
**LOS** line of sight.
1a. à portée optique.
1b. à vue directe.
1c. en visibilité directe.
**LOSAM** low-altitude surface-to-air missile.
missile surface-air à basse altitude.
**LOSC** Law Of the Sea Conference.
**LOSHADREP** local shipping advisory representative.
représentant local de la navigation commerciale.
**LOSS** Libraries of the Social Sciences.
**LOT** Lateral Olfactory Tract.
**LOT** Linear Optical Trajectory.
**LO-TO effect** Longitudinal-Optic-Transverse Optic effect.
*Condensed Matter Physics.*
**LOT position** Left Occipitotransverse position.
*Medicine.*
**LOTS** logistics over the shore.
opérations logistiques sur plage.
**LOVA** Loss-Of-Vacuum Accident.
**LOVAL** Larval Occluded Virus Alkali-Liberated.
*Virology.*
**LOWCAP** low altitude combat air patrol.
patrouille aérienne de combat à basse altitude.
**LOx** Liquid-Oxygen.
**LOX; L.O.X.** Liquid Oxygen Explosive.
**loz** liquid ozone.
**loz** The above acronym was coined accidentally using the Arabic word "loz" which means: almond (*Botany*).
**L.P.** Labour Party.
**LP** 1. landing point.
1. point de débarquement.
2. light patrol.
2. patrouille légère.
**LP** lap.
*Engineering; Materials Science; Metallurgy; Military Science.*
**L.P.; LP** Liberal Party.
**LP** Licitazione Privata.
Italian initialism meaning: Private Tender.
**L.P.** Life Policy.
*Insurance.*
**LP** Limited Partner.
*Business; Finance.*
**LP** Linear Programming.
*Mathematics.*
**LP** List Processing.
*Computer Programming.*
**L.P.; LP** London Port.
**L.P.** London Post.
**LP** Long Position.
**LP** Lord Provost.
**LP** Low Pressure.

**LP** Luna Piena.
Italian initialism meaning: full moon.
*Astronomy.*
**LPA** Link Pack Area.
**LPA** Lysophosphatidic Acid.
LPA is a bioactive lipid.
*Biochemistry; Medicine; Molecular Biology; Physiology.*
**LPAR** large phased-array radar.
1a. grand radar à balayage électrique.
1b. grand radar à éléments en phase.
**LPC** Linear Predictive Coding.
**LPD** landing transport, dock.
transport amphibie de chalands de débarquement et de personnel.
**LPD** Light Petroleum Distillate.
**LPE** Liquid-Phase Epitaxy.
*Solid-State Physics.*
**LP electrons** *p*-like Lone Pair electrons (of chalcogen atoms).
*Atom Technology.*
**Lperu** Lycopersicon peruvianum.
**LPF process** Leaching, Precipitation, and Flotation process.
*Mining Engineering.*
**LPG** Laboratory of Population Genetics.
**LPG** Lipophosphoglycan.
*Biochemistry; Biological Chemistry; Host Resistance; Molecular Pharmacology; Medicine.*
**LPG** Liquefied Petroleum Gas.
LPG is also known as: Compressed Petroleum Gas; Liquefied Hydrocarbon Gas.
*Petroleum Engineering.*
**LP gas** Liquefied Petroleum gas.
For further derails see under: **LPG**.
**LPH** amphibious assault ship, helicopter.
porte-hélicoptères d'assaut amphibie.
**LPH** Lipotropin Hormone.
LPH is also known as: Lipotropic Hormone.
*Biochemistry; Endocrinology.*
**LPI** Living Planet Index.
**LPI** low probability of intercept.
faible probabilité d'interception.
**LPI** Lunar and Planetary Institute (U.S.A.).
*Planetary Science.*
**LPJ-DGVM** LPJ Dynamic Global Vegetation Model.
*Biogeochemistry; ecosystems Analysis; Geography.*
**LPL** Lipoprotein Lipase.
*Heart Disease Genes; Population Genetics.*
**LPL** The airport code for Liverpool, G.B.
**LPLs** Lamina Propria Lymphocytes.
*Medicine; Primate Research.*
**LPM** Lateral Posterior Mesoderm.
*Anatomy; Developmental Biology; Medicine.*
**LPM; lpm** lines per minute.
**LPM** List Programming Language.
**LP mission** Lunar Prospector mission.
The LP mission was launched on 7th January 1998. It is the third mission in NASA's Discovery Program.
*Lunar Research.*
**Lpn** Lender participation notes.
*Finance.*
**LPN** Licensed Practical Nurse.
**LPO** Lattice-Preferred Orientation.
*Geology; Geophysics.*
**LPO model** Late Pleistocene Origins model.
**Lpp** Length between perpendiculars.
*Naval Architecture.*
**LPPs** Long-Period Pulses.
*Earthquake Research; Geology; Meteorology; Volcanology.*
**LPPS** low-pressure pump station.
station de pompage basse pression.
**LPR** Late-Phase Reaction.
*Asthma and Allergy; Clinical Immunology; Medicine.*
**LPR; lpr** le plus réduit.
*Business; Commerce.*
**LPRA** Library Publication Relations Association.
**LP record** Long-Playing record.
**LPS** Lipopolysaccharide.
LPS is a TLR ligand.
*Biochemistry; Immunology; Medicine.*
For further details se under: **TLR**.
**LPSC** Lunar and Planetary Science Conference (U.S.A.).
The 37 LPSC on Martian Meteorite ALH 84001 was held in Houston (U.S.A.).
**LPTB; L.P.T.B.** London Passenger Transport Board (G.B.).
**LPTM** Latest Paleocene Thermal Maximum.
*Earth Sciences; Geological Sciences; Marine Science.*
**LPTR** Livermore Pool-Type Reactor.
*Energy.*
**LPTs** Long-Period Tremors.
*Earthquake Research; Geology; Meteorology; Volcanology.*
**LPU** Language Processor Unit.
**LPU** Lavori di Pubblica Utilità (Italy).
**LPVT** Large Print Video Terminal.
**lpW; l.p.W.** lumen per Watt; lumens per Watt.
*Optics.*

**LQ** Letter-Quality.
*Computer Technology.*

**LQA** Livello di Qualità Accettabile.
Italian initialism meaning: Acceptable Quality Level.

**LQG problem** Linear-Quadratic-Gaussian problem.

**LQMA** Limite di Qualità Media Accettabile.
Italian initialism meaning: Average Acceptable Quality Limit.

**LQP** Letter-Quality Printer.
*Computer Technology.*

**LQR** Law Quarterly Review.

**LQTS** Long QT Syndrome.
*Artery-Clogging Plaques; Cardiology; Cardiovascular Electrophysiology; Genetics; Medicine.*

**LR** Label Record.
*Computer Technology.*

**Lr** The chemical symbol for Lawrencium.
Named for the **Lawrence** radiation laboratory (California, U.S.A.) founded by Ernest O. **Lawrence**.
*Chemistry; Symbols.*

**LR** Legal Reserve.

**LR** Legge Regionale.
Italian initialism meaning: Regional Law.

**LR** Lending Rate.
*Banking; Business; Commerce; Finance.*

**LR** Likelihood Ratio.

**LR** Listing Requirements.
*Finance.*

**LR** Lloyd's Register (G.B.).
*Insurance; Shipping.*

**LR** Loan Rate.
*Business; Finance.*

**LR** Logical Record.
*Computer Programming.*

**LR** long-range.
1a. à grande distance [télécoms].
1b. a long rayon d'action [aéronef].
1c. à long terme [prévision météo, financières].
1d. à longue portée [engin, missile].

**LRA** Lagged Reserve Accounting.

**LRA** 1. long-range attack.
1. attaque à grande distance.
2. long-range aviation.
2. aviation à long rayon d'action.

**LRACCC** Learning Resources Association of California Community Colleges (U.S.A.).

**LRAM** Long-Range Attack Missile.

**LR asymmetry** Left-Right asymmetry.
*Anatomy; Medicine.*

**LRBA** Ligue Royale Belge d'Athlétisme.
*Belgian League.*

**LRBGE** Laboratory of Receptor Biology and Gene Expression.
LRBGE is a Division of the Basic Sciences - U.S. National Cancer Institute.

**LRBM** Long-Range Ballistic Missile.

**LRC** Learning Resource Center.
Technical College (U.S.A.).

**LRC** logistic readiness centre.
centre de préparation logistique.

**LRC** London Rowing Club (G.B.).

**LRC** Longitudinal Redundancy Check.
*Computer Programming.*

**LRCC** Laboratoire de Recherches et de Contrôle du Caoutchouc (France).
French initialism of the: Rubber Research and Control Laboratory.

**LRCM** long-range cruise missile.
missile de croisière à longue portée.

**LRE** Linguistic Research and Engineering.
Research and technological development in the field of telematic systems in areas of general interest. LRE (1990-1994).
*E.C. Telematics Program.*

**LREEs** Light Rare Earth Elements.

**l.reg.** legge regionale.
Italian abbreviation meaning: regional law.

**L-RERP** Long-Range Effects Research Program.

**LRF** laser range-finder.
télémètre à laser.

**LRF** Lumber Recovery Factor.

**LRF** Luteinizing hormone-Releasing Factor.

**LRF-MD** Local Reaction Field-Molecular Dynamics.
*Chemistry.*

**LRI** Lateral Reticular nucleus, Internal division.
Department of *Anatomy*, Georgetown University School of Medicine and Dentistry (U.S.A.).

**LRI** Left-Right Indicator.

**LRI** limited range of intercept.
faible portée d'interception.

**LRI** Lupus Research Institute (U.S.A.).

**LRINF** long-range intermediate nuclear forces.
forces nucléaires intermédiaires à plus longue portée.

**LRM** lance-roquettes multiple.
1a. multiple launch rocket system (MLRS).
1b. multiple rocket launcher (MRL 2.).

**LRM** Liquid Reaction Molding.

**LRMP** long-range maritime patrol (aircraft).
PATMAR à long rayon d'action.

**LRMS** long-range missile system.
système de missile à longue portée.

**LRN** lay reference number.
numéro de référence de mouillage.
**LROD Experiment** Long-Range Overwater Diffusion Experiment.
**LRP** Long-Range Planning.
**LRP1** low-density lipoprotein receptor-related protein 1.
*Atherosclerosis Protection; Cell Biology; Molecular Genetics.*
**LRPDS** Long-Range Position-Determining System.
**LRPs** Luciferase Reporter Phages.
**LRQA** Lloyds Register Quality Assurance Ltd. (G.B.).
*Quality & Environment; Certification Services.*
**LRR** Long Range Radar.
**LRR** Long Regulatory Region (viral).
**LRR domain** Leucine-Rich Repeat domain.
*Chemical and Screening Science.*
**LRRP** long-range reconnaissance patrol.
patrouille de reconnaissance dans la profondeur.
**LRRP** Lowest Required Radiation/Radiating Power.
*Telecommunications.*
**LRRR** Laser Ranging Retroreflector.
**LRSOM** long-range stand-off missile.
missile à longue portée tiré à distance de sécurité.
**LRSP** long-range security programme.
programme de sécurité à long terme.
**LRT** Light-Rail Transit.
*Transportation Engineering.*
**LRTNF** long-range theatre nuclear forces.
forces nucléaires de théâtre à longue portée.
**LRU** Least Recently Used.
**LRU** Line Replaceable Unit.
**LRV** Lunar Roving Vehicle.
LRV is also known as: Lunar Rover.
*Space Technology.*
**LRX** Lateral Reticular nucleus, External division.
Department of *Anatomy*, Georgetown University School of Medicine and Dentistry (U.S.A.).
**LS** 1. landing site.
1. site de débarquement.
2. launching station.
2a. lanceur.
2b. site de lancement.
3. leaver section.
3. section à détacher d'un convoi.
4. Liechtenstein.
4. Liechtenstein.
**L.S.**; **l.s.** Law Society.
**LS** Left Septum.
**LS** Letters Shift.
*Telecommunications.*
**LS** Letter Stock.
*Business; Finance.*
**LS** Level Set.
*Computer Programming.*
**LS** Licei Scientifici (Italy).
**L.S.** Licentiate in Surgery.
**LS** Limit Switch.
**LS** Line Skew.
*Computer Technology.*
**LS** Linguistic Stock.
**LS** Listed Securities.
*Business; Finance.*
**LS** List Structure.
*Computer Programming.*
**LS** Little Stock.
**LS** Logical Security.
*Computer Technology.*
**L.S.**; **LS** London Society (G.B.).
**L.S.**; **l.s.** long sight.
**L.S.**; **l.s.** loudspeaker.
*Acoustical Engineering.*
**LS** Low Speed.
**LS** Lumbosacral.
**LSA** Large Science Aperture.
**LSA** Later Stone Age.
**L.S.A.** Left Sacroanterior.
**LSA** logistic support analysis.
analyse de soutien logistique.
**LSAC** Law School Admission Council.
**LSA diode** Limited Space-charge Accumulation diode.
*Electronics.*
**L.S. & D. charges** Landing, Storage and Delivery charges.
**LSB** Least Significant Bit.
*Computer Programming.*
**LSB** logistic support base.
base de soutien logistique.
**LSB galaxies** Low-Surface-Brightness galaxies.
*Astronomy.*
**LS buffer** Low Salt buffer.
**LSC** Leaf area-Specific hydraulic Conductance.
*Botany; Ecology; Tree Hydraulic Architecture.*
**LSC** Legge sullo Stato Civile.
*Italian Laws.*
**LSC** Loop Station Connector.
**L.Sc.A.** Left Scapuloanterior.
**LSC coordinate system** Landing Site Cartographic coordinate system.
**LSCE** Laboratoire des Sciences du Climat et de l'Environnement.
French initialism of the: Climate and Environmental Sciences Laboratory (France).
**LSCM** Laser Scanning Confocal Microscopy.

*Geomechanics; Earth and Space Sciences.*
**LSCO supeconductor** Lanthanum Strontium Copper Oxide superconductor.
*Superconductivity.*
**LSCP** Living Stock Collection Program.
NIH's (U.S.A.).
For further details see under: **NIH**.
**LSD** Language for Systems Development.
**LSD** League for Spiritual Discovery.
**LSD** Least Significant Digit.
*Computer Programming.*
**LSD** Line Sharing Device.
**LSD** Line Signal Detector.
**LSD** 1. logistic support detachment.
1. détachement de soutien logistique.
2. landing ship dock.
2. bâtiment transport de chalands de débarquement.
**LSD** Lysergic Acid Diethylamide.
LSD, which is also known as: Lysergide, is a hallucinogen.
*Organic Chemistry.*
**LSD** Pounds, Shillings and Pence (G.B.).
**LSDM** Lagrangian Stochastic Dispersion Model.
Named for the French mathematician Joseph **Lagrange**.
**LSDs** Lignostibbene Dioxygenases.
**LSE** logistic support element.
élément de soutien logistique.
**LSE**; **L.S.E.** London School of Economics (G.B.).
**LSECs** Liver Sinusoidal Endothelial Cells.
*Hepatocyte Growth; Molecular Oncology; Pathology; Protein Engineering.*
For further details see under: **HGF** and **VEGF**.
**LSEE** Loi Sur l' Emploi d'Etrangers.
French initialism meaning: Law relating to the Employment of Foreigners.
*Law.*
**LSEP** Legal Services for the Elderly Poor (N.Y., U.S.A.).
**LSF plan** Limited Salary Flexibility plan.
**LSG** Large-Scale Geostrophic.
*Geophysics.*
**LS Gazette** Law Society Gazette.
Since 1903.
**lshld** leasehold.
**LSI** Large-Scale Integration.
*Electronics.*
**LSI circuit** Large-Scale Integrated circuit.
**LSIR** Limb Scanning Infrared Radiometer.
**LSIRF** Lymphocyte-Specific Interferon Regulatory Factor.
LSIRF is a transcription factor. It is now called IRF4.
*Immunology; Medical Biophysics; Medicine; Oncologic Pathology; Oncology.*
**LSL** landing ship, logistics.
bâtiment de soutien logistique de débarquement.
**LSL** Link Support Layer.
**LSM** Landing Ship, Medium.
The LSM is a landing ship having a length of about 200 feet.
*U.S. Military and Navy.*
**LSMS** Living Standards Measurements Study.
The LSMS is a household survey conducted by the World Bank since 1985.
*World Bank Surveys.*
**LSND** Liquid Scintillator Neutrino Detector.
*Cosmology; Physics.*
**LSO** London Symphony Orchestra (G.B.).
**LSP** Language for Special Purposes.
*Linguistics.*
**LSP** Laser Scattering Patternator for liquid flow measurement of industrial sprays.
*European Community Project.*
**L.S.P.** Left Sacroposterior.
**LSP** logistic support plan.
plan de soutien logistique.
**LSPs** Land Surface Parameterizations.
*Atmospheric Research; Atmospheric Science; Biological Sciences; Environmental Science and Management; Land-Atmosphere Interactions; Meteorology; Plant Biology.*
**LSQA** Local System Queue Area.
**LSR** Local Standard of Rest.
*Astronomy; Astrophysics.*
**LSRO** Life Sciences Research Office.
**LSS** Lap Shear Strength.
*Materials Science.*
**LSS** Large-Scale Structure.
*Physics.*
**L.S.S.** Lifesaving Service.
**LSS** logistic support site.
site de soutien logistique.
**LS state** Low-Spin state.
*Molecular Chemistry.*
**LST** Landing Ship, Tank.
The LST is a military vessel used for landing troops and equipment on beaches.
**LST** Lap Shear Test.
*Materials Science.*
**LST** Latest Starting Time.
**L.S.T.** Left Sacrotransverse.
**L.st.** Lira sterlina.
Italian abbreviation meaning: pound sterling.

**LST** Local Sideral Time.
*Astronomy.*
**LST** Local Solar Time.
**LSt neurons** Lumbar Spinothalamic neurons.
Neurons that are part of the spinothalamic tract and send sensory information from the body to the brain.
*Medicine; Neuropsychiatry.*
**LSU** Large Subunit.
*Biochemistry.*
**LSU** Lavori Socialmente Utili (Italy).
**LSU** Library Storage Unit.
**LSU** Louisiana State University (U.S.A.).
**LSUMC** Louisiana State University Medical Center (U.S.A.).
**LT** Land Tax.
**LT** Laser Thermometer.
A newly produced (April 2003) thermometer to prevent contagion, and spreading of an infection, for instance like SARS. In view of the fact that it is not in direct contact, it is safe with respect to traditional thermometers.
**LT** Latina, Italy.
**LT** Lawn Tennis.
**l.t.** left tackle.
*Football.*
**L.T.** Legal Tender.
*Business; Finance.*
**LT** Legal Title.
*Business; Finance.*
**LT** Lesotho.
**LT** Less Than.
**L.T.** Letter of Transmittal.
**LT** Letter of Trust.
*Business; Finance.*
**L.T.** Letter-Telegram.
**Lt** (abbr.) Lieutenant.
**lt.** (abbr.) light.
*Architecture; Optics.*
**LT** Local Time.
**LT** London Transport (G.B.).
**LT** Long Term.
**lt** long ton.
*Metrology.*
**LT** Long Ton.
*Ordnance.*
**L.T.**; **Lt** or **lt.** Low-Tension.
**LT** Luxury Tax.
**LT** Lymphoid Tissue.
Lymphoid Tissue is also known as: Lymphotic Tissue.
*Histology.*
**LT** Lymphotoxin.
*Immunology.*
**LT** The airline code for LTU International Airways.
**LTA** Lawn Tennis Association.
**LTA** Lettera di Trasporto Aereo.
Italian initialism meaning: Air Waybill.
**LTA** local target area.
zone locale d'objectifs.
**LTA** London Teachers' Association (G.B.).
**LTB** London Transport Board (G.B.).
**LTBF** long-term build-up force.
force à long délai de montée en puissance.
**LTBMD** layered theatre ballistic missile defence.
défense multicouche contre les missiles balistiques de théâtre.
**LTBP** London Tanker Brokers Panel (G.B.).
*Tanker Freight.*
**LTBT** Limited Test Ban Treaty.
Traité d'interdiction partielle des essais (nucléaires).
**LTC** Less Than Carload.
**LTC** Lieutenant Commander.
**LTC** Long Term Contract; Long Term Credit.
*Business; Commerce; Finance.*
**LTC** long-term costing.
estimation de coûts à long terme.
**LTCB** Long Term Credit Bank of Japan.
**LTCG** Long Term Capital Gain.
*Banking; Business; Finance.*
**LTC-ICs** Long-Term Culture-Initiating Cells.
**LTCM** Long-Term Capital Management.
**Lt.Col.** Lieutenant Colonel.
**Lt. Com.**; **Lt. Cmdr.** Lieutenant Commander.
**LTCs** Local Training Centers.
**LTCs** L-Type voltage-activated Channels.
*Neuroscience; Neurobiology; Medicine; Transcription Factors.*
**Ltd.**; **ltd.** (abbr.) Limited.
Also: **Ld.**
**LTD** Line Transfer Device.
**LTD** Long Term Depotentiation.
*Physiology.*
**LTD** Long-Term Depression.
*Molecular Biology; Neurosciences.*
**LTDE** Learning Technology and Distance Education.
**LTDP** long-term defence programme.
programme de défense à long terme.
**LTE** Local Thermodynamic Equilibrium.
*Astrophysics.*
**LTER network** Long-Term Ecological Research network.
The LTER was created by the U.S. National Science Foundation in 1980.

*Chemistry and Biology of the Oceans; Ecological Processes.*
**LTF** Lymphocyte Transforming Factor.
**LTFF** long-term financial forecast.
prévisions financières à long terme.
**LTFP** 1. long-term force planning.
1. plans de forces à long terme.
2. long-term force proposals.
2. propositions de forces à long terme.
**LTG** local tactical grid.
carroyage tactique local.
**ltge.** (abbr.) lighterage.
*Industrial Engineering.*
**Lt.Gen.**; **LTG** Lieutenant General.
**Lt.Gov.** Lieutenant Governor.
**L.Th.** Licentiate in Theology.
**LTH**; **LtH** Luteotropic Hormone.
**Lt.Inf.** Light Infantry.
*Military.*
**LTIP** long-term infrastructure programme [formerly called ACELIP].
programme d'infrastructure à long terme [anciennement appelé ACELIP].
**LTL** Less-than-Truck-Load.
*Freight.*
**LTL** Licentiate in Theology.
**LTM** Licentiate in Tropical Medicine.
**LTM** Long-Term Memory.
Long-Term Memory is also known as: Long-Term Store; Secondary Memory.
*Behavior.*
**LT-MCD** Low-Temperature Magnetic Circular Dichroism.
**LTMFM** Low-Temperature Magnetic Force Microscope.
*Physics.*
**LTN** The airport code for Luton, London, G.B.
**ltng.arr.** lightning arrester.
*Electricity.*
**LTNPs** Long-Term Nonprogressors.
*AIDS Research; Molecular Biology.*
**LTP** Long Term Potentiation.
**LTP** Long Term Program.
**LTPA** long-term planning area.
domaine de planification à long terme.
**LTPD** Lot Tolerance Percent Defective.
*Industrial Engineering.*
**LTPG** long-term planning guideline.
directive de planification à long terme.
**LTQ** Lysine Tyrosylquinone.
**ltr.** (abbr.) letter.
For further details see under: **let**.
**LTR** Long Terminal Repeat.
*Molecular Biology.*
**LTR** long-term requirement.
besoin à long terme.
**LTRS** Letters Shift.
*Telecommunications.*
**LTRs** Long Terminal Repeats.
**LTS** Launch Telemetry Station.
**LTS** Launch Tracking System.
**LTS** long-term study.
étude à long terme.
**LTSEM** Low Temperature Scanning Electron Microscopy.
**LTT** limited technology transfer.
transfert de technologie limité.
**LTT** Lithium Thallium Tartrate.
**LTT** Long Term Trend.
**LTT** Lymphocyte Transformation Test.
*Chemotherapy; Medicine; Microbiology; Immunology.*
**LTTE** Liberation Tigers of Tamil Eelam (Sri Lanka).
**LTTM treatment** Low-Temperature Thermomechanical treatment.
**LTV ratio** Loan-To-Value ratio.
**lt.yr.** light-year; light years.
**LTZ** local target zone.
zone locale d'objectifs.
**l/u** laid up.
**LU** Light Unit.
*Space Greenhouses.*
**LU** Linear Uptake.
**LU** London University (G.B.).
**LU** Lucca, Italy.
**lu**; **lug** luglio.
Italian abbreviation meaning: July.
**Lu** The chemical symbol for Lutetium.
Lutetium is a metallic element having the atomic number 71, an atomic weight of 174.967, a melting point of 1660°C. Lutetium was discovered in Paris in 1907.
*Chemistry; Symbols.*
**LU** Luxemburg / Luxembourg.
Also: **Lux**.
**l.u.b.** least upper bound.
*Mathematics.*
**LUBL** Lombard & Ulster Banking (Ireland).
The Dublin-based LUBL is the leasing arm of Ulster Bank.
**L.U.C.** Limburgs Universitair Centrum (Belgium).
**LUCI** Liverpool University Cardiovascular Institute (G.B.).
**LUDES**; **Ludes** Libera Università Degli Studi di Scienze Umane e Tecnologiche.

*Italian University.*
**LUF** Lowest Usable Frequency.
**LUF** Luxemburg franc [obsolete].
Now: EURO/EUR (€). Became ECU (European Single Currency) with effect from January 2002.
**LUHF** Lowest Useful High Frequency.
*Telecommunications.*
**LUI** Language User Interface.
**L.U.I.M.O.** Libera Università Internazionale di Medicina Omeopatica "Samuel Hahnemann" (Naples, Italy).
Homeopathy is a therapy advanced by Dr. Samuel **Hahnemann** in the late 18th century.
*Homeopathy.*
**LUINA** Libera Università Italiana di NAturopatia (Italy).
*Italian University.*
**LUISS** Libera Università Internazionale di Studi Sociali.
*Italian Universities.*
**LUL**; **L.U.L.** Left Upper Lobe.
**LULU** Locally Unwanted Land Use.
**LULUCF** Land Use, Land Use Change and Forestry.
*Afforestation; Reforestation.*
**LUM** LUnar excursion Module.
Lunar excursion module is also known as: Lunar Module.
*Space Technology.*
**LUMCON** Louisiana Universities Marine CONsortium (U.S.A.).
**LUMEN** Libera Università di Medicina Naturale (Italy).
*Italian University.*
**LUMO** Lowest Unoccupied Molecular Orbital.
*Bioinorganic Chemistry.*
**lun.** lunedì.
Italian abbreviation meaning: Monday.
**LUOs** Laboratory Unit Operations.
**LUP** Late Upper Paleolithic.
*Anthropology; Island Genetics; Neandertal Arms; Primate Birth.*
**LUQ**; **L.U.Q.** Left Upper Quadrant.
**l.urb.** (abbr.) legge urbanistica.
*Italian Laws.*
**LUST** Libera Università di Studi Tributari.
*Italian Universities.*
**LUT** Local User Terminal.
**LUV Conference** Lisp Users and Vendors Conference.
**LUVs** Large Unilamellar Vesicles.
*Analytical Chemistry; Physical Chemistry.*
**Lux.** (abbr.) Luxembourg / Luxemburg.
Also: **LU**.
**LV** Left Value.
*Computer Programming.*
**LV** Lettera di Vettura.
Italian initialism meaning: Consignment Note; Waybill.
*Business; Commerce.*
**LV** Low Voltage.
*Electricity.*
**LVA** Large Vertical Aperture.
**LVA** Low Voltage-Activated.
**LVAs** Low-Velocity Anomalies.
*Seismology.*
**LVD** Laboratory of Viral Diseases.
The LVD is located on the U.S. NIH main campus.
For further details se under: **NIH**.
**LVD** Large Volume Detector.
**LVDT** Linear Variable-Differential Transformer.
*Electricity.*
**LVEF** Left Ventricular Ejection Fraction.
**LVF** Left Visual Field.
*Cognitive Neuroscience; Neuroscience.*
**LVF** Loyalist Volunteer Force (Ireland).
The LVF is a group outside CLMC.
For further details see under: **CLMC**.
**LVH**; **L.V.H.** Left Ventricular Hypertrophy.
*Medicine.*
**LVI** Lettre de Voiture Internationale.
French initialism meaning: International Consignment (or Delivery) Note.
**LVMH** Louis Vuitton Moët Hennessy.
Yearly Science for Art Prizes awarded to scientists.
*Art Prizes; Science.*
**LVN** Licensed Vocational Nurse.
**LVP** Lysine Vasopressin.
*Medicine.*
**LVs** Lateral Ventricles.
*Anatomy.*
**LVSC** London Voluntary Service Council (G.B.).
**LVT** Landing Vehicle, Tracked.
**LVZ** Low-Velocity Zone.
*Geology; Oceanography.*
**LVZ** Low-Viscosity Zone.
The asthenosphere.
**LW** Landing Weight.
**LW** laser weapon.
arme laser.
**LW** Long Wave.
*Hydrology* - Long Wave is also known as: Shallow-water Wave.
*Meteorology* - Long Wave is also known as: Planetary Wave; Major Wave.
*Telecommunications* - The term long-wave in

telecommunications refers to a wave having a length of over one thousand meters.
**LW** Low Water.
*Oceanography.*
**LWAT** Lynx and Wolverine Advisory Team (U.S.A.).
*Conservation Biology.*
**LWB** Lower Bound.
*Mathematics.*
**LWC** Language of Wider Communication.
**LWD** Low-Water Data.
**LWI** Lasing Without Inversion.
*Quantum Coherence; Physics.*
**LWL** Length (at) Water Line.
**LWL** Load Water Line.
*Naval Architecture.*
**L.W.M.; l.w.m.** Low Water Mark.
**L.W.O.S.T.** Low Water Ordinary Spring Tides.
**lwp** leave with pay.
**LWP** Load Water Plane.
*Naval Architecture.*
**LWR** 1. laser warning receiver.
1. récepteur d'alerte laser.
2. local wage rate (personnel).
2. (personnel à) statut local.
**LWR** Light-Water Reactor.
*Nucleonics.*
**LWS** Long-Wavelength Spectrometer.
**lwst** (abbr.) lowest.
**LWUA** Local Water Utilities Administration (The Philippines).
**lx** lux.
*Optics.*
**LXRα** Liver X Receptor α.
*Biochemistry; Lipid Research; Medical Nutrition; Nuclear Receptors; Oxysterol; Pharmacology.*
**LY** Last Year / Year's.
**LY** The airline code for El Al Israel Airlines.
**LY** Lucifer Yellow.
**LY** Libya.
**Ly-α** Lyman α.
*Astrophysics; Space Physics.*
**LYRIC** Language for Your Remote Instruction by Computer.
**lys.** (abbr.) lysine.
Lysine is an amino acid.
*Biochemistry.*
**LYSG** London Young Solicitors Group.
The Associazione Giovani Avvocati Milano (AGAM) and the London Young Solicitors Group (LYSG) represent respectively the young lawyers and solicitors of Milan and London.
**LysRS** lysyl-tRNA Synthetase.
*Microbiology.*
**LZ** landing zone.
1a. zone d'atterrissage.
1b. zone de débarquement.
**LZ** Leucine Zipper.
**LZT** Large Zenith Telescope.
Work on the LZT started in 1994. Operative in April 2003.
*Astronomy.*
**LZT** Lead Zirconate Titanate.
LZT is used mainly in computers memory units.
*Materials.*

# M

**M** Mach.
Also: Mach; mach.
Named for the Austrian physicist: Ernst **Mach**.
*Fluid Mechanics.*
**m** (abbr.) machine.
*Computer Technology; Mechanical Engineering; Mechanics.*
**M**; **m** Magistrate.
**m** (abbr.) magnetization.
magnetization is the process by means of which materials are magnetized.
*Electromagnetism.*
**M** Majesty.
**m** male.
*Biology; Botany; Engineering.*
**m** manual.
manual means carried out by hand.
*Engineering; Science.*
**m** mark.
*Computer Programming; Geology; Military Science; Ordnance; Telecommunications.*
**M** Marquess.
**m** masculine.
**m** mass.
*Mechanics; Metrology; Military Science.*
**m** matured.
Also: **mat.**
*Stocks.*
**M** Medical.
**M** megabyte.
*Computer Technology.*
**M**; **m** member.
Also: **mbr**.
*Anatomy; Engineering; Geology; Mathematics; Taxonomy.*
**m** (abbr.) memory.
*Computer Technology; Immunology; Psychology.*
**m** meridian.
*Astronomy; Cartography.*
**m** meter / metre.
metre derives from the Greek verb "to measure".
*Engineering; Metrology.*
**m** mile.
*Metrology.*
**M** Mill.
*Industrial Engineering; Mechanical Devices; Mining Engineering.*
**m** milli-.
*Mathematics.*
**m** million.
*Mathematics.*
**M** Minesweeper / mine sweeper.
For further details see under: **MS**.
**m** mist.
*Meteorology* - Beaufort letter.
**m** (abbr.) mode.
*Archaeology; Computer Programming; Computer Technology; Electromagnetism; Petrology; Physics; Statistics; Telecommunications.*
**m** mois.
meaning month in French.
**m** molar.
*Chemistry.*
**M**; **m** Molarity.
*Physical Chemistry.*
**M**; **m** Monday.
**M**; **m** money.
**m** (abbr.) monitor.
*Computer Programming; Computer Technology; Electronics; Engineering Surgery.*
**M** Monsieur.
Mr. in French.
**m** Moon / moon.
*Astronomy.*
**M**; **m** motorway.
**M**; **m** mountain.
*Geography.*
**M** to move (as of work).
*Time Study.*
**m** mucoid.
*Biochemistry.*
**m** (abbr.) multiplier.
*Electricity; Electronics; Mathematics.*
**m** muscle.
*Anatomy.*
**MA** 1. Madagascar.
1. Madagascar.
2. military assistant.
2. assistant militaire.
**MA** Maison d'Arrêt.
French acronym meaning: prison; jail; gaol.
**MA** Mandelic Acid.
Mandelic Acid, also known as: amygdalic acid is used mainly as a urinary antiseptic.
*Organic Chemistry.*
**MA** Manpower Administration.
**MA** Margin Account.
**MA** Maritime Administration.
**MA** Market Average.
*Business; Finance.*
**MA** (abbr.) Massachusetts (U.S.A.).
**MA** Massimo Avvalorabile.

Italian acronym meaning: Maximum Value of Issue.
**MA** Master of Arts.
**MA** Mechanical Advantage.
*Mechanical Engineering.*
**MA** Mental Age.
*Psychology.*
**MA** Methyl Acetate.
Methyl acetate is used mainly as a solvent for lacquers.
*Organic Chemistry.*
**MA** Military Accademy.
**MA** Military Attaché.
**MA** Military Aviation.
**MA**; **ma** Milliampere.
MA is one-thousandth of an ampere.
*Electricity.*
**Ma** Million years ago.
**M.A.** Ministry of Agriculture.
**M.A.** Modulazione di Ampiezza.
Italian acronym meaning: Amplitude Modulation.
**MA** Moving Average.
**MA** My Account.
**MAA** Mathematical Association of America (U.S.A.).
**MAA** Maximum Authorized Altitude.
**MAA** Methanearsonic Acid.
MAA is used as an herbicide.
*Organic Chemistry.*
**M.AA.EE.** Ministero degli Affari Esteri.
Italian initialism of the: Ministry of Foreign Affairs.
**MAAP** message de résultat d'appel préliminaire.
*Communications.*
**MAAs** Mycosporine-like Amino Acids.
**MAB** marine amphibious brigade.
brigade amphibie du corps des marines.
**MAB** Mediator's Advisory Board.
**MAB** Mediator's Auditing Board.
**mAb** monoclonal Antibody.
*Biotechnology.*
**MAB program** Man And the Biosphere program.
MAB is a U.N. 30-year-old program.
**MA branch** Meteorological Applications branch.
**mAbs** monoclonal antibodies.
**mac** (abbr.) macadam.
macadam is a material for making road surfaces.
*Civil Engineering.*
**mac.** (abbr.) maceration.
*Medicine.*
**mac** (abbr.) macro.
Also known as: macroinstruction.
*Computer Programming.*
**MAC** 1. major area commander.
1. grand commandant de zone.
2. maritime area commander.
2. commandant maritime de zone.
3. mine-action centre.
3. centre d'action antimines.
**MAC**; **M.A.C.** Maximum Allowable Concentration.
MAC is also known as: Maximum Admissible Concentration.
**MAC** Media Access Control.
**MAC** Message Authentication Code.
**MAC** Methyl Allyl Chloride.
Methyl allyl chloride is used mainly to produce pharmaceuticals and insecticides.
*Organic Chemistry.*
**MAC** Membrane Attack Complex.
**MAC** Military Airlift Command.
**MAC** Minimum Alveolar Concentration.
**MAC** Multiaccess Computer.
Multiaccess computer is also known as: Multiple-Access Computer.
*Computer Technology.*
**MACA** maritime air control authority.
1a. autorité contrôleur de l'aéronavale.
1b. autorité contrôleur des PATMAR.
**MACC** maritime coordination centre.
centre de coordination maritime (CCMAR).
**MACC** Midwest Athletes against Childhood Cancer.
Medical College of Wisconsin, U.S.A.
*Cancer Genetics; Molecular Oncogenesis; Pediatric Oncology.*
**MACE** Magnetic resonance Angiography Contrast Enhancement.
**MACE** multinational airlift coordination element.
élément multinational de coordination du transport aérien.
**Mach**; **mach** Also: M.
*Fluid Mechanics.*
**mach.** (abbr.) machine.
For further details see under: **m**.
**mach.** (abbr.) machinery.
Also: **M/CY**.
*Mechanical Engineering.*
**mach.** (abbr.) machinist.
**MACHA** Midwest Automated Clearing House Association.
**Mach.Dge.** (abbr.) machinery damage.
**MACH-NC** Meta Analysis of Chemotherapy in Head and Neck Cancer.
*European Community Project.*
**MACHO** MAssive Halo Object.

*Astronomy; Astrophysics; Cosmology; Dark Matter; Physics; Planetary Systems.*
**MACHO** Men Allied to Combat Hypocrisy and Oppression.
**mAChR** muscarinic Acetylcholine Receptor.
**MACH technology** Multilayer Actuator Head technology (Epson's).
**maclib** (abbr.) macro library.
*Computer Programming.*
**macp** (abbr.) macro processor / macroprocessor.
macroprocessor is also known as: macrogenerator.
*Computer Programming.*
**MACPED** mine antichar pointable à effet dirigé.
aimed controlled-effect antitank mine (ACEATM).
**macro** (abbr.) macroassembler.
*Computer Programming.*
**macro** (abbr.) macroprocessor.
For further details see under: **macp**.
**MACS** MAgnetic Cell Sorting.
*Magnetic Cell Isolation.*
**MACS** Multicenter AIDS Cohort Study.
Funded mainly by NIAID, U.S.A.
For further details see under: **NIAID**.
**MACTIS** Marine And Coastal Technology Information Service - U.N.
**MAD** 1. magnetic anomaly detector.
1. détecteur d'anomalie magnétique.
2. mutual assured destruction.
2. destruction mutuelle assurée.
**MAD** Michigan Algorithm Decoder.
**MAD** Mitosis Arrest Deficient.
*Biochemistry; Biomedical Research; Physiology.*
**MAD** Multiwavelength Anomalous Dispersion.
*Macromolecular Crystallography; Molecular Biology; Physical Biosciences.*
**MAD** Mutual Acceptance of Data.
*U.S.-E.C. Business; Transatlantic Issues.*
**MAD** The airport code for Madrid, Spain.
**MADC** maritime air defence cell.
cellule de défense aérienne des opérations maritimes.
**MADER** Management of Atmospheric Data for Evaluation and Research.
**MAD gene** Mitotic Arrest Defective gene.
*Molecular, Cellular, and Developmental Biology; Physiology.*
**MAD methods** Multiwavelength Anomalous Dispersion methods.
*Biochemistry; Biophysical Chemistry; Medicine; Structural Biology.*
**MADs** Mass Access Devices.
**MADT** Microalloy-Diffused Transistor.
*Electronics.*
**MADVEC** magnetic anomaly detector verification (run).
(passe de) vérification par détecteur d'anomalie magnétique.
**MAE** Magnetic Anisotropy Energy.
*Physics.*
**MAE** Memory Access Extension.
**MAE** Ministère des Affaires Etrangères.
French acronym of the: Ministry of Foreign Affairs. Foreign Office (G.B.). Department of State (U.S.A.).
**MAES** Michigan Agricultural Experiment Station.
At Michigan State University (U.S.A.).
*Projects; Programs.*
**MAESA** Measurements for Assessing the Effects of Stratospheric Aircraft.
**MAF** Macrophage Activating Factor.
*Immunology.*
**M.A.F.** Ministero dell'Agricoltura e delle Foreste (Italy).
Italian acronym of the: Ministry of Agriculture and Forestry.
**MAFAC** MArine Fisheries Advisory Committee (U.S.A.).
**MAFF** Ministry of Agriculture, Food and Fisheries (G.B.).
**MAFIA** Multiaccess executive with Fast Interrupt Acceptance.
**MAFIS** Malaysian Aquatic sciences and Fisheries Information System.
**mag.** (abbr.) magazine.
*Computer Technology; Ordnance.*
**mag.** (abbr.) magnetic; magneto.
*Electromagnetism.*
**mag.** (abbr.) magnetism.
*Physics.*
**mag.** (abbr.) magnitude.
In mathematics magnitude is also known as: absolute value.
*Astronomy; Geophysics; Mathematics.*
**MAG** Maximum Available Gain.
*Electronics.*
**MAG** 1. MNC Allotment Group.
1. Groupe d'attribution des GCO.
2. Movements, Transportation, Mobility Management Advisory Group.
2. Groupe consultatif sur la gestion des mouvements, des transports et de la mobilité.
**MAG** Molecular Applications Group (U.S.A.).
MAG was founded in 1990 by a Stanford University Professor.
**MAG** Mutua di Autogestione (Italy).

Italian acronym meaning: Self-Managed Co-operative Fund.
**MAG** Myelin-Associated Glycoprotein.
*Biochemistry; Biology; Biophysics; Medicine; Neuronal Regeneration; Neural Plasticity; Pathology.*
**MAGE** Marine Aerosol and Gas Exchange.
**MAG/ER experiment** MAGnetometer and Electron Reflectometer experiment.
*Lunar Research; Physics; Space Sciences.*
**MAGIE** MNC Advisory Group on Interoperability and Electronics.
Groupe consultatif des GCO sur l'interopérabilité et l'électronique.
**MAGOIM** MNC Advisory Group on Identification Matters.
Groupe consultatif des GCO sur les questions d'indentification.
**MAGPIE** Machine Automatically Generating Production Inventory Evaluation.
**MAGTF** marine air-ground task force.
force opérationnelle air-sol des marines.
**MAHRSI** Middle Atmosphere High Resolution Spectrograph Investigation.
MAHRSI is an instrument of the U.S. Naval Research Laboratory.
*Atmospheric Chemistry; Meteorology; Physics.*
**MAHs** Motor Activity Histograms.
*Anatomy; Cerebral Mechanisms; Neurobiology; Organismal Biology; Sensory Phisiology.*
**MAI** Manufacturers' Association of Israel.
**MAI** Member of the Anthropological Institute.
**MAI** Multilateral Agreement on Investment.
*U.S.-E.C. Business; Transatlantic Issues.*
**mai** The above acronyms were coined accidentally using the Italian word "mai" which means: never.
**MAIDS** Murine Acquired Immunodeficiency Syndrome.
MAIDS is a mouse disease similar to human AIDS.
*Immunobiology; Medicine; Pathology.*
**MAIM** maritime anti-invasion mine.
mine marine anti-invasion.
**MAIT**; **Mait** Manufacturers' Association for Information Technology (India).
**Maj** Major.
**maj.** (abbr.) majority.
**Maj. Gen.** Major General.
**MAL** mine actuation level.
niveau de déclenchement d'une mine.
**MAL** Maximal Acceptable Load.
**MAL** Museo civico Amedeo Lia (Italy).
*Museums.*
**mal** The above acronyms were coined accidentally using the French word "mal" which means: pain, evil; ache; trouble.
**MALA** Malawi Library Association.
**mala** The above acronym was coined accidentally using the Italian word "mala" (short for "malavita") which means: "the underworld".
**MALC** Midwest Academic Libraries Conference.
**MALDI-MS** Matrix-Assisted Laser Desorption Ionization / Mass Spectrometry.
**MALDI technique** Matrix Assisted Laser Desorption/Ionization technique.
MALDI is a technique that gives complete polymer characterization in a matter of minutes.
*Polymers.*
**MALDI/TOFMS** Matrix-Assisted Laser Desorption Ionization / Time-Of-Flight Mass Spectrometry.
*Bacteriology; Biochemistry; Biophysics; Microbiology.*
**MALG** Minnesota Antilymphocyte Globulin.
**MALL** Michigan Association of Law Libraries (U.S.A.).
**MaLR family** Mammalian apparent LTR-retrotransposon family.
*Developmental and Metabolic Neurology; Genetic Disease Research; Human Genome Research; Neurobiology; Neurological Disorders.*
**MALT** Master of Arts in Language Teaching.
**MALT** Mucosa-Associated Lymphoid Tissue.
*Geographic Medicine; Immunology; Infectious Diseases; Medicine; Microbiology.*
**MAM** Memory Allocation Manager.
**MAMBO** Mediterranean Association of Marine Biological Oceanography.
**man.** (abbr.) manual.
**man.** (abbr.) manufacture.
Also: **manf.**; **manuf.**; **mfr**.
**MAN** The airport code for Manchester, G.B.
**MAN** metropolitan area network.
réseau métropolitain.
**M&A** Mergers and Acquisitions (U.S.A.).
*Finance.*
**M&A** monitoring and assessment.
surveillance et évaluation.
**MANDATE** Multiline Automatic Network Diagnostic and Transmission Equipment.
**M. and M.** Mechanization and Modernization.
**M&N** May and November.
*Securities.*
**M & R** Maintenance and Repair.
**M & S** Maintenance and Supply.
**M&S** March and September.
*Securities.*

**M&S** Modeling and Simulation.
**M&T** movements and transports.
mouvements et transports.
**M&T Conference** Management & Technology Conference (U.S.A.).
**manf.** (abbr.) manufacture.
Also: **man.**; **manufr.**; **mfr**.
**manf.** (abbr.) manufacturer.
**manf.** (abbr.) manufacturing.
Also: **manuf**.
**Mang.B** Manganese Bronze.
*Metallurgy.*
**Man-Glc.** (abbr.) Mannose-Glucose.
**MANIAC** Mathematical Analyzer Numerical Integrator And Computer.
**maniac** The above acronym was coined using the English word "maniac" (*Psychology*).
**MANOVA** Multivariate ANalysis Of VAriance.
**MANPADS** man-portable air defence system.
système antiaérien portable.
**manuf.** (abbr.) manufacture.
Also: **man.**; **manf**.
**MAO** Methyl-Alumoxane.
*Chemistry.*
**MAOA** Monoamine Oxidase.
An enzyme which metabolizes several kinds of neurotransmitters in the brain.
*Psychology.*
**MAOA Panel** Meteorological Aspects of Ocean Affairs Panel.
Of the U.N. WMO.
For further details se under: **WMO**.
**MAOI** Monoamine Oxidase Inhibitor.
*Medicine; Pharmacology.*
**MAOT** maximum allowable operation time.
temps de fonctionnement maximal admissible.
**MAP** Macroassembly Program.
*Computer Programming.*
**MAP** Manufacturing Automation Protocol.
**MAP** Mean Arterial Pressure.
**MAP** Membership Action Plan.
Plan d'action pour l'adhésion.
**MAP** Memory Allocation and Protection.
**MAP** Microwave Anisotropy Probe.
MAP is a satellite launched aboard Delta II rocket in June 2001.
*Astronomy; Astrophysics; Space Science.*
**MAP** Ministero per le Attività Produttive.
Italian acronym of the: Ministry for productive activities.
**MAP** Ministry of Aircraft Production.
**MAP** Mitogen-Activated Protein.
*Biological Chemistry; Life Sciences.*
**MAP** Multiannual Program - E.C.
**MAP-2** Microtubule-Associated Protein 2.
**MAPE** Multinational Advisory Police Element.
Élement multinational de conseil en matière de police.
**M.A.P.E.A.** Movimento Animazione Persone Età Adulta (Italy).
**MAPEX** map exercise.
exercice sur cartes.
**MAPEX** Mid-America Payment EXchange.
**Maphilindo Confederation** Malaysia, the Philippines and Indonesia Confederation.
**MAPK** Mitogen-Activated Protein Kinase.
*Cancer; Molecular Biology; Genes Development.*
**MAPKK** Mitogen-Activated Protein Kinase Kinase.
**MA press** Multianvil press.
**MAPS** Mail Abuse Protection System (U.S.A.).
**MAPS** Measuring Air Pollution from Space.
**MAPS** Mesoscale Analysis and Prediction System.
**MAPS** Modern Accounts Payable System.
*Accounting; Business; Finance.*
**MAPS** Monetary And Payments System.
*Business; Finance.*
**MAPSS** Mapped Atmosphere-Plant-Soil System.
*Atmospheric Science; Climate Change; Ecology.*
**mar.**(abbr.) marine.
*Military Science; Oceanography.*
**mar.** (abbr.) maritime.
**mar.** (abbr.) married.
**MAR** Mass Accumulation Rate.
*Biodiversity; Limnology; Sedimentation.*
**MAR** Memory Address Register.
Memory address register is also known as: Address Register.
*Computer Technology.*
**MAR** Microanalytical Reagent.
**MAR** Mid-Atlantic Ridge.
*Geology.*
**MAR** Minimum Angle of Resolution.
**MARAIRMED** Maritime Air Forces, Mediterranean [obsolete - now called MARAIRSOUTH].
Forces aéronavales de la Méditerranée [obsolète - maintenant appelé MARAIRSOUTH].
**MARAIRNORTH** Maritime Air Forces, North [has replaced MAIRAIRNORTHWEST].
Forces aéronavales Nord [remplace MARAIRNORTHWEST].
**MARAIRNORTHWEST** Maritime Air Forces, North-Western Europe [obsolete - now called MARAIRNORTH].
Forces aéronavales du Nord-Ouest-Europe [obsolète - maintenant appelé MARAIRNORTH].

**MARAIRSOUTH** Maritime Air Forces, South.
Forces aéronavales Sud.
**MARC; Marc** Machine-Readable Cataloging.
**MARC** Meat Animal Research Center.
MARC is a research facility located in south-central Nebraska (U.S.A.).
*Basic Molecular Genetics; Biological Engineering; Mathematical Modeling; Population Biology.*
**MARC** Monitoring and Assessment Research Center (G.B.).
**M.Arch.** Master of Architecture (U.S.A.).
**MARCM** Mosaic Analysis with a Repressible Cell Marker.
*Biochemistry; Medicine; Physiology.*
**MARCONFOR** maritime contingency force.
force maritime de circonstance.
**MARCONFORAMPH** maritime contingency force, amphibious.
force maritime amphibie de circonstance.
**MARCONFORLANT** maritime contingency force, Atlantic.
force maritime de circonstance de l'Atlantique.
**MARCONFORPLAN** maritime contingency force plan.
plan de force de circonstance maritime.
**MARCs** Microsoft Authorized Resource Centers.
*IT Recruitment Agencies.*
**MARD** Marine Assessment Research Division.
MARD has been replaced by OERD.
For further details see under: **OERD**.
**MAREPS** Methodology for the Analysis of Rationality and Effectiveness of Prevention and health promotion Strategies.
*European Community Project.*
**MAREX** maritime exercise.
exercice maritime.
**marg.** (abbr.) margin; marginal.
**MARIC** MArine Resources Information Center (U.S.A.).
**mark.** (abbr.) market; marketing.
**mar.merc.** (abbr.) marina mercantile.
Italian abbreviation meaning: merchant marine.
**mar.mil.** (abbr.) marina militare.
Italian abbreviation meaning: navy.
**MARREP** maritime reporting.
comptes rendus maritimes.
**MARs** Matrix Attachment Regions.
**MARSA** Microfilm Association of the Republic of South Africa.
**MARSTAN** (Bi-Sc) maritime forces standard.
norme de forces maritimes (des SC).
**MART-1** Melanoma Antigen Recognized by Tcells-1.
*Tumor-specific Antigen.*
**MARV** manoeuvrable re-entry vehicle.
corps (vecteur) de rentrée manœuvrable.
**mas** (abbr.) macroassembler.
*Computer Programming.*
**MAs** Macronutrient Additives.
*Biochemistry.*
**MAS** Magic-Angle Spinning.
*Chemistry Standards and Technology; Materials Research; Mechanical Engineering.*
**MAS** Military Agency for Standardization [replaced by NSA 2.].
Bureau militaire de standardisation (BMS) [remplacé par l'AON 1.].
**mAs** milliampere-second.
*Nucleonics.*
**MAS** Mobile Atmospheric Spectrometer.
**MAS** Modis Airborne Simulator.
*Atmospheric Sciences; Oceanography.*
**MAS** Monetary Authority of Singapore.
**M.A.S.** motoscafo antisommergibile.
Italian acronym meaning: Motor Torpedo -Boat.
**MASC** Mountain Administrative Support Center.
**MASCA** Museum Applied Science Center for Archaeology.
At the University of Pennsylvania Museum of Archaeology and Anthropology (U.S.A.).
**MASCOT** Modular Approach to Software Construction Operation and Test.
**MASE program** Multiple Alignment Sequence Editor program.
**MASER** Microwave Amplification by Stimulated Emission of Radiation.
**MASGC** Mississippi-Alabama Sea Grant Consortium.
The MASGC is headquartered in Ocean Springs, Mississippi, U.S.A.
*Marine and Coastal Research.*
**MASH** Mobile Army Surgical Hospital.
**MASINT** measurement and signature intelligence.
renseignement de télémétrie et signature.
**MASK** Multiple Amplitude Shift Keying.
**MAS NMR** Magic Angle Spinning Nuclear Magnetic Resonance.
*Materials Research; Mesoporous Materials; Physics; Template Mechanisms.*
**MASO** Morpholino Antisense Oligonucleotide.
*Biology; Systems Biology.*
**MASP culture** Microaerophilus Stationary Phase culture.
*Veterinary Pathobiology.*

**MASQUES** Medical Application Software QUality Enhancement by Standards.
**MASS** 1. maritime air surface surveillance.
1. surveillance de surface par (avion) PATMAR.
2. maritime air surveillance support.
2. soutien surveillance par (avion) PATMAR.
**MASS** Multiple Access Switching System.
**mass** The above acronyms were coined using the English word "mass" (*Mechanics; Metrology; Military Science).*
**MASSC** Multi-Application Secure Smartcard.
The aim of MASSC is to develop advanced microelectronics for multifunctional cards.
*Pan-European Research Projects; Multifunctional Cards.*
**MASSTIC** maritime ACCS ship-shore tactical interface component.
composante maritime de l'interface tactique merterre de l'ACCS.
**MAST** Manned Astronautical Space Telescope.
**MAST** Mega Amp Spherical Tokamak.
Location: Culhan (near Oxford).
*Fusion Power.*
**MASTER** Modified Atmosphere Systems in varying TEmperature Regimes.
*European Community Project.*
**MASTER** Multiple Access Shared-Time Executive Routines.
**MAST project** MArine Science and Technology project - E.C.
**MAT** Master of Arts in Teaching.
**mat.** (abbr.) matured.
Also: **m**.
*Stocks.*
**mat.** (abbr.) maturity.
**MAT** Mean Annual Temperature.
**MAT** Medial Axis Transformation.
**MAT** Methionine Adenosyltransferase.
*Enzymology.*
**MAT** military air traffic.
circulation aérienne militaire (CAM 2.).
**mat** The above acronyms were coined accidentally using the Arabic word "mat" which means: he died.
**MATCH** medium-range antisubmarine torpedo-carrying helicopter.
hélicoptère à moyen rayon d'action armé de torpilles anti-sous-marines.
**MATCONOFF** material control officer.
officier de contrôle de matériel.
**MATELO** Maritime Air Telecommunications Organization.
Organisation des télécommunications de l'aviation maritime.
**MATE system** Modular Automatic Test Equipment system.
**MATEX** Macrotext (Editor).
**MATI** Mass-Analyzed Threshold Ionization.
MATI is a technique for generating state-selected molecular ions.
**MATIF** Marché à Terme d'Instruments Financiers.
French acronym meaning: Financial Futures Market.
*Business; Economics; Finance.*
**MATL** (abbr.) Material.
**MAT project** Measurements And Testing project - *European Community.*
*Gas-fired Boilers.*
**MATS** Military Air Transport Service.
**MATV** Master Antenna Television System.
*Telecommunications.*
**MAU** Medium Attachment Unit.
**MAU** million accounting units.
million d'unités de compte (MUC).
**MAV** mercaticien après-vente.
French acronym meaning: quality reporter.
*Business; Marketing.*
**MAV** Mediante Avviso (pagamento).
Italian acronym meaning: payment against notice.
**MAVOC** military aircraft voice weather code.
code météorologique phonie pour aéronef militaire.
**MAW** missile approach warner.
avertisseur d'approche de missile.
**max** (abbr.) maximum.
*Mathematics.*
**MAX** Millimeterwave Anisotropy Experiment.
(Balloon Experiment) Flown from Palestine (Texas) and Ft. Summer (New Mexico).
**MAXAT** MAXimum-Aperture Telescope.
The MAXAT workshop was held on 28$^{th}$/29$^{th}$ August 1998. It was organized by the AURA, Madison, Wisconsin, U.S.A.
*Astronomy; High-Resolution Spectra.*
For further details see under: **AURA**.
**max.cap.** (abbr.) maximum capacity.
**MAXIM** MicroArcsecond X-ray Imaging Mission.
*Astronomy; Cosmology; Cosmic Genesis; Physics.*
**MB** Marine Board (U.S.A.).
**MB** Medical Board.
**Mb** Megabase.
**mb** megaBIT.
For further details see under: **mbit**.
**MB** Megabyte.
*Computer Technology.*

**MB** Memory Bank.
*Computer Technology.*
**MB** Merchant Bank.
**MB** Métabolisme Basal.
French initialism meaning: Basal Metabolism.
*Physiology.*
**MB** military budget.
budget militaire.
**M.B.** Ministero del Bilancio.
Italian initialism of the: Ministry of Budget.
**MB** Monetary Base.
**M/B** Motor-Boat / motorboat.
*Naval Architecture.*
**MB** Municipal Bond.
**MB** Municipal Borough.
**MBA** Mantle Bouguer gravity Anomaly.
*Earth Sciences; Geological Sciences.*
**MBA** Marge Brute d'Autofinancement.
French initialism meaning: Cash-Flow.
**MBA** Master of Business Administration.
**MBA** Mortgage Bankers Association (U.S.A.).
**MBARI** Monterey Bay Aquarium Research Institute.
The MBARI of California, U.S.A., was founded in 1987; it is an independent laboratory dealing with scientific discoveries.
*Oceanography.*
**MBC** Maximum Breathing Capacity.
MBC is also known as: Maximum Ventilatory Capacity.
**MBC** Middle East Broadcasting.
**MBC** Military Budget Committee.
Comité du budget militaire (CBM 1.).
**MBC** Monetary Base Control.
**MbCO** Carbon Monoxide Complex of Myoglobin.
*Biochemistry; Biophysical Chemistry; Molecular Biology.*
**MBD** Million Barrels per Day.
**MBDA** Minority Business Development Agency.
**MBDOE** Million Barrels per Day Oil Equivalent.
**MBDS** Minimum Basic Data Set.
**MbE** Management by Exception.
**MBE** Molecular Beam Epitaxy.
*Solid-State Physics.*
**MBF** Marine Biology and Fisheries.
**MBF** medium bomber force.
force de bombardiers moyens.
**MBFR** mutual and balanced force reductions.
réductions mutuelles et équilibrées des forces.
**MBG** main body group [navy].
groupe du gros [marine].
**MBG** Missouri Botanical Garden (U.S.A.).
The MBG is one of the founders of the new St. Louis not-for-profit Center devoted to *basic plant science* which opened in 2000.
**MBGC** main body group commander.
commandant du groupe du gros.
**MBHC** Multi-Bank Holding Company.
**MbI** Management by Intimidation.
**MBI** Marine Biotechnology Institute (Japan).
**MBI** Mathematics and Biosciences in Interaction.
**MBI** Medicine and Bioinformatics.
**MBI** Michigan Biotechnology Institute (U.S.A.).
*Biocatalysis; Bioprocess Engineering; Chemistry; Fermentation.*
**MBIA** Municipal Bond Insurance Association.
**MBI project** Manchester Biosciences Incubator project (G.B.).
*Biological Sciences; Biotechnology Businesses.*
**MBIRN** Mouse Brain Imaging Research Network.
For further details see under: **BIRN**.
**mbit** (abbr.) megaBIT.
A megabit consists of about 1 million binary bits.
*Computer Technology.*
**MBL** Marine Biological Laboratory (U.S.A.).
**MBL** Marine Boundary Layer.
**MBL** Medical & Biological Laboratories (Japan).
**MBM manufacture** Meat and Bone Meal manufacture.
**MBMI** Mind/Body Medical Institute.
The MBMI was founded in Boston, U.S.A. in 1988. It is a nonprofit research and education center.
*Biomedical Research; Cardiovascular Research; Experimental Psychology; Psychiatry.*
**MBO** Management By Objectives.
*Industrial Engineering.*
**MBP** Maltose Binding Protein.
**MbP** Management by Performance.
**Mbp** Mega-base-pair.
**MBP** Myelin Basic Protein.
*Applied Neurobiology; Medicine; Molecular Biology.*
**MBPRB** Military Budget Priority Review Board.
Commission d'examen des priorités du budget militaire.
**Mbps** Megabits per second.
**mbr.** (abbr.) member.
For further details see under: **M**; **m**.
**MBR** Memory Buffer Register.
*Computer Technology.*
**MBRS program** Minority Biomedical Research Support program (U.S.A.).
**MBS** Mortgage-Backed Security.
*Finance.*
**MBS** Myosin-Binding Subunit.

*Biology.*
**MBSL** Multiple-Bubble Sonoluminescence.
*Applied Physics.*
**MB structure** Mushroom Body structure.
*Biomedical and Life Sciences; Genetics; Molecular Genetics.*
**MBT** Mahindra - British Telecom Ltd. - G.B. and India.
**MBT** main battle tank.
char de bataille.
**MBT** Mercaptobenzothiazole.
*Organic Chemistry.*
**MBT** Midblastula Transition.
*Cell Biology; Medicine; Molecular Biology.*
**mbt** minimum best torque (spark advance).
**MBTA** Massachusetts Bay Transportation Authority.
**MBTI** Molecular Bioscience and Technology Institute (U.S.A.).
**MBWA** Management By Walking Around.
**MC** Macerata, Italy.
**m/c** (abbr.) machine.
For further details see under: **m**.
**MC** Magnetic Card.
*Computer Technology.*
**M/C** Manchester (G.B.).
**MC** Marché Commun.
French initialism meaning: Common Market.
**MC** Marginal Cost.
**MC**; **M.C.** Marginal Credit.
**MC** Margin Call.
**MC** Margine di Contributo.
Italian initialism meaning: Contribution Margin.
**MC** Maritime Commission.
**mc** marked capacity.
*Railways.*
**MC** Marriage Certificate.
**MC** Master Control.
*Computer Programming; Telecommunications.*
**MC** Master of Ceremonies.
**MC** Medical Corps.
**MC** Mediocredito Centrale (Rome, Italy).
**Mc** megacycle.
**MC** Melanocortin.
**MC**; **M.C.** Member of Congress (U.S.A.).
**MC**; **M.C.** Member of Council.
**MC** Memory Card.
*Computer Technology.*
**MC** Memory Controller.
**MC** Methylene Chloride.
Methylene Chloride, also known as: Dichloromethane is used mainly in paint removers.
*Organic Chemistry.*
**MC**; **mc** metric carat.
**MC** Military College.
**MC** Military Committee.
Comité Militaire (CM 2.).
**MC** Military Cross.
**mC** millicoulomb.
**m/c** mio conto.
Italian initialism meaning: to my account; my account.
**MC** Monaco international vehicle registration letters.
**MC** Moneta di Conto.
**MC** Mortgage Company.
**MC** Motocannoniera.
**m/c** motor cycle / motorcycle.
*Mechanical Engineering.*
**MC** Multichannel Communication.
The term multichannel communication refers to communication occurring along two or several channels over the same path.
*Telecommunications.*
**MC** Multiple Choice.
*Linguistics.*
**MC** Municipal Code.
**MC** Myotonia Congenita.
*Clinical Neurology; Human Genetics; Medicine; Molecular Neurobiology.*
**MCA** Magnetocrystalline Anisotropy.
**MCA** Management Consultancies Association.
**MCA** Medicines Control Agency (G.B.).
*Safety of Drugs.*
**MCA** Metal Construction Association (U.S.A.).
The MCA sponsors Metalcon International.
For further details see under: **Metalcon International**.
**MCA** Middle Cerebral Artery.
*Cardiovascular Research; Neurology; Stroke Research.*
**MCA** Monetary Compensatory Amounts.
*European Law.*
**MCA** Monochloroacetic Acid.
**MCA** mot-code d'attribution [marine FR].
subject indicator code (SIC 1.).
**MCA** Multichannel Analyzer.
**MCACE** Measurement, Characterization and control of Ambulatory Care in Europe - E.C.
**MCAOC** mobile combined air operations centre.
centre combiné mobile d'opérations aériennes.
**MCAT** Maritime Central Analysis Team [obsolete].
Équipe centrale d'analyse des exercices maritimes [obsolète].
**MCAT** Medical College Admission Test.
**MCB department** Molecular and Cell Biology department (U.S.A.).

**MCB junction** Mechanically Controllable Break junction.
*Electrical Engineering.*
**MCBs** Membranous Cytoplasmic Bodies.
**MCC** 1. main control centre [SATCOM].
1. centre de commande principal [SATCOM].
2. maritime component command(er).
2. commandement (commandant) de composante maritime.
3. military control centre.
3. centre militaire de contrôle (CMC 1.).
4. movement control centre.
4. organisation des mouvements et transports.
5. movement coordination centre.
5. centre de coordination des mouvements.
**MCC** Medicines Control Council (South Africa).
The MCC is the statutory licensing Authority for medicines and drugs.
*Licensing Authorities.*
**MCC** Micro Compact Car.
**MCC** Midwest Climate Center (U.S.A.).
**MCC** Moth Cytochrome.
**MCCA** Mobile Communications Corporation of America (U.S.A.).
**MCCAP** maritime CIS contingency assets pool.
pool de moyens SIC maritimes de circonstance.
**MCCIS** Maritime Command and Control Information System [element of the NACCIS].
système maritime d'information de commandement et de contrôle [élément du NACCIS].
**MCCLPHEI** Massachusetts Conference Chief Librarians of Public Higher Education Institutions (U.S.A.).
**MC/CS** Military Committee in Chiefs of Staff Session.
Comité militaire en session des chefs d'état-major.
**MCCS** mine countermeasures command and support ship.
bâtiment de commandement et de soutien de la lutte contre les mines.
**M/cd** (abbr.) Machined.
**MCD** Magnetic Circular Dichroism.
**MCD** manipulative communications deception.
déception par manipulation des télécommunications.
**MCD** Massimo Comune Divisore.
Italian initialism meaning: Greatest Common Divisor.
*Mathematics.*
**mcd** millicurie-destroyed.
*Nucleonics.*
**MCD** Multicentric Castleman's Disease.
MCD is a polyclonal lymphoproliferation.
*Cancer Research; Medicine; Pathology.*
**MCDA** military and civil defence assets.
ressources militaires et de la protection civile.
**MCDB department** Molecular, Cellular, and Developmental Biology department.
Of the University of California, Santa Barbara (U.S.A.).
**MCE** Magnetocaloric Effect.
*Magnetic Refrigeration Techniques.*
**MCE** Master of Civil Engineering.
**MCE** Mercato Comune Europeo.
Italian initialism meaning: European Common Market.
**MCE** Movimento di Cooperazione Educativa.
*Italian Movement.*
**M cells** Migrating cells.
*Cell Biology; Immunology; Medicine.*
**MCF** Macrophage Chemotactic Factor.
**MCF** Mean Carrier Frequency.
*Electronics.*
**McF**; **mcf** one thousand cubic feet.
**mcfd** thousands of cubic feet per day.
**mCFP** mutants of Cyan Fluorescent Protein.
**MCG** Magnetocardiograph.
*Medicine.*
**MCG** Medical College of Georgia (U.S.A.).
Georgia's Health Sciences Research University (Since 1828). The MCG includes schools of medicine, dentistry, nursing, allied health science, etc.
**MCG** Mediterranean Cooperation Group.
Groupe de coopération méditerranéenne.
**mcg** microgram.
**MCGP** Mouse Cancer Genetics Program (U.S.A.).
**MCH** Machine Check Handler.
*Data Communications.*
**MCH** Mean Corpuscular Hemoglobin.
*Medicine.*
**MCH** Melanocyte-Concentrating Hormone.
*Metabolic Diseases; Obesity.*
**MCH** Methylcyclohexanol.
MCH is used as a solvent for cellulose esters.
*Organic Chemistry.*
**MCH** Miami Children's Hospital (U.S.A.).
**MCHC** Mean Corpuscular Hemoglobin Concentration.
*Medicine.*
**MchDge** (abbr.) Machinery Damage.
**M.Ch.E.** Master of Chemical Engineering.
**MCHF calculation** Multi-Configuration Hartree-Fock calculation.
**MCI** Machine Check Interruption.
*Data Communications.*
**MCI** Malleable Cast Iron.

*Metallurgy.*
**MCI** Master Control Interrupt.
*Computer Technology.*
**MCi** Megacurie.
**mCi** millicurie.
*Metrology.*
**MCI** Moteur à Combustion Interne.
French initialism meaning: Internal Combustion Engine.
**MCI** The airport code for Kansas City International Airport, Kansas City, Missouri, U.S.A.
**MC-ICPMS** Multiple-Collector Inductively Coupled Plasma Mass Spectrometer.
*Geological Sciences; Inorganic Chemistry; Isotope Geology.*
**MCL** Maximum Concentration Level.
**MCLK** Master Clock.
MCLK is also known as: Master Timer.
*Computer Technology.*
**MCM** Mechanical Current Meter.
**MCM** 1. Military Committee memorandum.
1. mémorandum du Comité Militaire.
2. mine countermeasures.
2a. contre-mesures mines.
2b. lutte contre les mines.
**m.c.m.** minimo comune multiplo.
Italian initialism meaning: lowest common multiple.
*Mathematics.*
**MCM** Monte Carlo Method.
**MCMEX** mine countermeasures exercise.
exercice de lutte contre les mines.
**MCMFN** see MCMFORNORTH.
voir MCMFORNORTH.
**MCMFORMED** Mine Countermeasures Force Mediterranean [obsolete - replaced by MCMFORSOUTH].
Force de lutte contre les mines de la Méditerranée [obsolète - remplacée par MCMFORSOUTH].
**MCMFORNORTH** Mine Countermeasures Force North [has replaced STANAVFORCHAN].
Force de lutte contre les mines du Nord [remplace STANAVFORCHAN].
**MCMFORSOUTH** Mine Countermeasures Force South [has replaced MCMFORMED].
Force de lutte contre les mines du Sud [remplace MCMFORMED].
**MCMG** Military Committee Meteorological Group.
Groupe météorologique du Comité Militaire.
**MC mission** Magnetospheric Constellation mission - NASA's.
The MC mission is planned for 2007.
**MCMOPDIR** MCM operations directive.
directive des opérations MCM.
**MCMR** mine countermeasures report.
compte rendu de lutte contre les mines.
**MCMV** mine countermeasures vessel.
bâtiment de lutte contre les mines.
**MCO** Mars Climate Orbiter.
**MCP** Major Capsid Protein.
**MCP** Marginal-Cost Pricing.
*Business; Economics; Commerce.*
**MCP** Master Control Program.
**μCP** Microcontact Printing.
*Chemistry.*
**MCP** 1. military cooperation programme.
1. programme de coopération militaire.
2. mobile command post.
2. poste de commandement mobile.
**MCP** Mobile Carrier Peak.
*Astronomy; Materials Science; Physics.*
**MCP-3** Monocyte Chemoattractant Protein-3.
*Biochemistry; Molecular Biology; Medical Sciences; Periodontal Physiology.*
**MCP amplifiers** Microchannel Plate amplifiers.
**MCP program** Microsoft Certified Professional program.
*Qualification Programs.*
**MCPS**; **mcps**; **mc/s** megacycles per second.
**MCPs** Methyl-accepting Chemotaxis Proteins.
*Cellular and Molecular Biology; Genomics; Immunology; Microbiology.*
**MC/PS** Military Committee in Permanent Session.
Comité militaire en session permanente.
**MCR** Metabolic Clearance Rate.
*Medicine.*
**MCR** 1. military-civil relations.
1. relations militaro-civiles.
2. military communications requirement.
2. besoin en télécommunications militaires.
**MC4-R** Melanocortin-4 Receptor.
*Metabolic Diseases; Obesity.*
**MCRMLP** Midcontinental Region Medical Library Program.
**MCRTF** military-civil relations task force.
groupe pour les relations militaro-civiles.
**MCS** Madras Civil Service.
**MCS** Malayan Civil Service.
**MCS** Management Consulting Service.
**MCs** Mantle Cells.
**MCS** Master Control System.
**MCS** Master of Commercial Sciences.
**MCS** Mesoscale Convective System.
**MCS** Message Control System.
**MCS** Monte Carlo Simulation.
**MCS** Multiple Console Support.

**MCSC** mine countermeasures command and control ship.
bâtiment de commandement et de contrôle pour la lutte contre les mines.
**MCSF** multinational cryptologic support facility.
installation multinationale de soutien cryptologique.
**MCT** Main Central Thrust.
**MCT** Mainstream Corporation Tax.
*Business; Finance.*
**MCT** 1. mobile command team.
1. équipe mobile de commandement.
2. movement control team.
2. équipe des mouvements et transports.
**MCT** Mode-Coupling Theory.
*Automation; Chemical Research; Electrometry; Solid-State Physics.*
**MCTD** Mixed Connective Tissue Disease.
MCTD is also known as: Sharp's syndrome.
*Medicine.*
**MCTI** Metal Cutting Tool Institute.
**MCU** Master Control Unit; Memory Control Unit.
**MCU** Microprogrammed Control Unit.
*Computer Technology.*
**MCV** mandat-carte de versement.
*Business; Finance.*
**MCV** Marge Coûts Variables.
*Economics; Finance.*
**MCV** Mean Corpuscular Volume.
MCV is also known as: Mean Cell Volume.
*Medicine.*
**MCV** Medical College of Virginia (U.S.A.).
**MCV** Mesoscale Convectively-generated Vortices.
**MCV** Molluscum Contagiosum Virus.
MCV is a viral infection of the skin transmitted by direct or indirect contact.
*Virology.*
**MCVD process** Modified Chemical Vapor Deposition process.
*Physics.*
**MCV/VCU** Medical College of Virginia / Virginia Commonwealth University (U.S.A.).
**MCWG** Military Cooperation Working Group.
Groupe de travail sur la coopération militaire.
**MCXD** Magnetic Circular X-ray Dichroism.
**M/CY** machinery.
Also: **mach.**
*Mechanical Engineering.*
**MCZ** Museum of Comparative Zoology (U.S.A.).
**MD** Doctor of Medicine.
**MD** Malicious Damage.
**MD** Management Development.
**MD** Managing Director.
**m.d.** mano destra.
Italian initialism meaning: right hand.
**md** (abbr.) marchand.
**MD** Mark Down.
**MD** Market Day.
**MD** (abbr.) Maryland (U.S.A.).
**MD** Master Data.
*Computer Programming.*
**MD** Maturity Date.
*Business; Finance.*
**MD** 1. mechanized division.
1. division mécanisée.
2. military district.
2a. district militaire.
2b. région militaire.
3. Moldova (formerly called Moldavia).
3. Moldova (anciennement appelée Moldavie).
**MD** Medical Department.
**MD**; **M.D.** Medical Doctor.
**MD** Memorandum of Deposit.
**Md** The chemical symbol for Mendelevium.
Named for the Russian chemist Dmitri Ivanovich **Mendeleev**.
*Chemistry; Symbols.*
**MD** Mental Defective.
**MD** Midnight Dumping.
**M.D.** Ministero della Difesa.
Italian initialism of the: Ministry of Defense.
**MD** Molecular Dynamics.
*Physical Chemistry.*
**Md.** money demand.
**MD**; **M/D**; **m/d** Months After Date.
**MD** Multiple Dissemination.
**MD** Muscular Dystrophy.
MD is also known as: Myodystrophy.
*Pathology.*
**MDA** 1. main defence area.
1. zone de défense principale.
2. mine danger area.
2. zone de danger mines.
3. multiple docking adapter.
3. adaptateur d'amarrage multiple.
**MDA** Malondialdehyde.
Malondialdehyde is a carbonyl compound. It is carcinogenic and mutagenic and is produced by liquid peroxidation.
*Biochemistry; Cancer Research; Clinical Physiology; Pharmacology.*
**MDA** Medical Devices Agency.
*British Agencies.*
**MDA** Mesocyclone Detection Algorithm.
**MDA** 3,4-Methylene Dioxyamphetamine.
**MDA** Monochrome Display Adapter.

**MDA**; **M.D.A.** Motor Discriminative Acuity.
**MDA** Multiple Docking Adapter.
**MDA** Muscular Dystrophy Association.
**MDAHG** Missile Defence Ad Hoc Working Group.
Groupe ad hoc sur la défense antimissile.
**M damage** Mobilization damage.
*Military Science.*
**MD&M West** Medical Design and Manufacturing West.
Conference & Expo. Held on $26^{th}$/$28^{th}$ January 1999 at Anaheim, CA, Convention Center.
*U.S. Conferences.*
**MDAP** Mutual Defense Assistance Program (U.S.A.).
**MDASM** medium-depth antisubmarine mine.
mine anti-sous-marine à profondeur moyenne.
**M-day** Mobilization day.
*Military Science.*
**MDB** Multilateral Development Bank.
**MDB** Multiterapia Di Bella.
Italian initialism coined on $22^{nd}$ January 1998 at a summit of scientists discussing the alternative cancer therapy of Professor Luigi Di Bella to be used on an experimental-basis on 2600 patients.
*Alternative Cancer Tharapies.*
**MDBs** Multilateral Development Banks.
The world's five Multilateral Development Banks have had an important role, since their creation, in helping poor countries foster sustainable economic growth and higher standards of living.
**MDC** Macrophage-Derived Chemokine.
**M.d.C.** Margine di Contribuzione.
Italian initialism meaning: Contribution Margin.
*Economics; Finance.*
**MDC** Max Delbrück Center for Molecular Medicine (Germany).
The MDC was the first of three national research centers to be established in the former East Germany. Named for the American biologist Max **Delbrück** (1906-1981).
*Molecular Medicine.*
**MDC** mesures de confiance.
confidence-building measures (CBM 2.).
**MDC** Momentum Distribution Curve.
*Materials Science; Superconductivity; Physics.*
**MDC** Movement for Democratic Change (Zimbabwe).
**MDCK epithelial cells** Madine-Darby Canine Kidney epithelial cells.
*Hong Kong Influenza A Virus (H5N1); Medical Sciences; Molecular and Cellular Physiology; Pathological Sciences.*
**MDCS** mesures de confiance et de sécurité.
confidence- and security-building measures (CSBM).
**MDD** Magnetic Disk Drive.
**MDD** Marque De Distributeur.
French initialism meaning: private label.
**MDD** Meteorological Data Distribution.
**MDF** 1. main defence forced.
1. force(s) de défense principale.
2. main distribution frame.
2. répartiteur principal (ou d'entrée).
3. modulation par déplacement de fréquence.
3. frequency shift keying (FSK).
**MDF**; **Mdf** Market Development Fund.
**MDF** Median Demagnetization Field.
*Geology; Geophysics.*
**Mdf** Medium density fireboard.
**MdF** Millions de Francs.
(before the advent of the EURO).
**MDF** Minimal Discharge Field.
*Medicine; Neurobiology; Physiology.*
**MDF system** Micro-Dose Focusing system - Zeiss's.
**MDG** Machining-intensive Durable Goods.
**MDGs** Millennium Development Goals.
Of the World Bank.
**MDH** Malate Dehydrogenase.
**MDI** Michelson Doppler Imager.
*Solar Physics.*
**MDI** Michelson Doppler Interferometer.
The MDI is an instrument aboard the SOHO satellite which detects oscillations on the sun's surface as well as in magnetic fields.
*Solar Physics.*
For further details see under: **SOHO**.
**MDI** Multiple Document Interface.
**MDIBL** Mount Desert Island Biological Laboratory (U.S.A.).
**MDL** minimum decode level.
niveau minimal de décodage.
**MDM** modulation par déplacement minimal.
minimum shift keying (MSK).
**MDMA** 3,4-Methylenedioxymethamphetamine.
**MDM Observatory** Michigan-Dartmouth-Massachusetts Institute of Technology Observatory (U.S.A.).
*Earth, Atmospheric, and Planetary Sciences.*
**MDMP** Mediterranean Dialogue Military Programme.
Programme militaire du Dialogue méditerranéen.
**mdn** (abbr.) median.
**MDN** 1a. ministère de la Défense [FR].
1b. ministère de la Défence nationale.
Ministry of Defence (MOD).

**MDNR** Michigan Department of Natural Resources. Michigan State University (U.S.A.).
**MDO** Monthly Debit Ordinary.
**MDP** meteorological datum plane.
plan de référence météorologique.
**MDP** Multidomain Polymer.
*Materials Science and Engineering; Polymer Science.*
**MDPR** message de demande de prise de ressource.
*Communications.*
**MDR** Minimum Daily Requirements.
*Nutrition.*
**MDR** Multidrug Resistance / Multiple Drug Resistance.
**MDR-TB** Multidrug-Resistant Tuberculosis.
*Communicable Diseases; Disease Control and Prevention.*
**MDRU** Medications Development Research Unit.
**MDS** Master of Dental Surgery.
**MDS** Minimum Discernible Signal.
*Electronics.*
**mdse.** (abbr.) merchandise.
**MD simulations** Molecular Dynamics simulations.
*Materials Structures; Physics.*
**MDS method** Multidimensional Scaling method.
*Chemistry; Chemical Kinetics; Electrophoresis; Physical Chemistry.*
**MDS system** Multiple Data Set system.
**MDT** Milizia Difesa Territoriale.
**MDTCA** Ministry of Domestic Trade and Consumer Affairs (Malaysia).
**MDVI** Movimento Di Volontariato (Italy).
*Italian Volunteers Movements.*
**MDW** The airport code for Midway Airport, Chicago, Illinois, U.S.A.
**ME; Me.** (abbr.) Maine (U.S.A.).
**ME** Master of Engineering.
**ME; M.E.** Mechanical Engineer; Mechanical Engineering.
**ME** Median Eminence.
*Posterior Pituitary Hormones.*
**ME; M.E.** Medical Examiner.
**ME** Medio Evo.
Italian acronym meaning: The Middle Ages.
**M.E.** Membro Effettivo.
Italian acronym meaning: Active Member.
**ME** Memory Element.
*Computer Technology.*
**ME** Mercantile Exchange.
**ME** Messina, Italy.
**ME** Metabolizable Energy.
*Nutrition.*
**Me** Methyl.
Methyl is the akyl group $CH_3$-, present in many organic compounds.
*Organic Chemistry.*
**ME** Middle East.
**ME** Middle English.
Middle English is the English language of the period c1150-c1475.
*Languages.*
**ME** Mining Engineer.
**ME** Ministère de l'education (France).
**ME** Montréal Exchange (Canada).
**ME** Most Excellent.
**ME** Moyenne Entreprise.
French acronym meaning: Medium-sized Company / Enterprise.
**MEA** Minimum En route Altitude.
*Navigation.*
**MEA** Monoethanoalamine.
*Organic Chemistry.*
**MEA** The airline code for Middle East Airlines.
**MEA** Multilateral Environmental Agreement.
**MEADS** medium extended air defence system.
système de défense aérienne élargie à moyenne portée.
**MEAS** mission-essential avionics spares.
rechanges d'avionique indispensables à la mission.
**MEB** marine expeditionary brigade [U.S.].
brigade du corps expéditionnaire des marines [US].
**MEB** Midlands Electricity Board (G.B.).
**MEBIOCE** Ultra high sensitivity integrated detection technology for cellular and bacteriological qualification and control with bioselective polymers.
*E.C. Projects; Medical Diagnostics.*
**MEBS** Master in Economia e Banca Siena.
At the Faculty of Economics "R.M. Goodwin" of the University of Siena, Italy. A collaboration between the University of Siena and the MPS SpA.
For further details see under: **MPS**.
**MEC** Marginal Efficiency of Capital.
**MEC** Member of the Executive Council.
**MEC** Mercato Europeo Comune.
Italian acronym meaning: European Common Market.
**MEC** Mixed Economic Commission.
**mecc.raz.** (abbr.) meccanica razionale.
Italian abbreviation meaning: theoretical mechanics; analytic mechanics.
**mech.** (abbr.) mechanical; mechanism; mechanics.
**MECO** Main Engine Cut-Off.
**meco** The above acronym was coined accidentally

using the Italian word "meco" which means: with me.

**MECs** (Thymic) Medullary Epithelial Cells.
*Immunology; Immunogenetics; Molecular Biology.*
For further details see under: **AIRE**.

**Med.**; **med.** (abbr.) medical; medicine.

**MED**; **M.E.D.** Minimal Effective Dose; Minimal Erythema Dose.

**MEDASSESSREP** medical assessment report.
compte rendu d'évaluation médicale.

**MEDCENT** Central Mediterranean Area.
Secteur Central de la Méditerranée.

**MEDEAST** Eastern Mediterranean Area.
Secteur orientale de la Méditerranée.

**MEDEVAC** medical evacuation.
évacuation sanitaire (EVASAN).

**MEDIA** MEDiterranean Innovation Array.

**MEDIACULT** International Research Institute for Media, Communication and Cultural Development (Austria).
Founded in 1969.

**MEDICA** Multimedial Medical Diagnostic Assistant.

**MEDLARS** MEDical Literature Analysis and Retrieval System.

**MEDLI** Medical and Scientific Library of Long Island (U.S.A.).

**MEDLINE** (abbr.) The online research database of the National Library of Medicine (U.S.A.).

**MEDNOREAST** North-Eastern Mediterranean Area.
Secteur Nord-Est de la Méditerranée.

**MEDOC** Western Mediterranean Area.
Secteur occidental de la Méditerranée.

**MEDR** medical returnee.
repatrié pour raisons médicales.

**MEDS** Marine Ecological Database System.

**MEDS** Marine Environmental Data Service (Canada).

**MEDS** Meteorological and Environmental Data Services (U.S.A.).

**MEDSITREP** medical situation report.
compte rendu de situation médicale.

**MEDSOUTHEAST** Southeastern Mediterranean Area.
Secteur Sud-Est de la Méditerranée.

**MEDSUPLAN** medical supply plan.
plan de ravitaillement médico-sanitaire.

**MEDTEC** Medical Equipment Design & Technology Exhibition & Conference (The Netherlands).

**MEERC** Multiscale Experimental Ecosystem Research Center (U.S.A.).

**MEF** 1. marine expeditionary force [US].
1. force du corps expéditionnaire des marines [US].
2. minimum essential facility.
2. installation essentielle minimale.
3. mission-essential force.
3. force essentielle à la mission.

**MEF 2** Myocyte Enhancer Factor - 2.
*Cardiac Morphogenesis and Myogenesis; Cardiology; Cell Biology; Internal Medicine; Molecular Biology; Oncology.*

**MEFs** Mouse Embryo Fibroblasts.
*Apoptosis; Cell Biology; Medical Sciences; Molecular Biology; Human Genetics; Pathology.*

**MEG** Magnetoencephalography.
*Medicine.*

**meg** (abbr.) megaohm.
*Electricity.*

**MEG** Metals Economics Group (Canada).

**MEGA** Molecular Evolutionary Genetics Analysis.
*Cellular Pathology; Molecular Pathology.*

**MEGS** Market Entry Guarantee Scheme.

**MEH** Module d'Extraction d'Horloge.

**MeHg** Methylmercury.
Methylmercury, in toxic doses, causes developmental and neurological disorders.

**MEIG** Maritime Exercise Information Group.
Groupe d'information sur les exercices maritimes.

**MEKA thermal plasma code** Mewe-Kaastra thermal plasma code.
*Astronomy; Astrophysics.*

**MEKK** MEK kinase.

**MEL** main events list [exercises].
liste des principaux évènements [exercices].

**Mél.** Message / Messagerie électronique.
French acronym meaning: e-mail.
*Telecommunications.*

**MEL** The airport code for Melbourne, Australia.

**MELAS** Mitochondrial Encephalomyopathy with Lactic Acidosis and Seizure.
*Degenerative Diseases; Medicine.*

**MELT experiment** Mantle ELectromagnetic and Tomography experiment.
*Geology; Oceanography; Seismology; Terrestrial Magnetism.*
For further details see under: **RIDGE**.

**MELU** Molecular Epidemiology Laboratory Unit (U.S.A.).

**MEM** Macrophage Electrophoretic Mobility.

**MEM** Maximum Entropy Method.
*Biological Chemistry; Environmental Sciences; Physical Science; Synthetic Chemistry.*

**mem.** (abbr.) memorandum.

**MEM** The airport code for Memphis, Tennessee, U.S.A.
**MEM** Minimum/Minimal Essential Medium.
**MEMC** Methoxyethylmercury Chloride.
**MEMO** Multimedia Environment for MObiles.
*European Community Project.*
**MEMS** Microelectromechanical / Micro-Electro-Mechanical Systems.
*Applied Physics; Chemical Engineering; Miniature Devices.*
**MEMW** MEMory Write.
**MEN 1** Multiple Endocrine Neoplasia-type 1.
*Biotechnology Information; Chemistry and Biochemistry; Gene Transfer Human Genome Research; Metabolic Diseases; Pathology.*
**MENA** Middle-East, North Africa.
Moyen-Orient-Afrique du nord.
**mens.** mensile.
Italian abbreviation meaning: monthly; month's pay / wages / salary.
**MEOR** Microbial Enhanced Oil Recovery.
*Microbial/Biochemical Processes (New Applications).*
**mep** mean effective pressure.
*Mechanical Engineering.*
**MEP** Member of the European Parliament.
**MEP** methyl ethyl pyridine.
**MEP** Ministry of Environmental Protection.
**MEP** multi-ethnic police.
police pluri-ethnique.
**MEPC** Marine Environment Protection Committee.
Of the International Maritime Organization.
**MEPCs** Miniature Excitatory Postsynaptic Currents.
**MEPs** Members of the European Parliement.
**mEPSPs** miniature Excitatory Postsynaptic Potentials.
*Medicine; Neurobiology and Behavior; Psychiatry; Surgery.*
**MEP state** Maximum Entropy Production state.
*Climate; Computational Mathematics; Meteorology; Physics.*
**MEPT** Mercury European Privatisation Trust.
**mEq.** (abbr.) milliéquivalent.
French abbreviation meaning: milliequivalent.
*Chemistry.*
**MEQC** Marine Environmental Quality Committee.
Of the International Council for The Exploration of the Sea.
**MER** Management par Ecoute et Rencontre.
French acronym meaning: Management by Wandering Around (MBWA).
**MER** maximum effective range.
portée efficace maximale.
**MER** Maximum Efficient Rate.
**mer.** (abbr.) meridian.
*Astronomy; Cartography.*
**MER** Methanol Extraction residue.
**MERB** Maritime Exercise Review Board.
Commission d'étude des exercices maritimes.
**MERC** Chicago Mercantile Exchange.
**merc.** (abbr.) mercantile.
**MERCASREP** merchant ship casualty report.
compte rendu d'avarie de navire de commerce.
**MERCAST** merchant ship broadcast.
émission de navire de commerce.
**MERCO** merchant ship reporting and control (message system).
(système de messages du) contrôle naval de la navigation commerciale.
**MERC program** Middle East Regional Cooperation program.
The MERC program is a joint research program involving Egyptians, Israeli, and Americans. It is funded by the U.S. Agency for International Development.
**MERCOMMS** merchant ship(ping) communications system.
système de télécommunications pour navires de commerce (ou navires marchands).
**Mercosur** Mercado Común del Sur.
Abbreviation meaning: Latin-American Common Market.
**MERCS** merchant ship crypto system.
système cryptographique de navire de commerce (ou navire marchand).
**MEREP** merchant ship report.
compte rendu du navire de commerce (ou navire marchand).
**MERIT Awards** Method to Extend Research In Time Awards.
*U.S. Awards.*
**MERLIN** Medical Emergency Relief International G.B.
*Epidemiology; Microbiology; Reemerging Diseases; Tuberculosis.*
**MERMLS** Mid-Eastern Regional Medical Library Service.
**MERRF disease** Myoclonic Epilepsy and Ragged - Red Fiber disease.
**MERSHIP** merchant ship.
1a. navire de commerce.
1b. navire marchand.
**MERSHIPWARN** merchant shipping warning.
avis à la navigation commerciale.
**MERZONE** merchant ship control zone.

1a. zone de contrôle naval.
1b. zone de contrôle naval de la navigation commerciale.
**MES** modulation par étalement du spectre.
spread-spectrum modulation (SSM 1.).
**MES** Multiple Earning Statement.
**MESA** Middle East Studies Association of North America.
**MESAB** Medical Education for South African Blacks.
For the fight against *AIDS; Malaria; Tuberculosis.*
**MESA program** Mathematics, Engineering, and Science Achievement program.
*U.S. Program.*
**MESAR** multifunctional electrically-scanned adaptive radar.
radar adaptif multifonction à balayage électronique.
**MESCs** Mouse Embryonic Stem Cells.
**MESG** Mediterranean Shipping Group.
Groupe méditerranéen de la navigation commerciale.
**MeSH** Medical Subject Headings.
*Cell Biology; Gene Expression; Gene Regulation; Genetics; Medicine.*
**MESOP** Management Enrichment Stock Ownership Plan.
**met.** (abbr.) metallurgical.
**met.** (abbr.) metaphor; metaphorical.
**met.** (abbr.) meteorological; meteorology.
**Met** Methionine.
*Biochemistry.*
**Met** (abbr.) The Metropolitan.
**met.** (abbr.) metropolitan.
**MET** Mid European Time.
**MeT** Mobile electronic Transactions.
**METACAN** METa-Analyses for the improved treatment of CANcer.
*European Community Project.*
**Metalcon International** International Exhibition and conference for metal construction products and services (U.S.A.).
Held annually, it is sponsored by the MCA.
For further details see under: **MCA**.
**métaph.** (abbr.) métaphore.
French abbreviation meaning: metaphor.
**METCON** control of meteorological information.
contrôle des renseignements météorologiques.
**METCON** (abbr.) METropolitan CONsortium.
**Met Hb** Methaemoglobin / Metahaemoglobin.
**METIM** MErcato Telematico delle Imprese Medie (Italy).
**METL** mission-essential task list [PCC].
liste des tâches essentielles à la mission [CCP].
**METOC** meteorological and oceanographic centre.
centre météorologique et océanographique.
**METON** METropolitan Optical Network.
*European Community Project.*
**METRO** MEssenger TRansport Organizer.
*Cancer; Developmental Biology; Molecular Genetics.*
**MetRS** Methionyl-tRNA Synthetase.
*Biology.*
**METSAT network** METeorological SATellite network.
**MetSO** Methionine Sulfoxide.
**MEU** marine expeditionary unit.
unité du corps expéditionnaire des marines.
**MEUR** million euros [single European currency - M€].
million d'euros [monnaie unique européenne - M€].
**Meuro** Milioni di euro.
Italian abbreviation meaning: Million Euros. Also: M€. The single European currency.
**MeV** Méga-électron-Volt.
French symbol meaning: Megaelectron Volt. Also: mev. Energy unit equal to $10^6$ electron volts.
*Physics.*
**MEW** Microwave Early-Warning.
*Engineering - Radar.*
**MEWSG** NATO Multiservice Electronic Warfare Support Group.
Groupe OTAN interarmées de soutien de la guerre électronique.
**MEX** MEWSG TRACSVAN exercise.
exercice de TRACSVAN du MEWSG.
**Mex** (abbr.) Mexican.
**MEX** The airport code for Mexico City.
**MEXH** Multi-Energy X-ray Holography.
*Solid-State Physics.*
**MexSp** Mexican Spanish.
*Languages.*
**MEZ** missile engagement zone.
zone d'engagement des missiles.
**MF** Master File.
*Computer Programming.*
**MF** Master of Forestry.
**MF** Medium Focus.
**MF**; **mf** Medium Frequency.
MF is the band of frequencies ranging from 300 to 3000 kilohertz.
*Telecommunications.*
**MF** microfiche.
The microfiche is used mainly in libraries.
*Graphic Arts.*

**MF** Middle French.
Middle French is the French language of the 14th, 15th, and 16th centuries.
*Languages.*
**MF** 1. military function.
1. fonction militaire.
2. modulation de fréquence.
2. frequency modulation.
**MF** Millifarad.
mF is equal to one-thousandth of a farad.
*Electricity.*
**MF** Mineworkers' Federation.
**M.F.** Ministero delle Finanze.
Italian initialism of the: Ministry of Finance.
**MF** Minister / Ministry of Food.
**MF** Modulazione di Frequenza.
Italian initialism meaning: Frequency Modulation.
*Telecommunications.*
**MF** More Fragments.
*Computers.*
**MF** Mutual Fund.
*Business; Finance.*
**MFB** Multicell Fluidized-bed Boiler.
**mfd** (abbr.) manufactured.
Also: **mfr.**
**MFE** Magnetically confined Fusion Energy.
Also: Magnetic Fusion Energy.
*Bomb Physics; Laser Fusion Research; Nuclear Fusion Research; Physics; Tokamaks.*
**MFEL** Medical Free Electron Laser.
**MF family** Major Facilitator family.
*Molecular and Cell Biology.*
**mfg.** (abbr.) manufacturing.
**MFI** Mean Fluorescence Intensity.
**MFL** Maximum Foreseeable Loss.
**MFM** Magnetic Force Microscopy.
*Physics.*
**MFN** Most Favoured Nation.
For further details see under: **NTR**.
**MFO** Multinational Force and Observers.
**MFP** Mobile Flux Platform.
**MFP** Multiform Printer.
**MFPS** Mathematical Foundations of Programming Semantics.
**MFr.** Mali franc.
*Currencies.*
**mfr** (abbr.) manufacture.
Also: **man.**; **manufr.**
**mfr.** (abbr.) manufactured.
Also: **mfd**.
**mfr** (abbr.) manufacturer.
Also: **manf.**
**MFR** Methanofuran.
**MFRS** maritime force requirement study.
étude des besoins de forces maritimes.
**MFS** Marfan's Syndrome.
Marfan's Syndrome is also known as: Arachnodactyly. Named for the French pediatrician Bernard-Jean Antonin **Marfan**.
*Genetics.*
**MFS** Main Field Site.
*Aquarium Research; Biogeology; Earth Sciences.*
**mfst.** (abbr.) manifest.
**MFT** Most Favorable Terms.
*Business; Commerce; Finance.*
**MF technique** Membrane Filtration technique.
*Microbiology.*
**MFUA** Medical Follow-Up Agency (U.S.A.).
The MFUA is funded by the U.S. NIH, the U.S. V.A., and the U.S. DOD.
*Medical Studies.*
For further details see under: **NIH**, **V.A.** and **DOD**.
**MG** Machine Gun.
Also: **mg**.
*Ordnance.*
**MG** Madigan Gulf (Lake Eyre).
**Mg** The chemical symbol for Magnesium.
Used mainly in batteries, alloys and pyrotechnics.
*Chemistry; Symbols.*
**MG** Manchester Guardian.
**MG** Medial Gastrocnemius.
MG is a sensory nerve in the calf muscle.
*Anatomy; Locomotor System; Neurophysiology.*
**Mg**; **Mg.** Megagram / Megagramme.
*Metrology.*
**MG**; **mg** (abbr.) microglobulin.
*Immunology.*
**mg** (abbr.) milligram / milligramme.
*Metrology.*
**MG** Minimum Garanti.
**MG** Mongolia.
**MG** Myasthenia Gravis.
*Medicine.*
**MGA** Magnetic Gradient Accelerator.
**MGA** Monochrome Graphics Adapter (Hercule's).
**MGA** Multiple Gas Analyzer.
**mgal** milligal.
*Metrology.*
**Mg-ATP** Magnesium salt of Adenosine Triphosphate.
**MGB** Medial Geniculate Body.
**MGC** Manual Gain Control.
*Radio.*
**Mg/Ca ratio** Magnesium-to-calcium ratio.
**$MgCl_2$** Magnesium Chloride.
*Inorganic Chemistry.*

**$MgCO_3$** Magnesite.
*Mineralogy.*
**$MgCO_3$** Magnesium Carbonate.
Magnesium Carbonate is used mainly in the manufacture of pharmaceuticals; cosmetics and food products.
*Inorganic Chemistry.*
**$MgCr_2O_4$** Magnesiochromite.
*Mineralogy.*
**MGCs** Multinucleated Giant Cells.
*HIV Encephalitis; Pathology.*
**MGD**; **mgd** Million Gallons per Day.
**MGD** Molybdopterin-Guanine Dinucleotide.
*Biochemistry; Biological Sciences; Biomedical Sciences.*
**mGDNF** mutant form of Glial cell line - Derived Neurotrophic Factor.
*Anatomy; Genetic Therapies; Medicine; Neurobiology.*
**MGED Society** Microarray Gene Expression Data Society.
*Cell Biology; Genetics; Gene Regulation; Gene Expression.*
**MGE program** Minority Graduate Education program (U.S.A.).
**$MgF_2$** Magnesium Fluoride.
$MgF_2$ also known as: Magnesium Flux, is used mainly in ceramics and optics.
*Inorganic Chemistry.*
**M.G.G.** Ministero di Grazia e Giustizia.
Italian initialism of the: Ministry of Justice. Lord Chancellor's Department (G.B.). Department of Justice (U.S.A.).
**MGH** Massachusetts General Hospital (U.S.A.).
**mgh** milligram-hour.
**MGI** Marine Geological Institute (Indonesia).
**MGID** military geographic information and documentation.
renseignements et documentation géographiques militaires (RDGM).
**MGk** Medieval Greek.
*Languages.*
**MGluR2** Metabotropic Glutamate Receptor 2.
*Biological Sciences; Bioregulation; Medicine; Neurophysiology.*
**MGM** Modified Gaussian Model.
*Geological Sciences; Geophysics.*
**MGMR** Ministry of Geology and Mineral Resources (China).
**mgmt.** (abbr.) management.
**MGN** Medial Geniculate Nuclei.
*Biomedical Sciences; Neurology; Psychology.*
**$Mg(NH_2)_2$** Magnesium Amide.
Magnesium Amide is used for polymerization purposes.
*Inorganic Chemistry.*
**MgO** Magnesium Oxide.
MgO is used mainly in food additives, in laxatives, and fertilizers.
*Inorganic Chemistry.*
**MGO** Methylglyoxal.
**MgO** Periclase.
A minor component of Earth's lower mantle.
*Mantle Convention; Mineral Physics.*
**$MgO_2$** Magnesium Peroxide.
$MgO_2$ also known as: Magnesium Dioxide is used mainly in medicine.
*Inorganic Chemistry.*
**$Mg(OH)_2$** Magnesium Hydroxide.
Magnesium Hydroxide also known as: Magnesium Hydrate is used mainly in food processing and in medicine.
*Inorganic Chemistry.*
**Mg-Proto** Magnesium-Protoporphyrin IX.
An intermediate in chlorophyll biosynthesis.
*Medicine; Plant Biology.*
**Mgr.**; **mgr.** (abbr.) manager.
**MGRR** Merry-Go-Round Reactor (water-cooled).
**MGRS** military grid reference system.
système de référence de carroyage militaire.
**MGS** Mars Global Surveyor.
For further details see under: **MOLA**.
**MGSA** Melanoma Growth Stimulatory Activity.
**M/G set**; **MG set** Motor-Generator set.
*Electricity.*
**$Mg_2SiO_4$** Forsterite.
*Mineralogy.*
**mgt.** (abbr.) management.
**$MgTiO_3$** Geikielite.
*Mineralogy.*
**MGUS** Monoclonal Gammopathy of Undetermined Significance.
*Hematology; Medicine; Myeloma Precursors; Oncology; Virology.*
**$MgWO_4$** Magnesium Tungstate.
Also known as: Magnesium Wolframate is used mainly in luminescent paint.
*Inorganic Chemistry.*
**MH** Maladie Héréditaire.
French initialism meaning: Hereditary Disease.
*Medicine.*
**MH** Maleic Hydrazide.
Maleic hydrazide is used as an herbicide.
*Organic Chemistry.*
**MH** Malignant Hypertension.
*Pathology.*

**MH** manhole.
Manhole is also known as: manhead.
*Engineering.*
**MH** 1. materials handling.
1. manutention des matériels.
2. minehunter.
2. chasseur de mines.
**MH** Medal of Honor.
The MH is a U.S. Military decoration.
**mh** millihenry.
*Electromagnetism.*
**MHA** 16-Mercaptohexadecanoic Acid.
*Materials Science; Nanotechnology; Physics.*
**MHA** Microhemagglutination Assay.
**MHC** Major Histocompatibility Complex.
*Immunology; Medicine.*
**MHC** 1. military high command.
1. haut commandement militaire.
2. minehunter, coastal.
2. chasseur de mines côtier.
**MHCs** Major Histocompatibility Complexes.
*Immunology; Medicine.*
**MHCS** Multicenter Hemophilia Cohort Study.
The Multicenter Hemophilia Cohort Study was sponsored by the U.S. NCI.
For further details see under: **NCI**.
**MHD** Magnetohydrodynamics.
Magnetohydrodynamics is also known as: Hydromagnetics; Magnetofluid Dynamics; Magnetogas Dynamics.
*Physics.*
**MHD**; **M.H.D.** Minimum Hemolytic Dose.
**MHD LT** Masthead Light.
*Navigation.*
**MHE** material handling equipment.
équipement de manutention des matériels.
**MHEA** Mechanical Handling Engineer's Association.
**MHF Experiments** Massive Hydraulic Fracture Experiments.
**MHG** Middle High German.
*Languages.*
**MHI** Marine Hydrophysical Institute (Sevastopol, Ukraine).
**MHLA** Manitoba Health Libraries Association (Canada).
**MHMS** Modular Hydrologic Modeling System.
**MHN** moving haven.
zone de sécurité mobile.
**MHQ** maritime headquarters.
1a. PC maritime.
1b. quartier général maritime.
**MHR** Major Homology Region.
**MHR** Member of the House of Representatives.
**MHS** Message Handling Service / System.
**MH(S)** Multifrequency Hypertermia (System).
**MHSLA** Michigan Health Sciences Library Association (U.S.A.).
**MHSLN** Midwest Health Sciences Library Network.
**MHSS** Military Health Services System (U.S.A.).
**MHV** Mouse Hepatitis Virus.
**MHV** Murine Hepatitis Virus.
**M.H.W.**; **m.h.w.** Mean High Water.
*Oceanography.*
**MHW** Ministry of Health and Welfare (Japan).
**MHWS** Mean High Water Springs (tides).
**MHW Thermoelectric Generator** Multihundred Watt Thermoelectric Generator.
*Thermoelectric Technology.*
**MHz** Megahertz.
MHz is a unit of frequency equal to $10^6$ hertz.
*Physics.*
**MI** Magistratura Indipendente (Italy).
**MI** 1. Malawi.
1. Malawi.
2. military intelligence.
2. renseignement militaire.
**MI** Malleable Iron.
*Metallurgy.*
**MI** Merit Increase.
**MI** (abbr.) Michigan (U.S.A.).
**mi** microinstruction.
*Computer Programming.*
**MI** Milano, Italy.
**mi** mile.
a unit of length.
*Metrology.*
**MI** Mineral Insulated.
**MI** Minority Interest.
*Business; Economics; Finance.*
**MI** Miscellaneous Income.
**MI** Mitotic Index.
*Cell Biology.*
**MI** Mitral Incompetence; Mitral Insufficiency.
*Medicine.*
**MI** Modulation Instability.
*Electrical Engineering; Physics.*
**MI** Mounted Infantry.
**MI** Myocardial Infarction.
*Medicine.*
**MIA** message initial d'adresse.
*Communications.*
**MIA** missing in action.
disparu au combat.
**MIA** Multiplex Interface Adapter.

**MIA** The airport code for Miami International, U.S.A.
**MIACA** Mission Interministérielle d'Aménagement de la Côte Aquitaine (France).
**MIAGE** Maîtrises d'Informatique Appliquées à la GEstion (France).
**MIAM** McGill Institute for Advanced Materials.
MIAM coordinates interactions and partnerships across faculties and departments at the McGill University, Quebec, Canada.
**MIAME** Minimal Information about A Microarray Experiment.
*Cell Biology; Genetics; Gene Regulation; Gene Expression.*
**MIAMIN** MIAmi International MINing Show.
Held at the Miami Beach Convention Center 8th/10th October 1998.
**MIAS** Marine Information and Advisory Service (G.B.).
**MIAS** Minimally Invasive Articular Surgery.
**MIATM** Missione Italiana di Assistenza Tecnico Militare a Malta.
**MIAU** million infrastructure accounting units.
million d'unités de compte d'infrastructure (MUCI).
**MIB** Indice Borsa Milano.
Italian acronym meaning: Milan Stock Exchange Index.
**MIB** Marketing of Investments Board.
**MIB** Maternal Imprinting Box.
*Molecular Pathology.*
**MIB** Microinstruction Bus.
**MIBG** Metaiodobenzylguanidine.
**MIBOR** Madrid Interbank Offered Rate.
**MIC** Management Investment Company.
**MIC** Meteorologist-In-Charge.
**MIC** Methyl Isothiocyanate.
Methyl Isothiocyanate, also known as: Methyl Mustard Oil, is used mainly as an insecticide.
*Organic Chemistry.*
**MIC** Microwave Integrated Circuit.
**MIC** Mikroelektronik Centret.
MIC is based at the Denmark Technical University.
**MIC** Minimum Inhibitory Concentration.
**MIC** Ministero dell'Industria e Commercio (Italy).
**MIC** modulation par impulsions et codage.
**MIC** Mortgage Insurance Company; Mortgage Investment Company.
**MIC** Museo Internazionale delle Ceramiche.
MIC is located in Faenza (Italy).
**MICA** Ministero dell'Industria, del Commercio, dell'Artigianato (Italy).
**MICAS** military intelligence combat aerial surveillance.
surveillance aérienne du combat pour le renseignement militaire.
**MICC** Mobile Integrated Communication in Construction.
*European Community Project.*
**MICE** Member of the Institute of Civil Engineers.
**MICEX** Moscow International Currency Exchange.
**MICR** Magnetic Ink Character Recognition.
*Computers.*
**MICRONET** Microelectronic devices, Circuits, and Systems for ultralarge-Scale integration.
*Electrical Engineering.*
For further details see under: **NCE**.
**MICS** Manufacturing Information and Control Systems.
**MICV** mechanized infantry combat vehicle.
véhicule de combat d'infanterie mécanisée (VCIM).
**M.I.D.** Master of Industrial Design.
**mid.** (abbr.) middle.
**Mid.** (abbr.) Midshipman.
**MIDA** position Mento-Iliaque Droite Antérieure.
French acronym meaning: Right Mentoanterior position.
**MIDAS** metal Ion-Dependent Adhesion Site.
*Biosciences; Biomedical Research; Immunology; Leukocyte Biology; Target Research; Oncology.*
**MIDAS** MIssile Defense, Alarm System.
*Military.*
**MIDAS net** Multimedia Information Demonstration And Support network - E.C.
**MIDC** Maharashtra Industrial Development Corporation (India).
MIDC is an organization committed towards the complete industrialization of the State.
**MIDI** Musical Instrument Digital Interface.
*Computer Programming.*
**MIDIST** Mission Interministérielle De l'Information Scientifique et Technique (France).
**MIDP**; **Midp** Motor Industry Development Programme.
Developed by the South African Government in 1995.
*South African Programs.*
**MIDP** position Mento-Iliaque Droite Postérieure.
French initialism meaning: Right Mentoposterior position.
*Medicine.*
**MIDS** multifunctional information distribution system.

système multifonction de diffusion de l'information.
**MIDU** Movimento Italiano per i Diritti Umani.
Italian acronym of the: Italian Movement for Human Rights (Italy).
**MIEM** Master of International Economics and Management.
**MIESR techniques** - Matrix Isolation and Electron Spin Resonance techniques.
**MIF** 1. maritime interdiction force.
1. force maritime d'interdiction.
2. modulation d'impulsions en fréquence(s).
2. pulse frequency modulation (PFM).
**MIF** Master Index File.
**MIF** Melanocyte Inhibiting Factor.
*Medicine.*
**MIF** Mercato Italiano dei Futures.
Italian acronym meaning: Italian Futures Market.
**MIF** Migration Inhibition Factor.
Migration Inhibition Factor is also known as: Migration Inhibitory Factor.
*Immunology.*
**MIF** Mortgage Insurance Fund.
**MIF files** Management Information Format files.
**MIG** Moody's Investment Grade.
**MIGA** Multilateral Investment Guarantee Agency.
MIGA is a member of the World Bank Group.
**MIGA** position Mento-Iliaque Gauche Antérieure.
French acronym meaning: Left Mento-Anterior position.
*Medicine.*
**MIGP** position Mento-Iliaque Gauche Postérieure.
French initialism meaning: Left Mento-Posterior position.
*Medicine.*
**MIGT** position Mento-Iliaque Gauche Transverse.
French initialism meaning: Left Mentum Transverse Presentation.
*Medicine.*
**MIG welding** Metal Inert Gas welding.
*Metallurgy.*
**MIHCK** MI Heavy Chain Kinase.
*Biology; Cell Biology; Pathology; Signal Transduction.*
**MII** Ministry of Information Industry (China).
**MIICS** MHC Class II Compartments.
For further details see under: **MHC**.
**MIJI** meaconing, intrusion, jamming and interference.
transplexion, intrusion, brouillage et interférence.
**MIL** main incidents list [exercises].
liste des principaux incidents [exercices].
**MIL** Marine Instrumentation Laboratory.
**MILCO** mine-like contact.
contact de type mine.
**MILCOM** Military Committee communication.
message du Comité militaire.
**MILEC** mine-like echo.
écho de type mine.
**MILF** Moro Islamic Liberation Front (The Philippines).
The MILF is one of two main groups fighting for an independent muslim state in the south of The Philippines.
**MILNET** (abbr.) MILitary NETwork.
MILNET separated from ARPANET in 1983.
For further details see under: **ARPANET**.
**MIL.OC.** (abbr.) Military Oceanography.
*Geophysics.*
**MILOPs** military operations.
opérations militaires.
**MILREP** military representative.
représentant militaire.
**MILSPEC** military specification.
spécification militaire.
**MILSTAND** military standard.
norme militaire.
**MIL-STD** see MILSTAND.
voir MILSTAND.
**MILSTRIP** military standard requisitioning and issue procedure.
procédure militaire standard de requisition et de distribution.
**MIM** Modem Interface Module.
**MIM** Multilateral Initiative on Malaria.
*Malaria Research.*
**MIM** Musée des Instruments de Musique (Brussels, Belgium).
**mim** The above acronyms were coined accidentally using the Arabic word "mim" which is the twenty-fourth letter of the Arabic alphabet.
**MIMD** Multiple Instruction, Multiple Data.
MIMD is a sort of parallel computer architecture.
**MIMICS** Microwave Monolithic Integrated Circuits.
MIMICS are used in cellular telephones.
**MIMIC technique** Micromolding In Capillaries technique.
*Materials Science.*
**MIMS** medical information management system.
système de gestion de l'information médicale.
**min.** (abbr.) minimo.
Italian abbreviation meaning: minimum.
**min.** (abbr.) minimum; minority.
**min.** (abbr.) minuto.
Italian abbreviation meaning: minute.

**MINA** Member of the Institution of Naval Architects.

**mina** The above acronym was coined accidentally using the Italian word "mina" which means in Italian: mine (*Explosives*).

**MINATOM**; **Minatom** Ministry of Atomic Energy (Russia).
For further details see under: **NCI**.

**MINCOMES** (abbr.) MINistero per il COMmercio EStero (Italy).
Italian abbreviation meaning: Ministry of Foreign Trade.

**MIND** Modular Interactive Network Designer.

**MINDD** MINimum Due Date.
*Business; Commerce; Finance.*

**MINE** Microbial Information Network in Europe.
*European Community Network.*

**MINEX** minelaying exercise.
exercice de mouillage de mines.

**MINEXREP** mine explosion report.
compte rendu d'explosion de mine.

**MINISID** MINiature Seismic Intrusion Detection.

**MINITEX** Minnesota Interlibrary Telecommunications Exchange (U.S.A.).

**Minn.** (abbr.) Minnesota (U.S.A.).
Also: **MN**.

**Min.Plen.** (abbr.) Minister Plenipotentiary.

**MINT** Managing Integration on New Technology.

**MINTS** Mutual Institutions National Transfer Systems (U.S.A.).

**MINUGUA** United Nations Verification Mission in Guatemala.

**MINURSO** MIssion des Nations Unies pour le Referendum dans le Sahara.

**MIO** maritime interdiction operation.
opération maritime d'interdiction.

**MIOS** maritime intelligence organization study.
étude sur l'organisation du renseignement maritime.

**MIP** β-Macrophage Inflammatory Protein.

**MIP** Managers' International Program.

**MIP** Marine Insurance Policy.

**MIP** Master di Potenziamento Imprenditoriale.
Of the School of Management - Polytechnic of Milan, Italy.

**MIP** Master in Ingegneria della Produzione (Italy).

**MIP** Mean Indicated Pressure.
*Physics.*

**MIP** Missouri Institute of Psychiatry (U.S.A.).

**MIP** Monthly Investment Plan.
*Business; Economics; Finance.*

**MIP** Mortgage Insurance Premium.

**MIPA** Metodologie e Innovazioni nelle Pubbliche Amministrazioni (Italy).

**MIPS** Martinsried Institute for Protein Sequences (U.S.A.).

**MIPS** Million Instructions Per Second.
*Computer Technology.*

**MIR** Maximum Incremental Reactivity.

**MIR** 1. military infrastructure requirement.
1. besoin militaire en matière d'infrastructure.
2. MNC interoperability requirement.
2. besoin des GCO en matière d'interopérabilité.

**MIRAS** Mortgage Interest Relief At Source.

**MIRCENS** Microbial Resources Centres - UNESCO network.

**MIR map** Multiple Isomorphous Replacement map.
*Biophysics; Biochemistry; Protein Engineering Research.*

**MiRNAs genes** micro-RNAs genes.
*Biology; Biomedical Research -Biotechnology; Botany; Genes Development; Plant Pathology.*

**MIRV** multiple independently-targetable re-entry vehicle.
corps de rentrée à têtes multiples indépendamment guidées.

**MIS** Management Information System.
*Industry.*

**MIS** Man In Space.
*U.S. Program.*

**MIS** Master in International Studies.

**MIS** Matrix Isolation Spectroscopy.
*Astrochemistry; Astronomy; Astrophysics; Molecular Astrophysics; Space Science.*

**MIS** Metal-Insulator Semiconductor.
*Solid-State Physics.*

**MIS** Minimally Invasive Surgery.
Compared with conventional surgery, MIS can reduce side-effects and post-surgical complications.

**MIS** Modern Investment Systems.

**MIS** Müllerian Inhibiting Substance.
*Human Ovarian Cancer.*

**MIS II** Marine Isotope Stage II.
*Geology; Geophysics; Climatology.*

**MISD stream** Multiple-Instruction, Single-Data stream.
*Computer Technology.*

**MISFET** Metal- Insulator-Semiconductor Field-Effect Transistor.

**MISLIC** Mid-Staffordshire Libraries in Co-operation.

**MISPEC** merit of individual system performance characteristics.

valeur des caractéristiques fonctionnelles des systèmes pris individuellement.
**MISR** Multi-angle Imaging Spectrometer.
**MISREP** mission report.
compte rendu (ou rapport) de mission).
**Miss.** (abbr.) Mississippi (U.S.A.).
Also: **MS**.
**MISSUM** mission summary.
synthèse de mission.
**MISTI** Multipurpose International Securities Trading Information.
**MISURC** Mosaico Informatizzato degli Strumenti Urbanistici Comunali (Italy).
**MIT** Massachusetts Institute of Technology (U.S.A.).
**MIT** Master Instruction Tape.
Master Instruction Tape is also known as: Master Program File.
*Computer Programming.*
**MIT** Modern Investment Theory.
*Business; Economics; Finance.*
**MIT** Monoiodotyrosine.
*Endocrinology.*
**MIT** Municipal Investment Trust.
**MITBASE** MITochondrial data BASE - E.C.
**MITER**; **Miter** Materiali Innovativi e TEcnologie Relative (Italy).
Istituto Nazionale di Coordinamento Materiali - CNR.
Italian acronym meaning: Innovative Materials and Relevant Technologies.
Of the Italian National Research Council.
**MITEs** Miniature Inverted-repeat Transposable Elements.
*Rice Nuclear Genome.*
**MITES** Minority Introduction to Engineering, Entrepreneurship, and Science (U.S.A.).
**MITI** Ministry of International Trade and Industry (Japan).
MITI was established in 1987.
**MI transition** Metal-Insulator transition.
*Astrophysics; Chemistry; Physics.*
**MITS** Mechatronic Invasive Tools for Surgery.
**mitt.** (abbr.) mittente.
Italian abbreviation meaning: addresser; forwarder; sender.
**MIUS** Modular Integrated Utility System.
**MIUU** Meteorological Institute of the University of Uppsala (Sweden).
**MIWC** see MWC.
voir MWC.
**MIZ** Marginal Ice Zone.
**MIZEX** Marginal Ice Zone EXperiment.
**MJD** Management Job Description.
**MJLC** 1. multinational joint logistic centre.
1. centre logistique interarmées multinational.
2. multinational joint logistic commander.
2. commandant logistique interarmées multinational.
**MJO** Madden-Julian Oscillation.
A 30/60 day wave in the atmosphere originating over the Indian Ocean.
Named after the researchers who discovered it about 35 years ago.
*Atmospheric Science; Climatology; Geophysics; Meteorology; Oceanography.*
**MJR** MJ Research - MA, U.S.A.
*Peltier-effect; Thermal Cyclers.*
**MJSD** March, June, September, December.
*Securities.*
**mk.** Mark.
Now: EURO/EUR (€). Became ECU (European single currency) with effect from January 2002.
*Currencies.*
**MKBS** Medical Knowledge-Based Systems.
*Medicine.*
**MKC** The airport code for Downtown Kansas City Airport, Kansas City, Missouri, U.S.A.
**mkr** (abbr.) maker.
**MKS**; **M.K.S.** meter-kilogram-second.
Also: **mks**; **m.k.s**.
**MKSA**; **mksa system** meter-kilogram-second-ampere system.
*Metrology.*
**mkt.** (abbr.) market.
**ML** 1. Mali.
1. Mali.
2. Multi-Layer (defence).
2. (défense) multicouche.
**ML** maximum likelihood.
Bayesian method to analyze DNA sequences.
**ML** Medieval Latin.
*Languages.*
**mL** millilambert.
**ml** millilitre / milliliter.
**ML** Monolayer.
Monolayer is also known as: Monofilm; Molecular Film; Monomolecular Film.
*Physical Chemistry.*
**m/l** more or less.
**ML** Motor Launch.
**MLA** Manitoba Library Association (Canada).
**MLA** Maryland Library Association (U.S.A.).
**MLA**; **Mla** Master Licence Agreement.
*Netware.*
**MLA** mean line of advance.

1a. axe moyen de progression.
1b. route moyenne.
**MLA** Medical Library Association.
**MLA** Michigan Library Association (U.S.A.).
**MLA** Minnesota Library Association (U.S.A.).
**MLA** Missouri Library Association (U.S.A.).
**MLA** Modern Language Association.
**MLA** Montana Library Association (U.S.A.).
**MLA** Music Library Association.
**MLAJ** Music Library Association of Japan.
**MLAP** Multilingual Action Plan - E.C.
**MLAT** Mutual Legal Assistant Treaty.
**MLB** Multilayer Board.
**MLB** multinational logistics base.
base logistique multinationale.
**MLB** The airport code for Melbourne, Florida, U.S.A.
**MLBT** mobile land battle target.
objectif terrestre mobile.
**MLC** Member of Legislative Council.
**MLC** Michigan Library Consortium (U.S.A.).
**MLC** military load classification.
1a. classement militaire.
1b. classification des ponts et véhicules.
**MLC** Mixed Leukocyte Culture; Mixed Lymphocyte Culture.
*Medicine.*
**MLC** Myosin Light Chain.
*Internal Medicine; Science and Technology; Signal Transduction.*
**MLC-1A expression** Myosin Light Chain-1A expression.
*Cardiac Morphogenesis and Myogenesis; Cardiology; Cell Biology; Internal Medicine; Molecular Biology; Oncology.*
**MLCNY** Medical Library Center of New York (U.S.A.).
**MLCT** Metal-to-Ligand Charge Transfer.
**MLD**; **M.L.D.** Median Lethal Dose.
*Pharmacology; Virology.*
*Military Science* - Regarding exposure of personnel to nuclear radiation or chemical agents.
*Toxicology* - MLD is also known as: Toxin Unit; Toxic Unit.
**MLD** Mixed-Layer Depth.
*Geology; Oceanography.*
**ML dome** Mallard Lake dome.
**MLE** Maximum-Likelihood-Estimatiom.
**MLE** Muconate Lactonizing Enzyme.
MLE is an enzyme involved in benzoate catabolism.
*Basic Medical Science; Biochemistry; Molecular Genetics; Pharmaceutical Chemistry; Pharmacy.*
**MLEs** *Mariner*-Like Elements.
The *mariner* elements in animals are collectively known as: *Mariner*-Like Elements.
*Microbiology; Organismic and Evolutionary Biology.*
**MLF** multilateral force.
force multilatérale.
**MLGH** Medical Library Group of Hawaii.
**MLGSCA** Medical Library Group of Southern California and Arizona (U.S.A.).
**MLIS programme** Multilingual Information Society programme.
*European Community Program.*
**MLKs** Mixed Lineage Kinases.
*Biological Chemistry; Signal Transduction.*
**Mlle** Mademoiselle.
meaning: Miss in French.
**M.LL.PP.** Ministero dei Lavori Pubblici (Italy).
Italian initialism of the: Ministry of Public Works.
**MLM** Military Liaison Office (Moscow).
Mission de liaison militaire (à Moscou).
**MLN** Mesenteric Lymph Nodes.
*Medicine.*
**MLNC** Missouri Library Network Corporation.
**MLNSC** Manuel Lujan Jr. Neutron Scattering Center (U.S.A.).
The Manuel Lujan Jr. Neutron Scattering Center is at Los Alamos National Laboratory's Neutron Science Center accelerator facility.
*Neutron Science.*
**MLO** Mauna LOa - Hawaii.
**MLO** military liaison officer.
officier de liaison militaire.
**MLP** Major Late Promoter.
*Biomedical Research; Biology.*
**MLP** Master Limited Partnership (U.S.A.).
*Finance.*
**MLP** Murein Lipoprotein.
**MLPB** montant limite du projet de budget.
budget submission figure (BSF).
**MLPS** Ministero del Lavoro e della Previdenza Sociale (Italy).
Italian initialism of the: Ministry of Labour and Social Security.
**MLR** Main Line of Resistance.
*Military Science.*
**MLR** Minimum Lending Rate.
*Banking.*
**MLR** Ministry of Land and Resources (China).
**MLR** Mixed Lymphocyte Reaction.
MLR is also known as: Mixed Leukocyte Reaction.
*Immunology.*

**MLR** Multiple Linear Regression.
*Antarctic Research; Marine Research; Atmospheric and Oceanic Sciences.*
**MLRS** multiple-launch rocket system.
lance-roquettes multiple (LRM).
**MLRV** Myrobolan Latent Ring Spot Virus.
*Fruit Pathology; Fruits Research.*
**MLS** Master Lab Station.
**MLS** Microwave Landing System.
*Navigation.*
**MLS** multi-level security.
sécurité multiniveau.
**MLSB** multinational logistic support base.
base de soutien logistique multinationale.
**MLSP** Maximum Life Span Potential.
For further details see under: **MLSPs**.
**MLSPs** Maximum Life Span Potentials.
*Biology; Physiology.*
**MLST** Multilocus Sequence Typing.
*Biological Sciences; Clinical Laboratory Sciences; Clinical Medicine; Epidemiology of Infections Diseases; Tropical Medicine; Staphylococcus aurens Disease.*
**MLT** mean lifetime.
durée de vie moyenne.
**MLT** Medical Laboratory Technician.
**MLTA** Manitoba Library Trustees Association (Canada).
**ML tree** Maximum Likelihood tree.
**MLU** mid-life update (or upgrade).
modernisation à mi-vie.
**MLV** Mottle Leaf Virus.
*Fruit Pathology; Fruits Research.*
**MLW** Mean Low Water.
*Oceanography.*
**mm.** made merchantable.
**M.M.** Magazzini.
Italian initialism meaning: stores; warehouses.
**MM** Marketing Mix.
**M.M.** Master Mason.
**M.M.** Master Mechanic.
**MM** Memory Management.
*Computer Technology.*
**MM** Memory Model.
*Artificial Intelligence.*
**M.M.** Mercantile Marine.
**MM** Mesoscale Model.
**MM** Messieurs.
meaning: Messrs.; Gentlemen in French.
**MM** Metropolitana Milanese (Italy).
Italian initialism of the: *Milan Subway.*
**MM** Middle Management.
**MM** Military Medal.
**MM** military mission.
mission militaire.
**mm.**; **mm** millimeter / millimetre.
*Metrology.*
**mM** millimolar.
**M.M.** Money Market.
**M.M.** Mucous Membrane.
*Histology.*
**MM** Multiple Myeloma.
MM is a cancerous growth of plasma cells in bone marrow and bone tissue which can spread to other tissues.
*Cancer; Medicine.*
**MM** The mariner's mirror.
**MMA** Methylmalonic Acidemia.
MMA is a recessive genetic disorder of amino acid metabolism.
**MMA** Methyl Methacrylate.
*Organic Chemistry.*
**MMA** Millimeter Array (U.S.A.).
MMA is a U.S. project (1998).
*Millimeter-Wave Astronomy.*
**Mma** Money market account.
**MMA** Monomethyl Aniline.
**MMA** Monomethylarsonic Acid.
**MMAC1** Mutated in Multiple Advanced Cancers.
*Cancer Research; Cell Biology; Gliomas; Molecular Biology; Tumor Suppressors.*
**MMAJ** Metal Mining Agency of Japan.
**MMBR** Microbiology and Molecular Biology Reviews (U.S.A.).
Of the American Society for Microbiology.
**MMC** Marine Mammal Commission.
**MMC** MERCOMMS management centre.
centre de gestion du MERCOMMS.
**MMC** Mitomycin C.
*Clinical Genetics; Fanconi Anemia; Medical Genetics; Medicine; Oncology; Pathology; Pediatrics.*
**MMC** Money Market Certificate.
*Business; Finance.*
**MMC** Monopolies and Mergers Commission (U.S.A.).
**MMCT** Metal-Metal Charge Transfer.
**MMCT technique** Microcell-Mediated Chromosome Transfer technique.
**Mme** Madame.
meaning: Mrs.; Madam in French.
**MME** Master of Mechanical Engineering.
**MME** Master of Medical Education.
**MME** Mouse Molecular Embryology.
**MME** Multi Mode Electrode.
**mmf** magnetomotive force.

*Electromagnetism.*
**mmf** micromicrofarad.
**MMF** mission militaire française.
French military mission /FMM/.
**MMF** Money Market Fund.
*Business & Finance.*
**MM.GG.** Magazzini Generali (Italy).
Italian initialism meaning: Bonded Warehouse.
*Customs.*
**MMHS** military message handling system.
système militaire de manipulation des messages.
**MMI** man-machine interface.
interface homme-machine.
**MMLV-RT** Moloney Murine Leukemia Virus - Reverse Transcriptase.
**MMM** Mesoscale and Micro-scale Meteorology.
**MMM**; **M.M.M.** Ministero della Marina Mercantile; Ministère de la Marine Marchande.
Italian and French initialism of the: Ministry of Merchant Navy / Shipping.
**MMMC** Minimum Monthly Maintenance Charge.
**MMN** Mismatch Negativity.
*Neurophysiology; Otolaryngology.*
**MMO** Methane Monooxygenase.
*Biochemistry; Enzymology; Molecular Biology.*
**MMOMS** Multi-Modality Organ Modelling System.
**MMOU** multilateral memorandum of understanding.
mémorandum d'entente multilatéral.
**MMP** Magnetotactic Many-celled Prokaryote.
MMP is a morphological type of magnetotactic bacteria.
*Biochemistry; Chemistry; Geology; Immunology; Magnetotactic Bacteria; Medicine; Microbiology; Physics; Preventive Medicine.*
**MMPA** Marine Mammal Protection Act (U.S.A.).
**MMP cancers** Microsatellite Mutator Phenotype cancers.
*Cancer Research.*
**MMP family** Matrix Metalloproteinase family.
*Anatomy; Medicine.*
**MMPI** Minnesota Multiphasic Personality Inventory.
The MMPI is a test used for personality assessment.
*Psychology.*
**MMPP** Mitochondrial Matrix Processing Peptidase.
*Biochemsitry; Medicine; Molecular Biology.*
**MMPs** Matrix Metalloproteinases.
The MMPs are involved in remodeling extracellular matrix.
*Aging; Neurodegenerative Diseases.*
**MMR** Methyl-directed Mismatched Repair.
*Molecular Biology; Mutator Phenotypes.*
**MMR** minimum military requirement.
besoin militaire minimum.
**MMR vaccination** Measles-Mumps-Rubella vaccination.
The MMR vaccination is used for the immunization of children.
*Immunology.*
**MMS** Methyl Methane Sulfonate.
**MMS** Minerals Management Service (U.S.A.).
**MMS** minimum manning strength.
effectifs minimums.
**MMS** Multimedia Messaging Service.
**M.M.Sc.** Master of Medical Science.
**MMSDs** Multiple Minor Symptoms Days.
**MMSP** Modelling in Materials Science and Processing.
**MMT** Multiple Mirror Telescope.
**MMTV** Murine Mammary Tumor Virus.
*Medicine; Pathology; Virology.*
**MMTV-LTR** Mouse Mammary Tumor Virus; Murine Mammary Tumor Virus - Long Terminal Repeat.
*Medicine; Oncology; Virology.*
**MMTV/v-Ha-ras** Mouse Mammary Tumor Virus / Harvey viral ras.
*Gene Expression; Receptor Biology.*
**MMU** Mass-Memory Unit.
*Computer Technology.*
**MMU** mobile meteorological unit.
unité météorologique mobile.
**MMV project** Medicines for Malaria Venture project.
The MMV project is developed by WHO.
*Malaria Research; Venture Capital Funds.*
For further details see under: **WHO**.
**MMW**; **Mmw** Make Multilanguage Web.
*Online Services.*
**MMWR** Morbidity and Mortality Weekly Report (U.S.A.).
A publication of the U.S. Centers for Disease Control and Prevention Atlanta, U.S.A.
**MN** Magnetic North.
*Geophysics.*
**Mn** The chemical symbol for Manganese.
*Chemistry.*
*Metallurgy* - used as an alloying element.
**MN** Mantova, Italy.
**MN** Master of Nursing.
*Medicine.*
**MN** Merchant Navy.
**MN** (abbr.) métanéphrine.

French initialism meaning: metanephrine.
*Biochemistry.*
**MN** (abbr.) Minnesota (U.S.A.).
Also: **Minn.**
**MN** Monaco.
**M/N**; **Mn**; **M/n** Motonave.
Italian initialism meaning: motor ship / boat; steamship.
**MN** Motor Neuron / Motoneuron.
*Physiology.*
**MN**; **Mn** multinational.
**MNA region** Middle east and North Africa region.
**MNATF** multinational amphibious task force.
force opérationnelle amphibie multinationale.
**MNAU** million NATO accounting units.
million d'unité de compte de l'OTAN.
**MNB** Moscow Narodny Bank.
Incorporated in the City of London since 1919.
*Corporate Finance; Project Finance; Russian Bank.*
**MNB** multinational brigade.
brigade multinationale /BMN/.
**$MnB_4O_7$** Manganese Borate.
Used mainly as a varnish.
*Inorganic Chemistry.*
**MNBT** mobile naval battle target.
objectif naval mobile.
**MNC** Major NATO Command (Commander) [obsolete - replaced by SC].
Grand Commandement (commandant) de l'OTAN /GCO/ [obsolète - remplacé par SC].
**$MnCl_2$** Scacchite.
*Mineralogy.*
**MNCN** Museo Nacional de Ciencias Naturales.
Spanish initialism of the: Spanish Natural History Museum.
The MNCN was founded in 1772 by King Charles III. It is located in downtown Madrid and has the most important natural history collections in Spain.
**$MnCO_3$** Manganese Carbonate.
$MnCO_3$ is used mainly as a food additive.
*Inorganic Chemistry.*
**$Mn^{+2}CO_3$** Rhodochrosite.
**MNCs** Mediterranean Non-member Countries.
**MNCs** Mononuclear Cells.
*Biology; Biophysics; Cell Biology; Medicine; Microbiology; Pathology.*
**MNCs** Multinational Corporations.
MNCs use dividend remittances and payments of royalty and engineering charges to measure their subsidiaries' cash flows, but measure operational cash flows differently for management evaluation purposes. Consistent with the provisions of SFAS N° 52, companies should revise their definition of cash flow to account for exchange rate movements and periodically adjust cash flows from investment base by the current translation adjustment residing in equity.
*Cash Flow.*
**MND** 1. mission need document.
1a. document énonçant les besoins de la mission.
1b. expression (ou énoncé) des besoins de la mission.
2. multinational division.
2. division multinationale /DMN/.
**MND** Motor Neuron Disease.
A common neurodegenerative disease.
*Cancer Research; Neurology; Neuropathology.*
**MN DDP** multinational detailed deployment plan.
plan de déploiement détaillé multinational.
**MNDO** Modified Neglect of Differential Overlap.
*Biochemistry; Chemistry; Optoelectronic Computing Systems; Physics.*
**MNEs** Multinational Enterprises.
**MNF** Métaux Non Ferreux.
French initialism meaning: nonferrous metals.
**MNF** multinational force.
force multinationale.
**$MnF_3$** Manganic Fuoride.
$MnF_3$ is also known as: Manganese Fluoride; Manganese Trifluoride.
*Inorganic Chemistry.*
**MN frequency** Micronucleus frequency.
*Human Nutrition.*
**mnfrs.** (abbr.) manufacturers.
**mng.** (abbr.) managing.
**MNGIE** Mitochondrial Neurogastrointestinal Encephalomyopathy.
The MNGIE is an autosomal recessive human disease.
*Gastrointestinal Dysmotility; Leukoencephalopathy; Myopathy; Ophthalmoplegia; Peripheral Neuropathy.*
**MNI** Mononucléose Infectieuse.
French initialism meaning: Infectious Monucleosis.
*Medicine.*
**MNL** The airport code for Manila, Philippines.
**MNLC** 1. maritime NATO logistic concept.
1. concept maritime de la logistique de l'OTAN.
2. multinational logistic command (commander).
2. commandement (commandant) logistique multinational.
**MNLC(A)** multinational logistic centre (air).
centre logistique multinational (air).

**MNLC(L)** multinational logistic centre (land).
centre logistique multinational (terre).
**MNLC(M)** multinational logistic centre (maritime).
centre logistique multinational (mer).
**MNMF** multinational maritime force.
force maritime multinationale.
**$MnO_2$** Manganese Dioxide.
Also known as: Manganese Black; Manganese Peroxide, is used mainly in batteries and matches.
**$Mn_2O_3$** Manganic Oxide.
*Inorganic Chemistry.*
**$Mn_2O_7$** Manganese Heptoxide.
*Inorganic Chemistry.*
**MNOS** Metal-Nitride Oxide Semiconductor.
*Solid-State Physics.*
**MNP** Microcom Network Protocol.
*Modems.*
**MNRAS** Monthy Notices of the Royal Astronomical Society.
**MNRF** Mexican National Research Foundation.
Established in March 1995. It is based in Mexico City.
**$Mn^{+2}S$** Alabandite.
*Mineralogy.*
**MnS** Manganous Sulfide.
MnS is used in the steel manufacturing industry.
*Inorganic Chemistry.*
**$MnS_2$** Hauerite.
*Mineralogy.*
**MNSE** multinational support element.
élément de soutien multinational.
**MnSOD** Manganese - Superoxide Dismutase.
**MNZ** Merino New Zealand.
*Research, Development & Marketing Organization.*
**MO** Magnetooptic; Magneooptical.
*Optics.*
**MO** Magnetorestrictive Oscillator.
*Electronics.*
**M.O.** Mail Order.
**MO** Mars Observer.
**MO** Massima Occupazione.
**MO** Master Oscillator.
*Electronics.*
**M.O.** Medical Officer.
**MO** Medio Oriente.
Italian acronym meaning: Middle East.
**Mo** Mega-octet.
*Electronics;* Megabyte in French.
**m/o** mio ordine.
Italian initialism meaning: my order.
**MO**; **Mo.** (abbr.) Missouri (U.S.A.).
**MO** Modena, Italy.
**Mo** The chemical symbol for Molybdenum.
Molybdenum is used mainly in resistors and audio magnets.
*Chemistry; Symbols.*
**M.O.** Money Order.
**mo.** (abbr.) month.
**MO** Moral Obligation.
*Business; Commerce; Finance.*
**MO** Morocco.
**MOA** Memorandum Of Agreement.
**MOB** Main Olfactory Bulb.
*Brain Science; Chemosensory Receptors; Medicine; Neurobiology of Synapse; Neuronal Recognition Molecules; Odorant Receptors; Olfaction; Physiology.*
**MOB** 1. main operating base.
1. base d'opérations principale.
2. maritime order of battle.
2. ordre de bataille Mer.
3. see MORBAT.
3. voir MORBAT.
**MOB** Methane-Oxidizing Bacteria.
*Microbiology; Microbial Ecology.*
**MOBEX** mobility exercise.
exercice de mobilité.
**MOBS** multiple orbital bombardment system.
système de bombardement multiple orbital.
**M.O.C.** Mineralometria Ossea Computerizzata.
**MOC** Ministry Of Construction.
**MOCN** Machine Outil à Commande Numérique.
**MOCNESS** Multiple Opening-Closing Net and Environmental Sensing System.
**MOC strength** (Atlantic) Meridional Overturning Circulation strength.
For further details see under: **WOCE**.
**MOCVD** Metal-Organic Chemical Vapor Deposition.
MOCVD is a semiconductor fabrication technique.
**MOD** Ministry Of Defence.
**mod.** (abbr.) model.
**MODE** Merchant-Oriented Data Entry.
**MODE** Mid-Ocean Dynamics Experiment.
**mode** The above acronyms were coined using the English word "mode".
*Archaeology; Computer Programming; Computer Technology; Electromagnetism; Petrology; Physics; Statistics; Telecommunications.*
**MODEM** (abbr.) MOdulator-DEModulator.
*Electronics.*
**ModGk** Modern Greek.
Modern Greek, also called New Greek, is the Greek language since c1500.
*Languages.*

**ModHeb** Modern Hebrew.
Modern Hebrew is the living language of Israel. It is a revised version of ancient Hebrew.
*Languages.*
**MODIO** conference of information officials in Ministries of Defence.
conférence des responsables de l'information des ministères de la Défense.
**MODY** Maturity-Onset Diabetes of Youth.
*Epidemiology; Genetics; Medicine.*
**MOE** Main d'Oeuvre Etrangère.
**MOE** Measure Of Effectiveness.
**MOE** Milanfair Overseas Exhibition.
**MOE** Multiple Of Earnings.
*Economics; Finance.*
**MOF** Ministry Of Finance (Japan).
**MOF** Multi-Option Facility.
**MoFe** Molibdenum Iron.
**M of F** Ministry of Food.
**MOFs** Metalorganic Frameworks.
*Chemical Engineering; Materials Science.*
**MOFTEC**; **Moftec** Ministry Of Foreign Trade and Economic Cooperation (China).
**MOG** Myelin Oligodendrocyte Glycoprotein.
*Autoimmune Diseases; Immunology; Neuroimmunology; Neurology; Pathology.*
**MOH** Medical Officer of Health.
**MOH** Ministry Of Health.
**MOHAVE Study** Measurement Of Haze And Visual Effects Study.
**MOI** Memorandum Of Intent.
**MOI** Ministry Of Information; Ministry Of the Interior.
**MOI** Multiplicity of Infection.
*Virology.*
**MOIC** military oceanographic intelligence centre.
centre de renseignement océanographique militaire.
**MOIC** MOvimento Italiano Casalinghe (Italy).
Italian acronym meaning: Italian Housewives Movement.
Also: **Moica**.
**MOL** Manned Orbiting Laboratory.
**MOL** Margine Operativo Lordo.
Italian acronym meaning: Gross Operational Margin.
**MOL** Muscle Of Lawrence (of male flies).
*Developmental Genetics; Genetics.*
**MOLA** Mars Orbiter Laser Altimeter.
An instrument aboard the Mars Global Surveyor spacecraft - MOLA arrived at Mars on 12th September 1997.
*Earth, Atmospheric and Planetary Sciences; Geology; Geophysics; Space Research; Terrestrial Magnetism.*
**MOLA map** Mars Orbiter Laser Altimeter map.
*Martian Topography.*
For further details see under: **MOLA**.
**molc** molar concentration.
**MOLD** Methylglyoxal-Lysine Dimer.
**MOM** Microsoft Office Manager.
**MOM** Modular Ocean Model.
**MOMENTS** MObile Media and ENTertainment Services.
*European Community Project.*
**MOMI**; **Momi** Museum of Moving Image (G.B.).
Re-opened in 2003.
**MoMLV** Moloney Murine Leukemia Virus.
*Medicine; Endocrinology.*
**MOMS** Manganese Oxide Mesaporous Structures.
*Chemical Engineering; Chemistry; Materials Science.*
**MOMUSYS** (abbr.) MObile MUltimedia SYStems.
*European Community Project.*
**Mon.** (abbr.) Monday.
**mon.** (abbr.) monetary.
**mon.** (abbr.) monitor.
For further details see under: **m**.
**MONEX** (abbr.) MONsoon EXperiment.
**MONICA** multinational MONitoring of trends and determinants In CArdiovascular disease - *European Community.*
**MONOCEPT** Monocrystalline Silicon Solar Cell Cost Effective Production Technology.
**Mont.** (abbr.) Montana (U.S.A.).
**Montr.** (abbr.) Montreal (Canada).
**$MoO_2$** Molybdenum Dioxide.
$MoO_2$ is used to make pigments.
*Inorganic Chemistry.*
**$MoO_3$** Molybdenum Trioxide.
$MoO_3$, also known as: Molybdenum Anhydride, is a toxic powder.
*Inorganic Chemistry.*
**$MoO_3$** Molybdite.
Molybdite is also known as: Molybdic Ocher; Molybdine.
*Mineralogy.*
**MOON** Management Of Optical Networks.
*European Community Project.*
**MOOTW** military operations other than war.
opérations militaires autres que celles de guerre.
**MOP** Maintenance Operation Protocol.
**MOP** Margin Of Profit.
*Business & Finance.*
**mop** (abbr.) molybdopterin.
**MOPA** Master Oscillator Power Amplifier.

**MOPA** Methoxyphenyl-Acetic Acid.
**MOPITT** Measurements Of Pollution In The Troposphere.
*Environmental Technology; Medicine; Science.*
**MOPL** MOvimento Primo Lavoro (Italy).
**MOPP** Mechanization Of Planning Processes.
**MOPRB** Manpower and Organization Policy Review Board.
Commission d'examen de la politique en matière de personnel et d'organisation.
**MOR** military operational requirement.
besoin militaire opérationnel.
**MORB** Mid-Ocean Ridge Basalt.
For further details see under: **MORBs**.
**MORBAT** missile order of battle.
ordre de bataille des missiles.
**MORBs** Mid-Ocean Ridge Basalts.
*Astronomy; Earth Sciences; Geochemistry; Geophysics; Planetary Sciences.*
**MORF4** MORtality Factor from chromosome 4.
*Cell Biology.*
**MORI** Market & Opinion Research International.
**MORL** Manned Orbiting Research Laboratory.
**MORO** Moon ORbiting Observatory (U.S.A.).
A proposed mission that lost the competition (1996).
**MORPs** Mid-Ocean Ridge Peridotites.
*Astronomy; Earth Sciences; Geochemistry; Geophysics; Planetary Sciences.*
**MORs** Mid-Ocean Ridges.
*Oceanography.*
**MORTREP** mortaring (or mortar firing) report.
compte rendu de tir de mortier.
**MOS** Management Operating System.
**MOS** Margin Of Safety.
*Business; Finance.*
**MOS** Marine Observation Satellite.
**MOS** Metal Oxide Semiconductor.
*Solid-State Physics.*
**MOS** minimum operating strip.
piste opérationnelle minimale.
**mos.** (abbr.) months.
**$MoS_2$** Molybdenite.
*Mineralogy.*
**$MoS_2$** Molybdenum Disulfide.
$MoS_2$, also known as: Molybdic Sulfide; Molybdenum Sulfide, is used mainly as a catalyst and lubricant.
*Inorganic Chemistry.*
**MOSFET** Metal-Oxide-Semiconductor Fiel-Effect Transistor.
The MOSFET consists of source and drain electrodes and a gate electrode.
*Applied Physics; Electrical and Computer Engineering.*
**MOSFET** Metal-Oxide-Semiconductor Floating Electrode Transistor.
*Electronics; Nanoengineering.*
**MOSFETs** Metal-Oxide-Semiconductor Field-Effect Transistors.
For further details see under: **MOSFET**.
**mOsm** milliosmole.
**MOSS** Market Oversight Surveillance System.
**MOST** Management Operation System Technique.
**MOST** Metal Oxide Semiconductor Transistor.
**MOST** Ministry Of Science and Technology (Korea).
**MOSTE** Ministry Of Science, Technology, and the Environment (Malaysia).
**MOT** Mercato delle Obbligazioni e dei Titoli di Stato (Italy).
*Banking; Finance.*
**MOT** Middle Of Target.
*Military.*
**mot.** motore.
Italian abbreviation meaning: motor, engine.
**MOT apparatus** Magneto-Optic Trap apparatus.
*Physics.*
**MO theory** Molecular Orbital theory.
**MOTS** military off-the-shelf.
militaire sur étagère (ou militaire standard).
**MOU** memorandum of understanding.
mémorandum d'entente.
**MOUSE** Minimum Orbital Unmanned Satellite of Earth.
**mouse** The above acronym was coined using the English word "mouse".
*Computer Technology; Vertebrate Zoology.*
**MOUTH** Modular Output Unit for Talking to Humans.
**mouth** The above acronym was coined using the English word "mouth".
*Anatomy; Acoustical Engineering; Geography; Mining Engineering; Zoology.*
**MOVEREP** movement report.
compte rendu de mouvements.
**MOVEX** movement exercise.
exercice de mouvements.
**MOVREP** see MOVEREP.
voir MOVEREP.
**MOVs** Metal Oxide Varistors.
**MOVSITREP** movement situation report.
compte rendu de situation des mouvements.
**MOVSUMREP** movement summary report.
compte rendu de synthèse des mouvements.
**MOX fuels** Mixed OXide fuels.

**MOZAIC program** Measurement OZone by Airbus-In-Service Aircraft program.
*Atmospheric Chemistry.*
**MP** Mail Payment.
*Commerce.*
**MP** Mammillary Protrusions.
**M.P.** Marginal Product.
**MP** Market Price.
*Commerce.*
**MP** Materia Plastica; Materiale Plastico.
Italian initialism meaning: plastic material.
**MP** Mathematical Programming.
**MP** maximum parsimony.
Bayesian method to analyze DNA sequences.
**MP** Mediocredito Piemontese (Italy).
*Banks.*
**m.p.** melting point.
*Thermodynamics.*
**MP**; **M.P.** Member of Parliament (G.B.).
**MP** Memory Protection.
*Computer Programming; Computer Technology.*
**MP**; **M.P.** Metropolitan Police.
**mp** microprocessor; multiprocessing.
*Computer Technology.*
**mp** microprogram.
*Computer Programming.*
**MP** Military Police.
**M.P.** Months after Payment.
**mp** multiprocessor.
Multiprocessor is also known as: multiprocessing system.
*Computer Technology.*
**MP** 3-Methylpentane.
3-Methylpentane is used mainly as a solvent.
*Organic Chemistry.*
**MPA** maritime patrol aircraft.
avion de patrouille maritime /PATMAR/.
**MPA** NATO Marine Patrol Aircraft.
**MPA** Marine Protected Area.
**MPAs** Marine Protected Areas.
**M.P.&C.** Management Planning and Control.
**MP applications** Multiprocessing applications.
**MPAs** Marine Protected Areas.
**MPB** Mobilization of Stem Cells to Blood.
*Development Biology; Pathology; Stem Cell Research.*
**MPC** 1. main planning conference.
1. conférence de planification principale.
2. message processing centre.
2. centre de traitement des messages.
**MPC** Man Process Chart.
**MPC** Marginal Propensity to Consume.
*Business; Finance.*
**MPC** Mathematics of Program Construction.
**MPC** Maximum Permissible Concentration.
MPC is also known as: Maximum Allowable Concentration.
*Medicine; Radiation.*
**MPC** Medial Premotor Cortex.
The MPC is a region of the brain mainly involved in preparing body movements but, according to research being carried out, it could be involved in sensory processing.
*Neuroscience.*
**MPC&A systems** Modern Materials Protection, Control, and Accounting systems.
**M-Pc complexes** Metallo-Phthalocyanine complexes.
*Applied Physics; Molecular Photochemistry; Nanophotonic Materials; Physical and Chemical Research; Quantum Electronics.*
**MPCs** Monolayer-Protected metal Clusters.
*Chemistry; Nanoparticles; Physics.*
**MPCs** Multimedia PCs.
**MPCS** multiple payload communications satellite.
satellite de télécommunications à charge utile multiple.
**MPCVD** Microwave Plasma-assisted Chemical Vapor Deposition.
Used to grow TGCs.
For further details see under: **TGCs**.
**MPD** Maximum Permissible Dose.
*Medicine* - Referring to the maximum radiation exposure of a person.
*Military Science* - Referring to the highest amount of radiation that military personnel can withstand.
**MPE** Maximum Possible Exposure (referring to radiation for man safety).
**MPE** mesures de protection électronique.
electronic protective measures /EPM/.
**MPE** Mission to Planet Earth.
MPE is also known as: **MTPE** (Mission To Planet Earth).
**MPEG**; **Mpeg** Moving Picture Expert Group.
*Digital TV.*
**MPers** Middle Persian.
*Languages.*
**MPF** Mandatory Provident Fund (Hong Kong).
*Pension Schemes.*
**MPF** Maturation Promoting Factor.
The MPF stimulates cell division in frog eggs.
*Basic Research; Cell Division Mechanisms; Zoology.*
**MPF** M Phase Promoting Factor.
*Biology.*
**MPF** multinational protection force.

force de protection multinationale.
**MPFSEE** Multinational Peace Force South-Eastern Europe.
Force multinationale de paix pour l'Europe du Sud-Est.
**MPFT** French-Chadian Paleoanthropological Mission.
**MPG** moyen polyvalent du génie.
multi-purpose engineer vehicle.
**MPH** Master of Public Health.
Also: **M.P.H**.
**Mphil** Master of Philosophy.
**mphps** miles per hour per second.
**MPI** Mannose Phosphate Isomerase.
**MPI** Marginal Prosperity to Invest.
*Business; Finance.*
**MPI** Marine Pollution Incident.
**MPI** Maximum Potential Intensity.
*Hurricanes.*
**MPI** Mean Point of Impact.
MPI is also known as: Center of Burst.
*Ordnance.*
**M.P.I.** Ministero della Pubblica Istruzione.
Italian initialism of the: Ministry of Education (Italy).
**MPIA** Max-Planck-Institut für Astronomie (Heidelberg, (Germany).
The MPIA runs the Calar Alto Observatory in Southern Spain.
**MPIF** Message Passing Interface Forum.
**MPIM** Max-Planck Institut für Meteorologie (Germany).
**MPL** Mars Polar Lander.
*Planetary Science.*
**MPL** Maximum Permissible Level.
*Medicine; Radiation.*
**MPL**; **mpl** motivated productivity level.
**MPL** Movimento Politico Lavoratori.
*Italian Movements.*
**MPL** Multischedule Private Line.
**MPM**; **mpm** meters per minute.
Also: **m.p.m**.
**MPM** Mid-Pacific Mountains.
**MPMG technique** Melt-Powder Melt-Growth technique.
**MPMS** mission planning and monitoring system.
système de planification et de suivi de mission.
**MPNAs** Modified Peptide Nucleic Acids.
*Genetics & Development.*
**MPN test** Most Probable Number test.
*Microbiology.*
**MPO** Metropolitan Planning Organization.
**MPO** Myeloperoxidase.
Myeloperoxidase is also known as: Verdoperoxidase.
*Biochemistry; Microbial Infections.*
**MPOs** Metropolitan Planning Organizations.
**MPP** Mitochondrial Processing Peptidase.
*Biochemistry; Life Science; Molecular Bioenergetics; Molecular Biology.*
**MPP architecture** Massively Parallel Processor architecture.
MPP architecture links together independent processors, each of which has its own memory, disks and operating systems.
*Computer Science.*
**MPPC** Multipotent Hematopoietic Progenitor Cell.
**MP2 perturbation theory** second-order Møller-Plesset perturbation theory.
*Chemistry.*
**MPPs** Multipotent Progenitors.
*Developmental Biology; Pathology; Stem Cell research.*
**MPQ** McGill Pain Questionnaire.
*Medicine; Neurogenetics; Psychiatry.*
**MPR** Monthly Program Review.
**MPS** Maintenance Painting Service.
**MPS** Marginal Propensity to Save.
*Economics.*
**MPS** Massive Parallel Systems.
**MPS** Materials Processing in Space.
Experiments of materials processing in space were conducted by NASA, ever since the late 1960s.
**MPS** Mathematical Programming Society.
**MPS** Mathematics and Physical Sciences.
**MPS** Median Period of Survival.
**MPS** mission planning system.
système de planification de mission.
**MPS** Monte dei Paschi di Siena (Italy).
Founded in 1472.
*Banks.*
**MPS** Multipurpose Ship.
*U.S. Navy.*
**MPSM** Master in Public Sector Management.
**MPSV** Myeloproliferative Sarcoma Virus.
**MPT** Ministry of Post and Telecommunications (China).
**MPT** Modern Portfolio Theory.
*Business; Finance.*
**MPTP** 1-Methyl-4-Phenyl-1,2,3,6-Tetrahydropyridine.
**MPU** Microprocessing Unit.
*Electronics.*
**MPX** (abbr.) multiplex.
**MQ** Memory Quotient.
For further details see under: **MQs**.

**mq.** metro quadrato.
Italian initialism meaning: square metre / meter.
**Mq** Miglio quadrato.
Italian abbreviation meaning: square mile.
**MQA** Modified Quinacridone.
*Chemistry; Materials Science; Molecular Materials; Physics; Thin-film Transistors.*
**MQCA** Magnetic QCA.
*Engineering; Nanoscale Science.*
For further details see under: **QCA**.
**MQD** Metallurgical Quenching Dilatometry.
*Materials Science and Engineering.*
**MQ register** Multiplier-Quotient register.
*Computer Technology.*
**MQs** Memory Quotients.
*Aging; Antiaging; Cognitive Neuroscience; Geriatrics; Gerontology; Hippocampal Pathology; Medicine; Mental Health.*
**MQSA** Mammography Quality Standards Act.
The MQSA was passed by the U.S. Congress in 1992.
*Radiological Health.*
**MQT** Macroscopic Quantum Tunneling.
*Physics.*
**MR** Maintenance Report.
**MR** Mandelate Racemase.
*Basic Medical Sciences; Biochemistry; Microbiology; Molecular Genetics; Pharmaceutical Chemistry; Pharmacy.*
**MR** Manufacturer's Representative.
*Business; Commerce.*
**MR** Map Reference.
**MR** Marginal Revenue.
*Business; Finance.*
**MR** 1. maritime reconnaissance.
1. reconnaissance maritime.
2. Mauritania.
2. Mauritanie.
3. medium range.
3a. à moyen rayon d'action [avion].
3b. moyenne portée [missile].
**MR** Market Ratio.
*Business; Finance.*
**M.R.** Master of the Rolls (G.B.).
**M/R** Mate's Receipt.
**MR** Memorandum Report.
**MR** Memory Reclaimer.
**MR** Mental Retardation.
*Chromosome Abnormalities; Brain Development Abnormalities.*
**Mr** Mister.
**MR** Moment Release.
**MR** Multiple Regression.
Multiple Regression is also known as: Linear Regression.
*Statistics.*
**MR(A)** military requirement (armament).
besoin militaire en matière d'armement.
**MRA** Mutual Recognition Agreement.
*U.S.; E.C. Business; Transatlantic Issues.*
**MRAAM** medium-range air-to-air missile.
missile air-air à moyenne portée.
**MRADs** Minor Restricted Activity Days.
**MRAG** medium-range air-to-ground.
air-sol moyenne portée /ASMP/.
**MRAH** memorandum receipt account holder.
agent comptable des biens.
**MRAM** Magnetic Random Access Memory.
*Applied Physics; Integrated Circuits; Nonvolatile Storage; Unlimited Read / Write Cycles.*
**MRAs** Mutual Recognition Agreements.
For further details see under: **MRA**.
**MRBM** medium-range ballistic missile.
missile balistique (à) moyenne portée.
**MRC** 1. major regional conflict.
1. conflit régional majeur.
2. movement report centre.
2. centre de compte rendu des mouvements.
**MRC** Marine Research Corporation.
**MRC** Marine Resources Center (U.S.A.).
**MRC** Medical Research Council.
*British Councils.*
**MRC** Molecular Research Center, Inc. (U.S.A.).
**MRCA** multi-role combat aircraft.
avion de combat polyvalent.
**MRCC** maritime rescue coordination centre.
centre de coordination du sauvetage en mer.
**MRCI approach** Multireference Configuration Interaction approach.
**MRDOS** Mapped Real-time Disk Operating System.
**MRE** Microbiological Research Establishment (G.B.).
**MRE** Ministère des Relations Extérieures (France).
**MRE account** Major Research Equipment account (U.S.A.).
The MRE account was set up by the U.S. National Science Foundation in 1994 to fund big science.
**MRF** Midbrain Reticular Formation.
**MRF** multiplexage par répartition en fréquence.
frequency-division multiplexing /FDM/.
**MRFIT** Multiple Risk Factor Intervention Trials.
The MRFIT was a study funded by the U.S. National Institutes of Health, that ended in the early 1980s.
*Heart Diseases; Low-Fat Diets.*

**MRFL** master radio frequency list.
liste principale des fréquences radio.
**MRF model** Medium-Range Forecast model.
**MRFSS** Marine Recreational Fishing Statistics Survey.
**MRG** modes réservés pour le temps de guerre.
war reserve modes /WRM/.
**MRI** Magnetic Resonance Imaging.
*Electromagnetism.*
**MRI** Memory Reference Instruction.
*Computer Programming.*
**MRI** Meteorological Research Institute (Japan).
**MRI** Midwest Research Institute.
For further details see under: **HVs** (Hybrid Vesicles).
**MRISC** Magnetic Resonance Imaging and Spectroscopy Center.
**M-RISP** Minority Research Infrastructure Support Program (U.S.A.).
**Mrk 501** Markarian 501.
*Galaxies.*
**MRL** 1. maritime rear link.
1. liaison maritime de l'arrière.
2. multiple rocket launcher.
2. lance-roquettes multiple /LRM/.
**MRLS** multi-rocket launcher system.
système de lance-roquettes multitube.
**MRMS** medium range missile system.
système de missile à moyenne portée.
**MRN** mine reference number.
numéro de référence de mine.
**mRNA** messenger RNA.
*Molecular Biology.*
For further details see under: **RNA**.
**MRO** 1. medical regulating officer.
1. responsible de la régulation médicale.
2. military response option.
2. réaction militaire possible.
**MROs** Maintenance, Repair and Operations.
**MRP** Manufacturers' Recommended Price.
**MRP** Manufacturing Resources Planning.
**MRP** Material Requirements Planning.
*Industrial Engineering.*
**MRPR** message de résultat de prise de ressource.
*Communications.*
**MRPs** Multidrug Resistance Proteins.
*Biochemistry; Cell Physiology; Medicine; Molecular Biology.*
**MRR** maritime radar reconnaissance.
reconnaissance maritime au radar.
**MRR** Medical Research Reactor.
**MRR** Molecular Receptive Range.
*Brain Science; Chemosensory Receptors; Medicine; Neurobiology of Synapse; Neuronal Recognition Molecules; Odorant Recptors; Olfaction; Physiology.*
**MRRD** Marine Resources Research Division (U.S.A.).
MRRD has been replaced by OERD - For further details see under: **OERD**.
**MRRF** Multinational Rapid Reaction Force.
force multinationale de réaction rapide.
**MRS** Materials Research Society.
*Chemistry; Physics; New Materials.*
**MRS** medium-range sonar.
sonar (à) moyenne portée.
**MRSA** Methicillin-Resistant *Staphylococcus Aureus.*
*Antimicrobial Agents; Chemotherapy; Clinical Immunology; Epidemiology; Infectious Diseases; Medicine; Microbiology.*
**MRSAM** medium-range surface-to-air missile.
missile surface-air (à) moyenne portée.
**MRS program** Monitored Retrievable Storage program.
*Nuclear Waste.*
**MRT** 1. manpower restructuring team.
1. équipe de restructuration des effectifs.
2. medical regulating team.
2. équipe de régulation médicale.
**MRT** Ministère de la Recherche et de la Technologie.
French initialism of the: Ministry of Research and Technology.
**MRT** multiplex par répartition dans le temps.
**MRU** Multicampus Research Unit (U.S.A.).
Of the University of California.
**MRV** multiple re-entry vehicle.
corps de rentrée à têtes multiples.
**MRX** Magnetic Reconnection Experiment.
*Plasma Physics.*
**MS** Magnetostriction.
*Electromagnetism.*
**M.S.** Mail Steamer.
**MS** Main Storage.
Main storage is also known as: Internal Memory, Internal Storage; Primary Memory; Main Memory.
*Computer Programming.*
**MS** Majority Stockholders; Major Stockholder.
*Business; Economics; Finance.*
**m.s.** mano sinistra.
Italian initialism meaning: left hand.
**MS** Manuscript.
**MS** March and September.
*Securities.*
**MS**; **ms** margin of safety.

*Business; Finance.*
**Ms** Massa Carrara, Italy.
**MS** Mass Spectrometer; Mass Spectroscope.
*Spectroscopy.*
**MS** Mass Spectrometry.
*Analytical Chemistry.*
**MS** Mass Storage.
Mass storage is also known as: Auxiliary Storage.
*Computer Technology.*
**MS** Master of Science.
Also: **MSC**; **Msc**.
**MS** Master of Surgery.
**MS** Mechanosensitive.
**MS** Metric System.
*Metrology.*
**MS** Microwave Scanner.
**MS** Mild Steel.
*Metallurgy.*
**MS** Military Standard.
**ms.** (abbr.) millisecond.
*Computer Technology.*
**MS** Minesweeper / mine sweeper.
*Naval Architecture; Ordnance.*
**M.S.** Ministero della Sanità (Italy).
Italian initialism of the: Health Ministry.
**M.S.** Ministry of Shipping.
**MS** Ministry of Supply.
**MS** Minority Stockholders.
*Business; Economics; Finance.*
**MS** (abbr.) Mississippi (U.S.A.).
Also: **Miss**.
**MS** Money Supply.
*Business; Finance.*
**MS** Months after Sight.
**MS** Motor Ship.
*Naval Architecture.*
**MS** Multiple Sclerosis.
*Chronic Illnesses; Medicine.*
**MS** Mutuo Soccorso.
Italian initialism meaning: Mutual Aid.
**MSA** Maritime Safety Agency (Japan).
**MSA** Member of the Society of Apothecaries.
**MSA** Member of the Society of Architects.
**MSA** Methanesulfonic Acid.
MSA is used as a catalyst in chemical reactions.
*Organic Chemistry.*
**MSA** Multilateral Steel Agreement.
**MSA** Multiplication Stimulating Activity.
**MSAG** Media Support Advisory Group.
Groupe consultatif pour le soutien des médias.
**MSAM** Medium Scale Anisotropy Measurement (Balloon Experiment).
Flown from the U.S. National Scientific Ballooning Facility in Palestine, Texas.
**MSAT** Minnesota Scholastic Aptitude Test (U.S.A.).
**MSAU** Multi-Station Access Unit.
**MSB** Millennium Seed Bank (G.B.).
*Cryobiology; Plant Species; Seed Preservation Technology; Seed Germination Technology.*
**MSB** minesweeper, boat.
embarcation de dragage.
**msb** most significant bit.
**MSB** Mutual Savings Bank.
**MSC** 1. Major Subordinate Command (Commander) [obsolete - replaced by RC 4.].
1. Haut Commandement (commandant) subordonné /HCS/ [obsolète - remplacé par RC 4.].
2. Maritime Subordinate Command (Commander) [obsolete - replaced by CC NAV].
2. Commandement (commandant) maritime subordonné [obsolète - remplacé par CC NAV].
3. minesweeper, coastal.
3. dragueur de mines côtier.
**MSC** Management Service Center.
**MSC** Mass Storage Control.
**MSC**; **MSc** Master of Science.
Also: **MS**.
**MSC** Medical Staff Corps.
**MSC** Message Switching Concentration.
*Data Communications.*
**MSC** Most Significant Character.
MSC is also nown as: Most Significant Digit; Most Significant Bit.
*Computer Programming.*
**M.S.C. Cystica** Meningitis Serosa Cystica.
M.S.C. Cystica is also known as: Meningitis Serosa Circumscripta.
**MscL** Mechanosensitive ion channels (Large).
*Chemical Engineering; Chemistry; Medicine; Physiology.*
**MSCP**; **mscp** Mean Spherical Candle Power.
**MSC project** Multimedia Super Corridor project (Malaysia).
**MSCs** Marrow Stromal Cells.
*Gene Therapy; Health Sciences; Medicine.*
**MscS** Mechanosensitive ion channels (Small).
For further details see under: **MscL**.
**MSCs** Mesenchymal Stem Cells.
*Stem Cell Research.*
**MSCS**; **Mscs** Microsoft Cluster Services.
**MSCTs** Miniature Synaptic Calcium Transients.
**MSD** Mean-Square Displacement.
**MSD** mine safety distance.
distance de sécurité "mines".
**MSD** Most Significant Digit.

MSD is also known as: Most Significant Character; Most Significant Bit.
*Computer Programming.*
**MSDN; Msdn** Microsoft Developer Network.
**ms-DNA** multicopy single-stranded DNA.
*Biochemistry; Biology.*
**MS-DOS** Microsoft Disk Operating System.
MS-DOS is a system developed by The Microsoft Corporation.
*Computer Technology.*
**MSDR** Master Sensor Data Record.
**MSE** 1. main staff element.
1. élément principal d'état-major.
2. mesures de soutien de guerre électronique.
2. electronic warfare support measures /ESM/.
**MSE** Mexican Stock Exchange.
**MSE** Middle gene Sporulation Element.
*Biochemistry; Biophysics; Genetics; Medicine.*
**MSE** Midwest Stock Exchange.
**MSEB** Maharashtra State Electric Board (India).
**MSEB** Mathematics Science Education Board (U.S.A.).
**m/sec.** metri al secondo.
Italian abbreviation meaning: metres / meters per second.
**MSEHPA** Model State Emergency Health Powers Act.
The U.S. MSEHPA has been written upon request of The Centers for Disease Control and Prevention.
**MSF; Msf** Medici Senza Frontiere.
**MSF** military sub-function.
sous-fonction militaire.
**MS-FBC** Multisolid Fluidized-Bed Combustion Process.
*Fluidized-bed Combustion Technology.*
**MSFZ** missile seeker free zone.
zone de liberté d'autodirecteur de missile.
**MSG** (abbr.) Message.
*Computer Programming; Telecommunications.*
**MSG** manpower scaling guide.
normes d'utilisation des effectifs.
**MSG** Monosodium Glutamate.
Monosodium Glutamate, also known as: Sodium Glutamate, is used as a flavour enhancer.
*Organic Chemistry.*
**MSGO** MNC Steering Group on Operations.
Groupe directeur des GCO sur les opérations.
**MSH** Melanocyte-Stimulating Hormone.
*Endocrinology.*
**MSHA** Mannone-Sensitive Hemagglutination.
*Extracellular Organelles; Genomics; Immunology; Microbiology.*
**MSHA** Mine Safety and Health Administration (U.S.A.).
**MSH-IF** Melanocyte-Stimulating Hormone-Inhibiting Factor.
**MSH-RF** Melanocyte Stimulating Hormone-Releasing Factor.
*Endocrinology.*
**MSI** Magnetic Source Imaging.
*Neuroscience; Brain-Imaging Techniques.*
**MSI** Medium-Scale Integration.
*Electronics.*
**MSI** Member of the chartered Surveyor Institution.
**MSI** Member of the Sanitary Institute.
**MSI** minesweeper, inshore.
dragueur de mines de petits fonds.
**MSI** Multi-Spectral Imager.
**MSJBS** Master of Science in Japanese Business Studies.
**MSK** minimum shift keying.
modulation par déplacement minimal /MDM/.
**MSKCC** Memorial Sloan-Kettering Cancer Center (U.S.A.).
**MSL** Marine Sciences Libraries.
**M.S.L.; m.s.l.** Mean Sea Level / mean sea level.
*Geography.*
**M.S.L.; m.s.l.** midsternal line.
**MSL proteins** Male-Specific Lethal proteins.
*Epigenetics.*
**MSM** Men who have Sex with Men.
**MSM** Morehouse School of Medicine (U.S.A.).
*Cardiovascular Research.*
**MSM '99 International Conference** International Conference on Modeling and Simulation of Microsystems (U.S.A.).
**MSMA** Monosodium Acid Methanearsonate.
MSMA is a crystalline solid having a melting point of 132-139°C. It is used mainly as an herbicide and as preplant treatment.
*Organic Chemistry.*
**MSN** Master of Science in Nursing.
**Msn; msn** (abbr.) Mission / mission.
**MSN** The airport code for Madison, Wisconsin, U.S.A.
**MSO** minesweeper, ocean.
dragueur de mines océanique.
**MSO** Multistage Operations.
**MSOW** modular stand-off weapon.
arme modulaire tirée à distance de sécurité.
**MSP** Monobasic Sodium Phosphate.
$NaH_2PO_4$ - Monobasic Sodium Phosphate is used mainly in dyeing and for baking powders.
*Inorganic Chemistry.*

**MSP approach** Multiple-Shielding Polarizability approach.
*Chemistry.*
**MSPB** Merit Systems Protection Board (U.S.A.).
**MSR** 1. main-supply route.
1. route principale de ravitaillement.
2. military standardization requirement.
2. besoin militaire de normalisation.
**MSR** Merchant Ship Reactor.
**MSR** Missile Site Radar.
*Engineering.*
**MSR** Molten-Salt Reactor.
*Nucleonics.*
**MSRB** Municipal Securities Rule-making Board (U.S.A.).
**MSRC** Marine Sciences Research Center.
University at Stony Brook, State University of New York.
*Coastal Oceanography; Marine Conservation; Marine Science; Marine Shellfish Biology; Population Dynamics; Shellfish Ecology.*
**MSRD** Marine Services Research Division (U.S.A.).
MSRD has been replaced by: **CARD**.
**MSS** Management Support System.
**MSS** Manufacturers Standardization Society.
**MSS**; **mss** Manuscripts.
**MSS** Mass Storage System (U.S.A.).
The MSS contains more than 30 terabytes of atmospheric and oceanographic data.
*Atmospheric Research; Oceanography.*
**MSS** Member of the Statistical Society.
**MSS** missile surface-surface.
surface-to-surface missile /SSM 2./.
**MSS** Multispectral Scanner.
**MSSD** Model Secondary School for the Deaf (U.S.A.).
**MSSF** Mechanical Social Systems Foundation (Japan).
**MS Society** Multiple Sclerosis Society.
**MSSQ** Methylsilsesquioxane.
**MS Stars** Main Sequence Stars.
*Astronomy; Mathematics; Physics.*
For further details see under: **TTS**.
**MS System** Master-Slave system.
*Computer Technology.*
**MST** Maladie Sexuellement Transmissible.
For further details see under: **MTS**.
**MST** Mesosphere - Stratosphere - Troposphere.
**MST** Methods for Systems Thinking.
**MST** Mountain Standard Time.
**MST area** Medial Superior Temporal area.
*Cognitive Science; Neurophysiology.*
**MSTC** missile and space test centre.
centre d'essais spatiaux et de missiles.
**MS theory** Maximum Stress theory.
*Materials Science.*
**MSTO stars** Main Sequence Turnoff stars.
*Astrophysics; Custers; Main-sequence stars; Thermonuclear fusion.*
**MSTS** Military Sea Transportation Service.
**MSTZ** missile seeker tight zone.
zone d'interdiction d'autodirecteur de missile.
**MSU** Michigan State University (U.S.A.).
**MSU** Microwave Sounding Unit.
For further details see under: **MSUs**.
**MSU** Montana State University (U.S.A.).
**MSU** multinational specialized unit.
unité multinationale spécialisée.
**MSUs** Microwave Sounding Units.
The MSUs are instruments carried by satellites that compile global temperature records.
*Atmospheric Research; Climate; Earth, Oceans and Space Studies; Global Change; Natural Resource Ecology.*
**MSV** minesweeper vessel.
bâtiment dragueur de mines.
**MSV** Murine Sarcoma Virus.
*Virology.*
**MSW** Magnetic Surface Wave.
**MSW** Master of Social Welfare; Master of Social Work.
**MSW** Municipal Solid Waste.
NREL's GIS produces color-coded maps that clarify complex relationships. In this study, analysts wanted to determine which areas of the United States could support power plants fueled by MSW.
*Geographic Information System maps.*
For further details see under: **GIS** and **NREL**.
**MSWD** Mean Square Weighted Deviation.
**MSY** Maximum Sustainable Yield.
*Ecology.*
**MSY** The airport code for New Orleans International, New Orleans, Louisiana, U.S.A.
**MSZ** mutual security zone.
zone de sécurité commune.
**MT** Machine Translation.
Machine translation is also known as: Mechanical Translation.
*Computer Technology.*
**MT** Magnetic Tape.
*Electronics.*
**MT** Magnetotelluric.
*Geology; Geophysics.*
**M.T.**; **mt**; **m/t** mail transfer.
**MT** Malta.

**MT** Master Terminal.
*Computer Technology.*
**MT** Matera, Italy.
**MT** Mean Time / mean time.
**MT** Measured Time.
**M.T.**; **mt.**; **m/t** mechanical transport.
**M.T.** Medical Technologist.
**MT** megaton, megatons.
**M.T.** Membrana Tympani.
**MT** Metallothionein.
*Biochemistry.*
**M.T.** metric ton.
M.T. is also known as: Megagram and Tonne. It is equal to 1000 kgs.
*Metrology.*
**MT** Microtubule.
*Biological Imaging; Cell Biology and Metabolism; Human Development.*
**MT** Military Training.
**M.T.** Ministero del Tesoro (Italy).
Italian initialism of the: Ministry of Treasury.
**MT** Ministry of Transport.
**MT** (abbr.) Montana (U.S.A.).
**M.T.**; **mt.**; **m/t** motor tanker.
**M.T.**; **mt**; **m/t** motor transport.
**M.T.**; **mt**; **m/t** (abbr.) mount.
*Engineering; Military Science; Ordnance.*
**mt.** (abbr.) mountain.
*Geography.*
**MTA** message transfer agent.
agent de transfert de messages /ATM 1./.
**MTA** Motion Time Analysis.
*Time Study.*
**mT air** maritime Tropical air.
**MT area** Middle Temporal area (of the brain).
For the detection and perception of motion.
**MTAs** Materials Transfer Agreements.
*Technology Transfer; Exchange of Materials.*
**μTAS** Micro Total Analysis Systems.
*Microfluidic Systems.*
**Mtase** Methyltransferase / Methyl transferase.
*Enzymology.*
**MTAv** Mother-Tongue-Avoidance.
*Linguistics.*
**MTB** Materials Transportation Bureau (U.S.A.).
**MTB** Motor Torpedo Boat.
MTB is also known as: Mosquito Boat; Petrol Torpedo Boat.
*Naval Architecture.*
**MTBE** Methyl Tertiary Butyl Ether.
**MTBF** Mean Time Between Failures.
*Computer Technology.*
**MTBR** mean time between repairs.
temps moyen entre réparations.
**MTC** Manhattan Theater Club (U.S.A.).
**MTC** Massachusetts Technology Collaborative.
*U.S. Technology Programs.*
**MTC** Microbiology and Tumor biology Center.
The MTC is a department of the Karolinska Institute (Stockholm, Sweden).
**MTC** Minimum Tax Credit (U.S.A.).
**MTC** Module Terminal de Commutation.
**MTC** M. Tuberculosis Complex.
*Biological Sciences; Cell Biology; Medicine; Molecular Bacteriology.*
**Mtcr** Missile technology control regime.
**MTCT** Mother-To-Child Transmission (of HIV).
For further details see under: **ARV therapy** and **HIV**.
**MTD** Maximum Tolerated Dose.
**mtDNA** mitochondrial DNA.
*Genetics.*
For further details see under: **DNA**.
**mtDNAs** mutant DNAs.
**MTDP** Molecular Targets Discovery Program.
Of the U.S. NCI.
For further details se under: **NCI**.
**MTEP** Milioni di Tonnellate di Equivalente Petrolifero.
Italian initialism meaning: Millions of Tons of Oil Equivalent.
**MTF** 1. medical treatment facility.
1. installation de traitement médical.
2. message text format.
2. format de texte de message.
**MTF** Modulation Transfer Function.
**MTFP** 1. medium-term financial plan.
1. plan financier à moyen terme /PFMT/.
2. mission-tailored force package.
2. ensemble de forces adapté à la mission.
**MTFS** Medium-Term Financial Strategy (G.B.).
**mtg.** (abbr.) meeting.
**Mtg.** (abbr.) mortgage.
Also: **mtge**.
**mtgd.** (abbr.) mortgaged.
**mtge.** (abbr.) mortgage.
Also: **Mtg**.
**mtgee.** (abbr.) mortgagee.
**mtgor.** (abbr.) mortgagor.
**MTH** medium transport helicopter.
hélicoptère moyen de transport.
**Mth.** (abbr.) month.
**MTHFR** 5,10-Methylene Tetrahydrofolate Reductase.
**mthly.** (abbr.) monthly.
**MTI** Moving Target Indicator.

*Electronics.*
**MTIP** 1. medium-term implementation plan.
1. plan de mise en œuvre à moyen terme.
2. medium-term infrastructure plan.
2. plan d'infrastructure à moyen terme.
**MTIWG** Military Transitional Issues Working Group.
Groupe de travail militaire sur les questions relatives à l'Alliance en période de transition.
**MTJ** Mendocino Triple Junction.
**MTL** minimum trigger level.
niveau minimal de déclenchement.
**MTL regions** Medial Temporal Lobe regions.
*Cognitive Neuroscience; Psychology.*
**mtlrRNA** mitochondrial large ribosomal RNA.
*Biological Sciences.*
For further details see under: **RNA**.
**mtls.** (abbr.) materials.
**MTM** Method-Time Measurement.
*Time Study.*
**MTMS** maritime tactical message system.
système de messages tactiques maritimes.
**MTN Blots** Multiple Tissue Northern Blots.
Clontech Laboratories (U.S.A.).
*Poly A* RNA Northern Blots.*
**MTN** Medium Term Notes (U.S.A.).
**MTNL** Mahanagar Telephone Nigam (India).
MTNL is state-owned.
**MTO** Medical Technical Officer.
**MTOC** Microtubule-Organizing Center.
*Cell Biology.*
**MTOE**; **Mtoe** Million tonnes of oil equivalent.
**mTOR** mammalian Target Of Rapamycin.
*Medicine; Molecular Pharmacology; Oncology; Signal Transduction; Rapamycin-sensitive Kinase.*
**MTP** Maritime Tactical Publication.
publication tactique maritime.
**MTP** Microsomal triglyceride Transfer Protein.
Defects in MTP cause abetalipoproteinemia disease.
*Discovery Chemistry; Medicine; Pharmaceutical Research; Pharmacokinetics.*
**MTPE** Mission To Planet Earth - NASA's (U.S.A.).
**Mt-PK** Myotonin-Protein Kinase.
**MTPR** Miniature Temperature Pressure Recorder.
**MTR** Material Testing Reactor.
*Nucleonics.*
**MTR** Miniature Temperature Recorder.
*Temperature Recorders.*
**M.Tr.** Ministero dei Trasporti (Italy).
Italian abbreviation of the: Ministry of Public Transport.
**MTR** missile tracking radar.
radar de poursuite de missiles.
**MTR** (abbr.) Motor.
**MTRP** medium-term resource plan.
plan de ressources à moyen terme /PRMT/.
**MTS** Maladie à Transmission Sexuelle; Malattia a Trasmissione Sessuale.
French and Italian initialism meaning: Sexually Transmitted Disease.
**MTS** Marine Technology Society.
**MTS** Mercato all'ingrosso dei Titoli di Stato.
*Banking; Finance.*
**MTS** Message Toll Service.
**MTS** Message Transfer System.
**MTs** Microtubules.
*Biological Imaging; Cell Biology and Metabolism; Human Development.*
**MTS** Multitrack Stereo.
*Acoustical Engineering.*
**MTSO** Mobile Telecommunications Switching Office.
**MTSU** Middle Tennessee State University (U.S.A.).
**MTT** mobile training team.
équipe mobile d'entraînement.
**MTT** Myoblast Transfer Therapy.
*Cell Therapy; Cell Transplantation.*
**MTTF** Mean Time To Failure.
*Engineering.*
**MTTR** Mean Time To Repair.
*Engineering.*
**MTTR** mean time to repair/replace.
1a. moyenne des temps des traveaux de réparation/remplacement.
1b. temps moyen de réparation/remplacement.
**MTTR** Mean Time To Restore.
*Transportation Engineering.*
**MTU** Methylthiouracil.
Methylthiouracil is used in the treatment of hyperthyroidism.
*Pharmacology.*
**MTX** Methotrexate.
A drug, also known as Amethopthin, used to treat leukemia and several other cancers.
*Pharmacology.*
**MTY** The airport code for Monterrey, Mexico.
**MU** Oman.
**M.u.** Mache unit.
**M/U** Making Up.
**mU** milliunit.
**M/U** Monetary Unit.
**MUA** Multi-Unit Activity.
**MUAT** mobile underwater acoustic unit.
dispositif acoustique sous-marin mobile.
**MUC** million d'unités de compte.

million accounting units.
**MUC** The airport code for Munich, Germany.
**MUCI** million d'unités de compte d'infrastructure.
1a. million infrastructure accounting units /MIAU/.
1b. million international acounting units.
**MUF** Material Unaccounted For.
*Evaluation.*
**MUF**; **muf** Maximum Usable Frequency.
*Telecommunications.*
**MUG** multi-user group.
1a. groupe d'utilisateurs multiples.
1b. groupe multiutilisateur.
**MUI** Indonesian Ulemas Council.
MUI is the highest Indonesian Muslim body authorized to release religious rulings or labels of "halal"(allowed) on processed food products distributed in the country.
**mul.** (abbr.) multiplexer.
*Electronics.*
**mult.** (abbr.) multiple.
*Electricity; Mathematics; Science.*
**mult** (abbr.) multiplier.
*Electricity; Electronics; Mathematics.*
**MULTICS** MULTiplexed Information and Computing System.
**multl** (abbr.) multiple.
For further details see under: **mult.**
**mun.** (abbr.) municipal.
Also: **munic**.
**MUNIS** MUNicipal Securities (U.S.A.).
**MUPO** Maximum Undistorted Power Output.
*Electronics.*
**MUPPIES** Middle-Aged Urban Professionals (U.S.A.).
**MURA** Midwestern Universities Research Association (U.S.A.).
**MURIM** MUltidimensional Reconstruction and Imaging in Medicine.
*Medicine.*
**MURR** Missouri University Research Reactor.
MURR operates a 10 MW light water moderated reactor that is operational more than 90% of real time.
*Research Reactors.*
**MURST** Ministero dell'Università e della Ricerca Scientifica e Tecnologica (Italy).
**MUS** Medical University of Silesia (Poland).
**MUs** Money Units.
**mus.** (abbr.) museum; music; musical.
**MUSA** Multiple - Unit Steerable Antenna.
*Electromagnetism.*
**MUSC** Medical University of South Carolina (U.S.A.).
**MUSES-B** Second Mu Space Engineering Satellite.
The MUSES-B was launched on 12[th] February 1997 and after its launch it was renamed HALCA.
For further details see under: **HALCA**.
**MUSIST** Multimedia User Interfaces for Interactive Services and TV.
*European Community Project.*
**MUST** Malaysian University of Science and Technology (Malaysia).
The MUST campus will be built over the next 5 years in an area 30 km. North of Kuala Lumpur.
*Advanced Manufacturing; Biochemistry; Materials; Microelectronics; Water Resources Management.*
**MUST** Manned Undersea Science and Technology.
**MUST** Multipurpose User-oriented Software Technology.
**MUSYC** MUltifunctional mini-robot SYstem for endoscopy - *European Community.*
**MUX** (abbr.) Multiplex.
*Cartography; Telecommunications.*
**MUX**; **mux** (abbr.) Multiplexer.
*Electronics.*
**MUZM** Makerere University Zoology Museum.
*Anatomical Sciences; Anthropology; Geochronology.*
**MV** 1. Maldive Islands.
1. îles Maldives.
2. military vigilance.
2. vigilance militaire.
**m.v.** market value.
*Business; Economics; Finance.*
**MV**; **m.v.** Mean Variation.
**MV** Measles Virus.
MV is also known as: Rubeola Virus.
*Virology.*
**MV** Megavolt.
The MV is equal to 1 million volts.
*Electricity.*
**Mv** The chemical symbol for Mendelevium.
For further details see under: **Md**.
**MV** Merchant Vessel.
**μV** microvolt.
μV is equal to one-millionth of a volt.
**mV**; **mv** millivolt.
*Electricity* - One-thousandth of a volt.
**MV** Minimum Vital.
**MV** Motor Vessel.
**MV** Motoveliero.
Italian initialism meaning: Auxiliary Sailing Ship.
**MVA** Manual Vacuum Aspiration.

*Biopsy and Uterine Evacuation; Medical Instruments.*
**MVA** Market Value Added.
Essentially, MVA is the measure of shareholder wealth because it compares resources invested by lenders and shareholders with their current value in the marketplace.
*Economics; Finance.*
For further details see under: **EVA**.
**MVA**; **Mva** Megavolt-Ampere.
**MVA** Modified Vaccinia Ankara.
*Medicine; Vaccine Vectors.*
**MVB** Multivesicular Bodies.
**MVBR** Multivibrator.
*Electronics.*
**mvc** manual volume control.
**MVC** Maximal Voluntary Contraction.
*Motor Units; Muscle Mass; Physiology.*
**MVE** Methyl Vinyl Ether.
**MVE** Murray Valley Encephalitis.
The Murray Valley Encephalitis is a brain inflammation that caused an epidemic in the early 1950s in the Murray Valley (Australia).
*Medicine.*
**MVM** Mariner-Venus-Mercury.
**MVPCB** Motor Vehicle Pollution Control Board.
**MVR** Minisatellite Variant Repeat.
*DNA Variation Analysis; Genetic Identification Tests.*
**MVS** Multiple Virtual Storage.
**MVSS** Motor Vehicle Safety Standard.
**MVT** Mot de Verrouillage de Trame.
**MVV** Maximum Voluntary Ventilation.
**Mw** Megawatt.
**mW**; **mw** milliwatt.
*Metrology.*
**MW** mine warfare.
guerre des mines.
**MW** Mount Washburn.
**MWA** 1. memorandum of working agreement.
1. mémorandum de mise en œuvre.
2. morale and welfare activities.
2. activités socio-récréatives.
**MWB** Metropolitan Water Board.
**MWC** Maximal Work Capacity.
**MWC** mine warfare coordinator.
coordonnateur de la guerre des mines.
**MWCF** Montana Women's Capital Fund (U.S.A.).
**MWDs** Molecular Weight Distributions.
**MW(E)**; **MWE**; **Mwe** Megawatt Electric.
*Nucleonics.*
**MWHQ** 1. main war headquarters.
1. quartier général de guerre principal (QGGP).
2. maritime war headquarters.
2. quartier général de guerre maritime (QGGM 1.).
3. mobile war headquarters.
3. quartier général de guerre mobile (QGGM 2.).
**MWIA** Medical Women's International Association (Germany).
The MWIA was founded in 1919 to facilitate contacts between medical women.
**MWL** Meteoric Waterline.
*Groundwater Research; Isotopic Signatures; Mineral Exchange.*
**MWM** Motif Window Manager.
**MWNTs** Multiwalled Nanotubes.
*Multiwalled Physics.*
**MW OP** mine warfare operation.
opération de guerre des mines.
**MWP** Mine Warfare Publication.
Publication lutte (guerre) des mines.
**MWR** morale, welfare and recreation (activities).
(activités) socio-récréatives.
**MWS** Microwave Spectrometer.
**MWS** missile warning system.
système d'alerte (aux) missiles.
**MWS** Multiwork Station.
**MWSR** Microwave Water Substance Radiometer.
**MW(Th)** Megawatt Thermal.
*Nucleonics.*
**MWTR** mine warfare testing range.
polygone d'essai de guerre des mines.
**MWV** Maximum Working Voltage.
*Electricity.*
**MWV** mine warfare vessel.
bâtiment de guerre des mines.
**MWV flow** Modulated Wavy Vortex flow.
**MWYr** Megawatt Year.
**Mx** Maxwell / maxwell.
*Electromagnetism.*
**MX** Mexico.
Also: **MEX**.
**Mx** (abbr.) Middlesex (G.B.).
**MY** Malaysia.
**my.** (abbr.) Mayer.
*Thermodynamics.*
**My** Million years.
**My** (abbr.) Myopia.
Myopia is also known as: Nearsightedness.
*Medicine.*
**myc.** (abbr.) mycology.
*Botany* - Mycology is the study of fungi.
**MyHC** Myosin Heavy Chain.
**MYIP** Yellow Fluorescent Protein molecules.
**MYR** mid-year review.
examen de mi-exercice.

**MZ** Monozygotic; monozygous.
**MZ** Motozattera.
Italian initialism meaning: motor raft; landing craft.
**MZ** Mozambique.
**M-Zone** Manufacturing Zone.

# N

**N** Nasal.
*Anatomy.*
**N** Neutron number.
*Nuclear Physics.*
**N** Newton.
*Metrology.*
**N** The chemical symbol for Nitrogen.
Nitrogen is used mainly as an inert gas and refrigerant.
*Chemistry; Symbols.*
**N** normal.
*Chemistry; Mathematics; Medicine; Meteorology; Organic Chemistry.*
**N** north.
**N** Norway's international vehicle registration letter.
**N** Nucleus.
*Astronomy; Cell Biology; Computer Programming; Hydrology; Nuclear Physics; Science.*
**NA** Naming Authority.
**NA** Napoli, Italy.
**NA** Narcotics Anonymous.
Founded in the U.S.A. in 1953 (self-help).
**NA** Net Assets.
*Business; Economics; Finance.*
**NA** Netherlands Antilles.
**NA**; **N.A.** Neutral Axis.
*Mechanics.*
**NA** New Account.
**N/a** no advice; non acceptance.
**NA** Nomina Anatomica.
Nomina Anatomica was adopted in 1955.
*Medicine.*
**NA** Noradrenaline.
**N.A.** North America.
**NA** Not Applicable.
**NA** Not Appropriated.
**NA** Not Authorized.
**NA** Not Available.
**NA**; **N.A.** Numerical Aperture.
*Optics.*
**NA** Nurse's Aide.
*Medicine.*
**Na** The chemical symbol for Sodium.
Sodium is used mainly as a polymerization catalyst and in cables (as a conductor).
**NAA** National Academy of Arbitrators (Washington, D.C., U.S.A.).
**NAA** National Association of Accountants (U.S.A.).
**NAA** Neutron Activation Analysis.
Neutron activation analysis is also known as: Activation Analysis.
*Nuclear Engineering.*
**NAA** National Aeronautic Association.
**NAA** North Atlantic Assembly.
Assemblée de l'Atlantique Nord (AAN).
**n.a.a.** not always afloat.
**NAAA** $\alpha$-Naphthaleneacetic Acid.
NAAA is used mainly to promote growth of roots in plant cuttings.
**NAABSA** Not Always Afloat, But Safe Aground.
**NAACP** National Association for the Advancement of Coloured People (U.S.A.).
**NAAEE** North American Association of Environmental Educators (U.S.A.).
**NAAG** NATO Army Armaments Group.
Groupe OTAN sur l'armement des forces terrestres.
**NAAL** Network of Alabama Academic Libraries (U.S.A.).
**NAALD** Nigerian Association of Agricultural Librarians and Documentalists.
**NAAQS** National Ambient Air Quality Standards.
*Environmental Health Sciences.*
**NAB** National Australia Bank.
NAB is the largest and strongest bank in Australia.
**NAB** NATO Appeals Board.
Commission des recours de l'OTAN.
**NAB** Neurobiology and Anesthesiology Branch.
**NAB** Neutralizing Antibody.
*Medicine.*
**NABA** Nuova Accademia di Belle Arti.
*Italian Academy.*
**NABE** National Association for Bilingual Education.
**NABE** National Association of Bar Executives.
Chicago, Illinois, U.S.A.
**NABE** National Association of Business Economists (U.S.A.).
**$NaBF_4$** Ferrucite.
Ferrucite is found on Mount Vesuvius (Italy).
*Mineralogy.*
**$NaBiO_3$** Sodium Bismuthate.
$NaBiO_3$, also known as: Sodium Metabismuthate, is used mainly in pharmaceuticals.
*Inorganic Chemistry.*
**NABO** North Atlantic Biocultural Organization.
NABO is headquartered at the City University of New York (U.S.A.).
**$NaBO_2$** Sodium Metaborate.
Sodium Metaborate is used as an herbicide.
*Inorganic Chemistry.*

**NABs** Neutralizing Antibodies.
Also: **Nas**.
*Medicine.*

**NABS** NATO airbase SATCOM (system).
(système) SATCOM des bases aériennes de l'OTAN.

**NABT** National Association of Biology Teachers.
The NABT was established in the U.S.A. in 1938.

**NAC** Narrow-Angle Camera.

**NAC** National Accelerator Center.
The National Accelerator Center is located near Cape Town (South Africa).
*Nuclear Physics.*

**NAC** Newly Associated Countries.
*European Community.*

**NAC** Non-Aligned Countries.

**NAC** North Atlantic Council.
Conseil de l'Atlantique Nord (CAN).

**nac** Nucleus Accumbens / nucleus accumbens.

**NACA** National Advisory Committee for Aeronautics (U.S.A.).
The NACA is the predecessor of NASA.
For further details see under: **NASA**.

**NACA** National Association for Court Administration (Virginia, U.S.A.).

**$NaCa(SO_4)_2$** Glauberite.
Glauberite is found in nitrate and salt deposits.
*Mineralogy.*

**NACC** North Atlantic Cooperation Council [obsolete - replaced by EAPC].
Conseil de coopération nord-atlantique (CCNA) [obsolète - remplacé par CPEA].

**NACCIS** NATO automated command and control information system [includes MCCIS].
système d'information de l'OTAN pour le commandement et le contrôle [comprend le MCCIS].

**NACDL** National Association of Criminal Defense Lawyers (Houston, Texas, U.S.A.).

**NACE** National Association of Corrosion Engineers (U.S.A.).

**nAChR** neuronal Acetylcholine Receptor.
*Neurobiology; Neurology; Neuroscience; Signal Transduction.*

**nAChR** Nicotic Acetylcholine Receptor.
*Chemistry; Chemical Engineering.*

**NACISA** NATO Communications and Information Systems Agency [obsolete - incorporated into NC3A].
Agence des systèmes de communication et d'information de l'OTAN [obsolète - intégrée dans la NC3A].

**NACISC** NATO Communications and Information Systems Committee [obsolete - see NC3B].
Comité des systèmes de communication et d'information de l'OTAN [obsolète - voir NC3B].

**NACISO** NATO Communications and Information Systems Organization [obsolete - see NC30].
Organisation des systèmes de communication et d'information de l'OTAN [obsolète - voir NC30].

**NaCl** Halite.
Halite is also known as: Rock Salt; Common Salt.
*Mineralogy.*

**NaCl** Sodium Chloride.
Sodium Chloride, common table salt, besides seasoning, is used particularly in medicine and for the production of chemicals.
*Inorganic Chemistry.*

**NACMA** NATO Air Command and Control System Management Agency.
Agence OTAN de gestion du système de commandement et de contrôle aériens.

**NACME** National Action Council for Minorities in Engineering (U.S.A.).

**NACMO** NATO Air Command and Control System Management Organization.
Organisation OTAN de gestion du système de commandement et de contrôle aériens.

**NACMO BOD** NATO ACCS Management Organization Board of Directors.
Comité de direction de l'Organisation OTAN de gestion de l'ACCS.

**NaCN** Sodium Cyanide.
NaCN is used in electroplating, and for many industrial uses.
*Inorganic Chemistry.*

**NACO** National AIDS Control Organization.
*Indian Organization.*

**NACOA** National Advisory Committee on Oceans and Atmosphere (U.S.A.).

**NACOLADS** National Council On Libraries, Archives and Documentation Services.

**NACOS** NATO courier service.
service courrier de l'OTAN.

**NACOSA** NATO CIS Operating and Support Agency.
Agence OTAN d'exploitation et de soutien des SIC.

**NAC peptide** Nonamyloid Componenet peptide.
*Medicine; Neuroscience; Pathology; Psychiatry.*

**NACRE** North American Coalition on Religion and Ecology (U.S.A.).

**nacre** The above acronym was coined accidentally using the word "nacre" also known as "mother-of-pearl".
*Invertebrate Zoology.*

**NACSI** NATO Advisory Committee on Special Intelligence.
Comité consultatif OTAN sur le renseignement spécial.
**NACSIS** NAtional Center for Science Information System.
*Japanese Centers.*
**NACUA** National Association of College and University Attorneys (U.S.A.).
**NAD** national armaments director.
directeur national des armements.
**NAD** Nicotinamide Adenine Dinucleotide.
NAD is a coenzyme that is involved in many enzymatic reactions.
*Enzymology.*
**NAD** Nitric Acid Dihydrate.
**NAD** No Appreciable Disease.
**NADA** National Automobile Dealers Association (U.S.A.).
**NAD(B)** National Air Data (Branch).
**NAD Bank** North American Development Bank.
**NADC** NATO Air Defence Committee.
Comité OTAN de défense aérienne.
**NADDO** NATO design and development objective.
objectif OTAN d'étude et de développement.
**NADEES** NATO air defence electronic environment system.
système d'infrastructure électronique de la défense aérienne de l'OTAN.
**NADEFCOL** NATO Defence College.
Collège de défense de l'OTAN.
**NADGE** NATO Air Defence Ground Environment.
infrastructure électronique de la défense aérienne de l'OTAN.
**NADIR** NILU's Atmospheric Database for Interactive Retrieval.
For further details see under: **NILU**.
**NADPH** Nicotinamide Adenine Dinucleotide Phosphate.
Also: **NAD/P**.
*Enzymology; Molecular Biology.*
**NADR** Naval Air Development Center.
**NADREPS** national armaments directors' representatives.
représentants des directeurs nationaux des armaments.
**NADREX** Major NATO Commanders' Exercise Directive [obsolete - replaced by EPG].
Directive d'exercice des Grands Commandements de l'OTAN [obsolète - remplacé par l'EPG].
**NADW** North Atlantic Deep Water.
**NAE** National Academy of Engineering (U.S.A.).
**NAE** national administrative expenses.
dépenses administratives nationales (DAN).
**NAE** Nuclear Astrophysics Explorer.
**NAEGIS** NATO Airborne Early Warning Ground Environment Integration Segment.
segment d'intégration entre l'infrastructure électronique et le système aéroporté de détection lointaine de l'OTAN.
**NAEMB** National Academy of Engineering Marine Board.
**NAEP** National Agency for Environmental Protection (Denmark).
**NAEP** National Assessment of Educational Progress.
*U.S. Education.*
**NAEW** see NAEW&CS.
voir NAEW&CS.
**NAEW&C FC** NATO Airborne Early Warning and Control Force Command [when referring to the headquarters, the E-3A Component and the E-3D Component].
Commandement de la Force aéroportée de détection lointaine et de contrôle de l'OTAN [englobe le quartier général, l'Élément E-3A et l'Élément E-3D].
**NAEW&C Force** NATO Airborne Early Warning and Control Force.
Force aéroportée de détection lointaine et de contrôle de l'OTAN.
**NAEW&CS** NATO Airborne Early Warning and Control System.
système aéroporté de détection lointaine et de contrôle de l'OTAN.
**NAEWF** incorrect - use NAEW&C Force.
incorrect - utiliser NAEW&C Force.
**NAEWFC** incorrect - use NAEW&C FC.
incorrect - utiliser NAEW&C FC.
**NAF** Non Appropriated Funds.
*Business; Economics; Finance.*
**NaF** Sodium Fluoride.
NaF is used mainly in toothpastes, and as an insecticide and fungicide.
*Inorganic Chemistry.*
**NAFAG** NATO Air Force Armaments Group.
Groupe OTAN sur l'armement des forces aériennes.
**NAFO** North-West Atlantic Fisheries Organization.
**NAFS** NATO Automated Financial System.
système financier automatisé de l'OTAN.
**NAFTA** North American Free Trade Agreement.
**NAG** national armament goals.
objectifs nationaux d'armement.
**NAG** Net Annual Gain.
*Business; Economics; Finance.*

**NAG** Numerical Analysis Group (Oxford, G.B.).
**NAGARA** National Association of Government Archivists and Records Administrators.
**NA gene** Neuraminidase gene.
**NAGP** National Animal Germplasm Program.
USDA's.
*Germplasm preservation of agricultural animal species.*
For further details see under: **USDA**.
**NAGPRA** Native American Graves Protection and Repatriation Act (1990) (U.S.A.).
**NAHB** National Association of Home Builders (U.S.A.).
**$NaHCO_3$** Nahcolite.
*Mineralogy.*
**NAHEMA** NATO Helicopter for the 1990s Design and Development, Production and Logistics Management Agency.
Agence de gestion OTAN pour la conception, le développement, la production et la logistique de l'hélicoptère OTAN des années 90.
**NAHSL** North Atlantic Health Sciences Libraries.
**NAI** 1. named area of interest.
1. zone d'intérêt désignée.
2. naval ammunition interchangeability.
2. interchangeabilitité des munitions navales.
**NAI** NASA Astrobiology Institute (U.S.A.).
For further details see under: **NASA**.
**NAI** New Atlantic Initiative.
Washington-based.
*U.S. Initiative.*
**NAIA** National Association of Intercollegiate Athletes (U.S.A.).
**NAIC** National Association of Investment Clubs (U.S.A.).
**NAICC** National Association of Independent Computer Companies.
**NAIMA** North American Insulation Manufacturers Association (U.S.A.).
**$NaIO_3$** Sodium Iodate.
Sodium Iodate is used mainly in disinfectants and in anticeptics.
*Inorganic Chemistry.*
**NAIRU** Non-Accelerating Inflation Rate of Unemployment.
**NAK**; **Nak** Negative Acknowledgement (ASCII).
*Computer Programming.*
**NAL** National Aerospace Laboratory (Japan).
For further details see under: **ISAS**.
**NAL** normal actuation level.
niveau normal de déclenchement.
**NAL**; **Nal** Novell Application Launcher.
**NALGO Association** National And Local Government Officers Association.
**NALL** Nigerian Association of Law Libraries.
**NALLA** National Long Lines Agency.
Bureau national des lignes à grande distance.
**NALS** national liaison staff.
personnel de liaison national.
**NALSS** naval advanced logistic support site.
site avancé de soutien logistique naval.
**NAM** National Association of Manufacturers (U.S.A.).
**NAM** Non-Aligned Movement (India).
*Political Parties.*
**NAMAT** naval and marine tactical code.
code tactique naval et maritime.
**NAMC** National Association of Credit Management (U.S.A.).
**NAMEADSMA** NATO Medium Extended Air Defence System Design and Development, Production and Logistics Management Agency.
Agence de gestion pour la conception, le développement, la production et la logistique du système de défense aérienne élargie à moyenne portée de l'OTAN.
**NAMEADSMO** NATO Medium Extended Air Defence System Design and Development, Production and Logistics Management Organization.
Organisation de gestion pour la conception, le développement, la production et la logistique du système de défense aérienne élargie à moyenne portée de l'OTAN.
**NAMFI** NATO missile firing installation.
polygone de tir de missiles de l'OTAN.
**NAMH**; **N.A.M.H.** National Association for Mental Health (U.S.A.).
**NAMI** National Alliance for the Mentally Ill.
Washington D.C.-based.
*U.S. Alliances.*
**NAMIC** National Arsenic Mitigation Information Center.
NAMIC opened in Dhaka on 1st October 1998 with help from the Swiss Government and the World Bank. Arsenic pollution was first detected in Bangladesh in 1993.
*Arsenic Pollution; Hydrogeology; Purification Methods.*
**NAMILCOM** North Atlantic Military Committee.
Comité militaire de l'Atlantique Nord.
**NAMMA** NATO Multi-Role Combat Aircraft Development and Production Management Agency [obsolete - replaced by NETMA].
Bureau de gestion OTAN pour la mise au point et

la production d'un avion de combat polyvalent [obsolète - remplacé par NETMA].

**NAMMO** NATO Multi-Role Combat Aircraft Development and Production Management Organization [obsolete - replaced by NETMO]. Organisation de gestion OTAN pour la mise au point et la production d'un avion de combat polyvalent [obsolète - remplacé par NETMO].

**NAMP** NATO annual manpower plan. plan annuel des effectifs de l'OTAN.

**NAMSA** NATO Maintenance and Supply Agency. Agence OTAN d'entretien et d'approvisionnement.

**NAMSB** National Association of Mutual Savings Banks (U.S.A.).

**NAMSO** NATO Maintenance and Supply Organization. Organisation OTAN d'entretien d'approvisionnement.

**$NaN_3$** Sodium Azide. $NaN_3$ is used mainly for airbag inflation. *Inorganic Chemistry.*

**$NaNbO_3$** Lueshite. *Mineralogy.*

**NAND** NOT AND. *Computer Technology.*

**N&M** November and May. *Securities.*

**NANTIS** Nottingham And Nottinghamshire Technical Information Service. *British Library Association.*

**NAO** National Audit Office (G.B.).

**NAO** North Atlantic Oscillation. NAO is a major source of interannual variability in atmospheric circulation. *Atmospheric Research; Climate; Geophysics; Hydrology; Meteorology.*

**NaOAc** Sodium Acetate. Used mainly in medicine, pharmaceuticals and as a food additive. *Organic Chemistry.*

**NAOC** National Astronomical Observatory Center (China). The NAOC was created by the Chinese Academy of Sciences in April 1999.

**NAOCC** NATO air operation coordination centre. centre de coordination des opérations aériennes de l'OTAN.

**NAOJ** National Astronomical Observatory of Japan.

**NAP** National Academy Press (U.S.A.).

**NAP** Net Aboveground Production. *Ecology.*

**NAP** Neutrophil Activating Protein.

**NAP** Nuclei Armati Proletari (Italy).

**nap** The above acronyms were coined using the English word "nap". *Botany; Textiles.*

**NAPAP** National Acid Precipitation Assessment Project. NAPAP started in the late 1980s. *Acid Rain.*

**NAPBC** National Action Plan on Breast Cancer (U.S.A.).

**NAPC** North American Paleontological Convention (U.S.A.). Held in Washington D.C. in June, 1996. *Evolution; Geology; Mammal Paleontology.*

**NAPF** National Association of Pension Funds (U.S.A.).

**NAPM** National Association of Purchasing Management (U.S.A.).

**NAPMA** NATO Airborne Early Warning and Control (AEW&C) Programme Management Agency. Agence de gestion du programme du système aéroporté de détection lointaine et de contrôle de l'OTAN.

**NAPMO** NATO Airborne Early Warning and Control Programme Management Organization. Organisation de gestion du programme du système aéroporté de détection lointaine et de contrôle de l'OTAN.

**NAPR** NATO armaments planning review. examen de la planification des armements de l'OTAN.

**NAPs** Network Access Points.

**NAR** No Action Required.

**nar** The above acronym was coined accidentally using the Arabic word "nar" which means: fire. *Chemistry; Engineering; Ordnance.*

**NARA** Narcotic Addict Rehabilitation Act. Enacted in 1966. *U.S. Acts.*

**NARA** National Aquatic Resources Agency. *SRI Lanka Agency.*

**NARE** North Atlantic Regional Experiment.

**NARELLO** National Association of Real Estate License Law Officials (U.S.A.).

**NARL** Naval Arctic Research Laboratory. *Arctic Science.*

**NARM** Naturally occurring and Accelerator-produced Radioactive Materials.

**NARS** National Agricultural Research Systems. *Plant-Breeding Programs.*

**NARTC** Nalidixic Acid-Resistant, Thermophilic strains of *Campylobacter* bacteria.

*Bacteriology.*
**NARUC** National Association of Regulatory Utility Commissioners (U.S.A.).
**NAS**; **N.A.S.** National Academy of Sciences (U.S.A.).
**NAS**; **Nas** National Advanced Systems.
**NAS** National Aircraft Standards.
**NAS** National Association of Scholars (U.S.A.).
**NAS** National Association of Schoolmasters.
**NAS** naval air station.
base aéronavale.
**NAS** Network Application Support.
**NAS** Network Attached Storage (Procom Technology).
**NAs** Neutralizing Antibodies.
Also: **NABs**.
**NAS** Non-indigenous Aquatic Species.
**NAS** Nonsense-associated Altered Splicing.
*T-cell Development.*
**N.A.S.** Nucleo Anti-Sofisticazioni (Italy).
Italian acronym meaning: Office for the Prevention of the Adulteration of Beverages and Foodstuffs.
**NAS** Nursing Auxiliary Service.
**nas** The above acronyms were coined accidentally using the Arabic word "nas" which means: people; persons.
**NASA**; **N.A.S.A.** National Aeronautics and Space Administration.
Washington D.C. (U.S.A.).
**NASA** National Association of Securities Administrators (U.S.A.).
**NASADAD** National Association of State Alcohol and Drug Abuse Directors.
Founded in the U.S.A. in 1978.
**NASC** North Atlantic Salmon Convention.
**NASCO** National Academy of Sciences Committee on Oceanography.
NASCO has been replaced by OAB.
For further details see under: **OAB**.
**NASCO** North Atlantic Salmon Conservation Organization (G.B.).
**NASD** National Association of Securities Dealers (U.S.A.).
**NASDA** NAtional Space Development Agency (Japan).
For further details see under: **ISAS**.
**NASDAQ** National Association of Securities Dealers Automated Quotations.
**NASDIM** National Association of Security Dealers and Investment Managers (U.S.A.).
**NASEO** National Association of State Energy Officials (U.S.A.).
**NASIP** NAEW system improvement plan.
plan d'amélioration du système NAEW.
**NASIS** NATO subject indicator system.
système OTAN d'indicateur(s) d'object.
**NAS(N)** National Air Surveillance (Network).
**$Na_2SO_4$** Thenardite.
*Mineralogy.*
**NASP** National Aerospace Plane.
**NASP** NATO ammunition supply point.
point OTAN de ravitaillement en munitions.
**NASSCOM**; **Nasscom** National Association of Software and Services Companies (India).
NASSCOM is a Delhi-based Association.
**NASUCA** National Association of State Utility Consumer Advocates (U.S.A.).
**NASULGC** National Association of State Universities and Land-Grant Colleges.
In Washington D.C., U.S.A.
**NASW** National Association of Science Writers (U.S.A.).
**nat.** (abbr.) national; native; natural.
**NAT** National AIDS Trust.
*British Trust.*
**nat.** (abbr.) naturalist.
**NAT**; **nat** Nitric Acid Trihydrate.
**NAT** No Action Taken.
**NATAS** National Appropriate Technology Assistance Service.
For further details see under: **EREC**.
**NATE** National Association for the Teaching of English.
**NATINAD** NATO Integrated Air Defense [obsolete - replaced by NATINEAD].
défense aérienne intégrée de l'OTAN [obsolète - remplacée par NATINEAD].
**NATINADS** NATO Integrated Air Defence System [obsolete - replaced by NATINEADS].
système de défense aérienne intégrée de l'OTAN [obsolète - remplacé par NATINEADS].
**NATINEAD** NATO Integrated Extended Air Defence [has replaced NATINAD].
défense aérienne intégrée élargie de l'OTAN [remplace NATINAD].
**NATINEADS** NATO Integrated Extended Air Defence System [has replaced NATINADS].
système de défense aérienne intégrée élargie de l'OTAN [remplace NATINADS].
**NATIP** NATO Information and Presss Office.
Bureau OTAN d'information et de presse.
**NATIS** NATional Information System (U.S.A.).
**NATIS** North Atlantic Treaty Information Service.
Service d'information de l'Organisation du Traité de l'Atlantique Nord.

**NATO** North Atlantic Treaty Organization.
Organisation du Traité de l'Atlantique Nord (OTAN).

**NATOCLIP** NATO commander's long-term infrastructure plan.
plan d'infrastructure à long terme des commandements de l'OTAN.

**NATO FORACS** NATO naval forces sensors and weapons accuracy check site.
site de contrôle de précision des armes et des détecteurs des forces navales de l'OTAN (FORACS OTAN).

**NAT radio sources** Narrow-Angle Tailed radio sources.
*Astronomy; Physics.*

**NATM** New Australian Tunnelling Method.
*Concrete.*

**NATS** National Air Traffic Service (G.B.).

**Natwest** (abbr.) National Westminster Bank (G.B.).

**NAU** NATO accounting unit [has replaced IAU].
unité de compte de l'OTAN [remplace UCI].

**NAU** Northern Arizona University (U.S.A.).

**NAV** Net Asset Value.
*Business; Economics; Finance.*

**NAVAID** (abbr.) NAVigational AID.

**NAVAREAS** (abbr.) NAVigation Areas.

**NAVBALTAP** Allied Naval Forces, Baltic Approaches [obsolete].
Forces navales alliées des approches de la Baltique [obsolète].

**NAVCAMSEASTPAC** Naval Communications Area (Master) Station Eastern Pacific.
station(-mère) de zone pour les transmissions navales dans le Pacifique est.

**NAVCAMSLANT** Naval Communications Area (Master) Station Atlantic.
station(-mère) de zone pour les transmissions navales dans l'Atlantique.

**NAVEX** naval exercise.
exercice naval.

**NAVNON** Allied Naval Forces, North Norway [obsolete].
Forces navales alliées du Nord de la Norvège [obsolète].

**NAVNORTH** Allied Naval Forces North [has replaced NAVNORTHWEST].
Forces navales alliées Nord [remplace NAVNORTHWEST].

**NAVNORTHWEST** Allied Naval Forces, North-Western Europe [obsolete - replaced by NAVNORTH].
Forces navales alliées du Nord-Ouest-Europe [obsolète - remplacé par NAVNORTH].

**NAVOCFORMED** Naval On-Call Force Mediterranean [obsolete - replaced by STANAVFORMED].
Force navale alliée disponible sur appel en Méditerranée [obsolète - remplacé par STANAVFORMED].

**NAVO Office** NAVal Oceanographic Office (U.S.A.).

**NAVSAT** (abbr.) NAVigation SATellite.

**NAVSONOR** Allied Naval Forces, South Norway [obsolete].
Forces navales alliées du sud de la Norvège [obsolète].

**NAVSOUTH** Allied Naval Forces, South.
Forces navales alliées Sud.

**NAVSPASUR** (abbr.) NAVal SPAce SURveillance System.
*Navigation.*

**NAWAC** National Aviation Weather Advisory Committee (U.S.A.).

**NAWAS** NAtional WArning System.

**NAWAU** National Aviation Weather Advisory Unit.
Of the U.S. FAA.
For further details see under: **FAA**.

**naz.** (abbr.) nazionale.
Italian abbreviation meaning: national.

**NB** Narrow band / narrow-band.
*Acoustical Engineering; Telecommunications.*

**n.b.** nave da battaglia.
Italian abbreviation meaning: battleship.
*Navy.*

**NB** Newborn.
*Medicine.*

**NB** New Brunswick (Canada).

**Nb** The chemical symbol for Niobium.
Niobium is a chemical element, having the atomic number 41, an atomic weight of 92.9064, and a melting point of 2468°C. It is used manily in steel alloys. Niobium is also known as Columbium.
*Chemistry - Symbols.*

**NB** No Bias.
*Electricity.*

**N.B.** Nota Bene.

**NB** Nucleus Basalis.
NB is a nucleus in the basal forebrain of a rat.
*Anatomy; Cell Biology.*

**NBA** National Bankers / Banking Association (U.S.A.).

**NBA** National Bankruptcy Act.
*U.S. Acts.*

**NBAA** National Business Aircraft Association.

**NBAC** National Bioethics Advisory Committee.
The U.S. National Bioethics Advisory Committee

has replaced in 1993 the President's Commission for the Study of *Ethical Problems* in *Medicine* and *Biomedical and Behavioral Research.*
**NBBB** National Better Business Bureau (U.S.A.).
**NBC** National Broadcasting Corporation (U.S.A.).
**NBC** National Building Code (U.S.A.).
**NBC**; **N.B.C.** Nuclear, Biological, and Chemical (weapons or missile warheads).
*Ordnance.*
**NBC ACC** nuclear, biological and chemical area control centre.
centre de contrôle de secteur nucléaire, biologique et chimique.
**NBCC** National Breast Cancer Coalition (U.S.A.).
**NBC CC** 1. nuclear, biological and chemical collection centre.
1. centre de collecte nucléaire, biologique et chimique.
2. nuclear, biological, chemical control centre.
2. centre de coordination nucléaire, biologique et chimique.
**NBCD** nuclear, biological and chemical defence.
défense nucléaire, biologique et chimique.
**NBC SCC** nuclear, biological and chemical subcollection centre.
centre secondaire de collecte nucléaire, biologique et chimique.
**NBC ZCC** nuclear, biological and chemical zone control centre.
centre de contrôle de zone nucléaire, biologique et chimique.
**NBD** National Bank of Detroit.
*U.S. Bank.*
**NBD** National Bank of Dubai.
Date of opening: January 2001.
**NB-DNJ** N-Butyldeoxynojirimycin.
**NBER** National Bureau of Economic Research (G.B.).
**$NBF_2$** Nucleotide-Binding Fold.
*Cell Biology; Medicine; Metabolism and Endocrinology.*
**NBG** National Bank of Greece.
*Greek Bank.*
**NBH** Neuroscience and Behavioral Health.
**NBI** nuclear burst indicator.
indicateur d'explosion nucléaire.
**NBIF** National Biotechnology Information Facility.
**NBII** National Biological Information Infrastructure (U.S.A.).
The NBII is a U.S. Geological Survey Project.
**NBIOS** Network Basic Input Output System.
*Electronics.*
**NBOs** Nonbridging Oxygens.
**NBP** Name Binding Protocol.
**NBP** National Bank of Poland.
*Polish Bank.*
**NBP** Net Biome Production.
*Climate.*
**NBPS** Non-Bank Private Sector (G.B.).
**NBQX** 6-Nitro-7-Sulphanoyl-Benzo(F) Quinoxalinedion.
**NBR** Nonborrowed / Non-borrowed Reserves.
**NBRF** National Biomedical Research Foundation.
**NBRT** National Board of Respiratory Therapy (U.S.A.).
**NBS** National Biological Service.
Formerly: National Biological Survey.
**NBS** National Biological Survey.
Renamed National Biological Service.
**NBS**; **N.B.S.** National Bureau of Standards.
**NBSS** National Bank Surveillance System (U.S.A.).
**NBSS** National Canadian Breast Screening Survey (Canada).
**NBSV** narrow-band secure voice.
cryptophonie à bande étroite.
**NBSVE** narrow-band secure voice equipment.
matériel de cryptophonie à bande étroite.
**NBTC** National Blood Transfusion Council (India).
The NBTC was created to regulate blood banking.
**NBTI** S-(4-Nitrobenzyl)-6-Thioinosine.
**NBV** Net Book Value.
**NC** Narrow Coverage.
*Business; Economics; Finance.*
**N.C.** National Congress.
**NC** 1. NATO Civilian.
1. civil à statut OTAN.
2. NATO Confidential.
2a. NATO Confidentiel.
2b. OTAN Confidentiel.
2c. Confidentiel OTAN [FR].
**NC** Neo/New - Classical.
*Economics.*
**NC** Net Capital.
*Business; Economics; Finance.*
**NC** Net Cost; No Charge.
*Business; Commerce.*
**NC** Network Computer.
**N/C** New Charter.
**NC** Nitrocellulose.
**NC** no charge.
**nc** noncallable.
*Business; Economics; Finance.*
**NC** Normal Control.
**NC** (abbr.) North Carolina (U.S.A.).
**NCA** Neurocirculatory Asthenia.
NCA is also known as: Da Costa's Syndrome.

*Medicine.*

**NCA** The Netherlands Center for Alternatives to Animal Use.
The NCA is a government-funded research and advocacy center in Utrecht, The Netherlands.
*Biomedical Research; Genetics; Medical Biology; Alternatives to Animal Use.*

**NC3A** NATO Consultation, Command and Control Agency.
Agence de consultation, de commandement et de contrôle de l'OTAN.

**NCAA** NATO Civil Aviation Agency.
Agence OTAN de l'aviation civile.

**NCAB** National Cancer Advisory Board (U.S.A.).

**NCAB** NATO Civil Aviation Board.
Bureau OTAN de l'aviation civile.

**NCAGS** naval cooperation and guidance for shipping [has replaced NCS 3.].
coopération et orientation navales pour la navigation commerciale [remplace NCS 3.].

**NCAGSEX** naval coordination and guidance for shipping exercise [has replaced NCSEX].
exercice de coordination et d'orientation pour la navigation commerciale [remplace NCSEX].

**NCAGSLO** naval cooperation and guidance for shipping liaison officer [has replaced NCSLO].
officier de liaison de la coopération et de l'orientation navales pour la navigation commerciale [remplace NCSLO].

**NCAGSORG** Naval Cooperation and Guidance for Shipping Organization [has replaced NCSORG].
Organisation de la coopération et de l'orientation navales pour la navigation commerciale [remplace NCSORG].

**NCAM** Neuronal Cell Adhesion Molecule.
*Cell Biology; Medicine; Molecular Neurobiology.*

**N-CAMs** Neural Cell Adhesion Molecules.

**NCAQ** National Commission on Air Quality (U.S.A.).

**NCAR** National Center for Atmospheric Research (U.S.A.).

**NCARC** NATO Conventional Armaments Review Committee.
Comité d'examen des armements conventionnels de l'OTAN.

**NCAUR** National Center for Agricultural Utilization Research (U.S.A.).

**NCAVC** National Center for the Analysis of Violent Crime (U.S.A.).

**NCB** National Coal Board.

**NCB** 1. 1. national codification bureau.
1. bureau national de codification (BNC).
2. national competitive bidding.
2. appel d'offres national (AON 2.).

**NCB** Nederlands Centrum Voor Buitenlanders (The Netherlands).

**NCB** Nippon Credit Bank (Japan).
NCB is the smallest of Japan's three long-term credit banks.

**NC3B** NATO Consultation, Command and Control Board.
Bureau de consultation, de commandement et de contrôle de l'OTAN.

**NCBI** National Center for Biotechnology Information (U.S.A.).
*Biotechnology Databases.*

**NCBs** National Central Banks.

**NCC** National Central Catalogue.

**NCC** National Consumer Council.

**NCC** National Council of Churches.

**NCC** National Computing Centre (G.B.).
*Mobile Computing.*

**NCCAM** National Center for Complementary and Alternative Medicine (NIH, U.S.A.).
Established in 1992, NCCAM's mission is to explore complementary and alternative healing practices in the context of rigorous science, educate and train complementary and alternative medicine researchers, and disseminate authoritative information to the public and professionals.
For further details see under: **NIH** and **OAM**.

**NCCAP** NATO CIS contingency assets pool.
pool de moyens SIC de circonstance de l'OTAN.

**NCCB** National Consumer Cooperative Bank (U.S.A.).

**NCCD** National Council on Crime and Delinquency (U.S.A.).

**NCCIS** obsolete - see NACCIS.
obsolète - voir NACCIS.

**NCCM** Natural Community Conservation Model (California, (U.S.A.).
*Biology; Ecology; Ecosystem; Endangered Species; Environment; Habitat Conservation; Zoology.*

**NC code** Numerical Control code.

**NCCP** nuclear command and control procedure.
procédure de commandement et de contrôle nucléaires.

**NCCS** NATO Command and Control System.
système de commandement et de contrôle de l'OTAN.

**NCCU** North Carolina Central University (U.S.A.).

**NCD** No Claims Discount.

**NCD** Non-Cumulative Dividend.
*Business; Economics; Finance.*

**NCDAI** National Clearinghouse for Drug Abuse Information.
The NCDAI was established in the U.S.A. in 1970.

**NCDC** National Climate Data Center (U.S.A.).
For further details see under: **NSRDB**.

**NCEA** National Council for Education Awards.
*Irish Councils.*

**NCEA-CIN** National Center for Environmental Assessment - Cincinnati, U.S.A.

**NCEAS** National Center for Ecological Analysis and Synthesis.
The NCEAS located in Santa Barbara, California, U.S.A. opened in mid-1995.
*Ecology - Environment.*

**NCED** National Center for Earth-Surface Dynamic.
At the University of Minnesota (U.S.A.).

**NCEF** National Clearinghouse for Educational Facilities (U.S.A.).

**NCEF transfer** National Commission on Electronic Funds transfer (U.S.A.).

**NCEH** National Center for Environmental Health (U.S.A.).

**NCEP** National Centers for Environmental Prediction (U.S.A.).

**NCEP** NATO civil emergency planning.
plans civils d'urgence de l'OTAN.

**NCE program** Networks of Centers-of-Excellence program (Canada).
The NCE are university-based research centers. Their purpose is to strengthen industrial research and development through joint projects with private companies.
*Ultralarge Scale Integration; Canadian Research Centers.*
For further details see under: **MICRONET**.

**NCEU** Nuovo Catasto Edilizio Urbano (Italy).
Italian initialism of the: New City Property Registry Office.

**NCF** National Communications Forum.

**NCF** NATO composite force [NAEW].
force mixte de l'OTAN [NAEW].

**NCF** Net Cash Flow.
*Business; Economics; Finance.*

**NCG** Nanochannel Glass.

**NCGR** National Center for Genome Resources.
The NCGR is based in Santa Fe, New Mexico.
*Bioinformatics.*

**N CHG** Normal Charge.
*Business; Commerce.*

**NCHGR** National Center for Human Genome Research.
Of the U.S. NIH.
*Genome Science and Technology; Human Genome Project.*
For further details see under: **NIH**.

**NCHS** National Center for Health Statistics (U.S.A.).

**NCI; N.C.I.** National Cancer Institute (U.S.A.).
Established in 1937, the NCI leads a national effort to reduce the burden of cancer morbidity and mortality. Its goal is to stimulate and support scientific discovery and its application to achieve a future when all cancers are uncommon and easily treated. Through basic and clinical biomedical research and training, the NCI conducts and supports programs to understand the causes of cancer; *prevent, detect, diagnose, treat and control cancer; and disseminate information to the practitioner, patient and public.*

**NCI** Nuclear Cities Initiative.
The NCI is a program launched by Minatom and U.S. DOE in July 1998 (date started 1999) to complement IPP.
*Nuclear Stockpile; U.S. / Russian Initiatives.*
For further details see under: **Minatom**; **DOE** and **IPP**.

**NC3-IC** NATO C3 integration centre.
centre d'intégration des C3 de l'OTAN.

**NCI-FCRDC** National Cancer Institute's Frederick Cancer Research & Development Center (U.S.A.).
The NCI-FCRDC is a GOCO complex.
For further details see under: **GOCO**.

**NCIIA** National Collegiate Inventors and Innovators Alliance.
The NCIIA is an interdisciplinary educational alliance founded in 1995 at Hampshire College (U.S.A.). Its mission is to nurture a new generation of innovators, by fostering and promoting the teaching of invention, innovation and entrepreneurship at colleges and universities nationwide. The NCIIA grants program funds curriculum and program development and independent student projects focusing on commercially directed innovation. Grants Workshop held at Anaheim, California, U.S.A. on 23rd January 1999.

**NCIS** National Criminal Intelligence Service (G.B.).

**NCIS** NATO common interoperability standards.
normes communes d'interopérabilité de l'OTAN.

**NCISE** National Center for Improving Science Education (U.S.A.).

**NCISS** NATO Communications and Information Systems School.
École des systèmes d'information et de communication de l'OTAN.

**NCITD** National Committee on International Trade Documentation (U.S.A.).
**NCL** National Consumers League (U.S.A.).
**NCLA** North Carolina Library Association.
**NCLC** North Country Library Cooperative.
**NCLE** National Congress on Language in Education (U.S.A.).
**NCLS** National Conference of Lawyers and Scientists (U.S.A.).
**NCM** Caudomedial Neostriatum.
The NMC is an auditory area in songbirds brains.
*Integrative Neuroscience; Physiology; Psychiatry.*
**NCM** National Coastal Monitoring (U.S.A.).
**NCMHD** National Center on Minority Health & Health Disparities (U.S.A.).
The NCMHD was founded on 22 November, 2000. Aims: to promote, lead, coordinate, support and assess the NIH effort to reduce and ultimately eliminate health disparities. In this effort NCMHD will conduct and support basic, clinical, social, and behavioural research, promote research infrastructure and training, foster merging programs, disseminate information, and reach out to minority and other health disparity communities. Projects include: Loan Repayment Program, Endowment Program and Project EXPORT.
For further details see under: **NIH** and **EXPORT**.
**NCMO** North-Central Missouri (U.S.A.).
**NCNMLG** Northern California and Nevada Medical Library Group (U.S.A.).
**NCN** 1. NATO circuit number.
1. numéro de circuit OTAN.
2. see NCN/NTR.
2. voir NCN/NTR.
**NCN/NTR** NATO communications network / near-term review.
réseau de télécommunications de l'OTAN / examen à court terme.
**NCNP** National Center of Neurology and Psychiatry (Japan).
**NCNR** National Center for Nursing Research (U.S.A.).
For further details see under: **NINR**.
**NCO** Nuova Camorra Organizzata (Italy).
**NC3O** NATO Consultation, Command and Control Organization.
Organisation de consultation, de commandement et de contrôle de l'OTAN.
**NCOIC** non-commissioned officer in charge.
sous-officier responsable.
**NCP** National Contact Point.
For further details see under: **NCPs**.
**NCP** National People's Congress (China).
**NCP** Network Control Program.
**NCP** Northern Contaminants Program.
For further details see under: **CACAR II**.
*Arctic Ecology.*
**NCPB** National Cancer Policy Board.
The NCPB is based at the U.S. NRC.
For further details see under: **NRC**.
**NCPC** National Capital Planning Commission (U.S.A.).
**NCPH** North Carolina Power Holdings (U.S.A.).
**NCPR** NATO Civilian Personnel Regulations.
Règlement du personnel civil de l'OTAN (RPCO).
**NC protein** Nucleocapsid protein.
*Biochemistry; Chemistry; Medicine.*
**NCPs** National Contact Points.
They offer a special port of call for SMEs and provide a wide range of support services. Set up under FP5 and will continue to operate under FP6.
For further details see under: **FP5** and **SMEs**.
**NCR** National Cash Register.
**NCR** NATO Commander's representative.
représentant du commandant OTAN.
**NCRF** nonclassical Receptive Field.
*Molecular Biology; Neuroscience; Psychology.*
**NcRNAs** noncoding RNAs.
*RNA Silencing.*
For further details see under: **RNA**.
**NCRP**; **N.C.R.P.** National Council on Radiation Protection.
**NCRR** National Center for Research Resources (NIH, U.S.A.).
Established in 1990, the NCRR advances biomedical research and improves human health through research projects and shared resources that create, develop, and provide a comprehensive range of human, animal, tehcnological, and other resources. The NCRR's support is concentrated in four areas: *biomedical technology, clinical research, comparative medicine,* and *research infrastructure.*
For further details see under: **NIH**.
**NCS** 1. NATO codification system.
1. système de codification de l'OTAN.
2. NATO Command Structure.
2. structure de commnadement de l'OTAN.
3. NATO Committee for Standardization.
3. Comité OTAN de normalisation.
4. naval control of shipping [obsolete - replaced by NCAGS].
4. contrôle naval de la navigation commerciale [obsolète - remplacé par NCAGS].
5. net control station.
5. station de contrôle de réseau.
**NCs** Neighborhood Clusters.

*Human Development; Sociology.*
**NCs** Network Computers.
**NCS** Neuronal Calcium Sensors.
**NCS** Non-Callable Securities.
*Business; Economics; Finance.*
**NCS** Noncrystallographic Symmetry.
*Crystallography.*
**NCSA** National Center for Supercomputing Applications.
**NCSA** National Computational Science Alliance (U.S.A.).
*Physical and Computational Sciences.*
For further details see under: **NPACI** and: **PACI**.
**NCSA** National Computer Security Association.
NCSA is a U.S. *Security Software* industry group.
**NCS BCS** National Conference of States on Building Codes and Standards (Herndon, Virginia, U.S.A.).
*U.S. Standards Issuing Organizations.*
**NCSC** National Council of Senior Citizens.
**NCSC** North Carolina Supercomputing Center (U.S.A.).
**NCSEX** naval control of shipping exercise [obsolete - replaced by NCAGSEX].
exercice de contrôle naval de la navigation commerciale [obsolète - remplacé par NCAGSEX].
**NCSL** National Conference of Standards Laboratories.
Boulder, Colorado, U.S.A.
**NCSLO** naval control of shipping liaison officer [obsolete - replaced by NCAGSLO].
officier de laison du contrôle naval de la navigation commerciale [obsolète - remplacé par NCAGSLO].
**NCSN** Northern California Seismic Network.
*Earth & Planetary Science; Geology; Seismology.*
**NCSO** naval control of shipping officer [obsolete].
officier du contrôle naval de la navigation commerciale [obsolète].
**NCSORG** Naval Control of Shipping Organization [obsolete - replaced by NCAGSORG].
Organisation du contrôle naval de la navigation commerciale [obsolète - remplacé par NCAGSORG].
**NCSRC** naval control of shipping regional commander [obsolete].
commandant régional du contrôle naval de la navigation commerciale [obsolète].
**NCSU** North Carolina State University (U.S.A.).
**NCT** National Center for Toxicogenomics (U.S.A.).
**NCT** Non-Competitive Tenders.
*Business; Commerce.*
**NCT** Nuovo Catasto Territoriale (Italy).
Italian initialism meaning: New Land Registry Office.
**NCTE** National Council of Teachers of English.
**NCTM** National Council of Teachers of Mathematics (U.S.A.).
**NCTR** National Center for Toxicological Research (U.S.A.).
**NCTR** non-cooperative target recognition.
reconnaissance des objectifs non coopératifs.
**NCUA** National Coal Utilisation Assessment (U.S.A.).
**NCV** Net Calorific Value.
*Energy.*
**NCV** No Commercial Value.
*Business; Commerce.*
**NCVA** National Council for Vocational Awards.
*Irish Councils.*
**NCVQ** National Council for Vocational Qualification (U.S.A.).
**NCWA** NATO civil wartime agency.
agence civile OTAN du temps de guerre (ACOG).
**NCWM** National Conference on Weights and Measures (U.S.A.).
**ND** National Debt.
**N.D.**; **ND** Navy Department (U.S.A.).
**Nd** The chemical symbol for Neodymium.
Neodymium is a metallic element having the atomic number 60, an atomic weight of 144.24 and a melting point of 1024°C. Neodymium is used mainly in alloys, and electronics.
*Chemistry; Symbols.*
**ND** Net Debt; New Deal.
**ND** Nobildonna.
Italian initialism meaning: Noblewoman.
**ND**; **n.d.** no date; not dated.
**ND** (abbr.) North Dakota (U.S.A.).
Also: **N.Dak**.
**NDA** Naphthalene-2,3-Dicarboxaldehyde.
**NDA**; **N.D.A.** National Dental Association (U.S.A.).
**NDA** New Drug Application.
**NDA** Nondestructive Assay.
The NDA is a method used to determine burnup and fissile content of irradiated *nuclear fuels*.
**NdA** Nota dell'Autore; Note de l'Auteur.
Italian and French initialism meaning: Author's Note.
**NDAC** Nuclear Defence Affairs Committee.
Comité des questions de défense nucléaire.
**NDAG** NATO Data Administration Group.
Groupe pour l'administration des données de l'OTAN.
**N.Dak.** North Dakota (U.S.A.).
Also: **ND**.

**NDB** National Development Plan.
Funded by the Irish Government.
**NDB** National Discount Brokers (Germany).
NDB was acquired by the Deutsche Bank in 2000.
**NDB** nuclear depth bomb.
grenade anti-sous-marine nucléaire.
**NDBC** National Data Buoy Center (U.S.A.).
**NDBO** National Data Buoy Office (U.S.A.).
**NDC** National Democratic Congress (Ghana).
**NDC** see NADEFCOL.
voir NADEFCOL.
**$NdCl_3$** Neodymium Chloride.
*Inorganic Chemistry.*
**NDE** Non Destructive Evaluation.
*Energy.*
**NdE** Nota dell'Editore; Note de l'Editeur.
Italian and French initialism meaning: Publisher's Note.
**NDEA** N-nitrosodiethylamine.
**NDF** Nucleosome Disruption Factor.
*Biochemistry; Gene Expression; Molecular Biology.*
**NDGA** Nordihydroguaiaretic Acid.
*Organic Chemistry.*
**NDI** non-development item.
article non destiné au développement.
**NDIC** NATO defence information complex.
ensemble des systèmes d'information pour la défense de l'OTAN.
**NDK** Nucleoside Diphosphokinase.
*Enzymology.*
**NDL** Non-Deposit Liabilities (G.B.).
*Banking.*
**NDLA** North Dakota Library Association (U.S.A.).
**NDMA** NATO data management authority.
autorité de gestion des données de l'OTAN.
**NDMAA** NATO Defence Manpower Audit Authority [has replaced NDMMSC].
Autorité chargé de l'évaluation des besoins en effectifs de défense de l'OTAN [remplace la NDMMSC].
**NDMC** NATO Defence Manpower Committee.
Comité des effectifs de défense de l'OTAN.
**NDMMSC** NATO Defence Manpower Management Survey Capability [obsolete - replaced by NDMAA].
Équipe d'étude de gestion des effectifs de défense de l'OTAN [obsolète - remplacé par la NDMAA].
**NDO** Naphthalene Dioxygenase.
*Biochemistry; Microbiology; Molecular Biology.*
**NDO** National Debt Office (Sweden).
**NDP** National Development Plan.
Funded by the Irish Government.
**NDP** Non Doversi Procedere (non luogo a procedere).
Italian initialism meaning: no suit.
*Law.*
**NDPR** NATO defence planning review.
examen des plans de défense de l'OTAN.
**NDR** Natural Disasters Roundtable (U.S.A.).
**NdR** Nota della Redazione; Note de la Rédaction.
Italian and French initialism meaning: Editor's Note.
**NDRI** National Disease Research Interchange.
Funded by the U.S. NIH, the NDRI supplies scientists worldwide with human tissues and organs donated for research.
For further details see under: **NIH**.
**NDRO** Nondestructive Readout.
**NDS** non-development software.
logiciel non destiné au développement.
**NDS**; **Nds** Novell Directory Services.
**NDS** Nuclear Diagnostic System.
**NDSC** Network for the Detection of Stratospheric Change (New Zealand).
**NDSEG Fellowships** National Defense Science and Engineering Graduate Fellowships (U.S.A.).
**NDSS** NATO depot support system.
système de soutien des dépôts de l'OTAN.
**NDSU** North Dakota State University (U.S.A.).
**NDT** Net Data Throughput.
**NDT** Neurodevelopmental Treatment.
**NDT** non-destructive testing.
essai non destructif.
**NdT** Nota del Traduttore.
Italian initialism meaning: Translator's Note.
**NDTE** North Dakota Tracer Experiment.
**NDT method** Non-Destructive Testing method.
**N du T** Note du Traducteur.
French initialism meaning: Translator's Note.
**NDVI** Normalized Difference Vegetation Index.
*Atmospheric Research; Earth, Oceans, and Space Studies; Natural Resource Ecology; Plant Biology; Evolution.*
**NE** National Exhibition.
**NE** Naval Engineer.
**NE** (abbr.) Nebraska (U.S.A.).
Also: **Neb**.
**Ne** The chemical symbol for Neon.
Neon is a gaseous element having the atomic number 10, an atomic weight of 20.180 and a melting point of -249°C. Neon is used mainly in fluorescent lighting, and lasers.
*Chemistry; Symbols.*
**NE** Net Earnings.
*Business; Economics; Finance.*

**NE** Neutrophil Elastase.
**NE**; **N/E** New Edition.
**NE** New England.
**NE** No Effects.
**N-E** Nord-Est.
meaning: North-East in Italian.
**NE** Norepinephrine.
Norepinephrine is also known as: Noradrenaline.
*Endocrinology.*
**N/E** not entered.
**NE** not equal.
**n.e.** not exceeding.
**NE** Nuclear Envelope.
*Cytomegalovirus; Electron Microscopy.*
**N:EA** Napoli: Europa Africa (Naples, Italy).
*Italian Organization.*
**NEA** National Endowment for the Arts (U.S.A.).
**NEA** Near-Earth Asteroid.
*Astronomy; Planetary Science; Physics.*
**NEAFC** North-East Atlantic Fisheries Commission.
**NEA material** Negative Electron Affinity material.
*Electronics.*
**NEACP** National Emergency Airborne Command Post (U.S.A.).
*Ordnance.*
**NEAPACC Project** North East Atlantic Paleoceanography and Climate Change Project.
*Earth Sciences; Geochemistry; Geophysics; Global Biogeochemistry.*
**NEAP probe** Near Earth Asteroid Prospector probe.
NEAP was built in 1998 and launched in mid-1999.
*Asteroids; Chemistry; Geology; Planetary Science.*
**NEAR spacecraft** Near Earth Asteroid Rendezvous spacecraft - NASA's.
NEAR returned to Earth in 1998, two years after its launch. On the 3rd January 1999, NEAR was put into a trajectory that float it back to asteroid Eros on 14th February 2000.
*Planetary Science.*
**NEAs** Near-Earth Asteroids.
*Astronomy; Earth, Atmospheric, and Planetary Sciences; Physics.*
For further details see under: **LINEAR project**.
**NEAT** National Electronic Autocoding Technique.
**NEAT** Nonexercise Activity Thermogenesis.
*Biochemistry; Endocrinology; Human Physiology; Medicine; Molecular Biology.*
**NEAT system** Near Earth Asteroid Tracking system - NASA's.
*Planetary Science; Solar Satellites.*
**NEB** National Enterprise Board.
**Neb.** (abbr.) Nebraska (U.S.A.).
Also: **NE**.
**NEB** New England Biolabs (U.S.A.).
**NEB** Noise Equivalent Bandwidth.
*Communications.*
**NEB** North Equatorial Belt.
**NEB** Nuclear Envelope Breakdown.
Also: **NEBD**.
*Embryology; Microtubule Polymerization; Nuclear Trafficking.*
**NEBs** Neuroepithelial Bodies.
**NEB technique** Nudged Elastic Band technique.
*Chemistry; Geochemistry; Physics.*
**NEC** National Economic Council (G.B.).
**NEC** National Electrical Code.
**NEC** National Enterprises Corporation (G.B.).
**NEC** North Equatorial Current.
**NEC** Northern European Command [obsolete].
Commandement du Nord-Europe [obsolète].
**NEC** Nuclear Energy Center.
**NEC** Nuclear Energy Commission.
**NEC** Nuclei Ecologici Carabinieri (Italy).
**NEC** Null Energy Condition.
*Physics.*
**NECB** NATO Exercise Coordination Board.
Commission de coordination des exercices de l'OTAN.
**NECC** North Equatorial Countercurrent.
*Oceanography.*
**NECHI** Northeastern Consortium of Health Information.
**NECOP program** Nutrient-Enhanced Coastal Ocean Productivity program.
**NECs** Neuroepithelial Cells.
**NED** NATO effective data.
date d'entrée en vigueur OTAN.
**NED** No Evidence of Disease.
**NEDB** NATO Emitter Database.
base de données OTAN sur les émetteurs.
**NEDC** National Economic Development Council (G.B.).
**NEDH** New England Deaconess Hospital.
**NEDO** New Energy and industrial technology Development Organization (Tokyo, Japan).
**NEDP** (BI-SC) NATO Exercise Directive and Programme.
Directive-programme des exercices de l'OTAN (des SC).
**NEE** Net Ecosystem Exchange.
**NEET** Nuclear Excitation by Electron Transition.
*Physics.*
**NEF** National Energy Foundation (G.B.).
**NEF** New Economics Foundation (G.B.).
**NEFA** Nonesterified Fatty Acids.

*Medicine.*

**NEFMA** NATO European Fighter Aircraft Development, Production and Logistic Management Agency [obsolete-replaced by NETMA].
Agence de gestion OTAN pour le développement, la production et la logistique de l'avion de combat européen [obsolète - remplacée par la NETMA].

**NEFMO** NATO European Fighter Aircraft Development, Production and Logistic Management Organization.
Organisation de gestion OTAN pour le développement, la production et la logistique de l'avion de combat européen.

**NEG** Numerical Experimentation Group.

**negb.** (abbr.) negotiable.

**Neg.Inst.** (abbr.) Negotiable Instrument.
*Business; Economics; Finance.*

**NEI** National Eye Institute (U.S.A.).
Established in 1968, the NEI, part of the NIH, is the U.S. Government's principal agency for conducting and supporting vision research. The NEI conducts research in the own laboratory and clinical facilities located on the NIH campus in Bethesda, Maryland and supports extramural research at universities, medical schools, hospitals, and other institutions throughout the United States and abroad. Major NEI program areas include the *retina*; the *cornea*; *cataract*; *glaucoma*; and *strabismus, amblyopia,* and *visual processing*; and *visual impairment and its rehabilitation.*
For further details see under: **NIH**.

**NEI** Nederlands Economisch Instituut (The Netherlands).
*Dutch Institutes.*

**nei** The above acronyms were coined accidentally using the Italian word "nei" which means: beauty-spots; birth-marks.

**NEIC** National Earthquake Information Center (U.S.A.).

**NEIS** National Earthquake Information Service (U.S.A.).

**NEJM** New England Journal of Medicine (U.S.A.).

**NEL** National Engineering Laboratory (G.B.).

**NEL** No Effect Level.

**NELA** National Electric Light Association (U.S.A.).

**NELA** New England Library Association (U.S.A.).

**NELIAC** Navy Electronics Laboratory International Algol Compiler.
*Computer Programming.*

**NELINET** New England LIbrary NETwork.

**NELLCO** New England Law Library COnsortium.

**NELS** National Educational Longitudinal Study (U.S.A.).

**NEM** N-Ethylmaleimide.

**NEMA** National Electrical Manufacturers Association (U.S.A.).

**NEMD** Nonequilibrium Molecular Dynamics.
*Physics; Shock Waves.*

**NeMO** New Millenium Observatory.
*Marine Science; Oceanography.*

**N.Eng.** Northern England.

**NEO** Near-Earth Orbit.

**NEO** non-combatant evacuation operation.
opération d'évaluation de non-combattants.

**néol** néologisme.
French abbreviation meaning: neologism.
*Linguistics.*

**NEON** National Ecological Observatory Network (U.S.A.).
NEON stations are equipped with sensor arrays, gene sequencers and computing power for petascale databases.
*Environmental Science.*

**NEOUCOM** Northeastern Ohio Universities College Of Medicine (U.S.A.).

**NEP** National Energy Programme (Canada).

**NEP** Net Ecosystem Production.
*Ecology.*

**NEP** noise equivalent power.

**NEPA** National Environmental Policy Act.
Advent: 1969.
*U.S. Acts.*

**NEPA** Nuclear Energy Propulsion Aircraft.

**NEPHGE** Nonequilibrium pH Gradient Electrophoresis.
*Cell Biology and Anatomy; Medicine.*

**NEPB** NATO Exercise Policy Board.
Commission sur les orientations des exercices de l'OTAN.

**NEPS** North European Pipeline System.
réseau de pipelines du Nord-Europe.

**NEQ** net explosive quantity.
poids (ou quantité) net(te) d'explosifs.

**NERC** National Ecology Research Center (U.S.A.).

**NERC** National Environmental Research Council (G.B.).
Swindon-based, NERC is one of five research councils funded by the Department of Education and Science.
For further details see under: **CEH** and **COAPEC**.

**NERC** Northern American Electric Reliability Council.

**NERI** National Environmental Research Institutes (Denmark).

**NERI** Nuclear Energy Research Initiative.
Created by the U.S. Department Of Energy.
*Cold Fusion Studies; New Technologies for Nuclear Waste Storage; New Reactor Designs; Physics; Proliferation; Resistant Reactors.*

**NERL** National Exposure Research Laboratory (U.S.A.).
At the U.S. EPA, NERL conducts research and development related to exposure of people and ecosystems to air, water, and soil pollutants.
For further details see under: **EPA**.

**NERMLS** New England Regional Medical Library Service.

**NERP** National Environmental Research Park.
The first NERP (at the Savannah River - South Carolina) was designated by the Atomic Energy Commission (now DOE, U.S.A.) in 1972.
*Ecology; Wildlife.*
For further details see under: **DOE**.

**NER-PRC** New England Regional Primate Research Center (U.S.A.).

**NER proteins** Nucleotide Excision Repair proteins.
*Biochemistry; Cancer Research; Developmental Biology; DNA damage; DNA transcription and Replication.*

**NERVA** Nuclear Engine for Rocket Vehicle Application.
*Nuclear Engineering.*

**NES** National Energy Strategy (U.S.A.).

**NES** NATO electronic warfare support measures system.
système OTAN de mesures de soutien de guerre électronique.

**NES** Non-English Speakers.

**NESC** National Electric Safety Code.

**NESCAUM** The Northeast States for Coordinated Air Use Management (U.S.A.).
An Association of state regulatory agencies in New York, New England, and New Jersey. The aim of the Association is to protect the environment and the public from exposure to high levels of air pollutants.

**NESDIS** National Environmental Satellite, Data, and Information Service.
Of the U.S. NOAA.
For further details see under: **NOAA**.

**NESHAP** National Emissions Standards for Hazardous Air Pollutants (U.S.A.).

**NESS** National Environmental Satellite Service.

**NESS** NATO electronic warfare support measures and strike system.
système OTAN de mesures de soutien de guerre électronique et d'intervention.

**ness** The above acronyms were coined using the English word "ness"
*Geology.*

**NEST** Nuclear Emergency Search Team (U.S.A.).
*Nuclear Defense.*

**nest** The above acronym was coined using the English word "nest".
*Computer Programming; Geology; Vertebrate Zoology.*

**NESTOR** NEutrinos from Supernovae and TeV sources, Ocean Range.

**NET** Next European Torus.

**NET** norme européenne de télécommunication.
European telecommunication standard (ETS).

**NET** Not Earlier Than.

**Netec** Network economy.
Also: Net economy.

**NETF** NATO expanded task force.
force opérationnelle OTAN élargie.

**NETMA** NATO EF 2000 and Tornado Development, Production & Logistics Management Agency [has replaced NAMMA and NEFMA].
Agence de gestion OTAN pour le développement, la production et la logistique de l'ACE 2000 et du Tornado [remplace la NAMMA et la NEFMA].

**NETMO** NATO EF 2000 and Tornado Development, Production & Logistics Management Organization [has replaced NAMMO and NEFMO].
Organisation de gestion OTAN pour le développement, la production et la logistique de l'ACE 2000 et du Tornado [remplace NAMMO et NEFMO].

**NETTOX** (abbr.) NETwork on TOXicants.
*European Community Project.*

**NEU** neutral merchant ship.
navire de commerce neutre.

**NeuAc** N-Acetylneuraminic Acid.
*Immunology; Virology.*

**NEWAC** NATO Electronic Warfare Advisory Committee.
Comité consultatif OTAN sur la guerre électronique.

**Newfld.** (abbr.) Newfoundland.
Also: **NF**.

**NEWTEST** high performance Neural Network signal processing for Wireless TErrestrial and Satellite Transmissions.
*European Community Project.*

**NEWVAN** NATO electronic warfare van.
module de guerre électronique de l'OTAN.

**NEZA** New Stock Exchange Market (Greece).

**NEXAFS** Near-Edge X-ray Absorption Fine Structure.
**NEXRAD** NEXt generation RADar.
**NExT** New Experiences in Teaching (U.S.A.).
*Mathematics Teaching; Pedagogic Reforms.*
**NF**; **nf** nanofarad.
**NF** Nephritic Factor.
*Medicine.*
**NF** Nerve Fiber.
*Cell Biology.*
**NF** Newfoundland.
Also: **Newfld**.
**NF** non focalizzata.
**NF** Non-Fundable.
*Business; Economics; Finance.*
**NF** Norman-French.
**NF** Norme Française.
**NF** Nouveau(x) Franc(s).
Now: EURO/EUR (€). Became ECU (European single currency) with effect from January 2002.
*Currencies.*
**NF1** Neurofibromatosis type 1.
An inherited disorder characterized by the development of multiple benign tumors in the nervous system that at times become malignant.
*Nerve Disorders.*
**$NF_3$** Nitrogen Trifluoride.
$NF_3$, also known as: Nitrogen Fluoride, is used mainly in chemical synthesis.
*Inorganic Chemistry.*
**NFA** National Futures Association (U.S.A.).
**NFA** New Financing Agreement.
Bosnia-Hercegovina (1988-Agreement).
**NFA** no-fire-area.
zone de sécurité.
**NF-AT cells** Nuclear Factor of Activated T cells.
*Blood Research; Cancer Biology; Cell Biology; Medicine; Molecular Biology; Pathology; Signal Transduction.*
**NFC** National Finance Center (U.S.A.).
**NFC** National Freight Corporation (U.S.A.).
**NFC** national fusion centre.
centre national de fusionnement de données.
**NFD** Negative File Database.
The NFD was built by Lightbridge of the U.S.A.
*Fraud Detection Systems.*
**NFF** No Fault Found.
**NFFE** National Foundation for Fairness in Education.
**NFFTIPO** Naval Fleet / Force Program Office (U.S.A.).
The NFFTIPO ensures a link between the Department of Navy S&T Program and Joint, Navy and Marine Corps Commands worldwide.
**NFH** NATO frigate helicopter.
hélicoptère pour la frégate OTAN.
**NFI** National FIsheries Center (U.S.A.).
**NFI** Neurofibromatosis.
NFI is laso known as: von Recklinghausen's disease.
**NFL** National Federation of Laymen.
**NFL** National Football League.
**NFL** National Forensic League.
**NFL** no-fire line.
ligne de sécurité.
**NFLS** naval forward logistic site.
site logistique naval de l'avant.
**NfMRIDC** National functional MRI Data Center.
Launched in fall 2000.
*U.S. Data Centers.*
For further details see under: **MRI**.
**NFO** NATO FORACS Office.
Bureau OTAN des FORACS.
**NFO microscopy** Near-Field Optical microscopy.
**NFOV infrared radiometer** Narrow Field Of View infrared radiometer.
**NFP** Not-For-Profit (colleges and universities).
For further details see under: **FASB** and **SFAS**.
**NFPA** National Fire Protection Association.
*Safety.*
**NFPA** National Fluid Power Association.
**NFR** NATO Financial Regulations.
Règlement financier de l'OTAN (RFO).
**NFR** Naturvetenskapliga Forskningsrådet (Stockholm, Sweden).
The NFR is the Swedish Natural Science Research Council.
**NFROT** National Framework for the Recognition Of Training.
**NFS** NATO force structure.
structure de forces de l'OTAN.
**NFs** Nested Fullerenes.
*Materials and Interfaces; Materials Science and Engineering.*
**NFS** Network File System.
**NFs** Neurofilaments.
*Cell Biology.*
**NFS** Not For Sale.
*Business; Commerce.*
**NFS** Nuclear Fission Safety.
Research and education program (1990-1994).
*Euratom Programs.*
**NFS** Nuclear Forward Scattering.
*Physics.*
**NFS** Numeration, Formule Sanguine.

French initialism meaning: Blood Count and Differential White Count.
*Medicine.*
**NFSAT** National Foundation of Science and Advanced Technologies - Armenia.
*Advanced Technologies; Armenian/U.S. Projects; Biosensors; Cocaine Antagonists.*
**NF Standards** National Formulary Standards.
**NFT** Networks File Transfer.
**NFTs** Narrow-Field X-ray Telescopes.
The NFTs are contained in the BeppoSAX: the Italian-Dutch satellite launched in 1996.
*Astrophysics; Italian/Dutch Satellites.*
**NFU** National Farmers' Union (G.B.).
**NFZ** no-fly zone.
zone d'exclusion (ou d'interdiction) aérienne.
**NG** National Gallery; National Government; National Guard.
**NG** 1. Naval group [has replaced IEG].
1. groupe naval [ remplace l'IEG].
2. Niger.
2. Niger.
**NG** New Guinea.
**NG** Nitroglycerine.
Nitroglycerine is used mainly as a high explosive.
*Organic Chemistry.*
**NGA** National Governor's Association (U.S.A.).
**NGA** National Graphical Association.
**NgB** Neuroglobin.
NgB is a recently discovered $O_2$-binding protein.
*Biomedicine.*
**NGCC plants** Natural Gas Combined Cycle plants.
*Energy.*
**NGCS** NATO General-Purpose Segment Communication System.
système de communication du segment à usage général de l'OTAN.
**NGDC** National Geophysical Data Center.
Of the U.S. NOAA.
For further details see under: **NOAA**.
**NGF** Nerve Growth Factor.
*Endocrinology.*
**NGFIA** Nerve Growth Factor - Induced A.
*Neuroscience.*
**NGHTS** Next Generation Highway Traffic System.
**NGI** Next Generation Internet (U.S.A.).
The NGI was announced in october 1996 by President Clinton. A test-bed for technology and applications.
**NGI initiative** Next Generation Internet initiative (U.S.A.).
*Electronic Superhighways; Joint Research.*
**NGNs** Next Generation Networks (Compaq).
**NGO** Non-Governmental Observer.
**NGO** Non-Governmental Organization.
**NGOs** Non-Governmental Organizations.
**NGP** Nomenclature Générale des Produits (France).
**NGP** Northern Great Plains.
**NGRI** Not Guilty by Reason of Insanity.
*Criminal Law; Criminology.*
**NGRS** National Geodetic Reference System.
**NGS** National Geodetic Survey (U.S.A.).
**NGS** National Geographic Society (U.S.A.).
**NGS** naval gunfire support.
appui-feu naval.
**NGST** Next Generation Space Telescope.
The NGST is a United States-Europe collaboration to build the successor to the Hubble Space Telescope. The 8m. primary mirror telescope will be launched in 2007.
*Astronomy; Astrophysics; Galaxy Evolution.*
**NGTs** Noble Gas Temperatures.
**NGU** Nongonococcal Urethritis.
NGU is a human urethral inflammation.
*Medicine.*
**NGVL** National Gene Vector Laboratories (U.S.A.).
*Human Gene; Therapy Trials; Vector Production.*
**N.H.** National Hosts.
*European Community Initiative.*
**NH** (abbr.) New Hampshire (U.S.A.).
**NH** New High.
**NH** Northern Hemisphere.
**NH** North Holland.
*Publishers.*
**NH** Not Held.
*Business; Commerce.*
**NHA** National Hydrogen Association (U.S.A.).
**NHANES** National Health And Nutrition Examination Survey (U.S.A.).
*Human Nutrition; Preventive and Behavioral Medicine; Obesity.*
**NHC** Non-Holding Company.
**$NH_4Cl$** Ammonium Chloride.
$NH_4Cl$ also known as: Sal Ammoniac is used mainly in medicine and in dry cells.
*Inorganic Chemistry.*
**NHDP** Nicotinamide Hypoxanthine Dinucleotide.
**NHE** Normal Hydrogen Electrode.
**NHE laboratory** New Hydrogen Energy laboratory (Japan).
NHE was shut down due to lack of support in commercial development.
*Cold Fusion.*
**NHEJ** Nonhomologous End-Joining.
*Biochemistry; Cancer Research; DNA damage; Developmental Biology; Oxidative Metabolism.*

For further details see under: **NER** and **IR**.

**NHEJ process** Nonhomologous End Joining process.
*Biophysics; Biotechnology; Cellular Biochemistry; Eukaryotes; DSBs repair.*
For further details see under: **DSBs**.

**NHG** Northern Hemisphere Glaciation.
*Oceanography; Paleoceanography.*

**NHGRI** National Human Genome Research Institute (U.S.A.).
Established in 1989, the NHGRI supports the NIH component of the Human Genome Project, a worldwide research effort designated to analyze the structure of human DNA and determine the location of the estimated 30,000 to 40,000 human genes. The NHGRI Intramural Research Program *develops and implements technology for understanding, diagnosing, and treating genetic diseases.*
For further details see under: **NIH**.

**NHI** National Heart Institute (U.S.A.).

**NHI** National Health Insurance.

**NHL** National Home Loans (G.B.).

**NHL** non-Hodgkin's Lymphoma.

**NHLBI** National Heart, Lung and Blood Institute (U.S.A.).
Established in 1948, the NHLBI, provides leadership for a national program in diseases of the heart, blood vessels, lung, and blood; blood resources; and sleep disorders. Since October 1997, the NHLBI has also had administrative responsibility for the NIH Woman's Health Initiative. The Institute plans, conducts, fosters, and supports an integrated and coordinated program of *basic research, clinical investigations and trials, observational studies, and demonstration and education projects.*
For further details seeunder: **NIH**.

**NHM** Natural History Museum (G.B.).

**NHMFL** National High Magnetic Field Laboratory.
The NHMFL was established in 1993 by Florida State University (U.S.A.).
*Condensed-Matter Physics; Magnet Science; Magnet Technology.*

**NHMO** NATO HAWK Management Office.
Bureau de gestion OTAN HAWK (BGOH).

**NHMRC** National Health and Medical Research Council (Australia).

**$NH_2OH$** Hydroxylamine.
Hydroxylamine, also known as: Oxammonium, is used mainly in organic synthesis.
*Inorganic Chemistry.*

**NHP** Nominal Horsepower.

**NHPLO** NATO HAWK Production and Logistics Organization.
Organisation de production et de logistique OTAN HAWK (OPLOH).

**NHPP** National Hormone and Pituitary Program (U.S.A.).
Through the NHPP, reagents are supplied free for research purposes.

**NHQC3S** NATO Headquarters C3 Staff.
Secrétariat des C3 du siège de l'OTAN.

**NHRE** National Hail Research Experiment.
Of the U.S. NCAR.
For further details see under: **NCAR**.

**NHS** National Health Service.

**NHSMAL** NHS-Maleimide.

**NHS VS** NHS-Vinylsulfone.

**NHTSA** National Highway Traffic / Transportation Safety Administration (U.S.A.).

**NI** National Income.

**NI** National Insurance.

**NI** Negotiable Instrument.
*Business; Economics; Finance.*

**NI** net income.

**Ni** Net interest.
*Business -Finance.*

**Ni** The chemical symbol for Nickel.
*Symbols; Chemistry.*

**NI** Nigeria.

**NI** Normal Information.

**NI** Northern Ireland.

**NIA** National Indoor Arena - Birmingham, G.B.

**NIA** National Institute on Aging (U.S.A.).
Established in 1974, the NIA leads a national program of research on the *biomedical, social, and behavioural aspects of the aging process; the prevention of age-related diseases and disabilities; and the promotion of a better quality of life* for all older Americans.

**NIA** Nuclear Installation Act (1965).

**NIAAA** National Institute on Alcohol Abuse and Alcoholism (U.S.A.).
Established in 1970, the NIAAA conducts research focused on improving the treatment and prevention of *alcoholism and alcohol-related problems* to reduce the enormous health, social, and economic consequences of this disease.

**NIACE** National Institute of Adult Continuing Education (G.B.).
*British Institutes.*

**NIAF** National Italian-American Foundation.

**NIAG** NATO Industrial Advisory Group.
Groupe consultatif industriel OTAN.

**NIAID** National Institute of Allergy and Infectious Diseases (U.S.A.).
NIAID has its roots in the Hygienic Laboratory established in 1887, the predecessor of the modern NIH. The Rocky Mountain Laboratory and the Biologics Control Laboratory, formed in 1902, merged with NIH's Division of Infectious Diseases and the Division of Tropical Diseases in 1948 to form the National Microbiological Institute. In 1955, Congress gave the Institute its present name to reflect the inclusion of allergy and immunology research. Projects, Programs, Aims: NIAID conducts and supports research that strives to understand, treat, and ultimately prevent the myriad infectious, immunologic, and allergic diseases that threaten hundreds of millions of people worlwide. Major areas of investigation: *Acquired Immunodeficiency Syndrome; Asthma* and *Allergic Diseases; Biodefense, Emerging Diseases; Enteric Diseases; Genetics* and *Transplantation; Immunologic Diseases; Vaccine Development.* Other areas of research include: *fungal diseases, hospital-associated infections, respiratory diseases,* and *antiviral and antimicrobial drug development.*

**NIAMS** National Institute of Arthritis and Musculoskeletal and Skin Diseases (U.S.A.).
Established in 1986, the NIAMS supports research into the causes, treatment, and prevention of arthritis and musculoskeletal and skin diseases, the training of basic and clinical scientists to carry out this research, and the dissemination of information on research progress in these diseases.

**NIAS** National Institute for Advanced Studies (India).

**NIAS**; **Nias** Novell Internet Access Server.

**NIB** National Investment Bank (The Netherlands).

**NIB** 1. NATO Intelligence Board.
1. Bureau OTAN du renseignement.
2. naval infantry brigade.
2. brigade d'infanterie de marine.

**NIBIB** National Institute of Biomedical Imaging and Bioengineering (U.S.A.).
Established in 2000, the NIBIB improves health by promoting fundamental discoveries, design and development, and translation and assessment of technological capabilities in *biomedical imaging* and *bioengineering*, enabled by relevant areas of *information science, physics, chemistry, mathematics, materials science,* and *computer sciences.*

**NIBN** National Institute for Biotechnology in the Negev.
At Ben-Gurion University of the Negev (Israel).

**NIBOR** New York Interbank Offered Rate.

**NIBSC** National Institute for Biological Standards and Control (G.B.).
*Biological Medicines.*

**NIC** National Income Commission.

**NIC** 1. national intelligence cell (or centre).
1. cellule (ou centre) national(e) de renseignement.
2. NATO International Civilian.
2. personnel (ou agent) civil OTAN à statut international.

**NIC** Network Information Center.

**NIC** Newly Industrialized Country.

**NIC** (abbr.) Nicaragua.

**NICC** Northern Ireland Curriculum Council (Ireland).

**NICE** National Institute of Clinical Excellence (G.B.).
The NICE advises on risks, benefits, cost-effectiveness and use of new drugs.

**NICEC** National Institute for Careers Education and Counselling.
*British Institutes.*

**NICHD** National Institute of Child Health and Human Development (U.S.A.).
Established in 1962, the NICHD's research on *fertility, pregnancy, growth, development, and medical rehabilitation* strives to ensure that every child is born healthy and wanted and grows up free from diseases and disability.

**NICL** National Ice Core Laboratory.
Lakewood, Colorado, U.S.A.

**$NiCl_2$** Nickel Chloride.
$NiCl_2$ is used mainly in chemical reagents and electroplating.
*Inorganic Chemistry.*

**NICMOS** Near Infrared Camera and Multi-Object Spectrograph.
The NICMOS is an instrument aboard the HST used to collect and analyze wavelengths of light that have never been seen from space before.
*Astronomy; Engineering; Planetary Science; Space Science.*
For further details see under: **HST**.

**NICOP** Northwest Interlibrary Cooperative of Pennsylvania (U.S.A.).

**NICs** National Insurance Contributions.

**NICS** NATO integrated communications system.
système de télécommunications intégré de l'OTAN.

**NICs** Newly Industrialized Countries.

**NICS COA** NICS Central Operating Authority [obsolete - see NACOSA].

Autorité centrale d'exploitation du NICS [obsolète - voir NACOSA].

**NICS OCO** NICS Operating and Control Organization [obsolete - see OCO].
Organisation de contrôle de l'exploitation du NICS [obsolète - voir OCO].

**NICSOI** NICS operating instruction.
instructions d'exploitation du NICS.

**NID** naval infantry division.
division d'infanterie de marine.

**NID** Next IDentifier.

**NID** NR-Interacting Domain.
For further details see under: **NR**.

**NIDA** National Institute on Drug Abuse (U.S.A.).
Established in 1973, the NIDA leads the nation in bringing the power of science to bear on drug abuse and addiction through support and conduct of research across a broad range of disciplines and rapid and effective dissemination of results of that *research to improve drug abuse and addiction prevention, treatment, and policy*.
For further details see under: **NIH**.

**NIDCD** National Institute of Deafness and Other Communication Disorders (U.S.A.).
Established in 1988, the NIDCD conducts and supports *biomedical research* and research training on normal mechanisms as well as *diseases and disorders of hearing, balance, smell, taste, voice, speech,* and *language* that affect 46 million Americans.

**NIDCR** National Institute of Dental and Craniofacial Research (U.S.A.).
The NIDCR, formerly NIDR, was established in 1948 to promote the general health of the American people by improving their oral, dental and craniofacial health. Through the conduct and support of research and the training of researchers, the NIDCR aims to *promote health, prevent diseases and conditions*, and *develop new diagnostics and therapeutics*. NIDCR distributes professional and consumer education materials free of charge, which cover a variety of subjects about oral health.

**NIDD** Non-Insulin-Dependent Diabetes.

**NIDDK** National Institute of Diabetes and Digestive and Kidney Diseases.
Bethesda, MD, U.S.A.
Established in 1948, the NIDDK conducts and supports basic and applied research and provides leadership for a national program in *diabetes, endocrinology,* and *metabolic diseases; digestive diseases* and *nutrition*; and *kidney, urologic,* and *hematologic diseases*. Several of these diseases are among the leading causes of disability and death; all seriously affect the quality of life of those who have them.

**NIDDM** Non-Insulin-Dependent Diabetes Mellitus.

**Nidil** Nuove identità di lavoro (Italy).
Italian acronym meaning: New Work identities.

**NIDR** National Institute of Dental Research (U.S.A.).
For further details see under: **NIDCR**.

**NIDS** NATO integrated data service.
service intégré de données de l'OTAN.

**NIDTS** NATO initial data (common user) transfer system.
système initial de transfert de données (à usage commun) de l'OTAN.

**NIE** National Institute for the Environment.

**NIE** The Netherlands Institute of Ecology.
NIE was founded in 1992 by the Royal Netherlands Academy of Arts and Sciences. NIE unites three Academy Institutes.

**NIEHS** National Institute of Environmental Health Sciences (U.S.A.).
Established in 1969, the NIEHS reduces the burden of human illness and dysfunction from environmental causes by defining how environmental exposures, genetic susceptibility, and age interact to affect an individual's health. NIEHS conducts and administers *research programs*.

**NIESR** National Institute of Economic and Social Research (G.B.).

**NIF** National Ignition Facility (U.S.A.).

**NIF** National Islamic Front - Sudan.

**NIF** NATO interoperability framework.
cadre d'interopérabilité OTAN.

**NIF** Noise Improvement Factor.
NIF is also known as: Improvement Factor; Signal-to-Noise Improvement Factor.
*Telecommuncations*.

**NIF** Note Issuance Facility.
*Banking; Business; Economics; Finance*.

**NIFO** Next In, First Out.

**NIFS** NATO Integrated Financial System [obsolete - replaced by NAFS].
système financier intégré de l'OTAN [obsolète - remplacé par le NAFS].

**NIFs** Not In Files.

**Nif system** Nitrogen-fixing system.
*Biochemistry*.

**NIFTI** NATO interoperability framework technical infrastructure.
infrastructure technique du cadre d'interopérabilité OTAN.

**NIG** NCN-IVSN gateway.
passerelle NCN/IVSN.

**NIG&P** Nanjing Institute of Geology and Paleontology (China).
*Geophysics; Paleogeology; Paleontology; Stratigraphy.*

**NIGEC** National Institute for Global Environmental Change (U.S.A.).
NIGEC was established in 1989.
*Global Environmental Change; Multidisciplinary Research.*

**NIGMS** National Institute of General Medical Sciences (U.S.A.).
Established in 1962, the NIGMS supports biomedical research that is not targeted to specific diseases. NIGMS funds studies on genes, proteins, and cells, as well as fundamental processes like communication within and between cells, how our bodies use energy, and how we respond to medicines. The results of this research increase our understanding of life and lay the foundation for advances in *disease diagnosis, treatment, and prevention*. The NIGMS also supports *research training programs* that produce the next generation of biomedical scientists, and it has special programs to encourage underrepresented minorities to *pursue biomedical research careers.*

**NIH** National Institutes of Health (U.S.A.).

**NIH** Not Invented Here.

**NIH-ADAMHA** National Institutes of Health and Alcohol, Drug, Abuse, and Mental Health Administration (U.S.A.).

**NII** National Information Infrastructure (U.S.A.).

**NII** Nuclear Installations Inspectorate (U.S.A.).
*Nuclear Plants.*

**$NiI_2$** Nickel Iodide.
*Inorganic Chemistry.*

**NIID** National Institute of Infectious Diseases (Japan).
The NIID is the national government's main facility for research on and surveillance of infectious diseases. It has replaced: JNIH.
For further details see under: **JNIH**.

**NIIG** NATO item identification guide.
guide OTAN d'indentification d'article.

**NIIN** NATO item identification number.
numéro OTAN d'indetification d'article.

**NIJ** National Institute of Justice (U.S.A.).

**NIKHEF** National Institute for Nuclear and High-Energy physics (Amsterdam, The Netherlands).

**NIL** Nearly Isogenic Line.
*Agronomy; Plant Breeding; Plant Genetics.*

**NILU** Norwegian Institute for Air Research (Norway).

**NIMA** NATO Information Management Authority.
Autorité de gestion de l'information de l'OTAN.

**NIMA** Never In Mitosis A.
*Cancer Biology; Pharmacology.*

**NIMBY** Not-In-My-Backyard (U.S.A.).
(against nuclear installations, incinerators, etc.).

**NIMCP** NATO information management control point.
point de contrôle de la gestion de l'information de l'OTAN.

**NIMH** National Institutes of Mental Health (U.S.A.).
Established in 1949, the NIMH provides national leadership dedicated to *understanding, treating, and preventing mental illnesses* through *basic research* on the *brain and behavior*, and through clinical, epidemiological, and services research.

**NIMIC** NATO Insensitive Munitions Information Centre.
Centre d'information OTAN sur les munitions à risques atténués.

**NIMP** NATO interoperability management plan.
plan OTAN de gestion de l'interopérabilité.

**NIMR** National Institute for Medical Research (G.B.).

**NIMR** Netherlands Institute for Metals Research - Delft, The Netherlands.

**NIMS** Near-Infrared Mapping Spectrometer.
*Astronomy; Lunar and Planetary Sciences; Space Science.*

**NIN** National Institute of Neuroscience (Japan).

**NINDS** National Institute of Neurological Disorders and Stroke (U.S.A.).
Established in 1950, NINDS's mission is to reduce the burden of neurological diseases a burden borne by every age group, every segment of society, and people all over the world. To accomplish this goal the NINDS *supports and conducts research*, both basic and clinical, on the *normal and diseased nervous system*, fosters the training of investigators in *basic and clinical neurosciences*, and seeks better understanding, diagnosis, treatment, and prevention of *neurological disorders.*

**NINES** Norfolk Information Exchange Scheme.

**$NiNi_2S_4$** Polydymite.
*Mineralogy.*

**NINR** National Institute of Nursing Research (U.S.A.).
NINR was established as the National Center for Nursing Research (NCNR) in 1986 and redesignated as NINR in 1993. NINR provides financial support for about 300 research projects across the U.S.A. and a few in other countries. NINR also provides research training at the predoctoral and

postdoctoral level; this research training is restricted to nurses and to citizens of the US and certain (U.S.) territories. Additionally, NINR provides career development awards to provide doctorally prepared nurses with additional skills they need as a researcher. NINR supports about 35 centers across the U.S.A. which *focus on reducing health disparities on vulnerable populations*; these centers serve to *stimulate research capability* in their host schools of nursing.

**NINR** Norwegian Institute for Nature Research.

**Ni-NTA** NI-Nitrilloacetic Acid.

**NIOF** National Institute of Oceanography and Fisheries (Egypt).

**NIOMR** Nigerian Institute for Oceanography and Marine Research.

**NIOSH** National Institute for Occupational Safety and Health (U.S.A.).
The U.S. NIOSH conducts research on health effects associated with the *coal conversion technology.*

**NIOZ** Netherlands Institute for Sea Research.

**NIP** NADGE improvement plan.
plan d'amélioration du NADGE.

**NIP45** NF-AT Interacting Protein 45.
For further details see under: **NF-AT**.

**NIPD** NATO interoperability planning document.
document OTAN de planification de l'interopérabilité.

**NIPR** New Ideas in Pollution Regulation - Of the World Bank.

**NIPS** National Institute for Physiological Sciences (Japan).

**NIR** Nuclear Installations Regulations (1971).

**NIRE** National Institute for Resources and Environment (Japan).

**NIR-IT** Network Information Retrieval (Italy).
Meeting held in Milan on 29th/31st March 1999.

**NIRLAB** Non Ionizing Radiation LABoratory.

**NIRNS**; **N.I.R.N.S.** National Institute for Research in Nuclear Science (G.B.).

**NIR radiation** Near-Infrared radiation.
*Electromagnetism.*

**NIRS** National Institute of Radiological Sciences (Japan).
Japan's HIMAC began operating at NIRS in 1995.
*Cancer Therapies; Radiation Oncology.*
For further details see under: **HIMAC**.

**NIS** Naval Investigative Service (U.S.A.).
NIS is one of the U.S. Department of Defense's investigative offices.

**NIS** 1. NATO identification system.
1. système d'identification de l'OTAN.
2. NATO International Staff.
2. Secrétariat international de l'OTAN.

**NIS** Newly Independent States.

**NISAT** Navigation Information System in Advanced Technology.

**NISCO** NATO Identification System Coordination Office.
Bureau de coordination du système d'identification de l'OTAN.

**NISGRT** NATO Inter-Staff Group on Reinforcement and Transportation.
Groupe mixte OTAN sur le renforcement et les transports.

**NISK** Norwegian Forest Research Institute (Norway).

**NIST** National Institute for Standards and Technology.
NIST was formerly known as the National Bureau of Standards.
*U.S. standards Issuing Organizations.*

**NISTEP** National Institute of Science and TEchnology Policy (U.S.A.).

**NIT** Negative Income Tax.

**NIT** New Investment Technology.
*Business; Economics; Finance.*

**NITD** The Novartis Institute for Tropical Diseases.
Private, nonprofit institute, set up by Swiss Novartis with support from the Singapore Government. It will be in temporary quarters until April 2004 and then will move to a new building in Biopolis.
*Dengue; Multidrug-resistant tuberculosis; Life Sciences.*

**$NiTe_2$** Melonite.
*Mineralogy.*

**NITEC** National Information Technology in Education Centre.
*Irish Centers.*

**NITEL** (abbr.) NIgerian TELecommunications Limited.

**NIVA** Norwegian Institute for Water Research.

**NIWA** Namibian Information Workers Association.

**NIWA** National Institute of Water and Atmospheric Research (New Zealand).

**NIWIP** NATO integrated warning improvement programme.
programme OTAN intégré pour l'amélioration de l'alerte.

**NIWS** NATO intelligence warning system.
système d'alerte du renseignement de l'OTAN.

**NJ** (abbr.) New Jersey (U.S.A.).

**NJCEC** NATO Joint Communications and Electronics Committee.

Comité mixte des télécommunications et de l'électronique de l'OTAN.
**NJFA** NATO Joint Frequency Agreement.
Accord mixte OTAN sur les fréquences.
**NJI** Network Job Interface.
**NJIT** New Jersey Institute of Technology.
The U.S. NJIT was founded in 1881. It is a public research university.
*Architecture; Computing; Engineering; Liberal Arts; Management; Mathematics; Science; Technology.*
**NJLA** New Jersey Library Association (U.S.A.).
**NJLN** New Jersey Library Network (U.S.A.).
**NJPAC** New Jersey Performing Arts Center (U.S.A.).
**NK** New Keynesian.
*Economics.*
**$NK_1$** Neuro Kinin-1.
**NKAT1** NK-Associated Transcript 1.
*Immunology.*
**NK cells** Natural Killer cells.
*Immunology.*
**NL** The Netherlands.
**NL** Net Liquidity.
*Banking; Economics; Finance.*
**NL** New Line (character).
**NL** Night Letter.
**NL** No-Load.
*Funds.*
**NL** Nouvelle Lune.
French initialism meaning: New Moon.
*Astronomy.*
**NLA** National Librarians Association.
**NLA** Navy Library Network.
**NLA** Nebraska Library Association (U.S.A.).
**NLA** Nevada Library Association (U.S.A.).
**NLA** Nigerian Library Association.
**NLC** Next Linear Collider.
*Particle Physics.*
**NLC** Northern Library Colloque.
**NLCC** national logistics coordination cell.
cellule nationale de coordination logistique.
**NLCs** Nematic Liquid Crystals.
*Applied Physics; Embryonic Science; Macromolecules.*
**NLD** National League for Democracy (Burma).
**NLG** Netherlands / Dutch Guilder.
Now: EURO/EUR (€). Became ECU (European single currency) with effect from January 2002.
*Currencies.*
**NLGI** National Lubrification Grease Institute (U.S.A.).
**NLL** National Legal Laboratories, Inc. (U.S.A.).
*Genetics; Identity Testing.*
**NLLDB** NATO lessons learned database [has replaced CREME].
base de données OTAN sur les enseignements (tirés) [remplace CREME].
**NLM** National Library of Medicine (U.S.A.).
Established in 1956, the NLM collects, organizes, and makes *available biomedical science information* to investigators, educators, and practitioners and carries out programs designed to strengthen medical library services in the United States. Its *electronic data bases*, including MEDLINE and MEDLINEplus are used extensively throughout the world by both health professionals and the public.
**NLO** 1. national liaison officer.
1. officier de liaison national.
2. naval liaison officer.
2. officier de liaison de la marine.
**NLO** No-Limit Order.
*Business; Commerce.*
**NLO** Nonlinear Optical Materials.
*Materials Science.*
**NLP** Natural Language Processing.
NLP uses computational methods to discern meaning from a text.
*Artificial Intelligence; Information Management; Information Retrieval and Dissemination.*
**NLPAD summaries** Natural Language processing of PAtient Discharge summaries.
**NLQ** Near Letter Quality.
*Computer Technology.*
**NLR** national liaison representative.
représentant de liaison national.
**NLRB** National Labor Relations Board (U.S.A.).
**NLS** National Library of Scotland.
**NLS** National Longitudinal Study (U.S.A.).
*Education.*
**NLS** Nuclear Localization Sequence.
*Molecular Biology*
**NLS** Nuclear Localization Signal.
*Biology; Biophysics; Medicine; Nuclear Transport; Physiology Biochemistry; Plant Biology.*
**NLSC** National Logistics Supply Center.
Of the U.S. NOAA.
For further details see under: **NOAA**.
**NLSC** national logistics support command.
commandement national du soutien logistique.
**NLSs** Nuclear Localization Signals.
For further details see under: **NLS**.
**NLSST** Nonlinear Sea Surface Temperature.
**NLT** NATO liaison team.

équipe de liaison de l'OTAN.
**NLT** Natural Language Technology.
**NLT** Not Later Than.
**NLT** Not Less Than.
*Business; Commerce; Finance.*
**NLW** non-lethal weapon.
arme non létale (ANL).
**NM** Narrow Market.
**NM**; **n.m.** Nautical Mile.
The International nautical mile is equal to 6076 feet, equivalent to 1852 meters.
*Metrology.*
**Nm** nave a motore.
**NM** (abbr.) New Mexico (U.S.A.).
Also: **N.Mex**.
**NM** New Moon / new moon.
*Astronomy.*
**NM**; **Nm** Newton meter.
Named for the English astronomer, mathematician and physicist Sir Isaac **Newton**.
**NM** Nictitating Membrane.
*Vertebrate Zoology.*
**NM**; **n.m.** No Mark.
Referring to bills of lading.
**NM** Nuovo Mercato (Italy).
Italian initialism meaning: New Market. The Italian New Market was launched in May 1999 and became operative in June 1999.
*Banking; Finance; Investments.*
**NMA** 1. national military authority.
1. autorité militaire nationale.
2. NATO military authority.
2. autorité militaire de l'OTAN.
**NMA** National Mining Association (U.S.A.).
**NMAB** National Materials Advisory Board (U.S.A.).
**NMACs** Near Midair Collisions.
**NMAF** NATO multinational area force.
force multinationale de zone de l'OTAN.
**NMB** NATO military body.
organisme militaire de l'OTAN.
**NMC** National Marine Center.
**NMC** National Meteorological Center (U.S.A.).
**NMC** 1. NATO Manual on Codification.
1. Manuel OTAN de codification.
2. NATO Military Committee.
2. Comité militaire de l'OTAN.
**NMC** Network Management Center.
**NMC** Network Measurement Center.
*Communications.*
**NMCC** national movement coordination centre.
centre national de coordination des mouvements.
**NMCCIS** NATO MCCIS.
MCCIS de l'OTAN.
**NM cells** Nonmigrating cells.
*Cell Biology; Immunology; Medicine.*
**NMDA** N-Methyl-D-Aspartate.
**NMDARs** N-Methyl-D-Aspartate Receptors.
*Medicine; Molecular Genetics; Cellular and Molecular Pharmacology.*
**NMDIS** National Marine Data and Information Service (China).
**NMD process** Nonsense-Mediated Decay process.
For further details see under: **PTCs**.
**NMD system** National Missile Defence System (U.S.A.).
**NMDZ** NATO maritime defence zone.
zone de défense maritime de l'OTAN.
**NMEFC** National Marine Environmental Forecasting Center (China).
**N.Mex.** New Mexico.
Also: **N.M**.
**NMF** Non-Member Firm.
*Business; Commerce; Finance.*
**NMFS** National Marine Fisheries Service.
The NMFS was formerly known as: BCF.
*Oceanography.*
For further details see under: **BCF**.
**NMHC** Nonmethane Hydrocarbon.
**Nmi** Nuovo mercato italiano (Italy).
**NMICC** NATO maritime intelligence coordination centre.
centre de coordination du renseignement maritime de l'OTAN.
**NMJ** Neuromuscular Junction.
**NMJs** Neuromuscular Junctions.
**NMLT** national medical liaison team.
équipe de liaison médicale nationale.
**NMMAPS** National Morbidity, Mortality, and Air Pollution Study (U.S.A.).
*Environment Analysis; Public Health.*
**NM metal** Non-Magnetic metal.
*Core Research; Nano Electronics Research; Physics.*
**NMMF** NATO multinational maritime force.
force maritime multinationale de l'OTAN.
**NMOS** NATO maritime operations intelligence system.
système de renseignement opérationnel maritime de l'OTAN.
**NMP** North Magnetic Pole.
**NMPA** NATO maritime patrol aircraft.
avion de patrouille maritime de l'OTAN.
**NMPIS** National Marine Pollution Information Systems (U.S.A.).

**NMPPO** National Marine Pollution Program Office (U.S.A.).
**NMR** 1. national military representative.
1. représentant militaire national (RMN).
2. NATO military requirement.
2. besoin militaire de l'OTAN.
**NMR** Nuclear Magnetic Resonance.
*Physics; Radiology.*
**NMRI** Navy Medical Research Institute.
**NMRR** Normal-Mode Rejection Ratio.
**NMS** National Market System (U.S.A.).
*Business; Commerce; Finance; Stock Exchange.*
**NMS** Normal Market Size.
*Stock Exchange.*
**NMSC** Nonmelanoma Skin Cancer.
*Cancer Research; Dermatology; Immunology; Medicine; Photobiology; Photochemistry.*
**NMSU** New Mexico State University.
**NMSZ** New Madrid Seismic Zone.
*Geosciences.*
**NMU** National Maritime Union.
**N.N.** Niente di Nuovo.
Italian initialism meaning: no news; nothing new.
Also: **n.n.**
**n.n.** non numerata/e.
Italian initialism meaning: not numbered (referring to pages).
**N/N** No Noting.
*Banking; Economics; Finance.*
**NN** Numeri.
Italian initialism meaning: Numbers.
Also: **n.n.**
**NNAC** neutral and non-aligned countries.
pays neutres et non alignés.
**NNAG** NATO Naval Armaments Group.
Groupe OTAN sur les armements des forces navales.
**NNCC** NACOSA network control centre.
centre de commande des réseaux de la NACOSA.
**NNCCRS** NATO nuclear command, control and reporting system [has replaced SCARS].
système OTAN de commandement, de contrôle et de compte rendu des forces nucléaires [remplace le SCARS].
**NNCS** NICS network control system.
système de commande du réseau NICS.
**N-N-E** Nord-Nord-Est.
North-North-East in Italian.
**NNF** National Nanofabrication Facility.
The NNF started about twenty years ago at Cornell University (U.S.A.).
*Micro-engineering.*
**NNG** NATO-national gateway.
passerelle OTAN-pays.
**NNI** Net-Net Income.
*Business; Economics; Finance.*
**NNISS** National Nosocomial Infections Surveillance System (U.S.A.).
**NNMC** National Naval Medical Center (U.S.A.).
**NNMS** new NATO military structure.
**N-N-O** Nord-Nord-Ovest.
North-North-West in Italian.
**NNO** numéro de nomenclature OTAN.
NATO stock number (NSN).
**NNOC** numéro de nomenclature OTAN commun.
NATO standard stock number (NSSN).
**NNP** Net National Product; New National Product.
**NNPS** NATO nuclear planning system.
système de planification nucléaire de l'OTAN.
**NNRLIS** National Natural Resources Library and Information System.
**NNS** Non-Native Speakers.
*Linguistics.*
**NNT** Nearest Neighbor Tool.
*Mathematical Methods.*
**NNTCN** non-NATO troop contributing nation.
pays non OTAN fournissant des troupes.
**NNTP** Network News Transfer Protocol.
**NNUN** National Nanofrabrication Users Network (U.S.A.).
NNUN is a collaboration of five university nanofabrication facilities.
**N/O** Name Of.
**NO** Navigation Officer.
**NO** Nefropatia Ostruttiva.
Italian acronym meaning: obstructive nephropathy.
*Medicine.*
**NO** Nitric Oxide.
*Inorganic Chemistry.*
**$NO_2$** Nitrogen Dioxide.
Nitrogen Dioxide is a brown gas that has a melting point of -9.3°C. It is used mainly in the production of nitric acid.
*Inorganic Chemistry.*
**$N_2O$** Nitrous Oxide.
$N_2O$, also known as: Nitrogen Monoxide, is used mainly as an anesthetic.
*Inorganic Chemistry.*
**No** The chemical symbol for Nobelium.
Named for the **Nobel** Institute for Physics in Stockholm, Sweden.
*Chemistry; Symbols.*
**N/O** No Orders.
*Business; Commerce.*
**N-O** Nord-Ouest.
North-West in French.

**NO** Norway.
Also: **N**.
**NO** Novara, Italy.
**$N_2O_5$** Nitrogen Pentoxide.
$N_2O_5$, also known as: Nitric Anhydride is used in chloroform solution.
*Inorganic Chemistry.*
**N/O** No Orders.
*Business; Commerce.*
**NO** Normally Open (contact).
*Electricity.*
**No.** (abbr.) Number.
**NOA** National Oceanography Association.
NOA has been replaced by NOIA.
For further details see under: **NOIA**.
**NOA** notice of availability.
avis de disponibilité.
**NOA** Nucleo Operativo Alcologia (Italy).
*Alcoholism.*
**NOAA** National Oceanic and Atmospheric Administration (U.S.A.).
**No Adv.** (abbr.) No Advice.
**NOAO** National Optical Astronomy Observatory.
*Astronomy; Optical Engineering.*
For further details see under: **AURA**.
**NOARL** Naval Ocean and Atmosphere Research Laboratory (U.S.A.).
**NOB** naval order of battle.
ordre de bataille naval.
**NOC**; **Noc** Nuclei Operativi di Controllo (Italy).
**NOC 2001** Network and Optical Communications.
6[th] European Conference held June 2001 in Ipswich, G.B.
*WDM Optical Switching; Photonic Networks.*
**NOCLA** Negros OCcidental Library Association.
**NOCN** National Ocean Communications Network (U.S.A.).
**NoCs** Network-oriented Computers.
**NODC** National Oceanographic Data Center.
**NOD mice** Nonobese Diabetic mice.
**NOE** nap of the earth.
au ras du sol.
**NOE** Net Operating Earnings.
*Business; Economics; Finance.*
**NOE** Nuclear Overhauser Effect.
**NOE** Nucleo Ecologico (Italy).
Of the "Carabinieri".
**Noè** The above acronyms were coined accidentally using the Italian word "Noè" which means: Noah.
**NOESY** NOE Spectroscopy.
For further details see under: **NOE**.
**NOF** National Oceanographic Facility.
**NOFA** Notice Of Funds Available (U.S.A.).
*Banking.*
**NOFUN** no first use of nuclear weapons.
non-recours en premier à l'arme nucléaire.
**NOGO** Negative Observations in Genetic Oncology.
*Journals.*
**NOHD** nominal ocular hazard distance.
distance oculaire critique nominale.
**NOI** notice of intention.
avis d'intention.
**NOIA** National Ocean Industries Association.
NOIA has replaced NOA.
For further details see under: **NOA**.
**noia** The above acronym was coined accidentally using the Italian word "noia" which means: annoyance; boredom; bother; tediousness.
**NOIC** National Oceanographic Instrumental Center.
**NOIS** NATO operational interoperability standard.
norme OTAN d'interopérabilité opérationnelle.
**NOK** Next Of Kin.
**NOK** Norwegian Krone.
Also: **NKr**.
**NOL** Net Operating Loss.
**NOLM** Nonlinear Optical Loop Mirror.
*Materials Science.*
**NOMAN** NTTS operation and management (system).
(système d') exploitation et de gestion du NTTS.
**NOMBO** non-minelike bottom object.
objet au fond atypique de mine.
**NOME** non-minelike echo.
écho atypique de mine.
**NOMES** NOuveau Mouvement Européen Suisse (Switzerland).
French acronym of the: New European Swiss Movement.
**NOMLAC** Newsletter On Military Law And Counseling (U.S.A.).
**NON** Northern Norway.
1a. nord de la Norvège.
1b. Norvège septentrionale.
**NONOP** non-operational.
non opérationnel.
**NOO** National Organization Order.
**NOP** Nominal Option Poll.
**n.o.p.** not otherwise provided for.
**NOP** 1. nuclear operations plan.
1. plan d'opération nucléaire.
2. nuclear operations procedures.
2. procédures d'opérations nucléaires.
**NOR** 1. NATO operational requirement.
1. besoin opérationnel de l'OTAN.
2. notice of revision.

2. avis de révision.
**NOR** Not Otherwise Rated.
*Stock Exchange.*
**Nor.** (abbr.) Norway; Norwegian.
**NORC** National Option Research Center.
Of the University of Chicago, U.S.A. NORC was established in 1941. During the war it carried out hundreds of surveys for government agencies. Since the war it has become a major *university-affiliated social research organization.*
**NORD** National Organization for Rare Disorders (U.S.A.).
**NORDA** Naval Oceanographic Research and Development Administration (U.S.A.).
**Norf.** (abbr.) Norfolk.
**NORFLT** Northern Fleet.
flotte du Nord (ou de l'Arctique).
**NORLANT** Northern Sub-Area Atlantic [obsolete].
Sous-secteur septentrional de l'Atlantique [obsolète].
**NORO** National Optical Astronomical Observatories (U.S.A.).
For further details see under: **AURA**.
**NORs** Nucleolar Organizer Regions.
**NORSAR** NORwegian Seismic ARray (Norway).
**Northants.** (abbr.) Northamptonshire (G.B.).
**Northumb.** (abbr.) Northumberland (G.B.).
**Norw.** (abbr.) Norwegian.
*Languages.*
**NORWELD** Northwest Library Districts.
**NOS** National Ocean Service (U.S.A.).
Of the U.S. NOAA.
For further details see under: **NOAA**.
**NOS** 1. NATO Office of Security.
1. Bureau de sécurité de l'OTAN.
2. NATO open systems.
2. systèmes ouverts de l'OTAN.
**NOS** Network Operating System.
**NOS** Nitric Oxide Synthase.
**NOS** nopaline synthase.
**NOS** Notice Of Sale.
*Business; Commerce.*
**NOS** Not Otherwise Specified.
**Nos.**; **nos.** (abbr.) Numbers.
**NOSC** Naval Ocean Systems Center.
**NOSCA project** New Optical Sensor Concept for Aeronautics project.
*European Community Project.*
**NOSIP** NATO open systems interconnection profile.
profil d'interconnexion des systèmes ouverts de l'OTAN.
**NOSREP** national overseas shipping representative.
représentant national outre-mer de la navigation commerciale.
**NOSS** National Oceanic Satellite System.
**NOT** Nordic Optical Telescope.
*Astrophysics; Space Research.*
**NOT** Nuclei Operativi Tossicodipendenze (Italy).
**NOTAL** not to all.
1a. pas à tous.
1b. diffusion partielle.
**NOTAM** notice to airmen.
avis aux navigants.
**NOTAR** no tail rotor.
sans rotor de queue.
**NOTS** NATO off-the-shelf.
OTAN sur étagère (ou OTAN standard).
**Notts.** (abbr.) Nottinghamshire (G.B.).
**nov** (abbr.) novembre.
Italian abbreviation meaning: November.
**NOW** National Organization for Women.
**NOW** Negotiable Order of Withdrawal (U.S.A.).
*Banking; Business; Finance.*
**NOW** New Opportunities for Women - E.C.
**$No_x$** Oxides of Nitrogen.
*Chemistry.*
**NOZE** National OZone Experiment.
**NP** Nanoparticle.
For further details see under: **NPs**.
**np** (abbr.) neap (tides).
*Oceanography.*
**NP** Nepal.
**np** neper.
Named for the Scottish physicist John **Neper**.
*Physics.*
**Np** The chemical symbol for Neptunium.
Named for the planet, **Neptune**, it is used mainly in neutron detection instruments.
*Chemistry; Symbols.*
**NP** New Page.
**NP** Net Position; Net Price.
*Business; Commerce.*
**NP** Net Proceeds; Net Profit.
*Business; Economics -Finance.*
**NP** Neuropsychiatric; Neuropsychiatry.
**n.p.** new paragraph.
**N.P.** Nobel Prize.
**n.p.** non-participating.
**NP** Non Pertinente.
Italian initialism meaning: impertinent; irrelevant.
**NP**; **Np** No Problem.
**NP** Normal Profit.
*Business; Commerce; Economics; Finance.*
**NP** Notary Public.
Also: **N.P.**

**NP** Note/s Payable.
*Business; Commerce.*
**NPA** National Personnel Agency (Japan).
**NPA** National Policy Agency.
**NpA** National port Authority.
**NPA** Nematode Polyprotein Allergen.
*Disease Reactions.*
**NPA** New Partnership Approach.
**NPACI** National Partnership for Advanced Computational Infrastructure (U.S.A.).
*Digital Libraries;* San Diego Center.
For further details see under: **PACI**.
**NPA rebels** New People's Army rebels (The Philippines).
**NPC** National Petroleum Council.
**NPC** 1. NATO Pipeline Committee.
1. Comité OTAN des pipelines.
2. NATO Programming Centre.
2. Centre de programmation de l'OTAN (CPO 1.).
**NPC** Nitrophenyl Carbonate.
**NPC** Noncumulative Preferred Stock.
*Business; Economics; Finance.*
**NPC** Non-Profit Corporation.
**NPC** Nouveau Plan Comptable.
**NPC** Nuclear Pole Complex.
*Cytomegalovirus; Electron Microscopy.*
**NPC2** Second NP-C genotype.
For further details see under: **NP-C disease**.
**NP-C disease** Niemann-Pick type C disease.
The NP-C disease is an autosomal recessive cholesterol storage disorder.
*Cell Biology; Human Genome Research; Inherited Diseases; Medicine; Neurological Disorders and Stroke; Neuroscience.*
**NPCMW** North Pacific Central Mode Water.
**NPCs** Nuclear Pore Complexes.
*Biomolecular Chemistry - Medicine.*
**NPEDP** (Bi-SC) NATO-plus Exercise Directive and Programme [includes PfP].
Directive-programme des exercices OTAN+ (des SC) [inclut le PPP].
**NPF** Nazione Più Favorita.
Italian initialism meaning: Most Favored Nation.
*International Business.*
For further details see under: **NTR**.
**Npf**; **npf** not provided for.
**NPF** Nuova Professione Forense.
**NPG** Nature Publishing Group.
**NPG** Nuclear Planning Group.
Groupe des plans nucléaires (GPN).
**NPG (HLG)** NPG High Level Group.
Groupe des haut niveau du NPG.
**NPGQC** National Plant Germplasm Quarantine Center (U.S.A.).
**NPGS** National Plant Germplasm System (U.S.A.).
*Germplasm Banks; Plant Genetics.*
**NPGs** New Projects Groups.
**NPHS** National Pregnancy and Health Study (U.S.A.).
*Medicine.*
**NPIS** NATO procedural interoperability standard.
norme OTAN d'interopérabilité des procedures.
**NPIW** North Pacific Intermediate Water.
**NPL** National Priorities List (U.S.A.).
**NPL** normal peacetime location.
emplanment normal du temps de paix.
**NPLO** NATO production and logistics organization.
organisation de production et de logistique de l'OTAN (OPLO).
**NPLs** Non-Performing Loans.
**NPM** Nuclear Planning Manual.
Manuel des plans nucléaires.
**NPN** Nonprotein Nitrogen.
*Biochemistry.*
**NPN** n-propyl nitrate.
**n.p.n.d.** no place, no date.
**NPOESS** National Polar Orbiting Environmental Satellite System (U.S.A.).
**NPOI** Navy Prototype Optical Interferometer.
The NPOI consists of six telescopes. It is located near Flagstaff, Arizona, U.S.A.
*Astronomy; Optical Images.*
**NPP** Net Primary Production.
*Biological Sciences; Climate; Marine and Coastal Sciences.*
**NPQ** Nonphotochemical Quenching.
*Plant Ecology; Plant Physiology.*
**NPR** National Performance Review.
**NPR** Noise-Power Ratio.
*Electrical Engineering.*
**NPR** Nuclear Posture Review.
**NPRC** Nonproliferation Program Review Committee.
*International Security and Arms Control; Nuclear Nonproliferation; Strategic Arms Reduction.*
**NPs** Nanoparticles.
*Primary and Metastatic Tumors.*
**NPS** National Park Service.
*Energy Use.*
**NPS** 1. NATO pipeline system.
1. réseau (ou système) de pipelines de l'OTAN.
2. NATO precautionary system.
2. système de mesures de précaution de l'OTAN.
3. NATO-provided software.
3. logiciel fourni par l'OTAN.

4. nuclear planning system.
4. système de planification nucléaire.
**NPS** No-Par Stock.
*Business; Economics; Finance.*
**NPSAC** NATO Precautionary System Alert Committee.
Comité d'alerte sur le système de mesures de précaution de l'OTAN.
**NPSC** NATO Precautionary System Conference.
Conférence sur le système de mesures de précaution de l'OTAN.
**NPSH** Net Positive Suction Head.
*Mechanical Engineering.*
**NPSM** NATO Precautionary System Manual.
Manuel du système de mesures de précaution de l'OTAN.
**NPT** 1. national shipping administration planning team.
1. équipe de planification de la direction nationale de la navigation commerciale.
2. Non-Proliferation Treaty.
2. Traité sur la non-prolifération (des armes nucléaires) (TNP).
**NPT** Neomycin Phosphotransferase.
*Medicine.*
**NPT** Normal Pressure and Temperature.
*Medicine.*
**NPT** Nuclear nonproliferation Treaty.
**NPT** Nutrizione Parenterale Totale.
*Medicine.*
**NP time** Nondeterministic Polynomial time.
*Computer Science Jargon; Mathematics.*
**NPTZ** North Pacific Transition Zone.
**NPV** Net Present Value.
*Accounts.*
**NPV** No Par Value.
*Business; Economics; Finance; Stock Exchange.*
**NPV** Nuclear Polyhedrosis Virus.
*Virology.*
**NPVS** No Par Value Stock.
**NPY** Neuropeptide Y.
*Biochemistry; Medicine; Peptide Neurotransmitters.*
**NQ** non-quota (post).
(poste) hors quota.
**NQA** niveau de qualité acceptable.
acceptable quality level (AQL).
**NQAA** national quality assurance authority.
autorité nationale pour l'assurance de la qualité (ANAQ).
**NQR detector** Nuclear Quadruple Resonance detector.
The NQR detects conceiled explosives (such as in luggage, bulk mail, etc.).
*Counterterrorism.*
**NR** 1. NATO Restricted.
1a. NATO Diffusion Restreinte.
1b. OTAN Diffusion Restreinte.
1c. Diffusion Restreinte OTAN [FR].
2. Nauru.
2. Nauru.
3. Northern Region [obsolete].
3. Région Nord (RN) [obsolète].
**NR** Nitrate Reductase.
NR is also known as: Nitratase.
*Enzymology.*
**NR** noise ratio.
**N.R.** Non-Resident.
**NR** no-refil.
*Medicine.*
**N.R.** No Risk.
Also: **NR**.
**NR** note receivable.
*Business; Commerce.*
**N.R.** Not Rated.
*Stock Exchange.*
**NR** Nuclear Receptor.
*Biochemistry; Molecular Neurobiology; Pathobiochemistry.*
**NRA** NATO Refugees Agency.
Agence OTAN pour les réfugiées.
**NRAO** National Radio Astronomy Observatory.
NRAO is operated by Associated Universities.
**NRB** National Rehabilitation Board (Ireland).
**NRC** National Reconditioning Order (U.S.A.).
Of the U.S. NWS.
For further details see under: **NWS**.
**NRC** National Research Council (U.S.A.).
**NRC** Net Replacement Cost.
**NRC** Nuclear Regulatory Commission (U.S.A.).
**NRCC** National Research Council of Canada.
*Canadian Council.*
**NRCC** National Resource Center for Cephalopods (U.S.A.).
**NRCD** National Reprographic Centre for Documentation.
**NRDC** Natural Resources Defense Council (U.S.A.).
**NRCDES** National Research Council Division of Earth Sciences.
**NRE** Negative Regulatory Element.
*Gynecology; Medicine; Newborn Medicine; Obstetrics; Pediatrics; Radiology; Veterinary Medicine; Veterinary Pathology; Viral Pathogenesis.*

**NRECA** National Rural Electric Cooperative Association (U.S.A.).

**NREL** National Renewable Energy Laboratory.
NREL was established by the Solar Energy Research Development and Demonstration Act of 1974. Originally called Solar Energy Research Institute, NREL began operating July 1977 and was designated a national laboratory of the U.S. DOE in September 1991.
*New Energy Technologies.*
For further details see under: **DOE**.

**NREN** National Research and Education Network (U.S.A.).
Ever since 1991, the goal of NREN, has been to *connect research centers, universities, and industry laboratories* in every state to lines capable of transmitting 1 gigabit (1 billion bits) of data per second by 1996.

**NRENs** National Research and Education Networks.
For further details see under: **NREN**.

**NRERDC** New and Renewable Research and Development Center (Kabul, Afghanistan).

**NRE Rupee Account** Non-Resident External Rupee Account (India).
*Investment Schemes.*

**NRF** NATO Response Force.
Force de réaction de l'OTAN.

**NRI** Neuroscience Research Institute.
Aston University Birmingham, G.B.
*Magnetoencephalography; Visual Psychophysics.*

**NRIM** National Research Institute for Metals.
*Japanese Institute.*

**NRIs** Non-Resident Indians.
NRIs is a term coined to describe persons of Indian origin living overseas.

**NRK** Normal Rat Kidney.

**NRL** Naval Research Laboratory.
The NRL is located in Washington D.C. (U.S.A.).

**NRL** Non-Resident Landlord (G.B.).

**NRLB** Northern Regional Library Bureau.

**NRLM** National Research Laboratory of Metrology (Japan).

**NRM** Natural Remanent Magnetization.
*Geophysics.*

**NRM** Normal Response Mode.

**NRM** Nucleus Raphe Magnus.

**NRNR Rupee Deposit** Non-Resident Non-Repatriable Rupee Deposit.
*Investment Schemes.*

**NRO funds** Non-Resident Owned funds.
*Banking.*

**NROSS** Navy Remote Ocean Sensing System (U.S.A.).

**NRPB** National Radiological Protection Board.
Headquartered at Chilton, Oxfordshire, G.B.
*British Boards; Radiation Standards; Radiological Protection.*

**NRPSs** Nonribosomal Peptide Synthetases.
*Bacteriology; Chemistry; Pharmacy; Polyketide Synthase.*

**NRR** net reproduction rate.

**NRRC** Nuclear Risk Reduction Centre.
Centre de réduction du risque nucléaire (CRRN).

**NRS** NATO range safety.
sécurité des champs de tir de l'OTAN.

**NRS** Normal Rabbit Serum.

**NRS** Nuclear Reaction Spectrometry.

**NRSA** National Remote Sensing Agency.

**NRSA** National Research Service Award - NIH's.
*U.S. Awards.*
For further details see under: **NIH**.

**NRSP** National Remote Sensing Program (U.S.A.).

**NRSV** Necrotic Ring Spot Virus.
*Plant Pathology.*

**NRT; nrt** net register tonnage.

**NRT** The airport code for Narita, Tokyo, Japan.

**NRTC** National Rural Telecommunications Cooperative.

**NRU** Natural Rate of Unemployment.

**NRV** Net Realizable Value.

**NRZ** Non-Return to Zero.

**NS** Native Speaker.
*Linguistics.*

**NS** 1. NATO Secret.
1a. NATO Secret.
1b. OTAN Secret.
1c. Secret OTAN [FR].
2. NATO shipping.
2. navigation commerciale de l'OTAN.
3. Surinam.
3. Surinam.

**NS** Nederlandse Spoorwegen (The Netherlands).

**NS** Net Sales.
*Business; Commerce.*

**NS** Neutron Spectrometer.
A cubical block of boron-loaded plastic scintillator divided into four individual sensors.
*Lunar Research.*

**NS** New Series.

**N.S.** New Style.

**Ns** Nimbostratus.
*Meteorology.*

**NS** Non Significatif.

**ns.** (abbr.) nostro.

Italian abbreviation meaning: our; ours.
**N.S.**; **n.s.** not specified.
**NS** Not Sufficient.
*Business; Commerce.*
**NS** Nova Scotia (Canada).
**NS** Nuclear Ship.
*Naval Architecture.*
$N_S$ Number of Sequences.
**NSA** National Security Agency (U.S.A.).
**NSA** 1. national shipping authority.
1a. autorité nationale chargée de la marine marchande.
1b. Direction nationale de la navigation commerciale.
2. NATO Standardization Agency [has replaced MAS and ONS].
2. Agence OTAN de normalisation (AON 1.) [remplace le BMS 2. et l'ONS].
**NSABP** National Surgical Adjuvant Breast and Bowel Project (U.S.A.).
*U.S. Biomedical Policy.*
**NSAC** Nuclear Science Advisory Committee (U.S.A.).
For further details see under: **NUSL** and **RIA**.
**NSAG** NATO Shipping Advisory Group.
Groupe consultatif OTAN de la navigation commerciale.
**nsAI** nonsteroid Anti-Inflammatory.
For further details see under: **AINS**.
**NSAIDs** Nonsteroidal Anti-Inflammatory Drugs.
*Alzheimer Disease Research; Cell Biology; Drugs Testing; Epidemiological Studies; Immunology; Medicine; Molecular Biophysics and Biochemistry.*
**NSAM** National Survey of Adolescent Males (U.S.A.).
The NSAM begun in 1995 and was conducted using the Audio-CASI Technology.
For further details see under: **Ausio-CASI Technology**.
**NSB** National Savings Bank (G.B.).
**NSB** National Science Board.
The NSB is the U.S. NSF's oversight body.
For further details see under: **NFS**.
**NSB** Naval Studies Board (U.S.A.).
**NSBA** Nebraska State Bar Association (U.S.A.).
**NSBRI** National Space Biomedical Research Institute - NASA's.
*Space Biomedical Research.*
**NSC** National Science Council (U.S.A.).
**NSC** National Security Council (U.S.A.).
*International Security and Arms Control; Nuclear Nonproliferation; Strategic Arms Reduction.*
**NSC** National Space Council (U.S.A.).
**NSC** 1. NATO Security Committee.
1. Comité de sécurité de l'OTAN.
2. NATO steering committee.
2. Comité directeur OTAN.
3. NATO Standardization Committee.
3. Comité OTAN de normalisation.
**NSC** Neural Stem Cell.
For further details see under: **NSCs**.
**NSC** Nuovo Strumento Comunitario - E.C.
**NSCAT** NASA's SCATterometer.
An instrument aboard ADEOS.
For further details see under: **ADEOS**.
**NSCC** 1. NATO supply classification code.
1. code de classification des approvisionnements OTAN.
2. NATO surveillance coordination centre.
2. centre OTAN de coordination de la surveillance.
**NSCL** National Superconducting Cyclotron Laboratory.
At Michigan State University (U.S.A.).
**NSCORT** NASA Specialized Center Of Research and Training (U.S.A.).
*Crystallography; Geology; Oceanography.*
**NSCs** Neural Stem Cells.
Adult NSCs in the SVZ (in mammals) give rise to the olfactory interneurons.
*Donor Cells; Rodents; Transplantation Genes.*
For further details see under: **SVZ**.
**NSDD** National Security Decision Directive (U.S.A.).
**NSDL** National Science Digital Library.
Of the U.S. NSF.
For further details see under: **NSF**.
**NSE** 1. NACOSA Support Element [has replaced ROC].
1. élément de soutien de la NACOSA [remplace le ROC].
2. national support element.
2. élément de soutien national.
**NSE** Nagoya Stock Exchange (Japan).
**NSE** National Stock Exchange (India).
The NSE was set up in late 1992. India's National Stock Exchange started equity trading in November 1994 using a screen-based system.
**nsec.**; **ns.** nanosecond.
A unit of time equal to one-billionth of a second.
*Metrology.*
**NSEL** National Stock Exchange of Lithuania.
**NSEP** National Security Education Program.
Of the U.S. Academy for Educational Development.
*NSEP Fellowships.*

**NSERC** Natural Sciences and Engineering Research Council (Canada).
**NSES** National Science Education Standards (U.S.A.).
**NSF** National Science Foundation (U.S.A.).
**NSF** N-Ethylmaleimide-Sensitive Factor.
*Brain Research; Medicine; Neurobiology; Neurochemistry.*
For further details see under: **SNAP**.
**NSFA** National Science Foundation Act.
**NSG** national support group.
groupe de soutien national.
**NSI** nuclear safety / security inspection.
inspection de sécurité nucléaire.
**NSI** Nuovi Stati Indipendenti.
Italian initialism meaning: Newly Independent States.
**NSIA** National Security Industrial Association (U.S.A.).
**NSIDC** National Snow and Ice Data Center (U.S.A.).
**NSIF** NATO special intelligence facility.
installation OTAN de renseignement spécial.
**NSI HIV strains** Non-Syncytium-Inducing HIV strains.
*Applied Pharmacology; Cancer Research; Epidemiology; Medicine; Pathology.*
For further details see under: **HIV**.
**NSILA** Non Suppressible Insulin-Like Activity.
NSILA is also known as: Insuline-like growth factors.
*Biochemistry.*
**NSIP** NATO Security Investment Programme.
Programme OTAN d'investissement au service de la sécurité.
**NSI phenotype** Non-Syncytium-Inducing phenotype.
*Hematology; Infectious Diseases; Pathology; Virology.*
**NSIRB** NATO Security Investment Review Board.
Commission d'examen des investissements de l'OTAN au service de la sécurité.
**NSI viruses** Non-Syncytium-Inducing viruses.
**NSL** Nicaragua Sign Language.
*Cognitive Science; Linguistics.*
**NSL** non-stocked item list.
liste des articles non détenus en stock.
**NSLA** Nova Scotia Library Association.
*Canadian Association.*
**NSLB** NATO Standardization Liaison Board.
Bureau de liaison OTAN pour la normalisation.
**NSLG** NATO Shipping Liaison Group.
Groupe de liaison OTAN de la navigation commerciale.
**NSLS** National Synchrotron Light Source.
The NSLS is located at the U.S. Brookhaven National Laboratory.
**NSN** NATO stock number.
numéro de nomenclature OTAN (NNO).
**NSO** NATO Standardization Organization.
Organisation OTAN de normalisation.
**NSOM** Near-field Scanning Optical Microscope.
*Optics.*
**NSP** 1. NATO standardization programme.
1. programme de normalisation de l'OTAN.
2. NATO strike plan.
2a. plan d'attaque (nucléaire) de l'OTAN.
2b. plan de frappe de l'OTAN.
3. nuclear strike plan.
3. plan d'attaque nucléaire.
**NSP** Net Secondary Production.
**Nsp** Network service provider.
**NSP** Neurological Shellfish Poisoning.
**NSP** Northern States Power Co. (U.S.A.).
**NSPF** Not Specifically Provided For.
**NSPS** New Source Performance Standards (U.S.A.).
**NSR** NATO staff requirement.
spécification opérationnelle OTAN.
**NSRC** National Science Resources Center (U.S.A.).
**NSRC** National Supercomputing Research Centre.
Of the National University of Singapore.
**NSRDB** National Solar Radiation Data Base.
NSRDB, created in 1992, contains data for the United States from 1961 to 1990 and is available from the NCDC.
For further details see under: **NCDC**.
**NSRS** National Spatial Reference System (U.S.A.).
**NSS** 1. NADGE system stock(age).
1. stock du système NADGE.
2. negotiation support system.
2. système interactif d'aide à la négociation.
**NS(S)** NATO School (SHAPE).
École OTAN du SHAPE.
**NSS** Neutron Scattering Society.
**NSS** Non-Sex-Specific.
*Cell Biology; Molecular Medicine; Nucleic Acids.*
**NSS** No Strain Structure.
*Epidemiology.*
**NSSDC** National Space Science Data Center (U.S.A.).
**NSSG** NATO Standardization Staff Group.
Groupe consultatif de normalisation OTAN.
**NSSL** NADGE system stock list.
catalogue de stock du système NADGE.
**NSSL** National Seed Storage Laboratory (U.S.A.).

**NSSL** National Severe Storms Laboratory.
Of the U.S. NOAA.
For further details see under: **NOAA**.
**NSSLA** Nova Scotia School Libraries Association.
**NSSN** NATO standard stock number.
numéro de nomenclature OTAN commun (NNOC).
**NSSS** nuclear steam supply system.
chaufferie nucléaire.
**NST** 1. NATO staff target.
1. objectif OTAN d'état-major.
2. nuclear and space talks.
2a. entretiens sur les questions (ou armes) nucléaires et spatiales.
2b. pourparlers sur les armes nucléaires et spatiales.
**NST** Nucleus of the Solitary Tract.
**NSTA** National Science Teachers Association.
**NSTC** National Science and Technology Council (U.S.A.).
**NSTDA** National Science and Technology Development Agency (Thailand).
**NSTR** nothing significant to report.
rien d'important à signaler.
**NSTX** National Spherical Torus Experiment.
Princeton, U.S.A.
*Fusion Power.*
**NSU** Nonspecific Urethritis.
NSU is also known as: Nongonococcal Urethritis.
*Medicine.*
**NSVN** NATO secure voice network.
réseau de cryptophonie de l'OTAN.
**NSVP** NATO secure voice programme.
programme de cryptophonie de l'OTAN.
**NSW** New South Wales (Australia).
**NSWC** Naval Surface Warfare Center (U.S.A.).
**NSWMA** National Solid Wastes Management Association (U.S.A.).
NSWMA is one of the sponsors of WasteExpo.
**NSX** Namibia Stock Exchange.
**NT** Nanotube.
*Physics.*
**N.T.** National Trust.
**N/T** navire-terre.
ship-shore.
**n.t.** net terms.
*Business; Commerce.*
**NT**; **N/T** Net Tonnage.
**NT** Network Terminations.
*Telecommuncations.*
**N/T** Non Trasferibile.
**NT** Northern Territory (Australia).
**Nt** note tipografiche.
**NT** Nuclear Transfer.
Also known as: Nuclear Transplantation.
*Biotechnology.*
**nt**; **nt.** nucleotide.
*Biochemistry.*
**NT** Nuisance Tax.
**N/T**; **N.T.** Nuovo Testamento.
Italian initialism meaning: New Testament.
**NT-3** Neurotrophin-3.
*Biology; Neurobiology.*
**NTA** New Transatlantic Agenda.
*Transatlantic Issues; U.S.-E.C. Business.*
**NTA** Nitriloacetic Acid.
**NTB** National Training Board.
**NTB** 1. NATO tactical broadcast.
1. système de radiodiffusion tactique de l'OTAN.
2. nuclear test ban.
2. interdiction des essais nucléaires.
**NTBG** National Tropical Botanical Gardens (U.S.A.).
**NTDI** NATO target data inventory.
liste OTAN des données d'objectifs.
**NTDS** naval tactical data processing system.
système d'exploitation naval des informations tactiques (SENIT).
**NTDs** Neural Tube Defects.
**NTE** Not To Exceed.
**NTF** National Tidal Facility (Australia).
**NTF** NATO task force.
force opérationnelle OTAN.
**NTF** $NH_2$-Terminal Fragment.
*Apoptosis; Genetics; Life Sciences; Medicine; Neurology.*
**NTF** No Trouble Found.
**NTFPs** Nontimber Forest Products.
**NTG** 1. NATO task group.
1. groupe opérationnel OTAN.
2. NATO Training Group.
2. Groupe d'entraînement OTAN.
**NTG patients** Nontoxic Goiter patients.
For further details see under: **HT** (Hashimoto's Thyroiditis).
**NTI** Nœud de Transit International (France).
**NTIA** National Telecommunications and Information Administration.
The NTIA is a section of the U.S. Department of Commerce.
**NTICS** National Training Information Central Support (G.B.).
**NTIMS** Negative Thermal Ionization Mass Spectrometry.
*Chemistry; Earth and Environmental Sciences;*

*Geological and Planetary Sciences; Isotope Geology.*
**NTIS** National Technical Information Service (U.S.A.).
**NTIS** NATO technical interoperability standard.
norme OTAN d'interopérabilité technique.
**NTM** notice to move.
avis de mouvement.
**NTMs** Normal Transmitting Males.
**NTN** National Trends Network (U.S.A.).
**NTP** National Toxicology Program (U.S.A.).
*NIEHS Programs; Risks to Human Reproduction.*
For further details see under: **NIEHS**.
**NTP** Normal Temperature and Pressure.
*Medicine.*
**NTP concentration** Nucleoside Triphosphate concentration.
*Bacteriology; Microbiology.*
**NTP(F)** Number of Terminals Per Failure.
**NTPs** $NH_2$-Terminal Peptides.
**NTR** Normal Trade Relations.
NTR has replaced MFN (Most Favoured Nation) which has been abolished by the U.S. Senate in mid-july 1998. The term MFN will continue to be employed by the rest of the world.
*U.S. Trading Designations.*
**NTS** NAMSA transportation system.
système de transport de la NAMSA.
**NTS** Nevada Test Site.
**NTS** Non-Transcribed Strand.
*Genetics; Life Sciences; Medicine; Microbiology; Radiation Oncology.*
**NTS** Nucleus Tractus Solitarius.
*Anatomy.*
**NTSC** National Television Standard Code.
**NT-SD** Network Test-System Division - Hewlett Packard's.
**NTT** New Technology Telescope.
The NTT was completed in 1990.
**NTT** Nippon Telegraph and Telephone Corporation (Japan).
**NTTS** NATO terrestrial transmission system.
système de transmissions terrestres de l'OTAN.
**NTUA** National Technical University of Athens (Greece).
*Turbomachinery; Greek Universities.*
**NTX** Noxious Toxin.
**NU** 1. nationality undetermined (post).
1. (poste) sans attribution de nationalité.
2. NATO Unclassified.
2a. NATO Sans Classification.
2b. OTAN Sans Classification.
2c. Sans Classification OTAN [FR].
3. Nicaragua.
3. Nicaragua.
**NU** Nations Unies; Nazioni Unite.
French and Italian acronym meaning: United Nations.
**NU** Natural Uranium.
**N.U.** Nettezza Urbana (Italy).
Italian acronym meaning: City Sanitation Department.
**NU** Nothing Unsatisfactory.
**NU** Nuoro, Italy.
**NUB** Natural Uranium Block.
**NUBE** National Union of Bank Employees.
**nube** The above acronym was coined accidentally using the word "nube" which means in Italian: cloud (also "nuvola").
**NUBL** Northwestern University Biotechnology Laboratory (U.S.A.).
**NUBLU** New Basic Logic Unit.
**NUC** NATO-Ukraine Commission.
commission OTAN-Ukraine.
**NUCOL** NUmerical COntrol Language.
**NUCSTAT** nuclear operational status report.
compte rendu opérationnel de situation nucléaire.
**NUE** Nitrogen-Use Efficiency.
*Botany.*
**NU.I.R.** NUcleo Intervento Rapido (Italy).
**NUM** National Union of Mineworkers (South Africa).
**NUMA**; **Numa systems** Non-Uniform Memory Access systems.
For further details see under: **SMP systems**.
**NUMC** NATO-Ukraine Military Committee.
Comité militaire OTAN-Ukraine.
**NuMI** Neutrinos at the Main Injector.
An experiment of the U.S. Department of Energy for neutrino sightings.
*High-Energy Physics.*
**NUPE** Nation Union of Public Employees.
**NuPECC** Nuclear Physics European Collaboration Committee.
NuPECC produces 5-year plans for nuclear physics and meets under the auspices of the European Science Foundation.
*Nuclear Physics.*
**NUR** National Union of Railwaymen.
**NUR** Natural Uranium Reactor.
NUR is also known as: Natural Fuel Reactor.
*Nuclear Engineering.*
**nur** The above acronyms were coined accidentally using the Arabic word "nur" which means: light (brightness).
**NURF** Nucleosome-Remodeling Factor.

*Biochemistry; Gene Expression; Medicine; Microchemistry; Molecular Biology; Transcription.*
**NURP** National Undersea Research Program (U.S.A.).
In 1990 more than 600 researchers won NURP grants for projects ranging from studies of coral reef ecosystems to exploration of submarine volcanoes.
*Undersea Research; Grants.*
**NURP(S)** numbered reference position (system).
(système de) positions de référence numérotées.
**NUS** National Union of Students (G.B.).
**NUS** National University of Singapore.
Founded in 1905.
**NUS; N.U.S.** National Utility Service (U.S.A.).
**NUSL** National Underground Science Laboratory.
NUSL is a facility endorsed by the U.S. Government's NSAC to study neutrinos. The laboratory is buried at 7 kilometers below ground.
For further details see under: **NSAC**.
**NUWC** Naval Undersea Warfare Center.
**NV** (abbr.) Nevada (U.S.A.).
**NV** Nonvegetarians.
*Human Nutrition.*
**NVA** National Vaccine Authority (U.S.A.).
*Immunization.*
**nvCJD** new variation Creutzfeldt-Jakob Disease.
*Prion Diseases.*
**NVA** night vision aid.
moyen auxiliaire de vision nocturne (ou de nuit).
**NVD** Night Viewing Device.
Used for seeing and photographing in the dark, also for the study of sleep patterns of human as well as nocturnal habits of reptiles, insects and mammals.
**NVD** night vision device.
dispositif de vision nocturne (ou de nuit).
**NVE** Network Visible Entry.
**NVG** night vision goggles.
lunettes de vision nocturne (ou de nuit).
**NVI** norme de vérification internationale.
international auditing guideline (IAG).
**NVOCC** Non-Vessel Owner Common Carrier.
**NVP** Nevirapine.
A regimen based on NVP reduces MTCT of HIV.
For further details see under: **MTCT**.
**NVQs** National Vocational Qualifications.
The introduction of the General System of NVQs started in 1986.
**NVS** Nonvoting Stock.
**NVSN** NATO voice switching network.
réseau téléphonique commuté de l'OTAN.
**NVTS** Network Virtual Terminal Service.
**NW** Net Worth.
*Business; Finance.*
**NW** North West.
**NW** The airline code for Northwest Airlines.
**NW** nuclear warfare.
guerre nucléaire.
**NWAPPS** North-West Approaches.
approches (maritimes) du Nord-Ouest.
**NWC** Net Working Capital.
**NWCR** National Weight Control Registry (U.S.A.).
*Obesity.*
**NWDC** National Wildlife Defence Council (U.S.A.).
**NWF** National Wildlife Federation (U.S.A.).
**NWIL** North-Western Illinois (U.S.A.).
**NWO** Netherlands Organization for Scientific Research (The Netherlands).
**NWOO** NATO wartime oil organization.
organisation pétrolière OTAN du temps de guerre.
**NWP models** Numerical Weather Prediction models.
*Atmospheric Research; Atmospheric Sciences; Environmental Science and Management; Land-Atmosphere Interactions; Meteorology.*
**NWRA** NATO wartime refugees agency.
agence OTAN pour les réfugiés en temps de guerre.
**NWRC** National Wetlands Research Center (U.S.A.).
**NWRC** National Wildlife Research Center (Saudi Arabia).
The NWRC is a division of the National Commssion for Wildlife Conservation and Development in Saudi-Arabia.
**NWRP** nuclear weapon release procedures.
procédures d'autorisation d'emploi d'armes nucléaires.
**NWS** National Weather Service (U.S.A.).
*Climate.*
**NWS** Nuclear-Weapon State.
**NWSBA** N.W. Suburban Bar Association (Illinois, U.S.A.).
**NWSGC** North West Structural Genomics Centre (G.B.).
Established in 2001.
**Nwt** Net Weight.
**NWT** New World Telephone (Hong Kong).
**NWT** North West Territories (Canada).
**NMTC** National Wind Technology Center (U.S.A.).
**NWWI** North-Western WIsconsin (U.S.A.).
**NY** Net Yield.
**N.Y.** New Year.

**NY** (abbr.) New York (U.S.A.).
**NYAS** New York Academy of Sciences.
The NYAS was founded in 1817 and has had as members people like Thomas Jefferson, Darwin and Einstein. It specializes in sponsoring multidisciplinary and cutting edge *meetings* and *conferences*. It also publishes The Annals of the New York Academy of Sciences, which dates back to 1823 and currently represents 28 books published each year that compile the best talks in frontier fields of scientific discourse given at outstanding conferences.
**NYBG** New York Botanical Garden (U.S.A.).
**NYBOT** New York Board Of Trade (U.S.A.).
**NYC** The airline code for New York City.
**NYCEP** New York Consortium in Evolutionary Primatology.
**NYD** New York Dock (U.S.A.).
**NYD** Not Yet Diagnosed.
**NYFE** New York Futures Exchange (U.S.A.).
**NYIF** New York Institute of Finance (U.S.A.).
**NYLA** New York Library Association (U.S.A.).
**NYME** New York Mercantile Exchange (U.S.A.).
**NYPD** New York Police Department (U.S.A.).
**NYPIRG** New York Public Interest Research Group (U.S.A.).
**NYSE** New York Stock Exchange (U.S.A.).
**NYSERDA** New York State Energy Research and Development Authority (U.S.A.).
**NYSILL** New York State Interlibrary Loan Networks (U.S.A.).
**NYU** New York University (U.S.A.).
**NYUMC** New York University Medical Center (U.S.A.).
**NZ** New Zealand.
**NZ** Not Zero.
**NZLA** New Zealand Library Association.
**NZMS** New Zealand Meteorological Service.
**NZOI** New Zealand Oceanographic Institute.
**NZ$** New Zealand Dollar.

**O** Ohio (U.S.A.).
Also: **OH**.
**o**; **o.** ohm.
Named for the German physicist Georg S. **Ohm**.
*Electricity.*
**o** open.
*Computer Programming; Electricity; Graphic Arts; Linguistics; Medicine; Physiology; Veterinary Medicine.*
**o** operand.
*Computer Programming; Mathematics.*
**o** operation.
Also: **op**.
*Computer Programming; Industrial Engineering; Military Science; Surgery.*
**o** operational.
*Engineering; Military Science.*
**o** operator.
Also: **opr**.
*Computer Programming* - In computer programming, the operator is the person dealing with the operation of computers.
*Engineering* - The operator is the person who deals with the operation and/or maintenance of devices, machines and the like.
*Telecommunications* - In this case, the operator is the person dealing with the operation of a telephone company switchboard.
**o**; **o.** order.
For further details see under: **ord**.
**o** output.
*Computer Technology; Electronics; Mechanical Engineering.*
**o** overcast.
*Meteorology; Mining Engineering.*
**O** Owner.
**O** The chemical symbol for Oxygen.
Oxygen is a gaseous chemical element having the atomic number 8, an atomic weight of 15.9994, and a melting point of -218.4°C. Oxygen makes up about 20% of the air by volume.
**$O_3$** Ozone.
Ozone is used mainly to purify drinking water.
*Chemistry.*
**OA** 1. objective area.
1. zone de l'objectif.
2. offensive action.
2. action offensive.
3. out of action.
3. hors combat.
**OA** Office Automation.
*Computer Technology.*
**OA** Office of Administration.
**OA** Okadaic Acid.
**o/a** on account of.
**OA** On or About.
**OA** Open Account.
*Business; Finance.*
**OA** Operational Analysis; Operational Auditing.
*Business; Finance.*
**OA** Osteoarthritis.
*Medicine.*
**oa** (abbr.) overall.
**OA** The airline code for Olympic Airways.
**OAA** Oxaloacetic Acid.
**OAB** Ocean Affairs Board (U.S.A.).
The OAB has replaced NASCO.
For further details see under: **NASCO**.
**OAC** Oceanographic Advisory Committee (U.S.A.).
**OAC** Office of Arms Control (U.S.A.).
**OAC** On Approved Credit.
*Business; Finance.*
**OACES** Ocean-Atmosphere Carbon Exchange Study.
**OACHA** Oregon Automated Clearing House Association (U.S.A.).
**OACI** Organisation de l'aviation civile internationale.
International Civil Aviation Organization (ICAO).
**OAEC** Organization of Asian Economic Co-operation.
**OAEs** Otoacoustic Emissions.
**OAF** Osteoclast-Activating Factors.
*Endocrinology.*
**OAK** The airport code for Oakland, California, U.S.A.
**OALA** Ohio Academic Libraries Association (U.S.A.).
**OALOS** Office for Ocean Affairs and the Law Of the Sea - U.N.
OALOS has been replaced by: **DOALOS**.
**OAM** Office of Alternative Medicine.
**OAM** Orbital Angular Momentum.
*Quantum Computation; Quantum Information; Quantum Optics.*
**O&G** Oil and Gas Technology.
**O&M** operation and maintenance.
exploitation et maintenance.
**O&M** Organization and Methods.
Also: **OM**; **O.M**.
**O&M** Organizzazione e Metodi.

Italian initialism meaning: Organization and Methods.
**O&S** operation(s) and support.
exploitation et soutien.
**OAO** Orbiting Astronomical Observatory.
**OAP** Observation Active Permamente.
French initialism meaning: Business Intelligence System.
**OAP** Occupational Ability Pattern.
**OAP** Œdème Aigu du Poumon.
French initialism meaning: Acute Pulmonary Oedema.
*Medicine.*
**OAP**; **oap** Old Age Pensioner.
**OAP** Oncovin, Ara-C, and Prednisone.
*Oncology.*
**OAR** Office of AIDS Research (U.S.A.).
**OAR** Office of Oceanic and Atmospheric Research (U.S.A.).
**OAR** Open Architecture for Reasoning.
**OAR** Ordering As Required.
*Business; Commerce.*
**OARDC** Ohio Agricultural Research and Development Center (U.S.A.).
**OAS** offensive air support.
appui aérien offensif.
**OAS** On Active Service.
**OAS** Organization of American States.
**Oas** Organizzazione dell'armata segreta.
Italian acronym of the: Organization of the Secret Army.
**OASDI** Old Age, Survivors & Disability Insurance.
**OASI** Old-Age and Survivors' Insurance (U.S.A.).
**OASIS** Oceanic and Atmospheric Scientific Information System.
**OAT** operational air traffic.
1a. circulation aérienne opérationnelle (CAO1.).
1b. circulation opérationnelle militaire (COM).
**OAU** Organization of African Unity.
**OAW** Oxyacetylene Welding.
*Metallurgy.*
**Ob.** (abbr.) obligation.
Also: **OBL**; **oblg**.
**OB** Obligation Bond.
*Business; Finance.*
**OB**; **ob.** (abbr.) obstetrician.
The obstetrician is a specialist in obstetrics.
*Medicine.*
**OB.**; **ob.** (abbr.) Obstetric; Obstetrical; Obstetrics.
*Medicine.*
**OB** Octave Band.
*Electronics.*
**OB** Oerlikon-Bührle (Switzerland).
Renamed Unaxis (2000). Transformed from armaments industry to *high-technology group.*
**OB** Olfactory Bulb.
*Brain Science; Chemosensory Receptors; Medicine; Olfaction; Neurobiology of Synapse; Recognition Molecules.*
**OB** Oligonucleotide-Binding.
*Biophysics; Biotechnology; Cellular Biochemistry; Molecular Medicine; Pharmacology.*
**o/b** on or before.
**OB** Opening of Books.
**O.B.** Operating Budget.
**OB** see ORBAT.
voir ORBAT.
**OB** Or Better.
**OB** Ordered Back.
*Business; Commerce.*
**OB** Order of the Bath.
**O.B.** Ordinary Business.
**OB** Osteoblasts.
*Cell Transplantation.*
**OB** Output Buffer.
*Computer Technology.*
**O/B** Outstanding Bill.
**OB** Overseas Borrowing.
**OBA** oxygen breathing apparatus.
appareil de respiration à oxygène.
**OBD** Output Bus Driver.
*Electronics.*
**OBEX** (abbr.) OBject EXchange.
**ob-gyn.** (abbr.) obstetrician gynecologist; obstetrics and gynecology.
**OBIS** Ocean Biogeographic Information System (U.S.A.).
A database project which is part of the International Census of Marine Life.
**OBI standard** Open Buying on the Internet standard.
OBI has been developed by a Consortium of 50 large U.S. Companies.
*Electronic Business-to-Business Technologies.*
**Obj.**; **obj.** (abbr.) objective.
**OBL.** (abbr.) Obligation.
Also: **Ob.**; **oblg**.
**obl** (abbr.) oblique.
*Botany; Mathematics; Science.*
**obl** (abbr.) oblong.
**OB/L** Ocean Bill of Lading.
Also: **Oc. B/L**.
*Business; Commerce.*
**OBL** Order Bill of Lading; Outward Bill of Lading.
**oblg.** (abbr.) obligate; obligation.
**OBM** orbital ballistic missile.

missile balistique orbital.
**OBM** Ordnance Bench Mark.
**OBP** Odorant-Binding Protein.
*Structural Biology.*
**OBR** Optical Bar-code Reader.
The optical bar-code reader also known as: Optical Bar-code Scanner is a device that reads coded details from labels or the like and is used mainly in retail stores.
*Computer Technology.*
**OBR** Overseas Business Report (U.S.A.).
**OBR** Outboard Recorder.
*Data Communications.*
**obs.** (abbr.) Observatory.
*Astronomy.*
**obs.** (abbr.) observer.
**obs.** (abbr.) obsolete.
*Biology; Science.*
**OBS** Obstetrician; Obstetrics.
*Medicine.*
**OBS** Ocean-Bottom Seismometers.
*Earthquakes Research; Earth Sciences; Earth Tides; Geology; Geophysics; Oceanography; Planetary Sciences; Seismic Tomography.*
**OBSs** Ocean-Bottom Seismometers.
For further details see under: **OBS**.
**OBU** Offshore Banking Unit.
**obv** (abbr.) obverse.
**OC.**; **oc.** (abbr.) Ocean.
**OC** Off Center.
**OC** Officer Commanding.
**OC** Officer Commissioner.
**OC** Officer Candidate.
**OC** On Center.
**OC** On Course.
**OC** Ondes Courtes.
French initialism meaning: Shortwaves / Short-waves.
*Electricity; Physics; Telecommunications.*
**O/C**; **o/c** Open Charter.
**OC** Open Circuit.
*Electricity.*
**OC** Operating Company.
*Business; Finance.*
**OC** Operating Cost.
*Business; Commerce.*
**OC** Opportunity Cost.
**OC** Organizational Chart.
**OC** Osteocyte.
*Histology;* The osteocyte is a bone cell.
**O/C**; **o/c** overcharge.
**OC** Over-the-Counter.
**OCA** 1. oceanic area [airspace area].
1. zone océanique [zone de l'espace aérien].
2. offensive counter-air (operation).
2. (opération) effensive contre le potentiel aérien.
3. operational control authority [NCS].
3. autorité de contrôle opérationnel [NCS].
**OCA/DCA** offensive counter air/defensive counter air.
(opération) offensive/défensive contre le potentiel aérien.
**OCAL** Online Cryptanalytic Aid Language.
**OCAS** Organization of Central American States.
**OCBC** Overseas-Chinese Banking Corporation.
**Oc. B/L** Ocean Bill of Lading.
Also: **OB/L**.
**OCBS** Oral and Craniofacial Biological Sciences.
**OCC** Office of the Comptroller of the Currency.
The OCC regulates nationally chartered banks in the U.S.A.
**OCC** Official Custodian Charities.
**OCCAM** Osservatorio per la Comunicazione Culturale e Audiovisiva del Mediterraneo.
Created in Milan, Italy, by UNESCO.
For further details see under: **UNESCO**.
**OCCR** Office Central de Chauffe Rationnelle (France).
**OCD** Obsessive - Compulsive Disorder.
The OCD also known as: Obsessive-Compulsive Neurosis affects young individuals aged 7 to 17.
*Psychiatric Drugs; Psychology.*
**OCD** Ocean Chemistry Division.
Of the AOML (U.S.A.).
For further details see under: **AOML**.
**OCDE** Organisation de Coopération et de Développement Economiques (France).
French initialism of the: Organization for Economic Co-operation and Development (OECD).
**OCDM** office of civil and defence mobilization.
bureau de la mobilisation civile et militaire.
**OCDM models** Open universe Cold Dark Matter models.
*Astronomy; Astrophysics; Physics.*
**OCE** officer conducting the exercise.
officier directeur de l'exercice.
**OCEANLANT** Ocean Sub-Area Atlantic [obsolete].
Sous-zone océanique de l'Atlantique [obsolète].
**OCEE** Oceanic Convergence zone - Eastern Edge.
*Atmospheric Science; Climatology; Geophysics; Zonal Displacements.*
**OCG** Oral Cholangiogram.
**OCGA** Office of Congressional and Government Affairs (U.S.A.).

**OCHA** Office for the Coordination of Humanitarian Affairs [has replaced UNDHA].
Bureau de la coordination des affaires humanitaires (BCAH) [remplace l'UNDHA].
**OCI** Ontario Cancer Institute (Canada).
**OCIA** Organic Crop Improvement Association.
The OCIA is located in Bellafontaine, Ohio, U.S.A.
**OC image** Opposite Circular image.
*Astronomy; Space Research; Space Science.*
**OCLC** Ohio College Library Center (U.S.A.).
**OCLC** Online Computer Library Center.
**OCLIPS** Operational CLImate Prediction and Services.
**OCLS** Office of Consolidated Laboratory Services (U.S.A.).
**OCM** Octyl Methoxycinnamate.
**OCM**; **Ocm** Online Customer Management.
**OCM** Optical Channel Monitor.
*Channels Measurement.*
**OCM** optical countermeasures.
contre-mesures optiques.
**OCM** Organizzazione Comune dei Mercati.
**OC meteorites** Ordinary Chondrite meteorites.
*Earth, Atmospheric, and Planetary Sciences.*
**OCNMAP** (abbr.) Ocean Map.
**OCN method** Optimal Climate Normals method.
**OCNS** Oklahoma Center for Neuroscience (U.S.A.).
**OCNs** Open College Networks.
**OCO** one-cancels-the-other (referring to orders).
**OCO** Operating and Control Organization [NACOSA].
Organisation d'exploitation et de contrôle [NACOSA].
**OCP** Onchocerciasis Control Program.
The OCP started in 1974 and will continue till 2012 in West Africa.
Onchocerciasis is also known as: Onchocercosis.
*Medicine.*
**OCPA** Overseas Chinese Physics Association.
**OC polarizations** Opposite-sense Circular polarizations.
**OCR** Office of Civil Rights.
**OCR** Office of Coal Research.
**OCR** Optical Character Reader.
*Computer Technology.*
**OCR** Optical Character Recognition.
The optical character recognition is also known as: Electrooptical Character Recognition and deals with the identification of handwritten or printed numerals and letters.
*Computer Technology.*
**OCRD** Ocean Climate Research Division.
Of the Pacific Marine Environmental Laboratory (U.S.A.).
**OCRGDF** Office Central de Répression de la Grande Délinquance Financière (France).
*Criminal Law.*
**OCRM** Office of Coastal Resource Management (U.S.A.).
**OCRTIS** Office Central pour la Repression du Traffic Illicite de Stupéfiants.
French initialism of the: Central Office for Illegal Drug Traffic Repression.
**OCS** Officer Candidate School.
**OCS** officer conducting the serial.
officier responsable d'une phase de l'exercice.
**OCS** Office of the Chief Scientist.
**OCs** Oral Contraceptives.
*Birth Control.*
**OCs** Ordinary Chondrites.
*Earth and Space Science; Mineral Sciences.*
**OCS** Organe Central de Signalisation.
**OCS** Outer Continental Shelf.
**OCSAB** Outer Continental Shelf Advisory Board (U.S.A.).
**OCSE** Organizzazione per la Cooperazione e lo Sviluppo Economico.
Italian acronym of the: Organization for Economic Cooperation and Development.
**OCSEAP** Outer Continental Shelf Environment Assessment Program.
**oct.** (abbr.) octal.
*Computer Programming.*
**Oct.** (abbr.) October.
**OCT** Optical Coherence Tomography/Tomology.
*Biomedical Optics; Neonatal and Developmental Medicine; Pathology; Tomographic Images; Tissue Optics.*
**OCT** Optimal Cutting Temperature.
**OCTRF** Ontario Cancer Treatment and Research Foundation (Canada).
*Cancer Education; Cancer Preservation; Cancer Research; Cancer Treatment.*
**OCTS** Ocean Color and Temperature Scanner.
*Biology; Botany; Earth Science; Environmental and Estuarine Studies; Marine Sciences.*
**OCTV** Open-Circuit Television.
**OCU** Over-the-counter Control Unit.
**OCV** Open Circuit Voltage.
**OD**; **O.D.** Doctor of Optometry.
**OD** Occhio Destro.
Italian initialism meaning: Right Eye.
**O/D**; **o.d.** On Deck.
**OD**; **O/D**; **o.d.** On Demand.
**OD**; **O.D.** Optical Density.

*Optics.*
**OD**; **O.D.** Ordnance Department.
**OD** Organizational Development.
**OD** Other Data.
**OD**; **O.D.** Outside Diameter.
*Design Engineering.*
**OD**; **O.D.** Outside Dimension.
**O/D**; **OD**; **o.d.** (abbr.) overdraft.
**OD**; **O.D.** Overdose.
An overdose is an excessive dose of a drug or a medical substance.
*Medicine.*
**od.** (abbr.) overdraw; overdue.
**ODA** Office Document Architecture.
**ODA** Overseas Development Administration.
Of the British Government.
**ODAF** Organizzazione per il Diritto degli Affari in Africa (Italy).
*Italian Organizations.*
**ODA Program** Official Development Assistance Program.
**ODA project** Optimum Design in Aerodynamics project.
*European Community Project.*
**ODB** voir ORBAT.
see ORBAT.
**ODBC** Open Database Connectivity.
**ODBE** ordre de bataille électronique.
electronic order of battle (EOB).
**ODC** Ornithine Decarboxylase.
**ODD** Oculodentodigital Dysplasia.
ODD is also known as OculoDentoDigital syndrome; Oculodentoosseous Dysplasia.
**ODE** Occasion d'Entendre.
Opportunity to hear.
**ODE** Ordinary Differential Equation.
*Mathematics.*
**OD fcc phase** Orientationally Disordered face-centered cubic phase.
**O.d.G.**; **OdG**; **o.d.g.** Ordine del Giorno.
Italian initialism meaning: Agenda; List of business; Order of the day.
**o.d.i.** opera dell'ingegno.
**ODI** Overseas Development Institute.
**ODL** Open and Distance Learning.
**ODL** organisation de défense littorale.
seaward defence organization.
**ODMR spectrum** Optically Detected Magnetic Resonance spectrum.
**ODNs** Oligodeoxynucleotides.
*Antisense Agents; Biology; Cellular Biology; Gene Expression; Molecular Biology.*
**ODO** Ospedali Domiciliari Oncologici (Italy).
**ODP** Ocean Drilling Program.
For further details see under: **CORK**.
**ODP** Orbit Determination Program (U.S.A.).
Of the JPL.
For further details see under: **JPL**.
**ODP** overall documentation plan.
plan d'ensemble de la documentation.
**ODPs** Ozone Depletion Potentials.
**ODS**; **Ods** Ordine di Servizio (Italy).
**ODS** Orofaciodigital Syndrome.
*Medicine.*
**ODSS** Ocean Dumping Surveillance System.
**ODT** 1-Octadecanethiol.
*Chemistry.*
**ODT** Optical Data Transmission.
**ODT** Optical Doppler Tomography.
*Biomedical Optics; Neonatal and Developmental Medicine; Pathology; Tomographic Images; Tissue Optics.*
**ODV** object de vérification.
object of verification (OOV).
**ODV** Occasion de Voir.
French acronym meaning: Opportunity to see.
**ODW** Omega Dropwindsonde.
**Oe** Oersted; oersted.
*Electromagnetism.*
**OE** Old English.
Old English is the English of any period before Modern English.
*Languages.*
**OE** Olfactory Epithelium.
*Brain Science; Neurobiology of Synapse; Chemosensory Receptors; Olfaction; Recognition Molecules.*
**OE** Operating Expense.
**OE** organizational element.
élément organique.
**OE** Original Equipment.
*Computer Technology.*
**OEC** Oxygen-Evolving Complex.
**OECD** Organization for Economic Co-operation and Development.
**OECE** Organizzazione Europea per la Cooperazione Economica; Organisation Européenne de Coopération Economique.
Italian and French acronym of the: Organization for European Economic Co-operation.
**OECQ** Organisation Européenne pour le Contrôle de la Qualité.
French initialism of the: European Organization for Quality Control.
**OECs** Olfactory Ensheathing Cells.
**OED** Oxford English Dictionary.

**OEDSF** Onboard Experimental Data Support Facility.

**OEDT** Osservatorio Europeo della Droga e delle Tossicomanie.

**OEEC** Organization for European Economic Co-operation.

**OEHHA** Office of Environmental Health Hazard Assessment.
*Breast Cancer; Cancer Research; Carcinogen Identification; Endometrial Cancer.*

**OEM** officier d'état-major.
staff officer (SO2.).

**OEM** Ondes Electro-Magnétiques.
French initialism meaning: Electromagnetic Waves.
*Electromagnetism.*

**OEM** Original Equipment Manufacturer.

**OEMP** Office of Environmental Monitoring and Prediction (U.S.A.).
Of the U.S. NOAA.
For further details see under: **NOAA**.

**OEO** Office of Economic Opportunity.

**OEP** Office of Emergency Preparedness (U.S.A.).

**OEP** Office of Environmental Policy (White House, U.S.A.).

**OER** Office of Energy Research (U.S.A.).
U.S. Department Of Energy.

**OERD** Ocean Environment Research Division (U.S.A.).
The OERD has replaced: MARD and MRRD.
For further details see under: **MARD** and **MRRD**.

**OERI** Osservatorio Europeo delle Relazioni Industriali.
*Industrial Relations.*

**OES** Office of Earth Science (U.S.A.).

**OES** Office of Endagered Species.

**OES bureau** Oceans and international Environmental and Scientific Affairs bureau.

**OF** Offshore Funds.
*Business; Finance.*

**OF** Old French.
Old French is the French language from the 9th to the 16th century.
*Languages.*

**OFC 2001** Optical Fiber Communication Conference (U.S.A.).

**OFCCP** Office of Federal Contract Compliance Programs (U.S.A.).
Of the United States Department of Labor.

**OFDA** Office of Foreign Disaster Assistance.
At the U.S. Agency for International Development.

**Off.**; **off.** (abbr.) Officer.

**off.** (abbr.) officina.
Italian abbreviation meaning: workshop; shop.

**off.mecc.** (abbr.) officina meccanica.
Italian abbreviation meaning: mechanical workshop.

**OFFs** Optical Fourier Transforms.
*Ocean Wave Detection.*

**OFHC** Oxygen-Free High-Conductivity.

**OFI** Office of the Federal Inspector (U.S.A.).

**OFII** Organization for International Investment (U.S.A.).
OFII represents 62 subsidiaries of foreign-based multinationals.
*International Investments Organization.*

**OFM** Order of Friars Minor.

**OFN** other forces for NATO.
autres forces pour l'OTAN.

**OFPL** (Ufficio Centrale per) l'Orientamento e la Formazione Professionale dei Lavoratori (Italy).
*Vocational Training.*

**OFS** Orange Free State.

**OFT** Office of Fair Trading (G.B.).
The OFT is the Body which monitors professional practices.

**OFT** Orbital Flight Test.

**OFTs** Optical Fourier Transforms.
*Ocean Wave Detection.*

**Oftel** (abbr.) Office of telecommunications.

**OFWS** Open-Field Walking Score.

**OG** Official Gazette.

**OG** Ordinamento Giudiziario (Italy).

**OGCM** Ocean General Circulation Model.
*Oceanography.*

**OGCN** Olympique Gymnaste Club de Nice.

**ogg.** (abbr.) oggetto.
Italian abbreviation meaning: object: (in correspondence): subject; re: (U.S.A.).

**OGJ** Oil & Gas Journal.

**OGL** Open General Licence.

**OGLE** Optical Gravitational Lensing Experiment.
*Astronomy; Astrophysics; Cosmology; Dark Matter; Physics; Planetary Systems.*

**OGM** Ordinary General Meeting.

**OGM** Organismi Geneticamente Modificati.
Italian initialism meaning: Genetically Modified Organisms.

**OGO** Orbiting Geophysical Observatory.

**OGP** Office of Global Programs (U.S.A.).
Of the U.S. NOAA.
For further details see under: **NOAA**.

**OGS** Oxford Glyco-Sciences (G.B.).
*Protein Analysis; Protein Profiles; Proteomics Research.*

**OH** (abbr.) Ohio (U.S.A.).

Also: **O**.
**OH** Ohmic Heating.
**OH** Oil Hardening.
*Metallurgy.*
**OHBM** Organization for Human Brain Mapping.
*Mapping Imaging.*
**OHC** Overhead Camshaft / overhead cam.
*Mechanical Engineering.*
**6-OHDA** 6-Hydroxydopamine.
**OHER** Office of Health and Environmental Research (U.S.A.).
**OHG** Old High German.
*Languages.*
**OHIM** Office for Harmonization in the Internal Market (Spain).
**OHIONET** Ohio Library Network (U.S.A.).
**OHLC** Open, High, Low and Close (realtime line).
Wall Street.
**OHMS** On Her Majesty's Service (G.B.).
**OHP** Observatoire de Haute Provence (France).
*Astronomy; Astrophysics.*
**OHP** Overhead Projector.
**OHR** Office of Human Resources (U.S.A.).
**OHR** Office of the High Representative [UN].
Bureau du Haut Représentant [à l'ONU, on écrit "Haut-Representant"].
**OHRP** Office of Human Research Potection.
At the Department of Health and Human Services (U.S.A.).
**OHSU** Oregon Health Sciences University (U.S.A.).
**OHTEX** Ocean Heat Transport Experiment.
*Japanese Experiments.*
**OHV engine** Overhead-Valve engine.
*Mechanical Engineering.*
**OI** Operating Income.
**OI** 1. operational instruction.
1. directive opérationnelle.
2. organisation internationale.
2. internationale organization (IO).
**OI** Optical Isomerism; Optical Isomers.
*Physical Chemistry.*
**OI** Optimum Interpolation.
**OI** Ordinary Interest.
**OI** Ordinateur Individuel.
French initialism meaning: Personal Computer.
**OI** Output Impedance.
*Electronics.*
**OIA** Office of International Affairs (U.S.A.).
**OIB** Ocean Island Basalt.
For further details see under: **OIBs**.
**OIBs** Ocean Island Basalts.
*Astronomy; Earth Sceinces; Geochemistry; Geophysics; Planetary Sciences.*
**OiC** officer in charge.
officier responsable.
**OICR** Organismi di Investimento Collettivo del Risparmio (Italy).
*Banking.*
**OIDA** position Occipito-Iliaque Droite Antérieure.
French acronym meaning: Right Occipito-Anterior position.
*Medicine.*
**OIDP** position Occipito Iliaque Droite Postérieure.
French initialism meaning: Right Occipito-Posterior position.
*Medicine.*
**OIDT** position Occipito-Iliaque Droite Transverse.
French initialism meaning: Right Occipitotransverse position.
*Medicine.*
**OIES** Office for the Interdisciplinary Earth Studies.
**OIF** Oocyte Imprinting Factor.
*Genetic Imprinting; Molecular Pathology.*
**OIG** Office of the Inspector General.
**OIG** Organizzazione Intergovernativa.
**OIGA** position Occipito-Iliaque Gauche Antérieure.
French acronym meaning: Left Occipito-Anterior position.
*Medicine.*
**OIGP** position Occipito-Iliaque Gauche Postérieure.
French initialism meaning: Left Occipito-Posterior position.
*Medicine.*
**OIGT** position Occipito-Iliaque Gauche Transverse.
French initialism meaning: Left Occipitotransverse position.
*Medicine.*
**OIL** Organizzazione Internazionale del Lavoro.
Italian acronym of the: International Labor Organization.
**O.I.L.** Organizzazione Italiana Lubrificanti (Italy).
*Italian Organization; Lubricants.*
**OIM** Organisation internationale pour les migrations.
International Organization for Migration (IOM).
**OIPA** Organizzazione Internazionale Protezione Animali.
Italian acronym of the: International Organization for Animals Protection (Italy).
**OIPTT** Office of Intellectual Property and Technology Transfer (U.S.A.).
*Intellectual Property; Technology Transfer.*
**OIRA** Office of Information and Regulatory Affairs (U.S.A.).
**OIRM** Organization of Islamic Revolution Mojahedin.

**OIs** Olivine-rich Inclusions.
*Earth and Planetary Sciences; Geochemistry; Geophysics.*
**Ois** Opportunistic infections.
*Molecular Histology; Oral Infections; Pathology.*
**OIT** Office of International Trade.
**OIT** Oregon Institute of Technology (U.S.A.).
**OIT** Organisation Internationale du Travail.
**OJCCT** Online Journal of Current Clinical Trials.
**OJP** Ontong Java Plateau.
*Geology; Geophysics; Oceanography.*
**OJR** Online Journalism Review.
**OJT** On-the-Job Training.
**OK** (abbr.) Oklahoma (U.S.A.).
Also: **Okla**.
**O.K.** Outer Keel.
**OKC** The airport code for Will Rogers World Airport, Oklahoma City, Oklahoma, U.S.A.
**OKE** Optical Kerr Effect.
*Chemistry; Non-linear Spectroscopy.*
**OKIOC** Offshore Kazakhstan International Operating Company (Kazakhstan).
OKIOC is the consortium formed to explore the Kashagan formation in the Northern Caspian Sea.
*Energy Resources.*
**Okla.** (abbr.) Oklahoma (U.S.A.).
Also: **OK**.
**ol.** (abbr.) olivine.
Olivine is also known as: Chrysolite.
*Mineralogy.*
**OLA** Ohio Library Association (U.S.A.).
**OLA** Ontario Library Association (Canada).
**OLA** Oregon Library Association (U.S.A.).
**OLA** Osteopathic Libraries Association.
**OLAFAS** on-line automated frequency assignment system.
système en ligne automatisé d'assignation de fréquences.
**OLAP** On-Line Analytical Processing.
*Data Modeling and Design; Multi-Dimensional Analysis Techniques.*
**OLC** Online Library Center.
Ohio-based (U.S.A.).
*Electronic Publishing.*
**OLCNSS** Oxford Lane Certified Network Security Specialist (Denver, Colorado, U.S.A.).
*Certified Information Technology Training.*
**OLC system** On-Line Computer system.
*Computer Technology.*
**OLCO** On-Line Cryptographic Operation.
Also: **OLO**.
*Telecommunications.*
**OLDB** On-Line Database.
*Computer Programming.*
**OLE** Object Linking and Embedding (Microsoft's).
*Software.*
**OLED** Organic Light-Emitting Device.
**OLED** Organic Light-Emitting Diode.
**OLEDs** Organic Light-Emitting Devices.
*Chemistry; Electrical Engineering; Photonics and Optoelectronic Materials.*
**OLEDs** Organic Light-Emitting Diodes.
**OLF** officier de liaison français.
French liaison officer (FLO 2.).
**OLIS** Oregon Legislative Information System (U.S.A.).
**OLO** On-Line Operation.
On-line operation is also known as: On-line Cryptographic Operation.
*Computer Technology.*
**OLP** On-Line Programming.
*Robotics.*
**OLR** Outgoing Longwave Radiation.
**OLRTS** On-Line Real-Time System.
*Computer Technology.*
**OLS** Ordinary Least Squares.
*Statistics.*
**OLTEP** Online Test Executive Program.
**OM** Oncostatin M.
**OM** Onda Media.
Italian initialism meaning: Average Wave; Medium Wave.
**OM** On Margin; Open Market.
*Business; Finance.*
**OM** Optical Microscopy.
*Optics.*
**OM** Optical Modulator.
The optical modulator is a device to impress data on a light beam.
*Telecommunications.*
**OM** Order of Merit.
**OM** Organic Matter.
**O.M.**; **OM** Organization and Methods.
Also: **O&M**.
**OM** Ospedale Militare.
Italian initialism meaning: Military Hospital.
**OM** Outer Membrane.
*Cell Biology.*
**OMA** Oceanography and Marine Assessment.
**OMA** Optical Multichannel Analyzer.
**OMA** The airport code for Eppley Airfield, Omaha, Nebraska, U.S.A.
**OMAE** Offshore Mechanics and Arctic Engineering.
**OMAM** Organizzazione Mondiale Assistenza Massonica.

*Freemasonry.*
**OMAR** Optical MArk Reading.
Also: **OMR**.
*Computer Technology.*
**OMB** Office of Management and Budget (U.S.A.).
**OMB** Ontario Municipal Board (Canada).
**OMC** Organisation Mondiale du Commerce; Organizzazione Mondiale per il Commercio.
French and Italian initialism of the: World Trade Organization.
**OMDS** Oral Medicine and Diagnostic Sciences (Department).
University of Illinois at Chicago (U.S.A.).
**OME** Open Microscopy Environment (G.B.).
*Data & Metadata Storage; Emaging Technology; Software Projects.*
**OMG** Object Management Group (G.B.).
The OMG was set up in 1989 to solve the problem of incompatible databases and promote object-oriented design standards for distributed computing. Its Corba Standard is the basis of most commercial middleware technologies.
*Biological Databases; Genomics; Object-oriented design Standards.*
For further details see under: **Corba Standard**.
**OMG** operational manoeuvre group.
groupement opérationnel de manœuvre (GOM).
**OMGE** Organisation Mondiale de Gastro-Entérologie (Germany).
Founded in 1935 to conduct research and contribute to the progress generally of the study of gastroenterology.
**Omgp** Oligodendrocyte myelin glycoprotein.
*Neuronal Plasticity; Neuronal Regeneration.*
**OMI** Operations and Maintenance Instructions.
**OMI** Organisation maritime internationale.
International Maritime Organization (IMO).
**OMI** Organizzazione Marittima Internazionale.
Italian acronym of the: International Maritime Organization.
**OMICROM** Osservatorio MIlanese sulla CRiminalità Organizzata a Milano (Italy).
*Organized Crime.*
**OMIM** Online Mendelian Inheritance in Man.
**OMM** Organizzazione Mondiale della Meteorologia; Organisation Météorologique Mondiale.
Italian and French initialism of the: World Meteorological Organization.
For further details see under: **WMO**.
**OMMSQA** Office of Modeling, Monitoring Systems and Quality Assurance (U.S.A.).
**OMNIS** Observatory for Multiflavor Neutrinos from Supernovae (U.S.A. and G.B.)
*Astrophysics; Physics.*
**OMO** Office of Marine Operations (U.S.A.).
**OMO funds** Open Market Option funds.
**OMP** Orotidine 5'-Monophosphate.
*Biochemistry; Chemistry.*
**OMPA** Office of Marine Pollution Assessment.
**OmpA** Outer membrane protein A.
*Cell Biology; Medicine; Physiology.*
**OMPI** Organisation Mondiale de la Propriété Industrielle.
**OMPs** OM Proteins.
*Molecular Microbiology.*
For further details see under: **OM**.
**OMPs** Outer Membrane Proteins.
**OMR** Optical Mark Reading.
Also: **OMAR**.
**OMRF** Oklahoma Medical Research Foundation (U.S.A.).
*Biochemistry; Fellowships; Immunology; Molecular/Cellular Biology; Training Programs.*
For further details see under: **JHS**.
**OMS** Orbital Maneuvering System.
**OMS** Organisation Mondiale de la Santé; Organizzazione Mondiale della Sanità.
French and Italian initialism of the: World Health Organization.
**OMS** Organisation Mondiale du Commerce.
French initialism of the: World Trade Organization.
**OMS** Ovonic Memory Switch.
*Electronics.*
**OMS materials** Octahedral Molecular Sieve materials.
*Chemical Engineering; Chemistry; Materials Science.*
**OMZ** Oxygen Minimum Zone.
*Climate Diagnostics; Earth Sciences; Geological Science; Paleoceanography.*
**ONC** Open Network Computing.
**ONC** operational navigational chart.
carte de navigation opérationnelle.
**ONC** Ordinary National Certificate.
**ONEM** Office National de l'EMploi (Belgium).
**ONERA** Office National d'Etudes et de Recherches Aérospatiales (France).
**ONG** Organizzazioni Non Governative; Organisations Non Gouvernementales.
Italian and French initialism meaning: Non-Governmental Organizations.
**ONIA** Office National Industriel de l'Azote (France).

**ONISEP** Office National d'Information Sur les Enseignements et les Professions (France).
**ONL** Outer Nuclear (photoreceptor) Layer.
*Biological Timing; Medicine; Neurobiology; Physiology.*
**ONLUS** Organizzazioni Non Lucrative di Utilità Sociale (Italy).
**o.n.o.** or near offer.
*Business; Economics; Finance.*
**ONP** Office National des Pensions (Belgium).
**ONP** Open Network Provision.
**ONPG** *Ortho*-Nitrophenyl β-Galactoside.
**ONPI** Office of News and Public Information (U.S.A.).
**ONR** Office of Naval Research (U.S.A.).
**ONS** Office for National Statistics (G.B.).
**ONS** Office of NATO Standardization [replaced by NSA 2.].
Secrétariat OTAN pour la normalisation [remplacé par l'AON 1.].
**ONSS** Office National de Sécurité Sociale (Belgium).
**ONST** outline NATO staff target.
ébauche d'objectif d'état-major de l'OTAN.
**Ont.** (abbr.) Ontario (Canada).
**ONT** The airport code for Ontario, California, U.S.A.
**ONT** out-of-national territory (forces).
(forces) hors du territoire national.
**ONU** Organisation des Nations Unies; Organizzazione delle Nazioni Unite.
French and Italian acronym of the: United Nations Organization.
**ONURC** opération des Nations Unies pour le rétablissement de la confiance en Croatie.
United Nations Confidence Restoration Operation in Croatia (UNCRO).
**ONUSAL** U.N. operation in El Salvador.
**ONUSI** Organizzazione delle Nazioni Unite per lo Sviluppo Industriale.
Italian acronym of the: United Nations Organization for Industrial Development.
**OO** Observation Officer.
**o.o.** on order.
**OO** Open Order.
*Business; Commerce; Finance.*
**OO** Operation Order.
*Military.*
**o/o** order of.
**OOA** out-of-area.
hors zone.
**OOB** see ORBAT.
voir ORBAT.
**OOC** Operational Oceanography Center (U.S.A.).
**OODBMS** Object-Oriented Database Management System.
**OOE** Office of Ocean Exploration - At the U.S. NOAA.
*Ocean Exploration.*
For further details see under: **NOAA**.
**OOO** Out Of Order.
**OOP** Object-Oriented programming.
*Software.*
**OO.PP.** Opere Pubbliche.
Italian initialism meaning: Public Works.
**OOS** Ocean Observing System.
**OOS** Office of Opportunities in Science (U.S.A.).
**OOSDP** Ocean Observing System Development Panel.
**OOTW** operations other than war.
opérations autres que celles de guerre.
**OOV** object of verification.
objet de vérification (ODV).
**OP; O.P.** Observation Post.
*Military Science.*
**op** (abbr.) open.
For further details see under: **o**.
**OP** Open Market.
*Business; Commerce; Finance.*
**OP** Open Policy.
**OP** Opening Price; Opening Purchase.
*Business; Finance.*
**op** (abbr.) operand.
*Computer Programming; Mathematics.*
**OP** Operating Profit.
*Business; Finance.*
**op** (abbr.) operation.
For further details see under: **o**.
**OP; O.P.** Operation Part.
Operation part is also known as: Operation Field.
*Computer Programming.*
**op** (abbr.) operator.
For further details see under: **o**.
**op** (abbr.) output.
*Computer Technology; Electronics; Mechanical Engineering.*
**op.** (abbr.) opposed; opposite.
**op.** (abbr.) opus.
**OPA** Offre Publique d'Achat.
French acronym meaning: Takeover Bid.
*Business; Finance.*
**OPA** Oil Pollution Act.
**OPA amicale** Offre Publique d'Achat amicale.
French acronym meaning: Friendly Takeover Bid.
*Business; Finance.*

**OPA/βME** *O*-phthaldialdehyde / β-Mercaptoethanol.

**OPA inamicale** Offre Publique d'Achat inamicale. French acronym meaning: Contested Takeover Bid; Hostile Takeover Bid.
*Business; Finance.*

**OPARISOD** OPen ARchitecture for Interactive Services On Demand.
*European Community Project.*

**OPAS** Offerta Pubblica di Acquisto e Scambio. Italian acronym meaning: Public Offer of Purchase and Exchange.
*Banking; Business; Finance.*

**OPAs** Optical Parametric Amplifiers.
*Optics; Quantum Electronics.*

**OPB** Occupational Pensions Board (U.S.A.).

**OPC** Ocean Products Center (U.S.A.).
Of the U.S. NOAA.
For further details see under: **NOAA**.

**OPC** Outboard Pleasure Craft.

**OPCOM** operational command.
commandement opérationnel.

**OPCON** operational control.
contrôle opérationnel.

**OPCPA** Optical Parametric CPA.
For further details see under: **CPA**.

**OPCVM** Organismes de Placements Collectifs en Valeurs Mobilières.

**OPD** Outpatient Department.

**OPDAR** Optical Direction And ranging Radar.
OPDAR is also known as: Optical Radar.
*Engineering.*

**OPDC** Ocean Pollution Data Center (U.S.A.).

**OPDEC** operational deception.
déception opérationnelle.

**OP DEF** (equipment) operational defect.
défaut de fonctionnement (du matériel).

**OPDS** Orthopyridyl-Disulfide.

**OPEC** Organization of Petroleum Exporting Countries.

**OPEN** Optical Pan European Network.
*European Community Project.*

**OPEP** Organisation des Pays Exportateurs de Pétrole.
French acronym of the: Organization of Petroleum Exporting Countries.

**OPES** Orbiter Pole Escape System.

**OPET** Organizations for the Promotion of Energy Technologies - E.C.
The network of the above organizations, which consists of 39 bodies throughout all of the Member States of the European Union, came into operation in January 1991. OPET aims to promote the wider use of new and innovative *Energy Technologies.*

**OPF** Official Personnel Folder.

**OPFOR** opposing forces.
forces d'opposition.

**OPG** Optical Parametric Generator.
*Applied Physics; Quantum Electronics.*

**OPGs** Optical Parametric Generators.
For further details see under: **OPG**.

**Oph clouds** Ophiuchus clouds.
*Astronomy; Astrophysics; Space Research.*

**OPI** Information Processing Centre (Poland).

**OPI** office of primary interest.
service principalement intéressé.

**OPIC** Overseas Private Investment Corporation.
*Project Financing.*

**OPINTEL** operational intelligence.
renseignement opérationnel.

**OPIs** Olivine-Pyroxene Inclusions.
*Earth and Planetary Sciences; Geochemistry; Geophysics.*

**opl** (abbr.) operational.
For further details see under: **o**.

**OPLAN** operation plan.
plan d'opération.

**OPLAW** operational law.
droits des conflicts armés appliqué aux opérations.

**OPLO** organisation de production et de logistique de l'OTAN.
NATO production and logistics organization (NPLO).

**OPLOH** Organisation de production et de logistique OTAN HAWK.
NATO HAWK Production and Logistics Organization (NHPLO).

**OPM** Office of Personnel Management.

**OPM** Opérateurs Principaux du Marché.
French initialism meaning: Main Market Operators.

**OPM** Options Pricing Model.
*Stock Exchange.*

**OPM** Other People's Money.
*Stock Exchange.*

**OPN** Olivary Pretectal Nucleus.
*Biology; Circadian Rhythms.*

**OPO** Optical Parametric Oscillator.
*Astronomy; Optics; Physics.*

**OPORD** operation order.
ordre d'opération.

**OPORDER** see OPORD.
voir OPORD.

**OPOs** Optical Parametric Oscillators.
For further details see under: **OPO**.

**OPP** operational planning process.
processus de planification opérationnelle.
**opp.** (abbr.) opposed.
**OPP** Order Penetration Point.
*Marketing.*
**OPPBTP** Organisme Professionnel de Prévention du Bâtiment et des Travaux Publics (France).
**oppn.** (abbr.) opposition.
**OPR** office of primary responsibility.
bureau de première responsabilité (BPR).
**opr** (abbr.) operand.
For further details see under: **op**.
**opr** (abbr.) operator.
For further details see under: **o**.
**OPR** *Ortho*-to-*Para* Ratio.
*Astrophysics; Evolution of Comets.*
**OPRR** Office for Protection from Research Risks (U.S.A.).
Of the U.S. Department of Health and Human Services.
**OPRB** ACE Operational Planning and Review Board.
Commission de planification et d'examen des opérations du CAE.
**OPREP** operation report.
compte rendu d'opération.
**OP/REP** see OPREP.
voir OPREP.
**OPS** Open Profiling Standard.
**OPs** Organophosphates.
While high concentrations of OPs are very toxic, U.S. researchers have found that low-levels of OPs produce long-term problems in cognitive areas of the brain.
*Neuropharmacology; Neuroscience.*
**OPS** Outpatient Service.
**OPS** Oxygen Plasma Source.
**OPSEC** operations security.
securité des opérations.
**OPSL-980** Optically Pumped vertical-cavity Surface-emitting Laser (that operates at 980 nm).
**OPSTR** operational strength.
effectif opérationnel.
**OPSYS** (abbr.) OPerating SYStem.
*Computer Technology.*
**OPT** Office de Promotion du Tourisme.
French initialism of the: Office for the Promotion of Tourism (Belgium).
**OPT** operational planning team.
équipe de planification opérationnelle.
**opt** (abbr.) optical; optic.
*Optics.*
**opt** (abbr.) optician.
*Engineering.*
**opt** (abbr.) optics.
*Physics.*
**OPT**; **Opt** Osservatorio nazionale dei Prezzi e delle Tecnologie biomediche.
*Projects.*
**OPU** Overseas Placing Unit (G.B.).
**OPUS** Office on Public Understanding of Science (U.S.A.).
**OPV** Offre Publique de Vente; Offerta Pubblica di Vendita.
French and Italian initialism meaning: Offer for Sale.
**OPV** Offshore Patrol Vessel.
**OPV** Oral Polio Vaccine.
**OPW** Orthogonalized Plane Wave.
*Physics.*
**opx** orthopyroxene.
Orthopyroxene is also known as: Orthorhombic Pyroxene.
*Mineralogy.*
**OQ** Oil Quenching.
*Heat Treatment.*
**OR** Odorant Receptor.
For further details see under: **ORs**.
**OR** Official Receiver.
**OR**; **O.R.** Operational Research; Operations Research.
*Mathematics; Science.*
**OR**; **O.R.** Operating Room.
**OR**; **Or.** (abbr.) Oregon (U.S.A.).
Also: **Ore.**; **Oreg**.
**Or.** (abbr.) Orient; Oriental.
**OR**; **O.R.** Orienting Response.
Orienting response is also known as: Orienting Reflex.
*Behavior.*
**OR** Oristano, Italy.
**OR** other ranks.
sous-officiers-militaires du rang.
**OR** Owner's Risk.
**ORA** Output Register Address.
**ora** The above acronym was coined accidentally using the Italian word "ora" which means: hour; time; now; at present.
**ORAC assay** Oxygen Radical Absorbance Capacity assay.
*Aging; Antioxidants; Human Nutrition.*
**ORALL** Ohio Regional Association of Law Libraries (U.S.A.).
**OR&F** Operations, Research and Facilities.
**ORAU** Oak Ridge Associated Universities.
ORAU is a not-for-profit corporation; a multi-uni-

versity consortium; and a U.S. Department of Energy management and operating contractor located in Oak Ridge, Tennessee. ORAU serves government, academia, and the private sector in science and technology. ORAU manages ORISE for the U.S. Department of Energy.
*Science & Technology.*
For further details see under: **ORISE**.

**ORB** Omnidirectional/Omni-directional Radio Beacon.

**ORB** Owner's Risk of Breakage.
*Insurance.*

**ORBAT** order of battle.
ordre de bataille.

**ORBAT TOA** ORBAT transfer of authority.
transfert d'autorité en fonction de l'ORBAT.

**ORBL** operational requirements baseline.
référence des besoins opérationnels.

**ORC** Optoelectronics Research Centre (G.B.).
University of Southampton. The OCR houses are one of the world's largest University Research Groups in photonics.
*Atom Optics; Fibre Lasers; Optical Telecommunications; Optical Sensors; Optical Switching & Routing; Photonics.*

**ORC** Origin Recognition Complex.
*Biology; Cell Biology.*

**ORD** Office of Research and Development (U.S.A.).

**ORD** operational requirements document.
expression (ou énoncé) des besoins opérationnels.

**ORD** Optical Rotary Dispersion.
*Optics.*

**ord.** (abbr.) order.
Also: **o**; **o**.
*Architecture; Chemistry; Mathematics; Physics; Systematics.*

**ord.** (abbr.) ordinary.

**ORD** The airport code for O'Hare International, Chicago, Illinois, U.S.A.

**ORDER** On-Line Order Entry System.

**ORE** operational readiness evaluation.
évaluation du degré d'aptitude opérationnelle.

**Ore.** (abbr.) Oregon (U.S.A.).
Also: **OR**; **Or.**; **Oreg**.

**ORE** Output Register Empty.

**Oreg.** (abbr.) Oregon (U.S.A.).
Also: **OR**; **Or.**; **Ore**.

**Oregon LA** Oregon Library Association (U.S.A.).

**ORF** Open Reading Frame.
*Molecular Biology.*

**org.** (abbr.) organ.
*Anatomy; Botany.*

**org**; **org.** (abbr.) organic.
*Agronomy; Biology; Chemistry; Medicine.*

**org.** (abbr.) organism.
*Biology.*

**org.** (abbr.) organization; organized.

**ORG** Organization Resources Counselors.

**ORGALIME** Organisme de Liaison des Industries Métalliques Européennes.
French acronym meaning: Liaison Body for the European Metal Industries.

**ORGDP** Oak Ridge Gaseous Diffusion Plant (U.S.A.).

**ORI** Ocean Research Institute (Japan).

**ORI** Office of Research Integrity.
Of the U.S. PHS.
For further details see under: **PHS**.

**ORI** operational readiness inspection.
inspection de l'état de préparation opérationnelle.

**O.R.I.A.** Organizzazione Rapporti Internazionali Artistici (Italy).
*International Relations.*

**orig.** (abbr.) original.

**ORISE** Oak Ridge Institute for Science and Education.
ORISE undertakes national and international programs in education, training, environmental and health sciences, and technical analyses and assessments.
For further details see under: **ORAU**.

**ORL** Oto-Rhino-Laryngologie.
French initialism meaning: Ear-Nose-Throat; Otorhinolaryngology.
*Medicine.*

**ORMAK** Oak Ridge Tokamak.

**ORMH** Office of Research on Minority Health.
Created by U.S. NIH in 1990 as an administrative home for minority health activities.
For further details see under: **NIH**.

**ORMS software** Operating Resource Management System Software.
By Ariba Technologies. California-based, U.S.A. Founded 1996.
*e-commerce software and services.*

**ORNL** Oak Ridge National Laboratory (U.S.A.).

**ORNs** Olfactory Receptor Neurons.
*Brain Science; Chemosensory Receptors; Medicine; Olfaction; Recognition Molecules.*

**ORO** Operations Research Office.

**oro** The above acronym was coined accidentally using the Italian word "oro" which means: gold.
*Chemistry; Metallurgy.*

**ORP** Office of Radiation Programs.
*Radiation-levels measurements.*

**ORP** operational readiness platform.
aire d'alerte.
**ORPRC** Oregon Regional Primate Research Center (U.S.A.).
**ORR** Onsager Reciprocal Relations.
*Thermodynamics.*
**ORRMIS** Oak Ridge Regional Modeling Information System.
**ORs** Odorant Receptors.
*Chemosensory Receptors; Olfaction.*
For further details see under: **7-TM proteins**.
**ors.** (abbr.) others.
**ORSA** Operations Research Society of America.
**orsa** The above acronym was coined accidentally using the Italian word "orsa" which means: she-bear; and (*Astronomy*): Orsa maggiore (The Great Bear).
**ORSTOM** Office de la Recherche Scientifique et Technique d'Outre-Mer (France).
**ORT** Organization for Rehabilitation through Training.
**ORTA** Office of Research and Technology Applications (U.S.A.).
**ORTGE** Office of Research, Technology, and Graduate Education (U.S.A.).
**orth.** (abbr.) orthodontics.
Orthodontics is the dentistry branch dealing with malocclusion of the teeth.
*Medicine.*
**orth.** (abbr.) orthopedics.
Orthopedics is the branch of surgery dealing with the treatment of deformities of the skeletal system.
*Medicine.*
**ORTP** operational readiness test programme.
programme d'évaluation de l'état de préparation opérationnelle.
**ORWH** Office of Research on Women's Health (U.S.A.).
Of the U.S. NIH.
For further details see under: **NIH**.
**ORY** The.airport code for Orly, Paris, France.
**O.S.** Occhio Sinistro.
Italian initialism meaning: left eye.
**OS** Offset.
*Botany; Cartography; Computer Programming; Geology; Graphic Arts; Mining Engineering; Ordnance.*
**OS** Old Series.
**O.S.**; **o/s** On Sample.
**OS** Opening Snap.
OS is also known as: Mitral Opening Snap.
*Medicine.*
**OS** Operating System.
*Computer Technology.*
**OS** Optical Scanning.
*Optics.*
**OS** Option Spreading.
**OS** Ordnance Service.
**O.S.** Ordnance Survey.
**Os** The chemical symbol for Osmium.
Osmium is a chemical element having the atomic number 76, an atomic weight of 190.2, and a melting point of 2700°C. Osmium is used mainly as hardener in alloys. The word Osmium derives from the Greek word "smell".
*Chemistry; Symbols.*
**O/S** Out of Stock.
**OS** Outsize.
**o/s** (abbr.) outstanding.
**OSA** Office for Special Affairs.
(Scientology Secret Police).
**OSA** Official Secret Act (G.B.).
**OSA** Open System Architecture.
**OSA** 1. operational support aircraft.
1. avion de soutien opérationnel.
2. operational support airlift.
2. transport aérien opérationnel de soutien.
3. operational support authority [ACE ACCIS].
3. autorité de soutien opérationnel [ACE ACCIS].
**OSA** Optical Society of America (U.S.A.).
**OSA** Optimization by Simulated Annealing.
**OSA** Order of St. Augustine.
**OSA** Organizzazione degli Stati Americani.
Italian acronym of the: Organization of American States.
**OSAA** Operational Satellite Active Archive (U.S.A.).
**OSAC** Overseas Security Advisory Council - U.S. Department of State.
**OSB** Ocean Studies Board (U.S.A.).
**OSB** Order of St. Benedict.
**OSB** Organ Systems Branch.
**OSC** Office of Special Counsel.
For Immigration Related Unfair Employment Practices, Washington D.C. (U.S.A.).
**OSC** on-scene commander.
commandant sur place.
**OSC** Orbital Sciences Corporation.
OSC is located in Fairfax, Virginia, U.S.A.
*Space Science.*
**OSC** Organic Sulfur Compounds.
**OSC** Overlapping Spreading Center.
*Earth Science; Geology; Geophysics.*
**OSCAR** Optically Scanned Character Automatic Reader.

**OSCAR** Orbiting Satellites Carrying Amateur Radio.
**OSCAR**; **Oscar** Osservatorio Sul Commercio delle ARmi (Italy).
**OSCC** Open Skies Consultative Commission.
Commission consultative "ciel ouvert".
**OSCE** Organization for Security and Cooperation in Europe / OSCE [formerly called CSCE].
Organisation pour la sécurité et la coopération en Europe (OSCE) [anciennement appelé CSCE].
**OSCE** Organizzazione per la Sicurezza e la Cooperazione in Europa.
Italian acronym of the: Organization for Security and Cooperation in Europe.
**OSCR** Ocean Surface Current Radar.
**OSD** Office of the Secretary of Defense (U.S.A.).
**OSDP** Operations System Development Program.
**OSE** 1. officer scheduling the exercise.
1. officier chargé de la mise sur pied de l'exercice.
2. open systems environment.
2. environnement de systèmes ouverts.
**OSE** Osaka Stock Exchange (Japan).
**OSEC** Office of Solar Energy Conversion.
Of the U.S. Department of Energy.
**OSEP** Office of Scientific and Engineering Personnel (U.S.A.).
**OSF**; **O.S.F.** Office of Space Flight.
**OSF** Order of St. Francis.
**OSGi** Open Services Gateway initiative.
An industrial Group that defines an open standard for connecting homes and small companies to Internet Services.
**OSHA** Occupational Safety and Health Act (U.S.A.).
**OSHA**; **O.S.H.A.** Occupational Safety and Health Administration (U.S.A.).
**OSI** Office of Scientific Integrity (U.S.A.).
**OSI** 1. interconnexion de systèmes ouverts.
1. open systems interconnexion.
2. on-site inspection.
2a. inspection sur place.
2b. inspection sur site.
3. other security interests.
3. autres intérêts dans le domaine de la sécurité.
**OSI** Open System Interconnection.
**OSI** Orientation Selectivity Index.
*Brain and Cognition Sciences; Neuroscience.*
**OSINT** open source intelligence.
renseignement de source ouverte.
**OSIR** Office of Scientific Integrity Review.
**OSIRIDE** Open Systems Interconnection su Rete Italiana Dati Eterogenea.
Of the Italian National Research Council.
**OSL** Optically Stimulated Luminescence.
*Geobiology; Geography; Physics.*
**OSL** The airport code for Oslo, Norway.
**OSLs** Organic Semiconductor Lasers.
*Electrical Engineering; Optoelectronic Materials; Photonics.*
**OSM** Oncostatin M.
**OSM** Open Service Model.
**OSMEG**; **Osmeg** OSservatorio MEtropolitano Giovani (Italy).
**OSMR** Oncostatin M Receptor.
*Immunology; Medicine.*
**OSN** Ocean Science News.
**OSNs** Olfactory Sensory Neurons.
*Chemosensory Receptors; Odorant Receptors; Olfaction.*
For further details see under: **7-TM proteins**.
**OSO** Office of Systems Operations.
**OSO** Orbiting Solar Observatory.
**OSOCC** on-site operations coordination centre.
centre de coordination des opérations sur le terrain.
**OSOR** operational stand-off range.
distance de sécurité opérationnelle.
**OSP** Office of Special Projects (U.S.A.).
**OSPARCOM** (abbr.) OSlo - PARis COMmision.
*International Marine Monitoring Programs.*
**OSPF** Open Shortest Path First.
*Computers.*
**OSR** Optical Solar Reflector.
**OSS** Observing Simulation System.
**OSS** Office of Space Science - NASA's.
**OSS** operational support system.
système de soutien opérationnel.
**OSS** Orbital Space Station.
**OSSC** on-scene surveillance coordinator.
coordonnateur local de la surveillance.
**OSSE** Oriented Scintillation Spectrometer Experiment.
*Astronomy; Space Physics.*
**OST** Ocean Surface Temperature.
**OST** Office of Science and Technology (G.B.).
**OST** Open Skies Treaty.
Traité "ciel ouvert".
**OSTP** Office of Science and Technology Policy (U.S.A.).
**OSU** oceanographic support unit.
unité de soutien océanographique.
**OSU** Ohio State University (U.S.A.).
**OSU** Oregon State University (U.S.A.).
**OSW** Office of Saline Water (U.S.A.).
**OSWS** Operating System Work Station.
**OT** Occupational Therapy.

The term occupational therapy refers to certain occupations that are taught as a therapeutic or rehabilitation means.
*Medicine.*
**OT** Office of Telecommunications.
**OT** Old Testament.
**OT** Olfactory Tubercle.
**O.T.**; **O/T** On Truck.
**OT** Operating Time.
*Electronics.*
**OT** Optic Tectum.
OT is a brain area which is the source of visual signals.
*Neurobiology.*
**OT** Orascom Telecom.
OT is the main shareholder in Egypt's largest mobile telephone operator.
*Mobile Telephones.*
**OT** Organigramme Technique.
French initialism meaning: Work Breakdown Structure.
**OT** Overseas Trade.
**ot.** (abbr.) overtime.
**OT** Oxytocin.
OT is a peptide hormone.
*Endocrinology.*
**OTA** Office of Technology Assessment.
U.S. Congress. OTA was created in 1972 and ceased to operate in November 1995.
**OTAD** over-the-air (key) distribution.
distribution (de clés) par radiocommunication.
**OTAN** Organisation du Traité de l'Alantique Nord.
North Atlantic Treaty Organization (NATO).
**OT&E** Operational Testing and Evaluation.
**OTAR** over-the-air rekeying.
mise à clé par radiocommunication.
**OTB** Off The Board.
*Business; Finance.*
**OTC** officer in tactical command.
officier assurant (exerçant) le commandement tactique.
**OTC** Organization for Trade Co-operation.
**OTC** Over-The-Counter.
*Stock Exchange.*
**OTD** Organ Tolerance Dose.
**OTDR** Optical Time-Domain Reflectometer.
**OTE** Hellenic Telecommunications Organization.
*Greek Organization.*
**O-TE** Observatory on Tele Education.
2 year project.
*E.C. Program Socrates.*
**OTEC** Ocean Thermal Energy Conservation / Conversion.
**OTF** Outdoor Test Facility.
NREL's OTF: for testing and evaluation of prototype cells, modules, and systems.
For further details see under: **NREL**.
**OTH** over-the-horizon.
transhorizon.
**OTHR** over-the-horizon radar.
radar transhorizon.
**OTHT** over-the-horizon targeting.
désignation d'objectifs transhorizon (DOTH).
**OTID** Office of Talent Identification and Development.
**OTP** Office of Telecommunications Policy.
**OTPP** Ocean Thermal Power Plant.
**OTR** (Registered) Occupational Therapist.
**OTS** Office of Technical Service.
U.S. Department of Commerce.
**OTS** off-the-shelf.
1a. sur étagère-standard.
1b. disponible.
1c. se série.
**OTS** Organismo Tecnico Scientifico.
Italian acronym meaning: Technical Scientific Body.
**OTS** Organization for Tropical Studies (U.S.A.).
**OTS** Overseas Trade Services.
This body, responsible for trade promotion, draws its staff from the U.K. Department of Trade and Industry and the Foreign Office.
**OTS** Ovonic Threshold Switch.
*Electronics.*
**OTSGs** Once-Through Steam Generators.
**OTSR** optimum track ship routing.
route optimale de navire.
**OTTO** Optical-To-Optical Interface device.
*Optics.*
**otto** The above acronym was coined accidentally using the Italian word "otto" which means: eight.
**OTU** Operational Taxonomic Unit.
*Systematics.*
**OTV** Orbital Transfer Vehicle.
**OU** Oklahoma University (U.S.A.).
**OU** Operational Unit.
The operational unit is also known as: Parastratigraphic Unit.
*Geology.*
**OUA** Organizzazione dell'Unità Africana.
**OUB** Overseas Union Bank (Singapore).
**OUG** operational user group.
groupe d'utilisateurs opérationnels.
**OULCS** Ontario University Libraries Co-operative System (Canada).
**OUP** Oxford University Press.

**oupt.** (abbr.) output.
For further details see under: **o**.
**OUR** Oxygen Uptake Rate.
*Biotechnology.*
**OUSR** Operating Units Status Report.
**OUTLIM facility** Output Limiting facility.
**OV** Osservatorio Vesuviano (Italy).
*Geophysics; Volcanology.*
**ov.** (abbr.) overflow.
Also: **ovf.**; **ovfl**.
*Civil Engineering; Computer Programming; Hydrology; Science.*
**OVA** (abbr.) Ovalbumin.
*Biochemistry.*
**ovbd.** (abbr.) overboard.
**OVC** (test) Observation de la Vision par Caméra.
French initialism meaning: Eye Camera.
**OVC** Ontario Veterinary College.
At the University of Guelph, Canada.
**OVCSEL** Organic Vertical-Cavity Surface-Emitting Laser.
*Electrical Engineering; Optoelectronic Materials; Photonics.*
**ovf.** (abbr.) overflow.
Also: **ovfl**.
*Civil engineering; Computer Programming; Hydrology; Science.*
**ovhd.** (abbr.) overhead.
*Chemical Engineering; Computer Technology; Industrial Engineering.*
**ovld.** (abbr.) overload.
*Computer Programming; Electronics; Geology; Psychology.*
**ovno** or very near offer.
**ovr.** (abbr.) overflow.
Also: **ov.**; **ovfl**.
For further details see under: **ovf.**
**OVRO** Owens Valley Radio Observatory (California, U.S.A.).
**OVVs** Optically Violent Variables.
**OWH** Ordinary Working Hours.
**OWL** Overwhelmingly Large.
*New Telescopes.*
**OWLA** Organization of Women for Legal Awareness.
**OWL collector Project** Orbiting Wide-angle Light collector Project.
The OWL collector Project consists of twin satellites. It will be launched in 2010.
*Astrophysics; Space Physics.*
**OWM** Old World Monkeys.
**Ox.** (abbr.) Oxford.
**OXCs** Optical Cross-Connect Switches.
**OXPHOS** (abbr.) OXidative PHOSphorylation.
*Biochemistry; Genetics; Molecular Medicine.*
**OY** Optimum Yield.
*Ecology.*
**oz.** ounce.
*Metrology.*
**oz.ap.**; **oz ap** ounce apothecary.
Also: **oz.apoth**.
*Metrology.*
**zs.**; **ozs** ounces.
**oz.t.**; **ozt** ounce troy.

# P

**P** page.
Also: **pg.**
*Graphic Arts; Computer Programming.*
**p** parity.
*Business; Economics; Finance.*
**p** partnership.
*Business; Finance.*
**P** Pascal.
For further details see under: **Pa.**
**p** (abbr.) patent.
*Botany; Medicine; Science.*
**p** payee.
*Business; Commerce.*
**p** penny, pence.
*Currencies.*
**p.**, **p** per- (prefix).
**P** The chemical symbol for Phosphorus.
Phosphorus is a nonmetallic element having the atomic number 15, an atomic weight of 30.98 and a melting point of 44.1°C. Phosphorus is used mainly in matches and fertilizers. It is an important element in the human diet. The word phosphorus derives from the word "light" in Greek.
*Chemistry; Symbols.*
**p** pint.
*Metrology.*
**p**; **p.** pitch.
*Botany; Materials.*
**P** port; post; Prince; Protestant; Public.
**P** Portugal's International vehicle registration letter.
**p** post.
*Civil Engineering; Computer Programming; Mining Engineering.*
**P** Posteggio.
meaning in English: Parking.
**P**; **P.** poise.
Poise is the unit of dynamic viscosity in the centimeter-gram-second system of units.
*Fluid Mechanics.*
**P**; **P.** position.
*Cartography; Industrial Engineering.*
**P.**; **P** positive.
*Chemistry; Electricity; Graphic Arts; Mathematics; Medicine; Mechanics; Physics.*
**P**; **P.** Power.
*Engineering; Physics; Mathematics; Optics.*
**P**; **P.** Presbyopia.
Presbyopia is the decreased capacity to focus the eye on near items as a result of aging.
Also: **Pr**.
*Medicine.*
**P** President.
**P**; **P.** pressure.
*Mechanics; Physics.*
**p.** procuration.
**p**; **p.** proton.
*Physics.*
**P**; **P.** pulse.
*Electricity; Physics; Physiology; Telecommunications.*
**p** purchaser.
*Business; Commerce.*
**P3** preservation, packaging and packing.
traitement, protecteur, conditionnement et emballage.
**PA** Palermo, Italy.
**PA** Panama's International vehicle registration letters.
**PA** Paper Advance.
*Data Communications.*
**PA** Paraguay.
**PA** Parallel Access; Parallel Addition; Parallel Algorithm.
*Computer Programming.*
**Pa.**; **Pa** Pascal.
Pascal is the basic unit of pressure in the motor-kilogram-second system. Named for the French philosopher, physicist and mathematician Blaise **Pascal**.
*Metrology.*
**PA** Patto Atlantico.
North Atlantic Treaty.
**pA** paying Agent.
**PA**; **Pa** (abbr.) Pennsylvania (U.S.A.).
**PA**; **pa** per annum.
**PA** Pernicious Anemia.
**P/A**; **PA** Personal Assistant.
**Pa** peso atomico.
Italian acronym meaning: atomic weight.
**PA** Phosphatidic Acid.
*Biochemistry.*
**PA**; **P.A.** Physician's Assistant.
**PA** Polyamide.
*Organic Chemistry.*
**PA** Porti Autonomi (Italy).
**PA** Posta Aerea.
Italian acronym meaning: Air-Mail / airmail.
**PA** posteroanterior.
*Anatomy.*
**PA**; **P.A.** Power Amplifier.
*Electronics.*
**PA** Power of Attorney.

**PA**.; **pa** Press Agent.
**PA** Press Association.
**PA** Private Account.
**Pa** The chemical symbol for Protactinium.
Protactinium is a chemical element having the atomic number 91, an atomic weight of 231.036, and a melting point of about 1500°C.
*Chemistry; Symbols.*
**PA** Protective Antigen.
A protein secreted by *Bacillus anthracis*.
*Anthrax Toxin; Biochemistry; Cell Biology; Medicine.*
For further details see under: **EF** and **LF**.
**PA**; **P.A.** Psychiatric Aide.
**PA** Pubblica Accusa.
Italian acronym meaning: Public Prosecutor.
**PA** Pubblica Amministrazione.
Italian acronym meaning: Public Administration.
**P.A.**; **P/A** Public Accountant.
**PA** Public Affairs.
**PA** Publishers Association.
**PAA** Polyacrylamide.
PAA, also known as Polyacrylamide Gel is used mainly as a food additive and adhesive additive.
*Organic Chemistry.*
**PAA** Polyacrylic Acid.
PAA is used mainly in paints and adhesives.
*Organic Chemistry.*
**PAAET** Public Authority for Applied Education and Training.
**PAAMS** Principal Anti Air Missile System.
**PAARL** Philippine Association of Academic and Research Libraries.
**PAB** Post-Apply Bake.
*Chemistry; Chemical Engineering; Macromolecules; Neutron Research; Plymers; Semiconductors.*
**PABA** p-aminobenzoic acid.
*Biochemistry.*
**PA band** Photoinduced Absorption band.
*Optical Science.*
**PABX** Private Automatic Branch Exchange.
**Pac.** (abbr.) Pacific.
**PAC** Padiglione Arte Contemporanea (Italy).
Italian acronym meaning: Contemporary Art Pavillon.
**PAC** Partnership Annual Conference [PfP - formerly called EAC].
conférence annuelle du Partenariat [PPP - anciennement appelé EAC].
**PAC** Patriot Advanced Capability.
**PAC** Piano di Accumulazione del Capitale.
Italian acronym meaning: Capital Accumulation Plan.
*Banking; Finance.*
**PAC** Politica Agricola Comune; Politique Agricole Commune.
Italian and French acronym meaning: Common Agricultural Policy.
**PAC** Political Action Committee (U.S.A.).
**PAC** Polyaluminium Chloride.
**P.A.C.** Produttori Artigiani Canturini (Italy).
**PAC** Programme Activity Centre (Kenya).
United Nations Environment Programme, *Global Environment Monitoring System.*
**PAC** Public Accounts Committee.
**PACAP** Pituitary Adenylate Cyclase-Activating Polypeptide.
*Biological Sciences.*
**PAC option** Put And Call option.
**PACE** Palestinian Association for Cultural Exchange.
In the West Bank town of Ramallah. Israeli-Palestinian projects funded by the U.S. Department of State.
*Archaeology.*
**PACE** Planetary Association for Clean Energy.
**PACE** pocket-sized automatic crypto equipment.
matériel cryptographique automatique de poche.
**PACE** Precision Analog Computing Equipment.
**pace** The above acronyms were coined accidentally using the Italian word "pace" which means: peace.
**PACHA** President's Advisory Committee on HIV / AIDS (U.S.A.).
**PACI** Partnerships for Advanced Computational Infrastructure.
PACI is the successor to a network of five NSF Supercomputing centers created in 1986 to provide access to supercomputers for researchers around the United States.
*Supercomputing Centers; U.S. Programs.*
For further details see under: **NPACI** nad **NSF**.
**PACIOLI** Panel in ACcounting for Innovation, Offering a Lead-up to the use of Information modeling.
*European Community Project.*
**PACL** Prairie Association of Christian Librarians.
**PACS** Pan American Climate Studies.
**PACs** P1 Artificial Chromosomes.
**PACS** Picture Archives and Communication System; Picture Archiving and Communications Systems.
PACS require: viewing stations, optical juke boxes to store the images, and broadband networks to transmit them.

*Telemedicine.*

**PACT** Programme of Assistance and Technical Cooperation in favour of Developing Countries.
*JRC European Communities.*

**PACVD** Plasma-Assisted Chemical Vapour Deposition.
PACVD is a development of Chemical Vapour Deposition in which plasma is used to yield results similar to those of ion implantation.
*Metal Implants.*

**PAD** Packet Assembler / Disassembler.

**PAD** provisional acceptance date.
date de réception provisoire.

**pad** The above acronyms were coined using the word "pad".
*Anatomy; Electronics; Engineering; Metallurgy; Zoology.*

**PADO** Pan-Atlantic Decadal Oscillation.
*Climate Science; Decadal Variations; Geophysics; Marine Geochemistry; Meteorology.*

**PADP** Panel on Air Defence Philosophy.
Commission sur la philosophie de la défense aérienne.

**PADRE** Portable Automatic Data Recording Equipment.

**padre** The above acronym was coined accidentally using the Italian word "padre" which means: father.

**PADTA** poste avancé de direction tactique air.
forward air control post (FACP).

**PADW** Paleo-Arctic Deep Water (frigid).
*Ocean Thermohaline Circulation; Paleogeography.*

**PADW** Panel on Air Defence Weapons.
Commission sur les armes de défense aérienne.

**PAF** Petroleum Advisory Forum.

**PAF** Platelet-Activating Factor.
*Endocrinology.*

**PAFEX** Process Analysis Field EXperiment.

**PAF systems** Power-Actuated Fastening systems.

**PAFTAD Conference** PAcific Trade And Development Conference.

**PaG.** Pennsylvania German.
*Languages.*

**PAGE** Polyacrylamide Gel Electrophoresis.

**PAGEOS** PAssive GEOdetic Satellite.

**pagg.** (abbr.) pagine.
Italian abbreviation meaning: pages.

**PAG molecules** Photoacid Generator molecules.
*Chemistry; Chemical Engineering; Macromolecules; Neutron Research; Polymers; Semiconductors.*

**PAH** p-aminohippuric (acid).
Also: **PAHA**.
*Biochemistry.*

**PAHO** Pan-American Health Organization.
PAHO was formerly known as the Pan-American Sanitary Organization.

**PAHR** Postaccident Heat Removal.

**PAHs** Polycyclic Aromatic Hydrocarbons.
*Chemistry; Earth and Planetary Sciences; Exobiology; Geophysics; Space Science.*

**PAI** Pathogenicity Island.
*Cancer Epidemiology; Clinical Microbiology; Molecular Microbiology.*

**PAIR** Precision Approach Interferometer Radar.

**PAIS** Palazzo delle Alternative e Iniziative Sociali (Italy).

**PAIS** Public Affairs Information Service.

**PAK** Pakistan's International vehicle registration letters.

**PAK2** P21-Activated Kinase-2.
PAK2 is an enzyme.
*Apoptosis; Medicine.*

**pal.** (abbr.) paleography.
The term paleography refers to the study of ancient writings.
*Anthropology.*

**Pal.** (abbr.) paleontology.
The term paleontology refers to the study of ancient life.
*Biology.*

**PAL** permissive action link.
1a. dispositif de sécurité et d'armement.
1b. système de verrouillage électronique.

**PAL** Philippines Airlines.

**PAL** Preapproved Loan.
*Business; Commerce; Finance.*

**P.A.L.** Promozione Avviamento al Lavoro (Italy).
*Transnational Projects.*

**PALACEs** Profiling Autonomous LAgrangian Circulation Explorers.
PALACEs were first deployed in 1990 by an Oceanographer of the Scripps Institution of Oceanography (U.S.A.).
*Chemistry and Biology of the Oceans.*

**PALD project** Policy Alternatives for Liverstock Development in Mongolia project.

**PALINET** Pennsylvania Area Library Network (U.S.A.).

**PALLAS** Paul Laser Cooling Acceleration System.
*Crystalline Ion Beams.*

**PAL system** Phase-Alternation Line system.
*Telecommunications.*

**PAM** Programma Alimentare Mondiale.
Italian acronym meaning: World Food Program.

*United Nations Program.*
**PAM** Pression Atmosphérique Moyenne.
**PAM** Programmable Algorithm Machine.
**PAM** Pulse-Amplitude Modulation.
**PAMPs** Pathogen-Associated Molecular Patterns.
*Medicine; Immunology.*
**PAMs** Pulmonary Alveolar Macrophages.
**PAN** Conservative National Action Party (Mexico).
**PAN** Périartérite Noueuse.
French acronym meaning: Periarteritis Nodosa, also known as: Polyarteritis Acuta Nodosa.
*Medicine.*
**PAN** Peroxyacetyl Nitrate / Peroxy Acetyl Nitrate.
*Chemistry.*
**PAN** Pesticide Action Network.
*U.S. Networks.*
**PAN** Pression Artérielle Normale.
**PANAFTEL Network** Pan African Telecommunication Network.
**PANAS** Positive And Negative Affectivity Scale.
*Medicine; Neurogenetics; Psychiatry.*
**P&A** personnel and administration.
personnel et administration.
**P&A** Promotion and Assistance.
**P&C** purchasing and contracting.
achats et marchés.
**P&CM** Project and Construction Management.
**P&D** Pick up and Delivery.
*Business; Commerce.*
**P&G** Procter & Gamble.
Research, Development, Manufacture and Marketing.
*Consumer Products.*
**P&H** Postage and Handling.
**P.&I.** Protection and Indemnity (Clubs or Associations).
**P&L** Profit and Loss.
*Accounts.*
**P&P (Committee)** Payments and Progress Committee.
Comité des paiement et de l'avancement des travaux d'infrastructure.
**P&S statement** Purchase and Sale statement.
**P&S syphilis** Primary and Secondary syphilis.
*Epidemiology; Medicine; Sexually Transmitted Diseases.*
**P&U** Pharmacia and Upjohn.
Pharmacia (Sweden) and Upjohn (USA-based) merged in 1995.
*Drugs.*
**PANEL** Protection Across NEtwork Layers.
*European Community Project.*
**PANK** Pantethemate Kinase.
*Biomedicine; Neurodegeneration Disorders.*
**PAO** Pression Artérielle Ophtalmique.
French acronym meaning: Ophtalmic Artery Pressure.
*Medicine.*
**PAO** Progetto di Adeguamento Organizzativo (Italy).
**PAO** property accounting officer.
1a. officier comptable des biens.
1b. agent comptable des biens.
**PAO** Publication Assistée par Ordinateur.
French acronym meaning: Desktop Publishing.
**$PAO_2$** Alveolar Partial Pressure in Oxygen.
*Medicine.*
**$PaO_2$** Arterial Partial Pressure in Oxygen.
*Medicine.*
**Pap**; **Pap. test** Papanicolaou test.
The Pap test, also known as pap strain or pap smear is used to diagnose uterine cancers. The Papanicolaou test was named for the (Greek-born) American physiologist George **Papanicolaou**.
*Pathology.*
**PAP** Password Authentication Protocol.
*Computers.*
**PAP** Poly (A) Polymerase.
**PAP** Port et Assurance Payés.
French acronym meaning: Carriage and Insurance Paid to.
*Economics; International Trade.*
**PAP** Prearranged Payments.
*Business; Commerce; Finance.*
**PAP** Pression Artérielle Pulmonaire.
French acronym meaning: Pulmonary Artery Pressure.
*Medicine.*
**PAP** Prêt d'Accession à la Propriété.
French acronym meaning: Home Loan.
**PAP** Prêts aidés pour l'Accension à la Propriété (France).
**PAP** Printer Access Protocol.
**PAPS** phased armaments programming system.
système de programmation échelonnée des armements.
**PAPS** Periodic Arrays of Pinning Sites.
*Physics.*
**PAQs** Partially Allocated Quotas.
**par.**; **par** (abbr.) paragraph.
Also: **para.**
**par.**; **par** (abbr.) parallel.
*Cartography; Computer Programming; Electricity; Geodesy; Mathematics; Physics.*
**PAR** Photosynthetically Active Radiation.
*Climate Change; Environment Research.*

**PAR** Plan d'Aménagement Rural (France).
**PAR** Precision Approach Radar.
*Navigation.*
**PAR** Pression Artérielle Rétinienne.
French acronym meaning: Ophtalmic Artery Pressure.
*Medicine.*
**PAR** Pseudoautosomal Region.
*Biology; Molecular and Cellular Biology.*
**PAR** The airline code for the city of Paris, France.
**PAR-1** Protease-Activated Receptor-1.
*Biochemistry; Cell Biology; Medicine.*
**para.** (abbr.) paragraph.
Also: **par.**; **par**.
**PARC** Palo Alto Research Center (U.S.A.) (Xerox's).
**PARC** Pulmonary and Activation-Regulated Cytokine.
**PARD** Periodic And Random Deviation.
**PARP** PfP planning and review process.
processus de planification et d'examen du PPP.
**PARP** Poly (Adenosine diphosphate-Ribose) Polymerase.
**PARP** Procyclic Acidic Repetitive Protein.
*Cell Biology; Molecular Biology; Molecular Parasitology; Pathogenicity; Trypanosome Biochemistry.*
**PARR** Postaccident Radioactivity Removal.
**PARS** Poly(ADP-Ribose) Synthetase.
**PARs** Protease-Activated Receptors.
**part.** (abbr.) participating; participation.
**part.** (abbr.) particular.
**Participex** Société de participations au developpement des entreprises régionales (France).
**PARTOL** (abbr.) PARallelism TOLerance.
**PAR wave** Photosynthetically Active Radiation wave.
*Atmospheric Sciences; Atmospheric Research; Biological Sciences; Land-Atmosphere Interactions; Meteorology; Plant Biology.*
**PAS** Patient's Aid Society (U.S.A.).
**PAS** Photoacoustic Spectroscopy.
**PAS** 1. protected aircraft shelter.
1. abri protégé pour aéronefs.
2. public address system.
2. système de sonorisation.
**PASA** *Para*-aminosalicylic Acid.
*Organic Chemistry; Pharmacology.*
**PASFIS** Philippines Aquatic Sciences and Fisheries Information System.
**PASG** Pneumatic Antishock Garment.
**PAS reaction** Periodic Acid-Schiff reaction.
*Biochemistry.*
**pass.** (abbr.) passenger.
**pass.** (abbr.) passive.
*Aviation; Medicine; Military Science; Science.*
**p/ass.** porto assegnato.
Italian abbreviation meaning: carriage forward.
**PASS** Pubbliche Amministrazioni per lo Sviluppo del Sud.
Italian acronym meaning: Public Administrations for the Development of the South.
**PASSEX** exercise arranged with forces on passage.
exercice organisé avec des forces de passage.
**Past.** (abbr.) Pasteurella.
*Bacteriology.*
**past.** (abbr.) pasteurize.
To pasteurize means to subject fluids, such as milk, to a pasteurization process in order to improve their keeping properties.
*Food Technology.*
**PA system** Public Address system.
*Acoustical Engineering.*
**PAT** Paroxysmal Atrial Tachycardia.
*Cardiology.*
**pat.** (abbr.) patent.
**pat** (abbr.) patient.
**PAT** Permanent (exercise) Analysis Team [will be replaned by JALLC].
Équipe permanente d'analyse (des exercices) [sera remplacé par JALLC].
**PAT** Pio Albergo Trivulzio (Milan, Italy).
The PAT is a charitable institution for elderly persons in Milan.
*Law* - Its manager, Mario Chiesa, was arrested in 1992 giving rise to the first case of corruption that led to thousands of others within the context of the so-called "Clean Hands Operation" performed by Italian Judges.
**PAT** Polyaminotriazole.
**PAT** Prearranged Transfers.
*Business; Commerce; Finance.*
**PATAD Conference** PAcific Trade And Development Conference.
**PATB** police antiterrorism brigade.
brigade de police antiterrorisme.
**PATCO** Professional Air Traffic Controllers Organization (U.S.A.).
**patd.** (abbr.) patented.
**PATH** Program for Appropriate Technology in Health (U.S.A.).
PATH is a program of a Seattle-based international nonprofit health research organization aimed at disseminating vaccines against: *Rotavirus; Hepatitis B*; *Streptococcus Pneumoniae; Haemophilus Influenzae* type b.

*Children's Vaccine Programs; Health Research.*
**pathol.** (abbr.) pathological; pathology.
*Medicine; Psychology.*
**PATHS** PAcific Transport of Heat and Salt.
Canada - Japan (U.S.A.).
**PATMAR** 1. patrouille maritime.
1. maritime patrol (MP).
2. avion de patrouille maritime.
2. maritime patrol aircraft (MPA).
**Pat.Off.** Patent Office.
**PAU** Power Amplifier Unit.
**PAUP** Phylogenetic Analysis Using Parsimony.
*Cellular Pathology; Molecular Pathology.*
**PAVAC** Pubblications and Audiovisual Advisory Council (U.S.A.).
**PAW** Plasma Arc Welding.
**PAWS** Progressive Animal Welfare Society.
*Animal Rights.*
**PAWS project** Protected Area and Wildlife System project (Kenya).
PAWS is a project financed by the World Bank and other donors.
**paws** The above acronyms were coined using the English word "paws".
**PAX** Private Automatic Exchange.
**PAXIS** Pilot Action of Excellence on Innovative Start-ups.
*European Community.*
**PAYE** Pay As You Earn (G.B.).
**PAYE** Pay As You Enter.
**paye** The above acronyms were coined accidentally using the French word "paye" which means: pay; wage; salary.
**PAYSOP** PAYroll-based Stock Ownership Plan.
**payt.** (abbr.) payment.
**Pb** Banque Parisbas.
*French Bank.*
**Pb** The chemical symbol for Lead.
*Chemistry; Engineering; Graphic Arts; Metallurgy.*
**PB** Paris Bourse.
*French Stock Exchange.*
**PB** particle beam.
faisceau de particules.
**PB** Pass-Book.
**Pb.** passività a breve.
Italian initialism meaning: Short-term liabilities.
**P.B.** Permanent Bunkers.
**PB** Permit Bond; Preference Bond.
**PB** Pharmacopoeia Britannica.
**P.B.** Premium Bonds.
**PB** Privredna Banka Zagreb d.d.
*Banks.*
**PB** pulpobuccoaxial.
**PB** Push Button.
*Mechanical Engineering.*
**PB** Pyridostigmine Bromide.
PB is a drug used to treat myastenia gravis.
*Pharmacology.*
**PBAA** Polybutadieneacryl Acid.
**PB&Cs** see PBCs.
voir PBCs.
**$Pb_9As_4S_{15}$** Gratonite.
*Mineralogy.*
**PBB** Polybrominated Biphenyl.
**PBB** Processus de Bount en Bout.
French initialism meaning: Straight Through Processing.
**$PbBr_2$** Lead Bromide.
*Inorganic Chemistry.*
**PBC** Planification des Besoins en Capacités.
French initialism meaning: Manufacturing Resources Planning.
**PBC** Power Buildup Cavity (Fabry-Perot's).
*Physics.*
**PBC** Pre-Boetzinger Complex (of the brainstem).
*Anatomy; Anesthesiology; Sensory-Physiology.*
**$PbCl_2$** Lead Chloride.
Lead Chloride is used mainly in the production of lead salts.
*Inorganic Chemistry.*
**$Pb(CN)_2$** Lead Cyanide.
Lead Cyanide is used in metallurgy.
*Inorganic Chemistry.*
**$PbCrO_4$** Crocoite.
Crocoite is also known as: Crocoisite.
*Mineralogy.*
**PBCs** planning boards and committees [CEP].
bureaux et comités d'étude [PCU].
**$PbCuSbS_3$** Bournonite.
*Mineralogy.*
**PBD** Paid Blood Donor.
**PBD** Polo-Box Domain.
*Binding Domains; Cell Division; Proteomic Screens.*
**PBD** 1,3,4-phenylbiphenyloxadiaxole.
**PBEC** Pacific Basin Economic Council.
**PBEIST** Planning Board for European Inland Surface Transport.
Bureau d'étude des transports intérieurs de surface en Europe.
**PBF** Power Burst Facility.
**$PbF_2$** Lead Fluoride.
Lead Fluoride is used mainly in optics.
*Inorganic Chemistry.*
**$Pb_4FeSb_6S_{14}$** Jamesonite.

Jamesonite is also known as: Gray Antimony; Feather Ore.
*Mineralogy.*
**PBG materials** Photonic Band Gap materials.
PBG materials are also known as: Photonic crystals.
*Physics; Technology.*
**PBI** Polybenzimidazole.
*Materials.*
**PBI** Protein-Bound Iodine.
*Biochemistry.*
**PBI** The airport code for West Palm Beach, Florida, U.S.A.
**$PbI_2$** Lead Iodide.
Lead Iodide is used mainly in photography, bronzing and printing.
*Inorganic Chemistry.*
**Pb-I-Pb junction** Lead-I-Lead junction.
**PBK** Powszechny Bank Kredytowy SA.
*Polish Bank.*
**PBL** Planetary Boundary Layer.
*Meteorology.*
**PBL** product baseline.
référence de production.
**PBLG** Poly-γ-Benzyl-L-Glutamate.
*Polymer Chemistry.*
**PBLs** Peripheral Blood Lymphocytes.
*Medicine; Microbiology.*
**PBMCs** Peripheral Blood Mononuclear Cells.
**$PbMoO_4$** Lead Molybdate.
*Inorganic Chemistry.*
**PBMR** provisional basic military requirement.
besoin militaire provisoire de base.
**PBN** α-Phenyl-t-Butyl-Nitrone.
**$Pb(N_3)_2$** Lead Azide.
Lead Azide is used in explosives.
*Inorganic Chemistry.*
**PbO** Lead Monoxide.
*Inorganic Chemistry.*
For further details see under: **PbO** (Litharge).
**PbO** Litharge.
Litharge, also known as: Yellow Lead Oxide, and used mainly in ceramics; paints and varnishes, has the same formula as Lead Monoxide but different physical properties.
*Inorganic Chemistry.*
**PBO** Penicillin in Beeswax.
**PBO** Plate Boundary Observatory.
Got under way in 2002.
**PBO** Preboreal Oscillation.
**$PbO_2$** Lead Dioxide.
Lead Dioxide, also known as: Lead Peroxide; Plumbic Acid, is used mainly as an oxidizing agent.
*Inorganic Chemistry.*
**$Pb_3O_4$** Lead Tetroxide.
Lead Tetroxide, also known as: Red Lead Oxide is used mainly in glazes, paints, and storage batteries.
*Inorganic Chemistry.*
**PBOCSt** p-*tast*-butoxycarboxystyrene.
*Chemistry; Chemical Engineering; Macromolecules; Neutron Research; Polymers; Semiconductors.*
**$Pb(OH)_2$** Lead Hydroxide.
Lead Hydroxide is also known as: Lead Hydrate.
*Inorganic Chemistry.*
**PBOS** Planning Board for Ocean Shipping.
Bureau d'étude des transports océaniques.
**PBP** Penicillin-Binding Protein.
For further details see under: **PBPs**.
**PBPB** Pyridinium Bromide Perbromide.
**PBPs** Penicillin-Binding Proteins.
*Antimicrobial Agents; Chemotherapy; Medicine; Microbiology; Clinical Immunology.*
**PBR** Payment By Results.
**PBRC** Pennington Biomedical Research Center (U.S.A.).
*Exercise Biochemistry; Diet-induced Obesity Physiology; Macronutrient Intake Regulation; Nutrient-gene Interactions; Phenotype Metabolic Diseases.*
**PBRTC** Plant Biochemistry Research and Training Center.
**PbS** Galena.
*Mineralogy.*
**PbS** Lead Sulfide.
Lead Sulfide, also known as: Plumbous Sulfide, is used mainly in semiconductors, and in ceramics.
*Inorganic Chemistry.*
**PBS** Phosphate-Buffered Saline.
**PBS** Phycobilisomes.
*Plant Biology.*
**PBS** Public Broadcasting System.
**$Pb_7Sb_8S_{19}$** Heteromorphite.
Heteromorphite is found in antimony mines.
*Mineralogy.*
**$PbSiO_3$** Lead Silicate.
Lead Silicate also known as: Lead Metasilicate, is used mainly in ceramics.
*Inorganic Chemistry.*
**$PbSi_2S_4$** Galeno bismutite.
*Mineralogy.*
**$PbSnS_2$** Teallite.
Teallite is found in tin veins.

*Mineralogy.*
**$PbSO_4$** Lead Sulfate.
Lead Sulfate is used in storage batteries.
*Inorganic Chemistry.*
**PbTe** Altaite.
*Mineralogy.*
**PbTe** Lead Telluride.
*Inorganic Chemistry.*
**$PbTiO_3$** Lead Titanate.
Lead Titanate is used as a paint pigment.
*Inorganic Chemistry.*
**$(Pb,Tl)_2As_5S_9$** Hutchinsonite.
Hutchinsonite is found in crystalline dolomite.
*Mineralogy.*
**Pb virus** *Penicillium brevicompactum* virus.
*Virology.*
**PBW** particle beam weapon.
arme à faisceau de particules.
**$PbWO_4$** Lead Tungstate.
Lead Tungstate, also known as: Lead Wolframate, is used as a pigment.
*Inorganic Chemistry.*
**$PbWO_4$** Raspite.
*Mineralogy.*
**PBWSE** Philadelphia-Baltimore-Washington Stock Exchange (U.S.A.).
**PBX** Plastic Bonded Explosive.
**PBX access line** Private Branch Exchange access line.
**PC** L-$\alpha$-Phosphatidylcholine.
**PC** Panama Canal.
**PC** Parallel Computer.
The parallel computer is also known as: Parallel Digital Computer, Parallel Processor.
*Computer Technology.*
**PC** Parte Civile.
*Law* - Italian initialism meaning: Plaintiff.
**PC** Patrol Craft.
**pc** paycheck / paycheque.
**P/C**; **p.c.** percent; percentage.
Also: **p/c**.
**p.c.** per conoscenza.
Italian initialism meaning: copy to (particularly in a letter, fax, etc.).
**PC** Personal Computer.
The term personal computer refers to a compact computer to be used in offices and homes. The personal computer was invented in the 1960s at the Stanford Research Institute.
*Computer Technology.*
**PC** Petty Cash.
*Business; Economics; Finance.*
**PC** Phosphocreatine.
*Biochemistry.*
**PC** Phycocyanin.
PC is one of the major species of phycobiliproteins.
*Plant Biology.*
**PC** Piacenza, Italy.
**pc.** (abbr.) piece.
**PC** Pitch Circle.
*Design Engineering.*
**PC** Police Constable.
**PC** 1. Political Committee [NAC].
1. Comité politique [CAN].
2. poste de commandement.
2a. command post (CP 2.).
2b. headquarters (HQ).
**PC** Polycarbonate.
Polycarbonate is used mainly in household appliances.
*Organic Chemistry.*
**PC** Polycomb.
For further details see under: **PcG proteins**.
**PC** Portland Cement / portland cement.
*Materials.*
**PC** Prezzo Convenuto.
Italian initialism meaning: price agreed; price fixed.
**pc.** (abbr.) price.
**PC** Prime Cost.
**PC** Printed Circuit.
*Electronics.*
**PC** Professional Corporation.
**PC** Profit Center.
**PC** Program Counter.
The program counter is also known as: Control Counter or register; Instruction counter or register; Sequence Counter or register.
*Computer Technology.*
**PC** Programmable Controller.
*Control Systems.*
**PC** Purified Concentrate.
*Medicine.*
**PC** Pyrometric Cone.
The pyrometric cone is also known as: Seger cone.
*Materials Science.*
**PCA** Passive Cutaneous Anaphylaxis.
Passive cutaneous anaphylaxis is also known as: Passive Anaphylaxis.
*Immunology.*
**PCA** Perchloric Acid.
$HClO_4$ - Used mainly as a catalyst, and as a reagent.
*Inorganic Chemistry.*
**PCA** Physician Corporation of America.

PCA provides healthcare services in Florida, Texas and Puerto Rico, through health care organizations.
*Healthcare Services.*
**PCA** Polar Cap Absorption.
*Physics.*
**PCA experiment** Proportional Counter Array experiment.
*Astronomy; Physics.*
**PCAs** Partnership and Cooperation Agreements.
**PCAST** President's Committee of Advisers on Science and Technology.
*U.S. Defense.*
**PCB** Page Control Block.
*Data Communications.*
**PCB** Personal Communication Board.
**PCB** Petty Cash Book.
**PCB** Physique-Chimie-Biologie.
French initialism meaning: Physics - Chemistry - Biology.
**PCB** Point de Couverture Brute.
French initialism meaning: gross rating point.
**PCB** Polychlorinated Biphenyl.
*Materials Science* - Polychlorinated biphenyl is used mainly in adhesives, paints, and inks. It is a toxic compound that may cause cancer.
New research fields: *Endocrinology; Sexual Development; Toxicology; Zoology.*
**PCB** Printed Circuit Board.
*Design Engineering.*
**PCC** 1. Partnership Coordination Cell.
1. Cellule de coordination du Partenariat (CCP 1.).
2. planning coordination conference.
2. conférence de coordination des plans.
3. Prague Capabilities Commitment.
3. Engagement capacitaire de Prague.
**p.c.c.** per copia conforme.
Italian initialism meaning: certified copy; true copy.
**PCC** Physical Coal Cleaning.
**PCC** Policy Coordination Council (U.S.A.).
**PCC** Pour Copie Conforme.
French initialism meaning: certified copy; true copy.
**PCC** Production Credit Corporation.
**PCC** Protein-Conducing Channel.
*Biochemistry.*
**P-CCMB** Pulmonary - Critical Care Medicine Branch.
Of the U.S. NHLBI.
For further details see under: **NHLBI**.
**PCCP** Physical Chemistry Chemical Physics.
A Journal jointly owned by eight European Chemical Societies.
*Periodicals.*
**PCD** Pitch Circle Diameter.
**PCD** Programmed Cell Death.
*Apoptosis; Cell Biology; Neurobiology.*
**PCE** Perchloroethylene.
PCE is a common groundwater pollutant.
*Civil and Environmental Engineering; Microbiology.*
**pce** (abbr.) piece.
**PCE** Polyarthrite Chronique Evolutive.
French initialism meaning: Rheumatoid Arthritis.
**PCE** Pyrometric Cone Equivalent.
**PCF** Patrol Craft, Fast.
**pcf** pounds per cubic foot.
**PCFG missile** Patrol Craft, Fast, Guided missile.
**PCG** Photocardiogram.
**PCG** Policy Coordination Group.
Groupe de coordination des orientations.
**PCG** Primary Congenital Glaucoma.
PCG is a devastating form of glaucoma that causes blindness in young children. It is characterized by corneal edema, intraocular pressure, ocular enlargement and photophobia.
*Medicine; Metabolism; Ophtalmology.*
**PcG proteins** Polycomb Group proteins.
*Biochemistry; Chemistry; Genetics; Homeotic Gene Transcription; Molecular Cell Biology; Molecular Medicine; Structural Biology.*
**PCGG** Philippine Commission on Good Government (Manila).
A body set up after the revolution.
**PCI** Partito Comunista Italiano (Italy).
**PCI** Permis de Conduire International.
French initialism meaning: International driving licence.
**pCi** picocurie.
pCi is a unit of radioactivity equal to one trillionth of a curie.
*Nucleonics.*
**PCI** Production-Complexity Index.
**PCI** Program Check Interruption.
**PCI** Program-Controlled Interrupt.
*Electronics.*
**Pcl.** (abbr.) parcel.
**PCM** Percentage-of-Completion Method (U.S.A.).
*Book-keeping.*
**PCM** Pericentriolar Material.
*Biochemistry; Cell Biology; Medicine; Molecular Biology.*
**PCM** Presidenza del Consiglio dei Ministri.
Italian initialism meaning: Prime Minister's Office.

**PCM** Pulse-Code Modulation.
**PCM** Punched-Card Machine.
**PCMCIA** Personal Computer Memory Card International Association.
**PCM conditions** Power-Cooling-Mismatch conditions.
**PCMDI** Program for Climate Model Diagnosis and Intercomparison.
Of the Lawrence Livermore National Laboratory, UC, U.S.A.
**PCMI** President's Council on Management Improvement (U.S.A.).
**PCMS** p-chloromercurphenisulfonic acid.
**PCMUE** président du Comité militaire de l'Union européenne.
Chairman of the European Union Military Committee (CEUMC).
**PCN** Personal Communications Network.
*Telecommunications.*
**PCNA** Proliferating Cell Nuclear Antigen.
*Biochemistry; Biophysics; Cancer Research; Developmental Biology.*
**PCNB** Pentachloronitrobenzene.
Pentachloronitrobenzene is used mainly as a fungicide.
*Organic Chemistry.*
**PCO** Polar Cap Observatory.
The PCO was built in 1999 near the magnetic North Pole in Canada. Date completed 2001.
*Atmospheric Science; Geophysics; Space Physics.*
**PCO** Put and Call Option.
**PCOM** Philadelphia College of Osteopathic Medicine (U.S.A.).
**PCP** Pentachlorophenol.
$C_6Cl_5OH$. Pentachlorophenol is soluble in water and alcohol and has a melting point of 190°C. It is used mainly as a fungicide, and bactericide.
*Organic Chemistry.*
**PCP** Peridinin-Chlorophyll-Protein.
PCP is so called because the protein is associated with the pigments chlorophyll and peridinin.
*Photosynthesis; Plant Biochemistry; Plant Biology; Structural Biology.*
**PCP** Phencyclidine Hydrochloride.
$C_{17}H_{25}HN{\bullet}HCl$. Phencyclidine Hydrochloride is used in veterinary medicine.
*Pharmacology.*
**PCP** Pneumatic Capsule Pipeline.
*Coal Transportation.*
**PCP** Pneumocystis Carinii Pneumonia.
Pneumocystis carinii pneumonia, also known as: Pneumocystic Pneumonia, is a lung infection.
*Medicine.*
**PCP** Primary Control Program.
**PCPBS** Para-chlorophenylbenzenesulfonate.
*Organic Chemistry.*
**PCPs** Pollen Coat Proteins.
*Plant Biology; Plant Sciences.*
**pcpt.** (abbr.) perception.
*Artificial Intelligence; Behavior; Physiology.*
**PCQ rating** Productivity Criteria Quotient rating.
**PCR** Pitch Circle Radius.
**PCR** Polymerase Chain Reaction.
PCR is a very useful process in biotechnology and in research.
*Biotechnology.*
**PCRM** Physicians Committee for Responsible Medicine (U.S.A.).
A Washington-based Group that opposes animal experiments and advocates preventive healthcare.
*HIV Cat Study.*
**PCRS** primary casualty receiving ship.
principal bâtiment récepteur de pertes.
**PCS** Permanent Change of Station.
**PCS** Personal Communications Service (Hong Kong).
The PCS was launched in July 1997.
**PCs** Photonic Crystals.
*Electronic Science; Engineering Science.*
**pcs.** (abbr.) pieces.
**PCS** point de contrôle des stocks.
inventory control point (ICP 2.).
**PCS** Position Control System.
**PCs** Post Computers.
**Pcs.** Preconscious.
*Psychology.*
**PCS** Preferred Capital Stock.
*Business; Finance.*
**pcs.** (abbr.) prices.
**PCS bands** Personal Communication System bands.
**PC/SC** Personal Computer / Smartcard.
**PCSC** Programme Change Sub-Committee.
Sous-comité des modifications du logiciel.
**PCSD** President's Council on Sustainable Development (U.S.A.).
**PCSE** Pacific Coast Stock Exchange (U.S.A.).
**PCS technology** Personal Communications Services technology.
PCS is clearer, faster and cheaper than digital technology. It allows data and voice transmission over the airwaves and dispenses with phone lines.
**PCT** Patent Cooperation Treaty.
**PCT** Peak-Clad Temperature.
**pct.**; **pct** (abbr.) percentage, percent.
**PCTA** Percutaneous Translumenal Coronary Angioplasty.

**PCTFE** Polychlorotrifluoroethylene.
**PCU** plans civils d'urgence.
civil emergency planning (CEP 2.).
**PCU** Programme Coordination Unit (Belgium).
Environmental Programme for the Danube River Basin.
**PCV** Packed Cell Volume.
**Pcx** Periscopic Convex.
**PD** Interpupillary Distance.
**PD** Padova, Italy.
**PD**; **pd** (abbr.) paid.
**Pd** the chemical symbol for Palladium.
Palladium is a metallic element having the atomic number 46; and a melting point of 1552°C. It is used mainly in electrical components, and catalysts. Named for the asteroid **Pallas**.
*Chemistry; Symbols.*
**Pd**; **p.d.** papilla diameter.
**PD** Parkinson's Disease.
PD is a neurodegenerative disorder causing muscular rigidity, postural abnormalities, dementia. Named after the English surgeon James **Parkinson** who described it.
*Clinical Neurogenetics; Genetic Diseases; Genome Research; Medicine; Neurological Disorders.*
For further details see under: **L-DOPA**.
**PD**; **pd** (abbr.) passed.
**PD** Passive Device.
*Computer Technology.*
**PD** Past Due.
*Business; Commerce.*
**PD** Payroll Deduction.
**PD** 1. periscope depth.
1. (à) immersion périscopique.
2. point detonating.
2. détonation.
**PD** Personnel Department.
**PD** Pierce's Disease.
*Plant Pathology.*
**pd.** pitch diameter.
**PD** Police Department.
**PD** Policy Division.
**PD** Population Doubling.
**PD** (en) Port Dû.
French initialism meaning: Carriage forward; freight forward.
*Commerce.*
**P.D.**; **pd** Port Duties.
**PD**; **pd** Position Description.
**PD**; **pd** Postal District.
**PD**; **P.D.** Potential Difference.
*Electricity.*
**pd**; **p.d.** prism diopter.
*Optics.*
**PD** Problem Determination.
**PD** Pulpodistal.
**PDA** Personal Digital Assistant.
*Mobile Devices.*
**PDA** Post-Deflection Acceleration / Postacceleration.
*Electronics.*
**PDA** Predicted Drift Angle.
**PDA** Public Display of Affection.
**PDAs** Personal Digital Assistants.
*Mobile Devices.*
**PDAS** Photodiode Array Spectrophotometer.
**PDB** p-dichlorobenzene.
**PDB** Pee Dee Belemnite.
*Isotope Sciences.*
**PDB** Polish Development Bank.
PDB was established in 1990. Since 30th June, 1995 PDB has been listed on the Warsaw Stock Exchange.
**PDB** Protein Data Bank.
*Web Sites.*
**Pdc** Direct-current power.
**PDC** 1. position depth charge.
1. charge ASM de localisation.
2. practice depth charge.
2. grenade ASM d'exercice.
**PDCA** Plan, Do, Check, Act.
**PDDA** power-driven decontamination apparatus.
1a. appareil de décontamination motorisé.
1b. appareil de décontamination à entraînement mécanique.
**PDE** Partial Differential Equation.
*Mathematics.*
**PDE** Phosphodiesterase.
PDE is an enzyme that lowers the level of cyclic AMP.
*Biochemistry; Neuroscience; Neurobiology; Quantitative Biology.*
**PDE** Preliminary Determination of Epicenters.
*Earth Sciences; Earthquakes; Planetary Sciences; Oceanography; Seismic Tomography.*
**PD-ECGF** Platelet-Derived Endothelial Cell Growth Factor.
Thymidine Phsophorylase is also called: PD-ECGF or ECGF-1.
*Biochemistry; Biophysics; Genetics; Neurology; Neuropathology.*
**PDES scheme** Parallel Discrete-Event Simulation scheme.
*Astronomy; Applied Physics; Physics.*
**PDF** Pigment-Dispersing Factor.

*Activity Rhythms; Circadian Rhythms; Clock Research; Neuropeptide Expression.*
**PDF** Portable Data Format; Portable Document Format.
**p.d.f.** probability density function.
**PDF** Produits de Dégradation de la Fibrine.
French initialism meaning: Fibrin Degradation Products, also known as: Fibrin Split Products.
*Medicine.*
**PDFD** Predemonstration Fusion Device.
**PdG** Palazzo di Giustizia.
Italian initialism meaning: The Hall of Justice; The Law Courts.
**PDG** Président-Directeur Général.
French initialism meaning: Chairman and Managing Director.
**PD game** Prisoner's Dilemma game.
*Evolutionary Behavior.*
**PDGF** Platelet-Derived Growth Factor.
*Endocrinology; Hematology.*
**PDGFRA** Platelet-Derived Growth Factor Recetor $\alpha$.
*Medicine; Medical Oncology; Pathology.*
**PDK** Publishing Development Kit (Microsoft's).
**PDK1** 3-Phosphoinositide-Dependent Protein Kinase 1.
*Signal Transduction.*
**PDL** program design language.
langage de conception de programmes.
**PDL** Protein Design Labs (U.S.A.).
PDL is a developer of humanized monochlonal antibodies.
**PDLCs** Polymer-Dispersed Liquid Crystals.
**PD level** Population Doubling level.
**PDM** Product Data Management.
Of SDRC (U.S.A.).
PDM is essentially a database that helps manufacturers manage all types of product-related data files and associated processes required to design, manufacture and maintain products throughout their entire life cycles.
**PDM** Pulse-Duration Modulation.
*Telecommunications.*
**PDMP** D-*threo*-1-Phenyl-2-Decanoylamino-3-Morpholino-1-Propanol.
**PDMS** point defence missile system.
système de missile de défense ponctuelle.
**PDMS** Polydimethylsiloxane.
*Materials Science.*
**PDM techniques** Phase-Difference Modulation techniques.
*Digital Communication Systems; Systems Engineering.*
**pdn.** (abbr.) production.
Also: **prod.**
**PDN** Public Data Network.
**pDNA** plasmid DNA.
*Medicine.*
**PDO** Pacific Decadal Oscillation.
*Climate Science; Decadal Variations; Geophysics; Marine Geochemistry; Meteorology.*
**PDO** Palladium Oxide.
**PDP** Parallel Distributed Processing.
*Artificial Intelligence.*
**PDP** Payroll Deduction Plan.
**PDP** Profit Direct du Produit.
French initialism meaning: Direct Profit Product.
**PDP** Program Development Plan.
**PDP** Programmed Data Processor.
**PDQ** Produzione Diversificata di Qualità (Italy).
**PDR** Pathogen-Derived Resistance.
*Biological Sciences; Plant Pathology.*
**PDR** Periscope Depth Range.
**PDR** Physician's Desk Reference.
**PDR** Precision Depth Recorder.
The precision depth recorder is also known as: Precision Graphic recorder.
*Engineering.*
**PDR** Processing Data Rate.
**PDRs** Photodissociation Regions.
*Astrochemistry; Astronomy; Astrophysics; Molecular Astrophysics; Space Science.*
**PDS** Partitioned Data Set.
**PDS** Party of the Democratic Left (Italy).
**PDS** Photodischarge Spectroscopy.
**PDS** post-design services.
suivi des matériels en service.
**PDSC** Pressure Differential Scanning Calorimetry.
**PDT** Democratic Labor Party (Brazil).
**PDT**; **P.D.T.** Pacific Daylight Time.
**pdt.** (abbr.) pendant.
French abbreviation meaning: during; over.
**PDT** Photodynamic Therapy.
The photodynamic therapy also known as: Photoradiation is used for neovascular age-related macular degeneration AMD.
**PDT** programme de travail.
programme of work (POW 2.).
**PDTC** Pyrrolidine Dithiocarbonate.
*Aging Research; Apoptosis; Cerebrovascular Research.*
**PDU** (Carbonization) Process Development Unit.
**PDU** Protocol Data Unit.
**PDUFA** Prescription Drug User Fee Act (1992) (U.S.A.).
**PDWS** point defence weapon system.

système d'arme de défense ponctuelle.
**PDX** The airport code for Portland, Oregon, U.S.A.
**PDZ** Puente Del Zacate.
*Chemistry; Geophysical Sciences; Meteorite Studies.*
**P.E.** Parlamento Europeo.
Italian initialism meaning: European Parliament.
**PE** 1. peace enforcement.
1. imposition de la paix.
2. peace establishment.
2. tableau d'effectifs du temps de paix (TEP).
3. Peru.
3. Pérou.
4. probable error.
4. erreur probable.
**PE** Peltier Effect.
Named for its discoverer, the French physicist Jean **Peltier**.
*Bimetal Junctions; Physics; Thermoelectricity.*
**PE** Pentaerythritol.
Pentaerythritol is used mainly in explosives, pharmaceuticals, and fertilizers.
*Organic Chemistry.*
**p.e.** per esempio.
Italian initialism meaning: for example, e.g.
**PE** Periplasmically Exposed.
*Biological Sciences; Chemistry; Developmental Neurogenetics; Medicine.*
**PE** Permanent Error.
Permanent error is also known as: Hard Error.
*Computer Programming.*
**PE** Peru's International vehicle registration letters.
**PE** Pescara, Italy.
**PE** Phase Encoding.
*Data Communications.*
**PE** Phycoerythrin.
PE is found in red algae. It is one of the major species of phycobiliproteins.
*Biochemistry; Plant Biology.*
**PE** Physical Education; Physical Examination.
**PE** Pidgin English.
**PE** Polyethylene.
Polyethylene in film-form is used to wrap food products, and has numerous industrial uses.
*Materials.*
**PE** Prepaid Expense.
**P.E.**; **p.e.**; **P.E.**; **pe** Printer's Error.
*Graphic Arts.*
**PE** Processing Elements.
**PE** Professional Engineer.
**PEA** peace establishment authority.
autorité responsible du tableau d'effectifs du temps de paix.
**PEA** Plan d'Epargne en Actions.
French acronym meaning: Personal Equity Plan.
*Business; Finance.*
**PEAM** Piano Energetico dell'Area Metropolitana della Provincia di Milano (Italy).
*Italian Energy Plans.*
**PEARL** Process and Experiment Automation Realtime Language.
**PEAR laboratory** Princeton Engineering Anomalies Research laboratory (U.S.A.).
*Parapsychology; Physics.*
**PEB** Post-Exposure Bake.
*Chemistry; Chemical Engineering; Macromolecules; Neutron Research; Polymers; Semiconductors.*
**PEBBLEs** Probes Encapsulated By BioListic Embedding.
*Analytical Chemistry; Applied Spectroscopy; Biosensors; Chemistry.*
**PEC** Paesi dell'Europa Centrale.
Italian acronym meaning: Central Europe Countries.
**PEC**; **pec** Photoelectric Cell.
The photoelectric cell is also known as: Photocell; Electric Eye.
*Electronics.*
**PECC** Pacific Economic Co-operation Council.
**PECO** Paesi dell'Europa Centrale e Orientale.
**PECO** pays d'Europe centrale et orientale.
countries of Central and Eastern Europe (CCEE).
**PECP** Plasmodesmal-Enriched Cell Wall Protein.
*Biological Sciences; Plant Biology.*
**PECSD** politique européenne commune en matière de sécurité et de défense.
Common European Security and Defence Policy (CESDP).
**PED** Pays En Développement.
French acronym meaning: Developing Nation; Developing Country.
**Ped.** pediatrics: pediatrician.
**PEDC** politique européenne de défense commune (PEDC).
Commun European defence policy (CEDP).
**PEDF** Pigment Epithelium - Derived Factor.
*Angiogenesis.*
**PEDV** Porcine Epidemic Diarrhea Virus.
**PEEM** Photoelectron Emission Microscopy.
**PEEMs** Photoelectron Emission Microscopes.
*Physical Chemistry.*
**PEEP** Positive End Expiratory Pressure.
*Medicine.*
**PEER** Peer Evaluation of Extramural Research.

**PEFCO** Private Export Funding COrporation (U.S.A.).
**PEG** Piano Esecutivo di Gestione (Italy).
**PEG** Pneumoencephalogram.
*Medicine.*
**PEG** Polyethylene Glycol.
Polyethylene glycol is used mainly in making pharmaceuticals, plasticizers, and cosmetics.
*Organic Chemistry.*
**PEI** Percutaneous Ethanol Injection.
*Ablation Techniques; Carcinomas.*
**Pei** Progetto educativo di istituto (Italy).
**PEL** Plan d'Epargne Logement (France).
**PELs** Permissible Exposure Limits.
**PEM** Polymer Electrolytic Membrane.
**PEMD** Program for Export Market Development (Canada).
**PEMFC** Polymer Electrolyte Membrane Fuel Cell.
European Commission 5th FP.
*Electricity Generation; Waste Gases.*
For further details see under: **5FP**.
**PEN** Pacific Exchange Network.
**PEN** Piano Energetico Nazionale.
Italian acronym meaning: National Energy Plan.
**PENTA** Paediatric European Network for the Treatment of AIDS.
*European Community Project.*
**PENTAFLUX Experiment** Fifth Flux Experiment.
**PEO** peace enforcement operation.
opération d'imposition de la paix.
**PEO** Polyethylene Oxide.
*Bioengineering; Cell Biology; Chemical Engineering; Dentistry.*
**PEP** Packet Exchange Protocol.
**PEP** Paesi a Economia Pianificata.
**PEP** Peak Envelope Power.
*Electronics.*
**PEP** Personal Equity Plan.
*Business; Finance.*
**PEP** Phosphoenolpyruvate.
**PEP** Plan d'Epargne Populaire.
French acronym meaning: Tax-Exempt Special Savings Account.
*Economics; Finance.*
**PEP** Plant Enhancement Programme.
**PEP** Pneumothorax Extra-Pleural.
**PEP** Political and Economic Planning.
**PEP** Prevention of Environmental Pollution - WHO's.
For further details see under: **WHO**.
**PEPC** Phosphoenolpyruvate Carboxylate (an enzyme).
*Agrobiology; Microbiology.*
**PEPCK** Phosphoenolpyruvate Carboxykinase (an enzyme).
*Biomedicine; Diabetes; Gluconeogenesis; Molecular Genetics.*
**PEPCO** Potomac Electric Power Co. (U.S.A.).
*Cogeneration units.*
**PEPE** Parallel Element-Processing Ensemble.
*Computers.*
**pepe** The above acronym was coined accidentally using the Italian word "pepe" which means: "pepper".
*Botany.*
**PEP (exogenous)** Prolyl Endopeptidase.
*Biochemistry; Chemistry; Immunogenic; Epitopes; Medicine.*
**PEPS** Permanent Ethnographic Probability Sample.
*Anthropology.*
**PEPs** Personal Equity Plans.
**PEPS** Premier Entré, Premier Sorti.
French acronym meaning: First-In, First Out.
*Business; Economics; Finance.*
**PEQUOD Project** Pacific EQUatorial Ocean Dynamics Project (U.S.A.).
**per.** (abbr.) periodo.
Italian abbreviation meaning: period.
**per.** (abbr.) perito.
Italian abbreviation meaning: expert.
**P/E(R)** Price-Earning Ratio.
*Management.*
**PER** Program Event Recording.
*Data Communications.*
**PER** Protein Efficiency Ratio.
*Nutrition.*
**PERA** Production Engineering Research Association (U.S.A.).
**pera** The above acronym was coined accidentally using the Italian word "pera" which means "pear".
*Botany; Materials.*
**per.agrim.** (abbr.) perito agrimensore.
Italian abbreviation meaning: surveyor.
**P-E ratio** Precipitation-Evaporation ratio.
The precipitation-evaporation ratio is also known as: Precipitation-Effectiveness Ratio.
*Meteorology.*
**PERB** Public Employment Relations Board (U.S.A.).
**per.call.** (abbr.) perito calligrafo.
Italian abbreviation meaning: handwriting expert.
**per.comm.** (abbr.) perito commerciale.
Italian abbreviation meaning: commercial expert / assessor.
**per.est.** (abbr.) per estensione.
Italian abbreviation meaning: by extension.

**perf.** (abbr.) perfect.
*Botany; Science.*
**perf.** (abbr.) perforated.
**PERFASS** personnel functional area sub-system.
sous-système de domaine fonctionnel "personnel".
**Perk.** Perquisite.
Perquisite is also known as: Fringe Benefit.
*Employment.*
**PERL** Practical Extraction Report Language.
*Scripting Languages.*
**PERM** Partnership for Ecosystem Research and Management (U.S.A.).
**PERMREP** permanent representative.
représentant permanent.
**per.nav.** (abbr.) perito navale.
Italian abbreviation meaning: ship surveyor.
**Pers.** (abbr.) Persian.
*Languages.*
**PERT** Program Evaluation and Review Technique.
PERT was developed by the U.S. Navy in 1958.
*Industrial Engineering.*
**pert.** (abbr.) pertaining.
**PERV** Porcine Endogenous Retrovirus.
*Liver Growth; Liver Repair; Hepathology; Porcine Endogenous Retrovirus; Virology; Xenotransplantation.*
**PERVs** Pigs Endogenous Retroviruses.
For further details see under: **PERV**.
**PES** 1. pointd'entrée / de sortie.
1. point of entry / exit (POE).
2. prepositioned equipment storage.
2. dépôt de matériel prépositionné.
**PES** Polyethersulfone.
*Materials.*
**PES** Potential Energy Surface.
*Chemistry; Chemical Physics; Supercomputers.*
**PEs** Processing Elements.
**PESC** Politica Estera e di Sicurezza Comune.
Italian acronym meaning: Common Security and Foreign Policy.
**PESD** politique européenne en matière de securité et de défense.
European Security and Defence Policy (ESDP).
**pet.** (abbr.) petroleum.
*Geology.*
**PET** Poly (Ethylene Terephthalate).
*Polymer Science.*
**PET** Positron Emission Tomography.
*Radiology.*
**PETA** People for the Ethical Treatment of Animals.
PETA was founded in 1980.
*Biomedical Sciences; Life Sciences; Surgery; Veterinary Medicine.*
**PETE** Partnership for Environmental Technology Education (U.S.A.).
**PETE model** Protective Equipment Test Effigy model.
Specified in EN168 (European Standard for *Eye Protectors*).
**PETN** Pentaerythritol Tetranitrate.
Pentaerythritol tetranitrate is insoluble in water, soluble in acetone, and has a melting point of 139°C. It is used in explosives.
*Organic Chemistry.*
**PETT** Position Emission Transaxial Tomography.
**PETT** Professeur de l'Enseignement Technique Théorique (France).
**PEV** Position Effect Variegation.
*Cell Biology; Developmental Biology; Gene Silencing; Medical Research; Molecular Biology.*
**PEV** Proposition Exclusive Vendeuse.
French initialism: Unique Selling Proposition.
**PF** Pattern Formation.
*Chaotic Dynamics; Developmental Biology.*
**PF** Pension Fund.
**p.f.** per favore.
Italian initialism meaning: please.
**PF**; **P.F.** Phase Factor.
**pF** picofarad.
Picofarad is a unit of capacitance equal to $10^{-12}$ farad.
*Electricity.*
**PF**; **P.F.** Power Factor.
*Electricity.*
**pf.** (abbr.) preferred.
Also: **Pref.**; **pfd**.
**PF** Project Financing.
*Business; Finance.*
**PF** protection factor [NBC].
facteur de protection [NBC].
**PF1** Polyadenylation Factor 1.
*Cell Biology; Pathology.*
**PFA** Pulverized Fuel Ash.
**PFB** Pentafluorobenzyl.
*Pharmacology.*
**PFB** Pressurized Fluidized Bed.
**PFBC/CTIU** Pressurized Fluidized-Bed Combustion/Component Test and Integration Unit.
*Combustion Technology.*
**PFC** Perfluorocarbon.
**PFC** Prefrontal Cortex.
*Brain Science; Neural Mechnisms.*
**PFC** Privately Financed Consumption.
*Business; Commerce.*
**PFC** Pulse-Flow Coulometry.

**PFCP** Primary Familial and Congenital Polycythemia.

**PfCSP** *P. falciparum* Circumsporozoite Protein.
*Malaria DNA Vaccine; Medical Research; Microbiology; New Vaccine Technologies.*

**pfd.** (abbr.) preferred.
*Stocks.*

**PFD** Prefoldin.
Prefoldin is a gene involved in microtubule biogenesis. It is also known as the Gim complex.
*Cellular Biochemistry; Microtubule Biogenesis.*

**PFE** Photoferroelectric Effect.
*Solid-State Physics.*

**PFE** purchaser-furnished equipment.
équipement (matériel) fourni par l'acheteur.

**PfEMP1** *Plasmodium falciparum* Erythrocyte Membrane Protein 1.
*Medicine; Target Antigens.*

**PFEP** Programmable Front-End Processor.

**PFGE** Pulsed-Field Gel Electrophoresis.

**PFI** Pipe Fabrication Institute (U.S.A.).

**PFI** Private Finance Initiative (G.B.).

**PFK** Phosphofructokinase.
*Cardiology; Medicine.*

**PFM** Pulse-Frequency Modulation.
*Telecommunications.*

**Pf Msta II** Progetto finalizzato Materiali speciali per tecnologie avanzate.
Of the Italian National Research Council.
*Projects; Special Materials for Advanced Technologies.*

**PFMT** plan financier à moyen terme.
medium-term financial plan (MTFP).

**PFNS** position-fixing navigation system.
système de navigation par positionnement.

**PFOS** Perfluorooctanesulfonate.

**PFP** N-Pentafluoropropionyl.

**PfP** Partnership for Peace.
Partenariat pour la paix (PPP 1.).

**PFP** People's First Party (Taiwan).

**PFP** Pin-Feed Printer.
The pin-feed printer makes use of pins for feeding perforated-edge paper.
*Computer Technology.*

**PFPE** Perfluoropolyether.

**PfP/SC** Political-Military Steering Committee on Partnership for Peace.
Comité directeur politico-militaire du Partenariat pour la paix.

**PFR** Prototype Fast Reactor.

**PFS** pre-feasibility study.
étude des préfaisabilité.

**PFU** Plaque-Forming Unit.
*Medicine; Pathology.*

**PFZ** Polar Front Zone.

**pg.** (abbr.) page.
Also: **P.**

**PG** Parental Guidance.

**PG** Paying Guest.

**PG** Perugia, Italy.

**pg.** (abbr.) picograrn / picogramme.
*Metrology.*

**PG** Picture Grammar.
*Computer Programming.*

**PG** Polizia Giudiziaria.
Italian initialism meaning: Criminal Police.

**PG** (abbr.) Portugal.

**Pg.** (abbr.) Portuguese.
*Languages.*

**PG** Postgraduate.

**PG** 1. prisonnier de guerre.
1. prisoner of war (POW).
2. project group.
2. groupe de projet.
3. proving ground.
3. polygone d'essai.

**P.G.** Procuratore Generale; Procura Generale.
Italian initialism meaning: Attorney-General; Attorney-General's Office.
*Law.*

**PG** Propylene Glycol.
PG is used mainly as a lubricant and bactericide, as well as in pharmaceuticals and suntan lotions.
*Organic Chemistry.*

**PG** Prostaglandin.
*Endocrinology.*

**PG** Provincial Government.

**PG13** Parental Guidance 13 (U.S.A.).
To decide whether a motion picture is appropriate for children under 13 years of age.

**PGA** Policy and Global Affairs (Division) (U.S.A.).

**PGA** Pteroylglutamic Acid (folic acid).

**PGA** Professional Golfers' Association (of America) (U.S.A.).
Since 1916.

**PGCs** Primordial Germ Cells.
*Animal Biology; Reproductive Biology; Veterinary Medicine.*
For further details see under: **HSCs** and **SSCs**.

**PGD** Phosphogluconate Dehydrogenase.

**PGD** plan général de défense.
general defence plan (GDP).

**PGD of DNA** Preimplantation Genetic Diagnosis of DNA.
For further details see under: **DNA**.

**PGE-2** Prostaglandin E2.

**PGEs** Platinum Group Elements.
**PGHM** Peloton Gendarmerie de Haute Montagne (France).
**PGH synthase** Prostaglandin H synthase.
*Biochemistry; Cell Biology; Immunology; Medicine; Molecular Biophysics.*
**PGI** Phosphoglucose Isomerase.
**Pgi** Progiciel de Gestion Intégré.
French initialism meaning: Enterprise Resource Planning Application.
**PGI** programme-generated income.
recettes propres du (ou au) programme.
**PGIP** Polygalacturonase-Inhibiting Protein.
*Plant Pathology.*
**PGK** Phosphoglycerate Kinase.
**PGM** precision-guided munition.
munition à guidage de précision.
**PGMEA** Propylene Glycol Methyl Ether Acetate.
**PGMs** Platinum Group Metals.
**PGO waves** Pontogeniculooccipital waves.
**PGP**; **pgp** Pretty Good Privacy.
*Software.*
**PGR** Postglacial Rebound.
*Geophysics; Space Geodesy.*
**PGR** Psychogalvanic Reaction.
**PGR** Psychogalvanic Reflex.
*Physiology.*
**PGR** Psychogalvanic Response.
**PG repeats** Polyglutamine repeats.
*Biomedicine.*
**PGRP** Peptidoglycan Recognition Protein.
Iantibacterial Immune Responses.
**PGRT** Petroleum and Gas Revenue Tax (Canada).
**PGS** Petroleum Geo-Services.
*Seismic Services.*
**PGS** Power Generation Satellite.
**PGS** Processeur de Gestion de la Signalisation.
**PGS** Protein G-Sepharose.
**PGSF** Public Good Science Fund.
Weelington, New Zealand.
**PGS missile** Patrol Hydrofil, Guided missile.
**PGT** Processeur de Gestion de Trame.
**ph** page heading.
*Data Communications.*
**ph** Pharmacopoeia.
*Pharmacology.*
For further details see under: **Phar.**
**ph** (abbr.) phase.
*Archaeology; Astronomy; Cartography; Chemistry; Materiais Science; Metallurgy; Physics.*
**ph** phosphor.
*Physics.*
**pH** potential hydrogen.
**PH** Public Health.
**PH** purpleheart.
Purpleheart is a type of wood used to make furniture.
*Materials.*
**$PH_3$** Phosphine.
Phosphine, also known as hydrogen phosphide, is used mainly in organic preparations.
*Inorganic Chemistry.*
**PHA** Bachelor of Philosophy.
**PHA** Phytohemagglutinin.
**PHA** Public Housing Administration.
**PHA** Public Housing Authority.
**PHA II** Pseudo-Hypoaldosteronism Type II.
*Hypertension.*
**PHABSIM** Physical HABitat SImulation Model.
PHABSIM was developed by the U.S. Fish and Wildlife Service in the 1970s.
*Biology; Fisheries Biology; River Ecology; River Morphology.*
**PHAPs** Putative HLA-DR-Associated Proteins.
Regulators of caspase-3 activation.
*Apoptosis; Tumor Suppressors.*
**Phar.**; **phar.** Pharmaceutical; Pharmacist; Pharmacy.
Also: **Pharm.**; **pharm.**
**Phar.**; **phar.** Pharmacology.
Also: **Pharm.**; **pharm.**
**Phar.** Pharmacopoeia.
The term pharmacopoeia refers to a list of drugs and drug uses. The first U.S. pharmacopoeia was published in the U.S.A. in 1820.
*Pharmacology.*
**PHARMA** PHArmaceutical Research and Manufacturers of America (U.S.A.).
**PHAs** Polyhydroxylalkanoates.
*Biodegradable Plastics; Biocatalysis of Macromolecules; Bioprocessing of Macromolecules.*
**PHAs** Potentially Hazardous Asteroids.
There are 171 PHAs currently known (2003).
**PHASIC** Photonic Hybrid Active Silica Integrated Circuit.
*Multistage Processes; Patented Fabrication Techniques.*
**PHB-V** Poly-β-Hydroxybutyrate-β-hydroxyvalerate.
**ph.bz** phosphor bronze.
Also: **Phos.B**.
*Metallurgy.*
**PHC** Personal Holding Company (U.S.A.).
**PHC** Pharmaceutical Chemist.
**PhD**; **Ph.D.** Doctor of Philosophy.

**PHDCN** Project on Human Development in Chicago Neighborhoods (U.S.A.).

**PHD fingers** Plant Homeodomain fingers.
*Biology; Development Genetics.*

**PH domain** Pleckstrin Homology domain.
*Biochemistry; Biophysics; Microbiology; Molecular Genetics; Neurology; Neuroscience; Psychiatry; Signal Transduction.*

**PHE** Plate Heat Exchanger.

**PHE** POL handling equipment.
matériel (ou équipement) de manutention des produits pétroliers.

**PHEM** Primitive HElium Mantle.
*Earth and Planetary Sciences; Isotope Chemistry.*

**PHFs** Paired Helical Filaments.
*Neuropathology.*

**PHG missile** Patrol Hydrofoil, Guided missile.

**PHIB** amphibious.
amphibie.

**PHIBEX** amphibious exercise.
exercice amphibie.

**PHIC** Poly (Hexyl Isocyanate).

**PHIDIAS** laser PHotopolimerization models based on medical Imaging - a Development Improving the Accuracy of Surgery.
*European Community Project.*

**PHIL** Programmable algorithm machine High-level Language.

**PHIRMA** PHotorealistic Image Rendering for MAnufactured objects.
*European Community Project.*

**PHLS** Public Health Laboratory Service.
A Centre of Excellence for expertise, reference and research on pathogens that affect human health (G.B.).

**PHN** Post-Herpetic Neuralgia.
*Medicine.*

**phon.** (abbr.) phonetics.
*Linguistics.*

**PHOs** Potentially Hazardous Objects.
*Asteroids; Comets.*

**PHOSt** poly(hydroxystyrene).
*Chemistry; Chemical Engineering; Macromolecules; Neutron Research; Polymers; Semiconductors.*

**photog.** (abbr.) photographer; photography.

**PHOTON** Paneuropean PHOtonic Transport Overlay Network.
*European Community Project.*

**PHOTOS** PHOtosensitive Technology for Optical Systems.
*European Community Project.*

**PHQ** peace headquarters.
quartier général du temps de paix (QGP).

**PHRA** Pennsylvania Human Relations Act.

**PHRI** Public Health Research Institute (N.Y., U.S.A.).
*Drug-resistant Strains; Epidemiology; Microbiology; Reemerging Diseases; Tuberculosis.*
For further details see under: **DOTS** and **MERLIN**.

**PhRMA** Pharmaceutical Research and Manufacturers of America.
PhRMA is a U.S. Association representing large drug companies.

**PHS** Personal Handiphone System.

**PHS** Public Health Service (U.S.A.).

**PHT** Patrol Hydrofil, Torpedo.

**phys.** physical; physics; physician.

**phys.** physiological; physiology.

**PHYA** PHYtochrome A.
*Botany.*

**$P_i$** Inorganic Phosphate.

**PI** Performance Index.

**PI** Perpetual Inventory.

**PI** Personal Income.

**PI** Phosphoinositide.

**PI** Philippine Islands.

**PI** Pisa, Italy.

**PI** Planet Imager.
NASA's PI will be launched in 2020.

**PI** Polyisoprene.
*Organic Chemistry.*

**PI** Principal Investigator.

**PI** Productivity Index.

**Pi** Progetto di istituto - Italy - Formerly Pei.
For further details see under: **Pei**.

**PI** Propidium Iodide.

**P.I.** Pubblica Istruzione.
Italian acronym meaning: Public Education.

**P.I.** Pubblico Impiego.
Italian acronym meaning: Civil Service.

**PI** public information.
1a. information publique.
1b. presse et information (ou presse - information).

**PI** Public Interest.

**PIA** Personal Investment Authority.
PIA became fully operational from 1st July 1993.

**PIA** 1. point d'identification et d'accueil.
1. identification / reception point.
2. public information adviser.
2. conseiller en information publique.

**PIA** Progiciel Industriel d'Acquisition.

**PIA** The airline code for Pakistan International Airlines.

**PIADC** Plum Island Animal Disease Center.

PIADC is the principal U.S. Department of Agriculture laboratory for research and diagnosis of animal diseases which are foreign to the United States.
**PIAM** (16th Annual) Program on Investment Appraisal and Management (U.S.A.).
Harvard University 23rd May / 23rd June 2000.
Inception in 1985.
*Project Appraisal; Seminars.*
**PIAT** Projector Infantry Anti Tank.
*Ordnance.*
**PIB** Produit Interieur Brut.
French acronym meaning: Gross Domestic Product.
**PIBAL; pibal Observation** Pilot-Balloon Observation.
*Meteorology.*
**PIBOR** Paris Interbank Offered Rate -France.
**PI-b-PEO block copolymers** Poly (Isoprene-*b*-ethyleneoxide) block copolymers.
*Chemistry; Materials Science; Polymers.*
**PIBS** Permanent Interest Bearing Shares.
*Finance; Investments.*
**PIC** Paid-In Capital.
*Business; Finance.*
**PIC** 1. Peace Implementation Council.
1. Conseil de mise en œuvre de la paix.
2. press information centre.
2. centre d'information de la presse.
**PIC** Personal Identification Code.
The personal identification code consists of a six-character number on a magnetic strip on a plastic card used for identification purposes by users accessing special-purpose computers.
*Computer Programming.*
**PiC** Phosphate Carrier.
*Mitochondrial Carriers.*
**PIC** Preinitiation Complex.
*Molecular Medicine.*
**PIC** Preintegration Complex.
*Genetics; Lentiviruses; Microbiology.*
**PICA** Project of Integrated Catalogue Automation.
**PICASSO** Practical and Intelligent CAD for ASSembly Objects.
*European Community Project; Assembly Design.*
**PICB** Progiciel Industriel Conversationnel de Base.
**PICC** point of ingress control centre.
centre de contrôle du point d'entrée.
**PIC simulations** Particle-In-Cell simulations.
*Physics.*
**PICTO** Programma per la gestione Integrata del Cambiamento Tecnico / Organizzativo (Olivetti) (Italy).
**PID** Panel Integrated Display.
**PID** Pelvic Inflammatory Disease.
*Medicine.*
**PIDS** Public Investment Data System.
**PIF** 1. peace implementation force.
1. force de mise en œuvre de la paix.
2. price increase factor.
2. coefficient de hausse de prix.
**PIF** Prolactin Inhibitory Factor.
PIF is also known as: Prolactin Release-Inhibiting Factor.
*Endocrinology.*
**PIFWC** person indicted for war crimes.
personne inculpée de crimes de guerre.
**PIGMAP** PIg Gene MAPping - E.C.
**PIH** Pregnancy-Induced Hypertension.
*Physiology.*
**PII** Progiciel Industriel d'Identification.
**PII regulations** Professional Indemnity Insurance regulations.
**PIK** Panel-Integrated Keyboard.
**PI3Ks** Phosphatidylinositol 3-Kinases.
*Biochemistry; Cancer Research; Molecular Biology.*
**PIL** Prodotto Interno Lordo.
Italian acronym meaning: Gross Domestic Product.
**PILOT** Payment In Lieu Of Taxes (U.S.A.).
**PILOT** Programmed Inquiry, Learning, Or Teaching.
*Computer Programming.*
**pilot** The above acronyms were coined using the English word "pilot".
*Aviation; Computer Programming; Mechanical Engineering; Telecommunications.*
**PIM** Piano Indicativo Mondiale.
**PIM** Piano Intercomunale Milanese (Italy).
**PIM** Plant Information Management.
**PIM** position and intended movement.
position et mouvement prévue.
**PIM** Pulse Interval Modulation.
**PIM Act** (Symantec's) Personal Information Manager Act.
*Portable Recorders.*
**PIMS** PfP information management system.
système de gestion de l'information du PPP.
**PIMs** Phosphatidylinositol mannosides.
PIMs are phosphoglycolipids.
*Immunology; Lymphocyte Biology; Rheumatology.*
**PIMS** Profit Impact of Market Strategies.
*Business; Economics; Finance.*
**PIMS** Program In Medical Sciences (U.S.A.).

At the Florida State University, Tallahassee, Florida.
**PIM technology** Processor-In-Memory technology.
*Computer Science; Petaflops Machines; Physics.*
**PIN** Pacific Island Network.
**PIN** Paleontology INstitute.
Of the Russian Academy of Sciences.
**PIN** Personal Identification Number.
**PIN** Prodotto Interno Netto.
Italian acronym meaning: Net Domestic Product.
**PINC** Property INvestment Certificate (G.B.).
**PIN construction** Positive-Intrinsic-Negative construction.
*Electronics.*
**PIOCS** Physical Input/Output Control System.
*Computers.*
**PIP** 1. package implementation plan.
1. plan de mise en œuvre des paquets (ou ensembles) de capacités.
2. project implementation plan.
2. plan de mise en œuvre du projet.
**PIP** Performance-Indexed Paper (U.S.A.).
*Business; Economics; Finance.*
**PIP** Petroleum Incentive Programme (Canada).
**PIP** Picture-In-Picture.
*Digital Special Effects.*
**PIP$_2$** Phosphatidylinositol-4,5-biphosphate.
*Medicine; Physiology; Protein Biochemistry.*
**PIPICO Affairs** Panel for International Programs and International Cooperation in Ocean Affairs.
Of the U.S. State Department.
**PIP**; **Pip Technology** Partner Interchange Process technology (3 Com.).
A Rosetta Net technology based on Xml.
*Business-to-Business Transactions.*
**PIPRA** Public-sector Intellectual Property Resource for Agriculture (U.S.A.).
*Patented Agricultural Technologies.*
**PIR** 1. periodic intelligence review.
1. examen périodique du renseignement.
2. pressure ignition rocket.
2. roquette percutante avec armement à dépression.
3. priority intelligence requirement.
3. besoin prioritaire en renseignement.
**PIR** Progiciel Industriel de Régulation (France).
**PIR** Protein Information Resource.
**PIRAS method** Polarized Infrared Absorption Spectroscopy method.
*Chemistry; Nanomaterials.*
**PI rate** Prime Interest ratee.
**PIRE puissance isotrope rayonnée équivalente**.
equivalent isotropically radiated power (EIRP).
**PIREPS** (abbr.) Piilot Reports.
**PIRGs** Public Interest Research Groups.
The PIRGs aim to mobilize college students to fight pollution; consumer fraud and other issues (U.S.A.).
**PIRMED** Programme Interdisciplinaire de Recherche sur les bases scientifiques du Médicament (France).
**PIR properties** Post-Inhibitory Rebound properties.
*Neural Science.*
**PIS** Peripheral Immune System.
**PISC** Programme for the Inspection of Steel Components.
*European Community.*
**PISITREP** public information situation report.
compte rendu de situation en matière d'information publique.
**PISTA** Polo Integrato di Sviluppo Torino Aeroporto (Italy).
**PIT** Plasma Iron Turnover.
**PIT** The airport code for Greater Pittsburgh, Pennsylvania, U.S.A.
**PITAC** President's Information Technology Advisory Committee (U.S.A.).
The PITAC is a 26-member panel (2003) of industry executives and computer scientists.
*Information Technology Research.*
**PITP** Phosphatidylinositol transfer protein.
*Medicine; Physiology; Protein Biochemistry.*
**PIU** Path Information Unit.
**PIV** Peak Inverse Voltage.
*Electronics.*
**PIXE** Proton-Induced X-ray Emission.
*Spectroscopy.*
**PJ** Palais de Justice.
French initialism meaning: the Hall of Justice; the Law Courts.
**P.J.**; **p.j.** Pièces Jointes.
French initialism meaning: enclosures.
**PJ** Police Judiciare.
French initialism meaning: Criminal Police.
**PJC** Permanent Joint Council [NATO - Russia].
Conseil conjoint permanent (CCP 3.) [OTAN - Russie].
**PJC-CS** Permanent Joint Council in Chiefs of Staff Session [NATO - Russia].
Conseil conjoint permanent en session des chefs d'état-major [OTAN - Russie].
**PJC-MR** Permanent Joint Council at Military Representatives' Level [NATO - Russia].
Conseil conjoint permanent au niveau des représentants militaires [OTAN - Russie].
**PK** 1. Pakistan.
1. Pakistan.

2. peacekeeping.
2. maintien de la paix.
**pk.** (abbr.) park.
**pk.**(abbr.) peak.
*Geology; Metrology; Science.*
**PK** Pyruvate Kinase.
**PKA** Primary Knock-on Atom.
**PKA** Protein Kinase A.
PKA is an enzyme that modulates the function of other proteins.
*Cellular Regulation; Neurosciences; Pharmacology; Physiology; Toxicology.*
**PKB** Protein Kinase B.
*Signal Transduction.*
**PKCI protein** Protein Kinase C Interacting protein.
*Biochemistry; Genomics; Molecular Biophysics.*
**pkg.** (abbr.) package.
Also: **pkge**.
*Computer Programming.*
**pkg.** (abbr.) packing.
*Acoustical Engineering; Crystallography; Engineering; Geology; Surgery.*
**pkg**; **pkg.** per kilogram.
**PKI** public key infrastructure.
infrastructure à clés publiques.
**PKL** (abbr.) Pickle.
*Plant Biology.*
**pkl mutation** pickle mutation.
*Arabidopsis Plants; Mutagenized Population Plants; Plant Biology.*
**PKN** Protein Kinase N.
**PKO** peacekeeping operation [UN].
opération de maintien de la paix [ONU].
**PK Ops** see PKO.
**PKP** predicted kill point.
point d'impact prévu.
**PKSs** Polyketide Synthases.
*Bacteriology; Biosynthetic Chemistry; Chemical Engineering; Lovastatin Biosynthesis; Pharmaceutical Sciences.*
**PKSs** Polyketide Synthases.
**PKU** Phenylketonuria.
PKU is a disease in which phenylalanine concentrations are high.
*Medicine.*
**PL** Paper Loss; Partial Loss.
**PL**; **P/L** Parts List.
**PL** 1. phase line.
1. ligne d'objectifs intermédiaires.
2. Poland.
2. Pologne.
**PL** Physical Layer.
*Computer Technology.*
**PL** (abbr.) place.
Place is also known as: Column (positional notation system).
*Mathematics.*
**PL** (abbr.) plan.
*Architecture.*
**PL** (abbr.) plane.
*Architecture; Aviation; Mathematics; Mechanical Devices; Medicine; Physiology.*
**PL** Pleine Lune.
French initialism meaning: Full Moon.
*Astronomy.*
**PL** Poids Lourd.
French initialism meaning; heavy lorry.
**PL** (abbr.) pole.
*Astronomy; Biology; Cell Biology; Crystallography; Electricity; Mathematics; Mechanics; Optics; Physics.*
**PL** (abbr.) plate.
*Anatomy; Building Engineering; Graphic Arts; Electricity; Geology; Medicine.*
**PL** (abbr.) plural.
**PL** Price Level; Price List.
**PL** Private Label (U.S.A.).
*Marketing.*
**PL** Private Loan.
*Business; Commerce; Finance.*
**PL** Profit and Loss.
**PL** Public Law.
**PL** pulpolingual.
**pla** passengers' luggage in advance.
**PLA** Pennsylvania Library Association (U.S.A.).
**PLA** Philippine Library Association.
**PLA** 1. plain language address.
1. adresse d'un message (ou adresse en clair).
2. plain language addressee.
2. destinataire en langage clair.
**PLA** Polylactic Acid.
**PLA** Port of London Authority.
**PLA** Prêts Locatifs Aidés (France).
**PLA** Programmable Logic Array.
*Electronics.*
**PLA** Public Library Association.
**PLA** Pulpolabial.
**PLA** Pulpolinguoaxial.
**PLAC** Plant Artificial Chromosome.
*Plant Biotechnology.*
**PLAL-Lys** Poly (Lactic acid-*co*-Lysine-*graft*-Lysine).
*Animal Science; Biomedical Engineering; Chemical Engineering.*
**PL&PD** Public Liability and Property Damage.
*Insurance.*

**PLANET** Photonic Local Access NETworks.
*European Community Project.*
**PLANMAN** Operator-driven technological information system for the continuous improvement of process planning.
The PLANMAN project was suggested by the Institute for Production Engineering and Machine Tools, at the University of Hanover. It was launched at the Septenber 1996 CIM Show (G.B.).
*European Community Project.*
**PLATLS** Philippine Association of Teachers of Library Science.
**PLATO systems** Photonic Links in ATM and Optical systems.
*European Community Project.*
**PLB** personal locator beacon.
balise de localisation individuelle.
**PLBR** Prototype Large Breeder Reactor.
**PLC** Public Limited Company (G.B.).
**PLCβ** Phospholipase Cβ.
**plcy.** (abbr.) policy.
**PLD** Pulsed Laser Deposition.
PLD is used for thin-film and multilayer research.
*Applied Physics; Materials Research; Physics; Spectroscopy.*
**PLDT** Philippine Long Distance Telephone.
PLDT is the country's dominant fixed-line telecoms operator.
*Telecommunications Carriers.*
**PLE** prudent limit of endurance.
limite de sécurité du temps de vol.
**plf**; **plff** (abbr.) plaintiff.
Also: **pltf**.
**PLGA** Poly (Lactic acid-*co*-Glycolic Acid).
*Animal Science; Biomedical Engineering; Chemical Engineering.*
**PlGF** Placenta Growth Factor.
*Medicine; Pathology.*
**pli** pounds per linear inch.
**Pl. law** (abbr.) Poiseuille's law.
Named for its discoverer, the French physiologist and physician Jean-Louis-Marie **Poiseuille**.
**PLM**; **Plm** Product Lifecycle Management (SAP's).
*Supply Chains.*
**PLN** Perusahan Listrik Negara (Indonesia).
PLN is the state-owned Indonesian electricity monopoly.
**PLN** Phospholomban.
A mutation in phospholamban can cause dilated cardiomyopathy and heart failure.
*Cell Biophysics; Genetics; Medicine.*
**PLO** Palestine Liberation Organization.
**PLO** Partnership liaison office.
bureau de liaison du Partenariat.
**PLO** Programmable Local Oscillator.
*Extraterrestrial Physics; Radar Astronomy; Space Physics.*
**PLOS** Public Library Of Science (U.S.A.).
**PLP** Packet Level Protocol.
**PLP** Progressive Labour Party (Bermuda).
**PLP** Proteolipid Protein.
*Immunology.*
**PLNs** Peripheral Lymph Nodes.
**PLR** Power-Line Radiation.
**PLRS** Position, Location, and Reporting System.
**PLS** position locator system.
système de localisation de position.
**PLSC** Plasma Science Committee (U.S.A.).
**PLSE** Pipe-Line Sud Européen.
**PLSS** Portable Life-Support System.
**PLSS** Precision, Location Strike System.
**PLT** 1. Partnership liaison team.
1. équipe de liaison du Partenariat.
2. planning and liaison team.
2. équipe de planification et de liaison.
**PLT** Photoluminescent Thermometer.
**PLT** Power Line Transmission.
**PLT** Princeton Large Torus.
*Neutral Beam Heating.*
**pltf** (abbr.) plaintiff.
Also: **plf**; **plff**.
**PLU** Primary Logical Unit.
**PLUM** Priority Low-Use Minimal.
**plum** The above acronym was coined using the English word "plum" (*Botany; Geology*).
**PLV** Publicité Lieu deVente.
French initialism meaning: Point-of-sale material.
**PLZT** Lead Lanthanum Zirconate Titanate.
PLZT is also known as: lanthanum-doped lead-zirconate-lead titanate.
**PM** Panama.
**PM** Particulate Matter.
*Physics.*
**PM** Permanent Magnet.
*Electromagnetism.*
**PM** Peso Molecolare.
Italian initialism meaning: molecular weight.
*Chemistry.*
**PM** Phase Modulation.
*Telecommunications.*
**PM** Plasma Membrane.
**P.M.**; **p.m.** Police Magistrate.
**PM** Polizia Militare; Police Militaire.
Italian and French initialism meaning: Military Police.
**P.M.**; **p.m.** Post Master / Postmaster.

**P/M** Powder Metallurgy.
*Metallurgy.*
**PM**; **pm** Premium.
**PM** Premium Money.
**PM** Preventive Maintenance.
*Industrial Engineering.*
**PM** Preventive Medicine.
*Medicine.*
**PM** Primary Market.
**PM** Primitive Mantle.
*Earth Sciences.*
**PM** Process Manager; Project Manager.
*Management.*
**Pm** The chemical symbol for Promethium.
Promethium is a chemical element having the atomic number 61, and an atomic weight of 147. It is produced by nuclear fission and is named for the ancient Greek god **Prometheus**.
*Chemistry; Symbols.*
**P.M.** Pubblico Ministero.
Italian initialism meaning: Public Prosecutor. In England: Director of Public Prosecutions.
*Law.*
**PM** Pulpomesial.
**PM** Pulse Modulation.
*Telecommunications.*
**PM** Purchase Money.
**PM** Push Money.
**$PM_{2.5}$** Particles smaller than 2.5 micrometers.
**PMA** Pharmaceutical Manufacturers Association.
**PMA** Phorbol 12-myristate 13-acetate.
**PMA** Prix Maximum Autorisé.
**PMA** project military adviser.
conseiller militaire pour le project.
**PMA** Pyromellitic Acid.
PMA is used mainly in the production of lubricants, and waxes.
*Organic Chemistry.*
**PMAA** Poly (Methacrylic Acid).
**PMBX** Private Manual Branch Exchange.
**PMC** Pacific Marine Center.
**PMCs** Primary Muscle Cells (of the ascidian larvae).
*Ascidian Larvae; Biology; Cellular Biology; Developmental Biology.*
For further details see under: **SMCs**.
**PMD** Pelizaeus-Merzbacher Disease.
*Applied Neurobiology; Medicine; Molecular Biology.*
**PMD** Polarization Mode Dispersion.
**PMD** Postmortem Dump.
*Computer Programming.*
**PMD** Programmed Multiple Development.
**PMd** dorsal Premotor Cortex.
*Medicine; Neurobiology; Physiology; Working Memory.*
**PMDA** Pyromellitic Dianhydride.
$C_6H_2(C_2O_3)_2$ - Pyromellitic Dianhydride is a white powder having a melting point of 286°C.
*Organic Chemistry.*
**PMDF** Project Master Data File.
**PME** Personnel Management Evaluation.
**PME** Petites et Moyennes Entreprises.
French initialism meaning: Small- and Medium-Sized Firms / Enterprises.
**PME** principal mission element.
élément principal de la mission.
**PMEL** (NOAA's) Pacific Marine Environmental Laboratory (Seattle, U.S.A.).
For further details see under: **NOAA**.
**PMF** Probable Maximum Flood.
**PMF** Produzione di Massa Flessibile.
Italian initialism meaning: Flexible Mass Production.
**PMG** Postrnaster General.
**PMG** programme management group.
groupe de gestion du programme.
**PMH** Past Medical History.
**pmh** per man-hour.
**PMH** Previous Medical History.
**pMHC antigen** self peptide-Major Histocompatibility Complex antigen.
*Chemical Biology; Immunology; Molecular Biology; Pharmaceutical Research.*
**PMHP** p-Methane Hydroperoxide.
**PMHS** Poly (3-Methyl-4-Hydroxy Styrene).
**PMI** Piccole e Medie Industrie.
Italian initialism meaning: Small- and Medium-Sized Industries.
**PMI** Point of Maximal Impulse.
*Cardiology.*
**PMIP** Paleoclimate Modeling Intercomparison Project.
**PML** Plymouth Marine Laboratory (G.B.).
**PML** Probable Maximum Loss.
**PML protein** Promyelocytic Leukemia protein.
*Cancer Research.*
**PMLs** Polymorphonuclear Leukocytes.
**PM-LSM method** Polarization-Modulation Laser-Scanning Microscopy method.
*Chemical Engineering; Chemistry.*
**PMM** Pentamethylmelamine.
*Oncology.*
**PMM** Purchase-Money Mortgage.
**PMMA** Parallel Money Market Assets.
*Economics.*

**PMMA** Polymethyl Methacrylate.
Polymethyl methacrylate is a thermoplastic polymer used mainly in lighting fixtures and surgical appliances.
*Organic Chemistry.*
**PMMB** Program in Mathematics and Molecular Biology (U.S.A.).
**PMN cells** Polymorphonuclear cells.
Polymorphonuclear cells are also known as: polymorphonuclear leukocytes.
*Immunology.*
**PMN granulocyte** Polymorphonuclear granulocyte.
The polymorphonuclear granulocyte is also known as: Neutrophil.
*Immunology.*
**PMO** Pièces et Main d'Oeuvre.
French initialism meaning: Labour and Spare parts.
**PMO** Postal Money Order.
**PMO** project management office.
bureau de gestion de projet (BGP).
**PMOS** p-channel Metal Oxide Semiconductor.
**PMOXA** Poly(2-Methyloxazoline).
**PMP** Physically possible Maximum Precipitation.
For further details see under: **PMPs**.
**PMPs** Physically possible Maximum Precipitations.
*Disaster Management; Flood risk estimates.*
**pmr** point of minimum radius - referring to a curve.
*Mathematics.*
**PMR** Pressure Modulator Radiometer.
**PMR** principal military requirement.
besoin militaire principal.
**PMR** Projection Microradiography.
*Physics.*
**PMR** Proportionate Mortality Ratio.
**PMR** Proton Magnetic Resonance.
**PMRC** Proctor Maple Research Center.
**PMR features** Private Mobile Radio features.
*Digital Mobiles.*
**PMRI** Percentage of the Maximum contraction Rate Increase.
**PMRS** Performance Management and Recognition System.
**PMRTP** Program for Minority Research Training in Psychiatry.
**PMS** Premenstrual Syndrome.
*Medicine.*
**PMS** Public Message Service.
**PMS** Punto Morto Superiore.
Italian initialism meaning: Top Dead Center.
**PMSC** Political-Military Steering Committee [of the Partnership for Peace] (now called PfP-SC).
Comité directeur polito-militaire [du partenariat pour la paix] (maintenant appelé PfP-SC).
**PMSF** Phenylmethylsulfonyl fluoride.
**PMSG** Pregnant Mare's Serum Gonadotropin.
**PMS notation** Processor-Memory-Switch notation.
*Computer Technology.*
**PMT** Photomultiplier Tube.
**PMTs** Photomultiplier Tubes.
*Astrophysics; Geography; Physics.*
**PMV** Private Market Value.
**PMv** ventral Premotor Cortex.
*Brain Research; Primates; Psychology.*
**PMVR** Prime Mover.
*Mechanical Engineering.*
**PMW** Project Manager Workbench.
**PN** Packet Network.
*Computer Science.*
**PN**; **P/N** Part Number.
**PN** Please Note.
**Pn** Pontine nucleus.
**PN** Pordenone, Italy.
**PN**; **P.N.** Practical Nurse.
**PN**; **P/N** Promissory Note.
**PNA** Pacific North Atlantic.
**PNA** Palestinian National Authority.
The PNA was created in 1994.
*Archaeology.*
**PNA** Peptide Nucleic Acid.
**PNAd** Peripheral Node Addressin.
**PNA hydrocarbon** Polynuclear Aromatic Hydrocarbon.
*Coal Conversion Processes.*
**PNACL** Pacific Northwest Association of Church Libraries.
**PNAP** p-nitroaceto-phenone.
**PNAS** Proceedings of the National Academy of Sciences (U.S.A.).
**PNA Sector** Pacific / North American Sector.
**PNB** Philippine National Bank.
The Philippines fifth-largest bank.
**PNB** Polo Nazionale Bioelettronica (Marciana, Italy).
*Bioelectronics.*
**PNB** Polynorbene.
*Applied Physics.*
**PNB** Produit National Brut.
French initialism meaning: Gross National Product.
**PNB** Punjab National Bank.
*Indian Bank.*
**PNBC** Pacific Northwest Bibliography Center.
**PNC** Perinucleolar Compartment.
*Biochemistry; Cell and Molcular Biology.*

**PNC** Phosphonitrilic Chloride.
**PNC effect** Parity Nonconservation effect.
*Physics.*
**PND** Percentuale Normalizzata sui Depositi.
Italian initialism meaning: Standardized Deposit Percentage.
**PNdB** Perceived Noise decibel.
*Acoustics.*
**PNE** peaceful nuclear explosion.
explosion nucléaire à des fins pacifiques.
**PNe** Planetary Nebulae.
The discovery of the PNe dates back to Charles Messier, the French astronomer who in 1784 compiled and published a catalogue of nebulae.
*Astronomy; Astrophysics; Physics.*
**PNET** Peaceful Nuclear Explosion Treaty.
Traité sur les explosions nucléaires à des fins pacifiques.
**P.N.F.** Partito Nazionale Fascista.
Italian initialism meaning: National Fascist Party.
**PNG** Papua New Guinea.
**PNGLA** Papua New Guinea Library Association.
**PNGV program** Partnership for a New Generation of Vehicles program (U.S.A.).
The PNGV program began in September 1993.
*Clean-car Technology; Futuristic Cars; Industrial Research.*
**PNI** Participate but do Not Initiate.
**PNIP** Presidio Nazionale Igiene e Prevenzione.
**PNIPAAM** (Polymers based on) Poly (*N*-Isopropylacrylamide).
*Materials Science.*
**PNL** Pacific Northwest Laboratory - Run by Battelle.
**PNL** Prodotto Nazionale Lordo.
Italian initialism meaning: Gross National Product.
**PNL** Programmazione Neurolinguistica; Programmation Neuro-Linguistique.
Italian and French initialism meaning: Neurolinguistic Programming.
**PNLA** Pacific Northwest Library Association.
**PNM** Public Service company of New Mexico.
**PNMT** Phenylethanolamine-N-Methyltransferase.
*Neurobiology; Stress Hormones.*
**PNN** Prodotto Nazionale Netto.
Italian initialism meaning: Net National Product.
**PNNL** Pacific Northwest National Laboratory.
The Battelle Memorial Institute operates PNNL for the U.S. Department of Energy.
**PNR** Piani Nazionali di Ricerca (Italy).
Italian initialism meaning: National Research Plans.
**PNR** Programmi Nazionali di Ricerca (Italy).
Italian initialism meaning: National Research Programs.
**PNS** Paraneoplastic Neurodegenerative Syndrome.
PNS is an autoimmune neurological disease.
*Medicine; Neurobiology; Neurology; Neuropathology.*
**PNS** Peripheral Nervous System.
*Anatomy.*
**PNS** The airport code for Pensacola, Florida, U.S.A.
**PNTR** Permanent Normal Trade Relation.
**PNUA** Programma delle Nazioni Unite per l'Ambiente.
Italian initialism meaning: United Nations Environment Program.
**PNUCID** Programma delle Nazioni Unite per il Controllo Internazionale della Droga.
*U.N. Programs.*
**PNUD** Programme des Nations Unies pour le Développement.
French initialism meaning: United Nations Development Program.
**PNUS** Programma delle Nazioni Unite per lo Sviluppo.
Italian initialism meaning: United Nations Development Program.
**PNX**; **px** Pneumothorax.
*Medicine.*
**PNYA** Port of New York Authority (U.S.A.).
**PO** Patent Office.
**Po** Polonium.
Its name derives from the Medieval latin name for **Poland**.
*Chemistry; Symbols.*
**PO** Portugal.
**PO** Posta Ordinaria.
Italian acronym meaning: Regular Mail; First Class Mail.
**P.O.**; **p.o.** Postal Order.
**PO** Post Office.
**PO** Prato, Italy.
**PO** Preauthorization Order.
*Business; Commerce.*
**PO** Public Offering; Purchase Order.
*Business; Finance.*
**P.O.A.** Pontificia Opera di Assistenza.
Italian acronym meaning: Papal Welfare Organization.
**POA** Power Of Attorney.
**POA-BF** Preoptic Area and adjacent Basal Forebrain.
*Neurology; Neuroscience; Neurobiology; Psychiatry.*
**POADS** Portuguese air defence sector [obsolete].

Secteur de défense aérienne du Portugal [obsolète].
**POAG** Primary Open Angle Glaucoma.
*Glaucoma; Medicine; Ophtalmology; Pediatrics.*
**POB** personnel on board.
personnel à bord.
**POB** Point Of Business.
**POB** Post Office Box.
**POB** Public Oversight Board.
**POC** (oceanic) Particulate Organic Carbon.
*Earth System Science.*
**POC** point of contact.
1a. point de contact.
1b. responsable à contacter.
1c. interlocuteur.
**POC** Portafoglio Obbligazioni Consigliate (Italy).
*Banking.*
**poc**; **p.o.c.** port of call.
**POC** Preservation Of Capital.
*Business; Economics; Finance.*
**POD** Pay/Payment On Delivery.
**POD** 1. point of disembarkation.
1. point de débarquement.
2. probability of detection.
2. probabilité de détection.
**POD** Port Of Debarkation.
**POD** Port Of Departure.
**POD** Postoperative Day.
**POD** Probability Of Detection.
**POD** Proton Omnidirectional Detector.
**POE** 1. point of embarkation.
1. point d'embarquement.
2. point of entry/exit.
2. point d'entrée/de sortie (PES).
**POE** Port Of Embarkation.
**POE** Port Of Entry.
**POEM Center** Photonics and Optoelectronic Materials Center.
At Princeton University, N.Y. (U.S.A.).
**POEMS** Polyoxyethylene monostearate.
**POEOP** Polyoxyethyleneoxypropylene.
**POES** Polar-orbiting Operational Environmental Satellite.
**Pof** Piano dell'offerta formativa (Italy).
**POF** Plastic Optical Fibres.
10th International Conference, September 2001, Amsterdam (The Netherlands).
*Cable Technologies; Fibre Technologies; Materials Technologies.*
**POGO** Polar Orbiting Geophysical Observatories.
**POGO** Programmer-Oriented Graphics Operation.
**POINT** POlo per l'INnovazione Tecnologica (Bergamo, Italy).
*Technological Innovation; Scientific and Cultural Development.*
**POIS** Point Of Information and Service.
**POL** petroleum, oil(s) and lubricants.
produits pétroliers.
**Pol.** (abbr.) Polish.
*Languages.*
**pol.** (abbr.) politica; politico.
Italian abbreviation meaning: politics; political.
**Pol.** (abbr.) Polizia.
Italian abbreviation meaning: Police.
**POL** Proudman Oceanographic Laboratory (G.B.).
**POLAD** political advisor.
conseiller politique.
**POLARA software** Programming Architecture for Laboratory Automation software.
*Biotechnology; Laboratory Automation Software; Pharmaceuticals, Food and Chemical Industries.*
**POLDER** POLarization and Directionality of the Earth's Reflectances.
**POLEX** (abbr.) POLar EXperiment.
**POLFER** (abbr.) POLizia FERroviaria.
Italian abbreviation meaning: Railway Police.
**POLHE** see PHE.
voir PHE.
**POLSTRADA** (abbr.) POLizia STRADAle.
Italian abbreviation meaning: Highway Police.
**poly.** (abbr.) polygon.
*Mathematics.*
**poly.** (abbr.) polytechnic / polytechnical.
*Science.*
**POM** Particulate Organic Matter.
**pom.** (abbr.) pomeridiano.
Italian abbreviation meaning: p.m.; after noon.
**POMAC** Pareto Optimal Model Assessment Cycle.
*Ecology; Statistics.*
**POMC signaling** Pro-opiomelanocortin signaling.
*Biomedical Research; Endocrinology; Genetics; Molecular Biology; Obesity.*
**POMCUS** prepositioned organizational material configured in unit sets.
prépositionnement de matériel de dotation organique en lots unitaires.
**POMS** Polar Operational Meteorological Satellite.
**POMs** Polyoxometalates.
*Chemistry; Materials Science; Paper Industry.*
**POMSS** prepositioned organizational material storage site.
dépôt de prépositionnement de matériel de dotation organique.
**PON** Particulate Organic Nitrogen.
**PON** Program Opportunity Notice.

PON is a program of the U.S. Department of Energy. Issued in 1980.
*Energy; Oceanography.*
**PONA analysis** Paraffins, Olefins, Naphthenes, Aromatics analysis.
*Analytical Chemistry.*
**POO** Post-Office Order.
**POP** performance-oriented packaging.
emballage performant.
**POP** Point Of Presence.
Also: **Pops**.
**POP** Point-Of-Purchase.
*Business; Commerce.*
**pop.** (abbr.) population.
*Archaeology; Ecology; Statistics.*
**POP** Produzione di Origine Protetta (Italy).
**POPDA** Polyoxypropylenediamine.
**POPE** Palmitoyl-Oleoyl-Phosphatidylethanolamine.
**POPG** Palmitoyl-Oleoyl-Phosphatidylglycerol.
**POPITT** Point Of Presence In The Territory.
**POPs** Persistent Organic Pollutants.
*Toxic Chemicals.*
**POR** Payable-On-Receipt; Pay On Return.
*Business; Commerce.*
**por** port of refuge.
**PORTS** Physical Oceanographic Real-Time System.
**PORTS** Port Objective for Real-Time Systems.
**POS** Patent Office Society (U.S.A.).
**POS** Plan d'Occupation des Sols.
French acronym meaning: Zoning Regulations.
**POS** Point Of Sale.
**POS** Polar Orbiting Satellite.
**pos.** (abbr.) position.
**POS** The airport code for Port Of Spain, Trinidad.
**POSA** payments outstanding suspense account.
compte d'imputation provisoire (ou paiement en instance de régularisation).
**POSB** Post-Office Savings Bank (G.B.).
**POSDCORB** Planning, Organizing, Staffing, Directing, COordinating, Reporting and Budgeting.
**POSH** Probability Of Severe Hail.
*Meteorology.*
**POSS** passive optical satellite surveillance (system).
(système) passif de surveillance optique des satellites.
**poss.** (abbr.) possible.
**POSTECH** Pohong University Of Science and TECHnology (Korea).
**Postel** Posta elettronica.
Italian abbreviation meaning: electronic mail.
**PoS terminal** Place of Sale terminal.
*Computer Technology.*
**pot.** (abbr.) potential.
*Mathematics; Physics; Science.*
**POT** Program for Operational Trajectories.
**POTAD** Program for Operational Transport And Dispersion.
**POTS** Pediatric OCD Treatment Study.
For further details see under: **OCD**.
**POTS** Plain Old Telephone Service.
**POV** privately owned vehicle.
véhicule privé.
**POW** 1. prisoner of war.
1. prisonnier de guerre (PG 1.).
2. programme of work.
2. programme de travail (PD T).
**POWER** People Organized and Working for Economic Rebirth.
**POWER** PROFS Operational Weather Education and Research.
For further details see under: **PROFS**.
**POWF** Physical One-way Function.
*Cryptography.*
**POW/PRG** Programme of Work Review Group.
Groupe d'examen du programme de travail.
**p.p.** pacco postale.
Italian initialism meaning: parcel post.
**pp**; **pp.** pages.
**PP** 1. paper play.
1. jeu (ou exercice) fictif.
2. Papua New Guinea.
2. Papouasie-Nouvelle-Guinée.
3. primary participant.
3. participant principal.
**PP** Paper Profit.
**PP** Parallel Processor.
*Computer Science.*
**PP**; **pp** Parcel Post.
**PP** Parity Price.
*Business; Commerce.*
**pp** partial payment.
**PP** Pension Plan.
**PP** Periodically Poled.
*Non-linear materials; Physics.*
**PP** Peripheral Processor.
*Computer Technology.*
**PP**; **pp**; **p.p.** Per Procura.
Italian initialism meaning: By proxy.
*Law.*
**PP** Peyer's Patches.
Peyer's patches are nodules of lymphoid tissue usually located in the ileum.
*Cancer; Histology; Medicine.*
**PP** Ping-Pong.

*Computer Programming.*
**PP** Polypropylene.
Polypropylene is used in industry mainly to make films, fibers, and toys.
*Organic Chemistry.*
**PP** Porto Pagato; Port Payé.
Italian and French initialism meaning: carriage paid.
*Economics; International Trade.*
**P.P.** posa piano.
Italian initialism meaning: handle with care (on parcels).
**p.p.** postage paid.
**pp.** (abbr.) prepaid; prepay.
**PP** Primary Production.
**PP** Principe du Prénom.
French initialism meaning: first name system.
**PP** Private Property.
**PP** Public Power Corporation.
**pp** purchase price.
**P2P** Person to Person.
**P3P** Privacy Preferences Project.
**PP-9** Protoporphyrin-9.
**PPA** Parahippocampal Place Area.
*Cognitive Science; Psychology.*
**PPA** parité de pouvoir d'achat.
purchasing power parity (PPP 2.).
**p.p.a.** per power of attorney.
**PPA** Probalistic Performance Assessment.
*Geologic Disposal; Geologic Repository; Nuclear Engineering; Radioactive Waste; Radiological Sciences.*
**PP2A** Phosphoprotein Phosphatase 2A.
*Signal Transduction.*
**PPARC** Particle Physics and Astronomy Research Council.
PPARs are regulators of lipid stoarge and metabolism.
*Astronomy; Particle Physics; Science Program; Signal Transduction; Space Science.*
**PPARs** Peroxisomal Proliferator Activated Receptors.
*Biochemistry; Medical Nutrition; Nuclear Receptors.*
**PPB**; **ppb.**; **p.p.b.** parts per billion.
**PPB** Planning, Programming, Budgeting.
*Business; Economics; Finance.*
**PPB** Progetto Preliminare di Bilancio (Italy).
Italian initialism meaning: Preliminary Draft Balance.
**PPBS** Planning-Programming Budgeting System.
**PPC** Petroleum Planning Committee.
Comité d'étude des produits pétroliers.
**PPC** Point de Pénétration des Commandes.
French initialism meaning: Order Penetration Point.
**PPC** Point-to-Point Communication.
*Telecommunications.*
**PPCG** Provisional Policy Coordination Group.
**ppd.** (abbr.) postpaid.
**ppd** (abbr.) prepaid.
**PPD** Purchasing Power of the Dollar.
*Business; Finance.*
**PPD** Purified Protein Derivative.
*Bacteriology; Cancer Biology; Epidemiology; Public Health; Social Hygiene; Virology.*
**PPF** Publicité de Petit Format.
French initialism meaning: Case-Shopping.
**PPF diet** Plant-Polyphenol Free diet.
*Human Nutrition.*
**ppg** picopicogram.
**PPG** Program for Population Genetics (U.S.A. - China).
The PPG was launched in May 1996.
*Medicine; Epidemiology; Genetics; Population Biology.*
**PPH** Phosphopyruvate hydratase.
**PPI** Populist Party (Italy).
A group of ex-Christian Democrats in the ruling Center-left coalition (1998).
**PPI** Producer Price Index.
**PPIases** Peptidyl-Propyl cis-trans Isomerases.
*Cancer Biology; Cell Biology; Eukaryotic Gene Expression; Histone Deacetylases; Medicine; Oncology; Signal Transduction.*
**PPI repeater** Plan Position Indicator repeater.
**PPL** Particulier à Particulier en Ligne.
French initialism meaning: Person to Person.
**PPLL measuring device** Pulse Phase-Locked Loop measuring device.
*Biology; Crystallography; Developmental Neurobiology; Developmental Neurosurgery; Physiology; Psychobiology.*
**PPLO** Pleuropneumonialike organism.
*Medicine; Microbiology.*
**ppm** pulse per million.
**ppm** pulse per minute.
**PPM** Pulse Phase Modulation.
**PPM** Pulse-Position Modulation.
**ppmv.** parts per million by volume.
**PPND subjects** Pallido-Ponto-Nigral Degeneration subjects.
*Geriatric Medicine; Gerontology; Medicine; Neurodegenerative Diseases; Neurology; Pathology.*
**P2P networking** Peer-to-Peer networking.

*Electronic Business.*
**PPO** Principe de la Porte Ouverte.
French initialism meaning: Open-Door System.
**PP.OO.MM.** Pontificie Opere Missionarie.
Italian initialism meaning: Papal Mission Welfare Organization.
**PPOs** Preferred Provider Organizations.
**PPP** Indonesia's minority Moslem-oriented United development party.
**PPP** 1. Partenariat pour la paix.
1. Partnership for Peace (PfP).
2. purchasing power parity.
2. parité du pouvoir d'achat (PPA).
**PPP**; **ppp** Point to Point Protocol.
*Computers.*
**PPP** Prior-Participating Preferred.
*Stocks.*
**PPP** Public-Private Partnership.
**PPP Clients** Planned Production Proforma Clients.
**PPPI** precision plan position indicator.
indicateur de gisement de précision.
**PPPL** Princeton Plasma Physics Laboratory (U.S.A.).
*Fusion Research.*
**PPP theory** Purchasing Power Parity theory.
**PPQ** Polyphenylquinoxaline.
**PPQ-b-PS** Poly (Phenylquinoline)-*block*-polystyrene.
*Chemical Engineering; Chemistry.*
**PPR** Package Power Reactor.
*Nuclear Physics.*
**PPR** Peste des Petits Ruminants.
The peste des petits ruminants also known as: Pseudorinderpest is a viral disease of sheep and goats.
*Veterinary Medicine.*
**PPR** Photopolarimeter Radiometer.
*Astronomy; Space Science.*
**PPRB** Project and Priority Review Board [MBC].
Commission d'examen des projets et priorités [CBM].
**p.pro** per procuration.
**PPS** Parliamentary (or Principal) Private Secretary.
**PPS** Participating Preferred Stock.
**PPS** Plant Protection System.
**PPS** Point-to-Point System.
**PPS** Polygons Per Second.
*Graphics Processors.*
**PPS** precise positioning system.
système de positionnement de haute précision.
**PPS** Prior-Preferred Stock.
**pps** pulses per second.
**PPSEP** Prenyl Protein-Specific Endoprotease.
*Biochemistry; Chemistry.*
**PPSMT** Prenyl Protein-Specific Methyltransferase.
*Biochemistry; Chemistry.*
**PPSPT** Prenyl Protein-Specific Palmitoyltransferase.
*Biochemistry; Chemistry.*
**PP.SS.** Partecipazioni Statali.
Italian initialism meaning: State Shareholdings.
**ppt** parts per thousand.
*Medicine.*
**ppt** parts per trillion.
*Medicine.*
**PPT** Pielografia Percutanea Translombare.
*Medicine.*
**Ppt**; **ppt.** (abbr,) precipitate.
*Chemistry; Meteorology.*
**PPT** Processing Program Table.
*Electronics.*
**PPTases** Protein Phosphatases.
**pptn.** (abbr.) precipitation.
*Chemistry; Immunology; Meteorology.*
**pptv** parts per trillion by volume.
**PPV** Poly(p-Phenylene Vinylene).
**PPV** Pubblicità sul Punto di Vendita.
Italian initialism meaning: Point-of-Sale Advertising.
**PPV technology** Panoramic Passive View technology.
*Aviation.*
**Ppy** Polypyrrole.
A conductive film material.
**PPyV** Poly-p-Pridylene-Vinylene.
PPyV is a yellow light-emitting polymer.
**PQ** Parametric Quantum.
*Physics.*
**PQ** Permeability Quotient.
**PQ** Programma Quadro.
*European Community.*
**PQ molecules** Plastoquinone molecules.
*Proton and Electron Transport.*
**PQQ** Pyrroloquinoline quinone.
**PR** Packet Radio.
*Computer Science.*
**pr** (abbr.) pair.
*Electricity.*
**pr** pair.
Also: Kinematic pair.
*Mechanical Engineering.*
**PR** Parallel Representation.
*Computer Programming.*
**PR** Parity Ratio.
**PR** Parma, Italy.
**P.R.** Partito Radicale.

Italian initialism meaning: Radical Party.
**PR** Pattern Recognition.
*Acoustical Engineering; Computer Programming; Psychology; Robotics.*
**pr.** (abbr.) payroll.
**PR** Personal Representative.
**P.R.** Piano Regolatore.
Italian initialism meaning: Town-Planning Regulations.
**PR** Pink Rock.
*Rock Types.*
For further details see under: **IMP**.
**PR** Physical Record.
*Computer Technology.*
**P.R.** Poste Restante.
**Pr** Praseodymium.
Praseodymium is used mainly in glazes, lasers, and thermoelectric materials.
*Chemistry; Symbols.*
**PR** Preliminary Report.
**Pr** Presbyopia.
*Medicine.*
For further details see under: **P**.
**pr** (abbr.) price.
**PR** Price Rate.
**PR** Primary Radar.
Primary radar is also known as: Primary Surveillance Radar.
*Engineering.*
**pr.** (abbr.) principal.
**pr** (abbr.) priority.
Also: **pri**.
**PR** Prix de Revient.
French initialism meaning: cost price.
**PR** Progress Report; Project Report.
**Pr** Propyl.
*Organic Chemistry.*
**PR** Pro Rata.
**Pr.** (abbr.) Provençal.
*Languages.*
**PR**; **P.R.** Pubbliche Relazioni.
Italian initialism meaning: public relations.
**PRA** Paint Research Association (G.B.).
**PRA** Planetary Radio Astronomy.
**PRA** Probabilistic Risk Assessment.
*Risk Analysis (Satellites).*
**P.R.A.** Pubblico Registro Automobilistico.
Italian acronym meaning: Office where Motor Vehicles are Registered.
**PRAC** Phosphoribosylformiminoimidazole Carboxamide.
**PRAD** Phosphoribosylaminoimidazole.
**PRAL** Patrulla de Reconocimiento de Alcance Largo (El Salvador).
**PRA method** Participatory Rural Appraisal method.
*Biodiversity.*
**PRAs** Probabilistic Risk Assessments.
**PRB** Polar Research Board (U.S.A.).
**PRB** (Financial) Policy Review Board.
Commission d'examen de la politique (financière).
**PRB** Poundreries Réunies de Belgiques (Belgium).
**pRB** Retinoblastoma protein.
*Basic Sciences; Biology; Biomedical Research; Cancer Research; Genetics.*
**PRB's** Population Reference Bureau's.
**PRC** The People's Republic of China.
**PRC** Phase-Response Curve.
**PRC** Price Regulation Committee.
**PRC1** Polycomb Reprensive Complex 1.
For further details see under: **PcG proteins**.
**PRD** Party of the Democratic Revolution (Mexico).
**PRD** Presidential Review Directive.
**PRD technique** Planar Reactive Deposition technique.
**pre.** (abbr.) prefix.
**prec.** (abbr.) preceded; precedent; preceding.
**PRECIS** Preserved Context Index System.
Used by the British National Bibliography ever since 1971.
**PRECISE** PRospects for Extra-mural and Clinical Information Systems Environments.
*Medicine.*
**PRE-EX** pre-exercise (conference).
(conférence) de pré-exercice.
**pref.** (abbr.) prefazione.
Italian abbreviation meaning: introduction; foreword; preface; proem; prologue.
**Pref.** (abbr.) preference; preferred.
**PR effect** Photorefractive effect.
*Optical Sciences.*
**Pre-IPC** pre-initial planning conference.
conférence de planification pré-initiale.
**PREM** Preliminary Reference Earth Model.
**prem.** (abbr.) premium.
**pre-mRNAs** precursors of messengers RNAs.
*Biomedical Research; Pathobiology.*
**PREP** Post-doctoral Research and Education Program.
PREP is funded by the U.S. NIH.
*U.S. Program.*
For further details see under: **NIH**.
**PREPs** Programmed Electronics Patterns.
**PREREADEX** pre-readiness exercise.
exercice de préparation au combat.
**Pres.** (abbr.) President.

**pres.** (abbr.) presumed.
**pre-tRNA** transfer RNA precursor.
*Biotechnology; Cellular Biology; Endonucleases; Molecular Biology.*
**prev.** (abbr.) previous.
**PREVENT** Pacific northwest REgional Visibility Experiment using Natural Tracers.
**PRF** Poisson Random Field.
Named after the French mathematician and physicist Siméon Denis **Poisson**.
*Biometrics; Evolutionary Biology; Genetics; Mathematics; Organismic Biology.*
**PRF** Prolactin-Releasing Factor.
*Endocrinology.*
**prf.** (abbr.) proof.
*Engineering; Food Technology; Graphic Arts; Mathematics.*
**PRF** Pulse Repetition Frequency.
Also: Pulse Repetition Rate.
*Electricity.*
**PRG** Piano Regolatore Generale (Italy).
*Building Areas.*
**PR genes** Pathogenesis-Related genes.
*Biochemistry; Cell Biology; Immunology; Medicine; Molecular Biophysics.*
**PRH** point de référence de l'hélicoptère.
helicopter reference point (HRP 1.).
**PRH** Prolactin-Releasing Hormone.
**PRI** Institutional Revolutionary Party (Mexico).
**P.R.I.** Partito Radicale Italiano.
Italian acronym of the: Italian Radical Party.
**P.R.I.** Partito Repubblicano Italiano.
Italian acronym of the: Italian Republican Party.
**PRI** Pharmaceutical Research Institute (U.S.A.).
**PRI** President of the Royal Institute (of painters in water colours).
**pri** primary winding.
Primary winding is also known as: primary coil.
*Electricity.*
**pri.** (abbr.) priority.
Also: **pr**.
**PRI** Project for a Retinal Implant.
A joint project of the Massachusetts Eye and Ear Infirmary (MIT) and the Harvard Medical School.
*Ophtalmology.*
**PRIDE** Parents' Resources Institute for Drug Education (U.S.A.).
**PRIH** Prolactin Release-Inhibiting Hormone.
**PRIMAVERA** Parks Resources Information MAnagement Via Environmental Remotely sensed data Analysis.
Launched in Rome on 16th October 1998.
*European Community Project.*
**primavera** The above acronym was coined using the Italian word "primavera" which means: (*Botany*) primrose; cowslip. Also: spring.
**PRIME** Practical Reuse Improvement MEtrics.
*European Community Project.*
**PRIME** Prediction and Retrospective Ionospheric Modelling over Europe.
*European Community Project.*
**prin.** (abbr.) principal.
**PRINTIT** Publishers Reusable Integrated Network Toolkits for Information Technologies.
*European Community Project.*
**PRL** Physical Review Letters.
**PRL** Plant Research Laboratory.
**PRL** Prolactin.
Prolactin is also known as: Lactogenic Hormone. PRL is present in the neural tissues of vertebrates and invertebrates.
*Endocrinology.*
**PRLA** Puerto Rico Library Association.
**PRLR** Prolactin Receptor.
For further details see under: **PRL**.
**PRM** Pattern Recognition Molecules.
**PRMT** plan des ressources à moyen terme.
medium-term resource plan (MTRP).
**PRNs** Package Recovery Notes.
Europe's first exchange for trading recyclable commodities was launched in London in November 1998. European Union Regulations require member States to recover 50-65% of waste packaging materials (2001) and recycle at least half that amount.
*Recycling.*
**Pr.O.** Press Officer.
**pro.** (abbr.) procurement.
**PRO** Public Records Office.
**P.R.O.** Public Relations Officer.
**PROBE** Pilot Radiation OBservation Experiment.
**proc.** (abbr.) procuration.
**prod.** (abbr.) product; production.
**prof.** (abbr.) professional; professor.
**proff.** (abbr.) professori.
Italian abbreviation meaning: professors.
**PROFS** Program for Regional Observing and Forecasting Services (U.S.A.).
**prof.ssa** (abbr.) professoressa.
Italian abbreviation meaning: lady-teacher; lady-professor.
**PROI** Project Return On Investment.
*Business; Finance.*
**proj.** (abbr.) project.
**PROM** Premature Rupture Of the amniotic Membrane.

*Perinatal Research.*
**PROM** Programmable Read-Only Memory.
*Computer Technology.*
**PROMEC Project** Power and Communications Sectors Modernization and Rural Services Project (Ecuador).
Of the World Bank / IDA.
**PROMETHEUS** Program for European Traffic with Highest Efficiency and Unprecedent Safety.
*1960/2003 Programs.*
**PROMIS** PROgrammable Multidimensional Injection System.
**PROMIS** PROMotori di Iniziative Sociali (Italy).
**PROMISE** Predictability and variability of monsoons, and their agricultural and hydrological impacts of climate change.
PROMISE is a major 3-year research programme funded by the European Commission under 5FP.
For further details see under: **5FP**.
**prop.** (abbr.) property.
**ProPlanT** Production Planning Technology.
**PRORA** PROcedura Rischi Anomali.
Italian acronym meaning: Anomalous Risks Procedure.
*Banking.*
**PROSUB** probable submarine.
sous-marin probable.
**PROSUMER** (abbr.) Producer-Consumer (U.S.A.).
**prot.** (abbr.) protein.
**ProT** Prothymosin-α.
*Apoptosis; Oncoproteins.*
**PROTAC** proposed tactical (amendment message).
(message de) proposition de modification tactique.
**PRO.T.E.O.** PROgetto Tecniche Ecologiche e Occupazione (Italy).
*Transnational Projects.*
**prov.** (abbr.) provincia.
Italian abbreviation meaning: district; province.
**provv.** (abbr.) provveditore.
Italian abbreviation meaning:.
*Commerce* - Purveyor.
*Military* - Quartermaster-general.
*Schools* - Superintendent.
**provv.** (abbr.) provvisorio.
Italian abbreviation meaning: provisional; provisory; temporary; interim.
**PROWL system** PROcedure Work Log system.
**prox.** (abbr.) proximate.
**PrP$^c$** normal, cellular Prion Protein.
*Biochemistry; Biophysics; Creutzfeldt-Jakob Disease; Prion Diseases.*
**PRR** Pattern Recognition Receptor.
**PRR** Pulse Repetition Rate.
Pulse Repetition Rate is also known as: Pulse Recurrence Rate, Pulse Repetition Frequency.
*Electricity.*
**Prr1** Poliovirus receptor-related protein 1.
*Medicine.*
**PRRs** Pattern Recognition Receptors.
**PRS** Power Relay Satellite.
**PRS** President of the Royal Society.
**PRS** Programma Regionale di Sviluppo.
Italian initialism meaning: Regional Development Program.
**PRT** Particolare Rilevanza Tecnologica.
Italian initialism meaning: Particular Technological Importance.
**PRTase** Phosphoribosyltransferase.
**PRTD** point de référence de transmission de données.
data link reference point (DLRP).
**PRTLI** Programme for Research in Third Level Institutions.
The PRTLI is administered by the Higher Education Authority of Ireland and started in 1999.
**PRTM** Printing Response-Time Monitor.
**Pruss.** (abbr.) Prussian.
*Languages.*
**PRV** Porcine Pseudorabies Virus.
*Medicine; Microbiology; Immunology; Oral Health.*
**PRWORA** Personal Responsibility and Work Opportunity reconciliation Act.
A U.S. 1996 Act.
*U.S. Welfare System.*
**PS** Packet Switching.
*Computer Science.*
**PS** Parallel Storage.
*Computer Technology.*
**P.S.** Partita Semplice.
Italian initialism meaning: Single entry.
**P/S**; **P.S.** Passenger Steamer.
**PS** Peel Strength.
*Engineering.*
**PS** Pesaro e Urbino, Italy.
**PS** Phonetic Search.
*Computer Programming.*
**PS** Phosphatidylserine.
**PS** Photosystem.
*Biochemistry.*
**ps** picosecond.
*Metrology.*
**ps.** (abbr.) pieces.
**ps.** (abbr.) poise.
*Fluid Mechanics.*
For further details see under: **P**.

**PS** Polystyrene.
Polystyrene is a nonpolar polymer glassy at room temperature. It is used mainly in packaging, and insulation.
*Organic Chemistry.*
**PS** Post Scriptum.
**PS** Power Steering.
*Mechanical Engineering.*
**PS** Power Supply.
*Electricity; Electronics.*
**PS** Preferred Stock.
**PS** Presenilin.
*Apoptosis; Genetics; Life Sciences; Medicine; Neurology.*
**PS** Price Spreading.
**PS** Profit Sharing.
*Business; Finance.*
**P.S.** Pubblica Sicurezza.
Italian initialism meaning: Police; Public Safety.
**P/S**; **P.S.** Public Sale.
**PSA** Pacific Science Association (U.S.A.).
**PSA** Precipitation Series Algorithm.
**PSA** Prostate Specific Antigen.
**PSA** 1. provisional site acceptance.
1. réception provisoire de la station (ou du site) (RPS).
2. provisional system acceptance.
2. réception provisoire du système.
**PSA** Public Service Advertising.
**PSAs** Production Sharing Agreements.
**PSA test** Prostate Specific Antigen test.
*Prostate Cancer.*
**PsbMV** Pea seed-borne Mosaic Virus.
*Virology.*
**PSBN**; **Psbn** Peoplesoft Business Network.
Peoplesoft was founded in 1987.
**PS-*b*-PAA** Polystyrene-*b*-Poly (Acrylic Acid).
*Chemistry.*
**PSBR** Public Sector Borrowing Requirement.
**PSC** Phylogenetic Species Concept.
*Phylogenomics.*
**PSC** Pittsburgh Supercomputing Center (U.S.A.).
**PSC** Polar Science Center (U.S.A.).
**PSC** Polar Stratospheric Cloud.
For further details see under: **PSCs**.
**PSC** 1. Political and Security Committee.
1. Comité politique et de sécurité (COPS).
2. Principal Subordinate Command (Commander) [obsolete - replaced by SRC].
2. Commandement (commandant) subordonné principal (CSP) [obsolète - remplacé par SRC].
**PSCM** Permanent-Split Capacitor Motor.
PSCM is also known as: Capacitor Start-Run Motor.
*Electricity.*
**PSc protein** Posterior Sex Combs proteins.
For further details see under: **PcG proteins**.
**PSCs** Polar Stratospheric Clouds.
*Atmospheric Physics; Climate; Geophysics; Meteorology; Middle Atmosphere Research; Space Research.*
**PSD** POL storage depot.
dépôt de stockage de produits pétroliers.
**PSD** Population and Sustainable Development.
*Biodiversity.*
**PSD** Prevention of Significant Deterioration.
**PSD-95** Postsynaptic Density Protein-95.
*Signal Transduction.*
**PSE** Pacific coast Stock Exchange.
**PSE** Packet-Switching Exchange.
**PSE** PfP staff element.
élément d'état-major du PPP.
**psec.** Picosecond.
*Metrology.*
**PSF** Pattern Sensitive Fault.
*Computer Programming.*
**PSF** peace support force.
force de soutien de la paix.
**psf** pounds per square foot.
*Metrology.*
**PSF** Program Support Facility.
**PSI** Pacific Stratus Investigation.
**PSI** Pacific Sulfur Investigation.
**PSI** Paul Scherrer Institute (Canton of Aargau, Switzerland).
The PSI is a multidisciplinary Federal Research Institute.
*Astrophysics; Biology; Energy & Environmental Research; Materials Science; Medicine; Particle Physics; Solid-state Physics.*
**PSI** Plasma Source Instrument.
*Geophysics; Space Science.*
**psi** pounds per square inch.
*Metrology.*
**psia**; **p.s.i.a.** pounds per square inch absolute.
**PSIC** Passive Solar Industries Council.
The residential builder's guidelines developed by Balcomb and the PSIC are being used by architects and engineers to create comfortable, affordable, *Energy-Conserving Buildings.*
**psid** pounds per square inch differential.
*Engineering.*
**psig** pounds per square inch gauge.
*Mechanics.*

**PSII photosynthesis** Photosystem II photosynthesis.
*Biochemistry; Molecular Biology.*
**PSK** Phase-Shift Keying.
*Telecommunications.*
**PSL** Polish Peasants' Party (Poland).
**PSLA** Pennsylvania School Library Association (U.S.A.).
**PSM** Presomitic Mesoderm.
*Developmental Biology.*
**PSMG** Primary coolant System Motor Generator.
**PSMSL** Permanent Service for Mean Sea Level (U.S.A.).
**PS muscle** Pleurosternal muscle.
**PSN** Piano Sanitario Nazionale (Italy).
Italian initialism meaning: National Health Plan.
**PSN** Piano Spaziale Nazionale (Italy).
Italian initialism meaning: National Space Plan.
**PSO** 1. peace support operation.
1. opération de soutien de la paix.
2. primary strike objective.
2. premier objectif de frappe.
**PSP** Paralytic Shellfish Poisoning.
**PSp** Pneumothorax Spontané.
*Medicine.*
**PSP** portée sonar prédite.
predicted sonar range (PSR).
**PSP** Pseudostatic Spontaneous Potential.
*Petroleum Engineering.*
**PSP** The airport code for Palm Springs, California, U.S.A.
**PSPA** peace support psychological activities [PSYOP(s)].
Activités psychologiques de soutien de la paix [PSYOP(s)].
**PSPB copolymers** Polystyrene-Polybutadiene copolymers.
*Chemical Engineering; Materials; Physics.*
**PSPC** Positional Sensitive Proportional Counter.
*Astronomy; Astrophysics.*
**PSR** predicated sonar range.
portée sonar prédicte (PSP).
**PSRA** programme spécial de revêtement d'aérodrome.
special aerodrome pavement programme (SAPP).
**PSRMLS** Pacific Southwest Regional Medical Library Service.
**PSRO** Professional Standards Review Organization.
**PSS** Parallel Search Storage.
*Computer Technology.*
**PSS** Pressure Suppression System.
**PSS** Public Services Satellite.
**PST** Pacific Standard Time.
**PST** portée sonar tactique.
tactical sonar range (TSR).
**PST** Profit-Sharing Trust.
**PSTC histograms** Peri-Stimulus-Time Cumulative histograms.
**PSTD** Programma Sviluppo delle Tecnologie Didattiche (Italy).
**PSTH** Peri-Stimulus/Peristimulus Time Histogram.
*Neurology; Neuroscience; Psychiatry.*
**PSTHs** Peri-Stimulus / Peristimulus Time Histograms.
*Neurology; Neuroscience; Psychiatry.*
**PSTN** Public Switched Telephone Network.
*Circuit-Switched Networks.*
**PSTV** Potato Spindle Tuber Viroid.
**PSU** Pennsylvania State University (U.S.A.).
**PSU** Primary Sampling Unit.
**PSV** Paleosecular Variation.
**PSVP** pilot secure voice project.
projet pilote de cryptophonie.
**PSW** Processor Status Word.
Processor status word is also known as: Status Mode.
*Computer Technology.*
**PSYOP** (abbr.) PSYchological OPerations.
PSYOP is also known as: Psychological Warfare.
*Military Science.*
**PSZ** Partially Stabilized Zirconia.
*Materials.*
**PSZN** Pubblicazioni della Stazione Zoologica di Napoli (Italy).
**PT** Lead Titanate.
For further details see under: **$PbTiO_3$**.
**PT**; **P.T.** Pacific Time.
**PT** Paper Tape.
*Computer Programming.*
**PT** Parallel Transfer; Parallel Transmission.
*Computer Technology.*
**pt.** (abbr.) part.
**p.t.** part time.
**pt** (abbr.) particular.
**pt.** (abbr.) patient.
*Medicine.*
**pt** (abbr.) payment.
**PT**; **P.T.** Physical Therapy.
*Medicine.*
**PT**; **P.T.** Physical Training.
**pt.** (abbr.) pint.
*Metrology.*
**PT** pipeline time.
temps d'acheminement.
**PT** Pistoia, Italy.
**PT** Planum Temporale.

*Anatomy; Medicine; Neurobiology; Otolaryngology.*

**Pt** The chemical symbol for Platinum.
The word platinum derives from the Spanish word "silver".
*Chemistry; Metallurgy; Symbols.*

**pt** (abbr.) point.
*Geography; Graphic Arts; Navigation; Mathematics; Military Science; Ordnance; Robotics; Transportation Engineering.*

**PT** Polythiophene.

**pt.** (abbr.) port.

**PT** Portugal Telecom.

**P.T.** Preferential Tariffs.

**P/T** Pressure / Temperature.

**Pt** Private trust; Profit taking.
*Business; Finance.*

**p/t** pronti contro termine.
Italian initialism meaning: Spot against forward; repurchase agreement; swap.
*Banking.*

**PT** Prothrombin Time.

**P.T.** Purchase Tax.

**PTA** Percutaneous Transluminal Angioplasty.
Percutaneous transluminal angioplasty is also known as: Balloon Angioplasty.
*Surgery.*

**pta.** (abbr.) peseta (Spain).
Now: EURO/EUR €). Became ECU (European Single Currency) with effect from January 2002.
*Currencies.*

**PTA** Phosphotungstic Acid.
Phosphotungstic Acid is also known as: Phosphowolframic Acid; Tungstophosphoric Acid.
*Inorganic Chemistry.*

**PTA** Plasma Thromboplastin Antecedent.

**PTA** Prepaid Ticket Advice.

**PTA** primary training activities.
activités d'entraînement de base.

**PTA** Purified Terephthalic Acid.

**PTA-test** Peroxidase Treponemal Antibody test.
*Medicine.*

**PTB** N-Phenacylthiazolium Bromide.
*Chemistry.*

**PTB** Protein Tyrosine Binding.
*Cancer Research; Cell Biology; Signal Transduction.*

**PtBA** Poly (*tert*-Butyl-Acrylate).

**PTB domains** PTyr-Binding domains.

**PtBMA** Poly (*tert*-Butyl-Methacrylate).

**PTB protein** Polypyrimidine Tract-Binding protein.
PTB is also known as: hnRNPI.
*Cell Biology; Molecular Medicine; Nucleic Acids.*

**PTBT** Partial Test Ban Treaty.
Traité sur l'interdiction partielle des essais (d'armes nucléaires).

**PTC** Phenylthiocarbamide.

**PTC** Plasma Thromboplastin.
*Medicine.*

**PTCL** Pakistan Telecommunications Corporation.
88% owned by the State.

**PTCs** Premature Termination (nonsense) Codous.
The PTCs in mDNA result in its accelerated degradation which is known as: NMD process.
*Immunology; Medicine; Microbiology.*
For further details see under: **mDNA** and **NMD process**.

**ptd.** (abbr.) painted; pointed; printed.

**PTD** Post-Tuning Drift.
*Electronics.*

**PTD** Protein Transduction Domain.
*Cell Biology.*

**PTE** Portuguese Escudo.
Now: EURO/EUR (€). Became ECU (European Single Currency) with effect from January 2002.
*Currencies.*

**PTE** Pretax Earnings.

**Pte** (abbr.) Private (Limited Company).

**PTEN** Phosphatase and TENsin Homolog Deleted on Chromosome.
*Cancer Research; Cell Biology; Gliomas; Molecular Biology; Tumor Suppressors.*

**PTFB** Plasma Thromboplastin Factor B.
*Medicine.*

**PTFE** Polytetrafluoroethylene.
Polytetrafluoroethylene is resistant to heat and chemicals. It is used mainly for electrical insulation.
*Materials.*

**PTG** période de tension ou temps de guerre.
time of tension or war (TTW 1.).

**ptg.** (abbr.) printing.

**PTGS** Posttranscriptional Gene Silencing.
*Biological Sciences; Gene Expression; Genetics; Molecular Biology; Molecular Genetics.*

**PTH** Parathyroid Hormone.
Parathyroid Hormone is also known as: Parathormone; Parathyrin.
*Endocrinology.*

**PTHrP** Parathyroid Hormone-related Protein.
The PTHrP is produced mainly in the perichondrium.
*Developmental Biology; Endocrinology; Genetics; Medicine.*

**PTI** Palomar Testbed Interferometer.
*Astronomy; Astrophysics; Planet Search.*

**PTKs** Protein Tyrosine Kinases.
*Biological Chemistry; Life Sciences.*
**PTLA** Philippine Theological Library Association.
**PTLO** Patent & Technology Licensing Office.
**PTM** Pulse-Time Modulation.
**PTMEG** Polytetramethylene Ether Glycol.
**PTMS** p-toluidine-m-sulfonic acid.
**PTO** Patent and Trademark Office (U.S.A.).
**PTO**; **P.T.O.** Please Turn Over.
**PTO** public telecommunications operator.
opérateur de réseau public de télécommunications.
**PTO** Public Trustee Office.
**PTOM** Paesi e Territori d'Oltremare.
Italian initialism meaning: Overseas Countries and Territories.
**PTP** Posto Telefonico Pubblico.
Italian initialism meaning: Public Telephone.
**PTP** Posttetanic Potentiation.
PTP is a common form of short-term synaptic plasticity that is considered to be presynaptic.
*Medicine; Neurology and Behaviour; Psychiatry; Surgery.*
**PTPs** Protein Tyrosine Phosphatases.
*Cancer Research; Pharmaceuticals; Signal Transduction.*
**PTRP** Post-Treatment Resource Program.
The Memorial Sloan-Kettering's Conference will be held on 18th October 2003.
*Cancer Survivorship.*
**PTSA** p-toluene Sulfonamide.
**PTSD** Posttraumatic Stress Disorder.
*Biological Sciences; Psychiatric Nosology.*
**PTS experiment** Pressurized Thermal Shock experiment.
**PTT** Partial Thromboplastin Time.
**PTT** Pulse Transit Time.
*Aging; Antiaging; Arteriosclerosis; Geriatrics; Gerontology.*
**PTTG** Pituitary Tumor-Transforming Gene.
*Biochemistry; Cell Cycle.*
**PTU** 6-Propyl-2-Thiouracil.
PTU is a compound that may induce goiter.
*Toxicology.*
**PTX** Pertussis Toxin.
PTX is a toxin produced by the bacterium that causes whooping cough.
*Immunology; Microbiology; Toxicology.*
**PTY** The airport code for Panama City, Panama.
**PTY**; **pty** (abbr.) Proprietary.
**PU** 1. Guinea Bissau.
1. Guinée-Bissau.
2. participating unit.
2. unité participante (UP 2.).
**PU** Peptic Ulcer.
*Medicine.*
**Pu** The chemical symbol for Plutonium.
Plutonium is a reactive metallic element having the atomic number 94, and a melting point of 640°C. Plutonium is used in nuclear weapons. Named for the planet **Pluto**.
*Chemistry; Symbols.*
**PU** Propellant Utilization.
**Pub.** (abbr.) public.
**Pub.** (abbr.) Published; Publisher.
**PUC** Public Utility Commission (U.S.A.).
**PUEO** Probing the Universe with Enhanced Optics.
*Curvature Systems; Optics.*
**pueo** The above acronym was coined using the Hawaiian word pueo which is the name of a Hawaiian owl.
**PUFA** Polyunsaturated Fatty Acid.
**PUFAs** Polyunsaturated Fatty Acids.
**PU foam** Polyurethane foam.
PU foam is used mainly for padding or insulation.
*Materials.*
**PUK** Patriotic Union of Kurdistan.
**PUK** Personal Unblocking Code.
*Cellular Phones.*
**Put** Piano urbano del traffico.
Italian acronym meaning: Traffic Urban Plan.
**put.** (abbr.) putative.
**P.V.** Par Value.
**PV** Pavia, Italy.
**PV** Potential Vorticity.
*Fluid Mechanics.*
**PV** Pression Veineuse.
French initialism meaning: Venous Pressure; Intravenous Tension.
*Medicine.*
**PV** Processo Verbale; Procès Verbal.
Italian and French initialism meaning: minutes; official records (legal); summary of the proceedings.
**p.v.** prossimo venturo.
Italian initialism meaning: next month.
**PVA** Polyvinyl Alcohol.
Polyvinyl alcohol is used mainly in adhesives, and as a thickener.
**Pvac** Polyvinyl acetate.
Pvac is used mainly in inks, latex paints, and adhesives.
*Organic Chemistry.*
**PVAMC** Portland Veterans Affairs Medical Center (U.S.A.).
**PVB** Polyvinyl Butyral.
Polyvinyl butyral is also known as: Butvar.

*Materials.*
**PVBC** Polyvinyl Benzyl Chloride.
**PVC** Polyvinyl Chloride.
*Organic Chemistry.*
**PVC** Pression Veineuse Centrale.
French initialism meaning: Central Venous Pressure.
*Medicine.*
**PVD** Pays en Voie de Développement.
French initialism meaning: Developing Nation; Developing Country.
**PVD** Peripheral Vascular Disease.
*Medicine.*
**PVD** The airport code for Providence, Rhode Island.
**PVDF** Polyvinylidene Fluoride.
Polyvinylidene fluoride is used mainly for protective coatings, and for gaskets.
*Organic Chemistry.*
**P/VDF-TrFE copolymer** Poly/Vinylidene Fluoride-Trifluoroethylene copolymer.
*Electrical Engineering; Materials Research; Ferroelectric Polymers.*
**PVD hard coatings** Physical Vapor Deposition hard coatings.
*Basic Energy Science; Materials Science; Physics of Thin Films; Superlattice Technology; Vacuum Coaters.*
**PVE** Polyvinyl (ethyl) Ether.
*Organic Chemistry.*
**PVEM** Green Ecologist Party of Mexico.
**P-V-E states** Pressure-Volume-internal Energy states.
*Shock Physics.*
**PVK** Poly(N-Vinylcarbazole).
**PVM** Polyvinyl Methyl Ether.
PVM is used mainly in pressure-sensitive adhesives, and in inks.
*Organic Chemistry.*
**PVMaT** Photovoltaic Manufacturing Technology.
PVMaT, administered for DOE by NREL, is a U.S. Government/industry partnership aimed at identifying and solving manufacturing problems that affect module cost and production. The program is coordinated through the joint efforts of DOE, NREL, Sandia National Laboratories, and the Solar Energy Industries Association.
*Photovoltaic Modules.*
For further details see under: **DOE** and **NREL**.
**PVMTI** Photovoltaic Market Transformation Initiative.
**PVN** Paraventricular Nucleus.
*Physiology.*
**PVO** Principal Veterinary Officer.
**PVO** private volunteer organization.
organisation bénévole.
**PVP** Polyvinylpyrrolidine.
**PVR** Peripheral Vascular Resistance.
*Aging; Antiaging; Geriatrics; Gerontology.*
**Pvr** Poliovirus receptor.
**PVR** The airport code for Puerto Vallarta, Mexico.
**PVS** Paesi in Via di Sviluppo.
Italian initialism meaning: Developing Countries; Less-Developed Countries.
**PVS** Photovoltaic System.
**PVS** Pressure Vessel Surveillance.
**PVST** port visit.
escale.
**PVT** par voie télégraphique.
**PVT** Pressure, Volume, Temperature.
**pvt** (abbr.) private.
**PVX** Potexvirus - Potato Virus X Group.
*Biological Sciences; Crop Research; Gene Silencing; Plant Recombination; Virology.*
**p.w.** per week.
Also: **pw**.
**pW** picowatt.
*Metrology.*
**PWA** Professional Women's Association (Rome, Italy).
**PWA** Provincial Waterworks Authority (Thailand).
**PWC** Pacific Wave Communications (U.S.A.).
Los Angeles-based.
*Polymer Broadband Modulation.*
**PWC** principal warfare commander.
commandant principal de lutte.
**PWF** Present Worth Factor.
*Business; Finance.*
**PWG** permanent working group.
groupe de travail permanent.
**PWHQ** primary war headquarters.
quartier général de guerre principal (QGGP).
**PWM** Poke-Weed Mitogen.
**PWM** The airport code for Portland, Maine, U.S.A.
**PWP** Partnership work programme (plan).
programme (plan) de travail du Partenariat.
**pwr**; **pwr.** power.
*Engineering; Mathematics; Physics; Optics.*
**PWR** Pressurized Water Reactor.
*Nucleonics.*
**PWRS** prepositioned war reserve stocks.
stocks de réserves de guerre prépositionnés.
**PWSB** Parrotfish White Spot Biting.
*Coral Disease.*
**PWSOIL database** Prince William Sound OIL database.

The PWSOL database contains analyses of hydrocarbons present in animals and plants.
**pwt.** Pennyweight.
*Metrology.*
**Px**; **px** patient; patients.
**PX** Physical Examination.
*Medicine.*
**px** pneumothorax.
*Medicine.*
**px.** prix.
French abbreviation meaning: price; cost; charge.
**PX** Private Exchange.
**Px** Prognosis.
*Medicine.*
**PXD** post-exercise discussion.
débat postérieur à l'exercice.
**PXE** post-exercise evaluation.
évaluation postérieure à l'exercice.
**PXE** Pseudo-Xanthoma Elasticum.
PXE is an inherited disease that causes calcification of connective tissue.
*Genetics.*
**PXR** post-exercise report.
compte rendu postérieur à l'exercice.
**PY** Paraguay International vehicle registration letters.
**PY** Prior Year.
**Pycno.** (abbr.) Pycnodysostosis.
Pycno. is a lysosomal disease resulting from gene defects.
*Human Genetics; Medicine.*
**py-GC-MS** pyrolysis-Gas Chromatography-Mass Spectrometry.
py-GC-MS provides a powerful means for the chemical characterization of invertebrate cuticles.
*Biogeochemistry; Chemistry; Fossil Anthropods; Geology; Organic Geochemistry.*
**pymt.** (abbr.) payment.
**PYP** Photoactive Yellow Protein.
*Biochemistry; Biology; Chemistry; Medicine; Molecular Biology; Pathology; Photobiology; Photochemistry.*
**Py-tract** Polypyrimidine-tract.
*Cell Biology; Molecular Medicine; Nucleic Acids.*
**PZ** (abbr.) pancréozymine.
French initialism meaning: pancreozymin.
Pancreozymin is also known as: cholecystokinin.
*Endocrinology.*
**PZ** 1. pick-up zone.
1a. zone d'enlèvement [logistique].
1b. zone de ramassage [personnel].
2. point zéro.
2a. ground zero (GZ).
2b. surface zero (SZ 1).
**PZ** Potenza, Italy.
**PZ** Progress Zone.
*Biology; Genetics; Medicine; Vertebrate Limb Development.*
For further details see under: **AER**.
**PZC** Point of Zero Charge.
*Business; Finance.*
**PZN-PT** Lead-Zinc-Niobate / Lead-Titanate.
**PZT** Lead Zirconate Titanate.

**q** quadrato.
meaning: square in Italian.
**q** qualcuno.
meaning: somebody; someone in Italian.
**q** quart.
Quart is a unit of volume.
*Mechanics.*
**q** quarter.
Quarter is a unit of mass.
*Mechanics.*
**q** (abbr.) quarterly.
Also: **qtly**.
Quarterly means: occurring four times a year.
*Accounting; Periodicals.*
**q** quartile.
*Statistics.*
**Q** Quebec (Canada).
Also: **Que**.
**Q** Queen.
Also: **Qu**.
**Q** Queensland (Australia).
Also: **Qld.**; **Que.**
**q** (abbr.) query.
Also: **qy**.
*Computer Programming.*
**q** question.
**Q** queue.
**q** quintal.
quintal is equal to 100 Kilograms.
*Metrology.*
**q** quire.
*Materials.*
**q** quota.
meaning: aliquot; proportion; quota; share in Italian.
**Q** Quotient.
*Mathematics.*
**QA** Qatar.
**QA** Quality Assurance.
**QA** Quick Assets.
*Business; Finance.*
**QALAS** Qualified Associate Land Agent's Society.
**QALY** Quality-Adjusted Life Years.
*Quality of Life; Health Care.*
**QAM** Quadrature Amplitude Modulation.
**QAM** Queued Access Method.
*Computer Programming.*
**QAMS** Quality Assurance of Medical Standards.
*Medicine.*
**Q&A** Questions and Answers.
**QARANC** Queen Alexandra's Royal Army Nursing Corps.
**QARNNS** Queen Alexandra's Royal Naval Nursing Service.
**QAs** Quadrature-phase Amplitudes.
*Physics.*
**QAS** Question-Answering System.
*Computer Programming.*
**QAT** qualification approval test.
essai d'homologation.
**QB** Qualified Bidders.
**q.b.** quanto basta.
Italian initialism meaning: as much as is sufficient.
**QB** Queen's Bench.
**QBD** Queen's Bench Division.
**QBO** Quasi-Biennial Oscillation.
The term quasi-biennial oscillation refers to a 13-month cycle wherein stratospheric winds change direction from east to west and vice versa.
*Geodesy; Geophysics; Meteorology.*
**QBS** Quantized Bottleneck States.
*Atomic and Molecular Sciences; Chemical Physics; Molecular Reaction Dynamics.*
**QBSF media** Quality Biological Serum-Free media.
*Cell Growth; Monoclonal Antibody Production.*
**q.c.** qualcosa; qualche cosa.
Italian initialism meaning: something.
**QC** Qualità Controllata (Italy).
**QC** Quality Circle.
**QC** Quality Control.
*Industrial Engineering.*
**QC** Quantum Cascade.
*Microstructural Sciences.*
**QC** Quantum Chemistry.
*Physical Chemistry.*
**QC** Quantum Computer.
**QC** Quasi Contract; Quasi Corporation.
*Business; Commerce; Finance.*
**QC** Queen's College; Queen's Counsel.
**QC** Quinary Code.
*Computer Technology.*
**QCA** Quantum-dot Cellular Automata.
*Electrical Engineering; Nanoscale Science; Physics; Technology.*
**QCB** Queue Control Block.
**QCD** Quantum Chromodynamics.
*Particle Physics.*
**QCDS** Quality, Cost, Delivery, Safety.
**QC lasers** Quantum Cascade lasers.
*Applied Physics; Chaotic Resonators; Microlasers.*
**QCM** Questionnaire / Questions à Choix Multiple.

**QCM measurements** (microgravimetric) Quartz Crystal Microbalance measurements.
*Chemistry.*
**QCPE** Quantum Chemistry Program Exchange (U.S.A.).
**QC-PRC assay** Quantitative Competitive Polymerase Chain Reaction assay.
**QCPSK** Quaternary Coherent Phase-Shift-Keyed.
**QCS** Quadri Comunitari di Sostegno - E.C.
**QCSE** Quantum-Confined Stark Effect.
*Optical Modulation Applications.*
**QCT** Quasi-Classical Trajectory.
**QD** Quad Density.
*Computer Technology.*
**QDA** Quantity Discount Agreement.
**QDS** Quality Dental Services (U.S.A.).
*Dental Bearings; Dental Gaskets.*
**QDs** Quantum Dots.
QDs are small electrically conducting regions containing from a small number to a few thousand electrons.
*Applied Physics; Electrical Engineering; Submicron Research.*
**QDS** Queue-Driven System.
*Computer Programming.*
**QDSL structures** Quantum Dot Superlattice structures.
*Applied Physics; Thermoelectric Materials.*
**Q1D structures** Quasi-one-dimensional structures.
**QE** Quoziente Emozionale.
Italian initialism meaning: Emotional Quotient.
*Psychology.*
**QED** Quantum Electrodynamics.
*String Theory.*
**QEDs** Quantum Emission Domains.
**QED test** Quantitative Enzymatic Diagnostic test.
**Qes** Quantum efficiencies.
*Solar Energy.*
**QF** Quality Factor.
*Nucleonics.*
**QF** Quick Firing.
**QF** The airline code for Qantas Airways Ltd.
**Q fever** Queensland fever.
*Medicine.*
**QG** Qualité Globale.
**QG** Quartier Generale; Quartier Général.
Italian and French initialism meaning: Headquarters.
*Military.*
**QGCA** quartier général de contrôle avancé.
advanced control headquarters (ACHQ).
**QGG** quartier général de guerre.
war headquarters (WHQ).
**QGGF** quartier général de guerre fixe.
static war headquarters (SWHQ).
**QGGFR** quartier général de guerre fixe de rechange.
static alternate war headquarters (SAWHQ).
**QGGM** 1. quartier général de guerre maritime.
1. maritime war headquarters (MWHQ 2.).
2. quartier général de guerre mobile.
2. mobile war headquarters (MWHQ 3.).
**QGGP** quartier général de guerre principal.
1a. main war headquarters (MWHQ 1.).
1b. primary war headquarters (PWHQ 1.).
**QGGPI** quartier général de guerre principal interarmées.
joint primary war headquarters (JPWHQ).
**QGGR** quartier général de guerre de rechange.
alternate war headquarters (AWHQ).
**QG NORD** Quartier général des Forces alliées du Nord-Europe [obsolète].
Headquarters Allied Forces North Europe (HQ NORTH) [obsolete].
**QGP** quartier général du temps de paix.
peace headquarters (PHQ).
**QHA** Quasi-Harmonic Approximation.
*Chemical Engineering; Materials Science.*
**QHCl** Quinine Hydrochloride.
**QHE** Quantum HALL Effect.
*Physics.*
**QHE operation** Quantum Heat Engine operation.
*Quantum Coherence; Physics.*
**QHM** Quartz Horizontal Magnetometer.
*Engineering.*
**QI** Quarterly Index.
**QI** Quotient Intellectuel; Quoziente di Intelligenza / Intellettivo.
French and Italian initialism meaning: Intelligence Quotient.
*Psychology.*
**QIL** Quad-In-Line.
**QIMR** Queensland Institute for Medical Research (Australia).
**QI of IQ** Quantum Interpretation of Intelligence Quotient.
**QIP** quadrilateral interoperability programme.
programme quadrilatéral d'interopérabilité.
**QISAM** Queued Indexed Sequential Access Method.
*Computer Science.*
**QKD** Quantum Key Distribution.
*Quantum Cryptography.*
**QL** Query Language.
*Computer Programming.*
**ql.** (abbr.) quintale.

Italian abbreviation meaning: quintal.
For further details see under: **q**.
**QLA** Quebec Library Association (Canada).
**Qld.** (abbr.) Queensland (Australia).
Also: **Q.**; **Que.**
**QLL** Quasi-Liquid Layer.
*Atmospheric Physics; Meteorology; Microphysics of Clouds; Physics.*
**QLM** Quasi-Lagrangian Model.
**qlty.** (abbr.) quality.
**qly.** (abbr.) quarterly.
For further details see under: **q**.
**QM** Quantum Mechanics.
Quantum mechanics is also known as: Quantum Theory.
*Physics.*
**QM** Queen Mother.
**QMC** Quartermaster Corps.
**QMD** Quantum Molecular Dynamics.
**QMF** Query Management Facility.
**QMG** Quartermaster General.
**QM mouse** Quasi-Monoclonal mouse.
*Immunology; Microbiology; Somatic Hypermutation.*
**QMR** Qualità Media Risultante.
Italian initialism meaning: Average Outgoing Quality.
**QMR** qualitative military requirement.
besoin militaire qualitatif.
**QM scattering calculations** Quantum Mechanical scattering calculations.
**QMS measurements** Quadruple Mass Spectrometer measurements.
*Astronomy; Physics.*
**Qn** quinolinium.
**qn.** (abbr.) quotation.
**qnty.** (abbr.) quantity.
**QOL** Quality Of Life.
**QOP** Quality Orientation Profile.
**QOS**; **QoS** Quality Of Service.
**QP** Quasi-Periodicity.
*Chaotic Dynamics.*
**QP** Query Program.
The query program enables a user to put questions to a database and to store the data obtained.
*Computer Programming.*
**QP** Quoted Price.
*Business; Commerce; Finance.*
**QPC** Quantum Point Contact.
*Condensed Matter Physics; Submicron Research.*
**QPC** Quasi-Public Company.
*Business; Commerce; Finance.*
**QPCs** Quantum Point Contacts.
*Physics.*
**QPCU** questionnaire des plans civils d'urgence.
civil emergency planning questionnaire (CEPQ).
**QPE ground state** Quantum Paraelectric ground state.
**QPEX** Quasi-Parallel EXecution.
*Computer Technology.*
**QPM** Quality Protein Maize.
*Nutrition; Protein Maize.*
**QPM schemes** Quasi-Phase-Matching schemes.
*Solid-State Microstructures.*
**QPOS** Quasi-Periodic Optical Superlattice.
*Solid-State Microstructures.*
**QPOs** Quasi-Periodic Oscillations.
*Astronomy; Astrophysics; Black Holes.*
**Q-PRIME** Quality-oriented software PRocess management In Medium Enterprises.
*European Community Project.*
**QPRK** Quadrature Partial-Response Keying.
*Telecommunications.*
**QPs** Quasi-Particles.
A quasi-particle has the features of a particle, but is not a true free particle.
*Physics.*
**QPSK**; **Qpsk** Quaternary/Quadrature Phase Shift Keying.
*Electronics.*
**qq.** (abbr.) questions.
**qqch.** quelque chose.
French abbreviation meaning: something.
**qqf.** quelquefois.
French abbreviation meaning: sometimes.
**qqn.** quelqu'un.
French abbreviation meaning: somebody; someone.
**QR** Qatar Riyal.
*Currencies.*
**qr.** (abbr.) quarter.
For further details see under: **q**.
**QR** Quotation Request.
**QRA** Quantitative Risk Assessment.
**QRA** quick reaction alert (aircraft).
(avion en) alerte de réaction rapide.
**QRF** quick reaction force.
1a. force de réaction rapide.
1b. force d'intervention rapide [FR].
**QRM** Quick Response Mechanism.
**QRO** 1. quick response option.
1. option de réponse rapide.
2. quick reation option.
2. option de réaction rapide.
**QRS** quick reference system.
système de référence rapide.

**qr.tr.** Quarter.
For further details see under: **q**.
**QRUMs** Quasi-Rigid Unit Modes.
*Physics.*
**QS** Qualitative Simulation.
*Artificial Intelligence.*
**QS** Quality Stock.
*Business; Commerce.*
**QS**; **Qs** Quantité Suffisante.
French initialism meaning: sufficient quantity.
**QS** Quarter Sessions.
*Law.*
**QS** Quiet Sleep.
Quiet Sleep is also known as: Non-Rapid Eye Movement Sleep.
*Neurology.*
**QS** Quinacrine Sterilization.
*Birth Control; Contraception; Laparoscopy.*
**QSAM** Queued Sequential Access Method.
*Computer Science.*
**QSG** Quasi Stellar Galaxy.
**QSO** Quasi-Stellar Object.
For further details see under: **QSOs**.
**QSOs** Quasi Stellar Objects.
QSOs are the brightest distant objects known. They are also known as: Quasars.
*Astronomy; Astrophysics; Space Physics.*
**QSP** quick-start package.
module de mise en train rapide.
**qt.** (abbr.) quantity.
**qt.** (abbr.) quart.
For further details see under: **q**.
**QT** Questioned Trade.
**qt.** (abbr.) quiet.
**QT** Quotation Ticker.
**QTAM** Queued Telecommunication Access Method; Queued Teleprocessing Access Method.
**qt.é** (abbr.) quantité.
French abbreviation meaning: quantity.
**QTLs** Quantitative Trait Locus / Loci.
*Animal Breeding; Biochemistry; Genetics; Genome Technology; Microbiology.*
**qtly.** (abbr.) quarterly.
For further details see under: **q**.
**QTML** Quick Time Media Layer.
*Integrated Programming Languages.*
**QTN** Quasithermal Noise.
*Aeronautics; Astronomy; Astrophysics; Physics; Space Science.*
**Q-T plateau** Qinghai-Tibetan Plateau.
*Environmental Science; Geological Sciences; Glaciology; Geocryology.*
**qtr.** (abbr.) quarter.
**qtz.** (abbr.) quartz.
*Mineralogy.*
**qu.** (abbr.) quality.
Also: **qual.**
*Science; Thermodynamics.*
**Qu.** (abbr.) Queen.
Also: **Q**.
**qu.** (abbr.) query; question.
**Qu** Quinoline.
Quinoline is used mainly in medicine and as a flavoring agent.
*Organic Chemistry.*
**Qu A** Anterior Quadrangular lobule.
*Clinical Psychology; Medicine; Neuroscience of Autism; Radiology.*
**quad.** (abbr.) quaderno.
Italian abbreviation meaning: copy-book; notebook; book.
**quad.** (abbr.) quadrangle.
*Architecture; Cartography; Mathematics.*
**quad.** (abbr.) quadrant.
*Anatomy; Electromagnetism; Engineering; Mathematics; Naval Architecture; Navigation; Mechanical Engineering; Physiology; Optics.*
**quad.** (abbr.) quadruplicate.
Also: **quadr.**; **quadrupl**. In quadruplicate means: an original plus three carbon copies or photocopies.
**qual.** (abbr.) qualitative.
**qual.** (abbr.) quality.
Also: **qu**.
*Science; Thermodynamics.*
**QUAMI** QUAlification for young MIgrants (Germany).
*Projects.*
**Quamta** Qualificazione manageriale e tecnica degli artigiani (Italy).
*Projects; Vocational Training.*
**quar.**; **quart.** quarter.
*Metrology; Naval Architecture.*
**quar.**; **quart.** (abbr.) quarterly.
For further details sec under: **q**.
**QUARTET** quick and ready to encrypt test terminal.
terminal d'essai de chiffrement rapide et prêt.
**QUASAR** QUAlità e Servizi per gli Appalti Pubblici (Italy).
**QUASCO** QUAlificazione e Sviluppo del COstruire (Italy).
**QUASH** QUality ASsurance of Sample Handling - *European Community.*
*Sample Handling and Storage.*

**QUASIMEME** QUality ASsurance of Information for Marine Environmental Monitoring in Europe.
QUASIMEME has built an effective European Marine Monitoring Network. The project was funded under the Standards, Measurements and Testing programme.
*European Community Project.*

**QUAUBAT** QUicker Assessment of lifetime of PV BATteries.

**QUE** Quality in Undergraduate Education (Indonesia).
QUE is funded by the World Bank.
*World Bank Programs.*

**Que.** Quebec (Canada).
Also: **Q**.

**Que.** Queensland (Australia).
Also: **Q.**; **Qld.**

**QUERCUS** QUalitative Experiments to determine the components Responsible and eliminate the Causes of Undesirable Sensory characteristics in drinks stoppered with cork.
*European Community Project.*

**QUEST** Center for QUantized Electronic STructures.

**QUI** Queen's University (Ireland).

**QUIC** QUantum Information and Computing.
QUIC at Caltech was founded by the Massachusetts Institute of Technology, and the University of Southern California (U.S.A.).

**QUIL** QUad In-Line.
*Electronics.*

**quint.** (abbr.) quintuplicate.
In quintuplicate means: an original plus four carbon copies or photocopies.

**QUIRT** QUality control In Radiation Therapy.
*Medicine.*

**quot.** (abbr.) quotation.
Also: **quote**.
*Business; Commerce.*

**quot.** (abbr.) quotazione.
Italian abbreviation meaning: quotation.

**quot.** (abbr.) quoted.
*Commerce.*

**QUOVADIS** QUality Of Video and Audio for DIgital television Services.

**Qu P** Posterior Quadrangular lobule.
*Clinical Psychology; Medicine; Neuroscience of Autism; Radiology.*

**QUT** Queensland University of Technology.
QUT is one of Australia's largest universities. The faculties of the university are: arts, environment and engineering, business, information technology, law and science.

**q.v.** qualche volta.
Italian initialism meaning: sometimes.

**QVC** Quality, Value, Convenience.
The above initialism was coined referring to shopping in the U.S.A.: customers watch the products on a screen and order by telephone.

**QW** Quad Word.
A quad word is actually a 16-bytes-long word.
*Computer Technology.*

**QW** Quantum Well.
*Quantum Engineering.*

**QWELD** Quality control procedure and normative for highly reliable flash butt WELDing.
*European Community Project.*

**QWH** Quantum-Well Heterostructure.
*Electrical Engineering; Optical Circuit Design; Optical Computing; Optoelectronic Technology; Photonic Circuits.*

**QWIP** Quantum-Well Infrared Photodetection.
*Microstructural Sciences.*

**QWL** Quality-of-Work Life.

**QWs** Quantum Wells.
*Quantum Engineering.*

**qy.** (abbr.) query.
Also: **q**.
*Computer Programming.*

# R

**R**; **r** (abbr.) radius.
*Anatomy; Mathematics.*
**r** (abbr.) raggio.
Italian abbreviation meaning: radius.
**R**; **r** railway.
*Transportation Engineering.*
**r** (abbr.) rain.
**R** Heavy Rain (Beaufort letter).
*Meteorology.*
**r** (abbr.) range.
*Cartography; Ecology; Engineering; Geography; Mathematics; Military Science; Navigation; Physics; Robotics; Statistics.*
**r** rare.
**R** rare earth.
*Chemistry.*
**R**; **r** ratio.
*Mathematics.*
**R** reach.
*Civil Engineering; Engineering; Geography; Industrial Engineering; Robotics.*
**r** (abbr.) read.
*Computer Technology; Electronics; Telecommunications.*
**r** (abbr.) reader.
Also: **rdr.**
*Computer Technology; Graphic Arts.*
**r** real.
**R** Réaumur (temperature scale).
Named for the French physicist René de **Réaumur** who invented it.
*Thermodynamics.*
**R** Receiver.
*Chemical Engineering; Electronics; Mechanical Engineering.*
**r** recommendation.
**r** recto.
*Graphic Arts.*
**R** refined.
*Chemical Engineering.*
**r** register.
*Computer Technology; Graphic Arts; Mechanical Engineering; Military Science; Telecommunications.*
**R**; **r** registered; rent.
**r** regulation.
**r** reliability.
*Engineering; Statistics.*
**R** report.
*Computer Programming.*
**r** request.
**r** (abbr.) research.
In science as well as in other fields research is the investigation conducted with a view to find new data and put it into use.
**R**; **r** reserved.
**r** (abbr) reset.
*Computer Technology.*
**r** resistor.
resistor is also known as: resistor element.
*Electricity.*
**R** response.
*Behavior.*
**R** return (referring to fares; tickets; etc.).
**r** revolution.
*Astronomy; Geology; Mechanics.*
**R**; **r** ricevuta.
Italian abbreviation meaning: receipt.
**r** right.
**R** river.
*Geography; Hydrology.*
**r** road.
*Civil Engineering; Geology; Mining Engineering.*
**r** rod.
*Bacteriology; Mechanical Devices; Nucleonics.*
*Geology* - In geology, rod is also known as: roller.
*Histology* - In histology rod is also known as: rod cell.
**R**; **r** roentgen.
roentgen is also known as: Röntgen.
*Nucleonics.*
**R** rolled.
**R** Romania's international vehicle-registration letter.
**r** rood.
*Metrology.*
**r** rough.
**r** routine.
In computer programming, routine is a series of instructions used to perform particular functions.
*Computer Programming.*
**r** run.
*Cartography; Chemical Engineering; Computer Programming; Engineering; Geology; Hydrology; Mechanical Engineering; Military Science; Naval Architecture; Ordnance.*
**R**; **r** rupee.
*Currencies.*
**RA** Argentina's international vehicle-registration letters.
**R/A** radius of action.
rayon d'action.
**RA** Radio Astronomy.

**Ra** The chemical symbol for Radium.
Radium is a radioactive element having the atomic number 88. It is used mainly in medicine and in radiography. The word radium derives from the Latin term "ray".
*Chemistry; Symbols.*
**RA** Random Access.
*Computer Technology; Telecommunications.*
**RA** Range Arithmetic.
Interval arithmetic is now known as: Range Arithmetic.
*Computer Programming.*
**RA** Ravenna, Italy.
**RA** Read Amplifier.
**RA** Rear Admiral.
*Military.*
**RA** 1. rear area.
1. zone arrière.
2. reinforced alert.
2. alerte renforcée.
**RA** Record Address.
**RA** Referees' Association.
**RA**; **R/A**, **R.A.** Refer to Acceptor.
*Business; Commerce; Finance.*
**RA** Registro Aeronautico.
Italian acronym meaning: Air Registry.
**RA** Relative Address.
Relative address is also known as: Floating Address.
*Computer Technology.*
**RA** Reliability Analysis; Reliability Assessment.
**RA** Remote Access.
*Computer Technology.*
**R.A.** Repurchase Agreement.
**RA** Research Articles.
**RA** Research Assistant.
**RA** Reserve Alcaline.
*Medicine.*
**RA** Resident Abroad (G.B.).
A magazine for Expatriates.
**RA** Restricted Account.
**RA** Retinoic Acid.
**RA** Return Address.
*Computer Programming.*
**RA** Revenue Act.
*U.S. Acts.*
**RA** Rheumatoid Arthritis.
Rheumatoid arthritis is also known as: Arthritis Obliterans.
*Autoimmune Diseases; Medicine.*
**R.A.** Right Ascension.
*Astronomy.*
**RA** Robustus Archistrialis.
**RA** Row Address.
*Computer Programming.*
**RA** Royal Academician; Royal Academy.
**RA** Royal Artillery.
**RAA** Regional Airlines Association (Canada).
**RAA** Remote-Access Admittance.
*Robotics.*
**RAA** Rhumatisme Articulaire Aigu.
French initialism meaning: Acute Articular Rheumatism.
*Medicine.*
**RAA** Royal Academy of Arts.
**RAAMS** remote anti-armour mine system.
système de mines antiblindage à distance.
**rAAV vectors** recombinant Adeno-Associated Virus vectors.
*Genetic Immunization; Gene Transfer.*
**RAB** Radio Advertising Bureau (U.S.A.).
**RAB** Registrar Accreditation Board.
The RAB is located in Milwaukee, Wisconsin, U.S.A.
**rab** The above acronyms were coined accidentally using the Arabic word "rab" which means: God, Lord, master.
**RAC** Radio Adaptive Communications.
**RAC** Random Access Controller.
**RAC** Recombinant DNA Advisory Committee.
The RAC of the U.S. NIH was created in 1974 and dealt with gene splicing. Since 1984 it deals mainly with human gene therapy.
For further details see under: **NIH**.
**RAC** Rectified Alternating Current.
*Electricity.*
**RAC** regional air commander.
commandant régional des forces aériennes.
**RAC** Royal Agricultural College; Royal Armoured Corps; Royal Automobile Club.
**RACA** regional airspace control authority.
autorité de contrôle de l'espace aérien.
**racc.** (abbr.) raccomandata.
Italian abbreviation meaning: registered letter.
**rACC** rostral Anterior Cingulate Cortex.
*Anaesthesia; Cognitive Neurophysiology; Intensive Care Medicine; Opioid Analgesia; Placebo Analgesia.*
**RACE** rapid off-line crypto equipment.
matériel de chiffrement rapide hors ligne.
**RACE** Research in Advanced Communication technologies in Europe.
**RACE** Routing And Cost Estimate.
**race** The above acronyms were coined using the English word "race".

*Anthropology; Biology; Civil Engineering; Design Engineering; Oceanography.*
**RAC environment** Rapid Application Customisation environment.
**RAC guidance** Radiometric Area-Correlation guidance.
**RACI** Ricerche Applicazioni Chimiche Industriali.
Italian acronym meaning: Industrial Chemical Applications Research.
**RACKs** Receptors for Activated C Kinases.
**RACON** radar beacon.
balise radar.
**RACP** regional airspace control plan.
plan régional de contrôle e l'espace aérien.
**RACS** Random Access Communications System.
**RACS** Random Access Computing System.
**RACS** Road Automobile Communication System.
**rad**; **rad.** radian.
*Mathematics.*
**rad.** (abbr.) radiation.
*Anatomy; Cartography; Evolution; Physics.*
**rad** radiation absorbed dose.
*Nucleonics.*
**RAD**; **rad** radius.
*Mathematics.*
**RAD** Random Access Device.
**RAD** Rapid Access Device; Rapid Access Data.
*Electronics.*
**RAD** Régiment d'Artillerie Divisionnaire (France).
**Rad** Registro anagrafico ditte.
Italian acronym meaning: Register of Firms.
**RAD** Restricted Activity Day.
**RAD** Ritenuta d'Acconto sui Dividendi.
Italian acronym meaning: Advance Withholding Tax on Dividends.
**RADA** Random-Access Discrete Address.
*Telecommunications.*
**RADA** Royal Academy of Dramatic Art.
**rada** The above acronyms were coined accidentally using the Italian word "rada" which means: road /roadstead.
*Geology.*
**RADAR** RAdio Detection And Ranging.
**RADAR** Results, Approach, Deloyment, Assessment and Review.
The five tenets of corporate excellence.
RADAR is an acronym of the: European Foundation for *Quality Management.*
**RADARSAT** (abbr.) RADAR SATellite (Canada).
**RADC** regional air defence commander.
commandant régional de défense aérienne.
**RADC** Rome Air Development Center (Italy).
**Rad CM** Radar Countermeasure.
*Military Science.*
**RADFREQ** radar frequency.
fréquence radar.
**RADHAZ** radiation hazards.
1a. dangers dus aux rayonnements.
1b. dangers de radiation (ou de rayonnement radioactif).
**RAD I** RADiographic Inspection.
*Metallurgy.*
**RADIAC** RadioActivity Detection, Identification And Computation.
**RADINT** radar intelligence.
renseignement radar.
**RADIUS** Remote Authentication Dial-In User Service.
*Servers.*
**RADIUS** Research And Development In the Unites States.
**RADM** Radar and Algorithm Display Model.
**RADM** Regional Acid Deposition Model.
**RADOC** regional air defence operations centre.
centre régional des opérations de défense aérienne.
**RADPROT** (abbr.) RADiation PROTection.
Research and Training program in the field of biology - health protection.
*Euratom Programs.*
**rad/s** radians per second.
Also: **rad/sec**.
**RADS** Real-time Analysis and Display System.
**RADWASTOM** Management and Storage of Radioactive Waste.
*Euratom Programs.*
**RAE** Research Assessment Exercise (G.B.).
**RAE** Russian Antarctic Expedition.
**RAF** Régiment d'Artillerie de Fortesse (France).
**RAF** Regolazione Automatica di Frequenza.
Italian acronym meaning: Automatic Frequency Regulation.
**RAF** Rendu A la Frontière.
French acronym meaning: Delivered At Frontier.
*Economics; International Trade.*
**RAF** resource allocation figure.
1a. montant de la dotation.
1b. montant des ressources à affecter.
**RAF** Royal Air Force (G.B.).
Also: **R.A.F.**
Created in 1918.
**RAFCO** Russian-American Fuel Cell Consortium.
*U.S.; F.S.U. projects.*
**RAFI** Rural Advancement Foundation International.
RAFI is a farmers' advocacy organization.
**RAFT** Restoration of muscle Activity Through

Functional electrical stimulation and associated Technology.

**Rag.**; **rag.** (abbr.) Ragioniere.
Italian abbreviation meaning: accountant.

**RAG** Recombination Activating Gene.
*Immunology.*

**RAH** Rome American Hospital (Italy).

**RAI** Research Activity Index (U.S.A.).
Developed in 1991 at the University of Arizona's Center for the study of Higher Education.

**RAID** Rapid Access to Intervention Development (U.S.A.).
RAID is a 1998 initiative of the U.S. NCI.
The goal of RAID is the rapid movement of novel molecules and concepts from the laboratory to the Clinic for proof-of-principle clinical trials.
*Preclinical Development.*
For further details see under: **NCI**.

**RAID** Redundant Array of Inexpensive Disks.

**rail.** (abbr.) railroad.
*Civil Engineering; Transportation Engineering.*

**rail.** (abbr.) railway.
Also: **R**; **r**; **Rly**; **rly.**; **rwy.**; **RY**; **ry**.
*Transportation Engineering.*

**RAIL** Recupero Alluminio In forma di Lattine (Italy).
*Aluminum Recovery.*

**RAIL** Robotic Aid to Independent Living.
*European Community Project.*

**RAIM** Red de Agentes de Igualdad para la Mujer.
Of the European NOW Projects.
*European Quality Agents.*
For further details see under: **NOW**.

**RAINBOW** Radio Access INdependent Broadband On Wireless.

**RAIR** Reflection-Absorption Infrared.

**RAIRE** Recognition Awards for the Integration of Research and Education.
U.S. National Science Foundation first Awards Electronic Program (July 1996).
*Awards.*

**RAISA** Ricerche Avanzate per Innovazioni nel Settore Agricolo (Italy).
*Agricultural Innovations.*

**RAI - TV** Radio Audizioni Italiane e Televisione.
Italian initialism meaning: Italian TV and Broadcasting Corporation.

**RAL** Rapid-Access Loop.
*Computer Technology.*

**RAL** Relational Algebraic Language.
*Computer Programming.*

**RAL** Rutherford Appleton Laboratory (G.B.).
*Neutron Research.*

**RALCC** regional airlift coordination centre.
centre régional de coordination des transports aériens.

**RAM** 1. radar absorbent material.
1. matériau non réflecteur.
2. ravitaillement à la mer.
2. replenishment at sea (RAS).
3. reliability and maintainability.
3. fiabilité et maintenabilité.

**RAM** Random-Access Memory.
Random-Access Memory is also known as: Random-Access Storage.
*Computer Technology.*

**RAM** Rapid Access Memory.

**RAM**; **r.a.m.** Relative Atomic Mass.

**RAM** Reserve Adjustment Magnitude.
*Business; Economics; Finance.*

**RAM** Rete Aziendale Mobile (Omnitel) (Italy).

**RAM** Reverse Annuity Mortgage.
*Business; Finance.*

**RAM** Rolling Aiframe Missime.

**RAM** Royal Academy of Music.

**RAMA** Régiment d'Artillerie de MArine (France).

**RAMAN** Regional Atmospheric Measurement and Analysis Network.

**ramark** (abbr.) radar marker.
*Navigation.*

**RAMCC** regional air movement coordination centre.
centre régional de coordination des mouvements aériens.

**RAMINO** Reliability Assessment for Maintenance INspective Optimization - C.E.C.

**ramino** The above acronym was coined using the Italian word "ramino" which means: copper pot.
Also: "rummy".

**RAMIT** rate-aided manually implemented tracking.
poursuite manuelle assistée (en vitesse angulaire).

**RAMM branch** Regional And Mesoscale Meteorology branch (U.S.A.).

**RAMPS** Rabbit Anti-Mouse Platelet Serum.

**RAMPS** rapid message preparation system.
système de préparation rapide des messages.

**RAMPS** Resource Allocation in Multi-Project Scheduling.

**ramps** The above acronyms were coined using the English word "ramps".
*Aviation; Engineering; Electrical Engineering.*

**RAMS** RAdiation Measuring Systems.
The radiation measuring systems are multiple instrument arrays.
*Atmospheric Sciences; Oceanography.*

**RAMS** Regional Atmospheric Modeling System (U.S.A.).
**RAM station** Regional Air Monitoring station.
**RAN** regional air navigation.
navigation aérienne régionale.
**RAN** Revenue Anticipation Note (U.S.A.).
**RAN** Royal Australian Navy (Australia).
**RAND** Research And Development.
Also: **R&D**.
**r and c** rail and canal.
*Transportation.*
**r. & cc** riot and civil commotion.
*Insurance.*
**R&D** Research and Development.
Also: **RAND**.
*Industry.*
**R&H** Refined and Hardened.
**R and I** recognition and identification (radar).
(radar de) repèrage et identification.
**r and l** rail and lake.
*Transportation.*
**R.&M.** Reliability and Maintainability.
**r and o** rail and ocean.
*Transportation.*
**R and R**; **R&R** Rest and Recuperation.
*Military Science.*
**R&SA** Royal & Sun Alliance.
*Insurers.*
**R&ST** Ricerca e Sviluppo Tecnologico.
Italian initialism meaning: Research and Technological Development.
**R & TD policy** Research and Technological Development policy.
**r and w** rail and water.
**Ran GDP** Ran Guanosine Diphosphate.
*Biochemistry; Cell Biology; Embryology; Medicine; Microtubule Polymerization; Mitosis; Molecular Biology; Nuclear Trafficking.*
**Ran GTP** Ran Guanosine Triphosphate.
*Biochemistry; Cell Biology; Embryology; Medicine; Microtubule Polymerization; Mitosis; Molecular Biology; Nuclear Trafficking.*
**RANN** Research Applied to National Needs.
A 1971 *U.S. Program.*
**RANs** Resource-Adjacent Nations.
**RANTES** Regulated on Activation, Normal T Expressed and Secreted.
RANTES is a chemotactic and proinflammatory soluble peptide.
*Malaria; Hematology.*
**RAO** Radio Astronomy Observatory.
**raob** (abbr.) radiosonde observation.
*Meteorology.*
**RAOC** regional air operations centre.
centre d'opérations aériennes régional (COAR).
**RAOC** Royal Army Ordnance Corps.
**RAOP** regional air operations plan.
plan régional d'opérations aériennes.
**RAP** Radiological Assistance Program.
The U.S. Radiological Assistance Program was created to assist in case of a potential nuclear accident in the United States.
**RAP** 1. recognized air picture.
1. situation aérienne générale.
2. reliable acoustic path.
2a. chemin acoustique sûr.
2b. chemin acoustique fiable.
**RAP** Research Associateship Program (U.S.A.).
**RAP** RNAIII Activating Protein.
*Internal Medicine; Medical Pathology.*
**RAPCON** radar approach control (centre).
(centre du) contrôle d'approche radar.
**RAPD** Randomly Amplified Polymorphic DNA.
For further details see under: **DNA**.
**RAPID** Rapid Access to Preventive Intervention Development.
RAPID is a 1999 initiative of the U.S. NCI.
For further details see under: **NCI**.
**RAPID Program** Research And Public Information and Dissemination Program.
RAPID was created in 1992. It is a scientific program run by the U.S. DOE and the U.S. NIEHS.
*Laboratory Studies; Scientific Programs.*
For further details see under: **DOE** and **NIEHS**.
**RAQ** Rendu A Quai.
French acronym meaning: Delivered Ex Quay.
*Economics; International Trade.*
**RAR** Radioacoustic Ranging.
Radioacoustic Ranging is also known as: Radioacoustic Sound Ranging; Radioacoustic Position Finding.
*Engineering.*
**RAR** Recettore per l'Acido Retinoico.
Italian initialism meaning: Retinoic Acid Receptor.
*Human Genetics; Medicine; Pathology.*
**RAR**$\alpha$ Retinoic Acid Receptor $\alpha$.
*Human Genetics; Medicine; Pathology.*
**RARC** Regional Administrative Radio Conference.
**RARDE** Royal Armaments Research and Development Establishment (G.B.).
**RARE** Réseaux Associés pour la Recherche Européenne.
For further details see under: **TEREHA**.
**RARE cleavage** RecA-Assisted Restriction Endonuclease cleavage.
*Biochemistry; Genetics.*

**RAREP** (abbr.) RAdar REPort.
RAREP is also known as: Rain Area Report.
**RARP** Reverse Address Resolution Protocol.
**RAS** Random-Access Storage.
For further details see under: **RAM**.
**RAS** Recruitment and Assessment Services.
**RAS** Rectified Air Speed.
**R.A.S.** Regione Autonoma Sarda.
Italian acronym of the: Autonomous Region of Sardinia.
**R.A.S.** Regione Autonoma Siciliana.
Italian acronym of the: Autonomous Region of Sicily.
**RAS** Remote Access System.
**RAS** Renin-Angiotensin System.
**RAS** replenishment at sea.
ravitaillement à la mer (RAM 2.).
**RAS** Rescue At Sea.
**RAs** Research Assistants.
**RAS** Rete Autonoma Studentesca (Italy).
**RAS** Riunione Adriatica di Sicurtà (Italy).
*Insurers.*
**RAS** Royal Agricultural Society; Royal Asiatic Society; Royal Astronomical Society.
**RAS** Russian Academy of Sciences.
**RASA** Russian Aviation and Space Agency.
**RASIT** radar de couverture de surveillance.
gas-filling surveillance radar.
**RASMC** Rat Aortic Smooth Muscle Cell.
For further details see under: **RASMCs**.
**RASMCs** Rat Aortic Smooth Muscle Cells.
*Anesthesiology; Biochemistry; Biophysics; Human Physiology; Medicine; Molecular Genetics; Pathology; Physiology.*
**RASP** recognized air-surface picture.
1a. situation générale air-surface.
1b. situation air-surface identifiée (ou renseignée) [marine].
**RASREQ** replenishment-at-sea request.
demande de ravitaillement à la mer.
**RASS** Radio Acoustic Sounding System.
**RASS** ROSAT All-Sky Survey.
*Astronomy; Astrophysics.*
For further details see under: **ROSAT**.
**RASSI** RApporto sullo Stato del Sistema Internazionale (Italy).
**RAST** Radioallergosorbent Test.
*Immunology.*
**RAST Systems** Recovery, Assist, Secure and Traverse Systems.
**RAT** Remote-Association Tests.
*Psychology.*
**RAT** Rocket-Assisted Torpedo.
*Ordnance.*
**RATAC** radar de tir d'artillerie de campagne.
field artillery fire-control radar.
**ratan** radar and television aid to navigation.
**RATCC** regional air traffic control centre.
centre régional de contrôle de la circulation aérienne.
**RATCHET** Regional Atmospheric Transport Code for Hanford Emission Tracking.
**RATG** Rabbit Antithymocyte Globulin.
*Medicine; Transplantation.*
**RATO**; **rato** Rocket-Assisted Take-Off.
*Aviation.*
**RATOG** Rocket Assisted Take-Off Gear.
**RATP** Régie Autonome des Transports Parisiens (France).
RATP is the operator of the Paris metro system.
*Metro System Operators.*
**RATT** radioteletype.
radiotéléimprimeur.
**raTTs** run-away T Tauri stars.
*Astronomy; Astrophysics.*
**RAWIN system** RAdar WINd system.
The RAWIN system provides air-wind data by radar observation of a balloon.
*Engineering; Radar Observations.*
**RAWMAT** (abbr.) RAW MATerials.
Research and Development program in the raw material sector.
*European Community Program.*
**RAX** Random-Access; Remote-Access.
*Computer Technology.*
**RAZ angle** Relative Azimuth Angle.
**RB** Railroad Bonds.
*Economics; Finance.*
**RB** Redeemable Bond.
*Business; Economics; Finance.*
**RB** Remote Batch.
**RB** Reserve Bank.
**RB** Retinoblastoma.
RB is a congenital neoplasm of the retina.
*Oncology.*
**RB** Return to Bias.
**RB** Revenue Bond.
*Business; Finance.*
**Rb** The chemical symbol for Rubidium.
Rubidium is a chemical element having the atomic number 37, and an atomic weight of 85.47. It is used mainly in photocells.
*Chemistry; Symbols.*
**RB** Run Book.
Run Book is also known as: Problem File; Problem Folder.

*Computer Programming.*
**RBA** Reserve Bank of Australia.
**RBA** Roads Beautifying Association.
**RBA** Royal Society of British Artists (G.B.).
**RBA** The Reserve Bank of Australia.
**RbBr** Rubidium Bromide.
Rubidium bromide is soluble in water and insoluble in alcohol and has a melting point of 693°C. It is used in medicine.
*Inorganic Chemistry.*
**RBBS** Remote Bulletin Board System.
**RBC** Red Blood Count.
**RBC** Royal Bank of Canada.
**RbCl** Rubidium Chloride.
*Inorganic Chemistry.*
**RBCs** Red Blood Cells.
RBCs are also known as: Red Blood Corpuscles; Red Corpuscles; Red Cells.
*Hematology.*
**RBD** Ras-Binding Domain.
*Cancer Research; Cell and Molecular Biology.*
**RBE** Relative Biological Effectiveness.
*Nuclear Engineering.*
**RBF** Renal Blood Flow.
*Medicine.*
**RbF** Rubidium Fluoride.
*Inorganic Chemistry.*
**RBH** Republic of Bosnia-Herzegovina.
**RBI** Reserve Bank of India.
**RBL** (Interest) Rate on Banking Lending.
**RBL** Real Time Blackhole.
**RBM** Roll Back Malaria.
A multiagency crusade that aims to cut malaria mortality in half over the next 10 years.
*Malaria Mortality Reduction.*
**RBO** radio beacon omnidirectional.
radiophare omnidirectionnel (RPO).
**RBOCs** Regional Bell Operating Companies.
*Mobile Communications; Telecommunications.*
**RbOH** Rubidium Hydroxide.
RbOH is also known as: Rubidium Hydrate.
*Inorganic Chemistry.*
**RBP** Restrictive Business Practices.
**RBP** Retinol-Binding Protein.
*Biochemistry; Genetics; Molecular Biology.*
**RBP Code** Restrictive Business Practices Code.
**RBS** radar bombardment system.
système radar de bombardement.
**RBS** Ribosomal Binding Site.
**RBS** Royal Bank of Scotland.
*Scottish Bank.*
**RBS** Royal Botanic Society.
**RBS** Royal Society of British Sculptors (G.B.).
**RBS** Rutherford Backscattering Spectrometry.
**RBSI** RIKEN Brain Science Institute (Japan).
RIKEN launched the RBSI in October 1997.
**$Rb_2SO_4$** Rubidium Sulfate.
Rubidium Sulfate is used in medicine.
*Inorganic Chemistry.*
**RBU** Rothschild Bioscience Unit (G.B.).
**RBV** Return-Beam Vidicon.
**R/C** Radio Controlled (referring to craft).
**RC** Radix Complement.
*Mathematics.*
**RC** Range Check.
*Computer Programming.*
**RC** Reader Code.
**RC** Real Circuit.
**RC** Receiver Card.
**R.C.** Re-crediting.
**RC** Recurring Charges.
*Business; Economics; Finance.*
**RC** Red Cross.
**RC** 1. reduced charge.
1. charge réduite.
2. régiment de chars.
2a. armoured regiment [GB].
2b. tank regiment [GB].
2c. tank battalion [US].
3. Région Centre [obsolète].
3. Central Region (CR) [obsolete].
4. regional command [has replaced MSC 1.].
4. commandement régional [remplace HCS].
5. regional conflict.
5. conflit régional.
6. repair coordinator.
6. coordonnateur de réparation.
7. required capability.
7. capacité requise.
**RC** Redundancy Check.
*Computers.*
**RC** Reggio Calabria, Italy.
**RC** Registered Check.
*Business; Economics; Finance.*
**RC** Registre du Commerce.
**RC** Reinforced Concrete.
*Civil Engineering.*
**RC** Remote Computer.
**RC** Remote Control.
*Control Systems; Electronics.*
**RC** Reserve Capital.
*Business; Finance.*
**RC** Reserve Currency.
*Business; Economics; Finance.*
**RC** Reset Cycle.

The term reset cycle means that a cycle is reset to its initial state.
*Computer Programming.*
**RC** Resistance Coupling.
RC is also known as: Resistive Coupling.
*Electronics.*
**RC** Resistor/Capacitor.
*Computers.*
**R.C.** Responsabilità Civile.
Italian initialism meaning: Civil Liability.
**RC** Risk Capital.
*Business; Economics; Finance.*
**RC** Run Chart.
The RC is also known as: Run Diagram.
*Computer Programming.*
**RC** Taiwan's international vehicle-registration letters.
**RCA** Radio Corporation of America (U.S.A.).
**RCA** Responsabilità Civile Auto.
Italian initialism meaning: Automobile Liability Insurance.
**RCA** Revealed Comparative Advantage.
*Bibliometric Analyses.*
**RCA** Royal Canadian Academy -Canada.
**RCA** The Central African Republic's international vehicle-registration letters.
**RCAC** Regional Citizen's Advisory Council (U.S.A.).
**RCAC service** Remote Computer-Access Communications service.
**RCAI** Research Center for Allergy and Immunology (RIKEN).
An institute established in 2002 fully supported by the Japanese Government.
**RC asphalt** Rapid-Curing asphalt.
**RC axis** Rostrocaudal axis.
**RCB** Rationalisation des Choix Budgétaires.
French initialism meaning: Planning, Programming, Budgeting.
*Business; Economics; Finance.*
**RCB** Renewable Chemicals from Biomass.
*European Community Project.*
**RCB** Congo - Brazzaville's international vehicle-registration letters.
**rCBF** regional Cerebral Blood Flow.
*Cognitive Neurology; Medicine; Psychiatry; Psychology; Radiology.*
**RCC** Radio Common Carrier.
**RCC** Regional Cancer Center - Kerala, India.
**RCC** Regional Climate Center.
**RCC** 1. regional control centre.
1. centre de contrôle régional.
2. rescue coordination centre.
2a. centre de coordination du sauvetage.
2b. poste de commandement de coordination du sauvetage.
**RCC** Remote Center Compliance.
*Robotics.*
**RCC** Renal-Cell Carcinoma.
For further details see under: **RENCA**.
**RCCA** Resistance-Capacitance Coupled Amplifier.
RCCA is also known as: Resistance-Coupled Amplifier.
*Electronics.*
**RCC&S** Riots, Civil Commotions & Strikes.
*Insurance.*
**RC circuit** Resistance-Capacitance circuit.
The resistance-capacitance circuit is also known as: RC network.
*Electricity.*
**RCD** Rabbit Calicivirus Disease.
*Epidemiology; Virology.*
**rcd.** (abbr.) received; record.
**RCD** Receiver-Carrier Detector.
**RC EAST** Regional Command (Commander) East [has replaced EASTLAND 2.].
Commandement (commandant) régional Est [remplace EASTLANT 2.].
**RCEP** Royal Commission on Environmental Pollution (G.B.).
**RCFs** Refractory Ceramic Fibers.
RCFs are man-made mineral fibers. They are used to insulate industrial furnaces and coke ovens.
*Asbestos; Induced Cancers Research.*
**RCG** Radioactivity Concentration Guide.
Of the U.S. DOE.
For further details see under: **DOE**.
**RCGL** Regulation of Cell Growth Laboratory.
A department within the CCR.
For further details see under: **CCR**.
**RCH** Chile's international vehicle-registration letters.
**RCH** Royal Children's Hospital (Australia).
For further details see under: **SASVRC**.
**RCHME** Royal Commission on the Historic Monuments of England (G.B.).
The RCHME was established in 1908.
**RCI** Radio Canada International (Canada).
**RCI** Relative Citation Impact.
*Bibliometric Analyses.*
**RCI** Royal Colonial Institute.
**rcl.** (abbr.) recall.
*Psychology; Telecommunications.*
**RCLED** Resonant-Cavity Light-Emitting Diode.
*Electrical Engineering.*
**RCM** Radar Countermeasures.

*Military Science.*
**RCM** Royal College of Music.
**RCMF** Radio Component Manufacturers Federation.
**RCMI** Research Centers in Minority Institutions (U.S.A.).
**RCN** Royal Canadian Navy (Canada).
**RC network** Resistance-Capacitance network.
*Electricity.*
**RC NORTH** Regional Command (Commander) North [has replaced AFCENT].
Commandement (commandant) régional Nord [remplace AFCENT].
**r colony** rough colony.
*Microbiology.*
**RC oscillator** Resistance Capacitance oscillator.
*Electronics.*
**RCPC** Regional Check Processing Center (U.S.A.).
**rcpt.** (abbr.) receipt.
**RCR** Respiratory Control Ratio.
**RCRA** Resource Conservation and Recovery Act (U.S.A.).
*Economics; Engineering; Environmental Engineering.*
**RCRC** Reinforced Concrete Research Council.
**RCS** Radar Cross Section.
**RCS** Registre du Commerce et des Sociétés.
French initialism meaning: Companies' Register / Register of Companies.
*Business; Commerce.*
**RCS** Regolamento di Contabilità di Stato.
**RCS** Remote Computing System.
*Computer Technology.*
**RCS** Residential Conservation Service.
*Energy.*
**RCS** Rizzoli Corriere della Sera.
Daily newspaper (Italy).
**RCS** Royal College of Surgeons.
*Medicine.*
**RCS** Royal Corps of Signals.
**RCSI** Royal College of Surgeons of Ireland.
*Bioinformatics; Chemical Synthesis; Genomics; Proteomics; Surgical Training.*
**RC SOUTH** Regional Commnad (Commander) South [has replaced AFSOUTH 2.].
Commandement (commandant) régional Sud [remplace AFSOUTH 2.].
**RC SOUTHEAST** Regional Command (Commander) South-East [interim title given to RC SOUTHLANT - has replaced IBERLANT].
Commandement (commandant) régional Sud-Est [titre provisoire donné au RC SOUTHLANT - remplace l'IBERLANT].
**RC SOUTHLANT** Regional Command (Commander) South Atlantic [has replaced IBERLANT].
Commandement (commandant) régional Sud de l'Atlantique [remplace l'IBERLANT].
**rct.** (abbr.) receipt; recruit.
**RCT** Red Colloidal Test.
*Medicine.*
**RCT** Region Control Task.
*Data Communications.*
**RCT**; **Rct** Rehabilitation Center for Torture Victims (Copenhagen, Denmark).
The RCT was created in 1982 from the Danish section of Amnesty International.
**RCT** Remote Capacitor Transistor.
**RCT** Remote Cash Terminal.
**RCT** Research Corporation Technologies.
The RCT is a nonprofit technology transfer corporation. It is based in Tucson, Arizona and acts on behalf of the University of Arizona, U.S.A. and the Max Planck Society.
*Technology Transfer.*
**RCTL** Resistor-Capacitor-Transistor Logic.
*Electronics.*
**rcv.** (abbr.) receive.
**RC WEST** Regional Command (Commander) West [has replaced WESTLANT].
Commadement (commandant) régional Ouest [remplace WESTLANT].
**RCZ** rear combat zone.
zone arrière de combat.
**RD** Réaction de Dégénérescence.
French initialism meaning: Reaction of Degeneration.
*Medicine.*
**RD** Reaction of Degeneration.
*Medicine.*
**rd** (abbr.) read.
*Computer Technology; Electronics; Telecommunications.*
**RD** réception (recette) définitive (RD).
final acceptance (FA 2.).
**R-D** recherche et développement.
research and development (R&D).
**RD** Regio Decreto.
Italian initialism meaning: Royal Decree.
**RD** Registered Dietitian.
*Medicine.*
**RD** Registration Date.
**r.d.** relative density.
relative density is also known as: specific gravity.
*Mechanics.*
**RD** Restituzione Diritti.

**rd.** (abbr.) road.
For further details see under: **r**.
**R.D.** Roads Department.
**rd**; **rd.** (abbr.) rod.
For further details see under: **r**.
**RD**; **rd** root diameter.
referring to gears.
*Mechanics.*
**RD**; **rd** (abbr.) round.
*Military Science; Navigation; Ordnance.*
**rd** running days.
**RD** Rural Dean; Rural Delivery.
**R.D.** Rural District.
**rd**; **rd.** (abbr.) rutherford.
rutherford is a unit of nuclear decay rate. Named for the Britsh physicist Ernest **Rutherford**.
*Nucleonics.*
**RDA** Recommended Dietary / Daily Allowance (U.S.A.).
According to the U.S. National Research - Food and Council Nutrition Board.
*Nutrition.*
**RDA** Regional Development Agency.
**RDA** Rendu Droits Acquittés.
French initialism meaning: Delivered Duty Paid.
*Economics; International Trade.*
**RDA** Representational Difference Analysis.
RDA is a technique which can identify abnormalities in DNA.
*Immunology; Medicine; Microbiology; Pathology.*
**RDA** Rural Development Administration (U.S.A.).
**RdAc** Radioactinium.
RdAc is found in many minerals.
*Nuclear Physics.*
**RD and d** Research, Development and demonstration.
**RD & P** Research, Development and Production.
**RDAs** Recommended Dietary Allowances.
For further details see under: **RDA**.
**RDAs** Regional Development Agencies.
**RDase** Reductase.
*Enzymology.*
**RDB** Research and Development Board (U.S.A.).
**RDBMS** relational database management system.
système de gestion de base de données relationnelle.
**RDC** Remote Data Concentrator.
**RDC** Repubblica Democratica del Congo.
**RDC** République démocratique du Congo [anciennement appelée Zaïre].
Democratic Republic of Congo / DRC [formerly called Zaire].
**RDC** Research Diagnostic Criteria.
**RDC** Running Down Clause.
*Insurance; Sea Transport.*
**RDC** Rural District Council.
**RDD** Rendu Droits Dus.
French initialism meaning: Delivered Duty Unpaid.
*Economics; International Trade.*
**RDD** required delivery date.
1a. date de livraison requise.
1b. date de livraison demandée.
**RDD** Research and Development Division.
**RDE** Receptor-Destroying Enzyme.
*Enzymology.*
**RDF** Radial Distribution Function.
*Physical Chemistry.*
**RDF** Radio Direction Finding.
*Navigation.*
**RDF**; **Rdf** Resource Description Format.
**R.d.G.** Risultato di Gestione.
Italian initialism meaning: Operating Profit.
**RDGE** Resorcinol Diglycidyl Ether.
$C_{12}H_{14}O_2$. RDGE is used for epoxy resins.
*Organic Chemistry.*
**RDGM** renseignements et documentation géographiques militaires.
military geographic information and documentation (MGID).
**RD HD**, **rd hd bolt** Round Head bolt.
*Mechanical Devices.*
**RDI** Recommended Dietary Intake.
*Human Nutrition.*
**RDI** Research and Development Intensity.
**RDI** Revue de Droit International; Rivista di Diritto Internazionale.
French and Italian initialism meaning: Journal of International Law.
**RDI** Royal Designer for Industry - Royal Society of Arts.
**RDILC** Revue de Droit International et de Législation Comparée.
**rDNA** ribosomal DNA.
For further details see under: **DNA**.
**rDNA technology** recombinant DNA technology.
**RDOS** Real-time Disc Operating System.
**RDOs** Rieske non-heme iron Dioxygenases.
*Biochemistry; Biocatalysis; Bioprocessing; Microbiology; Molecular Biology.*
**RDP** Radar Data-Processing.
**RDPR** Refer to Drawer, Please Re-Present.
**rdr.** (abbr.) reader.
For further details see under: **r**.
**RdRP** RNA-dependent RNA Polymerase.

*Gene Expression; Molecular Biology; Molecular Genetics.*
**RDS** Radio Dimensione Suono (Italy).
*Networks.*
**RDS** Rate-Determining Step.
*Chemistry.*
**R/Ds** Reference Doses.
**RDS** Remote Data Station.
Remote data station is also known as: Remote Data Terminal.
*Computer Technology.*
**RDS** Respiratory Distress Syndrome.
The respiratory distress syndrome is a complication in infants delivered prematurely, characterized by respiratory distress and a somewhat purple discoloration of the skin.
*Medicine.*
**Rds** roads.
**r.ds.** running days.
**RDS/TMC** Traffic Message Channel over Radio Data System.
*Transport Telematics.*
**R.D.T.** Rapid Diagnostic Test.
**RDT & E** Research, Development, Test and Evaluation.
**RDU** The airport code for Raleigh/Durham, North Carolina, U.S.A.
**RDV** see R/V.
voir R/V.
**rdy** (abbr.) ready.
**RE** Random Error.
Random Error is also known as: Sampling Error; Stochastic Error.
*Statistics.*
**RE** Rare Earth.
*Chemistry.*
**R/E** Rate of Exchange.
*Business; Economics; Finance.*
**RE** Read Enable.
*Computers.*
**RE** Read Error.
*Computer Technology.*
**RE** Real Estate.
**RE** Recursively Enumerable language.
*Computer Programming.*
**re.** (abbr.) reference; regarding.
**RE** Reggio nell'Emilia, Italy.
**re.** (abbr.) relating.
**RE** Renewable Energies.
**Re** Reynolds number.
Named for the British physicist Osborne **Reynolds**, who discovered it.
*Fluid Mechanics.*
**Re** The chemical symbol for Rhenium.
Rhenium is a metallic element having the atomic nurnber 75, and an atomic weight of 186.2. It is used mainly in electrical components and filaments.
*Chemistry.*
**R/E** Ricavo Effetti.
Italian acronym meaning: Receipts from Bills.
**RE** Rodding Eye.
*Buildings; Pipe Systems.*
**RE** Royal Engineers.
**RE** Royal Society of Painters and Etchers.
**Re** Rupee.
*Currencies.*
**re** with reference to.
*Commerce.*
**REA** Railway Express Agency.
**REA** rapid environmental assessment.
évaluation rapide de l'environnement.
**REA** Right Ear Advantage.
*Acoustics.*
**REA** Rural Electrification Administration.
**REAC/TS** Radiation Emergency Assistance Center/Training Site.
REAC/TS is one of the WHO's Centers.
*Nuclear Defense.*
For further details see under: **WHO**.
**REAG** Real Estate Advisory Group.
**REAPER** Red Europea de Accion Para Estudios Rurales.
*European Community Project.*
**REBs** Research Ethics Boards (Canada).
*Monitoring of Human Experimentation; Research Ethics.*
**REC** radio-electronic combat.
combat radioélectronique.
**REC** Registro Esercenti in Commercio.
**REC** REmote Console.
*Computer Technology.*
**RECCE** reconnaissance.
reconnaissance.
**RECCEXREP** reconnaissance exploitation report.
compte rendu d'exploitation de reconnaissance.
**recd**; **rec'd** (abbr.) received.
**RECF** receiving force.
force d'accueil.
**RECITAL** RElay Centre for Central Italy.
Tuscany and Umbria.
**RECO** reconnaissance.
reconnaissance.
**RECON** see RECCE.
voir RECCE.
**RECON** (abbr.) REmote CONsole.

**RECONEX** reconnaissance exercise.
exercice de reconnaissance.
**recpt.** (abbr.) receipt.
Also: **rect**.
**RECS** radio-electronic combat support.
appui au combat radioélectronique.
**RECSHIP** receiving ship.
bâtiment ravitaillé.
**RECSTA** receiving station.
station réceptrice.
**rect.** (abbr.) rectangle.
*Mathematics.*
**red.** Redeemable.
*Finance.*
**RED** Refunding Escrow Deposit (U.S.A.).
**REDSO/ESA** Regional Economic Developmental Services Office for East and Southern Africa.
*U.S. Aid.*
**REDVC** Russian-English Dictionary of Verbal Collocations.
**REE** Rare-Earth Element.
*Chemistry.*
**REED** Residential Energy Efficient Database.
*Indoor Air Quality.*
**REER** Regime Enregistré d'Epargne - Retraite (Canada).
French acronym meaning: Registered Retirement Savings Plan.
**REEs** Rare-Earth Elements.
*Chemistry; Geochemistry; Isotope Geology.*
**REES** Research Experience for European Students.
**REF** Rat Embryo Fibroblast.
**Ref**; **ref** (abbr.) reference.
**Ref**; **ref** (abbr.) refrigerated (ship).
**Ref.** (abbr.) Refunding.
*Business; Economics; Finance.*
**REF** Renal Erythropoietic Factor.
*Medicine.*
**REFCORP** REsolution Funding CORPoration.
**REFL** REFerence Line.
*Military Science; Navigation.*
**reflection HEED** reflection High-Energy Electron Diffraction.
*Physics.*
**REFM** Resource Ecology and Fisheries Management.
**reg.** (abbr.) register.
*Computer Technology; Graphic Arts; Mechanical Engineering; Military Science; Telecommunications.*
**Reg.** (abbr.) Registrar.
**reg.** (abbr,) registration.
**reg.** (abbr.) regulation.
*Biology; Control Systems; Electricity; Electronics.*
**reg** (abbr.) registered.
Also: **regd.**
**Reg.Gen.** (abbr.) Registrar-General.
**regs.** (abbr.) regulations.
**Regt** regiment.
régiment.
**REH** Rational Expectations Hypothesis.
*Economics.*
**REI** Rachat d'une Entreprise par des Investisseurs.
French acronym meaning: Leveraged Management Buy In.
*Business; Economics; Finance.*
**REI** Research and Education Institute (U.S.A.).
**REIC** Real Estate Investment Company.
**REIF** Real Estate Investment Funds.
**reimb.** (abbr.) reimburse; reimbursement.
**REIMEP** Regular European Interlaboratory Measurement Evolution Programme.
**REIS** Real Estate Information System.
**REIT** Real Estate Investment Trust.
**REITs** Real Estate Investment Trusts.
**REL** Rapidly Extensible Language.
Referring to English.
**rel.** (abbr.) related; relative; relating.
**rel.** (abbr.) release.
*Industrial Engineering; Mechanical Engineering; Ordnance.*
**REL** Répartition Electronique.
**RELMAP** REgional Lagrangian Model of Air Pollution.
**RELSAT** relay satellite.
satellite relais.
**RELUM** Highly reactive rare earth oxide powders for more efficient luminescent materials.
*European Community Project; Fluorescent Tubes.*
**REM** Radioactivity Environmental Monitoring.
**REM** Rapid Eye Movement.
*Physiology.*
**rem.** (abbr.) remboursable.
French abbreviation meaning: reimbursable; repayable.
*Commerce.*
**rem.** (abbr.) remboursement.
French abbreviation meaning: reimbursement; repayment; refundment.
*Commerce.*
**rem.** (abbr.) remittance.
Also: **remitt**.
**REM**; **rem** Roentgen Equivalent Man.
Named after the German physicist Wilhelm Konrad **Roentgen**.

*Ionizing Radiation; Population Studies; Radiation Effects Research; Radiation Risks.*
**REMACT** remedial action.
1a. action corrective.
1b. mesure corrective.
**REMI** Real Estate Mortgage Investment.
**REMI** Restriction Enzyme Mediated Integration.
**Re Mida** Rete Milanese per la didattica e l'apprendimento del 21° secolo.
A 1998-2001 Project promoted by the Comune di Milano and Milano per la Multimedialità.
*Teaching Technologies Development.*
**remitt.** (abbr.) remittance.
Also: **rem**.
**REMPI** Resonance-Enhanced Multiphoton Ionization.
*Chemistry; Organic Chemistry.*
**REMPI** REsonant Multiphoton Ionization.
*Molecular Physics.*
**REM sleep** Rapid Eye Movement sleep.
The rapid eye movement sleep is also known as: fast wave sleep; paradoxical sleep; active sleep; dreaming sleep; desynchronized sleep.
*Neurology.*
**REMUs** Remote Environmental Monitoring Units.
Created at the WHOI (U.S.A.).
*Chemistry and Biology of the Oceans.*
For further details see under: **WHOI**.
**RENCA** RENal-cell CArcinoma.
RENCA is also known as: Hypernephroma.
*Medicine.*
**REO** Real Estate Owned (U.S.A.).
*Law.*
**reo** The above acronym was coined accidentally using the Italian word "reo" which means: (*Law*) guilty; offender; culprit; criminal. Also: wicked; evil.
**REOP** Reasonable Expectation Of Privacy.
**REP** 1. radio-electronic protection.
1. protection radioélectronique.
2. report [suffix used in compound terms; e.g. LOGSUMREP].
2. compte rendu [suffixe utilisé dans les termes composés; cf. LOGSUMREP].
**rep.** (abbr.) repair.
**rep.** (abbr.) reparto.
Italian abbreviation meaning: department; division; ward (of hospital).
**rep.** (abbr.) reply.
reply is also known as: response.
*Telecommunications.*
**rep.** (abbr.) report; reporter.
**rep.** (abbr.) representative; representing.
**rep.** (abbr.) reprint.
Also: **R/P**.
**Rep**; **rep.** (abbr.) Repubblica.
Italian abbreviation meaning: Republic.
**rep.** (abbr.) republic.
**REP** Ricardian Equivalence Proposition.
*Economics.*
**REP elements** Repetitive Extragenic Palindromic elements.
*Genetics.*
**REPOS** Sale and Repurchase Agreements (U.S.A.).
**repos** The above acronym was coined accidentally using the French word "repos" which means: rest; nap; repose.
**repr.** (abbr.) representation.
*Artificial Intelligence.*
**repro.** (abbr.) reproduction.
**REPs** Repetitive Extragenic Palindromes.
**rept.** (abbr.) receipt; report.
**req.** (abbr.) request; required.
**RER** Rough Endoplasmic Reticulum.
*Cell Biology.*
**RE/RE** reinforcement / resupply (shipping).
(navigation de) renforcement / réapprovisionnement.
**RERF** Radiation Effects Research Foundation.
RERF was created in 1945 with a different acronym. It deals with the collection of information on cancer and other diseases due to ionizing radiation. RERF is funded by the United States and Japan.
**RERTR Agreement** Reduced Enrichment for Research Test Reactors Agreement.
RERTR is a 1978 Agreement.
*Nuclear Nonproliferation.*
**RES** Rachat d'une Entreprise par ses Salariés.
French acronym meaning: Leveraged Management Buy Out.
*Business; Economics; Finance.*
**RES** 1. radar environment simulation.
1. simulation de l'environnement radar.
2. radiation exposure state.
2. condition d'exposition aux radiations.
**RES** Renewable Energy Sources.
**res.** (abbr.) reserve.
*Aviation; Computer Programming; Military Science.*
**res.** (abbr.) restore.
*Computer Technology.*
**RES** Reticuloendothelial System.
*Anatomy.*
**RES** Royal Economic Society.
**RES** Royal Empire Society.

**RESA** REsearch Society of America (U.S.A.).
**resa** The above acronym was coined accidentally using the Italian word "resa" which means in Italian: surrender; yield; profit; return; restitution.
**RESCAP** rescue combat air patrol.
patrouille de combat de sauvetage.
**RESCO** recherche et sauvetage de combat.
combat search and rescue (CSAR).
**RESCUE** Relative Enhancer and Silencer Classification by Unanimous Enrichment.
*Biology; Cancer Research; Chemical Processes; Oligonucleotide Motifs.*
**RESOLV** REconstruction using Scanned Laser and Video.
*European Community Project.*
**RESPA** Real Estate Settlement Procedures Act.
*U.S. Acts.*
**RESPRO** Recycled paper mills Effluents to wood Substitutive PROducts.
*European Community Project.*
**R.E.S.Q.U.E.** Risparmio Energetico, Sostenibilità, Qualità, rapporti con gli Organi dell'Unione Europea (Italy).
*Energy.*
**resrt.** (abbr.) restart.
In computer technology, restart is also known as: Reboot.
*Aviation; Computer Technology.*
**RET** Reliable Earth Terminal.
**ret.** (abbr.) return.
*Architecture; Computer Programming; Design Engineering; Electronics; Geophysics.*
**retd.** (abbr.) retained; returned.
**retd** (abbr.) retired.
**RETRF** Rural Electrification and Telephone Revolving Fund.
**REU** Eurodollar Rate.
**REV** ravitaillement en vol.
air-to-air refueling.
**rev.** (abbr.) revenue; reverse; review; revision.
**rev.** (abbr.) revolution.
For further details see under: **r**.
**Rev. A/C** Revenue Account.
**Revd** Reverend.
**REW(S)** radio electronic warfare (service).
(service de) guerre radioélectronique.
**REX** Resonance Enhanced X-rays.
*Chemical Physics; Chemistry.*
**RF**; **rf** Radio Frequency.
Radio frequency is in the range from 10 kHz to 300,000 MHz.
*Telecommunications.*
**RF**; **rf** Radio Frequenza.
Italian initialism meaning: Radio Frequency.
For further details see under: **RF** (Radio Frequency).
**RF** Range Finder / rangefinder.
*Electronics; Optics; Ordnance; Telecommunications.*
**RF**; **rf** Rapid Fire.
*Ordnance.*
**RF** Rate Free.
**RF** reaction force.
force de réaction.
**RF** Receptive Field (visual).
**RF** Reducing Flame.
*Chemistry.*
**RF** Release Factor.
*Biochemistry.*
**RF** République Française.
French initialism meaning: French Republic.
**RF** Resistance Factor.
RF is also known as: Resistance Plasmid.
*Molecular Biology.*
**r.f.** revenu fixe.
**RF** Revolving Fund.
*Business; Economics; Finance.*
**RF** Rheumatoid Factor.
*Autoantibiotics; Immunology; Medicine; Microbiology.*
**RF(A)** reaction force (air).
force aérienne de réaction.
**RFA** Reciprocally Free of Average.
**RFA** 1. République fédérale d'Allemagne.
1. Federal Republic of Germany (FRG).
2. restricted fire area.
2. zone de tir restreint.
**RFA** Request For Applications.
**RFA** Royal Field Artillery.
**RFAF** Russian Federation Air Force.
armée de l'air de la Fédération de Russie.
**RF(A)S** reaction forces (air) staff.
état-major des forces aériennes de réaction.
**RFB** Request For Bid.
*Business; Economics; Finance.*
**RFBR** Russian Foundation for Basic Research.
The RFBR is the main agency for supporting peer-reviewed research.
**RFC** Reconstruction Finance Corporation (U.S.A.).
**RFC** Replication Factor C.
*Cancer Research; Developmental Biology.*
**RFC** Request For Comments.
**RFC** River Forecast Center (U.S.A.).
**RFC account** Resident Foreign Currency account (India).
*Investment Schemes.*

**RfD**; **Rfd** Reference Dose.
**RFD** Rural Free Delivery (U.S.A.).
**RFE/RL** Radio Free Europe/Radio Liberty.
The RFE/RL is the U.S. Congress-funded radio station.
**RFF** Resources for the Future (U.S.A.).
RFF is a Washington-based Research Organization.
Also: **RfF**.
**rfg.** (abbr.) refunding.
**RFG** revalidated force goal.
objectif de forces revalidé.
**RFHQ** reaction force headquarters.
quartier général des forces de réaction.
**RFI** Radio-Frequency Interference.
*Telecommunications.*
**RFI** Ready For Inspection (referring to shop production).
*Industry.*
**RFI** Request For Information.
**RFL** 1. restricted fire line.
1. ligne de tir restreinte.
2. restricted frequency list.
2. liste des fréquences restreintes.
**RFLP** Restriction Fragment Length Polymorphism.
**RFLPs** Restriction Fragment Length Polymorphisms.
*Cancer Research; DNA Changes; Human Evolution.*
**RFMF** Radio-Frequency Magnetic Field.
*DNA Hybridization; Nanocrystal-linked; Oligonucleotides.*
**RFNA** Red Fuming Nitric Acid.
**rFng** radical Fringe.
*Anatomy; Medicine; Neurobiology.*
For further details see under: **lFng** (lunatic Fringe).
**RFO** Règlement financier de l'OTAN.
NATO Financial Regulations (NFR).
**RFOM** restriction on freedom of movement.
entraves à la liberté de mouvement (ou de circulation).
**RFP**; **R.F.P.** Request For Proposal.
**RFP** Reverse-Field Pinch.
*Fusion; Plasma Science.*
**RFPA** Right to Financial Privacy Act.
*Treaties.*
**rf preheating** radio-frequency preheating.
*Engineering.*
**RFPs** Requests For Proposals.
**RFQ** Requests For Qualification.
**RFQ** Request For Quotation.
**rfrsh** (abbr.) refresh.
Also: **rfsh**.
*Computer Technology; Surgery.*
**RFS** Ready For Sea.
**RFs** Receptive Fields.
*Neuroscience.*
**RF-SET** Radio-Frequency Single-Electron Transistor.
*Applied Physics; Microelectronics; Nanoscience; Physics.*
**rFSH** recombinant Follicle-Stimulating Hormone.
**rfsh** (abbr.) refresh.
For further details see under: **rfrsh**.
**RF signal generator** Radio-Frequency signal generator.
*Electronics.*
**RFTS** Remote Fibre-Test System.
A group of products which enables to cut network down-time and guarantee quality of service. Of the Canadian *test and measurement* specialist EXPO.
**RFUCMS** Royal Force and University College Medical School (G.B.).
**RFW** radio frequency weapon.
arme à radiofréquences.
**RG** Ragusa, Italy.
**RG** Renseignements Généraux.
**RG** Report Generator.
*Computer Programming.*
**R6G** Rhodamine 6G.
*Chemistry.*
**RG** Rive Gauche (France).
**RG** Rough Grinding.
*Mechanical Engineering.*
**RG** The airline code for Varig, S.A.
**RGB** Red-Green-Blue.
*Computer Technology.*
**RGB stars** Red Giant Branch stars.
*Astronomy; Astrophysics; Nucleosynthesis in Stars.*
**RGC** (rat) Retinal Ganglion Cell.
For further details see under: **RGCs**.
**RGCs** Retinal Ganglion Cells.
The RGCs are nerve cells that transmit information from the eye to the brain.
*Circadian Clock; Circadian Light Responses; Cellular Biology; Development-Pathology; Medicine; Neurobiology.*
**rgd.** (abbr.) registered.
Also: **reg.**
**RGDIP** Revue Générale de Droit International Public.
*Publications.*
**RGI** Resource Group International (Norway).
*Offshore Engineering; Seafoods.*

**RGO** Royal Greenwich Observatory.
The RGO is located in Cambridge, G.B.
*Astronomy.*
**RGP** Rice Genome Research Program.
*Japane Programs; Rice Genome Research.*
**RGP** Remote Graphics Processor.
**RGS** 1. range gate stealing.
1. voleur de fenêtre de télémétrie.
2. remote ground sensor.
2. capteur au sol éloigné.
**RGS** Regulator of G protein-Signaling.
*Immunology; Medicine; Molecular Biology.*
**RGS** Ribbon Growth on substrate Silicon.
*Photovoltaics.*
**Rgt.**; **rgt.** (abbr.) règlement.
French abbreviation meaning: rule; code of practice. Also: payment; settlement; remittance.
**RGU system** Red, Green, and Ultraviolet system.
*Astronomy.*
**RGV** RELIT Grande Vitesse.
French initialism meaning: High-Speed DVP Securities Settlement System.
*Banking.*
For further details see under: **DVP** (Delivery-Versus-Payment system).
**RH** radar head.
tête radar.
**RH** Read Head.
*Computer Technology.*
**RH**; **rh** Relative Humidity.
*Meteorology.*
**RH** Releasing Hormone.
RH is also known as: Releasing Factor.
*Endocrinology.*
**Rh** The chemical symbol for Rhodium.
Rhodium is a metallic element having the atomic number 45, and an atomic weight of 102.9. The word rhodium derives from the Greek word "rose".
*Chemistry.*
**RH** Right Hand.
*Building Engineering; Mechanical Engineering.*
**RH** Rockwell Hardness.
*Engineering.*
**RHA** Road Haulage Association (Ireland).
**RHAW** radar homing and warning.
ralliement et alerte radar.
**RHD** Rabbit Hemorrhagic Disease.
A seminar on RHD was held in Adelaide (Australia) on 23rd September 1997.
*Ecology; Environmental Science; Virology.*
**RHD virus** Rabbit Hemorrhagic Disease Virus.
RHD is also known as: Rabbit Calicivirus Disease.
*Virology.*
**RHEED** Reflected High-Energy Electron Diffraction.
*Electrical and Computer Engineering; Materials; Quantized Electronic Structures.*
**Rh factor** Rhesus factor.
The term rhesus factor derives from: rhesus monkeys where it was first discovered.
*Genetics.*
**rhGH** recombinant human Growth Hormone.
*Health Sciences; Medicine; Pharmacology; Physiology; Primate Research.*
**RHI** Range Height Indicator.
*Engineering.*
**RHIC** Relativistic Heavy Ion Collider.
The RHIC will operate in 1997.
*High-Energy Physics; Nuclear Physics.*
**RHM** Roentgen-per-Hour-at-one-Meter.
*Nucleonics.*
**R-HOUR** hour at which retaliation is authorized.
heure à laquelle la riposte est autorisée.
**RHP** Resource-Holding Potential.
*Behavior.*
**RH panel** Radiation Hybrid panel.
*Biotechnology; Genetics; Human Genome; Medicine; Molecular Biology.*
**RHQ** 1. rear headquarters.
1. quartier général de l'arrière.
2. regional headquarters.
2. quartier général régional.
**RHQ AFNORTH** Regional Headquarters Allied Forces North.
Quartier général régional des Forces alliées Nord-Europe.
**RHQ AFSOUTH** Regional Headquarters Allied Forces South.
Quartier général régional des Forces alliées Sud-Europe.
**RHQ EASTLANT** Regional Headquarters East Atlantic.
Quartier général régional Est de l'Atlantique.
**RHQ SOUTHLANT** Regional Headquarters South Atlantic.
Quartier général régional Sud de l'Atlantique.
**RHQ WESTLANT** Regional Headquarters West Atlantic.
Quartier général régional Ouest de l'Atlantique.
**RH relations** Rankine-Hugoniot relations.
*Theoretical Geochemistry.*
**RHS** Right-Hand Side.
**RHS** Royal Historical Society.
**RHS** Royal Horticultural Society.
**RHS** Royal Humane Society.

**RHT** Rockwell Hardness Test.
*Engineering.*
**RI** Radio Influence; Radio Interference.
*Data Communications.*
**RI** Real Income.
*Business; Finance.*
**RI** Refractive Index.
*Optics.*
**RI**; **R/I**; **r.i.** reinsurance.
**RI** Reliability Index.
*Data Communications.*
**RI** Remote Inquiry.
*Computer Technology.*
**RI** Replicative Intermediate.
*Genetics.*
**RI** Repubblica Italiana.
Italian acronym meaning: Italian Republic.
**RI** Républicains Indépendants (France).
*Political Party.*
**RI** (abbr.) Rhode Island (U.S.A.).
**RI** Rieti, Italy.
**RI** Roslin Institute (G.B.).
*Farm Animal Biotechnology; Genetical Research.*
**RI** routing indicator.
1a. indicateur de routage.
1b. indicateur d'acheminement.
**RI** Royal Institute (of Painters in Watercolours).
**RI** Royal Institution.
**RIA** Radioimmunoassay.
*Immunology.*
**RIA** Rare Isotope Accelerator.
RIA is a facility endorsed by the U.S. Government's NSAC to study rare isotopes.
*Nuclear Physics.*
For further details see under: **NSAC**.
**RIA** Royal Irish Academy.
**RIAA** Recording Industry Association of America.
RIAA is the trade body which represents the U.S. record industry, and its Canadian counterpart.
*Acoustical Engineerings.*
**RIAs** Radioimmunoassays.
*Immunology.*
**RIB** Relevé d'Identité Bancaire (France).
French acronym referring to a form showing details of one's own bank account.
*Banking.*
**RIB** Resource Integration Board [MBC].
Commission d'intégration des ressources [CBM].
**RI.BA.** RIcevuta BAncaria.
Italian acronym meaning: Cash Order; Collection Order.
**RIBA** Royal Institute of British Architects (G.B.).
**RIC** Rare-earth Information Center.
**RIC** repatriation information centre.
centre d'information sur le rapatriement.
**ric.** ricevuta.
Italian abbreviation meaning: receipt.
**RIC** The airport code for Richmond, Virginia, U.S.A.
**RICA** Research Institute for Consumers' Affairs.
**RICA** Rete di Informazione Contabile Agricola (Italy).
Italian acronym meaning: Agricultural Bookkeeping Information Network.
**RI chromosome** Recombinant Inbred chromosome.
*Genetics; Genomic Research; Medicine; Molecular Genetics.*
**RICO Act** Racketeer Influenced and Corrupt Organizations Act.
*U.S. Acts.*
**RID** Radial Immunodiffusion.
**RID** Rapporti Interbancari Diretti (Italy).
Italian acronym meaning: Interbank Direct Relationships.
**RIDGE program** Ridge Inter-Disciplinary Global Experiments program.
RIDGE includes the MELT Experiment funded by the U.S. National Science Foundation.
For further details see under: **MELT Experiment**.
**RIDIRS** Resonant Ion-Dip IR Spectroscopy.
*Chemistry.*
**RIDIS** Réseau Ivorien de Documentation et d'Information Scientifique.
**RIE** Recognized Investment Exchange (G.B.).
**RIE** Research In Education (U.S.A.).
**RIET** Renault Industries Equipments et Techniques (France).
**RIE technique** Reactive Ion Etching technique.
*Chemical Engineering; Materials; Physics.*
**RIF** Reduction In Force.
**RIFM practices** Reduced Impact Forest Management practices (Brazil).
*Illegal Deforestation; Fire Risk Reduction.*
**RI/FS** Remedial Investigation / Feasibility Study.
**RIFs** Resource Impact Factors.
**RIG** Rate Integrating Gyroscope.
*Mechanical Engineering.*
**RIGS** Repeat-Induced Gene Silencing.
*Biology.*
**RIHANS** RIver and Harbor Aid to Navigation System.
**RII** Radar Intelligence Item.
*Electronics.*
**RILEM** Réunion Internationale des Laboratoires d'Essais et de recherches sur les Matériaux et les constructions (France).

French acronym of the: International Union of Testing and Research Laboratories on Materials and Structures. RILEM was founded in 1947.

**RILM** Répertoire International de Littérature Musicale.
French acronym meaning: International Repertory of Music Literature (New York, U.S.A.). Founded in 1966.

**RIM** Rab3A-Interacting Molecule.
A modular protein.
*Molecular Neurobiology; Presynaptic Plasticity Regulators.*

**RIM** Reaction Injection Molding; reaction-injected-molded.

**rim** The above acronym was coined using the English word "rim".
*Design Engineering; Geology; Metallurgy.*

**RIMA** Régiment d'Infanterie de MArine (France).

**R.I.Na** Registro Italiano Navale.
Italian acronym of the: The Italian ship-classification Society.
*Shipping.*

**RINA** Registro Italiano Navale e Aeronautico.
Italian acronym of the: Italian Air and Shipping Registry.

**Ri number** Richardson number.
Named for the English physicist Owen W. **Richardson** (1879-1959).
*Fluid Mechanics.*

**RIO** Rischi In Osservazione (Italy).
Italian initialism meaning: difficult loans; doubtful loans.
*Banking.*

**RIP** radar improvement plan.
plan d'amélioration des radars.

**RIP** rat insulin promoter.
*Metastasis Studies.*

**RIP** Relevé d'Identité Postale (France).
French acronym referring to a form showing details of one's own Post Office account.

**RIP** Rest In Peace.

**RIP** Riposi / Riposino in Pace.
Italian acronym meaning: Rest In Peace.

**RIP** RNAIII Inhibiting Peptide.
*Internal Medicine; Medical Pathology.*

**RIP** Routing Information Protocol.

**RIPA** Radio-Immuno-Precipitation Assay.
*Immunology.*

**RIPL** reconnaissance indication planning line.
ligne de planification des indices de reconnaissance.

**RIPM** Répertoire International de la Presse Musicale.

**RIP mapping** Replication Initiation Point mapping.
*Biology; Medicine.*

**RIP mutation** Repeat Induced Point mutation.

**RIPP** Russian-American Institute for President Programs.
RIPP deals with technology transfer and has offices in Moscow as well as in Washington D.C., U.S.A.
*Technology Transfer.*

**RiPPA** Ribonuclease Protection Proximity Assay.

**ripr.viet.** (abbr.) riproduzione vietata.
Italian abbreviation meaning: copyrighted, reproduction forbidden.

**RIR** repatriation information report.
compte rendu d'information sur le rapatriement.

**RIR** Request Immediate Reply.

**RIS** radar integration system.
système d'intégration des radars.

**RIS** Regional Innovation Strategies - E.C.

**RIS** Reparto Investigazioni Speciali/Scientifiche (Italy).

**RIS** Research Information System (U.S.A.).
The U.S. Research Information System deals with the classification of life sciences citation data and the organization of reference collections. RIS is located in Carlsbad, California.

**RIs** Research Institutes.

**RIS** Retroreflector In Space.
Instrument aboard ADEOS.
For further details see under: **ADEOS**.

**RISBDC** Rhode Island Small Business Development Center.
RISBDC is administered by Bryant College.

**RISC** Reduced Instruction Set Computer.
*Computer Technology.*

**Risc** Research institute on social change (France).

**RISC** RNA-Induced Silencing Complex.
*Biochemistry; Biological Sciences; Genetics; Medicine; Molecular Pharmacology.*
For further details see under: **RNA**.

**RISC** RNA Interference Specificity Complex.
A ribonuclease complex.

**RISC architecture** Reduced Instruction Set Computing architecture.
*Information and Communication Technology.*

**RISE** Regional Initiatives in Science Education (U.S.A.).

**RISE** Réseau International des Sciences de l'Environnement.
French initialism meaning: International Social Sciences and Environment Network.

**RISE** Resources for Involving Scientists in Education.

*U.S. Project.*
**rise** The above acronyms were coined using the English word "rise".
*Astronomy; Geology; Hydrology; Science.*
**RISE system** Rubber Insert Sleeves Expanding system.
**RISI** Regional Information Society Initiative - European Community.
The ARIANE project in the Calabria region (Italy) is funded by RISI.
**RISP** Ross sea Ice Shelf Project.
*New Zealand Projects.*
**RIST** Radio-Immuno Sorbent Test.
*Immunology.*
**rist.** (abbr.) ristampa.
Italian abbreviation meaning: reprint.
*Publishing.*
**RISTA** reconnaissance, intelligence, surveillance and target acquisition.
reconnaissance, renseignement, surveillance et acquisition d'objectif.
**RIT** Rail Inclusive Tour.
*Railways.*
**RIT** Rochester Institute of Technology.
**RITA** Resistance In The Army.
*U.S. Army.*
**R.I.T.A.** Ricerca Innovazione Tessile Abbigliamento (Italy).
*Textile Innovations.*
**RITC** rhodamine isothiocyanate.
**RITE** Regional Infrastructure for Telematics in Europe.
**RITE** Research Institute of Innovative Technology for the Earth (Japan).
**RITS program** Radiatively Important Trace Species program.
**RITTS** Regional Innovation and Technology Transfer Strategies and infrastructures.
*European Community Project.*
**RIVA** Rythme Idioventriculaire Accéléré.
French acronym meaning: Accelerated Idioventricular Rhythm.
*Medicine.*
**RIVES** Registro Italiano Veicoli Elettrosolari.
Italian acronym meaning: Italian Registry of Solar-Powered Vehicles.
**RIW** reliability improvement warranty.
garantie d'amélioration de la fiabilité.
**RJE** Remote Job Entry.
*Computer Technology.*
**RKA** Russian Space Agency.
**RKI** Robert Koch Institute - Berlin, Germany.
**RKKY interaction** Rudermann-Kittel-Kasuya-Yoshida interaction.
*Physics; Artificial Quantum Dot System; Kendo Effect; Electrical Engineering; Computer Engineering.*
**rkva** reactive-kilovolt-ampere.
**RL** Lebanon's International vehicle-registration letters.
**RL** Long Rate.
*Banking.*
**RL** Radio Liberty.
**RL** Regione Lombardia.
Italian initialism of the: Lombardy Region.
**RL** (abbr.) Release (referring to work).
**RL** Record Length.
Record Length is also known as: Record Size.
*Computer Programming.*
**RL** Relocatable Library.
**RL** Retinorecipient Laminae.
*Anatomy; Neurobiology.*
**RL** Rocket Launcher.
*Space Technology.*
**RL** Round Lot.
**RLCs** Regulatory Light Chains.
**RLF** Relaxin-like Factor.
A peptide hormone.
*Endocrinology; Fertility Research; Hormone Research.*
**RLF** Replication Licensing Factor.
*DNA Replication.*
**RLF** Retrolental Fibroplasia.
*Medicine.*
**RLF** Royal Literary Fund.
**RLG** Research Libraries Group.
**RLI** Royal Life International (G.B.).
*Insurers.*
**RLN** LORAN station.
station LORAN.
**RLO** Returned Letter Office.
**RLO** Round Lot Orders.
**RLPs** Ribosome-Like Particles.
**RLS** Reflective Light Sensor.
**RLSD** Received Line Signal Detector.
**RLT** regimental landing team.
groupe régimentaire de débarquement.
**RLT** Ricerca a Lungo Termine (Italy).
Italian initialism meaning: Long-Term Research.
**RLT** Rolling Liquid Transport.
*U.S. Army.*
**Rly**; **rly** (abbr.) railway.
Also: **rail.**; **rwy.**
**Rm** (abbr.) ream.
*Engineering; Materials Science.*

**RM** Registered Mail.
**RM** Registre des Métiers (France).
**RM** Règlement Mensuel (bourse des valeurs).
French initilism meaning: forward market (Bourse/Stock Exchange).
*Business; Economics; Finance.*
**RM** Removable Medium.
*Computer Technology.*
**RM** Reset Mode.
*Computer Technology.*
**RM** Resident Magistrate.
**RM** restriction of movement [formerly called ROM].
entrave à la liberté de mouvement (ou de circulation) [anciennement appelée ROM].
**R/M**; **RM** Restrizione Modificazione.
Italian initialism meaning: Restriction Modification.
*Molecular Biology.*
**RM** Rétrécissement Mitral.
French initialism meaning: Mitral Stenosis.
*Cardiology.*
**RM** Ricchezza Mobile.
Italian initialism meaning: Personal Property; Movable Wealth.
**RM** Risonanza Magnetica.
Italian initialism meaning: Magnetic Resonance.
*Physics.*
**Rm** (abbr.) room.
*Building Engineering; Geology; Mining Engineering.*
**RM** Root Module.
*Space Greenhouse.*
**RM** Rough Machining.
*Mechanical Engineering.*
**RM** Royal Mail.
**RM** Royal Marines.
**RM** Malagasy Republic's International vehicle-registration letters.
**RMA** reliability maintainability, availability.
fiabilité, maintenabilité, disponibilité.
**RMA** Rubber Manufacturers' Association.
**RMA position** Right Mentoanterior position.
**RMB Resources** Rand Merchant Bank Resources.
RMB Resources is a specialist division of RMB, focussing on the mining and oil and gas industries of sub Saharan Africa. The services provided by RMB Resources include the provision of advice in relation to *mergers, acquisitions* and *disvestments*, *project financing*, and the provision of debt and equity capital.
*Banking Services.*
**RMC** Rotating Modulation Collimator.
**RMC** Royal Military College.
**RMD** Ready Money Down.
*Business; Commerce; Finance.*
**Rmdr.** (abbr.) remainder.
*Mathematics.*
**RME** Receptor-Mediated Endocytosis.
*Biochemistry; Clinical Biochemistry; Genetics; Medical Research.*
**RMF** ready manoeuvre force.
force de manœuvre prête à l'action.
**RMI** Radio Magnetic Indicator.
**RMI** Republic of The Marshall Islands.
**RMI** Revenu Minimum d'Insertion (France).
French initialism referring to the minimum amount paid to an unemployed person in job training.
**RMI** Rocky Mountain Institute.
**RMIT** Royal Melbourne Institute of Technology (Australia).
The RMIT is the largest multi-level technological university in Australia.
**r.m.m.** relative molecular mass.
*Chemistry.*
**RMM** Mali's International vehicle-registration letters.
**RMN** représentant militaire national.
national military representative (NMR 1.).
**RMN** Résonance Magnétique Nucléaire; Risonanza Magnetica Nucleare.
French and Italian initialism meaning: Nuclear Magnetic Resonance.
*Physics; Radiology.*
**RMO** route management organization.
organisme de gestion des routes (maritimes).
**RMON specification** Remote MONitoring specification.
**RMP** recognized maritime picture.
1a. situation maritime générale.
1b. situation maritime renseignée.
**RMP position** Right Mentoposterior position.
**RMR** Resting Metabolic Rate.
*Nutrition.*
**RMS** Real Market Share.
*Business; Finance.*
**RMS** Recovery Management Support.
*Data Communications.*
**RMS** Remote Manipulator System.
**RMS**; **rms** Root-Mean-Square.
*Electrical Engineering.*
**RMS** Royal Mail Steamer (G.B.).
**RMS** Royal Meteorological Society.
**RMS** Royal Microscopical Society.
**RMSA** Rocky Mountain Superconductivity Alliance.

The RMSA was formed in late 1989 as an outgrowth of an NREL-hosted meeting of superconductivity researchers from Rocky Mountain region.
*Superconductivity.*
For further details see under: **NREL**.
**RMSE** Root-Mean-Square Error.
RMSE is also known as: Standard Deviation; Standard Error.
*Statistics.*
**RMS functions** Research Management and Support functions.
Of U.S. NIH.
For further details see under: **NIH**.
**rms value** roof-mean-square value.
**RMT presentation** Right Mentum Transverse presentation.
**RMV** Respiratory Minute Volume.
*Physiology.*
**Rn** The chemical symbol for Radon.
Used mainly in cancer treatment and in radiography.
*Chemistry; Symbols.*
**RN** Red Nucleus.
*Neurology.*
**RN** Région Nord [obsolète].
Northern Region (NR 3.) [obsolete].
**RN** Registered Nurse.
**RN** Registration Number.
**RN** Rimini, Italy.
**RN** Riserva Navale.
Italian initialism meaning: Navy Reserve.
**RNA** Ribonucleic Acid.
*Biochemistry.*
**RNAi** RNA interference.
*Biological Sciences; Biomedical Genetics; Genetics; Genes Development; RNAi-based therapies.*
**RNAP** RNA Polymerase (an enzyme).
*Biochemistry; Cellular and Molecular Biology; Molecular Genetics.*
**RNase** Ribonuclease.
*Enzymology.*
**RNB** Received-Not Billed.
**RNCS** regional naval control of shipping.
contrôle naval régional de la navigation commerciale.
**RND** Rendu Non Déchargé.
French initialism meaning: Delivered Ex Ship.
*Economics; International Trade.*
**RND** National Democratic Rally (Algeria).
**RND family** Resistance-Nodulation-Division family.
*Molecular and Cell Biology.*
**RNFL** Retinal Nerve Fiber Layer.
**RNG** Random Number Generator.
*Computer Programming.*
**RNG** Revenu Net Global.
**RNIS** réseau numérique à intégration de services.
integrated services digital network (ISDN).
**R.N.O.B.** Réserves Naturelles et Ornitologiques de Belgique (Belgium).
**RNODCs** Responsible National Oceanographic Data Centers (U.S.A.).
**RNP-CS** Ribonucleoprotein Consensus.
*Medicine; Molecular Biology.*
**RNPs** Ribonudeoprotein Particles.
*Biomolecular Chemistry; Medicine.*
**RNR** Zambia's vehicle-registration letters.
**RNU** Règlement National d'Urbanisme.
**RNY** Malawi's International vehicle-registration letters.
**RNZN** Royal New Zealand Navy (New Zealand).
**RO** Receive Only.
*Telecommunications.*
**R.O.** Receiving Office; Receiving Officer.
**R.O.** Receiving Order.
**R.O.** Record(s) Office.
**RO** Recruiting Officer; Relieving Officer; Returning Officer.
**RO** Regional Office.
**RO** Risultati Operativi.
*Marketing.*
**RO** Riyal Omani.
*Currencies.*
**RO** Ricerca Operativa.
Italian initialism meaning: Operational Research.
**RO** Rischio Ordinario.
Italian initialism meaning: Ordinary Risk.
*Insurance.*
**RO** 1. Romania.
1. Roumanie.
2. rotational (post).
2a. (poste) tournant.
2b. (poste) soumis à rotation.
**RO** Routine Order.
**RO** Rovigo, Italy.
**RO** Royal Observatory.
**ROA** radius of action.
rayon d'action.
**ROA** Return On Assets.
**ROA** Rules Of the Air.
**ROA** The airport code for Roanoke, Virginia, U.S.A.
**ROAD** Reparto Operativo Anti-droga (Carabinieri) (Italy).

**ROAM** Return On Assests Managed.
*Business; Finance.*
**ROA position** Right Occipito-Anterior position.
*Medicine.*
**ROAR** Reddito Operativo su Attività Reali.
Italian acronym meaning: Operating Income from Real Assets.
**ROB** Run On Bank.
**ROC** Reevaluation Of Capital.
**ROC** regional operating centre [NICS] [obsolete - replaced by NSE].
centre d'exploitation régional [NICS] [obsolète - remplacé par NSE].
**ROC** Relative Operating Characteristic; Receiver Operating Characteristic.
**ROC** Réponse Optimale au Consommateur.
French acronym meaning: Efficient Consumer Response.
**ROCE** Return On Capital Employed.
*Business; Economics; Finance.*
**ROCs** Receiver Operating Characteristics.
**ROD** 1. record of decisions.
1. compte rendu de décisions.
2. report of deficiency.
2. rapport de non-conformité.
**ROE** Rate Of Exchange.
*Business; Economics; Finance.*
**ROE** Return On Equity.
*Finance.*
**ROE** Royal Observatory, Edinburgh.
**ROE** rules of engagement.
règles d'engagement.
**ROEM** renseignement d'origine électromagnétique.
signals intelligence (SIGINT).
**ROEREQ** rule-of-engagement request.
demande de règles d'engagement.
**ROESY** Rotating frame Overhauser Effect Spectroscopy.
**ROFOR** (abbr.) ROute FORecast.
*International Code Words; Meteorology.*
**ROFOT** Route Forecast.
Win English system units.
*International Code Words; Meteorology.*
**ROG** Reactive Organic Gas.
*Chemical Engineering; Environmental Engineering Science.*
**R.O.G.** Receipt Of Goods.
Also: **ROG**; **r.o.g.**
**rog.** (abbr.) rogatoria.
Italian abbreviation meaning: rogatory letter; letters rogatory; request.
*Law.*
**ROH** Royal Opera House (G.B.).
**ROHUM** renseignement d'origine humaine [FR].
human intelligence (HUMINT).
**ROI** Rate Of Interest.
*Business; Commerce; Economics; Finance.*
**ROI** Return On Investment.
*Business; Economics; Finance.*
**ROI** Royal Institute of painters in Oils.
**Roi** The above acronyms were coined accidentally using the French word "Roi" which means: King.
**ROI capital** Return On Invested capital.
*Business; Economics; Finance.*
**ROIs** Reactive Oxygen Intermediates.
*Biochemistry; Biology; Biophysics; Medicine.*
**ROIs** Regions Of Interest.
*Clinical Psychology; Medicine; Neuroscience of Autism; Radiology.*
**ROK** Republic Of Korea.
**ROLINT** Rendimento Obbligazioni - Lira INTerbancaria.
Italian abbreviation meaning: Bond Yield - Interbank Lira. Last updated July 2001 - now obsolete.
*Business; Economics; Finance.*
**ROM** Read-Only Memory.
ROM is also known as: Read-Only Storage; Fixed Memory.
*Computer Technology.*
**ROM** Regional Oxidant Model.
**ROM** obsolete - see RM.
obsolète - voir RM.
**ROM** The airline code for the city of Rome, Italy.
**ROMP** Ring-Opening.
*Metathesis Polymerization; Chemical Engineering; Chemical Synthesis; Polymerization Processes.*
**ROMV** Return On Market Value.
*Business; Commerce; Economics.*
**RONA** Return On Net Assets.
**ROOI** Return On Original Investment.
*Business; Economics; Finance.*
**ROP** Run-Of-the-Paper.
**ROPOS** Remotely Operated Platform for Ocean Science.
**ROP position** Right Occipito-Posterior position.
*Medicine.*
**ROR** range-only radar.
radar de télémétrie.
**ROR** Rate Of Return.
**ROR** Right Of Rescission.
*Business; Economics; Finance.*
**ROR** vaccination contre Rougeole, Oreillons, Rubéole.

French acronym meaning: Measles-Mumps-Rubella vaccination.
*Immunology.*
**RORC** Royal Ocean Racing Club.
**RORO** Roll On / Roll Off.
*Ferry-boats.*
**RORSAT** radar ocean reconnaissance satellite.
satellite radar de reconnaissance océanique.
**ROS** Reactive Oxygen Species.
ROS are metabolic buy-products.
The main source of ROS is in the mitochondria.
*Anatomy; Biology; Longevity; Aging; Medical Sciences; Molecular Medicine; Physiology.*
**ROS** Read-Only Storage; Read-Only Store.
**ROS** Reparti Operativi Speciali (Arma dei Carabinieri) (Italy).
Italian acronym meaning: Special Operations Units (of the Carabineers Arm).
**ROS** report of survey.
1a. rapport d'expertise.
1b. procès-verbal de vérification.
**ROS** Return On Sales.
*Business; Commerce; Economics.*
**ROS** Rights Of Shareholders.
*Business; Economics; Finance.*
**ROS** Run-Of-Station.
**ROSAT** ROentgen SATellite.
For further details see under: **RASS**.
**ROSEBUD** Rare Object SEarches with Bolometers Underground (Spain).
Data taking commenced in 1998.
*Astronomy; Bolometers; Physics.*
**ROSS** Remote Oriented Simulation System; Route Oriented Simulation System.
*Data Communications.*
**ROSS** Russian ocean surveilance system.
système russe de surveillance océanique.
**ROT** Right Occipitotransverse position.
*Medicine.*
**ROTA** risks other than attack.
risques autres que ceux d'une attaque.
**ROTC** Reserve Officers Training Corps.
*Military Science.*
**ROV** Remotely Operated Vehicle.
**ROVs** Remotely Operated Vehicles.
*Unpiloted Submersibles.*
**ROZ** restricted operating zone.
zone d'opérations réglementée.
**RP** 1. Philippines.
1. Philippines.
2. réception /recette provisoire.
2. provisional acceptance.
3. release point.
3a. point de dislocation [mouvements terrestres].
3b. point de largage [transport aérien].
4. reporting post.
4. poste de détection.
5. rocket projectile.
5. fusée à tête inerte.
**RP** Radioscopie Pulmonaire.
*Medicine.*
**RP** Rapid Prototyping.
**RP**; **R.P.** Rates of Postage.
**RP** Reagente Puro.
*Chemistry.*
**RP** Real Property.
**RP** Received Pronunciation.
*Linguistics.*
**RP** Recommended (Retail) Price.
Also: **RPP**.
**RP** Reinforced Plastic.
*Materials.*
**RP** Relazioni Pubbliche.
Italian initialism meaning: Public Relations.
**R.P.** Re-order Point.
**RP** Reply Paid.
**RP** Report Program.
*Computer Programming.*
**R/P** Reprint.
Also: **rep.**
**RP** Rescue Party.
**RP** Retinitis Pigmentosa.
Retinitis Pigmentosa is an inherited retinopathy.
*Genetics.*
**R/P** Return of Post.
**R.P.** Return Premium.
**RP** Rhône-Poulenc (France).
*Life Sciences; Pharmaceuticals; Specialty Chemicals.*
**Rp** Ribosomal protein.
**RP** Riservata Personale.
referring to the initialism put on envelopes (personal).
**R2P2** rapid response planning process.
processus de planification des réponses rapides.
**RPA** Radiation Protection Adviser.
**RPA** Replication Protein A.
*Biochemistry.*
**RPA** Ricerca Progetti Ambiente (Italy).
*Environmental Projects.*
**RPB** Recognized Professional Body (G.B.).
*Investments.*
**RPC** 1. recognized air picture production centre.
1. centre de production de la situation aérienne générale.
2. Règlement du personnel civil.

2. Civilian Personnel Regulations (CPR).
**RPC** Remote Procedure Call.
*Computer Science.*
**RPC** Reports of Patent Cases.
*Patents* - Since 1884.
**RPCO** Règlement du personnel civil de l'OTAN.
NATO Civilian Personnel Regulations (NCPR).
**RPE** Rotating Platinum Electrode.
**RPE cells** Retinal Pigment Epithelial cells.
*Cell Biology; Neuroscience.*
**RPF** Renal Plasma Flow.
*Medicine.*
**RPF** Rwandese Patriotic Front.
**RPG** 1. (US-Canada) Regional Planning Group.
1. Groupe stratégique régional (US-Canada).
2. regional planning guide.
2. guide de planification régionale.
**RPG** Report Program Generator.
*Computer Programming.*
**RPGs** Research Project Grants.
Of U.S. NIH.
For further details see under: **NIH**.
**RPh** Registered Pharmacist.
**RPH** Remotely Piloted Helicopter.
**rpHPLC** reversed-phase High-Pressure Liquid Chromatography.
**RPI** Rensselaer Polytechnic Institute (U.S.A.).
RPI offers new degree programs in: *Ecological Economics; Environment Economics; Resource Economics.*
**RPI** Retail Price Index.
**RPI** Ribozyme Pharmaceuticals, Inc. (U.S.A.).
RPI deals with the development of *ribozyme-based products* for pharmaceuticals and agricultural applications.
**R2PI-TOFMS** A Resonant Two-Photon Ionization Time-Of-Flight Mass Spectroscopy.
**RPL** Robot Programming Language.
The robot programming language is used to control robots.
*Robotics.*
**RPL** Rocket Propulsion Laboratory.
**RPM** Regional Particulate Model.
**RPM**; **r.p.m.** Resale Price Maintenance.
**RPM**; **rpm** Revolutions per Minute.
*Mechanics.*
**RPMI** Roswell Park Memorial Institute.
**RpMV** Ring pattern Mosaic Virus.
*Fruits Research; Plant Pathology.*
**RPN** Reverse Polish Notation.
RPN is also known as: Postfix Notation.
*Computer Programming.*
**RP-Net** Rhône-Poulenc Network (France).
**RPO** radiophare omnidirectionnel.
radio beacon omnidirectional (RBO).
**RPOD** rail point of debarkation.
point de débarquement ferroviaire.
**RPP** Rastriya Prajatantra Party (Nepal).
**RPP** regional priority plan.
plan de priorité régional.
**RPQ** Request for Price Quotation.
**RPR** Gaullist Rally for the Republic (France).
*Political Parties.*
**RPRC** Regional Plant Resource Center (Bhubaneshwar, India).
**RPRC** Regional Primate Research Center (U.S.A.).
The RPRC is a group proposed to reshape or oversee certain aspects of AIDS research.
**RPR test** Rapid Plasma Reagin test.
*Medicine.*
**RPR (V)** Remotely Piloted Research (Vehicle).
**RPS** réception provisoire de la station (ou du site).
provisional site acceptance (PSA).
**rps**; **r.p.s.** revolutions per second.
**RPSA** Regional Private Sector Advisor.
*U.S. Aid.*
**RPSEP** Refurbishment of Power Station Electrical Plant.
**RPT** Registered Physical Therapist.
**RPT** Rhône-Poulenc Telecom (France).
**RPTKs** Receptor Protein Tyrosine Kinases.
*Axon Growth; Cell Biology; Medicine; Molecular Biology.*
**RPTP** Receptor Protein Tyrosine Phosphatase.
*Axon Fasciculation / Defasciculation; Cell Biology; Medicine; Molecular Biology.*
**RPTPs** Receptor Protein Tyrosine Phosphatases.
For further details see under: **RPTP**.
**RPV** Remotely Piloted Vehicle.
**RPWs** Relativistic Plasma Waves.
*Physics.*
**RQ** Puerto Rico.
**rq** radice quadrata.
Italian abbreviation meaning: square root.
*Mathematics.*
**RQ**; **R.Q.** Respiratory Quotient.
*Physiology.*
**RQL** Rejectable Quality Level.
**RR** Railroad.
*Civil Engineering; Transportation Engineering.*
**RR** Rate of Return.
*Business; Finance.*
**RR** Recovery Room.
*Medicine.*
**RR** Rediscount Rate.
*Business; Economics; Finance.*

**RR** regional reinforcement.
renforcement régional.
**RR** Registered Representative.
*Business; Finance.*
**RR** Registered Reserves.
*Business; Economics; Finance.*
**RR** Relative Risks.
*Medicine.*
**RR** Required Reserves.
**RR** Reserve Requirement.
*Business; Finance.*
**RR** Return Rate.
*Business; Finance.*
**R.R.** Ricevuta di Ritorno.
Italian initialism meaning: acknowledgement of receipt.
**RR** Risk Ratios.
**RR** Rolls Royce.
**RRA** Radio-Receptor Assay.
**RRA** Registered Records Administration (U.S.A.).
**R rays** Roentgen rays.
Named after the discoverer, the German physicist Wilhelm Konrad **Roentgen**.
*Radiology.*
**RRB** Railroad Retirement Board (U.S.A.).
**RR branch** Risk Reduction branch.
Of the U.S. Forecast Systems Laboratory.
**RRBs** Red Rectangle emission Bands.
*Astrochemistry; Astronomy; Astrophysics; Space Science.*
**RRC** Radioricevitore Cardiaco.
*Biomedical Technologies.*
**RRC** Report Review Committee (U.S.A.).
**RRC** Royal Red Cross.
**RRCC** Rete Romana Consumo Critico (Italy).
**RRDE** Rotating Ring-Disk Electrode.
**RRE** Raloxifene Response Element.
**RRE** Rev Response Element.
**RR estimate** Relative Risk estimate.
**RRF** Ragged Red Fibers.
**RRF** rapid reaction force.
force de réaction rapide.
**RRF** Release and Recycling Factor.
*Biochemistry.*
**RRF** Ribosome Recycling Factor.
**RRH** remote radar head.
tête radar éloignée (ou distante).
**RRKM theories** Rice-Ramsperger-Kassel-Marcus theories.
**RRL** radio relay link.
liaison hertzienne.
**RRL** Registered Records Librarian.
**RRL** Road Research Laboratory (G.B.).
**RRL system** Rabbit Reticulocyte Lysate system.
**RRM** Renegotiable-Rate Mortgage.
*Business; Economics; Finance.*
**RRM** Reports, Reviews and Meeting.
**r-RNA** ribosomal Ribonucleic Acid.
*Cell Biology; Human Development; Metabolsim.*
**RRP** rapid reinforcement plan.
plan de renforcement rapide.
**RRP** Recommended Retail Price.
**R.r.r.** Raccomandata con ricevuta di ritorno.
Italian initialism meaning: registered, return receipt requested.
*Mail.*
**RRR** rapid runway repair.
réparation rapide des pistes.
**RRS** Railroad Station.
**RRS** Royal Research Ship (G.B.).
**RR spectroscopy** Resonance Raman spectroscopy.
*Biochemistry; Chemistny; Molecular Biology.*
**RRSPs** Registered Retirement Savings Plans.
**RRT** Rail Rapid Transit.
*Transportation Engineering.*
**RRT** Registered Respiratory Therapist.
**RRTF** return and reconstruction task force.
groupe pour le reconstruction et le retour.
**RS** Radiographic Sensitivity.
*Nucleonics.*
**RS** Real Storage.
Real Storage is also known as: Real Memory.
*Computer Technology.*
**R.S.**; **r.s.** Recording Secretary.
**RS** Record Separator.
*Computer Technology.*
**RS** Redeemable Stock.
*Business; Economics; Finance.*
**RS** Registered Securities.
*Business; Finance.*
**RS** Republika Srpska.
(Serbian Republic).
**RS** Results Sign.
**RS** Revenue Sharing.
*Business; Finance.*
**R.S.**; **r.s.** Right Side.
**RS** Rischio Semplice.
Italian initialism meaning: Simple Risk.
*Insurance.*
**RS** Rostral Site.
*Histology.*
**RS** Royal Society.
**Rs** rupees.
*Currencies.*
**R.S.** Short Rate.
*Banking.*

**RSA** rear support area.
zone de soutien arrière.
**RSA** Rehabilitation Services Administration (U.S.A.).
**RSA** Royal Scottish Academician; Royal Scottish Academy.
**RSA** Royal Society of Antiquaries.
**RSA** Russian Space Agency.
**RSABG** Rancho Santa Ana Botanical Gardens (California, U.S.A.).
**RSA position** Right Sacro-Anterior position.
*Medicine.*
**RSB** regional shipping board.
bureau régional des transports maritimes.
**RSC** Reactor Safety Commission (Germany).
**RSC** 1. rear support command.
1. commandement du soutien (de la zone) arrière.
2. reinforcement support category.
2. catégorie "soutien du renforcement".
**RSC** Royal Society of Chemistry (G.B.).
**RSCC** 1. rear support coordination centre.
1. centre de coordination du soutien arrière.
2. regional stocks under CINCSOUTH control.
2. stock régionaux contrôlés par le CINCSOUTH.
**R SCU PA** Recombinant Single Chain Urokinase Plasminogen Activator.
*Medicine.*
**RSD** Relative Standard Deviation.
**RSD** Remote Sensor Disconnection.
**R.S.D.E.** Remote Sensing Data Engineering (Italy).
**RSE** Richmond Stock Exchange (U.S.A.).
**RSF** Remodeling and Spacing Factor.
*Biochemistry; Medicine; Transcription.*
**RSFQ logic** Rapid Single-Flux Quantum logic.
The first RSFQ system, which consists of an array of 15 logic elements converting analog signals to digital output, was tested in 1996.
*Computer Science; Microelectronics; Petaflops Machines; Physics.*
**RSFs** Rabbit Synovial Fibroblasts.
*Medicine.*
**RSFTA** réseau du service fixe de télécommunications aéronautiques.
aeronautical fixed telecommunication network (AFTN).
**RSG** 1. rear support group.
1. groupe de soutien arrière.
2. Research Study Group [CNAD].
2. Groupe d'étude pour la recherche [CDNA].
**RSGI** Random Sample Genome Initiative.
**RSGI** RIKEN Standard Genomics/Proteomics Initiative.
*Japanese Initiatives.*
**RSH** Radiation, Science and Health.
**RSI** radiation status indicator.
lettre de régime d'émissions.
**RSI** Repetitive Strain Injuries.
For further details see under: **RSIs**.
**RSI** Retour Sur Investissements.
French initialism meaning: Return on Investments.
*Business; Economics; Finance.*
**RSI** Risk Science Institute (U.S.A.).
**RSI** Royal Sanitary Institute.
**RSIs** Repetitive Strain Injuries.
The RSIs are maladies such as the ones that occur to persons banging keyboards. They include tendonitis; tensosynovitis; rotator cuff syndrome; and others.
**RSL** Royal Society of Literature.
**RSL** Royal Society of London (G.B.).
**RSL Technology** Remote Source Lighting Technology.
*Guided Missile Destroyers.*
**RSM** Regimental Sergeant-Major.
**RSM** Repubblica di San Marino (Italy).
**RSM**; **Rsm** Resource Specific Module.
**RSM** Royal School of Mines.
**R.S.M.** Royal Society of Medicine.
**RSMAS** Rosentiel School of Marine and Atmospheric Science (U.S.A.).
**RSMC** Regional Specialized Meteorological Center - Of the U.N. WMO.
For further details see under: **WMO**.
**RSMIS** Real estate and Space Management Information System.
**RSMS** Radio Spectrum Measurement System.
*Telecommunications.*
**RSMs** Reciprocal Space Maps.
**RSN** role specialist nation.
pays prestataire spécialisé.
**RSNA**; **R.S.N.A.** Radiological Society of North America.
**RSNC** Royal Society for Nature Conservation (G.B.).
**RSO** Radar à Synthèse d'Ouverture.
**RSO** Radiation Safety Officer.
**RSO** Railway Sub-Office.
**RSOM** reception, staging and onward movement.
accueil, stationnement transitoire et mouvement vers l'avant.
**RSp** Rapport Sinistres-Primes.
*Insurance.*
**RSP** 1. recognized sea picture.
1. situation maritime générale.
2. render(ing) safe procedure.
2. procédé de neutralisation.

**RSP** Red Sea Program.
The RSP is funded by the German Science Ministry. A collaboration between Israeli and Palestinian scientists led by the Center for Tropical Marine Ecology in Bremen, Germany and based at the Interuniversity Institute in Eilat, Israel.
**RSP** Right Sacroposterior Position.
*Medicine.*
**RSPA** Research and Special Programs Administration (U.S.A.).
**RSPBs** Royal Society for the Protection of Birds.
**RSPL** recommended spare parts list.
liste de pièces de rechange recommandées.
**RSPs** Research Support Programs.
**RSPT** real storage page table.
**RSQ** (abbr.) Rescue.
**RSQs** Range Size Quartiles.
**RSR** required supply rate.
taux de ravitaillement requis.
**RSR** Rotating Shadowband Radiometer.
**RSRA** Rotor Systems Research Aircraft.
**RSS movement** Rashtriya Swayamsevak movement (India).
The RSS movement was founded in the 1920s to promote Hindu identity and consciousness.
**RSSs** Recombination Signal Sequences.
*Diabetes and Digestive and Kidney Diseases; Molecular Biology.*
**rst**; **res.** (abbr) reset.
*Computer Technology.*
**RST** Ricerca e Sviluppo Tecnologico (Italy).
Italian initialism meaning: Research and Technological Development.
**RST** Ricerca Scientifica e Tecnologica (Italy).
Italian initialism meaning: Scientific and Technological Research.
**RSTA** reconnaissance, surveillance and target acquisition.
reconnaissance, surveillance et acquisition d'objectif.
**RSU** Rappresentanza Sindacale Unita (Italy).
**RSU** Remote Service Unit.
**RSU** Rifiuti Solidi Urbani.
Italian initialism meaning: City Solid Waste.
**RSV** Rat Sarcoma Virus.
**RSV** Respiratory Syncytial Virus.
*Virology.*
**RSV** Rous Sarcoma Virus.
*Oncology; Virology.*
**RSVLTR** Rous Sarcoma Virus Long Term Repeat.
**R.S.V.P.** Répondez S'il Vous Plaît.
French initialism meaning: please reply.
**RSVP** Resource Reservation Protocol.
The RSVP has been running on an experimental basis since 1994.
*Internet Reservation Systems.*
**RSZs** Replication Slow Zones.
*Genome Damage.*
**RT** radiotelegraphy.
*Telecommunications.*
**RT**; **R/T** Radio Telephone; radiotelephony.
*Telecommunications.*
**RT** Rapporti Tecnici.
Italian initialism meaning: Technical Reports.
**RT** Reaction Time.
RT is also known as: Latent Period.
*Physiology.*
**RT** Real-Time.
*Computer Technology.*
**R.T.**; **rt** received text.
**RT** Receiver and Transmitter.
*Radio.*
**RT** Reciprocal Translocation.
**RT** Recovery Time.
*Electronics; Nucleonics.*
**RT** Recreational Therapy.
*Medicine.*
**RT** Regressive Tax.
**RT** Relocatable Term.
*Computers.*
**RT** Remote Terminal.
*Computer Technology.*
**RT** Résistance Totale.
French initialism meaning: Total Resistance.
*Medicine.*
**RT** Respiratory Therapist.
*Medicine.*
**RT** Restraint of Trade.
*Business; Commerce.*
**RT** Reverse Transcriptase.
*Enzymology.*
**RT** Ricavi Tassati.
**rt.** (abbr.) right.
**RT** Room Temperature.
**R.T.**; **rt** round trip.
**rt.**; **rte** (abbr.) route.
**R.T.**; **rt** Rye Terms.
**RTA** Reciprocal Trade Agreement.
*Business; Economics; Finance.*
**RTA** Research and Technology Agency [has replaced AGARD/(DRG)].
Agence de recherche et de technologie (ART 1.) [remplace AGARD/(GRD)].
**RTAS** Real-time Technology and Application Symposium.
**RTB** Research and Technology Board.

Comité pour la recherche et la technologie.
**RTB** Rural Telephone Bank (U.S.A.).
**RTBA** Rate To Be Agreed.
**RTC** 1. radio transmission control.
1. contrôle des transmissions radio.
2. reduced tactical COMPLAN.
2. plan de transmissions tactiques restreint.
3. reserve and training command.
3. commandement des forces de réserve et de l'entraînement.
**RTC** réseau téléphonique commuté.
**RTC** Resolution Trust Corporation (U.S.A.).
**RTCA** Radio Technical Commission for Aeronautics.
**RTCP** Real-Time Control Protocol.
**RTD** Research, Technological development and Demonstration.
**RTD** Resistance Temperature Detector.
**RTD** Research and Technology Development.
**RTD curves** Residence Time Distribution curves.
**RTE** Reti Transeuropee.
Italian initialism meaning: Transeuropean Networks.
**RTECS** Registry of Toxic Effects of Chemical Substances (U.S.A.).
*Bibliographic Retrieval Services.*
**RTF** Radio-Télévision Française.
French initialism meaning: French TV and Broadcasting Corporation.
**RTF** Resistance Transfer Factor (R factor).
*Genetics.*
**RTF** Rich Text Format.
*Software.*
**RTG** Radioisotope / Radioisotopic Thermoelectric Generator.
*Nucleonics.*
**RTGS services** Real-Time Gross Settlement services.
**RTI** Referred To Input.
*Electronics.*
**RTI** Research Triangle Institute (U.S.A.).
*U.S. Government and Industry Contracts.*
**RTII** Réseau de Télétransmission Interbancaire International.
French initialism meaning: SWIFT.
*Business; Economics; Finance.*
**RTIO** Real-Time Input/Output.
**RTIRS** Real-Time Information Retrieval System.
**RTJ** Rodrigues Triple Junction.
*Geology; Geophysics.*
**RTKs** Receptor Tyrosine Kinases.
*Biological Chemistry; Life Sciences; Signal Transduction; Tumor Suppressor.*
**RTL** Real-Time Language.
**RTL** Real-Time Link.
**RTL** Resistor-Transistor Logic.
*Electronics.*
**RTL** rolling target list.
liste d'objectifs évolutive.
**RT laboratory** Reproductive Toxicology laboratory.
**RTM** Registered Trade Mark.
**RTN** regional telecommunications network.
réseau régional de télécommunications.
**rtn** (abbr.) return.
**RTNC** returned to national control.
retour sous contrôle national.
**rtng** (abbr.) returning.
**RTNS II** Rotating-Target Neutron Source II.
**RTO** Railway Transport Officer.
**RTO** Referred To Output.
*Electronics.*
**RTO** Regional Transmission Organization.
**RTO** Research and Technology Organization.
Organisation pour la recherche et la technologie.
**RTOS** Real-Time Operating System.
*Computer Technology.*
**RTOs** Regional Transmission Organizations.
**RTP** Real-Time Processing.
RTP is also known as: Real-Time Operation.
*Computer Technology.*
**RTP** Real-Time Program; Real-Time Programming.
*Computer Programming.*
**RTP** Research Training Program (U.S.A.).
**rtPA**; **RTPA** Recombinant Tissue-type Plasminogen Activator.
*Medicine.*
**RTPCR assay** Reverse Transcriptase Polymerase Chain Reaction assay.
*Cell Biology; Medicine; Molecular Genetics; Pathology.*
**RTR** Road Traffic Reports.
Since 1970.
**RTS** radar tracking station.
station de poursuite radar.
**RTS** Reactor Trip System.
**RTS** Real-Time System.
*Computer Technology.*
**RTS** Remote Terminal System.
**RTS** Request to Send.
**RTs** Reverse Transcriptases.
**rts** (abbr.) rights.
**RTS** Royal Toxophilite Society.
**RTS system** Remote Terminal Scanning system.
*Computer Technology.*
**RTSW** Real Time Software.
**RTT** Request To Talk.

**RTTS project** Regional Innovation and Technology Transfer Strategy project.
*European Union.*
**RTTY** Radioteletype.
**RTTY** radioteletypewriter.
The radioteletypewriter is a teletypewriter which operates over a radio channel instead of operating over wires.
*Telecommunications.*
**RU** Regno Unito.
Italian acronym meaning: United Kingdom.
**RU** Relazioni Umane.
Italian acronym meaning: Human Relations.
**RU** Request/Response Unit.
**RU** Rugby Union.
**RU** Rwanda's International vehicle-registration letters.
**RU** Are You ?.
**Ru** The chemical symbol for Ruthenium.
*Chemistry; Metallurgy; Symbols.*
**RUBISCO** ribulose-1,5-bisphosphate Carboxylase-Oxygenase.
*Microbiology; Biochemistry.*
**RuBPCase** Ribulose Biphosphate Carboxylase.
*Cell Biology; Chemical Biology.*
**RUC** Rapid Update Cycle.
**RUC** Reporting Unit Code.
**RUC** Royal Ulster Constabulary (Ireland).
RUC is the Northern Ireland police force.
**$RuCl_3$** Ruthenium Chloride.
$RuCl_3$, also known as: Ruthenium Trichloride, Ruthenic Chloride, is used in laboratory analysis.
*Inorganic Chemistry.*
**RUD** Recently Used Directory.
**RUE** Rational Use of Energy.
*Energy Conservation.*
**RUF** Resource Utilization Factor.
**RUF** Eevolutionary United Front - Sierra Leone.
**RUF** Revolving Underwriting Facility.
**RUG** Regional Unit Group.
**RUH** The airport code for Riyadh, Saudi Arabia.
**Rui** Residenze universitarie internazionali.
**RUM** Resource Utilization Monitor.
**RUMs** Rigid Unit Modes.
*Physics.*
**$RuO_4$** Ruthenium Tetroxide.
$RuO_4$ is used as an oxidizer.
*Chemistry.*
**RUP** Remote Unit Processor.
**RUPA** Rete Unitaria / Reti Unitarie delle Pubbliche Amministrazioni / della Pubblica Amministrazione (Italy).
**RUPPIES** Rich Urban Professionals (U.S.A.).
**RUQ** right upper quadrant.
**RuRed** Ruthenium Red.
Rhutenium Red is also known as: (ammoniated) Ruthenium Oxychloride.
*Inorganic Chemistry.*
**$RuS_2$** Laurite.
*Mineralogy.*
**RUSH** Remote Use of Shared Hardware.
*Data Communications.*
**RUT** Resource Utilization Time.
**R.V.** Ratable Value.
**RV** Rear View.
*Drawings.*
**RV** Recreational Vehicle.
**RV** Re-entry Vehicle.
**RV** Relief Valve.
RV is also known as: Blowoff Valve.
*Mechanical Engineering.*
**R/V** rendez-vous.
1a. point de rassemblement.
1b. point de regroupement.
1c. rendez-vous [marine].
**RV** Research Vehicle.
*Space Technology.*
**RV** Residual Volume.
**rv** (abbr.) reverse.
*Graphic Arts; Mechanical Engineering.*
**rv** (abbr.) revolution.
For further details see under: **r**.
**RVA** Recorded Voice Announcement.
**RVA**; **rva meter** Reactive volt-ampere meter.
The RVA meter is also known as: Varmeter.
*Engineering.*
**RVB quantum state** Resonating Valence Bond quantum state.
*Applied Physics; Materials Research; Physics.*
**RVD** Regulatory Volume Decrease.
*Medicine.*
**RVF** Rift Valley Fever.
RVF is a viral disease that affects humans and domestic animals in Saharan Africa.
*Bacteriology; Medicine; Pathology; Virology.*
**RVF** Right Visual Field.
*Cognitive Neuroscience; Neuroscience.*
**RVH** Right Ventricular Hypertrophy.
*Medicine.*
**RVI** Regulatory Volume Increase.
*Medicine.*
**RVI** Renault Véhicules Industriels (France).
**RVI** Reverse Interrupt.
*Data Communications.*
**RVL** Radar à Visée Latérale.
French initialism meaning: Side-Looking Radar.

**RVP** Reid Vapor Pressure.
*Petroleum Engineering.*
**RVPA** Retour Veineux Pulmonaire Anormal.
French initialism meaning: Anomalous Pulmonary Venous Drainage.
*Medicine.*
**RVR** runway visual range.
portée visuelle de piste.
**RVs** Re-entry Vehicles.
**RVS** Relative Value Studies.
**RVT** Reliability Verification Tests.
**rVV** recombinant Vaccinia Virus.
**RW** Radiological Warfare.
**RW** rainwater.
*Hydrology; Meteorology.*
**R/W**; **RW** Read/Write.
*Computers.*
**RW**; **R.W.** Right of Way.
*Road Traffic.*
**RW** Rubbery Wood.
**RW** Rwanda.
**RWAT** Rubber-Wheel Abrasion Test.
**R wave** Rayleigh wave.
*Geophysics.*
**RWCP** Real World Computing Partnership (U.S.A.).
*Information-Processing Technologies.*
**RWD** Rapid-Wasting Disease.
*Coral Disease; Scleractinian Corals.*
**RWED** Read, Write, Extend and Delete.
**Rw. Fr.** Rwanda Franc.
*Currencies.*
**RWI** radar warning installation.
installation d'alerte radar.
**RWI** Read-Write-Initialize.
**RWJPRI** R.W. Johnson Pharmaceutical Research Institute (U.S.A.).
*Health Care; Pharmaceutical Businesses; Screening Technologies.*
**RWM**; **R/WM** Read/Write Memory.
The Read/Write Memory enables reading as well as writing.
*Computer Technology.*
**rwnd.** (abbr.) rewind.
*Electronics.*
**RWO** Rain Water Outlet.
*Buildings.*
**RWO counter** Right Wrong Omit counter.
**RWO** Routine Work Order.
**RWP** Rain Water Pipe.
**RWP** real world parameter.
paramètre de la situation réelle.
**RWR** radar warning receiver.
récepteur d'alerte radar.
**RWR** Read Write Register.
**RWS** Rapid-Wasting Syndrome.
*Coral Disease; Scleractinian Corals.*
**RWX** Read Write Execute.
**rwy.** (abbr.) railway.
Also: **rail.**; **Rly.**; **rly.**; **RY**; **ry**.
**rx** (abbr.) receive; receiver.
**RXR** Retinoid-X Receptor.
For further details see under: **RXRs**.
**RXRs** Retinoid-X Receptors.
*Human Genetics; Lipid Research; Molecular Biology; Medicine; Nuclear Retinoid Receptors; Pathobiochemistry; Pathology.*
**RXTE** Rossi X-ray Timing Explorer - NASA's.
*Astronomy; Astrophysics.*
**RY**; **ry** railway.
Also: **Rly.**; **rly.**; **rail.**; **rwy**.
*Transportation Engineering.*
**RYC**; **ryc** referring to your cable.
**RYC** In Reply to Your Cable.
**RyRs** Ryanodine Receptors.
*Medical Biotechnology; Physiology.*
**RZB** Raiffeisen Zentralbank Österreich AG.
*Austrian Bank.*

# S

**$** Dollar (the Dollar mark).
**S** Saturation.
*Ecology; Electromagnetism; Electronics; Nucleonics; Optics; Physical Chemistry; Physics.*
**s** seasonal; second; seller; shilling; stockbroker.
**S; S.** Siemens.
*Electricity* - Siemens was formerly known as: mho; reciprocal ohm.
**S; s** sign.
**S; s** South, southern.
**S; S.** Steradian.
Steradian is a unit of measurement for solid angles.
*Mathematics.*
**S** Structure.
*Aviation; Chemistry; Engineering; Geology; Mineralogy; Science.*
**S** Sulfur.
Also: Sulphur.
*Chemistry; Mineralogy.*
**S** Sweden's International vehicle registration letter.
**SA** Sail Area.
**SA** Salary Administration (U.S.A.).
**SA** Salerno, Italy.
**SA** Salicylic Acid.
**SA** 1. Saudi Arabia.
1. Arabie Saoudite.
2. security authority.
2. autorité en matière de sécurité.
3. selective availability.
3. disponibilité sélective.
4. simple alert.
4. alerte simple.
5. situation awareness.
5. perception globale de la situation.
6. small arms.
6. armes de petit calibre.
7. special assignment.
7. mission spéciale.
8. staging area.
8. zone d'étape.
9. surface-to-air.
9. surface-air.
**SA** Savings Accounts.
**SA** Scheduling Algorithm.
*Computer Programming.*
**SA** Security Analyst.
**S/A** see SA 3.
voir SA 3.
**sa** semiannual / ly.
**SA** Sinoatrial.
*Anatomy.*
**S.A.** Società Anonima; Société Anonyme.
Italian and French acronym meaning: Joint Stock Company.
*Business; Economics; Finance.*
**SA** Spaced Antenna.
**SA** Special Assessment.
**SA** Strategia Aziendale.
Italian acronym meaning: company strategy.
**S.A.** Sua Altezza.
Italian acronym meaning: His/Her Highness.
**SA** Subject to Approval; Subject to Acceptance.
**S/A** Survivorship Agreement.
*Banking.*
**SAA** Satellite Active Archive (U.S.A.).
**SAA** Scuola di Amministrazione Aziendale (Italy).
**SAA** 1. security accreditation authority.
1. autorité d'homologation de sécurité.
2. small arms ammunition.
2. munitions d'armes de petit calibre.
3. submarine action area.
3. secteur d'action de sous-marins.
**SAA** Society of American Archivists.
**SAA** Special Arbitrage Account.
**SAAFA** Special Arab Assistance Fund for Africa.
**SAAO** South African Astronomical Observatory.
For further details see under: **SALT**.
**SAARC** South Asian Association for Regional Co-operation.
**SAAWC** secteur anti-air warfare coordination.
coordonnateur de secteur de lutte antiaérienne.
**SAB** Science Advisory Board (U.S.A.).
Of the U.S. EPA.
*Environment; Toxicology.*
For further details see under: **EPA**.
**SAB** Special Assessment Bond.
**SAB-MIS** Submarine Antiballistic Missile.
*Military.*
**SABRE** South Atlantic Bight Recruitment Experiment.
**SAC** 1. scene-of-action commander.
1a. commandant de la zone de contact.
1b. commandant sur le lieu de l'action.
2. subordinate area commander.
2. commandant régional subordonné.
3. supporting arms coordination.
3. coordonnatuer des armes d'appui.
**SAC** Scientific Advisory Committee.
**SAC** Scottish Automobile Club.
**SAC** Society for Analytical Chemistry.
**SAC** Staff Association Committee.

ESA Technical Center (The Netherlands).
**SAC** Standing Advisory Committee.
**SAC** Staphylococcus Aureus Cowan I.
*Cellular and Molecular Biophysics.*
**SAC** Strategic Air Command.
**SA Cat channels** Stretch-Activated nonselective Cation channels.
*Biology; Cell Biology; Cellular Regulation; Medicine; Physiology; Supermolecular Science.*
**S.acc.** Società in Accomandita.
Italian initialism meaning: Limited Partnership.
*Business; Economics; Finance.*
**SACC** South African Council of Churches.
**SACC** supporting arms coordination centre.
centre de coordination des armes d'appui.
**SACCAR** South African Center for Cooperation in Agricultural Research.
**S.acc.p.a.** Società in accomandita per azioni.
Italian initialism meaning: Partnership Limited by shares.
*Business; Economics; Finance.*
**SACE** Sezione Speciale per l'Assicurazione dei Crediti all'Esportazione (Italy).
**SACEUR** Supreme Allied Commander Europe.
commandant suprême des Forces alliées en Europe.
**SACEUREP** SACEUR Representative to MC.
représentant du SACEUR auprès du CM.
**SACEUREX** SACEUR exercise.
exercise du SACEUR.
**SACEX** supporting arms coordination exercise.
exercice de coordination des armes d'appui.
**SACLANT** Supreme Allied Commander, Atlantic.
commandant suprême allié de l'Atlantique.
**SACLANTCEN** SACLANT Undersea Research Centre.
Centre de recherche sous-marine du SACLANT.
**SACLANTREPEUR** SACLANT Representative in Europe.
représentant du SACLANT en Europe.
**SACLEX** SACLANT exercise.
exercice du SACLANT.
**SACLOS** semi-automatic command-to-line-of-sight.
commande semi-automatique sur la ligne de visée.
**SACNAS** Society for the Advancement of Chicanos and Native Americans in Science (U.S.A.).
**SACO** standing airspace coordination order.
message préétabli d'organisation de l'espace aérien.
**SACP** (défense) sol-air à courte portée.
short-range air defence (SHORAD).
**SACR** State Administration for Cultural Relics (China).
*Paleontology.*
**SAD** Seasonal Affective Disorder.
A sort of depression that takes place in winter and is delivered by a season change.
*Psychology.*
**SADC** sector air defence commander.
commandant de la défense aérienne de secteur.
**SADC** South African Development Community.
**SADCGEF** SADC / Global Environmental Facility - Malawi.
For further details see under: **SADC**.
**sae** self-addressed envelope; stamped addressed envelope.
**SAE** Society of Automotive Engineers.
**SAE** South African English.
*Linguistics.*
**SAED patterns** Selected-Area Electron Diffraction patterns.
*Chemistry; Geology; Geophysics; High Pressure Research; Materials Science; Mineral Physics; Naval Research; Space Sciences.*
**SAEMS** Saskatchewan Association of Educational Media Specialists (Canada).
**saf** (abbr.) safety.
**SAF** small arms fire.
tir d'armes de petit calibre.
**SAF** Structural Adjustment Facility.
For further details see under: **CCFF**; **EFF** and **ESAF**.
**SAF** Sub-Antarctic Front.
*Ocean Science.*
**SAFE** Safeguards Automated Facility Evaluation.
**SAFE** Safety Actions For Europe.
1996 / 2000 Program of non-legislative measures to improve health and safety at work.
*European Community Programs.*
**SAFER** Spectral Application of Finite Element Representation.
**SAFI** Semiautomatic Flight Inspection.
*Navigation.*
**safi** The above acronym was coined accidentally using the Arabic word "safi" which means: pure, nett.
**SAFISY** Space Agency Forum for the International Space Year.
**SAFL** St. Anthony Falls Laboratory (U.S.A.).
**SAfrD** South African Dutch (Afrikaans).
*Languages.*
**SAFS** San Andreas Fault System.
The SAFS, in Southern California, consists of the

San Andreas Fault, the San Jacinto Fault, and the Elsinore Fault.
**SAFS** Society for Academic Freedom and Scholarship (Canada).
**SAFTA** South American Free Trade Agreement.
**SAFZ** San Andreas Fault Zone.
*Geology.*
**SAG** Sindacato Autonomo Giustizia (Italy).
*Italian Union.*
**SAG** surface action group.
groupe d'action de surface.
**SAGA experiment** Soviet-American Gas and Aerosol experiment.
**SAGB** Senior Advisory Group on Biotechnology.
SAGB is a Brussel-based industry lobby group.
**SAGC** surface action group commander.
commandant du groupe d'action de surface.
**SAGE** Serial Analysis of Gene Expression.
A method developed by the Amersham Pharmacia Biotech and Science 1999 Grand prizewinner for Young Scientists.
*Expression Analysis; Genetics; Global Gene; Molecular Biology; Molecular Genetics; Molecular Oncology.*
**SAGE** Solar-Assisted Gas Energy.
**SAGE** Soviet-American Gallium Experiment.
SAGE is a collaborative research project between the United States and Russia. Ever since the mid-1980s it has been measuring neutrinos from the sun's nuclear processes. It is located in the Caucasus Mountains.
*Neutrino Physics.*
**SAGE** Stratospheric Aerosol and Gas Experiment.
**SAGE KE** Science of Aging Knowledge Environment.
Launched by **Science** in 2001.
*Aging and related disciplines; Web Sites.*
For further details see under: **AAAS**.
**SAGE system** Semiautomatic Ground Environment system.
*Military.*
**SAGENAP** Scientific Assessment Group for Experiments in Non-Accelerator Physics.
*U.S. Scientific Groups.*
**s.a.g.l.** Società a garanzia limitata.
Italian initialism meaning: Joint-Stock Company limited by guarantee.
*Business; Economics; Finance.*
**SAGUF** Swiss Society of Environmental Science (Switzerland).
**SAH** Subarachnoid Hemorrhage.
*Medicine.*
**SAHFE** Standardization of Hip Fracture audit in Europe - E.C.
**SAHPS** Solar energy-Assisted Heat Pump System.
**SAI** Società Attori Italiani (Italy).
**SAI** supreme audit institutions.
institutions supérieures de contrôle des finances publiques.
**6SAI** Sixth South African Infantry.
6SAI is a military base in the Eastern Cape Province (South Africa).
**SAIB** Sucrose Acetate Isobutyrate.
**SAIC** Science Applications International Corporation.
SAIC deals with legal matters and routine work involving U.S. Companies and Russian collaborators.
**SAIDI** Spaced Antenna Imaging Doppler Interferometer.
**Saie '99** Salone internazionale dell'industrializzazione edilizia (Italy).
Held at the Bologna Fair on 13/17th October 1999.
*International Shows.*
**Saigon Postel** Saigon Posts and Telecommunications (Vietnam).
Semi-private.
**SAILER** Staffing of African Institutions of Legal Education and Research.
SAILER was established in 1962. The project consisted primarily of fellowships granted to African teachers for graduate studies in the U.S.A.
**SAILIS** South African Institute for Librarianship and Information Science.
**SAINA** Sistema di Aree di Interesse Naturalistico-Ambientale.
**SAIW** Subantarctic Intermediate Water.
*Oceanography.*
**SAK** National Bank of Kuwait.
Established in 1952.
**SAL** Sérum Antilymphocyte.
French acronym meaning: Antilymphocyte Serum.
*Immunology.*
**SAL** Superficial Axon Layer.
*Molecular Pharmacology.*
**SAL** support airlift.
transport aérien de soutien.
**SALA** Savings And Loan Association.
**SALA** South African Library Association.
**sala** The above acronym was coined accidentally using the Italian word "sala" which means: hall; room; axle; parlour; operating-theatre; testing-room; pumproom.
**SALALM** Seminar on the Acquisition of Latin American Library Materials.

**S.A.L.E.** Simple Alphabetic Language for Engineers.
Also: **SALE**.
**SALIS** Substance Abuse Librarians and Information Specialists.
**SALS** Shanghai Academy of Life Sciences.
**SALT** Salute, Ambiente, Lavoro e Territorio (Italy).
**SALT** Script Application Language for Telix.
**SALT** South African Large Telescope.
The 11-meter SALT is located at SAAO. It is the largest single optical telescope in the Southern Hemisphere and its construction will be complete by 2003.
*Single Optical Telescope.*
For further details see under: **SAAO**.
**SALT** 1. Strategic Arms Limitation Talks.
1. négociations (pourparlers) sur la limitation des armes stratégiques.
2. Strategic Arms Limitation Treaty.
2. Traité sur la limitation des armes stratégiques.
**SAM** Montreal Automated System.
*Derivatives.*
**SAM** S-Adenosyl-L-methionine.
*Biochemistry; Chemistry.*
**SAM** Scanning Acoustic Microscope / Microscopy.
*Acoustical Engineering.*
**SAM** Scanning Auger Microanalysis.
*Materials Science and Engineering.*
**SAM** Self-Assembled Monolayer.
*Chemistry.*
**SAM** Service d'Aide Médicale.
**SAM** Servizio ricerche sociali ed AMbientali.
Italian acronym meaning: Social and Environmental Research Service.
**SAM** SLAM Associated Protein.
*Immunology.*
For further details see under: **SLAM**.
**SAM** Società Aerea Mediterranea (Italy).
**SAM** Squadra Antimostro.
Based in Florence, Italy.
*Criminal Law.*
**SAM** Strategic Analyzer Map.
**SAM** surface-to-air missile.
1a. missile surface-air.
1b. missile sol-air.
**SAMA** Saudi Arabia Monetary Agency.
*International Business.*
**SAMBA** Saudi AMerican BAnk.
**SAMBA** System for Advanced Mobile Broadband Applications.
*European Community Project.*
**SAM domain** Sterile Alpha Motif domain.
*Biochemistry; Chemistry; Molecular Medicine; Structural Biology.*
**SA method** Simple-Adjoint method.
**SAMFETs** Self-Assembled Monolayer Field-Effect Transistors.
*Applied Physics; Chemistry; Molecular Electronics; Supramolecular Architecture.*
**SAM-FS** Storage Archive Management File System (Sun's).
**SAMHSA** Substance Abuse and Mental Health Services Administration (U.S.A.).
For further details see under: **ADAMHA**.
**SAMO** Sensitivity Analysis of Model Output - European Community.
**SAMOC** surface-to-air missile operations centre.
centre d'opérations de missiles surface-air.
**SAM Program** Significance Analysis of Microarrays Program.
**SAMs** Self-Assembled Monolayers.
*Chemistry.*
**SAMS** The Scottish Association for Marine Science.
*Molecular Genetics; Maritime Algae.*
**SAMW** Sub-Antarctic Mode Water.
*Geological Sciences; Marine Science; Paleoceanography.*
**san.** (abbr.) sanitary.
*Medicine.*
**SAN** small access node.
petit nœud d'accès.
**SAN**; **San** Storage Area Network.
**SAN** Strong Acid Number.
*Chemistry.*
**SA(N)** surface-to-air missile (naval).
missile surface-air (marine).
**SAN** The airport code for Lindbergh Field, San Diego, U.S.A.
**SANDF** South African National Defence Force (South Africa).
*Language Policies.*
**S&E** Science and Engineering.
**S&FA** Shipping and Forwarding Agent.
*Business; Commerce.*
**SANR** Subject to Approval - No Risks.
**SAN resin** Styrene-Acrylonitrile resin.
*Organic Chemistry.*
**SANS** Small-Angle Neutron Scattering.
SANS is an analytic technique.
*Chemistry.*
**SANs**; **Sans** Storage Area Networks.
**SANS experiments** Small-Angle Neutron Scattering experiments.
*Materials and Nuclear Engineering; Polymers.*

**SANTA** Systematic Analog Network Testing Approach.
*Electronics.*
**SANZ** Standards Association of New Zealand.
**SAO** Signatory Affair Office.
Established by British Telecommunications in 1993.
**SAO** Smithsonian Astrophysical Observatory (U.S.A.).
**SAOA** sub-area originating authority.
autorité d'origine de sous-secteur.
**SAP** Sindacato Autonomo di Polizia (Italy).
*Italian Police Union.*
**SAP** Sintered Aluminium Product.
*Metallurgy.*
**SAP** situation awareness picture.
représentation de la perception globale de la situation.
**SAP** Soon As Possible.
**SAP** Start of Active Profile.
*Mechanics.*
**SAPIA** Società Anonima Promotrice Industrie Agrarie.
Italian acronym meaning: Joint-Stock Company for the Promotion of Farming Industries.
**sapl** sailed as per list.
**SA Plate motion** South American Plate motion.
*Geological Sciences; Terrestrial Magnetism.*
**SAPP** special aerodrome pavement programme.
programme spécial de revêtement d'aérodrome (PSRA).
**SAPRC** Statewide Air Pollution Research Center (U.S.A.).
**SA press** Single-Action press.
*Mechanical Engineering.*
**SAQs** Self-Administered Questionnaires.
SAQs are the traditional paper-and-pencil questionnaires.
For further details see under: **Audio-CASI technology**.
**SAR** Scaffold Attachment Region.
**SAR** Search And Rescue.
**SAR** Second Assessment Report.
Of the IPCC.
For further details see under: **IPCC**.
**Sar** Segmenting and reassembling.
**SAR** Semiannual Report.
**SAR** Specific Absorption Rate.
**SAR** Stenosi Arteria Renale.
**SAR** Stock-Appreciation Relief (G.B.).
**SAR** Stock Appreciation Rights.
**S.A.R.** Sua Altezza Reale.
Italian acronym meaning: His/Her Royal Highness.
**SAR** Synthetic Aperture Radar.
*Nuclear Defense.*
**SAR** Systemic Acquired Resistance.
*Crop Protection.*
**SARA** Superfund Amendments and Reauthorization Act.
A 1986 U.S. Act.
**SAREX** search and rescue exercise.
exercice de recherche et sauvetage.
**SARIR** search and rescue incident report.
compte rendu d'inciddent de recherche et sauvetage.
**SARL**; **s.a.r.l.** Société à Responsabilité Limitée.
French acronym meaning: Limited Liability Company.
**SAROP** search and rescue operation.
opération de recherche et sauvetage.
**SARPA** Security Advanced Research Projects Agency.
**SARPS** Standards And Recommended Practices (of ICAO).
**SARR** San Antonio Road Route.
**SARREQ** search and rescue request.
demande de recherche et sauvetage.
**SARS** Severe Acute Respiratory Syndrome.
*Coronavirology; Emerging Infections.*
**SARSAT** search and rescue satellite.
satellite de recherche et sauvetage.
**SARS-CoV** SARS-Coronavirus.
Discovered in March 2003 by laboratories in the United States, Canada, Germany and Hong Kong.
For further details see under: **SARS**.
**SARSIT** search and rescue situation summary report.
compte rendu succint de situation recherche et sauvetage.
**SART** search and rescue transponder.
transpondeur de recherche et sauvetage.
**SART** Society for Assisted Reproductive Technology (U.S.A.).
**SAS** Servizio Assistenza Stradale (Italy).
**SAS** Small Astronomy Satellite.
**S.a.s.** Società in accomandita semplice.
Italian acronym meaning: Limited partnership.
*Business; Economics; Finance.*
**SAS** Society for Applied Spectroscopy.
**SAS** special ammunition storage.
dépôt de munitions spéciales.
**SAS** Stability Augmentation System.
**SAS** Statistical Analysis System.
**SAS** Statement of Auditing Standards.

*Accounts.*

**SAS-C** Scientific Applications Satellite-C - U.S.A. and Argentina.
The SAS-C was launched aboard the U.S. shuttle at the end of 1998.
*Astrophysics.*

**Sase** Synthase-Synthase.

**SASE process** Self-Amplified Spontaneous Emission process.
*Free-electron Lasers; Nuclear Physics.*

**SASI** South African Standards Institution.
*Technology.*

**Sask** (abbr.) Saskatchewan (Canada).

**SASP** special ammunition supply point.
poste d'approvisionnement en munitions spéciales.

**SAS phenomenon** Systemic Acquired Silencing phenomenon.
*Botany; Plant Biology; Plant Physiology; Transgenic Plants.*

**SASPs** Specialized Acid-Soluble Spore Proteins.
The DNA structure is changed and prevented from reacting with damaging molecules when SASPs bind to it.
*Bacterial Spores; Biochemistry; Entomology; Evolutionary Biology.*

**SASS** surface-to-air (missile) in the surface-to-surface mode.
(missile) surface-air en mode surface-surface.

**SASSE** Space Adaptation Syndrome Supplemental Experiments.

**SASUWC** sector antisubmarine warfare commander.
commandant de secteur de lutte anti-sous-marine.

**SASVRC** Sir Albert Sakzewski Virus Research Centre (Australia).
Administered by the RCH.
*Medical Virology.*
For further details see under: **RCH**.

**SASWC** sector antisurface warfare coordinator.
coordonnateur de secteur de lutte antisurface.

**SAT** Scholastic Aptitude Test (U.S.A.).
*Education.*

**SAT** Servicio de Administracion Tributaria (Mexico).

**SAT** Servizi ad Alta Tecnologia (Italy).

**SAT** Standard Aptitude Test (U.S.A.).

**SAT** submarine advisory team.
équipe consultative sur les sous-marins.

**SAT** Sulfuric Acid Tetrahydrate.

**SAT** Surface Air Temperature.
For further details see under: **SATs**.

**SAT** The airport code for San Antonio, U.S.A.

**SATAN** Security Administration Tool for Analysing Networks.
SATAN was written and published by a computer scientist and a programmer at Sun Microsystems. It was distributed freely on the Internet in 1997.
*Software Programs.*

**SATAR** Satellite-Aerospace Research.

**SATCC** South Africa Transport and Communcations Commission.

**SATCOM** satellite communications.
télécommunications par satellite.

**SATCP** (défense) sol-air à très courte portée.
very short-range air defence (VSHORAD).

**SATNAV** satellite navigation.
navigation par satellite.

**SATRA** South African Telephone Regulatory Authority.

**SATs** Surface Air Temperatures.
*Geological Sciences; Geophysics; Meteorology; Physics; Seismology.*

**SAT-UNSAT phase boundary** (abbr.) Satisfiable-Unsatisfiable phase boundary.
*Algorithms; Artificial Intelligence; Computer Science; Discrete Algorithms; Theoretical Physics.*

**SAU** search and attack unit.
unité de recherche et d'attaque.

**SAUB** Struttura Amministrativa Unificata di Base (Italy).
Italian acronym meaning: Unified Administrative (Health) Service.

**SAUC** search and attack unit commander.
commandant d'unité de recherche et d'attaque.

**SAUS** School for Advanced Urban Studies (G.B.).

**S.Aus.**; **S.Austr.** South Australia.

**sav.** (abbr.) save; savings.

**SAV** Service Après-Vente.
French acronym meaning: After-Sale Service.

**SAV** State-of-the-Atmosphere Variables.

**s.a.v.** stock at valuation.

**SAV** The airport code for Savannah, California, U.S.A.

**SAVE** South Atlantic Ventilation Experiment.

**SAW** Software Audio Workshop.

**SAW** Subantarctic Water.

**SAW** Surface Acoustic Wave.

**SAWHQ** static alternate war headquarters.
quartier général de guerre fixe de rechange (QGGFR).

**SAXS** Small-Angle X-ray Scattering.

**S.A.Y.E.** Save As You Earn.
*Banking; Finance.*

**Sb** The chemical symbol for Antimony.

Used mainly in semiconductors and storage batteries.
*Chemistry; Symbols.*
**SB** Savings Bank; Savings Bond; Senior Bond.
**SB** Schiff Base (protonated).
*Chemistry; Physics.*
**SB** Simultaneous Broadcasting.
**SB** Smithkline Beecham (G.B. & U.S.A.).
*Genome-based Pharmaceutical R&D; Life Sciences.*
**sb.** (abbr.) stockbroker.
Also: **s**.
**SBA** Safe Buildings Alliance (U.S.A.).
A lobbying group of former asbestos producers.
**SBA** Strategic Business Area.
*Business; Finance.*
**SBA** Small Business Administration.
U.S. SBA's award is bestowed annually to federal prime contractors in the categories of research and development, manufacturing, service, and construction.
*U.S. Awards.*
**SBA** The airport code for Santa Barbara, California, U.S.A.
**SB&F** Science Books & Films.
SB&F is a review journal of the AAAS.
For further details see under: **AAAS**.
**SBB** La Société de Banque de Bourgogne.
**SBC** Swiss Bank Corporation (Switzerland).
SBC acquired the BSI in 1991.
For further details see under: **BSI**.
**SBCL** Special Buyer Credit Limit.
*Business; Commerce.*
**SBE sciences** Social, Behavioral, and Economic sciences.
**s.b.f.** salvo buon fine.
Italian initialism meaning: under usual reserve.
*Business; Economics; Finance.*
**SBG** Standard Battery Grade.
**SBH** Sequencing By Hybridization.
**$SbH_3$** Antimony Hydride.
$SbH_3$ is also known as: Stibine.
*Inorganic Chemistry.*
**SBHs** Supermassive Black Holes.
*Astronomy; Physics.*
**SBIC** Sustainable Buildings Industry Council (U.S.A.).
*Energy-efficient Homes.*
**SBIR program** Small Business Innovation Research program (U.S.A.).
The SBIR program was created by the U.S. Congress in 1982 with a view to assist small businesses in commercializing their ideas making use of the U.S. Federal Research & Development funds.
**SBM** State Bank of Mauritius.
**SBMA** Spinal-Bulbar Muscular Atrophy.
*Cancer Research; Neurodegenerative Diseases; Neuropathology.*
**SB model** Semi-Balance model.
**S.B.M. program** Small Business Management program (Italy).
**SBN** Servizio Bibliotecario Nazionale (Italy).
*Books Online.*
**SBN** The airport code for South Bend, Indiana, U.S.A.
**SBNMI** State Bureau of Non-ferrous Metal Industry (China).
**SBNT** Single-Breath Nitrogen Test.
**$Sb_2O_3$** Senarmontite.
Senarmontite is used mainly as a paint pigment.
*Mineralogy.*
**SBP** Sex-Biased Parasitism.
*Biological Sciences; Male-biased Mortality; Mammals.*
For further details see under: **SSD**.
**SBP** Substrate-Binding Protein.
**SBP** Swatantra Bharat Party (India).
**SBPs** Substrate-Binding Proteins.
**SBR** Styrene Butadiene Rubber.
*Organic Chemistry.*
**SBR** Subcommittee on Basic Research (U.S.A.).
**SBRI** Seattle Biomedical Research Institute (U.S.A.).
**SBRP** Superfund Basic Research Program.
**SBRS** Senior Biomedical Research Service.
*Biomedical Research.*
**SBS** Society for Biomolecular Screening (U.S.A.).
*Biomolecular Discovery.*
**$Sb_2S_3$** Antimony Trisulfide.
Antimony Trisulfide is used in matches.
*Inorganic Chemistry.*
**SBSL** Single-Bubble Sonoluminescence.
*Applied Physics; Energy; Physics of Shock Waves; Sonoluminescence.*
**$Sb_2S_2O$** Kermesite.
Kermesite is also known as: Red Antimony; Pyrostibite.
*Mineralogy.*
**SBT** special boarding team.
équipe de visite spéciale.
**SBTA** S-Band Test Accelerator.
*Particle Physics.*
**SBU** Strategic Business Unit.
*Business; Economics; Finance.*
**SBU** Ukranian Security Bureau.

Formerly the KGB.
**SBUV** Solar Backscatter Ultraviolet.
**SC** Safe Custody.
**SC** Safety Clause.
**SC** Satellite Communications.
*Telecommunications.*
**SC** Satellite Computer.
The Satellite Computer which is an auxiliary computer, is also known as: Satellite Processor.
*Computer Technology.*
**Sc** The chemical symbol for Scandium.
Named for Scandia / **Scandinavia**.
**$Sc_3$** Schmidt number 3.
*Physical Chemistry.*
**SC** Scientific Calculator.
The SC can carry out exponential and trigonometric operations besides arithmetic ones.
*Computer Technology.*
**SC** Scientific Computer.
The scientific computer can handle high-speed arithmetic as well as floating-point arithmetic.
*Computer Technology.*
**SC** 1. screen commander.
1. commandant de l'écran.
2. sea current.
2. courant marin.
3. Security Council (of the UN).
3. Conseil de Sécurité (des Nations Unies).
4. St. Christopher-Nevis.
4. Saint-Christophe-et-Nevis.
5. Stockholm Conference.
5. Conférence de Stockholm.
6. strategic command [has replaced MNC].
6. commandement stratégique [remplace GCO].
7. sub-committee.
7. sous-comité.
**S.C.** Sede Centrale.
Italian initialism meaning: Head Office.
**SC** Self-Compatible.
**SC; s/c** self-contained.
**SC** Semantic Count.
*Linguistics.*
**SC** Service Charge.
**SC** Seul Cours.
French initialism meaning: Sole Quotation.
**SC** Small Consumer.
**SC** Static Check.
*Computer Technology.*
**SC** Stock Certificate.
**sc** son compte.
French initialism meaning: his/her account.
**SC** Sous-Cutané.
French initialism meaning: Subcutaneous.
*Medicine.*
**SC** (abbr.) South Carolina (U.S.A.).
**SC** Space Council - NASA's.
**SC** Special Committee.
**SC** Spell-Checker.
SC is also known as: Spell-Check; Spelling Checker.
*Computer Programming.*
**SC** Spindle-shaped Cell.
*Biomedicine; Human Virology.*
**SC** Stem Cell.
For further details see under: **SCs**.
**S.C.** Subcutaneously.
*Medicine.*
**SC** Subsidiary Company.
**SC** Superconducting.
*Physics.*
**SC** Surcharge Combustible.
French initialism meaning: Bunker Adjustment Factor.
**SC** Synaptonemal Complex.
For further details see under: **SCP3**.
**SC** System Command.
*Computer Programming.*
**SCA** Shareholder Credit Accounting.
**SCA** Spinocerebellar Ataxias.
*Biomedicine.*
**SCA1** Spinocerebellar Ataxia Type 1.
A disease caused by a faulty dominant gene, passed from generation to generation.
*Gene Therapy; Neurology.*
**SCA conductor** Steel-Cored Aluminium conductor.
**SCADA** Supervisory Control And Data Acquisition.
**SCALL** Consortium of Psychoanalytic Libraries.
**SCAMS** SCAnning Microwave Spectrometer.
**SCAN** Southern California Answering Network (U.S.A.).
**SCAN** Subcontracting Assistance Network - European Community.
**scan** The above acronyms were coined using the English word "scan".
*Computer Technology; Electronics; Medicine; Telecommunications.*
**Scand** (abbr.) Scandinavian.
Scandinavian is the group of languages comprising Danish, Icelandic, Norwegian, Old Norse, Swedish, and the language of the Faeroe Islands; North Germanic.
*Languages.*
**scanning HEED** scanning High-Energy Electron Diffraction.
*Physics.*
**SCANSAR** Scanning Synthetic Aperture Radar.

**SCAP** SREBP Cleavage-Activating Protein.
*Genetics; Gerontology; Molecular Biology; Neurology; Medicine.*
For further details see under: **SREBP**.

**SCAR** Scientific Committee on Antarctic Research.
Founded in 1958 by ICSU after the close of the International Geophysical Year to continue the promotion of international co-operation in scientific research in the Antarctic.
For further details see under: **ICSU**.

**scar** The above acronym was coined using the English word "scar".
*Geology; Medicine; Mycology.*

**SCARS** status control alert reporting system [replaced by NNCCRS].
système d'alerte de contrôle et de compte rendu [remplacé par NNCCRS].

**SCATER** Security Control of Air Traffic and Electromagnetic Radiation.

**SC Atl** see SC Atlantic.
voir SC Atlantic.

**SC Atlantic** Strategic Command Atlantic [has replaced ACLANT].
Commandement stratégique de l'Atlantique [remplace ACLANT].

**SCATMIN** scatterable mine.
mine dispersable.

**SCATMINREC** scatterable minefield record.
enregistrement de champs de mines dispersables.

**SCATMINREP** scatterable minefield report.
compte rendu sur les champs de mines dispersables.

**SCATMINWARN** scatterable minefield warning.
avis de danger de champs de mines dispersables.

**SCATT** (abbr.) Scatterometer.
The scatterometer is a radar for terrain mapping.
*Engineering.*

**SCAUL** Standing Conference of African University Librarians.

**SCAULEA** Standing Conference of African University Librarians, Eastern Area.

**SCAULWA** Standing Conference of African University Librarians, Western Area.

**SCB** Society for Conservation Biology (U.S.A.).
Launched in 1985.

**SCB** Space Construction Base.

**SC backscatter** Same Circular backscatter.
*Astronomy; Space Research; Space Science.*

**SCC** Satellite Communications Controller.

**SCC** 1. SHAPE Command Centre.
1. centre de commandement du SHAPE.
2. surveillance coordination centre.
2. centre de coordination de la surveillance.
3. system coordinate centre.
3. origine des coordonnées du système.

**SCC** Short-Course Chemotherapy.

**SCC** Specialized Common Carrier.

**SCC** Stock Clearing Corporation.

**SCC** Storage Connecting Circuit.

**SCC** Stress Corrosion Cracking.
*Metallurgy.*

**SCCA** Sports Car Club of America (U.S.A.).

**scCO$_2$** Supercritical Carbon Dioxide.
*Chemistry.*

**SCCWRP** Southern California Coastal Water Research Project (U.S.A.).

**SCD** security coding device.
dispositif de codage de sécurité.

**SCD-1** Stearoyl-CoA Desaturase 1.
*Biochemistry; Clinical Medicine; Energy Expenditure; Molecular Genetics; Nutritional Sciences.*

**SCDE** Service Conseil Développement à l'Exportation (France).

**SCDM** Standard Cold Dark Matter.
*Astronomy; Astrophysics; Physics.*

**SC dome** Sour Creek dome.

**SCE** Safety Code for Elevators.
*Buildings.*

**SCE** Saturated Calomel Electrode.
*Engineering; Nanotubes.*

**SCE** see SC Europe.
voir SC Europe.

**SCEAL** Standing Conference of East African Librarians.

**SCEAR** Scientific Committee on the Effects of Atomic Radiation.
Of the United Nations.

**SCEC** Southern California Earthquake Center (U.S.A.).
*Seismology.*

**SCEM** 1. service central d'exploitation de la météo.
1. central meteorology processing centre.
2. sous-chef d'état-major.
2. assistant chief of staff (ACOS).

**SCEMA** sous-chef d'état-major adjoint.
deputy assistant chief of staff (DACOS).

**SCENE** Scientific Computational Environment for Numerical Experimentation.
*Software.*

**SCEPC** Senior Civil Emergency Planning Committee.
Haut Comité pour l'étude des plans d'urgence dans le domaine civil.

**SC Europe** Strategic Command Europe [has replaced ACE].

Commandement stratégique en Europe [remplace CAE].
**SCF** Stem Cell Factor.
*Cell Biology; Medicine; Oncology; Pathology.*
**ScF$_3$** Scandium Fluoride.
$ScF_3$ is used to make scandium metal.
*Inorganic Chemistry.*
**SCF box protein** Skp1-Cullin-F-box protein.
*Plant Breeding Research.*
**SC filters** Switched Capacitor filters.
**SCF levels** Self-Consistent Field levels.
*Chemistry.*
**scfm** standard cubic feet per minute.
**sCAI** starvation CAI.
For further details see under: **CAI**.
**SCGs** Susceptibility-Conferring Genotypes.
*Genetic Tests.*
**sch.** (abbr.) schedule.
**Sch** Schilling.
The currency unit of Austria (obsolete). Now: EURO/EUR (€). Became ECU (European Single Currency) with effect from January 2002.
*Currencies.*
**SCHIN** South Carbling Health Information Network.
**SCI** ship-controlled intercept.
interception contrôlée à partir de navires.
**sci.** (abbr.) science.
The word "science" derives from the Latin term "knowledge".
**SCI** Science Citation Index.
The SCI is established by the Institute for Scientific Information.
**sci.** (abbr.) scientific.
**SCIC** Servizio Comune Interpretazione e Conferenze (Italy).
**SCICO** Servizio Centrale Investigativo Criminalità Organizzata (Italy).
A recently coined Italian acronym. SCICO is a Service of the Italian Revenue Guard Corps / Tax Police.
**SCICOOP-CAN** SCIentific and Technological COOPeration between the European Community and CANada - E.C.
**SCID** Severe Combined Immunodeficiency Disease.
*Biological Chemistry; Life Sciences.*
**SCIFAC** (abbr.) SCIentific FACilities.
E.E.C. Plan to support and facilitate access to large-scale scientific facilities of European interest.
*European Community Plans.*
**SCILL** Southern California Interlibrary Loan (U.S.A.).
**SCIT** Special Commissioners of Income Tax.
*Law & Taxation* (G.B.).
**sCJD** sporadic Creutzfeldt-Jakob Disease.
*Biochemistry; Biophysics; Medicine; Neurology; Neuropathology; Pathology; Prion Diseases.*
**SCL** The airport code for Santiago, Chile.
**SCLA** South Carolina Libraries Association (U.S.A.).
**SCLCPs** Side-Chain Liquid Crystalline Polymers.
*Applied Physics; Chemistry; Defence Research; Liquid Crystals; Physics.*
**SCLs** Synthetic Combinatorial Libraries.
*Chemical Biology; Clinical Research; Medicine; Molecular Studies; Neurology; Peptide Research; Pharmacology.*
**ScM** Master of Science.
**SCM** School Of Chinese Medicine (Hong Kong).
**SCM** Sex Combs on Midleg.
For further details see under: **PeG proteins**.
**SCM** Single Column Model.
**SCM** State Certified Midwife.
**SCM** Succinimidyl Carboxymethyl.
**SCM** Supply Chain Management.
**SCMF** SACEUR's conceptual military framework.
cadre conceptuel militaire du SACEUR.
**SCMI** Samba Capital Management International.
SCMI is a fully-owned subsidiary of Saudi American Bank.
**SCMM** Standing Committe on Military Matters.
Commission permanente aux affaires militaires.
**SCMO** South-Central Missouri (U.S.A.).
**SCMS** Serial Copy Management System.
*Duplication.*
**SCN** standard consumption norm.
norme de consommation standard.
**SCN** Suprachiasmatic Nucleus.
A group of neurons at the base of the optic chiasma within the CNS.
*Biological Rhythms; Cell and Structural Biology; Integrative Neuroscience Research; Physiology; Circadian Rhythm.*
For further details see under: **CNS**.
**SCNd** dorsal Suprachiasmatic Nucleus.
**SC-NP** Semiconducting Nanopraticle.
*Conductivity.*
**SC-NPs** Semiconducting Nanoparticles.
*Conductivity.*
**SCNT** Somatic Cell Nuclear Transfer.
*Biotechnology; Clonig Research; Stem Cell Research.*
**SCO** selective contigency options.

possibilités d'opérations ponctuelles de circonstance.

**SCO** Servizio Centrale Operativo (Polizia di Stato) (Italy).
Italian acronym meaning: Central Operating Service (Italian State Police).

**Sco-Cen association** Scorpius and Centaurus association.
*Astronomy.*

**SCODP** Sustainable Community Oriented Development Programme.
A Kenyan NGO.
*African Food Security.*
For further details see under: **NGO**.

**SCOHLZA** Standing Conference Of Head Librarians in Zambia.

**SCOLCAP** Scottish Libraries Co-operative Automation Project.

**SCOLMA** Standing Conference on Library Materials for Africa.

**SCONUL** Standing Conference of National and University Libraries.

**SCOP database** Structural Classification Of Proteins database.
*Molecular Biology; Structural Biology.*

**SCOPE** San Clemente Ocean Probing Experiment.

**SCOPE** Scientific Committee On Problems of the Environment.
Located in Paris, France. Founded in 1969; interdisciplinary research in environmental field.

**SCOR** Scientific Committee on Oceanic Research.
Founded in 1957 to further international scientific activity in all branches of oceanic research; scientific advisory body to UNESCO and to Intergovernmental Oceanographic Commission.
SCOR has replaced **IACOMS**.

**SCOR** Société Commerciale de Réassurance (France).

**SCORE** Special Claim On Residual Equity.

**SCOSTEP** Scientific Committee On Solar-Terrestrial Physics.
An Inter-Union Commission founded in 1966 by ICSU that became a Scientific Committee in 1978 to promote and co-ordinate international interdisciplinary programmes in solar-terrestrial phyiscs and to work with other ICSU bodies in the co-ordination of symposia in the field of *solar-terrestrial physics*.
For further details see under: **ICSU**.

**Scot** Scottish.
Scottish, also known as: Scots, is the English dialect spoken in Scotland.
*Languages.*

**ScotGael** Scots Gaelic.
Scots Gaelic, also known as Scottish Gaelic is the gaelic of the hebrides and the Highlands of Scotland, spoken as a second language in Nova Scotia.
*Languages.*

**Scotix** Scottish Internet Exchange (Edinburgh, Scotland).
A facility created in 1999 to provide a hub for e-commerce and internet traffic.
*Scottish Facilities.*

**SCP** shipping control point.
point de contrôle de la navigation commerciale.

**SCP** Single-Cell Protein.
*Biotechnology.*

**SCP** Spherical Candlepower.

**SCP3** Synaptonemal Complex Protein 3.
*Aneuploidy; Chiasmata Formation; Murine Oocytes; Genomics; Molecular Sciences.*

**SCPA** Société Commerciale des Potasses et de l'Azote (France).

**SCPC** Single Channel Per Carrier.

**scpd** (abbr.) scrapped.

**SCP-ECG** Standard Communications Protocol for Computerized Electrocardiography.
*Medicine.*

**SC polarizations** Same-sense Circular polarizations.

**SCPP** Seasonal-to-interannual Climate Prediction Program.

**scr.** (abbr.) screwed.

**SCR** Selective Catalytic Reduction.
*Power Plants NO emissions.*

**SCR** Silicon-Controlled Rectifier.
SCR is also known as: Reverse-Blocking Triade Thyristor.
*Electronics.*

**SCR** United Nations Security Council Resolution.
résolution du Conseil de sécurité des Nations Unies.

**SCRA** Senior Clinical Research Associate.

**SCRA** single-channel radio access.
acces radio à voie unique.

**scramjet** supersonic combustion ramjet.
*Aviation.*

**SCREEN** Service CReation Engineering ENvironment.
*European Community Project.*

**SCRI** Supercomputer Computations Research Institute (U.S.A.).
*High Performance Computing.*

**SCRLC** South Central Research Library Council.

**SCRS** Secondary Control Rod System.

**SCRSS** Secretoria de Estado da Segurança Social (Portugal).
**SCS** Silicon-Controlled Switch.
SCS is also known as: Reverse-Blocking Tetrode Thyristor.
*Electronics.*
**SCs** Spindle-shaped Cells.
For further details see under: **SC**.
**SCS** Sport Club Sesto (Italy).
*Fitness.*
**SCS** Stem Cell Sciences (Melbourne, Australia).
*Cell Replacement Therapies; Gene Technology.*
**SCs** Stem Cells.
In vertebrates the three types of SCs are: ESC, NSC and HSC.
*Cellular Biology; Genetics; Molecular Biology.*
**SCSG** Superior Cervical Sympathetic Ganglia.
**SCSI** Small Computer Systems Interface.
*Computer Technology.*
**SCSIN** Service Central de Sûreté des Installations Nucléaires (France).
**SCS MEX** South China Sea Monson EXperiment.
Besides China and Taiwan, scientists from Brunei, Malaysia, Indonesia, Thailand, Vietnam, Philippines, Singapore, participate in the experiment.
*Atmospheric Science; China-U.S. Cooperation; Marine Climate Research; Meteorology; Ocean Monitoring; Oceanography.*
**SCSN** Southern California Seismograph Network (U.S.A.).
**SC state** Superconducting state.
**SCSU** Southern Connecticut State University (U.S.A.).
**SCT** Service Counter Terminals.
**SCT approximation** Small-Curvature Tunneling approximation.
*Chemistry; Physics.*
**SCT(L)** Short-Circuited Transmission (Line).
**SCU** Site Control Unit.
The SCU of a system is a program that assembles, classifies and stores data using information supplied from other parts of the system.
*Computer Programs.*
**SCUBA** Submillimeter Common User Bolometer Array.
SCUBA comprises a camera mounted on the 15 m. British-Dutch-Canadian James Clerk Maxwell Telescope. It is built by the Royal Observatory in Edinburgh.
*Astronomy.*
**SCUNIAL** Subcommittee of United Nations Inter-Agency Librarians.
**SCUP** Society for College and University Planning (U.S.A.).
*Educational Web Sites.*
**SCU-PA** Single Chain Urokinase Plasminogen Activator.
**S.C.V.** Stato della Città del Vaticano.
Vehicle-registration letters of the Vatican City.
**SCVs** Submesoscale Coherent Vortices.
*Geophysics; Subsurface Circular Eddies.*
**SCWO** Supercritical Water Oxidation.
*Organic Waste Disposal.*
**SCWS** Scottish Cooperative Wholesale Society.
**SCZ** ship control zone.
zone de contrôle des bâtiments.
**sd** (abbr.) sailed; signed.
**SD** Sales Department.
**SD** sea damage.
**SD** Secondary Distribution.
**s.d.** senza data.
Italian initialism meaning: no date.
**SD** Settlement Date.
**SD** short delivery.
**SD** Sight Draft.
*Business; Commerce.*
**SD** Skin Dose.
**s/d** soft-drawn.
*Metallurgy.*
**sd.** (abbr.) sound.
*Acoustics; Computer Science; Geography; Surgery.*
**SD** (abbr.) South Dakota (U.S.A.).
**SD** 1. soutien direct.
1. direct support (DS 3b.).
2. Stockholm Document.
2. Document de Stockholm.
**SD** Spreading Depression.
*Cortical Tissues; Mammalian Brain Cells; Tissue Depolarization.*
**S.D.**; **s.d.** Standard Deviation.
Standard deviation is also known as: Standard Error, Root-Mean-Square Error.
*Statistics.*
**SD** steel drum.
**SD** Stock Dividend.
**SD** Streptodornase.
*Enzymology.*
**SD** Surface Drainage.
*Hydrology.*
**SD** System Design.
System design in control systems is also known as: synthesis.
*Control Systems.*

**SDA** Scuola di Direzione Aziendale (Bocconi University, Milan, Italy).
**SDA** 1. secteur de défense aérienne.
1. air defence sector.
2. ships destination authority.
2. autorité de destination des navires.
3. system design and architecture.
3. conception et architecture du système.
**S.D.A.** Società Nazionale Dante Alighieri.
Italian acronym of the: Dante Alighieri National (Cultural) Association (Italy).
**SDA** Source Data Automation.
SDA is also known as: Automation Source Data.
*Computer Technology.*
**SDA** Specially Denaturated Alcohol.
**SDA** Specific Dynamic Action.
*Medicine.*
**SDAF** SACEUR's direct augmentation force.
force d'appoint directe du SACEUR.
**SD&I** system design and integration.
conception et intégration de système.
**SD&IC** software design & integration contract.
contrat d'étude et d'intégration du logiciel.
**SDAT** Senile Dementia of the Alzheimer's Type.
*Medicine.*
**SDB** Sales Daybook.
*Business; Commerce.*
**SDB** Sulfur-Disproportionating Bacteria.
*Marine Microbiology.*
**SDBL** Sight Draft Bill of Lading.
*Commerce; Shipping.*
**SDBL action** Sandblast action.
*Engineering; Geology.*
**SDC** Solenoid Detector Collaboration.
**SDC** strategic direction centre.
centre de direction stratégique.
**SDCE** Society of Die Casting Engineers (U.S.A.).
**SDD** Spin-Dependent Delocalization.
*Biochemistry; Chemistry and Chemical Biology; Enzyme Research.*
**SDDC** Sodium Dimethyldithiocarbamate.
$(CH_3)_2NCS_2Na$. Sodium Dimethyldithiocarbamate is used mainly as a fungicide, and corrosion inhibitor.
*Organic Chemistry.*
**SDE** Spatial Database Engine.
**SDE** Specific Dynamic Effect.
*Nutrition.*
**SDE-GWIS** Sigma Delta Epsilon-Graduate Women in Science (U.S.A.).
*Fellowships.*
**SDF** The airport code for Louisville.
**SDF-1** chemokine Stromal cell-Derived Factor-1.
*Cell Biology; Immunology; Medicine.*
**SDFI** State's Direct Financial Interest.
The SDFI controls much of Norway's natural gas reserves.
*Norway Controlling Bodies.*
**SDH/SONET capacity** SDH / Synchronous Optical NETwork capacity.
For further details see under: **SDH technology**.
**SDH technology** Synchronous Digital Hierarchy technology.
SDH is a transmission system that enables networks to be built quickly and maintained cheaply.
*Carrier Networks; Data Communications.*
**SDI** Selective Dissemination of Information.
**Sdia** Soap and Detergents Industrial Association (G.B.).
**SDIG** Société pour le Développement de l'Industrie du Gaz (France).
**SDK** Software Development Kit.
**SDL** standard distribution list.
liste de diffusion officielle.
**SDLA** South Dakota Library Association (U.S.A.).
**SDLC** Synchronous Data Link Communications.
**SDLC** Synchronous Data Link Control.
**SDM** Site-Directed Mutagenesis.
*Biochemistry; Molecular Biophysics.*
**SDMI** Secure Digital Music Initiative.
Formed in early 1999. It is an alliance of electronics, music and computing companies.
**SDMJ** September, December, March, June.
*Securities.*
**SDMP** software development and maintenance procedure.
procédure d'élaboration et de maintenance du logiciel.
**SDMS** Scanning Defect Mapping System.
NREL's SDMS is being used to analyze defects in large silicon wafers. It can also be easily adapted to analyze defects in other semiconductor materials or to monitor surface contamination of microelectronic circuits.
*Laser-Scanning System.*
For further details see under: **GaAs** and **NREL**.
**SDN** salle de destination des navires.
ship(ping) destination room.
**SDN** Società Delle Nazioni.
Italian initialism meaning: League of Nations.
**SDOA** Scuola di Direzione e Organizzazione Aziendale (Italy).
**SDoC** Supplier's Declaration of Conformity.
*Product Certification; Transatlantic Issues; U.S.-E.C. Business.*
**SDP**; **S.D.P.** Sacrodextra Posterior.

**SDP** Social Democratic Party (Germany).
**SDP** Sulfonyldiphenol.
**SDR** Sensor Data Record.
A record formatted for further computer processing.
**SDR** Sociétés de Développement Régional.
French initialism meaning: Regional Development Companies.
**SDR** Statistical Data Recorder.
**SDRS** satellite data relay system.
système de satellites de relais de données.
**S.D.Rs** Special Drawing Rights.
*Finance.*
**SDRU** Streptococcus and Diphtheria Reference Unit (G.B.).
*Diphtheria and Streptococcal Infections.*
**SDS** Sodium Dodecyl Sulfate.
**SDSA** Synthesis-Dependent Strand Annealing.
*Bloom Syndrome.*
For further details see under: **BS**.
**SDSA pathway** Synthesis-Dependent Strand-Annealing pathway.
*Biology; Biotechnology; Molecular Biology.*
**SDSC** San Diego Supercomputer Center (U.S.A.).
**SD scenario** Single-Degenerate scenario.
*Astronomy; Astrophysics.*
**SDS-PAGE** SDS-Polyacrylamide Gel Electrophoresis.
*Biochemistry.*
For further details see under: **SDS**.
**SDSS** Sloan Digital Sky Survey.
*Astronomy.*
**SDT**; **S.D.T.** Sacrodextra Transversa.
**SDT** Scalar Data Type.
*Computer Science.*
**SDT**; **Sdt** Servizio Di Traduzione.
Italian initialism meaning: Translation Service.
**SDV** Silica Deposition Vesicle.
For further details see under: **SDVs**.
**SDVs** Silica Deposition Vesicles.
Located in the cell cytoplasm.
*Biomineralization; Biosilica; Botany; Diatoms.*
**Se** The chemical symbol for Selenium.
Selenium is a nonmetallic element, having the atomic number 34, an atomic weight of 78.96 and a melting point of 217°C. It is used mainly in photoelectric cells, and in metallurgy.
*Chemistry; Symbols.*
**SE** Semantic Error.
*Computer Programming.*
**SE** 1. Seychelles.
1. Seychelles.
2. support element.
2. élément de soutien.
**SE** Shareholder Equity.
**SE** Sieve Element.
*Botany; Plant Biology; Plant Physiology.*
**SE** Slovak Enterprise.
**SE** Slovenske Elektrarne.
SE is the Slovak Electric Utility Company. SE was a state-owned company. Since November 1994 it is a joint-stock company. The name changed from SEP to SE.
**SE** Smooth Early.
*Monkeys Vocal Sounds.*
**SE** Software Engineering.
*Computer Programming.*
**S.E.**; **SE**; **se**; **s.e.** Southeast; Southeastern.
**S.E.** Standard Error.
For details see under: **S.D.** (Standard Deviation).
**S/E** Stock Exchange.
**SEA** Science and Educational Administration (U.S.A.).
**SEA** Single European Act - E.C.
The SEA came into force on 1st July 1987.
**SEA** Società Esercizi Aeroportuali (Italy).
**SEA** Staphylococcal Enterotoxin A.
*Immunology; Medical Biophysics; Medicine; Oncologic Pathology; Oncology.*
**SEA** State Earthquake Administration (China).
**SEA** Strategic Environmental Assessment.
**SEA** The airport code for Seattle/Tacoma International.
**SEAC** Safety and Environmental Assurance Centre (Unilever's).
**SEAC** Spongiform Encephalopathy Advisory Committee (G.B.).
*Creutzfeldt-Jakob Disease; Neuropathology; Prions.*
**SEAC** submarine exercise area coordination.
coordonnateur des secteurs d'exercice pour sous-marins.
**SEAD** suppression of enemy air defences.
mise hors de combat des moyens de défense aérienne ennemis.
**SEADEX** seaward defence exercise.
exercice de défense contre une menace maritime.
**SEAFIS** South-East Asian Fisheries Information System.
**SEAFLOE** Southeast FLorida Outfalls Experiment (U.S.A.).
**SEAL** South East Area Libraries.
**SEAL**; **seal team** Sea-Air-Land team.
**SEAMAP** Southeast Area Monitoring and Assessment Program (U.S.A.).

**SEAMEO** SouthEast Asian Ministers of Education Organization.
**SEAP** SEcreted form of Alkaline Phosphatase.
*Cell Biology; Molecular Biology.*
**SEAQ system** Stock Exchange Automated Quotation system (G.B.).
**SEARCHEX** sea/air search exercise.
exercice de recherche mer/air.
**SEAS** Shipboard Environmental data Acquisition System (U.S.A.).
**S.E.A.T.** Società Elenchi ufficiali degli Abbonati al Telefono (Italy).
Italian acronym of the: Telephone Directory Publishing Company.
**SEATO** South East Asia Treaty Organization.
**SEATS** Stock Exchange Alternative Trading Service (G.B.).
**SEATS** Stock Exchange Automated Trading System (Australia).
**SEB** Society of Experimental Biology (G.B.).
*Fruit Development and Ripening; Carbon Metabolism Regulation; Plant Reproductive Biology; Epigenetics; Plant Matabolism.*
**SEB** Source Evaluation Board.
**SE - Banken** Skandinaviska Enskilda Banken.
*Swedish Bank.*
**SEBC** Sistema Europeo delle Banche Centrali.
Italian initialism meaning: European System of Central Banks.
*Changeover to the EURO.*
**SEBI** Securities and Exchange Board of India.
**sec** (abbr.) secant.
*Cartography; Mathematics.*
**sec.** (abbr.) secolo.
Italian abbreviation meaning: century.
**Sec**; **sec.** (abbr.) second; section; secretary; secretarial.
**SEC** Secondary-Electron Conduction.
**SEC** Securities and Exchange Commission.
*Stock Exchange U.S.A.*
**SEC** Sistema Europeo di Contabilità.
Italian acronym meaning: European Bookkeeping System.
**SEC** Size-Exclusion Chromatography.
**SEC** South Equatorial Current.
*Oceanography.*
**SEC** Space Environment Center.
At U.S. NOAA.
For further details see under: **NOAA**.
**SEC** Strong Energy Condition.
*Physics.*
**SEC** submarine element coordinator.
coordonnateur de l'élément sous-marin.

**SECAN** Military Committee Communciation and Information Systems Security and Evaluation Agency.
Bureau de sécurité et d'évaluation des systèmes de communication et d'information du Comité militaire.
**SECGEN** Secretary General.
Secrétaire général.
**SECIT**; **Secit** SErvizio Centrale degli Ispettori Tributari (Italy).
**SECMA** Stock Exchange Computer Managers Association.
**SECO** Securities and Exchange Commission Organization.
**SecOP** security operating procedure.
procédure d'exploitation de sécurité.
**SECURE** Safe and Environmental Clean Urban REactor.
**Secy.** (abbr.) Secretary.
**sed**; **sed.** (abbr.) sediment; sedimentation.
*Chemistry; Geology; Metallurgy.*
**SED** Skin Erythema Dose.
*Nucleonics; Radiation Exposure.*
**SED rate** (abbr.) SEDimentation rate.
**SEDS** Students for the Exploration and Development of Space.
SEDS is a U.S. 20-year-old Organization.
*Astronomy.*
**SEE** Science and Everyday Experiences.
SEE is a weekly radio program produced by the AAAS in collaboration with the Delta Sigma Theta Sorority Inc., and the Delta Research and Education Foundation.
For further details see under: **AAAS**.
**SEE** Spazio Economico Europeo.
Italian initialism meaning: European Economic Space.
**SEEDS** Subarctic Pacific Iron Experiment for Ecosystem Dynamics Study.
*Aquatic Bioscience; Fisheries Science; Iron-enrichment Experiments; Radiological Sciences.*
**SEEN** Société Européenne de l'Energie Nucléaire.
**SEEPZ** Santacruz Electronic Export Processing Zone.
SEEPZ is Asia's largest software technology park, developed to boost India's electronic exports.
**Seeren** South-east European research and education networking.
Seeren includes the NRENs.
*European Community Initiatives.*
For further details see under: **NRENs**.
**SEER program** Surveillance, Epidemiology and End Results program.

Of the U.S. NCI.
For further details see under: **NCI**.

**SEFCAR** Southeast Florida and CAribbean Recruitment (U.S.A.).

**seg.** (abbr.) seguente.
Italian abbreviation meaning: following.

**SEG** Society of Economic Geologists.

**segg.** (abbr.) seguenti.
Italian abbreviation meaning: following (plural).

**SEHPP** Science and Environmental Health Policy Project.
*U.S. Project.*

**SEI** Slovak Energy Inspection.
*Energy Agencies.*

**SEI** Space Exploration Initiative (U.S.A.).

**SEI** Stockholm Environment Institute (Sweden).

**SEI** Sustainable Ecosystems Institute.
A nonprofit in Oregon, U.S.A.
*Ecological Issues; Forums.*

**SEIA** Solar Energy Industries Association (U.S.A.).

**SEIR** Southeast Indian Ridge.
*Geology; Geophysics.*

**SEJ** Sliding Expansion Joint.
*Piping.*

**SEL** The airport code for Seoul.

**SELA** Sistema Economico Latino Americano.
Italian acronym meaning: Latin American Economic System.

**SELA** Southeastern Library Association.

**SELENE** SELenological and Engineering Explorer (Japan).
SELENE is a joint mission to the moon by NASDA (Japan) and ISAS (Japan). Launched in 2003.
*Lunar Polar Orbiters; Relay Satellites.*
For further details see under: **ISAS** and **NASDA**.

**SELRC** Southeastern Library Resources Council.

**SEM** Scanning Electron Micrograph; Scanning Electron Microscope.
*Electronics.*

**SEM**; **S.E.M.** Scuola Europea di Musicoterapia (Italy).
*European Schools.*

**SEM** Shared Equity Mortgage.

**SEM** Système d'Exploitation et Maintenance.

**sem** The above acronyms were coined accidentally using the Arabic word "sem" which means: poison.
*Atomic Physics; Chemistry; Electronics; Nuclear Engineering; Toxicology.*

**Sem.** (abbr.) Seminary.

**Sem.** (abbr.) Semitic.
Semitic is a subfamily of Afro-Asiatic languages. It includes: Akkadian, Arabic, Aramaic, and Hebrew.

**SEMM** Single Electron MOS Memory.
*Electrical Engineering; Nanostructure.*
For further details see under: **MOS**.

**SEMPA** Scanning Electron Microscopy with Polarization Analysis.
*Metals; Physics.*

**SEMPER** Secure Electronic Marketplace for Europe.
SEMPER aims to harmonize approaches to security across Europe. It is sponsored by the European Union. Started in 1995, completed by the end of 1998.
*European Community Project.*

**SEMs** Scanning Electron Microscopes.
*Electronics.*

**SEMT** Société d'Etudes des Moteurs Thermiques (France).

**Sen.** (abbr.) Senior.

**Sen** The fractional currency unit of Indonesia.
*Currencies.*

**SENIT** système d'exploitation naval des informations tactiques.
naval tactical data processing system (NTDS).

**SENSATIONS** Standing with Electrical Neuromuscular Stimulation Applying Tactile and proprioceptive Information Obtained from Natural Sensors - E.C.

**SENYLRC** Southeastern New York Regional Library Council.

**S.E.O.** Salvo Errori e Omissioni.
Italian acronym meaning: Errors and Omissions Excepted.

**$SeO_2$** Selenium Dioxide.
$SeO_2$ is used mainly as an oxidizing agent.
*Chemistry.*

**SEOCS** Sun-Earth Observatory and Climatology Satellite.

**SEON** Solar Electro-optical Observing Network.

**SEOS** Synchronous Earth Observatory Satellite.

**SEP** Sclérose En Plaques.
French acronym meaning: Multiple Sclerosis.

**SEP** selective employment plan.
plan d'emploi sélectif.

**SEP** Slovensky Energeticky Podnik.
Now SE.
For further details see under: **SE**.

**SEP** Solar Electric Propulsion.

**SEP** Synthetic Erythopoiesis Protein.
SEP is a modified protein with a defined covalent structure.
*Biochemistry; Blood Research; Medicine.*

**SEPA** Scottish Environment Protection Agency.
**SEPA** Swedish Environmental Protection Agency (Sweden).
**sEPOR** soluble EPOR.
For further details see under: **EPOR**.
**SEPR** Southern East Pacific Rise.
*Geology; Geophysics; Oceanography.*
**SEP(S)** Solar Electric Propulsion (Stage).
**SEQUAL** Seasonal EQUatorial Atlantic Experiment (U.S.A.).
**SER** Safety Evaluation Report.
**ser.** (abbr.) serial; series.
**Ser** Serine.
$C_3H_7NO_3$. Serine is used mainly as a dietary supplement.
*Biochemistry.*
**SER** Smooth Endoplasmic Reticulum.
*Cell Biology.*
**SER** surface équivalente radar.
radar cross-section (RCS).
**SERC** Science and Engineering Research Council (U.S.A.).
**SERCA** Sarcoplasmic-Endoplasmic Reticulum $Ca^{2+}$ Adenosine Triphosphatase.
*Biomedical Sciences; Calcium Homeostasis; Molecular Medicine; Pathology.*
**SERDP** Strategic Environmental Research and Defense Program.
Created by the U.S. Congress in 1991.
*Commercial Research Projects; Environmental Preservation.*
**SEREB** Société pour l'Etude et la Réalisation d'Engins Balistiques (France).
**SERF** Solar Energy Research Facility (U.S.A.).
The unique, energy-efficient design of NREL'S Solar Energy Research Facility has ranked it among 77 winners in 1996. The SERF uses daylighting, compact fluorescent lights, window shades powered by photovoltaics, and other advanced features to reduce energy consumption.
*Awards.*
For further details see under: **NREL**.
**SERF model** Solar Electromagnetic Radiation Flux model.
**SERI** Schepens Eye Research Institute.
SERI is an affiliate of the Harvard Medical School (U.S.A.).
**SERI** Solar Energy Research Institute.
**SERL** Section on Energy and natural Resources Law.
Of the London International Bar Association.
**SERM** Selective Estrogen Receptor Modulator.
For further details see under: **SERMs**.
**SERMLP** Sourtheastern Regional Medicail Library Program.
**SERMs** Selective Estrogen Receptor Modulators.
*Aging Medicine.*
**SERP** Strategic Education Research Program (U.S.A.).
**SERPs** Strategic Education Research Partnerships (U.S.A.).
**SERS** Surface-Enhanced Raman Scattering.
*Chemistry.*
**SERT** Serotonin Transporter.
*Medicine; Neurology; Psychiatry.*
**SERT** SErvizio Ricupero Tossicodipendenti (Italy).
**SERT-IR** SERT-Immunoreactive.
*Medicine; Neurology; Psychiatry.*
For further details see under: **SERT**.
**serv.** (abbr.) service.
**SERV** Simian Endogenous Retrovirus.
*Biology; Retroviruses; Virology; Xenotransplantation.*
**SES** Senior Executive Service.
**SES** Socioeconomic Status.
*Human Development; Sociology.*
**SES** Standards Engineers Society.
**SES** Stock Exchange of Singapore.
**SeS** Superior Semilunar lobule.
*Clinical Psychology; Medicine; Neuroscience of Autism; Radiology.*
**SES** Surface-Effect Ship.
*Naval Architecture.*
**SESA** Society for Experimental Stress Analysis.
*Experimental Stress Analysis.*
**SESAME** Simultaneous Engineering System for Applications in Mechanical Engineering - European Community.
*Software Packages.*
**SESAME** Standardization in Europe on Semantical Aspects in MEdicine - E.C.
**SESAME** station d'écoute de satellite météorologique.
meteorological satellite monitoring station.
**SESLP** Sequential Explicit Stochastic Linear Programming.
**SESPA** Scientists and Engineers for Social and Political Action.
**SESs** Seismic Electric Signals.
*Seismology.*
**SESS** surface-effect surface ship.
bâtiment de surface à effet de surface.
**SET** Secure Electronic Transaction.
**SET** Single Electron Transistor.
*Applied Physics.*
**SET** Single-Electron Tunneling.

*Microelectronics.*
**SETAR** Service de l'Enseignement des Techniques Avancées de la Recherche.
French acronym meaning: Advanced Research Techniques Teaching Service.
**SETBIS** SEt Top Box for Interactive Services on demand.
*European Community Project.*
**SETC** State Economic and Trade Commission (China).
**SETCA**; **Setca** Syndicat des Employùés, Techniciens et Cadres (de Belgique).
*Belgian Unions.*
**SETI** Search for Extraterrestrial Intelligence.
Until 1993 SETI was funded by NASA. Now it is under private financing. The main branches of SETI are located at Harvard University and in Mountain View, California, U.S.A.
**SETO** Southern Europe Transport Organization.
Organisation des transports du Sud de l'Europe.
**SET protocol** Secure Encryption Transaction protocol.
The first purchase using the new Security Technology Standard took place in Denmark at the beginning of 1997.
*Electronic Commerce.*
**SETs** Secure Electronic Transactions.
**SETs** Single-Electron Transistors.
*Microelectronics; Nanoscience; Transistor Architecture; Solid-state quantum computers.*
For further details see under: **RF-SET**.
**SETSE** Single-Electron Transistor Scanning Electrometer.
*Applied Physics; Microelectronics; Nanoscience; Physics.*
**SET standard** Secure Electronic Transactions standard.
The SET standard was set up in 1996.
*Digital Certificates; Encryption Technologies; Internet Commerce.*
For further details see under: **SFNB**.
**sett.** (abbr.) settembre.
Italian abbreviation meaning: September.
**$E-U** Dollar Etats-Unis; Dollar Américain.
French initialism meaning: U.S. $.
*Currencies.*
**SEUHS** Southeastern University of the Health Sciences (U.S.A.).
**SEV** (abbr.) Sevenless.
**SEV** surface-effect vessel.
bâtiment à effet de surface.
**SEW** shared early warning.
mise en commun des informations de détection lointaine.
**SEWS** satellite early warning system.
système de détection lointaine par satellite.
**SF** Finland's international vehicle registration letters.
**SF** 1. saut de fréquence.
1. frequency hopping (FH).
2. South Africa.
2. Afrique du Sud.
**SF** Scale Factor.
*Engineering.*
**SF** Seasonal Fluctuation.
**SF** semifinished.
*Metallurgy.*
**SF** Serial File.
Serial File is also known as: Sequential Organization.
*Computer Programming.*
**SF** Short Focus.
**SF** Special Forces (U.S.A.).
**SF** Specializzazione Flessibile.
**SF** Spontaneous Fission.
*Nuclear Physics.*
**SF** Standard Form.
*Computer Programming.*
**SF** Statute of Frauds.
Also: **S/F**.
**SF** Submarine, Fleet.
*U.S. Navy.*
**SF-1** Steroidogenic Factor-1.
*Gynecology; Internal Medicine; Obstetrics; Pathology.*
**SF** Stock Fund.
**SF** Sundaram Finance Limited (India).
*Hire Purchase; Investment Banking; Asset Management; Leasing; Merchant Banking.*
**SF** Sylvian Fissure.
*Anatomy.*
**$SF_6$** Sulfur Hexafluoride.
$SF_6$ is used as a dielectric.
*Inorganic Chemistry.*
**SFA** Société Française d'Astronautique (France).
**SFAS** Statement of Financial Accounting Standards.
*SFAS N° 117* is meant to provide minimal requirements for financial statement presentation and does not preclude colleges and universities from providing additional information. Implementation of SFAS N° 117 promises many challenges to industry accountants and their auditors. The final product should promote understanding of financial statements within and among the NFP industries.

For further details see under: **FASB** and under **MNCs**.
**SFB** Special Research Programs (Austria).
**SFBR** Southwest Foundation for Biomedical Research (U.S.A.).
**SFC** Sales Finance Companies.
**SFC** Securities and Futures Commission.
SFC is China's Stock Market Regulator.
**SFC** Space Forecast Center (U.S.A.).
**SFC** Specific Fuel Consumption.
*Aviation; Mechanical Engineering.*
**SFC** Supercritical Fluid Chromatography.
**SFCC** San Francisco City Cohort (U.S.A.).
**SFE** Solvation component of the Free Energy.
*Pharmaceutical Chemistry.*
**SFE** Supercritical Fluid Extraction.
**S/Fee** Survey Fee.
**SFF** Swi Five Factor.
*Biochemistry; Pathology.*
**SFG** Superior Frontal Gyrus.
*Brain Sciences; Cognitive Neuroscience; Psychoacoustics.*
**SFH** Slow Frequency Hopping.
*Wireless Communications.*
**SFI** Santa Fe Institute (U.S.A.).
**SFI** Science Foundation Ireland.
The SFI was launched by the Government in 2000.
*Biology; Biotechnology; Awards.*
**SFI** Società Finanziaria Internazionale.
Italian initialism meaning: International Finance Corporation.
**SFI** Sports Fishing Initiative.
**SFM** Scanning Force Microscope.
**SFM** Sustainable Forest Management.
*Biodiversity; Conservation Practices; Ecosystems; Forest Management.*
**SFMR** Stepped Frequency Microwave Radiometer.
**SFNB** Security First Network Bank.
The SFNB (Atlanta, Georgia, U.S.A.) was one of the first banks to bring secure banking services to the Internet.
*Banks; Digital Certificates; Encryption Technologies.*
**SFO** Satellite Field Office.
**SFO** The airport code for San Francisco, U.S.A.
**SFOP** Strumento Finanziario di Orientamento della Pesca - *European Community.*
**SFOR** Stabilization Force.
Force de stabilisation.
**SFOSRC** South Florida Oil Spill Research Center.
**SFPE** Society of Fire Protection Engineers (U.S.A.).
**SFPM** Surface Feet Per Minute.
Referring to a tool cutting speed.
**sfr.** sotto fascia, raccomandato.
Italian initialism meaning: under cover, registered.
**SFR** status of forces report.
rapport sur l'état des forces.
**SFr** Swiss Franc.
*Currencies.*
**SFRs** Star-Forming Regions.
*Astronomy; Astrophysics.*
**SFS** Sodium Formaldehyde Sulfoxylate.
SFS is used mainly as a bleaching agent (for soap, etc.).
*Organic Chemistry.*
**sfs** sotto fascia semplice.
Italian initialism meaning: under cover, not registered.
**SFS** Statistical Fine Structure.
*Physical Chemistry.*
**SFS** see STRIKFORSOUTH.
voir STRIKFORSOUTH.
**SFSC** Southeast Fisheries Science Center.
**SFS program** Scholarship For Service program.
*Computer Security; Information Assurance.*
**SFSS** Satellite Field Service Station (U.S.A.).
Of the U.S. National Weather Service.
**SFST** Santa Fe Science and Technology.
**SFSTP** Société Française des Sciences et Techniques Pharmaceutiques (France).
**SFSU** San Francisco State University (U.S.A.).
**SFT** State Pollution Control Authority (Norway).
**Δ** San Francisco Veterans Affairs Medical Center (U.S.A.).
**SFWMD** South Florida Water Management District (U.S.A.).
*Agriculture; Biology; Ecology; Ecosystem Restoration; Engineering Environment; Hydrology; Wetlands.*
**Sg** *Schizaphis graminum.*
*Ecology; Evolutionary Biology; Endosymbiotic Bacteria; Molecular Evolution.*
**SG** Sea Grant.
**s.g.** secondo grandezza.
Italian initialism meaning: according to size.
**SG** Sécurité Générale (France).
**sg** (abbr.) seguente.
Italian abbreviation meaning: following; next.
**SG** specific gravity.
Also known as: relative density.
*Mechanics.*
**SG** spese generali.
Italian initialism meaning: operating expenses; overheads; overhead expenses; working expenses; indirect charges; running costs.

**SG** State Graph.
*Computer Technology.*
**SG** Structural Glass.
*Buildings.*
**SG2000** Sasakawa Global 2000.
*Agronomy; Agricultural Economics; Commercial Fertilizers; Technology.*
**SGA** Sale of Goods Act (G.B.).
**SGA** Société Générale Acceptance N.V.
**SGBD** système de gestion de bases de données.
database management system (DBMS).
**SGC** section de guidage et de commande.
guidance and control unit (GCU).
**SGC** Structural Genomics Consortium (Canada).
A 2003 public/private venture.
**SGCB** Secrétariat Général de la Commission Bancaire (France).
**SGF** Société Générale de Financement (du Québec) (Canada).
Founded in 1942 by its shareholder, the Québec Government, SGF is a financial holding that provides development capital.
*Business; Economics; Finance.*
**SGFS** Stratum Griseum et Fibrosum Superficiale.
*Anatomy; Neurobiology.*
**Sgg** (abbr.) Shaggy.
*Drosophila* protein also known as: $Zw^3$.
For further details see under: **$Zw^3$**.
**SGH** Singapore General Hospital.
**SGHWR** Steam-Generating Heavy Water Reactor.
**SGI** Schizophrenia Genetics Initiative (NIMH's).
For further details see under: **NIHM**.
**SGML** Standard Generalized Markup Language.
Codified in 1986 in the Standard ISO 8879/1986.
**SGNMOS** Screen-Grid n-channel Metal Oxyde Semiconductor.
**SGO** Surgeon General's Office.
**SGOR** Solution Gas-Oil Ratio.
**SGOT** Serum Glutamic Oxaloacetic Transaminase.
**sGP** secreted Glycoprotein.
*Ebola Virus.*
**SGP** Senior Politico-Military Group on Proliferation.
Groupe politico-militaire de haut niveau sur la prolifération.
**SGP** Southern Great Plains.
**SGPT** Serum Glutamic Pyruvic Transaminase.
**SGR** Self-Generation Recycle.
**SGR** Soft Gamma-ray Repeater.
For further details see under: **SGRs**.
**SGRs** Soft Gamma-ray Repeaters.
A type of rotating neutron stars.
*Astrophysics.*
**SGSA** submarine-generated search area.
zone de recherche générale par le sous-marin.
**SGT** satellite ground terminal.
terminal terrien de satellite.
**SGU** Geological Survey of Sweden (Sweden).
**SGU** Signal Generating Unit.
*Medicine; Microbiology.*
**SGX** Structural GenomiX.
*Crystallography; Protein Structures.*
**SH** Sérum Hépatite ou Hépatite à virus B.
French initialism meaning: Hepatitis B.
*Medicine.*
**SH** Serum Hepatitis.
**SH** Service Hydrographique.
**SH** Social History.
**SH** Southern Hemisphere.
*Climate Change.*
**SH** Stockholder.
*Business; Economics; Finance.*
**SH2** Src Homology 2 or 3.
*Biological Chemistry; Life Sciences.*
**ShA** Short Access.
*Drug Addiction; Drug Intake; Neuropharmacology; Psychopharmacology.*
**SHA** Sideral Hour Angle.
*Astronomy.*
**SHA** The airport code for Shanghai, China.
**SH ABS** (abbr.) shock absorber.
*Mechanical Engineering.*
**SHAPE** Supreme Headquarters Allied Powers Europe.
Grand Quartier général des Puissances alliées en Europe.
**SHAPEX** SHAPE exercise.
exercice du SHAPE.
**SHaPrP transgene** Syrian Hamster PrP transgene.
*Biochemistry; Biophysics; Neurology; Prion Diseases.*
**SHB** Svenska Handelsbanken.
*Swedish Bank.*
**SHBG** Sex Hormone Binding Globulin.
*Medicine.*
**SHC** Shriners Hospital for Children (U.S.A.).
**shd** (abbr.) shelter deck.
*Naval Architecture.*
**SHD** special handling detachment.
détachement de traitement spécial.
**SHD images** Super-High-Definition images.
*Multimedia Communications.*
**S/He** She/He.
**SHE** Standard Hydrogen Electrode.
**SHED** Solar Heat Exchange Drive.
**SHED** special handling and evaluation detachment.

détachement de traitement spécial et d'évaluation.
**SHED COINS** SHED communications and information systems.
système d'information et de communication du SHED.
**SHELREP** shelling report.
compte rendu de bombardement.
**SHEX** Sundays and Holidays Excepted.
Also: **S/HE**.
**SHF** Sensible-Heat Factor.
*Thermodynamics.*
**SHF** Super High Frequency.
Also: **SH(F)**.
**SHF technology** Shell Hydroformylation technology.
*Biodegradable Surfactants; Oxo-process.*
**Shh** Sonic hedgehog.
*Developmental Biology.*
**SHHT** Shut Height (referring to a press).
**Sh.I** Sheet Iron.
**SHIPREL** Reliability methods for SHIP structural design.
*European Community Project; Design Rules; Ship Design.*
**SHIPS** Statistical Hurricane Intensity Prediction Scheme.
**SHIVs** Simian / Human Immunodeficiency Viruses.
*Medicine; Constructed Viruses.*
**SHLC** Subject Headings Library of Congress.
**SHM** Simple Harmonic Motion.
SHM is also known as: Harmonic Motion.
*Mechanics.*
**SHM** Staggered Herringbone Mixer.
*Applied Sciences; Chemistry; Chemical Biology; Mathematics; Mechanical and Environmental Engineering; Microchannels.*
**SHMA** SH Annular Mode.
A large-scale pattern of variability.
*Climate Change.*
For further details see under: **SH**.
**SHMI** Slovak Hydrometeorological Institute.
The SHMI permanently and systematically measures water flows at various sites of Slovak rivers.
**SHM (of immunoglobulin genes)** Somatin Hypermutation (of immunoglobulin genes).
*Antigen Affinity; Antibody mutation in B cells.*
For further details see under: **AID**.
**SHO** Simple Harmonic Oscillator.
*Physics.*
**SHOPA** School & Home Office Products Association (U.S.A.).
**SHOP technology** Shell Higher Olefins Process technology.
**SHORAD** short-range air defence.
défense sol-air à courte portée (SACP).
**SHORADEZ** short-range air defence engagement zone.
1a. zone d'engagement des systèmes à courte portée.
1b. zone d'engagement de la défense aérienne à courte portée.
**SHORADS** short-range air defence system.
système de défense sol-air à courte portée.
**SHORAN** short-range air navigation (system).
(système de) navigation aérienne à courte portée.
**shotcrete** (abbr.) sprayed concrete.
shotcrete is used as a preliminary tunnel lining.
**SHOTS** Sheet fed Offset Training Simulator.
*European Community Project.*
**shp** shaft horsepower.
*Mechanical Engineering.*
**shpg** (abbr.) shipping.
**SHPP** Small Hydro Power Plants.
**SHR** Spontaneously Hypertensive Rats.
*Genetics.*
**SHRIMP** Sensitive High-Resolution Ion Microprobe (Canada).
*Geology; Paleobiology; Paleontology; Earth, Atmospheric and Planetary Sciences.*
**SHRIMP RG** SHRIMP Reverse Geometry.
*Environmental Sciences; Geology; Geochemistry.*
For further details see under: **SHRIMP**.
**shRNAs** short heterochromatic RNAs.
*Epigenome Plasticity; Molecular Biology; Molecular Pathology.*
**SHS** Self propagating High temperature Synthesis.
New materials for aluminum electrolysis cells produced by SHS.
*European Community Project.*
**SH-S** Sheet Steel.
**SHSS** Super High Speed Steel.
**Sh.tn** Short Ton.
*Weight Measure.*
**SI** Scale Invariance.
*Chaotic Dynamics.*
**SI** Seasonal Industry.
**SI** 1. Secrétariat international.
1. International Staff (IS 2.).
2. Slovenia.
2. Slovénie.
3. special instructions.
3. instructions particulières.
4. special intelligence.
4. renseignement spécial.
5. standardization and interoperability.
5. normalisation et interopérabilité.

**SI** Siena, Italy.
**Si** Silicon.
Used mainly as a semiconductor and in alloys.
*Chemistry.*
**SI** Simple Interest.
**SI** Sound Investment.
*Business; Finance.*
**SI** Standard Interface.
*Computer Technology.*
**SI** Système International.
French acronym meaning: International System.
*Measures.*
**SIA**; **Sia** Semiconductor Industry Association (U.S.A.).
**SIA** Sequential Injection Analysis.
SIA is a new variant of the technique called FIA. For further details see under: **FIA**.
**SIA** Small-amplitude Irregular Activity.
*Neuroscience.*
**SIA**; **S.I.A.** Società Italiana di Andrologia (Italy).
**SIA** Software Industry Association.
**SIAB** Scientific Integrity Advisory Board.
**SIAC** Securities Industry Automation Corporation (U.S.A.).
*Stock Exchange.*
**Siac** Società italiana assicurazione cavalli (Italy).
*Horse Insurance.*
**S.I.A.E.** Società Italiana Autori ed Editori.
Italian initialism of the: Italian Author's and Publisher's Association.
**SIAF** Scuola Italiana Aerobica e Fitness (Italy).
**SIAIC** Società Italiana di Allergologia e Immunologia Clinica.
Italian acronym of the: Italian Society of Allergology and Clinical Immunology.
**SIAM** Società di Incoraggiamento d'Arti e Mestieri (Italy).
A non-profit Association established in 1838 for the promotion of *Arts* and *Crafts*. Aims: founding and running *Applied Sciences Schools* for *Technical Vocational Training*.
**SIAM** Society for Industrial and Applied Mathematics.
**SIAP** sonobuoy interference avoidance plan.
plan pour prévenir l'interférence entre bouées sonores.
**SIB** Securities and Investment Board.
The SIB is G.B.'s main financial services regulator.
**SIB** Swiss school of International Banking and Finance (Switzerland).
**SIBIA** Salk Institute Biotechnology / Industrial Associates, Inc. (U.S.A.).
**SIBMAS** Société Internationale des Bibliothèques et Musées des Arts du Spectacle.
**SIBOR** Singapore Interbank Offered Rate.
**SIBS** Shangai Institutes for Biological Sciences.
Established in 1999.
*Biotechnology; Developmental Biology; Immunology; Neuroscience; Plant Science; Pharmaceutical Science; Proteomics; Stem Cell Research.*
**α-SiC** Moissanite.
Moissanite is also known as: Artificial Carborundum.
*Earth Sciences; Mineralogy; Planetary Sciences.*
**SIC** Servizio Ispettivo Centrale (Italy).
**SiC** Silicon Carbide.
Silicon Carbide is used mainly as an abrasive.
*Inorganic Chemistry.*
**SIC** Société Internationale de Chirurgie.
For further details see under: **ISS**.
**SIC** Specific Inductive Capacity.
SIC is also known as: Dielectric Constant; Relative Dielectric Constant; Relative Permittivity.
*Electricity.*
**SIC** Split Investment Company.
**SIC** Standard Industry Code.
*Computers.*
**SIC** 1. subject indicator code.
1a. code indicateur d'objet.
1b. code d'identification de sujets.
1c. mot-code d'attribution (MCA) [marine FR].
2. systèmes d'information et de communication.
2. communication and information systems (CIS 2.).
**SICADS**; **Sicads** Società Italiana di Chirurgia Ambulatoriale e Day Surgery (Italy).
**SICAV** Società di Investimento a Capitale Variabile; Société d'Investissement à Capital Variable.
Italian and French acronym meaning: Open-end investment company.
**SICB** Society for Integrative and Comparative Biology (U.S.A.).
**$Si(C_2H_5O)_4$** Ethyl Silicate.
Ethyl Silicate is used mainly in refractory bricks, and in cements.
*Organic Chemistry.*
**$SiCl_4$** Silicon Chloride.
Silicon Chloride, also known as: Tetrachlorosilane; Silicon Tetrachloride, is used in many industrial processes.
*Inorganic Chemistry.*
**SICMA** Scalable Interactive Continuous Media server-design and Application.
*European Community Project.*

**SICOM** Securities Industry COMmunications.
**S.I.COM.** Sistema Informativo COMunale (Milan, Italy).
**SIC system** Standard Industrial Classification System.
Of the U.S. Department of Commerce.
**SID** Servizio Informazioni della Difesa (Italy).
Italian acronym of the: Military Counter-Espionage Organization Formerly S.I.F.A.R.
*Military.*
**SID** Sistema d'Informazione Doganale (Italy).
Italian acronym meaning: Customs Information System.
**SID** Sudden Ionospheric Disturbance.
*Geophysics.*
**SIDA** position Sacro-Iliaque Droite Antérieure.
French acronym meaning: Right Sacroanterior position.
*Medicine.*
**SIDA** Sindacato Italiano Dottori Agrari.
*Italian Union.*
**SIDA** Syndrome Immunodéficitaire Acquis.
French acronym meaning: acquired immunodeficiency syndrome.
*Medicine.*
For further details see under: **AIDS**.
**SIDAAC** Snow and Ice Distributed Active Archive Center.
**S.I.D.O.** Società Italiana di Ortodonzia (Rome, Italy).
*Orthodontics.*
**SIDIP**; **S.I.D.I.P.** Scuola Italiana di DIscipline Psicocorporee (Italy).
*Italian Schools.*
**SIDP** position Sacro-Iliaque Droite Postérieure.
French initialism meaning: Right Sacroposterior position.
*Medicine.*
**SIDS** Sudden Infant Death Syndrome.
*Pediatrics.*
**SIE** sis-inducible element.
**S.I.E.C.A.** Sindacato Italiano Editori Compositori Autori (Italy).
Italian acronym of the: Italian Union of Publishers Composers Authors.
**SIEP** Service d'Information sur les Etudes et les Professions (Belgium).
**SIERE** Syndicat des Industries Electroniques de Reproduction et d'Enregistrement.
*French Unions.*
**SIF** selective identification feature [IFF equipment].
équipement (ou dispositif) d'identification sélective [matériel IFF].
**SIF** sis-inducible factor.
**S.I.F.** Società Internazionale di Finanziamento.
Italian acronym meaning: International Financing Company.
*Business; Economics; Finance.*
**$SiF_4$** Silicon Fluoride.
Silicon Fluoride, also known as: Tetrafluorosilane; Silicon Tetrafluoride is used mainly in chemical analysis.
*Inorganic Chemistry.*
**SIFAR** Servizio Informazioni Forze Armate.
Italian acronym meaning: Information Service of the Armed Forces now superseded by: Servizio Informazioni della Difesa.
For further details see under: **SID**.
**SIFF** Stock Index Futures Fund.
*Business; Finance.*
**SIG** Secretory Immuno-Globulin.
*Immunology.*
**sig.** (abbr.) signature.
**SIGA** position Sacro-Iliaque Gauche Antérieure.
French acronym meaning: Left Sacro-anterior position.
*Medicine.*
**SIGEX** signals exercise.
exercice de transmissions.
**Sigg.** (abbr.) Signori.
Messrs. In Italian.
**SIGG**; **Sigg** Società Italiana di Geriatria e Gerontologia.
Italian abbreviation of the: Italian Society of Geriatrics and Gerontology.
**SIG.GEN**; **Sig.Gen.** (abbr.) Signal Generator.
Also known as: Test Oscillator.
*Engineeering.*
**SIGINT** signals intelligence.
renseignement d'origine électromagnétique (ROEM).
**Sig Mis** (abbr.) Signature Missing.
**SIGO**; **S.I.G.O.** Società Italiana di Ginecologia e Ostetricia (Italy).
**SIGP** position Sacro-Iliaque Gauche Postérieure.
French initialism meaning: Left Sacroposterior position.
*Medicine.*
**Sig Unk** (abbr.) Signature Unknown.
**$SiH_4$** Silane.
Silane is also known as: Silicon Tetrahydride; Silicane.
*Inorganic Chemistry.*
**SiHoLS** Studies in the History of Language Sciences.
**$SiI_4$** Silicon Iodide.

$SiI_4$ is also known as: Silicon Tetraiodide.
*Inorganic Chemistry.*

**SII** Strategic Impediments Initiative.

**SIL** Société Internationale de Linguistique (Cameroon).
*Linguistics.*

**SIL** Speech-Interference Level.
*Acoustics.*

**SILA** Sindacato Italiano Lavoratori dell'Automobile.
*Italian Union.*

**SILAR process** Succesive-Ionic-Layer-Adsorption-and-Reaction process.
*Materials Science.*

**SILAS** Singapore Library Automation System.

**SILB** Sindacato Italiano Locali da Ballo (Italy).
*Italian Unions.*

**SILCEP** security investment, logistics and civil emergency planning [has replaced ILCEP].
investissement au service de la sécurité de la logistique et des plans civils d'urgence [remplace ILCEP].

**SILS** SILver Solder.
Silver Solder is also know as: Silver-Brazing Alloy.
*Metallurgy.*

**SILTAR** silent target.
objectif silencieux.

**SIM** Screen Image Buffer.
*Computer Technology.*

**S.I.M.** Servizio Informazioni Militari.
Italian acronym of the: Army Intelligence Service.
*Military.*

**sim.** (abbr.) simile.
Italian abbreviation meaning: similar; alike.

**SIM** Società di Intermediazione Mobiliare.
Italian acronym meaning: Stock Brokerage Company.

**SIM** Space Interferometry Mission - NASA's.
SIM's main purpose is to do astrometry (measuring stellar positions). It will also be used to measure the expansion rate of the universe and in view of its precision it will be used for a wide range of studies.
*Astrometry; Astronomy; Astrophysics; Planet Search.*

**SIM** submarine intended movement.
mouvement prévu de sous-marin.

**SIM** Système d'Information Mercatique.
French acronym meaning: Marketing Information System.

**SIM**; **Sim card** Subscriber Identity Module card; Subscriber information module card.
*Smartcards.*

**SIMD**; **Simd** Single-Instruction Multiple-Data (Pentium).

**SIME** Stress Induced Microspore Embryogenesis.

**S.I.M.G.** Società Italiana di Medicina Generale (Italy).

**SIMO** Scuola Italiana di Medicina Olistica.
*Italian Schools.*

**SIMODEC** Salon de la Machine-Outil de Décolletage (France).

**SIMP** Satellite Information Message Protocol.

**SIMPLE** Salt IMPLEmentation.
For further details see under: **SALT**.

**SIMS** Scanning Ion Microprobe Spectrometer.
*Planetary Science.*

**SIMS** School of Information Management and Systems.
Of the University of California at Berkeley, U.S.A.
For further details see under: **CRATOS**.

**SIMS** Secondary-Ion Mass Spectrometry.
*Materials Science; Naval Research; Space Science.*

**SIMS** Stable Isotope Mass Spectrometer.

**SIMT** Stuttgart Institute of Management and Technology (Germany).
SIMT opened in 1999 offering courses in international management, information technology, etc.
*University Reforms.*

**SIN** Servizi INdustriali.
Italian acronym meaning: Industrial Services.

**$Si_3N_4$** Silicon Nitride.
Silicon Nitride is used for many industrial purposes.
*Inorganic Chemistry.*

**SINAL** SIstema Nazionale per Accreditamento Laboratori di prova (Italy).

**SINAP** Sistema d'Informazione sugli Appalti Pubblici (Italy).
Italian acronym meaning: Public Tenders Information System.

**SINAPSI** Società INternazionale Analisti PSIcologi.
Italian acronym of the: Psychological Analysts International Society.

**SINCERT** SIstema Nazionale per la CERTificazione (Italy).

**SINCO**; **Sinco** Servizio INterno di COntrollo (Italy).

**SINE** Small Interspersed Nuclear Element.

**SINEs** Short Interspersed Nucleotide Elements.
*Biology; Genomic Biology; Medicine; Molecular Biotechnology; Neurology; Psychiatry.*

**SINI** Short INtegument.
SINI is a gene that has an essential role in regulat-

ing the development of ovules and the time of flowering.
*Botany; Molecular Biology; Plant Evolution; Plant Genetics.*
**SINET** Science Information NETwork (Japan).
**SINR** Swiss Institute for Nuclear Research (Switzerland).
**SINS** Ship's Inertial Navigation System.
**SINTAC** système intégré d'identification, de navigation, de contrôle de trafic, d'antiabordage et de transmission.
integrated identification, navigation, traffic control, collision prevention and communciations system.
**S.INTE.S.I.** Strumenti finanziari INTEgrati per lo Sviluppo Internazionale (Italy).
Of the Milan Chamber of Commerce.
**SINUS** Satellite Integration into Networks for UMTS Services.
*European Community Project.*
**SiNWs** Silicon Nanowires.
*Materials Sciences; Physics.*
**SIO** Scripps Institution of Oceanography (U.S.A.).
**SIO** Section interorganisations.
Inter-Organizations Section (IOS).
**SiO** Silicon Monoxide.
*Inorganic Chemistry.*
**SIO** Sistema Informativo Ospedaliero (Italy).
**SIO** Skidaway Institute of Oceanography (U.S.A.).
**$SiO_2$** Fused Quartz.
Fused Quartz is also known as: Quartz Glass.
*Materials.*
**$SiO_2$** Lechatellerite.
Named after the French chemist Henri **Le Châtelier**.
*Mineralogy.*
**$SiO_2$** Low Quartz.
Low Quartz is also known as: Alpha Quartz.
*Mineralogy.*
**$SiO_2$** Silica; Silicon Dioxide.
$SiO_2$ is used mainly to make ceramics; cosmetics; pharamceuticals and concrete.
*Mineralogy.*
**SIOs** Scattered, Icy Objects.
*Astronomy; Astrophysics; Physics; Space Science.*
For further details see under: **JFCs**.
**SIP** 1. SACLANT intelligence plan.
1. plan de renseignement du SACLANT.
2. Security Investment Programme.
2. Programme d'investissement au service de la sécurité.
**SIP** Sharebuilder Investment Plan.
**SIP** Single In-fine Package.
**SIP** State Implementation Plan (U.S.A.).
The U.S. State Implementation Plan has to be submitted to the U.S. EPA for approval in cases of violation of air quality standards.
*Chemistry; Environment; Nuclear Physics.*
For further details see under: **EPA**.
**SIP** Strongly Implicit Procedure.
**SIPA** Securities Investor Protection Act (U.S.A.).
**SIPA** Simposio Internazionale delle Pagine sull'Africa (2002).
**SI phenomenon** Self-Incompatibility phenomenon.
*Plant Biology; Plant Sciences.*
**SIPI** Scientists' Institute for Public Information.
**SIPP** Sodium Iron Pyrophosphate.
**SIPRI** Stockholm International Peace Research Institute.
Located in Solna, Sweden. Founded in 1966 for research into problems of peace and conflict with particular attention to the problems of disarmament and arms control.
**SIR** Safe Integral Reactor (G.B.).
**SIR** Shuttle Imaging Radar.
**SIR** Submarine Intermediate Reactor.
**SIR complex** Silent Information Regulator complex.
SIR mediates silencing of entire chromosome regions. It determines, in part, life-span.
*Biology.*
**SI response** Self-Incompatibility response.
*Biological Sciences; Plant Biology.*
**SIRF** Sistema Italiano Rilevamento Fulmini (Italy).
*Lightning Detection.*
**SIRGS** Sistema Infomativo Integrato della Ragioneria Generale dello Stato (Italy).
**SIRIO** Sistema Integrato in Rete per l'Incremento Occupazionale (Italy).
Title of transnational project: Training Patterns and Standards in Progress Applied to Actions in Favour of Disadvantaged Young People.
*Transnational Projects.*
**SIRIT** SIstema di Ricerca e Innovazione Tecnologica.
Italian acronym meaning: Research and Technological Innovation System. Of Padua University (Italy).
**siRNAs** small/short interfering RNAs.
*Biomedical Genetics; Molecular Carcinogenesis; Tumor Biology; Genes Development.*
**SIRPEL** Sistema Integrato per la Rilevazione Permanente della domanda di lavoro nell'Economia Lombarda (Italy).
**SIRS** Satellite Infrared Spectrometer.
**SIRS** Soluble Immune Response Suppressor.

*Medicine.*
**SIRTF** Space Infrared Telescope Facility (U.S.A.).
NASA launched SIRTF at the end of 2001.
*Space Science.*
**SIS** Servizio Italiano Scritto.
Italian acronym meaning: Written Italian Service. Coined in 1996 by a Professor of the University of Venice for undergraduate students who need a refresher course on Italian Grammar.
**SIS** Sistema Informativo Sanitario (Italy).
**SIS** Sistema Informativo Schengen.
**SIS** Servizio Ispettivo di Sicurezza (Italy).
**SIS** Society for Information Science.
**SIS** strategic intelligence summary.
rapport de synthèse de renseignement stratégique.
**SISAL** straight-in, silent and low (approach).
(approche) directe, silencieuse et à basse altitude.
**SIS-DCA** Società Italiana Studi Disturbi Comportamento Alimentare (Italy).
**SISDO** Sistemi Informativi Sviluppo Dell'Organizzazione (Italy).
**SISEX** Satellite Imaging Spectrometer EXperiment.
**SISF** Società Italiana di Scienze Farmaceutiche (Italy).
*Pharmaceutical Sciences.*
**SISRS** system interconnection security requirements statement.
énoncé des impératifs de sécurité applicables à l'interconnexion de systèmes.
**SISS** Scuola Internazionale Servizi di Sicurezza.
*International Schools.*
**SISS**; **S.I.S.S.** Società Italiana di Sessuologia Scientifica (Italy).
**SISSI** Sistema Informativo per il Servizio Sanitario Italiano (Italy).
A DEDALUS Project.
Dedalus, Florence, Italy. Founded in 1982.
**SIT** Self-Induced Transparency.
*Optics.*
**S.I.T.** Servizio di Immunoematologia e Trasfusione (Ospedale Niguarda) Milan, Italy.
*Immunohematology (Hospitals).*
**sit.** (abbr.) situation.
*Geography.*
**sit.** (abbr.) sitting-room.
**SIT** Système Interbancaire de Télécompensation (France).
French acronym meaning: Interbank Teleclearing System.
**SIT** System Improvement Time.
*Computer Technology.*
**SIT University** Seoul Information Technology University.
SIT debuted on 3rd March 2003.
**SITAR** Sistema Informativo Telematico sugli Appalti articolato in nodi Regionali (Italy).
**SITCEN** Situation Centre [NATO HQ].
Centre de situation [siège de l'OTAN].
**S.I.T.E.S.** Sindacato Italiano TEcnici Sanitari.
*Italian Unions.*
**SITREP**; **sitrep.** (abbr.) situation report.
**SITS** Salon International des Traitements de Surface et finition industrielle (France).
**sits.vac.** (abbr.) situations vacant.
**SITSUM** (intelligence) situation summary.
1a. synthèse de situation (renseignement).
1b. résumé de situation (renseignement).
**SIU** Southern Illinois University (U.S.A.).
**SIU** Système International d'Unités.
French acronym meaning: International System of Units.
**SIULP** SIndacato Italiano Unitario dei Lavoratori di Polizia (Italy).
*Italian Unions.*
**SIV** Simian Immunodeficiency Virus.
*Gynecology; Newborn Medicine; Pediatrics; Radiology; Veterinary Medicine; Veterinary Pathology; Viral Pathogenesis.*
**SI viruses** Syncytia-Inducing viruses.
**SJ** Soldered Joint.
*Buildings; Mechanics; Technology.*
**SJC** The airport code for San Jose, California, U.S.A.
**SJCRH** St. Jude Children's Research Hospital (U.S.A.).
**SJO** The airport code for San José, Costa Rica.
**SJU** The airport code for San Juan, Puerto Rico.
**sk** (abbr.) sack; sketch.
**sk.** (abbr.) safekeeping.
**SK** Search Key.
*Computer Technology.*
**SK** Starknumber.
**SK** Streptokinase.
*Enzymology.*
**SK** The airline code for SAS (Scandinavian Airlines System).
**SKAI** Square Kilometer Array Interferometer.
SKAI has a total surface area of 1 kilometer square. Radio astronomers from Australia, Canada, China, India and The Netherlands will begin construction in 2005.
*Astronomy Research; Radio Astronomy; Radio Telescopes; Magnetic Fields Mapping.*
**SK detector** Super-Kamiokande detector (Japan).
*Physics; Neutrino Physics.*

**SKELLEM** Sheffield, Keele, Liverpool, Leeds and Manchester University Libraries.
**SKEM** Scanning KErr Microscopy.
*Metals; Physics.*
**SKI** Sloan-Kettering Institute (U.S.A.).
**Skt** (abbr.) Sandkrit.
*Languages.*
**SL** 1. sea level.
1. niveau de la mer.
2. Sierra Leone.
2. Sierra Leone.
**SL** Skilled Labor.
**SL** Smooth Late.
*Monkeys Vocal Sounds.*
**SL** Sonoluminescence.
*Acoustics; Energy; Physics of Shock Waves; Radiation Hydrodynamics.*
**SL** System Library.
*Computer Programming.*
**SL** System Loader.
*Computer Programming.*
**SLA** Sales and Loan Association (U.S.A.).
**SLA** Saskatchewan Library Association (Canada).
**SLA** School Library Association.
**SLA** Scottish Library Association.
**SLA** Second Language Acquisition.
*Linguistics.*
**SLA** Sex and Love Addicted.
**SLA** Special Libraries Association.
**SLAC** Stanford Linear Accelerator Center.
In Menlo Park, California, U.S.A.
*Biological Molecules; Structural Analysis.*
**SLALOM** Semiconductor Laser Amplifier in a LOop Mirror.
*Digital Information Processing; Electronic Engineering.*
**SLAM** Signalling Lymphocyte Activation Molecule.
*Immunology.*
For further detils see under: **SAM**.
**SLAM; slam** Standoff Land Attack Missile.
*Ordnance.*
**SLAM** Supersonic Low-Altitude Missile.
*Military.*
**SLAR** side-looking airborne radar.
1a. radar aéroporté à antenne latérale.
1b. radar aéroporté à vision latérale.
**Slav** Slavic.
Slavic, also known as Slavonic, is a branch of the Indo-European family of languages, divided into East Slavic, West Slavic, and South Slavic.
*Languages.*
**SLBM** submarine-launched ballistic missile.
1a. missile balistique à lanceur sous-marin.
1b. missile balistique tiré de sous-marin.
**SLC** The airport code for Salt Lake City, Utah, U.S.A.
**SLC** Secondary Lymphoid tissue Chemokine.
**SLCM** 1. sea-launched cruise missile.
1. missile de croisière à lanceur naval.
2. submarine-launched cruise missile.
2a. missile de croisière à lanceur sous-marin.
2b. missile de croisière tiré de sous-marin.
3. surface-launched cruise missile.
3a. missile de croisière à lanceur naval.
3b. missile de croisière tiré de bâtiment.
**SLD** Left Democratic Alliance (Poland).
**sld** (abbr.) sailed.
*Shipping.*
**sld.** (abbr.) sold.
**SLE** SACLANT liaison element [in PCC].
élément de liaison du SACLANT [à la CCP].
**SLE** Systemic Lupus Erythematosus.
SLE is an inflammatory disease that afflicts particularly middle-aged women.
*Medicine.*
**SLE virus** St.Louis Encephalitis Virus.
*Virology.*
**SLI** Soutien Logistique Intégré.
French acronym meaning: Integrated Logistic Support.
**SLI** Specific Language Impairment.
**SLIC** Savings and Loan Insurance Corporation (U.S.A.).
**SLIR** side(ways)-looking infra-red (system).
(système) infrarouge à vision latérale.
**SLLA** Sierra Leone Library Association.
**SLM** Spatial Linear Model.
**SLM** staff-level meeting.
réunion à l'échelon de l'état-major.
**s.l.m.** sul livello del mare.
Italian initialism meaning: above sea level.
**SLMA** Student Loan Marketing Association (U.S.A.).
**SLMs** Spatial Light Modulators.
*Biochemistry; Chemistry; Optoelectronic Computing Systems.*
**SLO** Self-Liquidating Offer.
*Business; Commerce.*
**SLO** Stop-Loss Order.
*Business; Commerce.*
**SLO** Streptolysin O.
*Medicine; Physiology; Protein Biochemistry.*
**SLOC** sea lines of communication.
voies de communication maritimes.

**SLOSH model** Sea Lake and Overland Surges from Hurricanes model (U.S.A.).
**SLOT** submarine-launched one-way tactical (buoy).
(bouée) tactique à émission unilatérale larguée d'un sous-marin.
**SLO technique** Scanning Laser Optical trapping technique.
*Chemical Biology; Chemical Engineering; Colloidal Devices; Microfluidic Control; Physics.*
**SLP** Sea-Level Pressure.
The SLP is the atmospheric pressure at mean sea level.
*Climate / Ocean Variability; Ecosystem and Population Biology; Meteorology; Oceanography.*
**SLP** 1. standardized language proficiency.
1. aptitudes linguistiques normalisées.
2. standardized language profile.
2. profil linguistique normalisé.
**SLP** Superficie Lorda di Pavimento.
**SLPI** Secretary Leukocyte Protease Inhibitor.
*Cell Biology; Medicine; Physiology.*
**SLR** Satellite Laser Ranging.
*Geophysics; Space Geodesy.*
**SLR** Sea-Level Rise.
**SLSI** Super-Large-Scale Integration.
*Electronics.*
**slsman** (abbr.) salesman.
**slsmen** (abbr.) salesmen.
**slsmgr** (abbr.) salesmanager.
**SLSTINET** SriLanka Scientific and Technical Information Network.
**SLSTP** Space Life Sciences Training Program.
**SLS synthesis** Solution-Liquid-Solid synthesis.
*Chemical Biology; Chemistry.*
**SLTA** Saskatchewan Library Trustees Association (Canada).
**SLU** Southern Louisiana University (U.S.A.).
**SLU** Swedish University of Agricultural Sciences (Sweden).
**SLV** space-launched vehicle.
1a. véhicule à lanceur spatial.
1b. véhicule lancé de l'espace.
**SLVs** Single-Locus Variants.
For further details see under: **MLST**.
**SLW** Supercooled Liquid Water.
**SLWPG** Senior Level Weapons Protection Group.
Groupe de niveau élevé sur la protection des armements.
**SM** Sales Manager.
**Sm** The chemical symbol for Samarium.
Samarium is a rare-earth metal having the atomic number 62, and an atomic weight of 150.36.
*Chemistry; Symbols.*
**SM** 1. San Marino.
1. Saint-Marin.
2. scatterable mine.
2. mine dispersable.
**SM** Secondary Market.
**SM** Second Mortgage.
**SM** Sector Mark.
*Computer Technology.*
**SM** Somatomédine.
French initialism meaning: Somatomedin.
Also known as: Insulinlike Growth Factor.
*Endocrinology.*
**SM** Special Memorandum.
**SM** Stato Maggiore.
Italian initialism meaning: General Staff.
**SM** Stock Market.
**SM** Strategia di Marketing.
Italian initialism meaning: Marketing Strategy.
**S.M.** Sua Maestà; Sa Majesté/ée.
Italian and French initialism meaning: His/Her Majesty.
**S.M.** Sue Mani.
Italian initialism meaning: to be delivered personally (when "S.M." is indicated on a letter/envelope).
**SM** Surcharge Monétaire.
French initialism meaning: Currency Adjustment Factor.
**SMA** Shape Memory Alloy.
**SMA** Sistemi per la Meteorologia e l'Ambiente (Italy).
**SMA** Special Miscellaneous Account (U.S.A.).
*Stock Exchange.*
**SMA** 1. specific message address.
1. adresse spécifique de mesage.
2. specific military agreement.
2. accord militaire particulier.
3. system management authority [ACCIS].
3. autorité de gestion du système [ACCIS].
**SMA** Spinal Muscular Atrophy.
*Biochemsitry; Biophysics; Medicine.*
For further details see under: **SMN protein**.
**SMA** State Meteorology Administration (China).
**SMA** Sub-Millimeter Array.
SMA was completed in 2000.
*Millimeter Wave Astronomy.*
**SMAA** submarine movement advisory authority.
autorité consultative pour les mouvements de(s) sous-marins.
**SMAC Collaboration** Streaming Motions of Abell Clusters Collaboration.
*Astronomy; Astrophysics; Galaxy Clusters.*

**SMACNA** Sheet Metal and Air Conditioning Contractors' National Association (U.S.A.).
**SmA phase** smetic-A phase.
*Physics.*
**SMART** Simple Modular Architectural Research Tool.
*Epigenetics.*
**SMART1** Small Missions for Advanced Research in Technology.
ESA's SMART-1 will be launched in August 2003.
*Lunar Exploration Missions.*
For further details see under: **ESA**.
**SMARTS** SME And Regional Telecoms Support.
*European Community Project.*
**SMAs** Shape Memory Alloys.
Used mainly in spectacle frames, medical devices and space station connectors.
For further details see under: **SMPS**, **WEEE** and **ADSM**.
**SMASH** Storage for Multimedia Applications Systems in the Home.
*European Community Project.*
**SMASHEX** submarine search escape and rescue exercise.
exercice de recherche, d'évacuation et de sauvetage de sous-marins.
**SMAT** Surface Mechanical Attrition Treatment.
*Materials Science; Metal Research.*
**SMBA** Scottish Marine Biological Association.
*Marine Biology.*
**SMBH** Supermassive Black Hole.
*Astronomy; Physics.*
**SMC** Scientific Manpower Commission.
**SMC** Sheet Molding Compound.
*Plastic Industry.*
**SMC** Small Magellanic Cloud.
*Astronomy.*
**SMC** Smooth Muscle Cell.
For further details see under: **SMCs**.
**SMC** Structural Maintenance of Chromosomes.
*Biochemistry; Biomedical Sciences; Cell Biology; Molecular Biology.*
**SMCs** Secondary Muscle Cells (of the Ascidian Larvae).
*Ascidian Larvae; Biology; Cellular Biology; Developmental Biology.*
For further details see under: **PMCs**.
**SMCs** Smooth Muscle Cells.
*Atherosclerosis; Cell Biology; Molecular Genetics.*
**SM cycle** Sphingomyelin cycle.
*Anatomy; Cell Biology; Hematology; Medicine; Oncology.*
**SMD** Single-Module Detection.
*Chemistry; Energy.*
**SMD** Système Mondial de Distribution.
French initialism meaning: Global Distribution System.
**SMDC** software maintenance and development centre.
centre de développement et de maintenance du logiciel.
**SMDS** Switched Multimegabit Data Service.
*Broadband Technologies.*
**SME** Science, Mathematics & Engineering.
**SME** Sistema Monetario Europeo.
Italian acronym meaning: European Monetary System.
**SME** Society of Manufacturing Engineers (U.S.A.).
**SME** Society of Mining Engineers (U.S.A.).
**SME** Sous régime de la mise à l'epreuve (France).
**SMECI** SMEs Community Initiative -European Community.
**SMER** submarine escape and rescue.
évacuation et sauvetage des sous-marins.
**SMERAT** submarine escape and rescue assistance team.
équipe d'assistance à l'évacuation et au sauvetage des sous-marins.
**SMEs** Small and Medium sized Enterprises.
**SMF** Static Magnetic Field.
**SMF** System Management Facilities.
**SMF** The airport code for Sacramento Metropolitan Field, Sacramento, California, U.S.A.
**SMG** Scuola lombarda di Medicina Generale.
*Italian Schools.*
**SMG** special mobile group.
groupe mobile spécial.
**S.M.G.** Stato Maggiore Generale.
Italian initialism meaning: General Staff.
*Military.*
**SMI** Storage Management Initiative.
**SMIC** Study of Man's Impact on Climate (U.S.A.).
**SMIC mensuel** Salaire Minimum Interprofessionnel de Croissance mensuel.
French acronym meaning: Minimum Statutory Wage per Month.
**SMIG** Salario Minimo Interprofessionale Garantito.
Italian acronym meaning: Guaranteed Interprofessional Living Wage.
**SMIL; Smil** Synchronized Multimedia Integration Language.
**SML** Self-Mode Locking.
*Microstructural Sciences.*
**SML** Silent Mating Loci.
*Molecular Biology.*
**SMLWF** Self-Modulated Laser Wake Field.

*Physics.*

**S.M.M.** Master of Sacred Music.

**SMMAPP** standard manpower management and planning procedures.
procédures normalisées de gestion et de planification d'effectifs.

**SMMHC gene** Smooth Muscle Myosin Heavy Chain gene.

**sMMO** soluble Methane Monooxygenase.

**SMMR** Scanning Multichannel Microwave Radiometer.

**SMNs** Survival of Motor Neurons.
*Medicine; Spinal Muscular Atrophy.*

**$Sm_2O_3$** Samarium Oxide.
Samarium Oxide, also known as: Samarium Sesquioxide is used in ethanol production.

**SMO** Science Management Office.

**smog** The term smog was derived using the words: smoke and fog.

**SMOM** Sovrano Militare Ordine di Malta.
Italian acronym meaning: Sovereign Military Order of Malta.

**SMON** Subacute Myelo-Optico-Neuropathy.
The SMON disease is characterized by visual loss, muscle weakness and numbness.
*Alzheimer; Clioquinol (chelating antibiotic); Neurology.*

**SMOW** Standard Mean Ocean Water.

**SMP** self-maintenance period.
période d'automaintenance.

**SMP** Shape Memory Polymer.

**SMP** Sinistre Maximum Prévisible.
French initialism meaning: Maximum Foreseeable Loss.
*Business; Economics; Finance.*

**SMP architecture** Symmetric Multi-Processing architecture.
SMP architecture links processors together so that they all share memory, disks, and a single operating system, which shares out the work between them.

**SMPs** Shape Memory Alloy.
For further details see under: **ADSM**; **SMAs** and **WEEE**.

**SMPs** Shape Memory Polymers.

**SMP systems** Symmetrical Multiple Processor systems.
SMP systems, such as NUMA systems, link many processors together to push the power up.
For further details see under: **NUMA**.

**SMPTE** Society of Motion Picture and Television Engineers (U.S.A.).

**SMPY** Study of Mathematically Precocious Youth.

**SMR** Sensorimotor Range.
*Behavioral Medicine; Neuropsychiatry.*

**SMR** Standard Mortality Ratio.
Standard mortality ratio is also known as: Standard Morbidity Ratio.

**smRNA** small nuclear RNA.
*Genetics.*

**SMRT** Single Message Rate Timing.

**SMS** Short Message/Messaging Service.

**SMS** Single Molecule Spectroscopy.
*Physical Chemistry.*

**SMS** Synchronous Meteorological Satellite.

**SMSU** Southwest Missouri State University (U.S.A.).

**SMT** Standards, Measurement and Testing.
Research and Technological development program in the field of SMT.
*E.C. Programs.*

**SMT education** Science, Mathematics and Technology education (U.S.A.).

**SMTP** Simple Mail Transfer Protocol.

**SMT treatment** Subtilisin-digested Microtubules treament.
*MAPS binding.*
For further details see under: **MAPs**.

**SMUD** Sacramento Municipal Utility District.
The SMUD in California planned to replace (in 1993) up to 47,000 electric water heaters with solar water heaters before the turn of the century.
*Solar Water Heaters.*

**SN** 1. sending nation.
1. pays d'origine (ou pourvoyeur).
2. Singapore.
2. Singapour.

**SN** Sensory Neuron.
For further details see under: **SNs**.

**SN** Serial Number.

**S/N** Shipping Note.
*Commerce; Shipping.*

**SN** The airline code for Sabena World Airlines.

**SN** Substantia Nigra.

**Sn** Tin.
Used mainly as solder and in alloys.
*Chemistry.*

**SNA** sous-marin nucléaire d'attaque.
subsurface, nuclear (nuclear-powered) attack submarine (SSN).

**SNA** Système Nerveux Autonome.
French acronym meaning: Autonomic Nervous System.
*Physiology.*

**SNA** System of National Accounts.

**SNA** The airport code for John Wayne International Airport, Orange County, California, U.S.A.
**SNAC** Standing North Atlantic Council.
Conseil permanent de l'Atlantique Nord.
**SNADOC** Servizio Nazionale di Accesso ai Documenti (Italy).
**SNAFID** Slovakia National Agency for Foreign Investment and Development (Slovak Republic).
SNAFID was created by the Ministry of Foreign Affairs.
**SNAL** Sudan National Association of Libraries.
**SNAME** Society of Naval Architects and Marine Engineers (U.S.A.).
**SNAP** NSF Attachment Protein.
*Brain Research; Medicine; Neurobiology; Neurochemistry.*
For further details see under: **NSF**.
**SNAP** SACEUR's nuclear assessment procedures.
procédures d'évaluation nucléaire du SACEUR.
**SNAP** Sensory Nerve Action Potential.
**SNAP** Simplified Numerical Automatic Programmer.
**SNAP** S-Nitroso-N-Acetyl-Penicillamine.
*Biological Rhythms; Cell and Structural Biology; Integrative Neuroscience Research; Physiology.*
**SNAP** Standard Network-Access Protocol.
**SNAP** Surrey Nano-Satellite Applications Platform.
Launched into orbit on 28th June 2000.
*Multi-point Measurements; Nano-satellites; Space Exploration.*
**SNAP** Systems for Nuclear Auxiliary Power.
**snap** The above acronyms were coined using the English word "snap".
*Mechanical Devices; Meteorology.*
**SNARE** Soluble N-ethylmaleimide-sensitive factor Attachment protein Receptor.
*Biochemistry; Biophysics.*
For further details see under: **t-SNARE**.
**SNARP** SHAPE nuclear assessment and request procedure.
procédure SHAPE d'évaluation et de demande d'emploi de l'arme nucléaire.
**SNb** Segmental Nerve b.
**$SnBr_2$** Stannous Bromide.
Stannous Bromide is also known as: Tin Dibromide.
*Inorganic Chemistry.*
**$SnBr_4$** Stannic Bromide.
Stannic Bromide also known as: Tin Tetrabromide is used in mineral separation.
*Inorganic Chemistry.*
**SNC** Sistema di Contabilità Nazionale (Italy).
**SNC** Société en Nom Collectif.
French initialism meaning: general partnership.
**SNC** special naval chart.
carte marine spéciale.
**SNC** Syndicat National des Collèges.
*French Unions.*
**SNC** Système Nerveux Central.
French initialism meaning: Central Nervous System.
*Anatomy; Medicine.*
**$SnCl_4$** Stannic Chloride.
Stannic Chloride, also known as: Tin Chloride, is used mainly in ceramics and soaps.
*Inorganic Chemistry.*
**SNCM** Société Nationale Corse-Méditerranée.
**SNCO** senior non-commissioned officer.
sous-officier supérieur.
**SNE** Sector North-East [SFOR].
Secteur Nord-Est [SFOR].
**SNe** Supernovae.
*Astronomy; Astrophysics; Nucleosynthesis (in stars).*
**SNEC** Secrétariat National de l'Enseignement Catholique (Belgium).
**SNECMA** Société Nationale d'Etude et de Construction de Moteurs d'Aviation (France).
**Sne Ia** Type Ia Supernovae.
*Cosmology; Stellar Explosions.*
**SNF** 1. short-range nuclear force.
1. force nucléaire à courte portée.
2. standing naval force.
2. force navale permanente.
**SNG** Substitute Natural Gas.
**SNIA** The Storage Networking Industry Association.
SNIA represents over 300 vendors, it has completed the Bluefilm standard to allow San to interoperate.
For further details see under: **San**.
**SNIP** single net information and plotting.
réseau unique de renseignements et de signalisation des tenues de situation.
**SNLC** Senior NATO Logisticians Conference.
Conférence des hauts responsables de la logistique de l'OTAN.
**SNLE** sous-marin nucléaire lanceur d'engins.
sub-surface ballistic, nuclear (nuclear-powered ballistic missile submarine (SSBN).
**SNM** Special Nuclear Materials.
**SNMP** Simple Network Management Protocol.
**SNN** The airport code for Shannon, Republic of Ireland.
**SNO** S-Nitrosothiol.
**SNO** Sudbury Neutrino Observatory (Canada).

*Neutrino Detectors; Neutrino Oscillations; Physics; Solar Neutrinos.*
**$SnO_2$** Stannic Oxide.
Stannic Oxide also known as: Tin Dioxide; Tin Peroxide, is used mainly in perfumes, textiles, and ceramics.
*Inorganic Chemistry.*
**SNOBOL** String-Oriented-Symbolic Language.
*Computers.*
**SNOM** Scanning Near-field Optical Microscope.
*Imaging.*
**sno RNPs** small nucleolar Ribonucleoprotein Particles.
**SNOWCAT** support of nuclear operations with conventional air tactics.
appui des opérations nucléaires par les tactiques aériennes classiques.
**SNP** Sodium Nitroprusside.
For further details see under: **SCN**.
**SNP** Système Net Protégé (France).
French initialism meaning: Protected Net Settlement system (for large-value fund transfers).
**SNPC** Service National de la Protection Civile (France).
**SNPs** Single Nucleotide Polymorphisms.
The single nucleotide polymorphism is an alteration that takes place in a single nucleotide base in a DNA stretch.
*Biotechnology; Gene Expression; Genetics; Genome Mapping; Genomic Signposts; Human Genome; Life Sciences; Multigene Diseases; Pharmacogenomics.*
**SNR** Selective Noncatalytic Reduction.
**SNR**; **S/N R** Signal-to-Noise Ratio.
*Acoustics; Electronics.*
**SNR** Substantia Nigra pars reticulata.
**SNR** Supernova Remnant.
*Astronomy; Astrophysics; Theoretical Astrophysics; Physics.*
**snRNA** small nuclear RNA.
*Biomolecular Sciences; Molecular Biology.*
**snRNP** small nuclear Ribonucleoprotein.
**SNRs** Supernova Remnants.
For further details see under: **SNR**.
**SNs** Sensory Neurons.
*Biology; Psychology.*
**SNS** Somatic Nervous System.
*Physiology.*
**SNs** Source of Neutrons.
At Oak Ridge National Laboratory (U.S.A.). Will be completed in 2006.
*Neutron Scattering.*
**SNS** standard NATO bar code symbology.
système OTAN normalisé de symboles de codes à barres.
**$SnS_2$** Stannic Sulfide.
Stannic Sulfide also known as: Mosaic Gold; Tin Bronze; Artificial Gold; Tin Disulfide; is used mainly in imitation gilding.
*Inorganic Chemistry.*
**SNS** Struttura Nazionale di Sostegno (Italy).
**SNS** Sympathetic Nervous System.
*Anatomy.*
**SNSL** Siemens Network Services.
SNSL is the networking subsidiary of the German manufacturer Siemens Nixdorf.
*Network Management.*
**SNT** Sistema Nazionale di Taratura.
Italian initialism meaning: National Calibration / Rating System.
**SNU** Seoul National University (Korea).
**SNU** Solar Neutrino Unit.
**SO** Sales Office.
**SO** Seller's Option.
**S/O** Shipowner.
**SO**; **S/O** Shipping Order.
*Commerce; Shipping.*
**SO** small outline.
*Packaging.*
**SO** 1. Somalia.
1. Somalie.
2. staff officer.
2. officier d'état-major (OEM).
**SO** Sondrio, Italy.
**SO** Special Order; Standing Order.
**S.O.** Staff Office.
**SO** Stock Option.
**SO** Stratum Opticum.
*Anatomy; Neurobiology.*
**$S_2O$** Strontium Oxide.
Strontium Oxide, also known as: Strontium is used mainly in soaps and pigments.
*Inorganic Chemistry.*
**$SO_2$** Sulfur Dioxide.
Sulfur Dioxide is used mainly in pharmaceuticals and as a food additive.
*Inorganic Chemistry.*
**$SO_3$** Sulfur Trioxide.
Sulfur Trioxide also known as: Sulfuric Anhydride is used mainly in solar energy collectors.
*Inorganic Chemistry.*
**SO** System Operation.
*Computer Technology.*
**SOA** Secondary Organic Aerosol.
Like ozone, SOA is formed from the atmospheric oxidation of organic compounds.

*Chemical Engineering; Environmental Engineering Science.*

**SOA** Semiconductor Optical Amplifier.
*Digital Information Processing; Electronic Engineering.*

**SOA** speed of advance.
vitesse de progression.

**SOA** State Oceanic Administration (China).

**SOAs** Semiconductor Optical Amplifiers.
For further details see under: **SOA**.

**SOB** Shortness Of Breath.

**$SOBr_2$** Thionyl Bromide.
Thionyl Bromide is also known as: Sulfinyl Bromide.
*Organic Chemistry.*

**SOC** 1. sector operations centre.
1. centre d'opérations de secteur (COS 1.).
2. special operations command.
2. commandement des opérations spéciales.

**SOC** Sedimentary Organic Carbon.
*Earth System Science.*

**SOCA** Studies of the Ocular Complications of AIDS.
SOCA is a network of eleven clinics sponsored by the U.S. NEI.
*Ophthalmology.*
For further details see under: **NEI**.

**SOCA** submarine operations coordinating authority.
autorité de coordination des opérations sous-marines.

**$SOCl_2$** Thionyl Chloride.
Thionyl Chloride, also known as: Sulfur/Sulfurous Oxychloride is used mainly in pesticides.
*Organic Chemistry.*

**SOCMET** smoke and obscurant countermeasures materials evaluation test.
essai d'évaluation des fumées et obscursissants utilisés comme contre-mesures.

**SOCREDO** Société de Crédit et de Développement de l'Océanie.

**SOCs** Store-Operated Channels.
*Signal Translation.*

**SOCSOUTH** Special Operations Command, AFSOUTH.
Commandement des opérations spéciales de l'AFSOUTH.

**SOD** Seskatchewan Organic Directorate (Canada).
*Organic Farming.*

**SODI** Superoxide Dismutase (an enzyme).
Also: **SOD**.
*Amyotrophic Lateral Sclerosis; Enzymology; Genes; Neurodegenerative Diseases.*

**SOE** schedule of events [exercises].
calendrier des événements [exercices].

**SOEs** State-Owned Enterprises.

**SOF** Sound On Film.

**SOF** 1. special operations force.
1. force d'opérations spéciales.
2. status of forces.
2. statut des forces.

**SOF** State Ownership Fund - Bucharest.
*Romanian Funds.*

**SOFA** Society Of Financial Advisers.

**SOFA** Status of Forces Agreement.
Convention sur le statut des forces.

**SOFAR** SOund Fixing And Ranging.
*Geophysics.*

**SOFC** Solid Oxide Fuel Cel.
*Chemistry.*

**SOFE** Symposium On Fusion Engineering.
The 16$^{th}$ SOFE was held in Champaign, Illinois, U.S.A. in October 1995.

**SOFERMO** Société Française d'Etudes et de Réalisation de Machines et d'Outillage (France).

**SOFIA** Stratospheric Observatory for Infrared Astronomy.
*Astronomy; Physics; Planetary Sciences.*

**SOFIA** Sunflower Oil For Industrial Applications.
*European Community Project.*

**SOFT** Symposium On Fusion Technology.
The 19$^{th}$ SOFT was held in Lisbon, Portugal in September 1996.

**Sog** Short gastrulation.
*Developmental Biology.*

**SOG** speed made good over the ground.
1a. vitesse sur le fond.
1b. vitesse rapportée sur le sol.

**SOGEA** Scuola di Gestione Aziendale (Italy).

**SOHO** Small Office / Home Office.

**SOHO satellite** SOlar and Heliospheric Observatory satellite.
A joint NASA-ESA and satellite launched in late 1995.
*Astronomy; Atmospheric Physics; Space Physics; Physics of the Earth; Technology.*
For further details see under: **NASA**; **ESA**; **UVCS**.

**SOI** (prima) Settimana Oftalmologica Italiana.
Italian acronym meaning: (first) Italian Ophthalmologic Week (Italy, November 1998).

**SOI** 1. signals operating instruction.
1. instruction d'exploitation des transmissions.
2. standing operating instructions.
2. instructions permanentes.
3. statement of intent.
3. énoncé d'intention.

**SOI**; **Soi** Società Oftalmologica Italiana.
Italian acronym of the: Italian Ophthalmological Society.
**SOI** Southern Oscillation Index.
*Atmospheric Science; Climatology; Geophysics; Oceanography.*
**SOIN** Southern Indiana (U.S.A.).
**SOIREE** Southern Ocean Iron RElease Experiment.
A 13-day Experiment.
*ClimateChange; Physical and Chemical Ocanography.*
**SOI technology** Silicon-On-Insulator technology.
This technology, by IBM, reduces the amount of power that silicon chips need to operate.
*Microchip Technology; Nanomechanics.*
**SOJ** stand off jammer (or jamming).
brouilleur (ou brouillage) à distance de sécurité.
**Sol.**; **sol.** (abbr.) soluble; solution.
*Chemistry.*
**SOL** Standard Of Living.
**SOL** Statute Of Limitations.
**SOLAS** Safety Of Life At Sea.
**SOLEDs** Stacked Organic Light-Emitting Devices.
*Chemistry; Electrical Engineering; Photonics and Optoelectronic Materials.*
**SOLINET** Southeastern Library Network.
**solv.** (abbr.) solvent.
*Chemistry.*
**SOM** School Of Medicine.
**Som.** (abbr.) Somerset(shire) (England).
**SOM** Start Of Message.
**SOM** Supporting Online Material.
**SOMA** Short Oligonucleotide Mass Analysis.
*Gene Sequencing.*
**SOM algorithm** Self-Organizing Map algorithm.
**SOMECO** SOciété MEridionale de COntentieux (France).
**SOMMIT** Software Open MultiMedia Interactive Terminal.
*European Community Project.*
**SON** Spatial Ozone Network.
*Earth and Atmospheric Sciences; Forest Resources; Rural Air Quality.*
**SONOR** Southern Norway.
**SOON** Solar Observation Optical Network (U.S.A.).
**SOP** Senza Obbligo di Prescrizione (Italy).
**SOP** Ship-of-Opportunity Program (U.S.A.).
**SOP**; **S.O.P.** Standard Operating Procedure.
SOP is also known as: Standing Operating Procedure.
*Aviation.*
**SOP** Statement Of Policy.
**SOPA** Society for Professional Archaeologists (U.S.A.).
**SOR** Sell Or Return.
*Business; Commerce.*
**SOR** Society of Rheology.
*Rheology.*
**SOR** Specific Operating / Operational Requirement.
**SOR** 1. state of readiness.
1. état de préparation.
2. statement of requirements.
2. expression (ou énoncé) des besoins.
**SOR** Stimulus-Organism-Response.
**SO.RI.MA.** SOcietà RIcuperi MArittimi.
Italian acronym of the: Sea Salvage Company (Italy).
**SOS** Satellite Observing System.
**SOS** Save Our Souls (referring to the distress signal).
*International Morse Code.*
**SOS** Section Opérationnelle Spécialisée.
French acronym meaning: Specialized Operating Department.
**SOS** Silicon-On-Sapphire.
*Electronics.*
**SOS** Sucrose Octasulfate.
*Biochemistry; Molecular Biology; Molecular Biophysics; Organic Chemistry; Pharmacology.*
**SOSCOL** South Staffordshire College Libraries.
**Sos proteins** Son of sevenless proteins.
*Microbiology; Molecular Genetics.*
**SOSTAS** stand-off surveillance and target acquisition system.
système de surveillance et d'acquisition d'objectif(s) à distance de sécurité.
**SOSUS information** SOund SUrveillance System information.
*Covariation of Processes; Diking / Eruptive Events; Oceanic Crustal Formations; Oceanography.*
**SOT** Start Of Text.
**SOTAS** Stand-Off Target Acquisition System.
*Ordnance.*
**SOUTHLANT** South Atlantic [has replaced IBERLANT].
Sud de l'Atlantique [remplace l'IBERLANT].
**SOW** 1. scope of work.
1. portée (ou volume) des travaux.
2. statement of work.
2a. cahier des charges (CC 1.).
2b. énoncé des travaux.
**SOWEX** Southern Ocean Waves EXperiment (U.S.A.).
**SP** La Spezia, Italy.

**SP** Scalar Processor.
*Computer Science.*
**SP** Schering-Plough.
*Research Institutes.*
**SP** 1. secondary participants.
1. participants secondaires.
2. self-propelled.
2. autopropulsé.
3. sensitive point.
3. point sensible.
4. Spain.
4. Espagne.
5. start point.
5. point de départ.
6. supply point.
6a. point de distribution.
6b. point de ravitaillement.
**SP** Security Police.
**SP** Selling Price.
*Business; Commerce.*
**SP** Service Program.
Service Program is also known as: Service Routine; Service Utility Program.
*Computer Programming.*
**SP** Shore Patrol.
Military Police of the U.S. Navy.
**SP** Short Position.
**SP** Signal Peptidase.
**SP** Signal Processing.
*Computer Programming.*
**SP** Smokeless Powder.
In view of the fact that the smokeless powder produces a very small amount of smoke, it is used as a substitute for gunpowder.
*Explosives; Materials.*
**SP** Soil Pipe.
*Civil Engineering.*
**SP** Sole Proprietor.
**sp.** (abbr.) space.
**Sp** Spanish.
Spanish is a romance language. It is the language of Spain, used also in Latin America except Brazil.
*Languages.*
**Sp.** (abbr.) spare.
Also: **sp**.
**sp.** (abbr.) special.
*Stocks.*
**sp.** (abbr.) specific.
**sp.** (abbr.) specimen.
*Science; Systematics.*
**SP**; **sp** (abbr.) spese.
Italian abbreviation meaning: expenses; charges; costs.
**SP** Spot Price.
**SP** Stand Pipe / Standpipe.
*Engineering.*
**Sp** Starting price.
**SP** Strada Provinciale.
**SP** Stockless Production.
*Business; Commerce.*
**SP** Substance P.
**SP** Systems Programmer.
The systems programmer usually writes systems software.
*Computer Science.*
**SP** Systems Programming.
*Computer Programming.*
For further details see under: **SP** (Systems Programmer).
**Sp1** Specificity protein 1.
A sequences-specific transcriptional activator isolated from human cells in the 1980s.
*Molecular and Cell Biology; Neurodegeneration.*
**SPA** Scintillation Proximity Assay.
**S.p.A.** Società per Azioni.
Italian acronym meaning: Joint-Stock Company.
*Business; Economics; Finance.*
**S.P.A.** Società Pesca Atlantica.
Italian acronym of the: Atlantic Fishing Company.
**S.P.A.**; **SPA** Società Protettrice degli Animali; Société Protectrice des Animaux.
Italian and French acronym of the: Society for the Prevention of Cruelty to Animals.
**SPA** Succinimidyl Propionate.
**SPA basin** South Pole-Aitken basin.
**SPADATS** Space Detection and Tracking System.
*Space Technology.*
**SPADE** Stratospheric Photochemistry Aerosol and Dynamics Experiment (U.S.A.).
In October 1992 and May 1993.
For further details see under: **NOZE**.
**S.P.A.L.A.S.T.** Sindacato Provinciale Antuonomo Lavoratori Addetti Servizio Terziario (Italy).
*Italian Unions.*
**SPAN** Space Physics Analysis Network (U.S.A.).
**SPAR** Sandler Program for Asthma Research (San Francisco, California, U.S.A.).
**SPAR** seagoing platform for acoustic research.
plate-forme de haute mer pour recherches acoustiques.
**SpAr** Spanish Arabic.
*Languages.*
**SPARC** Scalable Processor ARChitecture.
*Computer* ***Technology***.
**SPARC** Scholarly Publishing and Academic Resources Coalition.

SPARC is a U.S.-Canadian group established in 1997 by the Association of Research Libraries.
*Academic Publishing.*
**SPARC** Sponsored Programs and Academic Research Center.
Of the University of Northern Colorado, U.S.A.
**SP$^3$ARK** Scientific Process, Practice, and Presentation: Applying Resources and Knowledge.
An educational reform initiative of the NYAS with support from the U.S. NSF. Launched in 1998.
For further details see under: **NYAS** and **NSF**.
**SPaSM code** Scalable Parallel Short-range Molecular Dynamics code.
**SPAWAR** space and naval warfare system command.
commandement des systèmes de guerre spatiale et navale.
**SPB duplication** Spindle Pole Body duplication.
**SPC** Science Program Committee.
Of the European Space Agency.
**SPC** Senior Political Committee.
Comité politique de niveau élevé.
**SPC** South Pacific Commission (U.S.A.).
**SPC** Storm Prediction Center (U.S.A.).
**SPCA** Serum Prothrombin Conversion Accelerator.
**SPCA**; **S.P.C.A.** Society for the Prevention of Cruelty to Animals.
**SP cells** Side-Population cells.
**SPC(R)** Senior Political Committee (reinforced).
Comité politique de niveau élevé (reforcé).
**SPCS** single payload communication satellite.
satellite de télécommunications à charge utile simple.
**SPCZ** South Pacific Convergence Zone.
**SPD** Social Democratic Party.
North-Rhine, Westfalia.
**SPDA** Single-Premium Deferred Annuity.
**SPDIF** Sony-Philips Digital Interface Format (connector socket).
*Sound Cards.*
**Spdl** (abbr.) spindle.
*Cell Biology; Mechanical Devices; Textiles; Virology.*
**SPDM** Special Purpose Dexterous Manipulator (Canada).
*Engineering; Robotic Hands; Space Science.*
**SPE** Society of Petroleum Engineers (U.S.A.).
**SPE** Society of Plastics Engineers (U.S.A.).
**SPE** Solid Phase Extracts.
**SPE** Solid Polymer Electrolyte.
**SPE**; **S.P.E.** SPecific dynamic Effect.
*Nutrition.*
**SPEAM** Sun Photometer Earth Atmospheric Measurements.
**SPEC** Scuola Professionale di Estetica e Cosmetologia (Italy).
*Italian Schools.*
**spec.** (abbr.) specifications.
*Engineering; Industrial Engineering.*
**SPEC** Systems and Procedures Exchange Center.
**SPECIAL** Service Provisioning Environment for Consumers' Interactive Applications.
*European Community Project.*
**SPECIAL** Space Processes and Electrical Changes Influencing Atmospheric Layers.
Established by the ESF and the Research Training Network CAL, and funded by the European Commission.
*Atmospheric Science; European Initiatives; Sprites Physics.*
For further details see under: **ESF** and **CAL**.
**specif.** (abbr.) specifically.
**SPECMAP** SPECtral MAPping Group (U.S.A.).
Developed by Researchers of the Brown University.
*Astronomical Cycles; Isotope Variations; Paleoclimatology.*
**SPECT** Single-Photon Emission Computed Tomography.
**SPEED transmission** Superhighway by Photonically and Electronically Enhanced Digital transmission.
*European Community Project.*
**SPEGEA** Scuola di Specializzazione in Gestione Aziendale (Italy).
**SPEM** Semispectral Primitive Equation Model.
**SPES** Stimulation Plan for Economic Science.
*European Community Plans.*
**Spett.**; **Spett.le** Spettabile.
Italian abbreviation usually put at the beginning of a letter corresponding to "dear Sir(s)/Madam"; or Messrs. when on an envelope.
**SPE** Society of Plastic Engineers.
**SPF** 1. sensor fusion post.
1. poste de fusionnement des capteurs.
2. special-purpose force.
2. force d'emploi spécial.
**SPF** Specific Pathogen Force.
*Immunology; Immunobiology.*
**SPF** S Phase-promoting Factor.
*Molecular Pathology.*
**SPF** Sun Protection Factor.
*Pharmacology.*
**SPF** Superplastic Forming.

Superplastic forming is a metal manufacturing process.
*Materials Science.*
**SPf66** Synthetic Peptide Vaccine.
*Malaria Research.*
**SPFA** Société des Professeurs de Français en Amérique.
**SPF colonies** Specific Pathogen-Free colonies.
*Biotechnology; Medicine; Xenotransplantation.*
**SPG** Society for the Propagandation of the Gospel.
**SPG** stockpile planning guidance.
directive sur la planification des stocks.
**SPG-2** Spastic Paraplegia-2.
*Applied Neurobiology; Medicine; Molecular Biology.*
**SPGC** Strong Perfect Graph Conjecture.
*Graph Theory; Linear Programming.*
**sp.gr.** (abbr.) specific gravity.
specific gravity is also known as: relative density.
*Mechanics.*
**SPH code** Smooth Particle Hydrodynamics code.
*Astronomy; Planetary Science.*
**sph.** (abbr.) spherical.
**SPHE** Society of Packaging and Handling Engineers (U.S.A.).
**sp.ht.** (abbr.) specific heat.
*Thermodynamics.*
**SPI** Service des Prototypes Industriels.
French acronym meaning: Industrial Prototypes Service.
**SPI** Sindacato Pensionati Italiani (Italy).
*Italian Unions.*
**SPI2** Salmonella Pathogenicity Island 2.
*Infectious Diseases; Medicine; Microbiology; Veterinary Science.*
**SPIA** Special Project on Impact Assessment.
Of CGIAR's TAC, the SPIA Study covers the period from 1960 to 2000.
*Economics; Food Crops.*
For further details see under: **CGIAR** and **TAC**.
**SPICE** Simulator Program for Integrated Circuit Emulation.
BIO/SPICE of the University of California at Berkeley, USA.
*Bioinformatics; Computer-Aided Simulation; Chemical Kinetic Systems; Cellular Pathways.*
**S.P.I.D.** Scuola Professionale Italiana Danza.
*Italian Schools.*
**SPIDER** Spectral Phase Interferometry for Direct Electric-field Reconstruction.
*Quantum Electronics; Optics.*
**SPIN** Southcentral Pennsylvania International Network (U.S.A.).
**SPINES** Summer Program In Neuroscience, Ethics and Survival (1998) (U.S.A.).
SPINES is administered by the American Psychological Association and the Association of Neuroscience Departments and Programs and is funded by the U.S. National Institute of Mental Health.
*Neuroscience Programs.*
**SPINS** special instructions [in the ATOS].
instructions particulières [dans les ATOS].
**SPIREX** South Pole Infrared EXplorer.
*Astronomy; Astrophysics.*
**SPIRIT** South Pole Infrared Imaging Telescope.
*Astronomy; Astrophysics; Protogalaxies.*
**SPL** Sound Pressure Level.
*Acoustics; Audiology; Communication Disorders; Communication Sciences; Hearing Sciences; Neuroscience; Physiology.*
**sPLA$_2$** soluble Phospholipase $A_2$.
For further details see under: **UG**.
**SPLEEM** Spin-Polarized Low-Energy Electromicroscopy.
For further details see under: **MCXD**.
**SPLI** Single-Premium Life Insurance.
**SPLP** (abbr.) splash-proof.
**sp.lt.** speed limit.
**SPLS** Single Particle Light Scattering.
**SPM** Scanned Probe Microscopy.
**S.P.M.** Scuola Professionale Marittima.
Italian initialism meaning: Seamen Vocational Training School.
**SPM** Self-Phase Modulation.
*Quantum Electronics; Optics.*
**S.P.M.** Sue Proprie Mani.
Italian initialism meaning: To be delivered in his/her own hands (when indicated on letters/envelopes).
**SPM** Summary for Policy-Makers (U.S.A.).
The U.S. Intergovernmental Panel on Climate Change at a meeting held in Madrid at the end of 1995 ratified the summary for Policy-Makers.
**SPM** Suspended Particulate Matter.
**SPMs** Scanning Probe Microscopes.
**SPMs** Statistical Parametric Maps.
*Medicine; Psychiatry; Psychology; Radiology.*
**SPN** Sacral Parasympathetic Nucleus.
*Anatomy; Cell Biology; Neurobiology.*
**SPO** Science Phasing Orbits.
*Spacecraft Orbital Phases.*
**S.P.O.** Scuola di Psicosociologia dell'Organizzazione (Italy).
*Italian Schools.*
**SPO** Serbian Renewal Movement.

**SPO** South POle.
**SPOAC** système de plans d'orientation pour les armements conventionnels.
conventional armaments planning system (CAPS).
**SPOD** seaport of debarkation.
port de débarquement.
**SPOE** seaport of embarkation.
port d'embarquement.
**SP OFF** (abbr.) SPecial OFFering.
*Stocks.*
**SPOIs** Spinel-Pyroxene-Olivine Inclusions.
*Astrophysics; Earth and Planetary Sciences; Geochemistry; Geophysics.*
**SPOOL** Simultaneous Peripheral Operation On-Line.
**spool** The above acronym was coined using the English word "spool".
*Computer Programming; Graphic Arts; Mechanical Engineering; Textiles.*
**SPOREFUN** Mass production of SPOREs FUNgal antagonists by solid-state fermentation-process design for optimal spore quality.
*European Community Project.*
**SPORES** Special Programs Of Research Excellence (U.S.A.).
Of the U.S. National Institutes of Health. Teams of scientists who dedicate themselves to translational research for the detection, prevention, diagnosis and treatment of human cancer.
*Translational Research.*
**SPOT** Satellite POsitioning and Tracking.
**SPOT** Système Pour l'Observation de la Terre.
French acronym meaning: Earth Observation System.
**SPP** Secondary Proliferative Population (of nonepithelial cells).
*Brain Development; Medicine; Neurobiology.*
**SPP** Signal Peptide Peptidase.
A hydrolase.
*Biochemistry; Intramembrane Proteolysis; Neurologic Diseases; Proteomics.*
**SPP** Single Peptide Protease.
**SPP** Sphingolipid metabolite Sphingosine-1-Phosphate.
*Biochemistry; Cell Proliferation; Medicine; Molecular Biology; Physiology.*
**SPP** Stock Purchase Plan.
*Business; Finance.*
**SPPS** Short Pulse Photon Source.
Proposed for the SLAC.
For further details see under: **SLAC**.
**SPPs** Signal Peptide Peptidases.
For further details see under: **SPP**.
**SPR** Substance P Receptor.
*Dentistry; Molecular Neurobiology; Preventive Sciences.*
**SPR detection** Surface Plasmon Resonance detection.
*Allergy and Infectious Diseases; Biology; Immunology; Molecular Biology.*
**SPREP** South Pacific Regional Environmental Programme (Western Samoa).
**SPRI** Scott Polar Research Institute (G.B.).
**SPRI** Solid-Phase Reversible Immobilization.
*Genome Research.*
**SPRINT** Strategic PRogramme for INnovation and Technology transfer.
*European Community Programs.*
**SPR-KKR** Spin-Polarized-Relativistic Korringa-Kohn-Rostocker.
*Physics.*
**SPS** Satellite Power Systems.
**SPS** Second Preferred Stock.
**SPS** 1. self-protection system.
1. système d'autoprotection.
2. special-purpose segment.
2. segment à usage spécial.
3. standard position system.
3. système de positionnement normalisé.
**SPS** Shuttle Pallet Satellite.
*Space Research.*
**SPS** Signal-Processing System.
*Computer Technology.*
**SPS** Solar Power Satellite.
**SPS** Spring Steel.
**SPS** Super Proton Synchrotron.
The SPS feeds electrons and positrons into CERN's LEP Collider. A 6-kilometer circle of magnets.
*High-Energy Physics.*
For further details see under: **LEP**.
**SPs** Surface Plasmons.
*Physics.*
**SPS Agreement** Sanitary and Phytosanitary Agreement.
Of the World Trade Organization.
**SPSE** Society of Photographic Scientists and Engineers (U.S.A.).
**SP stage** Single-Positive stage.
*Immunology.*
**SP-STS** Spin-Polarized Scanning Tunneling Spectroscopy.
*Applied Physics; Microstructure Research.*
**SPT** Serine Palmitoyl-CoA Transferase.
*Bioorganic Chemistry; Medicine; Molecular Pharmacology.*

**SPTF modifications** Sodium Pump Test Facility modifications.
**SPTs** Short-Period Tremors.
*Earthquake Research; Geology; Meteorology; Volcanology.*
**SPU** Solaris Processing Unit.
**SPV** Special Purpose Vehicle.
*Business; Finance; Securitization.*
**sp.vol.** (abbr.) specific volume.
*Mechanics.*
**SPV systems** Solar Photovoltaic systems.
**SPW** self-protect weapon.
arme d'autoprotection.
**SPZ** submarine patrol zone.
zone de patrouille de sous-marin(s).
**Sq.** (abbr.) Square (referring to an open space in a town).
**SQ** The airline code for Singapore Airlines.
**SQC** Statistical Quality Control.
**SQD** Signal Quality Detector.
**sq.ft.**; **sq ft** square foot/feet.
**SQG** Système de la Qualité Globale.
French initialism meaning: Total Quality Control System.
**sq.in.**; **sq in** (abbr.) square inch/inches.
*Metrology.*
**SQL** Structured Query Language.
**sq.m.**; **sqm** (abbr.) square meter/meters.
*Metrology.*
**sq.mi.**; **sq mi** (abbr.) square mile/miles.
*Metrology.*
**sqn.** (abbr.) squadron.
**sq.r.**; **sq r** (abbr.) square rod/rods.
*Metrology.*
**SQR** Succinate: Quinone oxidoreductase (enzyme).
*Energy Production; Intermediary Metabolism; Organism Biology; Structural Biology.*
**SQUALE** Security, Safety and QUALity Evaluation for dependable systems.
*European Community Project.*
**S QUARK** Strange Quark.
*Particle Physics.*
**SQUID** Superconducting Quantum Interference Device.
The superconducting quantum interference device is used mainly in highly sensitive magnetometers.
*Electronics; Microelectronics.*
**SQUIDs** Superconducting Quantum Interface Devices.
**SR** Sacra Rota (Italy).
**SR** Sarcoplasmic Reticulum.
*Cell Biology.*
**SR** Scanning Radiometer.
*Engineering.*
**SR** Scatter Read.
*Computer Programming.*
**SR** Sedimentation Rate.
*Pathology; Physical Chemistry.*
**S/R** Sell or Return.
*Business; Commerce.*
**SR** Service Renseignements.
French initialism meaning: Information Service.
**SR** Sex Ratio.
*Biology.*
**SR** Shift Register.
The shift register is capable of moving a sequence of stored bits to the right or left a specified number of positions.
*Computer Technology.*
**SR** 1. short-range.
1. courte portée.
2. Southern Region [obsolete].
2. Région Sud (RS) [obsolète].
3. strategic reconnaissance.
3. reconnaissance stratégique.
4. strategic reserve.
4. réserve stratégique.
**SR** Siracusa, Italy.
**SR** Solar Radiation.
**SR** Special Register.
**Sr.** (abbr.) Steradian.
For further details see under: **S**.
**SR** Stochastic Resonance.
The theory of stochastic resonance was developed 16 years ago by mathematicians and physicists.
*Bioengineering; Mathematical Physiology; Neuroscience; Nonlinear Dynamics; Physical Rehabilitation; Proprioception.*
**Sr** the chemical symbol for Strontium.
Strontium is a metallic element having the atomic number 38, and an atomic weight of 87.62. It is used mainly as an electron tube scavenger.
*Chemistry; Symbols.*
**SR** Studi di Rete.
**SR** Summary Report.
**SR** Surtax Rate.
**SR** The airline code for Swissair.
**SRA** Satellite Radar Altimetry.
**SRA** Scanning Radar Altimeter.
**SRA** Scientific Review Administrator.
**SRA** Self-Regulatory Agency (U.S.A.).
*Investments.*
**SRA** 1. shipping risk area.
1. zone de navigation à risque.
2. (force plan) suitability and (associated) risk assessment.

2. évaluation de l'adéquation du plan de forces et des risques (connexes).
**SRA** Signes de Reconnaissance et d'Appréciation.
French initialism meaning: Strokes.
**SRA** Strategic Rauil Authority (G.B.).
**SRAAM** short-range anti-air missile.
missile de défense aérienne à courte portée.
**SRAM** Short-Range Attack Missile.
*Ordnance.*
**SRAM** Static Random-Access Memory.
*Computer Programming.*
**SR&CC** Strikes, Riot and Civil Commotion.
*Insurance.*
**SRARM** short-range antiradiation missile.
missile antiradiation à courte portée.
**SRAs** Scientific Review Administrators.
**SRB** Senior Resource Board [MBC].
Bureau principal des ressources [MBC].
**SRB** Sulfate/Sulphate-Reducing Bacteria.
*Biogeochemistry; Geology; Geophysics; Marine Chemistry; Marine Microbiology; Physics.*
**SR band** Solar Schumann-Runge band.
*Astronomy; Phyiscs.*
**SRBCs** Sheep Red Blood Cells.
**SRBH** Serbian Republic of Bosnia-Herzegovina [obsolete].
République serbe de Bosnie-Herzégovine [obsolète].
**SRBM** Short-Range Ballistic Missile.
The short-range ballistic missile has a range of about 1100 kilometers.
*Ordnance.*
**SRC** Science Research Council (G.B.).
**SRC** Solvent-Refined Coal.
**SRC** sub-regional command [has replaced PSC].
Commandement sous-régional [remplace CSP].
**SRCC** Strikes, Riots, Civil Commotion.
*Insurance.*
**SRC-1 gene** Steroid Receptor Coactivator-1 gene.
*Cell Biology.*
**$SrCO_3$** Strontianite.
Strontianite is found in limestone.
*Mineralogy.*
**SRCP** Science and Religion Course Program.
**SRCs** SCID Repopulating Cells.
*Cell Biology; Immunology; Medicine.*
For further details see under: **SCID**.
**SRCs** Short-Range Correlations.
*Nuclear Physics.*
**SRE** Serum Response Element.
**SRE** Services Rendus aux Entreprises (France).
**SRE** single-round effectiveness.
capacité de destruction au premier coup.
**SRE** Système Réticulo-Endothélial.
French initialism meaning: Reticuloendothelial System.
*Anatomy.*
**SREBP** Sterol Regulatory Element Binding Protein.
For further details see under: **SREBPs**.
**SREBPs** Sterol Regulatory Element Binding Proteins.
*Genetics; Gerontology; Human Genome Research; Inherited Diseases; Medicine; Neurological Disorders and Stroke.*
**SR-ELDOR** Saturation-Recovery electron-electron Double Resonance.
*Molecular Dynamics (liquids).*
**SRF** Serum Response Factor.
*Molecular Cell Biology.*
**SRF** Smithsonian Research Foundation.
**SRF** strategic reserve force.
force de réserve stratégique.
**SRG** SACEUR Rover Group.
groupe itinérant du SACEUR.
**SRG** Steel Research Group (U.S.A.).
The SRG was founded in 1985.
**SRI** Stanford Research International (U.S.A.).
**SRIF** Somatotropin Release-Inhibiting Factor.
SRIF is also known as: Somatostatin.
*Endocrinology.*
**SR-IkBα** Super-Repressor form of IkBα.
*Cancer; Endodontics; Genetics; Medicine; Molecular Biology; Pharmacology.*
**SRK** S Receptor Kinase.
*Plant Biology; Plant Sciences.*
**SRL** Solvent Refined Lignite.
**SRL** Superconducting Research Laboratory (Japan).
For further details see under: **ISTEC**.
**SRM** short-range missile.
missile à courte portée.
**SRMs** Standard Reference Materials.
**SRMS** Structure Resonance Modulation Spectroscopy.
**SRN** system reference number.
numéro de référence de système.
**SRO** Scottish Renewables Obligation.
**SRO** Self-Regulatory Organization (G.B.).
**SrO** Strontium Oxide.
Strontium Oxide, also known as: Strontia, is used mainly in soaps and pigments.
*Inorganic Chemistry.*
**SRON** Space Research Organization of The Netherlands.
*Astrophysics.*
**SRP** Savannah River Plant.
**SRP** Signal-Recognition Particle.

The Signal-Recognition Particle is also known as: Signal-Recognition Protein.
*Biochemistry; Structural Biology; Biophysics.*
**SRP** Soluble Reactive Phosphorus.
**SRQ** Set of Relevant Questions.
**SRQ** The airport code for Sarasota/Bradenton, Florida, U.S.A.
**SRR** search and rescue region.
région de recherche et sauvetage.
**SRS** 1. satellite radar station.
1. station radar de satellite.
2. security requirements statement.
2. énoncé des impératifs de sécurité.
3. short-range sonar.
3. sonar à courte portée.
4. submarine rescue submersible.
4. submersible de sauvetage de sous-marin.
**SRS** Scientific Relations Specialist.
**SRS** (Norian) Skeletal Repair System.
The Norian Skeletal Repair System is a promising material developed in 1995 to repair bone fractures.
*Biomaterials.*
**SRS** Sonobuoy Reference System.
**SRS** Stimulated Roman Scattering.
*Roman-shifted Lasers; Physics; Optics.*
**SrS** Strontium Sulfide.
Strontium Sulfide, also known as: Strontium Monosulfide is used mainly in strontium compounds.
*Inorganic Chemistry.*
**SRS-A** Slow-Reacting Substance of Anaphylaxis.
*Medicine.*
**SRSG** Special Representative of the Secretary General - U.N.
**$SrSO_4$** Celestine.
Celestine, also known as: Celestite, is found mainly in hydrothermal vein deposits, and in sedimentary rocks.
*Mineralogy.*
**SRSOM** short-range stand-off missile.
missile à courte portée tiré à distance de sécurité.
**SRT** short-range transport aircraft.
aéronef de transport à court rayon d'action.
**SRT** Simple Reaction Time.
*Aging; Antiaging; Genetics; Gerontology.*
**$SrTiO_3$** Strontium Titanate.
Strontium Titanate is used mainly in electronics.
**SRTM** Shuttle Radar Topography Mission.
*Geophysics and Planetary Physics; Oceanography.*
**SRTP** Science Research Training Program.
Of the New York Academy of Sciences, the SRTP gives high school students the opportunity to explore science through summer internships with professional research scientists in academies, government, and industry.
For further details see under: **NYAS**.
**SRU** search and rescue unit.
unité de recherche et sauvetage.
**SRU** Seismic Research Unit.
University of the West Indies in Trinidad.
*Eruptive Activities; Geophysics; Seismic Research; Volcanic Hazards; Volcanology.*
**SS** Sassari, Italy.
**SS** Scientific System.
The scientific system deals mainly with computations.
*Computer Technology.*
**SS** Selling Short.
**SS** Senior Securities.
**SS** Servizio Segreto.
Italian initialism meaning: Secret Service.
**SS** Servizio Sociale.
Italian initialism meaning: Social Service.
**SS** Short Sale.
**SS** Social Security.
**SS** Stainless Steel.
Stainless Steel is commonly known as: Stainless Alloy.
*Metallurgy.*
**SS** Steamship.
Also: **s/s**.
*Naval Architecture.*
**SS** Stopped Stock.
**SS** Succinimidyl Succinate.
**SS** Surface-to-Surface.
**SS.A.** (Ordine Cavalleresco della) Santissima Annunziata.
Italian initialism meaning: (Order of Chivalry of the) Virgin Mary.
**SSA** Seismological Society of America (U.S.A.).
**SS&C** Scope, Sequence, and Coordination.
*U.S. Education Reforms.*
**SSAs** Stratospheric Sulfate Aerosols.
**SSB** Single-Sideband.
*Telecommunications.*
**SSB** Space Seismological Bureau.
**SSB** Space Studies Board (U.S.A.).
**SSB** State Seismological Bureau - Beijing (China).
*Earth Science; Earthquake Management; Geophysics; Physics of Earth Interior; Seismology.*
**SSB** State Statistical Bureau (China).
**SSB communication** Single-Sideband communication.
Also: single-sideband modulation.

*Telecommunications.*
**SSBI Survey** Spencer Stuart Board Index Survey.
**SSBN** subsurface ballistic, nuclear (nuclear-powered ballistic missile submarine).
sous-marin nucléaire lanceur d'engins (SNLE).
**SSBS** (missile) sol-sol, balistique, stratégique.
ground-to-ground strategic ballistic missile.
**SSBs** Single-Strand Breaks.
*Molecular Biology.*
**SSC** Solid-State Computer.
*Computer Technology.*
**SSC** Specialization in Social Cognition.
**SSC** Spermatogonial Stem Cell.
For further details see under: **SSCs**.
**SSC** Standard Saline Citrate.
**SSC** Stazione Sperimentale Combustibili (Italy).
**SSC** Superconducting Super Collider.
**SSC** surface search coordination.
coordination de la recherche de surface.
**SSCP analysis** Single-Strand Conformation Polymorphism analysis.
*AIDS Research; Life Sciences; Medicine; Pathology.*
**SSCs** Spermatogonial Stem Cells.
*Animal Biology; Reproductive Biology; Veterinary Medicine.*
**SSCs** State Scientific Centers (Russia).
The SSCs were launched in 1993.
**SSCV** Semi Submersible Crane Vessel.
**SSD** Sexual Size Dimorphism.
**SSD** Steady-State Distribution.
*Analytical Chemistry.*
**SSD** Sterol-Sensing Domain.
**SSD** Supersonic Diffuser.
*Mechanical Engineering.*
**SSD** Supplementary Special Deposit (G.B.).
*Banking; Business; Finance.*
**ssDNA** single-stranded DNA.
**SSE** Stredoslovenske Energeticke Zavody (Slovak Republic).
SSE located in Zilina, is one of the Energy Distribution Companies of the Slovak Republic, responsible for Central Slovakia.
**SSEA** Stage-Specific Embryonic Antigen.
*Gynecology; Human Blastocysts; Medicine; Obstetrics.*
**SSEC** Space Science and Engineering Center.
At the University of Wisconsin (U.S.A.).
**SSF** sub-strategic forces.
1a. forces sous-stratégiques.
1b. forces préstratégiques [FR].
**SSF** Supersonic Flow.
Supersonic Flow is also known as: Supercritical Flow.
*Fluid Mechanics.*
**SSFLC device** Surface Stabilized Ferroelectric Liquid Crystal device.
*Biochemistry; Chemistry; Optoelectronic Computing Systems.*
**SSG** Scientific Steering Group.
**SSHRC** Social Sciences and Humanities Research Council (Canada).
**SSI** Satellite Sequential Imaging.
**SSI** Sky Survey Instrument.
**SSI** standing signals instructions.
instructions permanentes des transmissions.
**SSI** Statewide Systemic Initiative.
**SSI** Supplemental Security Income (U.S.A.).
**SSIC** Sintered SIlicon Carbide.
Development on self-lubricating SSIC with optimized porosity and infiltration.
*European Community Project.*
**SSIE** Smithsonian Science Information Exchange.
**SSII** Société de Services et d'Ingénierie Informatique.
French initialism meaning: Computer Bureau Service; Software Company.
**SSI instrument** Solid State Imaging instrument.
*Astronomy; Lunar and Planetary Science; Space Science.*
**SSIO** Southern Subtropical Indian Ocean.
**SSI program** Statewide Systemic Initiatives program.
Of the U.S. National Science Foundation.
*Systemic Education Reforms.*
**SSI system** Solid State Imaging system.
Sensitive from 400 to 1000 nm.
*Medicine; Neurology; Psychiatry.*
**SSIT** Scuola Superiore per Interpreti e Traduttori (Italy).
*Italian Schools.*
**SSIZ** seasonal sea ice zone.
zone de glaces saisonnières.
**SSJ** self-screening jamming.
brouillage d'autoprotection.
**SSK** diesel.powered attack submarine.
1a. sous-marin d'attaque à propulsion diesel.
1b. sous-marin chasseur de sous-marin.
**SSKP** single-shot kill probability.
probabilité de destruction au premier coup.
**SSL; Ssl** Secure Socket Layer.
A protocol built into browsers that uses encryption to prevent the message being either read or changed.
*Digital Certificates; Protocols.*

**SSL** submarine safety lane.
chenal de sécurité de sous-marins.
**SSLI** Society of School Librarians International.
**SSLMIT**; **sslmit** Scuola Superiore di Lingue Moderne per Interpreti e Traduttori (Italy).
*Italian Schools.*
**SSLP** Simple Sequence Length Polymorphism.
For further details see under: **SSLPs**.
**SSLPs** Simple Sequence Length Polymorphisms.
*Genetics; Genomic Research; Medicine; Molecular Genetics.*
**SSM** Surface-to-Surface (guided) Missile.
*Ordnance.*
**SSMA** spread-spectrum multiple access.
accès multiple par étalement de spectre (AMES).
**SSME** Space Shuttle Main Engine.
**SS-N** naval surface-to-surface missile.
missile surface-surface à lanceur naval.
**SSN** subsurface, attack, nuclear (nuclear-powered attack submarine).
sous-marin nucléaire d'attaque (SNA).
**SSNM** Strategic Special Nuclear Material.
**SSO** 1. site security officer.
1. officier de sécurité du site.
2. space shuttle orbiter.
2. navette spatiale orbitale.
**SSO** Site-Specific Oligonucleotide.
**SSOM** Stritch School Of Medicine (U.S.A.).
Founded in 1909, the SSOM, at the Loyola University of Chicago, is one of the four Jesuit Catholic Medical Schools in the United States.
**SSP** scheduled strike programme.
programme de frappe préétabli.
**SSPE** Subacute Sclerosing Panencephalitis.
The subacute sclerosing panencephalitis is a sort of leukoencephalitis that affects particularly children.
*Pathology.*
**SSPS** Satellite Solar Power Station.
**SSPs** Self-assembling Supramolecular Pores.
*Analytical Chemistry; Physical Chemistry.*
**SSPS** Solar-based Solar Power Satellite.
**SSP2/TRAP** Sporozoite Surface Protein 2/Thrombospondin-Related Adhesive Protein.
*Life Cycles; Protective Immune Responses; Vaccines.*
**SSQ** Science and the Spiritual Quest.
SSQ is a four-year international project housed at the Center for Theology and the Natural Sciences in Berkeley, California, U.S.A.
**SSR** Secondary Surveillance Radar.
**SSR** Solid-State Relay.
*Electronics.*
**SSR** Subsynaptic Reticulum.
*Neuroscience.*
**SSR(A)** SACEUR's startegic reserve (air).
réserve stratégique du SACEUR (air).
**SSRA** submarine search and rescue authority.
autorité chargée de la recherche et du sauvetage de sous-marins.
**SSRC** Social Science Research Council (U.S.A.).
**SSRIs** Selective Serotonin Reuptake Inhibitors.
*Antidepressants; Psychiatry; Psychology; Psychopharmacology.*
**SSR(L)** SACEUR's strategic reserve (land).
réserve stratégique du SACEUR (terre).
**SSRP** Stanford Synchrotron Radiation Project (U.S.A.).
**SSRPs** Structure-Specific Recognition Proteins.
**SSRS** system-specific security requirements statement.
expression (ou énoncé) des besoins de sécurité propres au système.
**SSRZ** submarine search and rescue zone.
zone de recherche et sauvetage de sous-marins.
**SSS** ship-shore-ship.
navire-terre-navire.
**SSSA** Soil Sciences Society of America (U.S.A.).
*Soil Sciences.*
**SSSB** ship-shore-ship buffer.
tampon navire-terre-navire.
**SSSC** Solide State Sciences Committee (U.S.A.).
**SSSC** surface/subsurface surveillance coordinator.
1a. coordonnateur de la surveillance surface/sous-surface.
1b. coordonnateur de la veille surface et sous-surface.
**S/SSRRCS** surface/subsurface raid reporting control ship.
bâtiment contrôleur des comptes rendus d'attaque de surface ou sous la surface.
**SST** Sea Surface Temperature.
*Climate / Ocean Variability; Climate System Research; Ecosystem and Population Biology; Environmental Sciences; Oceanography; Space Studies.*
**SST** Slow-Scan Television.
*Telecommunications.*
**SST** Supersonic Transport.
**SSTA** Sea-Surface Temperature Anomaly.
**SSTC** State Science and Technology Commission (China).
**SSTR** Solid State Track Recorder.
**SSTs** Sea Surface Temperatures.
For further details see under: **SST**.

**SSUrRNA sequences** Small-Subunit ribosomal RNA sequences.
*Chemistry; Geology; Geophysics; Microorganisms.*
**SSV** soft-skinned vehicle.
véhicule non blindé.
**SSZ** surface security zone.
zone de sécurité de bâtiments.
**ST** Sales Tax.
**St** St. Lucia.
**ST** Search Time.
The search time is actually the time needed to find specific data in a computer storage device.
*Computer Technology.*
**ST** Sequence Type.
**ST** Spin Transition.
**ST** Spring Tide.
Occurring according to the moon phases.
*Oceanography.*
**st.** (abbr.) stamped.
**ST** State Table.
*Computer Technology.*
**ST** Stock Transfer.
**st.** (abbr.) stopped.
**St.** Street.
Also: **Str**.
**ST** Summer Time; Standard Time.
**STA** Science and Technology Agency.
**STA** 1. secondary training activities.
1. activités d'entraînement secondaires.
2. surveillance and target acquisition.
2. surveillance et acquisition d'objectifs.
**STA** Serum Thrombotic Accelerator.
**Stabex** Sistema di stabilizzazione dei proventi da esportazione (Italy).
**STADAN** Space Tracking And Data Acquisition Network (NASA's).
*Space Technology.*
**STAF**; **Staf** Servizio di Tutela dell'Amministrazione Finanziaria (Italy).
**STA fellowship program** Science and Technology Agency fellowship program.
The STA, an administrative organ of the Government of Japan, established the STA fellowship Program in 1988.
*Fellowships.*
**STAFFEX** staff exercise.
exercice d'état-major.
**Staffs** (abbr.) Staffordshire (G.B.).
**STAIF** Space Technology & Applications International Forum.
STAIF '99 was held on 31$^{st}$ January - 4$^{th}$ February 1999 in Albuquerque, New Mexico.
**STAIRS** Storage And Information Retrieval System.
**stan.** (abbr.) standard; standardization.
**STANAG** NATO standardization agreement.
accord de normalisation OTAN.
**STANAVFORCHAN** Standing Naval Force Channel [obsolete - replaced by MCMFORWORTH].
Force navale permanente de la Manche [obsolète - remplacée par MCMFORNORTH].
**STANAVFORLANT** Standing Naval Force Atlantic.
Force navale permanente de l'Atlantique.
**STANAVFORMED** Standing Naval Force Mediterranean [has replaced NAVOCFORMED].
Force navale permanente de la Méditerranée [remplace NAVOCFORMED].
**STAND** Science and Technology Agenda for National Development (The Philippines).
**STANDITT** STANDardization in the field of Information Technology and Telecommunications - E.C.
**STANIMUC** Servizio Tecnico Autonomo Normalizzazione Italiana Macchine Utensili e Collaudi (Italy).
STANIMUC is located in Turin, Italy.
*Italian Standards Issuing Organizations.*
**STANY** Security Traders' Association of New York (U.S.A.).
**STAP** Scientific and Technical Advisory Panel.
**Staph.** (abbr.) Staphylococcus.
The word Staphylococcus refers to the Greek term "a bunch of grapes" because under a microscope these bacteria appear as a group.
*Bacteriology.*
**STAR** Science To Achieve Results.
STAR is an initiative of the U.S. EPA.
*Astronomy; Physics; Planetary Sciences.*
For further details see under: **EPA**.
**STAR** Ship-Tended Acoustic Relay.
*Navigation.*
**STAR** Standard Terminal Arrival Route.
*Aviation.*
**STAR** State Acid Rain Program (U.S.A.).
**STAR** STorage And Retrieval.
**STAR** surveillance, target acquisition and reconnaissance.
surveillance, acquisition d'objectif et reconnaissance.
**star** The above acronyms were coined using the English word "star".
*Astronomy; Electricity.*
**StAR protein** Steroidogenic Acute Regulatory protein.

*Biochemistry; Medicine; Steroidogenesis.*
**S.T.A.R.S.** Satellite Televisione Applicazioni Ricerche Servizi (Italy).
**START** 1. Strategic Arms Reduction Talks.
1. pourparlers sur la réduction des armements stratégiques.
2. Strategic Arms Reduction Treaty.
2. Traité sur la réduction des armements stratégiques.
**START** System for Analysis, Research, and Training.
The System for Analysis, Research, and Training was created by the International Council of Scientific Unions in 1990.
*Environmental Research.*
**STARTEX** start of exercise.
début de l'exercice.
**STAS** submarine towed array system (sonar).
système (sonar) à antenne remorquée par sous-marins.
**Stasi** Ministry for State Security.
German Democratic Republic.
**stat.** (abbr.) statistics; status.
**STAT** Stratospheric Tracers of Atmospheric Transport.
**STATE** Sulfur Transformation And Transport Experiment.
**state** The above acronym was coined using the English word "state".
*Control Systems; Physics; Quantum Mechanics.*
**STATEC** Service central de la STAtistique et des Etudes EConomiques (Luxemburg).
**Static SP**; **SSP** Static Spontaneous Potential.
**STAT** (Cytoplasmic) Signal Transducers and Activators of Trascription.
*Biochemistry; Cell Biology; Medicine; Molecular Biology; Phyics; Surgery.*
**STAT 1** Signal Transducer and Activator of Transcription 1.
*Immunology; Norovirus resistance; Pathology.*
**STB** Special Tax Bond.
*Business; Finance.*
**stbd.** (abbr.) starboard.
*Navigation.*
**STC** Science and Technology Center.
For further details see under: **STCs**.
**STC** 1. sensitivity time control.
1a. régulation de la sensibilité en fonction du temps.
1b. à gain variable dans le temps (GVT).
2. SHAPE Technical Centre [obsolete - incorporated into NC3A].
2. Centre technique du SHAPE (CTS) [obsolète - intégré dans la NC3A).
**STC** Short-Term Credit.
*Business; Commerce; Finance.*
**STC** Sound Transmission Class.
**STC** Subject To Call.
**STC** Subtropical Convergence.
*Oceanography.*
**STC** Supplemental Type Certification.
**STCs** Science and Technology Centers.
Funded by the U.S. National Science Foundation.
*Biophotonics; Earth-surface Dynamics; Space Weather Modeling.*
**STD** Sexually Transmitted Disease.
*AIDS; HIV Carriers; Gynecological Infections.*
**std.** (abbr.) standard.
**STD** Subscriber Trunk Dialing.
**STD conditions** Standardized conditions.
**STDN** Space flight Tracking and Data Network.
**STD recorder** Salinity-Temperature-Depth recorder.
The salinity-temperature-depth recorder is also known as: CTD recorder.
*Engineering.*
**STDs** Sexually Transmitted Diseases.
For further details see under: **STD**.
**SteB** South Temperate Belt.
**STED** Solar Turboelectric Drive.
**STEM** Scanning Transmission Electron Microscope.
*Electronics.*
**STEM** Short-Team Energy Monitoring.
STEM is a new technique that quickly and easily predicts long-term energy performance such as annual heating requirements. STEM is a valid way to verify energy performance for third-party financing and utility rebate programs.
*Energy Monitoring.*
**STEP** Science, Technology and Economic Policy (Board) (U.S.A.).
**STEP** Sixth Term Examination Papers (G.B.).
**STEP** Stratosphere-Troposphere Exchange Project.
**STEP** Two Specific Research and Technological Development Programs in the field of environment.
*European Community Programs.*
**ster.** (abbr.) sterling.
Also: **stg.**
**Sterad.** (abbr.) steradian.
For further details see under: **S**.
**STES** Solar Total Energy Systems.
**St.Ex.** (abbr.) Stock Exchange.
**STF** Subtropical Front.
*Ocean Science.*

**STF** Systemic Transformation Facility.
For further details see under: **CCFF**; **EFF**; **ESAF** and **SAF**.

**STFs** Signal Transducing Factors.
*Immunology.*

**stg.** (abbr.) sterling.
Also: **ster**.

**STG** Superior temporal Gyrus.
*Brain Sciences; Cognitive Neuroscience; Psychoacoustics.*

**STH** Somatotrope Hormone.

**STIAC** Science, Technology and Innovation Advisory Council (U.S.A.).

**STIS** Space Telescope Imaging Spectrograph.
STIS is one of the instruments installed aboard the HST during the february 1997 servicing mission. STIS can collect spectral data from numerous objects simultaneously.
For further details see under: **HST**.

**stk.** (abbr.) stock.

**STKE**; **Stke** Signal Transduction Knowledge Environment.
A product of **Science** & Stanford University Libraries.
*Cellular Regulation; Electronic Journals; Electronic Libraries; Signaling Research.*
For further details see under: **AAAS**.

**STL** Science, Technology and Law.
*U.S. Programs.*

**STL** Space Technology Laboratory.

**STL** The airport code for St. Louis International.

**STM** Scanning Tunneling Microscopy.
*Chemical Sciences; Chemical Engineering; Nanoparticles characterization technique.*

**STM** Short-Term Memory.
Short-Term Memory is also known as: Primary Memory; Short-Term Store.
*Behavior; Biology; Memory Storage; Psychology.*

**STM programme** Standards, Testing and Measurements programme.
The E.C. QUASIMEME project was funded under the STM.
For further details see under: **QUASIMEME**.

**stmt.** (abbr.) statement.

**STN** Subthalamic Nucleus.
*Gene Therapy; Medicine; Molecular Medicine; Neurological Surgery.*

**STO**; **Sto** Servizio Terapia Occupazionale (Italy).

**STO** The airport code for Stockholm, Sweden.

**STOA program** Scientific and Technological Options Assessment program.
Of the European Parliament.

**STOBAR** Short Take-Off But Arrested Recovery.

**STOL** Short TakeOff and Landing.
*Aviation.*

**STOP** Stop the Trafficking Of Persons.
The STOP program - covering the period 1996/2000 - was launched to develop initiatives to eliminate trade in human beings, sexual exploitation and other crimes.
*European Community Programs.*

**STORMS** Software Tools for the Optimization of Resources in Mobile Systems.
*European Community Project.*

**STOVL** short take-off and vertical landing (aircraft).
(aéronef à) décollage court et atterrissage vertical (ADCAV).

**STP** Science and Technology Policy.

**STP** Self-Triggering Program.
*Computer Programming.*

**STP** Short Term Program.

**STP** Standard Temperature and Pressure.

**STP** Staurosporin.
A general kinase inhibitor.
*Biochemistry; Cell Biology.*

**STP** Surveillance Translocation Protein.
*Botany; Plant Biology; Plant Physiology.*

**STPP** Sodium Tripolyphosphate.
STPP is used mainly in water softening.
*Inorganic Chemistry.*

**STR** Self-Tuning Regulator.
*Control Systems.*

**Str** Short tandem repeat.

**STR** Société de produits chimiques des Terres rares (France).

**str.** (abbr.) strada.
Italian abbreviation meaning: street; road.

**str.** (abbr.) strait / straits.
*Geography.*

**str.** (abbr.) stream.

**Str.** Street.
Also: **St**.

**STR** Synchronous Transmitter Receiver.
*Data Communications.*

**STRATEVAC** strategic evacuation.
évacuation stratégique.

**STRATMAN initiative** (abbr.) Strategic Manufacturing initiative.
*U.S. NSF Program.*
For further details see under: **NSF**.

**strd** (abbr.) stranded.

**Strep.** Streptococcus.
Also: **Strep**; **strep**.
*Bacteriology.*

**STRESS** STRuctural Engineering System Solver.

*Computer Programming.*
**stress** The above acronym was coined using the English word "stress".
*Behavior; Materials Science; Mechanics; Physics; Psychology.*
**STRF** Spectrotemporal Receptive Field.
*Biomedical Engineering; Hearing Sciences; Neuroscience.*
**STRI** Smithsonian Tropical Research Institute (U.S.A.).
**STRIKEX** striking fleet exercise.
exercice de flotte d'intervention.
**STRIKFLTLANT** Striking Fleet Atlantic.
Flotte d'intervention de l'Atlantique.
**STRIKFORSOUTH** Allied Naval Striking and Support Forces Southern Europe [obsolete].
Forces navales alliées d'intervention et de soutien du Sud-Europe [obsolète].
**STRIPS** Stanford Research Institute Problem Solver.
*Artificial Intelligence.*
**STRKFLT** see STRIKFLTLANT.
voir STRIKFLTLANT.
**STrZ** South Tropical Zone.
**STS** Science, Technology, and Society.
**STS** Sequence Tagged Site.
*Genomic Research.*
**STS** Serologic Test for Syphilis.
*Medicine.*
**STS**; **S.T.S.** Society of Thoracic Surgeons.
**STS** Space Transportation System.
**STS** Student Travel Schools (Italy).
**STS** Superior Temporal Sulcus.
*Cognitive Neurology.*
**STScI** Space Telescope Science Institute (Baltimore, Maryland, U.S.A.)
*Astronomy.*
**STSs** Sequence-Tagged Sites.
*Biomedical Research; Human Genome Research; Molecular Biology.*
**STT** Small Tactical Terminal.
**STTL** Schottky Transistor-Transistor Logic.
*Electronics.*
**STTR program** Small business Technology Transfer Research program (U.S.A.).
**STU** secure telephone unit.
poste téléphonique protégé.
**STU** Società di Trasformazione Urbana (Italy).
**STUFT** ships taken up from trade.
navires de commerce réquisitionnés.
**STVIF** system test validation & integration facility.
centre de tests, de validation et d'intégration du système.
**STW** speed made good through the water.
vitesse sur l'eau.
**STW** Stichting Voor De Technische Wetenschappen (The Netherlands).
**STW** Subtropical Water.
**stwy.** (abbr.) stairway.
**STX** Start Of Text.
**SU** Signaling Unit.
**SU** Sudan.
**S.U.** Sûreté Urbaine.
French acronym meaning: Urban Security.
**SU** State University (U.S.A.).
**SU** Stati Uniti.
Italian acronym meaning: United States.
**SU** Strontium Unit.
*Nucleonics.*
**SU** The airline code for Aeroflot.
**SUA** Shipped Unassembled.
*Commerce; Shipping.*
**SUA** surface unit, attack (surface attack unit).
unité d'attaque de surface.
**sub.** (abbr.) sub-editor; submarine; subscription; subsidy; substitute; subvention.
**sub-** (prefix) under; below.
**SUBACLANT** Submarines, Allied Command Atlantic.
Forces sous-marines du Commandement allié de l'Atlantique.
**sub-Ch** sub-Chandrasekhar.
*Astronomy; Astrophysics.*
**SUBEASTLANT** 1. Submarine Forces, East Atlantic [has replaced SUBEASTLANT 2.].
1. Forces sous-marines Est de l'Atlantique [remplace SUBEASTLANT 2.].
2. Submarine Forces, Eastern Atlantic Area [obsolete - replaced by SUBEASTLANT 1.].
2. Forces sous-marines du Secteur oriental de l'Atlantique [obsolète - remplacé par SUBEASTLANT 1.].
**SUBEX** submarine exercise.
exercice de sous-marins.
**subg.** (abbr.) subgenus.
*Systematics.*
**SUBMISS** submarine missing.
sous-marin disparu.
**SUBNOTE** submarine notice (note).
avis de mouvement de sous-marins.
**SUBOPAUTH** submarine operating authority.
autorité responsable de la mise en œuvre des sous-marins.
**subQ** (abbr.) subcutaneous.
*Anatomy.*
**SUBROC** (abbr.) SUBmarine ROCket.

*Ordnance.*
**SUBSUNK** submarine sunk.
sous-marin coulé.
**SUBWESTLANT** Submarine Forces, Western Atlantic Area [obsolete].
Forces sous-marines du Secteur occidental de l'Atlantique [obsolète].
**suby.** subsidiary.
**SUC** Start-Up Costs.
*Business; Commerce.*
**SUCAP** surface combat air patrol.
patrouille aérienne de combat de surface.
**succ.** (abbr.) successori.
Italian abbreviation meaning: successors.
**succ.** (abbr.) succursale.
Italian abbreviation meaning: branch.
**SUCCESS** SUbsonic aircraft Contrail and Cloud Effects Special Study.
*Atmospheric Science; Earth Science; Planetary Physics; Space Physics.*
**SUCOC** succession of command.
succession du commandement.
**Suff.** (abbr.) Suffolk (G.B.).
**Su(Hw) protein** Suppressor of Hairy-wing protein.
*Biology; Molecular Genetics; Transcription.*
**SULFIXBACK** SULfide tailings integrated management: the FIXed stabilized BACKfill as an environmental and mining necessity.
*European Community Project.*
**SUM** Surface-to-Underwater Missile.
*Ordnance.*
**SUMER** Solar Ultraviolet Measurements of Emitted Radiation.
SUMER is one of 12 instruments of ESA/NASA SOHO Spacecraft.
For further details see under: **ESA**, **NASA** and **SOHO**.
**SUMS** Symposium for Undergraduates in the Mathematical Sciences.
Hosted by Brown University (U.S.A.).
For further details see under: **VIGRE Program**.
**SUNET**; **Sunet** Swedish University Network (Sweden).
*New Projects.*
For further details see under: **DAG**.
**SUNY** The State University of New York (U.S.A.).
**sup.** (abbr.) superior.
*Anatomy; Botany; Graphic Arts; Materials; Science.*
**superf.** (abbr.) superficie.
Italian abbreviation meaning: area; surface.
**SUPINTREP** supplementary intelligence report.
compte rendu supplémentaire de renseignement.
**SUPIR** supplemental programmed interpretation report.
compte rendu d'interprétation supplétif (ou auxiliaire).
**SUPPLAN** support plan [sometimes called SUPLAN].
plan supplétif [parfois appelé SUPLAN].
**SUR** Sulfonylurea Receptor.
*Biochemistry; Cell Physiology; Medicine; Molecular Biology.*
**sur.** (abbr.) surplus.
**SURCAP** surveillance combat air patrol.
patrouille aérienne de combat de surveillance.
**SURE** SUlfur Regional Experiment.
**SURF** standard underway replenishing fixture.
gréement, normalisé pour le ravitaillement à la mer.
**SURFMOVREP** surface movement report.
compte rendu de mouvements de surface.
**SURFRAD** (abbr.) SURFace RADiation.
**SURTAS** surveillance towed-array system.
1a. système d'antenne remorquée de surveillance.
1b. dispositif acoustique remorqué de surveillance.
**SUS** sonar underwater signal.
signal sonore sous-marin.
**SUSF** Stationary Ultrasonic Field.
*Atmospheric Physics; Meteorology; Physics; Sonoluminescence.*
**susp.** (abbr.) suspended.
*Stocks.*
**SUSY** (abbr.) SUperSYmmetry.
*Neutrinos.*
**SUV** Saybolt Universal Viscosity.
*Fluid Mechanics.*
**S.V.**; **s.v.** Sailing Vessel.
**SV** Savona, Italy.
**SV** Secular Variation.
Secular Variation is also known as: Geomagnetic Secular Variation.
*Geophysics.*
**S.V.** Signoria Vostra.
Italian initialism meaning: Your Lordship/Ladyship.
**SV** stop valve.
*Mechanical Engineering.*
**SV 40** Simian Virus 40.
*Biochemistry; Cell Biology; Caveolae; Virology.*
**SV2A** Synoptic Vesicle Protein 2A.
*Exocytosis; Calcium-dependent Neurotransmission.*
**SVBG** Stock Value Bank Guarantee.
For further details see under: **WISE**.
**SVC** Supervisor Call Instruction.

**SVC** Switched Virtual Circuit.

**SVCs** Second Viral Coefficients.
*Chemistry; Physical Chemistry.*

**SVD** Simultaneous Voice/Data.

**SVD analysis** Singular-Value Decomposition analysis.
*Chemistry; Biochemistry.*

**SVE** secure voice equipment.
matériel de cryptophonie.

**SVI** Spectral Vegetation Indices.
*Atmospheric Sciences; Land-Atmosphere Interactions; Meteorology; Plant Biology.*

**SVP** S'il Vous Plaît.
French initialism meaning: please.

**SVP** Society of Vertebrate Paleontology.

**SVR** Smart Video Recorder (Intel's).
Introduced in 1993. Won an Editor's Choice Award (in mid 1994) in "Reel to Reel".

**SVR** surface vessel radar.
radar de bâtiment de surface.

**S.V.S.S.** Servizi Volontariato Sostegno Sociale.

**SVTC** secure video teleconferencing.
vidéoconférence protégée.

**SVZ** Subventricular Zone.
A progenitor zone, which in adulhood continues to generate neurons.
*Brain Development; Medicine; Developmental Neurobiology.*
For further details see under: **NSCs**.

**SW** Salt Water; Saltwater.
*Biology; Hydrology.*

**SW** Short Wave; shortwave.
*Electricity; Physics.*

**SW** Software.
*Computer Programming.*

**SW** 1. special weapon.
1. arme spéciale.
2. surface warfare.
2. lutte (au dessus) de (la) surface (LASF).
3. Sweden.
3. Suède.

**SW** Special Weight.

**SW** Station Wagon.

**SW** Surface Water.
*Hydrology.*
In *Oceanography* Surface Water is also known as: Mixed Layer.

**Sw** Swedish.
Swedish is a Germanic language, the language of Sweden and parts of Finland. It is closely related to Danish and Norwegian.
*Languages.*

**SW** (abbr.) Switch.
*Civil Engineering; Computer Programming; Electricity; Robotics.*

**SW1** Schwassman-Wachmann 1.
*Astronomy.*

**SWA** Scientific Workers Association (India).

**SWALC** Southwest Academic Library Consortium.

**SWAMP** SouthWest Area Monsoon Project.
*U.S. Projects.*

**SWAPPS** South-West Approaches.
approches (maritimes) du sud-ouest.

**SWAS** Submillimeter Wave Astronomy Satellite (U.S.A.).
SWAS was launched by NASA on 5th December 1998. It observes the universe at submillimeter wavelengths.

**SWATH ship** Small-Waterplane-Area Twin-Hulled ship.
*Naval Architecture.*

**SWB** Subjective Well-Being (referring to people's).
*Psychology.*

**SWB Program** Science Without Borders Program.
Of the NYAS.
For further details see under: **NYAS**.

**SWC** anti-surface warfare commander.
commandant de la lutte de surface.

**SWC** Significant Wave Heights.

**SWCLC** Southwest Community Library Council.

**SWCNs** Single-Walled Carbon Nanotubes.
*Analysis; Chemistry; Ice nanotubes; Materials Science and Engineering.*

**SWCS** Soil and Water Conservation Society (U.S.A.).

**SWCX mechanism** Solar Wind Charge Exchange mechanism.
*Cometary X-rays; X-ray Images.*

**SWE** Society of Women Engineers.

**SWEEPEX** minesweeping exercise.
exercice de dragage de mines.

**SWEMP** Solid Waste / Environmental Management Project - Lebanon.

**SWEPS** South-West European pipeline system.
réseau de pipelines du sud-ouest de l'Europe.

**SWG** special working group.
groupe de travail spécial.

**SWH** Significant Wave Heights.

**SWHQ** static war headquarters.
quartier général de guerre fixe (QGGF).

**SWHSL** South East Wisconsin Health Sciences Library Consortium.

**SWICS** Solar Wind Ion Composition Spectrometer.

**SWIFT** Society for Worldwide Information and Fund Transfer.

**SWIFT** Society for Worldwide Interbank Financial Telecommunications.

**SWIL** South-Western Illinois (U.S.A.).

**SWIR** Southwest Indian Ridge.
*Geology; Geophysics; Lithosphere; Ocean & Earth Sciences; Oceanography.*

**SwissF** Swiss French.
*Languages.*

**SWISSPROT** Swiss database of PROtein Sequences.
SWISSPROT is one of the oldest protein sequence databases. In mid-1996 it was fully integrated with the European Molecular Biology Laboratory nucleotide database.

**SWITCHEX** circuit switching exercise.
exercice de commutation de circuits.

**SWLA** Southwestern Library Association.

**SWLC** Southwestern Library Council.

**SWMOVEX** special weapons movement exercise.
exercice de mouvement d'armes spéciales.

**SWNTs** Single-Walled carbon Nanotubes.
*Chemistry; Materials Science and Engineering; Nanoscale Science; Physics; Astronomy; Flow Sensors.*

**SWP** Safe Working Pressure.

**SWPS algorithm** Split Wigner Pseudo Spectral algorithm.
*Chemistry; Physical Chemistry.*

**SwRI** Southwest Research Institute.
In Boulder, Colorado, U.S.A.
*Planetary Geology; Planetary Science.*

**SWRLS** South Western Regional Library System.

**SWS** Short-Wavelength Spectrometer.

**SWS** Slow-Wave Sleep.
*Neuroscience; Neurobiology.*

**SWT** Seawater Tris.
*Biochemistry; Physics.*

**SWU** Separative Work Unit.
*Physics.*

**SX** Sundays Excepted.

**Sx** (abbr.) Sussex (G.B.).

**SXAPS** Soft X-ray Appearance Potential Spectroscopy.
SXAPS is an electron spectroscopic technique.

**SXI** Solar X-ray Imager.

**Sxl** Sex-lethal.
*Developmental Biology; Dosage Compensation; Evolutionary Biology; Molecular Biology; Molecular Research; Vertebrate Sex Determination.*

**SY** Seychelles.
International vehicle registration letters.

**SY** Steam Yacht.

**Sy** (abbr.) supply.

**Sy** (abbr.) Surrey (G.B.).

**SYD** South Yemen Dinar.
*Currencies.*

**Syd.** (abbr.) Sydney (Australia).

**SYD** The airport code for Sydney, Australia.

**sym.** (abbr.) symbol.
*Artificial Intelligence; Chemistry; Computer Programming; Linguistics.*

**sym.** (abbr.) symmetrical / symmetric.
*Chemistry; Science.*

**syn.** (abbr.) synchronous.

**syn.** (abbr.) synthetic.
*Chemistry; Engineering; Science.*

**SYNADEX** synthetic air defence exercise.
exercice synthétique de défense aérienne.

**sync./synch.** (abbr.) synchronization.
*Engineering; Horology.*

**SYNEX** synthetic exercise.
exercice synthétique.

**Syngas** (abbr.) synthesis gas.
*Chemical Engineering.*

**SYR** Syria's international vehicle registration letters.

**SYR** The airport Code for Syracuse,New York.

**sys./syst.** (abbr.) system.
*Engineering; Geology; Physics; Science.*

**SYSEVAL** system evaluation [air defence].
évaluation du système [défense aérienne].

**SYSGEN**; **sysgen** System Generation.
*Computer Programming.*

**SYSIN** (abbr.) SYStem INput.

**S.Y.T.** Scuola di Yoga Terapeutico (Italy).
*Yoga Schools.*

**SZ** Schizophrenia.
A psychiatric, debilitating disorder.
*Behavioral Sciecnes; Molecular Sciences; Neuroscience; Psychiatry.*

**SZ diode** Silicum-Zener diode.

**sz** size.
*Materials; Metallurgy; Science.*

**SZ** surface zero.
*Ordnance.*

**SZB** Slovak Guarantee Bank.

**S-Z effect** Sunyaer-Zeldovich effect.
*Astronomy.*

# T

**T**; **t** tank.
*Engineering; Ordnance.*
*Electronics;* In electronics, tank is also known as: tank circuit.

**T**; **t** tare.
*Engineering; Fluid Mechanics.*

**5T** Telematic Technology for Transport and Traffic in Turin.
*Telematic Applications.*

**T**; **t** telephone.
*Telecommunications.*

**t** temperature.
Also: **temp.**
*Medicine; Meteorology; Physiology; Thermodynamics.*

**T**; **T.** Tesla.
*Electromagnetism.*

**t** test.
Also: **tst**.
*Chemistny; Petroleum Engineering; Science.*

**T**; **t** Testament.

**T** Thailand's international vehicle registration letter.

**T** Thoracic.
*Medicine.*

**t** thunder.
*Beaufort Letter.*

**T**; **T.** Thymine.
Also: **Thy.**
*Biochemistry* - $C_5H_6N_2O_2$.

**T** Tome.
*Bibliography.*

**T**; **t** ton(s).
*Mechanical Engineering; Metrology; Naval Architecture; Nucleonics.*

**t** transaction.

**t** transmitter.
*Telecommunications.*

**T** The chemical symbol for Tritium.
Tritium is used in mononuclear research.
*Chemistry; Symbols.*

**T** tropical loading.
*Shipping.*

**t** true.
*Cartography; Mechanical Engineering; Science.*

**T**; **t** Tuesday.

**$T_3$** Triiodothyronine.
*Endocrinology.*

**$T_4$** Thyroxine.
*Endocrinology.*

**TA** Tangible Assets.
*Business; Economics; Finance.*

**TA** 1. tank army.
1. armée de chars.
2. tasking authority.
2. autorité responsible.
3. technical arrangement.
3. arrangement technique.
4. towed array.
4. antenne remorquée.

**Ta** The chemical symbol for Tantalum.
Tantalum is a chemical element having the atomic number 73, and an atomic weight of 180.95.
Tantalum is used mainly in the manufacture of surgical and dental instruments.

**TA** Taranto, Italy.

**TA** Tax Abatement.

**TA** Tax Amortization.

**TA** Teaching Assistant.

**TA** Technical Assistance.

**T.A.** Telegraphic Address.

**TA** Tension Artérielle.
*Medicine.*

**TA** Terephthalic Acid.
Used mainly to make polyester resins and as a poultry-feed additive.
*Organic Chemistry.*

**TA** Terminal Adapter.

**TA** Therman Analysis.
*Analytical Chemistry; Metallurgy.*

**TA** Tibialis Anterior.

**T.A.** Toxin-Antitoxin.
Also: **T.A.T**.

**TA** Track Address.
*Computer Technology.*

**TA** Transactional Analysis.
*Interpersonal Relationships; Psychology.*

**T.A.** Transferrable Account.

**TA** Travelling Allowance.

**TA**; **Ta** Twin Architecture.
*Enterprise Servers.*

**TAA** Tactical Air Army.
armée aérienne tactique.

**TAAC** Technology Assessment Advisory Council.

**TAAG** Toronto Area Archivists Group (Canada).

**tab.** (abbr.) table.
*Anatomy; Computer Programming; Geography; Mathematics; Mechanical Engineering; Mining Engineering.*

**TAB** Tax Anticipation Bill.

**TAB** Technical Abstract Bulletin (U.S.A.).

**TAB** Technical Assistance Board.

**TAB** Technology Assessment Board.

**TABA-AMCHAM** Turkish-American Business Association and AMerican CHAMber of Commerce (Istanbul).

**TABD** Transatlantic Business Dialogue.
A high-level group of U.S. and European Chief Executives that met in Cincinnati, Ohio, U.S.A. in November 2000.
*Transatlatic Issues; U.S./E.C. Business.*

**TA branch** Technical Applications branch.
Of the Forecast Systems Laboratory (U.S.A.).

**TAB vaccine** *Salmonella typhi* and *Salmonella paratyphi* A and B vaccine.
Also: Typhoid Vaccine.
*Immunology.*

**TAC** Tactical Air Command.
*Military.*

**TaC** Tantalum Carbide.
TaC is used in cutting tools.
*Inorganic Chemistry.*

**TAC** Technical Advisory Committee - CGIAR's.
For further details see under: **CGIAR** and **TAC**.

**TAC** Technical Assistance Committee.

**TAC** Technology Application Center.

**TAC** Tirage de loterie Avant Catalogue.
French acronym meaning: Sweepstake.

**TAC** Tomografia Assiale Computerizzata.
Italian acronym meaning: Computerized Axial Tomography.
*Radiology.*

**TACA**; **Taca** Trans Atlantic Conference Agreement.
*Shipping Conferences.*

**TACAIR** tactical air.
aérien(ne) tactique.

**TACAN**; **tacan system** Tactical Air Navigation system.
*Navigation.*

**TACC** tactical air control centre.
1a. centre de contrôle aérien tactique.
1b. centre de contrôle tactique air (CCTA).

**TACE** type "A" cost estimate.
estimation de coût de type "A" (ECTA).

**TACEVAL** tactical evaluation.
évaluation tactique.

**TACIS** EEC / Euratom Regulation concerning the provision of Technical Assistance to economic reform and recovery in the Independent States of the former Soviet Union and Mongolia.
*EEC/Euratom Regulations.*

**TACJAM** tactical jammer.
brouilleur tactique.

**$TaCl_5$** Tantalum Chloride.
Tantalum Chloride, also known as: Tantalic Chloride; Tantalum Pentachloride, is used mainly to produce pure metal.
*Inorganic Chemistry.*

**TACOM** tactical command.
commandement tactique.

**TACON** tactical control.
contrôle tactique.

**TACOS** tactical air combat simulation.
simulation de combat aérien tactique.

**TACP** 1. tactical air control party.
1. élément de contrôle aérien tactique.
2. tactical air control post.
2. poste de contrôle aérien tactique.

**TACS** 1. tactical air control system.
1. système de contrôle aérien tactique.
2. theatre air control system.
2. système de contrôle aérien de théâtre.

**TACSATCOM** tactical satellite communications.
télécommunications tactiques par satellite.

**TACTAS** tactical towed array system (sonar).
système (sonar) tactique d'antenne remarquée (ou TAS tactique).

**TAD** tactical air direction.
direction aérienne tactique.

**TAD** 6-Thioguanine, Ara-C (cytarabine), and Daunomycin.
*Oncology.*

**TAD** traitement automatique des données.
French acronym meaning: automatic data processing.

**TADB** terrain analysis database.
base de données d'analyse de terrain.

**TADC** tactical air direction centre.
centre de direction aérienne tactique.

**TADIL** tactical digital information link.
liaison de données numériques tactiques.

**TA DNA** Telomere-Associated DNA.
For further details see under: **DNA**.

**TAEG** Tasso Annuo Effettivo Globale (Italy).
*Banking; Finance.*

**TAF** Tactical Air Force.

**TAF** terminal airfield forecast.
prévision d'aérodrome.

**TAF** Toxoid-Antitoxin Floccules.

**TAFA** Tetrahydrofurfuryl Alcohol.

**TAFE** Technical And Further Education.

**TAFs** TBP-Associated Factors.
*Molecular and Cell Biology.*
For further details see under: **TBP**.

**TAFS** Technique d'Analyse Fonctionnelle Systématique.
French acronym meaning: Functional Analysis System Technique.

**TAFTA** Trans-Atlantic Free Trade Area.
**TAg** T Antigen.
*Biochemistry; Medicine; Metabolism; Oncology; Pathology.*
**TAG** Treatment Action Group (U.S.A.).
**TAGP** Trans-Asean Gas Pipeline.
**TAG project** Trans-Atlantic Geotraverse project.
Of the U.S. Atlantic Oceanographic and Meteorological Laboratory.
**TAH devices** Total Artificial Heart Devices.
*Biomedical Engineering; Mechanical Circultory Support Systems; Thoracic and Cardiovascular Surgery; Total Artificial Heart Devices; Transcutaneous Energy transmission Systems; Ventricular Assist Devices.*
**TAHRP** Trinational Animal Health Research Project.
*Egypt-Israel-U.S.A. Project.*
**TAI** target area of interest.
zone d'intérêt visée.
**TAIRA** Thermal Agro-Industrial Research Applications.
A pyrolysis network to review thermal processing of agricultural materials for production of chemicals and fuels.
**TALAR** TActical Landing Approach Radar.
*Navigation.*
**TALFF** Total Allowance Level of Foreign Fishing.
**TALIC** Tyneside Association of Libraries for Industry and Commerce.
**TALISMAN** Tracing Authors' rights by Labelling Image Services and Monitoring Access Network.
*European Community Project.*
**TALISMAN** Transfer Accounting, Lodging for Investors and Stock Management for jobbers (G.B.).
**TAlk** Total Alkalinity.
**TAM** tactical aerodynamic missile.
missile aérodynamique tactique.
**TAM** Telefono Anziani Maltrattati (Italy).
**TAM** Television Audience Measurement.
**Tam** Test Area Manager.
**TAM** Totale Annuo Mobile.
Italian acronym meaning: Mobile Annual Total.
**TAM** Triactinomyxon.
Whirling disease identified in Europe in 1893.
*Fish Biology; Fish Microbiology; Fish Pathology; Microbiology; Parasitology; Virology; Whirling Disease.*
**TAMM** Tetrakis(acetoxymercuri) Methane.
*Biology; Chemistry.*
**TAMU** Texas A&M University (U.S.A.).
**tan** (abbr.) tangent.
*Mathematics.*
**TaN** Tantalum Nitride.
*Inorganic Chemistry.*
**TAN** Tax-Anticipation Note.
**TAN** Tonically Active Neuron.
For further details see under: **TANs**.
**TAN** Total Acid Number.
*Chemistry.*
**T & A** Tonsilloadenoidectomy.
*Surgery.*
**T&AT** tank and antitank [artillery and ammunition].
char et antichar [artillerie et munitions].
**T&D** Transmission and Distribution.
**T&E species** Threatened and Endangered species.
The U.S. Federal Agency dealing with the protection of T&E species is the U.S. Fish and Wildlife Service.
**TANF** Temporary Assistance for Needy Families.
*U.S. Welfare System.*
**tang.** (abbr.) tangente.
Italian abbreviation meaning: tangent.
Also: **tg.**
*Mathematics.*
**TANs** Tonically Active Neurons.
*Behavioral Learning; Brain and Cognition Sciences; Neurobiology.*
**TAO** tactical air observation.
observation aérienne tactique.
**$Ta_2O_5$** Tantalum Oxide.
Tantalum Oxide, also known as: Tantalum Pentoxide; Tantalic Acid Anhydride, is used mainly in optical glass and lasers.
*Inorganic Chemistry.*
**TAO array** Tropical Atmosphere Ocean array.
*Atmospheric Science; Climatology; Geophysics; Meteorology.*
**TAOC** tactical air operations centre.
centre d'opérations aériennes tactiques.
**TAOO** theatre area of operations.
zone d'opérations de théâtre.
**TAP** Thinking Aloud Protocol.
**TAP** Trans-Alaskan Pipeline.
**TAP** Transporter associated with Antigen Processing.
**tap** The above acronyms were coined using the English word "tap".
*Electricity; Mechanical Devices; Mining Engineering; Telecommunications; Surgery.*
**TAPA** towed array patrol area.
zone de patrouille d'antenne remorquée.
**TAPESTRIES** The Application of Psychological Evaluation to Systems and Technologies in Remote Imaging and Entertainment Services.

*European Community Project.*
**TAPPI** Technical Association of the Pulp and Paper Industry.
*Paper Manufacturing.*
**tappi** The above acronym was coined accidentally using the Italian word "tappi" which means: bungs; caps; corks; plugs; stoppers.
**TAPs** Training Access Points (G.B.).
**TAR** tactical air reconnaissance.
reconnaissance aérienne tactique.
**TAR** Tension Artérielle Rétinienne.
**TAR** Terrain Avoidance Radar.
**TAR** Third Assessment Report.
Of the IPCC.
*Climate Change.*
For further details see under: **IPCC**.
**TAR** Thrust-Augmented Rocket.
**TAR** Transports Automobiles Routiers.
**TAR** Tribunale Amministrativo Regionale.
Italian acronym meaning: Regional Administrative Court.
**TARA** Tsukuba Advanced Research Alliance.
**TARANIS** Tool for the Analysis of Radiations from Lightnings and Sprites.
Proposed (2003) for France's CNES Microsatellite Program.
*Atmospheric Science; Microsatellite Programs; Sprites Research.*
For further details see under: **CNES**.
**TARC** Thymus and Activation-Regulated Cytokine.
*Chemokines; Immunology; Microbiology.*
**TARCAP** target combat air patrol.
patrouille aérienne de combat sur l'objectif.
**TARE** telegraph automatic relay equipment.
matériel de relais télégraphique automatique.
**TARGET** Trans-European Automated Real-time Gross-settlement Express Transfer.
The TARGET system came into force and started operating in Euro on 1st January 1999.
*Interbank Payment Systems.*
**TAROT** Trend Analysis by Relative Opinion Testing.
*Marketing.*
**TARU** The Action Research Unit (India).
A nongovernmental organization based in New Delhi.
**TARWI** target weather information.
renseignements météo sur l'objectif.
**Tas** (abbr.) Tasmania, Australia.
**TAs** Teaching Assistants.
**TAS** Telephone Answering Service; Telephone-Answering System.
**TAS** Telomere-Associated Sequence.
*Biochemistry; Molecular Genetics.*
**TA/s** Tentative d'Appel par seconde.
**TAS** towed array system (sonar).
système (sonar) à antenne remorquée.
**TAS** True Air Speed (referring to an aircraft).
**TAS** Turkmenistan Academy of Sciences - Republic of Turkmenistan.
**tas** The above acronyms were coined accidentally using the French word "tas" which means: heap; lot; mass; pile; stack.
**μTAS** microscale-Total Analytical Systems.
*Analytical Sciences; Bioengineering; Chemistry; Device Miniaturization; Medicine.*
**TASBI** Transatlantic Small Business Initiative.
*Translatlantic Issues; U.S./E.C. Business.*
**TASC** TAbular Sequence Control.
**TASC** Treatment Alternatives to Street Accidents.
**TASC** Tripartite Accounting Standards Committee (The Netherlands).
**TASC program** Trans-Atlantic Study of *Calanus finmarchicus* program.
*Oceanic capepod population; Oceanography; Polar and Marine Research.*
**TASD** Technical and Administrative Support Division.
Of the U.S. Pacific Marine Environmental Laboratory.
**TASE** Tel-Aviv Stock Exchange (Israel).
**Tase** Transferase.
Also known as: Transferring Enzyme.
*Enzymology.*
**TASES** Tactical Airborne Signal Exploitation System.
**TASI** Time-Assignment Speech Interpolation.
*Telecommunications.*
**TASLO** tactical air support for land operations.
appui aérien tactique des opérations terrestres.
**TASM** 1. Tractical air-to-surface missile.
1. missile tactique sir-surface.
2. TOMAHAWK anti-ship missile.
2. missile antinavire TOMAHAWK.
**TASMO** tactical air support for maritime operations.
soutien aérien tactique des opérations navales.
**TASO** The AIDS Support Organization (Uganda).
Founder: Noerine Kaleeba.
**TAT** Tariffa A Tempo.
Has Replaced TUT.
For further details see under: **TUT**.
**TAT** Thematic Apperception Test.
TAT is a projective test to assess the personality of a person by means of pictures to be interpreted.
*Psychology.*

**TAT** Trans-Activating Protein.
*Cell Biology.*
**TAT** Tyrosine Amino Transferase.
*Enzymology.*
**TAT cable** Transatlantic Telephone cable.
**TaTr** Tyrosine amino Transferase regulator.
**Tau clouds** Taurus clouds.
*Astronomy; Astrophysics; Space Research.*
**TAV** Tropical Atlantic Variability.
*Climate; Earth Sciences; Environmental Sciences.*
**tax.** (abbr.) taxation; taxes.
**Taxon.** (abbr.) Taxonomy.
Taxonomy is also known as: Taxology.
*Artificial Intelligence; Sistematics.*
**tb** tablespoon; tablespoonful.
Also: **tbs**; **tbsp**.
*Metrology.*
**TB** Technical Bulletin.
*Industry.*
**Tb** The chemical symbol for Terbium.
Terbium is a rare-earth element having the atomic number 65, and an atomic weight of 158.92.
*Chemistry; Symbols.*
**TB** Terminal Block.
*Telecommunications.*
**TB** Tone Burst.
TB is used mainly to test electroacoustical devices.
*Acoustical Engineering.*
**Tb** Traduction brute.
**TB**; **t.b.** Trial Balance.
*Commerce; Finance.*
**T/B** Tratta/Tratte su Banche.
Italian initialism meaning: Draft / Drafts drawn on banks.
*Commerce.*
**T.B.** Treasury Bill.
*Finance.*
**TB** Tuberculosis.
Tuberculosis is a chronic infectious disease. It is also known as: Consumption; Phthisis.
*Medicine.*
**T.B.A.** Television Bureau of Advertising.
**tba** to be advised; to be agreed.
**TBA**; **tba** To Be Announced.
**TBAF** Tetrabutylammonium Fluoride.
*Chemistry.*
**TB and S** Top, Bottom and Sides.
**TBARS** Thiobarbituric Acid-Reactive Substances.
*Lipid Peroxidation; Medicine.*
**TBB** Taux de Base Bancaire.
French initialism meaning: Bank Base Rate; Prime; Prime Rate.
**TBCE** type "B" cost estimate.
estimate de coût de type "B" (ECTB).
**TBD** To Be Determined.
**TBE** Tick-Borne / Tickborne Encephalitis.
TBE is a viral infection of the central nervous system which can lead to swelling of the brain and coma.
**TBF** Transferts Banque de France (France).
TBF started functioning in Euro on 1st January 1999.
**TBG** Thyroid-Binding Globulin.
*Medicine.*
**TBE** Total Binding Energy.
TBE is also known as: BE (Binding Energy).
*Physics.*
**TBF** Tunable Bandpass Filter.
For high accuracy tuning.
**TBG** Thyroxine-Binding Globulin.
*Endocrinology.*
**TBHQ** Tertiary Butylhydroquinone.
**T.Bil.** Total Bilirubin.
**TB/L** Through Bill of Lading.
**TBLC** Tampa Bay Library Consortium.
**TBM** tactical ballistic missile.
missile balistique tactique.
**TBMD** tactical ballistic missile defence.
défense contre les missiles balistiques tactiques.
**TBO** Time Between Overhaul.
**$Tb_2O_3$** Terbia.
Terbia is also known as: Terbium Oxide.
*Inorganic Chemistry.*
**TBOL** TES thermal BOLometer.
For further details see under: **TES** and **THEMIS**.
**T-BOND** (abbr.) Treasury Bond.
**TBP** TATA-box Binding Protein.
*Molecular and Cell Biology; Neurodegeneration; Genetics.*
**TBP** Thyroxine Binding Protein.
*Medicine.*
**TBP** Tri-(n-Butyl) Phosphate.
**TBPA** Thyroxine Binding Pre Albumin.
*Medicine.*
**TBR** Treasury Bill Rate.
*Business; Economics; Finance.*
**tbs** tablespoon, tablespoonful.
Also: **tb**; **tbsp**.
*Metrology.*
**TBS** Tecnologie Biomediche e Sanitarie.
**TBS** Theta Burst Stimulation.
*Neuroscience.*
**TBS** Tokyo Broadcasting System (Japan).
**TBT** Taux des Bons du Trésor.
**TBTA** Taux des Bons du Trésor Américain.
**TBW** Total Body Weight.

**T$_c$** Curie temperature.
Named after the French physicists Marie and Pierre **Curie**.
*Electromagnetism.*
**TC** Tape Crease; Target Computer.
*Computer Technology.*
**TC** Tax Certificate.
**T.C.** Taxes Comprises.
French initialism meaning: Taxes Included.
**TC** Teachers College.
**Tc** The chemical symbol for Technetium.
Technetium is an element having the atomic number 43. It is derived from the fission products of uranium and plutonium. It is used mainly in nuclear medicine.
*Chemistry; Symbols.*
**T.C.** Technical College.
**tc** Telecommunications.
The term telecommunications refers to communications over long distances.
*Electronics.*
**TC** Terminal Control.
*Space Technology.*
**TC** 1. Terminology Coordinator [NSA].
1. Coordonnateur de la terminologie [AON].
2. tidal current.
2. courant de marcé.
3. traduction en clair.
3. human-readable interpretation (HRI).
4. transit corridor.
4. couloir de transit.
5. United Arab Emirates.
5. Émirats arabes unis.
**TC** Terra-Cotta.
Terra-cotta is a clay material used mainly in the production of tile floors, roofing, and earthenware. Terra-cotta is an Italian term that means: "baked earth".
*Materials.*
**TC** Thermocale.
The TC is a thermochemical Database and Software system developed at the Stockholm Royal Institute of Technology.
*Materials Science and Engineering; Thermochemical Databases; Software Systems.*
**TC** Till Countermanded.
**T.C.** Time Charter.
**TC** Timer Clock.
*Computer Technology.*
**Tc** Tomografia computerizzata.
Italian initialism meaning: Computerized Tomography.
**T.C.** Town Clerk; Town Councillor.
**T.C.** Training Center.
**T.C.** Traveller's Cheque/Check.
**TC** Treasury Certificate; Trust Company.
**TCA** 1. track continuity area.
1. zone de continuité de piste(s).
2. trainer/cargo aircraft.
2. avion de transport de l'entraînement.
**TCA** 1,1,1-Trichloroethane.
TCA is a synthetic organic solvent and an environmental pollutant. It is used as an industrial solvent.
*Microbial Ecology; Molecular Genetics.*
**TCA** Tricyclic Antidepressants.
*Drugs.*
**TCA acid** Trichloroacetic acid.
Used mainly in medicine and pharmaceuticals.
*Organic Chemistry.*
**TCA cycle** Tricarboxylic Acid cycle.
Also: Citric Acid Cycle; Krebs cycle.
Named after the British biochemist Sir Hans Adolf **Krebs**.
*Biochemistry.*
**TCAG** TIGR Center for the Advancement of Genomics.
*Microbial Genomics; Clean Energy Products.*
For further details see under: **TIGR**.
**TCAM** Telecommunications Access Method.
**TCAs** Tricyclic Antidepressants.
*Psychiatry; Psychology; Psychopharmacology; Psychotherapies.*
**TCB** Tetracarboxybutane.
**TCB** Touring Club Royal de Belgique (Belgium).
**TCBC** Trichlorobenzylchloride.
**TCBM** Transcontinental Ballistic Missile.
*Ordnance.*
**TCC** Tethys Circumglobal Current.
*Oceanic Sciences; Paleobiogeography.*
**TCC** Trade Compliance Center (U.S.A.).
At the U.S. Commerce Department. The TCC monitors, investigates and evaluates foreign compliance with standards of conduct and international agreements.
**TCC** traffic coordination centre.
centre de coordination du trafic.
**TCCE** type "C" cost estimate.
estimation de coût de type "C" (ECTC).
**TCCS** Texas Center for Climate Studies.
Texas A&M University, Texas, U.S.A.
*Research Programs.*
**Tcd.** (abbr.) traced.
Also: **TRD**.
**TCD** Trinity College Dublin (Ireland).
**TCDCA** Taurine CDCA.
For further details see under: **CDCA**.

**TCDD** Tetrachlorodibenzodioxin.
**TCDM** Tilted Cold Dark Matter.
*Astronomy; Astrophysics; Physics.*
**TCDMS** Telecommunication/Data Management System.
**TCE** Trichloroethylene.
TCE is used mainly in dry cleaning and in organic synthesis.
*Organic Chemistry.*
**TCF** technical control facility.
installation (ou site) de contrôle technique.
**Tcf-Lef family** T cell factor-Lymphoid enhancer binding factor family.
*Medicine; Neurogenetics; Pathology.*
**TCFU** Total Colony Forming Units.
**TCGF** T-Cell Growth Factor.
**TCGF** Thymocyte stimulating Growth Factor.
*Medicine.*
**TCID** Tissue Culture Infectious Doses.
*Gynecology; Newborn Medicine; Obstetrics; Pediatrics; Radiology; Veterinary Medicine; Veterinary Pathology; Viral Pathogenesis.*
**TCM** Thermal Conduction Module.
**TCM** torpedo countermeasures.
mesures antitorpilles.
**TCM** Traditional Chinese Medicine.
*Cancer; Composite Herbal Formulas; Dermatology; Herbal Medicines; Resistance to Conventional Therapies.*
**TCMH** Teneur Corpusculaire Moyenne en Hémoglobine.
French initialism meaning: Mean Corpuscular Hemoglobin Content.
*Medicine.*
**TCMI** T-Cell-Mediated Immunity.
**TCN** troop contributing nation.
pays fournissant des troupes (ou pays contributeur).
**TCNQ** Tetracyanoquinodimethane.
**TCO** tactical control officer.
officier chargé du contrôle tactique (ou officier contrôleur tactique).
**TCO** Tin-based Composite Oxide.
**TCO**; **Tco** Total Cost of Ownership.
**TCOM** Texas College of Osteopathic Medicine.
At Fort Worth, Texas, U.S.A.
**t-commerce** television commerce.
**TCP** 1. tactical command post.
1. poste de commandmeent tactique.
2. traffic control post.
2. poste du contrôle du trafic.
**TCP** Technical Cooperation Program.
Of the U.S. DOD.
For further details see under: **DOD**.
**TCP** Tool-Center Point.
*Robotics.*
**TCP** Transmission Control Program.
In 1978 the TCP became TCP/IP.
For further details see under: **TCP/IP**.
**TCP** 2,4,6-Trichlorophenol.
TCP is used maninly as a fungicide and herbicide.
*Organic Chemistry.*
**TCP** Tricresyl Phosphate.
Tricresyl Phosphate is used mainly as a plasticizer, lubricant additive, and fire retardant.
**TCP** Tropical Cyclone Program.
Of the U.N. WMO.
For further details see under: **WMO**.
**TCP/IP** Transmission Control Program / Internet Protocol.
**TCPP** Tetra-p-Chlorophenylpyrrole.
**TCP phases** Topologically Close-Packed phases.
*Materials Science.*
**TCR** Taylor Creek Rhyolite.
*Geology; Physics.*
**TCR** T-Cell Receptor.
For further details see under: **TCRs**.
**TC relay neurons** Thalamocortical relay neurons.
**TCR process** Transcription-Coupled Repair process.
*Aging; Genetics; Life Sciences; Medicine; Microbiology; Radiation Oncology.*
**TCRs** T-Cell Receptors.
*Blood Research; Immunology; Medicine.*
**TCs** Technical Committees.
**TCS** Tecnologie per i Componenti e Sottosistemi.
**TCS** Tool-Coordinate system.
*Robotics.*
**TCS** Touring Club Suisse (Switzerland).
**TCSPC** Time-Correlated Single Photon Counting.
**TCS programme** Teaching Company Scheme programme.
**TCT** Tracheal Cytotoxin.
*Biologics Evaluation; Medicine; Microbiology; Molecular Biology; Whooping Cough Pathology.*
**TCTNB** Trichlorotrinitrobenzene.
**TCTP** Tetrachlorothiophene.
**TCU** Transmission Control Unit.
**TCV** Turnip Crinkle Virus.
*Virus-associated RNAs.*
For further details see under: **RNA**.
**TD** Take Down / Takedown.
*Computer Technology; Computer Programming.*
**TD** Tank Destroyer.
1. division de chars.
2. Trinidad and Tobago.

2. Trinité-et-Tobago.
**TD** Tardive Dyskinesia.
*Side-effects of drugs; Medicine.*
**T.D.** Telephone Department.
**TD** Test Data.
The term test data refers to data used to test computer systems.
*Computer Programming.*
**TD** Test Driver.
*Computer Programming.*
**TD** Theoretical Density.
**TD** Time Delay.
*Physics.*
**TD** Time Deposit.
**TD** Touchdown.
*Aviation.*
**TD** Transmitter-Distributor.
*Electricity.*
**TD**; **T.D.** Treasury Department.
**TD** Trust Deed.
*Business; Commerce; Finance.*
**TD** Tunisia Dinar.
**TDA** 1. tactical decision aid.
1. aide à la prise de décisions au niveau tactique.
2. temporary danger area.
2. zone de danger temporaire.
3. torpedo danger area.
3. zone de danger de torpillage.
**TDA** Tax Deposit Account.
**TDA** Tornado Detection Algorithm.
**TDA** Trade and Development Agency (U.S.A.).
**TDAE** Tetrakisdimethylaminoethylene.
**TDB** Technology Development Branch.
**TDB** Toxicology Data Bank.
**TDBL** Total Dendritic Branch Lengths.
*Cell Biology; Neuroscience.*
**TDBP** Tri-(Di-Butyl) Phosphate.
**TDC** Top Dead Center.
*Mechanical Engineering.*
**TDD** Teletype Device for the Deaf.
**TDE** Tetrachlorodiphenylethane.
**TDEM** Télédetection Électromagnetique.
**TDEV** Taxe Départementale d'Espaces Verts (France).
**TDF** territorial defence force.
force de défense territoriale.
**TDF** Testis-Determining Factor.
*Developmental Biology; Mammalian Sex Determination; Molecular Biology.*
**Tdh** Terre des hommes (Lausanne, Switzerland).
*Charitable Organizations.*
**TDH** Texas Department of Health (U.S.A.).
**TDHF** Time-Dependent Hartree-Fock.
**TDI** TACAN distance indicator.
indicateur de distance TACAN.
**TDI** Toluene 2,4-Diisocyanate.
TDI is used mainly to make elastomers.
*Organic Chemistry.*
**Tdk** Thymidine kinase.
*Genetics; Medical Research; Microbiology.*
**TDL** Test du Lendemain.
French initialism meaning: Day After Recall.
*Economics; Business; Finance.*
**TDL** Tunable-Diode Laser.
**TDLU** Terminal Ductal-Lobular Unit.
*Breast Cancer; Medicine; Pathology.*
**TDM** Time-Division Multiplexer.
*Telecommunications.*
**TDM** Tomodensitométrie.
French initialism meaning: Computer Tomography.
*Medicine.*
**TDMA** Time-Division Multiple Access.
*Cellular Phones.*
**TDNs** Total Digestible Nutrients.
*Agriculture.*
**T-DNA**; **tDNA** transfer DNA.
For further details see under: **DNA**.
**TDOA** Time Deposit Open Account.
**TDP** technical data package.
dossier technique.
**TDP** Technical Demonstration Program.
*Computer Security; Information Technology Development.*
**TDP** Telugu Desam Party (India).
**TDP** Thiamine Diphosphate.
**TDP** Traffic Data Processor.
*Computers.*
**TDQP** Trimethyldihydroquinoline Polymer.
**TDR** Time Delay Relay.
*Electricity.*
**TDR** Time-Domain Reflectometer.
The time-domain reflectometer is an instrument used to measure the electrical characteristics of components, lines, systems, and the like.
*Electronics.*
**TDR** Tropical Diseases Research.
*Parasitology.*
**TDR Program** Tropical Diseases Research Program (U.S.A.).
Of the WHO and the U.S. Department HHS.
For further details see under: **WHO**, **HHS** and **WB**.
**TDRSS** Tracking and Data Relay Satellite System.
**TDS** 1. tactical data system.
1. système de données tactiques.
2. target designation system.

2. système de désignation d'objectifs.
**TDS** Thermal Desorption Spectra.
*Physical Chemistry; Physics.*
**TDS** Thermal Desorption Spectrometry.
**TDS** Time-Dependent Sensitization.
*Psychiatry; Psychology; Psychopharmacology.*
**TDS** Transcranial Doppler-Sonography.
**Td-Scdma** Time division Synchronous-Cdma.
**TdT** Terminal deoxytransferase.
**TdT** (circuit de) Traitement de Trame.
**TDTS** tactical data transfer system.
système de transfert de données tactiques.
**TDU** Tongue Display Unit.
*Electrical Stimulators; Neuroscience; Surgical Tools.*
**TDW** Dead-Weight Tonnage.
**TDWR** Terminal Doppler Weather Radar.
**TDY** Temporary Duty.
**TDZ** torpedo danger zone.
zone d'efficacité des torpilles.
**TDZ** Touch-Down Zone.
*Navigation.*
**TE** Table of Equipment.
**TE** Tape Editor.
The tape editor is used to edit, and correct data on tapes.
*Computer Programming.*
**TE** 1. task element.
1. élément opérationnel.
2. training equipment.
2a. matériel d'instruction/d'entraînement.
2b. matériel didactique.
**TE** Taux d'Escompte.
**TE** Tax Exemption.
**Te** Tellurium.
Used mainly in alloys.
*Chemistry; Symbols.*
**TE** Tension Électrique.
**TE** Teramo, Italy.
**TE** Terminal Equipment.
*Telecommunications.*
**Te** Tetanus.
*Neurology; Pathology.*
**TE** Thermodynamic Equilibrium.
**TE** Thioesterase.
**TE** Timing Error.
*Computer Programming.*
**TE** Tissue Engineering.
**TE** Total Earnings.
**TE** Total Energy.
**TE** Totally Enclosed.
*Electricity.*
**TE** Trailing Edge.
*Aviation; Electronics.*
**TE** Transposable Element.
For further details see under: **TEs**.
**TE** Trazione Elettrica.
Italian acronym meaning: Electric Traction.
**TE** Trésorerie d'Exploitation.
**TEA** Tetraethylammonium.
**TEA** Transferred-Electron Amplifier.
**TEA** Triethanolamine.
$(HOCH_2CH_2)_3N$. Triethanolamine, also known as: Tris(2-Hydroxyethyl) Amine, is used mainly in cosmetics, wood scouring, and detergents.
*Organic Chemistry.*
**TEAC** Tetraethylammonium Chloride.
$(C_2H_5)_4NCl$. Tetraethylammonium Chloride also known as: TEA Chloride, is used mainly in medicine.
*Organic Chemistry.*
**TEAM** Team-based European Automotive Manufacture.
*European Community Project.*
**TEA pressure laser** Transversely Excited Atmospheric pressure laser.
*Optics.*
**TEAS** Trademark Electronic Application System.
**TEB** Tax-Exempt Bond.
*Business; Finance.*
**TeBG** Testosterone-estradiol-Binding Globulin.
**TEBP** Telomere End-Binding Protein.
*Biochemistry; Cell Biology; Chemistry; Human Genetics; Medicine; Molecular Biology; Molecular Genetics.*
**$TeBr_2$** Tellurium Dibromide.
Tellurium Dibromide is also known as: Tellurous Bromide; Tellurium Bromide.
*Inorganic Chemistry.*
**TEC** tableau d'effectifs du temps de crise.
crisis establishment (CE 4.).
**TEC** Techniques Européennes de Commutation.
**TEC** Terena Executive Committee.
For further details see under: **TERENA**.
**TEC** Thermionic Energy Converter.
**TEC** Texas Employment Commission.
The TEC is located in Austin, Texas, U.S.A.
**TEC** Total Electron Content.
**Te calorimeter** Tissue equivalent calorimeter.
**tech** (abbr.) technical; technician; technology.
*Engineering; Science.*
**TECH REPT** (abbr.) Technical Report.
**$TeCl_2$** Tellurium Dichloride.
$TeCl_2$ is also known as: Tellurous Chloride; Tellurium Chloride.
*Inorganic Chemistry.*

**TECODIS** TEleworking in COoperative Development of Industrial Software.
*European Community Project.*
**TECRO** Taiwan's Economic and Cultural Representative Office.
TECRO has replaced **CCNAA** (Coordination Council for North American Affairs).
**TECs** Thymic Epithelial Cells.
*Immunology.*
**TECs**; **Tecs** Training and Enterprise Councils (G.B.).
*Business Links Network.*
**TECSI** TECniques et Systèmes Informatiques.
**TECSICA** TEchnology and Characterization of SIlicon Carbide films for high temperature Applications.
*European Community Project.*
**TED** tableau d'effectifs et de dotation.
table of organization and equipment (TO&E).
**TED** Tax-Exempt Dividend.
*Business; Economics; Finance.*
**TED** Technology, Ethics and Dementia.
**ted.** (abbr.) tedesco.
Italian abbreviation meaning: German.
**TED** Tele-Education and Vocational Training for Disabled people.
A 3-year project of the European Program Leonardo da Vinci.
**TED** Tenders Electronic Daily.
**TED** Total Energy Demand.
**TED** Total Energy Detector.
**ted** (abbr.) traced.
**TED** Turtle Excluder Device.
**TEDA** Triethylenediamine.
**TED/GWP** Total Energy Demand/Gross World Product.
**TEDIS** Trade Electronic Data Interchange Systems.
*European Community Program.*
**TEDP** Tetraethyldithionopyrophosphate.
**TEE** Trans-Europe Express.
**TEED** Training, Enterprise and Education Directorate.
Department of Employment (G.B.).
**TEESURA** Techno Economic Evaluation and Sectorial User Requirements Analysis.
*European Community Project.*
**TEF** Test and Evaluation Facility.
**$TeF_6$** Tellurium Hexafluoride.
*Inorganic Chemistry.*
**TEFAF**; **Tefaf** The European Fine Art Fair (Maastricht, The Netherlands).
**TEFL** Teaching English as a Foreign Language.
**TEG** tableau d'effectifs du temps de guerre.
war establishment (WE).
**TEG** Taux Effectif Global.
French acronym meaning: Annual Percentage Rate.
*Business; Economics; Finance.*
**TEG** Tetraethylene Glycol.
TEG is used as a solvent.
*Organic Chemistry.*
**TEG** Thrombo-élastogramme.
*Medicine.*
**TEG** Triethylene Glycol.
TEG is used mainly as a humectant; solvent; and pesticizer.
**TEHP** Total Equivalent Horsepower.
**TEI** Traitement Electronique de l'Information.
**TEIS** Trans European Information Systems.
The Trans European Information Systems were set up by Olivetti, Bull and Siemens-Nixdorf in order to develop projects for compatible information systems in Europe based on common system and software applications.
**TEIs** Transmission Electron Images.
**Tel**; **tel** (abbr.) telegram; telegraph.
Also: **tg.**; **tlg.**
**Tel**; **tel** (abbr.) telephone.
The telephone was patented by Alexander Graham Bell, its inventor, on 7th March, 1876.
*Telecommunications.*
For further details see under: **tph**.
**TEL** Tetraethyl Lead.
The elimination of tetraethyl lead from gasoline reduces blood-lead levels particularly in infants.
*Economics; Engineering; Environmental Engineering.*
**TEL** transporter erector-launcher.
véhicule-rampe.
**TELAR** transporter-erector-launcher and radar.
véhicule de transport érecteur-lanceur et radar.
**telcos.** (abbr.) telecommunication companies; telecoms operators.
**TELECOMM** Telecomunicaciones de Mexico.
**TELEX** (abbr.) Telegraph Exchange.
**TELOPS** Telemetry Online Processing System.
**TEM** target engagement message.
message d'engagement de la cible (de l'objectif).
**TEM** Transmission Electron Microscope.
**TEM** Triethylenemelamine.
TEM, also known as: Tetramine, is used mainly in medicines.
*Organic Chemistry.*
**TEMA** Training, Education, and Mutual Assistance.
**TE mode** Transverse Electric mode.
*Optical Physics.*

**temp.** (abbr.) temperature.
Also: **t.**
*Medicine; Meteorology; Physiology; Thermodynamics.*
**temp.** (abbr.) temporary.
**TEMPO** Tetramethylpiperidinyloxy.
**TEM wave** Transverse Electromagnetic wave.
*Electromagnetism.*
**TEN** Toxic Epidermal Necrolysis.
TEN is also known as: Lyell's Syndrome; Toxic Bullous Epidermolysis.
*Biochemistry; Dermatology; Lyell's Syndrome; Pathology.*
**Tenn.** (abbr.) Tennessee, U.S.A.
**TENS** Transcutaneous Electrical Nerve Stimulator.
The transcutaneous Electrical Nerve Stimulator, also known as Transdermal Electrical Nerve Stimulator is actually a portable device that sends electric impulses on a body part to relieve pain.
*Medicine.*
**TENs initiative** Trans European Networks initiative.
*European Union Programs; Transport Networks.*
**TEO** Tecnologie Elettroottiche.
Italian acronym meaning: Electro-optical Technologies.
**TeO** Tellurium Monoxide.
*Inorganic Chemistry.*
**$TeO_2$** Tellurite.
*Mineralogy.*
**$TeO_2$** Tellurium Dioxide.
Tellurium Dioxide is also known as: Tellurous Acid Anhydride.
*Inorganic Chemistry.*
**TEOS** Tetraethoxysilane.
*Chemistry.*
**TEP** tableau d'effectifs du temps de paix.
peace establishment (PE 2.).
**TEP** Thioester-containing Protein.
For further details see under: **TEPs**.
**TEP** Tonnellate Equivalenti di Petrolio.
Italian acronym meaning: Tons of Oil Equivalent.
**TEP** Triethyl Phosphate.
Used mainly as a solvent.
*Organic Chemistry.*
**TEPA** Taiwan Environmental Protection Agency.
**TEPI** Total Expenditures Productivity Index (U.S.A.).
Developed at the University of Arizona's Center for the Study of Higher Education.
**TEPP** Tetraethyl Pyrophosphate.
TEPP is used as an insecticide.
*Organic Chemistry.*
**TEPs** Thioester-containing Proteins.
*Entomology; Epidemiology; Medicine; Microbiology; Molecular Biology; Molecular Parasitology.*
**TEPs** Traded Endowment Policies.
*Investments.*
**TER** Transepithelial Electrical Resistance.
**T-E ratio** Temperature-Efficiency ratio.
**TERAVISION** Terahertz Frequency Imaging and Biomedical & Other Applications.
An EC funded project involving academic and industrial collaboration from across Europe.
*Ultrafast Optoelectronics.*
**TERC** Twining Employment Resource Centre (G.B.).
**TERCOM** terrain contour matching (system).
(système de) suivi de terrain à corrélation topographique.
**TERCOM** TERrain COrrelation Matching.
**TEREC** Tactical Electronic REConnaissance.
**TERENA** Trans-European Research and Education Networking Association.
Formed in October 1994 by the merger of RARE and EARN.
For further details see under: **TEC**; **TTC**; **RARE** and **EARN**.
**TERI** Tata Energy Research Institute (New Delhi, India).
**TERI** Terrestrial Ecosystems Research Initiative - E.C.
*Environment and Climate Programs.*
**term.** (abbr.) termination.
*Computer Science; Electromagnetism; Materials Science.*
**TEROC** Tobacco Education and Research Oversight Committee (U.S.A.).
*Tobacco Studies.*
For further details see under: **TRDRP** (Tobacco-Related Disease Research Program).
**terr.** (abbr.) terreno.
Italian abbreviation meaning: ground; land; plot.
**terr.** (abbr.) territorio.
Italian abbreviation meaning: territory; possessions (pl.).
**TERT** (catalytic) TElomerase Reverse Transcriptase.
*Biochemistry; Molecular Genetics; Oncology.*
**$TeS_2$** Tellurium Disulfide.
Tellurium Disulfide is also known as: Tellurium Sulfide.
*Inorganic Chemistry.*
**TES** Thermal Emission Spectrometer.
**TES** Thermal Energy Storage.

**TES** Text-Editing System.
*Computer Programming.*
**Tes** Transposable elements.
*RNA Silencing.*
**TES** Tropospheric Emission Sensor.
*Environmental Technology; Medicine; Science.*
**TESL** Teaching English as a Second Language.
**TESLA** Tera-electron-volt Energy Superconducting Linear Accelerator.
*Particle Physics; Nuclear Physics; Superconducting Technology.*
**TESOL** Teachers of English to Speakers of Other Languages.
**tess.** (abbr.) tessera.
Italian abbreviation meaning: card; ticket; membership card.
**tess.** (abbr.) tessili (prodotti).
Italian abbreviation meaning: textiles.
**tess.** (abbr.) tessuti.
Italian abbreviation meaning: fabrics.
**TESSA** Tax-Exempt Special Savings Account.
**TESSACE** terrorism, espionage, sabotage and subversion directed against ACE.
terrorisme, espionage, sabotage et subversion dirigés contre le CAE.
**TET** Thermometric Enthalpy Titration.
**TETD** Tetraethylthiuram Disulfide.
**TETR** Tokamak Engineering Test Reactor.
**TETS** Transcutaneous Energy Transmission Systems.
For further details se under: **TAH devices**.
**TeTxLC** Tetanus Toxin Light Chain.
**TEU** tableau d'effectifs d'urgence.
emergency establishment (EE).
**TEV** Total Economic Value.
**TeV** Trillion electron-Volt.
**TE wave** Transverse Electric wave.
*Electromagnetism.*
**TEW project** Transport and Equatorial Waters project.
**TEX** Teletype EXchange.
**TEX** (abbr.) Telex.
**Tex.** (abbr.) Texas, U.S.A.
**TEXONO** Taiwan Experiment On Neutrinos.
A Taiwan-China Collaboration.
**TEXPROCIL** The Cotton Textiles Export Promotion Council of India (India).
**TEZ** total exclusion zone [SFOR].
zone d'exclusion totale [SFOR].
**TF** Tag Field; Tag Format.
*Computer Programming.*
**TF** 1. task force.
1. force opérationnelle.
2. temporary filled military post.
2. poste militaire pourvu temporairement.
3. terrain following [missile].
3. suivi de terrain [missile].
**TF** Temporary File.
The temporary file is created for temporary use and is destroyed afterwards.
*Computer Programming.*
**TF** Territorial Force.
*Military.*
**TF** Test File.
*Computer Programming.*
**TF** Tile Floor.
*Buildings.*
**TF** Till Forbidden.
**TF** Tissue Factor.
*Angiogenesis; Antiangiogenesis Drugs; Cancer Research; Medicine.*
**TF** Toroidal Field.
**TF** Torpedo Factory.
*Military.*
**TF** Transfer Factor.
Transfer factor is also known as: Transfer constant.
*Engineering.*
**TF** Transfer Function.
*Control Systems.*
**TF** Transition Function.
*Computer Technology.*
**TF** Tropical Fresh (water).
*Shipping.*
**TFA** toxic-free area.
zone exempte de toxiques.
**TFA** Trifluoroacetic Acid.
*Chemistry.*
**TFAP** Tropical Forestry Action Plan.
*Tropical Forest Conservation; Zoology.*
**TFBP** Thermal Fuels Behavior Program.
**TFCS** Treasury Financial Communication System (U.S.A.).
**TFE** Tetrafluoroethylene.
TFE is used as a monomer.
*Organic Chemistry.*
**TFE** Trifluoroethanol.
**TFEWR** Through-Focus Exit Wave Reconstruction.
*Applied Physics; Crystallography; Materials Science.*
**TFF** Tangential Flow Filtration.
**TFGT** Task Force on Genetic Testing.
The TFGT is a U.S. independent Government Advisory Group.
**TFI** The Fertilizer Institute.
**Tn** Transposon of fission yeast 1.
**TFL1** Terminal Flower 1.

*Botany; Plant Evolution.*
**TF line** Terrestrial Fractionation line.
*Earth and Space Sciences.*
**TFME** Thin-Film Mercury Electrode.
**TFMSA** Trifluoromethane Sulfonic Acid.
**TFOs** Triplex-Forming Oligonucleotides.
*Genetics; Molecular Medicine; Therapeutic Radiology.*
**TFR** terrain-following radar.
radar de suivi de terrain.
**tfr.** (abbr.) transfer.
Also: **trf.**; **trs.**
*Computer Programming; Mining Engineering; Navigation; Robotics; Transportation Engineering.*
**TFR** Trattamento Fine Rapporto.
Italian initialism meaning: retirement indemnity.
**TFS** tropospheric forward scatter.
tropodiffusion.
**TF subduction** Tonga-Fiji subduction.
*Geological Sciences; Tectonics.*
**TFT** Thin-Film Transistor.
*Organic Transistors.*
**TFT-LCDs** TFT-Liquid Crystal Displays.
For further details see under: **TFT**.
**TFTP** Trivial File Transfer Protocol.
**TFTR** Tokamak Fusion Test Reactor.
*Energy Research; Fusion.*
**TFTs** Thin-Film Transistors.
*Organic Transistors.*
**tg.** (abbr.) tangente.
Italian abbreviation meaning: tangent.
Also: **tang.**
*Mathematics.*
**TG** Tangible Goods.
**TG** Task Group (U.S.A.).
*Military.*
**TG** Telegiornale (Italy).
**tg.** (abbr.) telegraph.
Also: **Tel**; **tel**.
**TG** Terminal Guidance.
*Navigation; Space Technology.*
**TG** Text Generation.
*Artificial Intelligence.*
**TG** Thermogravimetry.
**TG** Togo's international vehicle registration letter.
**TG** Trésorerie Générale (France).
**TG** Trigeminal Ganglion.
**TG**; **t.g.** Type Genus.
*Systematics.*
**TGA** Thermogravimetric Analysis.
TGA is used in quantitative analysis.
*Analytical Chemistry.*
**TGA** Trace Gas Analysis.
**Tg animal** Transgenic animal.
The Tg animal is an animal with cloned genetic material.
*Molecular Biology.*
**TGC** Tripartite Gold Commission.
(Nazy Gold Fund).
**TGC** Tubular Graphite Cone.
For further details see under: **TGCs**.
**TGCs** Tubular Graphite Cones.
*Carbon Morphology; Quantum Structures; Surface Physics.*
For further details see under: **MPCVD**.
**TGED** Tarif Général Européen de Détail.
**TGEV** Transmissible Gastroenteritis Virus.
**TGF** Transforming Growth Factor.
*Biochemistry.*
**TGI** Tribunal de Grande Instance.
French initialism meaning: County Court.
**tgl** (abbr.) toggle.
*Electronics; Mechanical Devices; Mechanical Engineering.*
**TGM** 1. television-guided missile.
1. missile à guidage par télévision.
2. terminally-guided munition.
2. munition à guidage terminal.
**TGMH** Teneur Globulaire Moyenne en Hémoglobine.
For further details see under: **TCMH** (Teneur Corpusculaire Moyenne en Hémoglobine).
**Tg(MHu2M) mice** transgenic mice expressing a chimeric mouse-human PrP gene.
*Biochemistry; Biophysics; Neurology; Neuropathology; Pathology; Prion Diseases.*
**TGN** Trans-Golgi Network.
Named for the Italian physician Camillo **Golgi**.
*Biomedical Science; Blood Research; Cell Biology; Genetics; Medicine; Metabolism.*
**TGO** Transaminase Glutamique Oxacétique.
**TGOS** Transaminase Glutamique Oxacétique du Sérum sanguin.
**TGP** Transaminase Glutamique Pyruvique.
**TGPS** Transaminase Glutamique Pyruvique du Sérum sanguin.
**TGR** Telegiornale Regionale (Italy).
**TGS** Telegiornale Sportivo (Italy).
**TGS** telemetry ground station.
station terrienne de télémétrie.
**TGs** Trigeminal Ganglia.
*Biomedical Science; Medicine; Ophthalmology; Veterinary Science.*
**TGS** Triglycine Sulfate.
**tgt** (abbr.) target.
*Atomic Physics; Computer Programming;*

*Electronics; Medicine; Military Science; Radiology.*
**TGT** Thromboplastin Generation Test.
**TGWU** Transport and General Workers Union (G.B.).
**TGZM** Temperature-Gradient Zone Melting.
*Materials Science.*
**TH** Tax Haven.
*Business; Finance.*
**TH** 1. Thailand.
1. Thailande.
2. transport helicopter.
2. hélicoptère de transport.
**Th** Thalamus.
*Anatomy.*
**th** thermie.
thermie is a unit of heat energy.
*Thermodynamics.*
**Th** Thorium.
Used mainly as a nuclear fuel.
**TH** Tyrosine Hydroxylase.
**THAAD system** Theater High-Altitude Area Defense system (U.S.A.).
*Antimissile Projects; Ordnance.*
**THAM** Tris (hydroxymethyl) aminomethane.
**THAM** Tromethamine.
Tromethamine, also known as: Trisamine, Trimethylol, is used mainly in rubber accelerators, and in pharmaceuticals.
*Organic Chemistry.*
**THAA** Total Hydrolyzable Amino Acids.
**THC** Tetrahydrocannabinol.
*Organic Chemistry.*
**THC** Thermo-Haline Circulation (North Atlantic).
*Climate Change; Earth Science; Geology; Geophysics; Polar Science.*
**THC** Thermohaline Convection.
*Oceanography.*
**$ThC_2$** Thorium Carbide.
$ThC_2$ is used as a nuclear fuel.
*Inorganic Chemistry.*
**THC assemblies** Tentative Human Consensus assemblies.
**$ThCl_4$** Thorium Chloride.
Thorium Chloride, also known as: Thorium Tetrachloride, is used in incandescent lighting.
*Inorganic Chemistry.*
**THD** (abbr.) thread.
*Design Engineering; Geology; Hydrology; Mining Engineering; Textiles.*
**THD+N** Total Harmonic Distortion plus Noise.
**Th-Em** (abbr.) Thorium-Emanation.
*Chemistry.*
**THEMIS** THermal EMission Imaging System.
The Mars Odyssey THEMIS has been used for thermal observations.
*Astrogeology; Geological Sciences; Geophysics.*
**theor.** (abbr.) theorem.
*Mathematics.*
**THEP** TOGA Heat Exchange Program.
For further details see under: **TOGA**.
**THESEUS** Terminal at High speed for European Stock Exchange USers.
*European Community Project.*
**THF** Tetrahydrofuran.
THF is used mainly as a solvent.
*Organic Chemistry.*
**$ThF_4$** Thorium Fluoride.
Thorium Fluoride is used mainly in high-temperature ceramics.
*Inorganic Chemistry.*
**THF** Thymic Humoral Factor.
The thymic humoral factor is also known as: Thymolymphopoietic Factor.
*Endocrinology.*
**THG experiments** Third-Harmonic Generation experiments.
*Chemistry; Molecular Electronics and Photonics; Optics and Lasers Research.*
**THHF** Tetrahydrohomofolate.
**THIR** Temperature-Humidity Infrared Radiometer.
**thk** (abbr.) thick.
**THN** territorial host nation.
pays hôte souverain.
**$ThO_2$** Thorianite.
*Mineralogy.*
**$ThO_2$** Thorium Dioxide.
Thorium Dioxide, also known as: Thorium Oxide; Thoria; Thorium Anhydride, is used mainly in nuclear fuel, ceramics, and medicine.
*Inorganic Chemistry.*
**THORP** THermal Oxide Reprocessing Plant (G.B.).
**THORS facility** Thermal-Hydraulic Out-of-Reactor Safety facility.
**THP** Take-Home Pay.
**THP** Tetrahydropapaveroline.
**thp** thrust horsepower.
*Aviation; Naval Architecture.*
**THPC** Tetrakis (Hydroxymethyl) Phosphonium Chloride.
THPC is used as a fabric flame retardant.
*Organic Chemistry.*
**THPMA** Tetrahydropyranyl methacrylate.
**Thr** Threonine.
*Biochemistry.*
**THRI** Tobacco and Health Research Institute.

THRI is located in Lexington, the University of Kentucky, KY, U.S.A.
**$ThSiO_4$** Huttonite.
Huttonite is found in beach sands.
*Mineralogy.*
**ThT** Thioflavine T.
Used mainly in fluorescent paints and textiles.
**THT** Très Haute Tension.
**THTF** Thermal-Hydraulic Test Facility.
**Thz** Terahertz.
Terahertz is a frequency unit equal to $10^{12}$Hz.
*Physics.*
**TI** Tajikistan.
**TI** Target Identification.
referring to radar, etc.
**TI** Terapia Intensiva.
**TI** Texas Instruments (U.S.A.).
*Semiconductors.*
**Ti** Titanium.
Used mainly in the production of pure hydrogen and in alloys.
*Chemistry.*
**TIA** Tax Institute of America (U.S.A.).
**TIA** Thanks In Advance.
**TIA** The Internet Adaptor.
**TIA** Transient Ischemic Attack.
TIA is also known as: mini-ictus.
*Medicine; Neurology.*
**TIAA-CREF** The Teachers Insurance and Annuity Association - College equities REtirement Fund.
Established as a nonprofit service organization by the Carnegie Foundation for the Advancement of Teaching (U.S.A.).
**TIALDS** thermal imagery airborne laser designator system.
système aéroporté d'illumination laser à imagerie thermique.
**TIB** Technische Informations Bibliothek (Germany).
**$TiB_2$** Titanium Boride.
Titanium Boride is used mainly in metallurgy.
*Inorganic Chemistry.*
**T.I.B.** (Office du) Tourisme et d'Information de Bruxelles (Belgium).
**TIBA** Triidrobenzoic Acid.
**TIBOR** Tokyo Interbank Offered Rate.
**TIBP** Tri-(Iso-Butyl) Phosphate.
**TIC** 1. tactical intelligence centre.
1. centre de renseignement tactique.
2. toxic industrial chemical.
2. (produit) chimique industriel toxique.
**TIC** Technical Institute Council.
**TiC** Titanium Carbide.
Titanium carbide is used mainly in tungsten-carbide tools and arc-melting electrodes.
*Basic Energy Science; Inorganic Chemistry; Materials Science; Physics of Thin Films; Superlattice Technology; Vacuum Coaters.*
**TIC** Total Ion Chromatogram.
**TIC** Tripsin Inhibiting Capacity.
*Medicine.*
**tic** The above acronyms were coined using the English word "tic" (*Neurology*) which has the some meaning in French and Italian.
**$TiCl_3$** Titanium Trichloride.
Titanium Trichloride, also known as: Titanous Chloride is used mainly as a reducing agent.
*Inorganic Chemistry.*
**TIDE** tactical international data exchange.
échange de données tactiques internationales.
**TIDE** Technology Initiative for Disabled and Elderly people.
*European Community Initiatives.*
**TIDE** Thermal Ion Dynamics Experiment.
*Geophysics; Space Science.*
**TIE** Total Industrial Engineering.
**TIE** Total Interlibrary Exchange.
**tie** The above acronyms were coined using the English word "tie".
*Civil Engineering; Electricity; Engineering; Mining Engineering.*
**TIEHH** The Institute of Environmental and Human Health (U.S.A.).
**TIE receptors** Tyrosine kinase with Immunoglobulin and EGF-like domains receptors.
*Angiogenesis; Antiangiogenesis Drugs; Cancer Research; Medicine; Pharmaceuticals.*
**TIES** Telford Institute of Environmental Systems.
An interdisciplinary research centre based in the School of Environment and Life Sciences, University of Salford, G.B.
**TIES** Trophic Interactions in Estuarine Systems.
TIES is a U.S. National Science Foundation project. It was launched in 1995.
*Chemistry and Biology of the Oceans; Estaurine Ecology.*
**TIIF** tactical imaginery interpretation facility.
installation tactique d'interprétation photographique.
**TIF** Tasso di trasferimento Interno dei Fondi.
Italian acronym meaning: Rate of Internal capital transfer.
**TIF** Telephone Influence Factor.
*Telecommunications.*
**TIF** Trasporti Internazionali Ferroviari.

Italian acronym meaning: International Railway Transport.
**TIFF** Tagged Image File Format.
*Desktop Publishing Applications.*
**TIFR** Tata Institute of Fundamental Research (Mumbai, India).
**TIFR** Total Investment For Return.
*Business; Finance.*
**TIG** Time until IGnition.
TIG is also known as: Time of IGnition.
**TIGER** Topographically Integrated Geographical Encoding and Referencing.
TIGER is a system developed by the U.S. Bureau of Census and the U.S. Geological Survey.
*Map Files.*
**TIGET** Telethon Institute for Gene Therapy.
At the San Raffaele Hospital (Italy).
**TIGR** The Institute for Genomic Research.
The TIGR is based in Maryland (U.S.A.).
*Sequencing and Gene Analysis.*
For further details see under: **TCAG**.
**TIGR** Treasury Investment Growth Receipts (U.S.A.)
**TIGRIH** Towards Identifying the Gene Responsible for Idiopathic Haemochromatosis - E.C.
**TIGR protein** Trabecular Meshwork Inducible Gluco-corticoid Response protein.
*Genetics Research; Glaucoma; Molecular Biology; Molecular Genetics.*
**TI G welding** Tungsten Inert Gas welding.
*Technology.*
**$TiH_2$** Titanium Hydride.
Titanium Hydride is used mainly in metallurgy.
*Inorganic Chemistry.*
**TII; Tii** Technology Innovation-and-Information (Brussels).
**TIL** Tumor Infiltrating Lymphocytes.
**TILA** Truth-In-Lending Act (U.S.A.).
**TIM** Telecom Italia Mobile (Italy).
**T.I.M.E.** Technological Innovation Management Education.
**TIMPs** Tissue Inhibitors of Metalloproteinases.
**TIMS** Thermal Ionization Mass Spectrometry.
*Geology; Geophysics; Oceanography.*
**TIMs** Trust for Investments in Mortgages.
**TIMSS** Third International Mathematics and Science Study.
TIMSS is a huge test involving three grade levels and fifty countries.
*School Performance; Science Education Improvement.*
**TIN** Taxpayer Identification Number (U.S.A.).
**TiN** Titanium Nitride.
TiN is used mainly in alloys and semiconductors.
*Inorganic Chemistry.*
**TINA** There Is No Alternative (G.B.).
**tinc.** (abbr.) tincture.
Also: **tinct**.
*Materials.*
**$TiO_2$** Anatase.
$TiO_2$ is also known as: Octahedrite.
*Mineralogy.*
**$TiO_2$** Rutile.
*Mineralogy.*
**TIO** Taux Interbancaire Offert.
French acronym meaning: Interbank Offered Rate.
*Business; Economics; Finance.*
**TIO** Texas Institute of Oceanography (U.S.A.).
**$TiO_2$** Titanium Dioxide.
Titanium Dioxide, also known as: Titania; Titanic Anhydride; Titanium White, is used as a pigment.
*Inorganic Chemistry.*
**TiO** Titanium Oxide.
**$TiO_3$** Titanium Trioxide.
$TiO_3$ also known as: Pertitanic Acid; Titanello, is used mainly in dentistry.
*Inorganic Chemistry.*
**$Ti(OC_4H_9)_4$** Tetrabutyl Titanate.
Tetrabutyl Titanate, also known as: Titanium Butylate is used mainly as a catalyst.
*Organic Chemistry.*
**TIOT** Task Input/Output Table.
**TIP** target identification point.
point d'identification d'objectif.
**TIP** Tax-based Income Policy.
**TIP** Titre Interbancaire de Paiement.
French acronym meaning: Bank Giro Transfer.
**TIP** Total Individual Program.
A test to stop smoking.
**TIP** Traversing Incore Probe.
**tip** The above acronyms were coined using the English word "tip".
*Anatomy; Design Engineering; Electricity; Mechanical Engineering.*
**TIPH** Temporary International Presence in Hebron.
**TIPPSA** Technical Industrial Pharmacists and Pharmaceutical Scientists Association.
**TIPS** Terminal and host Interface Processors.
**TIPTOP** The Internet Pilot TO Physics.
A site that went up in 1994.
*Physics.*
**TIQ** Tetrahydroisoquinone.
**TIR** target-illuminating radar.
radar d'illumination d'objectif.
**TIR** Transport International Routier.

French acronym meaning: International Road Transport.

**TIRFM** Total Internal Reflection Fluorescence Microscopy.
*Biochemistry; Biological Sciences; Cellular Processes; Live Cell Imaging; Medicine.*

**TIRI** Taux Interne de Rentabilité Intégré (France).
*Banking.*

**TIROS** Television and Infrared Observation Satellite.

**TIS** Technological Information System.

**TIS** Trusted Information Systems.

**TIT** Test d'Immobilisation des Tréponèmes.
French acronym meaning: Nelson's Test; Treponema Pallidum Immobilization Test.
*Medicine.*

**TIT** Tokyo Institute of Technology (Japan).

**TIU** Toxicologically Insignificant Usage.

**TIWE** Tropical Instability Wave Experiment.

**TIWs** Tropical Instability Waves.
*Atmospheric Science; Climatology; Meteorology; Geophysics.*

**tjb** tonnes de jauge brute.

**TJS** tactical jamming system.
système de brouillage tactique.

**tk** (abbr.) tank.
For further details see under: **t**.

**TK** Thymidine Kinase.
*Enzymology.*

**tk** (abbr.) truck.
*Mechanical Engineering.*

**TKA** Thermokinetic Analysis.
*Analytical Chemistry.*

**TKD** Tokodynamometer.

**TKE** Turbulent Kinetic Energy.

**TKG** Tokodynagraph.

**TKP** Tripotassium Phosphate.

**TKPP** Tetrapotassium Pyrophosphate.

**tkr** (abbr.) tanker.
Tanker is also known as: tankship.
*Naval Architecture.*

**TKSC** TsuKuba Space Center (Japan).

**TKV** Thickveins.
*Basic Sciences; Cancer Research; Genetics.*

**TL** Tabular Language.
*Computer Programming.*

**TL** Tape Library.
*Computer Technology.*

**TL** Target Language.
The target language is usually the language into which texts are translated from the source language.
*Linguistics.*

**TL** Taxe Locale.

**Tl** Thallium.
Thallium is used mainly in optical glass, and in thallium salts. The word thallium derives from the Greek term "green stalk".
*Chemistry; Symbols.*

**TL** Thermoluminescence.
*Atomic Physics.*

**TL** Time Loan.
*Business; Economics; Finance.*

**TL**; **T.L.** Trade List.

**TL** Trading Limit.
*Business; Commerce.*

**T.L.** Truck Load.
referring to large shipments that fill an entire truck.
*Freight; Shipping.*

**TLA** Talk Listen Analyzer.
A product developed by U.K. vendor call scan.

**TLA** Tanzania Library Association.

**TLA** Tennessee Library Association (U.S.A.).

**TLA** Texas Library Association (U.S.A.).

**TLA** Thai Library Association.

**TLA** Theater Library Association.

**TLA** Turkish Library Association.

**$TlAsS_2$** Lorandite.
Lorandite is found in arsenic-antimony deposits.
*Mineralogy.*

**TlBr** Thallium Bromide.
TlBr, also known as: Thallous Bromide, is used mainly in infrared detectors.
*Inorganic Chemistry.*

**tlc.** (abbr.) telecomunicazioni.
Italian abbreviation meaning: telecommunications.

**TLC** Thin-Layer Chromatography.
The term thin-layer chromatography actually refers to chromatography carried out on thin layers of adsorbent material.
*Analytical Chemistry.*

**TLC** Total Lung Capacity.
*Physiology.*

**TlCl** Thallium Chloride.
Thallium Chloride also known as: Thallous Chloride is used mainly in suntan lamps.
*Inorganic Chemistry.*

**$Tl_2CO_3$** Thallium Carbonate.
Thallium Carbonate, also known as: Thallous Carbonate, is used mainly in artificial diamonds.
*Inorganic Chemistry.*

**TLCs** Thin-Layer Chromatograms.

**TLD** tRNA-Like Domain.
For further details see under: **tRNA**.

**TL dating** Thermoluminescent dating.

*Archaeology; Geology; Physics.*
**TLDs** Top Level Domains.
**TLE** Treaty-limited equipment.
équipement limité par le Traité (ELT 2.).
**TLF** TBP-Like Factor.
For further details see under: **TBP**.
**TLF** Trypanosome Lytic Factor.
*Biochemistry; Molecular Genetics; Medicine; Dentistry.*
**tlg.** (abbr.) telegram.
Also: **Tel**; **tel**.
**TLH** The airport code for Tallahassee, Florida, U.S.A.
**TlI** Thallium Iodide.
Thallium Iodide is also known as: Thallous Iodide.
*Inorganic Chemistry.*
**$TlNO_3$** Thallium Nitrate.
Thallium Nitrate, also known as: Thallous Nitrate, is used mainly in pyrotechnics.
*Inorganic Chemistry.*
**TLO** Technology Licensing Organizations (Japan).
*Technology Transfer.*
**$Tl_2O$** Thallium Monoxide.
Thallium Monoxide, also known as: Thallous Oxide, is used mainly in analysis for ozone.
*Inorganic Chemistry.*
**t.l.o.** total loss only.
**TlOH** Thallium Hydroxide.
Thallium Hydroxide is also known as: Thallous Hydroxide.
**TLP** Telefones de Lisboa e Porto (Portugal).
**TLP** truck loading point.
poste de chargement des camions.
**TLR** Times Law Report.
**TLR-4** Toll-Like Receptor-4.
The TLR-4, the first human Toll protein, was identified by U.S. Researchers.
*Molecular Biology; Immune Regulation; Immunology; Infectious Diseases; Innate Immune System; Medicine.*
**tlr** (abbr.) tailer.
*Electronics; Mechanical Engineering; Molecular Biology.*
**TLR** Tulane Law Review.
**TLRs** Toll-Like Receptors.
For further details see under: **TLR-4**.
**TLS** tactical landing strip.
piste d'atterrissage tactique.
**TLS** Tactical Landing System.
**$Tl_2S$** Thallium Sulfide.
Thallium Sulfide is also known as: Thallous Sulfide.
*Inorganic Chemistry.*
**TLS** Total Logistic Strategy.
**TLS** Two-Level System.
*Nanoscience.*
**$Tl_2SO_4$** Thallium Sulfate.
Thallium Sulfate, also known as: Thallous Sulfate, is used mainly to measure ozone levels.
*Inorganic Chemistry.*
**TLU** Table-Look-Up.
**TLUD** Table-Look-Up Device.
*Computer Technology.*
**TLV** Tracked Levitated Vehicle.
**TLV** The airport code for Tel Aviv-Jaffa, Israel.
**TLX**; **Tlx** Trading Lale Exchange.
**Tm** Capacité Tubulaire maximum.
French initialism meaning: maximum tubular excretory capacity.
*Medicine.*
**$T_m$** Melting Temperature.
**TM** tactical missile.
missile (ou engin) tactique.
**TM** Tape Mark.
Tape Mark is also known as: Destination Warning Mark; End-of-Tape Mark.
*Computer Programming.*
**T.M.** Technical Manual.
**TM** Tecnologie Multimediali (Italy).
**TM** Tempi e Metodi.
Italian initialism meaning: Time and Motion Study.
**TM** Thames Measurement.
**TM** Thematic Mapper.
**TM** Third Market; Third Mortgage.
**TM** Trascendental Meditation.
Used particularly by persons who make use of drugs.
**Tm** The chemical symbol for Thulium.
Thulium is a rare-earth element having the atomic number 69, an atomic weight of 168.93 and a melting point of 155°C. It is used mainly to make ferrites.
*Chemistry; Symbols.*
**TM** Top Management.
**T.M.** Tours Minute.
French initialism meaning: Revolutions per minute.
**TM** Trade Mark / Trademark.
*Commerce; Law.*
**TM** Turing Machine.
*Computer Technology.*
**TMA** target movement analysis.
analyse des mouvements de l'objectif.
**TMA** Thermal Mechanical Analysis.
**TMA** Trimetallic Anhydride.

**TMA** Trimethylamine.
Used mainly as an insect attractant and as a flotation agent.
*Organic Chemistry.*

**T-man** Treasury Man.
The T-man is a special agent of the U.S. Treasury Department.

**TMAOH** Trimethylammonium Hydroxyde.

**TMAP** Thermal Modeling and Analysis Project.

**TMAs** Tissue Micro Arrays.
*In Situ Analysis.*

**TMB** 1,3,5-Trimethylbenzene.

**TMBMS** Transportable Molecular Beam Mass Spectrometer.
A prime use for the TMBMS is to monitor pilot plants or larger-scale chemical processes. Another use is to monitor speciated hydrocarbons or chlorinated compounds in trial burns of hazardous wastes or other advanced destruction processes.

**tmbr** (abbr.) timber.

**TMBRB** Toxicology and Molecular Biology Research Branch.
NIOSH's within the CDC.
For further details see under: **CDC** and **NIOSH**.

**TMC** Trans-monolayer contact.
*Lipid bilayer vesicles; Membrane Fusion; Physics.*

**TMC** two-man control [NBC].
contrôle par deux personnes [NBC].

**TMCC** theatre movement coordination centre.
centre de coordination des mouvements sur le théâtre.

**TMCXD measurements** Transverse Magnetic Circular X-ray Dichroism measurements.
*Applied Physics; Physics.*

**TMD** 1. tactical missile defence.
1. défense contre les missiles tactiques.
2. theatre missile defence.
2. défense contre les missiles de théâtre.

**TMD** Transmembrane Domain.
For further details see under: **TMDs**.

**TMDL requirements** Total Maximum Daily Load requirements.
*Clean Water Act.*

**TMDs** Transmembrane Domains.
*Medicine; Structural Biology.*

**TMDSC** Temperature-Modulated DSC.
For further details see under: **DSC**.

**TMEDA** Tetramethylethylenediamine.
TMEDA is used mainly as a reaction solvent and a corrosion inhibitor.

**TMG** 1. tactical missile group.
1. groupe de missiles (ou d'engins) tactiques.
2. temps moyen (ou méridien) de Greenwich.
2. Greenwich mean time (GMT).

**T.M.G.** Tempo Medio di Greenwich.
Italian initialism meaning: Greewich Mean Time.

**TMI meltdown** Three Mile Island meltdown - Occurred in 1979.
*Nuclear Energy; Nuclear Engineering; Nuclear Safety.*

**$T_{MIN}$** Minimum Temperatures.
*Climate Change; Ecosystems.*

**TMJ syndrome** Temperomandibular Joint syndrome.
The TMJ syndrome is also known as: Myofascial Pain Dysfunction.
*Medicine.*

**TML** Test de Migration des Leucocytes.
French initialism meaning: Leukocytes Migration Test.
*Medicine.*

**TML** Tetramethyl Lead.
*Organic Chemistry.*

**TML(O)** Temporal Mode Laser (Optic).

**TMM** Total Manufacturing Management.

**TMMC** Tetramethyl ammonium Manganese Chloride.

**TM mode** Tranverse Magnetic mode.
*Optical Physics.*

**TMMPS** Tris(Methoxy)Mercaptopropylsilane.
*Chemistry.*

**TMO** Table Mountain Observatory.

**TMO** Telegraph(ic) Money Order.

**$Tm_2O_3$** Thulium Oxide.
Thulium Oxide, also known as: Thulia, is used to make thulium metal.
*Inorganic Chemistry.*

**TMOS** Tetramethoxysilane.

**TMOS** Tetramethylorthosilicate.
*Materials Research; Physics.*

**T.M.P.** (Associazione Italiana tra i) Tecnici delle Materie Plastiche (Italy).
*Plastic Materials Associations.*

**TMP** Terminal Monitor Program.
*Computers.*

**7TM proteins** Seven-Transmembrane proteins.
*Chemosensory Receptors; Odorant Receptors; Olfaction.*

**TMRCA** Time to Most Recent Common Ancestry.
*Genetics; Molecular Microbiology; Tropical and Emerging Global Diseases.*

**TmRNA** Incorporates both tRNA and mRNA functions in a single molecule.
For further details see under: **mRNA** and **tRNA**.

**TMPS** theatre mission planning system.
système de planification des missions de théâtre.

**TMPTMA** Trimethylolpropane Trimethylacrylate.

**TMRA** Technical and Miscellaneous Revenue Act (U.S.A.).

**TMRC** Tropical Medicine Research Cooperation (U.S.A.).
Of the U.S. Department of Health and Human Services.

**TMR grants** Training and Mobility of Researchers grants (U.S.A.).

**TMRI** Torrey Mesa Research Institute (Syngenta's).
*Rice Genome.*

**TMRM** Tetramethylrhodamine-Maleimide.

**TMRP** Tropical Meteorology Research Programme.
Of the U.N. WMO.
For further details see under: **U.N.** and **WMO**.

**TMR programme** Training and Mobility Researchers programme.
European Union 1994-1998. The TMR Programme has replaced the **HCM Programme** (Human Capital and Mobility Programme).

**TMRR** temporary minimum-risk route.
route temporaire à risque minimal.

**TMS** Telecommunications Message Switcher.

**TMS** The Metallurgical Society.

**TMS** Treasury Market Securities.

**TMS** Truth-Maintenance System.
TMS is also known as: Reason Maintenance System.
*Artificial Intelligence.*

**TMT** tanker mooring terminal.
terminal d'amarrage pour pétrolier.

**TMT** Thermomechanical Treatment.

**TMT sectors** Technology, Medic and Telecom sectors.

**TMTSF** Tetramethyl-Tetraselenafulvalene.

**TMU** Time-Measurement Unit.

**TMV** Tank Motor Vessel.

**TMV** Tobacco Mosaic Virus.
TMV is one of a series of virus diseases of tabacco and various other plants.
*Plant Pathology.*

**TN** Telephone Number.

**TN** (abbr.) Tennessee (U.S.A.).

**TN** Tonga.

**TN** Total Nitrogen.

**tn** (abbr.) train.
*Astronomy; Electromagnetism; Mechanical Engineering; Military Science; Mining Engineering; Ordnance; Psychology; Transportation Engineering.*

**TN** Transferable Notice.

**TN** Treasury Notes (U.S.A.).

**TN** Trento, Italy.

**T/N**; **t/n** Turbonave.
Italian initialism meaning: Turbine Steamship.
*Navigation.*

**TNA** Tetranitroaniline.

**TNB** Trinitrobenzene.
*Chemistry.*

**TNC** The Nature Conservancy (Guatemala).
*Conservation Biology; Conservation Initiatives; Ecology.*

**TNC** Trade Negotiating Committee.

**TNC** Transnational Corporation.

**TNCs** Transnational Corporations.

**TNF** 1. tactical nuclear forces.
1. forces nucléaires tactiques.
2. theatre nuclear forces.
2. forces nucléaires de théâtre.

**TNF** 2,4,7-Trinitrofluorenone.

**TNF** Tumor Necrosis Factor.
*Molecular Biology.*

**TNF+CHX** TNF plus Cycloheximide.

**TNFDM** (2,4,7-Trinitro-9-Flurenylidene) Malonitrile.

**TNFRs** Tumor Necrosis Factor Receptors.
*Genetics.*

**TNL** Test du Transfert normal des Lymphocytes.
French initialism meaning: Normal Lymphocyte Transfer Test.
*Medicine.*

**TNO** Centre for Coatings Research (The Netherlands).

**tNOs** trans-Neptunian Objects.
For further details see under: **JFCs** and **KBOs**.

**TNP** Traité sur la non-prolifération (des armes nucléaires).
Non-Proliferation Treaty (NPT).

**TNS** The Next Step.

**TNS** Total Network Solutions (G.B.).
*Confidential Information on the Network.*

**TNS** Transaction Network Service.

**TN stage** Triple-Negative stage.
*Immunology.*

**TNT** Trinitrotoluene.
Trinitrotoluene also known as: Methyltrinitrobenzene is used mainly as a chemical intermediate.
*Organic Chemistry.*

**TNV** Total Network Visibility.

**TO** Table of Organization (Organization Chart).

**T.O.** Telegraph Office; Telephone Office.

**TO** Telephone Order.

**TO** Tincture of Opium.

**TO** Togo.

**TO** Torino, Italy.

**TO** Treasury Obligations.
**TO**; **to** truncated octahedron.
**TO** Turn-Off.
**T.O.** turnover.
**TOA** Top Of the Atmosphere.
*Atmospheric Sciences; Cloud Microphysics; Geophysics.*
**TOA** transfer of authority.
transfert d'autorité.
**TOAD** Terahertz Optical Asymmetric Demultiplexer.
*Digital Information Processing; Electronic Engineering.*
**TO&E** table of organization and equipment.
tableau d'effectifs et de dotation (TED).
**TOB**; **T.O.B.** Take-Off-Boost.
**TOBASCO networks** TOwards Broadband Access Systems for CATV Optical networks.
*European Community Project.*
**TOC** Table Of Contents.
**TOC** 1. time of occurrence.
1. heure de l'incident (ou de l'événement).
2. transfer of command.
2. transfert de commandement.
**TOC** Total Organic Carbon.
*Biotechnology.*
**TOCS** Tropical Ocean Climate Study.
**TOCSY** TOtal Correlated Spectroscopy.
**TOD** 1. time of day.
1. heure du jour.
2. time of delivery.
2. heure de livraison.
3. time of detonation.
3. heure de l'explosion.
**TOE** Theory Of Everything.
The theory that unites all the fundamental forces of nature.
*Neutrinos.*
**TOE** Tons of Oil Equivalent.
**TOEFL** Test Of English as Foreign Language.
**TOFC** Trailers On Flat Cars.
**TOFC/CPFC** Trailer-On-Flatcar/Container-On-Flatcar.
**TOFSIMS** Time-Of-Flight Secondary Ion Mass Spectrometry.
**TOGA program** Tropical Ocean and Global Atmosphere program.
**TOGA technology** TOtal Gene Expression Analysis technology.
Of Digital Gene Technologies, Inc. of La Jolla, California, U.S.A.
**TOG method** Target Observer Gun method.
*Military.*
**TOH** Tyrosine Hydroxylase.
*Enzymology.*
**TOI** Table Of the Isotopes.
First published in 1940 by the American chemist Glenn Seaborg.
**TOI** time of injection.
heure d'introduction.
**TOI** Tour Operators Italiani (Italy).
**TOK** Theory Of Knowledge.
**TOL** (abbr.) tolerance.
*Agronomy; Design Engineering; Ecology; Engineering; Immunology; Pharmacology.*
**TOL** Tree Of Life.
*Systematic Biology.*
**TOL** The airport code for Toledo, Ohio, U.S.A.
**TOLD** take-off and landing data.
données sur le décollage et l'atterrissage.
**TOLEDs** Transparent Organic Light-Emitting Devices.
*Chemistry; Electrical Engineering; Photonics and Optoelectronic Materials.*
**TOL ZONE** (abbr.) Tolerance Zone.
*Mechanics.*
**TOM** Territoires d'Outre Mer.
French acronym meaning: French Overseas Territories.
**tom.** (abbr.) tomo.
Italian abbreviation meaning: tome.
*Bibliography.*
**TOMAS communications** (Intertrial) Testbed Of Mobile Applications for Satellite communications.
*European Community Project.*
**TOMOVES Experiment** VESuvius TOMOgraphy Experiment (Italy).
An Italian Vesuvius Project.
*Geophysics; Seismic Surveys; Seismic Tomography Techniques; Volcanology.*
**TOMS** Total Ozone Mapping Spectrometer.
An instrument aboard ADEOS.
For further details see under: **ADEOS**.
**tonn.** (abbr.) tonnage.
**TOO** To Order Only.
referring to goods.
*Business; Commerce.*
**TOP** Technical and Office Protocols.
**TOPEX** TOPographic ocean EXperiment - NASA's.
**TOPEX** Typhoon OPerational EXperiment.
Of the U.N. WMO.
For further details see under: **U.N.** and **WMO**.
**TOPO** Tri-*n*-Octylphosphine Oxide.
**topog.** (abbr.) topography.
*Cartography; Geology.*
**TOPS** Terminal OPerating System.

**TOPS** Total Ocean Profiling System.
**TOPS** Traffic Operator Position Systems.
**TOPSIS** Technique for Order Preference by Similarity to Ideal Solution.
*Economics Calculation Systems.*
**TOPSS** Traffic and Offshore Platform Safety System.
**5'TOP tract** 5 Terminal Oligopyrimidine tract.
*Biochemistry; Cancer Research; Molecular Biology.*
**TOPV** Trivalent Oral Poliovirus Vaccine.
**TOR** Target Of Rapamycin.
*Structural Biology.*
**TOR** 1. terms of reference.
1a. mandat.
1b. attributions.
2. time of receipt.
2. heure de réception.
**tor** (abbr.) torpedo.
Also: **torp**.
*Engineering; Ordnance; Vertebrate Zoology.*
**Torr.**; **torr** A unit of pressure.
Named after the Italian physicist and mathematician Evangelista **Torricelli** (1608-1647).
*Metrology.*
**TOS** Tape Operating System.
*Computers.*
**TOS** Transfer Orbit Stage.
**Tos** Type of service.
**tosc.** (abbr.) toscano.
Italian abbreviation meaning: Tuscan.
**TOSCA** TOTE system, computer-assisted.
système TOTE assisté par ordinateur.
**TOT** Terms Of Trade.
*Business; Commerce.*
**TOT** Time On Target.
*Military Science.*
**tot.** (abbr.) total.
**TOT code** Transfer Of Technology code.
**TOW missile** Tube-launched Optically tracked, Wire-command link missile.
*Ordnance.*
**tox.** (abbr.) toxicology.
**toy** twin-of-eyeless.
toy is an eye-forming fly gene.
*Biology; Developmental Biology; Developmental Genetics; Genetic Engineering.*
**TP** 1. Sao Tome and Principe.
1. Sao Tomé-et-Principe.
2. twinned post.
2a. poste de cumul.
2b. poste jumelé.
**TP** Tail Pressure.
referring to testing on animals.
**TP** Tangible Property.
**TP** Target Program.
*Computer Programming.*
**TP** Taux de Prothrombine.
French initialism meaning: Prothrombin Index.
*Medicine.*
**TP** Taxe Proportionnelle.
**tp** teleprinter.
*Telecommunications.*
**TP**; **tp** teleprocessing.
*Computer Programming.*
**TP** Terminal Point.
*Transportation Engineering.*
**TP** Testosterone Propionate.
**TP** Test Point.
*Electricity.*
**TP** Test Program.
*Computer Programming.*
**TP** Third Party.
*Insurance.*
**TP** Thymidine Phosphorylase.
For further details see under: **PD-ECGF**.
**Tp** timbre poste.
French initialism meaning: stamp; postage stamp.
**TP** Time Pulse.
**tp.** townshi p.
**TP** Trapani, Italy.
**TP** Trade Prices.
**TP** Trattativa Privata.
Italian initialism meaning: private negotiation; private dealing.
*Business; Finance.*
**TP** Travaux Pratiques.
**TP** True Position; True Profile.
**TPA** Tecnologie per Processi Aziendali.
Italian initialism meaning: Technologies for Company Processes.
**TPA** Terephthalic Acid.
TPA is used mainly as a poultry-feed additive.
*Organic Chemistry.*
**TPA** 12-0-Tetradecanoylphorbol-13-Acetate.
**TPA** The airport code for Tampa International, Florida, U.S.A.
**TPA** track poduction area.
zone de production des pistes.
**TPA** Two-Photon Absorption.
*Chemistry; Materials Science; Microdevices; Resins.*
**TP-AGB stars** Thermally Pulsing, Asymptotic Giant Branch stars.
*Astrophysics; Geophysical Sciences.*

**TPAP** testis-specific, cytoplasmic Poly(A)Polymerase.
*Male mice spermatogenesis.*
**TPA state** Terminal Proliferation Arrest state.
*Apoptosis; Medical Research; Senescence.*
**TPB** Tetradecylpyridinium Bromide.
**TPB** Tetraphenylbutadiene.
**Tpc** Tournament players championship.
*Golf.*
**TPCE** Tank Pressure Control Experiment.
**TPCK** N-Tosyl-L-Phenylalanine Chloromethyl Ketone.
**TPD** table of personnel distribution [manpower].
tableau de répartition du personnel.
**TPD** Temperature-Programmed Desorption.
**TPD** Tons Per Day.
**TPD** Transpolar Drift.
*Applied Marine Research; Geology; Geophysics; Glacial Marine Sedimentation; Marine Micropaleontology; Oceanography; Pleistocene Deglaciations.*
**TPE** Telomere Position Effect.
*Molecular Biology; Cell Biology; Medicine; Human Cells.*
**TPE** Terminaux de Paiement Electronique.
French initialism meaning: Electronic Payment Terminals.
**TPE spectrum** Two-Photon Excitation spectrum.
For further details see under: **TPA**.
**TPF** Terrestrial Planet Finder.
NASA's TPF will be launched in 2010.
*Extrasolar Planetary Systems.*
**TPF** Tetraphenylfuran.
**TPFD** time-phased force deployment.
déploiment échelonné des forces.
**TPG** Trésoriers-Payeurs Généraux (France).
**TPG** Triphenylguanidine.
**tph** (abbr.) telephone.
*Telecommunications* - Telephone is also known as telephone system. The word telephone derives from the Greek term "distant sound".
*Acoustical Engineering* - In acoustical engineering, telephone is also known as: telephone set.
For further details see under: **Tel**; **tel**.
**TPH** Tons Per Hour.
**TPH** Tryptophan Hydroxylase.
TPH belongs to a superfamily of aromatic amino acid hydroxylases.
*Pharmacology; Toxicology.*
**TPHA** Treponema Palladium Hemagglutination Assay.
TPHA is a test for venereal, congenital syphilis and other human diseases.
*Pathology.*
**TPI** Tax and Prices Index.
*Business; Commerce.*
**TPI** Technical Products International (U.S.A.).
*Fresh Tissue Sectioning; Technical Products.*
**TPI** Thai Petrochemical Industries.
**TPI** Threads per inch.
*Mechanics.*
**TPI** Tribunal pénal international pour l'ex-Yougoslavie.
International Criminal Tribunal for the former Yugoslavia (ICTY).
**TPI** Triose Phosphate Isomerase.
**TPIL** Transports Privés d'Intérêts Locaux (France).
**TPI-SAL** Telecommunications, Post Information technology - Sector Adjustment Loan.
*World Bank Project (Morocco).*
**TPI test** Treponema Pallidum Immobilization test.
The TPI test is a specific test for syphilis.
*Medicine.*
**TPL** Third Party Liability.
*Insurance.*
**TPL** Tonnellata di Portata Lorda.
Italian initialism meaning: Gross Ton Burden.
**TPLSM** Two-Photon Laser Scanning Microscopy.
*Cell Biology; Cellular Physiology; Molecular Biology; Molecular Physiology.*
**TPM** Teleprocessing Monitor.
*Computer Programming.*
**TPM** Third Party Maintenance.
**TP muscle** Tergo-Pleural muscle.
**TPN** Triphosphopyridine Nucleotide.
*Enzymology.*
**TPND** Theft, Pilferage and Non-Delivery.
*Insurance.*
**TPO positivity** Thyroperoxidase positivity.
For further details see under: **HT** (Hashimoto's Thyroiditis).
**TPOS** Tetrapropoxysilane.
**TPP** Tetraphenylporphine.
**TPP** Tetraphenylpyrrole.
**TPP** Thiamine Pyrophosphate.
*Biochemistry.*
**TPPE spectroscopy** angle-resolved Two-Photon Photoemission spectroscopy.
*Chemical Sciences; Spectroscopy.*
**TPPN** Trans-Pacific Profiler Network.
**TPPs** Trusted Third Parties.
**tpr** (abbr.) taper.
*Mechanics.*
**TPR** Temperature, Pulse, Respiration.
*Medicine.*
**TPR** Terrain Profile Recorder.

The TPR is also known as: Airborne Profile Recorder.
*Engineering.*
**TPR** test procedure record.
compte rendu de procédure d'essai.
**TPR motifs** Tetratricopeptide Repeat motifs.
*Biochemistry; Cell Biology; Medicine; Molecular Biology; Neurology.*
**TPS** Taxe sur les Prestations de Services.
French initialism meaning: Tax On Services.
**TPS** Telemetry Processing System.
**TPS** Transaction Processing System.
*Computer Technology.*
**TPS** Trigger-Price System.
*Economics; Finance.*
**TPSA** Telekomunikajca Polska (Poland).
*Fixed-line Carriers.*
**TPSS** target prioritization and selection system.
sous-système de détermination et de sélection des objectifs prioritaires.
**TPT** Tetraphenylthiophene.
**TPT** third-party targeting.
désignation d'objectif par relais.
**TPT** Third-Party Transaction.
**TP term** Two-Photon term.
**TPTMS** Tropical Pacific Thermal Monitoring System.
**TPU** Trasporto Pubblico Urbano.
Italian initialism meaning: Urban Public Transport.
**TPV devices** Thermophotovoltaic devices.
TPV devices convert heat energy to electricity using technology similar to solar cells. Applications of TPV for cogenerating heat and electricity include field hospitals and command centers for the U.S. Department of Defense.
**TPV Systems** Thermophotovoltaic Systems.
A TPV system consists of a heat source, an emitter, an optical element such as a filter or mirrored backing, the TPV converters, and a cell-cooling system that may include cogeneration for the recovered heat.
**TPW hypothesis** True Polar Wander hypothesis.
*Early Cambrian Geological Record.*
**TPX** Tokamak Physics Experiment.
The TPX - a fusion research facility - was closed down in 1995 by the U.S. Congress for economic reasons.
**T.Q.** Tel Quel.
Also: **t.q.**; **t/q**.
referring to tha rate of exchange.
**T.Q.** Total Quality.
**TQA** Teaching Quality Assessment (G.B.).
**T.Q.C.** Total Quality Control.
**TQM**; **Tqm** Total Quality Management.
**T Quark** Top Quark.
*Particle Physics.*
**TR** 1. tactical reconnaissance.
1. reconnaissance tactique.
2. theatre reserve.
2. réserve de théâtre.
**TR** Tape Reading.
**tr.** (abbr.) tare.
*Engineering; Fluid Mechanics.*
**TR** Taxation Reports; Tax Rate.
**TR** Tax Rate.
**TR** Technical Report.
**TR** Template Repeat.
**TR** Terni, Italy.
**TR** Test Run.
The test run is carried out by means of test information to ascertain whether a computer program is performing properly.
*Computer Programming.*
**TR** Thermoplastic Rubber.
**TR** Thyroid hormone Receptor.
*Cell and Structural Biology; Cellular and Molecular Pharmacology; Transcription.*
**TR**; **Tr** (abbr.) timer.
**TR** Tons Registered.
**TR** Total Reserves.
**TR** Toucher rectal.
*Medicine.*
**tr.** (abbr.) trace.
*Archaeology; Computer Programming; Electronics; Engineering; Geology; Mathematics; Meteorology; Science.*
**TR** Trade Representative.
**TR** Transfer Rate.
The transfer rate is the rate at which information can be transferred from an input/output device to a CPU.
*Computer Technology.*
For further details see under: **CPU**.
**TR** Transformer Rectifier.
*Electricity.*
**T-R** Transmission-Reception.
*Communications.*
**tr.** (abbr.) tratta.
Italian abbreviation meaning: draft.
*Commerce.*
**TR** Treasury Receipt.
**Tr**; **tr.** (abbr.) Trust; trust.
**Tr.** (abbr.) trustee.
Also: **Tree**.
**TR**; **T.R.** Trust Receipt.
**TRA** Taux Révisable Annuel.

**TRA** temporary reserved airspace.
espace aérien temporairement réservé.

**TRACE spacecraft** Transition Region And Coronal Explorer spacecraft.
*Astronomy; Astrphysics; Computational Sciences; Coronal Heating; Geophysics; Plasma Physics.*

**TRACIR** TRacking Air with CIrcularly polarized Radar.

**TRACMINER** TRACtion enhancing MINing Equipment Accessory.
*European Community Project.*

**TRACSVAN** transportable radar and communications simulation van.
module transportable pour la simulation d'émissions radar et de télécommunications.

**TRAC systems** Tecan Robotic Assay Composer systems.
*Molecular biology procedures automation.*

**trad.** (abbr.) traduttore / traduttrice; traduzione.
Italian abbreviation meaning: s/he translator; translation.

**TRAFFIC** Trade Records Analysis of Flora and Fauna in Commerce.
A group set up in London in 1975 with an Office in Washington, USA, financed by the WWF.
For further details see under: **WWF**.

**TRAFS** Torpedo Recognition and Alertment Functional Segment.
*U.S. Navy.*

**TRAI** Telecom Regulatory Authority of India.

**TRAINCOL** Advanced design of crash fail-safe train structures under service and impact conditions.
A four-year project that started in 1997.
*European Community Project.*

**TRAM** transmissions radioélectriques en l'air à destinataires multiples [terre-navire uniquement].
broadcast [shore-ship only].

**tran.** (abbr.) transaction.

**TRANET** (abbr.) Tracking Network.
*U.S. Navy.*

**TRANSEC** transmission security.
sécurité (ou sûreté) des transmissions.

**TRAP** Tactical Recovery of Aircraft Personnel.

**TRAP** Telomeric Repeat Amplification Protocol.

**TRAP** *trp* RNA-binding Attenuation Protein.
For further details see under: **AT**.

**trap** The above acronyms were coined using the English word "trap".
*Civil Engineering; Computer Programming; Electronics; Geology; Mechanical Devices; Mechanical Engineering; Solid-State Physics; Space Technology.*

**TRAPATT diode** TRApped Plasma Avalanche Transit Time diode.
*Electronics.*

**TRB** Transportation Research Board (U.S.A.).

**TRBF** Total Renal Blood Flow.

**TRC** Technology Reports Centre.

**TRC** Telecommunications Regulatory Commission (Sri Lanka).

**TRC** Truth and Reconciliation Commission (South Africa).

**TRD** (abbr.) traced.
Also: **Tcd**.
*Mechanics.*

**trdg.** (abbr.) trading.

**TRDRP** Tobacco-Related Disease Research Program.
TRDRP was created in 1989 by the University of California, U.S.A.
*Tobacco Studies.*

**TRE** Treaty-related equipment.
équipement couvert par le traité.

**treas.** (abbr.) treasurer.

**Treas.** (abbr.) Treasury.
*Finance.*

**TREAT** TRaining Environmental Adapted Techniques (Italy).
*Projects.*

**TREC** Text REtrieval Conference.
The TREC is an annual conference sponsored by the U.S. National Institute of Standards and Technology.
*U.S. Defence.*

**TREE** transient radiation effects on electronics.
effects transitaires des rayonnements sur les systèmes électroniques.

**TREE** Tropical Rainforest Ecology Experiment.

**Tree** (abbr.) Trustee.
Also: **Tr.**

**TRE** T-cell Replacing Factor.
*Immunology.*

**TRES** Trasporti Rapidi Economici e Sicuri.

**TRES** (abbr.) Tresylate.

**TREVI** Terrorismo, Radicalismo, Estremismo e Violenza Internazionale.

**TRF** tactical reconnaissance fighter.
chasseur de reconnaissance tactique.

**TRF** Thailand Research Fund.
The TRF was created in the early 1990s.

**TRF** Thyrotropin-Releasing Factor.

**trf.** (abbr.) transfer.
For further details see under: **trs**.

**TRF transformer** Tuned-Radio-Frequency transformer.

Also: **trf. transformer**.
*Electronics.*
**TRFs** Terminal Restriction Fragments.
*Cell Biology; Medicine; Neurosciences.*
**TRH** Thyrotropin-Releasing Hormone.
**TRI** Time-Reversal Invariance.
*Physics.*
**TRI** Toxics Release Inventory.
Of the U.S. EPA.
*Economics; Engineering; Environmental Engineering.*
For further details see under: **EPA**.
**TRI** The airport code for Tri-City Airport, Kingsport-Bristol-Johnson City, Tennessee, U.S.A.
**trib.** (abbr.) tribunale.
Italian abbreviation meaning: tribunal, law court.
**TRIC** TRacoma Inclusion Conjunctivitis.
*Medicine.*
**TRID** Trail Receptor without an Intracellular Domain.
*Cancer Research; Medicine.*
For further details see under: **DcR1**.
**TRIF** Tableau des Relations entre Intermédiaires Financiers (France).
**triflic acid** trifluoromethanesulfon ic acid.
**trig.** (abbr.) trigonometry; trigonometric; trigonometrical.
*Mathematics.*
**TRIGAT** third-generation antitank (missile).
(missile) antichar de la troisième génération.
**TRIGS** tactical reconnaissance information ground station.
station au sol d'informations provenant de la reconnaissance tactique.
**trim.** (abbr.) trimestrale.
Italian abbreviation meaning: quarterly; trimestral.
**trim.** (abbr.) trimestre.
Italian abbreviation meaning: quarter; term; three-month period.
**TRIM system** Transporation RIst Management system.
**TRIP** Thunderstorm Research International Program.
**TRIP** Transnational Research and Instruction Program.
*U.S. Programs.*
**triP** triphosphate.
**TRIPS** Trade-Related aspects of Intellectual Property Rights.
WTO's Agreemnt.
*Patent Laws.*
For further details see under: **WTO**.
**TRIP steels** Transformation-induced plasticity steels.
*Materials science; Metallurgical Process Engineering; Novel steels.*
**TRL** Tanabe Research Laboratories.
TRL is the U.S. Subsidiary of Tanabe Seiyaku.
**TRL** Turkish Lira.
*Currencies.*
**TRM** Thermoremanent Magnetization.
*Geophysics.*
**TRMM** Tropical Rainfall Measuring Mission - NASA's.
*Atmospheric Sciences; Cloud Microphysics; Earth Sciences; Geophysics.*
**tRNA** transfer RNA.
*Genetics; Molecular Biology; Biomedical Sciences; Microbiology.*
For further details see under: **RNA**; **tmRNA**; **mRNA**.
**TRNOE** TRansferred Nuclear Overhauser Effect.
*Chemical Biology; Chemistry; Molecular Biology.*
**TRO** Tool/Room Order.
*Mechanics.*
**TROICA project** Trans-Siberian Investigation of the Chemistry of the Atmosphere project.
*Atmospheric Chemistry; Projects.*
**TROPEX** (abbr.) TROPical EXperiment.
**TRP** Technology Reinvestment Program.
**TRP** time of reporting.
heure de compte rendu.
**trp.** (abbr.) trap.
*Civil Engineering; Computer Programming; Electronics; Geology; Mechanical Devices; Mechanical Engineering; Solid-State Physics; Space Technology.*
**Trp**; **trp** Tryptophan.
$C_{11}H_{12}N_2O_2$. Tryptophan is an amino acid used in mammalian diets.
*Biochemistry.*
**TRPL** (abbr.) Terneplate.
A sheet coated with terne.
*Metallurgy.*
**TRPRC** Tulane Regional Primate Research Center (U.S.A.).
Of Tulane University.
*SIV Pathogenesis; Vaccine Development.*
**TRR** target-ranging radar.
spécification des impératifs d'essais.
**TRR** Trade Regulation Rule.
*Business; Commerce.*
**TRRL** Transport and Road Research Laboratory.
Department of Transport (G.B.).
**TRS** test-requirement specification.

**TRS** Tough-Rubber-Sheathed (as a cable).
*Electricity.*
**TRS** Transcription Regulatory Sequences.
**trs.** (abbr.) transfer.
Also: **trf.**; **tfr.**
*Computer Programming; Mining Engineering; Navigation; Robotics; Transportation Engineering.*
**trs.** (abbr.) transpose.
**trs.** (abbr.) trustees.
Also: **ttees.**
**TRSA** Tax Reduction and Simplification Act (U.S.A.).
**TRSB** Time-Referenced Scanning Beam.
**TRU** target reporting unit.
unité chargée du compte rendu sur l'objectif.
**TRU waste** Transuranic waste.
**TRUF** Transferable Revolving Underwriting Facility.
**TRUST algorithm** Terminal Repeller Unconstrained Subenergy Tunneling algorithm.
*Computer Methods; Engineering Systems; Geophysics; Seismology.*
**TRX** tactical reconaissance all-weather (aircraft).
(aéronef de) reconnaissance tactique tout temps.
**Trx** Thioredoxin.
*Biochemistry.*
**trxG proteins** thrithorax Group proteins.
*Biochemistry; Biophysics; Genetics; Molecular Biology.*
**TrxR** Thioredoxin Reductase.
*Biological Chemistry; Biophysics; Medicine.*
**TS** Tape Skip.
*Computer Programming.*
**TS** Taper Shank.
*Mechanical Devices.*
**TS** Taxe de Séjour.
**TS** Tax Shelter; Tax Straddle.
**TS** Tecnologie del Software.
Italian initialism meaning: Software Technologies.
**TS** Temperature Switch.
**TS** Temporary Storage.
Temporary storage is also known as: Working Storage.
*Computer Technology.*
**TS** temps de saignement.
French initialism meaning: bleeding time.
**TS**; **ts** tensile strength.
*Materials Science; Mechanics; Textiles.*
**TS** Terminal Symbol.
*Computer Science.*
**TS** Thymidylate Synthase.
*Microbiology; Molecular Biology Evolution; Protozoa.*
**TS** Time Sharing.
**TS** Time Switch.
*Engineering.*
**TS** Tin-Steel.
**TS** Tool Steel.
*Materials Science.*
**TS** Tourette Syndrome.
*Clinical Brain Disorders; Neuroscience; Psychiatry.*
**TS** Transcribed Strand.
*Genetics; Life Sciences; Medicine; Microbiology; Radiation Oncology.*
**TS** Transcription Series.
**T/S** transhipment.
**TS** Treasury Stock.
**T.S.** Tribunale Speciale.
Italian initialism meaning: Extraordinary Court.
**T.S.** Tribunale Supremo.
Italian initialism meaning: Supreme Court.
**TS** Trieste, Italy.
**TS** Tunisia.
**Ts** turbine ship.
**T/S** Two-Stroke.
**TSA** Tax Sheltered Annuity.
**TSA** Toluenesulfonic Acid.
**TSA** Tumor-Specific Antigen.
**TSA** Tyramide Signal Amplification.
**TsAGI** Central Aerodynamic Institute.
The TsAGI is located in the closed city of Zhukovsky near Moscow.
*Russian Research Institutes.*
**T.S.B.** Trustee Savings Bank.
*Banking.*
**TSBF** Tropical Soil Biology and Fertility Programme.
*African Food Security.*
**TSC** The SNP Consortium.
*Human Genome; Life Sciences.*
For further details see under: **SNP**.
**TSC** Transmitter Start Code.
**TSC** Transportation Systems Center.
**TSCA** Toxic Substances Control Act (U.S.A.).
**TS cycle** Two-Stroke cycle.
*Mechanical Engineering.*
**TSD** Temperature-dependent Sex Determination.
**TSE** Tokyo Stock Exchange (Japan).
**TSE** Toronto Stock Exchange (Canada).
**TSE** Transmissible Spongiform Encephalopathy.
Also: Mad Cow Disease.
For further details see under: **TSEs**.
**TSER** Targeted Socio-Economic Research (1994-1998).
*European Community Programs.*

**TSEs** Transmissible Spongiform Encephalopathies.
TSEs are fatal, neurodegenerative diseases.
*Animal Health; Anti-TSE Drugs; Infectious Diseases; Viral Diseases; Zoology.*

**TSF** Thymocyte Stimulating Factor.
*Medicine.*

**TSG** tri-service group.
groupe interarmées.

**TSGCE** Tri-Service Group on Communications and Electronics.
Groupe interarmées sur les télécommunications et l'électronique.

**TSGT** transportable satellite ground terminal.
terminal terrien transportable de satellite.

**Tsh** Tanzanian shilling.
*Currencies.*

**TSH** Thyroid Stimulating Hormone.
*Endocrine Regulation; Medicine.*

**TSI**; **tsi** tons per square inch.
*Mechanics; Metallurgy.*

**TSI** Total Solar Irradiance.
*Climate.*

**TSI** Transportation Safety Institute (U.S.A.).

**tsk.** (abbr.) task.

**TSK model** Terrace-Step-Kink model.
*Engineering; Growth Atomistic Mechanisms; Materials Science; Physics.*

**TSL** Trafic de Surcharge Limité.

**TSL** Tri-State Logic.

**TSLC** TOGA Sea Level Center.
For further details see under: **TOGA**.

**TSM** Tail Service Mast.

**TSM** téléphone sous-marin.
underwater telephone (UWT).

**TSMS** tactical spectrum management system.
système tactique de gestion du spectre.

**TSN** Thermal Severity Number.
*Technology* - Referring to welds testing.

**t-SNARE** target membrane SNARE.
For further details see under: SNARE.

**TSO** Technical Standard Order.

**TSO** Time Sharing Option.

**TSO**; **Tsos** Transmission System Operators.

**TSO** Trattamento Sanitario Obbligatorio (Italy).

**TSP** Trisodium Phosphate.
*Chemistry.*

**TSP-1** Thrombospondin-1.
TSP-1 is a potent inhibitor of angiogenesis.
*Immunology; Medicine; Microbiology; Tumor Biology.*

**TSPA/VA** Total System Performance Assessment - Viability Assessment.
Completed by U.S. D.O.E. in 1998.
*Geologic Disposal; Geologic Repositories; Nuclear Engineering; Radioactive Waste; Radiological Sciences.*
For further details see under: **D.O.E.**

**TSPP** Tetrasodium Pyrophosphate.
*Inorganic Chemistry.*

**TSPS** Traffic Service Position System.

**TSR** tactical sonar range.
portée sonar tactique (PST).

**TSR** Technical Summary Report.

**TSRI** The Scripps Research Institute.
TSRI was established in 1961. It is located at La Jolla, California, U.S.A. and deals with basic research in *Chemistry, Structural Molecular and Cell Biology.*

**TSS** Tensile Shear Strength.
referring to adhesives.

**TSS** Tethered Satellite System.

**TSS** Time Sharing System.

**TSS** Toxic Shock Syndrome.
*Pathology.*

**TSS** Trade Support System.

**TSS** Transatlantic Support System.

**TSSG** Transfusion Safety Study Group (U.S.A.).

**TSST-1** Toxic Shock Syndrome Toxin-1.
*Human Immunology; Microbiology; Molecular and Cellular Biology.*

**TST** tactical support team.
équipe d'appui tactique.

**tst** (abbr.) test.
For further details see under: **t**.

**TST** Transition State Theory.
*Electrochemical Energy Systems; Electron Transfer; Photosynthesis.*

**TSTA** Tumor-Specific Transplantation Antigen.

**TSTF upconversion** Two-Step, Two-Frequency upconversion.
TSTF upconversion is a 3-dimensional display technology.
*Electrical Engineering; Mechanical Engineering.*

**tstr** (abbr.) transistor.
*Electronics.*

**TSU** Taiwan Solidarity Union.
New Party registered end July 2001.

**TSU** Towson State University (U.S.A.).

**TSUNAMI** Technology in Smart antennas for UNiversal Advanced Mobile Infrastructure.
*European Community Project.*

**T/S unit** Track/Store unit.

**TSV** (dispositif de) Télésurveillance.

**T.S.V.P.** Tournez, s'il vous Plaît.
French initialism meaning: Please Turn Over.

**T.T.** Telegraphic Transfer.

*Banking.*
**TT** Telephoto Transmission.
**tt** teletype.
*Telecommunications.*
**TT** Teller Terminal.
**TT** Terms of Trade.
*Business; Commerce.*
**TT** Tetanous Toxoid.
**T.T.** Time Taken.
**TT** Torpedo Tube.
*Ordnance.*
**TT** Tourist Trophy.
**TTA** Total Tangible Assets.
*Business; Commerce; Finance.*
**tTA gene** tetracycline-responsive Transactivator gene.
*Biochemistry; Medicine; Metabolism; Oncology; Pathology.*
**TT&C antenna** Telemetry, Tracking and Command antenna.
**TTBE regulation** Technology Transfer Block Exemption regulation.
Last revised by the European Commission in 1996.
**TTBT** Threshold Test-Ban Treaty.
Traité sur la limitation des essais en fonction d'un seuil.
**TTC** Telemetry, Telecommand and Control.
**TTC** Terena Technical Committee.
For further details see under: **TERENA**.
**TTC** Toronto Transit Commission (Canada).
**TTC**; **ttc** Toutes Taxes Comprises.
French initialism meaning: Inclusive of Tax.
**TTD** Temporary Text Delay.
*Computers.*
**TTD** Tetraethylthiuram Disulfide.
**TTD** Trichothiodystrophy.
A rare human disorder associated with defects in nucleotide excision repair.
*Biochemistry; Biophysics.*
**TTD list** Things-To-Do list.
*Psychology.*
**TTE** Total Tax Expenditures.
**ttees.** (abbr.) trustees.
Also: **trs**.
**TTF** Tetrathiofulvalene.
**tTF** truncated Tissue Factor.
*Clinical Immunology; Medicine; Pharmacokinetics; Pharmacology; Therapeutic Oncology Research.*
**tTgase** tissue Transglutaminase.
*Autoantigens; Biomedicine; Medicine; Ubiquitous enzymes.*
**TTI** Teletype Input.
**TTL** Test de la Transformation Lymphoblastique.
French initialism meaning: Blast Transformation of Lymphocytes.
*Medicine.*
**TTL** Transistor-Transistor Logic.
*Electronics.*
**TTNL** Test du Transfert Normal des Lymphocytes.
**TTO** Teletype Output.
**TTO** Ten-to-Twelve year Oscillation.
*Geodesy; Geophysics; Meteorology.*
**TTO** Transient Tracers in the Ocean (U.S.A.).
**TTP** Total Taxable Pay.
**TTR** Transthyretin.
Transthyretin was formerly known as prealbumin.
*Biochemistry; Genetics; Molecular Biology.*
**TTS**; **tts** Teletype Setter/teletypesetter.
*Telecommunications.*
**TTS** Transdermal Therapeutic System.
**TTS** T Tauri Stars.
TTS are young, low-mass, pre-MS stars.
*Astronomy; Astrophysics.*
**TTS plus system** Table Top Slide plus system.
**TTT diagram** Time-Temperature-Transformation diagram.
TTT diagram is also known as: Isothermal Transformation Diagram.
*Materials Science.*
**ttw.** (abbr.) teletypewriter.
Also: **TTY**.
**TTW** 1. time of tension or war.
1. période de tension ou temps de guerre (PTG).
2. transition to war.
2. passage à l'état de guerre.
**TTX** Terminal Télétex.
**TTX** Tetrodotoxin.
TTX is a potent neurotoxin that paralyzes nerves and muscles.
*Evolution; Physiology; Neuroscience.*
TTX is also known as: Fugutoxin; Tetraodontoxin.
*Toxicology.*
**TTY**; **tty** Tele-TYpe; Teletype.
*Telecommunications.*
**TTY** Teletypewriter.
Also: **ttw.**
*Telecommunications.*
**TU** Tape Unit.
Tape Unit is also known as: Tape Drive.
*Computer Technology.*
**TU** 1. task unit.
1. unité opérationnelle.
2. Turkey.
2. Turquie.

**TU** Terminal Unit.
referring to an air-conditioning system.
*Mechanical Engineering.*
**TU** Thermal Unit.
**T.U.** Testo Unico.
Italian initialism meaning: Unified body of laws; Consolidation Act.
**T.U.** Trade Union.
**TU** Trading Unit.
**TU** Transfer Unit.
*Chemical Engineering.*
**TU** Transmission Unit.
**Tu** Tubercle.
*Biology.*
**TU** Tuberculin Unit.
**TU** Tuesday.
**TUA** Tasso Ufficale sulle Anticipazioni.
Italian acronym meaning: Borrowing Rate of Interest.
*Banking; Economics.*
**TUA** Technology User's Agreement.
**TUAC** Trade Unions Advisory Committee to the OECD (France).
**TUC** Tempo Universale Coordinato.
Italian acronym meaning: Coordinated Universal Time; Universal Time Coordinated.
*Horology.*
**TUC** Trade Unions Congress; Trade Unions Council.
**TUC** Triangle University Computation Center (U.S.A.).
**TUE** Trattato sull'Unione Europea.
Italian acronym meaning: European Union Treaty.
**TÜFTAD** Turkish Association pf Pharmaceutical Technology Scientists (Turkey).
**TUG** Towed Universal Gilder.
*U.S. Army.*
**TUL** The airport code for Tulsa International Airport.
**TULPs** TUbby-Like Proteins.
*Biochemistry; Biology; Biophysics; Genetic Mutations; Hearing Loss; Medicine; Molecular Biology; Obesity; Retinal Degeneration; Structural Biology Program.*
**TUM** Technical University of Munich.
**TUNEL** Terminal deoxynucleotidyl transferase-mediated Nick-End Labeling.
**TUNL** Triangle Universities Nuclear Laboratory.
**Turk** Turkish.
Turkish is the language of Turkey; Ottoman Turkish.
*Languages.*
**TUS** Tasso Ufficiale di Sconto.
Italian acronym meaning: Bank Rate (G.B.); Official Rate of Discount (U.S.A.).
*Commerce.*
**TUS** The airport code for Tucson, Arizona, U.S.A.
**TUT** Tariffa Urbana a Tempo.
Italian acronym meaning: Local Dialling Charge.
Now called TAT.
For further details see under: **TAT**.
**TUTase** Terminal-U-Transferase.
**TV** Tasso Variabile.
Italian initialism meaning: Fluctuating Rate; Variable Rate.
**TV**; **tv.** (abbr.) television system / television set.
*Telecommunications.*
**TV** Test Voltage.
**TV** Tidal Volume.
*Physiology.*
**tv** tout venant.
**TV** Treviso, Italy.
**Tv** virtual temperature.
*Meteorology.*
**TVA** target value analysis.
Analyse de l'importance des cibles.
**TVA** Tassa sul Valore Aggiunto.
Italian initialism meaning: Value Added Tax.
**T.V.A.** Taxe à la Valeur Ajoutée.
French initialism meaning: Value Added Tax.
**TVA** Tax on Value Added.
**TVA** Televisione A Colori.
Italian initialism meaning: Colour Television.
**TVA** Tennessee Valley Authority (U.S.A.).
**TV BNL** télévision à bas niveau de lumière.
low-light television (LLTV).
**TVC** Television Camera.
*Telecommunications.*
**TVCA** Taipei Venture Capital Association.
**TVD** Total Variable Diminishing (difference scheme).
**TVI** technique de vérification informatisée.
computer-assisted audit technique (CAAT).
**TVL** Tenth-Value Layer.
*Radioactivity.*
**TVM** Track Via Missile.
*Ordnance.*
**TVM** Tubovesicular Membrane.
*Biology; Immunology; Medicine; Microbiology.*
**TVS** Tornado Vortex Signature.
**TW** Taiwan.
**TW** Tax Writeoff.
**TW** Terawatt.
Terawatt is a unit of power equal to $10^{12}$ Watts.
*Physics.*
**tw** (abbr.) twisted.

**TW** The airline code for Trans World Airlines (TWA).
**TWA** Transaction Work Area.
**TWA** Traveling Wave Amplifier.
Also: **TWTA**.
**TWA** Typewriter Adapter.
**TWAS** Third World Academy of Sciences.
Biannual meetings.
**TWERLE** Tropical Wind, Energy conversion and Reference Level Experiment (U.S.A.).
**TWI** Training Within Industry.
referring to personnel.
**TWIMC** To Whom It May Concern.
**TWOATAF** Second Allied Tactical Air Force Central Europe [obsolete].
2^e^ Force aérienne tactique alliée du centre-Europe [obsolète].
**TWP** Tropical Western Pacific.
**TWP** Twisted Pair.
*Electricity.*
**TWRI** Toronto Western Research Institute (Canada).
A multidisciplinary research centre affiliated with the University of Toronto located at the Toronto Western Hospital.
**TWT** Traveling-Wave Tube.
*Electronics.*
**T.W.T.** Tuscany Woodworking Technologies (Italy).
**TWTA** Travelling Wave Tube Amplifier.
Also: **TWA** (Travelling Wave Amplifier).
*Electronics.*
**TWX** Teletypewriter Exchange.
**tx** (abbr.) tax.
**tx** (abbr.) telex.
Telex is a teleprinter exchange service.
*Telecommunications.*
**TX** (abbr.) Texas (U.S.A.).
**TX** 1. transmitter.
1. émetteur.
2. Turkmenistan.
2. Turkménistan.
**$TxA_2$** Thromboxane $A_2$.
*Biomedicine; Hematology.*
**TXCam** TXCamelopardalis.
TXCam lies about 1000 light-years away.
*Astronomy; Astrophysics; Radio Polarization.*
**ty** (abbr.) type.
*Graphic Arts.*
**TYMV** Turnip Yellow Mosaic Virus.
**typ.** (abbr.) type; typical; typically.
**Tyr** (abbr.) Tyrosine.
*Biochemistry.*
**TYS** The airport code for Knoxville, Tennessee, U.S.A.
**TZ** Tanzania.
**TZM alloy** Titanium-Zirconium-Molybdenum alloy.
*Metallurgy.*
**TZP** Tetragonal Zirconia Polycrystal.
The TZP is a ceramic material used mainly in the manufacture of cutting implements.
*Materials Science.*

**U** uniform.
**U** Union.
*Computer Programming; Design Engineering; Mechanical Devices; Surgery.*
**u** (abbr.) unit.
*Engineering; Mathematics -Military Science; Physics.*
**U** Universal.
*Astronomy; Mechanical Engineering; Science.*
**u** universe.
In statistics, universe is also known as: statistical universe.
*Statistics.*
**U** University.
**u** update.
**u** upper / Upper.
Also: **up.**
*Geology.*
**u** uracil.
*Biochemistry.*
**U** The chemical symbol for Uranium.
Uranium is a metallic element having the atomic number 92, and an atomic weight of 238.03. Uranium is used mainly in nuclear fuel. Named after the discovery of the planet of **Uranus**.
*Chemistry; Symbols.*
**U**; **u** uridine.
Also: **Urd.**
*Biochemistry.*
**U** Uridylate.
**u** (abbr.) user.
*Computer Programming; Telecommunications.*
**U** Utah, U.S.A.
Also: **UT**; **Ut**.
**UA** unassigned.
**UA** Underwriting Account.
**UA** Unité Astronomique.
French initialism meaning: Astronomical Unit.
**U/A** Unit of Account.
**UA** University of Arizona (U.S.A.).
**UA** uranium appauvri.
depleted uranium (DU).
**U/A** Urinalysis.
The abbreviation urinalysis refers to urine analysis.
*Pathology.*
**UA** The airline code for United Airlines.
**UA** Universiteit Antwerpen (Belgium).
**UAA** University of Alaska, Anchorage.
**UAB**; **U.A.B.** Unemployment Assistance Board.
**UAB** Union des Automobilistes Bulgares.
**UAB** University of Alabama at Birmingham (U.S.A.).
**UACV** Unità Analisi Crimini Violenti (Italy).
Italian initialism meaning: Unit for the Analysis of Violent Crimes. Founded in 1995. Fully operative since 1997.
**UADS** User Attribute Data Set.
**UAE** United Arab Emirates.
**UAF** University of Alaska, Fairbanks.
**UAFA** Union Arabe du Fer et de l'Acier.
French acronym meaning: Arab Union for Iron and Steel.
**UAH** University of Alabama in Huntsville (U.S.A.).
**U.A.I.** Unione Astronomica Internazionale.
Italian initialism of the: International Union of Astronomers.
**UAL** Unione Aziende Lombarde (Italy).
Italian initialism of the: Lombard Companies Association (Milan, Italy).
**UAM** Underwater-to-Air Missile.
**UAMI** Ufficio per l'Armonizzazione nel Mercato Interno.
**UAMS** University of Arkansas for Medical Sciences (U.S.A.).
**UAMS** Upper Atmosphere Mass Spectrometer.
**UAP** Union des Assurances de Paris (France).
French acronym of the: Paris Insurances Union.
**UAP** Universal Availability of Publications.
**UAPA** United Amateur Press Association.
**UAR** Unit Address Register.
**UARC** University Affiliated Research Center (U.S.A.).
Set up by NASA near Ames.
**UARP** Upper Atmospheric Research Program - NASA's.
**UARS** Upper Atmosphere Research Satellite.
Launched in 1991. Shut down by NASA in August 2001 for economic reasons.
*Earth Sciences.*
**UART** Universal Asynchronous Receiver Terminal.
**UART** Universal Asynchronous Receiver/Transmitter.
*Computer Technology.*
**UAS** Uniform Accounting System.
**UAS** Unione Agenti SAI (Italy).
*Insurance; Unions.*
**UAS**; **uas** Upstream Activation Site.
UAS is also known as: Upstream Activator Sequence.
*Genetics.*

**UATI** Union Internationale des Associations et Organismes Techniques.
Located in Paris, France. Founded in 1951; activities: working groups and committees to identify, promote and co-ordinate actions of member associations in areas of common interest and to facilitate relations with international bodies, in particular UNESCO, UNIDO and ECOSOC.
**UAV** unmanned aerial vehicle.
véhicule aérien sans pilote.
**UAW** United Automobile Workers (U.S.A.).
**UB** University of Buffalo (U.S.A.).
**UB** Urinary Bladder.
*Anatomy.*
**UBA domain** Ubiquitin-Associated domain.
*Cancer Research; Pathology.*
**UBAF** Union de Banques Arabes et Françaises.
**UBC** Uniform Building Code.
**UBC** Universal Bibliographic Control.
*Bibliography.*
**UBC** Universal Block Channel.
**UBC** University of British Columbia (Canada).
**UBC enzyme** Ubiquitin-Conjugating enzyme.
*Biochemistry; Molecular Biology; Molecualr Biophysics.*
**UBF** Upstream Binding Factor.
*Cancer Research - Molecular and Cell Biology.*
**UBHC** Unit Bank Holding Company.
**U.B.I.** Unione Bibliografica Italiana.
Italian acronym of the: Italian Bibliographical Society.
**U.B.I.** Unione Bocciofila Italiana.
Italian acronym of the: Italian "Bocce" (Bowling) Fans Association.
**UBI** Unione Bonsaisti Italiani.
*Italian Unions.*
**UBIT** Unrelated Business Income Tax.
**UBLs proteins** Ubiquitin-like proteins.
*Molecular Biology.*
**UBM** UniCredit Banca Mobiliare.
Founded at the beginning of 2000.
*Investment Banking.*
**UBM** Unit Bill of Material.
**UBMTA** Uniform Biological Material Transfer Agreement (U.S.A.).
An agreement developed by the U.S. NIH.
*Biological Material Transfer.*
For further details see under: **NIH**.
**UBOT** Unfavorable Balance Of Trade.
**UBP** United Bermuda Party.
**UBQ** Ubiquinone.
Ubiquinone is also known as: Coenzyme Q.
*Enzymology.*
**UBQ proteins** Ubiquitin proteins.
*Molecular Biology.*
**UBR** Uniform Business Rate.
*Business; Finance.*
**UBS** Union Bank of Switzerland.
**UBS character** Unit Backspace character.
**UbxG** Ultrabithorax.
**UC; U.C.** Ufficiale di Complemento.
Italian initialism meaning: Reserve Officer.
**U.C.** Ufficio di Collocamento.
Italian initialism meaning: Labour Exchange.
**u.c.** under construction.
**U/C** underlying currency.
monnaie de départ.
**UC** Unfair Competition.
*Business; Commerce.*
**uc** unichannel.
**U.C.** Unità di Conto.
Italian initialism meaning: Unit of Account.
**UC** Unit Cost.
*Business; Commerce.*
**UC** Unité de Commande.
**UC** unité de compte.
accounting unit (AU 1.).
**UC** Unités de charge.
French initialism meaning: unit loading devices.
**UC** University of Calgari - Alberta, Canada.
**UC** University of California, Irvine (U.S.A.).
**uc** upper case.
Also: **u.c.**; **u/c**.
**u.c.** usual conditions.
**$UC_2$** Uranium Carbide.
$UC_2$, also known as Uranium Dicarbide, is used in nuclear reactor fuels.
*Inorganic Chemistry.*
**UCAID; Ucaid** University Corporation for Advanced Internet Development.
**UCAR** University Consortium for Atmospheric Research (U.S.A.).
A consortium of 59 North American Universities, located in Boulder, Colorado.
**U-CARE** Unexplained Cardiac Arrest Registry of Europe - *European Community.*
**UCAS** Universities and Colleges Admissions Service (G.B.).
**UCB** Ufficio Centrale Brevetti.
Italian initialism of the: Central Patent Office.
**UCB** Uganda Commercial Bank - Republic of Uganda.
**UCB** Union de Crédit pour le Bâtiment (France).
**Ucb** Unione credito bancario (Italy).
**UCC** Uniform Code Council (U.S.A.).
The UCC is located in Dayton, Ohio.

**UCC** Uniform Commercial Code.
**UCC** Union Confédérale des Ingénieurs et Cadres (de la CFDT).
*French Union.*
**UCC** University College Cork (Ireland).
**UCCC** Uniform Consumer Credit Code.
*Business; Finance.*
**UCCEGA** Union des Chambres de Commerce et Établissements Gestionnaires d'Aéroports.
*French Union.*
**UCCSN** University and Community College System of Nevada (U.S.A.).
**UCD** University College, Dublin (Ireland).
**UCD** University of California, Davis (U.S.A.).
**UCE** Unità di Conto Europea.
Italian acronym meaning: European Unit of Account.
**UCEI** University of California Energy Institute (U.S.A.).
UCEI was established in 1980 to provide in the University of California *Energy Research* and *Education Activities.*
**UCEO**; **U.C.E.O.** Union Chrétienne de l'Enseignement Officiel (Belgium).
**UCF** Universal Conductance Fluctuations.
*Physics.*
**UCG** Underground Coal Gasification.
**UCG** University College Galway (Ireland).
**UC HSC** University of Colorado Health Sciences Center (U.S.A.).
**UCI** Unicredito Italiano.
The merger (in 1998) of Credito Italiano; Rolo Banca 1473; Cariverona; Cassa di Risparmio di Torino e Cassamarca and during 1999 Cassa di Risparmio di Trento e Rovereto as well as Cassa di Risparmio di Trieste.
*Banking Integrations.*
For further details see under: **CI**.
**UCI** Union Cycliste Internationale.
**UCI** unité de compte d'infrastructure [obsolète - remplacée par NAU].
infrastructure accounting unit (IAU) [obsolete - replaced by NAU].
**UCI** University of California, Irvine (U.S.A.).
**UCID method** User-Centered Information Design method.
*Software Engineering.*
**UCIIM** Unione Cattolica Italiana Insegnanti Medi (Italy).
**UCIMA** Unione Costruttori Macchine Automatiche Confezionamento e Imballaggio.
Italian acronym of the: Automatic Packaging Machines Manufacturers Association (Italy).
**UCIMU**; **Ucimu** Unione costruttori italiani macchine utensili (Italy).
*Italian Unions.*
**UCIs** Undertakings for Collective Investments.
**UCITS** Undertakings for Collective Investment in Transferable Securities.
The E.U. directive for UCITS allows a fund authorized in one member state to be marketed throughout the E.U. subject to local marketing rules.
**UCL** Université Catholique de Louvain (Belgium).
**UCL** University College London (G.B.).
**$Ucl_4$** Uranium Tetrachloride.
*Inorganic Chemistry.*
**UCLA** University of California, Los Angeles (U.S.A.).
**UCLAF** Unione di Coordinamento della Lotta Antifrodi (Italy).
*Italian Unions.*
**UCLAF** Usines Chimiques des Laboratoires Français (France).
**UCLV** UCL Ventures.
UCLV manages UCL's Intellectual Property.
*Intellectual Property Licenses.*
For further details see under: **UCL**.
**UCM** Union syndacale des Classes Moyennes.
*Belgian Unions.*
**UCM** Unresolved Complex Mixture.
**UCMEA**; **U.C.M.E.A.** Ufficio Centrale di Meteorologia e di Ecologia Agraria.
Italian acronym of the: National Board of Meteorology and Agrarian Ecology (Italy).
**UCMEXUS** University of California Institute for Mexico and the United States.
**UCMP** Umeå Center for Molecular Pathogenesis.
Umeå University, Scandinavia.
The Center was founded in 1994.
**UCN** Ultra-Cold / Ultracold Neutron.
*Physics; Quantum effects of gravity.*
**UCN** Ultrafine Condensation Nuclei.
*Atmospheric Science.*
**UCNs** Ultracold / Ultra-Cold Neutrons.
**UCNW** University College of North Wales (Bangor, G.B.).
**Ucométal** Union commerciale Belge de métallurgie.
*Belgian Union.*
**UCOP** Unit Cost Of Production.
**UCP** Uninterruptible Computer Power.
**UCP1** first Uncoupling Protein.
The UCP1 was discovered by researchers at the CNRS (France) and at the University of Dundee (G.B.) in the mid-1970s. The UCP1 diverts energy from adenosine triphosphate synthesis to thermogenesis.

*Biomedical Sciences; Cell Biology; Metabolic Physiology; Neuroscience; Obesity.*

**UCPB** United Coconut Planters Bank (Manila).

**UCPMI** Union Centrale des Participations Métallurgiques et Industrielles.
*French Union.*

**UCPs** Uncoupling Proteins.
*Cell Biology; Metabolic Physiology.*

**UCR** Unconditioned Response.
UCR or UR is also known as: Unconditioned Reflex.
*Behavior.*

**UCR** Unione Costruttori Regolatori per Gas.

**UCR** University of California, Riverside (U.S.A.).

**UCR** University of Costa Rica.

**UCS** Unconditioned Stimulus.
*Behavior.*

**UCS** Uniform Cost Search.
*Artificial Intelligence.*

**UCS** Unione dei Capistazione (Italy).
Italian initialism of the: Station-Masters Union.

**UCS** Union of Concerned Scientists.

**UCS** Universal Character Set.
*Computers.*

**UCSB** University of California, Santa Barbara (U.S.A.).

**UCSC** University of California, Santa Cruz.

**UCSD** University of California, San Diego (U.S.A.).

**UCS diagram** Uniform-Chromaticity-Scale diagram.
*Optics.*

**UCSF** University of California, San Francisco (U.S.A.).

**UCSI** Unione Cattolica Stampa Italiana.
*Italian Union.*

**UCT** Universal Coordinated Time.

**UCT** University of Cape Town (South Africa).

**UCTDC** University of California Technology Development Company (U.S.A.).
The University of California Technology Development Company was created with a view to fund startup companies and help University of California researchers to develop inventions.

**U'CUT** (abbr.) Undercut.
*Anatomy; Engineering; Forestry; Metallurgy; Mining Engineering.*

**UCW** Unit Control Word.

**UD** Udine, Italy.

**UD** underwater diving.
plongée sous-marine.

**UD** Union Départementale (France).

**UD** Upper Deck.

**U.D.** Urban District.

**UDA** Ulster Defence Association (Ireland).

**UDAG** Urban Development Action Grants.

**UDAL** Unità Dialitiche di Assistenza Limitata (Italy).

**UDC** Universal Decimal Classification.

**UDCA** Union pour la Défense des Commerçants et Artisans (France).
French initialism of the: Union for the Defense of Dealers and Craftsmen.

**UDDI** Universal Description Discovery and Integration.
Microsoft, IBM and Ariba.
*Internet-based Directories.*

**U.D.E.** Unione della Difesa Europea.
Italian acronym of the: European Defence Union.

**UDE; U.D.E.** Unione Doganale Europea.
Italian acronym of the: European Customs Union.

**UDECO** Union de Crédit pour l'Environnnement et l'utilisation économique de l'énergie.
*Environment; Energy Savings.*

**UDF** Unducted Fan.

**UDF** Union des Fabricants (France).
French initialism of the: Manufacturers Union.

**UDF** Union pour la Démocratie Française.
French initialism of the: Union for French Democracy.
*Political Party.*

**UDF** United Democratic Front (South Africa).

**U.D.I.** Unione Donne Italiane.
Italian acronym of the: Association of Italian Women (Italy).

**U/die** Upper die.
*Press Working.*

**UDL** Uniformly Distributed Load.

**UDMH** Uns-dimethylhydrazine.

**UDOC** Ultrafiltered Dissolved Organic Carbon.

**UDOM** Ultrafiltered Dissolved Organic Matter.

**UDON** Ultrafiltered Dissolved Organic Nitrogen.

**UDP** Uniform Delivered Price.
*Business; Commerce.*

**UDP** Uridine Diphosphate.
*Biochemistry* - $C_9H_{14}N_2O_{12}P_2$.
*Biomedicine Research.*

**UDP** User Diagram Protocol.

**UDPG** Uridine Diphosphoglucose.
*Biochemistry.*

**UDP-Glc Nac 2-epimerase** Uridine Diphosphate-N-Acetylglucosamine 2-epimerase.
*Biochemistry; Cell Surface Sialylation; Glycobiology; Immunobiology; Molecular Biology.*

**UDR** Unione dei Democratici della Repubblica.

The UDR is the center-right party with 29 deputies founded by Francesco Cossiga, the former president, on 2nd July 1998 and led by him. (Italy).

**UDR** Union pour la Défense de la République.
French initialism of the: Union for the Defense of the Republic (France).

**UDSIS** Union Départementale des Syndicats Intercommunaux Scolaires.
*French Union.*

**UDT** underwater demolition team.
équipe de démolition sous-marine.

**UDU** Underwater Demolition Unit.

**UE** Unione Europea; Union Européenne.
Italian and French initialism of the: European Union.

**U.E.A.** Unione Europea Assicuratori.
Italian initialism of the: Insurers European Union.

**UEA** University of East Anglia (G.B.).

**UE and C** United Engineers and Constructors (U.S.A.).

**UEBL** Union Economique Belgique-Luxembourg.
French initialism of the: Economic Union Belgium-Luxemburg.

**UEC** Union Européenne des Experts Comptables Economiques et Financiers.
*European Unions.*

**UECE** University Entrance Center Examination.
University entrance exams in Japan.

**U.E.E.** Unione Economica Europea.
Italian initialism of the: European Economic Union.

**U.E.E.** Université Européenne d'Ecriture (Belgium).

**U.E.F.** Unione Europea dei Federalisti.
Italian acronym of the: European Union of Federalism Supporters.

**UEM** Unione Economica e Monetaria.
Italian initialism meaning: Economic and Monetary Union.

**UEM** United Engineer Malaysia.
*Malaysian Construction Groups.*

**UEMOA** Union Economique et Monétaire Ouest-Africaine.
French initialism of the: West African Economic and Monetary Union.

**UEO**; **U.E.O.** Unione Europea Occidentale; Union de l'Europe Occidentale.
Italian and French initialism of the: Western European Union.

**UEP**; **U.E.P.** Unione Europea dei Pagamenti; Union Européenne des Paiements.
Italian and French acronym of the: European Payments Union.

**UEPNO** Use of Enzymes in the Processing of New Oilseeds to industrial raw materials.
*European Community Project.*

**U.E.R.** Unione Europea di Radiodiffusione.
Italian acronym of the: European Broadcasting Union.

**UER** Unité d'Enseignement et de Recherche.
French acronym meaning: Teaching and Research Unit (France).

**UES** Upper Esophageal Sphincter.

**UET** Universal Engineering Tractor.

**UETP** University-Enterprise Training Partnerships.

**UF** United Front (India).

**UF** University of Florida (U.S.A.).

**UF** Urea Formaldehyde.

**UF** Used For.

**UF** User-Friendly.
*Computer Programming; Industrial Engineering.*

**$UF_4$** Uranium Tetrafluoride.
Uranium Tetrafluoride, also known as: Green Salt, is used in the production of uranium metal.
*Inorganic Chemistry.*

**$UF_6$** Uranium Hexafluoride.

**UFA** Until Further Advised.

**UFAC** Upholstered Furniture Action Council.
The UFAC is located in High Point, North Carolina (U.S.A.).

**UFAW** University Federation for Animal Welfare.

**UFCS** Union Féminine Civique et Sociale (France).

**UFD** User File Directory.

**uff.** (abbr.) ufficiale.
Italian abbreviation meaning: official; officer.
*Military.*

**uff.** (abbr.) ufficio.
Italian abbreviation meaning: bureau; office.

**UFF** Union des Femmes Françaises (France).
French initialism of the: French Women Union.

**UFF** Universal Flip-Flop.

**U.F.I.** Unione Fiere Internazionali.
Italian acronym of the: International Trade Fair Union.

**UFO**; **ufo** Unidentified Flying Object.
The unidentified flying object is also known as: Flying Saucer because it looks like a shining disk.
*Astronomy.*

**UFO** User Files On-line.

**UFPa** Universidade Federal Do Pará (Brazil).

**UFS** Universal Financial System.
*Business; Finance.*

**UFSCC** University of Florida Shands Cancer Center (U.S.A.).

**UFSIA** Universitaire Faculteitem St. Ignatius Antwerpen (Belgium).

**UFT** United Federation of Teachers.
**UFTAA** Universal Federation of Travel Agents' Associations.
**UG** Uganda.
**UG** Urogenital.
*Anatomy.*
**UG** User Group.
*Computer Programming.*
**UG** Uteroglobin.
UG or Blastokin was first discovered in the rabbit uterus.
*Animal Science; Cell Biology; Genetics; Heritable Disorders; Mammalian Genetics and Development; Veterinary and Tumor Pathology.*
**UGBN** Union Générale Belge de Nettoyage et de la Désinfection (Belgium).
*Belgian Unions.*
**U.G.C.** University Grants Committee (U.S.A.).
**UGGT** UDP-glucose: Glycoprotein Glucoryl Transferase.
For further details see under: **UDP**.
**U.G.I.** Unione Geografica Internazionale.
Italian acronym of the: International Geographic Union.
**UGI** Upper Gastrointestinal.
**UGM** Universidad Gabriela Mistral (Santiago, Chile).
UGM is Chile's first private university. Founded in 1981 UGM's programs include: master's degrees in economics; management for lawyers; finance and political philosophy.
**UGM** University of Gadjah Mada (Indonesia).
UGM is one of the nation's premier research universities.
**UGO** Unité de Grappe Opératrice.
*Communications.*
**UGPP** Uridine Diphosphoglucose Pyrophosphorylase.
**UGS** unattended ground sensor.
capteur au sol non surveillé.
**UGSP** Undergraduate Scholarship Program.
The UGSP is sponsored by the U.S. National Institutes of Health.
**UGT** User Group Table.
**UGTT** Union Générale des Travailleurs Tunisiens.
**UH** University of Hawaii.
**UH** University of Hertfordshire (G.B.).
**UH** University of Houston (U.S.A.).
**$UH_3$** Uranium Hydride.
$UH_3$ is used mainly as a reducing agent.
*Inorganic Chemistry.*
**UHC** Ultimate Holding Company.
*Business; Finance.*
**UHECRs** Ultra-High-Energy Cosmic Rays.
*Astrophysics; Space Physics.*
**UHF** Ultrahigh Frequency.
The ultrahigh frequency is the frequency band in the range from 300 to 3000 megahertz.
*Telecommunications.*
**UHKT** Institute of Hematology and Blood Transfusion (Prague, Czechoslovakia).
**UHL** User Header Label.
**UHMWP** Ultrahigh-Molecular-Weight Polyethylene.
*Plastics.*
**UHN** University Health Network.
Toronto-based, Canada.
**UHP** Ultrahigh Pressure.
**UHS/CMS** University of Health Science/Chicago Medical School (U.S.A.).
**UHT** Ultrahigh Temperature.
**UHTs system** Ultra High Throughput Screening system.
**UHV** Ultrahigh Vacuum.
*Physics.*
**U.I.** Unione Interparlamentare.
Italian initialism of the: Interparliamentary Union.
**UI** University of Indonesia.
**UI** User Identification.
*Computer Programming.*
**UIA** Union Internationale des Architectes.
French initialism meaning: International Union of Architects.
**UIA** Union of International Associations (Belgium).
**UIACP** Uniform International Authentication and Certification Practices.
Project E100 - sponsored by the International Chamber of Commerce - completed in April 1998.
*International Agreements; Security Procedures.*
**Uiae** Union industrielle pour l'Afrique équatoriale.
**UIAM** Unione Internazionale Assicurazioni Marittime.
Italian initialism of the: Marine Insurance International Union.
**U.I.C.** Ufficio Italiano Cambi.
Italian initialism of the: Italian Exchange Office.
**UIC** Union Internationale des Chemins de fer.
*International Union; Railways.*
**UIC** Unione Italiana Ciechi (Italy).
*Italian Unions.*
**UIC** unit identification code.
code d'identification d'unité.
**UIC** University of Illinois at Chicago (U.S.A.).
**UIC** Upper Inner Core.
*Earth and Environmental Sciences; Seismology.*
**U.I.C.C.** Unione Internazionale Contro il Cancro.

Italian initialism of the: International Union against Cancer.

**UICC** Union Internationale Contre le Cancer.
French initialism of the: International Union against Cancer.
Located in Geneva, Switzerland.

**UICN** Union Mondiale pour la Nature.
Located in Gland, Switzerland. Founded in 1948 to promote international co-operation in scientific research and in applying ecological concepts for conservation of nature and natural resources; to ensure the perpetuation of biological diversity and genetic resources of wild animals and plants in their natural environment; to disseminate information, ecological guidelines and techniques of conservation in preserving wildlife habitats and other natural landscape features for their ethical, aesthetic, scientific, educational and economic values; to facilitate the understanding of ecological principles and biological productivity for the long-term economic and social welfare of mankind.
*Scientific Research.*

**UICOM-UC** University of Illinois College Of Medicine at Urbana-Champaign (U.S.A.).

**UICs** Urea Inclusion Compounds.
*Chemistry; Chemical Engineering; Materials Science.*

**UID** (abbr.) Unidentified.

**UIF** Unione Industriali del Fermano.
Located at Fermo (AP), Italy.
*Italian Unions.*

**UIF**; **Uif** Unità di Intelligence Finanziaria.
Italian initialism meaning: Financial Intelligence Unit.
To fight money laundering.

**UIH** Union Instrumentale d'Hermance (Switzerland).

**UIL**; **U.I.L.** Ufficio Internazionale del Lavoro.
Italian acronym of the: International Labour Organization.

**UIL**; **U.I.L.** Unione Italiana del Lavoro.
Italian acronym of the: Italian Trade Union Federation.

**UILCER** Unione Italiana Lavoratori Chimica Energia E Risorse (Italy).
*Italian Unions.*

**UILDM** Unione Italiana Lotta alla Distrofia Muscolare (Italy).
*Muscular Dystrophy Union.*

**UILPS** Unione Italiana Lavoratori Polizia di stato.
*Italian Police Union.*

**UIP** Interdisciplinary University of Paris.

**UIPPI** Unione Internazionale per la Protezione della Proprietà Industriale.
Italian acronym of the: International Union for the Protection of Industrial Property, Paris convention 1883.

**UIR** Unione Italiana Ristoratori (Italy).

**UIR bands** Unidentified IR bands.
*Astrochemistry; Astronomy; Astrophysics; Molecular Astrophysics.*
For further details see under: **IR**.

**UIS** Unemployment Insurance Service (U.S.A.).

**U.I.S.** Unione Internazionale di Soccorso.
Italian acronym of the: International Aid Society.

**UIST Symposium** User Interface Software and Technology Symposium.

**UIT**; **U.I.T.** Unione Internazionale Telecomunicazioni; Union Internationale des Télécommunications.
Italian and French initialism of the: International Telecommunication Union.

**UITP** Union Internationale des Transports Publics (Belgium).
French initialism of the: International Union of Public Transport.
Founded in 1885 to study all problems related to the operation of public transportation.

**U.I.T.S.** Unione Italiana Tiro a Segno.
Italian acronym of the: Italian Rifle Association.

**UIV** Urographie Intraveineuse.
French initialism meaning: Intravenous Urography.

**UIV-FNCV** Unione Italiana Vini - Federazione Nazionale del Commercio Vinicolo.
Located in Milan, Italy.
*Wines Union.*

**UJ** Unconditional Jump.
UJ is also known as: Unconditional Branch; Unconditional Transfer.
*Computer Programming.*

**UJCL** Universal Job Control Language.

**U.J.I.** Universidad Jaume I (Spain).

**UJNR** United States - Japan cooperative program in National Resources.

**UJT** Unijunction Transistor.

**U.K.** United Kingdom.

**UK** University of Kentucky (U.S.A.).

**UK** Urokinase.
Urokinase is also known as: Plasminogen Activator.
*Enzymology.*

**UKADGE** United Kingdom Air Defence Ground Environment.
infrastructure électronique de la défense aérienne du Royaume-Uni.

**UKADR** UK Air Defence Region.

zone de défense aérienne du Royaume-Uni.
**UKAEA; U.K.A.E.A.** United Kingdom Atomic Energy Authority.
With effect from January 2000 the JET is run by the UKAEA on behalf of the European Commission's Euratom Program and the 17 European National Fusion Associations.
For further details see under: **JET**.
**UKAFF** U.K. Astrophysical Fluids Facility.
A national supercomputing facility based at the University of Leicester, G.B.
*Astrophysical Fluid Dynamics.*
**UKAPS; Ukaps** U.K. Association of Pharmaceutical Scientists (G.B.).
**UKAS** The United Kingdom Accreditation Service (G.B.).
UKAS is the U.K. national accreditation body responsible for assessing and accrediting the competence of organisations in the fields of *measurement, testing, inspection and certification of systems, products and personnel.*
**UKB** Universal Keyboard.
**UKDMC** U.K. Dark Matter Collaboration.
UKDMC runs a scintillation detector in Europe's deepest mine in Northern England. The UKDMC experiment takes place at the Rutherford Appleton Laboratory.
*Astronomy.*
**U.K. GER Office** United Kingdom Global Environmental Research Office.
**UKIRT** United Kingdom Infrared Telescope.
*Astronomy; Planetary Science.*
**UKITO** United Kingdom Information Technology Organization.
**UKMO** United Kingdom Meteorological Office (G.B.).
**UK/NL AMF** United Kingdom / Netherlands Amphibious Force.
Force amphibie Royaume-Uni / Pays-Bas.
**UKRA** United Kingdom Reading Association.
**UL** Underwriters Laboratories (U.S.A.).
**UL** upper layer (defence).
(défense de la) couche supérieure.
**UL** Upper Limit.
**UL** User Language.
**ULA** Uganda Library Association.
**ULA** Uncommitted Logic Array.
*Robotics.*
**ULA** Utah Library Association (U.S.A.).
**ULB** Université Libre de Bruxelles (Belgium).
**ULC** Unconfirmed Letter of Credit.
*Banking; Business; Commerce; Finance.*
**ULC** Urban Libraries Council.
**ULCC** Ultralarge Crude Carrier.
The ultralarge crude carrier is also known as: Supertanker.
*Naval Architecture.*
**ULD** Unit Logic Device.
**ULDs** Unit Loading Devices.
**ULIGs** Ultra-Luminous Infrared Galaxies.
Also: **ULIRGs**.
*Astronomy; Astrophysics.*
**ULIRGs** Ultra-Luminous Infrared Galaxies.
Also: **ULIGs**.
*Astronomy.*
**ULIS** Uniform Law on the International Sale of goods.
**ULLZZ** ultra-long-leg zigzag.
zigzag à tronçons ultra longs.
**ULMS** Undersea Long-range Missile System (U.S.A.).
**Ulsa** Ufficio lavoro sede apostolica (Italy).
**ULSAB project** Ultra-Light Steel Auto Body project (U.S.A.).
**ult.** (abbr.) ultimate; ultimately.
**ult.** (abbr.) ultimo.
Also: **ulto**.
**ULVZ** Ultralow-Velocity Zone.
The ULVZ consists of partially melted rock.
*Geophysics; Mineral Physics; Seismology.*
**u/m** undermentioned.
**U.M.** Unione Militare.
Italian initialism meaning: Military Union.
**UM** Union Minière (Belgium).
**UM** Unions Monétaires.
French initialism meaning: Monetary Unions.
**UM** University of Malaysia (Malaysia).
**UM** University of Manitoba (Canada).
**U.M.** University of Maryland (U.S.A.).
**UM** University of Miami (U.S.A.).
**UM** University of Missouri (U.S.A.).
**UM** User Mode.
*Computer Programming.*
**UMA** Union du Maghreb Arabe.
**UMA** unmanned aircraft.
avion sans pilote.
**UMA** Utenti Motori Agricoli (Ente) (Italy).
**UMARP** Upper Mantaro Archaeological Research Project.
**UMASS** University of Massachusetts (U.S.A.).
**UMBC** University of Maryland-Baltimore County (U.S.A.).
**UMBI** University of Maryland Biotechnology Institute (U.S.A.).
**UMC** United Methodist Church.

**UMC** University of Missouri-Columbia, Missouri (U.S.A.).
**UMD** University of Maryland (U.S.A.).
**UMD** University of Medicine and Dentistry (U.S.A.).
**UMD** Univesrity of Minnesota - Duluth (U.S.A.).
*Plant Biology; Population Biology; Plant Systematics.*
**UMDF** The United Mitochondrial Disease Foundation (U.S.A.).
*Mitochondrial Illness; Research Grant Programs.*
**UMDNJ** University of Medicine and Dentistry - New Jersey.
Medical School, Newark, NJ, U.S.A.
**UME** Unité Monétaire Européenne.
**UMF** unconventional military forces.
forces militaires non conventionnelles.
**UMH** Université de Mons-Hainaut (Belgium).
**UMI** Unione Magistrati Italiani (Italy).
Italian acronym of the: Italian Magistrates Union.
**UMI** Unione Matematica Italiana (Italy).
Italian acronym of the: Italian Mathematical Society.
**U.M.I.** Unione Monarchica Italiana (Italy).
Italian acronym of the: Italian Royalist Union.
**UMIST** University of Manchester Institute of Science and Technology (G.B.).
**UMKC** University of Missouri - Kansas City, U.S.A.
**UML** Unità Medica Libera (Italy).
**UMMC** University of Massachusetts Medical Center (U.S.A.).
**UMMI** Unione Medico Missionaria Italiana.
Italian acronym of the: Italian Medical Missionary Association; located in Rome, Italy.
**UMMS** University of Massachusetts Medical School (U.S.A.).
**UMOA** Union Monétaire Ouest-Africaine.
French acronym of the: West-African Monetary Union.
**UMOD** (abbr.) User MODule.
**UMP** Upper Mantle Project.
Of the International Council of Scientific Unions.
**UMP** Uridine Monophosphate.
*Biochemistry.*
**UMPTIDUMPTI** Using Mobile Personal Telecommunications Innovation for the Disabled in UMTS Pervasive Integration.
*European Community Project.*
**UMSO** Unione Mediterranea Saggiatori Olio (Italy).
**UMT** Union Marocaine du Travail.
*Morocco Union.*
**UMTS** Universal Mobile Telephony Services.
*Next-Generation Mobiles.*
**UN; U.N.** United Nations.
*Organizations.*
**UNA** Unione Nazionale dell'Avicoltura.
Italian acronym of the: Bird-Fancying National Union.
**unabr.** (abbr.) unabridged.
**UNADW** Upper North Atlantic Deep Water.
*Oceanography; Paleoceanography.*
**U.N.A.FLOR.** Unione Nazionale fra le Associazioni di produttori FLORovivaistici.
*Italian Unions.*
**UNAI** Unione Nazionale Amministratori di Immobili.
*Italian Unions.*
**UNAIDS** The United Nations' special program on AIDS.
UNAIDS replaced the GPA in 1994.
For further details see under: **GPA**.
**UNAM** National Autonomous University of Mexico (Mexico City).
**U.N.A.M.** UNione Arti Marziali (Italy).
*Italian Unions.*
**UNAPASS** Unione Nazionale Agenti Professionisti di Assicurazioni.
Italian abbreviation of the: National Association of Professional Insurance Agents (Italy).
**UNAPROA** Unione Nazionale tra le Associazioni di Produttori Ortofrutticoli, Agrumari e di Frutta in guscio.
*Italian Union.*
**U.N.A. PR. OL.** Unione Nazionale tra le Associazioni di PRoduttori di OLive (Rome, Italy).
*Italian Unions; Olive Producers.*
**UNARC** University of Alexandria, Institute of Graduate Studies and Research (Egypt).
**UNASAS** Unione Nazionale Accademia Scuola Acconciatori per Signora (Italy).
*Italian Academies.*
**UNASCA** Unione Nazionale Autoscuole Studi Consulenza Automobilistica (Italy).
*Italian Unions.*
**UNASP** Unione Nazionale Associazioni Sportive Popolari (Italy).
**U.N.A.T.** Unione Nazionale Artisti Teatrali.
Italian acronym of the: National Theatre Artists Association.
**UNATEX** Unione Associazioni Tessili.
*Italian Textile Associations.*
**UNATI** Union NAtionale des Travailleurs Indépendants (France).

French acronym of the: National Union of Independent Workers.
**UNAVIA** Associazione per la Normazione e la Certificazione nel Settore Aerospaziale.
UNAVIA is located in Rome, Italy.
*Italian Standards Issuing Associations.*
**UNC** University of North Carolina (U.S.A.).
**UNC** University of Northern Colorado (U.S.A.).
The UNC is a Carnegie Research Intensive Institution.
**UNCC** The United Nations Compensation Commission.
The UNCC was created in 1991.
**UNC-CH** University of North Carolina at Chapel Hill (U.S.A.).
**UNCED** United Nations Conference on Environment and Development.
**UNCG** University of North Carolina at Greensboro (U.S.A.).
**UNCI** Unione Nazionale delle Cooperative Italiane.
*Italian Union.*
**UNCITRAL** United Nations Commission on International Trade Law.
**UNCLOS** United Nations Convention on the Law of the Sea.
The marine mineral provision of UNCLOS was signed in 1982 and entered into force in 1994.
**UNCOL** Universal Computer-Oriented Language.
**UNCRO** United Nations Confidence Restoration Operation in Croatia.
opération des Nations Unies pour le rétablissement de la confiance en Croatie (ONURC).
**UNCW** University of North Carolina at Wilmington (U.S.A.).
**UNDHA** United Nations Department of Humanitarian Affairs [replaced by OCHA].
Département des affaires humanitaires des Nations Unies[remplacé par le BCAH].
**UNDOF** United Nations Disengagement Observer Force.
**UNDP** United Nations Development Program.
**UNE** University of New England (Australia).
**UNEF** Unified thread form Extra Fine.
**UNEF** Union Nationale des Etudiants de France.
French acronyrn of the National Union of French Students.
**UNEP** United Nations Environment Program.
For further details see under: **GEF**.
**UNEPTA** United Nations Expanded Program of Technical Assistance.
**UNESCO** United Nations Educational, Scientific and Cultural Organization.
**UNEXIM** United Export-Import Bank.
Moscow, Russia.
**UNF** Unified thread Form (Fine).
**UNF** Union Nationale des Femmes (France).
French initialism of the: Women National Union.
**UNFAO** United Nations Food and Agriculture Organization.
**UNFCCC** United Nations Framework Convention on Climate Change.
The UNFCCC has been ratified by 174 countries (1999).
*Climate; Greenhouse Gases.*
**UNFPA** United Nations Population Fund.
**UNGA** United Nations General Assembly.
**UNH** University of New Hampshire (U.S.A.).
**Unh** Unnilhexium.
**UNHCR** United Nations High Commissioner's Office for Refugees.
Haut-Commissariat des Nations Unies pour les réfugiés.
**UNI** Ente Nazionale Italiano di Unificazione.
UNI is located in Milan, Italy.
*Italian Standards Issuing Organizations.*
**U.N.I.** Unione Naturisti Italiani.
Italian acronym of the: Italian Naturist Association.
**UNI** Union Nationale des Intellectuels (France).
**UniBwM** University of Armed Forces Munich, Institute for Hydraulics (Germany).
**UNIC** Unione Nazionale Invalidi Civili (Italy).
**UNICE; U.N.I.C.E.** Union des Industries de la Communauté Européenne; Unione delle Industrie della Comunità Europea.
French and Italian acronym of the: European Community Industries Union.
**UNICEF** United Nations International Children's Emergency Fund.
**Unichar** (abbr.) Union Charbonnière Rhénane.
**UNICHIM** Associazione per l'Unificazione nel settore dell'Industria Chimica.
Italian abbreviation of the: Association for Standardization in the Chemical Industry Field (Italy).
*Italian Standards Issuing Associations.*
**UNICOL;Unicol** Universal computer-oriented language.
**UNICOST** (abbr.) UNItà per la COSTituzione.
**UNIDA** Unione Industrie Dolciarie e Alimentari (Italy).
**UNIDI** Unione Nazionale Industria Dentaria Italiana.
*Italian Dentistry Union.*
**UNIDIR** United Nations Institute for Disarmament Research (Geneva, Switzerland).

**UNIDO** United Nations Industrial Development Organization.
Headquartered in Vienna, Austria.
**UNIENET** United Nations International Emergency NETwork.
**UNIFER** Ente di Unificazione del Materiale Ferrotranviario.
UNIFER is located in Florence, Italy.
*Italian Standards Issuing Organizations.*
**UNIFIL** United Nations Interim Force In Lebanon.
**UNIKOM** United Nations Iraq-Kuwait Observers Mission.
**UNIL** UNIversité de Lausanne (Switzerland).
**UNIMAS**; **Unimas** UNIversity of MAlaysia at Sarawak (Malaysia).
**UNIONPLAST** Unione Nazionale Industrie Trasformatrici Materie Plastiche (Italy).
*Italian Unions; Plastic Materials.*
**UNIOSIND** Unione Sindacale Personale Direttivo Banche (Italy).
*Italian Banks Union.*
**UNIPEDE** UNIone dei Produttori E Distributori di Elettricità.
Italian acronym of the: Union of Electricity Producers and Distributors. A European Group (with Euroelectric).
**UNIPLAST** Ente Italiano di Unificazione nelle Materie Plastiche.
UNIPLAST is located in Milan, Italy.
*Italian Standards Issuing Organizations.*
**UNIPOL** Universal Procedure Oriented Language.
**UNIPRO** (abbr.) UNIversal PROcessor.
**UNIQUE** Uniform Inquiry Update and Edit.
**UNIRE** UNItà Ricerca Europea.
Italian acronym meaning: European Research Unit.
**UniS** Uni̲versity of S̲urrey (G.B.).
*Health, Food and Environment.*
**UNISIST** United Nations world Science Information System.
**UNISYS** UNited Information SYSstems.
**UNITA** UNione per l'Indipendenza Totale dell'Angola.
**UNITAR** United Nations Institute for Training And Research (Geneva, Switzerland).
**UNITEX** Associazione Nazionale per l'Unificazione nel Settore Tessile.
Italian abbreviation of the: National Association for Standardization in the Textile Field. UNITEX is located in Milan, Italy.
*Italian Standards Issuing Associations.*
**Unitop** U̲nion n̲ationale des i̲ndustries de t̲ransmissions o̲léohydrauliques et p̲neumatiques.
*French Union.*
**UN.I.TRA.** UNione Italiana TRAsportatori.
*Italian Union.*
**univ.** (abbr.) universal; universally.
*Astronomy; Mechanical Engineering; Science.*
**Univ.** (abbr.) University.
**Univa** U̲n̲ione i̲ndustriali della Provincia di V̲a̲rese.
*Italian Union.*
**UNIVAC** UNIVersal Automatic Computer.
**UNIVER** Union d'Intérêt pour la Valorisation de l'Espagne et la Retraite.
*French Union.*
**UNL** University of Nebraska-Lincoln (U.S.A.).
**U.N.L.A.** Unione Nazionale per la Lotta contro l'Analfabetismo (Italy).
Italian acronym of the: National Association for the fight against illiteracy.
**UNLOSC** United Nations Law Of the Sea Convention.
**UNLV** University of Nevada Las Vegas (U.S.A.).
**UNM** University of New Mexico (U.S.A.).
**UNMC** University of Nebraska Medical Center (U.S.A.).
**UNMICI** Unione Nazionale Mutilati Invalidi Civili d'Italia.
Italian acronym of the: National Association of Crippled and Disabled of Italy.
**UNML** Union Nationale des Mutualités Libérales (Belgium).
**UNMN** Union Nationale des Mutualités Neutres (Belgium).
**UNMO** United Nations military observer.
observateur militaire des Nations Unies.
**UNMOGIP** United Nations Military Observers Group in India and Pakistan.
**UNMOVIC** United Nations Monitoring, Verification and Inspection Commission.
referring to WMD in Iraq.
For further details see under: **WMD**.
**UNMPL** Union Nationale des Mutualités Professionnelles et Libres (Belgium).
**UNMS** Union Nationale des Mutualités Socialistes (Belgium).
**UNN** University of Nizhny Novgozod (Russia).
**UNO** United Nations Organization - The U.N.
**UNOLS** University-National Oceanographic Laboratory System.
UNOLS manages the U.S. academic fleet. It is a consortium of U.S. Institutions.
**UNOS** United Network for Organ Sharing.
UNOS is a U.S. private group.
*Transplantation.*
**Unp** Unnilpentium.

*Chemistry.*

**UNPA** United Nations protected area.
zone protégée par les Nations Unies (ZPNU).

**UNPC** Union Nationale des Professionnels de la Comptabilité.
*French Union.*

**UNPF** United Nations peace forces.
forces de paix des nations Unies (FPNU).

**UNPREDEP** United Nations Preventive Deployment Force.
Force de déploiement préventif des Nations Unies (FORDEPRENU).

**UNPROFOR** United Nations Protection Force [obsolete].
Force de protection des Nations Unies [obsolète].

**Unq.** unnilquadium.

**UNR** Union pour la Nouvelle République (France).

**UNR** University of Nevada Reno (U.S.A.).

**UNREP** underway replenishment.
ravitaillement à la mer.

**UNRISD** The United Nations Research Institute for Social Development (Geneva, Switzerland).

**UNRRA** United Nations Relief and Rehabilitation Administration.

**Uns** Unidentified Neurons.
*Brain Research; Pathophysiology; Physiology.*

**UNS** Unified thread form Special.

**Uns.** Unnilseptium.
*Chemistry.*

**UNSAS** Unione Nazionale Scuole per Attività Sociali (Italy).
voir SC3. [pas en usage à l'ONU].

**UN-SCEAR** United Nations Scientific Committee on the Effects of Atomic Radiation.
Established in 1955.
*Ionizing Radiation.*

**UNSCOM** United Nations Special Commission.
Established after the Gulf War in 1991. Entrusted by the U.N. Security Council to supervise the destruction of weapons of mass destruction in Iraq. The mandate was terminated in 1999.

**UNSCR** see SCR [not in use in the UN].
voir SCR [pas en usage à l'ONU].

**UNSIDER** Ente Italiano di Unificazione Siderurgica.
UNSIDER is located in Milan, Italy.
*Italian Standards Issuing Organizations.*

**UNSM** University of Nebraska State Museum.
Lincoln, Nebraska (U.S.A.).

**UNSTAT** United Nations Statistical Office, Environment Statistics Section.

**UNT** Unité Nutritive Transformable.
French initialism meaning: Total Digestible Nutrients.

**UNTAG** United Nations Transition Assistance Group.

**UNTDED** Uniform Trade Data Elements Directory.

**UNTDID** Uniform Trade Data Interchange Directory.

**UNTHSC-FW** University of North Texas Health Science Center at Fort Worth (U.S.A.).

**UNTS** United Nations Treaty Series.

**UNTSO** United Nations Truce Supervision Organization.

**UNU** United Nations University.
The University is an autonomous institution within the UN framework and is sponsored jointly by UN and UNESCO. UNU has no students or degree courses, it conducts various training activities in association with its programme and provides fellowships for post-graduate scientists and scholars from developing countries.
For further details see under: **UNESCO**.

**U.N.U.RI.** Unione Nazionale Universitaria Rappresentativa (Italy).
Italian acronym of the: Association of Italian University Students.

**UNUSS** Unione Nazionale Utenti Strutture Sanitarie.
*Italian Union.*

**UO** Unità Operativa; Unità Organizzativa.

**$UO_2$** Uraninite.
Uraninite is found mainly in sedimentary beds and hydrothermal veins.
*Mineralogy.*

**$UO_2$** Uranium Dioxide.
Uranium Dioxide, also known as: Yellowcake; Urania, is used in nuclear fuel rods.
*Inorganic Chemistry.*

**$UO_3$** Uranium Trioxide.
$UO_3$, also known as: Uranyl Oxide, is used mainly in pigments, and ceramics.
*Inorganic Chemistry.*

**$U_3O_8$** Tertiary Triuranium Octoxide.
$U_3O_8$ also known as: Uranyl Uranate; Uranous / Uranic Acid, is used mainly to prepare uranium compounds.
*Inorganic Chemistry.*

**UOA** Units Of Account.

**UoAs** Units of Assessment.

**$UO_2(CO_3)$** Rutherfordine.
*Mineralogy.*

**UofL** University of Louisville (U.S.A.).

**U. of S.A.** Union of South Africa.

**$UO_3{\cdot}2H_2O$** Schoepite.

*Mineralogy.*
**UOP** Unit Of Production.
**UOS** Unless Otherwise Specified.
**UOT** Unit Of Trading.
**UOV** Unit Of Value.
**UP** 1. Ukraine.
1. Ukraine.
2. unité participante.
2. participating unit (PU2.).
**U.P.** Ulster Parliament.
**UP** Underproof.
**UP** Unearned Premium.
**UP** United Press (U.S.A.).
**UP** United Provinces.
**UP** Unit Price.
**UP** Unrealized Profits.
**up.** (abbr.) upper.
Also: **u**.
**UP** Uroporphyrin.
*Biochemistry.*
**UP** User Prices.
**UP** User Program.
User program is also known as: User-Written Program, User-Written Code.
*Computer Programming.*
**UP** Utility Program.
**UPA** Uniform Partnership Act.
*Business; Finance.*
**U.P.A.** Unione Panamericana.
Italian acronym of the: Pan-American Union.
**UPA** Unique Product Advantage.
*Business; Commerce.*
**uPA** urokinase Plasminogen Activator.
**UPC** Uniform Practice Code.
**UPC** United Pan-Europe Communications (The Netherlands).
Dutch-based, UPC is the biggest European Cable operator.
**UPC** Universal Product Code.
The universal product code is usually a ten-digit bar code put on labels of packages identifying the manufacturer as well as the particular product. It is used at checkout counters in retail stores.
*Computer Technology.*
**UPE** Union Parlementaire Européenne.
**UPEB** Union of Banana Exporting Countries.
Founded in 1974. Members of the above Union are: Panama, Honduras, Guatemala, Colombia, Costa Rica, Venezuela and Nicaragua.
**UPF** Unit Power Factor.
*Electricity.*
**UPGMA** Unweighted Pair-Group Method with Arithmetic means.
**U.P.I.** Ufficio Privato Investigativo.
Italian acronym meaning: Private Detective Agency.
**UPI** Unione Province Italiane.
Italian acronym of the: Italian Provinces Union.
**U.P.I.** Unione Pubblicità Italiana.
Italian acronym of the: Italian Advertising Union.
**UPI** Union Paléontologique Internationale.
French acronym of the: International Paleontologic Union.
**UPI** United Press International.
**U.P.I.C.A.** Ufficio Provinciale Industria, Commercio e Artigianato (Italy).
**UPM** Undergraduate Program in Microbiology (U.S.A.).
**UPM** University Putra Malaysia.
**UPMC** University of Pittsburgh Medical Center (U.S.A.).
**UPMRC** Union of Palestinian Medical Relief Committees.
*First Aid Workers; Rehabilitation Clinics.*
**UPOs** Unstable Periodic Orbits.
**UPPE** Ultraviolet Photometric and Polarimetric Explorer.
**UPPIC** Union Interprofessionnelle Pour la Promotion des Industries de la Conserve.
*French Union.*
**UPR** Union Pacific Resources (U.S.A.).
*Oil Production.*
**UPR** University of Puerto Rico.
**UPR** Urétéropyélographie Rétrograde.
*Medicine.*
**UPS** Ufficio Provinciale di Statistica (Italy).
**UPS** Ultraviolet Photoelectron Spectroscopy.
Also: Ultraviolet Photoemission Spectroscopy.
**UPS** Uninterruptible Power Supply.
**UPS** Uninterruptible Power System.
Also: Uninterruptible Power Supply; Uninterruptible Power Source.
*Electricity.*
**UPS grid** Universal Polar Stereographic grid.
*Cartography.*
**UPSI** User Program Switch Indicator.
*Computers.*
**UPT**; **U.P.T.** Ufficio Provinciale del Tesoro.
Italian initialism of the: District Treasury Office.
**UPT** Ufficio Provinciale del Turismo (Italy).
**UPT** Undistributed Profits Tax.
*Business; Finance.*
**U.P.U.** Universal Postal Union.
**UPUCE** Ufficio delle Pubblicazioni Ufficiali delle Comunità Europee - E.C.

Italian acronym of the: Official Publications Office of the European Communities.

**UPVG** Utility PhotoVoltaic Group.
Two major results of the Tuscon meeting (in 1992) have been the formation of the UPVG and the creation of state working groups. A national steering committee guides and coordinates activities, which are dedicated to joint stakeholder actions leading to the commercialization of *utility-scale PV systems*.

**UQAM** Université du Québec à Montréal (Canada).
*Biotechnologies; Environmental Science; Mathematical and Computer Sciences; Health and Risk.*

**UR** Unconditioned Response.
UR is also known as: Unconditioned Reflex: **UCR**.
*Behavior.*

**UR** Under Rule.
*Stocks.*

**UR** Union of Soviet Socialist Republics [former USSR].
1a. ex-URSS.
1b. ex-Union soviétique.

**UR** Unit Record.
*Computer Programming.*

**UR** University of Rochester (U.S.A.).

**UR** Utility Routine.
UR is also known as: Utility Program.
*Computer Programming.*

**URA** University Research Association.

**URAL** Unione Regionale Albergatori della Lombardia (Italy).

**URAP wave experiment** Unified Radio And Plasma wave experiment.
*Aeronautics; Astronomy; Physics.*

**URC** underway replenishment coordinator.
coordonnateur du ravitaillement à la mer.

**URC** University Research Consortium.

**UR-CRIDF** Union Régionale - Centre Régional d'Information des Droits des Femmes.
Located at Besançon, France.
*Women Rights.*

**URCRM** Urals Research Center for Radiation Medicine.

**URCs** Ubiquitin Reaction Components.
*Adult Oncology; Biological Chemistry; Cancer Biology; Medicine; Molecular Pharmacology; Pediatric Oncology.*

**URCs** Uniform Resource Citations.
*Library and Information Science; Supercomputing Applications.*

**Urd.** (abbr.) uridine.
Also: **U**; **u**.
*Biochemistry.*

**UREF** unité de référence de grille.
grid reference unit (GRU).

**UREF** Universités des Réseaux d'Expression Française.
For further details see under: **AUPELF**.

**Urenio** Urban and regional innovation research unit.
At Aristotle University Thessaloniki.
For further details see under: **Verite**.

**UREPT** Unione Regionale degli Enti Provinciali per il Turismo della Lombardia.
*Italian Union.*

**URG** underway replenishment group.
groupe de ravitaillement à la mer.

**URGE** Unifying Research and Graduate Education (Indonesia).
URGE is funded by the World Bank.
*World Bank Programs.*

**URGV** Unité de Recherche en Génomique Végétale (France).
*Plant Genomics.*

**URI** University of Rhode Island.

**URI** Upper Respiratory tract Infection.

**URL**; **Url** Uniform Resource Locator.

**URM** Unité de Raccordement de Multiplex.

**URN**; **Urn** Uniform Resource Name.

**URNs** Uniform Resource Names.
*Library and Information Science; Supercomputing Applications.*

**urol.** (abbr.) urology; urological.

**URP** Ufficio Relazioni con il Pubblico.
Italian initialism meaning: Public Relations Office.

**URSI** Union of Radio Science.

**URSS** Union des républiques socialistes soviétiques [obsolète].
Union of Soviet Socialist Republic [obsolete].

**URT** Ufficio Regionale del Turismo (Italy).

**URTEL** (abbr.) Your Telegram.

**U.S.** Ufficio Stampa.
Italian initialism meaning: Press Agency.

**u.s.** ultimo scorso.
Italian abbreviation meaning: last; last month.

**US** ultrasuono.
Italian initialism meaning: ultrasound.
*Acoustics.*

**U.S.** Uncle Sam.

**US** Unconditioned Stimulus.
*Behavior.*

**US** Underlying Stock.

**US** Under Secretary.

**u/s** undersize.
*Materials Science.*

**U.S.** United States (of America).
Also: **U.S.A.**
**US** Unit Separator.
**US** Unlisted Security.
**US** Unregistered Stock.
**U.S.** unserviceable.
**US** Unstimulated Synapses.
**U.S.** Uscita di Sicurezza.
Italian initialism meaning: Emergency Exit.
**u/s** useless.
**US** The airline code for USAir.
**USA** United States Army.
**U.S.A.** United States of America.
Also: **U.S.**
**USABC** U.S. Advanced Battery Consortium (U.S.A.).
**USACE** U.S. Army Corps of Engineers.
Of the U.S. Department Of Defense.
**USAC-ICO** U.S. Advisory Committee for the International Commission for Optics (U.S.A.).
**USACM** U.S. Association for Computing Machinery (U.S.A.).
**USAEDH** U.S. Army Engineer Division Huntsville (U.S.A.).
**USA EHA** U.S. Army Environmental Hygiene Agency (U.S.A.).
**USAEP** U.S.-Asia Environmental Partnership.
**USAF** United States Air Force.
**USAFA** U.S. Air Force Academy.
**USAID** U.S. Agency for International Development.
**USAMRDC** U.S. Army Medical Research and Development Command.
**USAMRIID** U.S. Army Medical Research Institute of Infectious Diseases.
**USAMRMC** U.S. Army Medical Research and Material Command (U.S.A.).
*Hemorrhage Control; Freeze-dried-blood Storage Bags; Polymer Splints; Neuroprotection; Resuscitation.*
**USAN** United States Adopted Names.
**USARC** U.S. Arctic Research Commission (U.S.A.).
**USARCI** Unione Sindacati Agenti Rappresentanti di Commercio (Italy).
**USAS** U.S.A. Standard.
**USASI** United States of America Standards Institute (successor to A.S.A.).
*Technology.*
For further details see under: **ASA**.
**USB** Unité de Synchronisation de Boucle.
**USBE** Universal Serials and Book Exchange.
**USB interface** Universal Serial Bus interface.
**USC** Under Separate Cover.
*Mail.*
**U.S.C.** United States Code.
**USC** University of Southern California (U.S.A.).
**U.S.C.&G.S.** United States Coast and Geodetic Survey.
**USCF** United States Chess Federation.
**USCG** United States Coast Guard.
*Navy.*
**USCI** Unione Statistica dei Comuni Italiani (Italy).
**USCS** U.S. Commercial Standard.
**USD** U.S. Dollar / U.S. $.
*Currencies.*
**USDA; U.S.D.A.** United States Department of Agriculture.
**USDA/APHIS** U.S. Department of Agriculture's/Animal and Plant Health Inspection Service.
**USDHEW** U.S. Department of Health, Education and Welfare.
**US EPA** United States Environmental Protection Agency (U.S.A.).
**US EPA EMAP** United States Environmental Protection Agency, Environmental Monitoring and Assessment Program.
**USERID** (abbr.) User Identification.
**USES** United States Employment Service.
**USF** University of South Florida.
**USFCOM** University of South Florida College Of Medicine (U.S.A.).
**USFF** Undergraduate Student-Faculty Fellowships.
**USFPL** U.S. Forest Products Laboratory.
**USFs** Universal Stock Futures.
**USFS** U.S. Forest Service (U.S.A.).
Of the U.S. Department of Agriculture.
**USFWS** U.S. Fish and Wildlife Service.
**USG** (abbr.) Ultrasuonodiagnostica.
**USG** United States Government.
**USGCRP** U.S. Global Change Research Program (U.S.A.).
Set up in 1989 - Combined with CCRI.
*Climate-change Research.*
For further details see under: **CCRI**.
**USGRDR** U.S. Government Research and Development Reports (U.S.A.).
**USGS** U.S. Geological Survey (U.S.A.).
**USGW** Underwater-to-Surface Guided Weapon.
**U.S.I.** Ufficio Serico Italiano.
Italian acronym of the Italian Bureau for the Promotion of Silk Fabrics (Italy).
**USI** Unione Sindacale Italiana (Italy).
*Italian Union.*
**USI** Unité de Soins Intensifs.
French acronym meaning: Intensive Care Unit.

*Medicine.*
**USI** Urban Systemic Initiative.
*U.S. School Reforms.*
**USI** Utah Supercomputing Institute (U.S.A.).
**USIA** United States Information Agency.
**USIAS** Union Syndicale des Industries Aéronautiques et Spatiales.
*French Union.*
**USICA** United States International Communication Agency (U.S.A.).
**USIEF** United States-Israel Educational Foundation (U.S.A.).
**USIF** U.S.-India Fund.
For Cultural, Educational and Scientific Cooperation.
**USINACTS** USability IN ACTS.
*European Community Project.*
**USI program** Urban Systemic Initiatives program (U.S.A.).
A statewide program launched in 1994 by the U.S. NSF.
*Systemic Education Reforms.*
For further details see under: **NSF**.
**USIS**; **U.S.I.S.** United States Information Service (U.S.A.).
**USISTC** U.S. - Israel Science & Technology Commission (U.S.A.).
**USITA** United States Independent Telephone Association.
**USITC** United States International Trade Commission (U.S.A.).
**USJCMSP** U.S. - Japan Cooperative Medical Science Program.
**USL** For further details see under: **USSL**.
**USL** University of Southwestern Louisiana (U.S.A.).
**USLC-IUPAP** U.S. Liaison Committee for the International Union of Pure and Applied Physics (U.S.A.).
**USLTA** United States Lawn Tennis Association (U.S.A.).
**USM** Underwater-to-Surface Missile.
**USM** United States Mail.
**USM** United States Mint (U.S.A.).
**USM** Unlisted Securities Market (G.B.).
**USMC** United States Marine Corps.
**USMI**; **Usmi** Unione Superiore Maggiori d'Italia (Italy).
*Italian Union.*
**USN** United States Navy.
**USNCB** United States National Central Bureau (U.S.A.).
**USNC-IAU** U.S. National Committee for the International Astronomical Union (U.S.A.).
**USNC-IUHPS** U.S. National Committee for the International Union of the History and Philosophy of Science.
**USNC-IUPAC** U.S. National Committee for the International Union of Pure and Applied Chemistry.
For further details see under: **IUPAC**.
**USNC-IUPS** U.S. National Committee for the Intenational Union of Physiological Sciences (U.S.A.).
**USNC-IUPSYS** U.S. National Committee for the International Union for Psychological Sciences (U.S.A.).
**USNC-MATH** U.S. National Committee for Mathematics (U.S.A.).
**USNC-MI** U.S. National Commission on Mathematics Instruction (U.S.A.).
**USNCs** United States National Committees.
Groups of Engineers and Scientists who represent the United States in the Organizations that comprise the International Council for Science.
**USNC-SS** U.S. National Committee for Soil Science (U.S.A.).
**USNO** U.S. Naval Observatory.
**USNRC** U.S. Nuclear Regulatory Commission.
**UsnRNPs** Uridine-rich small-nuclear Ribonucleoporteins.
A family of RNA-protein complexes.
*Spinal muscular atrophy.*
**USO** Udaipur Solar Observatory.
USO was built in India in 1975. It deals with high-resolution optical studies of the sun.
**USO** Ultra-Stable Oscillator.
*Astronomy; Astrophysics; Geophysics; Radio Astronomy; Space Science.*
**USO** United Service Organization (Naples, Italy).
U.S. Military Base (Agnano).
**USOA** U.S. Opportunity Alert.
*Funding Information Service.*
**USP** Ultraspiracle.
*Biology.*
**USP** Unique Selling Proposition; Unique Selling Point.
**USP** University of the Science in Philadelphia (U.S.A.).
**USP**; **U.S.P.** U.S. Pharmacopoeia.
Also: **U.S. Pharm.**
**USPHS**; **U.S.P.H.S.** United States Public Health Service.
**USPI** Unione della Stampa Periodica Italiana (Italy).

**USPID**; **Uspid** Unione Scienziati Per Il Disarmo.
Italian acronyrn of the: Scientists Union for Disarmament.
**USPPI** Unione Sindacati Professionisti Pubblico Privato Impiego (Italy).
*Italian Union.*
**USPTO** United States Patent and Trademark Office.
The USPTO is located in Washington, D.C., U.S.A.
**USRA** United States Railway Association (U.S.A.).
**USRA** Universities Space Research Association.
USRA is a U.S. non-profit association of eighty universities.
**USRDA** U.S. Recommended Daily Allowances.
**Uss** Unconditioned Stimuli.
*Behavior.*
**USS** United Seamen's Service (Naples, Italy).
**USS**; **U.S.S.** United States Ship.
**USS** United States Standards.
*Technology.*
**USS** Unité Stratégique Sectorielle.
French initialism meaning: Strategic Business Unit.
**USSAF**; **U.S.S.A.F.** United States Strategic Air Force.
**USSB** United States Shipping Board (U.S.A.).
**U.S.S.I.T.** United States Southern Italy Trading (Naples, Italy).
**USSL** Unità Socio-Sanitaria Locale.
Italian initialism meaning: Local Health Centre/Executive Councils.
**USSR** ex-Union of Soviet Socialist Republics.
For further details see under: **UR** and **URSS**.
**UST** University System of Taiwan.
The UST was formed in 2002.
*Brain Research; Nanotechnology.*
**U stage** Universal stage.
Universal stage is also known as: Fedorov stage.
*Optics.*
**USTR** United States Trade Representative.
**USTTA** United States Travel and Tourism Administration (U.S.A.).
**usu.** (abbr.) usual; usually.
**USUHS** Uniformed Services University of the Health Sciences.
USUHS is located in Bethesda, Maryland, U.S.A.
**USUV** Usutu Virus.
A mosquito-borne pathogen of African birds which at times infects humans and mammals.
*Virology.*
**U.S.V.I.** Unione delle Società Veliche d'Italia.
Italian initialism of the: Association of Italian Sailing Clubs.
**USW**; **usw** Ultrashort Wave.
**USWA** United Steel Workers of America.
**U/T** Under Trust.
**UT** Union Technique.
**UT** Unit Test.
*Computer Programming.*
**UT** Universal Time.
*Horology.*
**UT** University of Tennessee (U.S.A.).
**UT** University of Texas (U.S.A.).
**u.t.** usual terms.
**UT**; **Ut.** (abbr.) Utah (U.S.A.).
Also: **U**.
**Ut.** (abbr.) Utility.
*Engineering; Computer Programming; Statistics.*
**UT1** Unit Telescope 1 (Chile).
*Astronomy.*
**UTA** Union des Transports Aériens.
**U.T.A.** Unione Traduttori Associati (Italy).
*Italian Translators Union.*
**UTA** United Telecom Aktiengesellschaft (Austria).
Headquartered in Vienna, its network is remotely managed from Stockholm.
**UT analogique** Unité Terminale analogique.
**UTC** universal time converted.
temps universel converti.
**UTC** Universal Time Coordinated or Coordinated Universal Time.
*Horology.*
**UTDC** Urban Transportation Development Corporation (Canada).
**UTE** Ufficio Tecnico Erariale.
Italian acronym meaning: Tax Technical Office.
**UTEP** University of Texas at El Paso.
**UTF** Ultra-High / ultrahigh Frequency.
*Telecommunications.*
**UTH** under-the-horizon.
sous l'horizon.
**UTHSCSA** University of Texas Health Science Center at San Antonio, Texas, U.S.A.
**UTI** Union Technique Interprofessionnelle.
*French Union.*
**UTI** Urinary Tract Infection.
*Medicine.*
**UTIs** Urinary Tract Infections.
*Microbiology.*
**UTIF** Ufficio Tecnico Imposte di Fabbricazione (Italy).
**UTK** University of Tennessee, Knoxville (U.S.A.).
**UTL** User Trailer Label.
**UTL** Utility boat, Light.
**UTM** Unité de Traction Mécanique.
**UTM** Universal Turing Machine.

*Computer Programming.*
**UTM** Utility boat, Medium.
**UTMB** University of Texas Medical Branch (U.S.A.).
Established in 1891.
*Ant-Pathogen Programs; Postdoctoral Felloships.*
**UTMDACC** University of Texas M.D. Anderson Cancer Center.
Located in Houston, Texas, U.S.A.
**UTM grid** Universal Transverse Mercator grid.
*Cartography.*
**UTMM** Ufficio Tecnico Marina Militare (Italy).
**U.T.O.** United Towns Organization.
**UTP** Uridine Triphosphate.
**UTPA** University of Texas - Pan American (U.S.A.).
**UTRC** United Technologies Research Center.
The UTRC is located in East Hartford, Connecticut (U.S.A.). UTRC has developed a computer model for detailed calculation of room airflow and comfort. Results will support UTRC in developing advanced *air-handling equipment* and systems that significantly improve indoor air quality. UTRC has also developed a device that hooks into a building's heating and ventilation system. Inside the device, air pollutants are bombarded with ultraviolet light in the presence of special catalysts. This technology is based on NREL work on processes that use light and catalysts to remove volatile organic compounds from contaminated air and water.
*Air Pollutants.*
For further detaikls see under: **NREL**.
**5'-UTR of mRNAs** 5' Untranslated Region of mRNAs.
For further details see under: **mRNAs**.
**UTRs** 3'Untranslated Regions.
*Medicine; Molecula Biology; Molecular Pharmacology; Oncology.*
**UTS** Ultimate Tensile Stress; Ultimate Tensile Strength.
*Materials Science.*
**UTS isotopique** Unité de Travail de Séparation isotopique.
*Nucleonics.*
**UTSW** University of Texas Southwestern Medical Center (U.S.A.).
**UTT** Utility Tactical Transport.
**UTW-EDS** Ultrathin Window Energy Dispersive x-ray Spectrometer.
*Nuclear Science.*
**UUM** Underwater-to-Underwater Missile.
**UUP** Ulster Unionist Party (Ireland) (pro-British).
**u.u.r.** under usual reserve.
**UUT**; **uut** unit under test.
**UV** Burkina Faso.
Burkina-Faso.
**UV**; **U.V.** Ultraviolet.
The term ultraviolet refers to ultraviolet radiation.
Also: **uviol**.
*Physics.*
**UV** Undervoltage.
*Electricity.*
**U.V.** Unione Valdostana.
Italian initialism of the: Aosta Valley Union.
**UvA** Universiteit van Amsterdam (The Netherlands).
**UVA** University of Virginia (U.S.A.).
**UV-B radiation** Ultraviolet-B radiation.
*Chemistry.*
**UVBY wavelengths** Ultraviolet, Violet, Blue, and Yellow wavelengths.
*Astronomy.*
**UVCF** Union des Villes et Communes de France.
**UVCS** Ultraviolet Coronagraph Spectrometer.
Aboard the SOHO Spacecraft.
*Astrophysics; Solar Physics.*
For further details see under: **SOHO**.
**UVF** Ulster Volunteer Force (Ireland).
For further details see under: **CLMC**.
**UVI** Ultra-Violet Imager.
*Geophysics.*
**U.V.I.** Unione Velocipedistica Italiana (Italy).
Italian acronym of the: Italian Cycling Association.
**uviol** ultraviolet.
*Physics.*
For further details see under: **U.V.**
**UVM** University of Vermont.
The UVM is located in Burlington, Vermont, U.S.A.
**UVR** Ultraviolet Rays.
**UV stabilizer** Ultraviolet stabilizer.
*Materials Science.*
**UVVIS camera** Ultraviolet-VISible camera.
**UV/VS** UV/Visible Spectrophotometers.
Also: **UV-VIS**.
For further details see under: **UV**.
**UW** Freedom Union (Poland).
**UW** unconventional warfare.
guerre non conventionnelle.
**u/w** underwriter; underwritten.
**UW** University of Washington (U.S.A.).
**UW** University of Wisconsin (U.S.A.).
**UW** Used With.
**UWA** University of Western Australia.

**UWA** User Working Area.
**UWEB** University of Washington Engineered Biomaterials (U.S.A.).
UWEB is a U.S. National Science Foundation-sponsored Engineering Research Center.
**UWFCT** Uganda Women's Finance and Credit Trust (Uganda).
**UWM** University of Wisconsin - Milwaukee (U.S.A.).
**UWT** underwater telephone.
téléphone sous-marin /TSM).
**UY** Uruguay.
Uruguay.
**ux** wife.
**UXB** Unexploded Bomb.
**UXO** Unexploded Ordnance.
**UZ** Uzbekistan.
Ouzbékistan.

# V

**V** Valley.
*Building Engineering; Electrical Engineering; Geology; Oceanography.*
**V.** valve.
*Anatomy; Invertebrate Zoology; Mechanical Devices.*
**V** The chemical symbol for Vanadium.
Vanadium is a rare element having the atomic number 23, and a melting point of 1900°C. It is used mainly in alloys.
*Chemistry; Symbols.*
**v** variable.
*Artificial Intelligence; Computer Programming; Mathematics; Meteorology; Science.*
**V** Vatican city's vehicle registration letter.
**v** vector.
*Aviation; Computer Programming; Mathematics; Medicine; Military Science; Molecular Biology; Physics; Robotics.*
**V** Vegetarians.
*Human Nutrition.*
**v**; **v.** vein.
*Anatomy; Botany; Entomology; Geology.*
**v** velocity.
*Mechanics.*
**v.** ventral.
*Anatomy; Botany.*
**v** verify.
*Computer Programming; Ordnance; Telecommunications.*
**v** version; versus.
**v** vertical.
*Geodesy; Science.*
**v** very; vicar.
**V**; **v** Vice or vice.
**V** Victoria; Victorian.
**v** village; virtual.
**V** Virus.
*Computer Programming; Virology.*
**v** viscount; vision.
**V** vocative.
**V**; **v** volt.
*Physics.*
**v.**; **v** voltage.
voltage is the potential difference or electromotive force measured in volts.
*Electricity.*
**v.**; **v** volume.
*Acoustical Engineering; Acoustics; Computer Technology; Mathematics; Transportation Engineering.*
**V1** primary Visual Cortex.
*Brain and Cognitive Sciences; Neuroscience.*
**VA** Valore Attuale.
Italian acronym meaning: Present Value; Actual Value.
**V.A.** Value Analysis.
Value Analysis is also known as: Value Engineering; Value Control.
*Industry.*
**VA** Varese, Italy.
**VA** velocità accelerata.
**VA** Ventilation Alvéolaire.
French acronym meaning: Alveolar Ventilation.
*Medicine.*
**va** very active.
**VA**; **V.A.** Veterans Administration.
**VA** Veterans Affairs (U.S.A.).
**VA** Vicar Apostolic; Vice Admiral.
**VA** Victoria and Albert.
*Royal Orders* (G.B.).
**VA**; **Va** (abbr.) Virginia, U.S.A.
**VA** Virtual Advertising.
**VA** Visual Acuity.
The term visual acuity refers to the sharpness of a visual image.
*Physiology.*
**VA** Visual Aid.
**VA**; **va** Volt-Ampere.
Volt-ampere is the unit in the IS.
*Electricity.*
**VA** Volume de l'Air (alvéolaire).
*Medicine.*
**VA** Votre Altesse.
French acronym meaning: Your Highness.
**VAADs** Vasoactive Amines Autoimmune Diseases.
**VAB** Vehicle Assembly Building.
**VAB** Vigilanza Antincendi Boschivi (Italy).
**VAB** Voice Answer Back.
**VABM** Value Added By Manufacturer.
*Business; Commerce.*
**VAC** Alternating Current Volts.
**vac.** (abbr.) vacancy.
*Materials Science; Solid-State Physics.*
**vac.** (abbr.) vacant.
**vac.** (abbr.) vacation.
The vacation period of law courts in Italy is called "periodo feriale"; "ferie" meaning vacation. Usually it is during the month of August.
*Law.*
**Vac.** (abbr.) vacuum.
*Physics; Quantum Mechanics.*

**VAC** Value-Added Carrier.
**VAC** Verified Audit Circulation (U.S.A.).
**VAC** Vincristine, Dactinomycin, and Cyclophosphamide.
*Oncology.*
**VacA** Vacuolating Cytotoxin.
*Gastroenterology; Immunology; Peptic Ulcer Disease.*
**VACE** Virtual Ampèrian Current Element.
*Magnetic Toroids.*
**VACM** Vector Averaging Current Meter.
**VAD** Velocity-Azimuth Display.
**VAD** Ventricular Assist Device.
The VAD provides support to the left ventricle: the locus of the most critical heart damage. Actually, it is a mechanical pump in use since the early 1990s.
For further details see under: **TAH devices**.
**VAD** Voice-Activated Dialing.
*Mobiles; Value-Added Services.*
**VAD** Voluntary Aid Detachment.
**VADC** Video Analog to Digital Converter.
**VADE** Versatile Automatic Data Exchange.
**VADs** Ventricular Assist Devices.
For further details see under: **VAD**.
**VAEC** Vietnam Atomic Energy Commission.
**VAF environment** Viral Antibody-Free environment.
**VAFTAD model** Volcanic Ash Forecast Transport And Dispersion model.
**VA-HUD** Veterans Affairs - Housing and Urban Development (U.S.A.).
**VAK** Virus-Activated Kinase.
*Antiviral responses; Medicine; Microbiology.*
**Val** (abbr.) Valine.
*Biochemistry* - $C_5H_{11}NO_2$.
**val.** (abbr.) valuation; value; valued.
**val** véhicule automatique léger.
**VALA** Victorian Association for Library Automation.
**VALIDATE** Verification And Launch of Integrated Digital Advanced Television in Europe.
*European Community Projects.*
**VALNET** Veterans Administration Libraries NETwork.
**VALS** Values And Life Styles.
*Marketing; Psychology.*
**VAMAS** Versailles project on Advanced MAterials and Standards.
**VAMC** Veterans Administration Medical Center (U.S.A.).
**VAMHCS** Veterans Administration Maryland Health Care System (U.S.A.).
**VAMI** Volontari Associati per i Musei Italiani.
Italian acronym meaning: Associated Volunteers for Italian Museums.
**VAMP** Vesicle-Associated Membrane Protein.
*Molecular and Cellular Physiology.*
**VAMP** Vincristine, Amethopterin, 6-Mercaptopurine, and Prednisone.
*Oncology.*
**VAN** Valore Attuale Netto.
Italian acronym meaning: Net Present Value.
**VAN** Value-Added Network.
**V&P** Vendor and Purchaser.
*Business; Finance.*
**V&V techniques** Verification and Validation techniques.
*Software Development.*
**VANGUARD** Visualisation Across Networks using Graphics and Uncalibrated Acquisition of Real Data.
*European Community Project.*
**VANIU** Valeur Actuelle Nette Intégrée Unitaire.
**VANS** Value Added Network Service - *European Community.*
**VANTAGE** VSAT ATM Network Trails for Applications Groups across Europe.
*European Community Project.*
**VAP** Vaccine Action Program.
*U.S.-India Programs.*
**VAPAHCS** VA Palo Alto Healthcare System.
**VAR** Vacuum Arc Remelt.
**VaR** Valore a Rischio.
*Banking; Finance.*
**var.** (abbr.) variable.
**var.**; **var** (abbr.) variant; variation; variety.
**var.** (abbr.) variegated.
*Biology.*
**var** various.
**VAR** visual-aural range.
*Navigation.*
**Var**; **var** volt-ampere reactive.
volt-ampere reactive is also known as: Reactive Volt-ampere.
*Electricity.*
**Varistor** variable resistor.
*Electronics.*
**VAR record** (abbr.) VARiant record.
*Computer Programming.*
**VARS** vertical and azimuth refernce system.
système de références verticale et azimutale.
**VAS** Value Added Service.
**VASFE** Vérification Approfondie de Situation Fiscale d'Ensemble (France).
*Banking.*
**VASI** Visual Approach Slope Indicator.

**VASIMR** VAriable Specific Impulse Magnetoplasma Rocket.
*Applied Plasma Physics; Fusion Technology.*
**VAS intensity units** Visual-Analog-Scale intensity units.
*Medicine; Neurogenetics; Pain Intensity; Psychiatry.*
**VASIS** visual approach slope indicator system.
indicateur visuel de pente d'approche.
**VASKhNIL** Lenin Academy of Agricultural Sciences.
**V.A.T.** Value Added Tax.
**Vat.** (abbr.) Vatican City.
Also: **V** and **VT**.
**VAT** Virtual Address Translator.
**VATE** Versatile Automatic Test Equipment.
**VATTR** Value Added Tax Tribunal Reports.
**VA/VL** Ventroanterior/Ventrolateral.
**VB** Valence Bond.
*Materials Science; Solid-State Physics.*
**VB** Variable-Block.
*Computer Programming.*
**VB** Vinylbenzoate.
**VB10** Van Biesbroeck 10.
The VB10 is a star which has a mass less than 1/10$^{th}$ that of the sun.
**Vba** visual basic for applications.
**VBA** Visual Business Area.
*Videoconference Networks.*
**VBA Journal** Vermont Bar Association Journal.
**VBC** véhicule blindé de combat.
1a. armoured combat vehicle.
1b. armoured fighting vehicle.
**VBCI** véhicule blindé de combat d'infanterie.
1a. armoured infantry combat vehicle (AICV).
1b. armoured infantry fighting vehicle (AIFV 1.).
**VBD** Voluntary Blood Donation.
**VBI** Virginia Bioinformatics Institute (U.S.A.).
At Virginia Polytechnic Institute and State University.
**VBL** véhicule blindé léger.
light armoured vehicle (LAV).
**VBLR** véhicule blindé lance-roquettes.
armoured vehicle-mounted rocket launcher (AVMRL).
**vBNS** very high-speed Backbone Network Service (U.S.A.).
A system developed for researchers in 1995.
**VBO-FEB** Verbond Van Belgische Ondernemingen.
Initialism of the Federation of Belgian Enterprises.
**VBPP** véhicule blindé poseur de ponts.
armoured vehicle-launched bridge (AVLB).
**VBTP** véhicule blindé de transport de personnel.
armoured personnel carrier.
**VBTT** véhicule blindé de transport de troupes.
armoured troop carrier.
**VC** St. Vincent.
**VC** Valor Civile.
Italian initialism meaning: Civic Valour.
**VC** Variable Costs.
*Business; Commerce.*
**VC** Vector Control.
**VC** Vegetative Compatibility.
**VC** Venture Capital/Capitalist.
*Business; Economics; Finance.*
**VC** Vercelli, Italy.
**VC** Veterinary Corps.
**VC** Vice-Chairman; Vice-Chancellor; Vice-Consul.
**VC** Victoria Cross.
**VC** Vietcong.
**VC** Vinyl Chloride.
VC also known as: Chloroethene; Chloroethylene is used mainly in organic synthesis and plastic adhesives.
*Organic Chemistry.*
**VC** Virtual Circuit.
**VC** Virtual Computer.
**VC** Vital Capacity.
*Physiology.*
**VC** Volume Control.
*Acoustical Engineering.*
**VC** Volume Courant.
French initialism meaning: Tidal Volume.
*Medicine.*
**VCA** Valve Control Amplifier.
**VCAC** véhicule de combat antichar.
antitank combat vehicle (ATCV).
**VCAH** Victorian College of Agriculture and Horticulture.
VACH is located in Melbourne (Australia).
*Agriculture; Horticulture.*
**VCAL** véhicule de combat à armement lourd.
heavy armament combat vehicle (HACV).
**VCAM-1** Vascular Cell Adhesion Molecule-1.
*Cell Biology; Immunology; Medicine; Molecular Biophysics and Biochemistry.*
**VCAPP Department** Veterinary and Comparative Anatomy Pharmacology and Physiology Department.
Washington State University (U.S.A.).
**VCC** 1. Verification Coordination Committee.
1. Comité de coordination de la vérification.
2. virtual command centre.
2. centre de commandement virtuel.
**VCC** Video Compact Cassette.
**VCD** Variable Capacitance Diode.

**VCF** Venture Capital Fund.
**VCF** Voltage Controlled Filter.
**VCG** Vectorcardiogram.
The vectorcardiogram is also known as: monocardiogram.
*Cardiology.*
**VCI** Value Chain Initiative.
Launched by Microsoft in 1997.
*Electronic Commerce; Online Transactions.*
**VCI** 1. véhicule de combat d'infanterie.
1a. infantry combat vehicle (ICV).
1b. infantry fighting vehicle (IFV).
2. volatile corrosion inhibitor.
2. inhibiteur volatil de corrosion.
**VCI** Veine Cave Inférieure.
French initialism meaning: Inferior Vena Cava.
*Medicine.*
**VCI** The German Chemical Industry Association.
**VCIM** véhicule de combat d'infantrie mécanisée.
mechanised infantry combat vehicle (MICV).
**vCJD** variant of Creutzfeldt-Jakob Disease.
The difference between vCJD and the classical CJD consists in the fact that the former develops much more quickly than the latter and strikes younger people. The symptoms are similar.
*Mad Cow Disease (New Studies).*
**$VCl_3$** Vanadium Trichloride.
Vanadium Trichloride is used to prepare vanadium compounds.
*Inorganic Chemistry.*
**$VCl_4$** Vanadium Tetrachloride.
Vanadium Tetrachloride is used to prepare vanadium compounds.
*Inorganic Chemistry.*
**V.C.M.** Vigilanza Città di Milano (Italy).
**VCO** Voltage-Controlled Oscillator.
*Electronics.*
**V-commerce** Voice-enabled e-commerce.
*Voice Recognition; Speech Synthesis; Software.*
**vcp** vacuum condensing point.
*Chemistry.*
**VCP** Voluntary Cooperation Program.
*Oceanography.*
**VCR** Variable Compression Ratio.
**VCR** Videocassette Recorder.
*Electronics.*
**VCS** Veine Cave Supérieure.
French initialism meaning: Superior Vena Cava.
*Medicine.*
**VCs** Venture Capitalists.
**VCSEL** Vertical-Cavity Surface-Emitting Laser.
VCSEL is a device developed in 1995 by Motorola. VCSELs present many advantages over edge-emitting lasers particularly in terms of fabrication costs.
*Materials Science; Semiconductor Lasers.*
**VCU** Virginia Commonwealth University (U.S.A.).
**VD** Vacuum Distillation.
Vacuum Distillation is also known as: Reduced-Pressure Distillation.
**VD** Valeur Déclarée.
French initialism meaning: Declared Value.
**VD** Vapor Density.
**VD** Various Dates.
**V.D.**; **VD** Venereal Disease.
VD is one of a series of diseases contracted through sexual contact.
*Pathology.*
**VD** Vente Directe.
French initialism meaning: Direct Marketing.
*Business; Commerce.*
**VD** Ventricule Droit.
French initialism meaning: Right Ventricle.
**VD** Vienna Document.
**vd** (abbr.) void.
*Astronomy; Computer Programming; Material Science; Physiology.*
**VD** Volume de Distribution.
*Medicine.*
**VD** Volume Discount.
*Business; Commerce; Finance.*
**VDAC** Voltage-Dependent Anion Channel.
*Biochemistry.*
**VDAP** Volcano Disaster Assistance Program.
USGS's.
*Monitoring of Volcanoes.*
For further details see under: **USGS**.
**VDAS** Virtual Direct-Access Storage.
*Computer Technology.*
**V - day** Victory Day.
**VDC** Direct Current Volts.
*Electricity.*
**VDCCs** Voltage-Dependent Calcium Channels.
*Circulatory Physiology; Medicine; Molecular Cardiology; Molecular Physiology.*
**VDD** very deep draught.
à très grand tirant d'eau.
**VDDS** very deep draught ship.
navire à très grand tirant d'eau.
**VDE** Variable Displacement Engine.
**VDE** Variable Display Equipment.
**VDEL** Venereal Disease Experimental Laboratory.
**VdF** Vigili del Fuoco.
Italian initialism meaning: firemen; fire brigade.
Also: **V.F**.
**VDFG** Variable Diode Function Generator.

*Electronics.*
**VDH** Valvular Disease of the Heart.
**VDMA** German Machine and Plant Building Association.
**VDMs** Virtual Dipole Moments.
**VDP** Video Display Processor.
**VDP** voluntary departure plan.
plan de départ volontaire.
**VDPS** Voice Data Processing System.
**VDR** Venereal Disease Research.
**VDR** Voltage-Dependent Resistor.
**VDRL** Venereal Disease Research Laboratory.
**VDS** Variable Depth Sonar.
*Engineering.*
**VDS** Voice/Data System.
*Telecommunications.*
**VDT** Variable Depth Transducer.
**VDT** Video Display Terminal.
**VDU** Visual Display Unit.
**VDWE method** Van Der Waals Epitaxy method.
Named for the Dutch physicist Johannes **Van der Waals**.
*Chemical Engineering; Electrical and Computer Engineering; Materials Science; Nuclear Engineering.*
**VE** Value Engineering.
**VE** Venezia, Italy.
**VE** Venezuela.
**VE** ventilatoire expiré (débit).
*Medicine.*
**VE** Vitelline Envelope.
*Molecular Biology.*
**Ve** Voltelettrone.
Italian abbreviation meaning: Electron Volt / Electronvolt.
*Physics.*
**VE** volume expiré.
*Medicine.*
**VE** Vortex Edge.
**VE** Vostra Eccellenza.
Italian initialism meaning: Your Excellency.
**VEB** Viral Epidemiology Branch.
**VECTAC** vectored attack.
1a. attaque téléguidée - attaque sur vecteur.
1b. attaque guidée.
**VED** visco-élasto-dynamique.
**VEE** Venezuelan Equine Encephalomyelitis.
**VEGF** Vascular Endothelial Growth Factor.
VEGF is an angiogenic protein also called Vascular Permeability Factor.
*Angiogenesis; Antiangiogenesis Drugs; Biochemistry; Biophysics; Cancer Research; Cell Biology; Hormone Research; Immunology; Medicine; Molecular Biology; Pharmaceuticals; Vasculogenesis.*
**VEI** Volcanic Explosivity Index.
**vel.** (abbr.) velocity.
**VEMS** Volume Expiratoire Maximale Seconde.
French acronym meaning: Timed Vital Capacity; Forced Expiratory Volume for the first second.
*Medicine.*
**Ven.** (abbr.) Venerabile.
Italian abbreviation meaning: Venerable.
**Ven.** (abbr.) Venetian.
**VENTEX** (abbr.) VENting EXperiment.
**VEP** Visual Evoked Potential.
**VER** vent effectif de retombée.
effective downwind (EDW).
**ver.** versamento.
Italian abbreviation meaning: payment.
**VER** Volume Expiratoire de Réserve.
*Medicine.*
For further details see under: **VRE**.
**VER** Voluntary Export Restraint.
**VERAs** VEgetable oil-based Release Agents.
*Health and Safety Hazards.*
**Verite** Virtual environment for regional innovation technologies.
Verite will be developed by Urenio and will offer information technology tools for innovation, improving the performance of regional bodies by giving them access to digital experts of innovation management techniques.
*European Commission.*
For further details see under: **Urenio**.
**vert.** (abbr.) vertebrate.
*Vertebrate Zoology.*
**vert.** (abbr.) vertical.
*Geodesy; Science.*
**VERTIC** VERification Technology Information Center.
**VERTICAL** VERtical cavity laser Technology for Interconnection and Access Links.
*European Community Projects.*
**VERTREP** vertical replenishment.
ravitaillement vertical.
**VES** Velocità di Eritrosedimentazione.
*Pathology.*
**VESA** Video Electronics Standards Association.
VESA is an organization comprising graphic *Adapter Manufacturers* and monitor makers.
**Vesc.** (abbr.) Vescovo.
Italian abbreviation meaning: Bishop.
**Vet** (abbr.) Veteran.
**vet.** (abbr.) veterinaria.
Italian abbreviation meaning: veterinary science.

**vet.** (abbr.) veterinarian.
**Vet**; **vet** (abbr.) Veterinary.
**VETS** Veterans' Employment and Training Service (U.S.A.).
**VEV** Voies d'Eau Vivantes.
*European Project.*
**v.f.** field of vision.
**VF** Version Française.
French initialism meaning: French Version.
**VF** Very Fair; Very Fine.
**VF** Video Frequency.
*Telecommunications.*
**V.F.** Vigili del Fuoco.
Italian initialism meaning: fire brigade; firemen.
Also: **V.d.F.**
**VF** Visual Field.
**VF** Voice Frequency.
*Telecommunications.*
**V.F.** Vocal Fremitus.
**VF** Vulcanized Fiber.
*Materials Science.*
**VFD** Value For Duty.
**VFFT** Voice-Frequency Facility Terminal.
**VFL** Variable Field Length.
**VFO** Variable Frequency Oscillator.
**VFR** Visual Flight Rules / visual flight rules.
**VG** Valeur Globulaire.
*Medicine.*
**VG** Ventricule Gauche.
French initialism meaning: Left Ventricle.
**VG** Very Good; Vicar General.
**VGA** Video Graphics Array.
*Computer Technology.*
**VGC** Viscosity-Gravity Constant.
*Petroleum Engineering.*
**VGCCs** Voltage-Gated Calcium Channels.
For further details see under: **UNs**.
**VGFE** Volvo Group Finance Europe B.V.
**VGFS** Volvo Group Finance Sweden.
**VGLI** Veterans Group Life Insurance (U.S.A.).
**VGM** Volume Globulaire Moyen.
French initialism meaning: Mean Corpuscular Volume; Mean Cell Volume.
*Medicine.*
**VGOS** Vocabulaire Général d'Orientation Scientifique.
French initialism meaning: General Dictionary of Scientific Orientation.
**VGP** Virtual Geomagnetic Pole.
**VGPM** Vertically Generalized Production Model.
*Marine and Coastal Sciences; Oceanography.*
**VGPO** velocity gate pull-off.
entraînement de la fenêtre de vitesse.
**VGS** velocity gate stealer.
voleur de fenêtre de vitesse.
**VGT** Volume Globulaire Total.
*Medicine.*
**VGW** variable geometry wings.
ailes à géométrie variable.
**VH** Vacuum Heating.
*Mechanical Engineering.*
**VH** Very High.
**VHA** vapour hazard area.
zone de danger vapeur.
**VH&DO** Vacuum Heating and Drying Ovens.
**VHC** Ventral Hippocampal Commissure.
*Cerebral Structure; Medicine; Molecular Biology; Physiological Sciences.*
**VHCT mice** VHC transected mice.
For further details see under: **VHC**.
**VHF** Very High Frequency.
Also: **vhf**; **v.h.f.**; **V.H.F.**
The very high frequency is the frequency band ranging from 30 to 300 megahertz.
*Telecommunications.*
**VHFO** Very High Frequency Oscillator.
**VHFR** Very High Frequency Receiver.
**vHL disease** Von Hippel-Lindau disease.
A congenital disease also known as: Retinocerebral Angiomatosis.
*Pathology.*
**VHN** Vickers Hardness Number.
*Materials Science.*
**VHP** Very High Precision.
**VHPCC** Very High Performance Computing and Communication.
**VHRR** Very-High Resolution Radiometer.
**VHS** Video Home System.
*Telecommunications.*
**VHSIC** Very High Speed Integrated Circuit.
**VI** Vested Interest.
*Business; Economics; Finance.*
**VI** Vicenza, Italy.
**VI** Virgin Islands.
**Vi** (abbr.) virulent.
*Medicine.*
**VI** Viscosity Index.
*Petroleum Engineering.*
**VI** Volume Indicator.
*Acoustical Engineering.*
**VIA**; **Via** Valutazione di Impatto Ambientale.
*Environment.*
**VIA magazine** Varian Instrument Applications magazine.
*Chromatography; Spectroscopy.*
**vib.** (abbr.) vibration.

*Mechanics.*
**VIBEX** Vehicle Industry Buyers EXpo.
VIBEX was held in Göteborg, Sweden on 12/13/14 May 1998.
**VIC** Very Important Country.
**Vic** (abbr.) Vicar; Vicarage.
**vic.** (prefix) vicinal.
*Organic Chemistry.*
**vic.** (abbr.) vicinity.
**vic.** (abbr.) vicolo.
Italian abbreviation meaning: alley.
**Vic** (abbr.) Victoria.
**Vic.Ap.** Vicar Apostolic.
**VICAP** VIolent Criminal Apprehension Program (U.S.A.).
**Vics** Vehicle information communication system.
The vehicle information communication system, a *beacon-based technology*, was sponsored by the Japanese Government in 1994.
**Vid.**; **vid.** (abbr.) video.
The term video derives from the Latin word "to see".
**VIDAC** Virtual Data Acquisition and Control.
**VIDAS** VIDeo ASsisted with Audio Coding and representation.
*European Community Project.*
**VIDAS** Volontari Italiani Domiciliari Assistenza ai Sofferenti (Italy).
**VIDEO** Visual Data Entry On-line.
**VIDES** Volontariato Internazionale Donne per Educazione e Sviluppo.
Italian acronym of the: International Women Volunteers for Education and Development.
VIDES is located in Rome, Italy.
**VIDO** Veterinary Infectious Disease Organization (Canada).
**VIE** The airport code for Vienna, Austria (Schwechat).
**VIG** Vaccinia Immune Globulin.
**vig.** (abbr.) vigente.
Italian abbreviation meaning: in force.
referring to laws.
**VIGRE program** Vertical Integration of Research and Education Program.
A 2002 Program of the U.S. NSF.
For further details see under: **NSF** and **SUMS**.
**VIL** Vertically Integrated Liquid.
**VIM** Ventilation Industrielle et Minière.
French acronym meaning: Industrial and Mining Ventilation.
**VIMS** Virginia Institute of Marine Science (U.S.A.).
*Algal Toxin Research; Aquatic Ecology; Fish Pathology.*
**VIMS** Visualizations In Materials Science.
**VIN** Vehicle Identification Number.
**VIO** Very Important Object.
**VIP** Vacuum Insulation Panel.
**VIP** Variable Interest Plus.
**VIP** Vascular Intestinal Peptide.
**VIP** Vasoactive Intestinal Polypeptide.
*Endocrinology.*
**VIP** Very Important Person.
**VIP** Visual Information Projection.
**VIQs** Verbal Intelligence Quotients.
*Cognitive Neuroscience; Hippocampal Pathology; Medicine; Mental Health.*
**VIR** Vavilov Institute of Russia.
*Electronics.*
**VIR** Visible and Infrared Radiometer.
**VIR** Volume Inspiratoire de Réserve.
*Medicine.*
**Vis** Viscount; Viscountess.
Also: **Visc.**
**vis** (abbr.) visibility.
**vis** (abbr.) visual.
The term visual refers to vision or sight.
*Physiology.*
**VIS** Volontariato Internazionale per lo Sviluppo.
Italian acronym of the: International Volunteers for Development; VIS is located in Rome, Italy.
**VISA strains** Vancomycin-Intermediate *Staphylococcus Aureus* strains.
*Antimicrobial Agents; Chemotherapy; Medicine; Microbiology; Clinical Immunology.*
**Visc.** (abbr.) Viscount; Viscountess.
Also: **Vis.**
**VISE** Vehicle Industry Suppliers Expo.
**VISET** VIsion System Experiment development Tests.
**VISPA** VIrtual Storage Productivity Aid.
**VISPE** Volontari Italiani per la Solidarietà ai Paesi Emergenti (Italy).
Italian acronym of the: Italian Volunteers for Solidarity to Emerging Countries; located at Casirate Olona di Lacchiarella, (near Milan) Italy.
**VISSR** Visible Infrared Spin-Scan Radiometer.
**VISTA** Visible and Infrared Survey Telescope for Astronomy.
VISTA is a 4-meter telescope that will be located in Chile. In every 10-minute exposure it will capture 100,000 galaxies and stars. It is planned for 2004.
*Astronomy; Physics.*
**VISTA** Volunteers In Service To America.
**vista** The above acronyms were coined accidentally

using the Italian word "vista" which means: eyesight; sight.
**VITA** Volunteers for International Technical Assistance.
**vita** The above acronym was coined accidentally using the Italian word "vita" which means: life.
**VITAL** Validation of Integrated Telecommunications Architectures for the Long-term.
*European Community Project.*
**VL-1** Viking 1 Lander.
**VLA** Vermont Library Association (U.S.A.).
**VLA** Very Large Array.
*Astrophysics.*
**VLA** Very Low Altitude.
**VLA** Virginia Library Association (U.S.A.).
**Vlan** Virtual lan.
**VLB** Very Long Baseline.
**VLBA** Very Long Baseline Array.
VLBA is a network of 10 identical radio telescopes that stretches across the United States.
*Astronomy; Astrophysics; Radio Polarization.*
**VLBI** Very Long Baseline Interferometry.
**VLBI technique** Very Long Baseline Interferometry technique.
For further details see under: **VSOP**.
**VLCC** Very Large Crude Carrier.
**VLCFAs** Very Long Chain Fatty Acids.
*ALD disease; Biochemistry; Medicine; Neurobiology; Neurology; Physiology.*
For further details see under: **ALD disease**.
**VLDB** Very Large Data Base.
**VLDL** Very-Low-Density Lipoprotein.
**V.le** (abbr.) viale.
Italian abbreviation meaning: avenue; boulevard.
**VLF; vlf** Very Low Frequency.
The very low frequency is the frequency band in the range from 3 to 30 kilohertz.
*Telecommunications.*
**VLL** Very Low-Luminosity.
*Astronomy.*
**VLLZZ** very-long-leg zigzag.
zigzag à tronçons très longs.
**VL nucleus** Ventrolateral nucleus.
**VLPD** Very Long-Period Displacement.
*Earthquake Research; Geology; Meteorology; Volcanology.*
**VLPO area** Ventrolateral Preoptic area.
**VLPs** Virus-Like Particles.
**VLR radar** Very-Long-Range radar.
*Electronics.*
**VLS growth** Vapor-Liquid-Solid growth.
*Chemical Biology; Chemistry.*
**VLSI** Very-Large-Scale Integration.
*Electronics.*
**VLSTRACK model** Vapor-Liquid-Solid TRACKing model.
**VLT** Very Large Telescope.
*Optical Astronomy.*
**VLVAs** Very Large low-Velocity Anomalies.
**V.M.** Valore Malleveria.
Italian initialism meaning: Value of Suretyship.
**V.M.** Valore Militare.
Italian initialism meaning: Military Valour.
**VM** Variabili di Marketing.
**VM** Vertical Merger.
*Business; Finance.*
**VM** Vietnam.
For further details see under: **VN**.
**VM** Virtual Machine.
*Computer Technology.*
**VM** Virtual Memory.
**vm** vitesse maximale.
**V.M.** Vostra Maestà.
Italian initialism meaning: Your Majesty.
**VMA** Valid Memory Address.
**VMb nucleus** basal Ventral Medial nucleus.
*Neuroscience; Neurophysiology.*
**VMC** Vermont Monitoring Cooperative (U.S.A.).
**VMC** Visual Meteorological Conditions.
**VMCM** Vector Measuring Current Meter.
**V.M.D.** Doctor of Veterinary Medicine.
**VMD** Veterinary Medicine Directorate (G.B.).
**VMDs** Volume Median Diameters.
**VMFI** visual mine firing indicator.
indicateur visuel de mise de feu.
**VMH** Ventromedial Hypothalamus.
*Obesity Research.*
**VMH** Victoria Medal of Horticulture.
**VM nucleus** ventromedial nucleus.
*Anatomy.*
**VMOS** Virtual-Memory Operating System.
**VMOS technology** Vertical Metal Oxide Semiconductor technology.
*Electronics.*
**VMPE** Virtual Memory Performance Enhancement.
**Vmps** Variable major proteins.
*Allergy; Infectious Diseases; Clinical Microbiology.*
**VMRC** Virginia Mason Research Center (U.S.A.).
**VMR combinations** Visual-Motor-Reward combinations.
*Brain Science; Neural Mechanisms.*
**VMS** Variable Message Signs.
*Transport Telematics; Traffic Management Software.*

**VMS** Vertical Market Structure.
*Business; Commerce; Finance.*

**VMS** Voice Message System.

**VMT** Vehicle-Miles Travelled.

**VMT** Virtual Memory Technique.
*Computer Programming.*

**VMx** Ventilation Maxima; Ventilation Maximale Volontaire.
French initialism meaning: Maximum Breathing Capacity.
*Medicine.*

**VMZ explants** Ventral Marginal Zone explants.
*Medical Science.*

**VN** Vietnam's international vehicle-registration letters.

**VN** vulnerability number.
indice de vulnérabilité.

**VNC** voluntary national contribution.
contribution nationale volontaire.

**VNCS** voluntary naval control of shipping.
contrôle naval volontaire de la navigation commerciale.

**V-(Ni, Fe)** Taenite.
Taenite is a mineral found in meteorites. It is a natural alloy of nickel and iron.
*Mineralogy.*

**VNIIEF** All-Russia Scientific Research Institute for Experimental Physics.
VNIIEF has built a niobium-based laser ISKRA-6. Its first module (Luch) was launched in 2001.
*Experimental Physics.*

**VNIITF** All-Russia Scientific Research Institute for Theoretical Physics.
VNIITF is a *nuclear weapons design* center in the closed city of Snezhinsk.

**VNO** Vomeronasal Organ.
In the mouse the VNO is a small cavity at the back of the nose.
*Chemoreceptor Organs; Chemosensory Receptors; Odorant Receptors; Olfaction; Recognition Molecules; Neuroscience.*

**VNODC** Vietnamese National Oceanographic Data Center.

**VNTRs** Variable Number Tandem Repeats.
*Biostatistics; DNA fingerprinting; Genetics.*

**VO** Vanadium Oxide.
*Inorganic Chemistry.*

**vo** verbal order.

**V.O.** Version Originale.
French initialism meaning: Original Version.

**VO** Very Old.

**VO** Veterinary Officer.

**VO** Victorian Order.

**VO** visitors and observers.
visiteurs et observateurs.

**v/o** votre ordre.
French initialism meaning: your order.

**$V_2O_3$** Vanadium Trioxide.
Vanadium Trioxide is used as a catalyst.
*Inorganic Chemistry.*

**$V_2O_4$** Vanadium Tetraoxide.
Vanadium Tetraoxide is used as a catalyst.
*Inorganic Chemistry.*

**$V_2O_5$** Vanadium Pentoxide.
$V_2O_5$, also known as: Vanadic Acid Anhydride, is used mainly in photography, and in ceramics.
*Inorganic Chemistry.*

**VOA** Variable Optical Attenuator.

**VOA** Voice Of America.
*Radio.*

**VOAs** Variable Optical Attenuators.
VOAs offer low losses in broadband window.

**VOB** visitors and observers bureau.
bureau des visiteurs et observateurs.

**voc.** (abbr.) vocabolo.
Italian abbreviation meaning: word; term.

**voc.** (abbr.) vocational.

**VOC** Volatile Organic Compound.
For further details see under: **VOCs**.

**vocab.** (abbr.) vocabulary.

**VOCAL** Vocabulary language.

**VOcdr** Voice coder.

**$VOCl_3$** Vanadium Oxytrichloride.
Vanadium Oxytrichloride is used mainly as a catalyst.
*Inorganic Chemistry.*

**VOCs** Volatile Organic Compounds.
The volatile organic compounds are the vapours given off by various chemicals used in industry, such as solvents, and contained in consumer products, such as house paints, petrol, and the like.
*Environmental Sciences.*

**VOD** vertical on-board delivery.
livraison à bord à la verticale.

**VOD** Video On Demand.

**VODAS** Voice-Operated Device Anti-Singing.
*Electronics.*

**VODER** Voice-Operation Demonstrator.
*Electronics.*

**VO engine** Vaporizing Oil engine.

**VOF** variable operating frequency.
fréquence de fonctionnement variable.

**VOGAD** Voice-Operated Gain-Adjusted Device.
*Electronics.*

**VOICI** Vegetable Oil for Innovation in Chemical Industries.

*European Community Project.*
**VoIP technology** Voice over Internet Protocol technology.
*Business Communications.*
**VOIR** Venus Orbiter Imaging Radar.
**VOIs** Volumes Of Interest.
*Clinical Psychology; Medicine; Neuroscience of Autism; Radiology.*
**vol.** (abbr.) volcano.
**vol.** (abbr.) volume.
*Acoustical Engineering; Acoustics; Computer Technology; Mathematics; Transportation Engineering.*
**vol.** (abbr.) volume.
Italian abbreviation meaning: volume.
**vol.** (abbr.) voluntary.
**Vol.** (abbr.) Volunteer.
**volc** (abbr.) volcanic; volcano.
**voll.** (abbr.) volumi.
Italian abbreviation meaning: volumes.
**VOM**; **vom** Volt-Ohm-Meter.
**VOP**, **V.O.P.** Valued as in Original Policy.
*Insurance.*
**VOP** Value Of Product.
*Business; Commerce; Finance.*
**VOR range** Very-high-frequency Omnidirectional Radio range.
*Navigation.*
**VOR-TEX** Verification of the Origins of Rotation in Tornadoes EXperiment.
*Analysis and Prediction of Storms; Mesoscale Meteorological Studies; Meteorology.*
**VOS** Value Of Stock.
*Business; Commerce; Finance.*
**VOS** Vertical Obstacle Sonar.
*Engineering.*
**VOS** Vessel Of Opportunity.
**VOS** Voluntary Observing Ship.
**VOSFA** Vegetable Oils with Specific Fatty Acids.
*European Community Project.*
**$VOSO_4$** Vanadyl Sulfate.
$VOSO_4$, also known as: Vanadium Sulfate; Vanadic Sulfate, is used mainly as a colorant and catalyst.
*Inorganic Chemistry.*
**vou.** (abbr.) voucher.
**VOX** Voice-activated.
*Electronics.*
**VP** Vaglia Postale.
Italian initialism meaning: postal money order.
**V.P.** Valore Plateale.
Italian initialism meaning: Apparent Value.
**VP** Vapor Pressure.
VP is also known as: Vapor Tension.
*Meteorology.*
**VP** Variable Pitch.
**VP** Variable Point.
*Computer Programming.*
**VP** Venous Pressure.
*Medicine.*
**VP** Vent Pipe.
*Mechanical Devices.*
**VP** Vice President.
Also: **V.P.**
**VP** Virtual Process.
*Quantum Mechanics.*
**VP branch** Verification Program branch.
Of the U.S. Forecast Systems Laboratory.
**VPC** Vente Par Correspondance.
French initialism meaning: Mail-Order Selling.
**VPF** Vascular Permeability Factor.
For further details see under: **VEGF** (Vascular Endothelial Growth Factor).
**VPg** Poliovirus virion protein, Genome-linked.
*Virology.*
**VPI** Vapor Phase Inhibitor.
**VPI** *Vibrio* Pathogenicity Island.
*Genomics; Immunology; Microbiology.*
**VPI** Virginia Polytechnic Institute (U.S.A.).
**VPI nucleus** Ventral Posterior Inferior nucleus.
*Neuroscience; Neurophysiology.*
**VPL nucleus** Ventral Posterior Lateral nucleus.
*Neuroscience; Neurophysiology.*
**VPM nucleus** Ventral Posterior Medial nucleus.
*Biomedical Technologies; Developmental Neuroscience; Physiology.*
**VPN**; **Vpn** Virtual Private Network.
**VPNs** Virtual Private Networks.
**VPP** Value Payable by Post.
**VPP** Variable-Pitch Propeller.
*Mechanical Engineering.*
**VPP** Vested Pension Plan.
**VPP** Virus Pneumonia of Pigs.
**VPR** Video Plankton Recorder.
The video plankton recorder is an instrument developed in 1992 by biologists at the U.S. WHOI.
*Biology; Oceanography.*
For further details see under: **WHOI**.
**VPRC** Volume of Packed Red Cells.
**VPR** Virtual Plan position indicator Reflectoscope.
*Navigation.*
**VPT** Vente Par Téléphone.
French initialism meaning: Telephone selling; telesales.
**VPT** Volume Plasmatique Total.

*Medicine.*
**VQA** Vendor Quality Assurance.
*Business; Commerce.*
**VQC** Vendor Quality Certification.
*Business; Commerce.*
**VQD** Vendor Quality Defect.
*Business; Commerce.*
**v.r.** vedi retro.
Italian abbreviation meaning: see overleaf; please turn over.
**VR** Verona, Italy.
**VR** Vested Rights.
*Business; Economics; Finance.*
**VR** Victoria Regina.
**VR** Virtual Reality.
*Artificial Intelligence; Computer Technology.*
**VR** Vocal Resonance.
**VR** Voltage Regulator.
VR is also known as: Voltage Corrector.
*Electronics.*
**VR** Volume Résiduel.
French initialism meaning: Residual Volume; Residual Air; Residual Capacity.
*Medicine.*
**VR1** Vanilloid Receptor subtype 1.
*Neurobiology.*
**VRA** Value Received Analysis.
*Business; Commerce.*
**VRC** Visible Record Computer.
**VRE** Volume de Réserve Expiratoire.
French acronym meaning: Expiratory Reserve Volume.
*Medicine.*
**V region** Variable region.
*Immunology.*
**VRFs** Visual Receptive Fields.
*Auditory Space Processing; Medicine; Neurobiology.*
**VRFWS** Vehicle Rapid Fire Weapon System.
**VRI** Virus Research Institute.
The VRI is located in Cambridge, Massachusetts, U.S.A.
**VRI** Volume de Réserve Inspiratoire.
French initialism meaning: Inspiratory Reserve Volume.
*Medicine.*
For further details see under: **IRV**.
**VRM** Variable-Rate Mortgage.
*Business; Finance.*
**VRM** Viscous Remanent Magnetization.
*Geophysics.*
**Vrm** Visitor relationship management.
**VRML; Vrml** Virtual Reality Mark-up Language.
**VRN** Variable-Rate Note.
**VROI** Value Return On Investment.
**VRS** Virus Respiratoire Syncytial.
French initialism meaning: Respiratory Syncytial Virus.
*Virology.*
**VR systems** Virtual Reality systems.
*Computer Technology.*
**VRT spectra** Vibration-Rotation-Tunneling Spectra.
**VR tube** Voltage-Regulator tube.
*Electronics.*
**VS** Valore di Stima.
Italian initialism meaning: Estimate Value.
Also: **Vs**, **V.S.**
**v.s.** vedi sopra.
Italian abbreviation meaning: see above.
**Vs** (abbr.) versus.
**VS** Vesicular Stomatitis.
*Veterinary Medicine.*
**VS** Veterinary Surgeon.
**v.s.** vibration seconds.
**VS** Vinyl Sulfone.
**VS** Virtual Storage.
**V/S** visual signalling.
signaux optiques.
**VS** Vitesse de Sédimentation.
French initialism meaning: Sedimentation Velocity.
*Analytical Chemistry.*
**vs**, **v.s.** volumetric solution.
**Vs**; **vs** Vostro.
Italian abbreviation meaning: Your, yours.
**VS** Voting Stock.
*Business; Commerce; Finance.*
**$V_2S_5$** Vanadium Sulfide.
$V_2S_5$, also known as: Vanadic Sulfide, is used to prepare vanadium compounds.
*Inorganic Chemistry.*
**VSAT technology** Very Small Aperture Terminal technology.
VSAT is used mainly to bring data from satellite to computer.
**VSB** Vestigial Sideband.
*Telecommunications.*
**VSBC** Very Small Business Computer.
**VSBR** Visuomotor Behavioral Rehearsal.
*Psychology.*
**VSC** Variable Speech Control.
*Electronics.*
**VSCC** Valence Shell Charge Concentrations.
**VSD** Ventricular Septal Defect.
**VSE** Vychodoslovenske Energeticke Zadovy - Slovak Republic.

VSE is one of the Energy Distribution Companies in the Slovak Republic responsible for East Slovakia.
**VSG** Variant Surface Glycoprotein.
*Biochemistry.*
**VSG** (Vitesse de) Sédimentation Globulaire.
French initialism meaning: Sedimentation Rate; Sed Rate.
*Medicine.*
**VSG model** Viscous Semi-Geostrophic model.
**VSHORAD** very short-range air defence.
(défense) sol-air à très courte portée (SATCP).
**VSHORADS** very short-range air defence system.
système d'arme de défense sol-air à très courte portée (système SATCP).
**VSM** Vascular Smooth Muscle.
**VSM instrument** Volcanic System Monitor instrument.
*Geophysics; Seismicity; Undersea Research.*
**VSMCs** Vascular Smooth Muscle Cells.
**VSNL** Videsh Sanchar Nigam Limited (India).
*International Telecom Services.*
**VSO** Very Superior Old.
referring to Brandy, etc.
**VSOP** Very Superior Old Pale.
**VSOP** VLBI Space Observatory Program.
The VSOP is a 25-telescope network.
*Active Galaxies; Astrophysics; Radio Astronomy; Supernovae.*
For further details see under: **VLBI**.
**VSP4D** Vesicle Surface Protein 4D.
*Cell Biology; Medicine.*
**V/STOL** Vertical Short Takeoff and Landing.
**VSV** Vesicular Stomatitis Virus.
*Virology.*
**VSV-G** Vesicular Stomatitis Virus G protein.
*Medicine.*
**VT** Vacuum Tube.
*Electronics.*
**VT** Valeur à Terme.
**VT** Variable Time.
**VT** Vatican City.
For further details see under: **V** and **Vat**.
**V.T.** Vecchio Testamento.
Italian initialism meaning: Old Testament.
**VT**; **Vt** (abbr.) Vermont, U.S.A.
**VT** Vertical Tabulation.
*Computer Programming.*
**VT** Video Terminal; Virtual Terminal.
**VT** Viterbo, Italy.
**VT** Voice Tube.
**VT** Volume courant Total.
*Medicine.*
**VT** Voting Trust.
**VTA** Variable Transfer Address.
**VTA** Ventral Tegmental Area (of the rat brain).
*Basic Neuroscience; Drug Addiction; Learning and Memory; Neurobiology; Psychiatry.*
**VTAM** Virtual Telecommunications Access Method.
**VTC** Volunteer Training Corps.
**VTC** Voting Trust Certificate.
*Business; Finance.*
**VTE** Vertical Tube Evaporator.
**vtg.** (abbr.) voting.
*Stock.*
**VTH** visualisation tête haute.
head-up display (HUD).
**VTO** Vertical Take-Off.
**VTOC** Volume Table Of Contents.
**VTOL** Vertical Takeoff and Landing.
*Aviation.*
**VTPR** Vertical Temperature Profile Radiometer.
**VTR** Videotape Recorder/Recording.
**VTS technology** Vessel Traffic Services Technology.
*Maritime Traffic Management.*
**VTUAV program** Vertical Takeoff and landing Unmanned Aerial Vehicle program.
**VTVM** Vacuum-Tube Voltmeter.
VTVM is also known as Tube Voltmeter.
*Engineering.*
**V.U.** Vigile Urbano.
Italian initialism meaning: Traffic Policeman.
**VU** vitesse uniforme.
**VU** Voice Unit.
**VU** Volume Unit.
*Acoustical Engineering.*
**VU** Vrije Universiteit - Amsterdam, The Netherlands.
**vulg** (abbr.) vulgar; vulgarly.
**VUP** Vivendi Universal Publishing.
**VUV continuum radiation** Vacuum Ultraviolet continuum radiation.
*Astronomy; Physics.*
**VV** Vaccinia Virus.
**vv** veins.
**VV** Vibo Valentia, Italy.
**v v** vice versa; volumes.
**v/v** volume per volume.
*Medicine.*
**VVSOP** Very Very Superior Old Pale.
**VV.UU.** Vigili Urbani.
Italian initialism meaning: Traffic Police.
**V.W.** Vessel Wall.
**VW** Volkswagen (Germany).

VM is Europe's biggest carmaker.

**vWD** von Willebrand Disease.
vWD also known as Pseudohemophilia, is a bleeding disorder characterized by increased binding of mutant vWF to GpIbα.
*Biochemistry; Biomedicine; Hematology; Medicine; Molecular Biophysics.*
For further details see under: **vWF** and **GpIbα**.

**vWF** von Willebrand Factor.
*Biochemistry; Biomedicine; Hematology; Medicine; Molecular Biophysics.*
For further details see under: **vWD**.

**vx** videotex.
videotex is also known as: videotext, viewdata.
*Telecommunications.*

**VXML**; **Voxml** Voice eXtensible Markup Language.
A standard VXML for using the human voice to browse the net.

**VYV** Vein Yellow Virus.
Of the peon-tree.

**VZ** Ventricular Zone.
*Brain Development; Medicine; Neurobiology.*

**VZIG** Varicella Zoster Immune Globulin.

**VZV** Varicella Zoster Virus.
VZV is also known as: Chickenpox Virus.
*Virology.*

**VZV Foundation** Varicella-Zoster Virus Foundation (U.S.A.).
*Fellowships; Grants.*

**W** Tungsten.
Tungsten is also known as: Wolfram.
*Chemistry.*
**W**; **w** wages.
**W** water; week; with; wide; wife; work; wrong.
**W** Wakefulness.
*Biomedicine; Psychiatry.*
**w** wait.
*Computer Science.*
**W** Wait Time.
For further details see under: **WT** (Waiting Time).
**W** Wales.
**W**; **w** watt.
Watt is a unit of power equal to one joule per second.
*Physics.*
**W** Wednesday; Welsh; West; Western.
**w** weight.
Also: **wgt.**; **wt**.
*Engineering; Mechanics; Metrology; Statistics.*
**w** width.
Also: **wdt**.
*Science; Telecommunications.*
**w** word.
*Linguistics* - One of the terms that make up a language dictionary.
*Computer Programming* - In computer programming word is also known as: computer word; machine word.
**w** write.
Also: **wrt**.
**WA** Namibia.
**WA** (abbr.) Washington (U.S.A.).
Also: **W**; **Wash**.
**WA** Weighted Average.
*Statistics.*
**W.A.** West Africa.
**WA** Western Atlantic.
**W.A.** Western Australia.
**WA** Williams Act.
Federal Legislation (1968, U.S.A.).
*Law.*
**WA** With Average.
**WAA** World Aluminum Abstracts.
**WAAC** Women's Army Auxiliary Corps.
**WAAF** Women's Auxiliary Air Force.
**WAB** When Authorized By.
**WAC** weather analysis centre.
centre d'analyse météorologique.
**WAC** World Aeronautical Chart.
**WACA** World Association of Center Associates.
Founded in 1979 to mobilize interested individuals not in the legal profession to promote the objects of the WJA.
For further details see under: **WJA** (World Jurist Association).
**WACCC** Worldwide Air Cargo Commodity Classification.
**WACH** West African Clearing House.
**WACK** Wait Acknowledge.
Also: **WAK**.
**WACL** Worcester Area Cooperation Libraries.
**WACLIM Data Service** West Africa CLIMate Data Service.
**WACS** wartime air courier services.
services de courrier aérien du temps de guerre.
**WAD**; **Wad** Web Aided Design.
**WADB** West African Development Bank.
**WADS** weapons access delay system [WS3].
système de restriction d'accès aux armes [WS3].
**WADS** Wide-Area Data Service.
*Telecommunications.*
**WAE** West African English.
*Languages.*
**WAEC** War Agricultural Executive Committee.
**WAES** Workshop on Alternative Energy Strategies.
**WAF** World AIDS Foundation (U.S.A.).
**WAFC** World Area Forecast Center.
**WAFS** Women's Auxiliary Fire Service.
**WAG** Gambia's international vehicle registration letters.
**WAG** Washington Advisory Group.
**WA HIV Cohort Study** Western Australian HIV Cohort Study.
Established in 1983.
*Biochemical Genetics; Clinical Immunology.*
**WAIR strategy** Wing-Assisted Incline Running strategy.
*Avian flight; Evolution of flight; Evolutionary Biology; Locomotor Performance.*
**WAIS** Wechsler Adult Intelligence Scale.
The Wechsler Adult Intelligence Scale is an intelligence test for adults.
*Psychology.*
For further details see under: **WISC**.
**WAIS** West Antarctic Ice Sheet.
*Geology; Geophysics; Glaciology; Marine Subglacial Sedimentation; Planetary Sciences; Polar Research.*
**WAIS** Wide Area Information Server.
*Supercomputing Applications; Library and Information Science.*

**WAJ** World Association of Judges.
Founded in 1966 to mobilize judicial leaders on important *transnational legal issues* and to improve the administration of justice.
**WAJCSC** W. Alton Jones Cell Science Center (U.S.A.).
**WAK** Wait Acknowledge.
Also: **WACK**.
**WAL** Sierra Leone's international vehicle registration letters.
**WAL** World Association of Lawyers.
Founded in 1975 to develop *transnational law* and improve lawyers' expertise in related areas.
**WALP** World Association of Law Professors.
Founded in 1975 to focus the attention of legal scholars and teachers on *transnational legal issues*, and improve scholarship and education in international legal matters, including training, practice, administration of justice, human rights, the environment and co-ordination of legal systems.
**WAM** WAve Model.
**WAME** World Association of Medical Editors.
The World Association of Medical Editors was formed in 1995.
*Ethics; Medicine; Physics.*
**WAMEX** West African Monsoon EXperiment.
**WAMI** Washington, Alaska, Montana and Idaho States (U.S.A.).
**WAN** Nigeria's international vehicle registration letters.
**WAN**; **Wan** Wide Area Network.
**WANA** West Asia / North Africa.
**WAND** Wireless ATM Network Demonstrator.
*European Community Project.*
**W&R** Wholesale and Retail.
*Business; Commerce.*
**WANO** World Association of Nuclear Operators.
The World Association of Nuclear Operators was formed by Industry in 1989.
*Nuclear Science.*
**WANs**; **Wans** Wide-Area Networks.
**WAP** Wireless Application Protocol.
Standard to allow Internet Services on *cellular phones.*
**WAPA** Western Area Power Administration (U.S.A.).
**WAPDA** Water And Power Development Authority (Pakistan).
**WARC** World Administrative Radio Conference.
**WARDA** West Africa Rice Development Association.
Ivory Cost. Founded in 1970.
**warda** The above acronym was coined accidentally using the Arabic word "warda" which means in Arabic: rose (the flower) (*Botany*).
**WARDAM** war damage [NPSM].
dommages causés en temps de guerre [NPSM].
**WARF** Wisconsin Alumni Research Foundation (U.S.A.).
**WARFS** WAter Resources Forecasting System.
**WARHD** (abbr.) Warhead.
*Military.*
**Warks** (abbr.) Warwickshire (G.B.).
**WARM** see WRM.
voir WRM.
**WaRPRC** Washington Regional Primate Research Center (U.S.A.).
**warr.** (abbr.) warrant.
**WAS** wartime authorized strength.
effectifs théoriques du temps de guerre.
**WASA** Worm's Air and Space Agency.
The WASA sponsors a show in the U.S.A. launched in January 1998 exploring *basic science concepts* at a preschool level.
**WASC** Western Administrative Support Center.
**WASDE** World Agricultural Supply and Demand Estimates.
Of the U.S.D.A.
For further details see under: **U.S.D.A**.
**Wash.** (abbr.) Washington, U.S.A.
Also: **W**; **WA**.
**WASP** White, Anglo-Saxon, Protestant.
**WASP**; **Wasp** Wireless Application Service Provider.
**WASTEC Association** WASte Equipment TEChnology Association (U.S.A.).
**WASWC** World Association of Soil and Water Conservation (U.S.A.).
**WAT** Word Association Test.
**WATERNET** Knowledge capture for advanced supervision of Water distribution Networks.
*European Community Project.*
**WATL** Worcestershire Association of Technical Libraries.
**WATOX** Western ATlantic Ocean Experiment.
**WAT radio sources** Wide-Angle Tailed radio sources.
*Astronomy; Physics.*
**WATS** Wide Area Telephone Service.
**WATS** World Air Transport Statistics.
*Airline Industry.*
**WATT** WWW Window for ACTS Trials and Testbeds.
*European Community Project.*

**WATTC** World Administrative Telephone-Telegraph Conference.
**W.Austr.**; **W.Aus.** Western Australia.
**WAVES** Women Accepted for Voluntary Emergency Service.
**waves** The above acronym was coined using the English word "waves".
*Fluid Mechanics; Military Science, Oceanography; Physics.*
**WAW** Warm Agulhas Water.
The Agulhas current is a swift current that flows along the southeast coast of Africa.
**WAW** The airport code for Warsaw, Poland.
**WAY** World Assembly of Youth (Belgium).
**W.B.** Warehouse Book.
**WB**; **W.B.** Water Ballast.
*Naval Architecture.*
**WB** Water Board.
**W.B.** Way-Bill.
Also: **Wb**.
**WB**; **W.B.** Weather Bureau.
**Wb** Weber.
Weber is the meter-kilogram-second unit of magnetic flux.
*Electromagnetism.*
**w.b.** westbound.
**WB** Whale Boat.
*Naval Architecture.*
**WB** Wheelbase / wheel base.
*Engineering Design.*
**WB** Wide Band.
*Acoustical Engineering; Electronics; Telecommunications.*
**WB** Work Bench.
**WB** World Bank.
The World Bank was established in 1944 at the Bretton Woods Conference and started operating in 1946. It is also known as the International Bank for Reconstruction and Development.
**$WB_2$** Tungsten Boride.
Tungsten Boride is used as a refractory.
*Inorganic Chemistry.*
**WBCs** White Blood Cells.
**WBCSD** World Business Council for Sustainable Development (Switzerland).
**WBCT** Whole Blood Clotting Time.
**WBDC** Women's Business Development Corporation (U.S.A.).
*Business; Finance.*
**WBDPC** Western Bancorp Data Processing Company.
**WBEM initiative** Web-based (or enabled) Enterprise Management initiative (Microsoft's).
**WBER** World Bank Economic Review.
**WBF** Wood Block Floor.
*Buildings.*
**WBRO** World Bank Research Observer.
**WBS** Work Breakdown Structure.
**WB temperature** Wet-Bulb temperature.
*Meteorology.*
**WC** Tungsten Carbide.
Tungsten Carbide is used mainly in ceramics, tools, and as an abrasive.
*Inorganic Chemistry.*
**WC** War Cabinet.
**WC** War Council.
**WC**; **wc** Water Closet.
**WC**; **wc** Water Column.
**WC** Watered Capital.
*Business; Economics; Finance.*
**W.C.** West Central.
**w.c.** with costs; without charge.
**WC** Working Capital.
*Business; Economics; Finance.*
**WC** Workmen's Circle (U.S.A.).
**W3C** World Wide Web Consortium (U.S.A.).
The W3C was founded in 1994 at the Massachusetts Institute of Technology's Laboratory for Computer Science.
**WCA** Women's Christian Association.
**WCA** Working-Capital Account.
*Business; Economics; Finance.*
**WCA** Workmen's Compensation Act.
**WCB** wartime contingency base.
base de circonstance du temps de guerre.
**WCBA** Westchester County Bar Association.
**WCC** Washtenaw Community College.
The WCC is located at Ann Arbor, Michigan, U.S.A.
**WCC** Westminster College of Computing (G.B.).
**WCC** White Collar Complex.
*Biochemistry; Genetics; Physiology.*
**WCCASIS** Western Canadian Chapter of the American Society for Information Science.
**W-CDMA** Wideband Code Division Multiple Access.
**WCDP** World Climate Data Program.
WCDP has been replaced by **WCP**.
Also: **WCSMP**.
**WCE** Whole-cell Crude Extracts.
*Biochemistry; Molecular Biology; Molecular Genetics.*
**WCES** Winter Consumer Electronics Show.
Held at Las Vegas NV Convention Center, U.S.A., $7^{th}/10^{th}$ January, 1999.
*International Annual Shows.*

**WCF** Wilson Creek Formation (late Pleistocene).
*Ash Layers; Geology; Paleogeography; Paleoclimatology; Paleoecology; Physics.*

**WCFI** Westpac Commodity Futures Index (Australia).
WCFI is specially designed to track, in real time, commodity prices important to Australia.

**WCIP** World Climate Impact studies Program.

**$WCl_6$** Tungsten Hexachloride.
Tungsten Hexachloride is used mainly as a catalyst.
*Inorganic Chemistry.*

**WCLA** Warren County Library Association.

**WCMC** World Conservation Monitoring Center.
The WCMC is an independent nonprofit organization based in Cambridge (G.B.).
*Botany; Ecology; Ecosystems.*

**WCMD** Wind Correlated Munition Dispenser.

**WCNDR** World Conference on Natural Disaster Reduction - U.N.

**WCO** weapon control order.
consigne de tir.

**WCO** World Customs Organization.
*Customs Administrations.*

**WCP** weapons collection point.
point de regroupement d'armes.

**WCP** World Climate Program.
WCP has replaced WCDP.
For further details see under: **WCSMP** and **WCDP**.

**WCRP** World Climate Research Program.
WCRP has replaced **GARP**.

**WCS** Wildlife Conservation Society - New York City, U.S.A.
*Biology; Ecology; Endangered Species.*

**WCS** Worm Community System.
The worm community system was developed in 1993 by a scientist of the University of Illinois, U.S.A.
*C. elegans Databases.*

**WCS** Writable Control Store.
The writable control store is a part of a CPU control store.
*Computer Technology.*
For further details see under: **CPU**.

**WCSMP** World Climate System Monitoring Program.
For further dertails see under: **WCP**.

**WCT** Water-Cooled Tube.

**WCWC** Western Canada Wilderness Committee.

**WCWI** West-Central WIsconsin (U.S.A.).

**WD** War Department.

**wd** (abbr.) warranted.
Also: **w/d**.

**WD** White Dwarf.
*Astrophysics; Binary Evolution.*

**WD** Winchester Disk.
*Computer Technology.*

**wd.** (abbr.) wind.
*Electronics; Meteorology.*

**W/D** Wire Diagrams.
*Electricity.*

**wd.** (abbr.) withdrawal; withdrawn.

**wd.** (abbr.) word.
For further details see under: **w**.

**W.D.** Works Department (U.S.A.).

**WDA** Welsh Development Agency (G.B.).
The WDA is a Government-funded body that has worked for 25 years to increase the economic prosperity of Wales.

**WDB** Women's Development Banking (South Africa).
*Business; Finance.*

**WDC** War Damage Commission.

**WDC** Wideband Directional Coupler.

**WDC** World Data Center.

**WDCGG** World Data Center for Greenhouse Gases.

**WDDES** World Digital Database for Environmental Sciences.

**WDIR** Working DIRectory.

**WDL** Workers' Defense League.

**WDM**; **Wdm** Wavelength-Division Multiplexing.
WDM is a technology for optical fibre transmission.
*Electrical Engineering; Quantum Optics.*

**WDMA** Wideband CDMA.
*Cellular Phones.*
For further details see under: **CDMA**.

**WDR** World Development Report 2003.
Of the World Bank. Released at the WSSD in Johannesburg, South Africa on 21st August 2002.
*International Health.*
For further details see under: **WSSD**.

**WDSS** Warning Decision Support System.

**wdt** (abbr.) width.
Also: **w**.
*Science; Telecommunications.*

**WDV** Written Down Value.

**WDX** Wavelength-Dispersive X-ray.

**WE** war establishment.
tableau d'effectifs du temps de guerre (TEG).

**WE** Wetlands Ecologist.

**WE** Window Editor.
*Computer Programming.*

**WEA** Workers' Educational Association (G.B.).

**WEAL** Women's Equity Action League.

Located in Washington D.C., U.S.A.
**WEAN** Women's Entrepreneurial Association of Nepal.
*Business; Finance.*
**WEC** wartime engagement criterion.
critère d'engagement du temps de guerre.
**WEC** Weak Energy Condition.
*Physics.*
**WEC** World Energy Conference.
Founded in 1924 in London as World Power Conference to consider the potential resources and all means of production, transportation, transformation and utilization of energy in all their aspects, and also to consider energy consumption in its overall relationship to the growth of economic activity; collects and publishes data; holds triennal congress; promotes regional symposia and technical studies.
*Energy Utilization; Energy Consumption.*
**WEC** World Energy Congress.
**WECA**; **Weca** Wireless Ethernet Compatibility Alliance.
A body that certifies devices for this type of network.
**WECAFC** WEstern Central Atlantic Fishery Commission.
Of the U.N. FAO.
For further details see under: **FAO**.
**WECES** Women European Complementary Education System.
*Projects.*
**WECS** Wind Energy Conversion System.
**WEE** Western Equine Encephalitis.
WEE is also known as: Viral Western Equine Encephalitis.
*Medicine.*
**WEEE** Waste Electrical and Electronic Equipment.
*Disposal; Recycling.*
**Wef** World economic forum.
Head Office: Switzerland.
**WEGO** Women's Entrepreneurial Growth Organization (U.S.A.).
*Business; Finance.*
**WEHI** Walter and Eliza Hall Institute (Australia).
*Pathobiology of Cerebral Malaria.*
**WELL** Whole Earth Lectronic Link.
Founded in 1985.
*Online Communities; Electronic Conferences.*
**Wemp** Women's entrepreneurship and management program.
Funded by the European Community 1996/1998.
**Wepro** Women entrepreneurs project.
*European Projects.*
**WERC** Waste-management Education and Research Consortium (U.S.A.).
WERC is managed by New Mexico State University.
**WESLINK** West Midlands Library and Information Network.
**WEST-FORNET** Western Forestry Information Network.
**WESTLANT** Western Atlantic Area [obsolete - see RC WEST].
Secteur occidental de l'Atlantique [obsolète - voir RC WEST].
**WestLB** Westdeutsche Landesbank (Germany).
**WET** West(ern) European Time.
**WET** Whole Earth Telescope.
WET is a series of medium-sized telescopes working together for the study of pulsations of a particular star.
*Astronomy; Asteroseismology.*
**wet** The above acronyms were coined using the English word "wet".
*Aviation; Chemistry; Meteorology; Physics.*
**WEU** Western European Union.
union de l'Europe occidentale (UEO).
**WEXCO** Increasing Wood EXterior joinery service-life by surface treatments and innovative COatings with reduced solvent emission.
*European Community Project.*
**WEZ** weapon engagement zone.
zone d'engagement d'arme.
**WF** warring factions.
factions belligérantes.
**Wf**; **wf** wharf.
*Shipping.*
**WF** Word Format.
*Computer Programming.*
**W.F.** Work Factor.
**wf** wrong font (typ. defect).
**WFA** World Federation of Advertisers (Belgium).
**WFC count rate** Wide Field Camera count rate.
*Aerospace Engineering; Space Physics.*
**W-FD** Water-Food-Deprived.
**WFHB** Women's Finance House Botswana.
*Business; Finance.*
**WFI** Water For Injection.
**WFL** Women's Freedom League.
**WFlem** West Flemish.
West Flemish is Flemish used in West Flanders.
*Languages.*
**WFMH** World Federation of Mental Health.
The WFMH was launched in Paris in 1948.
**WFO** Weather Forecast Office.
**WFP** World Food Programme - U.N.

For the fight against hunger.
**WFPC-2** Wide Field Planetary Camera 2.
In december 1995 the WFPC2 produced an image of the faintest galaxies ever seen.
*Astronomy; Galaxy Formation; Planet Observations; Sky Surveys; Space Science.*
**WFQ** Weighted Fair Queuing.
**WFREC** West Florida Research and Education Center (U.S.A.).
**W-FS** Water-Food-Satieted.
**WFS** Work Factor System.
**WFS** World Franchise Solutions (U.S.A.).
**WFSA** World Federation of Societies of Anaesthesiologists.
Founded in 1955 to make available the highest standards of anaesthesia to all people of the world.
**WF system** Work-Factor system.
**WFT** Women's Finance Trust (Sierra Leone).
*Business; Finance.*
**W.F.T.U.**; **WFTU** World Federation of Trade Unions.
**WFTZ** Women's Finance Trust of Zambia.
**Wfx** Workfolder for Microsoft Exchange.
**WFZ** weapons free zone.
zone de tir libre (ZTL).
**WG** Granada's international vehicle registration letters.
**W.G** Water Gauge.
Also: **w.g.**; **wg**.
*Engineering.*
**w.g.** weight guaranteed.
**WG** Welsh Gurrels.
**WG** Westminster Gazette.
**wg** (abbr.) wing.
**W.G.**; **w.g.** Wire Gauge / Wire Gage.
*Design Engineering; Engineering.*
**WG** working group.
groupe de travail (GT).
**WGA** Wheat Germ Agglutinin.
*Cell Biology; Developmental Biology.*
**WG activity** Wingless activity.
*Genetics; Medicine; Molecular Biology.*
**WGA-HRP** Wheat Germ Agglutinin conjugated to Horseradish Peroxidase.
*Bidirectional Tracers; Neuroscience.*
**WGAM** Working Group on Antarctic Meteorology.
Of the U.N. WMO.
For further details see under: **WMO**.
**WGCCD** Working Group on Climate Change Detection.
**WGD** Working Group on Data.
**WGmc** West Germanic.
West Germanic is a subbranch of Germanic. It comprises: English, Frisian, Flemish, Dutch, Plattdeutsch, Yiddish and German.
*Languages.*
**WGMS** Working Group on Marine Sediments.
Of the International Council for the Exploration of the Sea.
**WGNTE** Working Group of National Technical Experts.
Groupe de travail des experts techniques nationaux.
**WGs** Working Groups.
**WGS** world geodetic system.
système géodésique mondial.
**WGSAT** Working Group on SATellites.
Of the U.N. WMO.
For further details see under: **WMO**.
**WGSI** Working Group on Sea Ice.
**WGS sequences** Whole-Genome Shotgun sequences.
*Computational Genomics; Genetics; Medicine.*
**wgt** (abbr,) weight.
Also: **w**.
*Engineering; Mechanics; Metrology; Statistics.*
**WGZ bank** Westdeutsche Genossenschafts-Zentralbank (Germany).
**WH** warhead.
charge militaire.
**WH**; **wh** Watt-hour.
For further details see under: **whr**.
**wh** which; white.
**WHA** World Health Assembly (Geneva).
**Whf** (abbr.) wharf.
Also: **wh**.
**WHHL rabbit** Watanabe-Heritable Hyperlipidemic rabbit.
*Discovery Chemistry; Familial Hypercholesterolemia; Metabolic Diseases; Pharmaceutical Research; Pharmacokinetics.*
**WHI** Women's Health Initiative.
For further details see under: **HRT** and **WISDOM**.
**WHIM** World Humor and Irony Membership.
Arizona State University (U.S.A.).
**WHIMSY** World Humor and Irony Membership Serial Yearbook.
Arizona State University (U.S.A.).
**whl** (abbr.) wheel.
*Mathematics; Mechanical Engineering.*
**whm** watt-hour meter.
*Electrical Engineering.*
**WHNRC** Western Human Nutrition Research Center.

The WHNRC is located in San Francisco, California, U.S.A.
**WHNS** wartime host nation support.
soutien foruni par le pays hôte en temps de guerre.
**WHO** World Health Organization.
Agency of the U.N., established in 1948.
Also: **W.H.O.**
For further details see under: **U.N**.
**WHOI** Wood's Hole Oceanographic Institution (U.S.A.).
**whol** (abbr.) wholesaler.
*Business; Commerce.*
**WHQ** war headquarters.
quartier général de guerre (QGG).
**WHQEX** war headquarters exercise.
exercice d'activation des quartiers généraux de guerre.
**whr** watt-hour.
whr is a unit of energy equal to the energy consumed at a rate of one watt per hour.
*Electricity.*
**whs** (abbr.) warehouse.
Also: **whse**.
**WHS** Washington Headquarters Services (U.S.A.).
**WHSC** Wisconsin Health Sciences Librarians.
**whsl.** (abbr.) wholesale.
*Business; Commerce.*
**WHSLA** Wisconsin Health Sciences Library Association.
**wht** (abbr.) white.
**WHT** William Herschel Telescope.
*Astrophysics; Space Research.*
**wHTH motif** winged Helix-Turn-Helix motif.
**WHV** Woodchuck Hepatitis Virus.
**WHYCOS** World HYdrological Cycle Observing System.
**WI** Western Sahara.
**WI** West Indian; West Indies.
**WI** When Issued.
**WI** (abbr.) Wisconsin (U.S.A.).
Also: **Wis.** And **Wisc**.
**WI** Women's Institute.
**WI** Wrought Iron.
*Metallurgy.*
**WIA** Weather-Impacted Airspace.
**WIA** wounded in action.
blessé au combat.
**WIC** wartime identification code.
code d'identification du temps de guerre.
**WIC** Western International Communications.
WIC is a Canadian broadcaster.
**WIC** Women, Infants, and Children.
Special supplemental food program.
**WIDL** Web Interface Definition Language.
WIDL is a system for deciphering web pages.
**WIES** Wrigley Institute for Environmental Studies (U.S.A.).
Of the University of Southern California.
**WiFi** (abbr.) Wireless Fidelity.
**WiFS** (Sea-viewing) Wide Field-of-view Sensor.
*Environmental and Estuarine Studies; Marine and Coastal Sciences; Plant Biology.*
**WIG** wing-in-ground.
aile à effet de sol.
**WIG** Wolfram-Inert-Gas.
*Welding.*
**WIHG** Wadia Institute of Himalayan Geology (Dehradun).
WIHG is run by the government.
*Geology.*
**WII** Wildlife Institute of India (India).
**WIL** Wildlife Investigations Laboratory (U.S.A.).
**WIL** Women's International League.
**WILS** Wisconsin Interlibrary Loan Service.
**Wilts.** (abbr.) Wiltshire (G.B.).
**WIMP** Windward Island passages Monitoring Program.
**WIMPs** Weakly Interacting Massive Particles.
*Astronomy; Astrophysics; Cosmology; Physics.*
**WINGS** Warrants Into Negotiable Government Securities (U.S.A.).
**WIN program** Work INcentive program (U.S.A.).
**Wins** Windows naming system.
**WINS** Wireless In-house Network Studies - European Community.
**WIP** wartime intelligence plan.
plan de renseignement du temps de guerre.
**WIP** Work In Progress.
**WIPO** World Intellectual Property Organization.
Organisation Mondiale de la Propriété Intellectuelle. Publishes: "'Droit d'Auteur" (English Edition). Located in Geneva, Switzerland.
**WIPP** Waste Isolation Pilot Plant (New Mexico).
*Radioactive Waste Disposal.*
**Wis.** (abbr.) Wisconsin, U.S.A.
Also: **WI** and **Wisc**.
**WISC** Wechsler Intelligence Scale for Children.
The Wechsler Intelligence Scale for Children is an Intelligence Test for six to sixteen years old children.
*Psychology.*
For further details see under: **WAIS** (Wechsler Adult Intelligence Scale).
**wisd.** (abbr.) wisdom.
**WISDOM** Women's International Study of long Duration Oestrogen after Menopause.

*Oestrogen and Progestin Tests.*
For further details see under: **WHI**; **HRT**.

**WISE** Women in Science and Engineering.

**WISP** Winter Icing and Storms Project.

**WITEC** Women In TEChnology (G.B.).

**WJA** World Jurist Association.
Located in Washington, D.C., U.S.A.. Founded in 1963 to promote the continued development of *international law* and world order; biennial world conferences, World Law Day, demonstration trials, research programmes and publications have contributed to the growth of law and legal institutions by focusing on matters of international concern.

**WJAC** Women's Junior Air Corps.

**Wk**; **wk** (abbr.) week.

**wk** (abbr.) work.
*Industrial Engineering; Mechanical Engineering; Mechanics.*

**WKB method** Wentzel-Kramers-Brillouin method.
The WKB method is also known as: WKB approximation; phase integral method.
*Quantum Mechanics.*

**wkg** (abbr.) working.
*Mining Engineering; Navigation; Telecommunications.*

**wkly.** (abbr.) weekly.

**wkr** (abbr.) wrecker.

**wks.** (abbr.) weeks.

**wks** (abbr.) workshop.

**WL** Wagon Lit.

**WL**; **wl** Waterline / water line.
*Geology; Naval Architecture.*

**WL**; **wl** Wavelength.
The wavelength is the distance between two points of the same phase.
*Physics.*

**WL** West Longitude.

**WL** Window Level.

**WLA** Washington Library Association (U.S.A.).

**WLA** Wisconsin Library Association (U.S.A.).

**WLA** Women's Land Army.

**WLALW** World Laboratory Animal Liberation Week (U.S.A.).
The WLALW was held in the U.S.A. from 24th to 30th April, 1994.

**WLC** World Linear Collider.
A collaboration of laboratories around the world. Will be operative in 2014.
*Engineering; Physics; Supersymmetric particles.*

**WLF** Women's Liberal Federation.

**WLH** Willandra Lakes Hominid.
*Anthropology; Bioanthropology; Geochronology; Geology; Paleoanthropology.*

**WLL systems** Wireless Local Loop systems.
A technology that allows companies to set up basic telephony using satellite or cellular links.
*Wireless Telecommunications.*

**WLN** Washington Library Network.

**WLN** Western Library Network.

**WLO** Washington Liaison Office.
For further details see under: **JSPS**.

**WLR** Weekly Law Reports.

**WLVP** Wyeth-Lederle Vaccines and Pediatrics.
WLVP is a member of the Wyeth-Ayerst family. It is engaged in research development and manufacture of vaccines for prevention of viral and bacterial diseases.
*Immunizations.*

**WLWH** Workshop Library on World Humor.
The WLWH is located in Arizona State University (U.S.A.).

**WM** Watermark.
*Graphic Arts.*

**WM** water meter.
*Engineering.*

**Wm** Wattmeter.
Wm is an instrument used to measure electric power in watts.

**W/M** Weight or Measurement.
*Engineering.*

**WM** White Matter.

**WM** White Metal.
*Metallurgy.*

**WMA** World Medical Association.

**WMAP satellite** Wilkinson Microwave Anisotropy Probe satellite.
*Astronomy; Physics.*

**WMC** World Meteorological Center.
Of the U.N. WMO.
For further details see under: **WMO**.

**WMD** weapon of mass destruction.
arme de destruction massive.

**WMF**; **Wmf** World Monuments Fund.

**WMG** Warwick Manufacturing Group
Of the University of Warwick, G.B.
*Plasticisation of Thermoplastic Melts; Polymer Processing.*

**WMISH** Whole Mount In Situ Hybridization.
*Biology; Gene Expression; Systems Biology.*

**wmk.** (abbr.) watermark.

**WML**; **Wml** Wireless Mark-up Language.

**WMNC** Whole Mononuclear Cells.

**WMO** World Meteorological Organization.
Located in Geneva, Switzerland. Founded in 1951. Objects: world-wide co-operation in making *Meteorological* and *Hydrometeorological*

*Observations* and in strandardizing their publication, promotion of rapid weather information services, application of meteorology to human activities, encouragement of research and training in meteorology; promotion of activities in *Operational Hydrology*.

**WMRLB** West Midlands Regional Library Bureau.

**WMRS** White Mountain Research Station (California, U.S.A.).

**WMS** Wechsler Memory Scale.
*Cognitive Neuroscience; Medicine; Mental Health.*
For further details see under: **WAIS** and **WISC**.

**WN** The airline code for Southwest Airlines.

**WNA loading** Winter North Atlantic loading.

**WNBA** Women's National Basketball Association (U.S.A.).

**WNCBED** Western National Center for Biodefense and Emerging Diseases (U.S.A.).
The new WNCBED opened in early 2002.
*Biodefense; Bioterrorism; Emerging Diseases; Terrorist Weapons.*

**WNDP** With No Down Payment.
*Business; Commerce; Finance.*

**WNV** West Nile Virus.
*Biology; Migratory Birds; Zoology.*

**WNYLRC** Western New York Library Resources Council (U.S.A.).

**WO** Wait Order.

**W/O** Warrant Officer.

**W.O.** Wireless Operator.

**wo** (abbr.) without.
Also: **wt**.

**w/o** write-off.

**WO** Written Order.

$\mathbf{WO_3}$ Tungstic Oxide.
Tungstic Oxide is also known as: Anhydrous Wolframic Acid; Tungstic Trioxide; Tungstic Acid Anhydride; Tungstic Anhydride. $WO_3$ is used mainly in alloys, and as a pigment.
*Inorganic Chemistry.*

**w.o.b.** washed overboard.

**w.o.c.** without compensation.

**WOCA** World Outside Communist Area.

**WOCE** World Ocean Circulation Experiment.
*Observational Campaigns; Oceanography.*
For further details see under: **MOC**.

$\mathbf{WOCl_4}$ Tungsten Oxychloride.
Tungsten Oxychloride is used in incandescent lighting.
*Inorganic Chemistry.*

**WODC** World Ozone Data Center.

**W of A** Western railway of Alabama (U.S.A.).

**WOG**; **w.o.g.** with other goods.
*Commerce.*

$\mathbf{WO_3 \cdot H_2O}$ Tungstite.
*Mineralogy.*

**WOM** Write Only Memory.

**W.O.M.E.N.** WOmen for Management Enterprise Network.

**WON** Currency unit of South Korea.

**WOOPY** Well-Off Older Persons (U.S.A.).

**WOR** Without Our Responsibility.

**WORC** Women's Opportunities Resource Center (U.S.A.).

**Worcs** (abbr.) Worcestershire (G.B.).

**WORLDCOM** (abbr.) World Communications.

**WORM** Write Once Read Many times.
*Computer Technology.*

**WOROM** Write Only Read Only Memory.

**WOS** Wholly-Owned Subsidiary.
*Business; Commerce; Finance.*

**WOS** Wireless Office Systems.

**WOTAN** Wavelength agile Optical Transport and Access Network.
*European Community Project.*

**WOTAN** Weather Observation Through Ambient Noise.

**WOW** World Ocean Watch.

**WP** War Policy.

**WP** Waste Pipe.

**WP** Waterproof.
*Engineering.*

**W.P.** Weather Permitting.

**WP** Weatherproof.
The term weatherproof refers to materials that can withstand any type of weather.

**W.P.** Western Province.

**WP** Wettable Powder.

**WP** White Paper.
*European Union.*

**WP** White Phosphorus.
One of its main allotropic forms.
*Chemistry.*

**WP** Windfall Profit.
*Economics; Finance.*

**WP** Wire Payment.

**W.P.**; **w.p.** Without Prejudice.
*Law; Commerce.*

**WP** Word Processing; Word Processor.
*Computer Programming.*

**WP** Working Pressure.
*Engineering.*

**WP** Working Program.
*Computer Programming.*

**WP** Write Protection.
*Computer Programming.*

**WPA** Webb Pomerene Act.
*Law* - U.S.A. 1918.
**WPA** With Particular Average.
*Commerce.*
**WPC** Warrior Preparation Centre.
Centre de préparation des forces.
**WPD** Western Power Distribution.
U.S.-owned electricity group.
**WPDN** Wind Profiler Demonstration Network.
**WPFCC** Western Pacific Fisheries Consultative Committee.
**WPI** Wholesale Price Index.
**WPI** World Patent Index.
**WPI** World Precision Instruments (U.S.A.).
**WPIC** Western Psychiatric Institute and Clinic.
The WPIC is located in Pittsburg (U.S.A.).
*Behavioral Research; Psychiatry.*
**WPL** Wave Propagation Laboratory (U.S.A.).
**WPM**; **wpm** Words Per Minute.
*Telecommunications.*
**wpn** (abbr.) weapon.
*Military.*
**WPP** weapon production programme.
programme de production d'armes (ou d'armements).
**WPR** wartime personnel requirements.
besoins en effectifs du temps de guerre.
**WPR** Work Planning and Review.
**WPS** Windows Printing System.
**WPS** Word Processing System.
**WPS** Words Per Second.
**WPs** Work Packages.
**WPT** Windfall Profits Tax.
**WQ** Water Quenching.
*Metallurgy.*
**WR** Wagon-Restaurant.
*Railways.*
**WR** Warehouse Receipt.
**WR** War Reserve.
**WR** washroom; wardrobe.
**WRA** Waste Reduction Audit (U.S.A.).
**WRAC** Women's Royal Army Corps (G.B.).
**WRAF** Women's Royal Air Force (G.B.).
**WRAIR** Walter Reed Army Institute of Research.
**WRDC** World Radiation Data Center.
WRDC was established 30 years ago in Russia. It collects, archives, and disseminates *Solar Radiation Data* obtained at more than 1000 sites.
**WRI** World Resources Institute (Washington D.C., U.S.A.).
*Biodiversity; Conservation Biology.*
**WRIPS** Wave Rider Information Processing System.
**WRLS** Wales Regional Library Service.
**WRM** war reserve modes.
modes réservés pour le temps de guerre (MRG).
**WRNS** Women's Royal Naval Service.
**WRPT** (abbr.) Write Protection.
**WRS** war reserve stocks.
stocks de guerre.
**WRSIC** Water Resources Scientific Information Center.
**WRSK** war reserve spares kit.
lot de rechanges de réserve de guerre.
**WRT** With Respect To.
**wrt** (abbr.) write.
Also: **w**.
**WRU** Welsh Rugby Union.
**WRU** Who are you?.
*Data Communications.*
**WS** Tungsten Carbide.
Tungsten Carbide is used mainly in cutting tools.
*Inorganic Chemistry.*
**WS** Wall Street.
**ws.** (abbr.) warrants.
**WS** Watered Stock.
*Business; Finance.*
**WS** Water Soluble.
*Medicine.*
**WS** Werner's Syndrome.
Werner's syndrome is an inherited disease characterized by symptoms which resemble premature aging.
*Endocrinology; Geriatric Medicine; Geriatric Research; Medical Genetics; Medicine; Neurology; Pathology.*
**WS** 1. Western Samoa.
1. Samoa occidentales.
2. work sheet.
2. fiche de travail.
**WS** Wetted Surface.
**WS** Williams Syndrome.
WS is a genetic disorder in which complex language skills can develop despite general mental deficits.
*Cognition.*
**WS** Working Storage.
*Computer Technology.*
**WS** Work Space.
*Computer Programming; Robotics.*
**WS** Workstation / Work Station.
*Computer Technology; Industrial Engineering.*
**$WS_2$** Tungsten Disulfide.
Tungsten Disulfide is used mainly as an aerosol.
*Inorganic Chemistry.*
**$WS_2$** Tungstenite.

$WS_2$, also known as: Tungsten Disulfide, is used as a solid lubricant.
*Inorganic Chemistry; Mineralogy.*
**WS3** weapon survivability and security system.
système de survie et de sécurité des armes.
**WSA** Warramunga Seismic Array.
*Geology; Geophysics.*
**WSA** Women Scientists Advisors.
**WSCF** World Student Christian Federation.
Located in Switzerland. Founded in 1895. An ecumenical student, university and secondary school organization with participants from all major christian confessions; related groups in 100 countries.
**WSDCU** Wideband Satellite Delay Compensation Unit.
**WSE** Warsaw Stock Exchange.
**WSEO** Washington State Energy Office.
Project Rebound: a pilot program created by the Washington State Energy Office in 1988.
*Energy-Efficiency Projects.*
**WSF** Work Station Facility.
**WSFO** Weather Service Forecast Office.
**WSHLD** (abbr.) windshield.
**WSJ** Wall Street Journal.
**WSLC** weapon system life cycle.
cycle de vie du système d'arme.
**WSM** waterspace management.
gestion de l'espace marin (ou gestion de l'eau).
**WSMO** Weather Service Meteorological Offices.
**WSMR** White Sands Missile Range.
**WSO** Weather Service Office.
Of the U.S. NWS.
For further details see under: **NWS**.
**WSP** weapon system partnership.
association de système d'arme (ASA 3.).
**WSPC** weapon system partnership committee [NAMSO].
comité d'association de système d'arme (CASA 2.) [NAMSO].
**WSPU** Women's Social and Political Union.
**WSR-57** Weather Surveillance Radar 57.
**WSSD** World Summit on Sustainable Development.
For further details see under: **WDR**.
**WSSS** see WS3.
voir WS3.
**WSTB** Water Science and Technology Board.
**WSTT** Weather Scenario Test Tape.
**WSU** Washington State University (U.S.A.).
**WSU** Wayne State University (U.S.A.).
**WSU** Wichita State University (U.S.A.).
**WT** Waiting Time.
*Industrial Engineering* - In industrial engineering, waiting time is also known as: Idle Time.
*Computer Science* - In computer science, waiting time is also known as: wait time.
**wt.** (abbr.) warrant.
**WT** Watertight.
Also: **wt**.
*Engineering.*
**wt** weight.
Also: **wgt**; **w**.
*Engineering; Mechanics; Metrology; Statistics.*
**WT** Wild Type (fusion protein).
**WT** Wilms' Tumor.
A tumor of the Kidneys. Named for the German surgeon Max **Wilms**.
*Oncology.*
**WT** Winchester Technology.
*Computer Technology.*
**WT** Wireless Telegraphy.
**WT** Wire Transfer.
**Wt** without.
Also: **wo**.
**WTA** Willingness To Accept.
**WTAO** World Touring and Automobile Organization.
**WTBD** Work To Be Done.
**WTC** World Trade Center.
**Wtd.** (abbr.) Warranted.
**WTD** World Trade Directory.
**WTEC** World Technology Evaluation Center (U.S.A.).
**WT1 gene** Wilms Tumor 1 gene.
*Developmental Biology; Mammalian Sex Determination; Molecular Biology.*
**WTO** World Tourism Organization.
**WTO** World Trade Organization.
WTO has replaced GATT in 1995.
**WTO** Write-To-Operator.
**WTOR** Write-To-Operator with Reply.
**WTP** Willingness To Pay.
**WT plants** Wild-Type plants.
**wtr** waiter; winter; writer.
**WTRZ** (abbr.) Winterize.
**WTS** Women's Transport Service.
**WTT** Working Timetable.
**WTTC** World Travel and Tourism Council (Belgium).
**wTTS** weak-line T Tauri Stars.
T Tauri Stars without an active disk.
*Astronomy; Astrophysics.*
**WUDB** Work Unit Data Bank.
**WUI** Western Union International.
**WUMA** W Unsae MAjoris.
*Astronomy.*

**WV** St. Vincent's international vehicle registration letters.
**WV** Weight in Volume.
**WV** (abbr.) West Virginia (U.S.A.).
Also: **W.VA**; **W.Va**.
**W/V**; **w/v** wind velocity.
**WV** Working Voltage.
*Electricity.*
**WVF** Wavy Vortex Flow.
**WVLA** West Virginia Library Association.
**WVS** Women's Voluntary Services.
**WVU** West Virginia University (U.S.A.).
**WW** Warehouse Warrant.
**WW** Water Works / waterworks.
*Civil Engineering.*
**WW** Weight in Weight.
**WW** Window Width.
**WW** Word Wrap.
Word Wrap is also known as: Wrap Mode.
*Computer Programming.*
**WW**; **W.W.** World War.
**WWB** Women's World Banking.
*Business; Finance.*
**WWBG** Women's World Banking Ghana.
**WWBM** Women's World Banking / Malawi.
**WW board** Wire Wrap board.
**WW connection** Wire-Wrap connection.
*Electricity.*
**WWD** Weather Working Days.
**WWF** World Wildlife Foundation.
**WWF** World Wrestling Federation.
**WWF CBA** Women's World Finance Cape Breton Association (Canada).
**WWMCCS** Worlwide Military Command and Control System.
**WWNWS** World-Wide Navigation Warning Service.
**WWSSN** Worldwide Standardized Seismograph Network.
**WWW** World Weather Watch.
Of the U.N. WMO.
*Climate Change; Meteorology.*
For further details see under: **WMO**.
**WWW** World Wide Web.
Proposed by Berners - Lee (British Physicist) in 1990.
**WWWDM** WWW Data Management.
**WWWIC** WWW Implementation Coordination.
**WWW protocols** World Wide Web protocols.
*Library and Information Science; Supercomputing Applications.*
**WXTRN** Weak External Reference.
**WY** (abbr.) Wyoming, U.S.A.
Also: **Wy**; **Wyo**.
**WYSIWYG** What You See Is What You Get.
*Computer Science.*
**WZ** Swaziland.
Swaziland.

# X

**x** Chemical symbol for mole fraction.
**X** Christ; cross.
**X** excluded; extra.
**x** excluded; excluding.
**x** (abbr.) experiment.
*Science; Statistics.*
**x** (abbr.) express.
**X** Hoarfrost (Beaufort letter).
*Meteorology.*
**X** Siegbahn.
For further details see under: **XU**.
**X** Xenon.
*Chemistry.*
**XA** Auxiliary Amplifier.
**XA** Cross-Assembler.
**x.a.** excluding all (benefits).
*Business; Finance.*
**XAM** External Address Modifier.
**XANES** X-ray Absorption Near-Edge Structure.
**XAS** X-ray Absorption Spectroscopy.
**XASM** (abbr.) Cross Assembler.
**x.b.** ex bonus.
referring to shares.
*Business; Finance.*
**XBC** External Block Controller.
**XBM** Extended Basic Mode.
**XBT** Expendable Bathythermograph.
**X-C** excluding capitalization; ex capitalization.
**X-C** ex-coupon.
*Business; Finance.*
**X-ch** exchange.
*Business; Finance.*
**X-Cl** excess current liabilities.
**XCL** Exclearing House.
*Business; Finance.*
**X connection** Cross Connection.
**XCP** Ex-Coupon.
*Business; Economics; Finance.*
**XCP** Expendable Current Profiler.
**XCTD probe** Expendable Conductivity-Temperature-Depth probe.
**xcvr** (abbr.) transceiver.
transceiver is also known as: transmitter -receiver.
**xd.** excluding.
**x-d** ex distribution.
**X-D** ex-Dividend; excluding dividend.
Also: **ex-Div.**
*Business; Finance.*
**XDH** Xanthine Dehydrogenase.
**X-dis.** ex-distribution.
**X-disease** The X-disease is a virus disease.
**xdr** (abbr.) transducer.
Also: **xducer**.
*Acoustical Engineering; Engineering; Robotics.*
**X-Dsl** X-Digital subscriber line.
**Xe** The chemical symbol for Xenon.
Xenon is an element of the noble gas group having the atomic number: 54; and an atomic weight of 131.3. It is used mainly in luminescent tubes, and lasers.
*Chemistry.*
**xec.** (abbr.) execute.
**XEC** Extended Emulator Control.
**XEDAR** X-linked Ectodysplasin-A2 Receptor.
*Molecular Oncology; Protein Engineering.*
**xeq** (abbr.) execute.
**XF** Extra Fine.
**XFC** Extended Function Code.
**XFC** *Xenopus* Fibroblast Cells.
*Cell Biology.*
**X-FEL** X-ray Free-Electron Laser.
An X-FEL is a kilometer (or more) long, linear particle accelerator that produces a beam of electrons.
*Physics.*
**X-FELs** X-ray Free-Electron Lasers.
For further details see under: **X-FEL**.
**xfer** (abbr.) transfer.
**xfmr** transformer.
*Electricity.*
**xg** (abbr.) crossing.
**XG** Xyloglucan.
**xge** (abbr.) exchange.
*Computer Programming; Quantum Mechanics; Telecommitnications.*
**XGF mice** Ex-Germ-Free mice.
*Ecology; Medical Microbial Ecology; Medicine; Molecular Biology; Pharmacology.*
**XHVY** (abbr.) Extra Heavy.
**Xic** X inactivation center.
*Cell Biology; Developmental Biology; Human Genetics; Medicine.*
**XID** X-Linked Immunodeficiency.
**X.I.**; **x-in.** ex-interest.
**XL** Execution Language; Extra Large.
$\mathbf{X_L}$ The symbol for inductive reactance.
*Electricity.*
**XLA** X-Linked Agammaglobulinemia.
**XLCM** X-Linked Cardiomyopathy.
*Genetics; Heart Research.*
**XLFs** X-ray Luminosity distribution Functions.
*Astronomy; Astrophysics.*

**XLP** Extra Large scale Packaging.
**XL PCR analysis** Extralong PCR analysis.
*Aging; Medicine; Molecular Biology.*
For further details see under: **PCR**.
**Xm.** Christmas.
Also: **Xmas**.
**XM** Expanded Memory.
**XMCD** X-ray Magnetic Circular Dichroism.
**xmit** (abbr.) transmit; transmitter.
*Computer Programming; Physics; Telecommunications.*
**XML**; **Xml** Extensible Markup Language.
XML is the key to creating electronic exchanges.
**XMLD** X-ray Magnetic Linear Dichroism.
*Astronomy; Physics.*
**XMM mission** X-ray Multiple Mirror mission.
ESA's orbiting X-ray observatory launched 10th December 1999.
*Astronomy; Astrophysics; Engineering; Space; X-ray Astronomy.*
For further details see under: **ESA**.
**XMP** Xanthosine 5'-Monophosphate.
**xmsn** (abbr) transmission.
*Computer Programming; Electromagnetism; Electronics; Genetics Mechanical Engineering; Medicine; Virology.*
**xmtr** transmitter.
**Xn** Christian.
Also: **Xtian**.
**XN** Execution Node.
**XN** ex New.
**XNAs** Xeno-Reactive Natural Antibodies.
*Immunology; Pathology; Surgery; Transplantation Biology Xenotransplantation.*
**Xnty** Christianity.
**XO** Executive Officer.
**XO** Extra Old.
referring to brand labels.
**XO** Xanthine Oxidase.
Xanthine Oxidase is also known as: Schardinger enzyme.
*Enzymology.*
**XO** Xylenol Orange.
*Chemistry.*
**XOP** Extended OPeration.
**XOR** Xanthine Oxidoreductase.
*Physiology.*
**XP** Xeroderma Pigmentosum.
A rare inherited skin disease.
*NER deficiencies.*
For further details see under: **NER**.
**xpd** (abbr.) expedite.
**XPL** explosive.
*Military.*
**XPM** Expanded Metal.
**XPR** Ex PRivileges.
*Business; Finance.*
**XPS** X-ray Photoelectron Spectroscopy.
The X-ray Photoelectron Spectroscopy is also known as: Electron Spectroscopy for Chemical Analysis.
**xpt** (abbr.) crosspoint.
**XR** Exchange Reactor.
**X-R**; **xr** Ex-rights, exduding rights.
*Business; Finance.*
**XR** External Reset.
**XRD** X-Ray Diffraction.
The X-ray diffraction is also known as: X-ray microdiffraction.
*Physics.*
**XREF listing** Cross-REFerence listing.
**XREP** Extended REPorting.
**XREs** Xenobiotic Responsive Elements.
**XRF** X-Ray Fluorescence.
The X-ray fluorescence is also known as: X-ray emission.
*Atomic Physics.*
**XRLs** X-Ray Lasers.
*Physics; X-ray Lasers.*
**XRMD** X-Ray Microdiffraction.
**1XRTT** 1X Radio Transmission Technology.
**Xs** atmospherics.
**xs** (abbr.) excess.
**XSCID disease** X-linked Severe Combined Immunodeficiency disease.
*Gene Therapy.*
**XSECT** (abbr.) Cross Section; cross-section.
*Cartography; Geology; Graphic Arts; Mathematics; Nucleonics.*
**XSTR** (abbr.) Extra Strong.
**xstr** (abbr.) transistor.
*Electronics.*
**XSW method** X-ray Standing Wave method.
*Geoscience; Materials Science and Engineering.*
**Xt** Christ.
Also: **X**.
**XTA** X-Band Tracking Antenna.
**xtal** crystal.
**XTC** External Transmit Clock.
**XTEN** Xerox TElecommunications Network.
**XTE satellite** X-ray Timing Explorer satellite - NASA's.
*Astrophysics.*
For further details see under: **NASA**.
**Xtian** Christian.
Also: **Xn**.

**xtlo** crystal oscillator.
*Radio.*
**XTM** X-ray Tomographic Microscope.
*X-ray Tomographic Studies.*
**xtmr** (abbr.) transformer.
*Electromagnetism.*
**XTP** Expendable Temperature Profiler.
*Applied Ocean Physics; Oceanography; Ocean Engineering.*
**Xtra** (abbr.) Extra.
**Xts College** Christ's College (at Cambridge).
**XU** X Unit.
X Unit is also known as: X-ray unit; siegbahn.
*Physics.*
**xu** Fractional currency unit of Vietnam.
*Currencies.*
**xvers** (abbr.) transverse.
*Anatomy; Cartography.*
**xvtr** (abbr.) transverter.
**X-war.** Ex-warrants.
*Business; Finance.*
**X wave** Extraordinary Wave.
*Geophysics; Optics.*
**XX** Double Excellent.
**XX** without securities or warrants.
*Business; Finance.*
**XXY trisomy** Klinefelter Syndrome.
*Genetics; Human Syndromes.*
**XYAT** X-Y Axis Table.
**XYP** X-Y Plotter.

**Y** Dry Air (Beaufort letter).
*Meteorology.*

**Y** Wye.
*Electricity* - Wye is also known as: Y, yoke.

**y** yield.
*Agronomy; Engineering; Mechanics.*

**Y** The chemical symbol for Yttrium.
Yttrium is a rare-earth metallic element having the atomic number 39, an atomic weight of 88.905, and a melting point of 1500°C. It is used mainly in alloys and in the nuclear field.
*Chemistry; Symbols.*

**YAC** Yeast Artificial Chromosome.
*Biophysics; Genetics.*

**YACC** Yet Another Compiler-Compiler.
*Computer Science.*

**YAG laser** Yttrium-Aluminum-Garnet laser.
*Optics.*

**YAG sintering agent** Yttrium-Aluminum-Garnet sintering agent.
*Materials Science.*

**YAHOO** Yet Another Hierarchical Officious Oracle.

**YAP** Yield Analysis Pattern.

**YAR** York/Antwerp Rules.
Also: **YA rules**.
*Shopping.*

**YARU** Yale Arbovirus Research Unit (U.S.A.).
*Arbovirology.*

**YA rules** York/Antwerp rules.
Also: **YAR**.
*Shopping.*

**YB** Year Book.
*Legal.*

**Yb** The chemical symbol for Ytterbium.
Ytterbium is a metallic element having the atomic number 70, an atomic weight of 173.04, and a melting point of 824°C. Ytterbium is used mainly in lasers, and X-ray tubes.
*Chemistry; Symbols.*

**YBCO** Yttrium, Barium, Copper, and Oxide.

**YBIL** Year Book of International Law.

**$Yb_2O_3$** Ytterbium Oxide.
Ytterbium Oxide also known as: Ytterbia, is used mainly in ceramics; alloys and glasses.
*Inorganic Chemistry.*

**YBP** Years Before Present.
Also: **yrBP**.

**Y/C** Yale College (U.S.A.).

**YC** Youth Council.

**YCC** Youth Conservation Corps.

**YCF** Yacht Club de France.

**YCI** Yacht Club Italiano.

**$YCl_3 \cdot 6H_2O$** Yttrium Chloride.
Yttrium Chloride is used in analytical chemistry.

**YCSA** Young Clinical Scientist Award.
Sponsored by FAMRI.
*Smoking-related Disorders.*
For further details see under: **FAMRI**; **CIA** and **CoE**.

**Yd**; **yd** (abbr.) yard.
*Architecture; Metrology; Naval Architecture.*

**YD** Yemen dinar.
*Currencies.*

**YD** Younger Dryas.
The YD was a return to glacial conditions during the last deglaciation.

**YD-PB transition** Younger Dryas - Preboreal transition.
*Geology; Geophysics; Deglacial Records; Quaternary Geology.*

**YE** Yemen.

**YED** Year-End Dividend.
*Business; Economics; Finance.*

**YEE** Young Enterprise Europe.

**YEEP** Youthful Energetic Elderly Persons.

**YEG** The airport code for Edmonton (Alberta) International, Canada.

**Yel.**; **yel** (abbr.) yellow (color).

**YES** Yamaha Education Suite.
*Trademarks.*

**YES** Young Engineer's Satellite.
*Space Science; Space Telecommunications; Telecommunication Engineering.*

**YES liquid culture** Yeast Extract medium Supplemented liquid culture.
*Biochemistry; Molecular Genetics.*

**YFD** Yard Floating dry Dock.
*U.S. Navy.*

**YFE** Youth For Europe.
EEC action program for the promotion of youth exchanges in the Community.
*European Community Programs.*

**YG** Yield Grade.

**YHA** Youth Hostels Association.

**YHJLS** Yorkshire and Humberside Joint Library Service.

**YHZ** The airport code for Halifax (Nova Scotia) International, Canada.

**YIAL** Yellow Island Aquaculture Limited.
A commercial salmon farm in British Columbia, Canada.
*Captive Salmon; Egg-size Evolution.*

**YIF** Young Investigator Fellowship (U.S.A.).
**YIG** Yttrium - Iron Garnet.
*Electronics.*
**YIR** yearly infrastructure report.
rapport annuel sur les projets d'infrastructure.
**YKI** Institute for Surface Chemistry (Sweden).
**YL** Yellowstone Lake.
**yld.** (abbr.) yield.
*Agronomy; Business; Engineering; Finance; Mechanics.*
**YMCA** Young Men's Christian Association (G.B.).
**YLKI** Indonesian Consumers Institute.
**YMS** Yield Measurement System.
**YMQ** The airport code for Montreal, Quebec, Canada.
**YN** Yes-No.
**YNP** Yellowstone National Parks.
The soils at YNP have annual temperature fluctuations that range from about 20°C to 50°C.
*Ecology; Environment; Plant Physiology.*
**YO** Yugoslavia.
Former Republic of Yugoslavia.
**YOB** Year Of Birth.
**YOE** Year Of Entry.
**YONAH** Years Of the North Atlantic Humpback.
*Marine Biology.*
**YOW** The airport code for Ottawa, Ontario, Canada.
**YP** Yard Patrol (craft).
*U.S. Navy.*
**YP** Yield Point.
*Engineering; Mechanics.*
**YPD** Yeast Protein Database.
**$YPO_4$** Xenotime-(Y).
$YPO_4$ is a radioactive mineral found particularly in pegmatites and in acidic igneous rocks.
*Mineralogy.*
**YP system** Yellowstone Plateau system.
*Geology.*
**yr** (abbr.) year; younger; your.
**YR** Yemen Riyal.
*Currencies.*
**YRA** Yacht Racing Association.
**YRLB** Yorkshire Regional Library Bureau.
**yrs** (abbr.) years; yours.
**YS** Yield Spread.
*Business; Economics; Finance.*
**YS** Yield Strength.
*Mechanics.*
**YSC** Yokohama Science Center (Japan).
**YSF** Yield Safety Factor.
**YSN** Young Scientists' Network (U.S.A.).
**YSOs** Young Stellar Objects.
*Astronomy.*
**YSU** Youngstown State University (U.S.A.).
**YSZ** Yttria-Stabilized Zirconia.
*Materials Science.*
**yt** yacht.
*Naval Architecture.*
**YTB** Yield To Broker.
*Business; Commerce; Finance.*
**YTC** Yield To Call.
**YTD** Year To Date.
**YTM** Yield To Maturity.
*Business; Economics; Finance.*
**YU** Serbia and Montenegro Federal Republic.
**YVR** The airport code for Vancouver International, Canada.
**YWCA** Young Women's Christian Association.
**YWG** The airport code for Winnepeg, Manitoba, Canada.
**YWIA** You are Welcome In Advance.
**YYC** The airport code for Calgary, Alberta, Canada.
**YYS** Yo-Yo Stocks.
*Business; Finance.*
**YYZ** The airport code for Pearson International, Toronto, Canada.

# Z

**Z** Atomic Number.
*Physics.*
**z** haze (Beaufort letter).
*Meteorology.*
**Z** Zambia.
**Z** Zenith Distance.
For further details see under: **ZD**.
**z** zero; zone.
**ZAMS stars** Zero-Age Main Sequence stars.
*Astronomy; Astrophysics.*
**Z angle** Zenith angle.
Also: Zenith Distance.
**Zanz** (abbr.) Zanzibar.
**ZAP** Zymark Automation Planner.
*Interactive Software Programs.*
**ZAR** Zone d'activité de routine [du CECLANT].
CECLANT Routine Activity Area /CRAA/.
**ZBB** zero-based Budgeting.
**ZC** Zionist Congress.
**ZC** Zoological Gardens.
**ZCG** Zeolite Crystal Growth.
**ZChN** Christian National Union (Poland).
**ZCPR** Zürich Civil Procedure Rules.
**ZCTU** Zimbabwe Congress of Trade Unions.
**ZD** Zenith Distance.
ZD is also known as: Zenith Angle.
*Astronomy.*
**ZD** Zéro Défaut.
French initialism meaning: Zero Defect.
**ZD** Zone de Défense.
French initialism meaning: Defence Zone / Area.
**ZDA** zone de défense aérienne.
1a. air defence area (ADA 1.).
1b. air defence zone (ADZ).
**ZEF** Center for Development Research (Germany).
**ZELL** Zero-Length Launch.
**ZEP** Zero Emission Plant.
The first fossil-fueled ZEP pilot plant will be built by U.S. DOE by 2010.
For further details see under: **DOE**.
**ZEPs** Zero Emission Plants.
For further details see under: **ZEP**.
**ZETA** Zero Energy Thermonuclear Assembly.
**zeta** The above acronym was coined accidentally using the Italian word "zeta" which is the last letter of the Italian alphabet.
**ZF** Zero Frequency.
*Physics.*
**ZFC curve** Zero Field-Cooled curve.
*Chemistry; High Magnetic Field; Physics.*
**ZG** Zoological Gardens.
**z.hr.** zero hour.
**ZI** Zero-Impact.
**ZI** Zin Institute.
**ZI** Zonal Index.
*Meteorology.*
**ZI** zone d'intérêt.
area of interest (AOI 2.).
**ZI** Zone Inderdite.
**ZI** Zone Industrielle.
**ZI** Zone of the Interior.
**ZIA** Zone of Interior Armies.
**ZIF** Zero Insertion Force.
*Semiconductors.*
**Zinj.** (abbr.) Zinjanthropus boisel.
*Anthropology.*
**Zi test** Z test for instances.
*Statistics.*
**ZJS** Zürich Judicial System.
**ZKE** Zonal Kinetic Energy.
*Meteorology.*
**ZLA** Zambia Library Association.
**ZLA** Zimbabwe Library Association.
**ZM** Zona Militare; Zone Militaire.
Italian and French initialism meaning: Military Area.
*Military.*
**ZMBH** Zentrum für Molekulare Biologie (Germany).
At Heildelberg University.
**ZMNH** Zentrum für Molekulare Neurobiologie (Germany).
At University of Hamburg.
**Zn** The chemical symbol for Zinc.
Zinc is a metallic element having the atomic number 30, an atomic weight of 65.38, and a melting point of 419°C. It is used mainly in anodes, alloys, and dry cells.
*Chemistry; Symbols.*
**$ZnAl_2O_4$** Gahnite.
Gahnite is found mainly in crystalline schists.
*Mineralogy.*
**$ZnBr_2$** Zinc Bromide.
Zinc Bromide is used mainly in photography.
*Inorganic Chemistry.*
**$ZnCl_2$** Zinc Chloride.
$ZnCl_2$ is used mainly in medicine and textiles.
*Inorganic Chemistry.*
**$ZnCO_3$** Smithsonite.
Smithsonite is also known as: Szaskaite; Zinc Carbonate.
*Mineralogy.*

**$ZnCO_3$** Zinc Carbonate.
$ZnCO_3$ is used mainly in cosmetics; pharmaceuticals and medicine.
*Inorganic Chemistry.*

**$ZnF_2$** Zinc Fluoride.
$ZnF_2$ is used mainly in ceramics; electroplating and wood preserving.
*Inorganic Chemistry.*

**(Zn, Fe)S** Sphalerite.
Sphalerite is also known as: Zinc Blende; Blende.
*Mineralogy.*

**ZnO** Zinc Oxide.
Zinc Oxide is used mainly as a dietary supplement, and in cosmetics, pigments, and skin ointments. It is also known as: Chinese White; Zinc White.
*Inorganic Chemistry.*

**$Zn_3P_2$** Zinc Phosphide.
$Zn_3P_2$ is used mainly as a rodenticide.
*Inorganic Chemistry.*

**ZnS** Zinc Sulfide.
Zinc Sulfide is used mainly in rubber; plastics, and as a fungicide.
*Inorganic Chemistry.*

**ZnSe** Zinc Selenide.
ZnSe is used mainly in infrared optics.
*Inorganic Chemistry.*

**ZnTe** Zinc Telluride.
ZnTe is used mainly as a photoconductor.
*Inorganic Chemistry.*

**Zod.** (abbr.) Zodiac.

**ZOL** Zeolite with an Organic Lattice.
For further details see under: **ZOLs**.

**ZOLs** Zeolites with an Organic Lattice.
*Chemical Engineering; Materials Science.*

**zool** (abbr.) zoological; zoology.

**ZOPFAN** Zone Of Peace, Freedom And Neutrality.

**ZPA** Zone of Polarizing Activity.

**ZPCI** Zone Plate Coded Imaging.

**ZPEs** Zero Point vibrational Energies.
*Atmospheric Kinetics; Geological and Planetary Sciences; Heavy Isotopomers; Photochemistry.*

**ZPG** Zero Population Growth.

**ZPL** Zero Phonon Line.

**ZPNU** zone protégée par les Nations Unies.
United Nations protected area (UNPA).

**ZPO** Zoom Projection Optics.

**ZPRs** Zona Pellucida Remnants.
*Medicine; Genetics; Pathology.*

**Zr** The chemical symbol for Zirconium.
Zirconium is a metallic element having the atomic number 40, an atomic weight of 91.22, and a melting point of 1850°C. Zirconium is used mainly in alloys, and explosives.
*Chemistry; Symbols.*

**$ZrB_2$** Zirconium Boride.
$ZrB_2$ also known as: Zirconium Diboride, is used mainly in cutting tools.
*Inorganic Chemistry.*

**$ZrCl_4$** Zirconium Tetrachloride.
Zirconium tetrachloride which is also known as: Zirconium chloride, is used mainly in the manufacture of water repellent textiles and for many industrial purposes.
*Inorganic Chemistry.*

**$ZrH_2$** Zirconium Hydride.
$ZrH_2$ is used mainly in metallurgy.
*Inorganic Chemistry.*

**ZRH** The airport code for Zurich, Switzerland.

**ZrN** Zirconium Nitride.
Zirconium Nitride is used mainly in refractories.
*Inorganic Chemistry.*

**$ZrO_2$** Baddeleyite.
*Mineralogy.*

**$ZrO_2$** Zirconium Oxide.
Zirconium Oxide, which is also known as: Zirconia; Zirconia Anhydride; Zirconium Dioxide, is used mainly in ceramic glazes, for many industrial purposes and in medicine.
*Inorganic Chemistry.*

**ZRR** zone de responsabilité du renseignement.
1a. area of intelligence responsibility (AIR 2.).
1b. intelligence area of responsibility (IAR).

**$ZrW_2O_8$** Zirconium Tungstate.

**ZS** Zoological Society.

**ZSE** Zapadoslovenske Energeticke (Zadovy, Slovak Republic).
ZSE, located in Bratislava, deals with *Energy Distribution.*

**ZSL** Zoological Society of London (G.B.).

**ZSNF** Zone de sécurité nationale française [marine].
French National Safety Area (FNSA) [navy].

**ZST** zone de sécurité terrestre.
ground safety zone (GSZ).

**ZT** Zeitgeber Time.

**ZT** Zone Torride.

**ZTA** Zimbabwe Tobacco Association.

**ZTL** zone de tir libre.
1a. free-fire area (FFA).
1b. weapons free zone (WFZ).

**ZTMA** Zero-Temperature Metropolis.
Algorithm.
*Algorithms; Artificial Intelligence; Computer Science; Discrete Algorithm.*

**ZUA** Zone d'Usage Agricole.
**ZUP** Zone à Urbaniser par Priorité (France).
**Zw³** Zeste-white 3.
*Cell Biology; Developmental Biology; Medicine; Molecular Biology; Pharmacology.*
For further details see under: **Sgg**.
**ZWFT** Zimbabwe Women's Finance Trust.
*Business; Finance.*
**ZZ lamellar morphology** Zigzag lamellar morphology.
**zz lightning** (abbr.) zigzag lightning.
*Geophysics.*